THE OXFORD HANDBOOK OF

SAMUEL TAYLOR COLERIDGE

THE OXFORD HANDBOOK OF

SAMUEL TAYLOR COLERIDGE

Edited by

FREDERICK BURWICK

OXFORD

UNIVERSITY PRESS

OXFORD
UNIVERSITY PRESS

Great Clarendon Street, Oxford OX2 6DP

Oxford University Press is a department of the University of Oxford.
It furthers the University's objective of excellence in research, scholarship,
and education by publishing worldwide in

Oxford New York

Auckland Cape Town Dar es Salaam Hong Kong Karachi
Kuala Lumpur Madrid Melbourne Mexico City Nairobi
New Delhi Shanghai Taipei Toronto

With offices in

Argentina Austria Brazil Chile Czech Republic France Greece
Guatemala Hungary Italy Japan Poland Portugal Singapore
South Korea Switzerland Thailand Turkey Ukraine Vietnam

Oxford is a registered trade mark of Oxford University Press
in the UK and in certain other countries

Published in the United States
by Oxford University Press Inc., New York

British Library Cataloguing in Publication Data
Data available

Library of Congress Cataloging in Publication Data
Data available

Typeset by SPI Publisher Services, Pondicherry, India
Printed in Great Britain by
CPI Antony Rowe, Chippenham, Wiltshire

ISBN 978–0–19–922953–6

3 5 7 9 10 8 6 4 2

Acknowledgements

....

Hundreds of scholarly works have laid the foundation for the present *Oxford Handbook of Samuel Taylor Coleridge*. Of particular value are Earl Leslie Griggs's edition of the letters (1956–1971), and the edition of the notebooks (1957–2002), commenced by Kathleen Coburn and carried forward by Merten Christensen and Anthony John Harding. But the grandest development in Coleridgean scholarship has been *The Collected Works of Samuel Taylor Coleridge* (1969–2002). The major task of this *Handbook* is to address the vast scope, to assimilate, and to elucidate the manifold facets of Coleridge's literary career. The most profound acknowledgment, then, is owed to the dedicated and capable editors who have provided these indispensible editions. Happily, a few scholars who were involved in the editing of Coleridge's works have also been able to contribute to the *Handbook*. A second round of gratitude must therefore go to the thirty-four authors who accepted the formidable task of synthesizing their expertise in Coleridge's works and providing the chapters for this volume. They were given a rigorous schedule, and as editor I am extremely grateful for their dedication in meeting deadlines and their patience with the final revisions. In coping with the proof-reading and revisions, my fellow contributors will join me in thanking Claire Thompson and Andrew Hawkey for their meticulous attention to the text. My final word of thanks is to Andrew McNeillie for inviting me to undertake this project. In spite of its being far more work than I had anticipated, I must also say that it has been a rewarding learning experience.

Contents

PART II   THE PROSE WORKS

PART III   THE POETIC WORKS

PART IV   SOURCES AND INFLUENCES

PART V   RECEPTION

ABBREVIATIONS

CC	*The Collected Works of Samuel Taylor Coleridge*	
CL	*Collected Letters*	(6 vols.) ed. by Earl Leslie Griggs, Oxford: Clarendon Press, 1951–71
CN	*Notebooks* (5 vols. in 10)	Vol. 1, 1794–1804. (1957), ed. by K. Coburn, 1957; Vol. 2, 1804–8, ed. by K. Coburn, 1961; Vol. 4, 1819–26, ed. by K. Coburn and M. Christensen, 1990; Vol. 5, 1827–34, ed. by K. Coburn and A. J. Harding, 2002
CNS	*Coleridge's Notebooks: A Selection*	ed. by Seamus Perry, Oxford: Oxford University Press, 2002
Lects 1795	*Lectures 1795: On Politics and Religion*	Vol. 1, ed. by L. Patton and P. Mann, 1971
Watchman	*The Watchman*	Vol. 2, ed. by L. Patton and P. Mann, 1970
EOT	*Essays on his Times in the Morning Post and The Courier*	Vol. 3 (3-vol. set), ed. by V. Erdman, 1978
Friend	*The Friend*	Vol. 4 (2-vol. set), ed. by B. E. Rooke, 1969
Lects 1808–19	*Lectures 1808–1819: On Literature*	Vol. 5 (2-vol. set), ed. by R. A. Foakes, 1987
LS	*Lay Sermons*	Vol. 6, ed. by R. J. White, 1972
BL	*Biographia Literaria*	Vol. 7 (2-vol. set), ed. by W. J. Bate and James Engell, 1983

AR	*Aids to Reflection*	Vol. 9, ed. by J. B. Beer, 1993
CCS	*On the Constitution of the Church and State*	Vol. 10, ed. by John Colmer, 1976
SW&F	*Shorter Works and Fragments*	Vol. 11. (2-vol. set), ed. by H. J. Jackson and J. R. de. J. Jackson, 1995
Lects Phil	*Lectures 1818–1819: On the History of Philosophy*	Vol. 8 (2-vol. set), ed. by J. R. de J. Jackson, 2000
M	*Marginalia*	Vol. 12, Part I, Abbt to Byfield, ed. by G. Whalley, 1980; Part II, Camden to Hutton, ed. by George Whalley, 1984; Part III, Irving to Oxleye, ed. by H. J. Jackson and G. Whalley, 1992; Part IV, Pamphlets to Shakespeare, ed. by H. J. Jackson and George Whalley, 1998; Part V, Sherlock to Unidentified, ed. by H. J. Jackson and G. Whalley, 1999; Part VI, Valckenaer to Zwick, ed. by G. Whalley and H. J. Jackson, 2001
Logic	*Logic*	Vol. 13, ed. by James Robert de Jager Jackson, 1981
TT	*Table Talk*	Vol. 14 (2-vol. set), ed. by C. Woodring, 1990
Op Max	*Opus Maximum*	Vol. 15, ed. by T. McFarland, 2002
PW	*Poetical Works*	Vol. 16 (6-vol. set), Part I, Poems (Reading Text), ed. by J. C. C. Mays, 2001; Part II, Poems (Variorum Text), ed. by J. C. C. Mays, 2001; Part III, Plays, ed. by J. C. C. Mays and J. Crick, 2001

Contributors

Christoph Bode is Chair of Modern English Literature at Ludwig-Maximilians-Universität Munich, Germany. His major fields are British and European Romanticism, twentieth-century English and American Literature, Critical Theory, and Travel Writing. He is President of the German Society for English Romanticism and was, for many years, European Convener for the Wordsworth Summer Conference in Grasmere. In 2006 he was elected Centenary Fellow of the English Association, and in 2007 he was awarded a Christensen Fellowship by St Catherine's, Oxford. Author of nineteen books, his most recent ones are: *Historicizing/Contemporizing Shakespeare* (co-ed., 2000); *Re-mapping Romanticism: Gender, Texts, Contexts* (co-ed., 2001); *Romantic Voices, Romantic Poetics* (co-ed., 2005); *Der Roman* (2005); *British and European Romanticisms* (co-ed., 2007). He is currently engaged in writing a two-volume monograph on discursive constructions of identity in British Romanticism.

Frederick Burwick, Professor Emeritus at University of California, Los Angeles (UCLA), has taught courses on Romantic drama and directed student performances of a dozen plays. Author and editor of twenty-four books and over a hundred articles, his research is dedicated to problems of perception, illusion, and delusion in literary representation and theatrical performance. His book, *Illusion and the Drama* (1991), analyses theories of the drama from the Enlightenment through the Romantic period. His *Poetic Madness and the Romantic Imagination* (1996) won the Barricelli Book of the Year Award of the International Conference on Romanticism. He has been named Distinguished Scholar by both the British Academy (1992) and the Keats–Shelley Association (1998). Recent publications include *Romantic Drama: Acting and Reacting* (2009) and his electronic edition of *The Theatre Journal of John Waldie* (2008).

Paul Cheshire is a trustee of the Friends of Coleridge and author of a number of articles on Coleridge and his contemporaries. He has also written on the influence of seventeenth-century hermetic philosophy on Milton, and is engaged in researching the life and thought of a hermetic philosopher of the Romantic period, William Gilbert, author of *The Hurricane, a Theosophical and Western Eclogue* (1796). In addition to printed output he is editor of two websites: www.friendsofcoleridge.com and www.williamgilbert.com. He lives and works in Bath, England.

Pamela Edwards studied Philosophy at the University of British Columbia and Intellectual History at Simon Fraser University in Canada before writing her doctoral thesis on Coleridge's Political Thought at University College London. She has published numerous scholarly essays and reviews in journals and edited volumes including the JBS, *Enlightenment and Dissent* and the *Journal of the History of Political Thought*, Blackwell's *Companion to Eighteenth Century Britain*, and with Frederick Beiser *The Cambridge History of Nineteenth-Century Philosophy*. She is the author of *The Statesman's Science: History, Nature and Law in the Political Thought of Samuel Taylor Coleridge* which was published by Columbia University Press in 2004. From 2002 to 2007 she was a member of the History Department of Syracuse University. She is now Director of Academic Initiatives for The Jack Miller Center, an independent educational non-profit organization based in Philadelphia and focusing on the history and political thought of the American founding.

George Erving is Assistant Professor of English, Humanities, and Honors at the University of Puget Sound, where he is working on a book project regarding the early Coleridge and Unitarians. He has published 'The Politics of Matter: Newtonian Science and Priestleyan Metaphysics in Coleridge's "Preternatural Agency"' (2008), 'Mimetic Desire and the Problem of Subjectivity: Rene Girard and the Legacy of Alexandre Kojeve' (2003), and 'The Breakdown of Moral Order in Coleridge's *Osorio*' (2001).

Angela Esterhammer is Professor of English Literature at the University of Zurich and Distinguished University Professor at the University of Western Ontario. She has held visiting faculty positions at the Universities of Munich and Toronto, and the Free University of Berlin. Her publications include *Creating States: Studies in the Performative Language of John Milton and William Blake* (1994), *R. M. Rilke's Two Stories of Prague* (1994), *The Romantic Performative: Language and Action in British and German Romanticism* (2000), *Romanticism and Improvisation, 1750–1850* (2008), the edited volume *Romantic Poetry* (2002), and articles on English and European literature from the seventeenth to the twentieth century. She is a co-founder of the North American Society for the Study of Romanticism (NASSR) and a member of the Executive Council of the International Comparative Literature Association.

Murray J. Evans is Professor and Chair in the English Department at the University of Winnipeg, Canada. His teaching areas include medieval literature and medievalism, Coleridge, children's literature, and literary theory. He has published articles on Malory and the Malory manuscript, Chaucer and post-modern literary theory, *Piers Plowman*, C. S. Lewis's *Narnia* books, and Coleridge's *Opus Maximum*. His book, *Rereading Middle English Romance* (1995), explores the importance of medieval manuscript anthologies to our understanding of individual romances and of romance as a genre. A completed book manuscript—*Coleridge's Sublime Rhetoric in the* Opus Maximum: *System, Self and Trinity*—is under consideration for publication. With a degree in piano performance, he also enjoys playing and performing, particularly from nineteenth-century piano repertoire.

David Fairer is Professor of Eighteenth-Century English Literature at the University of Leeds. His most recent book is *English Poetry of the Eighteenth Century, 1700–1789* (2003). He is also the author of *Pope's Imagination* (1984), *The Poetry of Alexander Pope* (1989), and, as editor, *Pope: New Contexts* (1990). He has edited *The Correspondence of Thomas Warton* (1995) and the first complete printing of Warton's *History of English Poetry* (1998). With Christine Gerrard he has edited *Eighteenth-Century Poetry: An Annotated Anthology* (2003). He has also written widely on Sensibility and eighteenth-century Romanticism, including essays on Gray, the Wartons, Sterne, Chatterton, Leapor, Burke, Blake, Lamb, Coleridge, Southey, and Wordsworth. His monograph, *Organizing Poetry: The Coleridge Circle 1790–1798* is to be published by Oxford University Press in 2009.

Richard Gravil is author of *Romantic Dialogues: Anglo-American Continuities 1776–1862* (2000) and of two holistic studies of Wordsworth, *Wordsworth's Bardic Vocation, 1787–1842* (2003) and *Wordsworth's Variety* (forthcoming). He was the founding co-editor, with Chris Gair, of *Symbiosis: a Journal of Anglo-American Literary Relations*. As founder and commissioning editor of Humanities-Ebooks, LLP, he is responsible for digitizing the Owen and Smyser *Prose Works of William Wordsworth* (2008/2009). On behalf of the Wordsworth Conference Foundation, of which he is also a Trustee, he organizes the Wordsworth Summer Conference and the Wordsworth Winter School. His editorial work includes *Coleridge's Imagination* (1985 and 2007) with Nicholas Roe and Lucy Newlyn; *The Coleridge Connection* (1990), with Molly Lefebure; *Master Narratives* (2001) and *The Republic of Poetry: Transatlantic Continuities from Bradstreet to Plath* (a special issue of *Symbiosis*, 2003).

Nicholas Halmi is University Lecturer in English Literature of the Romantic Period, University of Oxford, and Margaret Candfield Fellow, University College, He is the author of *The Genealogy of the Romantic Symbol* (2007), editor of the forthcoming Norton Critical Edition of *Wordsworth's Poetry and Prose*, co-editor of the Norton Critical Edition of *Coleridge's Poetry and Prose* (2003), and textual editor of the *Opus Maximum* in *The Collected Works of Samuel Taylor Coleridge* (2002).

Anthony John Harding is co-editor, with the late Kathleen Coburn, of Volume 5 of the Bollingen edition of *The Notebooks of Samuel Taylor Coleridge* (2002). This work was partly funded by a Social Sciences and Humanities Research Council of Canada research grant. His other recent publications include *Coleridge's Responses,*

Volume 2: *Coleridge on the Bible* (2007); *Coleridge and the Inspired Word* (2003); *The Reception of Myth in English Romanticism* (1995); and the chapter 'Biography and Autobiography' in *Romanticism: An Oxford Guide*, ed. Nicholas Roe (2004). Dr. Harding has a BA Hons. from the University of Manchester, and Ph.D. from Cambridge University. He is Professor Emeritus of the University of Saskatchewan, and lives in Wolfville, Nova Scotia.

Douglas Hedley is senior lecturer in Philosophy of Religion in the Faculty of Divinity, Cambridge University and Fellow of Clare College. He studied philosophy and theology at the universities of Oxford and Munich. He taught at the University of Nottingham before being appointed lecturer at Cambridge in the Philosophy of Religion in 1996. He was Directeur d'études invite at the École Pratique des Hautes Études, Sorbonne, Paris in 2003. In 2006 he was Teape Lecturer in India in Bangelore, Delhi, Kolkotta and Hyderabad. His major works are *Coleridge, Philosophy and Religion* (2000) and *Living Forms of the Imagination* (2008).

Jeffrey Hipolito earned his Ph.D. in English Literature from the University of Washington in 2001. He has published on Coleridge in *European Romantic Review* and *Journal of the History of Ideas*, and teaches English and Philosophy at Everett Community College. He is currently at work on a book-length study of the interrelation of poetics and ethics in Coleridge thought.

H. J. Jackson, who teaches English and Book History at the University of Toronto, is the editor or co-editor of six volumes in the standard Bollingen edition of Coleridge's works (including four out of the six volumes of his marginalia), and the author of two books about readers' notes, *Marginalia* (2001) and *Romantic Readers* (2005).

Andrew Keanie is a lecturer at the University of Ulster, Northern Ireland. He is the author of articles on S. T. Coleridge and Hartley Coleridge, and student guides to *Wordsworth* (2000), *Coleridge* (2002) and *Byron* (2005), as well as *Wordsworth and Coleridge: Views From the Meticulous to the Sublime* (2007). He is also the author of the first full-length book on Hartley Coleridge since 1931, *Hartley Coleridge: A Reassessment of his Life and Work* (2008). He is a poet and musician, and lives in Derry with his wife and daughter.

Peter J. Kitson is Professor of English at the University of Dundee. He is the author of *Romantic Literature, Race and Colonial Encounter* (2007); (with T. Fulford and D. Lee) *Literature, Science and Explorations: Bodies of Knowledge* (2004); the editor (with T. Fulford) of *Travels, Explorations and Empires* (8 vols, 2001–2002) and (with D. Lee) *Slavery Abolition and Emancipation* (8 vols, 1999). Kitson is President of the English Association (2007–10) and President of the British Association for Romantic Studies (2007–10).

Julian Knox is a doctoral candidate at the University of California, Los Angeles, completing a dissertation on intersecting discourses of the visual arts, translation, and the body in Coleridge's poetical, philosophical and critical writings. He has presented papers on Coleridge at conferences in Cannington, Grasmere and Bologna. His article on Coleridge's translation of Schiller's *Wallenstein*, 'Coleridge's Transnational Translation', appears in *Home and Abroad: Transnational England, 1750–1850*, ed. Monika Class and Terry Robinson. His study of the translation and reception of Schiller on the English stage will appear in the forthcoming *Blackwell's Encyclopedia of Romanticism*.

Michael John Kooy is Associate Professor in the Department of English and Comparative Literature, University of Warwick, and Programme Director of Warwick's Centre for Research in Philosophy, Literature and the Arts. He is the author of *Coleridge, Schiller and Aesthetic Education* (2002) and essays on Romantic period aesthetics, philosophy and politics.

John-David Lopez teaches in the English Department at the University of California, Los Angeles, where he has recently completed his Ph.D. He is the author of 'Recovered Voices: The Sources of *The Siege of Valencia* (*European Romantic Review*, January 2006) and is currently completing his first book, *The Lover and the Fighter: British Romanticism and the Construct of the Modern Latino*.

Charles Mahoney is Associate Professor of English and Interim Associate Director of the Humanities Institute at the University of Connecticut. He is the author of *Romantics and Renegades: The Poetics of Political Reaction* (2003), editor of Leigh Hunt, *Later Literary Writings* (2003), co-editor (with Michael O'Neill) of *Romantic Poetry: An Annotated Anthology* (2008), and editor of *The Blackwell Companion to Romantic Poetry* (forthcoming, 2009). He is currently at work on a study of Romantic lyric poetry and lyric theory entitled *Revolutionary Measures: Romanticism, Formalism, Criticism*.

Robert M. Maniquis teaches in the English Department at the University of California, Los Angeles. He is the author of many essays on Enlightenment and Romantic literature as well as of *Lonely Empires: Personal and Public Visions of Thomas De Quincey, the English Opium-Eater*, and editor of such volumes as *The Encyclopedie and the French Revolution* (with Clorinda Donato); *The French Revolution and the Iberian Peninsula* (with Oscar Marti and Joseph Perez), *British Radical Culture of the 1790s*, and *Defoe's Footprints* (with Carl Fisher).

Tilar J. Mazzeo is Assistant Professor of English at Colby College and most recently the author of *Plagiarism and Literary Property in the Romantic Period* (2007).

James C. McKusick is Professor of English and Dean of the Davidson Honors College at the University of Montana. He completed his BA in English and Comparative Literature at Dartmouth College and his Ph.D. in English at Yale University. His books include *Faustus: From the German of Goethe, Translated by Samuel Taylor Coleridge*, co-edited with Frederick Burwick (2007); *Green Writing: Romanticism and Ecology* (2000); *Literature and Nature: Four Centuries of Nature Writing*, co-edited with Bridget Keegan (2001); and *Coleridge's Philosophy of Language* (1986). He has published articles and reviews in such journals as *Eighteenth-Century Studies*, *English Literary History*, *European Romantic Review*, *Keats–Shelley Journal*, *Modern Philology*, *Nineteenth-Century Contexts*, *Romantic Circles*, *Studies in Romanticism*, and *The Wordsworth Circle*. He currently serves as President of the Wordsworth–Coleridge Association and Executive Director of the John Clare Society of North America.

Christopher R. Miller is Associate Professor of English at Yale University and the author of *The Invention of Evening: Perception and Time in Romantic Poetry* (2006). He is completing a new book on surprise in the poetry and prose fiction of the long eighteenth century.

Raimonda Modiano is Professor of English and Comparative Literature and Co-Director of the Textual Studies Program at the University of Washington. She is the author of *Coleridge's Concept of Nature* (1985) and co-editor of Coleridge's marginalia on German works for *Marginalia*, Volumes 2–6 in *The Collected Works of Samuel Taylor Coleridge*. She also co-edited (with Nicholas Halmi and Paul Magnuson) the Norton Critical Edition of *Coleridge's Poetry and Prose* (2004), and (with Leroy Searle and Peter Shillingburg) the collection *Voice, Text and Hypertext: Emerging Practices in Textual Studies* (2004).

Michael O'Neill is a Professor of English and a Director of the Institute of Advanced Study at Durham University, and the author of many publications on Romantic and post-Romantic poetry. His most recent book-length publications are *The All-Sustaining Air: Romantic Legacies and Renewals in British, American, and Irish Poetry* (2007) and, with Charles Mahoney, *Romantic Poetry: An Annotated Anthology* (2007).

Morton D. Paley is the author of a number of books about British Romantic art and literature, of which the most recent are *Samuel Taylor Coleridge and the Fine Arts* and *The Traveller in the Evening: The Last Works of William Blake*. Others include *Coleridge's Later Poetry*, *Portraits of Coleridge*, *Apocalypse and Millennium in English Romantic Poetry*, and *The Apocalyptic Sublime*. He has been a Guggenheim Fellow (twice), Senior Fulbright Lecturer at The University of Heidelberg, and an Emeritus Fellow of the Andrew F. Mellon Foundation. He has received the Distinguished Scholar Award of the Keats–Shelley Association of America, and a festschrift entitled *Romanticism and Millenarianism* has been published in his honour. He is co-editor of *Blake: An Illustrated Quarterly*.

Seamus Perry is a Fellow of Balliol College, where he is Tutor in English Literature, and a Lecturer in the Faculty of English, University of Oxford. He is the author of *Coleridge and the Uses of Division* (1999), *Samuel Taylor Coleridge* (in the British Library Writers' Lives series, 2002), and *Alfred Tennyson* (2005); the editor of *Coleridge's Notebooks: A Selection* (2002) and *Coleridge on Writing and Writers* (2008); and the co-editor, with Nicola Trott, of *1800: The New Lyrical Ballads* (2001). He is an editor of the Oxford journal *Essays in Criticism*.

Nicholas Roe is Professor of English at the University of St Andrews, Scotland. He is the author of *Wordsworth and Coleridge: The Radical Years* (1988), *John Keats and the Culture of Dissent* (1997), *The Politics of Nature* (2002), and *Fiery Heart: The First Life of Leigh Hunt* (2005). His edited books include *Keats and History* (1995), *Samuel Taylor Coleridge and the Sciences of Life* (2001) and *Leigh Hunt: Life, Poetics, Politics* (2003). He was a founding editor of the scholarly journal *Romanticism* in 1995, and also edits the *Keats–Shelley Review*. His current projects include a biography of John Keats for Yale University Press, a collection of essays on *English Romantic Writers and the West Country*, and the Keats volume for the Longman Annotated English Poets series. Nicholas Roe is a Trustee of the Keats–Shelley Memorial Association, and Chairman of the Wordsworth Conference Foundation.

Matthew Scott is a Lecturer in English and American Literature at the University of Reading. Recent publications include essays on Wordsworth, Keats, and Edward Said. He is an editor of *Wordsworth and American Literary Culture* (Palgrave, 2005) and is currently writing a monograph on Transatlantic Romanticism.

Elinor Shaffer, FBA is Senior Research Fellow of the Institute of Germanic and Romance Studies, University of London, and Life Member of Clare Hall, Cambridge. She is Director of the Research Project on the Reception of British and Irish Authors in Europe. The Project has so far published fifteen books, most recently *The Reception of S.T. Coleridge in Europe* (2007), edited with Edoardo Zuccato. She is the author of *'Kubla Khan' and The Fall of Jerusalem. The Mythological School in Biblical Criticism and Secular Literature 1770–1880* (1975), and numerous chapters in books and articles on Coleridge, including 'Coleridge and Kant's "Giant Hand"', in *Anglo-German Affinities and Antipathies* (2004); 'Goethe's "Confessions of a Beautiful Soul" and Coleridge's "Confessions of an Inquiring Spirit"', in *Goethe and the English-Speaking World* (2002); 'The Hermeneutic Community: Coleridge and Schleiermacher', in *The Coleridge Connection* (1990); 'Irony in Biblical Criticism' in *Samuel Butler: Victorian against the Grain* (2007). She edited *Comparative Criticism* (1979–2004) for the British

Comparative Literature Association, which she helped to found in 1975. She has taught at universities in England, the United States, Germany and Switzerland.

Anya Taylor is Professor of English at John Jay College of Criminal Justice, CUNY. She is the author of *Erotic Coleridge: Women, Love, and the Law against Divorce* (2005); *Bacchus in Romantic England: Writers and Drink 1780–1830* (1999); *Coleridge: On Humanity* (1995); *Coleridge's Defense of the Human* (1985); *Magic and English Romanticism* (1979), and numerous articles on Romantic and modern writers.

David Vallins is a Professor in the English Department of the Graduate School of Letters at Hiroshima University, Japan, and previously taught at universities in Britain and Hong Kong. His monograph, *Coleridge and the Psychology of Romanticism*, was published by Macmillan in 2000, and he has also edited *Coleridge's Writings: On the Sublime* (2003). His essays on Akenside, Coleridge, Mary Shelley, Emerson, Virginia Woolf, and other authors have appeared in a number of books and journals, including *Journal of the History of Ideas*, *ELH*, *Modern Philology*, *Prose Studies*, and *Symbiosis*. His essay on 'Affective Spaces and Romantic Consciousness' in Radcliffe, Wordsworth, and Mary Shelley will appear in David Herman (ed.), *The Emergence of Mind: Representations of Consciousness in Narrative Discourse in English, 700–the Present* (2009).

Neil Vickers is Senior Lecturer in English at King's College London. He has published widely on Romantic period authors. His book *Coleridge and the Doctors* was published in 2004.

Eric G. Wilson is Thomas H. Pritchard Professor of English at Wake Forest University. He is author of several books on British and American Romanticism, including *Coleridge's Melancholia*, *The Spiritual History of Ice*, and *Emerson's Sublime Science*. His more recent work has focused on the persistence of Romanticism in modern popular culture, mainly in film. This work has resulted in *The Strange World of David Lynch* and *Secret Cinema*. His most recent research has produced *Against Happiness*, an exploration of the role of melancholy in contemporary American culture.

INTRODUCTION

FREDERICK BURWICK

FORTY years in production, the Bollingen edition of the Collected Works of Samuel Taylor Coleridge was completed in 2002. The Coleridge *Notebooks* (1957–2002) were also produced during this same period, five volumes of text with an additional five companion volumes of notes. The Clarendon Press of Oxford published the letters in six volumes (1956–71). The Coleridge scholar today has ready access to a range of materials previously available only in library archives on both sides of the Atlantic. In spite of the new insight provided by these volumes into the range and complexity of Coleridge's literary career, there has yet been no adequate guide to their potential value. With a voracious appetite for books, Coleridge characterized himself as 'a library cormorant'. Thomas McFarland, editor of Coleridge's *Opus Maximum* (2002), the last volume to appear in the Bollingen edition, said that Coleridge was a 'graveyard for biographers' because no single author could begin to comprehend the extensive knowledge invested in the vast array of his literary, critical, philosophical, and theological pursuits. A *Handbook*, bringing together the wisdom of thirty-five Coleridge scholars, will provide the proper tool for assimilating and illuminating Coleridge's rich and varied accomplishment, as well as offering an authoritative guide to the most up-to-date thinking about his achievements.

Each of the thirty-seven chapters provides an ample summary of its topic and also a depth of probing analysis. The principal aim of this *Oxford Handbook* is to provide a guide to Coleridge studies with comprehensive reference to the Collected Works, the Notebooks, and Letters as well as to current scholarship.

PART I BIOGRAPHY

This part covers aspects of Coleridge's life not addressed, or not addressed in the same manner, in the subsequent parts. Coleridge's early years at Ottery St Mary, Christ's Hospital, and Jesus College Cambridge, and his later collaboration with William Wordsworth are topics that are also relevant to the commentary on *Biographia Literaria* in Part II on the Works. The difference, of course, is that the chapter on *Biographia Literaria* will focus on Coleridge's critical principles rather than on the experiences crucial to the biographical context. Similarly, biography will also be addressed in Part V on the Reception. But again, there is governing difference in the focus. Especially important to this first part is the coverage of Coleridge's relationship with friends, collaborators, patrons, and publishers as well as his relationship with his wife, with other women in his life, and with his children Hartley, Derwent, and Sara Coleridge. Following a commentary on Coleridge's later years, this part closes with a study of Coleridge's self-representation in his poetry and other works, letters, and notebooks.

PART II THE PROSE WORKS

In addressing the works of Coleridge, the chapters in this part provide an integration rather than a reworking of what already exists in the Introduction to each of the sixteen (in thirty-four) volumes of the *Collected Works*. To fulfil the purpose of the *Handbook*, these chapters clarify the interconnections and relate the parts to the whole of Coleridge's career. Emphasis here is given to his work as editor, chapterist for the periodicals, lecturer, writer on politics and religion, literary critic, and philosopher.

PART III THE POETIC WORKS

This part is dedicated to perspectives on Coleridge's achievement as a poet. As a critic, Coleridge defined many of the criteria and terms of genre, which for the past century have directed the reading and interpretation of his poetry. In recent years, however, his own pronouncements on the nature and constraints of language have been challenged and reassessed. Similarly, debate has stirred about the implications of his privileging symbol over allegory. Essays in this part examine what Coleridge called a 'conversation poem', and what he identified as his concern with supernaturalism in his contributions to the *Lyrical Ballads*. When Coleridge and Wordsworth first came together, they were both writing plays: Wordsworth his *The Borderers*, and Coleridge his *Osorio*, later revised as *Remorse*, which met with remarkable stage success at Drury Lane in 1813. Following that success, Coleridge went on to write another play, *Zapolya*, in 1816. Following the study of Coleridge's practice as playwright, this part concludes by examining his lifelong commitment to translation, especially of contemporary German literature.

PART IV SOURCES AND INFLUENCES

Significant sources and influences on Coleridge's writings have long fascinated critics, and the commentary has ranged from condemnation for plagiarism to praise for myriad-minded weaving together of a manifold cultural materials. The attack on Coleridge's plagiarism commenced in 1840 with James Frederick Ferrier, who discovered Coleridge's use of passages from Friedrich Schelling while he was busily borrowing from the same source in his 'The Philosophy of Consciousness' (1838/9). John Livingston Lowe, in *The Road to Xanadu* (1927), revealed that 'Kubla Khan' was an encyclopedic repository of sources. *The Coleridge Connection* (1990), edited by Richard Gravil and Molly Lefebure, examined the 'symbiotic nature' of Coleridge absorption of ideas from his readings and from his friends and collaborators. This part opens with chapters on Coleridge's borrowings from biblical and classical tradition, and moves on to his indebtedness to English and European authors, and his incorporation of themes and motifs adapted from philosophy, science, and the arts.

PART V RECEPTION

The previous part addressed the influences on Coleridge. Part V opens with an appraisal of Coleridge's literary influence throughout the world following his death. The second chapter examines the revisions of his published works and the editing of the many previously unpublished manuscripts. As more and more of his letters, notebooks, and other documents came to light, the insight into Coleridge's life and accomplishment evolved and changed. That process of change will be examined first in an overview of the numerous biographies, from Thomas De Quincey (1839/51) to Richard Holmes (1990/7), and again in the course of the critical reception from his own day to the present.

PART I

BIOGRAPHY

CHAPTER 1

···

COLERIDGE'S
EARLY YEARS

···

NICHOLAS ROE

what I am depends on what I have been; and you, MY BEST FRIEND! Have
a right to the narration...and it will perhaps make you behold with no
unforgiving or impatient eye those weaknesses and defects in my
character, which so many untoward circumstances have concurred to
plant there.

S. T. Coleridge to Thomas Poole, 6 February 1797 (*CL*, i. 302)

THE sun went down at a little before quarter to six on the evening of Friday, 5
October 1781, as the Revd. John Coleridge rode home to Ottery St Mary. He had
been to Plymouth, enlisted his son Frank as a midshipman, and now paused at
Exeter to dine with his old friends the Harts. As darkness gathered, they pressed
him to stay the night. John appeared to be in 'high health and good spirits', and it
was only eleven moonlit miles to Ottery on roads that he knew well. He ventured
onward, arrived late at the vicarage, drank a bowl of punch, and went to bed. At
three in the morning his youngest son, eight-year-old Sam, was jolted awake by a
shriek, and said three words: 'Papa is dead.'[1]

'I was plucked up and transplanted from my birth place and family, at the death
of my dear father', he remembered: 'Providence (it has often occurred to me) gave
the first intimation, that it was my lot, and that it was best for me, to make or find
my way of life a detached individual, a Terrae Filius, who was to ask love or service

---

[1] *CL*, i. 355; *Coleridge: The Early Family Letters*, ed. James Engell (Oxford, 1994), 6. Hereafter *EFL*.

of no one.'[2] The Romantic idea that Coleridge shared the Ancient Mariner's unhappy lot was one of his own most beguiling inventions, dating from his teenage years at Christ's Hospital (1782–91). The 'Sonnet: On Quitting Christ's Hospital' (July–August 1791) recalls how Coleridge had been 'torn / By early Sorrow from [his] native seat' (12–13) at Ottery, only to experience 'as great a pang' on parting from scenes 'much-lov'd' at school (11–12; *CP*, I. i. 54–5). Repeated displacements in Coleridge's life eventually disclosed a higher purpose:

> To me th'Eternal Wisdom hath dispens'd
> A different fortune and more different mind—
> Me from the spot where first I sprang to light,
> Too soon transplanted, ere my soul had fix'd
> Its first domestic loves; and hence through Life
> Chasing chance-started Friendships.
>
> ('To the Rev George Coleridge', 15–20; *CP*, I. i. 326–8)

Prematurely unfixed from his domestic 'spot' at Ottery, Coleridge sees how an interplay of design and hazard had shaped a life of 'chasing chance', metaphysical speculation, and poetry. Passages in his 'Monody on the Death of Chatterton', 'Frost at Midnight', *Osorio*, 'A Letter to ——', and 'Dejection: an Ode' all return to the moment of Coleridge's 'detachment' to wander the world like

> a little Child
> Upon a heathy Wild
> Not far from home—but it has lost its way....
>
> ('A Letter to ——', 211–12; *CP*, I. i. 686)

—and each poem finds through the 'midnight' contemplation of his own misfortunes cause for 'tender gladness' in another's capacity for joy.

'Too soon transplanted'. Such was the explanation that Coleridge himself offered for his passionate devotion to a succession of men and women—Mary Evans, Robert Southey, Sara Fricker, William and Dorothy Wordsworth, Sara Hutchinson—all of whom seemed to offer an assurance of 'domestic love'. Perhaps, too, his poem 'To the Rev George Coleridge' gestures to his awareness that these 'chance' friendships inevitably passed, leaving others to live with the consequences as Coleridge 'roam'd through life / Still most a stranger' (40–1). So the myth of a damaged childhood became Coleridge's *apologia* for his feelings of lack, need, and longing for the nurture of the sick room (*CL*, i. 348; Gillman, 33). Deprivation and a wish for inclusion encouraged his lifelong imaginative and intellectual endeavour to 'idealize and to unify', and propelled him into various more mundane communities and collaborations including Unitarianism, Pantisocracy, and the

---

[2] James Gillman, *The Life of Samuel Taylor Coleridge* (London: William Pickering, 1838), i. 11–12 n. Hereafter Gillman.

co-authored *Lyrical Ballads* (BL, i. 304). When Coleridge told Thomas Poole his love of 'the Whole' grew from reading that habituated his mind '*to the Vast*', Poole knew already that those books had been a refuge from childhood miseries (*CL*, i. 354, 347). The reality of Coleridge's childhood, however, was not a scene of unrelenting deprivation, in that the occasion for Coleridge's reflection on '*the Vast*' was a memory of 'delight & admiration' occasioned by a walk with his father.

Born in January 1719 at Crediton, Coleridge's father was the son of John Coleridge (1697–1739), 'a respectable Woolen-draper', and Mary Wills (1698–1776) (*CL*, i. 302–3). On 24 May 1743 he married Mary Lendon, embarked on a three-year career as a schoolmaster, and then, aged twenty-eight, matriculated at Sidney Sussex College, Cambridge, where he became a distinguished scholar of Classics and Hebrew and might have had a Fellowship.[3] In later life he wrote several works: 'Miscellaneous Dissertations', 'Sententiae excerptae, for the use of his own School', and *A Critical Latin Grammar* published in 1772 that Coleridge considered his father's 'best work' (*CL*, i. 310). John left Cambridge and returned to the West Country where, after his first wife's death (1751), he married Ann Bowdon (1727–1809) of a family that 'inherited a house-stye & a pig-stye in the Exmore Country... [and] nothing better since that time' (*CL*, i. 302). More worldly than her amiable, absent-minded husband, Ann was an attentive manager of her family with considerable 'maternal ambition' for her children (*CL*, vi. 643). She was 'an admirable Economist', enjoyed gossip, and relished a tipple of 'decent brandy'—a taste that Coleridge inherited: 'Drink gin if brandy can't be had, / But if it can drink brandy.'[4]

In 1760 the Coleridges settled at Ottery St Mary in East Devon, a prosperous town of some 2000 inhabitants, where the River Otter meanders along water meadows from its source in the Blackdown Hills to the sea at Budleigh Salterton. John had been appointed headmaster of the King Henry VIII Grammar School and vicar of St Mary's, a large, ornate church on a ridge above the town centre. Modelled on Exeter Cathedral, St Mary's was part of an ecclesiastical college that flourished until 1545 when it closed after the dissolution of the monasteries. Located deep in the Devonshire countryside, amid a labyrinth of miry lanes, Ottery was only three miles from the nearest town, Honiton, and the coach road from Exeter to London. It was by no means an isolated community—in the civil war Sir Thomas Fairfax set up a garrison here—although at 230 miles from the capital it was solidly provincial. Elia's recollection of Coleridge at Christ's Hospital—a 'poor friendless boy' from 'far away'—obligingly echoed Coleridge's idea that he had been 'a playless day-dreamer' drawn back in imagination to the remote scenes of the 'sweet-birthplace' he had lost.[5]

---

[3] This account of STC's parental background draws on Rosemary Ashton's entry on John Coleridge for the New DNB, and STC's own recollections for Thomas Poole at *CL*, i. 302–3.

[4] Gillman, 6; *TT*, i. 183; 'Fireside Anacreontic', *CP*, ii. ii. 998; *CL*, i. 310.

[5] 'Christ's Hospital Five and Thirty Years Ago', *The Works of Charles and Mary Lamb*, ed. E. V. Lucas (7 vols., London, 1903–5), ii. 13.

A prominent, respected citizen of Ottery, John Coleridge was friendly with the local grandees Sir Stafford Northcote, who lived nearby at the Chanter's House, Ottery, and the MP Sir Francis Buller (a former pupil). He had three daughters by his first marriage, Mary, Sara, and Elizabeth. From his marriage to Ann, nine more children survived infancy: John (1754–87), 'a successful Officer, & a brave one' (*CL*, i. 310); William (1755–80), a schoolmaster; James (1759–1836), an army officer and 'man of reflection' (*CL*, i. 54, 310); Edward (1760–1843), 'Ned', the 'wit' of the family (*CL*, i. 41, 54, 310); George (1764–1828), Master of the King's School, Ottery; Luke (1765–90), 'bred as a medical Man', an 'uncommon Genius . . . & a good man' (*CL*, i. 311); Anne (1767–91), 'Nancy', 'beautiful and accomplished' (*CL*, i. 102, 311); Francis (1770–92), midshipman and army officer, he 'loved climbing, fighting, playing, & robbing orchards' (*CL*, i. 311, 348). Their youngest child, born in the morning of Wednesday 21 October 1772, was christened Samuel Taylor Coleridge, 'my God-father's name being Samuel Taylor Esq.' (*CL*, i. 311). As the seventh of John's surviving sons, he was one of the elect.

And Coleridge's early childhood was apparently blessed. 'My Father was very fond of me, and I was my mother's darling', he recalled on 9 October 1797, and then deflected his narrative in the direction he now preferred: 'in consequence, I was very miserable' (*CL*, i. 310–11, 347). Parental favour roused the jealousy of his brother Frank, and drew 'thumps & ill names' from their nurse Molly Newbery. 'Frank had a violent love of beating me', Coleridge told Poole, as if developing another scene of domestic misery. This time, however, he was drawn to a more affectionate presence like his father's: 'whenever that was superseded by any humour or circumstance, [Frank] was always very fond of me' (*CL*, i. 347–8). As Coleridge languished with 'a dangerous putrid fever' it was his 'poor Brother Francis' who, 'in spite of orders to the contrary', stole up to his room and comforted his little brother by reading Pope's Homer (*CL*, i. 348). When Coleridge wrote this in October 1797 his poor brother had been dead for five years, and he would have been well aware, too, that he was writing at the sixteenth anniversary of their father's death.

Elsewhere, an alternative narrative overlays brotherly devotion and parental fondness: 'by poor Frank's dislike of me when a little Child I was even from Infancy forced to be by myself' (*CN*, ii. 2647): Coleridge's belief that he had been perse-cuted and banished was imperative for the myth that he constructed about himself as a poet, a myth that mirrored the fate of his fellow west-country poet, Thomas Chatterton, the 'loveliest child of spring' whose 'early bloom' had also been blighted. Coleridge's poetic ambitions rivalled Chatterton's 'heaven-born Genius', and his deliciously gloomy speculation that they might share a 'kindred doom' was shadowed by the memory of his father's dream and its baleful consequences: 'stern FATE transpierc'd with viewless dart / The last pale HOPE, that shiver'd at my heart!' ('Monody on the Death of Chatterton', 51, 113, 116–17; *CP*, I. i. 139–44).

At two years he was sent with other Ottery children to Old Dame Key's village school, where he learned the alphabet, reading, and spelling (*CL*, i. 312). Like any boy he enjoyed cakes from the baker, and, more unusually, acquired a lifelong taste for bacon and beans. Around this time, too, he endured an agonising, Promethean release into language, occasioned—of course—by the neglect of one who should have been nurturing him: 'I was carelessly left by my Nurse—ran to the Fire, and pulled out a live coal—burnt myself dreadfully—while my hand was being Drest by a Mr Young, I spoke for the first time (so my Mother informs me) & said—"Nasty Doctor Young"!' (*CL*, i. 312). Scathed by fire, to the end of his life Coleridge retained a '*broad Devonshire*' accent—a 'native voice' as distinctive as Robert Burns's, as compelling as the Ancient Mariner's.[6]

By turns fretful, timorous, moping, 'inordinately passionate', and a 'tell-tale', at six years Coleridge felt himself despised and driven from the company of his school fellows 'to life in thought and sensation' (*CL*, i. 347; Gillman, 10). He avoided other children by reading—at his aunt's shop in Crediton; lying by the wall; in a play-ground corner—and devoured tales of Tom Hickathrift, Jack the Giant-killer, Belisarius, and the castaways Robinson Crusoe and Philip Quarll. The Arabian Nights stirred feelings of desire and dread, and these books were to be encountered only in broad daylight, 'whenever the Sun lay upon them' and banished his fear of spectres. His father found out the books' effects ('anxious & fearful eagerness' combined with indolence) and burned them, whereupon Coleridge says he became 'a dreamer'—drawn more and more into the world of imagination where the sun and 'th'enchantment of that sudden beam' continued to work their magic.[7] With 'a memory & understanding forced into almost an unnatural ripeness', he basked in the flattery of doting adults—the eloquence that branded him one of 'different mind' could also draw the attention he craved (*CL*, i. 347–8). Among the Ottery 'nymphs' he recalled from this time were tall Sarah Kestell, daughter of the surgeon John Kestell; Mrs. Hodge, whose eyes were 'divinely bright'; Miss Vaughan, whose sight was 'bleary'; pimpled Mrs. Bacon, and scrofulous Miss Bisson, 'sighing over a marriage, alas, hoped for in vain' (*CP*, I. i. 86).

What was Coleridge's world like on 21 October 1780, his eighth birthday? His oldest brother, John, a Lieutenant in the Indian army, wrote home about exotic places that are curiously suggestive of *Kubla Khan*, 'Monghyr famous for its wild romantic situation...About 2 miles from the garrison there is a Hotwell in which the water continually boils. The Natives esteem it sacred and flock thither from all parts of the Country to receive a holy sprinkling' (*EFL*, 32 and n.). William matriculated at Christ Church, 3 June 1774, aged 16, and the next year James left home for the army. Edward entered Pembroke College, Oxford, 17 December 1776,

---

[6] *The Farington Diary*, ed. James Greig (8 vols., London, 1903–5), ii. 210.
[7] *CL*, i. 347; *Friend*, i. 148; *Religious Musings*, 99, *CP*, I. i. 179).

aged 15, and George had followed him as recently as 27 April 1780. While Coleridge would never meet his older brother John, and had 'scarcely seen either James or Edward' (*CL*, i. 53), he was close to George—'my earliest Friend'—Luke, Anne, and Frank, 'the only one of my Family, whom similarity of Ages made more peculiarly my Brother' (*CL*, i. 53).

By now he was at the Grammar School, where he 'outstripped all of my age' (*CL*, i. 348), and on Sundays went to St Mary's to hear his father preach. As the Revd. John Coleridge thundered out the scriptures in the original Hebrew, his country congregation listened intently, necks craned, mouths agape, 'evidently impressed with something of a sense of the grand and holy'.[8] Coleridge was captivated too, and his own style of preaching and lecturing would echo his father's: William Hazlitt remembered that in the Unitarian meeting house at Shrewsbury Coleridge's voice resounded 'loud, deep, and distinct' like 'the music of the spheres'.[9]

Hazlitt wrote that recollection for Leigh Hunt's *Examiner* in 1817, and could not have known that when Coleridge heard his father preach at St Mary's, in the south transept was the gilded face of a great fourteenth-century astronomical clock depicting the spheres of the geo-centric, Ptolemaic universe. From this moment onwards Coleridge associated biblical language, prayer, guilt, and salvation with revolutions of 'the starr'd Azure'.[10] On the Ottery clock the sun, moon, and stars move around the earth—the fixed centre of the universe—as they appear to do in the *Ancient Mariner*:

> The Sun came up upon the left,
>   Out of the Sea came he . . .
>
>   (1798 text, 25–6; *CP,* I. i. 374)
>
> The moving Moon went up the sky
>   And no where did abide:
> Softly she was going up
>   And a star or two beside . . .
>
>   (1798 text, 263–6; *CP,* I. i. 392)

The sun, moon and a star or two accompany the mariner throughout his voyage, plotting his passage through guilt and despair to a chastened acceptance of the 'uncertain hour, / Now oftimes and now fewer' (1798 text, 582–4; *CP,* I. i. 416) when 'anguish comes'. At that moment of forlorn self-knowledge the sound of a 'little Vesper-bell' marks the canonical and celestial hour that bids the mariner to prayer, and to the contemplation of eternity.

---

[8] *TT,* i. 182.
[9] 'Mr. Coleridge's Lay-Sermon', *The Examiner* (12 January 1817), 28–9.
[10] *Religious Musings*, 19; *CP,* I. i. 175.

Perhaps it was the fine summer of 1780 that laid down the memories of 'sweet scenes of childhood' Coleridge drew upon in his poems: adventures along the River Otter, with its 'crossing plank', willow-trees, and 'bedded sand', to play at skimming stones ('Sonnet: To the River Otter', *CP*, I. i. 299–300) or the church bells pealing 'all the hot Fair-day' in June—'Pixie Day', when the Pixies were banished from the town to the Pixies' Parlour, a tiny sandstone cave in a hillside overlooking the river ('Frost at Midnight' and 'Songs of the Pixies', *CP*, I. i. 452–6, 107–12).[11] These spots—sunlit, gleaming, shadowy, dark—were frequented again and again by Coleridge as a boy, and he would return to them in images of the 'sacred river' and 'caverns measureless' that he associated with the mysterious sources of imaginative power.

The River Otter was also connected with more disturbing events: a jealous, violent eruption in the Coleridge family that soon engulfed the town. This occurred shortly after Coleridge's eighth birthday, possibly on one of the rain-drenched days between 29 and 31 October 1780.[12] His account for Thomas Poole is particular: 'I had asked my mother one evening to cut my cheese *entire*, so that I might toast it: this was no easy matter, it being a *crumbly* cheese', Coleridge recalls:

I went into the garden for some thing or other, and in the mean time my Brother Frank *minced* my cheese 'to disappoint the favorite'. I returned, saw the exploit, and in an agony of passion flew at Frank—he pretended to have been seriously hurt by the blow, flung himself on the ground, and there lay with outstretched limbs—I hung over him moaning & in a great fright—he leaped up, & with a horse-laugh gave me a severe blow in the face— I seized a knife, and was running at him, when my Mother came in & took me by the arm— / I expected a flogging—& struggling from her I ran away, to a hill at the bottom of which the Otter flows—about one mile from Ottery.—There I stayed; my rage died away; but my obstinacy vanquished my fears—& taking out a little shilling book which had, at the end, morning & evening prayers, I very devoutly repeated them—thinking *at the same time* with inward & gloomy satisfaction, how miserable my Mother must be!   (*CL*, i. 352–3)

The boys' squabble over food and maternal affection is transformed when Frank's 'horse-laugh' unleashes more destructive energies. Coleridge the moping school-boy picks up the knife and runs at his brother, only to be grasped by his mother who immediately becomes the target of his rage and, having run away, of his 'gloomy satisfaction' at the thought of her misery. As he hunkered, angry and obstinate, night fell—and there was no moon. Within half an hour neighbours were searching for him; he was '*cry'd* by the crier' at Ottery and villages nearby; a reward was offered; ponds and river were dragged; and soon 'half the town were up

---

[11] For the summer weather, June–August 1780, see 'Meteorological Journal Kept at the House of The Royal Society By Order of the President and Council', *Philosophical Transactions of the Royal Society of London*, 71 (1781), 199–226.

[12] October 1780 was predominantly a dry month, with three days of sustained rain on 29–31 October; 'Meteorological Journal', *Philosophical Transactions*, 71 (1781), 199–226.

all one night!' (*CL*, i. 353). As Coleridge recalls his feelings, echoes of the blasted heath in *King Lear* transform the hillside scene:

> I watched the Calves in the fields beyond the river. It grew dark—& I fell asleep—it was towards the latter end of October—& it proved a dreadful stormy night— / I felt the cold in my sleep, and dreamt that I was pulling the blanket over me, & actually pulled over me a dry thorn bush, which lay on the hill—in my sleep I had rolled from the top of the hill to within three yards of the River, which flowed by the unfenced edge of the bottom.—I awoke several times, and finding myself wet & stiff, and cold, closed my eyes again that I might forget it.
>
> (*CL*, i. 353)

The storm, cold, blanket, and thorn echo the third act of *King Lear* as reminders that Coleridge ('poor Tomkyn') had received 'too little care', that man is no more than a 'bare, forked animal' like a horse or the calves beyond the river. As the boy slept, he rolled towards the bank of the Otter; here, however, Coleridge's 'wild streamlet of the west' with gleaming beds of sand is 'the unfenced edge of the bottom'—a measureless gulf, a cold unfathomable universe.

An hour or so before sunrise, Coleridge saw shepherds and workmen at a distance, and then 'luck' brought Sir Stafford Northcote to the fields. He heard the boy crying, and carried him home to his father, 'calm, and the tears stealing down his face', and his mother, who was 'outrageous with joy'. The boy was put to bed and 'recovered in a day or so', although his night wandering would afflict him with ague for years to come (*CL*, i. 354). He survived, only to learn that on 21 November 1780 his brother William had died of a 'putrid fever' on the eve of his marriage to Jane Hart of Exeter (*CL*, i. 310). Sixteen years later Jane married George Coleridge.

This night escapade and associated guilt were seared into Coleridge, to reappear in his writings in the theme of fratricide, scenes of storm and tempest, and the figure of the lost child (*EFL*, 8–10; Holmes 17–18). The letter to Poole of 16 October 1797 is a first sketch of the 'little child' on the 'heathy wild' who will reappear in the poems and in a notebook entry from July 1803: 'heard a noise which I thought Derwent's in sleep—listened anxiously, found it was a Calf bellowing—instantly came on my mind that night, I slept out at Ottery' (*CN*, i. 1416). Coleridge's sense of an 'unfenced edge' proved lastingly significant too. As a young man he would be drawn to the dangerous edge of things—Unitarian dissent, radical politics, advanced science, experimental poetry—even a short-lived army career; in later life, no longer lured to such extremes, his state of mind could at times recall the little boy on the hillside at Ottery, pinioned between 'fears' and the edge of oblivion he now sought through drink and opium 'that [he] might forget'. For the moment, in October 1780, the eight-year-old stopped 'within three yards', waking only to close his eyes again, as the Ancient Mariner 'clos'd [his] lids and kept them close'.

A few days later came a seemingly benign occasion of night wandering with his father:

At eight years old I walked with him one winter evening from a farmer's house, a mile from Ottery—& he told me the names of the stars—and how Jupiter was a thousand times larger than our world—and that the other twinkling stars were suns that had worlds rolling round them—& when I came home, he shewed me how they rolled round— /.   (*CL*, i. 354)

Worlds rolling round. Coleridge's 'delight & admiration' as he heard his father accompanied a discovery as momentous as the 'roll from the top of the hill' that brought him to the brink. Without feeling 'the least wonder or incredulity', and almost as if it were a homecoming, he entered the twinkling abyss of the post-Copernican universe where 'other... stars were Suns that [have] worlds rolling round them' and the glory of the heavens no more than a glittering 'mass of *little things*'. Accustomed to '*the Vast*', Coleridge experienced no sense of the 'wild surmise' that Keats associated with the discovery of a 'new planet'. Whereas Keats felt himself able to exist amid uncertainties and doubts, he recognized that Coleridge was 'incapable of remaining content' and would pursue a metaphysical explanation of 'mystery'.[13] So *Religious Musings* banishes a godless universe of '*little things*', like a spectre from the enchanter sun, as Coleridge asserts 'Our noontide Majesty, to know ourselves / Parts and proportions of one wond'rous whole!' (127–8). 'This fraternizes man', Coleridge adds, 'this constitutes / Our charities and bearings' (129–30; *CP*, I. i. 180).

Coleridge's 'one life' has often been linked with his interests in science and Unitarianism, and it was also a compensation for the family love from which he had been 'torn'. Transplanted from the 'spot' that should have 'fix'd' his 'domestic loves', he was now 'center'd' in God: 'to perfect LOVE / Attracted and absorb'd ... We and our Father ONE!' (39–40, 45; *CP*, I. i. 176–7). While the death of his father was associated with traumatic 'detachment', Coleridge endeavoured to experience life—albeit fitfully, vicariously, subliminally—as it had been before that moment. This is why the date 4 October acquired an almost mystical significance, for it was the day on which—so Coleridge was told—his father paused at the Harts' house at Exeter and told them of his dream of death. At that moment, Coleridge's life had also been held in the balance: his father might yet decide to rest for the night at Exeter, and arrive back at Ottery the next morning, shortly after sunrise, in a different universe.

As it was, in April 1782, aged nine years, Coleridge took the coach to London where Judge Buller's influence had procured a 'Presentation' to enter Christ's Hospital. Once Coleridge had left Ottery, his relationship with his mother became colder and he did not return there for seven years. After a 'spoilt & pampered' stay with his mother's brother, Mr. Bowdon the tobacconist, he was sent to the school for 'younger Blue coat boys' at Hertford, and then, in September 1782, a little short of his tenth birthday, he was 'drafted up to the great school' that would be his home

---

[13] *The Letters of John Keats*, ed. Hyder Rollins (2 vols., Cambridge, Mass., 1958; rpt 1972), i. 193–4.

for the next nine years (*CL*, i. 388). The poem 'Easter Holidays', written at Christ's Hospital, alludes to his feelings of misfortune and loneliness (*CP*, I. i. 8–10), and further painful losses were shortly to follow. News of his brother John's death—possibly by suicide—came in 1787 (*EFL*, 12, 87 and n.); Luke died in 1790, and Ann (Nancy) the following year (*CP*, I. i. 38). Then, in 1793, word came from India that Frank had shot himself 'in a delirious fever' (*CL*, i. 311).

'O! what a change!', Coleridge recalled, 'Depressed, moping, friendless, poor orphan, half starved' (Gillman, 11–12). His letters and notebooks contain similarly indignant recollections of Christ's Hospital, and yet, as with his Ottery childhood, life at Christ's Hospital was not entirely 'solitary gloom' (*CP*, I. i. 13). Among his school fellows were some who would remain friends for life: Charles Lamb, George Dyer, Thomas Middleton, Robert Allen, John Gutch, and the brothers Charles and Valentine le Grice. His friend William Evans introduced him to his 'amiable family', and 'Brother Coly' promptly fell in love with his eldest sister Mary, the first of many intense yet unsatisfactory relationships with women (*BL*, i. 17 and n.).

Founded by royal charter in 1562, in Coleridge's time Christ's Hospital provided a free education for the sons of poor citizens, preparing them for lives as tradesmen, merchants, naval officers, clergymen, and scholars. Situated close to Newgate Prison, St Bartholomew's Hospital and Smithfield Market, Christ's Hospital has been hailed as the 'fam'd school' of 'youthful bards'[14] principally because of Coleridge's recollections in 'Frost at Midnight' and *Biographia Literaria*, Elia's 'Christ's Hospital Five and Thirty Years Ago', and Leigh Hunt's *Autobiography*. In the 'cloisters dim' Coleridge read Virgil, and discovered Bowles's sonnets, saturating his imagination in the classics and a contemporary poet remarkable for creating a 'sweet and indissoluble union between the intellectual and the material world' (Gillman, 19; *BL*, i. 13).[15] There were nearly seven hundred pupils, accommodated in twelve wards or dormitories. Leigh Hunt recalled that these had 'rows of beds on each side, partitioned off, but connected with one another, and each having two boys to sleep in it'. In the middle were bins for bread, and overhead hung a large chandelier. Each ward was in the care of a nurse, who was responsible for the boys' welfare—including the vigorous application of 'sulphur ointment' to cure ringworm ('the tad').[16]

Coleridge was woken by a bell at six o'clock in summer (seven in winter) to wash in cold water. Another bell summoned the boys to breakfast, and then on to school until eleven o' clock. There was an hour's play before the bell for lunch, the main meal of the day. 'Our diet was very scanty', Coleridge tells us: 'Every morning a bit of dry bread & some bad small beer—every evening a larger piece of bread, & cheese or

---

[14] 'Christ's Hospital', Leigh Hunt, *Juvenilia, or a Collection of Poems* (3rd edn, London, 1801), 20.

[15] See Coleridge's 'Preface' to his *Sonnets from Various Authors* (1796), 1.

[16] *The Autobiography of Leigh Hunt* (3 vols., London, 1850), i. 102, hereafter Hunt, *Autobiography*; *CL*, i. 388–9.

butter . . . For dinner—on Sunday, boiled beef & broth—Monday, Bread & butter, & milk & water—on Tuesday, roast mutton, Wednesday, bread & butter & rice milk, Thursday, boiled beef & broth—Friday, boiled mutton & broth—Saturday, bread & butter, & pease porritch'. The boys' appetites were '*damped* never satisfied' (*CL*, i. 389) and because there were no vegetables the diet was unhealthy. Afternoon classes ran from one o'clock until four in the winter (five in summer), then there was bread and cheese for supper at six and, in winter, bed straight afterwards.[17]

Sundays were passed in Christ-Church, Newgate Street. Seated high up in galleries beside the organ, hungry, bored by the somnolent drawl of the sermon, the boys passed the time with jokes, mimicking the preacher, and jabbing and kicking one another. This deadly Sunday routine was not calculated to win souls for the Church of England, and almost certainly encouraged Coleridge's attraction to Unitarian dissent and controversial ideas in religious, scientific and political life. Beyond the school walls momentous events in France were shaking the political and religious establishment. Soon after 14 July 1789, Coleridge wrote his 'Ode on the Destruction of the Bastile' welcoming 'glad Liberty . . . / With every patriot Virtue in her train!' (43–4, *CP*, I. i. 20–1). His poem echoed widespread excitement at the French Revolution and what it might promise for Britain, and indicated the direction in which Coleridge's political opinions would now develop.

There were brighter moments, associated with the few occasions the boys were allowed beyond school bounds. When Coleridge strolled down the Strand making swimming motions with his hands, to imitate Leander crossing the Hellespont, he brushed against a gentleman who mistook him for a pick-pocket. Coleridge's classical explanation so delighted the gentleman that he bought him a subscription to a circulating library in Cheapside, whereupon he read through the entire catalogue 'folios and all' (Gillman 17, 20).[18] All of the boys enjoyed 'skulking' beyond school walls in summer to swim in the New River (Gillman, 17–18).

The curriculum had a practical emphasis and its culture was meritocratic: 'the cleverest boy was the noblest, let his father be who he might'.[19] The pupils were divided into five schools, 'a Mathematical, a Grammar, a drawing, a reading, & a writing School—all very large buildings' (*CL*, i. 388). The reading and writing schools taught basic literacy, and the practical skills necessary for trade and commerce; the Mathematical and Drawing Schools trained boys for the navy and East India Company. The Lower and Upper Grammar Schools gave boys a classical education to equip them for careers in the law and the Church. The Upper School comprised two classes, called Little and Great Erasmus; over them were more senior scholars, known as Deputy Grecians, and at the pinnacle of the School were the Grecians, who were destined for University.

---

[17] For a full account of life at Christ's Hospital for Coleridge, Lamb, and Leigh Hunt, see *Fiery Heart: The First Life of Leigh Hunt* (London, 2005), 33–45.

[18] See Holmes, 28, for this moment as 'curiously prophetic' of Coleridge's literary career.

[19] Hunt, *Autobiography*, i. 97.

Coleridge was at first regarded as 'dull and inapt' (Gillman, 19) until Thomas Middleton found him reading Virgil for pleasure, and reported this to the head-master of the Grammar School, the sadistic James Boyer, who started to take notice. Leigh Hunt portrayed Boyer as 'a short stout man, inclining to punchiness, with large face and hands, an aquiline nose, long upper lip, and a sharp mouth. His eye was close and cruel.'[20] He 'was strictly a flogging master' who shook, punched, pinched, and threw books at his pupils. Hunt lost a tooth to one of Boyer's rages, and hinted that the master's ill-treatment of a sickly boy hastened his untimely death (Gillman 24; *FH*, 37). Whenever Boyer flogged Coleridge, he gave him an extra swipe 'because [he was] such an ugly fellow!' (Gillman, 20), yet he also had the foresight to preserve some of Coleridge's earliest poems in his 'Liber Aureus' of pupils' verses. *Biographia Literaria* shows that in later life Coleridge thought well of Boyer for moulding his taste in classical literature; for teaching him 'that Poetry, even that of the loftiest, and, seemingly, that of the wildest odes, has a logic of its own, as severe as that of science'; and for 'thoroughly [drilling him] in Greek & Roman History, and in Ancient Geography &c' (*BL*, i. 8–9; *CL*, vi. 843). Coleridge's fancy that he might apprentice himself to a shoemaker was angrily dismissed by Boyer; Saturdays walking the wards with his brother Luke at the London Hospital were more acceptable, and soon the would-be cobbler was 'wild to be apprenticed to a surgeon'. Then he took a further, decisive step, and 'bewildered [himself] in metaphysicks, and in theological controversy' (Gillman, 21–3; *BL*, i. 15).

By 1790 Coleridge was seventeen years old and a Grecian. He left Christ's Hospital on 7 September, and received a £40 exhibition to Cambridge in the following January. Having been admitted to Jesus College as a Sizar, 5 February 1791, Coleridge passed the summer at Tiverton, Exeter and Ottery. A sonnet, 'As late I journey'd', linked this return to native scenes with his sister Nancy's recent death (12 March), and looked forward to 'New Scenes of Wisdom . . . / . . . as my days advance!' (10–11, *CP*, I. i. 15). By October he was resident in College, a freshman surprised to discover that neither the Master nor the tutors had returned from the summer vacation (*CL*, i. 15).

He settled in quickly. November brought the award of a Rustat Scholarship, worth the considerable sum of £27 (*CL*, i. 17). He wrote to his brother George describing an exemplary routine of 'Mathematical Lectures, once a day—Euclid and Algebra alternately' and reading classics after tea: 'If I were to read on as I do now—there is not the least doubt, that I should be Classical Medallist, and a very high Wrangler—but *Freshmen* always *begin* very *furiously*. I am reading Pindar, and composing Greek verse, like a mad dog' (*CL*, i. 16–17). Middleton, now in his third year at Pembroke, was an important contact and mentor. In buoyant mood,

---

[20] Hunt, *Autobiography*, i. 116.

Coleridge announced his intention to compete for the 'Brown's Prize ode'—and went on to win a prize for his Greek ode on the slave trade (*CL*, i. 17; *CP*, I. i. 72–84). More ominously, he added that the dampness of his rooms had caused 'a most vio[lent] cold in [his] head', for which he was soon taking opium (*CL*, i. 16–18). A 'potently medicinal' Christmas was passed with the Evans family in London. Back in Cambridge and in high spirits, he wrote to Mary, 'I keep a Cat', and described Cambridge to her sister Anne as 'very fertile in alleys, and mud, and cats, and dogs, besides men, women, ravens, clergy, proctors, Tutors, Owls, and other two legged cattle' (*CL*, i. 19, 25, 31).

George worried about the company his brother was keeping. On 24 January Coleridge wrote to him: 'Mr Frend's company is by no means invidious', adding that the Master of the college, Dr Pierce, 'is very intimate with him' (*CL*, i. 20). Why did Coleridge need to reassure him? Cambridge had long been a centre for religious dissent, and the French Revolution gave impetus to the dissenters' campaign for political and civil rights, liberty of conscience, and parliamentary reform.[21] George already knew that Frend was the mathematics fellow at Jesus College; that he was a prominent and outspoken Unitarian, whose views had lost him his tutorship to the 'ecclesiastical tyranny' of the university; and that Coleridge had assiduously attended his lectures. As the political mood of Cambridge followed the whole country in becoming less tolerant of reformers and dissenters, Frend became a hero for idealistic undergraduates. Coleridge was drawn to Frend too, although for him Frend's attraction was more personal and shared some of the dangerous edginess in another of his role models, Thomas Chatterton. As a beleaguered and persecuted figure, a lone star, Frend represented all that Coleridge felt about himself—transplanted, detached, excluded—and with eager self-recognition he embraced Unitarianism and political reform. In a word, the 'furious freshman' had made common cause with the exiled family of dissent.

The storm broke in February 1793, when Frend published his pamphlet *Peace and Union Recommended*. The previous month had seen the French king Louis XVI executed at Paris, and Britain was now at war with France. Frend's willingness to draw comparisons between regicide France and Britain in 1793 was provocative, as was his observation that 'No Englishman need be alarmed at the execution of an individual at Paris':

Louis Capet was once king of France . . . He was accused of enormous crimes, confined as a state prisoner, tried by the national convention, found guilty, condemned, and executed. What is there wonderful in all of this?[22]

---

[21] See *Wordsworth and Coleridge. The Radical Years* (Oxford, 1988; rpt. 2003), 84–117. Hereafter RY.

[22] William Frend, *Peace and Union, Recommended to the Associated Bodies of Republicans and Anti-Republicans* (St Ives, 1793), 45.

Frend was in fact horrified at French violence and 'open violations of justice', but in 1793 his support for reform, apparent indifference to Louis' execution, and opposition to the war made him a marked man. He was banished from college, and on Friday 3 May appeared before a University court to the cheers of supportive undergraduates—including Coleridge—and was charged with violating the University statute 'De concionibus' which forbade comment, written or spoken, 'against the religion, or any part of it, received and established in our kingdom'.[23] As a report in the *Morning Chronicle* makes clear, Coleridge's antics in the gallery recalled schoolboy pranks at Christ Church, Newgate Street:

On the day of Mr. FREND'S defence, the young men in the gallery occasionally expressed by their usual tokens their approbation of the defendant, and their scorn for his accusers... This... kindled vehement indignation in the Seniors. Mr. FARISH, the Proctor, called out to Dr. MILNER, 'Mr. Vice-Chancellor, I see a young man clapping his hands in the gallery.' 'I hope you know him,' quoth Mr. Vice-President, 'Yes, Sir,' said the Proctor, and hurried into the gallery to seize the supposed delinquent. As soon as he had apprehended his man, he said, 'Sir, you were clapping your hands;' to which the young gentleman replied, with a smile, 'Ah! Sir, I wish I could,' which increased the zealous Proctor's wrath, and it might have gone hard with the luckless undergraduate, if he had not shewn that his left arm was disabled...[24]

Frend spoke for three hours in his own defence on Friday 24 May, and the 'delinquent' who applauded and then changed places with the 'luckless undergraduate' was Coleridge.[25] Later that day Frend was found guilty; refused to retract a word of what he had written in *Peace and Union* (he would 'sooner cut off this hand than sign the paper'); and was banished from the University. Later that year the gates of Jesus College were chained to prevent him entering.

Moving to London, Frend was soon active in reformist circles in the London Corresponding Society. On Friday 27 February 1795 he hosted a tea party at which William Wordsworth met William Godwin, author of *Political Justice*, and like-minded reformers such as Thomas Holcroft and George Dyer. Wordsworth was meeting individuals who already knew—and perhaps spoke about—Coleridge. Back at Cambridge, Coleridge would soon be aware of 'the emergence of an original poetical genius above the literary horizon'; 'During the last year of my residence at Cambridge', he recalled, looking back to 1794, 'I became acquainted with Mr. Wordsworth's... "Descriptive Sketches"' (*BL*, i. 77). In other respects the months after Frend's trial were restless and unhappy ones for him. Writing to George in February 1794, he explained how a 'multitude of petty Embarrassments' had depleted his funds:

[23] B. R. Schneider, *Wordsworth's Cambridge Education* (Cambridge, 1957), 115.

[24] *Morning Chronicle* (28 May 1793). Quoted in RY, 105.

[25] Henry Gunning, *Reminiscences of the University, Town and County of Cambridge, from the Year 1780* (2 vols., London, 1854), i. 299–300.

So small a sum remained, that I could not mock my Tutor with it—My Agitations were delirium—I formed a Party, dashed to London at eleven o'clock at night, and for three days lived in all the tempest of Pleasure—resolved on my return—but I will not shock your religious feelings—I again returned to Cambridge—staid a week—such a week! Where Vice has not annihilated Sensibility, there is little need of a Hell! On Sunday night I packed up a few things,—went off in the mail—staid about a week in a strange way, still looking forwards with a kind of recklessness to the dernier resort of misery—An accident of a very singular kind prevented me—and led me to adopt my present situation. (*CL*, i. 68)

Coleridge had run away a second time, and once again found himself in an awkward scrape at a riverside. He was writing to George from Henley-on-Thames, where he was billeted as a horse-soldier under the name Silas Tomkyn Comberbache. Petty embarrassments overlay the deeper turmoil he had found in his 'tempest of Pleasure': 'I am not, what I was: *Disgust*—*I feel*, as if it had—jaundiced all my Faculties' (*CL*, i. 67). He was more forthcoming to William Godwin, who made notes on Coleridge's trajectory from classical prize-winner to penniless private:

1793 wins a prize for the best Greek ode—never told his love—loose in sexual morality— spends a night in a house of ill fame, ruminating in a chair: next morning meditates suicide, walks in the park, enlists, sleeps 12 hours on the officer's bed, & upon awaking is offered his liberty, which from a scruple of honour he refuses—marched to Reading—dinnerless on Christmas day, his pocket having been picked by a comrade

1794 discharged by lord Cornwallis, after having been 4 months a horse-soldier—returns to Cambridge[26]

Whether or not Coleridge spent that night 'ruminating in a chair', he attempted to salvage a sense of personal 'honour' with the 'scruple' that kept him in the army. Behind the whole sorry story are memories of his two dead brothers John and Frank, as Coleridge miserably contemplates committing suicide too.

On his return to Jesus College, Coleridge was summoned before the Master and Fellows and sentenced to 'a month's confinement to the precincts of the College' (*CL*, i. 80). He resolved to make a walking tour to Wales with a friend, Joseph Hucks, and left Cambridge on 15 June to walk across country to Oxford. Here Coleridge's old Christ's Hospital friend Robert Allen introduced him to Robert Southey, and soon the new friends were planning an idealistic community to be set up in America: they called it Pantisocracy. Another chance-started friendship, and a scheme of transatlantic transplantation, seemed to offer Coleridge the assurance of the 'domestic love' he longed for. In elaborating a theory of Pantisocracy for Southey, he drew upon some of his earliest experiences:

The nearer you approach the Sun, the more intense are his Rays—yet what distant corner of the System do they not cheer and vivify? The ardour of private Attachments makes Philanthropy a necessary *habit* of the Soul. I love my *Friend*—such as *he* is, all mankind

---

[26] Godwin's MS notes on Coleridge's life up to 1799, quoted in RY, 109–10.

are or *might be*! The deduction is evident—Philanthropy (and indeed every other Virtue) is a thing of *Concretion*—Some home-born Feeling is the *center* of the Ball, that, rolling on thro' Life collects and assimilates every congenial Affection.   (*CL*, i. 86)

Coleridge's universe of affection is based in part on memories of the old astronomical clock at Ottery, of his father explaining the stars, and it is cheered and vivified by a sunburst of love: 'I love my *Friend*—such as *he* is, all mankind . . . *might be*!' And yet the 'deduction' is not evidently a 'congenial' one. 'Some home-born Feeling is the *center* of the Ball', Coleridge declares, wishfully, for the Ottery hillside and the river below had shown him how 'rolling on' can lead to an edge, beyond which finding a way through life is to experience detachment and solitude, rather than concretion and assimilation. Just as the earth was formerly thought the fixed centre of the universe, so the 'sweet scene' at Ottery had once seemed the home-born heart of Coleridge's childhood world—and from that '*center*' he had been 'plucked up and transplanted'. Christ's Hospital, the Evans family, Jesus College, and the army had followed, and now Coleridge had moved on again. Would 'the pure system of Pantocracy' become the 'home-born *center*' of universal philanthropy? Even as he assured Southey that '*Pantisocracy* in its most perfect Sense is practicable' (*CL*, i. 114) Coleridge, Terrae Filius, son of the earth, already knew otherwise.

Works Cited

ASHTON, ROSEMARY. 2004. Entry on John Coleridge in the *Oxford Dictionary of National Biography*.

COLERIDGE, SAMUEL TAYLOR. 1983. *Biographia Literaria*, ed. James Engell and Walter Jackson Bate, The Collected Works of Samuel Taylor Coleridge, 7, gen. eds. Kathleen Coburn and Bart Winer. Bollingen Series 75, 2 vols., Princeton.

—— 1956–61. *Collected Letters of Samuel Taylor Coleridge*, ed. Earl Leslie Griggs, 6 vols., Oxford.

—— 1969. *The Friend*, ed. Barbara Rooke, The Collected Works of Samuel Taylor Coleridge, 4, gen. eds. Kathleen Coburn and Bart Winer. Bollingen Series 75, 2 vols., Princeton.

—— 1957–2002. *The Notebooks of Samuel Taylor Coleridge*, ed. Kathleen Coburn et al. 5 vols. in 10 books, Princeton.

—— 2001. *Poetical Works*, ed. J. C. C. Mays, The Collected Works of Samuel Taylor Coleridge, 16, gen. eds. Kathleen Coburn and Bart Winer. Bollingen Series 75, 3 vols. in 6 parts, Princeton.

—— 1796. *Sonnets from Various Authors*.

—— 1990. *Table Talk*, recorded by Henry Nelson Coleridge and John Taylor Coleridge, ed. Carl Woodring, The Collected Works of Samuel Taylor Coleridge, 14, gen. eds. Kathleen Coburn and Bart Winer. Bollingen Series 75, 2 vols., Princeton.

ENGELL, JAMES (ed.). 1994. *Coleridge: The Early Family Letters*. Oxford.

FREND, WILLIAM. 1793. *Peace and Union, Recommended to the Associated Bodies of Republicans and Anti-Republicans*. St Ives.

GILLMAN, JAMES. 1838. *The Life of Samuel Taylor Coleridge*. London.

GREIG, JAMES (ed.) 1903–5. *The Farington Diary*. 8 vols. London.

GUNNING, HENRY. 1854. *Reminiscences of the University, Town and County of Cambridge, from the Year 1780*. 2 vols. London.

HAZLITT, WILLIAM. 1817. Mr. Coleridge's lay-sermon, *The Examiner*, 12 January.

HOLMES, RICHARD. 1989. *Coleridge: Early Visions*. London.

HUNT, JAMES HENRY LEIGH. 1850. *The Autobiography of Leigh Hunt*. 3 vols. London.

—— 1801. *Juvenilia, or a Collection of Poems*. 3rd edn., London.

LAMB, CHARLES. 1903–5. 'Christ's Hospital Five and Thirty Years Ago', *The Works of Charles and Mary Lamb*, ed. E. V. Lucas. 7 vols. London.

'Meteorological Journal Kept at the House of The Royal Society By Order of the President and Council', *Philosophical Transactions of the Royal Society of London*, 71: 1781.

Morning Chronicle. 1793. 28 May.

ROE, NICHOLAS, 2005. *Fiery Heart: The First Life of Leigh Hunt*. London.

—— 1988. *Wordsworth and Coleridge. The Radical Years*. Oxford.

ROLLINS, HYDER (ed.) 1958. *The Letters of John Keats* 2 vols., Cambridge, Mass.; rpt 1972.

SCHNEIDER, B. R. 1957. *Wordsworth's Cambridge Education*. Cambridge.

COLERIDGE AND WORDSWORTH: COLLABORATION AND CRITICISM FROM *SALISBURY PLAIN* TO *AIDS TO REFLECTION*

RICHARD GRAVIL

FRIENDSHIP

THE 'symbiosis' of Wordsworth and Coleridge, to use Thomas McFarland's meta-phor, is a well-attested phenomenon. When this celebrated friendship was at its height it involved intimate and creative gift exchange both in world view and in the craft of verse. Two of the very greatest poems of 1798—*Tintern Abbey* and *Frost at Midnight*—are luminous instances of this gift exchange. The conversation between such later poems as *Intimations* and *Dejection* and *Resolution and Independence* is also audible by any competent reader. In the years 1797–1800 the friendship extruded at least two poems by a species of osmosis: one, *The Three Graves*, contains extensive passages by both poets (Parrish 1986) while another, *The Monk*, has appeared in both authors' collected works, because it is written in a style that might have been produced by either (Erdman 1986). But that is about as far as critical agreement goes. This nurturing friendship led to a painful and quasi-permanent breach, which tends to divide readers into warring camps, unable to agree on who gave what to whom, and when; or who let down whom, and who was most responsible for the rupture.

The long-term outcome of the friendship may even have been a weakening of each poet's confidence in his own voice. Wordsworth's 'descent upon Coleridge' is fairly well documented: the fact that this is the version of events assiduously promoted by Coleridge himself should give one pause, but one can feel that Wordsworth's insensitivity to Coleridge's imagination contributed to its extinction.[1] It has been argued, on the other hand, that Coleridge wrote little of permanent value before the friendship began—Coleridge's early poetry speaks to very few—and that he rarely wrote considerable poetry when not in Wordsworth's immediate orbit (Coleridge makes the same point in his *Dejection* ode, remembering that golden time when 'fruits, and foliage, not my own, seemed mine' (*PW* [*CC*] 1: 700). As for Wordsworth, there has always been a critical tendency to attribute any new thinking on Wordsworth's part to Coleridge's influence. As H. M. Margoliouth put it—and he is not alone—without Coleridge, Wordsworth would 'have had no philosophy worthy of the name' (1953: 78). To others, however, the assumption that any new idea in Wordsworth's poetry 'must have' come from Coleridge leads to damaging oversight of the empiricist and sometimes materialist strain in Wordsworth's own thinking. One can also argue that Wordsworth's drift from experimental Romantic towards premature Victorian was brought about by Coleridge's ill-conceived advice.

The critical debate on the symbiosis of Wordsworth and Coleridge flourished in the 1970s and early 1980s, in such studies as Norman Fruman, *Coleridge: The Damaged Archangel* (1971); Stephen Parrish, *The Art of the 'Lyrical Ballads'* (1973); Mary Jacobus, *Tradition & Experiment in Wordsworth's Lyrical Ballads (1798)* (1976); John Beer, *Wordsworth in Time* (1979); Thomas McFarland, *Romanticism and the Forms of Ruin* (1981), particularly its first chapter on 'The Symbiosis of Coleridge and Wordsworth'; and Don H. Bialostosky, *Making Tales: The Poetics of Wordsworth's Narrative Experiments* (1984). It reached its zenith—in terms of a grasp of the day-to-day play of echo and allusion—in two consummate assessments, by Lucy Newlyn and Paul Magnuson.[2] These studies, however, take almost

---

[1] Coleridge told Godwin in March 1801 that any biographer of himself should say that 'Wordsworth descended on him . . . [and] by showing to him what true poetry was, he made him know, that he himself was no Poet' (*CL* 2: 714).

[2] See also Gravil (1984), Gravil (1985), and Modiano (1989). The present chapter draws on Gravil (1985).

diametrically opposite views of the proper way to understand the relationship. Paul Magnuson's *Coleridge and Wordsworth: A Lyrical Dialogue* (1988) adopts an extreme formulation of the 'symbiosis' position. Cued by a remark by Coleridge to Cottle in May 1798 (*CL* 1: 411), Magnuson charts the 'lyrical dialogue' as if their poems constitute 'one work' (1988: 4), implying that it is illegitimate to read them any other way. He marginalizes *Lyrical Ballads*, and does so on revealing grounds: 'I have not considered [them] as of major significance in the dialogue, except for "Tintern Abbey"... because... the major poetry written at the time the shorter ballads were written is of vastly more importance'—a claim that privileges Coleridge's view of what is, and is not, 'important' in Wordsworth. Lucy Newlyn, on the other hand, emphasizes Coleridge's early suspicion of a 'radical difference' in their views of poetry. Her *Coleridge and Wordsworth: The Language of Allusion* (1986) points also to Wordsworth's dogged resistance to Coleridgean values (126), and the way his creativity is released in C's absence (172). Her account of *The Prelude* emphasizes Wordsworth's struggle for autonomy and how his autobiography attributes all of his growth points—some plausibly, some not—to a time before his meeting with Coleridge.

The story begins in June 1797, when after two brief encounters elsewhere in the West Country, Coleridge made his celebrated visit to Racedown, as a result of which the Wordsworths moved to Somerset the following year to be closer to this engaging new friend. Coleridge at the time of the Racedown visit was the better-known poet, and a celebrated lecturer and journalist, and was half way through a tragedy, *Osorio*. Wordsworth had already written two versions of his 'Salisbury Plain' poem, his own tragedy *The Borderers*, and some portion of *The Ruined Cottage*, moving in giant bounds from a Spenserian, to a Shakespearean, to a uniquely Wordsworthian mode of treating such themes as the psychology of guilt, sorrow, and human suffering—themes Coleridge was struggling to embody in *Osorio*. The completion of *Osorio* and its radical deepening owe much to that visit to Racedown, when Coleridge heard *The Borderers* and read its prefatory essay on the psychology of crime (Newlyn 1986: 9–15). Contrariwise, a year later, Coleridge's similar progression from the rhetoric of *Religious Musings* and *The Destiny of Nations*, through the somewhat stiff blank verse of *The Eolian Harp*, to the perfected ruminative tone of *Frost at Midnight*, will give Wordsworth the vehicle he needs for *Tintern Abbey*. Without Wordsworth's memories of childhood, Coleridge would not have had the imagery for the final movement of his poem; without Coleridge, Wordsworth might not have evolved the appropriate form for his very different view of the interaction between landscape, spirit and the human mind. The gift exchange is beyond doubt. Yet the most ambitious attempt to blend their talents and their methods, in co-authoring *The Ancient Mariner*, was—thanks to deep divergence in their approaches both to symbol and to characterization— wholly abortive and ultimately destructive. Despite contributing much of the plot, the slaying of the albatross, the idea of spectral persecution and the only description of the mariner himself, 'our respective manners', Wordsworth later said, 'proved so widely different' that he would be merely a 'clog' on the enterprise (Wordsworth 2007: 12).

A mildly amusing failure became much less amusing when Wordsworth, following the broadly hostile reception of the 1798 version of Coleridge's poem, not only demoted it from first to penultimate place in volume 1 of the second edition of *Lyrical Ballads*, but included a hurtful justification of its relegation: 'The Poem of my Friend has indeed great defects; first, that the principal person has no distinct character...: secondly, that he does not act...: thirdly, that the events having no necessary connection do not produce each other; and lastly, that the imagery is somewhat too laboriously accumulated'. The poem does, Wordsworth concedes, contain 'many delicate touches of passion', 'beautiful images', 'unusual felicity of language', and versification both 'harmonious and artfully varied'.[3] Seventeen years later, in *Biographia Literaria*, Coleridge responded with a large scale tabulation of Wordsworth's defects and excellences, in much the same ratio. In December 1818, he still remembered and resented the Wordsworth household's 'cold praise and effective discouragement of every attempt of mine to roll onward in a distinct current of my own—who *admitted* that the Ancient Mariner [and] the Christabel... were not without merit, but were abundantly anxious to acquit their judgements of any blindness to the very numerous defects' (*CL* 4: 888).

'Not without merit', however, is less than candid, as is the case with much of the sniping in this relationship. In fact, both Wordsworths professed themselves 'exceedingly delighted' with *Christabel* when they heard what there was of it in October 1800 (*DWJ*, 5 October) and they were ferocious in proclaiming its superiority to Scott's later imitation (*EY* 632–3). There were just two problems. First, the volume was at press, the poem was not finished, and (despite Wordsworth assuming some of Coleridge's debts in an effort to enable him to proceed with it) there was no prospect of three further cantos being produced in time. And second, the volume for which it was intended was now overwhelmingly Wordsworth's, Coleridge having written none of his assigned titles ('done nothing' as Dorothy put it). Nevertheless, the exclusion of *Christabel* from *Lyrical Ballads* (1800), and its substitution by *Michael*, has entered the mythology of Wordsworth–Coleridge relations as the primary evidence for the notion that Wordsworth destroyed Coleridge as a poet.[4] Wordsworth in 1800 was moving firmly towards a pastoral

---

[3] *Lyrical Ballads* (1800, Volume 1: n. pag.). The note follows a three-page defence of *The Thorn* at the close of the volume. J. C. C. Mays has remarked that this 'still remains the most cogent criticism of the poem' (*PW* 1: 366).

[4] See Buchan (1963: 346–66) for an instance of this view. For a popular version see Adam Sisman's professedly 'non-partisan' account: 'Ambition blinded [Wordsworth] to the predicament of his friend, who had helped him in so many ways to reach the commanding point where he now stood. Coleridge's prostration made it easy for Wordsworth to walk all over him' (Sisman 2006: 315).

mode of writing, as Coleridge flirted more and more with the Gothic, and it is entirely possible that both poets came to the reluctant conclusion that *Christabel* would (even supposing that Coleridge could be induced to finish it) be discordant within the new collection.

One can read *Christabel* as a poem so interrogative of narrative cliché that it suits the purpose of an intrinsically parodic volume extremely well, though such readings are very recent (see, as an exemplary case, Swann 1991). Like *The Thorn*, and *Old Man Travelling*, and *Goody Blake*, and *The Idiot Boy*, *Christabel* challenges contemporary reading assumptions. Yet the projected endings later described by Coleridge adumbrate a poem not only far too long for a joint collection but threatening to revert from interrogation of, to complicity with, all the clichés of story-telling.[5] The matter is not decidable. But interestingly, symptomatically perhaps, in all the partisan discussions that have taken place of this matter, two points are forgotten. Wordsworth continued to encourage Coleridge to finish *Christabel*. And both poets seem to have believed that a five-book poem was on the point of being realized, and that it would be published lavishly by Longman and Rees (*EY*, 321 n). 'Christabel is to be printed at the *Bulmerian* press, with Vignettes' writes Wordsworth to Thomas Poole on 9 April 1801, adding: 'I long to have the book in my hand it will be such a Beauty' (*EY*, 324). Both may have agreed at the time that the poem, precisely *because* Coleridge was swimming 'in a current of my own', as he later put it, would disrupt the now decidedly pastoral ideology of *Lyrical Ballads*. But like many literary myths this one is far too deeply ingrained in the culture ever to be successfully challenged.

That Wordsworth—or some hidden element in the chemistry of the relationship—stifled Coleridge's poetic voice may be true. But the idea that Coleridge was the weaker personality, which is in some sense assumed by most accounts of their relationship, is bizarre. Coleridge, after all, pursued his own path through life, subordinating many lives—including his own family's—to his own needs, and came to be regarded as the arbiter of Wordsworth's merit. Wordsworth accepted Coleridge's status in that regard, to a degree which borders upon self-immolation and devoted the major part of his lifetime to a labour ordained for him by Coleridge. He undertook to write, at Coleridge's behest, a long philosophical poem expressive of the younger poet's views to which he strove (not always unsuccessfully) to subordinate his own.

Indeed, Coleridge, having once decided that Wordsworth would make the ideal conduit for his own speculative interests, quickly set about reforming him to that end. Coleridge's 'Wordsworth' is a creation of Coleridge's need, an ideal Wordsworth liberated from the accidents of the existing Wordsworth's particular

---

[5] See for instance Gillman (1838), 301–2.

concerns. Wordsworth may have been a Shakespeare without the 'inequalities' (*CL* 1: 325, June 1797), and an amiable 'Giant' (*CL* 1: 391, March 1798) but the amiable giant needed considerable reformation if he was to become capable of Coleridge's ambition for him—capable as Coleridge says towards the close of *Biographia* (a decade after Coleridge had heard *The Prelude*) 'of producing...the FIRST GENUINE PHILOSOPHIC POEM'.

The process of transforming Wordsworth began early, but did not run smoothly. At least 'a *Semi*-atheist' in 1796, Wordsworth has progressed by May 1798 to being one who 'loves and venerates...Christianity', though Coleridge admits 'I wish, he did more' (*CL* 1: 216, 410). In May 1799, with Wordsworth out of his therapeutic reach, Coleridge is lamenting that the amiable giant 'has hurtfully segregated & isolated his being' (to Poole, *CL* 1: 491). This develops into an anxiety, by October 1803—when the contrast between Wordsworth's domestic happiness and Coleridge's discontent is extreme—'lest a Film should rise, and thicken on his moral Eye' (*CL* 2: 1013). The Notebooks are still more illuminating. Consider this revealing metaphor of a Wordsworth safely immured and subject to almost monastic discipline:

I am sincerely glad that he has bidden farewell to all small poems—& is devoting himself to his great work—grandly imprisoning while it deifies his Attention & Feelings within the Sacred Circle and Temple Walls of great Objects & elevated conceptions.   (*CN* 1: 1546)

In the same month, October 1803, in a further passage on his frustration with Wordsworth's faults Coleridge decides that to idealize is an 'instinct of all fine minds'.

And what was all this?—Evidently the instinct of all fine minds to *totalise*—to make *a perfectly congruous whole* of every character—& pain at the being obliged to admit incongruities.   (*CN* 1: 1606)

Wordsworth's incongruities proved harder to eradicate than Coleridge first supposed, and a later and painfully moving entry (October 1805) combines a comparison between Wordsworth and Empedocles, with a desire that Wordsworth might be perfected by an infusion of Coleridge's own spirit:

To W. in the progression of Spirit / once Simonides, or Empedocles or both in one? O that my spirit purged by Death of its weaknesses, which are alas! my identity might flow into thine, and live and act in thee, and be Thou.   (*CN* 2: 2712)

Such desires are more than latently aggressive, they are the sublime of egotism. What Wordsworth is not supposed to do, whether progressing towards his ideal form or not, is find the self-confidence to pronounce, for himself, let alone to Coleridge, on 'points of morals, wisdom and the sacred muses' (*CN* 2: 2750). And when he does so, in the Preface of 1815, Raimonda Modiano argues in this volume, the rebuke takes the form of *Biographia Literaria*.

DIVERGENT 'IMAGINATIONS'

Since I have written elsewhere on the forensic tone and critical obtuseness of *Biographia* where Wordsworth's more experimental poems are concerned (Gravil 1984), and since Stephen Parrish (1973) and Don Bialostosky (1978, 1984) have treated the subject definitively, I will merely summarize the matter here. Wordsworth's response to *Biographia* is recorded by Crabb Robinson: it had 'given him no pleasure. The praise he considered extravagant, and the censure inconsiderate' (*Diary*, 4 December 1817; *On Books*, 1: 213). This response is taken by many scholars as proof of Wordsworth's ingratitude: of course—it is implied—Wordsworth regarded any censure as inconsiderate, however much praise accompanied it. But he was not alone. Crabb Robinson seems to have harboured doubts about Coleridge's judiciousness—'of Wordsworth, I believe, Coleridge judges under personal feelings of unkindness' (*Diary*, 21 December 1822; *On Books*, 1: 288). The waywardness of the *Biographia* critique in the eyes of some informed contemporaries is confirmed by William Whewell's remark in July 1817: 'Even yet I doubt whether Wordsworth would allow that man to understand his poems who talks of them as Coleridge does' and (intriguingly, in view of the *Christabel* affair) 'How the man who wrote the critique on Wordsworth could write "Christabel" I cannot conceive' (Woof 2001: 984). The effect of a consecutive reading of the critical passages in the *Biographia* seems to have convinced even John Shawcross—whose 1907 edition points candidly to several of Coleridge's distortions—that 'something ... must have occurred to pervert Coleridge's vision, if he could really believe that in his criticisms in the *Biographia Literaria* he was serving Wordsworth's cause (and his cause was his own also) to the best of his ability' (Coleridge 1907, xcv). With the main judgement here I am in full agreement: the parenthesis, however, is highly questionable.

The poem to which Coleridge's method proves least adequate is, not surprisingly, Wordsworth's dramatization of the consciousness of an ancient mariner in *The Thorn*. What is good in *The Thorn*, Coleridge contends, is those parts 'which might as well or still better have proceeded from the poet's own imagination'. Those parts attributed to 'the supposed narrator' are felt to be 'sinkings from the height to which the poet had previously lifted them' (*BL* 2: 36–8). The lines Coleridge wishes to excise—'the last couplet of the third stanza; the seven last lines of the tenth; and the five following stanzas, with the exception of the four admirable lines at the commencement of the fourteenth'—establish the narrator's obsession with measurements, his peculiar mode of entrapping the curiosity of his interlocutor, his role as purveyor of rumour, his echoes of communal attitudes to Martha's plight, and the revelation, in stanza fifteen, that the story of Martha Ray is in large part a tissue of poisonous conjecture. By wishing that all of the poem were told by the poet himself, Coleridge shows himself unable to grasp that the primary subject of this poem is (as Wordsworth's own published note makes amply clear) the narrator's humanly disabling imagination. Indeed, Coleridge's failure to examine the poem as a whole, or to look at its parts in the light of that whole, in clear defiance of the principle outlined in his *Logic*,[6] is probably grounded in the fact that one radical difference between Wordsworth and Coleridge lies in their understanding of imagination. *The Thorn* is one of several lyrical ballads (*Old Man Travelling* is another) which embody a critique of Coleridge's understanding of imagination, and in this case Wordsworth's note (provokingly adjacent to his note on the defects of *The Ancient Mariner*) makes that critique dangerously, perhaps offensively, explicit. A man who sees a heap of moss as an infant's grave may be echoing the original act of creation in the Infinite I AM (not that Coleridge in 1798 had taken refuge in such hermetic formulae) but he is quite as likely to be pathologically deluded. Nor is Coleridge's treatment of *The Thorn* a unique failure of critical intelligence. The *Anecdote for Fathers*, *Simon Lee*, *Alice Fell* (one of Lamb's favourites), *The Beggars*, and *The Sailor's Mother* are all adjudged good only in those lines where the poet allegedly 'interposes the music of his own thoughts'. The remarkable methods employed in these poems of encounter do not register on Coleridge's apparatus. Even 'The Idiot Boy', Coleridge agrees can plausibly be described as 'a laughable burlesque on the blindness of anile dotage' (though it remains, on grounds unspecified, 'that fine poem').

One should not be surprised, therefore, to discover in a letter of November 1817, that Coleridge's dislike of the *Lyrical Ballads* goes back at least to 1798: 'To the faults and defects [of Wordsworth's poems] I have been far more alive than his detractors, even from the first publication of the Lyrical Ballads—tho' for a long course of years my opinions were sacred to his own ear' (*CL* 4: 780). When he writes to Godwin in March 1801, that he would judge 'of a man's heart and intellect' by the degree of admiration accorded to Wordsworth's poetry, it is the blank verse of 1800 that he has in mind. It pained him that Lamb and Fox failed this moral test; Fox perversely preferring 'The Idiot Boy', 'Goody Blake', 'The Mad Mother', and 'We Are Seven'. In July 1802, he is complaining to Southey about the daring humbleness of language and versification, matter-of-factness, and prolixity in some recent poems, and suspecting that 'somewhere there is a radical difference in our theoretical opinions concerning poetry' (*CL* 2: 830). By October 1803, despite the sacredness of such opinions to Wordsworth's own ear, he is confessing to Poole his 'feelings of hostility to the plan of several of the Poems in the L. Ballads' (*CL* 2: 1013).

Chapter 22 of *Biographia*, to make amends for a gratuitous display of Wordsworth's characteristic defects over the previous 100 pages (the defects are inconstancy of style, matter-of-factness, prolixity, bombast, and 'an undue predilection

---

[6] Good criticism, Coleridge says, depends on the insight that 'an examination and appreciation of the end, [is] necessarily antecedent to the formation of the rules, supplying at once the principle of the rules themselves and of their application to the given subject' (*Logic* 67).

for the dramatic form'), concludes by enumerating, in some fourteen pages, his correspondent 'excellencies'. These consist in 'an austere purity of language both grammatically and logically'; 'a correspondent weight and sanity of the Thoughts and Sentiments' (some of which Coleridge extracts, like any reviewer of the period); 'the sinewy strength and originality of single lines and paragraphs, and the frequent *curiosa felicitas* of his diction' (a modest achievement compared with Milton's 'glorious paragraphs and systems of harmony'); 'the perfect truth of nature in his images and descriptions' (an excellence cancelled out by Wordsworth's correspondent defect, namely his supposed 'matter-of-factness'); and 'a meditative pathos as a contemplator of human suffering, rather than a fellow-sufferer' (a self-interested judgement, arising directly from Coleridge's most rancorous notebook entries). Until we come to 'the gift of IMAGINATION in the highest and strictest sense of the word' the list is faintly damning, and whatever that gift consists in it is not what Wordsworth meant by it.

This is no place to debate the meaning of 'IMAGINATION in the highest and strictest sense of the word' or whether Coleridge's succinct definitions in chapter 13 have any bearing on this remark in chapter 22, or indeed are meant to have any bearing at all on critical practice. With Mary Warnock (1976: 72–130) I incline to the view that Wordsworth's theory of imagination (which is found in *The Prelude*, not in his prose: see *Prelude* (1805) 2: 237–80, 295–302; 321–41, 377–95 and the strictures in 8: 511–623) is both prior to and more coherent than Coleridge's. Wordsworthian Imagination is, in the first instance, as in Coleridge's definition of secondary imagination, a power that 'dissolves, diffuses, dissipates'; it is a solvent. To avoid confusion, however, Wordsworth has the good sense to call *primary* imagination, by which we constitute our world, by another name altogether—namely, 'the first poetic spirit of our human life'. In Coleridge's definitions secondary imagination is of the same 'kind' as primary imagination but coexists 'with the conscious will'. In Wordsworth's account it tends to willfulness. Wordsworth's poetry recognizes that what Coleridge came to call secondary imagination, the power of the mind to obliterate or suspend what is presented to it, in favour of its own constructs, or merely 'to idealize and to unify' is both existentially definitive, *and* constitutive of anxiety.[7] That is why Wordsworth's discussion throughout *The Prelude* is sceptical of imaginings which refuse to be anchored to empirical realities, and critical of imaginations which abuse the lordship and mastery of mind, *especially* perhaps when they exercise what Coleridge called 'the instinct of all fine minds to totalize' (*CN*, 1: 1606).

Three points in *Biographia* may tell us what Coleridge finds imaginative in Wordsworth. First and most notoriously—so notoriously that it is often felt to be bad manners to refer to it—chapter 22 offers as both as 'an instance and an

---

[7] For Coleridge on consciousness in this sense see Anthony Harding, 'Coleridge, the Afterlife and the Meaning of "Hades"', *Studies in Philology* 96:2 (1999), 204–23, 217, 218–19.

illustration' of imagination 'in the highest and strictest sense of the word', that the poet 'does indeed to all thought and to all objects'

> add the gleam,
> The light that never was, on sea or land,
> The consecration, and the poet's dream.

This state of illusion, or 'dream-gleam', unfortunately, is what Wordsworth wrote the *Elegiac Stanzas* to repudiate. Second, from what he says in chapter 18 (70–1), Coleridge appears to admire as imaginative that similar 'visionary state' into which his sensibility had thrust the poet in the first stanza of *The Sailor's Mother*: in this stanza Wordsworth's imagination struggles to idealize and unify the figure of the sailor's mother as a 'Majestic' Roman matron—listening, as it were, to 'the music of his own thoughts'—before empirical data awaken him to the woman's reality. Thirdly, and most curiously he claims in chapter 4 to have first understood the nature of imagination when exposed to a recitation of *Salisbury Plain*.

Salisbury Plain is the subject of a most surprising eulogy in *Biographia*, the most sustained passage of praise for Wordsworth in the volume. What impressed Coleridge on first hearing was:

the union of deep feeling with profound thought; the fine balance of truth in observing with the imaginative faculty in modifying the objects observed; and above all the original gift of spreading the tone, the atmosphere, and with it the depth and height of the idea world around forms, incidents, and situations, of which for the common view, custom had bedimmed all the luster, had dried up the sparkle and the dew drops . . .

Such powers characterize a mind (he is now quoting himself from *The Friend*) 'that feels the riddle of the universe and may help to unravel it'. From this he proceeds to 'the character and privilege of genius', and from this to the suspicion—still dated from his earliest meditations on Wordsworth's excellence as displayed in *Salisbury Plain*—that 'fancy and imagination were two distinct and widely different faculties' (*BL* 1: 80–2).

Of course there is in the 'Salisbury Plain' poetry evidence of imaginative power. The problem is: how can Coleridge describe it in the terms he uses? Here is part of a representative stanza from the 1793–4 text (Wordsworth 1975, 23):

> He stood the only creature in the wild
> On whom the elements their rage could wreak,
> Save that the bustard of those limits bleak,
> Shy tenant, seeing there a mortal wight
> At that dread hour, outsent a mournful shriek
> And half upon the ground, with strange affright,
> Forced hard against the wind a thick unwieldy flight.

Wordsworth here contrives to render the strange flight of the bustard and the distraught consciousness of the man in the same moment. It is an early instance of his power to make consciousness inundate landscape. It is not, however, an example of how to spread 'the tone, the atmosphere, and with it the height and depth of the ideal world around forms, incidents, and situations' which is what Coleridge finds, or claims to remember having found, somewhere (characteristically unspecified) in a poem where no other reader has found any such thing. Curiously, the imagination in this instance lies in the dramatization of a consciousness akin to but not identical with the poet's own, which is one aspect of Wordsworth's art that Coleridge specifically deprecates as a species of ventriloquism (*BL* 2: 135).

Disappointment with *The Prelude* and *The Excursion*

Most of us, I imagine, would, since his agile essay on the subject, answer W. B. Gallie's 1947 question, 'Is *The Prelude* a philosophical poem?' in the affirmative. In *To William Wordsworth* Coleridge comes close to agreeing. In sober prose, however, he categorically and repeatedly refused it that accolade.

In a remarkable letter to Wordsworth expressing disappointment with *The Excursion* (30 May 1815) Coleridge first quotes lines 12–47 of *To William Wordsworth*, so that we cannot doubt his total recall of *The Prelude* and its effect, then flatly proclaims '*This* I considered as "the Excursion".' The second instalment of *The Recluse* he had, he claims, anticipated

as commencing with you set down and settled in an abiding Home and that with the Description of that Home you were to begin a *Philosophical Poem*, the result and fruits of a Spirit so fram'd & so disciplin'd as had been told in the former.   (*CL* 4: 574)

This, unlike *The Prelude*, he had expected to exhibit 'the matter and arrangement of Philosophy':

I supposed you first to have meditated the faculties of Man in the abstract . . . demonstrating that the Senses were living growths and developements [*sic*] of the Mind & Spirit in a much juster as well as higher sense, than the mind can be said to be formed by the Senses.

It is hard to say whether Coleridge felt in 1815 that *The Prelude* had in any sense addressed itself to this question, or even marshalled some potentially useful phenomenological data, but the passage leaves no doubt that it lacks either 'the matter' or 'arrangement' of philosophy.

In 1804 Coleridge had prophesied immortality to *The Recluse* as long as it turned out to be 'a Faithful Transcript of [Wordsworth's] own most august & innocent life, of his own habitual Feeling and Modes of seeing and hearing' (To Sharp, *CL* 2: 1034). There is no proviso here about the poem needing the 'matter' and 'arrangement' of philosophy. By 1815, however, its purpose had become explicitly the enunciation of Coleridge's view of life. And this remained the case. He claimed in his *Table Talk*, for 21 July 1832, that the point of *The Recluse* was to infer and reveal 'the proof of, and necessity for, the whole state of man and society being subject to, and illustrative of, a redemptive process in operation', or 'in substance, what I have been all my life doing in my system of philosophy' (*TT* [*CC*] 2: 177).

The remainder of Coleridge's 1815 specification for the philosophical poem, it can hardly be said too emphatically, is not merely tangential to Wordsworth's proper concerns as a poet of the human mind, but wholly and radically incompatible with the argument of *The Prelude* and of the so-called 'Prospectus' to *The Recluse*. Wordsworth—and one must take the letter seriously and read it attentively if one is to grasp the fundamental intellectual dyspathy between two poets whose brilliant friendship had little to do with philosophical concurrence—was, in Coleridge's recollection,

to have affirmed a Fall in some sense, as a fact...the reality of which is attested by Experience & Conscience...and not disguising the sore evils, under which the whole Creation groans, to point out however a manifest Scheme of Redemption from this Slavery...and to conclude by a grand didactic swell on the necessary identity of a true Philosophy with true Religion...(*CL* 4: 575)

Nobody but Coleridge has ever supposed that Wordsworth, as opposed to Coleridge's 'Wordsworth', found the reality of a 'Fall' attested by conscience; or heard the whole Creation groaning for deliverance, or found manifest a scheme of redemption; or felt convinced of 'the necessary identity of true Philosophy with true Religion'.

My suggestion that Coleridge denied to *The Prelude* the status of 'a Philosophical poem' conflicts with one's sense that he valued it above *The Excursion*, and saw in it philosophic themes philosophically handled. We have not only the late observation that it was 'superior...upon the whole, to the Excursion' (a not unqualified commendation found in the *Table Talk*, 21 July 1832, as above), but also the fresher testimony of January 1807, in his poem *To William Wordsworth: composed on the night after his recitation of a poem on the growth of an individual mind*. Wordsworth's 'prophetic lay', he then recorded, was a pioneering investigation of human growth, of nature and nurture, of perception and of the creativity of perception, which probably sounds adequately philosophical to most of us:

> Of the foundations and the building up
> Of a Human Spirit thou has dared to tell
> What may be told, to the understanding mind
> Revealable.

> (*PW* 1: 816)

By calling *The Prelude* 'a poem on the growth of an individual mind' and by referring to its story as prophetic, not historic, Coleridge recognizes that while he has been listening to a poetic *Bildungsroman*, and a crisis narrative, he has also been listening to an account of human possibilities which is intended to be normative, not idiosyncratic. He gives particular weight to what he sees as the poem's closing theme: 'Then (last strain) / Of Duty, chosen Laws controlling choice, / Action and joy!' And insofar as the concept of 'duty' could be expressed by both poets in such Kantian terms as Wordsworth's obedience 'to paramount impulse not to be withstood' or to 'a moral law established by himself (Wordsworth 1974, 2: 24), Coleridge—properly, I suggest—recognizes in Wordsworth's concluding argument his own thinking.

What he could not have approved is Wordsworth's failure to recognize divine agency in *The Prelude* as a whole or its closing meditation in particular. An apt commentary on the Snowdon meditation, which was not written as such but may nonetheless express Coleridge's sense of it, was penned by Thomas Carlyle:

According to Fichte, there is indeed a 'Divine Idea' pervading the visible Universe; which visible Universe is indeed but its symbol and sensible manifestation, having in itself no meaning, or even true existence independent of it. To the mass of men this Divine Idea of the world lies hidden: yet to discern it, to seize it, and live wholly in it, is the condition of all genuine virtue, knowledge, freedom; and the end therefore of all spiritual effort in every age.[8]

One might see both Coleridge and Wordsworth meeting on this Fichtean ground, except that Wordsworth's version of this 'genuine virtue, knowledge, freedom' is defiantly presented as the gift of material Nature, of imagination working in creative alliance with all that it beholds. Nature as merely 'the language which thy God utters', the Nature of *Frost at Midnight*, remained for Wordsworth an inassimilable notion, and at the close of *The Prelude*, Nature herself is still capable of inspiring insights into what he sometimes called 'the Soul of things', sometimes the 'Soul of all the worlds', which to Wordsworth—nurtured in empirical intercourse with palpable rocks, water, stones, and trees—is the common ground of Nature and of Man.[9]

When Coleridge listened in January 1807 to Wordsworth reading his long poem, he had recently written to Thomas Clarkson in terms which leave us in no doubt at

---

[8] Thomas Carlyle, 'The State of German Literature', *Edinburgh Review*, 1827. The next sentence offers Carlyle's version of a 'clerisy', more in Emersonian than in Coleridgean mould: 'Literary men are the appointed interpreters of this Divine Idea; a perpetual priesthood, we might say, standing forth generation after generation, as the dispensers and living types of God's everlasting wisdom.'

[9] 'There was a time', Wordsworth 1995, 6; *Excursion*, 9: 15.

all what his real judgement must have been of Wordsworth's misty allusions to the deity in both instalments of 'The Recluse':

But all the actions of the Deity are intensely real or substantial / therefore the action of Love, by which the Father contemplates the Son, and the Son the Father, is equally real with the Father and the Son ... and neither of these Three *can* be conceived *apart*, nor *confusedly*—so that the Idea of God involves that of a Tri-unity; and as that Unity or Indivisibility is the intensest, and the Archetype, yea, the very substance and element of all other Unity and Union, so is that Distinction the most manifest and indestructible of all distinctions—and Being, Intellect, and Action, which in their absoluteness are the Father, the Word, and the Spirit will and must for ever be and remain the 'genera generalissima' of all Knowledge. (Letter to Clarkson, 13 October 1806, *CL*, 2: 1195–6)

By way of corrective, perhaps, he concludes his account of Wordsworth's hymn to self-sufficiency with the words 'I found myself in prayer.'

When Wordsworth published *The Excursion* in 1814 he gave little sign of having made up his mind about personified transcendence, indeed he robustly advertised his continuing ambivalence in the 'Prospectus'. While this claimed in line 15 that his theme included 'melancholy Fear subdued by Faith', the implications of this capitalized 'Faith' are instantly nullified. For him, we learn in lines 33–4, Jehovah and all his angels are but another provisional myth by which people have figured to themselves the unfigurable—'I pass them unalarmed'. In the end, Wordsworth simply would not totalize. The great project succeeded in part: the poet of *The Excursion* is one who has largely deserted the 'Lanes and allies' of the affective life in which it pained Coleridge to see him wander, and abandoned his propensities for the dramatic mode and the matter-of-fact. He still decides, in a way that would have irked Coleridge, to approach the great truths of human life empirically, by examining concrete instances of rural existence—sociological instances, as Regina Hewitt argues (1997)—but he views those instances through a clerical prism. This prism, however, was not enough.

To grasp the significance of Coleridge's disappointment in *The Excursion* and his decision to broadcast that disappointment in *Biographia*, one needs to triangulate Coleridge's response with those of Jeffrey and Lamb. What Francis Jeffrey deplores in his famous review of *The Excursion* (beginning 'This will never do...') is the poet's incorrigibility. In 1802 the Edinburgh despot had denounced the Lakers for their 'splenetic and idle discontent with the existing institutions of society', and for failing to grasp that the standards of poetry 'were fixed long ago, by certain inspired writers, whose authority it is no longer lawful to call into question'.[10] In 1814 he sees *The Excursion* as more of the same: as reaffirming the poet's class hostility, his lack of decorum, his defiant prosaisms and—worst of all for this Caledonian positivist—his uncorrected flights of mysticism. In this, Lamb's response confirms Jeffrey, though positively in tone. Prior to *Prometheus Unbound* or *The Prelude*, however

---

[10] *Edinburgh Review*, No. 1, October 1802, 63.

difficult this may be to grasp today, *The Excursion* was Romanticism's primary exposition. 'Its leading moral', says Lamb, 'is to abate the pride of the calculating understanding, and to reinstate the imagination and the affections in those seats from which modern philosophy has laboured too successfully to expel them.'[11]

It was also controversially democratic. According to Jeffrey in 1802, the author of *Lyrical Ballads* had failed to grasp that 'the love, or grief, or indignation of an enlightened and refined character, is not only expressed in a different language, but *is in itself a different emotion* from the love, or grief, or anger of a clown, a tradesman, or a market wench. The things themselves are radically and obviously distinct.'[12] Consistently with this essentialism Jeffrey now complains that, though the tale of Margaret has considerable pathos, one has first to get over 'the repugnance excited by the triteness of its incidents and the lowness of its objects', not to mention that it is narrated by *a Pedlar*. What most now prize as one of the great tragic poems in the language, powerful in its reliance on naturalistic detail and its entire avoidance of sentimentality, Jeffrey criticized for its 'Mawkish sentiments' and for 'detail of preposterous minuteness'.[13]

On this point, Coleridge's public verdict in *Biographia Literaria* not only colludes with Jeffrey, but does so by plagiarizing him. First, however, he makes a feint of solidarity with the poet. Where Jeffrey asks 'Did Mr Wordsworth really imagine, that his favourite doctrines were likely to gain anything in point of effect or authority by being put into the mouth of a person accustomed to higgle about tape, or brass sleeve-buttons?' Coleridge points out, properly enough, that the tape and buttons come from Jeffrey's imagination, not the poet's (*BL* 2: 118). Nevertheless, Coleridge asks, 'Is there one word...attributed to the pedlar in *The Excursion* characteristic of a pedlar? One sentiment that might not more plausibly...have proceeded from any wise and beneficent old man of a rank or profession in which the language of learning and refinement are *natural* [my emphasis] and to be expected?' The choice of profession involves Wordsworth, Coleridge says, in 'minute matters of fact, not unlike those furnished for the obituary of a magazine by the friends of some obscure ornament of society lately deceased in some obscure town'. Then he quotes precisely the passage selected by Jeffrey to ridicule such matter-of-factness (134–5). On the business of whether there is 'one human heart', or whether a pedlar can have such 'language, feelings, sentiments and information' (134) as this pedlar possesses, Coleridge and Jeffrey are as one. Pedlars, like shepherds, Jeffrey and Coleridge are agreed, are members of 'a known and abiding class' (*BL* 2: 47), whose characteristics are essentially fixed. A plausible pedlar could not have the same feelings as a man of culture, or for that matter, speak the same

---

[11] *Quarterly Review*, Vol. 12, October 1814, 107.
[12] *Edinburgh Review*, No. 1, 66, my emphasis.
[13] *Edinburgh Review*, Vol. 24, November 1814, 7.

language, for the best part of language is the product of philosophers, not of 'clowns or shepherds' (2: 40).

Book 9 of *The Excursion*, nevertheless, constitutes Wordsworth's most overt attempt to fulfil Coleridge's designs, however much covert resistance is built into its curiously binary construction—the last book follows the unusual form of thesis, antithesis, and vague hints of a deferred synthesis. The Wanderer and the Pastor, supposedly allies in the attempt to rehabilitate the Solitary, come to express contrary views of human life and possibilities, polarized between the (Lambish) natural Quakerism of the one and the (Coleridgean) pietism of the other. Put briefly, the Wanderer—suddenly rejuvenated—preaches by and large an Alfoxden vision of 'the one Life', and of how we have all of us 'one human heart'. He invokes that active principle which circulates through all things and is 'the Soul of all the worlds', which nameless 'something far more deeply interfused' (inspired more by Lucretius, Virgil, Newton, and the *philosophes* than by anything in Coleridge's philosophy) underwrites the humanist faith of *Tintern Abbey* and the ascent of Snowdon. In this faith, all man needs to listen to is what emerges from himself, and the only law he needs to obey is 'the law / Of life, and hope and action' (*Excursion* 9: 127–8). From this premise the Wanderer develops a view of human life as progressive, offering a sort of vision of permanent revolution: a programme based on the familiar *Prelude* idea that our real home is 'the world which is the world of all of us', and that our desire is for 'something evermore about to be'. The Pastor, contrariwise, sees human beings as bewildered and dark, able to hope for nothing better than law and order, peace and quiet, and (the sooner the better) ultimate release.

AIDS TO REFLECTION; OR, INTIMATIONS AS ANTIDOTE TO TINTERN ABBEY

It is possible of course that Coleridge's confident 1804 prophesy for 'The Recluse', that a 'faithful transcript' of Wordsworth's habitual feelings would be tantamount to a versification of Coleridge's own leading ideas was encouraged by a poem first copied into a manuscript volume for Coleridge to take to Malta in 1804, published in 1807 simply as 'Ode', and later sub-titled *Intimations of Immortality from Recollections of Early Childhood*.

For many readers of Wordsworth, *Intimations* is an anomaly with the oeuvre. For Coleridge (as for Emerson and Hopkins, among other Platonist admirers) it was the inescapable text. The climactic eleventh essay of Coleridge's series 'On the Grounds of Morals and Religion' in *The Friend* takes as its starting point the ninth stanza of the ode, with its mysterious thanks and praise for

> Those shadowy recollections,
> Which, be they what they may,
> Are yet the fountain light or all our day.

Coleridge's soaring (and not always intelligible) commentary on those 'shadowy recollections' (presumably, for the poem itself does not specify, recollections of 'God who is our home') leads to the suggestion that 'enlightening enquiry' will lead man at last 'to comprehend gradually and progressively the relation of each to the other, of each to all, and of all to each' (*Friend*, 1: 511). His essay finds in the notion of a 'world of spirit'—which to Coleridge is the ode's subject—nothing less than 'the substantiating principle of all true wisdom, the satisfactory solution of all the contradictions of human nature, of the whole riddle of the world' (1: 524). Such mental bombast reminds one that Coleridge allegedly discovered in 'Salisbury Plain', in 1796, an imaginative power 'that feels the riddle of the universe and may help to unravel it'.

In *Biographia*, however, Coleridge is in fact surprisingly reticent on the subject of the ode's merits. Its fifth and ninth stanzas (more dismemberment) are singled out for effusive praise, but, Coleridge says, will be found intelligible only by a small class of readers, those who have 'been accustomed to watch the flux and reflux of their inmost nature, to venture at times into the twilight realms of consciousness, and to feel a deep interest in modes of inmost being, to which they know that the attributes of time and space are inapplicable and alien, but which cannot be conveyed, save in symbols of time and space' (2: 153). For such readers, the sense of the Ode as a whole is '*perfectly plain*' (2: 147)—so plain that he feels no need to expand upon it.

Coleridge is presumably attending to Wordsworth's implied or even elided argument for personal immortality—there is no overt argument in *Intimations of Immortality* except in the title, which appears to have been an afterthought[14]— which can only be 'there' for one who is predisposed to a Christian Platonism, or, to tie that down a little, for one who reads the poem in the light of Plato's *Phaedo*, the *Enneads* of Plotinus, and the 32 tidy lines of Henry Vaughan's poem about pre-existence and post-existence, *The Retreat* (1650). For the content of that implied argument I refer the reader to an important essay by Anya Taylor, which pointed out that Coleridge accepted the comfortable argument for Immortality shared by Anselm, Ficinus, and David Hartley, that 'our feelings must have a purpose', and our appetites an adequate object.[15] This curious logic—'I desire, therefore gratification must exist'—seems to have satisfied both Coleridge and Wordsworth.

---

[14] In *Poems in Two Volumes* it was titled simply 'Ode'. Only the sequence of poems—the Ode follows elegies for Charles James Fox and for John Wordsworth (in Peele Castle)—establish the speaker as one who has 'kept watch o'er man's mortality' and who is prepared to entertain the idea that death means, in some sense, returning to the author of our being. Most helpfully, the Fox elegy asks why we should mourn if death means merely 'That man, who is from God sent forth, / Doth yet again to God return?'.

[15] 'Religious Readings of the Immortality Ode', *SEL*, 26:4 (1986), 639, 638. See also my more extended treatment of the argument of the Ode in *The First 'Poem to Coleridge': a Dialogic Reading of Wordsworth's 'Intimations' Ode*, Tirril: Humanities-Ebooks, 2007.

Certainly Wordsworth in 1810 seems to have trusted in what he refers to as 'a fore-feeling of immortality'.[16]

Coleridge was both the earliest advocate of this poem and its greatest calumniator. Ralph Waldo Emerson would have read and pondered Coleridge's citations from the ode in *The Friend* and *Biographia*, and may have re-read the ode with the benefit of having also read *Aids to Reflection* in Marsh's 1829 edition. Unlike Coleridge, however, Emerson or his formidable aunt Mary may have noticed that the poem's epigraph from Virgil—'*Paulo majora canamus* / let us sing a nobler song'—draws attention to the part of the poem that Coleridge had publicly derided as 'mental bombast' and makes it the crux of the poem. The 4th *Eclogue*, like *Intimations*, celebrates a gifted child, nurtured by 'the smile / Of parent's eyes'. Hartley's prototype in Virgil's *Eclogue* is perceived as one with whom 'the iron age will pass away / The golden age in all the earth be born'. Stanza 8 of the *Ode* offers a somewhat Nietzschean vision of the child as a new beginning, a sacred yes, a self-propelling wheel, 'yet glorious in the might / Of heaven born freedom on thy being's height', and read in the light of Virgil's millennialist, utopian argument, it becomes pivotal. Emerson reads *Intimations* not only as a plain and persuasive attribution of Reason—or the gifts of Reason—to Infancy but as a poem whose lament for the yoke of years, and the kinds of prison-house to which we too easily consign ourselves, calls attention to the endless renewal of possibility that is also man's birthright. He reads it, that is to say, as an American.

In accepting stanza 8, with its attribution of Reason to infancy, Emerson is contesting Coleridge's famous dismissal of that same stanza as 'mental bombast'. The passage Coleridge pillories most in *Biographia* is the address to the child as 'thou best philosopher / . . . Mighty prophet! Seer blest! / On whom those truths do rest, / Which we are toiling all our lives to find! / Thou, over whom thy immortality / Broods like the day, a master o'er the slave, / A presence that is not to be put by!' On these lines—which inspired Emerson, Bronson Alcott, and Elizabeth Palmer Peabody to reform the educational system of Boston—Coleridge merely quibbles about the 'the propriety making a 'master *brood* o'er a slave' or the day brood *at all*'. He asks 'what does this all mean? In what sense is a child of that age a philosopher' or how does it deserve those 'splendid titles'? Is the child-philosopher inspired 'by reflection? by knowledge, by conscious intuition, or by any form of modification of consciousness?' and 'At what time were we dipped in the Lethe, which has

---

[16] The first Essay upon Epitaphs uses this phrase, which is based on William Camden's *Remaines concerning Britain* (1605), although Wordsworth attributes it to 'Weever's Discourse on Funeral Monuments'. Camden refers to 'the presage or fore-feeling of immortality, implanted in all men naturally'. See Wordsworth *Prose Works* 2: 50, and 101 n. Read in a certain light, Wordsworth's lines in the Simplon Pass passage of Book 6 of *The Prelude* may express the same view: 'Our destiny, our nature, and our home, / Is with infinitude, and only there'. This certainly suggests a programme of endless becoming, but not necessarily in an afterlife. After all, the same poem, more characteristically perhaps, depicts this world as 'the place where, in the end, / We find our happiness or not at all' (*Prelude* 10: 726–7).

produced such utter oblivion of a state so godlike?' 'In what sense can the magnificent attributes, above quoted, be appropriated to a child, which would not make them suitable to a bee, or a dog, or a field of corn? . . . The omnipresent Spirit works equally in them, as in the child; and the child is equally unconscious of it as they.' And so forth. The jibe is four pages long, and again worthy of Francis Jeffrey.

The attack is, no doubt, driven partly by guilt, at his own dereliction of his children, partly by envy of Wordsworth's virtual fathering of Hartley Coleridge in the years of the estrangement, and partly by resentment of Wordsworth's poetic appropriation of Coleridge's bombastic pride in the perceptions and mental feats of his children. So the resentment is understandable: but Coleridge, above all, knows—or ought to know—perfectly well what the term 'broods' means in Wordsworth's poetry, as in 'Thou, over whom thy immortality / Broods like the day'. It had been used in the opening stanza of another poem for Coleridge, the woundingly titled 'Resolution and Independence', which contains the surprising metaphor 'over his own sweet voice the stock dove *broods*'. Wordsworth had explained in his own critical essay of 1815 (two years before *Biographia*) how the metaphor 'broods' conveys in that instance the idea of 'a still and quiet satisfaction, like that which may be supposed inseparable from a continuous process of incubation'. To brood may mean 'give thought to' but it also means, more literally, 'to incubate'. And the argument of the ode—as Coleridge will certainly understand in 1825 if he does not yet grasp it in 1817—is that the very instinct or 'preassurance' of immortality is what incubates and brings forth a wider apprehension of our spiritual nature. It is our sunlight. And our spiritual nature *is* to our mortal nature as a master to a slave, and is most precisely 'A presence that is not to be put by!' This is, ironically, the point at which Wordsworth's ode makes its most Coleridgean point and most fully deserves the approbation it receives (without explanation) in the very next chapter of *Biographia*.

Coleridge's two primary tributes to *Intimations*, in *Biographia* and in volume 3 of the 1818 edition of *The Friend*, prepare for the role of the Ode in *Aids to Reflection* where—however—it is never mentioned. The unstated *ad hominem* argument of *Aids to Reflection*, the last of Coleridge's attempts to remake the oeuvre of his friend in his own image, is that of Wordsworth's two great lyrical utterances (*Tintern* and *Intimations*)—one, under the influence of 'Behmen' and Priestley, has been poisonous in its effects and influence; the other, rightly understood, contains its antidote.

Aids to Reflection (1825) shows clearly for the first time how Coleridge, like Emerson, might have read *Intimations* as a defence of Reason-in-us. In a meditation on infancy, Coleridge marries the seventh stanza of the ode (with its mysterious talk of our 'first affections' and 'shadowy recollections') to the 'Blest the infant babe' passage of Book 2 of *The Prelude*, a manoeuvre which every reader of the ode is likely to replicate. *Aids*, however, annexes Wordsworth's naturalistic and matriarchal treatment of infancy to Coleridge's patriarchal sense of 'fundamental truth':

The great fundamental Truths and Doctrines of Religion, the existence and attributes of God, and the Life after Death, are in Christian countries taught so early, under such circumstances, and in such close and vital association with whatever makes or marks *reality* for our infant minds, that the words ever after represent sensations, feelings, vital assurances, sense of reality—rather than thoughts, or any distinct conception. (*Aids to Reflection* [*CC*] 237)

In the Ode, Wordsworth points back to 'those first affections' and 'those shadowy recollections' (though neither phrase has been used before) as both the 'master light of all our seeing' and 'truths that wake to perish never'. Coleridge makes it much easier to see how 'sensations, feelings' or feeling sensations can be synonymous with 'truths'. For, he goes on (the sentence is a little elliptical):

Associated, *I had almost said identified*, with the parental Voice, Look, Touch, with the living warmth and pressure of the Mother, on whose lap the Child is first made to kneel, within whose palms the little hands are folded, and the motion of whose eyes it's eyes follow and imitate—(yea, what the blue sky is to the Mother, the Mother's upraised Eyes and Brow are to the child, the Type and Symbol of an Invisible Heaven!)—from within and without, these great First Truths, these good and gracious Tidings, these holy and humanizing Spells, in the preconformity to which our very humanity may be said to consist, are so infused, that it were but a tame and inadequate expression to say, we all take them for granted.   (237–8)

The multiple echoes are unmistakable, though Wordsworth is not mentioned, once. Apart from the blending of first affections and 'great First Truths', the phrase 'Type and Symbol' recalls Wordsworth's very Coleridgean 'Types and Symbols of Eternity' in *Prelude* 6: 571 (the Simplon Pass). The substitution of 'infused' for the more Wordsworthian 'interfused' suggests that Coleridge is correcting not only *Tintern Abbey*'s 'far more deeply interfused', but (and much more relevantly) Wordsworth's doctrinal error in the 'blest the infant babe' passage, *Prelude* 2: 262ff.: 'Along his infant veins are interfused / The gravitation and the filial bond / *Of nature* that connect him *with the world*' (my italics). This child, in Coleridge's corrective vision, is being prepared by the mother to hear that eternal language which the Father utters.

Among those 'great First Truths' (that in the ode 'wake to perish never') is the notion of life after death. This was one of the three beliefs essential to Coleridge's religious life from an early date.[17] Yet it is not until *Aids to Reflection* that Coleridge expands on the universality of this belief, and its status, implied in *Intimations*, as a

---

[17] See Thomas McFarland (ed.), *Opus Maximum* (Princeton: Princeton University Press, 2002), cxii–iv, and especially (quoting *CL* 6: 577): 'The "main points" of his faith, as he said, were only three: "a personal God, a surviving principle of Life, & that I need & that I have a Redeeemer"' (*OM* cxiv).

postulate of the spiritual life.[18] What Wordsworth expressed, even in the 1843 Fenwick Notes, only as 'a sense of the indomitableness of the spirit within me' Coleridge formally announces in *Aids* as one of the three beliefs peculiar to Christianity: namely 'The belief in the reception (by as many as "shall be heirs of salvation") of a living and spiritual Principle, a Seed of Life capable of surviving this natural life, and of existing in a divine and immortal state' (*Aids*, 197).

Elaborating on this belief he writes:

I am persuaded, that as the belief of all mankind, of all tribes, and nations, and languages, in all ages, and in all states of social union, it must be referred to far deeper grounds, common to man as man; and that its fibres are to be traced to the *tap-root* of Humanity.... The Bull-calf *buts* with smooth and unarmed Brow. Throughout animated Nature, of each characteristic Organ and Faculty there exists a pre-assurance, an instinctive and practical Anticipation; and no pre-assurance common to a whole species does in any instance prove delusive... Nature is found true to her Word.   (*AR*, 351–3)[19]

That final phrase—rephrasing Wordsworth's 'Nature never did betray the heart that loved her' (*Tintern Abbey*) in a more philosophical tone—is aptly indicative of Wordsworth's role in *Aids* where each allusion to him takes the form of a correction.

Sometimes the correction is implicit and by way of theological imprimatur to a secular error, as in a passage attributed to Leighton: 'The Grave is thy bed of rest, and no longer the *cold* bed: for thy Saviour has warmed it, and made it fragrant' (*Aids*, 303), where the theology makes palatable Wordsworth's previously censured depiction of the grave as 'a place of thought where we in waiting lie'.[20] Elsewhere it is quite overt. The peroration of *Aids* begins by quoting the man Wordsworth once referred to as 'the philosophic Priestley'—

God (says Dr Priestley) not only does but *is* every thing.... And what has been the consequence? An increasing unwillingness to contemplate the Supreme Being in his *personal* Attributes: and thence a Distaste to all the peculiar Doctrines of the Christian Faith, the Trinity, the Incarnation of the Son of God, and Redemption. (403)

—and then backhandedly identifies *Tintern Abbey* as the misguided enunciation of doctrines that it has become Coleridge's mission to contest:

---

[18] What one does find at an early date is the routine reward-and-punishment conception of the afterlife offered to Thelwall in 1796, and so scorned by Keats, that 'when we appear to men to die, we do not utterly perish; but after this Life shall continue to enjoy or suffer the consequences & natural effects of the habits we have formed here whether good or evil' (*CL*, 1: 280).

[19] See also the prettier instances, whereby 'the wings of the air-sylph are forming within the skin of the caterpillar' and the 'chrysalis of the horned fly [leaves] room in its involucrum for antennae yet to come' (*BL* 1: 242)—which anticipations of a future state are presented as analogous to what Wordsworth calls 'the vision and the faculty divine' (241).

[20] *BL* 2: 141 objects specifically to *a child* ('who by the bye at six years old would have been better instructed in most Christian families') conceiving of death as lying *awake* in the grave. In February 1804, shortly before receiving his manuscript copy of *Intimations*, Coleridge wrote in his Notebook

Some I have known, constitutionally religious—I speak feelingly; for I speak of that which for a brief period was my own state[21]—who under this unhealthful influence have been so estranged from the heavenly *Father*, the *Living* God, as even to shrink from the personal pronouns as applied to the Deity. But many do I know, and yearly meet with, in whom a false and sickly Taste co-operates with the prevailing fashion: many who find the God of Abraham, Isaac, and Jacob, far too *real*, too substantial; who feel it more in harmony with their indefinite sensations

> 'To worship Nature in the hill and valley,
> Not knowing what they love:—'[22]

and (to use the language but not the sense or purpose of the great Poet of our Age) would fain substitute for the Jehovah of their Bible

> 'A sense sublime
> Of something far more deeply interfused,
> Whose dwelling is the Light of setting suns,
> And the round Ocean and the living Air;...'
>
> WORDSWORTH

And this from having been educated to understand the Divine Omnipresence in any sense rather than the alone safe and legitimate one, the presence of all things to God! (*AR*, 404–5)

Wordsworth, too, in middle years, denied having meant to present himself at as a worshipper of nature in what was merely 'a passionate expression uttered incautiously in the Poem upon the Wye',[23] but there is little doubt that he did so present himself, or that he was such a worshipper, or that *Tintern*'s 'false and sickly Taste' and 'indefinite sensations' was indeed a key text in the 'prevailing fashion' which it became the purpose of Coleridge's life to resist.

The Friend, to which Wordsworth contributed his own 'Essays upon Epitaphs', had begun this corrective process. In *The Friend*, the close of Coleridge's greatest meditation on *Intimations* had invoked Sir Thomas Browne to correct *Tintern Abbey*. There is but one principle, Coleridge says, which can lift the burden of the mystery, or in his own terms 'which alone reconciles the man with himself, with others and with the world; which regulates all relations, tempers all passions, and gives power to support all suffering' (*Friend*, 1: 523). This principle is not—contra

---

that 'We are not inert in the Grave—St Paul's Corn in the ground proves this scripturally' and asks 'What if our growth then be in proportion to the length & depth of our Sleep—with what mysterious grandeur does not this Thought invest the Grave?' (*CN* 2: 1896). It seems not unlikely that Coleridge planted in Wordsworth the seed whose secularized fruit he so deplores in *Biographia*.

[21] It is a curious manoeuvre: Coleridge's tactical confession of a 'brief period' of heresy both magnifies Wordsworth's more habitual error while minimizing his period of subjection to Wordsworth's spell.

[22] Quoted anonymously from Coleridge's own *Osorio*, 1: 244–5.

[23] To Catherine Clarkson, January 1815, *MY*, 2: 188.

Tintern Abbey—that 'never failing principle of joy' to be found by the worshipper of Nature. 'For it belongs not to the earth'. Rather, it is 'the principle of religion, the living and substantial faith "which passeth all *understanding*"'. His next sentence concludes the meditation on the ode by paraphrasing the argument of the ninth stanza ecstatically as promoting the 'elevation of the spirit *above the semblances of custom and the senses to a world of spirit, this life in the idea*, even in the supreme and godlike, which alone merits the name of life and without which our organic life is in a state of somnambulism' (1: 524, my italics). The paraphrase is repeated, more sharply, in *Aids to Reflection*. Shortly after quoting *Tintern*'s allegedly inadvertent heresy, Coleridge's peroration quietly annexes *Intimations* 9 once again, giving its revolt against the outward senses a still more doctrinal inflection:

> Now I do not hesitate to assert, that it was one of the great purposes of Christianity, and included in the process of our Redemption, *to rouse and emancipate the Soul from this debasing Slavery to the outward Senses, to awaken the mind to the true Criteria of Reality.* (*Aids*, 406, my emphases)

There, at last, is the simple and direct expression of the redemptive argument that Wordsworth failed to articulate in *The Prelude* and *The Excursion*. Rightly understood (according to Coleridge, and whether Wordsworth grasped this or not) the ode is where the spiritual man rises up against the natural man rooted in what *Tintern* calls 'the language of the sense'.

It is not known whether Wordsworth ever read his copy of *Aids to Reflection* (there was one in the Rydal Mount library), or what he thought of it, but in 1832 he did make a substantive change to his conclusion to *The Prelude* concerning his and Coleridge's message to future ages as joint 'Prophets of Nature':

> Prophets of Nature, we to them will speak
> A lasting inspiration, sanctified
> By reason ~~and by Truth~~, blest by faith'.[24]

In such revisionary instances, during the long gestation of his poem, Wordsworth gives substance to Shawcross's curious parenthesis—'(and his cause was his own also)'—remaining true, for better, for worse, to his poetic symbiont.

WORKS CITED

BEER, JOHN. 1979. *Wordsworth in Time*. London: Macmillan.
BIALOSTOSKY, DON H. 1984. *Making Tales: The Poetics of Wordsworth's Narrative Experiments*. Chicago and London: University of Chicago Press.

[24] Wordsworth 1995, 536–7, 664 n.

—— 1978. Coleridge's interpretation of Wordsworth's Preface to *Lyrical Ballads*. *PMLA*, 93 (5): 912–24.

BUCHAN, A. M. 1963. The influence of Wordsworth on Coleridge (1795–1800). *University of Toronto Quarterly*, 32: 346–66.

BURWICK, FRED, ed. 1989. *Coleridge's 'Biographia Literaria': Text and Meaning*. Columbus, OH: Ohio State University Press.

CARLYLE, THOMAS. 1827. The State of German Literature. *Edinburgh Review*.

COLERIDGE, S. T. 1907. *Biographia Literaria*, ed. John Shawcross. Oxford.

—— 1956–71. *Collected Letters of Samuel Taylor Coleridge*, ed. Earl Leslie Griggs. Oxford: Clarendon Press.

—— 1957–. *The Notebooks of Samuel Taylor Coleridge*, ed. Katheen Coburn. New York, NY: Bollingen Foundation.

ERDMAN, DAVID. V. 1985. The Otway connection, in Gravil et al. 1986: 143–60.

FRUMAN, NORMAN. 1971. *Coleridge: The Damaged Archangel*. New York: George Braziller.

GALLIE, W. B. 1947. Is The Prelude a philosophical poem?, *Philosophy* 22.

GILLMAN, JAMES. 1838. *The Life of Samuel Taylor Coleridge*, vol. 1 (no vol. 2). London: W. Pickering.

GRAVIL, RICHARD. 1985. Imagining Wordsworth: 1797, 1807, 1817 In Gravil et al. 1985: 129–42.

—— 1984. Coleridge's Wordsworth, *TWC*, 15 (2): 38–46.

—— 2007. *The First 'Poem to Coleridge': a Dialogic Reading of Wordsworth's 'Intimations' Ode*. Tirril: Humanities-Ebooks.

—— NEWLYN, LUCY, and ROE, NICHOLAS, eds. 1985. *Coleridge's Imagination*. Cambridge: Cambridge University Press. Reprinted 2007.

HEWITT, REGINA. 1997. *The Possibilities of Society: Wordsworth, Coleridge, and the Sociological Viewpoint of English Romanticism*. Albany, NY: State University of New York Press.

JACOBUS, MARY. 1976. *Tradition & Experiment in Wordsworth's Lyrical Ballads 1798*. Oxford: Clarendon Press.

McFARLAND, THOMAS. 1981. *Romanticism and the Forms of Ruin: Modalities of Fragmentation*. Princeton, NJ: Princeton University Press.

MAGNUSON, PAUL. 1988. *Coleridge and Wordsworth: A Lyrical Dialogue*. Princeton, NJ: Princeton University Press.

MARGOLIOUTH, H. M. 1953. *Wordsworth and Coleridge 1795–1834*. London: Oxford University Press.

MODIANO, RAIMONDA. 1989. Coleridge and Milton: The Case against Wordsworth in the *Biographia Literaria*, in Burwick 1989: 150–70.

NEWLYN, LUCY. 1986. *Coleridge, Wordsworth, and the Language of Allusion*. Oxford: Clarendon Press.

PARRISH, STEPHEN. 1973. *The Art of the 'Lyrical Ballads'*. Cambridge, Mass.: Harvard University Press.

—— 1986. 'Leaping and Lingering': Coleridge's lyrical ballads, in Gravil et al. 1985: 102–16.

ROBINSON, HENRY CRABB. 1938. *Henry Crabb Robinson on Books and their Writers*, ed. Edith J. Morley. 3 vols. J. M. Dent and Sons.

SISMAN, ADAM. 2006. *The Friendship: Wordsworth and Coleridge*. London: Harper.

SWANN, KAREN. 1991. Teaching *Christabel*: gender and genre. In *Approaches to Teaching Coleridge's Poetry and Prose*, ed. Richard E. Matlak. New York, NY: MLAA.

WARNOCK, MARY. 1976. *Imagination*. London and Boston: Faber & Faber.

WOOF, ROBERT. 2001. *William Wordsworth: The Critical Heritage, 1793–1820*. London and New York: Routledge.

WORDSWORTH, WILLIAM. 1974. *The Prose Works of William Wordsworth*, ed. W. J. B. Owen and Jane W. Smyser. 3 vols. Oxford: Clarendon Press.

—— 1800. *Lyrical Ballads 1800*. London.

—— 1967. *The Letters of William and Dorothy Wordsworth: The Early Years*, ed. Ernest de Selincourt, 2nd edn rev. Chester L. Shaver. Oxford: Clarendon Press.

—— 1969. *The Letters of William and Dorothy Wordsworth: The Middle Years*, ed. Ernest de Selincourt, 2nd edn rev. Mary Moorman. Oxford: Clarendon Press.

—— 1975. *The Salisbury Plain Poems*, ed. Stephen Gill. Ithaca, NY and Sussex: Cornell University Press and Harvester.

—— 1995. *The Prelude: the Four Texts (1798, 1799, 1805, 1850)* ed. Jonathan Wordsworth. Harmondsworth: Penguin.

—— 2007. *The Fenwick Notes of William Wordsworth*, ed. Jared Curtis. 2nd edn, revised and corrected. Tirril: Humanities-Ebooks.

CHAPTER 3

COLERIDGE'S PUBLISHER AND PATRON: COTTLE AND POOLE

JOHN-DAVID LOPEZ

WHEN S. L. Bensusan took up the task of writing a biography of Coleridge in the early part of the last century, he did so with a certain amount of circumspection and maybe a degree of distaste. Coleridge, Bensusan points out, lived a life that is difficult to chart in terms of progress. His life unfolded in fits and starts, openings without finishes, fragments of genius squandered. The life Bensusan was to record was, in short, less than inspiring. At the crux of Bensusan's discomfort with his task lay what might be called Coleridge's second worst habit: financial dependency. In Bensusan's view, 'the trouble with him (Coleridge) was not to get money for his work, but to give work in return for other people's money' (26). Coleridge's willingness to be financially dependent on his friends coupled with his inability to reward with industry his various patrons and publishers, left him a somewhat sorry subject for life study; Bensusan's biography of Coleridge thus reads largely as lament:

A shrewd, practical man with half his attainments could have turned them to better advantage. His health was never really robust, and he suffered from the fatal sickness of self-pity. He accepted the charity of friends and asked for more; though he seems to have had few personal extravagances, the income that kept his friends free from financial strain, would not have been enough for his support. None of his biographers know what he did with his money on the rare occasions when it was plentiful; there is ample reason to believe that he would have been equally puzzled to make out a balance-sheet . . . his private letters reveal too frequently an utter absence of personal dignity. (10)

It would be low manners and high pedantry to dredge up this biographical oddity if it were indeed an oddity, but Bensusan's discomfort with the record of Coleridge's relations with his friends, patrons and publishers serves as the template for a long series of biographical winces at Coleridge's pecuniary habits. At the commencement of our current century, Kelvin Everest in *The Cambridge Companion to Coleridge* wields language and sentiment not much removed from that deployed by Bensusan a century earlier. Remarking on Coleridge's brief foray into the horse guard, Everest notes that 'the episode sounds an ominous note in Coleridge's biography; regular collapse into craven dependency and transparent untruth was to become its only predictable constant' (19). The strain of Coleridge's financial dependence also runs through Molly Lefebure's account of his life: 'STC was increasingly incapable of fulfilling either social or professional commitments; his existence became a never-ending squalor of procrastination, excuses, lies, debts, degradation, failure' (25). But here Coleridge's financial dependency is handled somewhat differently, as Lefebure seeks to subsume one dark habit into another. Offering an answer to Bensusan's query as to where Coleridge put his money in those 'rare times of plenty', Lefebure notes that 'the constant procurement of opium was a drain on his pocket that kept him chronically short of money' (26). If Bensusan and Everest regard Coleridge's reliance on charity with simple disgust, Lefebure suggests that Coleridge's financial dependency is rooted in a deeper and more shameful dependency on opium. There has, of course, been another strategy employed by Coleridge's biographers in relation to his financial struggles, perhaps more charitable than the other two. This has been simply to regard the financial elements of Coleridge's life as beneath literary concern.

The critical tendency where Coleridge's financial habits are concerned has thus been threefold: to express disgust at his shortcomings, to lament Coleridge's financial weakness as part of a pattern of other weaknesses, or to turn a blind eye out of pity. All of these approaches are unsatisfying. All proceed from the assumption that Coleridge was simply weak and out of control where his finances were concerned, and that examination of his financial habits is therefore unnecessary, unfair and likely in poor taste. This ignores the fact that Coleridge devoted an extraordinary amount of intellectual energy to resolving the tangled ethics of largely economic issues such as gratitude, obligation, philanthropy, and private property. As Nick Roe has shown, the question of gratitude alone was enough to separate Coleridge irrevocably from Godwin in the 1790s. To ignore, or sweep away with simple value judgements, Coleridge's actual financial interactions is to deprive Coleridge studies of a possible avenue of understanding of the deeply conflicted economic idealism alive and at work in Coleridge's life. My aim here is to develop a more detailed (and perhaps more sympathetic) understanding of Coleridge's relationships with his various financial benefactors. Understanding these relationships in the broader context of Coleridge's beliefs may emancipate to some extent the critical understanding of 'poor Coleridge' in his dealings with his circle of friends, supporters, subscribers, and publishers. It may also cast some light on Coleridge's stubborn and enduringly ideal understanding of distribution of wealth and economic hierarchy.

William Christie notes that the borders between patron and friend were notoriously obscure in the Romantic period:

> There was patronage, there was friendship, and there was charity, and the lines between them were not always clear. Whatever we choose to call each individual gesture, however, Coleridge benefited financially from all of them. (61)

What is perhaps missing here is the agency behind this blurring of distinctions. Coleridge, out of ideological necessity, did much to muddy these connections. As a staunch Republican with a distaste for vertical hierarchy, the young Coleridge was, more than almost any man of his era, both ideologically incompatible with the concept of patronage and an uneasy participant in the vicissitudes of the literary marketplace. The fiery republicanism of the early years left little room for a mode of economic transaction so clearly monarchical/feudal in its structure as patronage. The idea of a great man dispensing financial rewards in exchange for a place of honor in the literary output of his client was necessarily repulsive to a poet committed to seeing the old social order cast into the dust. Neither was it natural for Coleridge to produce verse for another man's financial interest, to have his creative endeavors treated as an instrument of capital investment that must repay an initial outlay of cash with predictable, bankable, productivity. What Coleridge sought in his relationships with his would-be sponsors, be they patrons or publishers, was equality of footing. The vertical, paternal aspects of patronage were antithetical to Coleridge's Republican and Pantisocratic beliefs, and had to be replaced with horizontal, friendly relationships; the authority of fathers had to be replaced with the sympathetic affection of brothers. Likewise, the patriarchal control of the copyright holder needed to be defused with elements of brotherly affection based on sympathy, gratitude and freely bestowed philanthropy. One way the verticality of these relationships was subverted by Coleridge was in a blurring of these boundaries through the development of friendships with those ostensibly in power. A frequently taken shortcut to this result was in drawing 'patronage' from sources already friendly.

Coleridge's efforts to destabilize the boundaries between patron and artist involved developing a sympathetic relationship between writer and patron/publisher, where both parties brought something of equal value to the bargain through benevolent sympathy with each other's aims. If Coleridge created beauty and a supporter paid his bills, both men gained: the first by living a life unencumbered by grosser pursuit, the second by having access to a world of beauty otherwise closed to his senses five. Coleridge's ultimate failure to effectively merge the concept of friendship with patron and publisher was a disaster of the first order for him. The failure to develop an ideal and sustaining economy resulted in a lifetime of financial insecurity, badly damaged confidence, and harried obligation, all of which were detrimental to the development and expression of his art. But in the moments in which he was successful, we see glimpses of a happier possibility, most notably in the years at Stowey.

I focus my arguments initially on Coleridge's relationship with Joseph Cottle, his struggles to apply Pantisocratic notions to this first patron/publisher relationship, and the damaging effects of this failed relationship. I then describe Coleridge's search for his preferred economic model, the circle of like-minded subscribers, which he initially sought in the development of *The Watchman* with its hand-picked readership, and later, albeit temporarily, found in the sensitive friendship of Thomas Poole. Coleridge's later financial career can in many senses be understood as an oscillation between these two economic models. On the one hand there is the persistent inability to meet the demands of the patron/publisher, repeated again and again (as in the case of the Wedgwood annuity). On the other hand, are the faltering steps taken towards the temporary bliss of arranging an ideal economy cheerfully divorced from the larger economic realities of nineteenth-century England, one based on mutualism and sympathy, which while pleasing and positive, is hopelessly fragile. This is the model pursued in Coleridge's attempts at building a community of sympathetic subscribers, as has been much studied in relation to the Friend.[1] This model may also be related to Coleridge's attempts in later life to fashion a lasting economy of sympathy through his manner of living as an amanuensis of the families of others rather than in his own economic household. In all of this, Coleridge's lifelong struggles with pounds and pence illuminate his struggle with reconciling economic idealism and the vicissitudes of the economic realities of his day. In his failed patron relationship with Cottle, Coleridge's deep antipathy to vertical concepts of economic hierarchy offer a pattern for understanding a life-long inability to flourish in a client–financier relationship. In the more successful relationship with Thomas Poole, Coleridge's ability to flourish in a sympathetic, horizontal relationship emerges with startling clarity.

The first man to reward Coleridge's poetic talents with financial recompense was Joseph Cottle, who celebratedly offered Coleridge 30 guineas for his first volume of poetry in Bristol in 1795. What is less celebrated is that this was actually the second financial boon Cottle offered Coleridge. Cottle had met Coleridge and Southey a

---

[1] See Lucy Newlyn's 'Coleridge and the Anxiety of Reception'; Tim Fulford's *Coleridge's Figurative Language*; and Paul Hamilton's *Coleridge's Poetics*. See also Deirdre Coleman's *Coleridge and The Friend* for a discussion of the tyranny of audience in this same regard.

few weeks earlier, and was much impressed with his new acquaintances, but there was a worry in his heart. Coleridge and Southey were at this moment ardent Pantisocrats, and their stay in Bristol, they held, was to be temporary in the extreme. Henceforth, if Cottle would maintain the friendship, he would have to find some way of reaching the bright young things on the banks of the Susquehanna.

To what extent Cottle's fear of Coleridge and Southey's withdrawal was based on his own potential loss and to what extent it was based on Cottle's concerns about the unexamined hazards of the younger men's plan is unclear. In any event, Cottle was an early opponent of Pantisocracy, and was soon relieved to discover that he had little to fear in the way of Pennsylvania exerting a brain drain on Bristol:

The solicitude that I felt lest these young and ardent geniuses should in a disastrous hour, and in their mistaken apprehensions, commit themselves in their desperate undertaking, was happily dissipated by Mr. Coleridge applying for a loan of a little cash—to pay the voyager's freight? Or passage? No,—LODGINGS...Never did I lend money with such unmingled pleasure, for I now ceased to be haunted day and night with the spectre of the ship! (10–11)

Cottle's glee at offering up five pounds to the landlord of 48 College Street on behalf of his new friends is equivocal. In a generous mood, it can be taken as the sheer delight of a man delivered from his fears over the safety and wellbeing of his friends. In a more hard-nosed moment, it can be taken as the pleasure of a businessman who knows himself in control of a situation. Like much of Cottle's prose, the word 'dissipated' here cuts two ways, as the financial weakness of Coleridge and his circle leads Cottle to a clear understanding of his own ability to influence and shape his young friends' future course, as is evident in the next lines in Cottle's memoir:

Till this time, not knowing what the resources of my young friends were, I could not wholly divest myself of fear; but now an effectual barrier manifestly interposed itself to save them from destruction. And though their Romantic plan might linger in their minds, it was impossible not to be assured that strong good sense would eventually dissipate their illusions. Finding that there was a deficiency in that material, deemed of the first consequence in all civilized states, and remembering Burgh's feeling lamentation over the improvidence, or rather the indifference with which many men of genius regard the low thoughts that are merely of a pecuniary nature, I began to revolve on the means by which the two poets might advantageously apply their talents. (11)

It is initially unclear from Cottle's diction just whose 'strong good sense' would lead the poets to proper employ of their talents, but the last sentence makes it clear that it is Cottle who will direct the enterprise, and that the financial need of the young men offered him his avenue. The 'Romantic plan' of Pantisocracy must yield to the realities of the marketplace, and Cottle understood these realities far better than the young 'geniuses' did.

Cottle's memoir proceeds to tell how he offered Coleridge the 30 guineas history has remembered. Cottle takes obvious pleasure in recounting how he initially offered Coleridge 20 guineas then in a fit of generosity, improved his offer:

Others publish for themselves, I will chiefly remember you. Instead of giving you twenty guineas, I will extend it to thirty, and without waiting for the completion of the work, to make you easy you may have the money as your occasions require. The silence and the grasped hand showed that at that moment one person was happy. (12)

Cottle's turn of phrase here is interesting. He clearly implies that Coleridge's gratitude is too profound for words at this unlooked for windfall, and so it likely was. But Cottle's insistence that 'one person was happy' seems odd here, given his own clear pleasure in the act of patronage. Perhaps this phrase arises from some instinct to cloak the deep joy he felt at having, essentially, purchased himself a client artist of formidable gifts. What is clear is that Cottle had gained intelligence as to Coleridge's financial needs and acted on that knowledge promptly, putting 35 guineas to work. Whether those guineas went to work for Cottle's own interest or altruistically for the young poet's (or for both) is unclear.

Much depends then on what light we choose to see Cottle in. If he is the sympathetic benefactor he portrays himself, with the happiness of 'one man' in mind (and that man is Coleridge), then Coleridge's failures to meet Cottle part way are sadly baffling. If, however, Cottle is not quite a magnanimous philanthropist and is proceeding on some other motive, perhaps Coleridge's inability to produce for him becomes more intelligible. Likely the best opportunity to evaluate Cottle's motives where Coleridge is concerned lies in evaluating the motivations he had for publishing his memoir in the first place. The memoir in its initial form appeared only three years after Coleridge's death, and brought great unhappiness to Coleridge's family. Cottle's purposes in putting his private view of Coleridge before the public have been variously analyzed. Richard Holmes finds a 'pious Cottle' who 'dutifully' called Coleridge's darker habits into the light.[2] Alternatively, Molly Lefebure questions Cottle's motives and notes the anxiety with which Coleridge's friends and family sought to influence the content or halt the publication of Cottle's memoir. Lefebure and Holmes both concentrate their attention on the revelations therein regarding Coleridge's opium use, which were certainly the most sensational material in the memoir. But Cottle himself was also quite anxious to

---

[2] Here Holmes follows Cottle himself, who claims to have based his decision to publish Coleridge's most private letters on lines Coleridge had written to Josiah Wade: 'After my death I earnestly entreat that a full and unqualified narrative of my wretchedness, and its guilty cause, may be made public, that at least some little good may be effected by its direful example.' If this line is to be taken as authorization of the use of personal papers for a cautionary memoir, it was Wade who was thereby authorized by Coleridge, not Cottle. There may have been in Coleridge's mind a significant difference in the sympathy with which Wade would have carried out such an endeavor and that with which Cottle actually delivered it.

favorably dispose his reader to his intentions of exposing Coleridge's financial dependencies to public scrutiny.

Perhaps knowing the violence he could potentially do to Coleridge's legacy, Cottle goes to great lengths to excuse himself for laying before the public Coleridge's sloppy financial habits. He points out in a lengthy 'apology' that 'pecuniary difficulties, especially such as occur in early life, and not ascribable to bad conduct, reflect no discredit on men of genius' (9) but if this disclaimer was meant as a defense of Coleridge, it is utterly inept as Coleridge's financial difficulties extended far beyond youth, were 'ascribable to bad conduct', etc. In fact, Cottle's disclaimer merely acts to neatly exclude Southey from the opprobrium he heaps upon Coleridge alone. Cottle concludes that his deliberations on the morality of sharing Coleridge's financial weakness with the world convince him 'not to withhold from false delicacy, occurrences, the disclosure...by which all the features of Mr Coleridge's character will be exhibited to the inspection of the inquisitive and philosophical mind'. (10) Cottle then proceeds to spread out before his readers the lurid details of Coleridge's insolvency, beginning with the aforementioned note requesting five pounds for lodging, which is reproduced in its entirety despite its banal and prosaic nature. Subsequently, Cottle lays before his reader in agonizing detail dozens of Coleridge's various pleas for financial assistance in a manner that seems calculated to alternately provoke pity, moral outrage, and low mirth in his readers. In a particularly telling example, Cottle gives us the following view of his role as Coleridge's support at the time of the young poet's move to Clevedon:

Two days after his marriage, I received a letter from Mr. Coleridge (which now lies before me) requesting the kindness of me to send him down, with all dispatch, the following little articles. 'A riddle slice; a candle box; two ventilators; two glasses for the wash stand; one tin dust pan; one small tin tea kettle; one pair of candlesticks; one carpet brush; one flower dredge; three tin extinguishers; two mats; a pair of slippers; a cheese toaster; two large tin spoons; a bible; a keg of porter; coffee; raisins; currants; catsup; nutmegs; allspice; cinnamon; rice; ginger; and mace.' With the aid of the grocer, and the shoemaker, and the brewer, and the tinman, and the Glassman, and the brazier, &c., I immediately sent him down all that he had required and more. (40)

Cottle's motives for reproducing letters of this type can only be speculated upon. But the very fact that Cottle's memory of such details was so long, and that his interest a mere three years after Coleridge's death lay in calling such details to the public's attention, indicates the degree to which he was conscious of Coleridge's obligations to him and how much he felt slighted by Coleridge's inattention. And where Cottle was so acutely aware of what was owed him, is there any doubt that the mantle of debt was unnoticed by Coleridge?

Regardless of Cottle's motives, his patronage of a poet who could not square his beliefs with patronage was proved ultimately to be a damaging event in Coleridge's development as an artist.[3] As Coleridge became increasingly aware of his debts to Cottle and his seeming inability to extricate himself from them, the relationship became a paralytic trap for him. But it was not always so. Originally, the relationship with Cottle seemed full of promise to Coleridge. In a playful note in the early summer of 1795, Coleridge wrote:

Dear Cottle, By the thick smoke that precedes the volcanic eruptions of Etna, Vesuvius, and Hecla, I feel an impulse to fumigate, at [now] 25, College-Street, one pair of stairs room; yea, with our Oroonoko, and if thou wilt send me by the bearer, four pipes, I will write a panegyrical epic poem upon thee, with as many books as there are letters in thy name. Moreover, if thou wilt send me 'the copy book,' I hereby bind myself, by tomorrow morning, to write out enough copy for a sheet and a half. God bless you! S.T.C.

The lighthearted way in which Coleridge negotiates his relationship with Cottle here indicates his early view of patronage. The small scale of Cottle's gifts to him (four pipes and a copy book) versus the promised vast panegyric eruption gently ironizes both men's gifts. It indicates a playful awareness that Cottle is supporting Coleridge, and therefore due his verse, as indicated in the promise of work to be done. It also ironizes in a friendly way the dynamics of their relationship, de-emphasizing the business of copyright holding and deadlines behind a playful demand for tobacco and a conflation of the joy of smoking and the joy of writing. This blurring of the boundaries of friendship and patronage may go some way to explaining Coleridge's comfort in writing to Cottle constantly for money, goods, etc. His understanding of their relationship is that his creativity will be freely given just as Cottle's purse will be, and the joy of their interactions and the bounties of their sympathetic friendship will justify and satisfy them both.

This may seem willfully naïve, and Coleridge's beliefs in this period have certainly brought their share of cynical attention.[4] But it must be remembered that in 1795, Coleridge's main intellectual concern was the development of the project of Pantisocracy, and his concept of how human beings ought to economically govern themselves exposes the full scale of the divide between his 'Romantic plan' and Cottle's more calculating take on reality. In a letter written to Charles Heath on August 29th, 1794, Coleridge offers a clear view of his economic perspective:

With regard to pecuniary matters it is found necessary, if twelve men with their families emigrate on this system, (Pantisocracy) that 2000L should be the aggregate of their

---

[3] The effect for Southey was radically different. Southey was grateful throughout his life to Cottle, and with good reason. Cottle had noticed his talent and given him a chance to earn by it, as he had for Coleridge as well. But Southey's economic disposition was far better adapted to mainstream values than was Coleridge's, and this made all the difference in the relationships that unfolded between the publisher and his two very different poets. Cottle himself must have been quite hurt considering the very different reception his attentions drew from Coleridge than from Southey.

[4] For instance Oswald Doughty's comment in Perturbed Spirit that 'Lack of money had deeply afflicted both Coleridge and Southey—so money they agreed in despising.' (62)

contributions; but infer not from hence that each man's quota is to be settled with the littleness of arithmetical accuracy. No; *all* will strain *every* nerve, and I trust the surplus money of some will supply the deficiencies of others. (54) (emphasis his throughout)

This letter, signed by 'Your fellow Citizen, S.T. Coleridge' lays plain Coleridge's belief in an egalitarian economics that were at the heart of the Pantisocratic system. This concept of pooled wealth, shared by all according to need, produced by each according to ability, stands in stark contrast to the economic understanding of Cottle, the experienced man of business. The idea of debt, or of obligation based on debt, plays no part in Coleridge's ideal concept of an economy '*frendotatoi meta frendous*'—most friendly where all are friends.

Just how alien the terms of Cottle's literary 'friendship' were to Coleridge's ideals is perhaps rendered most clear in Cottle's potentially significant offer of support to Coleridge: his promise to pay a guinea and a half for every hundred lines of poetry Coleridge could produce. This offer represented the precise economic situation Coleridge hoped to move away from through Pantisocracy; this was the very definition of 'each man's quota...settled with the littleness of arithmetical accuracy'. That Coleridge accepted Cottle's terms (and his money) should not be lost in all this. Nor should Bristol be mistaken for the Susquehanna, the British actual economy for the Panitsocrat's ideal one. But neither should it be lost that a fissure in understanding of basic economic realities divided these two men fundamentally and was bound to pose perils to the relationship which was unfolding between them, a relationship which spiraled into increasingly difficult terms with great rapidity.

The deep cleft between the economic visions of Cottle and Coleridge is further illustrated by their differing receptions of the significance of Cottle's offer to buy Coleridge's poetry by the line, a difference not unnoticed by Cottle himself:

I thought it would afford a small relief to tell him that I would give him one guinea and a half (after his volume was completed,) for every hundred lines he might present to me, whether rhyme or blank verse. This offer appeared of more consequence in the estimation of Mr C, than it did in his who made it; for when a common friend familiarly asked him 'how he was to keep the pot boiling when married?' he very promptly answered that Mr. Cottle had made him such an offer that he felt no solicitude on the subject. (39)

Cottle's parenthetical here is telling. The obvious business stipulation, that the pay-per-line arrangement would commence after he received the volume for which he held a copyright, demonstrates that the offer involved multiple levels of leverage. It was both a guarantee of access to future produce and an inducement to complete a previously agreed upon contract that Cottle was beginning to regard as a likely default. Cottle's awareness of Coleridge's limited production capacity also set an effective ceiling on future payments; by this point it was clear to Cottle that Coleridge would not produce quarto upon quarto even if he had been offered three guineas a sheet. Hence it was clear to Cottle that this offer could not cost him too much, given Coleridge's uneven ability to produce. For Coleridge, however, how different seemed this offer! A recognition of his talent, flattering in the extreme, the generous offer of a friend more blessed in financial circumstances than he, the promise of support for an otherwise financially isolated young man. He would give freely of his talent, which was sure to flow, and Cottle would give freely of his purse. It was promise enough to marry on.

Proof of the deep damage that could be done to Coleridge's relationships by divergent economic understandings, as well as a final indication of the collision course Cottle's and Coleridge's conflicting understandings of economic matters had put them on, can be seen in Coleridge's degenerating relationship to a man he cared for more for than he ever would for Cottle. Coleridge's letter to Southey on 13 November, 1795, shows the deeply damaging effects that Coleridge's idealized form of economics could have when placed in conflict with more ordinary viewpoints. Coleridge, confronted by Southey's withdrawal from the Pantisocratic scheme, exposes the depth of his belief in egalitarian economics, and the depth of his betrayal at Southey's 'apostacy' from such beliefs:

Remember when we went to Ashton on the Strawberry Party. Your conversation with George Burnet on the day following he detailed to me. It scorched my throat. Your private resources were to remain your individual property, and everything to be separate except on five or six acres. In short, we were to commence Partners in a petty Farming Trade. This was the Mouse of which the Mountain of Pantisocracy was at last safely delivered! I received the account with Indignation and Loathings of unutterable Contempt.

Southey's withdrawal from the scheme of shared property central to Coleridge's vision of ideal society was tantamount to an end to their friendship and plans. Coleridge concludes: 'O Selfish, money-loving Man! what principle have you not given up . . . O God! That *such a mind* should fall in love with that low, dirty, gutter-grubbing Trull, WORLDLY PRUDENCE!!'

If Coleridge's deep relationship with Southey could founder, at least in part, on the divergence in their views over worldly wealth and its uses, the consequences for his comparatively fledgling friendship with Cottle should provoke no surprise.

That Coleridge wore the mantle of patronage increasingly uneasily is apparent in a series of letters he wrote to Cottle after the initial exchange of pounds and pence. In his memoirs, Cottle recites with exacting detail the various evasions Coleridge resorted to during the period in which he procrastinated the production of the promised volume, which eventually appeared on 16 April 1796. A short sampling will do some good. First, the optimistic note of July 1795: 'My dear friend, The printer may depend on copy on Monday morning, and if he can work a sheet a day, he shall have it.' Next, the evasive tone of early March 1796:

My dear Cottle, My eye is so inflamed that I cannot stir out. It is alarmingly inflamed. In addition to this, the Debates which Burnet undertook to abridge for me, (for the Watchman) he has abridged in such a careless, slovenly manner that I have been obliged to throw them into the fire, and am now doing them myself!

Finally the submissive obsequiousness of the latter part of that same month:

My dear very dear Cottle, I will be at your shop at half past six—if you will give me a dish of Tea—and between that time and eleven o'clock at night I will write out the whole of the notes and preface—As I give you leave to turn the lock and key on me . . . You may depend on it, I will not be a minute past my time—if I am, I permit you to send a note to Michael Castle [with whom Coleridge was to dine] requesting him to send me home to fulfill my engagements, like an honest man—S. T. Coleridge.

The degeneration of the two men's relations is clear, but so too is the damage done to the psyche of the junior partner, so too is the reduction of one man into a servile state, utterly incompatible with the visions of freestanding equality he so cherished. Coleridge's request that Cottle put him under lock and key clearly indicates the loss of freedom he felt under the terms of his obligation to his patron. His lamely self-effacing attempt at humor in his acknowledgement of his own inability to ensure a timely arrival, his buffoonish request for a cup of tea, and his wish to be 'like an honest man' show the servility to which the collar of unmet obligation had reduced him in his own view.

It is best not to make much of the shifting terms of salutation in the above letters, but it is worth noting that Coleridge initially chooses to regard Cottle as a friend, not a patron or holder of copyrights, and this is no accident. As a friend, Cottle fits the model of financial support most comfortable to Coleridge, the notion of a sympathetic comrade who, out of a magnanimous philanthropy of a pure and unalloyed type, based on greatness of soul and love of fellow man, and perhaps gratitude for another's talents, extends the comforts of his own good fortune to his neighbor, who happily (and effortlessly—and here is a big problem) shares the fruits of his own endowments. But the vicissitudes of Coleridge's increasingly conflicted relationship with Cottle gradually disabuse the poet of the possibility of maintaining a friendship so fundamentally uneven in distribution of power (read money). The result is a growing uncertainty about the nature of his relationship with Cottle, an uncertainty which is plainly exposed in a letter to Cottle on 22 February:

I think I should have been more thankful if He had made me a journeyman shoemaker, instead of an author by trade . . . I am forced to write for bread! Write the flights of poetic enthusiasm, when every minute I am hearing a groan from my wife. . . . The present hour I am in a quick-set hedge of embarrassment, and whichever way I turn a thorn runs into me! Nor is this all. My happiest moments for composition are broken in upon by the reflection that I must make haste. I am too late! I am already months behind! I have received my pay beforehand! Oh, wayward and desultory spirit of genius! Ill canst thou brook a task-master! The tenderest touch from the hand of obligation, wounds thee like a scourge of scorpions . . . I am writing as fast as I can. Depend on it you shall not be out of pocket for me! I feel what I owe you, and independently of this, I love you as a friend, so much, that I regret, seriously regret, that you have been my copyholder.   22 February 1796 (68)

Coleridge's painful awareness of his inability to simultaneously respect his friend while disappointing his 'copyholder' lays plain the tension in his mixed relationship with Cottle. Coleridge tries vainly to hold the feelings of owing and loving independently; his only sure conclusion is that mixing business concerns with love was a terrible error. But there is more in this letter than evidence of Coleridge's growing awareness of the failure of his friendly economics where Cottle is concerned. There is also in this letter the revelation that the very structure of patronage is destructive to Coleridge's capacity to work.

It takes a certain amount of wishful thinking to claim that any one factor might loom large in Coleridge's lifelong paralysis before impending tasks, but Coleridge's claim—that he cannot write his poetry under the duress of debt, obligation, and knowledge of a lack of proprietary relation to his work—makes good sense. As Coleridge gathered his creative energies to the task of weaving the gossamer strands of an ideal world, only faintly and partially formed in his mind in Pantisocratic terms, where gratitude and philanthropy and universal spirit and truth connect man with man, the gross cables of deadline and debt tethering him to Cottle might certainly have bitten hard into his flesh ('My happiest moments for composition are broken in upon by the reflection that I must make haste.'). The productive calm of an afternoon of contemplation, slowly gathered, scattered in a fit of worry ('I am too late! I am already months behind! I have received my pay beforehand!'). The tragic parting of forces on their way, and Coleridge left to bemoan a poem lost: 'Oh, wayward and desultory spirit of genius! Ill canst thou brook a task-master! The tenderest touch from the hand of obligation, wounds thee like a scourge of scorpions.'

In this image of scorpions, as well as in his reference to being in a 'quickset hedge of embarrassments', Coleridge links this letter to one he had written ten days earlier to Josiah Wade, in which the same images appear. In this letter he laments 'friendships lost by indolence, and happiness murdered by mismanaged sensibility!' It is true that Coleridge thought himself to have lost many friends to his indolence (most conspicuously Southey) but Cottle likely is in his mind here, given the proximity of the two letters in composition and the shared imagery. Coleridge concludes his letter to Wade with a forlorn poem on the hapless state of authors in the world, who alone among God's creatures seem set up to face the hostile world without defenses. In his concluding couplet, Coleridge writes, 'Vampire Booksellers drain him to the heart, and Scorpion Critics cureless venom dart!' There is a repositioning here of the scorpion to the critic and the vampire to the scourge of obligation, but the images are linked in Coleridge's mind. The patronage of Cottle is enervating, and the vampiric draining of energies might be particularly crippling given the shallow reserves of the victim.

In 1796, with a growing awareness of the debilitating effects of his patronized relationship with Cottle, Coleridge tried a new avenue to self-support: the launch of a subscriber-based periodical, *The Watchman*. It has been frequently wondered at by Coleridge's contemporaries, including Cottle, and by generations of scholars afterwards that a person of Coleridge's disposition (read laziness) should have sought wellbeing from any form of work so deadline driven as journalism. But perhaps within the context of his disappointed relationship with Cottle, Coleridge's motivations for launching *The Watchman* are drawn into sharper focus. *The Watchman* was a venture which, if successful, would financially have liberated Coleridge and put his means of production back into his own hands. *The Watchman* presented to Coleridge in 1796 the grand possibility of economic independence. The only difficulty was the replacement of a patron with an audience, but Coleridge had a plan to make that audience less menacing and anonymous.

Lucy Newlyn, among others, has pointed out that Coleridge felt a certain degree of anxiety in the presence of an anonymous audience. In her discussion of the later periodical venture *The Friend*, Newlyn argues in her introduction to *The Cambridge Companion to Coleridge* that Coleridge sought a deeper connection and intimacy with his readers, and therefore sought to establish a new form of audience based not on anonymous relations between writer and consumer, but on real, shared, sympathetic concerns:

> Friendship was not just a favorite figure for domestic and literary fraternity. It was the organizing principle in a hermeneutic enterprise designed to unite writers and their readers...Coleridge saw the bond of sympathy between author and reader in terms of a communitarian spirit, which had its roots in Christianity. The models for his reading circles can be traced back to Pantisocracy and its seventeenth century analogues, as can the spirit which motivates his literary dialogues and publishing ventures including *The Friend* itself. Just as the ideal of easy, intimate exchange was embodied into the idiom of the 'Conversation' poems, so in *The Friend* it was sublimated into a style designed to transform public taste. The spiritual community Coleridge sought early on in Pantisocracy was later projected onto the idea of a 'clerisy' of dedicated writer-readers. (Newlyn 2002, 5–6)

Coleridge sought to create in his readership what he had failed to create with Cottle: a symbiotic, sympathetic, easy community based on intimate exchange. Even as Coleridge had tried to refashion the patron relationship to suit his needs, he now turned his attention to reinventing the reader–writer relationship. So as not to be exposed to the raw vicissitudes of plebeian demand, Coleridge sought to select his own audience. He traveled the country in order to personally build a circle of subscribers, at least to some extent known to him. His interest in being in touch with his readers is familiar to his interest in leveling his relationship with Cottle: friendship between writer and reader precludes any grossness in the exchange of words for coins. Coleridge wished at this stage of his career to divest himself of any significant underwriter; he sought to exchange an increasingly oppressive source of income (Cottle) for the relative freedom and anonymity of a thousand small supporters, each subscribing at a small rate per annum.

Initially, of course, he required start-up capital, for which he turned to Josiah Wade. It is interesting that Coleridge turns away from Cottle at this moment. To have Cottle underwrite the venture directly would be only to continue his uncomfortable patronized relationship. Instead, he looked to borrow from a different friend, one he felt less encumbered by, and whom he would repay, as soon as the venture flew.

Coleridge knew that Cottle would feel the rupture in their relationship, and wrote to him immediately after his new financiers had gathered to discuss the project:

My Dear friend, I am fearful that you may have felt hurt at my not mentioning to you the proposed 'Watchman,' and from my not requesting you to attend the meeting. My dear friend, my reasons were these. All who met were expected to become subscribers to a fund; I knew there would be enough without you, and I knew, and felt, how much money had been drawn away from you lately.

The letter is something of a declaration of independence for Coleridge. A new pathway to financial support seemed open to him, one that did not depend on maintaining equality of footing with one man whose financial blessings might tilt the scale against friendship and in favor of obligation. Here Coleridge sought a circle of subscribers interested in his mind, and each willing to defray some part of the financial obligations of daily support; each subscriber would help to scrape away at the banal preoccupations of economic life for Coleridge. In each subscription, he saw the possibility of having the lower concerns absorbed, of being free to live without the baseness of putting materiality first, and without the harmful fantasy of assuming that another man might willingly assume all of that drudgery for him.

Unfortunately, the venture failed in nearly every respect. In a letter to Thomas Poole on 30 March 1796, the difficulties of the new concern are beginning to weigh, but are still tolerably under control:

Since you last saw me, I have been well nigh distracted—The repeated & most injurious Blunders of my printer out of doors, and Mrs Coleridge's increasing danger at home added to the gloomy prospect of so many mouths to open and shut, like puppets, as I move the string—in the eating and drinking way. . . I have received many abusive letters—post-paid, thanks to the friendly Malignants—but I am perfectly callous to disapprobation, except where it lessen profit.—There indeed I am all one Tremble of Sensibility, Marriage having taught me the wonderful uses of that vulgar commodity, yclept Bread.—The Watchman succeeds so as to yield a bread-and-cheesish profit.

The great burden of fiscal responsibility is wearisome, but prospects still seemed good for success. The language of business that pervades the letter suggests the depth of the effort Coleridge was making to take the reins of his financial life. But by 11 April, the picture was radically shifted in another letter to Poole:

You wish to have long Essay—so should I wish—; but so do not my subscribers wish. I feel the perplexities of my undertaking increased daily... In short, a Subscriber instead of regarding himself as a point in the circumference entitled to some diverging ray, considers me as the circumference and himself as the Centre to which *all* the rays ought to converge.— To tell you the truth, I do not think the Watchman will succeed—hitherto I have scarcely sold enough to pay the expences... to toil uncertainly for bread weighs me down to Earth.

Here are all of Coleridge's castles in the air crashing down. First there is the realization that audiences are not so easily made sympathetic as Coleridge would have liked. His hope of keeping his subscribers subordinate to his intellectual interests is clearly unraveling and he is experiencing a loss of creative control in the hopes of maintaining his audience. Furthermore, it is becoming increasingly clear that despite all of his spirited efforts, the venture is collapsing. Financial independence proves as elusive as authorial control. The dream of a new literary independence is in rapid collapse, and the pressures of quotidian need are dragging Coleridge down from his idealist flight to the hard realities of life on the ground.

Finally, the financial concern collapsed utterly, and threw him right back into debt to Cottle, who became his main source of the money to keep paper bills paid and print shops working. At the end of the *Watchman* experiment, Coleridge found himself where he had started: in debt, without prospects of literary freedom, and in doubt about his own abilities to make a go of things on his own, as is made clear in a third letter to Poole on 5 May 1796:

After No. 12, I shall cease to cry the state of the political atmosphere—It is not pleasant, Thomas Poole! To have worked 14 weeks for nothing—for nothing—nay, to have given the Public in addition to that toil five & 40 pounds!... Oh Watchman! Thou hast watched in vain—said the prophet Ezekiel, when, I suppose, he was taking a prophetic glimpse of my sorrow-sallowed Cheeks.—My Plans are reduced to two—, The first impracticable—the second not likely to succeed.[5]

The two plans Coleridge was reduced to were to try to publish a translation of Schiller or, alternatively, 'to become a Dissenting Parson & abjure Politics and carnal literature'. For the second path, Coleridge acknowledged that he had no inclination, and he acknowledged that to preach in the absence of a certain calling was a crime, but contrasted that crime to 'the greater wrongness of the Alternative', that is remaining with his family in a state of poverty.

The failure of *The Watchman* saw Coleridge's hopes greatly reduced. The avenue of patronage seemed closed to him by the failure of his relationship with Cottle. The alternative of a circle of sympathetic readers was equally defunct, buried in the ashes of *The Watchman*. Carlisle put the choice between patronage and publishing in pithily clear terms a few decades later:

---

[5] In fact, *The Watchman* only reached Number 10.

neither had very high attractions; the Patron's aid was now wellnigh *necessarily* polluted by sycophancy before it could come to hand; the Bookseller's was deformed with greedy stupidity, not to say entire wooden-headedness and disgust.

Coleridge was like a moth fluttering between two candles and burning himself in both. But a new, third opportunity was about to arise, one with a greater degree of compassion and sympathy than what had previously existed, and it would be presented, like so many other good things in Coleridge's life, by Thomas Poole.

In his reply to Coleridge's despairing letter, Poole offered the poet an escape from his straitened circumstances. Perhaps moved by the abject waste entailed in Coleridge's thought of entering the clergy without a calling and sacrificing 'carnal literature', Poole hit on a solution that was at once a salve to Coleridge's circumstances and his conscience. Poole contacted a circle of Coleridge's admirers and quietly asked them to contribute 5 guineas each, 'as a trifling mark of their esteem, gratitude, and admiration' of the young poet. The money was to be paid annually by the group's treasurer, originally John Cruikshank, later Joseph Prior Estlin. Perhaps no approach could have been more perfectly suited to Coleridge's needs. The small scale of contributions split among many meant that no one person was incommoded unduly by their support of Coleridge, but it also meant that there was no one person to whom Coleridge needed to feel particularly obliged. The money was provisioned for Coleridge not for any specific project (the completion of a volume of poetry or the delivery of a periodical) but for the general benefit of the poet's intellectual endeavors. This freed Coleridge to work on what he saw fit, without the feeling of schedule, obligation, or compulsion that he had earlier found so antithetical to his process of composition while working to fulfill his contract with Cottle. The language of Poole's offer conveys a deep understanding of Coleridge's economic ideology. Here is money given simply for the pleasure of seeing a great mind liberated from petty necessity, simply from an overflow of 'esteem and gratitude' for the intellectual gifts of a friend. The final delicacy of not placing the money directly in Coleridge's hand, but of having a 'treasurer' handle the annuity made the act of giving indirect, and erased the feeling of sycophantic unease with the patron.

The deep level of understanding Poole showed was not lost on Coleridge, who wrote on 18 May 1796 a far happier letter than he had in some time:

Poole! The Spirit, who counts the throbbings of the solitary heart, knows that what my feelings ought to be, such they are... Perhaps I shall not make myself intelligible—but the *strong and unmixed Affection*, I bear to you seems to exclude all Emotions of *Gratitude*, and renders even the principle of *Esteem* latent and inert; it's Presence is not perceptible, tho' it's absence could not be endured... I will make every possible Exertion; my Industry shall be at least commensurate with my Learning and Talents: if these do not procure me and mine the necessary Comforts of Life, I can receive as I would bestow, & in either case, receiving or bestowing, be *equally* grateful to my Almighty Benefactor... I should blame you for the exaggerated terms in which you have spoken of me in the proposal—did I not perceive the motive.—you wished to make it appear an *offering* not a *favor*—& in excess of delicacy have, I fear, fallen into some grossness of flattery.—God bless you—my dear, very dear Friend . . . Mrs Coleridge loves you—& says she would fall on your neck and kiss you . . .

The bonds of patronage so clearly evidenced in Coleridge's dealings with Cottle are here nowhere to be seen. The 'feelings' which suffuse Coleridge are only what they 'ought to be', and are only intelligible to a higher order of being than author or sponsor can ever hope to be. Gratitude and Esteem become invisible presences here, swept under by the strong tide of affection. Feelings of thankfulness and respect are rendered latent and secondary to love, in a powerful affirmation of the hierarchy of feeling Coleridge had sought between men in his Pantisocratic scheme. Here is Coleridge's perfect relationship between two men, freely offered gifts, freely accepted, without accountancy even in the way of increased gratitude and esteem: affection trumps all. It is out of this affection that Coleridge pledges to produce. 'Exertion and industry' follow as a natural consequence of the sympathetic understanding between the two men. Finally, the act of giving and receiving are rendered equal. Here is symbiotic reciprocity, the false binary between gift and receipt is broken down by the powerful upswell of unifying affection, and whatever gratitude is due is due not to man, but to God for being the first Author of affection.[6] The great lengths Poole has gone to erase the feeling of obligation and subvert the power dynamic of gifting is noticed by Coleridge in the distinction between 'favor' and 'offering'; the former is given in hopes of return, the latter freely, openly, and trustingly. In the end it is left to 'Mrs Coleridge' to offer the kisses of gratitude; between the two friends there can be no such requirement.

Poole's relief of Coleridge's circumstances marks something new. This was not merely a solution to the problems of bread and cheese. For Coleridge it was an act so perfectly in consonance with his most inward beliefs and ideals, that it marked a resuscitation of his former self. The bitterness of his disappointments with Southey and the deep scars left on his psyche from the loss of his Pantisocratic dream were suddenly offered salve. In a resilient rebirth, his faith in an idealized possibility for humanity and himself was reborn. This is made manifest in a letter he wrote to Poole after the latter had proposed that Coleridge move to Stowey and take a cottage there:

To live in a beautiful country & to inure myself as much as possible to the labors of the field, have been for this year past my dream of the day, my Sigh at midnight—but to enjoy these blessings *near you*, to see you daily, to tell you all my thoughts in their first birth, and to hear your's, to be mingling identities with you, as it were;—the vision-weaving *Fancy* has indeed often pictured such things, but *Hope* never dared whisper a promise!—Disappointment! Disappointment! Dash not from my trembling hand this bowl, which almost touches my lips! Envy me not this immortal Draught, and I will forgive thee all thy persecutions—forgive thee! Impious!—I will *bless thee*, black-vested Minister of Optimism! Stern Pioneer

---

[6] It is worth noting that Coleridge was as good as his word. In times of plenty he was generous to a fault. When the Morgans suffered financial collapse, Coleridge made a gift to them of a large part of the proceeds from *Remorse*, sold all of his books, and took out a subscription on their behalf.

of Happiness!—Thou hast been '*the Cloud*' before me from the day I left the flesh-pots of Egypt & was led thro' the way of the wilderness—the *cloud*, that has been guiding me to a land flowing with milk & honey—the milk of Innocence, the honey of friendship! I wanted such a letter as yours.

This is in essence the revivification of the Pantisocratic dream. The hole left in Coleridge's heart on Southey's departure is suddenly filled. What Poole has offered Coleridge, in his scheme for the annuity and in his invitation to come and live in Stowey is essentially what Coleridge had sought 'this year past': an opportunity to live in freedom, to meld with others and lose the distinction between individuals. It is the dream of the 'Eolian Harp', it is the vision of 'Kubla Khan'. The latter poem is particularly resonant here, as Coleridge feels himself about to quaff the milk of paradise, the immortal draught poised at his lips. Previous frustration is converted into the temporary agent of change, change which has led Coleridge from the wilderness of frustration in Bristol back into the garden of friendship, unity, and affection.

It is widely acknowledged that the Stowey years were the best years for Coleridge's poetry, and possibly for his happiness. Too little of the credit for this has gone to Poole, whose patient, even friendship is subsumed in the incandescence of that other celebrated friendship of this period. As Kelvin Everest has it,

Under Wordsworth's influence Coleridge's abstract intellectual interests were joined with a truly remarkable transformation of his talents as a poet. In the mainly quiet retirement of life in the Quantocks the two poets exchanged ideas and practice, often in the course of long country walks . . . the poetry that Coleridge produced in the period of his intimacy with the Wordsworths in Nether Stowey constitutes perhaps his least disputable claim to greatness. (Everest, 22)

It is hardly my purpose to subtract one iota from the legacy of Wordsworth's friendship with Coleridge, but it should not be forgotten that it was Poole's friendship with Coleridge that created the peaceful circumstances at Stowey that Coleridge required in order to fully develop his powers. This is not to say that Coleridge's time in Stowey was all pleasure, or that his friendship with Poole was all sunshine and delight. But that brief moment of two years in which the two men reached a level of understanding that bridged the cavernous rift between artist and supporter led to what was for Coleridge, as for lovers of Romantic poetry, a land of milk and honey.

Works Cited

Bensusan, S. L. 1913. *Coleridge*. London: T. C. and E. C. Jack; New York: Dodge Publishing Company.

Christie, William. 2006. *Samuel Taylor Coleridge: A Literary Life*. Basingstoke and New York: Palgrave Macmillan.

COLEMAN, DEIRDRE. 1988. *Coleridge and The Friend* (1809–10). Oxford: Oxford University Press.

COLERIDGE, SAMUEL TAYLOR. 1965. *Biographia Literaria,* ed. George Watson. New York: Dutton.

COTTLE, JOSEPH. 1847. *Reminiscences of Samuel Taylor Coleridge and Robert Southey.* London: Houlston and Stoneman.

DOUGHTY, OSWALD. 1981. *Perturbed Spirit: The Life and Personality of Samuel Taylor Coleridge.* Rutherford, NJ: Farleigh Dickinson University Press.

EVEREST, KELVIN. 2002. The Life. In *The Cambridge Companion to Coleridge,* ed. Lucy Newlyn. Cambridge and New York: Cambridge University Press.

FULFORD, TIM. 1991. *Coleridge's Figurative Language.* Basingstoke: Macmillan.

GRIGGS, EARL LESLIE. 1956–1971. *The Collected Letters of Samuel Taylor Coleridge.* Oxford: Clarendon Press.

HAMILTON, PAUL. 1983. *Coleridge's Poetics.* Oxford: Basil Blackwell.

HOLMES, RICHARD. 1998. *Coleridge: Darker Reflections.* London: Harper Collins.

LEFEBURE, MOLLY. 1974. *Samuel Taylor Coleridge, A Bondage of Opium.* London: Gollancz.

NEWLYN, LUCY. 1995. Coleridge and the Anxiety of Reception. *Romanticism,* No. 1. Spring.

—— 2002. 'Introduction', *Cambridge Companion to Coleridge.* Cambridge and New York: Cambridge University Press.

ROE, NICHOLAS. 1988. *Wordsworth and Coleridge: The Radical Years.* Oxford: Clarendon Press.

SANDFORD, MARGARET E. 1888. *Thomas Poole and His Friends.* London and New York: Macmillan.

CHAPTER 4

....

COLERIDGE'S MARRIAGE AND FAMILY

....

NEIL VICKERS

IT is difficult to write about Coleridge's marriage and family relationships. All marriages are to some extent opaque and there is real presumption in even attempting to understand them from the outside. The matter is complicated further in Coleridge's case by the fact that shortly after his death in 1834, at Wordsworth's and Southey's suggestion, his wife, Sara, burned 'sackfuls and sackfuls' of family letters (Lefebure, 17). The destroyed correspondence included not only most of the letters the couple had sent each other over a period of almost 40 years but also a large number of letters to or from members of the Southey and Wordsworth households. Those that were not consigned to flames often record only Coleridge's point of view. Such is the case with many of Coleridge's surviving letters and Notebook entries and also correspondence from partisan observers such as William and Dorothy Wordsworth. (Southey's letters constitute an important exception to this rule as they take Sara's side pretty consistently.) Some of Sara's letters to Tom Poole have survived and were published in 1933 by Stephen Potter. These give a lively picture of her personality and of some of her difficulties with Coleridge. In 1843, Henry Taylor, Southey's first biographer, approached Sara for her recollections of Southey and her husband. She drafted a fragmentary MS headed 'Mrs Codian. Remembrancies of RS and STC', now held at the University of Texas. It remains unpublished, though small sections appeared in Molly Lefebure's biography of Mrs Coleridge. But the fact remains that the textual materials we have do not give Sara enough of a voice.

A more intractable obstacle is Coleridge himself. At his best Coleridge was generous, open-hearted, full of curiosity about other people, and he had a gift for friendship, particularly with men. But he suffered prolonged periods of severe anxiety and depression during which he became dissatisfied with and hostile towards those closest to him. After 1801, when he lost his health for good, these depressions, compounded by severe physical debility and discomfort, sharply affected his relations with other people and especially with his wife. He acknowledged this in a letter he wrote her in 1808: 'I have never known any woman for whom I felt equal personal fondness . . . Till the very latest period, when my health & spirits rendered me dead to everything, I had a PRIDE in you, . . . I never saw you at the top of a hill, when I returned from a walk, without a sort of pleasurable feeling in the sight . . .' (*CL* 3: 77). But with his health gone, admiration subsided: as he told a correspondent eight days earlier, 'The *sight* of that woman would be the death of me' (*CL* 3: 73).

Coleridge's family life was difficult.[1] During his troubled middle years, friends often commented that he was not cut out to be a husband or a father. Ronald Wendling has written movingly about Coleridge's 'psychological homelessness' (51–4). Coleridge himself was in no doubt where the cause lay: in his childhood. He had been plucked from the family home in Devon at the age of nine and sent to Christ's Hospital. Over the next ten years, he returned home perhaps twice. Crabb Robinson records that his brothers felt degraded by his charity school uniform and that after a first visit the family made no further effort to bring him home (Morley, 1: 105–6). In the early 1780s he enjoyed a connection with his mother's brother, a tobacconist; but it did not last. Coleridge told Poole that his uncle was a 'sot' (*CL* 1: 388). During his teens he enjoyed the company of two of his brothers: Luke and George. Luke took him to the London hospital to 'walk the wards' with him and for a time Coleridge was 'wild to be apprenticed to a surgeon' (Gillman, 23). George, who had been appointed to a curacy in Hackney, he called his 'father, brother, everything' (*CL* 1: 3). Coleridge's relations with his two other surviving brothers, Edward and James, were more distant. With Edward he seems to have had almost no connection. He was somewhat in awe of his military brother James, writing to him infrequently and in a tone that suggests he did not expect to be taken altogether seriously. To the end Coleridge retained an idealized view of his father as a Parson Adams figure. Towards his mother his feelings were hostile. She seems to have been a cold woman. The best thing he could tell Poole about her was that she was an 'admirable economist' (*CL* 1: 348). James Engell, in his introduction to a very important volume of Coleridge family correspondence, has noted a

---

[1] Except where otherwise stated, all biographical information in this essay derives from Rosemary Ashton's biography of Coleridge.

tendency among several of Coleridge's brothers to sign their letters to her, 'Dutifully' (16–17). The few letters Coleridge wrote to her—he seems to have stopped in the early 1790s—emphasize duty rather than love. He did not attend her funeral.

Mrs Coleridge was 45 or 46 when Samuel was born and by the time he was sent off to Christ's Hospital he was the last child on her hands. In the wonderful autobiographical letters he sent to Thomas Poole in 1797, Coleridge remembered his Ottery years as dominated by rivalry with his brother Frank, two years his elder. The family kept a housekeeper who had nursed Frank but not Samuel and Coleridge believed that the family housekeeper, Molly, had encouraged Frank to be jealous of him. (Significantly, he also believed he was his mother's favourite.) To Poole he described a well-known incident in which he was given a piece of cheese by his mother which Frank then stole from him. Samuel then lunged at his brother with a knife and Frank feigned death. Terrified, Samuel ran away to the river Otter where he spent the night cold and damp. His only pleasure, he said in 1797, was imagining how miserable his mother must be (*CL* 1: 352). The incident is important because to it Coleridge traced his susceptibility to rheumatic fever, which was to flare up again when he moved to the Lakes and the Wordsworths in 1800. He was found the next day and the breach with Frank healed. Coleridge told Gillman that his character had been fixed during his Ottery years: 'from certain jealousies of old Molly, my brother Frank's dotingly fond nurse...I was in earliest childhood huffed away from the enjoyments of muscular activity from play, to take refuge at my mother's side, on my little stool, to read my little book, and listen to the talk of my elders. I was driven from life in motion, to life in thought and sensation' (Gillman, 10).

Many of Coleridge's biographers have drawn attention to Coleridge's fondness for households in which there were at least two women to look after the menfolk. They see this as evidence of his desire to resume the life he had lost on being sent to Christ's Hospital. As James Engell has pointed out, the 'pattern of a pair of brothers bonded to a pair of women, especially sisters, was first established when he and Frank were at home with their mother and the dear nurse Molly' (15). Stephen M. Weissman, the author of the only psycho-biography of Coleridge, has noted that on at least four occasions, Coleridge fell in love with one of a pair of sisters the other of whom was linked to the main man in his life. A practising psychoanalyst, Weissman suggests that one of Coleridge's great and perhaps unconscious aims as a lover was to be reunited with the brothers he lost and in some cases never knew from his family of origin. Engell has pointed out that there was a tradition in Coleridge's family of marrying sisters. Samuel's brothers William (1758–80) and Luke (1765–90), both of whom died young, had been engaged to two sisters, the Misses Hart of Exeter. Luke's marriage went ahead but William died the night before his wedding. George, Samuel's 'Brother and Father', married William's bride twenty years later.

On 4 October 1781 Coleridge and his father accompanied Frank to Plymouth where the latter was enlisted as a midshipman on a naval ship bound for India, the

Gibraltar. Coleridge would never see Frank again. His father died on the night of their return. The fourth of October was the last day he saw either of them alive and it precipitated far-reaching changes in the life of young Samuel, most saliently his expulsion to London. A Victorian critic wisely remarked that Coleridge's life is best seen as a series of leavetakings. The leavetakings that were set in train by the events of 4 October 1781 were to be lived out again and again in his life. Throughout his life Coleridge's friends often complained that 'out of sight, out of mind' was a habit deeply ingrained. It was as if they had died in his mind.

Coleridge first met his wife in Bristol in the summer of 1794. The summer had begun with a walking tour of Wales with his old school-friend Joseph Hucks. The two men stopped en route in Oxford where, through Hucks's friend Robert Allen, he made the acquaintance of Robert Southey. They stayed in Oxford for almost three weeks and resumed their journey on 5 July (*CL* 1: 82n.). The Welsh tour lasted three weeks and Coleridge returned to Bristol on 4 or 5 August. The next few weeks were perhaps the most eventful of his life. He and Southey devised a plan to start a settlement on the banks of the Susquehanna in Pennsylvania, in which individual property would be abolished. The scheme, known as Pantisocracy ('the equal government of all') would be put into practice by twelve young couples. According to Coleridge, its 'leading idea' was 'to make men *necessarily* virtuous by removing all Motives to Evil—all possible Temptations' (*CL* 1: 114).

As Pantisocracy required the cooperation of women, wives were needed. Southey introduced his new friend to the Fricker sisters. These young women were the daughters of a Bristol merchant who had fallen on hard times and they were well-educated—Southey once stated that he had been 'partly educated' with them but did not say when or where (Lefebure, 23). Southey was already attached to Edith Fricker and Coleridge soon began paying attention to her older sister Sara. By the end of the month, on the strength of an acquaintance lasting under three weeks, Coleridge was engaged to her.

On his return to Cambridge Coleridge wrote an effusive letter to Southey:

America! Southey! Miss Fricker!—Yes—Southey—you are right—Even Love is the creature of strong Motive—I certainly love her. I think of her incessantly & with unspeakable tenderness—with that infinite melting away of the Soul that symptomatizes it.   (*CL* 1: 103)

The day after he wrote these words he received a letter from Southey which appears to accuse him of breaking a promise to write to Miss Fricker and, by implication, of deserting her. He wrote his friend a reassuring letter. Coleridge in turn suspected Southey of going cold on Pantisocracy. Both men's doubts proved prescient. On 21 October, Coleridge told Southey of a letter he had received from Mary Evans, the sweetheart of his schooldays, apparently written with the aim of getting him to renounce pantisocracy (James Dykes Campbell suggested that she was acting on behalf of Coleridge's older brother George). The letter seems to have awakened feelings of love for Mary that he had set aside and for the next few months she eclipsed Sara Fricker in his affections: 'I love her Southey! almost to madness' (*CL* 1: 65). He also let Southey know that in order to forget Mary he had tried to fall under the spell of a Miss Brunton, a member of a travelling troupe of actors from Norwich. But he had been sedulous in the defence of Pantisocracy. Some time in early November Coleridge wrote to Mary asking her if it was true that she was engaged to be married and declaring his love for her (he did not mention that he was himself engaged). Her next letter has not survived but it gave him no grounds to hope he would marry her. He burnt her letters and asked her to 'forget' his. On 9 December, with the Pantisocratic scheme in trouble for other reasons, he made it clear that he wanted to disengage himself from Sara. He told Southey that he had 'mistaken the ebullience of *schematism* for affection . . . The most criminal action of my Life was the first letter I wrote to [Sara]. I had worked myself to such a pitch, that I scarcely knew I was writing like an hypocrite' (*CL* 1: 132). Strikingly he failed to draw any practical conclusions from this self-analysis. He continued on 29 December: 'To marry a woman whom I do *not* love, to make her the Instrument of low Desire—and on the removal of a desultory Appetite, to be perhaps not displeased at her Absence! . . . Mark you, Southey!—*I will do my Duty* (*CL* 1: 145). And so he did. In January, Southey went down to London as he put it 'to reclaim his stray' and Coleridge returned with him to Bristol and to Sara.

We are bound to ask why Coleridge went through with the marriage. The answer is necessarily complex. Sara's biographer, Molly Lefebure, has rightly pointed out that if he had told her that he didn't want to marry her she could hardly have forced him to do so (52). Moreover, she had other suitors (*CL* 1: 151). Lefebure suggests that Coleridge fell dramatically in love with Sara on his return in early 1795. Her only documentary source for this view is the exceedingly unreliable De Quincey who was reporting hearsay long after the fact. Contemporary letters and Notebook entries don't bear him out.

The point that requires to be made about Coleridge's attitude to his wife is that from the very beginning he was ambivalent about her. His ambivalence encompassed love, especially in the first years of their marriage. But it also involved an antipathy that he never relinquished. In considering Coleridge's decision to press ahead with the marriage a number of factors should be borne in mind. Often in Coleridge's life when he had to make a decision about an individual he staked everything he had. In different ways this shaped his relations with Southey, Wordsworth, and Gillman. Something of this sort seems to have happened with Sara too. He was also probably physically attracted to Sara and was gratified to discover that she was physically attracted to him. It is clear that in the course of 1795 his regard for Sara grew much stronger so that by November of that year he could tell Southey 'I love and am beloved' (*CL* 1: 164; the remarkable thing is how slow this declaration was in coming). Marriage to Sara offered him much-needed stability in his life. Barely three months earlier, his brothers had managed to get him discharged from the army on grounds of insanity. (In later years Coleridge regarded himself as having been on the very brink of insanity at that time (*CN* 2: 2398).) The stability he sought was the stability of an entire family: the Pantisocratic family but also the extended families that would have as their common focus the Fricker sisters. As his relations with the Evans, the Morgans, and the Gillmans all show, Coleridge was capable of forming passionate attachments to families in a very short space of time. Again, something of this sort seems to have happened with the Fricker sisters. Further, Coleridge wanted to retain the regard of the friend who meant most to him, Robert Southey. He had hoped to elicit from Southey a corresponding sense of duty towards Pantisocracy and towards himself. (He did, briefly. In March Southey amended the Pantisocratic scheme: it would now be centred on Wales rather than Pennsylvania; but because of obstacles his family placed in the way of his marrying Edith, Southey eventually withdrew from the scheme in late August.) In addition, Coleridge felt he had a moral and intellectual duty to marry her. How could he desert his fiancée when part of the point of marrying her was to prove that a class of men existed, to which he belonged, that would redeem mankind by rising above mere selfishness? (This sort of vanity was very much to the fore in early 1795. In a letter to his old Christ's Hospital friend George Dyer, he claimed that Sara had 'rejected the Addresses of two men, one of them of large Fortune—and by her perseverant attachment to me disobliged her relations in a very uncomfortable Degree'. A 'short time must decide whether she marries me whom she loves' or 'a man whom she strongly dislikes' (*CL* 1: 151). Coleridge presented himself as disinterestedly saving her from a worse fate than himself.) More speculatively, perhaps marriage to Sara—taking place against the background of Southey's marriage to Edith and Robert Lovell's to Martha—evoked a pleasing echo of his three brothers' marriages to the Misses Hart. Finally it was consilient with an aspect of his relationship with his mother towards whom he felt more duty than love (Engell, 17).

The couple were married on the *fata morgana* of 4 October 1795 in a church which, ominously, was closely associated with Thomas Chatterton. The early years of the marriage seem to have gone well enough. If Sara had any reservations about Coleridge in those days, they are unknown. Coleridge for his part ceased to talk as if he had been dragooned into a marriage not of his own making. The couple started a family: Hartley was born on 19 September 1796 and Berkeley in May 1798. Coleridge published his first volume of verse and enjoyed the most creative period of his life as a poet.

But Coleridge and Sara also had problems. Chief among these was that of finding a secure source of income and the related question of whether Coleridge would try to enter a regular profession. He lost money on *The Watchman*, his first major attempt to earn a living, and he had to be rescued by subsidies from friends and a grant of £10 from the Royal Society of Literature. The effect on him was searing. He never again wished to depend for his living on writing alone. Thomas Poole and a group of friends came forward with an annuity of £35 a year. In May of that year

Coleridge told Poole of two ambitions, one to spend a prolonged period in Germany translating Schiller's works, the other to 'become a Dissenting parson and abjure Politics & carnal literature'. The first required a significant outlay and had to be deferred indefinitely. The second he was more ambivalent about, seeing it more as a 'least bad' option than as something to be positively desired. Through the good offices of Dr Thomas Beddoes, Coleridge was offered an editorial post on the *Morning Chronicle* but he declined it as he did not wish to leave the West Country. He was also offered a lucrative position as a tutor to the children of a Mrs Evans in Darley near Derby though the offer was withdrawn on the advice of her relations. Coleridge and the heavily pregnant Sara visited her in August and were presented with £90 and 'all her baby clothes'. The following month he went to Birmingham to meet the family of Charles Lloyd, a young poet of means whom he had met on his *Watchman* tour earlier in the year. Lloyd's father agreed to pay Coleridge £80 a year to provide his son with board, lodging and inspiring companionship. In December he asked Poole to buy a cottage in Nether Stowey with a small plot of land attached. Poole was at first reluctant—the cottage was small and damp (Sara called it a 'hovel') and he may also have worried about the implications of becoming Coleridge's landlord. But Coleridge prevailed and the couple moved in at the beginning of 1797. Coleridge hoped to reduce their living expenses further by farming the plot of ground that came with the cottage. His main hopes, however, remained pinned on literature. At the invitation of Richard Brinsley Sheridan he began writing a play for Drury Lane from which he hoped to earn £500. He also began to write reviews for London periodicals. None of these schemes quite worked out as planned: *Osorio*, his play, was rejected; he quarrelled with Lloyd who left early and reviewing didn't pay much. By the end of 1797 he was telling friends that with great reluctance he was determined to become either a journalist or a minister. Among those to whom he confided his lack of enthusiasm were the Wedgwood brothers, Tom and Josiah. Hearing that he was about to accept the incumbency of a Unitarian congregation they sent him a draft for £100 which he sent back to them, on the grounds that to accept it was merely to put off a decision he would have to take sooner or later. They then offered him an annuity for life of £150, which he accepted. One hundred and fifty pounds was a significant sum but not quite enough to live on. By the end of the first year he had drawn on £40 from the next year's instalment and borrowed further money from Poole and Godwin.

Coleridge's objections to clerical and journalistic careers were eloquent and are perhaps to be admired the more given how racked he was by anxieties about making a living. Something he did not quite face up to was that his money worries were partly the result of his reluctance to confine his talents to any single track. Rosemary Ashton has observed that Coleridge took the Wedgwood annuity 'to mean no less than that he should enlighten mankind on every subject of inquiry'. No wonder, says Ashton, that he 'so embroiled himself as to render himself incapable of repaying the Wedgwoods' generosity on a smaller, more reasonable scale by work with which they and everyone else would have been perfectly satisfied. But we have the easy wisdom of hindsight' (120).

We can only speculate as to what Sara made of their financial prospects. We know that she wanted him to write more. Writing to his friend Charles Danvers in January 1802, Southey remembered that 'In the first years of their marriage she often put him out of temper by urging him to write. & she at last left it off as useless and only productive of dissention' (Pratt, 16). Cherry Durrant suggests that it would have been logical for Sara to see the Wedgwood annuity as a mixed blessing as it gave Coleridge the freedom not to make a more ambitious long-term set of arrangements (63). And the Wedgwood annuity did not in fact free them from deepening debt.

Coleridge's mental state was a second source of difficulty in the marriage. His letters and Notebooks show that he was depressed much of the time, often severely. There is a very moving Notebook entry dated 1805 in which he says this:

It is a most instructive part of my Life, the fact that I have always been preyed on by some Dread, and perhaps all my faulty actions have been the consequence of some Dread or other on my mind/ . . . So in my childhood & Boyhood the horror of being detected with a sorehead . . . then a short-lived Fit of Fears from sex—then horror of DUNS, & a state of struggling with madness from an incapability of hoping that I should be able to marry Mary Evans (and this strange passion of fervent though wholly imaginative and imaginary Love uncombinable by my utmost efforts with <any regular> Hope . . . Then came that stormy time/ and for a few months America really inspired Hope, & I became an exalted Being—then came Rob. Southey's alienation/my marriage—constant dread in my mind respecting Mrs Coleridge's Temper . . . and finally stimulants in the fear & prevention of violent Bowel-attacks from mental agitation/ then almost epileptic night-horrors in my sleep.   (CN 2: 2398)

Coleridge's psychological frailty elicited from his friends an extraordinarily protective attitude. It is striking that when Berkeley Coleridge fell ill (while Coleridge was abroad in Germany), Poole instructed Sara not to make too much of it, for fear of upsetting Coleridge to the point where his work would suffer. And when he died, Sara waited for Poole to write to Coleridge with the sad news. 'I shall not yet write to Coleridge', she reassured Poole, 'and when I do—I will pass over all disagreeable subjects with the greatest care, for I well know their violent effect on him' (Potter, 3). Coleridge's children were a constant source of anxiety to him. He often imagined that they had died. His first son Hartley was born while he was away. The news inspired him to write two sonnets, one of which imagines that the boy might be dead by the time he reached home.

The arrival of William and Dorothy Wordsworth in nearby Alfoxden in 1797 has been presented (by De Quincey and others) as a blow to the Coleridges' marriage.[2] It is a claim based more on speculation than evidence. It is clear that many of

---

[2] See e.g., Lefebure (91–8).

Coleridge's friends were disturbed by the extent of his admiration for Wordsworth. Poole for instance mentioned his fears of 'amalgamation' (Sandford, 1: 278.) It is possible and perhaps likely that Sara shared in this anxiety. However, there is no evidence of any hostility between Sara and the Wordsworths when they all lived in Somerset. Oswald Doughty has made much of the fact that portions of Dorothy's Alfoxden journal have not come down to us, conjecturing that Dorothy fell in love with him then (140). If she was, Coleridge does not appear to have suspected it.

Coleridge's voyage to Germany from September 1798 to September 1799 inaugurated a difficult period for Coleridge and Sara. Sara did not accompany her husband to Germany as originally planned. She had given birth in May 1798 to Berkeley Coleridge. Coleridge in consultation with Poole seems to have decided that it would be better if she and the children stayed in Somerset under Poole's guardianship. It was to prove a catastrophic decision. Poole's recently-widowed sister-in-law Mrs Richard Poole offered to have a number of local children inoculated against smallpox by giving them cowpox vaccine. Hartley and Berkeley were put forward. Hartley developed the red marks associated with the treatment but five-months' old Berkeley at first did not. Following a second dose, he came down with a bout of cowpox that almost killed him. He was blind for a time. Berkeley died in February 1799 of consumption caught, it is believed, from the Coleridge's woman-servant, known as Nanny. The news was kept from Coleridge on Poole's insistence until late March of 1799. Sara expressed the hope that he would come home by May but in fact Coleridge decided to stay on in Germany until the end of July to undertake a tour of the Harz mountains which he hoped to turn into a book.

Neither the marriage nor his friendship with Poole fully recovered from these events. The couple quarrelled shortly after Coleridge's return which had been further delayed by his decision to return via Sockburn in the far north of England where he met Wordsworth and his cousins the Hutchinsons. (It was on this occasion that Coleridge first met Sara Hutchinson.) Soon afterwards he decided to uproot his family from Stowey and move to the Lakes to be near Wordsworth. No record survives of Sara's feelings about the move. She was cut off from her sisters and the friends she had made in Stowey. When they left Somerset in July of 1800, she was seven months pregnant. Their third child Derwent was born on 14 September of that year. She wrote glowingly about Greta Hall, their new home, to Mrs George Coleridge (Lefebure, 127).

The first few months in the Lakes went well; but by the end of the year Coleridge's health began to decline. Though he did not know it, he had lost his health for good at the age of only 28. By April, he had convinced himself that he was dying (*CL*, ii, 724). The Wordsworths shared this fear. They also surmised that marital unhappiness was preventing him from making a proper recovery. As Dorothy noted in a letter to Mary Hutchinson of 29 April 1801: 'Mrs C. is in excellent health. She is indeed a bad nurse for C., but she has several great merits. She is very much to be pitied, for when one party is ill-matched the other necessarily must be so too. She would have made a very good wife for many another man but for Coleridge!! Her radical fault is want of sensibility and what can such a woman be to Coleridge?' (*W Letters*, 2, 330–1). With the Wordsworths' help, Coleridge formed a plan to go abroad again, this time to the Azores. Getting away from Sara was doubtless one of his motives. It came to nothing. Most of Coleridge's biographers agree that it was during these months that he became addicted to opiates which were almost certainly the cause of the 'gout' and 'scrofula' he complained of over the next three years. (It is unlikely that he understood the connection.) It was also during these months that Coleridge's ambivalence towards his wife tipped over into frank hatred. A second visit to Sockburn and to Sara Hutchinson resulted in three Notebook entries in which he alludes to the latter as his 'infinitely beloved Darling' (*CN* 1: 984–6). He was very depressed. For Sara there was the added burden of knowing that he blamed her for his depression. He had married her in a fit of enthusiasm and was discovering that he had made a disastrous choice. Of course, his accusation was not entirely untrue and in all sorts of ways they were incompatible. But some of his disappointment with Sara was a disappointment that he was to experience with almost everyone he was close to. (He would, for instance, in time express a comparable resentment towards Wordsworth, for taking advantage of his inspiring companionship while as he saw it giving him nothing in return.) To his Notebook he confided the following observation in September 1801:

Sara's…interesting to trace its source in…coldness perhaps & paralysis in all tangible ideas and sensations—all that forms *real Self.* Hence the Slave of her she creates her own self in a field of Vision & Hearing, at a distance, by her own ears & eyes. Nothing affects her with pain & or pleasure as it is but only as other people will say it is—nay by an habitual absence of reality in her affections I have had an hundred instances that the being beloved, or the not being beloved, is a thing indifferent; but the *notion* of not being beloved—that wounds her pride deeply.   (*CN* 1: 979)

This Notebook entry along with some others supports a conjecture by Molly Lefebure that about this time the Coleridges' sexual relationship broke down, perhaps as a result of his infatuation with Sara Hutchinson (145).[3] It is significant because it is the first time he voices what will become a constant grievance: that Sara could not respond to him authentically. The idea that Sara was overly sensitive of other people's opinions does seem to have a foundation in truth. While Coleridge was in Germany she wrote this to Poole:

By what I could perceive by Mr Ward's manner on Sunday I judge my intended visit to Mrs K—had been a subject of disapprobation to some persons. '*Mrs Poole approves* of your

---

[3] Coleridge strongly hints that this was the case in a letter he sent to Wedgwood in October 1802 (*CL* 2: 876).

going' said he, 'for I suppose you will be no great expence to them'—'certainly not—but she very earnestly invites me to come, and I think I shall accept it'—but upon reflection I shall not and have this evening written to them to be excused. I hope she will not take it amiss. (Potter, 3)

Coleridge now began to claim to speak openly of his desire to separate from his wife. Rumours that they were on the point of separating reached Bristol by the end of the year and Southey was forced to comment on these in a letter:

He complained that she irritates him & makes him so ill that he can do nothing. this is a wretched excuse for idleness. ill he assuredly is & that illness has perhaps changed his temper. he is in debt to the booksellers—to Johnson, to Longman—this preys upon him— he has not resolution enough to clear it off by exertion—letters come to him which he often will not open—still they vex him—& he can vent the vexation only upon his wife. Edith has heard him talk to her seriously of seperating [*sic*]—Mrs Coleridge never knows whether he means it or not—. she *now* knows not that his conversation with Davy, Tobin &c is about his wifes ill temper—in order that it may reach Wedgwood thro those channels.   (Pratt, 16)

Southey's closing insinuation—that Coleridge felt he needed Wedgwood's per-mission to leave his wife—is shrewd. If he had simply abandoned his family, the Wedgwoods might have felt compelled to withdraw the annuity. A legal divorce would have been a possibility only if she had committed adultery; but she was faithful. He and his wife had no other income. The question became harder to ask in the Spring when Sara fell pregnant again. (To Poole: 'Mrs Coleridge is indisposed and I have too much reason to suspect that she is breeding again/ an event that was to have been deprecated' (*CL* 2: 799).) At some point over the summer the Coleridges had a row that he said resulted in his succumbing to violent stomach spasms and prostration. Sara, he told Wedgwood, was 'shocked beyond measure' and promised 'to set about an alteration in her external manners & looks & language' (*CL* 2: 876).

If any woman wanted an exact and copious Recipe, 'How to make a Husband compleatly miserable', I could furnish her with one—with a Probatum est, tacked to it.—Ill tempered Speeches sent after me when I went out of the House, ill-tempered Speeches on my return, my friends received with freezing looks, the least opposition or contradiction occasioning screams of passion, & the sentiments which I held most base, ostentatiously avowed—all this added to the utter negation of everything a Husband expects from a Wife—especially, living in retirement—& the consciousness, that I was myself growing a worse man.   (*CL* 2: 876)

Coleridge also sent Sara an ignoble letter of remonstrance, attacking her character. 'Permit me, my dear Sara! Without offence to you, as Heaven knows! It is without any feeling of pride in myself, to say—that in sex, acquirements, and in the quantity and quality of natural endowments whether of Feeling, or of Intellect, you are the Inferior. Therefore, it would be preposterous to expect that I should see with your eyes, & dismiss my Friends from *my* heart just because you have chosen not to give them any Share of your Heart; but it is not preposterous, in me, on the contrary I have a right to expect & demand your heart' (*CL* 2: 888). The Coleridge's next child, Sara *fille*, was born on 23 December 1802. The Notebook entry following her birth reads: 'Conductor & *thunder-rod* of my whole Hatred' (*CN* 1: 1311).

In 1803, Coleridge's physical condition deteriorated further and he took out a life assurance policy valued at £1000. He continued to insist that he needed a warm climate. He resolved on a plan whose full ramifications he concealed from those most directly concerned. He persuaded Southey to come and live in Greta Hall and then he would go abroad. Southey's wife Edith was of a nervous disposition and Coleridge heartened Southey with the thought that Sara's company would lift her spirits. The two Pantisocrats meanwhile would engage in literary projects. The Southeys were expected in Keswick in early September but disaster intervened. Their only child Margaret died suddenly from 'water on the brain from teething' (probably tubercular meningitis) just as they were about to head north. In a letter of condolence Coleridge shows less concern with the Southeys' loss than with the possibility that they would remain in Bristol. Fortunately for the Coleridges, they came at the end of September. Coleridge immediately began making plans to go abroad, with everyone's blessing. Though Sara did not realize it, the marriage was to all intents and purposes now over. He would never again return to Greta Hall in the guise of a husband.

On his return from Malta in 1806, Coleridge told his London acquaintances that he was now resolved to separate from Sara. 'He dare not go home', Wordsworth told Sir George Beaumont, 'he recoils so much from the thought of domesticating with Mrs Coleridge, with whom, though on many counts he much respects her, he is so miserable that he dare not encounter it. What a deplorable thing!' (*W Letters*, 3: 78). It is clear that he wanted others to prepare Sara for a discussion about separation. The couple eventually met in November. Faced with Coleridge's claims that to live with her would probably result in his death, Sara agreed to a separation on 'friendly' terms. At first Coleridge proposed to take Hartley and Derwent. Sara and little Sara would remain with Southey. (George Coleridge, who disapproved of the separation, feared that his brother would leave Hartley and Derwent with him at the Ottery school and told him he was giving it up.) The financial terms of the settlement were obscure. In Malta he had made over the whole of the Wedgwood annuity to Sara.[4] The Wordsworths, finding Dove Cottage too small for their requirements, wanted to move. Coleridge encouraged them to take over the lease of Greta Hall, assuring them that Southey wanted to move back to Bristol, apparently assuming that the two Saras were now part of the Southey household. When news of this plan reached Southey he decided to remain in the house: 'That be hanged for a tale!' (Lefebure, 176).

---

[4] Letter from Sara Coleridge to Mrs George Coleridge, quoted in Lefebure (165).

In the end the boys were sent to the Reverend Dawes' school in Ambleside as weekly boarders and Sara, the most intellectually gifted of the three, remained at home where she was tutored by her mother, her aunts, and her 'uncle Southey'. Over the next few years the balance in Coleridge's ambivalence towards his wife became more positive. Especially striking is the following, which he sent to Morgan in Latin:

This is something worthy of note: my wife is chaste, modest, prudent, an excellent mother, outstanding equally in looks and manners, and seems to me even more beautiful today than she seemed in our first embraces. And I am the man you know whose own nature has filled his whole heart and all his feelings with passion, in whose very innards there is some kind of sick necessity to love somebody and be loved by someone in return—a man taken by native and congenital inclination with sweethearts, women's charms, and the sweet whisperings of intercourse both physical and mental, one ready to do anything that a husband might rightly desire or that I cannot prevent myself desiring—and yet, as though my wife had been my sister in the womb, I freeze and shudder at the very thought of conjugal intercourse. Thank God, she too doesn't want or desire it!'   (*CL* 3: 377)[5]

Following the rupture with Wordsworth in 1810, in 1812 Coleridge spent six weeks in Keswick in the vain hope that proximity might enable a reconciliation with his old friend. (He refused to go to the Wordsworths and they refused to come to him.) But he appears to have announced to his wife that he wished the family to live together again and that he would make arrangements for them to join him in London. Sara told Poole that she

listened . . . with incredulous ears, while he was building these 'airy castles' and calmly told him that I thought it was much better that I and the children should remain in the country until the Boys had finished their School-education and then, if he found himself in circumstances that would admit of it, & would engage not to leave us all alone in that wide city, I would cheerfully take leave of dear Keswick, and follow his amended fortunes. In the meantime, a regular correspondence was to be kept up between himself, and me, and the children; and never more was he to keep a letter of mine, or the Boys, or Southey's unopened.

(Potter, 17)

Coleridge never again returned to the Lakes. The correspondence was kept up briefly. Coleridge sent Sara £100 from the £400 he got from *Remorse*. This was especially welcome as a few months earlier Josiah Wedgwood had written to him to say that he could no longer afford his half of the annuity. Coleridge wrote back graciously releasing Wedgwood; but he did not mention his family. The annuity had in principle been Sara's from 1803, though Coleridge continued to be its first recipient. 'Mr Wedgwood, I daresay, little guesses the *increase in anxieties* his withdrawing his half of the annuity has caused me', Sara wrote to Poole. A few

---

[5] I thank Armand D'Angour of Jesus College, Oxford for this translation. Fruman conjectures that Coleridge's prolonged use of laudanum might have made him impotent (424–5).

years later, at the instigation of someone other than Coleridge, Wedgwood arranged for his brother's share to be paid directly to Sara.

1814 marked the low point in Coleridge's struggle with opium and he ignored the entreaties of Southey, Wordsworth and Poole to appeal for money to send Hartley to university. The financial arrangements were eventually made in spite of Coleridge. In 1815 he contacted the family to offer to coach Hartley in Greek during the summer. Hartley stayed with his father at the home of the Morgans in Calne in Wiltshire for four months.

Sara next saw her husband in January 1823 when she visited him at Moreton House with their daughter, Sara. The two women stayed with the Gillmans for three weeks before moving to Coleridge's nephew, John Taylor Coleridge. Although Sara told Poole that the visit had 'gone off to the greatest satisfaction of all parties', Henry Nelson Coleridge (who would soon become secretly engaged to Sara *fille*) informed his brother that 'He and his wife are kind but I suppose it is only surface work', adding 'Mr and Mrs C. do not even use the same sleeping room. Hum!' (Mudge, 32).

Sara left Greta Hall in 1830 to go and live with her daughter and son-in-law in Hampstead about three miles from Coleridge in Highgate. For the remaining four years of Coleridge's life, the couple saw each other from time to time when Coleridge's children and grandchildren visited him. Sara's letters to Poole become markedly favourable in reference to her husband during these final few years.

Lefebure's 1986 biography of Sara begins with the observation that she was 'among the most maligned of great men's wives' (15). Recent biographers have been much more sympathetic to Sara, in no small measure because of Lefebure's book. One trait to emerge is her marvellous sense of humour; Southey mentioned it often and it features in many of the Coleridge children's letters. (Coleridge is almost the only friend who never mentions it.) An excellent linguist, she invented a rich slang, which Southey dubbed her 'lingo *grande*'. He gave his friend Grosvenor Bedford a specimen of it in a letter of 1821: 'you are a stumparumper because you are a shortycum; and you are a wattlykin, a tendrum, a detestabumpus, and a figurumpus. These are the words which came from her chapset when she speaks of you, and you need not be told what they signifump' (Lefebure, 21). Lefebure shrewdly suggests that lingo *grande* was part of Sara's character armour, giving her a release from the tensions of constant anxiety (222). 'Mrs Codian', we may think, found solace in her code.

HARTLEY

Coleridge's relations with his children were necessarily constrained. When he left the family home in late 1803, Hartley was six, Derwent three, and Sara not even one.

Inevitably then it was with Hartley that he was most involved. Reggie Watters has written movingly about the way in which Hartley transformed Coleridge's whole view of childhood. Readers of Coleridge's verse will be aware of the extent to which Hartley came to embody his hopes of overcoming the damage he felt he had endured in his own childhood. Though Coleridge was virtually imprisoned in Christ's Hospital Hartley is promised in *Frost at Midnight* that he shall 'wander like a breeze' (*PW* 16.1.1: 456). The closing lines of *The Nightingale* suggest that it along with other poems will memorialize moments of profound significance for both father and son:

> once, when he awoke
> In most distressful mood (some inward pain
> Had made up that strange thing, an infant's dream—)
> I hurried with him to our orchard-plot,
> And he beheld the moon, and, hushed at once,
> Suspends his sobs, and laughs most silently,
> While his fair eyes, that swam with undropped tears,
> Did glitter in the yellow moon-beam! Well!
> It is a father's tale; But if that Heaven
> Should give me life, his childhood shall grow up
> Familiar with these songs, that with the night
> He may associate joy...
>
> (*PW* 16.1.1: 520)

The episode on which this is based is described in a Notebook entry of early 1804: 'Hartley fell down & hurt himself—I caught him up crying & screaming—& ran out of doors with him—The Moon caught his eye—he ceased crying immediately—& his eyes & the tears in them, how they glittered in the Moonlight!' (*CN* 1: 2192). Like countless other Notebook entries from this period, it is testimony to Coleridge's interest in making childhood experience the object of quasi-scientific experiment. In 1797 he became involved in discussions with Tom Wedgwood about the best way to bring up a child. Wedgwood told Godwin he wanted 'to find some master-stroke which should anticipate a century or two on the lazy-paced progress of human improvement'. In his view, a child should be confined to a 'nursery [with] plain, grey walls with one or two vivid objects for sight and touch'; however, 'the gradual explication of nature would be attended with great difficulty; the child must never go out of doors or leave his own apartment' (Erdman, 427). Wordsworth and Coleridge were predictably appalled! Coleridge followed the works of like-minded experimenters keenly. 'I pray you, my Love!' he wrote to his wife from Germany, 'read Edgeworth's Essay on Education—read it heart and soul—& if you approve of the mode, teach Hartley his Letters' (*CL* 1: 418).

A letter by Coleridge of 1803 gives an affectionate picture of the boy aged seven, which, by its emphasis on his eccentricities, presaged future portraits: 'Hartley is what he always was—a strange strange Boy—*exquisitely wild*! An utter Visionary! like the Moon among thin Clouds, he moves in a circle of Light of his own making—he alone, in a Light of his own. Of all human beings I never yet saw one so utterly naked of Self—he has no Vanity, no Pride, no Resentment, and tho' *very passionate*...Southey says, that the Boy keeps him in perpetual Wonderment' (*CL* 2: 1014). When Southey first moved to the Lakes he nicknamed Hartley Moses. After his parents separated he renamed him Job.

In 1807, shortly after his parents had agreed to separate, Hartley spent six months with his father. Derwent called that time 'the *annus mirabilis* of my brother's childhood' (xxxiii). He visited the tower of London with Scott and Wordsworth ('though Wordsworth's "economy" would not allow us to see the Jewel Office' (cciii)). 'At a very early period of his childhood' he invented an imaginary kingdom of Ejuxria (xli) peopled with generals and statesmen and featuring historic public events. Derwent and others felt that he lived in his imagination a little too much: 'He was, I am persuaded, utterly unconscious of invention...I have reason to believe that he continued the habit mentally...after he left school...in this as in many other ways continuing as a child' (xlv). Derwent also recalled that during their time as boarders at Ambleside, Hartley would regale his fellow pupils with the tale of 'a subtle intellectual villain, Scauzan, and his father, a man of gigantic stature outlawed and persecuted through the machinations of his son' (lix). Derwent commented that 'The struggles between parental affection and resentment against the injuries of his son were...powerfully depicted...The interest excited was occasionally so great as to become painful.' Another comment by Derwent suggests his brother identified strongly with Coleridge: 'While at school a certain infirmity of will, the specific evil of his life, had already shown itself. His sensibility was intense and he had not the wherewithal to control it. He shrank from mental pain.—he was beyond measure impatient of constraint' (lxiv). (Here he echoes Coleridge's remark in a draft letter to Dawes that 'I have in Hartley's case unwittingly fostered that cowardice as to mental pain which forms the one of the two calamitous defects in his disposition.')

In 1819 following a successful undergraduate career, Hartley was elected fellow of Oriel College, Oxford. Coleridge's natural delight was short-lived. In May the following year Hartley was deprived of his fellowship for 'sottishness, a love of low company and general inattention to college rules' (Griggs, 306). Coleridge numbered the misfortune amongst the 'four griping and grasping Sorrows' of his life (*CL* 5: 249). Draft letters survive in which he sought to explain his son's character to the Provost of the college, even quoting lines from 'Christabel' and Wordsworth's lines describing him as 'a spirit of joy dancing upon an aspen leaf'! He went up to Oxford to try to persuade the college to moderate the sentence but the fellows were unmoved. Hartley moved to London in 1820 and tried for a time to support himself by literary journalism. Coleridge plainly felt oppressed by Hartley's oddities and eventually urged him to return to Ambleside and become a schoolmaster with Mr Dawes. Sara was opposed to the plan, fearing that if it didn't work out, Hartley would become a burden to Southey or Wordsworth. Both men had already taken on their share of worrying about Hartley. It was Coleridge's turn to help him now. Coleridge was furious, complaining to a friend 'It will not be long, I trust, before Hartley may be set off for the North—much against the wish of his selfish *worreting* ever-complaining never-satisfied Mother. He might go to perdition body and soul, the trouble, embarrassment and anguish remaining on my shoulders, rather than be saved at the risk of any occasional annoyance to her, or of Mr Wordsworth's disapprobation' (*CL* 5: 248). Coleridge wrote to Mr Dawes himself and arranged for Hartley to move back to Ambleside as Dawes' assistant. Father and son corresponded until the mid-1820s and never saw each other again.

DERWENT

Coleridge's relationship with Derwent was less intense and on the whole, healthier. They spent little time together during Derwent's childhood: Derwent did not relive over and over any *annus mirabilis* as his brother had done. And while Coleridge was pleased by his son's physical resemblance to him, he never claimed to see in him a mirror of himself, as he had with Hartley: 'a nice little fellow', he remarked to Sara in 1810, 'and no Lackwit either' (*CL* 3: 286). Hartley is addressed or invoked in some of Coleridge's major verse but Derwent figures only in the amusing rhymed stanza that begins 'Trochee trips from long to short' (*CL* 3: 5–6). By the time Derwent was of university age, Coleridge was in better physical health and resolved to help him go to Cambridge. John Hookham Frere, once associated with the *Anti-Jacobin*, came forward with £300 though more slowly than expected: Derwent spent two years working as a tutor to a Lancashire family while he waited. Crabb Robinson who met him when he was seventeen said he was 'no scholar' (Morley, 1: 189–90).[6] Perhaps that was true but it should be said that, like his sister, Derwent was a brilliant linguist, with a command not only of Latin, Greek and the major European modern languages but in time also of Zulu, Arabic, Hawaiian, and Magyar. Derwent's biographers say that he resented his father for chastising him about getting into debt while making so little effort himself to support him. He graduated with a third class degree in 1823. On going down, he called on his father in Highgate and told him he had become an atheist. Coleridge attributed this apostasy to the society he kept in Cambridge which included Macaulay (a lifelong friend), John Moultrie and Charles Austin. For the next three years Derwent neither saw nor

---

[6] Robinson formed a bad impression of all the inmates of Greta Hall, especially Mrs Coleridge.

wrote to his father. Relations were re-established early in 1826 when Derwent announced that he was returning to Cambridge to take holy orders. He soon fell out again with both his parents when he got engaged to a Plymouth girl, Mary Pridham. They were opposed not to his fiancée but to the fact that he had no means of supporting a family. It was no doubt feelingly that Coleridge wrote the following lines to Derwent:

The most heart-withering Sorrow that can betide a high, honourable, morally sensitive and affectionate-natured Man, (a guilty conscience excepted) is: to have placed himself incautiously in such a relation to a Young Woman as neither to have it in his power to discontinue his attentions without dishonour & remorse, nor to continue them without inward repugnance, and a future *life* of Discomfort, of vain Heart-yearnings and remediless Heart-wastings distinctly before his eyes—as the alternative!—Either Misery of Remorse, or Misery of Regret!   (*CL* 6: 546–7)

Derwent waited a short time but got married anyway, taking up a curacy in Helston in Cornwall. The two men saw each other again in 1831 when Derwent came to London to explore the possibility of taking on a school in Harrow (CL 6: 854). Nothing came of the plan. They met for the last time in 1833 at a meeting in Cambridge of the British Association for the Advancement of Science. Derwent kept the Coleridgean flame alight through his work in education in which he sought to put some of his father's ideas into practice (Hainton and Hainton, 172–209). However, Derwent's daughter Christabel recalled her father saying that it was Wordsworth who had done more to form his mind than anyone else (ibid. 18).

SARA FILLE

Bradford K. Mudge has said of Coleridge's daughter Sara that 'she was the child least Coleridge's own' (32). He had spent months with Hartley and he had taken an interest in Derwent's education. But for Sara he had done almost nothing. When the separation occurred, he planned to take Hartley and Derwent to live with him but to leave Sara with her mother. While they were growing up, he wrote occasionally to his sons but almost never to Sara. This disregard is ironic given that Sara would do more than anyone else in the nineteenth century to secure his reputation against detractors. He saw her from time to time at Allan Bank in 1809 and 1810 while he was writing *The Friend* (he taught her and her mother Italian). But he first got to know her properly in 1823 when she and her mother made their trip to London and Ottery.

Sara did not have the advantages of her brothers, being schooled entirely at home. From an early age Sara was felt to be intellectually brilliant but also constitutionally weak (Potter, 26). The Wordsworths thought that the inmates of Greta Hall overemphasized Sara's academic prowess and assumed it was to make her financially independent. 'Should it be necessary', Wordsworth wrote, 'she will be well fitted to become a governess in a nobleman's or gentleman's family' (*W Letters*, 3: 209). At Southey's suggestion, she and Derwent began translating Martin Dobrizhoffer's book on Paraguay, *Historia de Abiponibus* (1784) but Derwent withdrew when Frere's money became available to him. (Dorothy thereafter referred to Sara as 'The Maid of Paraguay'.)

Sara's first visit to London resulted in her engagement to Henry Nelson Coleridge, son of the Colonel. Both sets of parents opposed the marriage, because of Henry's uncertain prospects and on grounds of consanguinity. These objections were dropped by 1827 and the couple married in 1829. Coleridge was too ill to attend the wedding, which took place in Keswick. Wordsworth's and Southey's daughters acted as bridesmaids and Southey gave her away. As a wedding gift Coleridge gave his daughter the copy of Virgil's *Hexaglotta* he had been given by William Sotheby. The inscription celebrates Sara's 'unusual attainments in ancient and modern Languages', which, Coleridge suggests, are to be admired the more for their 'co-existence in the same Person with so much piety, simplicity and un-affected meekness—in short, with a mind, character and demeanour so perfectly feminine' (*CL* 6: 692). As Mudge points out, the inscription assumes that marriage would mark the end of Sara's intellectual career when in fact it was just beginning. She assumed a subaltern editorial role in her husband's edition of Coleridge's *Literary Remains* and his *Table Talk* but her editions of *Biographia Literaria* (1847) and his *Essays on His Own Times* (1851)—completed after Henry's death—set new standards for editorial scholarship in the nineteenth century. Sara was the most unconditional Coleridgean of Coleridge's children. Sadly, her identification with him extended to narcotics. In spite of everything she knew about her father's fate, in or about 1824 she began taking laudanum for melancholy (Mudge, 36); by the mid 1830s she was as addicted to it as her father had been.

Charles Lamb once quipped that Coleridge 'ought not to have a wife and children; he should have a sort of diocesan care of the world, no parish duty' (Morley, 1: 289). It is hard to disagree. Throughout his life he made several attempts to integrate into other families: the Evans, the Frickers, the Pooles, the Wedgwoods, the Wordsworths, the Morgans, and finally the Gillmans. In each he sought what he despaired of finding in his own family: unconditional acceptance. His most successful 'family' relationship was perhaps with the Gillmans, for it was with them that he was allowed to occupy the role he had sought all his life, that of a child. In their care, he was more able to help and appreciate his own family than he had been at any time since his return from Germany. But the family he created with Sara remained a source of torment as well as pleasure to him. Hartley, it seems clear, was damaged by the intensity of his relationship with his brilliant ruined father; Derwent, we might think, saw Coleridge more clearly. Coleridge admired his daughter but he does not seem to have recognized the full extent of her intellectual powers. If real family relationships do not show him at his best, it might be remembered that his most successful relationships were with men who became in effect surrogate brothers to him. Southey, Wordsworth, Morgan and Gillman all answered this description. Likewise, the imagined communities with which Coleridge's name is associated—Pantisocracy, the Clerisy—strongly emphasized a fraternal dimension, indicating, we might think, an uncommon degree of insight concerning his own needs, emotional as well as intellectual. This, of course, is the paradox on which so many of Coleridge's biographers have come to grief, the fact that he could be so self-knowing and so self-defeating at the same time. It is as an honorary brother that Coleridge is best remembered. His wife and his family did not get enough of the best of him.

WORKS CITED

ASHTON, R. 1996. *The Life of Samuel Taylor Coleridge: A Critical Biography*. Oxford: Blackwell.

COLERIDGE, HARTLEY. 1851. *Poems by Hartley Coleridge. With a Memoir of his Life by his Brother*. 2 vols. London: Edward Moxon.

COLERIDGE, SAMUEL TAYLOR. 1956–71. *Collected Letters of Samuel Taylor Coleridge*. 6 vols. ed. Earl Leslie Griggs. Oxford: Clarendon. (= *CL*)

—— 1956–2002. *Collected Notebooks of Samuel Taylor Coleridge*. 5 vols., ed. Kathleen Coburn and Anthony John Harding. London: Routledge. (= *CN*)

—— 2001. *Poetical Works*, ed. J. C. C. Mays. Vol. 16 of *The Collected Works of Samuel Taylor Coleridge*. Princeton: Princeton University Press. (= *PW*)

DOUGHTY, OSWALD. 1980. *Perturbed Spirit: The Life and Personality of Samuel Taylor Coleridge*. Rutherford, NJ: Farleigh Dickinson University Press.

DURRANT, CHERRY ANNE. 1994. *The Lives and Works of Hartley, Derwent and Sara Coleridge*. unpublished Ph.D. dissertation, University of London.

ENGELL, JAMES (ed.). 1994. *Coleridge, The Early Family Letters*. Oxford: Clarendon Press.

ERDMAN, D. V. 1956. Coleridge, Wordsworth, and the Wedgwood Fund. Part I. Tom Wedgwood's 'Master Stroke'. *Bulletin of the New York Public Library*, 60: 425–43.

FRUMAN, NORMAN. 1984. *Coleridge: The Damaged Arch-Angel*. London: Allen & Unwin.

GILLMAN, JAMES. 1838. *The Life of Samuel Taylor Coleridge*. London: W. Pickering.

GRIGGS, EARL LESLIE and GRIGGS, GRACE. 1936. *Letters of Hartley Coleridge*. London: Oxford University Press.

HAINTON, RAYMONDE and HAINTON, GODFREY. 1996. *The Unknown Coleridge: The Life and Times of Derwent Coleridge 1800–1883*. London: Janus.

LEFEBURE, MOLLY. 1986. *The Bondage of Love: A Life of Mrs Samuel Taylor Coleridge*. London: Gollancz.

MORLEY, EDITH J. (ed.). 1938. *Henry Crabb Robinson On Books and their Writers*, 3 vols. London: J.M. Dent.

MUDGE, BRADFORD K. 1986. *Sara Coleridge, a Victorian Daughter: Her Life and Essays*. London: Yale University Press.

POTTER, STEPHEN. 1934. *Minnow among Tritons: Mrs S. T. Coleridge's Letters to Thomas Poole 1799–1834*. London: Nonesuch Press.

PRATT, LYNDA. 2002. Of All Men the Most Undomesticated: Coleridge's Marriage in 1802: An Unpublished Letter by Robert Southey. *Notes and Queries*, 49: 15–18.

SANDFORD, MARGARET E. 1888. *Thomas Poole and His Friends*. 2 vols. London: Macmillan.

WATTERS, REGGIE. 1997. 'A Limber Elf': Coleridge and the child. *The Coleridge Bulletin*, 9: 2–24.

WEISSMAN, STEPHEN M. 1986. *His Brother's Keeper: A Psychobiography of Samuel Taylor Coleridge*. Madison, Wis.: International Universities Press.

WENDLING, RONALD C. 1995. *Coleridge's Progress to Christianity: Experience and Authority in Religious Faith*. Lewisburg, PA: Bucknell University Press.

WORDSWORTH, W. and WORDSWORTH, D. 1967–93. *The Letters of William and Dorothy Wordsworth*. 7 vols, ed. Ernest de Selincourt. Chester Shaver and Alan Hill. Oxford: Clarendon Press.

CHAPTER 5

COLERIDGE'S TRAVELS

TILAR J. MAZZEO

IN a letter written in the autumn of 1800, Coleridge confidently wrote to offer William Godwin a bit of advice: 'you have not', he warned the philosopher, 'read enough of Travels, Voyages, & Biography' (Griggs, 1956, vol. 1, p. 636). Perhaps Godwin's reading was deficient. Or perhaps what we have here is simply Coleridge playing to his strengths in characteristic fashion. After all, it was a good bet that there would be few correspondents who had read in the genre of travel writing as voraciously as Coleridge. In fact, although we more often remember Coleridge for the youthful voyage that he did not take—the abortive Pantisocracy adventure—travel was an essential feature of Coleridge's life and of his verse, especially in the period from 1789 to 1806. His voyages and 'tours', as he called them, took him, over the course of a dozen years, from the pastoral scenes of Wales and the Scottish highlands to Germany, Sicily, and Malta, and his letters and journals are brimming with the details of itineraries that he planned eagerly in his imagination, travels that might have taken him from the Scandinavian Arctic Circle to the more nearly equatorial climes of the West Indies and almost a dozen ports of call in between.

EARLY CONTEXTS

Coleridge's passion for travel and travel writing began, predictably enough, in his small-town childhood, where he passed the first decade of his life never voyaging farther than Sidmouth, Crediton, and Exeter, all within a dozen miles of his native Ottery. From the beginning, travel for him was a textual experience. Giving an account of his childhood to his friend Thomas Poole, Coleridge remembered especially his early delight at discovering on the shelves of his aunt's shop in Crediton a copy of Defoe's travel novel *Robinson Crusoe* (Griggs, 1956, vol. 1, p. 347). More importantly, however, there were the letters sent home from abroad by his brothers John and, later, Frank. Like so many other modestly genteel families at the beginning of Britain's great imperial century and like his contemporaries William Wordsworth and Jane Austen, in particular, Coleridge had brothers who went east to make their fortunes. John sailed for Calcutta as a solider in 1771, a year before Coleridge's birth, so that the young Samuel never knew a time when long-awaited missives from distant ports-of-call were not central to family life. In fact, by the time of Coleridge's adolescence, the expectation was that Samuel would follow his brothers to India when he was old enough. After the death of his father in 1781 and the family's subsequent descent into poverty, especially, there were few obvious professional opportunities beyond the clergy or the east open to him.

Had Coleridge joined his brothers in India as planned, his travels would have been far different ones. As Bernard Smith demonstrated in an early article on Coleridge's fascination with exploration and exploration literature, part of his education at Christ's Hospital in London was aimed at preparing boys for service in colonial outposts and naval careers. His mathematics teacher was William Wales, a man who had achieved modest fame as Captain Cook's meteorologist aboard the *Resolution,* and many of the boys remembered Wales' accounts of adventure on the high seas and his role as a recruiting agent for clever young men suited to the farther study of navigation (Smith, 1956, p. 117). Travel was emphasized in the less scientific elements of the school's curriculum, as well. George Whalley has observed that in its literary studies 'Christ's Hospital [had a] custom of improvising tales of travel and adventure, presumably on the pattern of Defoe and his imitators' (1950, p. 330).

In the end, it was mostly down to chance that Coleridge was not sent to sea when he came of age. In 1787—just at the age when the family might reasonably have found a position for the fifteen-year-old Samuel—his brother John fell victim to the dangers of life in India and died. As a result, Coleridge was sent a few years later not to India but to Cambridge, with an eye toward training him to enter the clergy like his father, and it was there that his passion for travel found its first and most abiding outlet in poetry. Thomas Middleton lent Coleridge a book of verse by William Lisle Bowles entitled *Sonnets Written Chiefly on Picturesque Spots, during a Tour* (1789), and the result was Coleridge's first serious engagement with writing poetry. The book—which described Bowles' travels in Wales, Scotland, France, and Germany—also inspired many of the actual voyages that Coleridge would undertake in the years to come, and in many ways its themes (and the sonnet form) were central to his development as a poet in the 1790s.

WALES (1794)

Coleridge's most intense period of engagement with travel and travel writing began in 1794, during the summer after his third year at Cambridge, when he and some of his classmates planned an extended pedestrian tour of Wales. As Richard Holmes has noticed, walking tours 'were then a new fashion with strong democratic overtones' (1990, p. 60), and it was a particular fashion among liberal young university men with Jacobin sympathies. Coleridge's radical Cambridge acquaintance William Frend had recently returned from just such a tour of France. And, although the two poets had not yet met, William Wordsworth had already completed a walking tour of the Lake District, Yorkshire, and Derbyshire in 1789, of France, Switzerland, and Italy in 1790, and of Wales in 1791, in addition to having published his first book of verse—aptly titled *An Evening Walk: An Epistle in Verse Addressed to a Young Lady from the Lakes of the North of England* (1793). The stage for this most famous of literary friendships was already set, and the political sympathy suggested by shared pedestrian travels would always be an important part of it.

In preparation for his tour of Wales in the summer of 1794, Coleridge bought himself a new walking stick, and in July he set off with three companions—Hucks, Berdmore, and Brookes—intending to journey from Cambridge to Wales, passing through Oxford and Bristol en route. In Oxford, however, Coleridge was importantly diverted. On June 17, he met Robert Southey for the first time, and the planned tour was delayed for three weeks while Coleridge relished this new friendship. Both young men were also fascinated by the recent news that the radical agitator Joseph Priestley had emigrated to the United States that spring and established on 300,000 acres in Pennsylvania a settlement for the 'friends of liberty' (Park, 1947, p. 15). Filled with idealism and democratic passion, Coleridge and Southey soon concocted a plan to join Priestley in America and to establish the communitarian experiment that they would call Pantisocracy.

Coleridge finally set out from Oxford on his walking tour of Wales in early July, promising to send his fellow Pantisocrats bulletins from the road. But this was not the only writing that Coleridge planned to do. He also intended, like Bowles, to use the occasion to write poems, and there is some suggestion that Coleridge hoped to publish an account of the tour: for, as Coleridge wrote to Southey, 'I have bought a little Blank Book, and portable Ink Horn—as I journey onward, I ever and anon pluck the wild Flowers of Poesy' (Griggs, 1956, vol. 1, p. 84). Although Coleridge sent back a number of short poems in his letters, including minor verse compositions such as 'Perspiration: A Travelling Eclogue', 'Sonnet on Pantisocracy', 'To a Young Ass', and 'Lines on the "Man of Ross"', his travel account of the Welsh tour was never published. The following year, however, his companion Joseph Hucks did publish his journal of the trip under the title *A Pedestrian Tour through North Wales in a Series of Letters* (1795).

According to Hucks' estimate, the companions walked 629 miles in just over two months (Jones and Tydeman, 1979, p. lxxi), following an itinerary from Oxford that led them from Hereford to Gloucester and Shropshire, and into Wales at Llanfyllin, and his journal records the details of Coleridge's ascents of Penmaen-mawr, Snowdon, and Cader Idris. Coleridge also recorded his recollections of the tour in at least three places: in his unpublished notebooks, in the detailed letters to Southey and Henry Martin, written to 'give you some little account of our journey' (Griggs, 1956, vol. 1, p. 88), and in some passages of 'The Rime of the Ancient Mariner', where the details of the Mariner's thirst and the line 'they for joy did grin' have been traced to their origin in the group's ascent of Penmaenmawr on a hot July afternoon (ibid. 90–5).

PANTISOCRACY AND EMIGRATION (1794–1795)

On 5 August, at the end of the walking tour, Coleridge rejoined Southey and Robert Lovell in Bristol to make plans in earnest for their emigration to America, initially scheduled to take place in the spring of 1795. There, Coleridge met for the first time the radical printer Joseph Cottle and, more fatefully, his future wife Sara Fricker and her family. Again consciously following the fashion of radical tourism, Coleridge and Southey immediately decided to set off on a second walking tour that summer, departing Bristol in mid-August for an excursion through Somerset on foot, with Southey's dog Rover in tow, to the Cheddar Gorge and into the Quantocks (Holmes, 1990, p. 70). There, at Nether Stowey, Coleridge met Thomas Poole—who just two years earlier had completed his own extensive walking tour of the English Midlands, where he had traveled to see first-hand the deplorable conditions of the poor. The walking tour with its 'democratic overtones' emerges as central to the shared cultural moment that drew these young men into a community.

The idea of traveling in order to establish a community was the explicit purpose of the failed Pantisocracy scheme, as well. Most immediately, of course, the planned emigration would draw the participants into a shared social experiment and Coleridge into a disastrous marriage. The group, which was to have included at its core Coleridge, Southey, and the Fricker and Lovell families, planned to take up farming on the banks of the Susquehanna River in rural Pennsylvania. Although the plans never came to fruition, Pantisocracy was an important point of entry for

Coleridge into a larger political and literary culture during the 1790s. Like the democratic overtones of the walking tour, emigration to the now independent and democratic American states figured prominently in the radical imagination during the last decade of the century and generated its own close-knit community, whose members included some of the most controversial and politically adventurous figures of the decade: the Girondist émigré J. P. Brissot de Warville, author of Poole's favorite guide *New Travels in the United States of America* (1789); Joseph Priestley's son-in-law, Thomas Cooper, whose *Some Information Respecting America* (1794) Coleridge preferred; even Gilbert Imlay's *A Topographical Description of North America* (1792) and, later, Mary Wollstonecraft's despairing response to it in *Letters Written during a Short Residence in Sweden, Norway, and Denmark* (1796). The impact of these travelogues on his later career as a poet is clear. As John Livingston Lowes demonstrated years ago in his landmark study *The Road to Xanadu*, many of these and Coleridge's other readings in exploration literature from this period found their way into the language and imagery of his most famous compositions, including 'Kubla Khan' and 'The Rime of the Ancient Mariner'.

This period of collaboration with Southey was immensely productive for Coleridge in many ways; perhaps most importantly, as Whalley suggests, in these early years of their mutual self-fashioning as authors, 'Southey... stimulated Coleridge's interest in the poetic possibilities of travel literature' (Whalley, 1950, p. 330). Reminders of travel and exploration were all around them. From the window of his lodgings in Bristol, where Coleridge soon established himself, he could see 'the masts of ships—slavers, merchantmen, and men-of-war' (ibid. 331), and old library records at the Bristol Literary Society show that Coleridge, Southey, Joseph Cottle, and Charles Lloyd were avidly reading travelogues that ranged from J. Hector St John de Crèvecoeur's *Letters of an American Farmer* (1782) to *The Journal of the Life and Travels of John Woolman* (1774) (Eugenia, 1930, pp. 1069–84).

By the summer of 1795, however, the focus of Coleridge's readings in travel literature had shifted. As the plans for a North American Pantisocracy finally collapsed after months of increasing conflict and agonizing indecision, it was now titles like Byran Edward's *The Civil and Commercial History of the West Indies* (1794) that engaged Coleridge's imagination (Eugenia, 1930, p. 1070). He was slowly being drawn into an increasingly West Indian circle, and, off-and-on over the course of the next several years, despite his radical politics and abolitionist friends, Coleridge would fantasize about a new scheme of emigration to the Caribbean. It was the beginning of an intense fascination for Coleridge with the imperialist and colonialist modes that might have been his adolescent future, and, for much of the next decade, he would engage with equal enthusiasm in two seemingly irreconcilable forms of travel—the Jacobin-inflected pedestrian tour and the colonial administrator.

THE *WATCHMAN* TOUR AND THE BRITISH MIDLANDS (1796)

Ironically, it was also in the context of West Indian colonial society that Coleridge would first meet the comparatively worldly and well-traveled William Wordsworth, at the home of John Pinney, a wealthy sugar merchant with plantations on Saint Nevis. At the moment of this famous encounter, Coleridge was now a married man and increasingly committed to making a career for himself in writing—especially in writing with an alternately poetic and political focus. His first idea was to found a newspaper dedicated to espousing the era's new democratic ideals, and his efforts to launch *The Watchman* in the winter of 1796 were once again couched in the cultural rhetoric of the radical pedestrian tour. On 9 January, following in the footsteps of Poole, who had toured the region to study the conditions of poverty only a few years earlier, Coleridge set off on a five-week excursion through the Midlands, from Worcester and Birmingham to Sheffield. This trip would be followed in the summer by another two-month tour, this time with Sara in tow, to Matlock and its surrounding valleys. Then, for a time, the traveling stopped. For nearly a year, the Coleridges would settle into a quiet domestic routine in the Quantocks, where they moved in the summer of 1796 to live near Poole and where Charles Lamb and William and Dorothy Wordsworth soon joined them. The next thirteen months—much of it coinciding with the so-called *annus mirabilis*—would be the only hiatus from intense travel for the next decade, and during it Coleridge and Wordsworth would write many of the poems that comprised the *Lyrical Ballads*.

SOMERSET AND PASTORAL INTERLUDE (1796–7)

Even if the period 1796–7 was spent in domestic retirement, travel writing was one of the many interests that Coleridge, Wordsworth, and Poole shared. In directing Coleridge toward the poetics of travel, Wordsworth was far more influential even than Southey had been. In his study of *Wordsworth's Reading, 1770–1799* (1993), Duncan Wu offers a prodigious list of books on travel and exploration that Wordsworth had read or collected by the time of his celebrated poetic collaboration with Coleridge. In the Wordsworth library were books ranging from the pragmatic guides to France and Switzerland, collected during his earlier walking tours on the continent, to the voyages of discovery described in William Bartram's *Travels through North and South Carolina* (1794), Samuel Hearne's *Journey from the Prince of Wales Fort in Hudson Bay to the Northern Ocean* (1795), or George Shelvocke's *Voyage Round the World by Way of the Great South Sea* (1726). The latter were books resonant of the far-flung colonial travels that might have been Coleridge's professional destiny, and these were the voyages that he particularly relished now. Wordsworth, on the other hand, preferred the literature of picturesque Britain and, especially, the travel accounts describing the nostalgic scenes of his native Lakes; his collection included titles such as John Brown's *A Description of the Lakes at Keswick (and the Adjacent Country) in Cumberland* (1767), James Clark's *A Survey of the Lakes of Cumberland, Westmoreland, and Lancashire* (1789), William Gilpin's *Observations on the River Wye* (1789), Robert Heron's *Observations Made in a Journey through the Western Counties of Scotland* (1793), William Hutchinson's *An Excursion to the Lakes in Westmoreland and Cumberland* (1774), Richard Warner's *A Walk through Wales* (1798), Thomas West's *Guide to the Lakes* (1789)—and, importantly for Coleridge, of course, William Lisle Bowles' *Sonnets Written Chiefly on Picturesque Spots during a Tour* (1789).

This difference in preferences—Coleridge for the exotic geography of empire and Wordsworth for the lost scenes of his childhood—is apparent in the verse of each poet, and it may help to account for some of the aesthetic conflict between them that emerged in the years to come, especially in the context of the *Lyrical Ballads*. After all, many of Coleridge's most important poems written during his time at Stowey cannot be disentangled from the contemporary literature of travel and exploration or his aesthetic engagement with it. 'Kubla Khan' and 'The Rime of the Ancient Mariner', in particular, are deeply informed by Coleridge's readings in this genre. 'Kubla Khan', composed during the course of Coleridge's long solitary walk along the coast to Lynton, was literally composed as part of another version of the familiar pedestrian tour, but the poem also had some of its most important imaginative sources in books such as James Bruce's *Travels to Discover the Source of the Nile* (1790), Samuel Purchas's *Purchas, his Pilgrimage* (1614), and Mary Wollstonecraft's *Letters Written during a Short Residence in Norway, Sweden, and Denmark* (1796) (Lowes, 1927, p. 8). John Livingstone Lowes has identified allusions in Coleridge's poetry to a long list of travel sources that includes: James Rennell's *Memoir of a Map of Hindoostan* (1788), James Cook's *Voyage to the Pacific Ocean* (1784), Captain William Dampier's *New Voyage Around the World* (1729), Richard Hawkins's *Observations of Sir Richard Hawkins, Knight, in his Voyage into the South Sea* (1622), Falconer's *Shipwreck* (1762), Frederick Martens's *Voyage into Spitzbergen and Greenland* (1732), Augustus, Count de Benyowsky's *Memories and Travels of Mauritius* (1790), John Churchill's *Collection of Voyages* (1744), Basil Ringrose's *Dangerous Voyage and Bold Attempts...in the South Sea* (1741), Nicolas Downton's *Letters Received by the East India Company from his Servants in the East* (1710), William Bligh's *Mutiny on the Bounty* (1789), Sir Walter Raleigh's *First Voyage to*

Guiana (1765), François Bernier's *Voyage to Surat* (1745), and Thomas Taylor's *Description of Greece* (1794).

Were it not for Coleridge's and Wordsworth's shared interest in travel, in fact, the *Lyrical Ballads* might never have been published at all. The idea for the volume had its origins in a planned tour to Germany that the friends were hoping to take together by 1797. As Richard Holmes has observed, the 'Rime of the Ancient Mariner' was originally intended for publication in the *Monthly Magazine* in order 'to defray the expenses of their...tour' (Holmes, 1990, p. 171). By mid-March of 1798, Coleridge and Wordsworth had extended the idea and were hoping instead to persuade Cottle to publish a joint volume of their poems, with an eye toward raising the necessary thirty guineas (ibid. 187). Cottle obliged, although he later had reason perhaps to regret his ready compliance: when the friends were courting the radical publisher Joseph Johnson, whom they hoped might make up one of their traveling party, they tactlessly asked Cottle to give his rights to the book to his competitor (Todd, 1952, p. 509).

GERMANY (1798–1799)

On 16 September 1798, before even seeing the reviews of the *Lyrical Ballads*, Coleridge and William and Dorothy Wordsworth departed for Germany from Yarmouth, leaving Sara with the Coleridge children in Stowey. Choosing Germany as a destination now seems a somewhat curious choice, perhaps especially for a winter tour, but it was once again an itinerary inflected by the current fashion that connected Jacobin politics with certain forms of tourism. As F. M. Todd notes, 'After 1793 many Jacobins looked to Germany for the planting "in hardier soil" of the tree of liberty to which the French had proved so false', and the German universities, in particular, were associated with disaffected and radical young Englishmen (1952, p. 508). A letter published in *The Anti-Jacobin Review and Magazine* reveals precisely how the travels of Coleridge and Wordsworth were read in terms of contemporary political culture. 'I hear lately,' the author of the letter from 'An Honest Briton' writes,

of two gentlemen, formerly well-known at Cambridge; who, feeling the restraints of law and religion somewhat irksome, left the university and became philosophers. It seems these worthy men...agreed with four others to go to America and put their philosophy in practice. It was agreed that each of the six should engage a woman to accompany them and that these women should be common to the whole. Two of these gentlemen who, it seems, were the projectors of this admirable colony for America, and who are writers in the

'Morning Chronicle', and other publications of Jacobinical notoriety, came afterwards to Germany[.]   ('An Honest Briton', 1800, vol. 6, p. 562)

The letter, although confusing Wordsworth's role in the failed Pantisocracy project, clearly connects both American emigration and German travels with French republican sympathies. Perhaps most surprisingly, it suggests the extent to which certain forms of tourism were read as public political activity.

For Coleridge and Wordsworth, the political implications of their travel choices at this particular juncture were probably heightened somewhat unusually. The trip to Germany followed closely on the heels of their scandalous friendship with John Thelwall, who had celebrated his escape from the gallows on charges of treason in the summer of 1797 by setting off 'on a long "pedestrian tour" from London to the West of England and Wales...[intending to record] every fact connected with the history and actual condition of the labourious classes' (Thompson, 1994, pp. 104–5). As E. P. Thompson notes, Thelwall's tour had importantly included a visit to see Coleridge en route, and the entire circle at Stowey was acutely aware that Thelwall's arrival placed them under disturbing governmental scrutiny. It was the more cautious Poole who finally persuaded Wordsworth not to offer Thelwall longer-term accommodation at Alfoxden. As a result, Thelwall took up residence instead in the Wye river valley of Wales, and it was there, in the months immediately before their departure for Germany, that the friends—sometimes covering as many as twenty-five miles a day by foot or boat—visited Thelwall and that Wordsworth composed his memorable 'Lines Written above Tintern Abbey' (1798) (McNulty, 1945, p. 293).

It is not entirely clear how long the three travelers intended to remain in Germany. William and Dorothy talked of perhaps staying for several years, while Coleridge told his wife that he would stay a mere three months—just long enough to gather materials for the travel journal that he had been commissioned (and already paid) by publishers Longman to deliver. Those three months soon stretched into ten months for Coleridge. More curious to their friends back home was the fact that, after all the shared preparations, the joint spirit of the adventure did not last long. After spending just two weeks together in Hamburg at the end of September, William and Dorothy headed off alone to Goslar and the remote Harz Mountains. As Coleridge explained in a letter sent home to Poole, 'Wordsworth & his Sister have determined to travel on into Saxony to seek cheaper places' (Griggs, 1956, vol. 1, p. 419). Feeling unaccountably more flush, Coleridge went on to Ratzeburg, where he threw himself into a whirl of tourism and social activity. Throughout the fall and winter, he sent home a series of long and affectionate letters, posted twice a week to Sara and Poole, in which he described his impressions of Germany in voluminous detail. Later, Wordsworth would include some of Coleridge's memories of winter ice-skating in the first book of *The Prelude* (ll. 467–72).

After passing a solitary winter in Ratzeburg, Coleridge visited William and Dorothy in early February of 1799, on a six-day trip to the Harz. Once again, however, the friends chose not to renew the domestic intimacy they had established in Somerset, perhaps because William and Dorothy had already decided that they could not be happy in Germany and planned to leave as soon as that year's unusually ferocious winter made travel back to Britain possible (Todd, 1952, p. 510). A week later, Coleridge had established himself at the University of Göttingen, where he would spend the spring. By mid-April, William and Dorothy had had enough and arrived in Göttingen en route back to Britain. Surprisingly— and with what was perhaps not the wisest domestic judgement—Coleridge decided to stay on, despite having just received news of the death of his son Berkeley back in Stowey. Instead, Coleridge once again set off on a pedestrian tour, this time headed for the Harz Mountains with seven new friends. The companions climbed Brocken and visited Rübeland, Wernigerode, and Goslar, and on the tour Coleridge participated in another of the period's popular travel conventions: inscribing poems in hotel albums. As one of his companions later remembered, Coleridge was also soon enthusiastically proposing 'a pedestrian tour together through parts of Demark, Sweden, and Norway' (Carlyon, 1836–58, vol. 1, pp. 161–2). It was no doubt an itinerary suggested by his keen enjoyment of Mary Wollstonecraft's Scandinavian travel journal, with all its radical connotations.

Coleridge never made it to Scandinavia, of course. The companions soon postponed the trip until the following summer, and Coleridge 'promised . . . to return to make the projected tour with us the ensuing spring' (qtd. Holmes, 1990, p. 237). By July 1799, he was back in Somerset. For Coleridge as a writer, Germany had not been a resounding success. The poems written during his travels are largely unfamiliar to general readers and include verses—many adapted from German poems—such as 'I stood on Brocken's Sovran height and saw', 'Lines describing the Silence of a City' (possibly Hamburg or Ratzeburg), 'Something Childish, but very Natural', 'Home-sick, Written in Germany, Adapted from Bürde', 'Lines Written in an Album at Elbingerode, in the Harz Forest', 'To a Cataract, from a Cavern near the Summit of a Mountain Precipice, from Stolberg', 'The Visit of the Gods, Imitated from Schiller', and 'Ode to Georgiana, Duchess of Devonshire on the 24th Stanza in her *Passage over Mount Gothard*'. This habit of imitation would ultimately culminate in the now controversial publication of 'Hymn Before Sun-Rise in the Vale of Chamouny' (1802), silently adapted from the work of Friederike Brun.

The proposed German travelogue—despite the advance payment—was never published in the way that his publisher had been expecting. Coleridge later described to his friend Josiah Wedgwood

the loathing, which I once or twice felt, when I attempted to write it, merely for the Bookseller, without any sense of the moral utility of what I was writing. . . . tho' nearly done I am exceedingly anxious not to publish, because it brings me forward in a *personal* way, as a man who related little adventures of himself to *amuse* people—& thereby exposes me to sarcasm ... & is besides *beneath me*[.]   (Griggs, 1956, vol. 2, p. 706)

He eventually offered Longman, instead, the publication of *Christabel*, but the publisher was not enthusiastic. Significant parts of Coleridge's German notebooks were published later in *The Friend* (1809–10); extracts were also presented publicly in his 1808–9 lectures at the Royal Institute and in the 1811–12 lectures at the London Philosophical Society (Coleman, 1988).

TOURISTS IN THE LAKE DISTRICT (1799)

After returning to Britain, William and Dorothy went to Sockburn to stay with friends, and within months of his return Coleridge had joined them, with an eye toward accompanying Wordsworth and Cottle on a tour of the Lake District and then on into Yorkshire. Coleridge and Wordsworth would travel by foot, and Cottle, suffering from lameness, would follow along on a sturdy mare named Lily. After three days, Cottle recognized the ridiculous nature of the undertaking and returned home, and Wordsworth's brother John instead joined the party, with the three of them touring in October and November picturesque scenes at Ullswater, Borrowdale, and Grasmere. James A. Butler has observed that 'their trip was very much a standard tourist jaunt through the Lakes' (1996, p. 2), and, astonishingly given the languishing German volume, Coleridge 'seems to have been eager to exploit the fad for travel literature, desiring to make the trip answer "in a pecuniary way" by publishing his "travelling conversations" ' (Butler, 1996, p. 3). In fact, Coleridge went beyond merely contemplating it. By the next year, he was writing to Samuel Purkis: 'I have concluded a bargain with Longman, who is to give me a 100£ for my Tour of the North of England' (Griggs, 1956, vol. 2, p. 580). Longman, undoubtedly, was not yet aware that the German volume was not forthcoming, and Coleridge would also never publish his account of this tour.

In mid November of 1799, Coleridge parted company with Wordsworth and his brother and went to visit Dorothy, and it was there that he met Sara Hutchinson. It was, at least on Coleridge's part, a romance that had travel writing at its center. Soon, Coleridge was staying up late with Sara reading aloud to her from Bartram's travels and sending her letters filled with extracts from Richard Warner's *Tour through the North Counties* (1802). From 1800–4 his plans for travel were at a fevered pitch that was matched only by his intense passion for the young woman. He wanted to go somewhere and rather desperately, but his plans were constantly shifting. He was more or less simultaneously writing to Poole with dreams of reviving their old plans for American emigration, hoping to persuade Wordsworth to join him in relocating to John Pinney's estates in the West Indies, and sharing with Southey ideas for travels in Constantinople or Egypt (Holmes, 1990, p. 303). He visited Sir James Mackintosh to ask 'his endeavors to procure me a place under him in India' (Griggs, 1956, vol. 2, p. 1041), and to James Coleridge he would write, 'I am determined to pass the next year or two of my Life either at Madeira, or Teneriffe, or Lisbon—with my Family' (ibid. 896). Other times he talked of Cornwall, Ireland, or Naples. Before it was over, he would even propose to his wife, from whom he was bitterly estranged, 'a two years' residence in Montpellier' (ibid. 786) in the south of France, where Southey might join them.

SALUBRIOUS CLIMES: THE CARIBBEAN AND THE CONTINENT (1800–2)

In the beginning, it was emigration to a tropical island in the West Indies that captured Coleridge's imagination most fully, and he immersed himself in books like Captain Thomas James's *Strange and Dangerous Voyage of his Intended Discovery of the North-West Passage into the South Sea* (1704), Antonio de Herrera y Tordesilla's *General Description of the Vast Continent and Island of America, Commonly Call'd the West Indies* (1740), César de Rochefort's *History of the Caribby Islands* (1666), and Gonzalo Fernández de Oviedo y Valdés's *Generall Historie of the Indies* (1625) (Lowes, 1927, pp. 128, 162, 317). In one astonishing letter, he writes— with what one hopes is pointed irony—'St Nevis is the most lovely as well as the most healthy Island in the W. Indies—Pinny's Estate is there— . . . & perhaps, Pinny would appoint us sine-cure Negro-drivers at a hundred a year, or some other snug & reputable office' (Griggs, 1956, vol. 2, pp. 747–8). Wordsworth, at least, believed that Coleridge was serious enough about this planned emigration that he wrote Pinney asking about the possibility, and Wordsworth's sea-faring brother John was being queried for advice on the island climates. Already struggling with his opium addiction and an inability to complete remunerative writing projects, Coleridge increasingly saw travel to an inexpensive colonial outpost as a way of easing his financial pressures.

By the autumn of 1801, however, as it became increasingly clear that his rich friend Tom Wedgwood was terminally ill and as Coleridge's own mental and physical state was becoming precariously fragile, the plan shifted again. A failing Wedgwood, anxious to find a more salubrious climate, invited Coleridge to accompany him on an invalid's tour of France, Switzerland, and Italy. Perhaps as a test of their compatibility, Coleridge spent the winter of 1802, at Wedgwood's invitation, touring the West Country and Wales with him, and Coleridge was once again soon negotiating with booksellers for an advance on a proposed travelogue of the continent. Perhaps as a result of the trial period together, Wedgwood delayed the departure repeatedly, and Coleridge might have lost interest were it not for the fact that Poole then made the same trip over the summer and came back in good spirits. 'Poole', Coleridge later wrote to Southey, 'is nearly well: his account of his Travels & Conversations in France and Switzerland are exceedingly interesting & instructive' (Griggs, 1956, vol. 2, p. 924).

When Wedgwood was still delaying their departure in the winter of 1803, Coleridge finally began impatiently making plans to travel alone, and once again he relied on his friends to provide some inspiration. As chance would have it, in 1803 and 1804 Coleridge had two friends who were talking about Mediterranean islands. George Bellas Greenough—one of his classmates at Göttingen and a companion of the pedestrian tour of the Harz in 1799—had recently published a travelogue of Sicily, prompting Coleridge to arrange a meeting with his old compatriot and to assure him that, 'If your cheek burnt about 1/2 past 8 on Sunday Night, it was owning to a spirited Eulogy of Davy on your Sicilian Tour and description of Aetna, which he declared to be in his opinion unrivalled—*a*— nay—*the* Masterpiece' (Griggs, 1956, vol. 2, p. 1050). Coleridge also learned that another friend, John Stoddart, was planning an extended residence in Malta, where he was taking up a new appointment as King's and Admiralty Advocate (Sultana, 1969, p. 71). Stoddart suggested that Coleridge accompany him and his family, but by summer Coleridge was dithering, torn between two destinations. Malta—the so-called 'key to India'—represented the opportunity to find paid employment in colonial administration. The other option was a reiteration of the familiar pedestrian tour. Inspired, ironically, by the recent publication of Stoddart's *Remarks on Local Scenery and Manners in Scotland in the Years 1799 and 1800* (1801), Coleridge was drawn to the rural scenes of the Scottish highlands.

Scotland (1803)

In the end, Stoddart sailed for Malta, and Coleridge set off in mid-August for a tour of Scotland with William and Dorothy, using Stoddart's presentation copy as their guide. While the friends originally set off in a rustic and inexpensive jaunting car, intent on visiting the rural scenes of 'North Britain', they soon found it an inconvenient mode of transportation. They also soon found each other's company not entirely congenial. After traveling north from Glasgow, into the highlands, and making it as far as Loch Lomond, Coleridge and the Wordsworth siblings went their separate ways at Arrochar, a rupture apparently precipitated by William's annoyance with his invalid friend (Walker, 2002, p. 14). And perhaps Coleridge was overstating his ailments, after all. For the next seventeen days, Coleridge went on a solitary walking tour that took him to Edinburgh and throughout the highlands, visiting sites at Iveruglas, Glen Coe, Letterfinlay, and Loch Ness. By his own estimate, he walked 263 miles during one eight-day stretch (Griggs, 1956, vol. 2, p. 1005), and much of his tour was informally preserved in his letters and notebooks. Dorothy Wordsworth later published her recollection of the tour in Scotland, including the time with Coleridge, in her travelogue *Recollections of a Tour Made in Scotland, A.D. 1803* (1874).

ITALY AND MALTA (1804–6)

The anti-climactic nature of the Scottish tour and the growing tensions in his friendship with Wordsworth meant that soon Coleridge was considering both Malta and Sicily again. At the end of March in 1804, Coleridge sailed from Portsmouth for Malta, where he intended to arrive unannounced to take up residence with Stoddart and his family. The journey to Malta took nine weeks by sea, and, passing the coast of Portugal in mid-April, en route to the Straits of Gibraltar, Coleridge was reminded of Southey's travel account of the region. A month later, passing the west coast of Sicily, he had in hand a copy of his friend Patrick Brydone's *Tour through Sicily and Malta* (1774).

Coleridge arrived in Malta on 18 May 1804 and immediately began keeping what he called 'my Maltese journal,' perhaps once again with an eye toward a published account of his travels (Sultana, 1969, p. 142). He also found employment in the civil sector of the island's colonial administration, securing with Stoddart's assistance a position as private secretary to Sir Alexander Ball, the Governor of Malta. The duties, however, were evidently light, and Coleridge set out in early August for a three-month 'hasty tour of Sicily' (ibid. 193) that included a particularly memorable ascent of the volcanic Mount Etna. He also began writing for Ball and the government various political pamphlets and position papers on topics of strategic interest, and his research soon included travel narratives with a decidedly military emphasis, including an influential account of Malta's role in the expansion of the British empire, Sir Mark Wood's *Remarks during a Journey to the East Indies* (1803) (Mazzeo, 2001, pp. i–xxviii).

By the winter of 1805, Coleridge had been promoted to the Governor's public secretary, and, had he been content in Malta or with the position, Coleridge might have found himself launched on a comfortable career in colonial administration. Soon, however, Coleridge was disenchanted and restless. Less than nine months later, he resigned his post, planning to return to Sicily for a second tour and then to continue onward to tourist destinations on the Italian mainland. Arriving on Sicily at the end of September, he was particularly enchanted with the eastern end of the island, writing in his travel journal of Taormina: 'The view surpasses perhaps all I have ever seen' (qtd. Sultana, 1969, p. 373). He made the ascent of Etna a second time that autumn and passed a large part of his time in the nearby cities of Catania and Messina, setting sail for Naples finally toward the end of November.

As Edouardo Zuccato has observed, 'Coleridge's tour of Italy was unusual' (1996, p. 6). Not only did it take place 'at a time when the Continent was closed to English people as a consequence of war with France', but also 'Italy was for him more Mediterranean than it was for most British travelers' (ibid. 6–7). Neither Sicily nor Malta figured prominently on the conventional itinerary of the Grand Tour. Malta, at best, was a way station for travelers heading farther east to Greece and the Ottoman Empire, and, unlike France, Switzerland, or Germany, the island had none of the continent's radical connotations. Strategically positioned in the Mediterranean and critically important for Britain's access to the overland route to India during the Napoleonic Wars, Malta was a garrison rather than an idyllic winter retreat. Sicily, on the other hand, already suffered from the same cultural stereotypes that came to define the Italian *mezzogiorno* as a whole in the nineteenth century: most tourists viewed it as an impoverished and backward region lacking even the modest comforts of northern Italian cities. Not coincidentally, those who traveled to Sicily generally did so, like Coleridge, because they had other reasons for being on nearby Malta.

In sailing for Naples, however, Coleridge was now back on the beaten path for British tourists, even if he was traveling in a direction that reversed the itinerary of his contemporaries on the Grand Tour (Zuccato, 1996, p. 6). Among his guidebooks were conventional titles such as John Moore's *View of the Society and Manners in Italy* (1795) and Henry Swinburne's *Travels in the Two Sicilies* (1783). At Naples, he booked himself into a tourist's hotel with views of Vesuvius (Sultana, 1969, p. 376), and after a tour of the Apennines in early December he celebrated the New Year in Rome. By the spring, Coleridge had seen only a small number of the conventional highlights of an Italian tour, and he probably intended to travel for some months longer. The progress of the Napoleonic Wars, however, made residence in Italy increasingly dangerous for British subjects. Those tensions came to a peak in May, when the British were expelled from the Papal territories, and Coleridge was forced to move north, first to Florence and then Pisa, finally securing passage back to Britain from Leghorn on 23 June.

During his time in Italy and Malta, Coleridge had chronicled his travels in a series of journals and notebooks, and he may have once again intended to turn them to account as a publication. Unfortunately, most of those recollections were lost. During the return voyage to Britain, the Spanish navy boarded their ship, and, because those notebooks also included drafts of the political papers and strategic researches that he had completed for Sir Alexander Ball, he was forced to throw a significant part of them overboard. Many of his finished political papers survived, including his *Observations on Egypt* (1804), which he claimed was 'gained from the books or the conversation of intelligent Travellers' (Sultana, 1969, p. 189). He also wrote an essay on 'Malta, Egypt, &c' (1805) for *The Courier* and poems that included 'To Captain Findlay' (1804), 'Apostrophe to Beauty in Malta' (1805), and 'On Death at Pisa' (1806).

GERMANY (1828)

Coleridge arrived back in Britain in August of 1806, and, apart from a brief tour in 1807 to revisit familiar sites in Stowey and Ottery, Coleridge rarely traveled again. He settled into life as the Sage of Hampstead and struggled to cope with the increasingly debilitative nature of his opium addiction. His only excursions now were long walks on the Heath, where John Keats—himself just returned from a tour of Scotland—remembered meeting Coleridge in April of 1819 (Holmes, 1999). For Coleridge, travel once again became the primarily textual experience that it had been in his boyhood. And there were still plenty of travel books around him, including a steady stream of titles published by his old friends. Southey published his *Letters from England* (1807), and in the years to come Wordsworth would write his *Guide to the Lakes* (1810), *The River Duddon, A Series of Sonnets. . . . to which is Annexed, A Topographical Description of the Country of the Lakes in the North of England* (1820), and his *Memorials of a Tour, 1820* (1822). Coleridge's own poetic compositions from the latter part of his life also testify to his abiding interest in travel writing as a genre. In his collected works, readers still find minor pieces such as 'Lines on the Usury of Pain' (1819), suggested by William Burchell's *Travels in the Interior of Southern Africa* (1822), and 'The Delinquent Travellers', with its references to *The Private Journal of Captain G. F. Lyon . . . during the Recent Voyage of Discovery under Captain Parry* (1824).

To this settled life after 1807, there was one exception. In the summer of 1828, Coleridge returned to Germany on a seven-week tour of the Rhine with Wordsworth and Wordsworth's daughter Dora. There would have been little to remind either of Coleridge or Wordsworth of their first adventure in Germany more than thirty years before. Then, Coleridge and Wordsworth had been following the fashionable itinerary of young radicals, drawn to the northern intellectual centers of Göttingen and Jena. This time, they were following—although perhaps Wordsworth would have been chagrined to acknowledge it—a renewed fashion for 'romantic' tourism in the Rhineland, recently made popular by the publication in 1816 of the third canto of Lord Byron's *Childe Harold's Pilgrimage*.

The Rhine had been a minor picturesque destination in the 1790s, described most famously in Ann Radcliffe's *A Journey Made in the Summer of 1794 . . . with a Return Down the Rhine, to which are added Observations during a Tour to the Lakes of Lancashire, Westmoreland, and Cumberland* (1795), but it was a mode of travel more associated with the respectably genteel (and often feminine) than with radical democratic politics. When Byron traveled through Belgium and along the Rhine (which included parts of France, Holland, and Germany) after the end of the Napoleonic Wars, he lent new glamour to these scenes. The result was a revived interest in the area's castles and rural scenery that persisted throughout the 1820s— an interest reflected in the spate of travel books describing the region during the decade, titles such as Charles Tennant's *A Tour through Parts of the Netherlands, Holland, Germany, Switzerland, Savoy, and France* (1824), J. I. Gerning's *A Picturesque Tour along the Rhine* (1820), James Holman's *The Narrative of a Journey . . . through France, Italy, Savoy, Switzerland, [and] Parts of Germany Bordering on the Rhine* (1822), Charles Dodd's *An Autumn Near the Rhine* (1821), Seth Stevenson's *A Tour in France, Savoy, Northern Italy, Switzerland, Germany . . . Including Some Observations on the Scenery of . . . the Rhine* (1827), and, even earlier, Percy Bysshe and Mary Shelley's *History of a Six Weeks' Tour through a Part of France, Switzerland, Germany, and Holland* (1817).

It was this fashionable tourist's itinerary that Coleridge and his companions were following in the summer of 1828. Their route took them not to Hamburg but instead to Ostend, Bruges, and Ghent, into Brussels, Spa, and even Aix-la-Chapelle. They saw Cologne and Bonn and sailed down the Rhine to Utrecht, Amsterdam, and Rotterdam (Griggs, 1956, vol. 6, p. 749). 'Mr Wordsworth', Coleridge joked, with '. . . . his fair Daughter had by pure force of attraction carried me on, o'er Ditch and Dell, River and Plain, not to speak of German Mountains and Dutch Steeples and Rhenish Towers, like the Prodigal Son' (ibid. 6, p. 748). On the tour, Coleridge wrote his lines 'Two Expectations from Cologne' (1828) on the road from Cologne to Bonn, but this time there is no hint that he imagined turning his travels to account in published form. Christopher Wordsworth recorded the only complete account of the shared tour in his *Memoirs of William Wordsworth* (1851).

WORKS CITED

ANONYMOUS. 1800. An honest Briton. *Morning Chronicle*, 6 (28 April): 562.

BUTLER, JAMES A. 1996. Tourist or native son: Wordsworth's homecomings of 1799–1800. *Nineteenth-Century Literature*, 51 (1) (June): 1–15.

CARLYON, CLEMENT. 1836–58. *Early Years and Late Reflections*. 2 vols. London: Whittaker.

COLEMAN, DEIRDRE. 1988. *Coleridge and The Friend 1809–1810*. Oxford: Oxford University Press.

EUGENIA [Sister]. 1930. Coleridge's scheme of Pantisocracy and American travel accounts. *PMLA*, 45 (4 December): 1069–84.

GRIGGS, EARL LESLIE. 1956. *Collected Letters of Samuel Taylor Coleridge*. 6 vols. Oxford: Clarendon Press.

HOLMES, RICHARD. 1999. *Coleridge: Darker Reflections*. New York: Random House.

—— 1990. *Coleridge: Early Visions*. New York: Viking.

HUCKS, JOSEPH. 1979. *A Pedestrian Tour through North Wales in a Series of Letters* (1795). Rpt. Alan R. Jones and William Tydeman, eds. Cardiff: University of Wales Press.

LOWES, JOHN LIVINGSTONE. 1927. *The Road to Xanadu: A Study in the Ways of the Imagination*. Boston: Houghton Mifflin.

MAZZEO, TILAR. 2001. *Travels, Explorations, and empires, 1770–1835: The Middle East*. Vol. 4. London: Pickering and Chatto.

McNULTY, JOHN BARD. 1945. Wordsworth's tour of the Wye: 1798. *Modern Language Notes*, 60 (5) (May): 291–5.

PARK, MARY CATHRYNE. 1947. *Joseph Priestley and the Problem of Pantisocracy*. Philadelphia: University of Pennsylvania.

SMITH, BERNARD. 1956. Coleridge's Ancient Mariner and Cook's second voyage. *Journal of the Warburg and Courtauld Institutes*, 19 (1–2) (Jan.–June): 117–54.

SULTANA, DONALD. 1969. *Samuel Taylor Coleridge in Malta and Italy*. Oxford: Blackwell.

THOMPSON, E. P. 1994. Hunting the Jacobin Fox. *Past and Present*, 142 (Feb.): 94–140.

TODD, F. M. 1952. Wordsworth in Germany. *The Modern Language Review*, 47(4) (Oct.): 508–11.

WALKER, CAROL KYROS. 2002. *Breaking Away: Coleridge in Scotland*. New Haven: Yale University Press.

WHALLEY, GEORGE. 1950. Coleridge and Southey in Bristol, 1795. *The Review of English Studies*, New Series, 1(4) (Oct.): 324–40.

WORDSWORTH, CHRISTOPHER. 1851. *Memoirs of William Wordsworth*. New York: Ticknor, Reed, and Fields.

WU, DUNCAN. 1993. *Wordsworth's Reading, 1770–1799*. Cambridge: Cambridge University Press.

ZUCCATO, EDOUARDO. 1996. *Coleridge in Italy*. Cork: Cork University Press.

CHAPTER 6

COLERIDGE'S SELF- REPRESENTATIONS

ANYA TAYLOR

INSPIRED by the ferment of philosophical discussion about persons initiated by Hume, by the proliferation of autobiographical narrations initiated by Rousseau, and by his own curiosity, Coleridge recorded the 'inexhaustively re-ebullient' forms of his consciousness (*BL* 1, 300). His observations did not eddy into solipsism but came to focus on the search for 'Integrity'(*Friend* 1, 45) as a center from which to discover principles in the world at large. He sought a continuity in recollected glimpses of his life—the child asleep by the cold river, the *philosophe* on shipboard, the lover leaping into the ocean, the official in convoy to Malta to learn command, the sage entertaining his disciples—even as he studied politics, medicine, religion, and art. To connect his experiences, opinions, and impressions in writing was to assert his own coherence as a person. His discoveries appear as intertwined texts to his readers, but he lived his identity as a physical being at the center of the texts.

MULTIPLICITY

For Coleridge, experiencing the self was from the start intensely dramatic and wondrous. In one of his earliest letters he invited his friend Mrs Evans and her daughters to 'have the very first row in the front box of my Heart's little theatre—and—God knows! *you are not crowded*. There, my dear Spectators! you shall see what you shall see—Farce, Comedy, & Tragedy—my Laughter, my Chearfulness, and my Melancholy. A thousand figures pass before you, shifting in perpetual succession—these are my Joys and my Sorrows, my Hopes and my Fears, my Good tempers, and my Peevishnesses...my whole heart shall be laid open like any sheep's heart' (*CL* 1, no. 12, p. 21). He exults in the multiplicity that he discovers in 'this play house' or anatomical theatre, where the facets of his personality perform as actors or submit to dissection like cadavers. As he will for decades to come, he welcomes fellow observers to join him in watching the spectacle. At nineteen he already knows that this 'I' is kaleidoscopic, inclusive, and expansive. His early poems show this multiplicity, moving adventurously among satire (*PW* no. 29), lament at partings (*PW* no. 33), intimate memories (*PW* nos. 25 and 26), love ditties (*PW* no. 20), and political harangues (*PW* no. 13). His thought is playful in many senses, experimental, theatrical, open-ended. He explores his consciousness with the same avid curiosity with which he explores the effect of the slave trade on English sailors, the shapes of mountains and crags in Glencoe, the odd effect of hats on women, the tenses in Greek language, and superstitions in religious beliefs.

Such experiences of multiplicity help in his ongoing debate with eighteenth century philosophers on the nature of consciousness. From observing his own mind in action, he rejects the notion that the mind is blank or scattered. He sometimes addresses Hume directly in his notebooks as when he asks, 'On the simplicity or manifoldness of the human Being? In what sense is it one? Sense, Appetite, Passion, Fancy, Imagination, Understanding, & lastly the Reason & Will?' (*CN* 1712; and see also *CN* 2370) or when he attacks Locke in his letters to Wedgwood claiming that Locke's terms for '*we, Soul, Mind, Consciousness, & Ideas*' were jumbled together 'in a complete Whirl-dance of Confusion'(*CL* 2, no. 383, p. 696, letter 383). Even the inspirational Kant gets rebuffed, as when Coleridge notes his 'feeling' that Reason and Will do not always move in the same direction: 'Now I do not feel this perfect synonimousness in Reason & the Wille. I am sure, Kant cannot make it out. Again & again, he is a wretched Psychologist' (*CN* 1717). To his notebooks he muses, 'so I think oftentimes...that multitude & division are not (o mystery) necessarily subversive of unity. I am sure, that two very different meanings if not more lurk in the word, *one*'(*CN* 2332).[1]

His multiplicity, originating from inward energy, from ebullience and enthusiasm (Beer, *Poetic Intelligence*, p. xii), is proof to himself that materialistic philosophers who imagine passive or fractured selves base their conceptions on their own very different experiences of themselves. 'Materialists unwilling to admit

---

[1] Hume, *Treatise*, 1, 4, 5, and 6; McFarland, *Pantheist Tradition*, 221–55; Taylor, 'Persons and Things', 163–80; Leader, 316–22; Alan Richardson calls Romanticism 'a cultural movement throwing notions of conscious volition and the integral self into crisis' (p. 63). On egotism, see Bygrave, 3–28.

the mysterious of our nature make it all mysterious—nothing mysterious in nerves, eyes, &c: but that nerves think &c!!—Stir up the sediment into the transparent water, & so make all opaque' (*CN* 920). He tests philosophies through self-reflection, claiming that 'a moment's self-introition' verifies a philosophical position more truly than altering and dislocating sentences by 'dialectic art'(*CN* 1758). The 'mysterious in our nature' generates his creativity and will come to generate his theory of how that creativity arises.

Within his capacious subjectivity Coleridge enacts the multiple Coleridges that he discovers within himself. He darts his being through the personae of mystic, lover, prophet, diplomat, moralist, father, convivial humorist, man of pleasure, and man of despair. Even in sorrow he continues to admire 'my own mind so populous, so active, so full of noble schemes, so capable of realizing them/ this heart so loving, so filled with noble affections . . .' (*CN* 1577). When in retreat from a painful bout of rheumatism he nevertheless records myriad sources of pleasure as he watches his consciousness: 'My enjoyments are so deep, of the fire, of the Candle, of the Thought I am thinking, of the old Folio I am reading—and the silence of the silent House is so *most* & *very* delightful—that upon my soul! The Rheumatism is no such bad thing as *people make for*' (*CL* 1, no. 298, p. 539), a scintillation of impressions akin to those that Virginia Woolf celebrated a century later. He writes to William Sotheby, 13 July 1802 (*CL* 2, no. 444, p. 808) that the experiences of their first meeting 'all flowed in upon me with unusually strong Impulses of Pleasure / and Pleasure, in a body & soul such as I happen to possess, "intoxicates more than strong Wine"'. When he hears his five-year-old son Hartley pointing 'out without difficulty that there might be five Hartleys, Real Hartley, Shadow Hartley, Picture Hartley, Looking Glass Hartley, and Echo Hartley' (*CL* 2, no. 379, p. 673), he recognizes a kindred multiplicity, though he laments that Hartley later develops into a youth without a central core of being to unite those facets (Taylor, *Bacchus*, pp. 126–56). While his own divided being is often a cause of anguish, as recounted by McFarland ('Coleridge's Anxiety'), it nevertheless provides rousing stories to engage his correspondents.

The investigation of his multiple consciousnesses, interesting in itself, also indicates that there is a consciousness recording this consciousness and thus a center. His experience of his own layered subjectivity served as a living proof that consciousness was neither single nor passive but rather so deeply complex as to require the invention of a new vocabulary. Seeking a language to capture the subtleties within, he studied mystics, seventeenth-century English Platonists, and contemporary German philosophers and thus expanded his distinctions among terms designating the faculties and powers of the self (McKusick, p. 40). To existing terms such as mind, heart, reason, understanding, sense, spirit, and soul, he added his own inventions such as 'subconsciousness'and 'consciousness within a consciousness'(*CN* 2914 and 2999a; for other layers see *CN* 4186 f. 35). Lockridge claims that Coleridge coined the term 'self-realization', and pursued the self's organic growth through its forms as 'self-immersion' and 'self-actualization', laying the foundation for the twentieth century psychology of self-actualization (Lockridge, p. 149). Richardson credits him with 'psychosomatic' (p. 44). Coleridge even invented organs in the human body, which he called 'organs of spirit' (*BL* 1, 242). While denouncing egotism, he grounded his being in an 'I am I', a spirit, a soul, words that had emotional, empirical, biblical, and transcendental resonances. The transcriptions from Schelling in *BL*, chapter 12, reveal the importance for Coleridge of Schelling's work in locating the intersection of self-consciousness and 'the sacred power of self-intuition'and thus affirming the primacy and power of the subject (*BL* 1, 251–73 and Engell's notes). Guided by the German philosophers, though not always acknowledging their help, he works through 'the science of BEING' (*BL* 1, 252) to his 'SUM or I AM' finally to arrive at 'the heaven-descended KNOW THYSELF' (*BL* 2, 252). As late as 1830 he is still defining the nature of his self-consciousness and struggling to understand 'the suspensive duplicity of the "I" in Man' and 'the twofold "I"' (*CN* 6449 and 6477).

Coleridge's invitation to the Evans women to watch the theatre of his heart could serve as a metaphor for the honesty of the self-presentations in his notebooks, letters and poems. Coleridge is unusual for his time and perhaps for all time in openly describing his emotions and distresses to his friends, distresses often recounted with a touch of self-amusement. In five letters to Thomas Poole he shapes the narrative of his boyhood among fierce older siblings (*CL* 1, nos. 174, 179, 208, 210, 234). He writes in Latin to Robert Southey about his frustrations in marriage, screening his distress from his wife (*CL* 1, 569 and 571). While he exclaims at his delights, he also presents himself in surprising detail as a suffering person, whose body erupts and repels him, and whose mind is often 'paralytic' from 'self-dissatisfaction' (*CL* 3, no. 721, p. 131). He tells Mathilda Betham that he represses his emotions in times of turmoil: 'the more I force away my attention from any inward distress, the worse it becomes after—& what I keep out of my mind or rather *keep down* in a state of under-consciousness, is sure to act meanwhile with it's whole power of poison on my Body' (*CL* 3, no. 815, p. 310). This analysis to a near stranger bursts forth from his own effort to understand the pressures on his consciousness of this 'under-consciousness' that baffles his will. He apologizes to Daniel Stuart for his inability to assert himself: 'O dear friend! It would be far, far better for me if I had a little more of that vanity, a little more interest in the opinions, people entertain of my talents &c' (*CL* 3, no. 781, p. 232). He is not too ashamed to explain to his friend J. J. Morgan what it feels like to be an addict (*CL* 3, nos. 927 and 928; see on 'Will-Maniacs', Taylor, *Bacchus*, pp. 110–19). In his letters he represents himself to others in moods of anguish and buoyancy, making light of pain, making much of pain, elaborating to entertain them. Sometimes his confessions seem like lies as when he moans in 1811 about Wordsworth's betrayal and then is observed by the Lambs reveling like Bacchus (*CL* 3, no. 815, p. 309, note 1 and *Lamb Letters*, 3, 61–2). Integrity is not simple oneness but interplay of voices within a continuous consciousness. (For the intricacy and intensity of his love life see Taylor, *Erotic Coleridge*, and Ch. 4 by Neil Vickers.)

He confesses to weaknesses and desires that most men keep to themselves. In his frankness he opened his nature to criticism from observers who would otherwise not have noticed these weaknesses. This passionate precision about his feeling spills over into poems that reveal his anguish to the reading public. The 1803 poem 'Pains of Sleep' (*PW* no. 335), published in 1816 for all to read, arises in the context of several letters about his suffering during a walking trip through Scotland (*CL* 2, nos. 513, 514, 515). In the poem, part of letter 516 to Robert Southey, he continues the analysis in verse form, describing a sequence of three nights when his usual prayerful stillness was disrupted by torments deserved only by the truly wicked: 'Fantastic passions! mad'ning brawl! / And shame and terror over all!' (lines 18, 25–6). These hallucinations assault him from outside his essentially innocent being: 'But wherefore, wherefore fall on me? / To be beloved is all I need, / And whom I love, I love indeed' (lines 50–2; see Mays' headnote to *PW* no. 335). In trying to walk free of an addiction that he recognized only later (see *CL* 2, p. 984, note 1), Coleridge posits a 'me' tormented unjustly by outside forces that are driven, unbeknownst to him, by his own opium use. Coleridge's descriptions of the abyss of self-loss (emphasized by McFarland in 'Anxiety' and by Lockridge in *Coleridge the Moralist*) do not present the whole picture, however; for side by side with expressions of despair are letters and poems of zestful humor as well as love poems that indicate some reciprocity, hinting at resilience.

ONENESS AND IDENTITY

Coleridge seeks the cohesive force that binds the multiple aspects of the self together, the power that makes the multiplicity a *one*, *multum in unum*. His concern with finding the center of the person begins early and gains sharp focus in 1820: 'What is the definition, not verbal but real, of PERSONALITY? What constitutes a PERSON?' (*CN*, 4728). His focus is often on the will, which can choose to do something other than what it did do and can refuse to obey reason. (For the will, see Lockridge, pp. 61–7.) This search for the center organizes the many directions of his inquiries so that they do not seem to be random jottings to fill the loneliness of his life, but evidences of a self acting in a characteristic way that adds up to a totality of the person 'STC'.

This multiplicity spins on a central core, which Coleridge describes as a sense of warmth or a deep steady feeling of being himself, and which he calls variously a self, a soul, a person, a spirit, an intelligence. To Thelwall he describes the feeling of having a core of being, as he clarifies it for himself: 'I feel strongly and I think strongly; but I seldom feel without thinking, or think without feeling. . . . My philosophical opinions are blended with or deduced from, my feelings: & this, I think, peculiarizes my style of Writing' (*CL* 1, no. 164, p. 279). The experience of being an 'I myself I' is more intense than any intellectual conception of it: 'Now (let me) think of *myself*—of the thinking Being—the Idea becomes dim whatever it be—so dim that I know not what it is—but the Feeling is deep & steady—and this I call *I*—identifying the Percipient & the Perceived' (*CN* 921). Seamus Perry calls this characteristic musing an 'act of introspective self-reflection' that 'relocates life from outside to within the self' (*Notebooks*, p. 165).

The warmth of his physical experience of self is a distinctive affirmation of his personal identity. He contrasts his feelings with those of his estranged wife, who is cold and dependent on outside verification for her sense of self: 'As I seem to exist, as it were, almost wholly within myself, in *thoughts* rather than in *things*, in a particular warmth felt all over me, but chiefly felt about my heart & breast; & am connected with *things without* me by the pleasurable sense of their immediate Beauty of Loveliness, and not at all by my knowledge of their average value in the minds of people in general; & with *persons without* me, by no ambition of their esteem . . . by general kindliness of feeling . . . by an intense delight in fellow-feeling . . .' (*CL* 2, no. 467, and see *CN* 979 on her external sense of self, contrasted with his inwardly experienced self). Thus he represents himself to himself in his notebooks as physically 'warm' in the center of his 'heart & breast', appreciative of the beauty of the outside world, and affectionately receptive to other persons in themselves. Despite his frequent self-criticism, in this case he prefers his own self-generated warmth to his wife's superficial assessments of what others will say, a difference in values that chills their marriage from the start (see *Erotic Coleridge*, pp. 21–42). His wife's 'being' 'has been unfortunately little more than a far-stretched Series of Et Ceteras', while his own is complex, warm, and passionate. He feels himself to be a person, and is indifferent to his outward image: 'Does not this establish the existence of *a Feeling* of a Person quite distinct at all times, & at certain times *perfectly separable* from, the Image of the Person?' (*CN*, 2061). The image of the person, the surface toward the world, is not the same as the feeling of the person within.[2] Coleridge suggests that being a person is either a gift or an achievement, and that some people may not have selves at all but mere facades.

Coleridge establishes that he has a self by the warm, deep, and steady feeling that 'I call *I*' (*CN* 921); he experiences this self as one and also as many, and he revels in its multifariousness. Joy at his own being erupts in a series of little known poems from the years after falling in love with Sara Hutchinson in late 1799. Poems such as

---

[2] Charles Taylor, in *Sources*, p. 33, argues that 'selves are beings of the requisite depth and complexity to have an identity. Self-image . . . is not seen as something which is essential to human personhood.'

'After Bathing', 'A Soliloquy of the Full Moon', and 'Answer to a Child's Question' (*PW* nos. 275, 290, 291) exult in the identity of the 'I am I' and display the pleasure that he believes is essential to his nature. In these three poems the bird sings, he sings, the moon sings. In lines to Sara Hutchinson ('A Day-Dream', lines 19–22) he describes his 'depth of tranquil bliss' when she lay on his 'warm breast', his love affirming his sense of being a self. He exults, 'God is *with* me! God is *in* me! / I *cannot* die; for Life is Love!' (*PW* 276, lines 23–4). Such joy in being, however shadowed by later feelings that he 'alone & utterly hopeless for myself' (*CN* 3231), continues in the 'infinite self-rejoicing' of the 'Essays on the Principles of Method' (*Friend* 1, 521). As Seamus Perry observes, for Coleridge, '"To Be" is not just a copula but a spiritual end' ('Autonomy', p. 249). The self generates what is human, creative, and meaningful. In its very activity it disproves the shallow view that the mind is passive to external influences, a philosophy that would imagine a world deprived of artists such as Washington Allston, Southey, and Byron, and turn the 'I' into a random shadow cast by an impersonal universe, into a 'poor, worthless I' (*BL* 1, 119–20).

Coleridge derides philosophers who think that the activities of the intelligence are impelled by 'mere articulated motions of the air', and gives as proof of its power the spontaneous acts of genius. This is an area where his own experience again has provided memories of ebullience rising from within the self, with or without impulsion from the will.

In his two most famous supernatural poems the 'I' asserts its power, even to do evil, and struggles for preeminence among other voices. 'Kubla Khan', despite pretending to arise from a subconscious dream, takes the form of an orderly diagram of the multi-layered creative 'I'. Following the boom of the emperor's decree, the tumult of natural explosions, and the rapture of the Damsel's vocalization, the voice of the poet, belated and contingent, enters the symphony as a solo. The poet does not presume to rival these powerful creativities but artfully to take their sound into his own diminished human realm if he can. The self-abasing 'I' sings in the subjunctive voice: 'Could I revive within me / Her symphony and song, / To such a deep delight 'twould win me, / That with music loud and long, / I would build that dome in air...' The singer wishes to build, and the wish is accomplished line by line as the details accumulate: 'That sunny dome! Those caves of ice!' In an optimistic reading the 'I' succeeds in transforming sounds 'heard' into domes and caves that his listeners can immediately 'see':

> And all who heard should see them there,
> And all should cry, Beware! Beware!
> His flashing eyes, his floating hair!
>
> (*PW* no. 178, lines 42–50)

This song-generated vista inspires yet another layer of voices in his audience. The 'I' becomes a 'he', known and feared by others. The 'he' steps back and joins the roll of creative predecessors that the 'I' originally honored. Though some readers believe the wish falls short, the 'I' can be read as completing an exultant poem on the basis of the wish for completion (O'Neill, p. 89). The 'I' constructs a self to be seen from the outside as a 'he' possessed with power, even as the poet's humble preface, in a different voice, undercuts the experiential sense of the poem's wholeness.

In 'The Rime of the Ancient Mariner' the individualized voice of the guilty 'I' sounds amid a chorus of other voices. Richard Haven notes the reiterative announcements of the 'I' as agent: 'I shot the albatross'; 'I had done a hellish thing'; 'I looked upon the rotting sea'; 'And I blessed them unaware'; 'I dreamt'; 'I moved'; 'I heard'; 'I woke'; 'I have strange power of speech' (PW no. 161; Patterns, pp. 29–30). The 'Rime' plays with shifting voices, even within the Mariner's own voice, where the mariner is by turn objective, shocked, confessional, anguished, dreamily unconscious, skeptical, pious, and resigned, while other voices, of spirits, crewmembers, priest, and wedding guest swirl around him (See Schulz). At the edge of his complex narration a scholarly voice with modulations of its own interprets the text from an orthodox religious standpoint. This marginal voice intones in counterpoint in a different key, and pressures meaning into directions perhaps at odds with the meaning of the questionable text, holding all meaning in suspension but not thereby erasing it. The 'I' speaks as an agent, the other voices echo and respond. Coleridge's being flows in and out as narrator and agent without boundaries. The late 'The Improvisatore; or Jo Anderson my Jo' (PW no. 623) calls attention, even by its title and dramatic setting, to its own changing voices and to the principle of combining spontaneity with skilled orations; it moves from lyric, to mini-drama, to prose disquisition, to solitary lament.[3] See entry by Michael O'Neill.

The ebullient self moves through many fictive personae in the forms of lovers, murderers, ruined girls, abandoned figures, guilt ridden wanderers, and Bibical exiles as in 'The Wanderings of Cain' (PW no. 160). It shifts from the outer I to the inner I, the narrator and the story he tells; in 'Love' Coleridge is the lover wooing with the tale, as well as the frenzied seeker in the plot, he is the failure and the success, the rejected and the accepted. He is the author and the friend of 'Phantom or Fact' (no. 667), imagining the self from different points of view. He is the text and the marginal comment to his own text. He is Christabel betrayed, subdued and silenced, and he is Christabel's father betraying her to re-establish an intense earlier friendship at any cost. After sending Wordsworth his rhapsodic poem 'The Nightingale', which dedicates his son Hartley to a childhood amid nature's music and moonlight, he suddenly shifts voice into the jaunty humor typical of his epigrams, asking Wordsworth to tell him what he thinks his 'bird's worth' (PW, nos. 180 and 181). While some of the poems present versions of himself (Paley, p. 80), others take

[3] See Taylor, 'Romantic Improvvisatori', 501–21; Esterhammer, Spontaneous Overflows, 1–40.

the more difficult way that Coleridge recommended to Sotheby: it 'is easy to cloathe Imaginary Beings with our own Thoughts & Feelings; but to send ourselves out of ourselves, to *think* ourselves in to the Thoughts and Feelings of Beings in circumstances wholly & strangely different from our own/ *hoc labor, hoc opus/* and who has atchieved it? Perhaps only Shakespere' (*CL* 2, no. 444, p. 810).

Coleridge attempts in numerous metaphors to convey a sense of the vivacious identity of the self. 'I have rather made up my mind that I am a mere *apparition*—a naked Spirit!—and that Life is I myself I! which is a mighty clear account of it' (*CL* 1, no. 170, p. 295). He calls the soul a cricket chirping in fire (*CN* 3379). He writes to a young woman that 'I resemble a Bottle of Brandy in Spitzbergen—a Dram of alcoholic Fire in the center of a cake of ice' (*CL* 6, 532). He describes the self as an inviolable treasure vault. He calls the spirit 'an Island Harbourless, and every way inaccessible' (M 1, 70). Along with metaphors, analogies to animals intensify his self-descriptions. A few of his metaphors compliment his own mental agility: 'Oft like a winged Spider, I am entangled in a new Spun web—but never fear for me, 'tis but the flutter of my wings–& off I am again!—' (*CL* 1, no. 323, p. 578). But usually animal images portend self-criticism. When he compares himself to an animal (an ostrich or a bustard or a toad, for example) he calls his comparison an analogy so as to avoid any overlap between his human self and the animal world. Sometimes he calls himself a beast when his will has ceased to function: he feels his spirit so trapped that 'at every Gyre its wings beat against the personal Self' (*CN* 2541, 2531). He describes the squeals and purrs of the pinched soul (*BL* 1, 119) as if the soul were a cat, an image for the softenings down of man to brute creation, which he fears in himself, trying to preserve a chasm between man and brute.[4] He acknowledges the fear of 'a cold dark speck at the heart' or 'the secret lodger' that might greet investigations in the self (*AR*, 24). Such metaphors acknowledge the dark self he might find.

INNER DEBATES

Developing a science of self out of his 'own mind's self-experience in the act of thinking' (*BL* 1, 124), Coleridge represented his inner debates as 'divisions' that allow him to hold more than one possibility in suspension.[5] More stable than the scintillation of multiplicity, divisions permit dialogue about choices, a

[4] *CN* 2555; for the need for a chasm, a sense of distinct difference of kind, see Taylor, *Coleridge's Defense*, 35–55.

[5] Perry, *Uses of Division*, shows that alternative positions in life, poetry, and philosophy coexist under the rubric 'and yet'.

psychomachia that enlivens notes and letters to others as he sets forth his alterna-tives. In contemplating his decision to christen his blithe son Hartley he recreates his inner debate: 'Then I say, Shall I suffer the Toad of Priesthood to spurt out his foul juice in this Babe's Face?' (*CL* 1, no. 352, p. 625). He wonders to himself about his uncontrollable passion: 'Why do I feel jealous, if the last letter had not happened to be full of explicit love & feeling' (*CN* 1603), implying that Sara Hutchinson wrote to him often in amorous terms in the many letters burned after her death by her sister Mary. He represents himself to himself in direct address, chastising, enquiring, cross examining: 'My instincts are so far dog-like / I love beings superior to me better than my Equals—but inferior is so painful to me, that I never in common Life, feel a man my Inferior except by after-reflection. What seems vanity in me is in great part attributable to this Feeling but of this hereafter I will cross examine myself' (*CN* 2726). He tells himself that he judged Pitt harshly, not admitting his success against the slave trade for fear of being wrong in his earlier condemnation of him (*CN* 1605, 1606). He recognizes that some strong feelings are intensified by bringing up old hurts: 'Unspoken Grief is a misty medley, of which the real affliction only plays the first fiddle—blows the Horn, to a scattered mob of obscure feelings &c. [rousing] all the little relicts of pain & discomfort, bodily and mental, that we have endured even from infancy' (*CN* 1599). He urges himself to a 'fervent prayer' (*CN* 1647). He berates himself as a sot drinker of egged Brandy (*CN* 2570). He asks himself with exasperation, 'Why do I always?' (*CN* 1731). While staying with the Morgans in Bristol, he advises himself on how to interpret 'a short *meaning* Look, or rapid *Eye-smile*' passing between the sisters and warns himself, 'O No no! let me not think it— let me not add any imaginary anguish to the too large Pile of agonizing Realities!— and yet–/ (*but enough!*)' (*CN* 3235, 3236, and 3237). Note how the dialogue within himself proceeds: the reassuring voice tells himself to stop imagining trouble, the skeptical voice says trouble may be lurking, a third voice calls a halt to the debate to make peace. A dialogue can resemble 'Blows given by a person to himself, to his hands, breast, or forehead, in the paroxysms of *Self-reproof*', so belligerent 'as to make the body itself feel the *condemnation* which the mind feels so deeply'. Such conflict can be the foundation for 'spiritual revolution' (*CN* 2541, April 1805). Repeatedly he asks himself, why am I the kind of man I am, what 'skein of necessity' (*CN* 4109) has formed me?

Inner dialogue in notebooks occasionally flows into public form in poems of dialogue such as 'The Foster Mother's Tale: A Dramatic Fragment' (no. 152), 'The Suicide's Argument, with Nature's Answer' (no. 490), 'The Improvisatore, or Jo Anderson my Jo' (no. 623), or the late poem 'Phantom or Fact: A Dialogue in Verse' (no. 667);[6] it plays into his propensity for dramatic presentation of the situat-ions and opinions of others, empathizing with their plights. He attends to the voice of conscience, softly whispering (*CN* 3281). The inner debates console,

---

[6] See Taylor, 'Coleridge on Persons in Dialogue'.

amuse, and heal. Their subdivisions increase levels of consciousness, working toward the goal stated in a letter to Thomas Clarkson, that 'the great end and purpose of all [the soul's] energies and sufferings is the growth of that reflex consciousness' (*CL* 2, no. 634, p. 1197).

Looking within, he finds feelings and ideas blending, parts doubling. But when he imagines the inner life of other men, like Wordsworth and Southey, or Rousseau and Napoleon, he sees them as monumental, the watchtower of the absolute self, single, monadic, governed by clearly willed goals, steady and consistent, integral in their identity, but also therefore subject to the compromises of prudence or hypocrisy (Bygrave, pp. 150–84). They are so inflexibly themselves that they sometimes wear masks. Face to face with these manly monoliths, Coleridge feels himself to be womanly and pliant. While varied Coleridges enunciate political intricacies, chant magically powerful verses, solace suffering friends, satirize bombast and fraud, explore the facets of heartbreak, and make people laugh, this chameleon-like change-ableness weakens him in relation to men with more certain senses of themselves. He represents himself as weak in relation to Wordsworth in 'Ode to William Words-worth', where, after listening all night to Wordsworth reading aloud *The Prelude* (1806), he bows down before the procession of Wordsworth's honors. Secret under-tones, however, reveal a critique of the great poet for lacking the author's sensitivity, suggesting an underlying preference for his own way of being despite its flaws.[7]

Who is this self with coherence and continuity? Some critics have found a distinctive voice-print in the sequence of the six conversation poems written between 1797 and 1804, noting common themes in the narrative voices of the speaking 'I's. These narratives recreate in verse the sound of the syntactically intricate self-examinations in the notebooks and letters; in their 'intimate collo-quial candor' they revel in the 'playfulness' of the mind in activity (Parker, pp. 66–89). The fictive 'I's have sometimes been read as forming a composite person with shared characteristics revealed in repeated allusions and images—enclosures, the sounds of birds, harps, winds, moonlight, exclamations to loved ones addressed in the intimate tones common to the notebooks or letters, acts of listening or breaking silence, the overflow of radiance to others[8]—a composite person that seems not only to have unity but also to grow. For as a group the conversation poems show a developing emphasis on the generating force of the will, moving from passive receptivity in 'The Eolian Harp' to a gradual realization that 'the idling Spirit / By its own moods interprets every where / Echo or mirror seeking of itself' ('Frost at Midnight', lines 20–2).[9]

---

[7] Thomson, '"O Friend! O Teacher! God's great Gift to me!": Coleridge about Wordsworth'. In *Still Shines When You Think of It: A Festschrift for Vincent O'Sullivan*, eds. Bill Manhire and Peter Whiteford, 118–30.

[8] Harman notes in the conversation poems the 'power of discourse to generate interest where there was none', p. 903.

[9] Burwick, 'Coleridge's Conversation Poems: Thinking the Thinker', 168–82.

Taken side by side, two of the most mysterious conversation poems, 'A Letter to —— [SH]'and 'Dejection: An Ode' (*PW* nos. 289 and 293) dramatize the differences in representing the private and the public self, the inner and the outer 'I'. In the first the subject examines his choices and confesses them to the woman he openly loves. In the second, the subject purges these feelings to create an Ode to appear in the public press on the topic of personal energy on two levels, the primary imagination that allows the person to experience the wholeness of his or her life, and the secondary imagination that allows the artist to create with outwardly acting power. The original form of the poem to Sara Hutchinson flows out of a series of letters between them, implied in the poem but no longer extant. In the 'Letter to —— [SH]' these letters are mentioned, hers so painful that his heart is wrenched, his that preceded it making her physically sick. Written in the night as he lies awake, the 'Letter to SH' reveals how intimate they are, how frequently they write and talk, how much pain their inability to live together gives them, and how much their lives are intertwined.[10] Preparing this 'Letter to SH' for publication Coleridge must omit the references to his unhappy marriage, the burden of his children, his professional disappointments, and present the general outlines of loss of enthusiasm for the world in a lofty and impersonal voice. 'Dejection: An Ode' is the philosophical resolution of tormented passion; it distills immediate feeling into a stately public assessment of the role of self-generating imagination in creating one's own happiness. The anguished lover triumphs over sorrow by creating 'a genial, companionable counterpart for his own solitary, singing self' (Parker, p. 58). In this movement from private to public versions Coleridge creates a willed authority (Leader, p. 138), and presents himself to different audiences with startlingly different results.

DIALOGUES WITH OTHERS

As he speaks to himself as to an Other, he also speaks to others and merges himself with them with the generosity to allow others to be other that Paul Magnuson has noted (p. 166). Recognition of the otherness of others marks the onset of self-consciousness and heralds love.[11] Coleridge speaks to SH as to his other half; she is the soother of absence but is often present, taking dictation in his twilit room. On an arduous climbing trip in August, 1802, Coleridge keeps a 'Sheet Letter' for her describing his feats leaping down cliffs. She transcribes it in her journal, leaving out

---

[10] For varieties of love in these two poems, see Barth, 89–102.

[11] For this moment of recognition see *OM* p. 132; on love for others, see Davidson, 149–50; Harding, 1–6; Taylor, *Erotic Coleridge*, 166–85.

one drawing that she claims she has not ingenuity enough to trace (*CL* 2, nos. 450, 451, 453). Because he is writing to his dear friend he relishes the detail; he expands in humor and descriptive prowess knowing that she wants to know it all. By contrast, he summarizes the trip in one paragraph to Southey (*CL* 2, no. 452). Coleridge asks Sara Hutchinson through his notebook in spring, 1803, 'Why we two made to be a Joy to each other, should for so many years constitute each other's melancholy—O! but the melancholy is Joy' (*CN* 1394). Poignantly, in the summer of 1803, he makes passionate proposals to her while recognizing that as long as his wife lives he cannot marry her (*CN* 1421). Is he speaking to her as she sits beside him or as she forms a part of his consciousness? That she is an aspect of his consciousness is suggested by this note: 'In loving her thus I love two Souls as one' (*CN* 2530). He thinks of the two of them as 'two Birds of Passage, reciprocaly [*sic*] resting on each other in order to support the long flight, the awful Journey' (*CN* 2556). He writes to her as a life companion, accepting the physicality of his love for her: 'Why then should I fear or blush to say, I *love* you—love you always, and if I sometimes feel desire at the same time, yet Love endures when no such feeling blends with it—yet I desire because I love, & not Imagine that I love because I desire' (*CN* 3284, May 1808).

For ten years much of his self-analysis is bound up with his feelings about Sara Hutchinson as she becomes the 'You' that is his better self speaking to him inside his mind or in person. Written a month or two after he met her, the poem 'Love' depicts their closeness as physical beings sensing each other's movements and as partners listening to each other's stories.[12] The poem forms an intricate narrative inside a narrative, as the lover woos his lady by telling her a tale of a cold lady who caused the death of her lover. Shifting back and forth from the outer to the inner tale, stirring emotion with his calculated music, and watching his lady's reaction to his story, the lover is rewarded by a sensuous embrace as the lady resolves not to drive her lover to death in the manner of the inner fiction. This rhythmically repetitive poem, famous in its own time, hinted in public at his love for a woman not his wife (*PW* no. 253). 'The Night-Scene', 'The Day-Dream', 'The Keepsake', 'The Picture', 'Phantom', and 'Recollections of Love' (*PW* nos. 272, 294, 299, 300, 347, 354) also indicate her presence if not at his side at least as an undershadow of his thoughts. Like the river Greta, his love has been 'ceaseless', 'Sole voice, when other voices sleep, / Dear under-song in Clamor's hour' (*PW* no. 354, lines 28–30). She is present in his 'Heart's Self-commune and Soliloquy' and lies 'in all my many thoughts, like Light' (*PW* no. 406, lines a 3 and b 4). She is an aspect of himself, for together they circle within 'that subtle Vulcanian Spider-web Net of Steel—strong as Steel yet subtle as the Ether... in which my Soul flutters inclosed with the idea of [Sara's]' (*CN* 3708). Even when she leaves to live with her brother Tom, she persists

---

[12] For the subtle layers of this poem see Mays, 'Coleridge's "Love" ': 'All he can manage, more than he could', pp. 49–66; O'Neill (pp. 71–3) describes this 'deceptively simple poem' in action, 'checking forward momentum, revolving on its own axis, and swaying to and fro'; Taylor, *Erotic Coleridge*, pp. 77–101, examines the influence of Dante's Paolo and Francesca tale on the framing structure of the poem.

in his definitions of love as a warm presence and as an object of address, inspiring a late series of love poems, including 'Farewell to Love' and 'The Blossoming of the Solitary Date-Tree' (*PW* nos. 387 and 396).

He merges with other powerful selves whom he loves, for instance, imagining his soul after death assuming Wordsworth's identity: 'O that my Spirit purged by Death of its Weaknesses, which are alas! my *identity* might flow into *thine*, & live and act in thee, & be Thou.' (*CN* 2712, and also 3235, 3236, 3237). His symbiotic relation with Wordsworth is the subject of Ch. 2 by Richard Gravil. Others also become part of his identity as he of theirs. He writes in a late notebook, 'I + *He* = *Ye*, all men become Ye to me, I composing part of them & they part of me' (*CN* 4636).

However, as abject as he occasionally becomes, he also takes pride in his own sincerity and indifference to censure (*CL* 2, 761). He is defiant to his wife about his right to love, about bringing Sara Hutchinson with him when he comes home (*CL* 2, no. 470). Despite much self-reproof he frequently likes himself. 'Egotistic Talk *with me* very often the effect of my Love of the Persons to whom I am talking / My Heart is talking of them / I cannot talk continuously of them to themselves—so I seem to be putting into their Heart the same continuousness as to me, that is in my own Heart as to them' (*CN* 1772). Blending with the loved other person, he extends the boundaries of his own consciousness.

Some surprising discoveries in the new *Poetical Works* are the many poems that reveal a social Coleridge who amuses men and women in varied social venues. Jokes and mockeries emerge from a part of his personality that has been obscured by a long critical focus on somber experiences. To Thomas Poole he recalls 'what Jokes we made / Conundrum, Rebus, Crambo, and Charade' ; he remembers how he 'with my own laughter stifled my own wit!' ('Fragment of an Epistle to Thomas Poole', *PW* no. 120). In letters, too, his conviviality rebounds in puns, for instance, in thanking Thomas Ward for pens, he runs through penance, penality, penurous, peninsula, penal, penetrant, pensive, pendulous, and finally Penumbra (*CL* 1, no. 295). A letter about returning an old shirt to the cantankerous Richard Words-worth (*CL* 1, no. 289) puts words into Poole's voice, 'My Friend, the Bard, alias, S. T. Coleridge, has just received a damn'd disagreeable dunning dirty dribbling Letter about a beggarly shirt &c &c &c.' When Coleridge writes to his wife from Ratzeburg, 3 Oct. 1798, he describes his new European friends on the tossing shipboard 'spouting, singing, laughing, fencing, dancing country dances—in a word being Bacchanals' . The Dane flatters STC with 'the most highest super-lativities an Englishman can conceive' . This long dialogue between STC and the Dane (*CL* 1, no. 256) allows him to imitate the Dane's speech—'Vat imagination! Vat language! Vat fast science! Vat eyes!—vat a milk vite forehead—O my Heaven! You are a God!'; lets his wife know about his own eminence and popularity; and reveals the hypocrisy of the Dane who orders his mulatto servant to get him brandy and sugar even as he tells STC that all men are equal. The angles of the dialogue presenting Coleridge's relations with others in a convivial community have their parallel in poems in dialogue that also set up a dramatic situation and reveal Coleridge's empathy with others. Other social angles of himself appear in drinking songs such as 'Drinking versus Thinking' (*PW* no. 279; see *Bacchus*, pp. 94–100), corresponding to some of his apologies for drinking to excess, as to Godwin, when, under the influence of 'titubancy', he followed an Idea 'thro thick & thin, Wood & Marsh, Brake and Briar' because 'the whole Thinking of my Life will not bear me up against the accidental Press & Crowd of my mind, when it is elevated beyond it's natural Pitch' (*CL* 1, no. 325).

While 'self-image' is not essential to selfness, Coleridge does sometimes work to describe for absent friends how he looks. Such self-portraiture demands objectivity but often depends on his attitude towards himself at the moment. In early letters he tells Mary Ann Evans that he is dashing, and his wife that he is getting handsome, a view corroborated by his study-boy (cited Beer, p. 39). On shipboard to Germany his black garb marks him as a 'priest', but he calls himself '*un philosophe*'. He sees his face as flaccid and revelatory of his weak character (*CL* 1, no. 156, p. 259). Despite C's interest in drawing precise landscape and cloud formations, he does not often mention how people look or how he looks unless he is mocking himself.

HALFNESS OF PERSON

Amid the whirl of multiple consciousnesses, the mariner's desolate cry 'Alone, alone, all, all alone' inspires other ways of representing the self. In times of loneliness Coleridge represents his inner self as incomplete and yearning for completion either from another human being or from a comforting God. This shift from fullness to need creates its own energy. One of the earliest formulations of this incomplete self is 'The Blossoming of the Solitary Date-Tree' (*PW*, no. 396), which arises from Coleridge's discovery of the botanical peculiarity that some plants need a nearby plant to propagate. In these five stanzas the poet describes himself as so full of love and joy that his emotions are overflowing. But this overflow is balked by the absence of Sara Hutchinson, an absence that empties his joy of meaning: 'It is Joy's greatness and it's overflow / Which, being incompleat, disquieteth me so' (lines 6–7). Not being 'Whole', he hears his own sweet songs in a vacuum, their sweetness 'only sweet for their sweet Echo's sake' (lines 9 and 31–2). He sees himself as a man inherently full of mirth and love but frustrated in its fulfillment: 'Why was I made for Love, yet Love denied to Me?' (line 35). The poem describes a temporary absence that could be resolved by one individual person's presence. When Sara Hutchinson leaves him in 1810 and his other infatuations (as with Charlotte Brent and Mrs Anne Gillman) simmer, he dwells on the meaning of this incompleteness in later notebooks, poems, and prose writings, for it can be desolate or liberating, fixated or searching. Influenced by Plato's *Phaedrus*, where each human being yearns for another being to complete him (*CN* 4730), Coleridge sees halfness as the impetus to love and to the realization that man is a fallen being in need of divine help. Halfness opens the heart to others and anticipates a future life.

Enhancing this view with entomological metamorphoses, which he studied already in 1803 (*CN* 1, 1378), Coleridge argues that all creatures are created with space to develop, as the horned beetle leaves room for a future he cannot imagine. In the *Biographia* he lays claim to an exclusive philosophic imagination available only to the few. These few acquire 'the sacred power of self-intuition' because they understand the symbol of the 'air-sylph' and know that an analogous process is working within them. They 'feel in their own spirits the same instinct, which impels the chrysalis of the horned fly to leave room in its involucrum for antennae yet to come. They know and feel, that the potential works in them, even as the actual works on them' (*BL* 1, 241–2; see note 1). The image of the half-empty chrysalis awaiting its future wings clarifies the plight of the philosophical consciousness, feeling the incompleteness of the spirit and dissatisfied with the self as it is. The need to fill the empty half generates the series of words for yearning, craving, and desire, those 'self-reflexive proofs of immortality' that we 'seek and find within ourselves' (Taylor, *Coleridge's Defense of the Human*, pp. 145–65). Another term for halfness is 'self-insufficingness', which Coleridge develops at length in 1826 in 'The Improvisatore or, "John Anderson, My Jo, John"' (*PW* no. 623). In this poem he presents himself in the role of a 'Friend' to the family, an elderly man who has lost the love of his life. He tells the young women that the yearning in his heart is 'that *willing* sense of the insufficingness of the *self* for itself, which predisposes a generous nature to see, in the total being of another, the supplement and completion of its own—that quiet perpetual seeking which the presence of the beloved object modulates, not suspends, where the heart momently finds, and finding, again seeks on …' In late notebooks as well (*CN* 4728, 4730) Coleridge praises desire, need, and yearning as the impetus behind the spiritual life of human beings.[13] He sees this incompleteness of self as central to the human condition. The half self opens a way to immortality when it craves after the completing half. Intense love desires 'to be united to some other Individual (conceived as alone capable of perfecting my Being) by all the means which Nature, Reason, & Duty, permit or dictate' (*CN* 4730).

Pursuing his ideas about self, soul, person, free agency, and origination, Coleridge finds that incompleteness is mysteriously a ground of hope, because by recognizing

---

[13] Peter Larkin, in 'Repetition', pp. 146–59, discovers that yearning is already adumbrated in the 1798 ending of 'The Rime of the Ancient Mariner'. See Perkins for 'Personeity' and the divine.

their insufficingness human beings leave room for it to be filled. In 1828 he drew with Joseph Henry Green a design of the whole human consciousness. Big letters announce 'SCHEMA OF THE TOTAL MAN' (*SW&F*, 2, 1385). Here self-consciousness, all in all for Locke, occupies just one quadrant of the oblong design of intelligent being; it stands opposite the now equally important quadrant called 'Craving' with 'Desire of Being, Affection, and Desire of Having' just under it, Love and Appetite above and below it. Self-consciousness is no longer enough to define the person; the person must also know himself or herself to be incomplete and to yearn for completion by another self or divine spirit. The self becomes more dynamic in this quest. The cluster of terms around this right hand quadrant seeks beyond the wonder of sheer existence praised in the *Biographia* and the *Friend* to explore the image of the chrysalis preparing instinctively for change. The wondrous being seeks what is not, or what is not yet, in the human spirit. The self is multiple, integral, divided, dialogic, and continuous, but it also leaves an open space for future development as a different sort of being. It wants what it does not yet contain.

Works Cited

Barth, J. Robert, S. J. 1988. *Coleridge and the Power of Love*. Columbia: University of Missouri Press.

Beer, John. 1977. *Coleridge's Poetic Intelligence*. London and Basingstoke: Macmillan Press.

Burwick, Fred. 2008. Coleridge's conversation poems: thinking the thinker, *Romanticism*, 14: 168–182.

Bygrave, Stephen. 1986. *Coleridge and the Self: Romantic Egotism*. New York: St. Martin's Press.

Davidson, Graham. 1990. *Coleridge's Career*. New York: St. Martin's Press.

Esterhammer, Angela. 2004. *Spontaneous Overflows and Revivifying Rays: Romanticism and the Discourse of Improvisation*. Vancouver, BC: Ronsdale Press.

Harding, Anthony John. 1974. *Coleridge and the Idea of Love: Aspects of Relationship in Coleridge's Thought and Writing*. London: Cambridge University Press.

Harman, B. 1978. Herbert, Coleridge, and the vexed work of narration. *MLN*: 888–911.

Haven, Richard. 1969. *Patterns of Consciousness: An Essay on Coleridge*. Amherst: University of Massachusetts Press.

Hume, David. 1969. *A Treatise of Human Nature*, ed. Ernest G. Mossner. Middlesex: Penguin Books.

Lamb, Charles and Mary. 1975. *The Letters*, ed. Edwin W. Marrs, Jr. Ithaca and London: Cornell University Press.

Larkin, Peter. 2007. Repetition, difference and liturgical participation in Coleridge's 'The Ancient Mariner', *Literature and Theology*, 21 (2): 146–59.

Leader, Zachary. 1996. *Revision and Romantic Authorship*. Oxford: Oxford University Press.

LOCKRIDGE, LAWRENCE. 1977. *Coleridge the Moralist*. Ithaca and London: Cornell University Press.

MAYS, J. C. C. 1993. Coleridge's 'Love' : All he can manage, more than he could. In *Coleridge's Visionary Languages: Essays in Honour of J. B. Beer*, ed. Tim Fulford and Morton D. Paley. Cambridge: D. S. Brewer, pp. 49–66.

McFARLAND, THOMAS. 1969. *Coleridge and the Pantheist Tradition*. Oxford: Clarendon Press.

—— 1981. Coleridge and Anxiety, *Romanticism and the Forms of Ruin: Wordsworth, Coleridge, and the Modalities of Fragmentation*. Princeton: Princeton University Press, pp. 104–36.

McKUSICK, JAMES. 1992. 'Living Words' : Samuel Taylor Coleridge and the genesis of the OED, *Modern Philology* 90.

MAGNUSON, PAUL. 1988. *Coleridge and Wordsworth: A Lyrical Dialogue*. Princeton: Princeton University Press.

MODIANO, RAIMONDA. 1989. Coleridge and Milton: The case against Wordsworth in the *Biographia Literaria*. In Fred Burwick, ed., *Coleridge's Biographia Literaria: Text and Meaning*. Columbus: Ohio State University Press, pp. 150–70.

O'NEILL, MICHEAL. 1997. *Romanticism and the Self-Conscious Poem*. Oxford: Clarendon Press.

PALEY, MORTON. 1999. *Coleridge's Later Poetry*. Oxford: Oxford University Press.

PARKER, REEVE. 1975. *Coleridge's Meditative Art*. Ithaca and New York: Cornell University Press.

PERKINS, MARY ANNE. 1994. *Coleridge's Philosophy: The Logos as Unifying Principle*. Oxford: Clarendon Press.

PERRY, SEAMUS. 1994. Coleridge and the end of autonomy. In Nick Roe, ed., *Coleridge and the Sciences of Life*, pp. 246–68.

—— 1999. *Samuel Taylor Coleridge and the Uses of Division*. Oxford: Clarendon Press.

—— 2002. ed. *Coleridge's Notebooks: A Selection*. Oxford: Oxford University Press.

RICHARDSON, ALANZ. 2001. *British Romanticism and the Science of Mind*. Cambridge: Cambridge University Press.

SCHULZ, MAX F. 1963. *The Poetic Voices of Coleridge: A Study of His Desire for Spontaneity and Passion for Order*. Detroit: Wayne State University Press.

TAYLOR, ANYA. 1991. A father's tale: Coleridge foretells the life of Hartley, *SiR* 30: 37–56.

—— 1999. *Bacchus in Romantic England: Writers and Drink 1780–1830*. Basingstoke: Palgrave.

—— 1986. *Coleridge's Defense of the Human*. Columbus: Ohio State University Press.

—— 1991. Coleridge on persons and things, *ERR* 1 (2): 163–80.

—— 1989. Coleridge on persons in dialogue, *MLQ* 50 (40): 357–74.

—— 2000. Romantic *Improvvisatori*: Coleridge, L. E. L., and the difficulties of loving', *PQ* 79 (4): 501–21.

—— 2005. *Erotic Coleridge: Women, Love, and the Law against Divorce*. Palgrave: Macmillan.

TAYLOR, CHARLES. 1989. *Sources of the Self: The Making of the Modern Identity*. Cambridge, Mass.: Cambridge University Press.

THOMPSON, HEIDI. 2007. 'O Friend! O Teacher! God's great Gift to me!': Coleridge about Wordsworth. In *Still Shines When You Think of It: A Festschrift for Vincent O'Sullivan*, eds. Bill Manhire and Peter Whiteford. Wellington: Victoria University Press, pp. 118–30.

PART II

THE PROSE WORKS

CHAPTER 7

....

COLERIDGE'S LECTURES 1795: ON POLITICS AND RELIGION

....

PETER J. KITSON

COLERIDGE'S career as lecturer, journalist, and commentator on political and religious matters began when he arrived in the thriving commercial city of eighteenth-century Bristol in January 1795. Bristol claimed to be the second city of the nation and its colonial possessions, and it boasted a vibrant public life with several newspapers, theatres, and a large lending library. It had strong links with the American colonies, returning MPs who opposed the war waged against them almost twenty years earlier, and was second only to London as a port engaged in the transatlantic slave trade. The city also had a strong and active dissenting community composed of Independents, Baptists, Presbyterians, Quakers, and Unitarians. Coleridge, at this time in his life, was a Unitarian dissenter and political radical, sympathetic to the ideals of the French Revolution, and an opponent of Britain's participation in the war against the new French Republic. He had come to Bristol at the behest of his close friend and collaborator, the poet Robert Southey, a native of the city. Coleridge had met Southey in Oxford in 1794 and the two men quickly became friends, united by their shared interests in radical politics and poetry. Together they had planned to found a Utopian community on the banks of the Susquehanna River in Pennsylvania. The scheme was known as 'Pantisocracy' and was to involve twelve married couples who would keep all things in common and share labour equally. By early 1795 Southey had persuaded Coleridge that an immediate plan for emigration to the United States was impracticable and that the expedient of settling on a farm in rural Wales as a preparation for the full scheme had been accepted. Coleridge's primary motive in coming to Bristol was to collaborate with Southey in earning the necessary funds to achieve this through giving a series of public lectures on political, historical, and religious subjects. Coleridge's collaboration with Southey also involved the writing of an historical epic, *Joan of Arc*, and his courting and marrying of Sara Fricker, the sister of Southey's fiancée, Edith (Holmes 1989, pp. 89–106).

Coleridge began his lectures in January and February of 1795 and Southey followed in March. Coleridge's lectures were political and religious, while those of Southey were historical. During January and February Coleridge gave three political lectures; these were published as *A Moral and Political Lecture* and *Conciones ad Populum* later in the year. The former appeared as a publication in its own right but was then revised and republished as the 'Introductory Address' to the more substantial *Conciones*, Coleridge's first significant political publication (Patton and Mann 1971, pp. xxvi, xxxii–xxxiii). Coleridge gave only three of his projected longer series of political lectures having, he wrote to George Dyer in March, been 'obliged by the persecutions of Darkness to discontinue them' (*CL* 1, 155). Subsequently, he gave a course of 'Six Lectures on Revealed Religion, its Corruptions, and its Political Views'. They were probably delivered on Tuesday and Friday afternoons in the Card Room of the Assembly Coffee House in late May and early June (Patton and Mann 1971, pp. xxv–xxvi). These lectures were never published by Coleridge and survive only in a transcript of the original manuscript by his grandson, E. H. Coleridge. They were published for the first time in 1971. In addition to those two series of lectures, Coleridge also delivered a 'Lecture on the Slave Trade' on 16 June (which he reprinted in fourth number of *The Watchman* the following year). As well as the ten lectures that we are certain Coleridge delivered, there exists a prospectus for six lectures comparing the English Revolution of the mid-seventeenth century with the French Revolution. His publisher, Joseph Cottle, also reported that Coleridge lectured on the contemporary political subjects of the Hair-Powder Tax and the Corn Laws. It is, however, doubtful that any of these other lectures were actually given (Patton and Mann 1971, pp. xxvii–xliii). Coleridge left Bristol for nearby Clevedon after his marriage to Sara Fricker on 4 October 1795, but he returned in November to take part in the opposition to the new repressive measures of Pitt's government, the Two Bills, which curtailed the freedom to meet to discuss political matters and extended the legal definition of treason. He gave his 'Lecture on the Two Bills' on 26 November. This was published as the pamphlet *The Plot Discovered* in December 1795.

Coleridge's political position at this time was that of democrat, republican and dissenter, what was commonly referred to at the time as an 'English Jacobin' after the extremist French republican political faction, the Jacobins, led by Maximilien Robespierre which had executed Louis XVI, organized the mass political persecution of 'The Terror', and prosecuted the war against Britain and the European powers with considerable vigour. It was a term used loosely and pejoratively by the conservative opposition, though many radicals accepted it. Coleridge never appears to have been comfortable with the term, either at the time or later in life, his political sentiments being closer to the moderate French republican faction of the Girondists, whose adherents were largely executed in the Jacobin Terror. Coleridge preferred the generic appellation of one of the 'Friends of Freedom' which more accurately sums up his political position, as one rooted in the traditions of English political and religious dissent, rather than of French revolutionary politics (Kitson 1992, pp. 205–30; 1991, pp. 36–62; Leask 1988, pp. 19–33; Morrow 1990, pp. 11–31; White 2006, pp. 119–51). Nevertheless in giving his political lectures at a time when the war with revolutionary France was going badly, Coleridge was associating himself both ideologically and personally with a range of oppositional thinkers, such as the more notorious London political lecturer, John Thelwall, who shortly after became his very close friend and associate (Roe 1988, pp. 145–98). His political lectures certainly occasioned much opposition. He wrote to Dyer that 'the opposition of the Aristocrats' was 'furious and determined' with 'Mobs and Mayors, Blockheads and brickbats, Placards and press gangs' conspiring against him. (*CL* 1, 152)

CONCIONES AD POPULUM (1795)

Coleridge's *Conciones* was published in November 1795. It was comprised of an 'Introductory Address' and a section 'On the Present War'. The former was a revised version of his first political lecture and the second was probably a version of either or both the second and third of the three lectures. The second part of the *Conciones* contained a spirited attack on the government of William Pitt and its prosecution of, what was for Coleridge, an unjust and unnecessary war. Coleridge argued that, as there had been no attempts to negotiate with revolutionary France, it was hard to fathom how the present war could be described as necessary, and therefore it could not be termed a just war. Pitt's pretext that the atheism and guilt of the revolutionaries precluded the possibility of meaningful negotiations was undermined somewhat by the lack of piety of Britain's allies: 'the MERCIFUL Catherine, the HONEST King of Prussia, and that most CHRISTIAN Arch-pirate, the Dey of Algiers.' (*Lects 1795*, pp. 54–5) Similarly, the excuse that the French had committed so many excesses as to place them beyond the pale of civilized government was contradicted by the British government's conduct of the American War when its generals egged on the native Indians to 'banquet on blood' (pp. 56–8). Britain also had a share in the excesses of the French. Her ally the Duke of Brunswick had promised the execution of all those taken in arms as well as the entire French National Assembly, a threat which had driven the French to desperate and extreme measures. It was thus the interference of the European powers that had provoked the Terror in France and they must take a share of any guilt.

Coleridge's attack on the war policy of the Pitt government is fairly typical of much radical criticism of the time. What is unusual is its tone, which, at times, approximates to that of a prophetic denunciation. In lines which recall Blake's apocalyptic description of the nations's capital in his poem 'London', Coleridge argues that the government crackdown on the radicals and its use of spies and informers have poisoned and corrupted the national psyche. Appropriating Ezekiel 29.9 and Isaiah 8.19 he writes:

There have been multiplied among us 'men who carry tales to shed blood!' Men who resemble the familiar Sprits described by Isaiah, as 'dark ones, that peep and that mutter!' Men, who may seem to have been typically shadowed out in the Frogs that formed the second plague of Egypt: little low animals with chilly blood and staring eyes, that 'come up into our houses and our bed-chambers!' These men are plenteously scattered among us: our very looks are deciphered into disaffection, and we cannot move without treading on some political spring-gun.   (p. 60)

Coleridge also criticizes the established Church for its support of the war as anti-Christian. The religion it espouses is not that of peace, the religion of the 'meek and lowly Jesus' but that of 'Mitres and Mysteries, the Religion of Pluralities and Persecution' (pp. 66–7). Coleridge's radicalism is thus based on his oppositional religious dissent that opposed the union of religious and political establishments for a purer form of Protestantism in which 'every true Christian is the Priest' (p. 68). In a letter to John Thelwall a year later Coleridge would claim that Christianity was 'a religion for Democrats' and one 'which teaches in the most explicit terms the rights of Man, his right to Wisdom, his right to an equal share in all the blessings of nature' (CL 1, p. 282).

The relationship between Coleridge's religious and political dissent is defined even more clearly in the 'Introductory Address' to Conciones. Even at this early stage in his writing, Coleridge is concerned to address the general principles which should underlie his political ideas, a facet of his political writing that can be seen in his later works such as The Friend (1811) and On the Constitution of the Church and State (1830). He insists on the 'necessity of bottoming on fixed Principles' so that the liberty may be 'grounded on secure foundations'. (Lects 1795, p. 33) Even in 1795, Coleridge stressed the inefficacy of political action without a prior moral revolution:

The annals of the French Revolution have recorded in Letters of Blood, that the Knowledge of the Few cannot counteract the Ignorance of the Many; that the Light of Philosophy, when it is confined to a small Minority, points out the Possessors as the Victims, rather then the Illuminators, of the Multitude.

In France the enlightened reformers, when faced by the rage and power of the mob, had either tried to resist it, and paid the price with their heads, or, like the Jacobins, attempted to manipulate the people for their own ends and committed, what was for Coleridge, the 'gigantic Error' of 'making certain Evil the means of contingent Good' (pp. 33–4). Remarkably, for this time, Coleridge presents an analysis of the revolutionary Jacobin government that is complex and not unsympathetic. He credits Robespierre with good intentions that remained unfulfilled. The 'distant prospect' of his revolutionary ideals appeared 'grand and beautiful' but he 'fixed his eye on it with such intense eagerness as to neglect the foulness of the road'. To prevent tyranny he, himself, became a tyrant and his system of Terror gave to the republic an energy without which it would not been able to preserve itself. Unfortunately, it also gave the European powers an excuse to intervene (pp. 35–6).

Coleridge discriminates between the various classes of the Friends of Freedom in Britain whom he describes as the indecisive, the mob, the levellers and the 'small but glorious band' of 'thinking and disinterested Patriots' who are:

Accustomed to regard all the affairs of man as a process, they never hurry and they never pause. Theirs is not that twilight of political knowledge which gives just enough light to place one foot before the other; as they advance the scene still opens upon them, and they press right onward with a vast and various landscape of existence around them.

This was to become one of the central ideas in his later political philosophy, that political change (or, alternatively, conservation) must be led by an elite of progressive thinkers whose ideas will accommodate the populace to reform. In was the germ of the concept of the 'Clerisy', the guardians of the nation's cultural inheritance that he would develop in *On the Constitution of the Church and State*. For Coleridge the unmediated access of the poor and brutalized to radical and reformist ideas was extremely dangerous. He criticizes the radical political philosopher, William Godwin, for assuming that advanced ideas will somehow gradually diffuse themselves among the people. He argues that the true philosopher must be personally among the poor and possess the 'zeal of the Methodist'; one who will teach them 'their duties that they may be made susceptible of their rights' (p. 43). In stressing duties rather than rights, Coleridge makes it clear that politics must be underpinned by Christianity:

'Go, preach the GOSPEL to the Poor.' By its Simplicity it will meet their comprehension, by its Benevolence soften their affections, by its Precepts it will direct their conduct, by the vastness of its Motives ensure their obedience.   (pp. 43–4)

Coleridge as a religious radical, very clearly, separates himself from the deistic, materialist and atheistic radicalism of those such as Thomas Paine, William Godwin and John Thelwall in arguing that the gospel can bring about social and political reform. He argues that religion will provide the possibility of future rewards for the just which mitigate social inequality on earth, as well as 'habituating' the mind 'to anticipate an infinitely great Revolution hereafter' thus preparing the poor for the 'sudden reception of a less degree of amelioration in this World' (p. 137). In this, Coleridge is drawing upon a tradition of religious and political dissent, which derives from the Reformation. Although it might appear that Coleridge's radicalism may be muted by his appeal to religious conversion and piety, in fact, it allowed him to more effectively criticize those reformers who plead 'for equalization of *Rights*, not of *Condition*' (p. 48).

In the *Conciones ad Populum* Coleridge sets out his religious dissent, one which is differentiated from that of other materialistic and atheistic reformers and one which is motivated by a concern to improve the moral and social condition of the people. Although his political and religious views changed dramatically between 1795 and 1805, nevertheless certain ideas remained constant, such as the importance of clear principles, the crucial role of the Christian religion in informing political action, and the vital nature of the role played in politic organizations by an elite of philosophic reformers able to mediate fundamental political tenets to the populace.

'Lectures on Revealed Religion' (1795)

The 'Lectures on Revealed Religion' were delivered by Coleridge under the patronage of several prominent Bristol citizens, including the Unitarian minister of Lewin's Mead Chapel, John Prior Estlin, a Mr Morgan (a wine merchant), and the Cottle brothers, Robert, Amos and Joseph. They were probably delivered at the Card Room of the Assembly Coffeehouse on the Quay (Patton and Mann 1971, pp. xxxv). They serve to define Coleridge's religious stance of a politically engaged Unitarian Christian. In the prospectus to the Lectures, Coleridge claimed that they were 'intended for two Classes of Men—Christians and Infidels' (p. 83). The two positions he thus wanted to combat were atheism and established Christianity. However, for the Unitarian Coleridge, the Christianity, which he espoused, was very different from the orthodox belief of the Anglican Church. Unitarians believed in the importance of reason and scripture. They identified among corruptions that had warped and deformed Christianity such doctrines as the Trinity, the Atonement and Original Sin. It was their belief that Jesus Christ was a paragon of human virtue, but not possessed of the divine essence and simply a man. They wished to return Christian doctrine to the purity of the Gospels and the early Church. As such they were unable to conform to the Thirty Nine Articles required by Church of England and, according to the Test (1673) and Corporation (1661) Acts, excluded from holding public office. Because of his Unitarianism, which he seems to have adopted while at Cambridge, Coleridge was unable to take his degree.

The 'Lectures' set out to develop a form of religious radicalism which conforms to much contemporary dissenting ideology as typified by its most important eighteenth-century spokesman, Joseph Priestley, upon whose works they heavily rely; however Coleridge's particular brand of religious radicalism went far beyond that of middle-class dissent of the 1790s (Kitson 1991, pp. 39–44; 1993a, pp. 97–102; White 2006, pp. 19–27). True to his Pantisocratic principles, Coleridge countenanced a redistribution of property, something that propertied and commercial dissenters would find anathema. He begins the first lecture with a striking 'Allegorical Vision' in which he imagines himself in the 'Valley of Life' where he is constrained to enter a large and gloomy temple crowded with 'tawdry ornament and fantastic deformity' and home to strange and fantastic ceremonies. The temple houses men in black robes who collect a tenth part of everything within their reach (the Anglican practice of tithes). Before he can be presented to the Goddess of the temple, he must be sprinkled with water (baptism) and confront 'phosphoric inscriptions' which are comprehensible as individual words but meaningless when strung into sentences (the doctrine of the Trinity). His guide tells him he must 'Read and believe' for what he sees are mysteries: the riddle of the three in one. A small group within the temple decide to flee proclaiming they are in the 'Temple of Superstition'. Encountering 'a woman clad in white garments of simplest Texture' who calls herself 'Religion' half way around the valley, some run, but a few, struck by her general demeanour and difference from the other goddess, stay and follow. She leads Coleridge to an eminence where he can command a view of the Valley of Life. From here he sees how the different parts of the valley all connect. Religion then gives him an 'optic Glass' (Revelation) which assists 'without contradicting' his natural vision (reason) and enables him to see 'far beyond the Valley'. Religion thus complements and supplements human reason and is not antithetical to it. Here Coleridge depicts a pure and uncorrupted Christianity free from the accretions of the established Churches (Anglican and Catholic) (pp. 90–1). Those fleeing from the Temple of Superstition complete almost a whole circle and find themselves in a 'dusky cave' (atheism) located in the grounds of the very temple from which they had fled. The cave is unnaturally cold and is occupied by an old man who sits surveying the irregularities of nature with his microscope:

He spoke in diverse Tongues and unfolded many Mysteries, and among other strange Things he talked much about an infinite Series of Causes—which he explained to be—a string of blind men of which the last caught hold of the skirt of the one before him, he of the next, and so on till they were all out of sight; and all that they all walked straight without making one false step.

Here Coleridge parodies the materialist argument of those such as William Godwin and Erasmus Darwin, that the world is created from an endless series of accidental causes: that the world is created from chance. Thus, for the Unitarian Coleridge, superstition and atheism are the left and right boot of the same monster, Mystery, whereas Unitarianism is the golden mean because it unites reason with revelation, the head with the heart (pp. 91–3; Kitson 1993b, pp. 1–14).

Coleridge wished to ground his dissent on alternative lines to those such as Godwin who stressed the importance of human reason in deciding all issues. Notoriously, Godwin had argued that domestic affections, such as ties of kinship or bonds of gratitude should play no part in our judgments, the only crucial things were that we act truthfully and use our reason to arrive at a just position. He argued, for instance, in his *Political Justice* (1793), that if faced with the choice of saving our own mother or some distinguished thinker from a fire, we should use our reason and conclude that the philosopher was of more use to humanity in general and thus rescue him, allowing our mother to perish horribly in the flames. Coleridge objected to both Godwin's atheism and his denial of the importance of human feelings and relationships. He compares the arid rationalism, as he sees it, of Godwin's political philosophy to the example of Christ:

Jesus knew our Nature—and that expands like the circles of a Lake—the Love of our Friends, parents and neighbours lead[s] us to the love of our Country to the love of all mankind. The intensity of private attachments encourages, not prevents, universal philanthropy—the nearer we approach to the Sun, the more intense his Rays—yet what corner of the System does he not cheer and vivify?   (p. 163)

Godwin had also attacked the institution of marriage in *Political Justice* which he regarded as an irrational system of monopoly in human beings weakening the impartiality of justice. For Coleridge this philosophy taught that 'filial Love is a Folly, Gratitude criminal, Marriage Injustice, and a promiscuous Intercourse of the Sexes our wisdom and duty' (p. 164). Coleridge repeated this argument in his essay on 'Modern Patriotism' in *The Watchman* (1796) where he denounced 'Mr Godwin's Principles as vicious and his book as a Pandar to Sensuality' (*CC* 2. 196, pp. 98–100, 194–98).

In the 'Lectures' Coleridge presents a synthesis of much eighteenth-century dissenting theology. He draws on the argument for design for the existence of a deity where 'the evident contrivance and fitness of things for one another which we meet throughout all parts of the Universe seems to make the belief of a Deity almost an Axiom' (p. 93). This was an argument he would later dismiss with contempt, but he had no qualms about its use in 1795. He argues that the phenomena of nature are inexplicable without the notion of a deity and that atheistic reasoning only serves to confirm the limited nature of our intellects for though we may not comprehend divinity we can still conceive of its existence (p. 97). Coleridge defines two species of atheism, the first of which attempts 'to explain the formation of the Universe from the accidental play of Atoms acting according to mere mechanical laws, and derived the astonishing aptitude and ineffable Beauty of Things from a lucky hit in the Blind Uproar'. To argue this Coleridge believes is as rational as arguing that 'a vast number of Gold & Brass particles accidentally commoved by the Wind would after infinite Trials form themselves into a polished and accurate Watch or Time-piece' (pp. 98–9). Others argue that each particle or atom is embued with 'certain plastic Natures' acting as the 'unthinking Souls of each atom'. Although Coleridge rejects this latter pantheistic hypothesis, it was one that he would flirt with in his poem 'The Eolian Harp' later that year (Piper 1964, pp. 32–40; Everest 1989, p. 206) To argue this way, following the 'modern sages', Godwin and Darwin, is to reject final causes and 'exclude our God and untenant the Universe' (*Lects 1795*, p. 100). This was a complaint that Coleridge had also made against the science of Isaac Newton, which stressed a concentration on understanding second causes.

Coleridge believed that the major obstacle to theism was the problem of the existence of evil. This was something he wrestled with throughout his life but, in 1795, he adopted an optimistic solution. The optimistic solution to the problem is an old one and, notably, was found in the work of the philosophers Leibniz and Shaftesbury. Coleridge's more immediate sources were the eighteenth-century associationist philosopher, David Hartley, and his admirer Priestley. From Hartley and Priestley Coleridge took the idea that knowledge is created by the external world and its action on our senses. Ideas are thus no more than mental copies of physical sensation; the order to which they are presented to the mind is governed by the order in which the sensations that caused them occurred. Knowledge and thought are entirely governed by the association of ideas according to their spatial and temporal contiguity. From this associationist premise, Hartley and Priestley developed the doctrine of Necessity; that is, that all our actions are determined by the environments in which we are placed. As such environments were arranged by God, then all actions and events were part of a predetermined and benevolent purpose. In December 1794, Coleridge had written to Southey that he was a 'Necesitarian—and (believing in an all-loving Omnipotence) an Optimist'. So much so that his friends had begun to call him 'Dr Pangloss' after the unrelentingly optimistic philosopher of Voltaire's satirical novel *Candide* (1759), a portrait of Leibniz (*CL* 1, pp. 145, 168). Coleridge accepts that logically God must be totally benevolent, therefore all evil must be illusory. As the 'end determines the nature of the means', Coleridge claims that he can discover 'nothing of which the end is not good' (*CC* 1, p. 105). He instances the evil of the toothache that proceeds from poor hygiene and arouses sufferers to effect its removal. Pain is thus a stimulus to remove some moral evil, and, therefore, ultimately a good. So convinced an optimist was Coleridge in 1795 that he avowed that 'there is not one Pain but which is somehow or other the effect of moral Evil' (pp. 106–7). He soon abandoned this fallacious belief in the light of his own personal distresses, such as the death of his infant child Berkeley, as well as major historical and natural catastrophes. By the time of *The*

Friend he had come to fully appreciate that there existed 'Evil distinct from Error and from Pain...which is not wholly grounded in the limitations of our understandings' (*CC* 4, ii, p. 9). Certainly by 1801, Coleridge claimed to have overthrown the philosophies of Necessity and the association of ideas for one based the activity of the mind in the creation of knowledge and the crucial importance of free will.

The 'Lectures on Revealed Religion' provide a summary of Coleridge's Unitarian theology in 1795, most of which he would have decisively abandoned by 1805. Unitarianism was, in very many ways, a minimal creed. In the fourth lecture, Coleridge summarizes its essential points as:

That about 1800 years ago there lived a man called Jesus Christ, that did a great many wonderful things, such as healing incurable diseases, restoring suspended animation, and foretelling events long before they happened, that this good and kind man was put to Death unjustly, but that God Almighty brought him to Life on the Third Day after his crucifixion.

If asked what this 'good and kind man' taught, Coleridge believed that true Christians should identify the key teachings as follows:

That we should do to others as we would have others do to us—that wicked thoughts if indulged, are as bad as wicked actions, but above all he ordered us to love our enemies and bless them that hate us—and that we should believe in one God and call him Our Father and that all Religion which was pleasing to the God and Father consisted in this. To visit the fatherless and widows in their affliction, and to keep ourselves unspotted with the vices of the world.

Christ did not rely on the severity of the law to enforce these precepts but taught that those who observed his teachings 'would be happy for ever after—and that they who were wicked in this world would suffer for it in the next' (pp. 174–5). This is basic Unitarian theology as promulgated by Priestley. Christ is regarded simply as a human being who performed miracles and was resurrected as a proof of his divine mission. Humanity thus has proof that virtue will be rewarded and a spur to good actions, which 'by the magic power of association', will become something we seek for its own pleasures (p. 114). As a further proof of the truth of Christianity, Coleridge instances its success. It would take a divine miracle to explain the spread of Christianity if the doctrine were not true (p. 161). The problem for Unitarians, and other protestant dissenters, was that since the time of Christ a number of accretions had encrusted and corrupted his teachings. Coleridge sums up these teaching as:

That there is one God infinitely wise, powerful and good, and that a future state of Retribution is made certain by the Resurrection of Jesus who is the Messiah—are all the *doctrines* of the Gospel. That Christians must behave towards the majority with loving kindness and submission preserving among themselves a perfect Equality is a Synopsis of its Precepts.   (p. 195)

Corruptions began with the conversion of the Greeks to Christianity, and, in particular, the contribution of the Gnostic Christians who first developed the 'idolatrous doctrine of the Trinity' and the 'more pernicious dogma of Redemption'. (pp. 196–200, 212). Coleridge once again presented the standard Unitarian argument against the doctrines of redemption and Atonement as formulated by Priestley. He revolts at the 'most irrational and gloomy Superstition' that the brutal sacrifice of a human being could in any way influence a benevolent God. This was incompatible with the notion of 'God as all-loving Parent' and how could the sufferings of one being for a few hours provide an 'adequate Satisfaction for the Sins of the whole World?' (pp. 202–6) Christ voluntarily submitted to a cruel death so that he 'might confirm the Faith and awaken the Gratitude of Men'. Coleridge would come to abandon this view. In July 1802, he wrote to his orthodox brother George affirming his belief in original sin, the consequences of which humanity was redeemed not as the Unitarians affirm, by 'Christ's pure morals and excellent Example', but in rather 'a mysterious manner as an effect of his Crucifixion'. This is a matter of faith and not of reason (*CL* 2, p. 807). The 'Lectures' argue that the orthodox doctrine of the Trinity was another corruption of the early Christian teachings and was not to be found in scripture. Glossing John 1. 1–5, Coleridge defines the Greek word 'logos' or 'word', interpreted by the orthodox as the pre-existing Christ, simply as 'intelligence':

St John asserts, that in the *beginning* there was Intelligence, that this Intelligence was together with God, not an emanation from him, and that this Intelligence was God himself...and that this same Intelligence was imparted by immediate Inspiration to the man Jesus, who dwelt among us.   (p. 200)

The 'thrice strange Union of Father, Son and Holy Ghost in one God' was little more than the 'simple notion' that God is 'Love, and Intelligence and Life...a Trinity in Unity equally applicable to man or Beast!' (p. 207) Much of the confusion is attributed to the Christian neo-Platonists who wished to reconcile Platonic thought with Christianity and imported Plato's trinity of attributes of Life, Power and Benevolence into their notion of divinity (p. 208). Coleridge likewise came to reject this anti-trinitiarianism, along with his Necessitarianism and his political radicalism. In his *Biographia Literaria* of 1817 he claimed that it was his doubts concerning the 'incarnation and the redemption by the cross' which prevented him from accepting the Trinity as anything other than 'a fair scholastic inference from the being of God as a creative intelligence' (*CC* 7, i, pp. 204–5). In 1830 he confirmed his belief that the Trinity was 'the Will—the Reason or Word—the Love or Life and as the three were distinguished so should they be united' (*CC* 14, i, p. 127).

The 'Lectures' as well as setting out Coleridge's theological position also defined his political ideas and for most dissenters the two were inextricable. In the *Conciones ad Populum* he had stressed the importance of the elect of reformers who were to guide the masses to political freedom by preaching the gospel to the poor. In the sixth lecture he appeals to the New Testament precedent of the small number of Apostles whom he compares to a grain of mustard seed and to the leaven in the meal. This Christian concept of an elect or faithful remnant informs both his Pantisocratic ideas (with it twelve families) and his dissenting position:

Luke 13 v. 18. 21. Contains two prophetic similitudes. 'It is like a grain of mustard seed and it grew and waxed into a great Tree, ['] and ['it is like a very little leaven which a woman took and hid in three measures of meal till the whole was leavened!' It is natural for seeds which at length rise to great Trees to lie long in the ground before their vegetation is perceptible and to increase very slowly for a considerable Length of Time—a small Quantity of Leaven also enclosed within a great bulk of meal must of necessity operate very slowly and a cold unfavourable season would restrain the vegetative [. . .]   (CC 1, p. 229)

The leaven and the mustard seed stand for the 'small but glorious band' of true friends of freedom who will gradually and peacefully transform society during the cold season of William Pitt's repressive rule.

It is, however, in his ideas concerning property, that Coleridge departs most radically from both the Unitarian consensus and that of secular reformers, such as Thomas Paine and John Thelwall. Coleridge expressed his view to Thelwall that property was 'beyond doubt the Origin of all Evil' (CL 1, p. 214) and that Pantisocracy would make men virtuous by removing the temptation to accumulate. In the sixth lecture Coleridge refers explicitly to the example of the early Church which followed Christ's examples and kept the community of property: 'In Acts II. 44. 45 we read "And all that believed were together, & had all things in common—and sold their possessions & goods and parted them to all men, as every man had need" '. This part of Christian doctrine he adds was soon corrupted. Coleridge also argued that the Hebrew constitution enforced the equalization of property. He claimed that this was a wise and benevolent law because it prevented the concentration of power in too few hands: 'Property is Power and equal Property equal Power.'

['] The Land shall not be sold, for the Land is mine, saith the Lord, and ye are strangers and sojourners with me.['] There is nothing more pernicious than the notion that any one possesses an absolute right to the Soil, which he appropriates—to the system of accumulation which flows from this supposed right we are indebted for nine-tenths of our Vices and Miseries. The Land is no one's—the Produce belongs equally to all, who contribute their due proportion of Labour.   (CC 1, pp. 125–7)

One wonders what the response of Coleridge's propertied audience was to this passage in his lecture? Coleridge actually wishes to go beyond the Jewish commonwealth's equalization of property and argues for the 'abolition of individual Property' as 'perhaps the only infallible Preventative against accumulation' although he adds that the Jews were then too ignorant a people to achieve this

(p. 128). The 'Lectures' argues that universal equality and the abolition of individual property were the great objects of Christ's divinely inspired mission:

Jesus Christ therefore commanded his disciples to preserve a strict equality—and enforced his command by the only thing capable of giving it effect. He proved to them the certainty of an hereafter—and by the vastness of the Future diminished the Tyranny of the Present. If not with hereditary faith but from the effect of our examination and reflection we are really convinced of a state after Death, then and then only will Self-interest be wedded to Virtue.   (p. 218)

In appealing to the texts of the Old and New Testament to justify his belief in the abolition of individual property, Coleridge was going much further than most of the radicals of the time were ever prepared to contemplate. Joseph Priestley explicitly and, somewhat unconvincingly, dismissed the scriptural basis for the abolition of individual property. In his *Letters to the Right Honourable Edmund Burke* (1790) he denied that there was 'any obligation on Christians to *throw their goods into common.* Whatever was done of this kind, appears...to have been perfectly voluntary' (1817–32, p. 199). John Thelwall desired the equality of rights and not of property which he argued was totally impracticable in the present state of society:

...if once you could be seduced to attempt a system so wild and extravagant, you could only give to rascals and cut-throats an opportunity, by general pillage and assassination, of transferring all property into their own hands, and establishing a tyranny more intolerable than anything of which you now complain.   (1796, p. 14)

Coleridge's theory of property went far beyond the revolutionary aspirations of Thelwall and Paine, or the propertied dissent of Priestley and the Unitarians. The nearest contemporary equivalents were the radical followers of the working class radical Thomas Spence or the seventeenth-century Diggers led by Gerrard Winstanley (Kitson 1991, pp. 39–44). The extent to which Coleridge would have wished to alter the relations of property in European states is not spelt out, but it would seem that the Pantisocratic project was an attempt to opt out of the social and political relationships of contemporary Britain and to build a smaller scale alternative polity that, like the leaven in the bread, slowly work to build another model of social and political organization. Coleridge's faith in the equalization of property in the Jewish theocracy or community of property in Pantisocracy did not last. By December 1799 his essay 'On the French Constitution' showed that he had abandoned his Pantisocratic ideals:

For the present race of men Government must be founded on property; that *Government is good in which property is secure and circulates*; that *Government the best, which, in the exactest ratio, makes each man's power proportionate to his property.*   (*CC* 3, i, p. 32)

This understanding also grounded the theories of his later political statement, *On the Constitution of the Church and State,* where he argues that a balance must be struck between the interests of progression (the commercial classes) and of permanency (the landed classes) and that the state must represent both these interests, and not simply individuals.

'LECTURE ON THE SLAVE TRADE' (1795)

In June 1795 Coleridge gave his 'Lecture on the Slave Trade' on the very Quay close to ships themselves destined for the Guinea Coast to pick up slaves to transport to the Caribbean. The 'Lecture' is heavily dependent on the writings of Thomas Clarkson and C. B. Wadstrom which he borrowed from the Bristol Library Society (*Lects 1795*, p. 274) but typically inflected by Coleridge's own concerns. He argues that the transatlantic slave trade is entirely useless, built on the production of luxury goods, such as sugar, rum, coffee, indigo, cotton and mahogany, of which none are necessary and only mahogany and cotton useful. The trade destroys the bodies and minds of those engaged in it. A fourth of the crew of every Bristol slave ship will die on the voyage and those crew who survive 'employed as the immediate Instrument of buying, selling and torturing human Flesh, must from the moral necessity of circumstances become dead to every feeling of confession' (p. 238). Against those who argue that Africans are uncivilized and barbaric, Coleridge represents them as enjoying a quasi-Pantisocratic pastoral simplicity. Coleridge clearly sees Africa through the filter of his own times, and uses African society as a tool to criticize British materialism. Africans possess an 'acuteness of intellect' lacking in the European mechanic. Behind Coleridge's opposition to the slave trade is one of his fundamental ethical principles, which he would shortly find confirmed in his reading of Kant, that 'a person can never become a Thing, nor be treated as such without wrong' (*CC* 4, ii, p. 125). Coleridge's 'Lecture' is perhaps most interesting because of his much discussed virtuoso deconstruction of the binary opposition of African savagery and European civilization:

A part of that Food among most of you is sweetened with the Blood of the Murdered. Bless the Food which thou hast given us! O Blasphemy! Did God give Food mingled with Brothers blood! Will the Father of all men bless the Food of Cannibals—the food which is polluted with the blood of his own innocent Children? Surely if the inspired Philanthropist of Galilee were to revisit earth and be among the feasters as at Cana he would not change water into Wine but haply convert the produce into the things producing, the occasioned into the things occasioning.

Rather than 'sweetmeats' and 'music' our imaginations would be presented with 'tears, Blood, and Anguish . . . and the loud Peals of the Lash' (p. 248). Coleridge's ingenious trope is clearly fashioned to impress his urban audience with his rhetorical sophistication. Here the Unitarian attacks the Anglican practice of the Sacrament but also accuses the sugar-consuming Europeans of cannibalism, a practice that European travel accounts from Columbus onwards had attributed to the savage races. Although Coleridge is mainly concerned with defining his own Unitarian version of dissent in attacking the Anglican sacraments and representing the modern-day miracles of a messiah who is no more than 'an inspired Philanthropist' he does make his audience aware of both the horrors of the slave trade and the complicity of all consumers.

THE PLOT DISCOVERED (1795)

The final Bristol lectures that Coleridge gave in 1795 were occasioned by two bills introduced by the Pitt government to extend the legal definition of treason to curtail the right of free assembly to discuss political grievances: the Treasonable Practices and the Seditious Meetings Bills. They became law on 18 December 1795. The legislation had been prompted by a series of incidents of unrest, prompted by popular dissatisfaction with poor harvest and the by economic sufferings resulting from the war, and culminating in an attack on George III's carriage by a mob demanding 'No Pitt' and 'Bread' (Kitson 1991, pp. 36–9). Coleridge hurried back from his honeymoon cottage in Clevedon to take part in the opposition to the bills delivering a lecture on their consequences in Bristol on 26 November, which was published sometime in December (after the bills became law) as *The Plot Discovered.*

The Plot Discovered shows Coleridge the political pamphleteer at his very best. The work represents a powerful presentation of the republican and parliamentarian case, heavily influenced by the major writers of the commonwealth period of British history: John Milton, James Harrington, and Algernon Sidney (Kitson 1992, pp. 205–30). Coleridge in essence accuses Pitt of attempting a *coup d'état* (the 'plot' he has discovered) in abrogating the Bill of Rights of 1689 which guaranteed the subject's right to petition the Monarch and the subject's right to bear arms for defence as well as detailing constitutional requirements where the actions of the Crown require the consent of the governed as represented in Parliament. Coleridge argues that the Two Acts are a 'repeal of the Constitution' and 'Parliament cannot annul the Constitution' (*CC* 1, pp. 300–1). Much of the pamphlet is taken up with detailed constitutional history which Coleridge took chiefly from the work of the Whig political theorist, James Burgh, and is a much less radical statement of his political opinions than either the *Conciones ad Populum* or the 'Lectures on Revealed Religion'. It presents no social and political programme, merely arguing for the key constitutional freedoms of the right to petition, the freedom of the press, and the freedom of speech which the government wished to curtail or remove. Coleridge argues that there are three kinds of government: 'Government *by* the people, Government *over* the people, and Government *with* the people (p. 306). The first occurs when all are actually present in the workings of government, the ideal of Pantisocracy. The English constitution should be an example of the third kind of government but is close becoming a form of despotism, where 'the people at large have no voice in the legislature' (pp. 306–7). What saved a corrupt eighteenth-century government from despotism was the very freedom of the press that Pitt was attempting to remove. The 'Liberty of the Press' gives an '*influential* sovereignty' to the people by which their voice is heard 'gradually increasing till they swell into a deep and awful thunder, the VOICE OF GOD' (pp. 309–12).

Coleridge's Bristol Lectures of 1795 are important in defining the religious and political ideas that he held while a young man and which underpin the ideas expressed in much of his poetry of the time. They show that his ideas were an idiosyncratic mixture of scriptural, republican and democratic thought which he sought to differentiate as much from the commercial propertied dissent of his Unitarian fellow-believers as from deistic, atheistic and materialist reformers such as Godwin, Paine and Thelwall. Coleridge religious radicalism also owes much to those great seventeenth-century writers of the English Revolution, John Milton and James Harrington and the experiments in the community of property practised by Gerrard Winstanley and his 'Digger' followers. Coleridge was to abandon much of his religious radicalism between 1798 and 1805, including his advocacy of communitarianism, his anti-trinitarianism, and his opposition to the war against France, which he argued, with some justice, had become transformed into a struggle against French imperialism. Nevertheless there is still much continuity between his early dissenting belief and his later philosophical conservatism, such as the crucial importance of religion (though that of the established Anglican Church rather than Unitarian dissent), an understanding of the crucial relationship between property and power, and the advocacy of the role of an educated elite, or clerisy, to guide and improve the moral and cultural life of the nation.

WORKS CITED

EVEREST, KELVIN. 1979. *Coleridge's Secret Ministry: The Context of the Conversation Poems, 1795–1798*. Brighton: Harvester.

HOLMES, RICHARD. 1989. *Coleridge: Early Visions*. London: Hodder and Stoughton.

KITSON, PETER J. 1991. 'The Electric Fluid of Truth': The ideology of the Commonwealthsman in Coleridge's *The Plot Discovered*. In Peter J. Kitson and Thomas N. Corns, ed., *Coleridge and the Armoury of the Human Mind*. London: Frank Cass, pp. 36–62.

—— 1992.'Sages and patriots that being dead do yet speak to us': Readings of the English Revolution in the late eighteenth century, in James Holstun, ed. *Pamphlet Wars: Prose of the English Revolution*. London: Frank Cass, pp. 205–30.

—— 1993*a*. 'Our Prophetic Harrington': Coleridge, Pantisocracy and Puritan Utopia,' *The Wordsworth Circle* 24 (2): 97–102.

—— 1993*b*. 'The Whore of Babylon and the Woman in White: Coleridge's radical unitarian language,' in T. J. Fulford and Morton D. Paley, ed., *Coleridge's Visionary languages*. London: Boydell and Brewer, pp. 1–14.

LEASK, NIGEL. 1988. *The Politics of Imagination in Coleridge's Critical Thought*. London: Macmillan.

MORROW, JOHN. 1990. *Coleridge's Political Thought: Property, Morality and the Limits of Traditional Discourse*. London: Macmillan.

PATTON, LEWIS and MANN, PETER. 1971. 'Editors' Introduction'. *Lectures 1795 On Politics and Religion. CC* I, pp. xxiii–lxxx.

PIPER, H.W. 1962. *The Active Universe*. London: Athlone.

PRIESTLEY, JOSEPH. 1817–32. *Letters to the Right Honourable Edmund Burke*. (1790), in J. T. Rutt, ed., *Theological and Miscellaneous Works*, vol. XXII, 25 vols. London.

ROE, NICHOLAS. 1988. *Wordsworth and Coleridge: the Radical Years*. Oxford: Clarendon Press.

THELWALL, JOHN. 1796. *Peaceful Discussion, and not tumultary violence the means of redressing national grievance*. 2nd edn. London.

WHITE, DANIEL. 2006. *Early Romanticism and Religious Dissent*. Cambridge: Cambridge University Press.

CHAPTER 8

COLERIDGE AS EDITOR: *THE WATCHMAN* AND *THE FRIEND*

MICHAEL JOHN KOOY

COLERIDGE's involvement in public affairs was always fraught. At several periods of his life he sought deliberately to play a public role, notably as a political lecturer in Bristol, a civil servant in Malta and as a leader writer for two London daily newspapers. But in each of these endeavours, the direct experience of the rough and tumble of political life, while exhilarating, remunerative and to an extent professionally satisfying, nonetheless left him with a nagging feeling of disenchantment. *The Watchman* (1796) and *The Friend* (1809–10, 1818), though produced in very different political circumstances by a man whose own political views had also changed profoundly, nonetheless similarly arose out of, and sought to address, this complex feeling of disenchantment by appealing to fixed principles. Like Wordsworth's *The Recluse*, which would give hope to those who had been disappointed by the Revolution, Coleridge's journals would, at distinct times of crisis, inject political debate with high moral purpose, historical perspective, and philosophical reflection in order to give strength to those whose millenarian hopes had not been realized. In different ways, both carried forward the political idealism

I would like to thank Peter Larkin for his contributions to my research in this area.

released by the Revolution—in their unflagging hope for the possibility of political change and in their claim for independence from party politics. Above all, both journals offered probing contributions to contemporary debates about slavery, reform, commerce, and war, from the distinctive perspective of post-Enlightenment political theology.

This claim about the peculiarity of Coleridge's two single-authored journals is only possible given that both works have recently been rescued from obscurity. How, and why, did this come about? This question is important, because the recuperation of texts is hermeneutically invested: the way these two texts have re-entered Romantic studies after a long time in the wilderness has profoundly influenced how we read them. So, before turning to the works themselves, I shall ask why and how it is that we now read them at all.

Re-politicizing Coleridge

Coleridge once said wryly of *The Friend* that it was a secret he had entrusted to the public and that, 'unlike most secrets, it hath been well kept' (Allsop 1836, 1: 233). The mixture here of self-blame and resentment of the public exemplifies Coleridge's long-held attitude towards his own political journals and had an immense influence on how they were posthumously received. Both *The Watchman* and *The Friend* were conceived and published in direct response to specific national crisis conditions. For *The Watchman* in 1796, these consisted in the profound demoralization of the liberal opposition in the face of the highly effective 'Gagging Acts' (which tightened the law on treason and banned large political gatherings), William Pitt's continued pursuit of an aggressive war policy against Revolutionary France, and the repeated failure of legislation to abolish the slave trade and repeal the Test and Corporation Acts. For *The Friend* in 1809–10, the conditions were different but equally pressing: the national loss of nerve to pursue the war against Napoleonic France and the lingering uncertainty about how to pursue reform at home. And in 1818, it was postwar anomie that demanded attention, along with its interrelated causes: economic depression and class division. In each case, Coleridge threw himself energetically into the task. In early 1796 he travelled extensively throughout the Midlands drumming up support for his new journal (Roe 2003, Whittaker 2003), and then worked tirelessly from Bristol in the months that followed, corresponding with his printer, managing his subscription list and, above all, producing lively editorials. In 1809–10, with Sara Hutchinson and the Wordsworths at Allan Bank, he repeated the performance for *The Friend*: again, the

hunt for subscribers, the interminable negotiations with his printer and distribu-
tors, the fight with self-imposed deadlines, but also the energetic efforts to produce
timely, high quality, if sometimes disorderly, essays for his readers, the likes of
which simply did not exist in late Georgian Britain. And yet when the time came to
recall these efforts in *Biographia Literaria*, Coleridge could not bring himself to
communicate either the sense of urgency that had driven him on either occasion,
or the political content of his two works. Instead, it was the spectacle of their failure
that he put before his readers. He entertainingly recalled the 1796 *Watchman* tour
and, with less good humour, the complicated and ultimately self-destructive
publishing arrangements of *The Friend*, leading up to jokes about the perceived
worthlessness of both journals. Several numbers of *The Friend* had been retained by
the practical Earl of Cork for, Coleridge supposed, 'the culinary or post-culinary
conveniences of his servants' (*BL* 1: 176), while *The Watchman* was put to another
domestic purpose, this time by Coleridge's own servant:

I observed her putting an extravagant quantity of paper into the grate in order to light the
fire, and mildly checked her for her wastefulness; la, Sir! (replied poor Nanny) why, it is only
'WATCHMEN' (*BL* 1: 187)

Coleridge's self-deprecating analysis of his two political journals—so different from
his consistent appreciation of his other political activities, including newspaper
journalism and public service in Malta—served a distinct purpose. By emphasizing
the purity of his motives and the futility of his efforts, he managed to avoid the
awkwardly radical political content of *The Watchman* and to emphasize retrospect-
ively the philosophical purity of *The Friend* rather than its polemical political force.

   The reasons for belittling the politics of his journals I don't need to labour.
The double charge of apostasy and obscurity, of which Coleridge had, by the time
of *Biographia Literaria*, developed so deep-seated a fear, invited such defensive
exaggerations and misrepresentations. What's more important is how powerfully
stable this de-politicizing of his two journals became. *The Watchman* was never
republished in its entirety until relatively recently. The only excerpts to appear
throughout the whole of the nineteenth and most of the twentieth century were
those selected by Sara Coleridge for inclusion in the first volume of *Essays on His
Own Times*, excerpts that offered a reasonably good representation of the radical
Coleridge as a political essayist, but necessarily failed to convey the ensemble effect
of *The Watchman*'s poems, reviews, news digests and squibs. Sara Coleridge pre-
sented *The Watchman* to nineteenth-century readers rather as Coleridge did in
Biographia Literaria 35 years earlier: as political juvenilia that, unlike the later
Morning Post or *Courier* journalism, or for that matter the 1818 *Friend*, did not
demand sustained analysis. This view persisted through biographies, monographs
and scholarly articles well into the twentieth century. *The Watchman* was finally
republished in full in 1970, but then its appearance was owing less to academic
interest in its subject matter than to the powerful and prestigious publishing

venture by the Bollingen Foundation (Schultz 1971). Even Lewis Patton's scrupulous editing could not reverse the widespread consensus that *The Watchman* was political-poetic juvenilia. Critical readers reared on I. A. Richards' *Coleridge on Imagination* did not know what to do with the journal, and so tended to ignore it.

The story of *The Friend* is comparable. Here, the disorderly and polemical nature of the 1809–10 periodical edition was lost from view in a process that similarly began with Coleridge himself. His own completely revised 1818 edition grouped the floating material of the original periodical into three broad categories, dropped some of the filler and out-of-date references, strategically placed light material ('Landing Places') between the more taxing sections, and rounded off the whole with an entirely new section on Method. True, Coleridge's *rifacciamento* clearly focused on a new political problem: not war, but postwar anomie, and with remarkable acuity. But its Burkean rhetoric and obsession with order distracted posthumous readers from its radical subtext (I'll return to this below). While *Biographia* demoted *The Watchman* from a political journal into juvenilia, the 1818 *Friend* was seen to transform the 1809–10 edition into a lay sermon. And without exception, all editors of *The Friend* have followed Coleridge's lead, from the early nineteenth-century editions to the now standard edition in the Collected Works series, edited by Barbara Rooke and published in 1969. The latter included the 1809–10 edition in a one-volume appendix. Critical readers, accordingly, tended to focus on the 1818 edition and to emphasize its philosophical order and thoughtful conservatism (Muirhead 1930, Colmer 1959, Jackson 1969, also Cain 2003), sometimes at the expense of its complex political engagements. By comparison, contemporaneous Coleridge texts, such as *Biographia Literaria* and the notebooks, have been treated to much more generous critical attention.

Coleridge's work as a political journalist would have remained in the shadows, then, in spite of the Bollingen editions, if the critical landscape had not changed radically with the turn to history in literary studies. It's one of the ironies of scholarship that New Historicism, which in its early manifestations aimed in a disapproving spirit to *politicize* Coleridge's bourgeois imagination (McGann 1983, Leask 1988), ended up affirming the importance of his political writing. Through the work of Nicholas Roe (1988), and others (Cookson 1982, Jasper 1989, Kitson 1993, Magnuson 1998), Coleridge's radicalism, epitomized in his Bristol lectures and *The Watchman*, lost the juvenile colouring it had acquired since *Biographia* and instead gained respect for its rhetorical sophistication and thoughtful Jacobinism. For its part, *The Friend* lost its status as a self-contained *Lay Sermon*, as critics including Deirdre Coleman (1988), John Morrow (1990), Elinor Shaffer (1990), Jerome Christensen (1995), Lucy Newlyn (2000), Philip Connell (2001), and Paul Hamilton (2003) emphasized how Coleridge as a political journalist carried on a public, and quintessentially Romantic, quarrel with the Enlightenment values of cosmopolitanism, natural rights, and democracy during a period of wartime fear and scarcity, flattering and ignoring his exasperated audience by turns.

But while the turn to history has given us the critical tools to assess more fully the context and rhetoric of Coleridge's political journalism, in some respects its reach has not gone far enough. To its credit, it has helped identify political radicalism as one of the distinguishing features of early British Romanticism, in clear contradistinction from German and French variants, with their overwhelmingly statist and royalist leanings. It has also cast doubt on the notion, much favoured by earlier commentators, of Coleridge's progressive development out of a puerile radicalism into a thoughtful and mature Anglican conservatism. Instead, the change was by fits and starts, and filtered through budding nationalism, the exigencies of print culture and his own travels abroad. But the current historicist recuperation of Coleridge's political journalism has nonetheless left a number of lacunae as well as generating new hermeneutic difficulties.

One concerns the rhetoric and formal arrangements of Coleridge's political journals. Materialist and historicist readings of this work, focusing on its changing political commitments, have tended to exaggerate the rhetorical differences between *The Watchman* and *The Friend* as further evidence of apostasy (though see Mahoney 2004). In fact, the rhetorical continuities between both texts, in spite of their plainly different political agendas, demand a fuller explanation than so far has been given. Second, war. The recent recovery of Coleridge's political journalism has emphasized the British domestic political agenda, primarily focused on questions about parliamentary reform, abolition of the slave trade, censorship and citizenship. But as work elsewhere in Romantic studies has persuasively argued (Bainbridge 2003, Favret 1994, Shaw 2000 and 2002, Watson 2004) the domestic and international political agendas influenced each other, and in the case of Coleridge's political journalism this is no less so. This, too, is awaiting its fuller treatment. And thirdly, the recent recovery of Coleridge's political journalism has been reluctant to take seriously the theological content of Coleridge's political journalism, often assuming instead that the theological is either a function of the political (Canuel 2002) or non-political by definition. These assumptions have obscured the complexity of one fundamental aspect of all Coleridge's political journalism, indeed, their primary motivating force, namely, his political theology.

In the rest of this chapter I shall focus on the last of these topics. My approach privileges the relationship between the secular and the theological in Coleridge's journalism. Controversially, I suggest that Coleridge's political theology determines his place on the political spectrum, and not the other way around, as much commentary tends to assume. The young Coleridge's views about the relationship between *caritas* (selfless love) and politics in *The Watchman* is not, in my view, a function of his radicalism; rather, his radicalism is a function of his theology. This approach remains historical. My interest is to show how Coleridge tries to articulate political theological responses to a variety of contemporary crisis situations (revolution, war, anomie). These responses fluctuate between different forms of Christian materialism on the one hand (modelled on the perfectionism of Unitarianism and then, later, the incarnation of Trinitarian theology) and a secular-inflected idealism (derived from Kant) on the other. The story is by no means uniform, and one of the results of this approach is that it brings out similarities and differences in Coleridge's political journalism that otherwise remain muted.

THE WATCHMAN: RADICAL POLITICAL THEOLOGY

One of the unexpected outcomes of *The Watchman* was that it brought the young Coleridge to the attention of one of the most prominent atheist Jacobins of the period, John Thelwall (Roe 1988). The two entered into a lively correspondence that carried on well after *The Watchman* ceased publication in May 1796. Thelwall, who knew personally, and to his cost, the combined power of church and state to suppress dissent, challenged Coleridge to defend his Christianity as 'a religion for Democrats', which in December of that year he did:

It certainly teaches in the most explicit terms the rights of Man, his right to Wisdom, his right to an equal share in all the blessings of Nature; it commands it's disciples to go every where, & every where to preach these rights; it commands them never to use the arm of flesh, to be perfectly non-resistant; yet to hold the promulgation of *Truth* to be a Law above Law, and in the performance of this office to defy 'Wickedness in high places,' and cheerfully to endure ignominy, & wretchedness, & torments, & death, rather than *intermit* the performance of it; yet while enduring ignominy, & wretchedness, & torments & death to feel nothing but sorrow, and pity, and love for those who inflicted them; wishing their Oppressors to be altogether such as they, 'excepting these bonds.'—Here is *truth* in theory; and in practice a union of energetic *action*, and more energetic *Suffering*. For activity amuses; but he, who can *endure* calmly, must possess the seeds of true *Greatness*. For all his animal spirits will of necessity fail him; and he has only his *Mind* to trust to. —These doubtless are morals for all the Lovers of Mankind, who wish to *act* as well as *speculate*. . . (*CL* 1: 282).

Coleridge's response to Thelwall aims to reconcile Christianity with political radicalism. He does this in two ways: first by collapsing the discourse about equality within primitive Christianity into the Jacobin discourse about the rights of man, and laying great store by its promulgation; and secondly by emphasizing the virtue of suffering in the absence of such rights (another theme familiar from primitive Christianity), the millenarian expectation of vindication effectively doing away with the need to take up arms to fight for them.

This political theology, neatly displayed in the letter to Thelwall, is the subtext of *The Watchman*. At a point of political crisis, a time when the opposition was wilting under the pressure of the Two Acts and despairing in the face of the continued war policy and the failure of reform and emancipation legislation, Coleridge offered the hope of a political theology that combined high-minded denunciations of instituted power with an emphasis on the political virtue of self-emptying, or kenosis, modelled on the figure of Christ, from the sight of which the abusers of power would be shamed into repentance.[1] The crux of this politically inflected kenosis is *The Watchman*'s view of the socio-political importance of personal religion. This is stated programmatically in Coleridge's 'Introductory Essay' where, to the surprise of the atheists among his readers, he ascribed the inevitable increase of political enlightenment to 'the progress of the Methodists' (*Watchman* 12). Their religious enthusiasm, so far from leading to prejudice and quietism, produces instead the 'sobriety', zeal for 'instruction', hatred of 'political abuses', and above all 'pious horror' of violence, that, diffused among the people, will in the course of time bring tyranny to its knees and deliver liberty to all. What's radical about this political theology, distinguishing it alike from early libertarian as well as constitutionalist defences of political and religious freedom, is that the passage from 'enlightenment' to the enjoyment of 'liberty' is not mediated by self-assertion and violence, but instead by self-abnegation. The less one fights for one's rights, the more certainly they will be achieved:

Yes! They [the Methodists] shudder with pious horror at the idea of defending by famine, and fire, and blood, that Religion which teaches its followers—'if thine enemy hunger, feed him; if he thirst, give him drink: *for by so doing thou shalt melt him into repentance*' (*Watchman* 13)

What's *The Watchman*'s contribution here? Not the emphasis on speaking truth to power, which is common enough among both non-conformists as well as secular radicals in the 1790s. Nor the disavowal of violence *per se*, which, as scholars like Cookson (1982) and others have shown, also claimed wide support across the religious and non-religious spectrum. No, *The Watchman*'s point of originality is to offer a theological justification for the surprising view that kenosis, or self-emptying, has profound, beneficial political consequences. Combining a Puritan emphasis on introspection and education with a Catholic concern for the well-being of the collective, Coleridge argues that *caritas* is a political virtue, not only a private affair about one's own beliefs and salvation: it puts pressure on state policy and brings about systemic change in the inherited political and social hierarchies.

---

[1] The term kenosis figures prominently in Christology, where it is used in a variety of ways to describe the self-humbling implicit in divine incarnation. It also is interpreted to imply Christian *praxis* (see Moule 1970). I employ the term by analogy to the political, to describe a (visionary) politics whereby the state empties itself of pretensions to omnipotence in order to enable new forms of community.

By way of kenosis, the personal becomes political, precisely because it disavows a Calliclean or 'realist' view of politics as the exercise of naked will.

This emphasis on the political virtue of personal *kenosis* runs through all of *The Watchman*'s major interventions in contemporary political debate. In the essay on abolition, in the fourth number (a reworking of his 1795 lecture, discussed by Peter Kitson in Ch. 7, this volume), Coleridge outlines a method of direct consumer action that would have positive political consequences. Dismissing the use of legislative instruments to abolish the slave trade, he instead calls for a middle-class boycott of sugar. Let consumers prove their *caritas* by giving up sugar and thereby drive the slave plantations out of business, instead of enjoying sugar with culpable naiveté: 'She sips a beverage sweetened with human blood, even while she is weeping over the refined sorrows of Werter or of Clementina. Sensibility is not Benevolence... Benevolence impels to action, and is accompanied by self-denial' (*Watchman* 139–40).

The emphasis on the political value of private acts of *caritas* also lies at the heart of Coleridge's famous quarrel with Godwin. Though, as Coleridge himself later admitted (*CL* 3: 315), *The Watchman*'s critique of *Political Justice* is regrettably superficial—and, we should add, *ad hominem* to a fault—it nonetheless correctly discerns the dualism operating at the centre of Godwin's secular theory of political anarchism, which pitted private interests against public good. Godwin demanded, like the Jacobins during the worst moments of the Terror, the suppression of the former for the sake of the latter. In response, Coleridge appeals to Bishop Berkeley's *Maxims Concerning Patriotism* (1750) which emphasized, in accordance with his own political theology, the interdependence of personal virtue and public good (*Watchman* 98–9). *The Watchman* even finds an unexpected ally for its political theology in the style of Edmund Burke. Coleridge's famous critique of Burke's *Letter... to a Noble Lord* begins with an appreciation of his style, in which personal feeling and an idiosyncratic use of metaphor distinguish his reasoning from the mere declamation of both the Tories and the radicals:

Mr. Burke always appeared to me to have displayed great vigor of intellect, and an almost prophetic keenness of penetration: nor can I think his merit diminished, because he has secured the aids of sympathy to his cause by the warmth of his own emotions, and delighted the imagination of his readers by a multitude and rapid succession of remote analogies. It seems characteristic of true eloquence, to reason *in* metaphors; of declamation, to argue *by* metaphors.   (*Watchman* 31)

Among the chief faults of Burke's *Letter*—and a sign for Coleridge of its bad faith— was its abandoning of a rhetoric grounded in personal life in favour of one based on abstraction, which would lead inevitably to 'the throb and tempest of political fanaticism' (31). Coleridge admired Burke's former style, not because it was Burke, but because it was personal, its idiosyncratic use of metaphor and frequent self-inscriptions the mark of its political integrity. It was an integrity that didn't last.

'Alas!' Coleridge wrote, 'we fear that this Sun of Genius is well nigh extinguished: a few bright spots linger on its orb, but scarcely larger or more numerous than the dark *maculæ* visible on it in the hour of its strength and effulgence' (*Watchman* 31). This is a playfully over-written piece of prose. But behind the irony here (*The Watchman* displaying a rhetoric that out-Burkes Burke) lies a serious claim that runs throughout Coleridge's early journalism: that his own characteristic emphasis on the personal—his use of metaphor, his mixture of poetry and prose, his foregrounding of human interest and experience—are the marks of his own political integrity.

The Watchman's political theology also motivated its approach to geo-politics. States, and not just individuals, should practise a kenotic politics. Britain failed to do so, and would feel the consequences, its aggressive policy aimed at containing Jacobinism arising from a misplaced fear and narrow self-interest. It was bound to backfire, as the new French Republic, instead of concentrating on internal reform and the arts of peace, now had no other choice but to expand its defensive military operations and threaten British interests in return (*Watchman* 241–2). But France, too, was failing, and on the same grounds. When the French turned down British overtures for peace in 1796, *The Watchman* responded with a 'Remonstrance to the French Legislators' that faulted their narrow self-interest. The retention of the Netherlands, which the French government considered non-negotiable, was for *The Watchman* indefensible as a policy because the consequences would be disastrous for all concerned: 'misused success is soon followed by adversity, and ... the adversity of France may lead, in its train of consequences, to the slavery of all Europe' (*Watchman* 273). A kenotic policy, on the other hand, would bring infinitely greater reward: giving up the Netherlands in exchange for a politically and economically beneficial end to hostilities. 'Legislators of France! If your system be true, a few years only of Peace would so increase your population and multiply your resources, as to place you beyond all danger of attack' (*Watchman* 272).

The Watchman's political theology, with its emphasis on the value of kenosis, and its stress on the political value of personal acts of *caritas*, went a long way in fulfilling its aim of reconciling Christianity with political radicalism. But its work was not unproblematic. For one, Coleridge's radical political theology was weakened by the Hartleyan necessitarianism he was also committed to at this time. Even while commending policies that amounted to giving up power rather than seizing it, the young Coleridge couldn't help but regard the greatest outrages of his day as necessary episodes in the providential unfolding of history. Everything had a purpose, discernible or not, and looking on the bright side sometimes meant turning a blind eye to the dark. *The Watchman* stood for the freedom of the press, but nearly in the same breath he admitted that the Two Acts, though 'breaches of the Constitution', nonetheless might usefully 'render the language of political publications more cool and guarded, or even confine us for a while to the teaching of first principles, or the diffusion of that general knowledge which should be the basis or substratum of politics' (*Watchman* 13–14). War was also problematic from this regard. Even as he counselled peace, Coleridge remained fascinated by the providential usefulness of war. As he expressed in *Religious Musings*, in an excerpt that found a place in *The Watchman*, war brought with it ingenuity:

> ... all the sore ills
> That vex and desolate our mortal life.
> Wide-wasting ills! yet each th'immediate source
> Of mightier good! Their keen necessities
> To ceaseless action, goading human thought
> Have made Earth's reasoning Animal her Lord,
> And the pale-fear'd Sage's trembling hand
> Strong as an Host of armed Deities!
>
> (*Watchman* 131)

But there were political gains, too, from conflict: 'Continuance of the War likely to produce an abolition of Property', he confided to his notebook around this time (*CN* 1: 103). The worse the experience of war, the greater the people's feeling of political alienation, and the more likely would come the revolution: this was the thinking behind *The Watchman*'s Gothic account of battlefield horror in no. 7 (238–41). These thoughts were sweetly seditious. But they also took the punch out of *The Watchman*'s calls for peace.

But the most interesting problem encountered by *The Watchman*'s political theology concerned audience. Ironically, the more Coleridge clung to his message—to disseminate 'political information' (*Watchman* 5) in the name of freedom and to emphasize the power of political kenosis to effect reform—the more difficult it was to reach an audience in 1790s England, and this for two reasons. First, the weakened and divided state of the opposition itself. Coleridge aimed *The Watchman* at the 'Friends of Freedom, of Reason, and of Human Nature' as the Prospectus put it (*Watchman* 5). But as Coleridge discovered in the course of writing *The Watchman*, his audience was much more diverse than he had anticipated, divided both geographically and religiously into different constituencies with distinct, though sometimes overlapping, priorities: metropolitan Whigs interested in policy debate, provincial radicals hungry for news, non-conformist Christians seeking gradual reform and atheists or agnostics planning revolution. Having secured subscribers from all these groups, Coleridge tried to adapt his political theology to each, but ended up offending all. The essay against fasts in the second number pleased Coleridge's secular readership with its anticlericalism, but its light tone and its ironic use of Scripture (it provocatively began with the words of Isaiah, 'Wherefore my Bowels shall sound like an Harp', *Watchman* 51) shocked his religious readers and, as he later said with a touch of hyperbole, must have cost him 500 subscriptions (*BL* 1: 184). Coleridge's rough handling of Godwin's *Political Justice* had the reverse effect: moderate non-conformists warmed to *The Watchman*'s domestic piety, but atheist and deist radicals found its glib dismissal of rationalism surprising and just a little distasteful. The geographical divide was equally problematic. For his provincial readers Coleridge included plenty of 'political information' copied or précised from the London dailies and even made efforts to include stories of local interest (such as the arrest and trial of the Birmingham radicals Binns and Jones) but for metropolitan readers this information arrived late in London, by which time it was no longer news. They preferred original matter, such as essays and reviews, which Coleridge did not always manage to get into every number, owing to time constraints and the fear of prosecution. In the end, Coleridge admitted defeat. He could not continue to fulfil the competing demands of these different constituencies, nor, indeed, did he want to—and at the tenth number *The Watchman* gracefully took leave of his readers (374–5) and folded.

But there was another reason, apart from these practical difficulties. As historical research has shown, the Terror, war and then the Two Acts not only weakened and divided the opposition but exerted deeper structural changes to the public sphere that were only partly understood at the time, though their consequences were felt immediately: a breakdown in the consensus about rational debate, the diminished authority of disinterested political commentary, and the increased regulation of information. Crucially, with regard to political debate, these changes led to an important shift in authorial activity. In the absence of a republic of letters, writers seeking power and influence abandoned classical rhetorical methods aimed at persuasion in order to adopt novel strategies aimed at maintaining hermeneutic control (Barrell 2000, Mee 2003). The radical Coleridge did not follow suit. The achievement of *The Watchman* is not only the variety and energy of its approach to radical political themes but its hermeneutic openness, amply evident in the lead essays and reviews, which appeal to the reader's imagination without recourse to manipulation. In a context where power is achieved by controlling meaning, *The Watchman*'s hermeneutic openness is an act of self-humbling. Here, even at the level of form, Coleridge's radical theology leaves its mark.

THE FRIEND (1809–10): CREATIVE VIOLENCE

Like *The Watchman*, Coleridge's 1809–10 *Friend* aimed to intervene decisively in contemporary political debate, though by June 1809, when the first number appeared, 13 years after the *Watchman*, its author had undergone a decisive transformation in his political views. The invasion scares of the late 1790s, the expansion of the Napoleonic empire in the early 1800s, and a testing period working for the

British government on the embattled island of Malta awoke his latent nationalism while discrediting in his mind the Revolution's promises of liberty and prosperity. Additionally, Coleridge's conversion to Trinitarian Christianity within the context of Kantian dualism further pushed radical millenarian and perfectionist aspirations from his political horizon during these intervening years. As I'll argue in this section, the most decisive impact of these changes was on Coleridge's political theology.

Coleridge recorded his changing political views in articles published in *The Morning Post* and later in the *Courier* (discussed by Angela Esterhammer, Ch. 9, in this volume), but the exigencies of writing for a London daily led him to seek another outlet for his views, one that would allow him to reflect on abstract political questions in the intimacy of a self-selecting group of readers drawn from, though by no means identical to, the general reading public. In *The Friend* Coleridge repeats *The Watchman*'s independent publishing strategy, complete with endless worries about printers, paper, subscriptions, and postal distribution, while setting out a highly idiosyncratic counter-revolutionary political philosophy.

The Friend's continual prioritizing of principles over policies and events was not an avoidance of history, as New Historicist analysis suggests, but itself a response to the particularly acute form of political crisis that in Coleridge's view was paralysing Britain in 1809. The crisis was two-pronged. First, there was the blatant and wholly unwelcome fact of French imperial hegemony on the continent; second, there was the clear indication that at home the will to fight had diminished, and that some military and civilian leaders were ready to contemplate appeasement. *The Friend* addressed both. Regarding the first, Coleridge argued, contrary to the ultra Tories, that recent French militarism sprang not from an innate expansionism (such as had driven the wars of the eighteenth century) but rather from the misdirection of radical energies that had not properly been contained, at their inception in the 1790s, within robust political institutions: failing to find expression in politics, the people found it on the battlefield (*Friend* 2: 62–3). Coleridge then extrapolated from this a lesson about democracy as such. All of *The Friend*'s arguments regarding democratic reform—on Rousseau (numbers 8 and 9) and Cartwright (number 10) principally—attempt to institutionalize radical energy precisely out of the fear that otherwise it would turn into military aggression. The aim was to give the democratic impulse a grounding not in natural right but in historically determined social and political institutions, principally education and property, that would allow for its gradual pacific expansion, pre-empting the need for abrupt episodes in which 'the people' make their mark directly on history with violent and self-destructive consequences. The desire to re-direct radical energy within liberal institutions distinguishes *The Friend*'s project in important ways from other counter-revolutionary ones, including Burke's, whose paternalistic antiquarianism aimed rather to discredit radicalism in the name of history as such, and that of reactionaries like de Maistre, whose authoritarianism sought to subjugate it through fear of the mythical authority of the monarch.

The weakness of British resolve, the other pole of *The Friend*'s agenda, required more complex treatment, since it was a systemic, as well as an acute political problem. What Britain lacked, in *The Friend*'s view, was a conception of itself as a national polity that took into account the irreversible advances in commerce, technology and general knowledge ushered in by the Enlightenment—what Coleridge called 'the Powers that awaken and foster the Spirit of Curiosity and Investigation' (2: 86)—while retaining a sense of Britain's unique moral and spiritual vocation as a Protestant nation. In the absence of such a conception, according to *The Friend*'s way of thinking, Britain in 1809 risked falling under the sway of either reactionary aristocrats pursuing a war of attrition against the French empire or free-thinking pragmatists ready to make peace with it: one counselled war without reason, the other reason without war, so Britain would lose in either case. In contrast to both the Tory and the radical traditions, with their focus on constitutional history and natural right respectively, *The Friend* aimed to derive a modern conception of Britain from two alternative sources, namely the English republican tradition, with its emphases on civic participation, education, national self-defence, and the harmonious functioning of the three estates, and the new political economy, with its emphasis on the free circulation of capital as the generator of wealth. *The Friend*'s innovation was to reconcile these traditions in what one might call 'liberal republicanism'. Abandoning the Country tradition of his early years, with its characteristic hostility to commerce as a corrupting influence on civic action, Coleridge came increasingly to see commerce as Adam Smith did: as a way to exercise civic responsibility (Connell 2000, Malachuk 2000, though compare Edwards 2004). From these resources, *The Friend* projected a hybrid conception of the British polity according to which the state would be directed by a representative elite of legislators, charged with providing not only self-defence and economic stability but also education and leisure, while the people participate in national life via culture, technology and the market. Such a conception of the state—rather than the historically grounded heirarchies of the Tories (*vide* Burke) or the destabilizing utopias of the reformers (*vide* Rousseau)—would be worth fighting for. This was *The Friend*'s distinctive response to the war crisis.

Coleridge's 'liberal republicanism', with its powerful combination of wealth, national freedom and tradition, provided the goal to which the radical energies of the 1790s could be redirected, but war provided the occasion to realize it. As Coleridge discovered in the years leading up to *The Friend*, the emergency conditions of war, if properly managed, could become the crucible in which the old would be burned away and the new national polity could take shape. In what is surely its most controversial move, *The Friend* accordingly embraced a theory of 'creative violence' according to which the testing and costly experience of war would provide the necessary social, political and intellectual conditions for the emergence of the nation-state in its new form: 'if Peace has its stagnations as well as War, does not War create or re-enliven numerous branches of Industry as well as Peace?' (*Friend* 2: 160).

The Friend's 'liberal republicanism' marked a distinct break with the democracy and aspheterism of *The Watchman* (Malachuk 2000). More fundamentally, though, in embracing a theory of 'creative violence' *The Friend* turned its back on the principal themes of Coleridge's earlier political theology, namely the concern with the political implications of personal acts of *caritas*, the kenotic movement towards respecting the interests of other states, and the hermeneutic openness of political communication. Instead of seeking to incorporate these elements into a richer 'liberal republicanism', mindful of its own secular limits and open to theological critique, Coleridge opted to suspend them. *The Friend*'s 'liberal republicanism' trumped his political theology.

Let me point to one important instance of how this took place: in *The Friend*'s approach to the relationship between morality and politics. Coleridge began the journal by asserting the standard Augustinian view that practical political decision-making should be grounded on moral reflection. An honest man knows, he declared, 'that by sacrificing the law of his reason to the maxims of pretended Prudence, he purchases the sword with the loss of the arm which is to wield it' (*Friend* 2: 40). And yet by the seventh number he had severed the connection. In the context of his argument against the utopianism of the Revolutionary period rationalists, Coleridge declared himself an 'ardent Advocate for deriving the origin of all Government from human *Prudence*' (2: 140). This was the reasoning:

the moral Laws of the intellectual Worlds, as far as they are deducible from pure Intellect, are never perfectly applicable to our mixed and sensitive Nature, because Man is something besides Reason; because his Reason never acts by itself, but must cloath itself in the Substance of individual Understanding and specific Inclination, in order to become a Reality and an Object of Consciousness and Experience   (*Friend* 2: 132)

The awkwardness engendered by his dualism quickly came to the fore in *The Friend* when Coleridge addressed two specific, nationally prominent political issues. In number 22 he defended the British breaking of the Peace of Amiens in 1803 for the sake of Malta on the grounds that this pretext, though clearly insignificant in its own right, was of the utmost importance when considered prudentially from the perspective of the British right to defend her own interests (2: 302). He also defended the right of the British government in time of war to launch a pre-emptive attack on a neutral party (the Danish fleet at Copenhagen in 1807) on the prudential grounds that the fleet may have constituted a future threat (Coleman 1988, 164–93). In both cases it was necessary for Coleridge to minimize the relevance of moral considerations to the political process, the latter being largely determined by 'the imperious circumstances, which render a particular measure advisable' (*Friend* 1: 328). This weakening of the link between politics and ethical reflection is occasionally echoed elsewhere in *The Friend*, notably in its embracing of Political Economy in the essay on taxation in number 12 (Connell 2001) and its tendency towards hermeneutic closure in the Life of Ball in numbers 21–2, 26–7 (Fulford 1999 and Kooy 1999 and 2003*b*).

This dualism found sanction in Coleridge's interpretation of Kant's distinction between Understanding (interpreting what we have acquired through the senses) and Reason (intuiting regulative ideas), as John Milbank has argued (1988, 61–2). German Idealism's prudential approach to the political arose from a scheme/content dualism, which divided the work of imagination from the work of governing. Hence the conception of politics no longer as a process of human imaginative *poesis* indirectly imitative of divine making, but rather as a technocratic management of crisis situations. This conception of politics buttressed *The Friend*'s 'liberal republicanism', with its emphasis on the irreducible right of the state to self-preservation and the nationally vivifying effects of 'creative violence'.

Where is political theology in all of this? To the extent that it appears in *The Friend*, political Christianity figures either in reductive terms, as a private belief system that is largely indifferent to political debate, or in nakedly nationalist terms, as a mythic Anglicanism opposed to continental Catholicism. In either case, *The Friend*'s Christianity offers few resources to think critically about the contemporary crisis conditions of military threat and national disunity. That is not to say that it disappears: in *The Friend*'s commitment to freedom of the press, traced back to Milton's political theological polemic, *Areopagitica* (numbers 3–5), its emphasis on education as the means to expanding political participation (number 6), and its *avant la lettre* liberal conception of role of government to enhance, and not just preserve, civil society (number 15), one sees the tentative formation of a post-Revolutionary Christian communitarianism. But these elements tend to be subordinated to *The Friend*'s secular liberal and nationalist concerns. One might say that political theology remains a thorn in the side of *The Friend*'s 'liberal republicanism', one that Coleridge must continually negotiate his way around. This, I think, accounts for the spectacular doubling of the 1809–10 *Friend*'s political rhetoric that has been much commented upon (Christensen 1979 and 1995, Coleman 1988, Reed 1980, Shaw 2002): its dominant political thinking (the 'liberal republicanism'), straining to separate itself from its theological conscience, not always convincingly. Interestingly, all these elements of the earlier political theology would regain prominence in the 1818 *Friend*.

THE FRIEND (1818): CHRISTIAN COMMUNITARIANISM

The abandonment of *The Friend* in 1810 left Coleridge with stacks of unsold printed copies. In 1812 he combined these with revised reprints of the earlier numbers to form a single-volume work for immediate sale. Only a few hundred were sold, but the idea of reissuing the work stayed with him and in *Biographia Literaria*, two years after the end of the war, Coleridge announced he was working on a completely revised edition (*BL* 1: 218). The '*rifacciamento*', as he called it (*Friend* 1: 3), included much of the same material, trimmed and tailored with an eye no longer to war but to another threat, the anomie and simmering radicalism of the immediate postwar period: 'though the one storm has blown over... the hollow murmur of the Earthquake within the Bowels of our own Commonweal may strike a direr terror than ever did the Tempest of foreign Warfare' (*Friend* 1: 126), Coleridge warned darkly.

The 1818 *Friend*'s response to the postwar crisis period is complicated. Rhetorically, it orientates itself unambiguously against the new radicalism: alarmist and condescending by turns, the 1818 *Friend* often reads like a Burkean fulmination against modernity in the name of inherited hierarchies and new forms of legal and social regulation. In terms of its argument, however, the 1818 *Friend* is much more diverse, and by no means straightforwardly 'Tory' or 'conservative', or even whole-heartedly committed to social regulation, as some commentators have suggested. The secular inflected 'liberal republicanism' of the 1809–10 edition, with its appeal to violence, fascination with the market economy and commitment to 'national unity', remains amply evident, notably in the recycled essays on taxation, on war and international law and in the 'Life of Ball'. But theological concerns that pull in an opposite direction also have an increasing presence in the 1818 *Friend*, evident in the revised essays on the freedom of the press, education and the political role of the conscience.

These concerns are amplified by the new material Coleridge added to the 1818 edition. The new material shifts *The Friend*'s burden of argumentation away from the themes of his wartime 'liberal republicanism' and towards a novel conception of Christian communitarianism as an answer to postwar anomie. Two of the most substantial additions need mentioning here. One is the section on Law and Religion (*Friend* 1: 94–9), which was added to essay 5 of the 1809–10 *Friend*. Here Coleridge posits Law and Religion as polar forces of the same power, opposites rather than contraries (*Friend* 1: 94). Abandoning his earlier Idealist dualism between politics (Understanding) and conscience (Reason), Coleridge now argues that Law without Religion (modern liberalism) is as politically disingenuous as Religion without Law (theocracy). Coleridge's paean to the conscience ends the section:

[Reason] is of universal validity and obligatory on all mankind. There is one heart for the whole mighty mass of Humanity, and every pulse in each particular vessel strives to beat in concert with it. . . . That man's Soul is not dear to himself, to whom the Souls of his Brethren are not dear. As far as they can be influenced by him, they are parts and properties of his own soul, their faith his faith, their errors his burthen, their righteousness and bliss his righteousness and his reward—and of their Guilt and Misery his own will be the echo.

(*Friend* 1: 97)

For the 1818 *Friend*, conscience is no longer the private moral reflection character-
istic of a narrow Protestant liberalism, but the catalyst for communitarian solidar-
ity more characteristic of what would later be called Christian socialism.
Community arises from the experience of expressing shared values, not (as the
1809–10 *Friend* would have it) from the experience of fighting for them. Coleridge
is not a socialist, but his strong hint here of a theologically grounded politics
of solidarity in which imagining otherness ('the Souls of his Brethren') defeats self-
interest ('their Guilt and Misery his own') gives unexpected new life to the
cosmopolitanism of *The Watchman* while also looking ahead to the Christian
socialism of the mid nineteenth century.

The second, much longer, addition to the 1818 *Friend* were the Essays on the
Principles of Method, an original work of applied logic first written for the
Encyclopaedia Metropolitana and representing a lifetime's reflection on philosoph-
ical method (Jackson 1969, Myers 1987). Coleridge prefaced it with three essays on
Morals and Religion. While the essay on Method credibly advances on the 1809–10
Friend's longstanding interest in form and organization, the prefatory essays on
Morals and Religion revise the politics of the 1809–10 *Friend* in important ways. In
contrast to his earlier 'liberal republicanism', with its investment in military
competition and attraction to unregulated market economics, the 1818 *Friend*
resurrects the pacific and communitarian themes of *The Watchman*. Coleridge
quotes approvingly and at length the moderate Civil War commentator William
Sedgwick: 'I fear no party, or interest, for I love all, I am reconciled to all, and
therein I find all reconciled to me' (*Friend* 1: 414); he also critiques the technocratic
view of political decision making as 'mere prudence' (415) and condemns the
'false honor' that leads to conflict (426–7). Coleridge even turns against his
favourite seventeenth-century divine, Jeremy Taylor, citing with profound disap-
proval Taylor's use of Christian apologetics to defend 'a point of state expedience'
(433–4). The most clear statement of Coleridge's late political theology occurs in his
critique of Plato's Callicles and his politics of will, which the 1818 *Friend* sees as the
corrupt centre of what we now call the classical liberal state:

> … when the pure will … is ranked among the *means* to an alien end, instead of being itself
> the one absolute end, in the participation of which all other things are worthy to be called
> good—with this revolution commences the epoch of division and separation. Things are
> rapidly improved, persons as rapidly deteriorated; and for an indefinite period the powers
> of the aggregate increase, as the strength of the individual declines … religion and morals
> cannot be disjoined without the destruction of both: and that this does not take place to the
> full extent, we owe to the frequency with which both take shelter in the heart, and that men
> are always better or worse than the maxims which they adopt or concede.   (*Friend* 1: 444)

With their critique of the politics of will, the essays on Morals and Religion
constitute a profound shift in substance and tone from the 1809–10 *Friend*'s
concessions to prudence and violence. So far from offering solutions to national

crisis, both are now seen as socio-political determinants of that crisis. The 1818 *Friend* does not offer a univocal response to modern anomie, not least because its rhetoric tends undeniably towards Burkean nostalgia. But its profound antagonism to the secular conception of the political as the technocratic management of competing interests nonetheless stands out as instructive and of immense importance historically. In appealing to a theologically grounded conception of the good, and emphasizing the communitarian aspect of political life that that conception of the good gives rise to, the 1818 *Friend* offers resources for understanding and counteracting contemporary anomie in terms that neither radicals nor Tories had the courage or conviction to articulate.

Coleridge placed immense value on this addition to *The Friend*: 'in point of *value*', he wrote to his son Derwent in late 1818, '[these] pages...outweigh all my other works, verse or prose' (CL 4: 885). But the circumstances of publishing were—again!—against him, and the 1818 *Friend* sold only 250 copies before the publishers went into bankruptcy (*Friend* 1: lxxxv). Nonetheless, *The Friend* managed to reach a wide audience later in the century, in Britain, America, and abroad (Rémusat 1856, Shaffer 2007). A measure of both the 1818 *Friend*'s return to the themes of the *Watchman* and its influence on mid nineteenth-century thinkers can be had from the Christian socialist F. D. Maurice:

> In his "Friend" I seem to discover the very same man whom I had known amidst the storms of the revolutionary period. Nor do I find him less impatient of mere rules and decrees than he was then; only the impatience has taken a new form....Its merit is, that it is an enquiry, that it shews us what we have to seek for, and that it puts us into a way of seeking. Hence it was and is particularly offensive to more than one class of persons...to explain how a book, which is said to have no sympathy with the moving spirit of this age, should have affected the most thoughtful of our young men, this is a work of difficulty, which I hope that some of our Reviewers will one day undertake. I am not attempting to solve any such problems, but am merely accounting for its influence upon my own mind, an influence mainly owing to those very peculiarities which seem to have impaired or destroyed its worth in the opinions of wiser people.   (quoted in *Friend* 1: civ)

Maurice's homage to the restlessness of *The Friend* reminds critical readers today that Coleridge's late political theology, so far from exhausting itself in postwar grumbling, remained a provocative and inspiring presence for later generations of Christian progressivists (Prickett 1976). It also suggests how *The Friend*'s political theology sought to protect Christianity from the secular liberal attempt to purge the political of the sacred. In this respect, it seems wholly credible that Coleridge's later political theology anticipated some of the polemical strategies of later advocates of Christian modernity, including Kierkegaard and even Charles Péguy (Manent 1998).

WORKS CITED

ALLSOP, THOMAS, ed. 1836. *Letters, Conversations and Recollections of Samuel Taylor Coleridge*, 2 vols. London: Edward Moxon.

BAINBRIDGE, SIMON. 2003. *British Poetry and the Revolutionary and Napoleonic Wars*. Oxford: Oxford University Press.

BARRELL, JOHN. 2000. *Imagining the King's Death: Figurative Treason, Fantasies of Regicide, 1793–1796*. Oxford: Oxford University Press.

CAIN, JEFFREY. 2003. An experiment in honesty: Samuel Taylor Coleridge's *The Friend*. *Modern Age*, 45 (4): 295–304.

CANUEL, MARK. 2002. *Religion, Toleration, and British Writing, 1790–1830*. Cambridge: Cambridge University Press.

CHRISTENSEN, JEROME C. 1979. Politerotics: Coleridge's rhetoric of war in *The Friend*. *Clio*, 8 (3): 339–63

—— 1995. The method of *The Friend*. In *Rhetorical Traditions and British Romantic Literature*, ed. Don H. Bialostosky and Lawrence D. Needham. Bloomington: Indiana University Press, 11–27.

COLEMAN, DEIRDRE. 2002. The journalist. *The Cambridge Companion to Coleridge*, ed. Lucy Newlyn. Cambridge: Cambridge University Press, 126–41.

—— 1988. *Coleridge and the* Friend *(1809–10)*. Oxford: Clarendon Press.

COLMER, JOHN. 1959. *Coleridge: Critic of Society*. Oxford: Clarendon Press.

CONNELL, PHILIP. 2001. *Romanticism, Economics and the Question of 'Culture'.* Oxford: Oxford University Press.

COOKSON, J. E. 1982. *Friends of Peace: Anti-War Liberalism in England, 1793–1815*. Cambridge: Cambridge University Press.

EDWARDS, PAMELA. 2004. *The Statesman's Science: History, Nature, and Law in the Political Thought of Samuel Taylor Coleridge*. New York: Columbia University Press.

FAVRET, MARY. A. 1994. Coming home: the public spaces of Romantic war. *Studies in Romanticism*, 33: 539–48.

FULFORD, TIM. 1999. Romanticizing the Empire: the naval heroes of Southey, Coleridge, Austen, and Marryat. *Modern Language Quarterly*, 60 (2): 161–96.

HAMILTON, PAUL. 2003: Coleridge and the 'Rifacciamento' of Philosophy. *European Romantic Review*, 14 (4): 417–31.

JACKSON, J. R. DE J. 1969. *Method and Imagination in Coleridge's Criticism*. Cambridge: Harvard University Press.

JASPER, DAVID. 1989. Preserving freedom and her friends: a reading of Coleridge's *Watchman*, *Yearbook of English Studies*, 19: 208–18.

KITSON, PETER. 1993. 'The Whore of Babylon and the Woman in White: Coleridge's radical Unitarian language. In *Coleridge's Visionary Languages: Essays in Honour of John Beer*, ed. Timothy Fulford and M. D. Paley. Cambridge: D. S. Brewer, 1–14.

KOOY, MICHAEL JOHN. 1999. Coleridge, Malta and the 'Life of Ball': How Public Service shaped *The Friend*. *The Wordsworth Circle*, 30: 102–8.

—— 2003*a*. Disinterested patriotism: Bishop Butler, Hazlitt and Coleridge's quarto pamphlet of 1798. *Coleridge Bulletin: The Journal of the Friends of Coleridge*, 21: 55–65.

—— 2003*b*. Differences Between friends: Coleridge, Ball, and the politics of eulogy. *European Romantic Review*, 14 (4): 441–51.

LEADER, ZACHARY. 1998. Coleridge and the uses of journalism. *In Grub Street and the Ivory Tower: Literary Journalism and Literary Scholarship from Fielding to the Internet*, ed. Jeremy Treglown and Bridget Bennett. Oxford: Oxford University Press.

LEASK, NIGEL. 1988. *The Politics of Imagination in Coleridge's Critical Thought*. London: Macmillan.

McGANN, JEROME. 1983. *The Romantic Ideology: A Critical Investigation*. Chicago: Chicago University Press.

MAGNUSON, PAUL. 1998. *Reading Public Romanticism*. Princeton: Princeton University Press.

MAHONEY, CHARLES W. 2002. *Romantics and Renegades: The Poetics of Political Reaction*. Basingstoke: Palgrave.

MALACHUK, DANIEL S. 2000. Coleridge's republicanism and the aphorism in *Aids to Reflection*. *Studies in Romanticism*. 39 (3): 397–417.

MANENT, PIERRE. 1998. Charles Péguy: between political faith and faith. *In Modern Liberty and its Discontents*, trans. Daniel J. Seaton and Paul Mahoney. Lanham: Rowman & Littlefield, 79–81.

MEE, JON. 2003. *Romanticism, Enthusiasm and Regulation: Poetics and the Policing of Culture in the Romantic Period*. Oxford: Oxford University Press.

MILBANK, JOHN. 1987. Divine logos and human communication: a recuperation of Coleridge. *Zeitschrift für systematische Thelologie und Religionsphilosophie*, 29: 56–74.

—— 2004. The gift of ruling: secularization and political authority. *New Blackfriars*, 85: 212–38.

—— 2006. *Theology and Social Theory: Beyond Secular Reason*, 2nd edn. Oxford: Blackwell.

MORROW, JOHN. 1990. *Coleridge's Political Thought: Property, Morality, and the Limits of Traditional Discourse*. New York: St. Martin's Press.

MOULE, C. F. D. 1970. Further reflections on Philippians 2: 5–11. *In Apostolic History and the Gospels*, ed. W. W. Groque and R. P. Martin. Grand Rapids, MI: Eerdmans, 265–76.

MUIRHEAD, JOHN. 1930. *Coleridge as Philosopher*. London: George Allen & Unwin.

MYERS, VICTORIA. 1987. Coleridge's *The Friend*: an experiment in rhetorical theory. *Journal of English and Germanic Philology*, 86 (1): 9–32.

NEWLYN, LUCY. 2000. *Reading, Writing, and Romanticism: The Anxiety of Reception*. Oxford: Oxford University Press.

OWEN, W. J. B. 1971. Review of *The Friend*, ed. Barbara E. Rooke, in *The Review of English Studies*, New Series, 22: 85, 95–8.

PRICKETT, STEPHEN. 1976. *Romanticism and Religion: The Tradition of Coleridge and Wordsworth in the Victorian Church*. Cambridge: Cambridge University Press.

REED, ARDEN. 1980. Coleridge, the sot, and the prostitute: a reading of *The Friend*, Essay XIV. *Studies in Romanticism*, 19: 109–28.

RÉMUSAT, CHARLES DE. 1856. Controverse religieuses en Angleterre, deuxième partie: Coleridge–Arnold. *Revue des deux mondes*, 26 (5): 492–529.

ROE, NICOLAS. 2003. Coleridge's *Watchman* Tour. *Coleridge Bulletin*, New Series 21: 35–46.

—— 1988. *Wordsworth and Coleridge: The Radical Years*. Oxford: Clarendon Press.

SCHULZ, MAX. F. 1971. The new Coleridge. *Modern Philology*, 69 (2): 142–51.

SHAFFER, ELINOR. 1990. Coleridge and Schleiermacher. *In The Coleridge Connection: Essays for Thomas McFarland*, ed. Richard Gravil and Molly Lefebure. London: Macmillan.

SHAW, PHILIP, ed. 2000. *Romantic Wars: Studies in Culture and Conflict, 1793–1822*. Aldershot: Ashgate.

SHAW, PHILIP, 2002. *Waterloo and the Romantic Imagination.* Basingstoke: Palgrave.

WATSON, J. R. 2004. *Romanticism and War: A Study of British Romantic Period Writers and the Napoleonic Wars.* Basingstoke: Palgrave Macmillan.

WHITTAKER, ROBIN. 2003. Tourist, tradesman—or troublemaker? Coleridge's visit to Worcester, 1796. *Coleridge Bulletin,* New Series 21: 47–54.

CHAPTER 9

COLERIDGE IN THE NEWSPAPERS, PERIODICALS, AND ANNUALS

ANGELA ESTERHAMMER

COLERIDGE the periodical writer cuts quite a different figure from Coleridge the philosopher or theologian, and from the Coleridge normally encountered by students in courses on Romantic poetry. In periodical publications, Coleridge appears—sometimes sequentially and sometimes simultaneously—as a political journalist, a social commentator, an extemporizer of epigrams, and a contributor of sentimental verse to annual anthologies. All this activity is crucial to his place in literary and cultural history, not only because it was so extensive, but because it is inseparable from his creative temperament and from the way his contemporaries perceived him. This aspect of Coleridge's career addresses the issue raised by Marilyn Butler when she questions the reason for Coleridge's high profile and lasting influence: 'Coleridge is universally felt to be a great writer, but it is hard to define his greatness precisely in terms of what he wrote' (69). His significance in the history of literature and culture, in other words, does not seem entirely accounted for by the rather small corpus of great poetry and large amount of amorphous, tortuous prose that he produced. Butler suggests that the often overlooked component may be Coleridge's 'characteristic posture' as a public intellectual: he is the first exemplar of the 'modern journalist', a figure who represents 'one of the innovations of [the Romantic] period' (70–1). If this is so, then studying Coleridge's periodical writing in light of the audiences for whom it was written and by whom it was consumed should provide vital insight into both the man and his times.

This chapter will explore Coleridge's role as a public man of letters by highlighting two factors that seem crucial to his own conception of that role. One is the act of what I will call 'public writing'; the other concerns the relation between writing and temporality. 'Public writing' is the textual counterpart to 'public speaking', and both these activities were essential to Coleridge's self-development during the 1790s. Public writing involves formulating one's thoughts and articulating them in language in the face of a large and diverse audience; it involves a high degree of self-consciousness about the effect one's words will have, and a self-reflexive awareness of how, even during the process of composition, the public context affects what gets formulated, written, and published. The second factor—temporality—points to the constraints of time and occasion that are involved in writing 'periodically'. Most obviously, there is the pressure of composing to deadline, a constraint on the process of composition that can render it prone to cliché, provisionality, and the re-use and commodification of pre-existing material. Evident in Coleridge's journalistic prose of the 1790s, these qualities are also reflected in the poetry he later published in periodicals of the 1820s, which consist of 'lines', 'effusions', and, in one case, a full-scale thematization of spontaneous composition in a text entitled 'The Improvisatore'. Periodical publication in the daily newspaper, in monthly magazines, or in annuals also commits the writer to *occasionality*: to a sense of the moment, a dependence on material events, and a need to respond to these events as they happen. This occasionality is reflected in the title 'The Men and the Times' that Coleridge used for a couple of his essays in the *Morning Post* in 1803. It was also his proposed title for the volume in which he intended, at one time, to collect his journalistic prose. Although he never realized the plan himself, Sara Coleridge collected and published much of her father's newspaper journalism in a three-volume edition entitled *Essays on His Own Times* (1850). Under the similar title *Essays on His Times*, supplemented by additional items newly discovered or newly attributed to Coleridge since his daughter's edition, Coleridge's newspaper writings have entered the *Collected Coleridge*, where the three volumes dedicated to his journalism give access to a distinctive aspect of his career.

Coleridge published in newspapers, magazines, and annuals throughout his life; indeed, the poetry volumes of the *Collected Coleridge* reveal that most of his poetry first appeared in one or another periodical publication. But two epochs of intense involvement with periodicals call for special attention: 1797–1803, when Coleridge was writing prose and poetry regularly for the London daily papers, and the 1820s, when the growth in popularity of literary magazines and annuals coincided with his need for a new audience. Before focusing on those two periods, however, it is worth gaining an overview of the full extent of Coleridge's involvement with periodical publications. His earliest poetry appeared in the *Morning Chronicle*, a radical London newspaper, the first clearly identified contribution being the ode 'To Fortune, on Buying a Ticket in the Irish Lottery' on 7 November 1793. The poem was signed 'S. T. C.' and prefaced by an introductory note in which Coleridge already signalled his ambivalent attitude toward the publication venue by addressing the editor of the *Chronicle* 'with more respect and gratitude than I ordinarily feel for Editors of Papers' (*PW* 16.2.1: 123). Other poems, including a series of 'Sonnets to Eminent Characters', followed in the same paper during 1794 and 1795, along with occasional publications in the radical *Cambridge Intelligencer* and *Telegraph*, and the liberal *Monthly Magazine*. Coleridge's reasons for writing for newspapers and magazines during these years were both ideological and pragmatic, one of the most pointed examples of the latter being his scheme to sell *The Rime of the Ancient Mariner* to the *Monthly Magazine* for five pounds, in order to raise money for a walking tour in Wales. More ideologically, he claims in the Prospectus to *The Watchman* that it is the urgent mission of all 'Friends of Freedom, of Reason, and of Human Nature' to 'supply or circulate political information' (*Watchman* 5), and he acknowledges the 'almost winged communication of the Press', referring to newspapers as 'the vast conductors...by the which the electric fluid of truth was conveyed from man to man, and nation to nation' (*Lects. 1795*, 313). Motivated by these views, and by his need for a means of support, Coleridge sought in 1796 to join the staff of the London *Telegraph*, and at one point apparently accepted James Perry's invitation to become co-editor of the *Morning Chronicle*, although the job never materialized. His attempt to publish an independent periodical of his own, *The Watchman*, also belongs to this period, its ten issues appearing between March and May of 1796.

In November 1797, at age twenty-five, Coleridge accepted an invitation to became a regular writer for the *Morning Post*, one of the most important London newspapers; by the end of Coleridge's involvement with it in the early 1800s, it was the paper with by far the largest circulation. According to Coleridge himself, the *Morning Post* had to address the tastes of a readership consisting of '[Lond]on Coffee house men & breakfast-table People of Quality' (*CL* 1: 627), although it is worth contrasting his perception of the target audience with that of Mary Robinson, who wrote in 1800 that 'the daily prints fall into the hands of all classes'.[1] Mary Robinson and Robert Southey regularly contributed poetry to the *Morning Post*; Wordsworth did so on a few occasions. From 1797 to 1803, Coleridge's poetry often appeared in the *Post*; in addition, for a significant portion of those years he was the paper's main writer of editorials and essays on foreign and domestic politics, and for a few months its parliamentary reporter. When Coleridge's friend and editor Daniel Stuart sold the paper in 1803, Coleridge moved with him to an evening daily, the *Courier*. Although Coleridge was very heavily involved in newspaper journalism as the deputy editor of the *Courier* in 1811–12, he generally had an on-again, off-again relationship with the paper until 1818. This was a less satisfying professional role for Coleridge than his involvement with the *Morning Post*, in part

---

[1] 'Present State of the Manners and Society of the Metropolis', *Monthly Magazine* (November 1800), 305; quoted in Craciun, 21.

because of ongoing differences with the *Courier*'s managing editor. It was also a role less respected by Coleridge's readers, then and now, because the *Courier* was regarded as a paper in the pay of the Tory government. At the same time, Coleridge was trying to keep his own periodical, *The Friend*, afloat, and Deirdre Coleman suggests that the *Courier* functioned for him mainly as an outlet, or even a dumping-ground, for writing that was too committed to politics and current affairs to be suitable for *The Friend* (Coleman, 137). As will be discussed later in this chapter, after Coleridge's relationship with the *Courier* ended and *The Friend* folded, both in 1818, he began a phase of involvement with some of the new literary magazines and the annual gift-books that dominated the periodical scene in the early nineteenth century.

Like other aspects of Coleridge's life and career, his engagement with the periodicals is marked by inconsistency and paradox. He disparages his own journalistic activity, often suggesting that he only resorts to it because he badly needs the money. Yet he glories in the increased readership and the direct political influence that he claims to achieve through his almost daily appearances in the *Morning Post* in the years around 1800. He complains of the drain on his time from writing editorials, political commentary, and parliamentary reports for the London papers, yet it is while he is writing such pieces that he produces the greatest poetry of his life—a significant amount of it first published in those same papers. If this ambivalence mirrors Coleridge's personal conflicts, it also corresponds to a prevailing attitude among 'literary' authors toward newspapers and magazines at the end of the eighteenth century, when the growing number of these publications and their effect on society were forces to be reckoned with.[2] 'Journalism was not a respectable career in the late eighteenth century', notes one recent study of Coleridge's journalistic activity (Hessell, 46); yet Wordsworth, Hazlitt, Lamb, Mary Robinson, and many other well-known literary figures wrote for the newspapers, all the while expressing conflicted attitudes toward this very activity.

Most modern critics of Coleridge's journalism have focused on what it reveals about his political commitments—or, more precisely, about the apparent lack of commitment demonstrated by his oscillation between radical and conservative positions during his stints at the *Morning Post* and the *Courier*, as well as his more definitive abandonment of radicalism for conservatism over the longer term. On one hand, Coleridge's biographer Richard Holmes credits him with showing a new maturity and sobriety in his opinions during his stint as an editorial writer for the *Morning Post*. Coleridge shaped the new, moderate stance of the paper, according to Holmes, by attacking fanaticism and extremism on both sides of the political spectrum and calling for 'the creation of a moderate, centralized body of liberal

---

[2] Cf. Jon Klancher's seminal study *The Making of English Reading Audiences, 1790–1832*. While Klancher concentrates on the rise of weekly and monthly periodicals more than daily newspapers, his argument about the role of all these publications in factionalizing society into middle-class, mass, and radical readerships demonstrates their potentially disruptive and disturbing effect on Romantic readers and writers.

opinion' (Holmes, 255). But most critics are less sanguine about Coleridge's retreat from radicalism. E. P. Thompson memorably expressed astonishment and revulsion at Coleridge's journalism in a 1979 review essay, after David V. Erdman's edition of the *Essays on His Times* made the full extent of these articles available to modern readers for the first time. According to Thompson, Coleridge 'is chiefly of interest, in his political writings, as an example of the intellectual complexity of apostasy' (149). 'These articles . . . are, in the main, both irresponsible and unprincipled', he continues; 'they are also badly written' (152). Thompson's scorn for these journalistic performances is barely alleviated by his awareness that Coleridge's shifts of political position largely reflect the oscillating stance of the papers he wrote for,[3] or that the papers' oscillation was motivated by government censorship and attempts to avoid prosecution. According to Thompson, Coleridge let himself be used by the unprincipled editors of the *Post* and the *Courier*; indeed, he allowed himself 'to be turned on and off like a tap' because 'he needed the money' (153). Alan Liu offers a less affect-laden response to Coleridge's journalism and the practice of the *Morning Post*—commenting (in stark contrast to Thompson's remark that the articles are 'badly written') that 'what is ultimately most remarkable about Coleridge's writings in the *Post* is the brilliancy of their rhetoric' (425). Yet Liu also interprets the political content of the articles negatively as apostasy and opportunism—albeit an epoch-making kind of opportunism in which we can now locate the origin of the modern posture of journalistic impartiality.

The notion of *impartiality* first surfaces in Coleridge's own, retrospective view of his 1790s journalism. In his recollections in *Biographia Literaria*, he congratulates himself for developing a journalistic stance whose appeal to readers manifested itself directly in terms of a substantial increase in circulation:

The rapid and unusual increase in the sale of the Morning Post is a sufficient pledge, that genuine impartiality with a respectable portion of literary talent will secure the success of a newspaper without the aid of party or ministerial patronage. But by impartiality I mean an honest and enlightened adherence to a code of intelligible principles previously announced, and faithfully referred to in support of every judgment on men and events; not indiscriminate abuse, not the indulgence of an editor's own malignant passions, and still less, if that be possible, a determination to make money by flattering the envy and cupidity, the vindictive restlessness and self-conceit of the half-witted vulgar[.]   (*BL* 1: 214)

But 'apostasy', too, is Coleridge's own term. It is an accusation he hyperconsciously seeks to avoid when he realizes that readers will think he has changed his position (cf. *On the Constitution*, 8). More generally, the image contained in the word 'apostasy'—literally, 'standing apart'—is integral to Coleridge's journalistic self-representation. His most frequent and famous by-line in the *Morning Post*

[3] Cf. Erdman, 'Coleridge as Editorial Writer', 186: 'Before [April 1798] the *Morning Post* was committed to peace and reform; some time in 1802–1803 it became committed to war; when it was sold in 1803 it had become pretty obviously a government paper, with particular attachment to the Prince of Wales. In the middle period it was an oscillating paper—and Coleridge was in his element.'

and other periodical publications is ΕΣΤΗΣΕ or 'Es tee see': a pun on the initials 'S. T. C.' that Coleridge himself translated '*He hath stood*—which in these times of apostacy [*sic*] from the principles of Freedom, or of Religion in this country, & from both by the same persons in France, is no unmeaning Signature' (*CL* 2: 867). Coleridge's frequent plays on 'stance' and 'apostasy' invite rebuttals in kind from his contemporaries, as well as from modern critics of his journalism. Thus Jerome Christiansen and Alan Liu both identify apostasy, understood as a philosophical position or a habit of thought, as the inherent structural principle of Coleridge's journalistic essays. 'As a political philosopher *qua* political philosopher', Christiansen writes, 'Coleridge was always slightly away from a political position; never a Jacobin revolutionary or a Burkean compromiser, he was always technically an *apostate*. Coleridge's career does show a continuity: once an apostate always an apostate' (464). After a lucid analysis of Coleridge's writing style and patterns of thought in the *Morning Post* essays, Alan Liu also concludes that Coleridge made a career of being an apostate: one who 'hath stood' in several different spots, sometimes even elaborating two opposed positions at once. 'Coleridge's political journalism', according to Liu, 'elaborates what is essentially a logic of dialectic, of an ever-moving structure of thesis and antithesis' (421). But Liu goes one step further to suggest that, in the refulgent rhetoric of Coleridge's *Morning Post* essays, the display of 'dialectical imagination' (423) outdoes itself and overflows into 'poetic representation' (425–6). In other words, Coleridge is ultimately not so much taking a stand as '*performing* the act of taking a stand'. With this recognition of the performative aspect of Coleridge's journalism, as manifested in the prominent self-consciousness of his *Morning Post* contributions, we return to the concept of 'public writing' and the question of Coleridge's self-representation as a public intellectual.

While the political stance of Coleridge's journalism has been productively explored by the critics mentioned above, among others,[4] less attention has been paid to Coleridge's appearance in the periodicals in relation to his evolving sense of language as public performance. To explore this aspect of his periodical prose and poetry, it is necessary to consider in greater detail how Coleridge's contributions would have appeared to Romantic-era newspaper readers, and how this context might have proleptically influenced the composition of these same contributions as

---

[4] In addition to extensive scholarship on Coleridge's politics during the 1790s, important studies of his journalistic activity include Deirdre Coleman's overview of Coleridge as 'The Journalist' in *The Cambridge Companion to Coleridge*. Coleman concentrates mainly on Coleridge's independent periodical projects, *The Watchman* and *The Friend* (see Michael John Kooy's essay in the present volume). In 'Coleridge and the Uses of Journalism', Zachary Leader writes primarily about Coleridge's own attitude toward his journalistic activity, comparing the disparate comments he made about it at different points in his career, and concluding that his recognition of periodical writing as an inferior activity actually enhanced his aptitude for the more elevated pursuits of poetry and philosophy. A recent dissertation by Nicola Anne Hessell focuses on Coleridge's contributions to the *Morning Post* in 1799–1800, seeking to place these in the context of 'the practical and occupational constraints that governed newspaper journalism in the late eighteenth and early nineteenth centuries' (6).

instances of 'public writing'. Published every day except Sunday, the *Morning Post* was a closely printed four-page news-sheet that, like other contemporary dailies, featured extremely miscellaneous commercial, intellectual, and social content. The first page began by listing that evening's performances in the London theatres, and continued with advertisements of all types, from real estate, to new products and books on the market, to personals, to job listings; more ads filled up the end of the paper, on the second half of page four. Pages two and three, and part of page four, contained essays on foreign and domestic affairs, original poetry (sometimes), reviews of plays, concerts, lectures, and other performances, society news, shipping news, crime news and bankrupts, and a few notices of births, marriages, and deaths. The commercial 'outside' of the paper (pages one and four) thus provided a cover, of sorts, for the more content-laden sections inside on pages two and three. The editorial on page two, usually called the 'leading paragraph' or 'leader', was key; as Hessell notes, 'It was extremely important for any daily newspaper to have an effective leading article, which was one of two features (the other being the quality of parliamentary reporting) by which a daily was judged' (20). This leader, which was normally unsigned, is the piece that Coleridge most often contributed when he wrote for the *Post* and the *Courier*. On other days, readers might find poetry by Coleridge, usually published under a pseudonym, in the 'Original Poetry' section that followed the leading paragraph.

The *Morning Post* for the autumn months of 1802 makes a valuable case-study of Coleridge's presence in the London periodicals between 1797 and 1818, even if his involvement during these few months was too intense to be quite typical. These issues of the *Post* demonstrate the diversity and (conversely) the recurring themes of Coleridge's periodical writing, as well as the magnitude of his presence in the public eye during the era when he was most heavily involved in the London periodical scene. During the fall of 1802, one of the four thousand or so subscribers to the *Morning Post*, or the much larger number of readers who happened to pick up a copy in a household or a coffee-house, would read something by Coleridge in it every second or third day. It might be a poem as weighty as the 'Dejection' ode, or else punning epigrams and other light verse, translations and adaptations of German poetry, reports and analyses of current events in France, commentary and critique of domestic politics, or, in November and December, the five-part romantic adventure of the 'Maid of Buttermere'.

While this array of contributions displays Coleridge's range, a number of themes recur throughout the disparate material, including a persistent consciousness of the impact of public utterance, and the significance of public self-representation in language. The *Morning Post* of 14 October 1802 featured a revised reprint of Coleridge's 'France: An Ode', which had originally appeared in the *Post* under the title 'The Recantation' on 16 April 1798. On its first appearance, the poem already announced itself as a public speech-act. It bore an editorial head-note underlining the significance of 'Mr. COLERIDGE's decision to utter his critique of France in the public press: 'What we most admire, is the *avowal* of his sentiments, and public censure of the unprincipled and atrocious conduct of France' (*PW* 16.2.1: 585; italics in original). The revised version, appearing almost exactly four and a half years later, also carried a head-note emphasizing, first, the provisional state of the poem as originally published in 1798, and, second, the timeliness of the re-publication:

The following ODE was first published in this paper (in the beginning of the year 1798) *in a less perfect state*. The *present state* of France, and Switzerland, gives it so peculiar an interest *at this present time*, that we wished to re-publish it, and accordingly have procured from the Author, a corrected copy.   (*PW* 16.2.1: 586; italics added)

The head-note thus seizes on an opportune moment for re-publication, in light of the state of the poem as well as the state of European politics. Underlining the sense that the poem is intended as a momentous public statement is the fact that it carries Coleridge's full signature: 'An Ode: By S. T. Coleridge'. The declaration of authorship contrasts prominently with the pseudonym ΕΣΤΗΣΕ with which he signed most of his poetic contributions to the *Morning Post* at the time, and with the anonymity of his editorials.

'France: An Ode' is, to a large extent, a poem about the sources and effects of verbal declarations, especially those that seek to define 'liberty' in an age of political turmoil. Behind the ode lies an awareness that public political discourse—such as the new French constitution, or the official correspondence between the British government and Bonaparte, topics on which Coleridge had published several editorials in 1798–1800—use words like 'liberty', 'rights', 'people', and 'nation' *performatively*. That is, they bring new definitions for these words into being in the process of uttering them, while at the same time concealing this process of re-definition and pretending, instead, that the words represent independently exist-ing, objective constants that authorize or legitimate the declaration. 'France: An Ode' critiques these attempts to appropriate the definition of liberty insofar as Coleridge addresses himself *to* Liberty, thus implicitly positing 'Liberty' as an external power beyond the control of his discourse. Throughout the poem, he dissociates liberty from societal institutions and their speech-acts, asserting instead that it is a language of nature apprehensible only by the spirit. The ode thus distinguishes the '*spirit* of . . . Liberty' (line 21), evoked by conversation with the elements of nature, from 'the *name* / Of Freedom', ironically inscribed on chains with which the French have bound themselves: 'In mad game / They break their manacles, and wear the name / Of Freedom graven on an heavier chain' (lines 86–8).[5] Coleridge's contempt for the mere 'name' of freedom, here emphasized by the half-rhyme of 'name' and 'chain', picks up on other contemporary references to the abuse of inflammatory but empty terms—notably, the term 'Jacobin' in the

---

[5] Unless otherwise indicated, Coleridge's poetry is quoted in the versions that appeared in the periodicals under discussion.

essay that Coleridge was preparing for the *Morning Post* at same time, which will be discussed below. 'France: An Ode' offers the poet's conversation with nature as a corrective to the misapplied speech-acts that brought about the French Revolution, the ensuing wars, and the French invasion of Switzerland. Its concluding stanza dissociates liberty from imperialist and institutional discourses—from the 'victor's strain', from 'priestcraft' and 'blasphemy'. While admitting that he himself once sought liberty in these forms of human utterance and power ('with profitless endeavour / Have I pursued thee many a weary hour', lines 89–90), Coleridge now locates 'LIBERTY' in an unpeopled landscape, representing it not as a word that is heard, but a spirit that is felt:

> And there I felt thee! On yon sea-cliff's verge,
>   Whose pines just travell'd by the breeze above,
> Had made one murmur with the distant surge—
>   Yes! as I stood and gaz'd, my forehead bare,
>   And shot my being thro' earth, sea, and air,
> Possessing all things by intensest love—
>   O LIBERTY! my spirit felt thee there! (lines 99–105)

If this is the tendency of the poem's rhetoric and its reflection on political abuses of language, though, the context of the ode's appearance in the daily newspaper complicates its message.[6] Writing publicly in the London newspaper in 1802, Coleridge is the antithesis of a solitary figure in a landscape, lost in spiritual contemplation of liberty. Instead, the rhetorical context is that of a newspaper negotiating its stance within a volatile and potentially dangerous political landscape, and the poet is a professional writer all too conscious that in order to wrest the definition of 'liberty' from foreign or domestic antagonists, he must himself exercise verbal authority in a public statement. Rather than locating Liberty beyond the factionalism of human discourse, the ode ultimately seems to rescue liberty from the control of collective discourses, not to say the frenzy of the French revolutionary mob, by appropriating it to an authoritative individual voice—that of the poet-journalist. This movement from collective to individual authority realizes the terms set out in the 'Argument' that precedes the poem's five stanzas in the *Morning Post*, which describes the poem as

An address to Liberty, in which the Poet expresses his conviction, that those feelings, and that grand *ideal*, of freedom, which the mind attains by its contemplation of its individual nature, and of the sublime surrounding objects . . . do not belong to men, as a society, nor can possibly be either gratified, or realised, under any form of human government; but

---

[6] This aspect of my reading of 'France: An Ode' is in sympathy with Paul Magnuson's interpretation of Coleridge's poetry in the context of 'public Romanticism'—that is, with attention to 'the meanings of [a poem's] themes and figures that exist in the public discourse before the poem is written' ('Politics', 3). The periodical publication venues of Coleridge's poetry are central to Magnuson's argument in *Reading Public Romanticism*.

belong to the individual man, so far as he is pure, and inflamed with the love and adoration of God in Nature.   (*PW* 16.2.1: 587)

If the claim, here, is that the individual mind must be at liberty to discover liberty for itself, rather than allowing a definition of 'liberty' to be imposed by the rhetoric of factions or institutions, the reality of the context is that the individual writer—conspicuously named 'S. T. Coleridge'—takes responsibility for defining it in a carefully positioned and timely declaration. The public context of newspaper publication, which re-orients yet re-affirms the public context that attaches to the genre of the ode since its Classical origins, is reinforced by the courtroom metaphor in the poem's sub-text. Ultimately, the scene of discourse that 'France: An Ode' evokes is that of a courtroom trial, in which the poet is called to account for previous offences against the spirit of liberty. In the first two stanzas, he asks the natural world to 'bear witness' for him; in stanza three, he formally recalls his own speech-acts so that he can formally recant them; in stanza four, he petitions Liberty to forgive his misinformed words and thoughts. Last but not least, the re-published ode is followed in the *Morning Post* of 14 October 1802 by extracts from 'a Poem by the same Author'—namely, 'Fears in Solitude', which was also first published in 1798. These extracts are patently chosen so as to reinforce the public representation of the 'Author' as a loyal British subject and a steadfast Christian. Thus, the diction and imagery of 'France: An Ode', the choice of excerpts from 'Fears in Solitude', the framing of both poems with an 'Argument' and head-notes, and the use of the authorial signature all reflect a consciousness of how the words will be read in *this* newspaper at *this* political moment. The poems manifest all the features of public writing.

A week after the re-publication of 'France: An Ode' and 'Fears in Solitude', the *Morning Post* ran an anonymous editorial by Coleridge under the title 'Once a Jacobin Always a Jacobin'. This essay echoes the political message of the two poems—that is, a *volte-face* from Coleridge's earlier radicalism—as well as their self-conscious reflection on the language of public declarations. The title itself ironically quotes an insult hurled at suspected radicals by the reactionary press and by government ministers, and Coleridge immediately makes clear that he is paraphrasing William Pitt himself, accusing him of uttering 'once a Jacobin always a Jacobin' as an unproven 'blank assertion' (*EOT* 1: 367). 'What *is* a Jacobin?' Coleridge then asks, rhetorically, and his answer in this essay is that all too often 'Jacobin' is no more than 'a term of abuse, the convenient watch-word of a faction' (*EOT* 1: 367). It is a signifier detached from any signified, that derives its force from the self-interest and assumed authority of the speaker. Coleridge confidently shows how words *act* instead of signifying, how the utterance 'once a Jacobin always a Jacobin' has been used for the sake of its perlocutionary force by eliding the vagueness of its locutionary significance—in other words, how affect has entirely displaced meaning. To counter this injurious application of the performative

'Jacobin', Coleridge fills three newspaper columns with his own definition of the term, listing and elaborating the 'definite ideas' that, he claims, responsible users of the word attach to it. Supplying eight numbered points that make up the 'Jacobin's Creed', Coleridge explicitly undertakes a desynonymization of 'Jacobin' from the neighbouring words 'Republican', 'Demagogue', and 'Democrat'. His article astutely distinguishes between the meaning and the force of an utterance, and warns about the damage to civil society when force—which is to say, an illegitimate 'meaning' that derives solely from the power and menace of the speaker—is allowed to displace true meaning, which should derive from definite, articulate ideas. What Coleridge thereby (necessarily) conceals is the extent to which his (or any) definition still depends on alternative forms of authority—in this case, the anonymous public voice of the leader-writer of a London daily. *He* is, after all, the one now defining what a 'Jacobin' is in his public writing. When such a writer proclaims the definition of a Jacobin 'in *our* sense of the term' (*EOT* 1: 368), he is replacing one authority with another; his voice manifestly gains in conviction over the course of the article until, he writes, 'we dare be confident, that no other sense can be given' to the word Jacobin than that 'which we have here detailed' (*EOT* 1: 370–1). Even more insidiously, the 'we' that undertakes to re-define the term then disappears entirely behind an anonymous assertion of the new definition. Thus Coleridge's language, in turn, assumes the authority to transform postulates into assertions and subjective utterance into general truth.

Coleridge's own conviction that the 'Jacobin' essay constituted a significant public statement—even an innovation in journalistic practice—is shown by his decision to reprint an excerpt from it in *The Friend* (no. 10, 1809), and his reference to it in chapter ten of *Biographia Literaria*. In the *Biographia*, it is the first example he offers to show how his *Morning Post* essays 'contributed to introduce the practice of placing the questions and events of the day in a moral point of view' (*BL* 1: 217). 'I dare assume to myself', Coleridge continues, 'the merit of having first explicitly defined and analyzed the nature of Jacobinism; and that in distinguishing the jacobin from the republican, the democrat, and the mere demagogue, I . . . rescued the word from remaining a mere term of abuse.' To the extent that Coleridge achieves such a rehabilitation of words in his periodical essays, it depends on a heightened awareness of the public uses and abuses of language, and on an exercise of the often anonymous authority of the newspaper editorialist.

'Once a Jacobin Always a Jacobin' appeared between the first and second installments of what became a five-part series in the *Morning Post* (11 October to 31 December 1802) on the celebrated case of the 'Beauty of Buttermere'. These reports, sent by Coleridge from Keswick, chronicled a local scandal in the Lake District, but they soon took on the character of a serialized romance—a 'novel of real life', as Coleridge himself called it (*EOT* 1: 374). The story is one of identity theft and seduction, featuring a con man who, falsely assuming the name of a gentleman and Member of Parliament, deceived the virtuous daughter of an innkeeper in the village of Buttermere into a bigamous marriage, before being exposed and arrested. While the romance, sensationalism, and suspense of the unfolding story caused it to be picked up by several other newspapers besides the *Morning Post*, and made it 'the talk of London' in the fall of 1802 (Holmes, 339), the imposter, John Hatfield, may have interested Coleridge, albeit unconsciously, as a darker reflection of himself. Described as commanding 'an astonishing flow of words' and 'conversation...of that sort, which is the most generally delightful' (*EOT* 1: 406), the imposter presents himself to Keswick society under a pseudonym, using his conversational skills to obtain love and money. In some lights, Hatfield might look like a criminal-comical counterpart to Coleridge himself, a pseudonymous or anonymous writer scheming to attract a sympathetic audience for himself and subscribers for his newspaper.

Thus, in a variety of forms across the disparate topics and genres treated in Coleridge's *Morning Post* contributions in the autumn of 1802, we see him reflecting publicly on the significance of public declarations and self-(mis)representations. Richard Holmes suggests that this orientation may be determined by Coleridge's nature as well as his environment: his 'ebullient temperament, his exuberance and exhibitionism', according to Holmes, perfectly suited the primary occupations he undertook during his twenties—journalism and lecturing (176). Character and occupation spurred one another: Coleridge's talent for verbal and other kinds of performance, his 'public character', made him a rather successful and substantially original kind of journalist, while his extensive engagement with the London periodical papers fuelled his pre-existing interest in public discourse and its effects. Seizing the moment when newspapers and literary magazines began to intervene seriously in their times, Coleridge's journalism constitutes an occasion-bound, audience-oriented mode of writing.

A remark by Daniel Stuart, owner of the *Morning Post*, suggests that Coleridge needed the venue of the daily papers as much as they needed him. 'To write the leading paragraph of a newspaper', Stuart wrote,

> I would prefer him [Coleridge] to Mackintosh, Burke, or any man I ever heard of. His observations not only were confirmed by good sense, but displayed extensive knowledge, deep thought and well-grounded foresight; they were so brilliantly ornamented, so classically delightful. They were the writings of a Scholar, a Gentleman and a Statesman, without personal sarcasm or illiberality of any kind. But when Coleridge wrote in his study without being pressed, he wandered and lost himself.   (quoted in *EOT* 1: lxvii)

Often quoted as a measure of Coleridge's reputation as a journalist, this comment also bears witness to Coleridge's psychological need for the double demands of time pressure and a public venue, not only in order to *express* his ideas, but in order to develop them in the first place. Stuart suggests elsewhere that many of Coleridge's leading paragraphs originated orally in conversations between Coleridge and himself, and were written down just in time to go to press in the evening (cf. *EOT* 1: lxii–lxiii). Later, Coleridge also referred explicitly to the continuity between his conversation and his newspaper writing, offering to submit to the *Courier* occasional pieces prompted by his own reading of the newspaper, paragraphs 'which I might as well write as talk' (*CL* 4: 891). Evidently his ability to light on and develop ideas orally in the presence of a listener or audience, which he is practising throughout these years in his often extemporized public lectures, carried over directly into his journalism.

Despite Coleridge's hierarchical valorization of what he called 'truly *genial*' writing over newspaper work (*BL* 1: 224), the awareness of a newspaper-reading public was congenial to his habits of mind. Coleridge encountered the members of this public every day when he lived in London; the readership of the next morning's or evening's paper was a constant, expectant presence, at only a slightly further remove than the audience in a lecture hall awaiting the next words of Coleridge the speaker. The consciousness of an audience gives Coleridge's appearances in the periodicals, like his appearances in the lecture hall, a performative quality manifested in the distinctive features of public writing: the sense of declarative authority that it has in common with political, governmental, or other institutional utterances, and, on the other hand, the provisional quality of writing that is obliged to be both temporal and timely (in all the various senses of those words). In the periodicals, Coleridge frames his words in the face of an expectant public, knowing that he may be held to account for those words even as he is holding government ministers to account for their proclamations, speeches, and correspondence.

Coleridge's predilection for extempore composition was also a good fit with the conditions of the periodical press. The regular, frequent, and inflexible deadlines imposed by the daily press submit the development of ideas and the organization of language to the immediate constraints of time, especially in the case of editorials, which are based on the news as it happens and therefore cannot be prepared in advance. The temporality of writing might be disrupted by delays in the arrival of new information, forcing the editorial writer to re-work older news while still attempting to give readers the impression that something fresh and significant is being said. As Hessell notes, the unpredictable rhythm of 1790s journalism created an 'episodic temporal structure' that favoured writing about the same events or issues repeatedly in provisional form—and, she continues, this made the daily newspaper 'almost an ideal forum for [Coleridge's] talents as a writer, mirroring and maximizing some of his characteristic strengths in conversation and literature' (Hessell, 75). At the same time, the newspaper must, by rousing its readers' anticipation and suspense, induce them to buy future issues. The *Morning Post* is full of notices that such-and-such an article, essay, or continuation of a series, will appear 'to-morrow' (Erdman's edition of *Essays on His Times* reproduces these notices whenever they relate to pieces by Coleridge)—although many 'to-morrows' often pass before the promised piece actually appears. While such promises and delaying tactics may appear typically Coleridgean, they are also the intrinsic rhythm of the medium for which he was writing during the 1790s and early 1800s.

Yet the demanding temporality of periodical writing often weighed on Coleridge's mind. He felt his job at the *Morning Post* to be time-consuming work, writing to Thomas Wedgwood in October 1802 that it took up three days a week (*CL* 2: 876), and complaining that he felt enslaved to it. 'We Newspaper scribes are true Galley-Slaves', he laments, and, shortly after, 'I shall give up this Newspaper Business—it is too, too fatiguing' (*CL* 1: 569)—although he also notes that 'Newspaper writing is comparative extacy [*sic*]' compared to the drudgery of translation (*CL* 1: 583). After launching *The Watchman*, Coleridge made the wry discovery that 'it is one of the disadvantages attendant on my undertaking, that I am obliged to *publish* extempore as well as compose' (*CL* 1: 191). Writing for the *Morning Post*, he increasingly finds that the pressure of writing to deadline necessitates an adjustment to a new mode of composition, one that tempts the writer to choose shallow humour and pettiness over intellect and truth. 'The few weeks that I have written for the Morning Post', Coleridge admits to Josiah Wedgwood in 1798,

I have felt this—Something must be written & written immediately... and if any idea of ludicrous personality, or apt antiministerial joke, crosses me, I feel a repugnance at rejecting it, because *something must be written*, and nothing else suitable occurs. The longer I continue a hired paragraph-scribbler, the more powerful these Temptations will become.   (*CL* 1: 365)

Zachary Leader, in a recent article on Coleridge as a journalist, explores the distinction that developed for Coleridge between rapidly composed, provisional, timely, and pragmatic newspaper-writing, and the more elevated pursuits of poetry and philosophy. 'I think there are but 2 good ways of writing—one for immediate, & wide impression, tho' transitory—the other for permanence—/ Newspapers the first—the best one can do is the second', Coleridge writes to Thomas Poole in 1800 (*CL* 1: 582). The poetry that Coleridge contributed to the papers generally was not subject to the same deadline pressure as his prose articles; his verse submissions were more likely to be previously written pieces that he sent in when something was needed for the poetry corner. Still, some of Coleridge's poetry manifests characteristics typical of 1790s newspaper verse. 'The Apotheosis, or, The Snow-Drop', for instance, which was written in response to a poem of Mary Robinson's and published in the *Morning Post* on 3 January 1798, participates in the stylized, public, poetic dialogue associated with the Della Cruscans, whose verses filled the London papers in the late 1780s and 1790s. Coleridge's contributions to the newspaper's poetry corner tend toward timely topics, verses triggered by chance encounters, word-play, and brief, conversational forms such as epigrams. In a letter to William Sotheby in 1802, Coleridge refers to the verse he published in the newspapers as mere 'Experiments' and as 'peritura charta'—perishable or ephemeral writings (*CL* 2: 857). Yet these 'ephemera' include poems that have entered the Romantic canon as enduring and iconic, rather than provisional, such as 'Dejection: An Ode' or 'The Keep-sake'.

In 1800, fourteen of Coleridge's *Morning Post* poems and a few of his epigrams were reprinted in a different kind of periodical publication: the second volume of the *Annual Anthology* edited by Robert Southey. Begun in 1799 on the model of the *Musenalmanach* anthologies being produced in Germany by Bürger, Schiller, and Voss, this was intended as an annual publication for which Southey solicited previously unpublished contributions as well as poems that had been published in the *Morning Post*. But the *Annual Anthology* failed to survive beyond its second volume. Instead, the era of successful 'annuals' addressed to a new, carefully targeted, female audience would begin some twenty years later, and would be an important determining factor in Coleridge's poetic activity during the last decade of his life.

Coleridge's last identifiable publication in the London *Courier* came in 1818, but his reputation as a journalist was such that the *Courier* as well as other periodical publications continued to try to solicit contributions from him. His involvement with periodical literature in the early nineteenth century is bound up with the rapidly changing landscape of the periodical press during this period, including the launch of new, monthly publications aimed at a middle-class, metropolitan audience.[7] John Scott, the editor of one of these new start-ups, the *London Magazine*, wrote to his publisher in 1819 stressing '*the necessity of securing*' Coleridge as a contributor on political issues, but Coleridge regretfully declined the offer on the grounds that he was already committed to *Blackwood's Edinburgh Magazine* at the time (*CL* 4: 975–6). On Coleridge's side, the involvement with *Blackwood's* was motivated by financial necessity, but it turned out unhappily. Although *Blackwood's*, when it was founded in 1817, claimed to offer a new kind of literary reviewing not dominated by political partisanship, it soon became known for biting, often partisan attacks and parodies. It printed a damning review and personal attack on Coleridge himself in October 1817, following the publication of *Biographia Literaria* and *Sibylline Leaves*. Two years later, however, *Blackwood's* appeared to reverse its attitude toward Coleridge, printing a highly laudatory essay on him by John Lockhart. At the same time, in the fall of 1819, Coleridge found himself in a severe financial crisis due to the bankruptcy of the publisher Rest Fenner, who owed him unpaid royalties and held the copyright to his works. *Blackwood's Magazine* was accordingly one of the venues to which he looked in a desperate search for new publishers. He contributed a poem and essay to the magazine in 1819, a series of five letters totalling twenty pages in October 1821, and the essay 'The History and Gests of Maxilian' in January of 1822, along with a

---

[7] Cf. Klancher, Parker, and Higgins on the socio-economic, cultural, and technological developments that caused new weekly and monthly literary magazines to spring up and to form new audience groupings during this era.

last sonnet in June of 1832. Dorothy Wordsworth, for one, found these publications 'dull and unintelligible', and expressed doubt that they could even have been written by Coleridge (Strout, 117).

The annuals or gift-books of the 1820s and 1830s were a different story. As with Southey's abortive *Annual Anthology* a generation earlier, they built on a concept imported from Germany. Rudolph Ackermann's publication of the *Forget-Me-Not* beginning in 1823 launched a fashion for annual anthologies of poetry and engravings, reflected in the increasingly rapid introduction of new publications as well as in burgeoning sales figures. These were generally volumes of small format and affordable price, yet lavishly produced and bound, suitable as presents for middle-class female readers and therefore typically appearing for purchase during the Christmas season. The gender and class ideology perpetuated by the annuals has been cogently analysed recently by, among others, Morton Paley and Peter J. Manning. 'The annuals merchandised not goods *per se* but the elusive promise of refinement', writes Manning (68); their content was sentimental, emphasizing themes of friendship and romantic love but avoiding overt eroticism. These publications also played a part in the emerging culture of celebrity during the late-Romantic and early Victorian periods. The editors sought out contributors who were well-known poets or else titled nobility; they paid high prices for contributions, competed with one another for exclusive publication rights, and not infrequently resorted to unscrupulous tactics to one-up the competition.

The sudden rise in popularity of the annuals was a development in the poetry market with which all the ageing Lake Poets had to come to terms. Robert Southey acknowledged that they had displaced the type of poetry volume that he had been used to: 'The Annuals are now the only books bought for presents to young ladies, in which way poems formerly had their chief vent' (5: 336). Wordsworth generally kept his distance from them, but agreed to contribute to the *Keepsake for 1829*, a particularly lavish publication with big-name authors who were generously compensated. Manning analyses the financial motives behind Wordsworth's involvement with this publication as an indication of the overall commercialization of the literary marketplace in the early Victorian period, but he finds it equally important that annuals like the *Keepsake* offered poets of Wordsworth's generation 'the stimulus of renewed exchange with an audience, fresh starts rather than reworked collected editions' (Manning, 61). Once he himself had signed on, Wordsworth helped win over Coleridge to contribute to the same volume, as Coleridge relates in a letter:

Mr. Fred. Renyolds [editor of the *Keepsake*] called on me with a letter of introduction from Wordsworth, in which Wordsworth informed me, that he had been induced, as likewise Southey and Sir Walter Scott, to furnish some poems to a Work undertaken by Mr Heath with Mr R. as his Editor—that the unusually handsome terms would scarcely have overcome his reluctance, had he not entertained the hope that I might be persuaded to give my name.... In short, he hoped that I would write. (*CL* 6: 761)

Coleridge did write, although he was not rewarded, since Reynolds failed to pay him for his contributions even though Coleridge agreed to contribute exclusively to the *Keepsake* that year (Paley, 16).

But this was not Coleridge's first involvement with annuals, and, in general, he seems to have been more open to them than other poets of his generation and stature. From 1826 onward, he published some twenty poems in annuals that included the *Literary Souvenir*, the *Literary Magnet*, the *Amulet*, the *Keepsake*, and *Friendship's Offering*. He also corresponded with the editors of the *Amulet* and the *Literary Souvenir* in the late 1820s about the role of their publications in educating young people (Sonoda, 62). The *Bijou*, on the other hand, treated Coleridge unscrupulously, publishing some of his poems without consent. In these publications, the activity of 'public writing' for a sizeable target audience, and the distinctive temporality of periodical publication, take different forms than in Coleridge's newspaper days. Like anyone who wrote for the annuals of the 1820s and 1830s, Coleridge would have been aware of a very specific audience of middle-class female consumers with interests in polite literature, sentiment, emotion, and exotic settings. Sometimes the idiosyncrasies of the publication venues are distinctly reflected in the theme or setting of the poems Coleridge wrote for them, as with the Christmas motif in 'Impromptu on Christmas-Day' or 'The Improvisatore'. Coleridge's difference in age and gender from the readers of these publications helped cast him in the role of instructor, mentor, or sage; the educative and cultivating purpose inherent in the annuals thus suited Coleridge's own inclination late in life. By way of this role, Coleridge's contributions to the annuals brought him into a relationship with a younger generation of readers. Indeed, the gift-book consumers were the largest audience his poetry had ever had, and they were a notably different readership from that of his journalism or his poetry of the 1790s; as Paley notes, 'his new readers must necessarily have regarded him as a contemporary poet rather than one of a past generation' (19).

Several of Coleridge's late poems foreground the educative purpose and the awareness of a female audience—qualities determined by the distinctive publication venue—by mirroring within the poem itself the type of communication that is meant to take place between poet and reader. An especially common scenario in these late poems is the 'scene of instruction' in which the poet responds philosophically to a question posed by a naive, usually female auditor (e.g., 'Reproof and Reply', 'Duty Surviving Self-love', 'Reply to a Lady's Question', and 'Love and Friendship Opposite', which was originally published in *Friendship's Offering for 1833* under the title 'In Answer to a Friend's Question'). Other poems thematize the conversation between Coleridge and the editor of the annual, in that they depict the editor inviting the poet to develop his ideas on a given topic. Most obviously, 'The Garden of Boccaccio', commissioned for the 1829 *Keepsake*, contains within the poem a scene in which the poet is inspired to write when a female friend shows him an engraving by Thomas Stothard—an engraving that was, in fact, printed alongside Coleridge's poem in *The Keepsake*.

Coleridge's contribution to the *Amulet* for 1828, a piece of combined prose and poetry entitled 'The Improvisatore', incorporates both these scenarios: a scene of instruction, and the invitation to compose a poem. In 'The Improvisatore', two young women, Catherine and Eliza, encounter a fifty-something gentleman, identified only as 'the Friend' and nicknamed 'the Improvisatore', who instructs them on the definition of true love, then extemporizes a poem for them on the constancy of love over time. It is easy to see Coleridge and his *Amulet* readers in the roles of the 'Friend' and the two young women, respectively. The Friend or Improvisatore represents an authoritative voice, albeit a different one from Coleridge's newspaper persona of a generation earlier. This time, his authority derives from the wisdom of experience, by virtue of which he is able to put words to a sensation that Catherine and Eliza can feel inwardly, but for which they lack 'the *word* that would make it understand itself' (*PW* 16.1.2: 1058). He is also, in several senses, a performer, who is called 'Improvisatore' because of his habit of 'perpetrating charades and extempore verses at Christmas times' (*PW* 16.1.2: 1057). In the prose section of 'The Improvisatore', which is written in the form of a dialogue among the two young women and the Friend, the Friend demonstrates his talent by paraphrasing verses extempore from a variety of literary works on the theme of love: one of Moore's *Irish Melodies*, a play by Beaumont and Fletcher, poems by Nicholas Rowe and Robert Burns.

At the end of 'The Improvisatore', the Friend composes his own four-strophe poem 'ex improviso'. Its verse-form is an irregular mixture of couplet rhymes, alternating rhymes, and tercets, and there is similar variation in the metre, with five-stress, four-stress, and three-stress lines, and a single two-stress line. But the four-stress line predominates, making the poem resemble the verse-form of Letitia Landon's popular recent publication *The Improvisatrice* (1824), while the form and turns of thought in the four strophes are reminiscent of an irregular ode, the 'public' form that Coleridge had often used in his earlier poetry. While its imagery is almost metaphysical, the poem's most remarkable feature is that it explicitly meditates on the *idea*—or, rather, the 'fancy' (lines 2–4)—of being in love. Encouraged by the young ladies to confess that he has personal experience of true love, the Improvisatore instead avers that he 'fancied that he had' it. The question of whether the feeling was 'real or a magic shew' is left curiously unresolved, even though the poem ends on a note of 'CONTENTMENT.' By extemporizing a poem on nothing but a fancied feeling, the Improvisatore heightens the sense that the verses themselves— rhymes, rhythms, images, and conceits pulled spontaneously out of the air—are all there is. According to Coleridge, 'The Improvisatore' itself was a provisional composition *ex nihilo*, sent to the editor of the *Amulet* the day it was written, before the author himself had come to a 'comparative appreciation of it' (*CL* 6: 699). In its theme and its mode of composition, then, this late text recapitulates the idea of rapid composition before an audience, a talent shared by the oral extemporizer, the brilliant conversationalist, and the periodical writer.

Coleridge's very different performances and self-presentations in the London newspapers of the 1790s and the gift-books of the 1820s have in common the self-conscious orientation toward an expectant audience that is one of the distinctive features of periodical publication. In different ways, the newspapers and the annuals invite and encourage the rapid development of ideas and the instant formulation of phrases in response to a deadline and a timely trigger, be it a political event, a social occasion, or a conversational gambit that awaits a response. Thus, these venues foster forms of prose and poetry that highlight public speech (the ode, the scene-of-instruction poem) or extempore creativity (the impromptu, the epigram, 'lines suggested by...', or the more elaborate mimesis of extempore poetry represented by 'The Improvisatore'). In Coleridge's case, these qualities of periodical literature are particularly relevant because they capitalized on, and allowed Coleridge himself to capitalize on, his innate talents and tendencies toward performing for an audience and developing ideas in the midst of conversation. Despite his ambivalence towards them, Coleridge's appearances in the periodicals thus represent a felicitous conjunction of his creative disposition with the ascendant publication venues of the earlier and later Romantic periods: first the London daily newspapers and, later, the monthly periodicals and annual gift-books. In these compositions, we see the man and his times reciprocally determining his creative and cognitive modes, and the forms in which they achieve public expression. Coleridge's engagement with the periodicals therefore contributes substantially to his role as the first professional man of letters, and helps explain why such a professional would emerge at such a time.

Works Cited

Butler, Marilyn. 1981. *Romantics, Rebels and Reactionaries: English Literature and its Background, 1760–1830.* Oxford: Oxford University Press.

Christiansen, Jerome. 1982. Once an apostate always an apostate. *Studies in Romanticism* 21: 461–4.

Coleman, Deirdre. 2002. The Journalist. *The Cambridge Companion to Coleridge*, ed. Lucy Newlyn. Cambridge: Cambridge University Press, pp. 126–41.

Coleridge, Samuel Taylor. 1983. *Biographia Literaria*, ed. James Engell and W. Jackson Bate. Vol. 7 of *The Collected Works of Samuel Taylor Coleridge*. Princeton: Princeton University Press. (=*BL*)

—— 1956–71. *Collected Letters of Samuel Taylor Coleridge.* 6 vols., ed. Earl Leslie Griggs. Oxford: Clarendon. (=*CL*)

—— 1978. *Essays on His Times.* ed. David V. Erdman. Vol. 3 of *The Collected Works of Samuel Taylor Coleridge*. Princeton: Princeton University Press. (=*EOT*)

COLERIDGE, SAMUEL TAYLOR. 1971. *Lectures 1795: On Politics and Religion*, ed. Lewis Patton and Peter Mann. Vol. 1 of *The Collected Works of Samuel Taylor Coleridge*. Princeton: Princeton University Press.

—— 1976. *On the Constitution of Church and State*, ed. John Colmer. Vol. 10 of *The Collected Works of Samuel Taylor Coleridge*. Princeton: Princeton University Press.

—— 2001. *Poetical Works*, ed. J. C. C. Mays. Vol. 16 of *The Collected Works of Samuel Taylor Coleridge*. Princeton: Princeton University Press. (=*PW*)

—— 1970. *The Watchman*, ed. Lewis Patton. Vol. 2 of *The Collected Works of Samuel Taylor Coleridge*. Princeton: Princeton University Press.

CRACIUN, ADRIANA. 2002. Mary Robinson, the *Monthly Magazine*, and the free press. *Prose Studies* 25: 19–40.

CURRY, KENNETH. 1948. The contributors to *The Annual Anthology*. *Papers of the Bibliographical Society of America*, 42: 50–65.

ERDMAN, DAVID V. 1969. Coleridge as editorial writer. In *Power & Consciousness*, ed. Conor Cruise O'Brien and William Dean Vanech. London: University of London Press and New York: New York University Press, pp. 183–201.

HESSELL, NICOLA ANNE. 2003. Coleridge as journalist, 1799–1800. Diss. Toronto.

HIGGINS, DAVID. 2005. *Romantic Genius and the Literary Magazine: Biography, Celebrity, Politics*. London: Routledge.

HOLMES, RICHARD. 1989. *Coleridge: Early Visions*. London: Hodder & Stoughton.

KLANCHER, JON P. 1987. *The Making of English Reading Audiences, 1790–1832*. Madison: University of Wisconsin Press.

LEADER, ZACHARY. 1998. Coleridge and the uses of journalism. In *Grub Street and the Ivory Tower: Literary Journalism and Literary Scholarship from Fielding to the Internet*, ed. Jeremy Treglown and Bridget Bennett. Oxford: Clarendon Press, 22–40.

LIU, ALAN. 1989. *Wordsworth: The Sense of History*. Stanford: Stanford University Press.

MAGNUSON, PAUL. 1991. The politics of 'Frost at Midnight'. *The Wordsworth Circle*, 22: 3–11.

—— 1998. *Reading Public Romanticism*. Princeton: Princeton University Press.

MANNING, PETER J. 1995. Wordsworth in the *Keepsake, 1829*. In *Literature in the Marketplace*, ed. John O. Jordan and Robert L. Patten. Cambridge: Cambridge University Press, 44–73.

PALEY, MORTON D. 1994. Coleridge and the Annuals. *Huntington Library Quarterly*, 57: 1–24.

PARKER, MARK. 2000. *Literary Magazines and British Romanticism*. Cambridge: Cambridge University Press.

SONODA, AKIKO. 2005. Coleridge's later poetry and the rise of literary annuals. *Coleridge Bulletin*, NS, 26 (Winter): 58–74.

SOUTHEY, ROBERT. 1849–1850. *The Life and Correspondence of Robert Southey*, ed. Charles Cuthbert Southey. 6 vols. London: Longman, Brown, Green & Longmans.

STROUT, ALAN LANG. 1933. Samuel Taylor Coleridge and John Wilson of *Blackwood's Magazine*. *PMLA* 48: 100–28.

THOMPSON, E. P. 1997. A compendium of cliche: the poet as essayist. In *The Romantics: England in a Revolutionary Age*. New York: New Press, 143–55.

CHAPTER 10

COLERIDGE'S *LECTURES 1808–1819: ON LITERATURE*

MATTHEW SCOTT

BETWEEN September 1805, when he left his position as Acting Public Secretary in Malta, and 17 August 1806, the date of his eventual landing in Kent after a long and dreaded sea voyage from Leghorn, Coleridge undertook a circuitous and protracted tour of Italy which provided him with opportunities both to reflect at length upon Classical and Renaissance art and also to meet a number of the key literary and cultural figures who would do much to condition his intellectual development over the coming years. These included the painter Washington Allston, Ludwig Tieck (with whom he discussed August Wilhelm Schlegel) and Wilhelm von Humbolt. Rather typically for Coleridge, the tour was marred by its contradictory legacy. Although there are sadly few entries remaining from his notebook records, he seems undoubtedly to have felt a certain cultural awakening after the travails of Malta; yet Coleridge returned home exhausted, opium-dependent and in poor health. Desperately short of money and without immediate hope of employment, he felt isolated and resolved pretty soon to break permanently from Sara. He remained, however, on good terms with several old friends who were now key figures in or around London including Daniel Stuart, the proprietor of the *Courier*, and Humphrey Davy, the newly appointed professor of chemistry at the Royal Institution. Despite finding no immediate work with the former (at whose offices in the Strand he was shortly to lodge), it was almost certainly at the instigation of the latter that Coleridge was asked in September 1806 to undertake a series of general lectures on 'the Principles common to all the Fine Arts' (*CL* 2, 1181), These were scheduled to take place in the November of that year and would have required him to return from a visit north to Keswick almost as soon as he had arrived, thereby conveniently effecting the separation from his wife. However, it seems that such was the state of his mental and physical health at the time that although Coleridge did travel south again he decided eventually, in part on the advice of friends, to abandon the plan for this intriguing series of talks and instead took up the offer of temporary (and rather disastrous) accommodation with the Wordsworths and Sara Hutchinson at a farmhouse in Coleorton, Leicestershire that had been lent to them by Sir George Beaumont.

By the following summer, Coleridge had returned to Nether Stowey where he was staying once again with Thomas Poole, following a rather difficult visit to Ottery earlier in the year. During this period, he met Thomas De Quincey for the first time and it was in September that Davy contacted him once again with a proposal for another sequence of lectures. This time Coleridge responded in haste, giving Davy a significantly detailed proposal that greatly modifies the original plan. To speak on his 'sentiments respecting the *Arts*' in general, Coleridge wrote, presumably with the memory of his recent Italian tour in mind, would be over ambitious given his poor health, as it would require him to seek out 'books of Italian prints, &c.' And he determined instead to use literary material closer to hand (Shakespeare, Spenser, Chaucer, Milton, Dryden and Pope) with a view to drawing out the still considerable matter of 'the general and most philosophical [...] Principles of Poetry'. The letter to Davy is an often baffling list of half-formed and unexplained ideas for his lectures, richly suggestive but complex: 'the genius & writings of Shakespere, relatively to his Predecessors & Contemporaries [...] Chaucer: tho' the character of the latter, as a manner-painter, I shall have so far anticipated in distinguishing it from & comparing it with, Shakespere [...] Dryden, & Pope, including the origin, & after history of poetry of witty logic' (*CL* 3, 29–30). As vague as it must have seemed to Davy, his initial proposal appears to be for a sequence of close analyses of poets with whose work Coleridge was extremely familiar; one cast within a broad historical purview. In the end, however, although his first series of lectures—the 1808 Lectures on the Principles of Poetry—contains many of his most brilliant literary critical apercus, it falls some way short of such a simple analysis, and this is a quality common to the literary lectures more generally. In this essay, I shall suggest that we should not view these many lectures in their entirety somehow as a failure adequately to deliver on a straightforward pedagogic promise but rather celebrate their difficult diversity, accounting for it both in the occasionally strange circumstances under which the work was undertaken and also in Coleridge's very individual style. His literary lectures as a whole resist easy summary and yet are all the more rewarding as a result. They require us first to take account of him as a lecturer before his audience, their reception itself going some way to explaining the difficult textual form that we have as a record for them, and then to proceed to a discussion of their most important ideas, one which deals with his significant borrowings and the legacy of the whole in the history of criticism.

CIRCUMSTANCES OF THE LITERARY LECTURES

Among the most memorable moments in the lectures are certainly their acts of close reading, especially of Shakespeare, but it is as well to emphasize immediately that Coleridge's lectures never really adhere to the conventions of an historical overview designed to familiarize the audience with the chronologically surveyed literature of the past. His method of lecturing and mode of organizing his material, combined with a naturally extempore cast of mind, ensures that Coleridge's line of argument is often difficult to follow and that much of what is distinct and valuable in these extraordinary contributions to literary aesthetics is thrown up by the apparently arbitrary association of ideas when material previously worked out in notes is suddenly brought to bear upon an unexpected sequence of thoughts. And although they approach Coleridge's in their importance to the history of literary criticism, the more conventional lectures of his contemporary William Hazlitt give us some impression of how unusual Coleridge's must have seemed to his audiences. Where Hazlitt tends to follow a common theme throughout each course, proceeding in roughly chronological manner with obvious teleological purpose, Coleridge is disorganized but dazzling and difficult, and never afraid of the most daring or expansive claims. In part, this is explained by his very unconventional method and the circumstances under which the lectures were often given but it also runs to the core of Coleridge's literary critical project—in as much as we can speak of its having an unity—that he should seek answers to the larger theoretical issues that his own intellectual development had begun to expose in the years leading up to the decade of the lectures. Hazlitt builds squarely upon the tradition of English literary scholarship, greatly developing for example the eighteenth-century preoccupation with character in his *Characters of Shakespeare's Plays*. Coleridge, by contrast, works far more clearly within a European tradition alive to broad intellectual questions about the nature of taste and creativity. We sense the presence of such figures past as Samuel Johnson, Joshua Reynolds and Adam Smith in Coleridge's reading but only as far as their ideas are complicated by notions that he has inherited from first Immanuel Kant, Johann Gottfried Herder, Friedrich Schiller, Gotthold Ephraim Lessing and later—with greater controversy—Friedrich Wilhelm Joseph Schelling, Jean Paul Richter, and the Schlegels.

Of course, at the time of writing his letter to Davy, Coleridge could have had no idea that he was embarking upon such a lengthy career as a lecturer, one that would have him deliver over a hundred in twelve courses between 1808 and 1819. But he would have had an idea that this was a realistic way in which to earn an income of sorts and he already had some experience of lecturing over a decade earlier in Bristol, when his subject had been politics and religion. By the end of the 1800s, Coleridge's interests had shifted considerably, as is evinced by the philosophical project of the *Friend*, which preoccupied him with some difficulty for several years after 1809. And although he wrote briefly for the *Courier* from 1811, his years of attending closely to the social events of the time had passed gradually into the rather introspective life of arcane scholarship and philosophical speculation that would detain him more and more completely for the rest of his life. He was writing very little new poetry and was strangely reluctant and slow to follow up his various literary plans for translation or the revision of his earlier work. In the middle of the decade of the lectures, Coleridge did indeed turn back to his play *Osorio*, revising it into the moderately successful *Remorse*, and then in a burst of energy between 1815 and 1817, he produced *Christabel*, *Sibylline Leaves*, *Zapolya*, *Biographia*, and *The Lay Sermons*. But these were not a departure from the concerns of the literary lectures and the latter two especially built significantly upon ideas that emerge centrally in the lectures. By late 1818 and early 1819, however, when he delivered the last of his courses on Shakespeare, Coleridge was alternating them with an obscure, derivative and historically remote sequence on the history of philosophy, and it is not too dramatic to state that his interest in literary and aesthetic matters had begun to wane by this time as it was replaced, in ever more turgid form, by subjects relating to theological and philosophical disputation. In sum, it is a reasonable contention that during the eleven years, from 1808, in which he was lecturing on literature, Coleridge's creative attention was focused more often upon this enterprise than on any other; that in short it took up the bulk of his considerable intellectual energy during this intermittently fertile if troubled period.

Most especially, Coleridge's problems at this time lay with his health and it is remarkable in fact that he managed to achieve what he did. The first series was initially somewhat delayed when Humphrey Davy became ill after his experiments with potassium in 1807 but by the time Coleridge began the course early in 1808, his own health was fast deteriorating. Although there is, of course, no uniform picture to present throughout the period, the conditions of this first series are particularly striking not least because we have such a vivid (if not wholly reliable) account of them from Thomas De Quincey, who wrote in 1834:

His appearance was generally that of a person struggling with pain and overmastering illness. His lips were baked with feverish heat, and often black in colour; and, in spite of the water which he continued drinking through the whole course of his lecture, he often seemed to labour under an almost paralytic inability to raise the upper jaw from the lower.   (*Lects 1808–19*, 1, 147).

This pretty nasty attack must be seen within its proper context, which is of course the undermining of a former mentor with whom one has tired. But it does serve to remind us that Coleridge's health did impact very strongly upon the lectures and indeed contributed to their rather mixed reception. The records that we have of the lectures derive not only from Coleridge's own notes but also frequently from multiple testaments from those who heard and reported on them. This suggests that they were often eagerly received if not always fully understood. In particular, in the case of the 1808 Lectures on the Principles of Poetry, the 1811–12 Lectures on Shakespeare and Milton, and the 1818 Lectures on the Principles of Judgement, Culture and European Literature we have a very decent sense of what was said and if De Quincey's account is to be given any credence then it must be balanced against the fact that in sum the lectures remain an extraordinary venture into literary aesthetics. Having said this, there were clearly some unfavourable reactions and De Quincey himself cannot be dismissed. Indeed, he remains key to grappling with the legacy of the lectures since it was he who first accused Coleridge of plagiarism, an issue that remains of fundamental importance in any assessment even now of their original achievement. R. A. Foakes treats the subject carefully in the introduction to the Bollingen edition, noting the use by Coleridge of material from four German writers: Richter, Schelling, and both Schlegels. Of these, it is the presence of ideas borrowed from A. W. Schlegel's lectures *Ueber dramatische Kunst und Litteratur* for his Coleridge's own defence of Shakespeare that remains most problematical.

SHAKESPEARE AND MILTON

The reader of such remains as we have of Coleridge's literary lectures is unlikely, I think, to come away with the immediate impression that these are as a whole the work of one of the great progenitors of close practical criticism. In this regard, certainly, the record of the lectures is to be distinguished from the second volume of *Biographia Literaria* and allied more closely with the work of the author of the *Essays on the Principles of Genial Criticism*. The letter to Davy, cited at the start of this discussion, goes on describe the broader, philosophical and theoretical ambitions of Coleridge's proposed series and it is important to keep in mind a distinct sense of his lectures having a difficult (and occasionally contradictory) dual purpose; they are at once acts of close reading, a revelation or evocation of the matter of art and literature, and also difficult, occasionally straining exercises in the divination of aesthetic principles, a searching around for the quintessence of aesthetic experience, one that bears contiguity with other (largely German) Romantic hopes of discovering a universal key in art to questions of taste, pleasure and moral sense. Following a discussion of Shakespeare, it is to these that I wish to turn for the remainder of this chapter.

Inevitably, the value that we ascribe to the enterprise as a whole must rest upon what we make of Coleridge's contribution to the study of Shakespeare because it is to him that he returns most frequently and from this material that Coleridge's reputation as a literary critic continues to remain most current. Several of his editors have remarked a little impressionistically that Coleridge is able somehow to bring Shakespeare's writing to life in ways that do not appear to be available to his near contemporaries such as Johnson, Hazlitt and Schlegel. Alfred Harbage writes for example: 'When we read Coleridge, we think what a wonderful artist is Shakespeare. Coleridge's is the criticism with immediacy, the power to evoke the works criticized; when he speaks, Shakespeare is there' (*Lects 1808–19*, I, xl). This is pretty fustian praise, which reads Coleridge precisely in his own critical terms, but it does—just about—describe one of the recurrent qualities of some of the best elements of the lectures, when he attempts to read Shakespeare's language closely to unpick its almost unique density of texture. One of the reasons for which Coleridge returns so frequently to Shakespeare is that he comes to stand as an exemplar for 'the poet' in general; the body of work offering continual evidence against which to test grander claims about the nature of literary artistry. And in this regard, close reading is both an admirable and necessary tool because it enables Coleridge to show his audiences what it is that he intends by the term 'poetry'. Alongside Milton, Shakespeare takes centre stage for the first time in the great sequence of lectures given to the London Philosophical Society in 1811–12, and a key point that he makes repeatedly in these lectures is one about the inclusive nature of Shakespeare's poetic genius. In terms that Harbage has clearly internalized, Shakespeare, Coleridge suggests, speaks directly to us because he forces us to think poetically as we read him.

In Lecture 4, Coleridge introduces a key distinction in his general definition of the poet, one that works rather like his linguistic practice of desynonymization elsewhere in his critical theory, to articulate a division around which to arrange the material of his practical criticism. This is between the two types of poet represented respectively by Shakespeare and Milton. He speaks of Shakespeare 'on one of the two Golden Thrones of the English Parnassus, with Milton on the other', and the distinction serves to provide us with two versions of the Romantic poet par excellence (*Lects 1808–19*, I, 244). Shakespeare is a chameleon who can speak in any voice and turn himself with convincing conviction into any character. Milton meanwhile speaks with one glorious voice turning everything he touches into a version of himself, a product of his own one mind. Searching around for a word to describe Milton's work and the common quality shared by the whole, he employs an odd term (one just about traceable in eighteenth-century thought), which lends a sense that the poetry is abstract, difficult, classically and intellectually refined. Milton, he says, makes one 'Ideality', a word that is later taken up by the phrenologists to describe the organ of poetic creativity (*Lects 1808–19*, 1, 145). This is a fine idea suggesting imaginative transcendence over the mucky business of the body, which is so often Shakespeare's concern, and it also hints at a link to Wordsworth, who is charged in *Biographia* with casting his subjects solely upon his own terms. Shakespeare is a different order of artist, one who is magical in his diversity and range:

He darting himself forth, and passing himself into all the forms of human character & human passion. The other attracted all forms & all things to himself into the unity of his own grand ideal. Shakespeare became all things well into w^h he infused himself, while all forms, all things became Milton—the poet ever present to our minds & more than gratifying us for the loss of the distinct individuality of what he represents.   (*Lects 1808–19*, 1, 253)

So persuasive was this idea that we find it repeated in directly comparable terms in Hazlitt's Lectures on the English Poets some six years later when John Keats was in the audience, and of course similarities to the critical theory of the latter—to negative capability, the Shakespearean life of allegory, and the Wordsworthian egotistical sublime—are too obvious to need further elaboration. Above all, one has the sense that Coleridge saw his task in regard to Shakespeare as one of tireless defence. There are moments of purely speculative conjecture, which serve to animate a figure whom he was desperate to deliver from the weight of earlier discredit, which had him as a rude, uneducated and not entirely respectable figure: '[H]e first studied deeply, read & thoroughly understood every part of human nature, which he joined with his poetical feeling, till at length it gave him that wonderful power over which he had no equal' (*Lects 1808–19*, 1, 253). And the feeling that Shakespeare somehow embraced human life and was an empathetic celebrant of diverse experience runs over into a fundamental aesthetic tenet of the defence, that the greatest works of art are organic rather than mechanical in form. By this he intends that they attain a kind of vital logic of their own, and that they could not have been other than they are. This feels like an immensely Coleridgean idea not least because it is a dyad in which a quality of vitality is opposed to the dull, dead letter of fancy. That the conception is in fact Schlegel's throws up a few problems but, we can, I think, find similar and indeed innovative versions of this idea drawn out in the other key critical ideas that recur interestingly over the course of the literary lectures.

POETRY AND PLEASURE

Defining poetry in Lecture III of the 1811–12 Lectures on Shakespeare & Milton, Coleridge appeals to a quality of unity that differentiates it from other forms of creative writing. He may have Wordsworth's Preface to *Lyrical Ballads* in mind as his definition extends to an opposition between Poetry and Science:

Poetry is a species of composition, opposed to Science as having intellectual pleasure for its Object and attaining its end by the Language natural to us in states of excitement; but distinguished from other species, not excluded by this criterion, by permitting a pleasure from the Whole consistent with a consciousness of pleasurable excitement from the component parts, & the perfection of which is to communicate from each part the greatest immediate pleasure compatible with the largest Sum of Pleasure on the whole.

(*Lects 1808–19*, 1, 218)[1]

It is a given, for Coleridge, that in the reading of poetry we derive pleasure but such a statement does not go far enough. He is determined to assess exactly how the pleasurable reaction works, suggesting both that the reader responds to the work in its entirety (rather than, say, to a peculiar aspect which happens to produce an isolated subject-centred reaction) and that the reaction of the reader is intellectual, in the sense that it introduces activity of mind. Such an aesthetic response is complimented by the fact that it is mirrored in the poet himself, who in the act of composition is in such a state of excitement and enlivened sensibility that the poem comes into being in an act of 'vital', organic creation (*Lects 1808–19*, 1, 304–5)[2]:

A more vivid reflection of the Truths of Nature & the Human Heart united with that constant exertion of Activity which modifies & corrects these truths by that sort of pleasurable Emotion, which the exertion of all our faculties give in a certain degree, but which the full play of those Powers of Mind, which are spontaneous rather than voluntary, in which the Effort required bears no proportion to the activity enjoyed—/—This is the state which permits the production of a highly pleasurable Whole.   (*Lects 1808–19*, 1, 217)

Coleridge suggests that a successful poem appears to the reader as a truth-revealing entity of its own, an autonomous 'whole'. Its truth differs fundamentally from the scientific in that the means of poetry lies in the production of intellectual pleasure in the reader, but this again does not go far enough. A poem pretends to create a reality of its own, separate from if connected to nature, an idea drawn out in a different discussion of the relationship between poetry and science from the 'Essays on the Principles of Method'. There he writes that '[i]f in Shakespeare we find

---

[1] Coleridge is perhaps thinking of Wordsworth's discussion of the similarity between prose and poetry, see William Wordsworth, *Prose Works*, 3 vols, eds. W. J. B. Owen and Jane Worthington Smyser (Oxford: Clarendon Press, 1974), 1, 134.

[2] Coleridge does, of course, go beyond Schelling here by allowing for the possibility of struggle in creation, but even then the act is vital and aims at unity.

nature idealized into poetry, through the creative power of a profound yet obser-
vant meditation, so through the meditative observation of a Davy, a Woollaston, or
Hatchett [...] we find poetry, as it were, substantiated and realised in nature'
(*Friend*, 1, 471). The movement from nature to the page via the imagination is
reversed in science where that which the imagination devises first from meditation
later finds its mirror in nature.

For Coleridge, the pleasure that we derive from art lies directly in our appre-
hension of an autonomous object, which obeys its own laws and yet which
somehow corresponds to the world that we ourselves know. It is exactly this
that he is pointing to when he writes of the Shakespearean play as an organic
unity in which we respond to characters as wholes within a larger and complete
body:

in Sh.—the Play is a *syngenesia*, each [character] has indeed a life of its own & is an
individuum of itself; but yet an organ to the whole—as the Heart & the Brain—&c /. *The
Heart &c of that particular Whole.—S. a comparative Anatomist.*   (*Lects 1808–19*, 2, 151)

The pleasure that we derive from reading Shakespeare is that of interacting with a
unified artwork, but it is also directly related to the imaginative activity that we
undertake in responding to the combination of pleasure and imagination that has
composed the work in the first place. In Lecture IV of the 1811–12 Lectures on
Shakespeare and Milton, Coleridge suggests that in the act of reading Shakespeare,
we are encouraged to imaginative and moral activity. Of the couplet from Sonnet
33, 'Full many a glorious morning have I seen / Flatter the mountain-tops with
soverign [*sic*] eye', he writes:

Here is a union of thoughts, that bringing all into one, you see not only the sun rising over
the mountains, but you have also the *moral* feeling with wh the rapidity of the poet's mind
had connected it [...] You feel him to be a poet inasmuch as, for a time, he has made you
one—an active creative being.   (*Lects 1808–19*, 1, 231 (my italics))

The poem is self-contained in its description of nature, and obeys the specific laws
of the poet's imagination. However, Coleridge is keen to point out that there is a
level of correspondence between the poetic description of nature and our own
subjective experience. In reading, we come to terms with the description offered by
the poet and in so doing find our own imaginative capacity enlivened. There is,
however, another element at work here. Coleridge specifically refers to the moral
feeling that we experience in interacting with the poetic creation. He is certainly
not suggesting that we have been taught a moral lesson in reading the sonnet but
he does appear to believe that in the imaginative strength that we derive from
Shakespeare, there is an accompanying feeling that relates directly to our moral
nature. It will become ever more central to his project to explain the ways in
which poetic and indeed artist representations more generally relate to immanent
reality.

COLERIDGE'S THEORY OF MIMESIS

Coleridge's own thoughts on mimesis in art are developed over many years and show obvious debts to and indeed plagiarism from both the reading of A. W. Schlegel and F. W. J. Schelling. Towards the end of his life, Coleridge compares a portrait exactly mirroring its subject with that which provides a mere imitation. The fundamental difference between the two is the production of pleasure in the viewer when he looks at the imitation:

It is a poor compliment to pay a painter to tell him that his figure stands out from the canvas, or that you start at the likeness of the portrait. Take almost any daub, and cut it out of the canvas and place the figure looking in or out of the window, and any one may take it for life—or take one of Mrs. Salmon's wax queens or generals, and you will feel the difference between a Copy, as they are, and an Imitation of the Human Form, as a good portrait ought to be. (*TT*, 1, 408–9)

He goes on to say: 'Look at that flower vause of Van Huysam—and at these wax peaches and apricots. The last are likest to the original, but what pleasure do they give? None.' The distinction is, however, not so simple as Abrams's mirror and lamp opposition. The flower vase of Van Huysam provides as near a likeness to the original as most of us can bear, being late Dutch realism at its height.[3] It is certainly mimetic. But his point is surely that such a painting depends upon a code of the artist's own creation by which nature or reality is transformed into a picture before us. We must engage with this code to some degree if we are to understand the picture as such and thereby understand its relation to reality. In the case of wax peaches, however, there is no such undertaking: the viewer is meant to mistake the wax for the peach and attempt to take a bite.

Central to his literary lectures, the distinction between copy and imitation preoccupies Coleridge over many years. Focusing by necessity on questions of visual perception, this distinction applies to poetry only with some difficulty but it is fundamental to what Coleridge has to say in the lectures about theatre and dramatic representation. The obvious exception is Coleridge's criticism of Wordsworth's choice of characters in *Biographia*, which gives rise to perhaps his most famous critical statement about aesthetic illusion. There, Coleridge argues that the experience of illusion is destroyed when the aesthetic experience is made to compete with real facts and truths at the same time. It might be said that he is arguing for an autonomous aesthetic on the basis of the case that when art is independent of reality, it is able to provide the viewer or reader with an experience that is true or false on its own terms, even if it is one that ultimately illuminates the real.

---

[3] This distinction is particularly interesting since Coleridge elsewhere derides Dutch Painting as copy, see *Lects 1808–19*, I, 307.

From such an argument derive the apparently paradoxical statements that Shakespeare is both 'the Poet of nature—pourtraying [*sic*] things as they exist', and that 'his characters from Othello or Macbeth down to Dogberry are ideal: they are not things but the abstracts of the things which a great mind may take into itself and naturalize into its own heaven' (*Lects 1808–19*, II, 121; 1, 351). The 'reality' of Shakespeare's characters proceeds somehow from their ideality. When we go back to the real, it is, in some key sense, illuminated by the fact that we have willingly allowed ourselves to be taken in by a fictionalized, ideal representation of that reality. Coleridge is obviously engaged in an attempt to counter Platonic arguments against imitation. In privileging imitation over copy, he sets himself against Plato, but uses the same terms in his argument. Imitation's proximity to reality is guaranteed by the fact that such symbolic representations are somehow closer to a Platonic ideal form. In some cancelled lines from *Remorse*, Coleridge makes this suggestion in relation to the paintings of Titian:

> [Titian], like a second and more lovely nature,
> By the sweet mystery of lines and colors
> Changed the blank canvass to a magic mirror,
> That made the Absent present; and to Shadows
> Gave light, depth, substance, bloom, yea, thought and motion. (*PW*, III, 1269)

It is worthwhile to dwell on this for a moment since late in life Coleridge is recorded as having said of the progress of painting:

People may say what they please about the gradual improvement of the Arts. It is not true of the substance. The Arts and the Muses both spring forth in the youth of nations like Minerva from the front of Jupiter—all-armed; [...] Painting went on in Power till in Raphael it reached the apex, [...] After this the descent was rapid, till sculptors began to work inveterate likenesses of perriwigs in marble—as see Algarroti's tomb in the cemetery at Pisa—and painters did nothing but copy, as well as they could, the external face of Nature. ¶ Now in this age, we have a sort of reviviscence not, I fear of Power—but of a Taste for the Power of the early times. (*TT*, 1, 170–1 (25 June 1830))

Coleridge argues that art followed a teleological progress towards its greatest flowering. In this case, as in Lecture III of the 1811–12 Lectures on Shakespeare and Milton, he singles out Raphael (*Lects 1808–19*, 1, 221).[4] The importance of Raphael's painting, however, is not that it produces a mirror of reality, for he immediately contrasts it with seventeenth and eighteenth century modes of painting and sculpture which were realist. Instead, Raphael like Shakespeare produces an art that is inherently symbolic and yet somehow closer to reality than direct realism. When Hazlitt is recalling Coleridge in *My First Acquaintance with the Poets*, he remembers that he 'spoke with rapture of Raphael, and compared the women at Rome to figures that had walked out of pictures'.[5] Somehow, we must

---

[4] See also *CN* III, 3827, where Raphael is bracketed with Handel and Milton.

[5] *The Complete Works of William Hazlitt*, ed. P. P. Howe, 21 vols. (London: Dent, 1930–4), XI, 33–4.

suppose, the reality of the women in Rome is captured for Coleridge more completely by the painting that does not attempt to mirror reality, than could ever be the case in any purely mimetic representation. Furthermore, in a passage in the *Philosophical Lectures*, Coleridge makes exactly this point again in relation to Raphael:

There the mighty spirit still coming from within had succeeded in taming the untractable matter and in reducing external form to a symbol of the inward and imaginable beauty. We feel it to this day; we feel it for this reason, because we look at the forms after we have long satisfied all curiosity concerning the mere outlines; yet still look and look and feel that these are but symbols.   (*LHP*, 1, 239)

He goes on to suggest that there is something enduring about the symbol that allows us to continue to muse on it without fully understanding why it is so significant to us. In the end, he decides that it must be because the symbolic power of the artistic representation affects us in the same way as nature itself. If we muse upon a Raphael painting, it is because 'there is a divine something corresponding to something within, which no image can exhaust but which we are reminded of when, in the south of Europe we look at the deep blue sky'. The effect of such a representation is that we sink deeper and deeper into it and into ourselves: it is, in effect, not a substitution for external nature, but for our own nature. We are returned through art to ourselves, and through ourselves to a feeling of the presence of the divine.[6]

This cyclical, subjective process is certainly Coleridgean as is the presence of divinity in art. In his 'Desultory Remarks on the Stage' (a supplement to the series of 1808), Coleridge describes art as imitating 'Reality under a *Semblance* of Reality.' This is pithy but difficult and suggests that in pictorial representation, the artist should not attempt to produce a mirror of reality but rather to reflect the representation of reality. His thoughts on pictorial representation obviously cross over into his writing on the stage. In the marginalia to Payne Knight, which Frederick Burwick argues are probably Coleridge's thoughts despite their being in Wordsworth's hand, the same argument is advanced in relation to viewing a tragedy.[7] We do not derive pleasure in watching a play from the belief that we are seeing an actual representation of reality, he notes, for if this were the case then we would not differentiate between watching a tragedy and seeing an execution. The example is Burke's who suggests that the emotions induced in tragedy are, in some sense, a lower form and substitution for those induced by a real tragic situation. For Coleridge, the argument is simply absurd: 'whatever may be our

---

[6] As early as 1805, Coleridge associates the sky with a unity of sight and feeling. He writes: 'deep Sky is of all visual impressions the nearest akin to a Feeling / it is more a Feeling than a Sight / or rather it is the melting away and entire union of Feeling & Sight', *CN*, II, ¶ 2453.

[7] Frederick Burwick, *Illusion of the Drama: Critical Theory of the Enlightenment and Romantic Era* (University Park, PA: Pennsylvania State University Press, 1991), 210.

sensations when the attention is recalled to a scenic representation how farsoever we may lose sight of its being a mimic show, we know perfectly at the time, when we are going to see it [...] that it is nothing better or worse' (*CM*, III, 404). This conviction feeds into Coleridge's definition of drama in Lecture IV of the 1808 series, in which it is defined not as a copy of nature but as an imitation and it is worthwhile to look into this distinction more fully.

IMITATION AND COPY

At the heart of Coleridge's discrimination is the supposition that the mirror merely copies while the imitation is a self-conscious representation in which the artifice of the work is exposed. He had been developing these thoughts for some years, as is clear from a Notebook entry as early as November 1804, in which he defends opera against the charge that it is a lower form of dramatic entertainment because less real:

> To defend the *Opera* = all the objections against *equally* applicable to Tragedy & Comedy without music, & all proceed on the false principle, that Theatrical representations are *Copies* of nature whereas they are imitations. (*CN*, II, ¶ 2211)

Coleridge is extremely wary of dramatic entertainment that lulls the audience into a state of false belief that what they are watching is reality. It is precisely because we can live in the artifice of art for the duration of our response to it that affords it the restorative capacity that it has.

He elaborates this thesis most clearly in the late lecture notes known as 'On Poesy or Art', which lean very extensively upon Schelling. Lecture XIII of the 1818 series begins expansively: '*Art* (I use the word collectively for Music, Painting, Statuary, and Architecture) is the Mediatress, the reconciliator of Man and Nature.' (*Lects 1808–19*, II, 217) And he goes on to provide an argument for the way in which art develops from the primitive writing by and through which man is 'translated' into nature. This description of the passage from primitivism is familiar enough, and leads onto a position in which Coleridge can define art as man's attempt to imitate nature. However, it is obviously a more complicated business than this for through art man has been translated into nature and yet art itself is somehow an imitation of that nature. Ultimately the discussion leads onto his most difficult attempt to desynonymise the terms *copy* and *imitation*; first, however, he states:

> [O]f all the other species, which collectively form the *Fine Arts*, there would remain this as the common definition—that they all, like Poetry, are to express intellectual purposes,

Thoughts, Conceptions, Sentiments that have their origin in the human Mind, but not, as Poetry, by means of articulate Speech, but as Nature, or the divine Art, does, by form, color, magnitude, Sound, and proportion, silently or musically.

Foakes points out a telling similarity to a passage in Schelling's *Philosophische Schriften*: 'like poetry, the arts are capable of expressing intellectual thoughts, conceptions originating in the mind, but not through speech, rather as silent nature does, through form, through pattern, through sensuous works independent of herself'.[8] And it is very much with Schelling as his master that Coleridge returns to the opposition between copy and imitation, now more complicated than his earlier formulations. In a related but little known fragment, 'On Aesthetic Problems', Coleridge had written that 'The fine Arts are works of Imitation—mimetic—how in Imitation as contra-dist. from Copy, Difference is as *essential* as Likeness.' (*SW*, 1, 348) This is something of a modification of earlier ideas for imitation is now characterized by difference. We cannot be tricked by it but have to believe in it as an act of faith. In 'On Poesy or Art', Coleridge provides the analogy of a wax seal. A copy is the imprint that is made in the wax by the seal. The seal itself is the imitation. Burwick fairly poses the question of what the seal is in fact imitating but if we are to take Coleridge on his own terms then we must conclude that the seal is expressive and well as iconic and provides an analogy to the human mind in the act of representing experience, rather than the product of representation itself. The copy is merely the representation of that which has already been through the artistic process that reconfigures mental experience into new physical form. It is therefore an extreme example of bad faith in art, the rejection of artistic expression in favour of facsimile reproduction.

ILLUSION AND DELUSION

Coleridge defines the copy as a naive attempt to represent nature *tout court*: it draws the viewer in so that he cannot distinguish between reality and representation. In short, the viewer is placed in a state of involuntary delusion in which nature and representation are given equivalent status. Under such circumstances, the viewing mind accords no privilege to the medium of representation. Art is, in Platonic terms, simply a second and less perfect reality. In the copy, there is for Coleridge no presumption of a relationship between the subject representing and

---

[8] Schelling, *Philosophie Schriften*, 344–5, trans. Foakes, *Lects 1808–19*, II, 219. Frederick Burwick, 'Coleridge and Schelling on Mimesis', in *The Coleridge Connection: Essays for Thomas McFarland*, ed. Richard Gravil and Molly Lafebure (Houndsmiths, Basingstoke: Macmillan, 1990) pp. 178–99, 184.

the object represented. This is a constant fear, as is made evident in a notebook entry on Berkeleyean Idealism:

Berkely's [*sic*] Idealism may be thus illustrated: Our perceptions are impressions on our mind standing to the external cause in the relation of the picture on the Canvass [*sic*] to the Painter, rather than in that of the Image in the Mirror to the Object reflected   (*CN*, 111 ¶ 3605)

The universal ground for having faith in the objects represented by the mind on the canvas derives directly from the understanding of the co-incidence of subject and object. In another notebook entry Coleridge defines this faith in representation by explaining that the distinction between illusion and delusion does not arise from an understanding of the fact that the imitation is close to nature, but rather from the fact that the imitation is grounded in the self of the poet representing nature:

It is not the desire of attaching *Outness,* and *externality* to our representations which is at the bottom of this Instinct; on the contrary this very attachment of Outness originates in this Instinct—But it is to possess *a ground* to know a fixed Cause generating a certain reason.   (*CN*, 111, ¶ 3592 f 134)

The example Coleridge goes on to give is one in which the metaphor 'Clouds mountain-shaped' establishes a poetic link between clouds and mountains that is not pre-established in nature. He presupposes a symbiotic relationship between mind and nature in poetic representation. To say that clouds are simply not the same as mountains clearly misses the point of the poem, which is to express an intuition rather than merely to mirror.

Here the presence of the will is significant and in further distinguishing between involuntary and voluntary delusion, Coleridge makes the distinction between illusion and delusion itself. In the act of illusion, we realize that we are being tricked and are able to analyse the effects of illusion upon us; in a passive state of delusion we are not even aware that we are in being tricked. This seems to be a simple distinction, but is actually rather central to the analysis of aesthetic effect. The awareness of illusion is precisely that which enables analytical aesthetics to begin to investigate the artwork. For a later art critic like Gombrich, understanding the way in which art works its aesthetic effect upon us is dependent upon the fact that even though we are in a compact with illusion when we look at artworks, we are nevertheless conscious of this. To look away is to realize that we have just been experiencing an illusion. We cannot do both at once, but we can be aware of both at once. For art to be interpreted, we have to suspend our analytic disbelief for the moment of observation.[9]

---

[9] The fact that we cannot step outside an illusion to be both aware of it and under its spell is made by both E. H. Gombrich and Paul Feyerband in very different contexts. For Gombrich, representation relies upon a pact with illusion, in which techniques of representation enable the viewer to be taken into a world of illusion. The pact relies upon the viewer's understanding of the compacts at work and his

In terms of Coleridge's own thoughts on theatrical illusion, the will is, of course, again central. In the letter to Stuart of 13 May 1816, he continues from his discussion of dream images in which the will is suspended to make a comparison with the theatre:

Add to this a voluntary Lending of the Will to this suspension of one's own operations (i.e. that of comparison and consequent decision concerning the reality of any sensuous Impression) and you have the true Theory of Stage Illusion—equally distant from the absurd notion of the French Critics, who ground their principles on the presumption of an absolute *De*lusion, and that of Dr. Johnson who would persuade us that our Judgements are as broad awake during the most masterly representation of the deepest scenes of Othello, as a philosopher would be during the exhibition of a Magic Lanthorn with Punch & Joan, & Pull Devil Pull Baker, &c on it's painted Slides.   (*CL*, 4, 641–2)

Coleridge moves beyond Johnson, in the suggestion that faith in the spectacle can indeed be sustained by viewer, and beyond the French critics, in asserting that we are never deluded into the belief that it is in fact reality. He never suggests that delusion is a possibility in theatrical representations, as he does both in reference to the directly mimetic arts of sculpture and painting, and to ordinary perception. He goes so far, in the 'Desultory Remarks', as to complain that theatrical representations, which aim at direct mimesis, are simply misguided. The example that he gives is of a staged forest. If it is represented as an actual forest we will be neither deceived by it, nor derive pleasure from the scene because it will not provide us with the necessary material for imaginative engagement. If, however, we are presented with a 'picture' of the forest, there is no attempt to deceive us at all:

[A] Forest-scene is not presented to the Audience as a Picture, but as a Forest: and tho' in the *full* sense of the word we are no more *deceived* by the one than by the other, yet are our feelings very differently affected, and the Pleasure derived from the one is not composed of the same Elements, as that afforded by the other—even on the supposition, that the *quantum* of Both were equal. In the former, case it is a *condition* of all genuine delight, that we should *not* be ~~deceived~~luded/ *see Adam Smith's Posthumous Essays.* In the latter, (inasmuch as its principle End is not in or for itself, as <is the case> in a Picture, but to be an assistance and means of an End out of itself), its very purpose is to produce as much Illusion as its nature permits.   (*Lects 1808–19*, 1, 133–4)

Coleridge makes a central point here in the suggestion that 'picture' should be privileged over 'scene'. The picture is nothing more than a conventional iconic representation of the reality of the forest. It is a symbol that signifies 'forest' to the

willing participation in the act of viewing a reality. Paul Feyerabend has demonstrated how this pact lies at the heart of simple empirical observation. His example is looking at a simple figure like the Necker cube. E. H. Gombrich, *Art and Illusion. A study in the psychology of pictorial representation*, 5th edn (London: Phaidon Press, 1979), 5, and Paul Feyerabend, *Against Method* (London: Verso, 1986), 227.

audience. In placing this above the scenic representation, Coleridge not only states a case for idealized theatre but also presupposes the importance of the mental interaction of the audience. Seeing a symbolic forest, we must suppose, engages the audience themselves in an imaginative act of representing nature to themselves. In the remainder of the note, Coleridge makes this point explicitly:

In t Thisese and in all other Stage Presentations, are to produce a sort of temporary Half-Faith, which the Spectator encourages in himself & and supports by a voluntary contribution on his own part, because he knows that it is at any all times in his power to see it the thing as it really is. I have often noticed, that little Children are actually deceived by Stage-Scenery, but never are by Pictures: tho' even these produce an effect on their impressible minds, which they do not on the minds of Adults. The Child if strongly impressed, does not indeed positively think the picture to be Reality; but yet he does not think the contrary. [...] Now what Pictures are to little Children, Stage-Illusion is to Men, provided they retain any part of their Child's sensibility: except that in the latter instance, this suspension of the Act of Comparison, which permits this sort of negative Belief, is somewhat more assisted by the Will, than in a Child respecting a Picture.   (*Lects 1808–19*, 1, 134–5)[10]

The interaction of the audience with the play is explicitly a reciprocal relationship. The Spectator's half-faith implies a knowledge that what is seen is only fiction. It is, however, the fiction of the poet's or the playwright's imaginative invention, which cannot hope to be directly communicated to the audience without a 'voluntary contribution' from them. Coleridge is clearly calling for empathy from the audience in his assertion of the need to be in a state of half-faith but he is also suggesting that it is through an imaginative contribution from the spectator, or presumably from the reader, that theatre or poetic fiction attains the status that he accords it.

Writing to Charles Matthews, Coleridge extends his comments on stage illusion to the actors themselves. He writes: 'A good actor is Pygamlion's Statue, a work of exquisite *art, animated* & gifted with *motion*; but still *art*, still a species of *Poetry*'. (*CL*, 111, 501 (30 May 1814)) Coleridge's famous comments about Kean attack him precisely because he does not follow these rules.[11] The actor should provide the audience with the same experience as the work of art itself, so that the spectator can be drawn into the representation in order to complete the character for himself.

[10] Coleridge makes a similar point about the comparison between the child and the man in judgements of morality in *The Friend*, 1818. There again the question of delusion is raised.
'Every parent possess the opportunity of observing, how deeply children resent the injury of delusion; and if men laugh at the falsehoods that were imposed on themselves during their childhood, it is because they were not good and wise enough to contemplate the past in the present, and so to produce by a virtuous and thoughtful sensibility that continuity in their self-consciuousness, which Nature has made the law of their animal life.' See *Friend*, 1, 40.
[11] Kean is original; but he copies from himself. His rapid descents from the hyper-tragic to the infracolloquial, though sometimes productive of great effect, are often unreasonable. To see him act, is like reading Shakespeare by flashes of lightning. See *TT*, 1, 41 (27 April 1823).

Coleridge's theatre criticism certainly depends upon a developing nostalgia for the ideal over the real, but this is not everything. Such a theory of illusion grows out of the understanding of perception in idealist terms. The spectator as well as the artist is half-creator of what he sees and represents. Every act of interpreting a representation is its own act of creation.

WORKS CITED

ABRAMS, M. H. 1953. *The Mirror and the Lamp. Romantic Theory and the Critical Tradition.* Oxford: Oxford University Press.

BURKE, EDMUND. 1987. *A Philosophical Enquiry into the Origins of our Ideas of the Sublime and the Beautiful*, ed. James T, Boulton, 2nd edn. Oxford: Oxford University Press.

BURWICK, FREDERICK. 1990. Coleridge and Schelling on Mimesis. In *The Coleridge Connection. Essays for Thomas McFarland*, eds. Richard Gravil and Molly Lefebure. Houndsmills, Basingstoke: Macmillan, 178–99.

—— 1996. Ekphrasis and the mimetic crisis of Romanticism. In *Icons–Texts–Iconotexts: Essays on Ekphrasis and Intermediality*, ed. Peter Wagner. Berlin: Walter de Gruyter, pp. 78–104.

—— 1991. *Illusion and the Drama: Critical Theory of the Enlightenment and Romantic Era.* University Park, PA: Pennsylvania State University Press.

—— 1995. Reflections in the mirror: Wordsworth and Coleridge. In *Reflecting Senses: Perception and Appearance in Literature, Culture and the Arts*, eds. Frederick Burwick and Walter Pape. Berlin: Walter de Gruyter. 122–40.

—— 1996. The Romantic concept of mimesis: *Idem et Alter*. In *Questioning Romanticism*, ed. John Beer. Baltimore: Johns Hopkins University Press, 179–208.

FEYERABEND, PAUL. 1986. *Against Method.* London: Verso.

FOAKES, REGINALD A. 1995. Wordsworth, Coleridge, and illusion. In *Reflecting Senses: Perception and Appearance in Literature, Culture and The Arts*, eds. Frederick Burwick and Walter Pape. Berlin: Walter de Gruyter, 141–59.

GOMBRICH, E. H. 1979. *Art and Illusion. A Study in the psychology of pictorial representation*, 5th edn. London: Phaidon Press.

GRAVIL, RICHARD, and LEFEBURE, MOLLY. eds. 1990. *The Coleridge Connection. Essays for Thomas McFarland.* Houndsmills, Basingstoke: Macmillan Press.

—— NEWLYN, LUCY, and ROE, NICHOLAS. 1985. *Coleridge's Imagination.* Cambridge: Cambridge University Press.

HAMILTON, PAUL. 1983. *Coleridge's Poetics.* Oxford: Blackwell.

HAZLITT, WILLIAM. 1930–34. *The Complete Works of William Hazlitt*, ed. P. P. Howe, 21 vols. London: Dent.

PLATO. 1963. *The Collected Dialogues including the Letters*, eds. Edith Hamilton and Huntington Cairns, Bollingen Foundation, N.Y. Princeton, NJ: Princeton University Press.

SAUER, T. G. 1981. *A. W. Schlegel's Shakespearean Criticism in England, 1811–1846.* Bonn: Bouvier Verlag Herbert Grundmann.

SCHLEGEL, A. W. 1815. *A Course of Lectures on Dramatic Art and Literature by Augustus William Schlegel*, trans. John Black, 2 vols. London.

WORDSWORTH, WILLIAM. 1974. *Prose Works*, 3 vols, eds. W. J. B. Owen and Jane Worthington Smyser. Oxford: Clarendon Press.

ZUCCATO, EDOARDO. 1996. *Coleridge in Italy.* Cork: Cork University Press.

CHAPTER 11

COLERIDGE AS LITERARY CRITIC: *BIOGRAPHIA LITERARIA* AND *ESSAYS ON THE PRINCIPLES OF GENIAL CRITICISM*

RAIMONDA MODIANO

BIOGRAPHIA LITERARIA is without question Coleridge's most controversial, most widely read and provocative work. Since its publication in 1817, the book has attracted polarized critical reactions, from extravagant praise to downright mean-spirited ridicule, from awe to barely hidden contempt. While some have perceived the *Biographia* as 'the greatest book of criticism in English' (Arthur Symons) and its author as the 'acknowledged "father" of theory itself' (Trott 1998: 69), fantasizing about the day when every person pursuing a university education would be provided with a copy of this indispensable text (George Saintsbury), F. R. Leavis, writing in the early 1940s, at a time when the New Critics nearly made Saintsbury's wish come true, declared Coleridge's 'currency as an academic classic' to be 'something of a scandal' (*BL*, i. xli–ii; Wellek 1972: 221).

Scandal has indeed accompanied the reception of the *Biographia* ever since Thomas De Quincey exposed Coleridge's plagiarisms from Schelling, opening the door to a series of ever more vituperative revelations of his unacknowledged borrowings from German writers. But it is not just plagiarism, a natural subject of controversy, that has polarized critics, but virtually anything having to do with the *Biographia*: its compositional history; its structure, with some critics seeing this work as no less than 'a miracle of rare device' (Wheeler 1980) and others as one of Coleridge's 'rubble-heap works' (McFarland 1981: 21); its genre, which raises the question as to whether the denomination of 'autobiography' is the right fit for it; and its contribution to canons of literary criticism and an evaluation of Wordsworth as critic and poet. While one does not expect consensus among critics about any work, it is fair to say that the disagreements and acrimonious debates about the *Biographia* have been unusually and relentlessly divisive. The much prized Coleridgean ideal of 'extremes meet' is a rare find in the critical literature on the *Biographia*. In this domain more often than not extremes do **not** meet. In this essay, I shall review some of these controversies, beginning with the compositional history of the *Biographia*, a seemingly less inflammatory subject in Coleridge criticism than plagiarism, but in fact intimately connected to it. I shall also discuss Coleridge's conception of the enterprise of literary criticism in the *Biographia* in relation to what he elusively called 'genial criticism' in his 1814 *Essays on the Principles of Genial Criticism*. This work is rooted not only in Kant's *Critique of Judgment*, but also in the aesthetic theory of Richard Payne Knight, a source occluded by Coleridge, and largely unacknowledged by critics. I argue that in spite of Coleridge's distaste for Knight's associationist philosophy, Coleridge regarded him as a serious rival in aesthetics, because Knight in fact articulated, however inconsistently, a proto-Kantian theory of the universality of taste, anticipating Coleridge's own directions. Knight also defended the essential difference between poetry and prose, identifying in Milton's practice of mixing prosaic with elevated verse the same defect for which Coleridge criticized Wordsworth in the *Biographia*.

HISTORY OF COMPOSITION

The birth of the *Biographia* was by all measure an extraordinary event for Coleridge. That he wrote it at all after years of misery caused by opium addiction, health problems, and disappointment over his unfulfilled creative potential is a matter of wonder. Between March 1815, when he first decided to publish an edition of his collected poems with a preface, and the end of July, Coleridge managed to dictate to John Morgan a large manuscript, which was sent to the Bristol printer Gutch on 19 September 1815, complete with the philosophical chapters. The event which precipitated this unparalleled speed of composition was the appearance of Wordsworth's 1815 edition of poems and its Preface, which posed a fundamental threat to Coleridge's identity as philosopher and critic. However, as eager as Coleridge was to get the *Biographia* out expeditiously, the book was not published until July 1817, as Coleridge, responding to requests from the printers, had to divide the single prose volume into two, and later add one hundred and fifty pages to the second volume to make it equal in length to the first (*BL*, i. lix–xv).

The controversy I am about to outline concerns the specific chapters Coleridge might have completed by the end of July 1815, and between 29 July and 19 September when the manuscript was dispatched to the printers. This controversy is handicapped from the start by the absence of a substantial evidentiary record regarding the order in which Coleridge composed various chapters. With no manuscript surviving, this record amounts to a total of three letters: (1) a letter written by Coleridge to R. H. Brabant of 29 July 1815 which records the transformation of his Preface into an 'Autobiographia literaria', including 'a full account of the Controversy with Wordsworth' (*CL*, iv. 578–9); (2) a letter by Morgan to Hood of 10 August 1815, which describes Coleridge's manuscript as containing 'a metaphysical part of about 5 or 6 sheets', in addition to a completed section of '57 sides' and one nearly complete of '100 sides' (*CL*, iv. 585 and n. 2); and (3) a letter by Coleridge to Gutch of 17 September 1815, which specifies that the '57 sides' sent to him by Morgan contained chapters 1 to 3 of the *Biographia* and that the 'philosophic Part' was written after 10 August (*CL*, iv. 584–7).

For Engell and Bate, who follow the view of both Earl Leslie Griggs and Daniel Fogel (1977), these documents tell the following story: that by the end of July 1815, Coleridge had completed chapters 1 through 4, possibly part of chapter 5, chapters 14 through part of 22 on the critique of Wordsworth, and a conclusion, 'some of what later became chapter 24'. On the other hand, the philosophical chapters were 'of minor significance by August 10' as, according to a footnote added later, Coleridge was 'still in the midst of Chapter 12', which he finished along with chapter 13 by 19 September (*BL*, i. li–viii). This theory has been contested by Norman Fruman and Nigel Leask, who oppose the 'rushed writing' perspective on the philosophical chapters, claiming that they were composed much earlier and with considerable leisure. Fruman (1985: 160–5) believes that Morgan's estimate of the size of the manuscript completed by 10 August is inaccurate and that chapters 12 and 13 could not have been completed between 16 and 19 September, a period when Coleridge was most likely engaged in the correction of Morgan's transcript rather than in 'frantic composition'. Leask (Coleridge 1997: xlv–viii) also argues that the bulk of the *Biographia* was completed by the end of July 1815, but adds a new twist to this view, claiming that the chapters Coleridge wrote in August and September were those 'of an anecdotal, autobiographical or polemical (rather than philosophical/critical) character' (xlvii).

It is difficult to take sides with any of these points of views or decide which one is the more probable and authoritative. Fruman is certainly entitled to question Engell's and Bate's contention that the dense philosophical chapters 12 and 13 were written in three days, particularly as the main evidence for this view is a footnote with an uncertain date. However, Fruman's speculation that Morgan's letter to Gutch provides inaccurate information about the size of Coleridge's manuscript looks suspiciously convenient to bolster his theory that the full manuscript of the *Biographia*, except for final corrections, was completed by 10 August. There is also no real evidence to support Leask's theory that 'the anecdotal, autobiographical and polemical chapters' (i.e., chapters 10 and 11 of volume one and 15 and 16 of volume two) were written after the hard work on the 'philosophical/critical' chapters was completed. In fact, one could argue that chapter 15, on the 'characteristics of original genius' based on an analysis of Shakespeare's works, sets up important standards used by Coleridge to diagnose the defects of Wordsworth's poetry in chapter 22, while chapter 16, on the merits of fifteenth and sixteenth-century poets, redefines the ideal of simplicity in a way that makes it congruent with 'dignified conversation' rather than Wordsworth's version of the 'real language of men' (Modiano 1989*a*). These chapters, therefore, are integral to, and could have been written during the same period as the chapters focused on the critique of Wordsworth.

In the final analysis, as Leask aptly summarizes (Coleridge 1997: xlviii), the burden of proof for the composition of the *Biographia* consists in 'Coleridge's word' in his letter of 17 September 'against Coleridge's word' in his letter of 29 July. But if this is true, why have a controversy at all, and is this really a controversy about the dating of various chapters of the *Biographia*? Upon closer scrutiny, it becomes apparent that this debate is underwritten by a deeper and, for Coleridge admirers, more painful issue concerning Coleridge's plagiarisms, which has afflicted the reception of the *Biographia* ever since De Quincey launched the charge in *Tait's Magazine* in 1834. Engell and Bate present the rush with which Coleridge finished the *Biographia* under considerable financial pressures and psychological distress as a sympathetic 'explanation' of his plagiarisms, clearly with the view of taking the sting out of the duplicity of this practice (*BL*, i. lviii). Fruman, on the other hand, favors the idea of an early and leisurely composition of the *Biographia*'s philosophical chapters, so as to place the burden of plagiarism on an endemic flaw of Coleridge's character, rather than particular circumstances. Leask, who attempts to be even-handed and mediate between the two positions, in the end sides with Fruman's point of view.

We are told by critics that the issue of plagiarism, so 'hotly contested' in the late 1960s and early 1970s in the arduous debates between Fruman and McFarland,[1] 'has

---

[1] On the plagiarism debate, see McFarland (1969 and 1974), Fruman (1971 and 1989), Matlack (1993), and Andrew Keanie's essay in this volume.

more or less burnt itself out' (Trott 1998: 68–9), as critical interest has shifted from 'tracing Coleridge's indebtedness to placing him within the larger European intellectual community' as a contributor to the 'dissemination of philosophical knowledge' (Schulz 1985: 411). However, as the composition controversy about the *Biographia* proves, the focus on plagiarism is alive and well, and likely to emerge under different guises.

STRUCTURE AND GENRE

The compositional history of the *Biographia* has a direct bearing on discussions of its structure and genre. Given the haste with which Coleridge put together the manuscript largely by dictation, it would appear that Coleridge's own assessment of this work as an 'immethodical . . . miscellany' (*BL*, i. 88) was not far off the mark. But while critics have often characterized the *Biographia* as afflicted by 'dissociation, fragmentation, and incoherence' (Ruf 1992: 542), or 'the profusion of the peripheral' with no center in sight, (Christensen 1981: 96, 120–1), to this day many have defended its unity, regarding the 'accusations of incoherence and disorganization' to be 'misguided' (McGann 1989: 237). Much of the disagreement among critics as to whether the *Biographia* is or is not a methodical work, depends in large measure on three factors: (1) whether critics regard the material added by Coleridge during the printing process from work written for different occasions as mere 'padding', or congruent with Coleridge's opinions throughout the *Biographia*, as Shawcross argued (Coleridge 1907: xcii);[2] (2) whether critics view the relationship between Coleridge's philosophical speculations in volume one and the applied criticism of volume two as connected or disconnected;[3] and (3) whether they react positively or negatively to Coleridge's long promised but curtailed exposition of the theory of the imagination at the end of chapter 13, including the invented letter from a friend.

---

[2] This view is also endorsed by McGann (1989: 247–9), who claims that Coleridge's review of Marturin's play *Bertram* shows his 'literary criticism operating at its most polemical moral level', and by White (2003: 467), who demonstrates that the inclusion of 'Satyrane's Letters' was meant 'partly to exemplify and partly to mock both the autobiographical "I" and the transcendent "I AM"'.

[3] Hamilton notes (1983: 10) that Coleridge's failure to produce the promised treatise on the imagination in chapter 13, and thus establish the connection between his philosophy and practical criticism, 'has helped critics from Arnold to Leavis', to 'Empson, and the American "new critics"' to 'overestimate the importance of a pure practical criticism, and even to believe in the possibility of its self-sufficiency'.

A telling example of how a critic's view of the structure of the *Biographia* depends on an evaluation of Coleridge's theory of the imagination can be glimpsed from two studies published by Kathleen Wheeler and Eugene Stelzig in 1980, each offering opposite perspectives on the *Biographia*, as well as the dominant critical culture of the time. Wheeler (1980: 126), reacting against the view of the *Biographia* as 'an unsystematic disconnected jumble of unrelated elements', points out the seamless continuity between the treatment of philosophy in volume one and of poetry in volume two, singling out the theory of the imagination in chapter 13 as 'literally, as well as essentially, the structural pivotal point or the hinge which holds the two volumes together' (131) and as 'an expression of the design of the work as a whole' (127). Wheeler sees organicism not only as *Biographia*'s overriding philosophy, but also as its great feat of execution. By contrast, Stelzig (1980: 83) argues that Coleridge's theory of the imagination 'has been taken all too seriously by most modern scholars and critics' and that the *Biographia* is 'propped up from the start to collapse disastrously by the end of volume I'. Stelzig does not share Wheeler's enthusiasm for the self-conscious, masterful design of the *Biographia*, or chapter 13 in particular, a chapter which in his view is 'both farcical and anti-climactic', presenting a theory of the imagination that can at best be described as a 'failed epiphany' (93–4). These polarized views leave us in somewhat of a quandary regarding the dominant critical culture about the *Biographia* in the late 1970s, for what are we to believe? If Stelzig is correct, the majority of critics up to 1980 held an overly idealistic view of the structure of the *Biographia*, best exemplified by Wheeler's position, and if Wheeler is correct, the majority of critics up to 1980 held an overly pessimistic view of the structure of this work, best exemplified by Stelzig's position.

While nowadays, in the aftermath of deconstruction and new historicism, the notion of organic unity is largely discredited as a false and politically problematic conceit, the issue of the coherence or incoherence of the *Biographia* has not disappeared in Coleridge studies, with critics still offering perspectives on both sides of the original controversy. A related issue, the specific genre of the *Biographia*, could significantly influence the outcome of this debate, if, for example, one could prove that, irrespective of the extraneous material plugged into the *Biographia* at various stages of composition and publication, there is an underlying narrative form that holds everything together. But the question of the genre of the *Biographia*, in particular its status as autobiography, is by no means settled in Coleridge studies, with Coleridge being the first to disclaim this identity by changing the title from the original 'Autobiographia literaria' (*CL*, iv. 578) to *Biographia Literaria*, and promising readers a proper autobiography in the future (*BL*, ii. 237). And yet, contrary to Coleridge's view, many critics have argued that the book 'belongs squarely' to the genre of autobiography and that Coleridge's preference for the word 'biography' over 'autobiography' was motivated by his desire to replace a term which conveyed egotism with one that, as understood by

Samuel Johnson, implied 'Truth, impartiality, and setting the record straight' (Jackson 1997: 57).[4]

The question of the generic status of the *Biographia* is further complicated by the fact that autobiography is a host genre 'open to all forms of human experience' and writing (Jackson 1997: 67–8). It blends naturally with the genre of *apologia*, which was commonly used in eighteenth-century satiric literature (Vogel 1989: 34–5). 'All autobiography', writes Haeger (1989: 77), 'is apologia', a view contrary to Hazlitt's who saw a tension between the two terms, complaining that, instead of an autobiography, Coleridge produced an 'apologia', 'not so properly an account of his Life and Opinions, as an Apology for them' (Jackson, J. R. de J. 1970–91: i. 295). The etymological history of the term *apologia* reveals a double meaning that is particularly suited to the *Biographia*, signifying both a public defense against an unfair charge and an admission of offense. In the opening pages of the *Biographia*, Coleridge uses 'apologia' or in his designation, 'exculpation'[5] in the former sense, alluding to the numerous undeserved charges leveled against him by anonymous critics. To a large extent, *Biographia* features a defense of the man of letters in the public arena against hostile detractors, and aims to establish a new model of a literary review, entirely cleansed of personal biases, and based on the most scrupulous 'application of the rules, deduced from philosophical principles, to poetry and criticism' (*BL*, i. 5). Coleridge's discomfort with the possible designation of his work as 'autobiography' stems from his desire to avoid anything that could be inferred as bearing on personal motivations in his handling of the controversy with Wordsworth on poetic diction. However, given what we know about the sense of urgency with which Coleridge produced the *Biographia* in response to Wordsworth's 1815 volume, it is not surprising that the spirit with which he conducted his evaluation of his friend was hardly that of 'utmost impartiality', nor that Wordsworth registered Coleridge's presumed 'defense' of him against the anonymous critics as an 'offense'.[6] In the end, Coleridge did not, as he had hoped, 'settle' the controversy with Wordsworth on poetic diction, but in fact, as the current critical debates indicate, secured its longevity.

---

[4] Kearns (1995: 109–10) has also defended the appropriateness of viewing the *Biographia* as autobiography, but paradoxically, at moments which disrupt the narrative coherence conventionally associated with autobiographic writing. For the view that the *Biographia* is a 'mixture of autobiography and philosophy', see Haeger (1989: 77), and Wallace (1983), who warns, however, that this mixture creates 'awkward moments' and disorientation for 'even the most careful reader' (14).

[5] As noted by Leask (*BL* (1997): xxviii–xxx), exculpation, which is distinct from both 'confession and straight autobiography', is 'a central—maybe even the dominant and unifying—concern of the book'.

[6] As mentioned by Crabb Robinson, Wordsworth was as offended by Coleridge's 'extravagant' praise of him in the *Biographia*, as by his 'inconsiderate' criticisms (Gravil 1984: 38).

COLERIDGE'S CRITIQUE OF WORDSWORTH

In the late 1970s and early 1980s, Coleridge's assessment of Wordsworth in the *Biographia* came under sharp critical scrutiny, losing much of the authority and appeal it had previously enjoyed, even among critics such as Fruman and Wellek, who could hardly be suspected of partiality for Coleridge.[7] In an attempt to overturn the unfavorable view of Wordsworth generated by Coleridge, critics have mounted a vigorous campaign to exonerate Wordsworth of all the flaws singled out by Coleridge in the *Biographia*, exposing his critique as largely inaccurate, transparently hostile, and based on principles that were incongruous with Wordsworth's views on poetry and poetic practice. As a result, Coleridge has been accused by critics of misunderstanding, or worse, understanding rather precisely,[8] but willfully misrepresenting just about everything regarding his friend's theory and poetry. He misunderstood Wordsworth's conception of the 'language of real men' as presented in his Preface to the *Lyrical Ballads*;[9] he misunderstood the meaning of the word 'essential' in Wordsworth's provocative claim that there is no difference between the language of poetry and of prose (Bialostosky 1978: 920); he misunderstood Wordsworth's genuine 'passion for meter';[10] he misunderstood the 'truly revolutionary' status of Wordsworth's claim in the 1802 Preface that the poet is 'a man speaking to men'[11]; and he misunderstood the significance of Wordsworth's preference for narrators, which he characterized as a 'species of ventriloquism' arising from Wordsworth's inability to achieve, like Shakespeare, a genuine identification with his characters (Parrish 1973). Given these revelations, critics began to inquire 'how one can account for criticism so inconsiderate, and occasionally obtuse, emanating from a man as wonderfully gifted as Coleridge' (Gravil

---

[7] Bialostosky (1978) reviews and takes issue with early favorable opinions of Coleridge's chapters on Wordsworth. The controversy about his article that ensued in *PMLA* (see Bialostosky 1979*a* and 1979*b*) demonstrates how difficult it was in the late 1970s to question the authority of Coleridge's critical opinions.

[8] According to Simpson (1989: 213), it is 'inappropriate' to define Coleridge's 'negative judgments about Wordsworth' a 'misunderstanding', as his 'understanding seems very exact indeed', stemming from conservative political beliefs, a view also shared by Leask (1993: 54), who regards Coleridge's critique of Wordsworth as that of 'a Tory and Anglican Coleridge ... for reasons which ... were not motivated simply by aesthetic preferences'.

[9] Bialostosky (1978) argues that Coleridge's misrepresentation of what Wordsworth meant by 'the language of real men', derives from his error of using a grammatical concept of language, focused on words and their syntactical order, to interpret Wordsworth's rhetorical model, focused on the differences between the literal and figurative uses of language within a particular community.

[10] O'Donnell (1995) offers a detailed analysis of Wordsworth's dependence on meter and its relationship with diction 'to create a sense of the difference between the language of "real life" and the language of poetry' (24).

[11] Ruoff (1972) argues that while Coleridge privileges the written text in line with Neo-classical and Romantic formalist poetics, Wordsworth initiated a more radical, modern program that grounds poetic language in the spoken word.

1984: 38), and what might 'have occurred to pervert Coleridge's vision', as Shawcross suggested earlier on, though with considerable reluctance (Coleridge 1907: i. xciv–vi).

The particular event that led to Coleridge's vituperative attack on Wordsworth can be pinned down without difficulty and actually assigned a precise date. It was Wordsworth's 'Preface' to the 1815 edition of his *Poems*, which, as pointed out by Engell and Bate (*BL*, i. cxxxv) was the 'effective cause of the *Biographia*'. Although the roots of the *Biographia* can be traced further back into history, both with respect to its autobiographical form (*CN*, i. 1515), and Coleridge's plan to establish his version of the 'Canons of Criticism respecting Poetry' in reaction to Wordsworth (*CL*, ii. 830), without the appearance of Wordsworth's 1815 volume, Coleridge's own projected Preface may never have grown into 'an Autobiographia literaria' (*CL*, iv. 578), but would have remained yet another item on a long list of unrealized works.

The intensity of Coleridge's response to Wordsworth's 1815 Preface can be judged from his insistent instructions to the printer that the *Biographia* should be set in the same size and type as Wordsworth's 1815 Preface, and should not be confused with Wordsworth's 1800 Preface to the *Lyrical Ballads* (*BL*, ii. 284–5). This nervous demand on Coleridge's part about his preferred visual layout for the *Biographia* suggests that the 1815 rather than the 1800 Preface is the real source of the intemperate 'tone in which Coleridge approaches the dismemberment of Wordsworth's theory and practice in the public arena' (Gravil 1984: 38). The main provocation for Coleridge was by no means the audacity, for example, of Wordsworth's argument in the 1800 Preface that there was no 'essential' difference between the language of poetry and prose (an idea which at the time could have been prompted by Coleridge himself or Thelwall for that matter),[12] but rather Wordsworth's self-representation in the 1815 Preface not only as a literary giant in the distinguished lineage of Shakespeare and Milton, but, more ominously for Coleridge at that time, as an able philosopher, engaging fundamental concepts from Coleridge's own arsenal, such as the prized distinction between fancy and imagination.

As Johnston (1984: 333–62) convincingly demonstrates, the philosophical stature that Wordsworth assumes in the 1815 Preface is connected with the demise of his ambitious project *The Recluse*, partly due to the vicious criticisms heaped on *The Excursion* after its publication in 1814. As a result, the hopes for recognition Wordsworth had entertained regarding the grandiose philosophic scope and unified three part architectonic of *The Recluse* were now pinned onto his new but more manageable venture: the 1815 collection of poems, the Preface and 'Essay, Supplementary'. What was left of *The Recluse*, therefore, namely its meaning as 'symbol of the

---

[12] As O'Donnell (1995: 26–7) has shown, Thelwall had actually expressed a more radical view to Wordsworth about the lack of distinction between 'a *verse mouth* and a *prose mouth*' than Wordsworth was willing to entertain.

philosophic consistency of Wordsworth's genius', becomes Wordsworth's 'principal strategy' in the Preface, which consists of a shrewd defense of 'the coherence of his works' (334–5). Wordsworth's elaborate arrangement of his poems according to faculties of the mind, which gestures toward a recognizable Kantian schema, however vaguely and imprecisely,[13] indicates that the 'primary assumption of the 1815 preface is that a coherent arrangement of texts implies a coherent system of thought, in order that a collection of "poems, apparently miscellaneous" may be seen to exemplify the philosophical basis of the author's genius' (335–6).

Wordsworth's display of philosophic prowess in his 1815 Preface revived in Coleridge an earlier conflict born during their tortured collaboration on the *Lyrical Ballads*. In 1800, Wordsworth's assumption of single authorship of the second edition of the *Lyrical Ballads*, coupled with his notoriously uncharitable note on 'The Rime of the Ancient Mariner', left Coleridge with a keen sense of poetic failure and the decision to surrender poetry altogether to Wordsworth, confining his own efforts to the area of metaphysics, or what he mournfully called 'abstruse research' in 'Dejection: An Ode'. By a curious parallelism with an ironic twist, a sense of poetic failure caused by the critical response to *The Excursion*, likewise led Wordsworth to abandon a major poetic project, *The Recluse*, and make headway in philosophy instead, with no apparent sense that he was in any way unfit for the task.

For Coleridge, therefore, the challenge posed by Wordsworth's 1815 Preface was very real and very alarming. What concerned Coleridge in particular was Wordsworth's appropriation without acknowledgement of a significant number of Coleridge's own philosophic concepts, including the definition of the imagination as a 'modifying' and unifying power, as recoiling from 'everything but the plastic, the pliant and the indefinite' and as aligned with the eternal (Modiano 1989*b*). The only time Wordsworth refers to Coleridge as a source is with regard to Coleridge's view of fancy, which Wordsworth proceeds to criticize as 'too general', thus implying, as Johnston (1984: 337) rightly argues, that 'a Wordsworthian system has corrected a Coleridgean one, or supplanted one that Coleridge had failed to supply'. Perhaps such Wordsworthian provocations might have been less offensive to Coleridge if Wordsworth had not at the same time declared his independence from his former collaborator, bluntly banishing Coleridge's poems from his 1815 volume in exchange for the contributions of a 'Female Friend', and invoking the dispensation of 'propriety' to excise Coleridge out of his career (Owen and Smyser 1974: iii. 26, 39).

In view of these facts, it is not surprising that Coleridge took great offense at Wordsworth's 1815 Preface and was moved to respond. The seriousness of the threat

[13] As Engell and Bate argue (*BL*, i. 22 n. 3), Wordsworth's classification of his poems according to the faculties of the mind is influenced by Coleridge, and any such classification bears the mark of Kant. See Coleridge's statement that 'the only nomenclature of criticism should be the classification of the faculties of the mind' (*Lects 1808–19*, i. 564) and his remark in 1811 that, like Schlegel, he had studied 'the philosophy of Kant, the distinguishing feature of which [is] to treat every subject in reference to the operation of the mental Faculties, to which it specially appertains' (*CL*, iii. 360).

posed by Wordsworth is evident in the meticulousness and vehemence with which he undertook the demolition of Wordsworth's self-aggrandizing claims to 'undying remembrance' both as poetic and philosophic genius. Every move Wordsworth makes in the 1815 Preface is counteracted by Coleridge with a strategic counter-move. While Wordsworth retired the 1800 Preface to the end of the second volume, Coleridge makes it the very centerpiece of his critique in the *Biographia*, using it to undo Wordsworth's self-flattering presentation in the 1815 Preface as a dedicated philosopher, all clad in Kantian garb with a coherent system of classification. To Wordsworth's 'slim' performance in his 1815 Preface, Coleridge counterposes his own, conspicuously lengthy intellectual biography, which occupies the bulk of volume one of the *Biographia* and features Coleridge's arduous journey through the entire history of philosophy, from classical to contemporary; from empiricist, to rationalist, to transcendentalist; from British to continental. To Wordsworth's meandering theory of the imagination and his emphasis on imagination's capacity of 'consolidating numbers into unity, and dissolving and separating unity into number', Coleridge responds by outlining a much more complex dual structure at the heart of the imagination, as represented by the primary and secondary imagination, focusing on the connection of the former with the I AM, in a concise formula whose triumph is achieved in no mean measure through the simplicity and conciseness with which it distills dense philosophic material from numerous sources.

Coleridge's need to demonstrate the superiority of his philosophic stature over Wordsworth's was triggered not only by Wordsworth's trespassing into Coleridgean territory on subjects such as the nature of the imagination and its distinction from fancy, but also by the uninhibited way in which Wordsworth proclaims his place among famous conquerors and poets, using ideas garnered from Coleridge to propel himself to the very summit of literary achievement. In his Preface, Wordsworth boldly places himself in the company of Milton and Shakespeare, arguing that like his predecessors, he deserves 'to be holden in undying remembrance' (Owen and Smyser 1974: iii. 35). In his 'Essay, Supplementary', furthermore, he refers to the unmerited hostility toward and incomprehension of the merits of Milton's and Shakespeare's works by their contemporaries as proof that his own 'positions', frequently attacked by critics, were 'not erroneous' (Owen and Smyser 1974: iii. 71). In order to bolster the image of Shakespeare as an ideal mirror for his own self-regard, Wordsworth opposes the view of Shakespeare as a 'wild irregular genius', so popular among his own 'fellow-countrymen', proposing instead an approach to Shakespeare based on an organic model, whereby the apparent heterogeneity of Shakespeare's materials can be seen as belonging to 'a unity of their own' (Owen and Smyser 1974: iii. 69). In a footnote, Wordsworth appropriately acknowledges Coleridge's course of lectures at the Royal Institution, which are the direct source of his discussion of Shakespeare here, but while he applauds Coleridge's furor at the 'insensibility' of his countrymen in misunderstanding Shakespeare, he makes no mention that it was Coleridge who pushed for a new understanding of Shakespeare in terms of an organic model, albeit by paraphrasing or plagiarizing Schlegel.

In many respects the project of the *Biographia* is to defeat Wordsworth's assumption that he belongs to the company of Milton and Shakespeare by tightening the association of these two writers with an organic model of artistic creation and using that very model to expose Wordsworth's failure as both thinker and writer. In chapter 1 of the *Biographia*, Coleridge sets up the prerogative of organicism from the outset in an admittedly 'bold' formulation that invokes the authority of Milton and Shakespeare, asserting that 'it would be scarcely more difficult to push a stone out from the pyramids with the bare hand, than to alter a word, or the position of a word, in Milton or Shakespeare' (*BL*, i. 23). Viewed against the norm of organic unity, Wordsworth's poetry fares poorly, and Coleridge misses few opportunities to highlight the pervasive disunity at the heart of Wordsworth's poems. The five major defects in Wordsworth's poetry pointed out by Coleridge in chapter 22 of the *Biographia*— '*disharmony* in style' manifested in sudden moves from 'striking' to 'undistinguished' language (*BL*, ii. 121–6); matter-of-factness, which pulls the mind away from the contemplation of a whole, focusing the attention on disparate parts only (*BL*, ii. 126–35); the misuse of 'the *dramatic* form', which creates an incongruity between the 'thoughts and diction' of the poet and his characters or a 'species of ventriloquism' (*BL*, ii. 135); the disproportion of feelings to 'the objects described' (*BL*, ii. 136); and last '*mental* bombast' or the 'disproportion' of thought to expression (*BL*, ii. 136–41)—are all in the final analysis, as critics have often noted, sins of discontinuity that run counter to an organic ideal of art.[14] By invoking the example of Milton in this chapter to cure Wordsworth of matter-of-factness, and teach him the difference between genuine creation and 'minuteness of description', Coleridge demonstrates that while Milton and Shakespeare belong together, as creators of consummate art based on organic principles, Wordsworth cuts an awkward figure in this illustrious lineage.

Many critics have expressed a manifest distaste for Coleridge's theory of organic art on the ground that it misrepresents the actual 'processes by which poems have to be produced' (Bloom 1972: 265); that it conflicts with Coleridge's own practice in the *Biographia* which tends 'toward dissonance and fragmentation' as opposed to unity (Ruf 1992: 545); that it has no bearing on 'the history of the development of an accurate Shakespearean text' (Fruman 1971: 162–3; Davidson 1971: 171–6), nor for that matter on Milton's work, often viewed by others as inorganic (McLaughlin 1964); that it is willfully suspended in his evaluation of Wordsworth, as Coleridge 'makes no effort to examine' any of Wordsworth's poems 'as a whole, and to look at its parts in the light of that whole' (Gravil 1984: 41); that it does not apply to Wordsworth's theory of poetry, which emphasizes 'difference and variety' rather than unity (O'Donnell, 1995: 50–2); and that it is a conservative ideological construct in line with Edmund Burke, legitimating 'the hegemony of the few *over* the many' (Simpson 1989: 220–4). In an attempt to defend Coleridge against such

---

[14] As Simpson (1989: 215) points out, 'Almost all of Coleridge's objections to Wordsworth depend upon the degree to which certain features of his poetry inhibit or refuse the illusion of organic form.'

objections, Buell (1979: 400, 407–10) proposes that the *Biographia*, whose central subject is 'the unfolding of a mind in the act of self-definition', should be read as 'an implied' and apparently self-conscious 'critique' by Coleridge of the theory of organic unity. This theory, Buell argues, 'might be regarded as a necessary myth for Coleridge the thinker, at variance with his instincts' as well as his digressive, informal, and 'rambling' practice 'as a writer'.

While it is reasonable to question whether Coleridge was whole-heartedly attached to the notion of organic unity or merely used it as an effective tool against Wordsworth, and while one can observe in the *Biographia* alternative models of measuring artistic success put forward by Coleridge (below, 229), to regard organic theory as a 'myth' reveals more our own contemporary discomfort with such absolutist aesthetic standards than Coleridge's. For Coleridge, the notion of organic theory was, to use an appropriate Kantian language, *'an ideal without a flaw'* (*Critique of Pure Reason*, 531). Just as in Kant, the futile effort of reason to prove the existence of supersensible ideas such as God or freedom of will does not cancel but safeguards the ideal itself, which at the very point of the defeat of reason is celebrated as 'a concept which completes and crowns the whole of human knowledge' (531), so likewise, for Coleridge, deviations from or violations of the norm of organic unity in practice either by himself or Wordsworth do not amount to skepticism about the norm itself. Coleridge articulated the theory of organic unity long before Wordsworth became a target of his critique, so one cannot suspect mere pragmatic reasons on Coleridge's part for his ubiquitous use of it in the *Biographia*. The theory is at the core of Coleridge's concept of the imagination and of genius, which in large measure are the central subjects of the *Biographia*. It also underwrites Coleridge's endeavor to establish the discipline of literary criticism on sound philosophic principles, or better yet 'genial' principles. This project has an earlier incarnation in Coleridge's *Essays on the Principles of Genial Criticism*, a work published only a year before the composition of the *Biographia* with which, as we shall see, it shares an intriguing history, ultimately connected with the critique of Wordsworth.

Essays on the Principles of Genial Criticism

Coleridge's *Essays on the Principles of Genial Criticism*, first published in *Felix Farley's Bristol Journal*, appear to be the natural predecessor of the *Biographia*, as suggested by Coleridge's letter to Byron of 1815, where he described what eventually became the *Biographia*, as 'a general Preface...on the Principles of philosophic and genial criticism relatively to the Fine Arts in general; but especially to Poetry'

(*CL*, iv. 561). Coleridge maintained a high regard for the *Essays*, to which he referred as 'the best compositions' he had 'ever written' (*CL*, iii. 535), and as late as 1834, he expressed his desire to 'recover them', fearing that they would be lost for good (*TT*, i. 453). Coleridge's wish was granted posthumously, as in 1836 and 1837, the text was republished three times (by Thomas Allsop, T. Brokenhurst, and Joseph Cottle), but with numerous inaccuracies that would have shocked the author. These inaccuracies found their way into Shawcross's edition of the *Essays* appended to the *Biographia*, which, until their republication in their original form in the Collected Coleridge edition in 1995 (*SW&F*, i. 353–86), was the most widely used edition by critics, apparently without any awareness of the multiple textual errors it contained, including a most curious dislocation of lines from Coleridge's 'Dejection: An Ode'.[15]

The occasion for the *Essays* was provided by the exhibition in 1814 of the paintings of Washington Allston, whom Coleridge met in Rome in 1805 and who moved to London in 1811.[16] Coleridge's ostensible purpose in writing the *Essays* was to draw attention to Allston's paintings in order to help the artist restore his depleted finances and his reputation as a painter, which had been badly damaged by malicious reviewers (*CL*, iii. 534). In a letter to J. J. Morgan of July 1814, Coleridge justified his decision to publicize 'a bold Avowal of' his 'sentiments' as well as 'principles' concerning the fine arts 'by continued reference to Allston's Pictures', on the ground that he 'could not bear the Thought of putting in an ordinary Puff on such a man' (*CL*, iii. 520). The resulting *Essays*, did fulfill Coleridge's ambition to produce no 'ordinary Puff', but it is by no means clear in what way the *Essays* could have served Allston's interests, as references to the painter are infrequent, and only two of his paintings are discussed.

Two figures loom large in Coleridge's *Essays*, Immanuel Kant and Richard Payne Knight. Their conjunction spells out the contrast Coleridge proposes to show between an empirically-based theory of beauty linked to 'accidental associations', and a theory that conceives of beauty as 'pleasing for its own sake', and as impervious to personal attachments or interests. However, beyond this obvious contrast, Kant and Knight share a common feature—or shall we say fate—within the confines of Coleridge's *Essays*: neither of them is ever mentioned by name. The omission of Kant's name can be easily explained. If Coleridge mentioned Kant just once, he would have to mention him again and again, and reveal that, as Wellek (1931: 111–14) pointed out, the conceptual foundation of the *Essays* is essentially Kantian, including the distinction between the beautiful, the agreeable, and the good, the definition of beauty as consisting in a purely formal unity of parts within

---

[15] Shawcross (Coleridge 1907: ii. 313) notes the ridiculous manner in which Coleridge transposed lines from 'Dejection: an Ode', without realizing that, as Nabholtz (1986: 119, n. 26; 1987: 191) documented, he created the 'the very confusion about which he complains'.

[16] On Coleridge's relationship with Washington Allston, see *SW&F*, i. 354 and n. 5, *CL*, iii. 520–1 and *CN*, ii. 2796, 2831.

a whole, the universality of the judgments of taste, and the view that the beautiful consists in 'the perceived harmony of an object . . . with the inborn and constitutive rules of the judgment and imagination' (*SW&F*, i. 382–3). Even the meaning of the term 'genial criticism', which has been a puzzle to critics, is, as I shall demonstrate, of Kantian vintage.

If the omission of Kant's name in the *Essays* can be attributed to Coleridge's desire to conceal his debt to the German philosopher, the suppression of Knight's name is more intriguing and requires critical scrutiny. Coleridge might have had personal reasons to refrain from identifying Knight as the author of *An Analytical Inquiry into the Principles of Taste* (1805), against which he directed an abundance of vituperative comments and not a single word of approbation.[17] In 1804, Coleridge had visited Knight twice in the month of March to secure a letter of introduction for his trip to Malta. To attack Knight, therefore, would have appeared to Coleridge as an objectionable gesture of ingratitude and a breach of civility. Furthermore, Knight was already at the centre of heated controversies, triggered at one end by the publication of his work *The Worship of Priapus* (1786), which made the provocative claim that Christianity's main symbol, the cross, was derived from ancient fertility rites, and at the other end by the unpopular position he took on the subject of the Elgin marbles, which he regarded as second-rate Roman copies of Greek antiquities (Messmann 1974: 141–65). In 1810, Knight was also involved in a series of controversies, being attacked by the sculptor John Rossi for opposing his commission to work on some monuments, by Edward Copleston for criticizing the scholarship at Oxford University, and by Benjamin Robert Haydon for his negative review of the painter James Barry (Messmann 1974: 141–2). In this context, engaging Knight personally and vituperatively would have been both in bad taste and ineffective, adding a mere drop in a pretty large bucket of cumulative public opprobrium.

But there is another reason why Coleridge used the generic phrase 'English critic' (*SW&F*, i. 363) when criticizing Knight. In spite of all the controversies surrounding him, Knight remained a very respected and sought-after figure in literary and artistic circles. In 1814, 'he continued to be a conspicuous figure in London', dining with Byron and Thomas Lawrence and attending an exhibition at the British Institution, where he gave a guided tour to the Princess of Wales (Messmann 1974: 145). Furthermore, Knight's *Analytical Inquiry* remained a highly influential book, gaining the reputation of establishing the canon on taste, and, through its use of Scottish aesthetics, becoming 'the most sophisticated work on the subject to be produced in England during the period' (Funnell 1982: 83). In 1808, when Coleridge gave his first lecture on the principles of poetry, he recognized that the

---

[17] Coleridge's hostile reaction to Knight can be glimpsed from his marginalia to the third edition of his *Analytical Inquiry* (1806), written in Wordsworth's hand but believed to have been dictated by Coleridge (*M*, iii. 400–13).

work, which, by that time had reached its fourth edition, 'has excited no ordinary degree of attention' (*Lects 1808–19*, i. 31), an opinion corroborated by Sidney Smith who wrote from London that 'Knight's book has attracted amazing attention' (Funnell 1982: 83).[18]

Because critics have generally focused on the Kantian side of Coleridge's *Essays* or the syncretism of Kantian and neo-platonic elements in this work, they have missed the extent to which much of the manner and the matter of the *Essays* were triggered by Coleridge's intense response to Knight's *Analytical Inquiry*. This is evident in Coleridge's first lecture on the principles of poetry in the 1808 series where he copied a long passage from Knight's *Analytical Inquiry* and proceeded to develop a Kantian response to Knight's claims (*Lects 1808–19*, i. 31–6). The same passage from Knight and Coleridge's Kantian elaboration appear in more developed form in the *Essays*. This history makes clear that in the domain of aesthetics it was Knight who was Coleridge's rival, not Kant. Kant merely provided the solution, an authoritative one no doubt, to Coleridge's emerging ambition to displace Knight—to whom he referred disdainfully but meaningfully as the 'taste-meter to the fashionable world' (*SW&F*, i. 363)—and become the new authority on 'fixed' canons of art criticism for his generation.

The reason why Knight became a threat to Coleridge was not because Knight presented a concept of taste based on association. Rather, the problem for Coleridge was the same that alarmed him about Wordsworth when he read his 1815 Preface, namely Knight's movement toward a Kantian position. Although one can point to numerous passages in Knight where he presents judgments of beauty as relative, varying among different cultures or individuals, as Funnell (1982: 83) rightly contends, for 'Knight, associationism, like Burke's sensationism, could not on its own serve as an exhaustive explanation of the nature of "Taste"'. More importantly, Knight actually gestures toward a theory of the universality of taste. At the very start of his treatise, noting that individuals can determine their feelings in the matter of taste only by 'their congruity with those of the generality of his species', Knight (1805: 4–5) asks:

Is there then no real and permanent principle of beauty? No certain or definable combination of forms, lines, or colours, that are in themselves gratifying to the mind, or pleasing to the organs of sensation? Or are we, in this respect, merely creatures of habit and imitation; directed by every accidental impulse, and swayed by every fluctuation of caprice or fancy? It will be said, perhaps, in reply, that we must not found universal skepticism in occasional deviations, or temporary irregularities: for...there are certain standards of excellence, which every generation of civilized man...has uniformly recognized in theory, how variously soever they have departed from them in practice. Such are the precious remains of Grecian sculpture, which afford standards of real beauty, grace, and elegance in the

---

[18] On the critical reception of Knight's treatise, see Messmann 1974: 105–8.

human form, and the modes of adorning it, the truth and perfection of which have never been questioned...

Messmann's statement that Knight 'attempts to formulate a universal standard of taste' (1974: 103) strikes me as accurate. A proper reading of Knight, therefore, would include a focus on his search for a quasi Kantian/Coleridgean formula for taste and his agony of not finding it. As Messmann elaborates, 'Knight illustrates the eighteenth-century Newtonian tendency to search for immutable laws, hoping to find some permanent rules governing taste, yet really despairing of ever discovering them' (118).

One of Coleridge's recurrent critiques of Knight was that he did not differentiate between the 'pleasures derived from the palate and from the intellect', and that for him 'a taste *for* Milton' was 'essentially the same as the taste *of* mutton' (*SW&F*, i. 363). Coleridge clearly relished this phrase, which he repeated in several contexts, but as ingenious as the phrase is, linking two similarly sounding words to accentuate their utter incompatibility in meaning, it constitutes a cheap shot at Knight whose argument is more complex than Coleridge indicates. In a long passage from *An Analytical Inquiry* (9–13), the same Coleridge used for his 1808 lecture on the principles of poetry, Knight complained about the indiscriminate application of the word 'beauty' 'to almost every thing that is pleasing, either to the sense, the imagination, or the understanding; whatever the nature of it be, whether a material substance, a moral excellence, or an intellectual theorem'. He attacked Burke's view that beauty should be confined to sensible objects, arguing that the term could be used 'with equal propriety' not only with reference to 'the beauties of symmetry and arrangement' but also 'those of virtue, charity, holiness, &c.' Furthermore, while Knight does claim that there is no distinction in the application of the term 'beautiful' to sensory objects or to formal ('symmetry and arrangement') and moral qualities ('virtue, charity, holiness'), he does not mean to sink the latter to the level of the former. Rather, Knight is trying to show that in effect the beautiful, as Coleridge wrote, following Kant, 'must belong to the intellect' (*SW&F*, i. 381), whether this involves objects of sight and hearing or abstract qualities such as virtue and holiness. This is why Knight disputes the view that the beautiful is used in relation to 'objects of intellect' in a figurative sense, because figuration 'employs the image or idea of one thing to illustrate another', whereas

when we speak of the *beauty of virtue*, we mean the pleasing result of well-balanced and duly proportioned affections; and when we speak of the *beauty of the human form*, we mean the pleasing result of well-balanced and duly proportioned limbs and features. In both instances the word is equally applied to the results of proportion, without reference to any other image; and though, in the one, the *general subject* be mental, and in the other corporeal, the *particular object*, in both, is an abstract idea, and consequently, purely intellectual; nor is the expression more figurative in the one than in the other. (11–12)

This passage, as Knox (2004) has persuasively shown, underwrites Coleridge's first 1808 lecture, particularly his claim that

in its metaphorical Sense as applied to the fine arts, Taste implies an intellectual perception of any object ... for otherwise we should confound the metaphorical with the primary sense of the word—a blunder, which, if I mistake not, lies at the bottom of a whole system on the Principles of Taste—tho' common language might have suggested, that we taste a Ragout, but we do not taste the Paradise Lost, but *have a Taste* for it.   (*Lects 1808–19*, i. 30)

Here we have an earlier and, arguably tastier version of the Milton/mutton pun with an obvious reference to the title of Knight's treatise. Even as Coleridge deviates from Knight's formula by stressing the role of the mind in regulating the senses, the backbone of his discussion, as Knox argues, is still recognizably Knight's.[19] Coleridge's eagerness to see Knight's system collapse through a main blunder at the very point where Knight is struggling to articulate the intellectual source of the beautiful, is a telling example of Coleridge's main worry regarding his rival, which is not associationism but Knight's possible discovery of the internal ground that secures the legitimacy of 'principles of taste'.

   Coleridge's marginalia to Knight's treatise suggest that a great deal of his ire against Knight was triggered by his disparaging views of Milton. Undoubtedly, Knight's categorization of Milton as a poet who 'wrote from the head rather than the heart' (126), coupled with Knight's statement that Milton's deficiency of 'enthusiastic sentiment' manifested itself in the disproportion of 'gloomy grandeur and sour morality' (117), would have intensely provoked Coleridge. As early as 1802, Coleridge detected in Bowles rather than Milton 'a perpetual trick of *moralizing* everything' and contrasted Bowles to Milton, who possessed the 'native Passion' characteristic of 'a great Poet' (*CL*, ii. 864). There is, however, another aspect of Knight's critique of Milton that must have resonated with Coleridge, particularly by 1815, when he began the criticism of Wordsworth for the *Biographia*. Knight conducts his critique in the context of a larger argument about the difference between the language of poetry and prose, which Coleridge would take up in the *Biographia*. Knight claims that authentic verse must rise 'above the ordinary tone of common speech' and poetry, unlike prose, does not tolerate excessive variety. Therefore, Milton's abuse of irregularity, particularly with regards to pauses, is precisely what 'gives the character of prose to his verse, and deprives it of all that fire and enthusiasm of expression, which Pope has happily preserved in his translation of the corresponding passages of the Iliad' (118). In his critique of Milton, Knight also anticipates Coleridge's attack on Wordsworth's celebration of the language of rustics, a language which, according to Coleridge, lacks 'method'

---

[19] I am grateful to Julian Knox for sending me a copy of his conference paper on Knight (2004), as well as a longer version in which he demonstrates that Knight was a 'source of aesthetic paradigms from which Coleridge would extensively draw', including his theory of stage illusion which was central to his lectures on Shakespeare.

because it is not 'grounded on the habit of foreseeing, in each integral part . . . the whole that he intends to communicate' (*Friend*, i. 449). Knight writes that verse requires a 'methodical arrangement' of sounds and pauses to sustain 'a continued character of enthusiastic expression', which is 'above the ordinary tone of common speech'. He notes that it 'is only by a constant preconception of what is to follow, that the poetical flow of utterance and elevation of tone are sustained; for, unless the reader be generally apprized of what is to come, by what has gone before, he is like a person walking blindfolded over an uneven road' (116).

It should be clear by now that there is a link between Knight and Wordsworth, and between Coleridge's *Essays* and the *Biographia*. In the *Essays*, Wordsworth is invisible but present implicitly in Coleridge's citation of lengthy passages from his poem 'Dejection: An Ode', a poem written in response to the first four stanzas of Wordsworth's 'Intimations' ode and born out of a period of intense literary competition with his friend. But the association of Knight with Wordsworth has an even earlier history. It began in March 1804, when Coleridge met Knight for the first time, as recorded in the following memorable opening of a letter to George Beaumont:

> I called on Mr. Knight, on Tuesday Noon/he was engaged with a gentleman in looking over his collection. Bye the bye (whether it were that the sight of so many Bronzes all at once infected my eye, as by long looking at the setting Sun all objects become purple, or whether there really be a likeness) Mr. Knight's own face represented to my fancy that of a living Bronze. It is the hardest countenance, I ever beheld, in a man of rank and letters, but the myrtle, no less than the yew-tree, starts up from the fissures of the crag, and the Vine, that rejoices the hearts of Gods and Men, spreads its tendrils & ripens it's clusters on the naked rock.—In the following moment the likeness of his face to that Mask-portrait of Wordsworth at Keswick struck me with greater force; and till I had left the House, I did not recollect, that Lady Beaumont had observed the same. (*CL*, ii. 1078)

This passage contains within it two metamorphoses, one building upon the other. The first is the transformation of Knight from a human being into a lifeless object which becomes animated through this very process: a *living* Bronze. We might speculate that Coleridge's sense of helplessness at being ignored initially by the influential 'man of rank and letters' triggers his attempt to seize, master, and diminish his stature. Later in the letter, he refers to Knight's manners as 'embarrassing' but excusable, given Coleridge's 'own *unbellerorphontic* countenance and mien.' From this position of physical and social inferiority, Coleridge rises above Knight, imprisoning him in the image of a bronze statue. His very question, presented parenthetically—was this a mere delusion of sight or did Knight's countenance 'really' resemble a bronze?—reveals Coleridge's discomfort at his own bold act of transforming a live man into a statue, which in the end only enhances his anxieties, as Knight's countenance looks terrifying in its inanimate state, its severity imprinted permanently in the metallic hardness of a bronze. Coleridge's hasty exit from the unendurable fixity of Knight's countenance into the fertile and dynamic world of nature, capable of covering and thus redeeming the austerity of any 'naked rock' with lush mantles of hope-inspiring vines for the benefit of men and gods alike, foregrounds Coleridge's next metamorphosis, which is not simply of Knight into Wordsworth, but of an inanimate representation of Knight into an inanimate 'Mask-portrait' of Wordsworth. The presumption of likeness between Knight and Wordsworth must have struck Coleridge as sufficiently problematic to require confirmation from an objective witness, Lady Beaumont. But what did Lady Beaumont confirm, the likeness of Knight to Wordsworth or to a portrait of Wordsworth? There is no indication that she would have experienced, like Coleridge, the first transformation of Knight into a bronze, upon which the second transformation of Knight into Wordsworth is predicated.

As this passage so vividly conveys, for Coleridge, Knight is a double of Wordsworth, and linked with him in a chain of potential substitutions. While in *Essays*, Knight is Coleridge's unnamed rival, in the *Biographia*, this role is openly occupied by Wordsworth. Knight does not, however, disappear from the *Biographia*, but lurks in the shadows on more than one occasion. Knight's repeated claims without much documentation that Milton's poetry has many 'beauties' that counterbalance his defects of versification are mirrored in Coleridge's vague assessment of the 'beauties' of Wordsworth's poetry in chapter 22 of *Biographia*. More importantly, Knight's charge that Milton's verse displays a mixture of prosaic lines and 'splendid parts' (121) is precisely Coleridge's argument in demonstrating that Wordsworth fails to produce organically integrated poetry. In a sense, Knight acquires a new role in the *Biographia*: he becomes Coleridge's ally in the project of demonstrating that there is a *real* difference between the language of poetry and the language of prose and that, as Coleridge presumably learned from his stern teacher James Boyer, poetry 'even that of the loftiest, and seemingly, that of the wildest odes, had a logic of its own, as severe as that of science'(*BL*, i. 9). The domineering Knight, once reduced to a bronze statue, actually empowers Coleridge to downsize the 'Giant' Wordsworth after all, who in the *Biographia* is put through the wringer of a meticulously crafted critique, from which he emerges much diminished both as poet and critic.

Genial Criticism

In *Essays*, Coleridge inaugurates a distinctive type of criticism, connected with his subsequent evaluation of Wordsworth in the *Biographia*, which he calls 'genial' criticism, a tantalizing designation, used rather sparingly by Coleridge and insufficiently discussed by critics. What exactly did Coleridge mean by 'genial criticism' in contradistinction to other prevailing critical practices? It is important to note that Coleridge used the term 'sound criticism' in the title of the first essay ('On the Principles of Sound Criticism'), changing it to 'genial' in the second and third essay. We can infer, therefore, that the type of criticism he has in mind is not based solely on 'sound' principles of a philosophic nature, but has an added dimension that the word 'genial' is meant to capture.

As the titles indicate, the essential feature of 'genial criticism' consists in the deduction of evaluative principles 'from those which animate and guide', or as Coleridge revises the title in the second essay, 'from the laws and impulses which guide the true ARTIST in the production of his works' (*Essays*, 356, 361). This suggests that critics can succeed at their trade only if they take their cues from the artists themselves, a view advocated by Coleridge in his statement that 'the specific object of the present attempt is to enable the spectator to judge in the same spirit in which the Artist produced, or ought to have produced' (360). Based on this statement, critics have speculated that for Coleridge 'genial' means 'pertaining to genius' (Fogel 1962: 175 n. 64), or 'sympathetically evaluating Genius' (Orsini 1969: 168). There is, however, a fundamental tension, and typically a constellation of philosophic sources, in Coleridge's simple formula for 'genial criticism', which hinges on whether the implied sympathetic bond between critic and artist is interpreted as one of complete identity (as suggested by Plotinus's view that the act of seeing presupposes the 'congenerous' union of 'the beholder' with 'the object beheld' (*SW&F,* i. 386), and Fichte's similar conception of the intimate relationship between a spectator and an artist of genius), or as implying some degree of distance for a more objective assessment not only of what authors have 'produced' but also what they 'ought to have produced'. Coleridge's formula also highlights another potential division regarding the role of the critic in relationship to genius. While his statement that a critic must abide by the 'same spirit the Artist produced' grants full authority to genius, who, as Kant stipulated, 'gives the rule to art' (Kant 1951: 150), his view that one should evaluate what an artist 'ought to have produced' clearly empowers the critic, and aligns Coleridge with 'that leading hermeneutic principle enunciated by Schleiermacher', which he practiced abundantly in his critique of Wordsworth, that 'one can know the author better than he knows himself' (Shaffer 1990: 214).

The most important influence on Coleridge's concept of 'genial criticism' was Kant's *Critique of Judgment*, a connection critics have neglected, focusing instead on Kant's predominant role in shaping Coleridge's theory of the beautiful, taste and aesthetic pleasure. Coleridge derived from Kant several components of his philosophy of genial criticism, in particular the view that a critic can access the rules that guided an artist in their creation and, like the artist, can even be elevated to the status of genius. Coleridge also found in Kant a philosophic framework that identified the 'spirit' animating the work of genius as the power of imagination.

According to Kant, although genius is innate and irreducibly original, 'does not know himself how he has come by his ideas' and cannot hand down to others 'precepts that will enable them to produce similar products', he can nonetheless 'excite like ideas in his pupils'. Kant candidly admits that 'it is hard to explain' how 'this is possible', but moves away from this moment of uncertainty to establishing the ground on which the activity of the pupils can be legitimated, which consists in understanding the difference between imitation and copy. Kant claims that pupils studying the works of a genial artist can draw from them 'the rule on which' they 'may try their own talent by using it as a model, not to be *copied* but to be *imitated*'. Now a model, according to Kant, is precisely that which is '*exemplary*' and does not 'spring from imitation, but must serve as a standard or rule of judgment for others'. It appears therefore, that it is through imitation (but not copying) that one can access the standard of exemplary art, which, paradoxically, asserts its freedom from imitation (*Judgement*, 150–2).

In section 49 (Kant 1951: 162–3), Kant recasts the distinction between imitation and copy first, in relation to the proper response of a genius to another (curiously using the term 'imitation' in the sense of copying when he notes that 'the product of a genius...is an example, not to be imitated...but to be followed by another genius, whom it awakens to a feeling of his own originality'), and second, in relation to two types of critics: those who by imitation develop a 'methodical system of teaching according to rules...derived from the peculiarities of the products of' genius, to whom Kant has no objection, and another group whom Kant castigates fiercely for their practice of copying 'everything down to the deformities, which genius must have let pass only because he could not well remove them without weakening his idea'. In Coleridgean language, the error of the second group of critics stems from their lack of understanding that imitation, as opposed to mere copying, involves difference and not just likeness with an original (*BL*, ii. 72–3 and n. 4).

In the process of differentiating between genuine imitation and slavish copying, Kant in effect erases the boundary that separates pupil, artist or critic in their relationship to a 'genial' predecessor. All three figures are bound by the same constraint, namely that the only thing genius can impart to another is the injunction of originality. This leaves open the possibility that a critic can attain the status of genius in relation to another genius as easily as an artist, an empowering perspective that, as we shall see, Coleridge exploits fully in the *Biographia*. Furthermore, Kant notes that the activity of copying is the surest way of destroying that which 'is genius and constitutes the spirit of the work' (162), thus equating 'genius' with 'the spirit' inhabiting an artist's product, a term which in the same section Kant defined as 'the animating principle of the mind' (157). It is apparent, therefore, that the vocabulary and philosophical underpinnings of Coleridge's *Essays*, as well as his statement that his goal was to develop critical principles in congruence with the 'spirit in which' artists 'produced' and the 'laws and impulses' which 'animate and guide' them, come straight out of section 49 of Kant's *Critique of Judgment*.

In this section, Kant notes that there are worthy products of art that may be 'neat and elegant', 'exact and well arranged', 'solid and at the same time elaborate, but without spirit' (156), an argument also made by Fichte nearly verbatim in his essay *Ueber Geist und Buchstab in der Philosophie* (Concerning the Spirit and Letter within Philosophy), composed in 1794 and published in 1798. For Kant, a work that contains spirit activates the whole mind through an 'animating principle', or what Fichte, in his slightly revised version of Kant, calls 'animating power' (belebende Kraft). This principle is 'no other than the faculty of presenting *aesthetical ideas*', namely the imagination (157). Kant gives the imagination a much more expanded role here than in the earlier sections of the 'Analytic of the Sublime', where its misguided effort to reach a supersensible totality through objects of sense functioned primarily to secure the triumph of reason, and make 'intuitively evident' to the mind 'the superiority of the rational determination of our cognitive faculties to the greatest faculty of our sensibility' (96). In section 49 on the other hand, the imagination is envisioned as creative and potent, bringing 'the faculty of intellectual ideas (the reason) into movement' (158).

It is important to note that reason is not activated by perceiving its 'superiority' to the imagination, but on the contrary, its similarity to it. By generating 'aesthetical ideas', the imagination provides a mirror through which reason can regard its own activity. Just as the ideas of reason are supersensible, and cannot be grounded in a concept, so likewise the aesthetical ideas 'strive after something which lies beyond the bounds of experience' and cannot be contained by 'any definite thought' or rendered 'intelligible by language' (157). Paradoxically, the triumph of the imagination in the domain of aesthetics is predicated on a commensurate failure of embodiment, and the imagination's provision of an 'objective correlative' for the ideas of reason, must be understood to contain the very limitations and inadequacy of such an enterprise.[20] However, Kant actually celebrates what among many romantics becomes a dirge about (in Coleridge's rendition) 'the inadequacy of <Words to Feeling>, of the symbol to the Being', rendering words 'powerful only as they express their utter impotence' (*CN*, ii. 2998).

Kant's view of the 'animating spirit' of the mind pertains exclusively to the mental activity of genius in the act of creation, an activity that is sealed off from others and inexplicable even to the creator of beautiful art, who 'does not know himself how he has come by his ideas' and cannot 'communicate' to others 'precepts that will enable them to produce similar products' (151). Kant does maintain, however, as seen above, that artists can inspire and convey their 'aesthetical' ideas to pupils, but only if 'nature has endowed them with a like proportion

---

[20] One of the most problematic aspects of Kant's conception of aesthetical ideas concerns the fact that they do not offer an objective ground to ideas of reason. They are a 'counterpart' of the ideas of reason, precisely because they are supersensible. Thus, the task Kant bequeathed to the Romantics was, as Halmi (2007: 61) notes, 'to find a securer basis on which to claim that the numinousness of aesthetic ideas ... actually inhered in the objects they presented to the senses'.

of their mental powers' (152). In the end, in Kant's formula, only a genius can receive the mandate of another genius, which is essentially the mandate of originality.

Unlike Kant, Fichte (1846) democratizes considerably the transmission of the ideas of genius to even the most ordinary of readers. In 'Concerning the Spirit and Letter within Philosophy', Fichte claims that it is the responsibility of geniuses to generate works of art to which spectators are irresistibly drawn, losing their separateness from the authors, thinking and composing simultaneously with them, yet remaining unaware of their own part in what is essentially an act of joint creation. This is the reverse of the misrecognition Longinus (1991: 10) uncovered in the effect of sublime writing, where auditors think that they are the creators of what they have just heard. Even as Fichte, like Kant, differentiates between the spirit of a work and the accidental forms in which it finds expression, claiming that no language has been found to describe what lies in the soul of an artist (294), in his view artists encounter no obstacle in influencing readers. In fact, true artists write with the spectators in mind who are the final destination of their work (273). Every artist, Fichte claims, 'builds his public' and 'works for posterity' (297).

In the context of these two different conceptions of genius and definitions of the animating spirit in a work of art, we can define more precisely what Coleridge means by genial criticism. First, Kant's claims offer Coleridge a highly advantageous role in the way he conceives of the enterprise of criticism in his *Essays*. Coleridge's statement that the object of the *Essays* was to 'enable the spectator to judge in the same spirit in which the Artist produced' implicitly raises the status of the critic to that of a genius and a mediator between the artist and the public. Genial criticism, then, is criticism not only about a genius, but also by a genius, for in accordance with the Kantian standpoint, it takes a genius to recognize another and be inspired by his example. The critic is thus in a privileged position to extract from the products of genius the very standards by which he will evaluate the artist's work. Second, given that for Kant the animating spirit of a work of genius is the imagination, we can surmise that genial criticism will concern itself with this power, which, as Coleridge defined it in chapter 14 of the *Biographia*, 'brings the whole soul of man into activity' (*BL*, ii. 15–16). But finally, neither the Kantian nor the Fichtean position appears to be conducive to Coleridge's project of judging an author in terms of what he 'ought' to have produced rather than what he produced. Within the Kantian framework, such a presupposition is preposterous, as it is genius who sets the rules for art and thus, a true genius is beyond critique. Similarly, in the case of Fichte, the complete union of the artist with a spectator to whom he or she hands the key to unlock the work, prevents the separation needed to make the work of genius an object of analysis by the spectator. In Fichte, genius is all knowing. It is only spectators who can find out something about themselves they did not know before.

In the *Biographia*, Coleridge integrates a number of features of 'genial criticism', as defined in the *Essays*, with varying emphases, depending on the writers that become the focus of his investigation. The term 'genial' surfaces in the *Biographia* on several occasions in connection with genius, the power of imagination, criticism (*BL*, i. 224, 264; ii. 83), but, perhaps most obtrusively, in Coleridge's attempt to deflect foreseeable charges of plagiarism from Schelling by pointing to the 'genial coincidence' between their ideas, stemming from their mutual interest in Kant (*BL*, i. 160–1). However, the empathic element between critic and author implied by the term, especially in its Plotinian version of the merging of the observer with the object observed, diminishes considerably, particularly in places where Coleridge dwells at length on what a writer 'ought to have produced', as in the critique of Wordsworth. In such instances, a more philosophically detached spirit of 'sound' analysis, as implied by the title of the first of the *Essays*, comes into play.

The change is recorded in the opening paragraph of the *Biographia*, where Coleridge defines his critical project as one based on rules 'deduced from philosophical principles' and applied to the fine arts 'with utmost impartiality' (*BL*, i. 5). This brand of criticism may be more amenable to 'objective' rather than 'sympathetic' critical evaluation, but it does combine rather well with two ingredients of Coleridge's formula for genial criticism, both derived from Kant, namely: the view that only a genius can deliver authentic criticism about a genius, and that such criticism depends in large measure on a clear philosophic understanding of the function of the imagination. It is no mere coincidence that in the opening chapter of the first volume of the *Biographia*, Coleridge establishes his credentials as a poetic genius, while in the volume's concluding chapter, after an amply documented intellectual biography, he presents a theory of the imagination as proof of his philosophic genius, which 'no less than a poetic genius . . . is differenced from the highest perfection of talent, not by degree but by kind' (*BL*, i. 299–300).

In chapter 1 of the *Biographia*, Coleridge's claim to possessing poetic genius is made under the guise of a candid admission concerning the flaws of his early compositions. Citing the criticisms addressed by reviewers about his overuse of double epithets in his first volume of poetry (1796), Coleridge points to his effort to redress the problem 'with no sparing hand', but explains that 'these parasite plants of his youthful poetry had insinuated themselves into' his 'longer poems with such intricacy of union', that he was forced to 'omit disentangling the weed, from the fear of snapping the flower' (*BL*, i. 6–7). Thus, while appearing scrupulously self-critical and ready to accept the reviewers' charges without any defensiveness, Coleridge actually invalidates these charges by embracing the Kantian view that the products of genius will often exhibit flaws, even 'deformities', which are intrinsically linked with his ideas and 'the inimitable rush of his spirit' (Kant 1951: 162). Fichte likewise claimed that a genius, who gives birth to content and form simultaneously, was liable to engender, like nature itself, 'excrescences' (Auswüchse) that 'could not be removed without detriment to the whole' (297–8).

In his effort to point to the genial quality of his early compositions, Coleridge also introduces a representation of genius as a developing artist, who reaches the stage of organic art through a process of self-correction, a possibility that is not apparent in Kant's or Fichte's theories. In a strategic footnote at the beginning of the *Biographia (BL,* i. 6), Coleridge points out that, although Shakespeare and Milton began their careers with 'a superfluity of double epithets', they were able to create works of impeccable unity, in which no single word or 'the position of a word' could be changed 'without making the author say something else, or something worse, than he does say' (*BL,* i. 23). At the end of the chapter, Coleridge places himself squarely in this illustrious literary company, by referring to the quick progress he made in abandoning a 'florid diction' in the 'compositions of' his 'twenty-fourth and twenty-fifth year'. In chapter 4, Coleridge also tests the standard of evolving mastery characteristic of genius against Wordsworth, not surprisingly with less positive results. Here he traces the progress of Wordsworth's verse, from the 'strained thought, or forced diction' of 'Descriptive Sketches' to the 'union of deep feeling with profound thought' in 'Salisbury Plain', with the ostensible purpose of demonstrating 'how soon genius clears and purifies itself from the faults and errors of its earliest products' (*BL,* i. 78). But by placing this claim inside the frame of the agonizing, sacrificial transformation of a caterpillar into a but-terfly, which, in keeping with an earlier notebook entry, he also associates with disease (*BL,* i. 78; *CN,* 3: 3474), Coleridge casts a dark shadow over Wordsworth's emergence as a fully developed genius. Furthermore, the eulogy of 'Salisbury Plain' not only misrepresents the poem entirely by emptying it of all its Gothic horror and human tragedy and turning it into another version of 'Tintern Abbey', but effec-tively undermines Wordsworth's claim to the status of genius, by demonstrating that his subsequent contributions to the 'Lyrical Ballads', nearly a third of which by Coleridge's calculation displayed glaring flaws, revealed the pattern of his career to include regress rather than steady progress, as was the case with Milton and Shakespeare (Modiano 1997).

As critics have often noted, chapter 4, which includes this demystification of Wordsworth under the guise of flattery, represents a central 'landing place' in the conceptual structure of the *Biographia,* capturing its concerns as a whole. It is here that Coleridge begins the critique of Wordsworth's Preface to and poems of *Lyrical Ballads* in earnest, simultaneously enshrining and undermining his former collaborator, and defines the imagination as a faculty connected with 'the ideal world' that modifies and harmonizes objects of sense and renders familiar objects unfamiliar. It is also here that Coleridge begins 'a more intimate analysis of the human faculties' (*BL,* i. 82) in order to get to the root of the distinction between imagination and fancy. Finally, the chapter contains a significant discourse on genius cited from the 1809 *Friend* and pasted to the eulogy of 'Salisbury Plain,' which, rather than reinforcing the merits of Wordsworth's poem, represents 'both a defense and promotion of Coleridge's *own* genius', and of his 'authority to determine genius and the power to communicate its truth to the world' (Christensen 1978: 226). Coleridge's definition of genius here is identical with his definition of the role of the imagination. Like the imagination, genius has the power of stripping objects of their familiarity in order to reveal 'the sense of wonder and novelty' which 'for the common view, custom had bedimmed all the lustre' (*BL*, i. 80–1). As pointed out by Jenkins (1984: 123), by the time Coleridge composed the *Biographia*, the 'growth of genius as a concept' in his poetic theory and his evolving concept of the imagination became so closely 'interwoven' as to automatically signal each other's attributes.

For Coleridge, understanding the link between genius and imagination and the distinction between imagination and fancy, was fundamental to a proper 'theory of the fine arts, and of poetry in particular', which, as Coleridge elaborates, would

furnish a torch of guidance to the philosophical critic; and ultimately to the poet himself. In energetic minds, truth soon changes by domestication into power; and from directing in the discrimination and appraisal of the product, becomes influencive in the production. To admire on principle, is the only way to imitate without loss of originality.   (*BL*, i. 85)

This passage exhibits a characteristic feature of Coleridge's performance in the *Biographia*, namely the suspension of the boundary separating the identity of critic, philosopher and poet. Although Coleridge often defined the aims of poetry and philosophy as distinct, one having as its object pleasure, the other truth, in fact, as Vallins (2000: 88–95) notes, their functions are often analogous if not identical. In chapter 14, for example, it is not only the poet who is celebrated for the ability to generate 'a spirit of unity', that 'blends' and reconciles 'opposite or discordant qualities', but likewise the philosopher, who mindful of the fact that 'distinction is not division' separates 'notions of any truth' into 'distinguishable parts', only to 'restore them in our conceptions to the unity, in which they actually co-exist' (*BL*, ii. 11, 15–17). This view is further developed in chapter 15, devoted to Shakespeare, where Coleridge singles out 'DEPTH, and ENERGY of THOUGHT' as one of the salient characteristics of genius, claiming that 'No man was ever yet a great poet, without being at the same time a profound philosopher' (*BL*, ii. 25–6).

But what about the 'philosophical critic'? Here we have another merger which might read: 'No man was ever a great critic, without being at the same time a profound philosopher.' In chapter 13, the term 'philosophic critics' refers to critics 'of all ages' and 'all countries' who are in universal agreement about what constitutes great poetry, namely an organically linked whole, and what defeats poetry, namely, 'striking lines or distichs, each of which absorbing the whole attention of the reader to itself disjoins it from its context' (*BL*, ii. 13–14). In chapter 4, however, the focus appears to be different, moving 'philosophic criticism' closer to the pole of 'genial criticism', as suggested by the reference to the admiration owed to artists one chooses to imitate.

It is not altogether clear whether the term 'energetic minds' designates critics or poets, or critics that become poets by virtue of 'that sublime faculty, by which a great mind becomes that which it meditates on' (*CN*, iii. 3290). Coleridge may also draw here on sections 46 through 49 from the *Critique of Judgment*, where Kant shows that an artist, by imitating rather than copying the products of genius, not only can, but also must create works of radical originality. In this context, it becomes clear that the essential ingredient that unites the identities of critic, philosopher, and poet is genius, and that 'the true sources of *genial* discrimination' for all is the imagination (*BL*, ii. 82–3). Once again the discourse on genius and the discourse on the imagination prove to be inextricably linked.

The subject of the *Biographia* has always been genius and the revelation of Coleridge's greatness as writer, philosopher and critic of genius. The stage is set from the beginning for the centrality of this subject, which appears not only in the opening chapter where Coleridge highlights his similarity to Milton and Shake-speare, but also in chapter 2, where he professes his indifference 'to literary wrongs' (*BL*, i. 45) in keeping with the true character of genius, which he presents as a self-absorbed visionary, impervious to anger or the negative opinions of others (Modiano 1989*a*: 164–6). But it would be wrong to infer from these examples that Coleridge monopolizes the designation of genius and reserves it for himself alone. In fact, his very status as 'genial' critic depends on an assessment of other geniuses. Even as Coleridge declares genius to be 'a very rare plant' (*BL*, ii. 132), he bestows the term lavishly on an array of philosophers and writers, including Wordsworth, indeed especially on Wordsworth, who 'in imaginative power,' he claims, 'stands nearest of all modern writers to Shakespear and Milton; and yet in a kind perfectly unborrowed and his own' (*BL*, ii. 151). At last, Coleridge granted Wordsworth his wish to be classed as an original genius in the company of Shakespeare and Milton, as enunciated in his 1815 Preface, but this wish depends in fact on the authority of Coleridge's own assertion. As Christensen (1978: 227) notes, 'Wordsworth's genius is presented as whole and complete . . . in every sense of the word, by Coleridge', for only Coleridge, the critic, who apparently knows Wordsworth better than he knows himself, can access 'the truth' of Wordsworth's genius and 'assert what in Wordsworth's poetry is truly Wordsworthian and what is not'.

It is legitimate, however, to ask whether the kind of criticism Coleridge produces about Wordsworth can still be called 'genial', given that, as Parrish (1973) com-plained, it displays not just a failure of understanding the particularities of Words-worth's poetic theory and practice, but more glaringly, a failure of sympathy. Undoubtedly, the spirit of a 'congenerous' union of critic and author is effaced in Coleridge's critique, aimed at holding Wordsworth accountable for what he 'ought' to have produced. The 'ought' in Coleridge's practical criticism of Words-worth sustains the ineluctable severity that it has in Kant's usage of the term in the moral sphere, and as in Kant, measures the distance between flawed actions and their ideal counterpart. Perhaps for this reason, Coleridge was conspicuously averse to having his work judged according to what he 'ought' to have produced. In a passage (*BL*, i. 220–2) which hardly displays the serenity of genius in the face of adversarial criticism, but records instead the 'serious injury' Coleridge received from the perception that he 'dreamt away' his 'life to no purpose', a perception made public 'in the bulkiest works of periodical literature', he writes,

By what I *have* effected, am I to be judged by my fellow men; what I *could* have done, is a question for my own conscience.

This statement is followed by a dolorous quotation from Coleridge's 'To a Gentleman', which captures the sense of annihilation experienced by Coleridge after Wordsworth's recitation of 'The Prelude', articulating the very perception of wasted talents that had been picked up by the public: 'Sense of past youth, and manhood come in vain / And genius given and knowledge won in vain'. At such moments of raw pain and undisguised suffering, Coleridge discloses the origin of the *Biographia* in his tangled relationship with Wordsworth, and its primary purpose: to leave behind the 'voice of mourning' and the figure of a diseased metaphysician, as Wordsworth represented him in Book 6 of *The Prelude*, and emerge fully integrated as a genius of philosophy and criticism.

WORKS CITED

BIALOSTOSKY, D. H. 1978. Coleridge's interpretation of Wordsworth's Preface to *Lyrical Ballads*. *PMLA*, 93: 912–24.

—— 1979a. Forum on 'Coleridge's interpretation of Wordsworth's Preface'. *PMLA*, 94: 326–7.

—— 1979b. Forum on 'Coleridge's interpretation of Wordsworth's Preface'. *PMLA*, 94: 479–82.

BLOOM, H. 1972. Coleridge: The anxiety of influence. In G. H. Hartman, ed., *New Perspectives on Coleridge and Wordsworth*. New York: Columbia University Press, pp. 24–67.

BUELL, L. 1979. The question of form in Coleridge's *Biographia Literaria*. *ELH*, 46: 399–417.

BURWICK, F., ed. 1989. *Coleridge's 'Biographia Literaria': Text and Meaning*. Columbus, OH: Ohio State University Press.

CHRISTENSEN, J. 1978. The genius in the *Biographia Literaria*. *Studies in Romanticism*, 17: 215–31.

—— 1981. *Coleridge's Blessed Machine of Language*. Ithaca, NY: Cornell University Press.

COLERIDGE, S. T. 1907. *Biographia Literaria*, ed. J. Shawcross. London: Oxford University Press.

—— 1983. *Biographia Literaria*, ed. J. Engell and W. J. Bate. Princeton, NJ: Princeton University Press.

—— 1997. *Biographia Literaria*, ed. N. Leask. London: J. M. Dent.

DAVIDSON, C. 1971. Organic unity and Shakespearian tragedy. *Journal of Aesthetics and Art Criticism*, 30: 171–6.

FICHTE, J. G. 1846. Ueber Geist und Buchstab in der Philosophie. In J. H. Fichte (ed.), *Sämmtliche Werke*. Berlin: Verlag von Veit und Comp. 8 vols. Vol. viii. 270–300.

FOGEL, D. M. 1977. A compositional history of the *Biographia Literaria*. *Studies in Bibliography*, 30: 219–34.

—— 1962. *The Idea of Coleridge's Criticism*. Berkeley and Los Angeles: University of California Press.

FRUMAN, N. 1971. *Coleridge, the Damaged Archangel*. New York: George Braziller, Inc.

—— 1985. Review essay: aids to reflection on the new *Biographia*. *Studies in Romanticism*, 24: 141–73.

—— 1989. Editing and annotating the *Biographia Literaria*. In F. Burwick (ed.), 1–19.

FUNNELL, P. 1982. Visible appearances. In M. Clarke and N. Penny (eds.), *The Arrogant Connoiseur: Richard Payne Knight 1751–1824*. Manchester: Manchester University Press, 82–92.

GALLANT, C. ed. 1989. *Coleridge's Theory of Imagination Today*. New York: AMS Press.

GRAVIL, R. 1984. Coleridge's Wordsworth. *The Wordsworth Circle*, 15: 38–46.

HAEGER, J. H. 1989. Anti-materialism, autobiography, and the abyss of unmeaning in the *Biographia Literaria*. In F. Burwick (ed.), 75–87.

HALMI, N. 2007. *The Genealogy of the Romantic Symbol*. Oxford: Oxford University Press.

HAMILTON, P. 1983. *Coleridge's Poetics*. Stanford, CA: Stanford University Press.

JACKSON, H. J. 1997. Coleridge's *Biographia*: When is an autobiography not an autobiography? *Biography: An Interdisciplinary Quarterly*, 20: 54–71.

JACKSON, J. R. DE J. ed. 1970–91. *Coleridge: The Critical Heritage*. 2 vols. New York: Barnes & Noble; London: Routledge.

JENKINS, P. M. 1984. *Coleridge's Literary Theory. The Chronology of Its Development, 1790–1818*. New York: Exposition Press, Inc.

JOHNSTON, K. R. 1984. *Wordsworth and 'The Recluse'*. New Haven: Yale University Press.

KANT, I. 1976. *The Critique of Pure Reason*, trans. N. K. Smith. London: Macmillan Press, Ltd.

—— 1951. *Critique of Judgment*, trans. J. H. Bernard. New York: Hafner Press.

KEARNS, S. M. 1995. *Coleridge, Wordsworth and Romantic Autobiography*. London: Associated University Presses, 109–32.

KNIGHT, U. 1805. *An Analytical Inquiry into the Principles of Taste*. London.

KNOX, J. 2004. Principles unfixed: Science and imagination in Coleridge's 1808 and 1811–12 Lectures. Paper presented at the Coleridge Summer Conference, Cannington, United Kingdom.

LEASK, N. 1993. Pantisocracy and the politics of the 'Preface' to *Lyrical Ballads*. In A. Yarrington and K. Everest (eds.), *Reflections of Revolution. Images of Romanticism*. London: Routledge, 39–58.

LONGINUS. 1991. *On Great Writing (On the Sublime)*, trans. G. M. A. Grube. Indianapolis and Cambridge: Hacket Publishing Company, Inc.

MATLACK, R. E. 1993. *Licentia Biographica*: or, biographical sketches of Coleridge's literary life and plagiarisms. *European Romantic Review*, 4: 57–70.

McFARLAND, T. 1969. *Coleridge and the Pantheist Tradition*. Oxford: Clarendon Press.

—— 1974. Coleridge's plagiarisms once more: a review essay. *Yale Review*, 63: 254–86.

—— 1981. *Romanticism and the Forms of Ruin: Wordsworth, Coleridge and the Modalities of Fragmentation*. Princeton, NJ: Princeton University Press.

McGANN, J. 1989. The *Biographia Literaria* and the contentions of English Romanticism. In F. Burwick (ed), 233–54, 306–8.

McLaughlin, E. T. 1964. Coleridge and Milton. *Studies in Philology*, 61: 545–72.

Messmann, F. J. 1974. *Richard Payne Knight. The Twilight of Virtuosity*. The Hague: Mouton.

Modiano, R. 1989a. Coleridge and Milton: The case against Wordsworth in the *Biographia Literaria*. In F. Burwick (ed), 150–70, 286–90.

—— 1989b. Coleridge and Wordsworth: The ethics of gift exchange and literary ownership. In C. Gallant (ed.), 243–56.

—— 1997. Recollection and Misrecognition: Coleridge's and Wordsworth's Reading of 'The Salisbury Plain' Poems. *The Wordsworth Circle*, 28: 74–82.

Nabholtz, J. R. 1986. *'My Reader My Fell-Labourer'. A Study of English Romantic Prose*. Columbia: University of Missouri Press, 119–28.

—— 1987. The text of Coleridge's *Essays on the Principles of Genial Criticism*. *Modern Philology*, 85: 187–92.

O'Donnell, B. 1995. *The Passion for Meter. A Study of Wordsworth's Metrical Art*. Kent, OH: Kent State University Press.

Orsini, G. N. G. 1969. *Coleridge and German Idealism*. Carbondale, Ill.: Southern Illinois University Press.

Owen, W. J. B. and Smyser, J. W. eds. 1974. *The Prose Works of William Wordsworth*. 3 vols. Oxford: Clarendon Press.

Parrish, S. M. 1973. *The Art of the 'Lyrical Ballads'*. Cambridge, MA: Harvard University Press.

Ruf, F. J. 1992. Coleridge's *Biographia Literaria*: extravagantly mixed genres and the construction of a 'harmonized chaos'. *Soundings. An Interdisciplinary Journal*, 75: 537–53.

Ruoff, G. W. 1972. Wordsworth on language: toward a radical poetics for English Romanticism. *The Wordsworth Circle*, 3: 204–11.

Schulz, M. F. 1985. Samuel Taylor Coleridge. In F. Jordan (ed.), *English Romantic Poets. A Review of Research*. New York: Modern Language Association of America, 427–47.

Shaffer, E. S. 1990. The hermeneutic community: Coleridge and Schleiermacher. In R. Gravil and M. Lefebure (eds.), *The Coleridge Connection. Essays for Thomas McFarland*. London: Macmillan, 200–29.

Simpson, D. 1989. Coleridge on Wordsworth and the form of poetry. In C. Gallant (ed.), 211–25.

Stelzig, E. L. 1980. Coleridge's failed quest: the anticlimax of fancy/imagination in *Biographia Literaria*. *University of Mississippi Studies in English*, 1: 82–96.

Trott, N. 1998. Samuel Taylor Coleridge. In M. O'Neill (ed.), *Literature of the Romantic Period. A Bibliographic Guide*. Oxford: Clarendon Press, 68–79.

Vallins, D. 2000. *Coleridge and the Psychology of Romanticism*. London: Macmillan.

Vogler, T. 1989. Coleridge's Book of Moonlight. In F. Burwick (ed.), 20–46.

Wallace, C. M. 1983. *The Design of 'Biographia Literaria'*. London: Allen and Unwin.

Wellek, R. 1931. *Immanuel Kant in England, 1793–1838*. Princeton, NJ: Princeton University Press.

—— 1972. Coleridge's philosophy and criticism. In F. Jordan (ed.), *The English Romantic Poets. A Review of Research*. New York: Modern Language Association of America, 209–58.

Wheeler, K. 1980. *Sources, Processes and Methods in Coleridge's 'Biographia Literaria'*. Cambridge: Cambridge University Press.

White, D. E. 2003. Imagination's date: a postscript to the *Biographia Literaria*. *European Romantic Review*, 14: 467–78.

CHAPTER 12

COLERIDGE ON POLITICS AND RELIGION: *THE STATESMAN'S MANUAL, AIDS TO REFLECTION, ON THE CONSTITUTION OF CHURCH AND STATE*

PAMELA EDWARDS

COLERIDGE, from his earliest writings on politics and religion, had grounded his accounts of government and civil society in philosophical and theological understandings of truth. He had first undertaken such an approach in his *Moral and*

Political Lecture as well as in his *Lectures on Revealed Religion* of 1795. Likening the ship of state to a 'crazy bark' (*Lects 1795*, 5) in a storm-tossed sea, Coleridge had emphasized the need 'of bottoming on fixed principles' (*Lects 1795*, 33). In no small part, he was indebted to Edmund Burke for this maxim. But rather than Burke's more direct gesture toward the certain fixed principles of law, Coleridge was deliberately vague as to what those 'fixed principles', indeed just what his 'grand and comprehensive truth' (*Lects 1795*, 33), might be.

While many have recognized the theological foundations of Burke's natural law jurisprudence, less has been said about Coleridge's view of the law. Yet in his more mature political and theological writings nature and law were fused in an account of sacred history. Three works are key to understanding Coleridge's political and religious thought in this regard. *The Statesman's Manual* of 1816 begins to develop an account of the moral consequences and imperatives of human agency as providential history. The spiritual nature of the will and its essential consequences for the meaning of human freedom is established in the *Aids to Reflection* of 1825. Finally the significance of these two works as providing the template for Coleridge's institutional theory of government is brought to fruition with the publication, late in 1829, of *On the Constitution of Church and State According to the Idea of Each*. Taken together they represent Coleridge's final efforts to articulate his earliest attempts to ground the civil law in the law of nature, or to place it in its Platonic and Baconian form,[1] the Ideas of Nature.

In *Church and State*, Coleridge makes three important arguments which culminate in an empirically grounded idealist account of institutional governance. The first of these is that the State, properly understood, is an organic and dynamic whole comprising the past and the present through the dynamic tension between the principles of permanence and progression. In this regard, the State, in its fullest sense, comprehends the narrower spheres of politics and religion in their institutional forms as church and state. The second argument Coleridge makes is a necessary presumption for the first. As an expression of sacred time and secular space, the State is the living embodiment of an inspiring or animating Idea. It is the expression of concrete things; the culmination of the material conditions of history and human action. In short, the State is the organic manifestation of the living law. But acknowledging the theological or moral foundations of all jurisprudence as 'science of law', Coleridge maintained that the common law was imbued with a living spirit and that through a providential and inspired history, it was also the incarnation of the word. The final plank of Coleridge's argument in *Church and State* is an extension of the first two premises. It is predicated on an understanding of Burke's generational continuity, of the organic bond between the living, the dead

---

[1] 'Hence Plato often names ideas laws; and Lord Bacon, the British Plato, describes the Laws of the material universe as the Ideas in nature.' *C&S* 13.

and the as yet unborn. It is an inherently evolutionary account of history as the natural progress and perfection of human and social organization. But again this is a Platonic or Plotinian[2] and not a Lucretian[3] account of nature. It is the Platonism of Giordano Bruno,[4] and if we take Coleridge's reading, of Francis Bacon in the *Novum Organum*. It is vibrant, dynamic, and plastic nature; not mechanical, atomistic, and static; not dead matter. This vitalist account of natural philosophy is, in turn, the key to understanding Coleridge's conception of what law and history, truth and providence might mean. What in short is the ultimate aim or purpose of earthly time?

While there were certainly glimmerings of these ideas in Coleridge's earliest writings on politics and revealed religion, he does not bring them in line with any coherent or systematic effort at writing either a theory of history or of creating a comprehensive political philosophy until after 1815. Several significant watersheds account for this change. The first of course was his much celebrated encounter with the German learning, during and in the wake of his sojourn at Göttingen in 1799. The second was the progress of the war with Imperial France and his own forays as a political journalist and commentator, and as a minor government agent in Malta. The final was, in the aftermath of Waterloo, his intense concern from 1816–17 as to the moral and philosophical, no less the social and economic, crisis of the 'condition of England'. It is in this context, of Coleridge's Condition of England crisis, that he undertook to write his *Lay Sermons*.

The *Lay Sermons* are an attempt to make explicit the relationship between politics and religion which he had first suggested in 1795. His *Lectures on Revealed Religion* were highly political and were the most radically inflected writings of his early career. However they were moderated by his 'addresses to the people' which advocated a moral and indeed Christian foundation for political reform. In the *Lay Sermons*, Coleridge does not so much 'preach the gospel to the poor' as advocate the Bible as sound policy to the great. He also gives an interesting account of the hierarchy of social relationships and their consequences for political power and historical agency.

Projecting three *Lay Sermons*, to be addressed to the three orders of society, Coleridge completed only two. The first, published in 1816, is *The Statesman's Manual*, tellingly addressed to the higher orders of society. The second *Lay Sermon*,

---

[2] Coleridge elided the views of Plato and Plotinus contending that ideas were constitutive rather than regulative.

[3] The principal source of the Epicurean system of ethics and physics, Lucretius' *De Rerum Natura*, established the philosophical grounds for materialism, mechanism and atomism, suggesting these as the foundations of evolutionary advancement.

[4] Coleridge was deeply influenced by Bruno, *On Cause, Principle and Unity*, associating him with Shakespeare and Milton as an exemplar of human genius (*CN* ii, 2026 n. 7). He connected Bruno's Platonism with Bacon's *Novum Organum* as to their respective accounts of active nature or the *natura naturans*. *C&S* 13.

published in 1817, was subtitled 'Blessed are ye that sew beside all waters' and was addressed to the middle classes. The third work was intended but, also tellingly, never written for the poor and laboring classes. And so it is ultimately a paternalistic account of the relationship between the orders which informs Coleridge's understanding of the governed and the governing classes. This is not intended as a rebuke, but rather to emphasize his apprehension of the dualistic nature of the problem of political order with regard to its active elements. The poor are of enormous moral and indeed political consequence in Coleridge's view of a just and virtuous society. But they are in his more positive account of just governance portrayed as the more passive of the historical agents. Excepting their role as violent and unreflective instruments of brute force, whether as the raw revolutionary power of Burke's swinish multitude or as the *deus ex machina* of a vengeful providence, the lower orders are a reactive rather than active source of historical and hence political agency in Coleridge's account.

While Coleridge had argued that the 'best as well as the most benevolent' reformer must unite 'the zeal of the Methodist with the views of the Philosopher'; that he should be 'personally among the poor, and teach them their *Duties* in order that he may render them susceptible of their *Rights*' (*Lects 1795*, 43) he did not necessarily mean that the poor should read and interpret Scripture for themselves. In *The Statesman's Manual*, subtitled 'The Bible the Best guide to Political Skill and Foresight: A Lay Sermon Addressed to the Higher Classes', Coleridge established the order of interpretive as well as political authority in the secular sphere. While he acknowledged the universal efficacy of Scripture for all classes of society, he was not confident that every individual would equally attend to his 'inestimable privileges'. That such privilege while available to even 'the Humblest and least advanced of our countrymen' did not ensure a corresponding sense of responsibility. One could not assume that 'the labouring classes, who in all countries form the great majority of the inhabitants' would recognize the 'sufficiency of scripture in all knowledge requisite in a right performance of . . . duty' (*LS* 6). Coleridge was unclear but suggestive here. To do one's 'duty as a man and a Christian' (*LS* 6) did not partake of the same language as that which had contemplated the duty of the virtuous citizen of the republic. The Christian language of private men attached to Coleridge's account of the labouring poor. But for the higher orders of society the ancient classical language of the *res public* is preserved; a public language of duty and obligation, of virtue and trust, for public men. Private moral expectation, or more pointedly, a charitable disposition to hope, characterized Coleridge's account of the lower orders of society. If such as these, could simply fulfill their private obligations as men and Christians, it would be well. Such people were not called to public life. Coleridge makes the point emphatically, 'More than this is not demanded, more than this is not perhaps generally desirable' (*LS* 6).

But whether in private or public life, the overarching theme of Coleridge's *Statesman's Manual*, despite what may at first glance appear to be its top-down approach, is that freedom, and through its exercise the Will, is what makes us essentially human. Our capacity to think, to reflect, in essence to know and therefore to be, is the foundation and the end of all human action and history. Coleridge established this principle of a moral or first freedom as the sinecure of all other rights and freedoms early in his account. Even the principle of the right of property where, he observed, in Great Britain 'even the poorest amongst us contends with the richest' for its common defense; even this worldly principle revealed a fundamental human truth. 'These rights are the necessary spheres and conditions of free agency,' Coleridge argued. 'But free agency contains within it the idea of the free will,' he continued, and with that, all the complexities of human nature and the order of a divine providence are revealed to man. 'In this he intuitively knows the sublimity and the infinite hopes, fears, and capabilities of his own nature' (*LS* 27). Coleridge had made many efforts at writing history in his career, although few had come to fruition. In the grand tradition of Plutarch, Machiavelli, Bolingbroke, and even Hume, he understood the significance of history writing as both moral example and cautionary tale. But unlike these profane and retrospective historians, whether skeptical or apologetic, Coleridge believed that history writing could also contain an oracular or prophetic power.[5] Beyond this, history rightly understood as a science, could explain the deepest recesses of the human heart. In his short and fragmentary piece 'The Study of History preferable to the Study of Philosophy', Coleridge had argued that it was 'only in the mirror of history, that man can contemplate his true proportions' (*SW&F*).

Despite a willingness to acknowledge the insight and prudential wisdom of profane histories—histories which might provide insight but could not provide foresight—histories such as Hume's were not what Coleridge had in mind. The new skeptical histories of the enlightenment made the same error, but in the opposite extreme, as those produced by Herodotus and the pagan mythologists of the ancient world.[6] Hume's method was a product of the new skeptical empiricism

---

[5] Indeed Coleridge would argue that in contemplating the mirror, one understood the relative dimensions of distance and imagination to and reality and truth. The purpose of reflection was not only self knowledge but foresight. 'A man without forethought scarcely deserves the name of a man, so forethought without reflection is but a metaphorical phrase for the instinct of a beast.' *AR* 13.

[6] Coleridge was influenced by the new higher criticism of the Bible, but had concerns that the purely empirical pursuit of Evidences would be as destructive and fruitless a form of interpretation as the view that the text was literal, inspired in every word by God. The proper exegesis would be able to distinguish the metaphorical and allegorical from the historical elements and recover the revelatory power through an account of an emergent human history. In this approach Lessing is critically important, but also Vico. The resolution of these elements as a dialectic of truth and understanding may be derived from Vico's *Scienza* I: 50–1 tr.: 'all divine and human learning has three elements: knowledge, will and power whose single principle is the mind, to which God brings the light of eternal truth', which Coleridge quoted in the preface of *Aids to Reflection*. For a discussion of Coleridge's debt to Vico see 'The Coleridge's, Dr. Prati and Vico', *MP* xli (1943): 113.

of the Scots enlightenment. It was derived out of immediate and limited experience and so it was a thing of the understanding. Coleridge was deliberate in his objection to Hume and to his method. 'The inadequacy of the mere understanding to the apprehension of moral greatness we may trace in this historian's cool systematic attempt to steal away every feeling of reverence for every great name by a scheme of motives, in which as often as possible the efforts and enterprises of heroic spirits are attributed to this or that paltry view of the most despicable selfishness' (*LS* 24). In contradistinction to these profane and sensual histories, rooted as they were in the understanding, Coleridge posited a sacred history, inspired and revelatory of the moral law of reason.

His template for this sacred and oracular history was the Bible. Only in the Bible did the ancient and the modern come together in a prophetic and poetic philosophy of history. Its purposes were not merely inspirational or allegorical; they were in the deepest sense scientific. 'The imperative and rational form of the inspired Scripture as the form of reason itself in all things purely rational and moral'(*LS* 20). Coleridge made the case that the Bible was not only a spiritual guide to wisdom, it was the most practical of political and moral primers as well. It was a guide to right action and good government. It was a scientific treatise on human nature, encompassing the science of the legislator within the science of history. In short, the Bible stood for the ages as a true political science and therefore as the best corrective to the false political economy of the present age. What is best in 'Thucydides, Tacitus, Machiavel, Bacon and Harrington' can be found in a purer and more complete form in the Bible, Coleridge contended. (*LS* 18) Even Hume's *Histories*, despite their skeptical intentions, confirmed the same great truths about freedom and human agency as those revealed in the sacred history of scripture.

Coleridge's account of scripture as sacred history replicated his dynamic and dualistic account of the incarnate truth. History, like law, was reason made manifest. It was also imperfectly realized in any discrete moment in time. In this regard the Old Testament and the Law of Moses suggested principles of permanence in the enduring continuities of land and law. In the opening pages of the *Statesman's Manual*, Coleridge quoted from Milton's *Paradise Regained*, signaling his preference for the Old Testament prophets, over the Greek philosophers, as teachers of political wisdom. The reason was as clear as Milton had pronounced it, he maintained, 'As men divinely taught and better teaching the solid rules of civil government, in their majestic unaffected style, than all the oratory of Greece and Rome' (*LS* 9). In the Hebraic and not the Hellenistic learning were the purest and simplest principles of good government to be found. 'In them is plainest taught and easiest learnt what makes a nation happy and keeps it so, what ruins kingdoms and lays cities flat' (*LS* 9). The New Testament of the evangelists and the apostles confirmed a faith in the actions and intentions of the present. It looked toward a future world based on the faith, conscience, and right reason of individual men. It initiated a dynamic and progressive theodicy in which the human heart and the hope of salvation promised heaven on earth. For Coleridge, the incarnation of the word was the manifestation of reason through human action in the world. But individual human agents lived fragmentary existences, they could not perfect themselves in secular space.

In diagnosing the crisis of his age, Coleridge pointed to the 'restless cravings for the wonders of the day' (*LS* 9). This unrestrained passion for novelty and fame, or that 'appetite for publicity [which] spreads like an efflorescence on the surface of our national character' must be put to right. 'The antidote and . . . means must be sought for in the collation of the present with the past' (*LS* 10). Coleridge concluded that it was in the Bible that the best and truest 'collation' might be found. It was in scripture that men might discover and practice 'the habit of thoughtfully assembling the events of our own age to those of the ones before us' (*LS* 10). Caught up in the flux of their own individual interests and places people were spiritually and morally rootless. Attached only to the selfish and worldly, in short the fragmentary spatial limitations of the present, they are unable truly to see or to comprehend the significance of their own circumstances. As a consequence of this lack of perspective, attachment and appetite cloud and distort reason.

Coleridge's historicist phenomenology of mind adds a curiously Augustinian note to his Godwinian account of progress, benevolence, and disinterest. The problem for Coleridge in Godwin's accounts of *Political Justice* had been at least in part a consequence of a materialist reading of the doctrine of disinterest; one which conceived of human beings as wholly independent rational agents. Coleridge had criticized Godwin in 1796 both for that materialism,[7] but also for the view that benevolence existed without attachment. Coleridge had argued instead that benevolence was a 'thing of concretion'; that it flowed from a 'home-born feeling' (*Lects 1795*, 46). Individuals could not, he objected, follow Godwin's self-willed path to rational improvement without some larger force. Individual reason was simply insufficient to the task of universal understanding and, through that, a benevolent, or 'good', will. However, as part of a larger human and spiritual continuity they might, as part of the fabric of cumulative experience and wisdom, acquire perfection in sacred time. Once again Coleridge emphasized that the present is rooted in the past and the promise of the New Testament was a fulfillment of the prophetic covenants of the old. Consequently the *Statesman's Manual* draws most directly on the history of the Old Testament. It also makes clear that it is the obligation of the Statesman to commit to the reasoned and reflective study of this history of all histories. 'If' the collation of the past with the present 'be the moral advantage derivable from history in general', then surely it is 'the moral duty' of the higher orders of society, 'of such as possess the opportunities of books, leisure and

---

[7] See Coleridge's *Watchman* Essay on 'Modern Patriotism', which associated Godwinian principles with a fashionable and popular account of reform (*Watchman* 98–9), and his reply to Gaius Gracchus which described Godwin's principles as 'vicious and his book a pander to sensuality' (*Watchman* 196). Coleridge later adjusted his view and counted Godwin a friend, defending him against Malthus.

education', to 'view with pre-eminent interest' that history 'distinguished from all other history by [its] claim to Divine Authority' (*LS* 10).

But Coleridge's sacred history is not to be understood as some allegorical and coded reverie of the past, remote and esoteric in its relevance for worldly politics. Scripture, he suggested, comprises a sacred History that both records in the Old Testament the significance of God's superintendancy in the past actions and judgements of men, and with that meaning vindicated by the New Testament, prophesies the secular histories of worldly power and contest. In short, Coleridge argued that it was to the great 'events and revolutions' of the past that the statesman might look to read the 'especial manifestation of divine interference'. That is, if he understood how to read Scripture along side the events of this world, as a science of history.[8]

It was the great advantage of the Jewish religion to have understood the law in this way. 'The Hebrew legislator', Coleridge remarked, and 'the other inspired poets, prophets, historians and moralists of the Jewish Church have two peculiar advantages in their favour.' The first of these, Coleridge declared, is that the Law of Moses is explicitly grounded in a grand comprehensive truth. 'Their particular rules and precepts flow directly and visibly from universal principles as from a fountain' (*LS* 16). This, then, is the central claim at the core of Coleridge's *Statesman's Manual* and why the Bible differs as history and as law from 'all the books of Greek Philosophy'. Again, Coleridge offers two distinctions. The first of these is that the incarnation of the living God, more than the claim to divine nature, is the active embodiment of the *jus divinium*. It is the word made flesh; as the inspiration of the living law it establishes 'a direct relationship between the State and its magistracy to the Supreme being' (*LS* 6). The Old Testament established for all time the theological foundation not only of the natural but of the civil law. 'It is the vital and indisputable part of all moral' and, Coleridge might have added, *therefore* 'all political wisdom' (*LS* 36).

But just as the Old Testament established the foundations of the law as a principle of authority and order, so the New Testament 'sets forth the means and conditions of spiritual convalescence with all the laws of conscience relative to our future state and permanent being' (*LS* 136). This, Coleridge observed in his second lay sermon, suggested more than the advancement of Christian polity on the tribal and aristocratic kingdoms of the ancient Hebrews. It suggested, in its emphasis on the laws of the conscience rather than the laws of the kings, a progressive and providential dynamic in the wisdom of the gospels. Taken as a whole, 'So does the

---

[8] Coleridge was preoccupied by the example of the Hebrew Constitution and its application to Albion as the New Jerusalem. From his readings of Warburton's *Divine Legation of the Laws of Moses* to his deep study of Lessing and Eichhorn's histories and criticisms of the Old Testament, Coleridge searched for the first principles of government through the foundations of the original covenant if not contract. By the composition of the *AR* and *C&S*, he was also reading Moses Mendelssohn and Hyman Horowitz on the history of the ancient Hebrews.

Bible present to us the elements of public prudence, instructing us in the true causes, the surest preventatives, and the only cures of public evils' (*LS* 136).

Coleridge's account of the Bible as 'the best guide to political wisdom and foresight' suggests the retrospective and oracular nature of his double vision. Linking the future to the past, it offered both prospects from the ever present and immediate bridge of revelation. It is as sacred history the model of what Coleridge extolled as the science of history; as history studied in the light of philosophy. Such a history is the highest form of political science, the science of reading both the complexities and simple purities of human nature in action in time. As he would later observe in *Church and State* 'History studied in the light of Philosophy [is] the great drama of an ever-unfolding Providence' (*C&S*, 32).

It is in the *Aids to Reflection* that Coleridge attempted to give deeper substance to the metaphysical and epistemological foundations of his 'Spiritual Philosophy'. Among its many advertised claims, was that it be an 'aid to the formation of a manly character' (*AR* 1). It was to accomplish this task by clearly distinguishing morality from prudence and establishing the foundations of true theology in distinction to false religion. It drew heavily on the works of Warburton[9] and Law,[10] but chiefly was an extended reflection on the thought of the seventeenth-century divine Archbishop Leighton. Coleridge's own account of Leighton's works, tellingly offered in the aftermath of a discussion of freedom, causation, and the will, is as a 'Scotch Bishop's platonico-calvinistic commentary on St. Peter' (*AR* 81). However, it would be wrong to see this work merely as a 'monody on Leighton'. It is Coleridge's effort to explain the operation of the Idea in History and to establish its foundational significance as a principle of dynamic renewal; as the word in the world. While he made preliminary remarks about reason, freedom and the will in *The Statesman's Manual*, these defining critical elements of his theory of history are more fully articulated and integrated as interdependent ideas in the *Aids*. It is therefore appropriate that Coleridge's first aphorism of his preliminary *Introductory Aphorisms*—his prolegomena to future metaphysics as it were—is an observation on the significance of novelty and convention or tradition in philosophy.

It is, Coleridge argued, 'the highest prerogative of genius' (*AR* 11) to find new meaning in old wisdom. Or, as he states it explicitly, the greatest power and purpose of the mind is 'to produce the strongest impression of novelty, while it rescues admitted truths from the neglect caused by the very circumstance of their

---

[9] William Warburton (1698–1779), Bishop of Gloucester, *The Divine Legation of the Law of Moses*. While disagreeing with most of Warburton's conclusions, Coleridge used this as a resource for his discussion of the Mosaic dispensation. Coleridge also engaged, here and in *Church and State*, with Warburton's alliance theory.

[10] William Law (1686–1771), *The Spirit of Love, The Spirit of Prayer, A Serious Call to a Devout and Holy Life*. Coleridge used the idea of assimilation by faith which echoed Law's account. Also close overlaps in the passages quoted and conclusions drawn from the fourth Gospel with regard to spiritual awakening or quickening—'Christ as the inward light and life of my soul' (*The Spirit of Prayer*, ii: 4).

universal admission' (*AR* 11). This is a fascinating insight into the strange and paradoxical tension between the profundity and banality of truth. Coleridge here examines and reveals the single and fatal flaw at the heart both of human nature and political societies. In doing so he also identifies the chief impediment to the advancement of civil societies through an unbroken progression. The drive in history is not to remember but to forget. Several popular aphorisms come to mind, chief among them the old adage that 'familiarity breeds contempt'. Most clichés are true, that is why they become clichés. But as they become mere cant or convention they lose their power as truths. This power is both rhetorical and oracular for Coleridge; it contains both persuasive and revelatory force. As Truth loses its 'luster' (*AR* 12) it loses its power to compel action. People acknowledge the surface conventions long after their inner substance has been forgotten.

In identifying the poetic and philosophical conundrum inherent in his account of truth, Coleridge pointed to the driving force behind his own dynamic philosophy of history. 'Extremes meet', he mused (*AR* 11). The more profound the tension in Coleridge's paradox, the more dynamic and fecund are the possibilities of consciousness and action. The more profound the truth, the more prone it is to reduction as banal convention. Losing its 'lustre', it is buried under the sands of cumulative assumption. So it is with 'the most awful and interesting of truths', Coleridge lamented, that we lose 'the power of truth'. When luster and power had faded, old truths became frail and palsied things, indistinguishable from lies; 'bedridden in the dormitory of the soul, side by side with the most despised and exploded errors' (*AR* 11). How then to recover the 'Lustre' of truth? How, Coleridge asked, to 'restore a common place truth to its *uncommon* luster' (*AR* 12)? His answer brings the focus of the problem directly to bear on the question of history and the driving force behind historical agency. To recover the '*uncommon* luster' of truth, Coleridge insisted, 'you need only translate it into action' (*AR* 12).

The cornerstone of Coleridge's spiritual, moral, and political philosophy is that the cause of action in living beings is the will. Of mechanics and the nature of being, Coleridge observed 'Whatever is representable in the forms of Time and Space is Nature.' But, he continued, 'Whatever is represented in Time and Space, is included in the mechanism of Cause and Effect . . . conversely, whatever . . . has its principle in itself, so far as to originate its actions, can not be contemplated in any of the forms in Time and Space—it must therefore be considered as spirit or spiritual' (*AR* 80). This self-originating spirit, or free agency, is the essence of morality. Indeed, Coleridge's larger contention is that without freedom, morality is impossible; prudence and utility, but not morality. Those ideas arise from mechanical understandings of causation. They may be calculated consequentially, but not morally. Coleridge, continuing his discourse on nature and the will, admits that while he could not comprehensively define the nature of the living will, he could define it through inference by what it was not. Both the critical method and the transcendentalism of this account of moral action are deeply Kantian.[11] The will is not merely pattern and order in nature—the contiguity of Humean association. It cannot be understood mechanically; as in Newton's billiard balls or—as Coleridge poetically styles the mere appearance of cause and order—as the 'shifting current of a stream'. The Will, then, is above nature and not below it. It transcends the forms of 'Time and Space which is Nature'. The will, Coleridge concluded, is super-natural.

The supernatural condition of the will is the basis of Coleridge's contention that humans are the highest and most divinely inspired of living beings. What sets man above brute creation is the will. Coleridge rejected the Lucretian accounts of human nature most forcefully expressed in Aristotle's *Politics*. Rejecting 'the Philosopher's' claim that man is nature's 'noblest animal', Coleridge states explicitly, 'if there be aught *Spiritual* in Man then the Will must be such' (*AR* 135). Coleridge tied the point directly to the vitalist debate. Rejecting the view of Lawrence that life was a consequence of the principle of organization, Coleridge contended that 'there is more in man than can be rationally referred to the life of nature and the mechanism of organization' (*AR* 135) 'The Will', Coleridge contended, 'is in an especial and pre-eminent sense the spiritual part of our humanity' (*AR* 136).

The language which Coleridge had used to give account of the will, as a spiritual and supernatural force, had linked his vitalist ideas about the distinctive pre-eminence of human life to his political and moral account of reason in history. The animating spirit was the inspired word. Reason, and as an extension of reason, law, is what created living, vibrant, or plastic nature.[12] But it is also what ordered and regulated it. '[T]he regulator was not separated from the mainspring.' As Coleridge had argued in *The Statesman's Manual*, 'Reason, whose knowledge is creative, and antecedent to things known, is distinguished from the understanding, or creaturely mind of the individual the acts of which it records and arranges.' (*SM* 20)

The critical task of separating the spiritual from the creaturely nature in man was the first step in Coleridge's effort to understand, more pointedly, how the divine reason animated or inspired the humanity in man. Hence, much of Coleridge's energy in the *Aids to Reflection* focused on the Logos as originating and creative reason.[13] The human corollary of this first form, and the signal act of the Christian

---

[11] Coleridge's use or translation of Kant's philosophy has dominated the criticism of his works from the start. Famously as the foundation of the plagiarism charge in Rene Wellek's *Immanual Kant in England* (Princeton, NJ: Princeton University Press, 1931), as part of a larger synthetic use of German Idealism in *Coleridge and German Idealism* (Carbondale: Southern Illinois University Press, 1969) and more recently, as original philosophical composition in a surge of philosophical articles, of which Thomas R. Simons' 'Coleridge beyond Kant and Hegel: Transcendental Ethics and the Dialectic Pentad' is particularly helpful (*Studies in Romanticism* (September 2006)).

[12] As Coleridge explained in Aphorism IX, 'Life is the one universal soul, which by virtue of the enlivening Breath and the informing Word, all organized bodies have in common. This therefore all animals possess and man is an animal. But in addition God transfused into man a higher gift, and specially embreathed:...a (self-subsisting) soul...and man became a living soul. He did not merely possess it, he became it.' (*AR* 15)

[13] For an extended philosophical discussion of Coleridge's understanding of the Logos see Mary Anne Perkins, *Coleridge's Philosophy: The Logos as Unifying Principle* (Oxford: The Clarendon Press, 1994).

faith, was to be found in Scriptural accounts of the incarnation and the resurrection as well as the meaning of redemption in the Gospel of John. In his efforts to recover the Bible as sacred and revealed history,[14] Coleridge engaged at some length with the effect higher German criticism of the New Testament, notably Eichhorn,[15] had on the authenticity of John. Coleridge accepted Eichhorn's defense of the authenticity of the fourth gospel suggesting that this vindicated the historicity of John. Paley,[16] with whom Coleridge vigorously contended, had drawn prudential and utilitarian implications out of the idea that an organic and providential history could be read out of scripture. But Coleridge drew the opposite conclusions from the same premises, maintaining the realist's account of reason as the foundation of an evolutionary historical progress. Turning directly to the question of the redemption, Coleridge expressed his Platonic understanding of the trinity.[17] He again emphasized the primacy of the idea in his account of the relationship between faith and reason. 'Revelation must have assured it', he insisted, as the grounds 'given in the redemption of mankind by Christ, the savior and mediator' (AR 184). Christ is usually described as the savior of mankind. Coleridge described him as mediator, as the integrative link between the word and the world, an 'office' utterly incompatible 'with a mere creature' (AR 184). It is the philosophical unity of the Platonic trinity that makes redemption possible. Human reason is not sufficient to the divine reconciliation of spirit and flesh. It must be regenerated and made new by the incarnate word. That for Coleridge is the essence of the resurrection, and the meaning of Christ's 'mediation'. 'My words,

[14] Elinor Shaffer discussed Coleridge's use of the active imagination, in reconciling an inspirational power in scripture with its disparate historical elements in 'Kubla Khan' and the Fall of Jerusalem (Cambridge: Cambridge University Press, 1975). Shaffer has also emphasized Coleridge's rejection of the idea of plenary inspiration, while sustaining the possibilities of Scripture as sacred History, in her discussion of the importance of the Confessions of an Inquiring Spirit in reading the AR, as part of a larger discussion of ideology and the critical tradition in interpretations of the late Coleridge ('Ideologies in reading the Late Coleridge: Confessions of an Inquiring Spirit', Romanticism on the Net, 17 February 2000.

[15] Johann Gottfried Eichhorn (1752–1827). While also reading Michaelis on the New Testament and deeply in Lessing's biblical criticism, Eichhorn's histories of both the Old and New Testaments provided Coleridge with an extensive account of the historical debate amongst the German critics. In AR Coleridge engages in particular with Eichhorn's account of the fourth Gospel and the question of the historical authority for sacrament, specifically Baptism. The larger significance of the debate was as to the nature of the Logos. Coleridge's objection was that while Eichhorn had vindicated John as a historical matter he failed to grasp its meaning (CM ii: 464).

[16] William Paley, A View of the Evidences of Christianity (3 vols., 1794). Paley contended that the essence of Christianity could be reduced to the facts of Christ's life and advanced a philosophy of prudence. Paley, like Malthus, is considered a theological utilitarian. Moral action is calculated through outcomes and not through freedom of the will. Coleridge's objections were both plentiful and vigorous, but in particular, he contended that Paley's arguments reduced men to their 'creaturely natures', making them indistinguishable as moral agents from 'dogs and horses'.

[17] For a detailed and sustained argument regarding Coleridge's platonic trinitarianism in the Aids to Reflections see Douglas Hedley, Coleridge, Philosophy and Religion: Aids to Reflection and the Mirror of the Spirit (Cambridge University Press, 2000).

said Christ, are Spirit' (*AR* 407). Just as the word was made flesh, so the flesh is made spirit. This Platonic and synthetic view of Christology is also suggestive of Coleridge's ongoing efforts at reconciling the idea of revealed religion with that of natural religion. In doing so he established the foundations of his dynamic philosophy.

The concluding passages of the *Aids to Reflection* make the arguments implicit in the work's many aphorisms clear. The idea of reason is both speculative and practical. The will is an expression of practical reason, although its constitution is an extension of the principles of speculative reason, or pure reason as Kant would have it. It is, as such, an idea which flows out of an idea. It is the expression of spirit in action and therefore the primary driver in history. Awakening and kindling the inner light, the divine reason within, the inspiring spirit, this has been the great purpose of Christianity. Coleridge contended that this project, included in the process of redemption, was intended 'to rouse and emancipate the Soul from this debasing Slavery to the outward senses, to awaken the mind to the true Criteria of reality, viz. Permanence, Power, Will manifested in Act, and Truth operating as life' (*AR* 406). It is the template for not only spiritual renewal, but moral and political reform. To rephrase Coleridge's final account of Christianity's great and, one might add, historic purpose: to emancipate the soul, liberating it from the cave of the senses; to enlighten the mind to the reality of truth; concluding that 'Truth and Permanence act through the Will as a Power in Action and as the ground of life'. In *On the Constitution of Church and State According to the Idea of Each* (1829), Coleridge considered the principles of permanence and progression as the twin interests of moral and political societies and the twin principles of human history. In doing so he not only sought to establish an institutional theory of government grounded in the grand and comprehensive truths of revealed religion, but to translate truth into a principle of action and thereby restore its luster.

The immediate concerns addressed by Coleridge in *Church and State* are those most closely associated with the project of disestablishment as a cornerstone of 'liberal reform' in the aftermath and long delayed resolutions of the Irish Union. The text, quite clearly, is also a timely intervention into the debate on political economy and, most explicitly, a response to the bill for Catholic Emancipation. The simplest explanation of *Church and State* has been to view it as a pamphlet intended to defend landed wealth and privilege, against the corrosive and destabilizing influence of the new commercial society;[18] permanence as a bulwark against progression. But neither of these interests, as limited or discrete interests, mattered to Coleridge as such. They are each, equally, interdependent principles of historical agency. Considered as such they constitute Coleridge's effort to look deeply into the nature of things and to reveal the workings of a providential history.

---

[18] John Morrow, *Coleridge's Political Thought: Property, Morality, and the Limits of Traditional Discourse* (London: MacMillan, 1990).

Much of Coleridge's attention in the introductory sections of *Church and State* is directed toward establishing the critical and conceptual foundations of his analysis of the constitution. These preliminary observations, on the Idea in history and the meaning of moral, spiritual, and therefore political freedom are extensions and echoes of his account of reason and the will in the *Lay Sermons* and in the *Aids to Reflection*. The Idea is to be understood as an objective reality. Like Plato's *Laws* it is independent of and external to subjective experience. Yet the Idea suffuses and animates the world of sense and mind. Concepts, as distinct from Ideas, are derived out of experience, they are generated by 'a conscious act of the understanding' (*C&S* 13). The Idea for Coleridge, like the Reason for Kant, is antecedent to experience. It is therefore the grounds of the understanding, the first form of knowledge. In its spiritual and religious meaning it is the Word. In its political and social implication it is the constitution. Coleridge insisted that he would not distinguish the constitution from an Idea, for, as he remarked, 'the constitution is an Idea in itself' (*C&S* 18). But, he added, it is 'an idea arising out of the idea of a State' (*C&S* 19).

A 'Constitution is the attribute of a State' (*C&S* 23). Here Coleridge means State in the larger sense of realm or body politic or political society. This form of society as active, lived experience, generates certain structures and divisions of interest which in turn suggest certain forms of organization. The State in this larger sense has within it a principle of unity, whether pure as in monarchy, or through the interdependency of balanced and opposing interests as in the English Church-State. The equipoise or integrative equilibrium suggested by the interplay between the two structural components of spiritual authority in the church and civil authority in government Coleridge described as reflecting the 'two antagonistic powers or opposite interests of the State under which all other state interests are comprised'. These formative ideas are 'Permanence and Progression' (*C&S* 24). Taken as historical forces they are expressions of the interplay between enduring structures of power and freedom and free agency expressed as willed action.

In Coleridge's account, the Idea acts on the will and in the will. The constitution is both the ordering principle of the body politic and the fibres, nerves and tissues of the living State. Here, as so often, Coleridge's language slips into the 'medico-philosophical'. Theology, natural philosophy, and the question of civil polity are alike aspects of a 'comprehensive theory of life'.[19] Coleridge's model for a Platonic British Science is to be found in Francis Bacon's *Novum Organum*. 'Lord Bacon' or 'the British Plato', he tells us, 'describes the Laws of the material universe as the Ideas in nature' (*C&S* 13). It is not surprising then that Coleridge's associations move swiftly, identifying the crisis of the age in that false style of 'liberal' reform

---

[19] For an account of the relationship between Coleridge's medico-philosophy and his institutional theory of Government see Pamela Edwards, *The Statesman's Science: History, Nature and Law in the Political Thought of Samuel Taylor Coleridge* (New York, NY: Columbia University Press, 2004).

which denies the possibility of human moral freedom. Jonathan Edwards[20] and the politics of dissent, Coleridge quietly elided, as suggesting cognate concepts to those associated with William Lawrence[21] and materialist accounts of the theory of life. Calvinism and theological determinism are here linked to skeptical materialism and the doctrine of necessity; a religio-political imperative linking Hackney to Edinburgh (*C&S* 17).

As he had done in *The Statesman's Manual*, Coleridge took great pains in *Church and State* to establish the priority of these ideas. The Idea comes before the understanding and its conscious acts of conception in all things. But even ideas have a formative priority. The Idea of the State is anterior to the Idea of the constitution. The Idea of permanence is the first principle of the State, or as Coleridge observed, permanence is 'the first of the two great paramount interests of the social state' (*C&S* 15). Consequently, the idea of progression is the second great interest; it follows or flows out of the idea of permanence. It is, in Coleridge's dynamic account of this contiguous and comprehensive unity, both an extension and an opposition to its originating principle. Like the head and tail of a serpent, it stretches out and coils back on its self. (*C&S* 24)

Coleridge offered the image of the serpent as an illustration of the difference between opposites and contraries. But it is also a powerful image to apply to his understanding of the temporal axis, which links the present to the past. When considering the State his preference is the tree metaphor. The sacred tree was an image he had used repeatedly in his accounts of the history of civil polities, 'like that tree in Daniel'.[22] The tree grew on or after a germinating seed, its branches reaching up and out in complex and unexpected patterns and yet as natural extensions of the living wood. But it is an English acorn that grows the British oak tree. The tap root of the British oak of state was sunk deep in ancient ground,

---

[20] Jonathan Edwards (1629–1712), *A Careful and Strict Inquiry into the Modern Prevailing Notions of that Freedom of Will, which is supposed to be Essential to Moral Agency* (5th edn., 1790). Coleridge's notebook response to Edward's Calvinism: 'His world is a machine'. *CN* iv: 5077.

[21] William Lawrence and John Abernathy were both students of the great anatomist John Hunter. Lawrence was a materialist in his interpretation of Hunter's Theory of Life. Abernathy published and lectured against Lawrence, defending the vitalist position. By 1819 the Theory of Life controversy had drawn politicians and clergy into the debate. Coleridge, taking the vitalist line, wrote his own *Hints toward the formation of a More Comprehensive Theory of Life* which was published posthumously. Coleridge associated the Lawrentian view with the 'mechano-corpuscular fallacy' of Locke.

[22] Coleridge had first used this image in his 'Moral and Political Lecture' in 1795, but frequently alluded to it. Referring to the 'fixed principles' and 'grand comprehensive truth' which must be the grounding foundation of reform Coleridge wrote: 'In a deep and strong soil must that blessing fix its roots, the height of which like that tree in Daniel, is to reach to heaven, and the sight of it to the ends of all the earth' (*Lects 1795*). He echoed this with regard to the history of civil society in *The Statesman's Manual*. Of the historical development behind 'the happy organization of a well governed society', he observed 'with blood was it planted . . . the wild boar has whetted its tusks on its bark. The deep scars are still extant on its trunk, and the path of the lightening may be traced among its higher branches. And even after its full growth in the season of its strength, 'when its height reached to heaven, and the sight thereof to all the earth . . .' (*LS* 23).

established by the Law of Alfred and the providence and precepts of the primitive Church.[23] Of the English Constitution, Coleridge observed: '*Lex Sacra, Mater Legum*' (*C&S* 21). But perhaps the serpent and the oak are related ideas; at least in so far as they suggest something of Albion's pre-Lapsarian garden. Deep knowledge and inspiration are both interdependent sources of prophetic truths: ancient wisdom and oracular fire. The Serpent's coil expressed a different aspect of vital power than the tree. Snakes move quickly, slowly undulating or suddenly darting as they will. The complexity of a great and ancient oak, which carries with it the record of its slow evolution, is visible but not always seen.[24]

Much as he had discussed the nature of truth and its revelatory power in both *The Statesman's Manual* and the *Aids to Reflection,* Coleridge devoted some effort in *Church and State* to explaining why truth can be mistaken for error and how Statesmen and Citizens need to be educated to both recognize and cognize the underlying and defining power of reason in time. As a certain temperament of independence and reflective power are required for this, Coleridge considered the importance of a national church both as repository of cultural memory and as an independent estate of the realm free from the pull of interest. Establishing his priority of principle once again, Coleridge, in contra-distinction to canon-law convention, identified the church not as the first but as the third great estate of the realm; the first being the hereditary interest of permanence, the second being the circulative principle of progression. The third estate is the synthetic and dynamic fulcrum between the first two interests, containing and reconciling within itself elements of both. Sometimes the head and sometimes the tail, the Church secured that wealth which, being neither the heritable portions, nor the real property of the barons, nor the personal wealth or movables of the burgesses, was a national reserve. This great reserve or Nationalty, when combined with the wealth of the barons and the burgesses as the Propriety, constituted the Commonwealth.

The purpose of the Nationalty was for the maintenance of a learned elite. In the past this had been the priests and the prophets, then the clergy. However, as in the *Statesman's Manual,* Coleridge pointed to the deep significance of the clerical elite (as to the higher orders of society) not as a matter of their formal status as officiates of ritual, but as those whose temperament and leisure allowed for a contemplative

---

[23] Rooting Albion's Oak in the Idea of the Ancient Constitution, Coleridge personified that cumulative repository of action and judgment, the Common Laws of England. While he conferred a sacred majesty on the idea of the King and identifies Alfred as the fount of the British constitution (*C&S* 19), it is no particular head but the cumulative and temporal body of the state to which he gives life: '...law not to be derived from Alfred, or Alured, or Canute or any other elder or later promulgators of particular laws, but which might say to itself, when reason and the Laws of God first came, then came I with them' (*C&S* 22).

[24] Here the knowledge is associated with vision: of the eye, of light, of the mirror, of reflection, it is key to understanding Coleridge's account of evolutionary consciousness in Sacred History. Recalling his *AR*, 'nothing is wanted but the eye, which is the light of this house, the light which is the soul. This seeing light, this enlightening eye, is reflection' (*AR* 15).

life. Coleridge's innovation in *Church and State* was to advance his theory of the clerisy as comprising a learned and philosophically reflective elite who would act, not only as the educators and guardians of the people, but as their moral exemplars. The clerisy would be drawn from the learned of all professions who would not only undertake to civilize, but rather, to foster progressive moral improvement through the cultivation of the nation. As Coleridge emphatically remarked, 'a nation can never be a too cultivated but may easily become an over-civilized race' (*C&S* 49). In this sense, Coleridge distinguished between knowledge, scientific or technical, as a form of mastery or skill, and wisdom, where deep understanding was transparent to reason, and which signaled the progress of a genuine moral assent.

The distinction between cultivation and civilization is closely tied to Coleridge's account of the two great interests. Land cultivates and commerce civilizes, would be the simple division here. But again this is a distinction of substance rather than surface for Coleridge. The landed interest is the natural and rational source of permanence because land is the connective link to the past and a repository of collective wisdom. Commerce and the life of the city represent movable wealth, cosmopolitanism, and the world in dynamic flux. It is a world where things are constantly being broken up and reconfigured. It is therefore a principle both of immediacy and of futurity. Civilization in this account is associated with the rise of progress in the arts and sciences, it is a consequence and not a cause of the expansion of the understanding. Cultivation represents a deeper moral principle, it is grounded in the purest precepts of intuitive reason. Together, cultivation and civilization as active principles suggest the genuine moral advancement of human beings and human societies toward some final teleological resolution. But this will only be possible if equipoise can be achieved. Only if civilization is grounded and tempered by cultivation, Coleridge argued, only if permanence is softened by progression, can history be resolved in human perfection.

Coleridge's account of these principles is deeply wedded to his view of the possibility of a national education and its significance for civil as well as moral freedom, for rights as well as duties. Theologians had dominated the clergy, rather than constituted a branch of the clerisy, because it was, in an earlier less civilized age, natural that theologians take the lead. Again harnessing the tree analogy, Coleridge described theology as a 'science' and as 'the root and the trunk of the knowleges that civilized man' (*C&S* 47). While 'Philosophy or the doctrine and discipline of Ideas', was 'the *prima-scientia*', 'the ground-knowledge' (*C&S* 47). Much of Coleridge's argument centered on the idea of the institutional form of a national church, rather than as a defense of the Church of England as such. He stated that he did not refer to the particular history of the English Church but to the Idea of the Church. But, he also observed that while a national church need not be a Christian Church, indeed that the Jewish Church had been a national church, 'Christianity or the Church of Christ is a blessed accident, a providential boon' (*C&S* 55). Referring to particular histories nonetheless, Coleridge observed 'the numerous blessings of the English Constitution', 'where the principles of Protestantism have conspired with the freedom of the government to double all its salutory powers by the removal of its abuses' (*C&S* 75). English Protestantism engendered 'the gratitude of scholars and philosophers', securing through the Nationalty of the established Church, the freedoms and attainments of its clerisy.

Through his specific recurrence to English History, Coleridge implicitly raised the question, how is the structure of an English Protestant Church the perfect vessel for the freedom and progress inherent in a National Church? The great advantage of a National Church was twofold, he argued. First, the Church functioned as a conduit for advancement between the orders. Coleridge maintained that the 'Nationalty... continues to feed the higher ranks by the drawing up whatever is worthiest from below' (*C&S* 74). This had the double advantage of leavening the lump of permanence while at the same time inspiring and contenting the middling and lower orders, 'maintain[ing] the principle of hope in the humblest of families while it secures the possessions of the rich and the noble' (*C&S* 74). The second great advantage returned Coleridge to his thesis of education and moral improve-ment, or civilization and cultivation. 'The other' advantage 'is to develop in every native of the country, those faculties... and that knowledge and those attainments, which are necessary to qualify him for a member of the state, the free subject of a civilized realm' (*C&S* 74). Here, the assumptions about the priority of political and social order, and the relationship between private conscience and public duty, which had characterized Coleridge's account of civic education in *The Statesman's Manual* are echoed. Coleridge advocated a degree of education conducive to an individual's inclusion as a free member of a civilized polity. That is, that each man may know 'his duty as a Christian and a Citizen' (*LS* 6); more than this, as he had once conjectured, may not be demanded or, perhaps, desired. In *Church and State*, Coleridge advo-cates for the public at large only that knowledge that would distinguish a 'civilized man from the barbarian, the savage and the animal' (*C&S* 74).

Finally, Coleridge's account of education, improvement and freedom returns him to the efficacy of religion, or the only means 'universally efficient' (*Lects 1795*, 44), for reform. But by 1829 Coleridge's conception of religion had been translated into Christianity, which he described as 'the great redemptive process which began in the separation of light from chaos (*Hades or the Indistinction*) and has its end in the union of life with God' (*C&S* 113). He therefore considered the best way to accomplish the genuine regeneration of human society—its vital spiritual tissues and fibers—to be through the moral renewal of individuals. But this can only be accomplished through true institutions and not through the implementation of false revolutionary doctrines or false theological dogmas. History, reason, and providence will accomplish this work in sacred time. As to the Constitution of Church and State, it must be according to the Idea of Each. Permanence and Progression are understood by Coleridge to be forces of truth and enduring structure; like the immutable laws of nature which contend with the dynamic and living power of freedom or agency. One of the enduring questions in reading *Church and State* is whether it is a work of political or religious philosophy. The answer must surely be yes. It is Coleridge's last effort to bring to fruition, in light of a particular question of praxis, his synthetic philosophy. But in view of his contention that the 'Study of History, [is] preferable to the study of Philosophy', it is also Coleridge's effort to account for sacred time in secular space, to consider the condition of free living individual men in an ongoing, dynamic, and teleologically emergent providential history. As for the closing question of method, Coleridge answered it with a question, 'By what name shall I seek the historiographer of reason?' (*C&S* 59).

Works Cited

EDWARDS, PAMELA. 2004. *The Statesman's Science: History, Nature and Law in the Political Thought of Samuel Taylor Coleridge*. New York, NY: Columbia University Press.

FISCH, M. 1943. The Coleridges, Dr. Prati, and Vico. *Modern Philology*, 41 (2) (November): 111–22.

HEDLEY, DOUGLAS. 2000. *Coleridge, Philosophy and Religion: Aids to Reflection and the Mirror of the Spirit*. Cambridge: Cambridge University Press.

MORROW, JOHN. 1990. *Coleridge's Political Thought: Property, Morality, and the Limits of Traditional Discourse*. London: Macmillan Press.

ORSINI, G. N. E. 1969. *Coleridge and German Idealism*. Carbondale, Ill.: Southern Illinois University Press.

PERKINS, MARY ANNE. 1994. *Coleridge's Philosophy: The Logos as Unifying Principle*. Oxford: Clarendon Press.

PERRY, SEAMUS. 1999. *Coleridge and the Uses of Division*. Oxford: Clarendon Press.

SHAFFER, ELINOR. 1975. *'Kubla Khan' and the Fall of Jersusalem*. Cambridge: Cambridge University Press.

—— 2000. Ideologies in reading the late Coleridge: confessions of an inquiring spirit. *Romanticism on the Net*, 17 February.

SIMONS, THOMAS R. 2006. Coleridge beyond Kant and Hegel: transcendental ethics and the dialectic pentad. *Studies in Romanticism*, 45 (3).

WELLEK, RENE. 1931. *Immanuel Kant in England*. Princeton NJ: Princeton University Press.

COLERIDGE'S LECTURES 1818– 1819: *ON THE HISTORY OF PHILOSOPHY*

JEFFREY HIPOLITO

THE cliché of the Romantic poet—fiery creative genius in youth and either dead while young or aged into reactionary irrelevance—still looms large in the popular mind. Despite this image, the most philosophically adventurous and imaginative span in Coleridge's career is the ten-year period from 1815 to 1825, or from his 43rd to 53rd years. This period begins with *Biographia Literaria*, for better or worse the most influential book of literary criticism in British history (see Raimonda Modiano's essay in this volume); it ends with *Aids to Reflection*, the work that did much to shape the American Transcendentalist movement and perhaps had the greatest impact on theology by a British writer in the nineteenth century (see the essay by Pamela Edwards). Between these two epoch-making books Coleridge wrote his *Lay Sermons*, revised and republished *The Friend*, worked on his *Logic*, and made significant progress on the *Opus Maximum*, among other things.

It is no secret to experienced readers of Coleridge, then, that this was for him a period of tremendous intellectual ferment; yet, as Elinor Shaffer puts it, 'we have no accurate or adequate conception of the late Coleridge from 1819 to his death in 1834' (Shaffer 2000). How can this be? Or, to put the question in a way that more clearly points to the topic of this essay, why have so few people read carefully the *Lectures on the History of Philosophy* that Coleridge delivered over fourteen weeks from 16 December 1818 to 29 March 1819? After all, they have been publicly available since Kathleen Coburn published them in 1949. However, even as great a Coleridge scholar as Owen Barfield ran aground on the philosophical lectures—his landmark *What Coleridge Thought* proposes to be, precisely, an account of 'What Coleridge Thought towards the End of his Life' (5), but the notes he developed as an editor of the philosophical lectures undercut much of what he wrote in that book. No longer does he see Coleridge as expounding a deductively grounded 'coherent system' (5) rooted in chapter 12 of the *Biographia Literaria*, as he now recognizes that for Coleridge 'the business of *modern* philosophy is not the discovery of fresh truths but the refutation—not of false philosophy; that had already been done by the ancients themselves—but of the "effects" of false philosophy on the general mind' (*LHP* 2: 874). That as careful a reader as Barfield could find his image of Coleridge overthrown by the philosophical lectures indicates both their importance and their obscurity.

The need to attend to them looms still larger when one recognizes that they are the first major attempt by a Briton to make important philosophical claims about, and from within, a purportedly comprehensive history of philosophy; indeed, that the lecture cycle ranks with those of Hegel and Schelling as the most ambitious of the age—surpassed only by Hegel's in its historical scope—provides them with considerable historical importance in their own right. Whatever the causes of their neglect, the fact remains that the most substantial critical discussion of them is still the editor's introductions by Coburn to the Pilot Press edition and Barfield and Jackson to the Bollingen editions,[1] as well a brief discussion by McFarland in his introduction to the Bollingen edition of the *Opus Maximum*. The lectures are one of the few places in Coleridge's *oeuvre* that can still be considered virgin soil. My main task in this chapter will accordingly be to place the lectures in the context of Coleridge's thought *circa* 1 January 1819, the beginning of the period that is so little understood, even by Coleridge critics.

Coleridge explains how *he* thinks we should interpret his philosophical lectures in a letter to Robert Southey in early 1819. He plans to publish them, he tell Southey, 'because a History of *Philosophy*, as the gradual evolution of the instinct of Man to enquire into *the Origin* by the efforts of his own reason, is a desideratum in Literature—and secondly, because it is almost a necessary Introduction to my *magnum opus*, in which I had been making considerable progress till my Lectures'

---

[1] Barfield was the original editor of the Bollingen edition, but handed it over to Jackson. Substantial portions of Barfield's introduction are published as an appendix.

(*CL* 4: 917). One notes first that this 'almost...necessary' history of philosophy does not emphasize a sequence of metaphysical systems as increasingly proximate (or increasingly distant) steps towards (or away from) a grand truth. He does not say that '*the Origin*' has been reached, much less that he finds or presents it in his lectures. Rather, he focuses on the 'the efforts of...reason', driven on by a pre-rational cognitive itch it can't help but scratch. Moreover, the nebulous picture of 'the gradual evolution of the instinct of man to enquire' suggests that he is not as interested in '*the Origin*' as he is in the origin of inquiry into it. Coleridge does not pause to illuminate these points, but simply proceeds to mention that the lectures are not an atomic unit; they are an essential part of his larger attempt to delineate his 'system' as a whole in the *Opus Maximum* (see Murray Evans's essay in this volume).[2]

The same letter to Southey goes on to explain the basic outline of his philosophical 'system' (leaving aside the specific meaning that term has for Coleridge), and forces Southey to piece together on his own how the lectures are an 'almost necessary' introduction to it:

> I give 4 and oftener five hours [dictation] twice a week, and Mr Green...writes down what I say—so that we have already compassed a good handsome Volume—and hitherto we have neither of us been able to detect any unfaithfulness to the four Postulates, with which I commenced—1. That the System should be *grounded*. 2. That it should not be grounded in an *abstraction*, nor in a *Thing*. 3. That there be no chasm or saltus in the deduction or rather production. 4. That it should be bonâ fide progressive, not in circulo—productive not barren.   (*CL* 4: 917)

Philosophy is not deductive or inductive, then, but 'productive'—what Southey made of this is an open question. Furthermore, Coleridge simultaneously demands a 'ground' and denies its usual descriptive designators. Locke's 'substratum', Hume's 'impressions', Descartes's 'cogito', Spinoza's 'substance', Kant's 'Ding an sich', Fichte's 'Ich', Schelling's 'Absolute'—the list could go on—are all immediately ruled out because for Coleridge in early 1819 each analyzes unambiguously into either a 'thing' or an 'abstraction'. (In fact, Coleridge consistently held from at least the early 1800s that things and abstractions can each be analyzed into one another anyway.) His distance from his British contemporaries is a given, he implies, but lest we harbor suspicions that he remains tied to his German contemporaries, as his reference to the history of philosophy as reason's gradual self-discovery might suggest, he emphasizes that there will be no gap between the transcendental deduction and the mass of particulars because there will be no *de*duction at all. Instead he intends a philosophical '*pro*duction' (my emphasis) from his new ground, albeit one without gaps or jumps, and without the usual self-confirming

---

[2] Coleridge's reference in the letter is clearly to *Opus Maximum*, not the larger general project, usually referred to as the *magnum opus*.

foundational presuppositions. He does not say what the new ground is, how production differs from deduction (or induction), or how production can be chasm-free (answers to the first two are implied in his model of inquiry, while the last hints at the 'logic of premises' Coleridge was developing in his *Logic* at this time—see the chapter by Murray Evans in this volume). Putting together the two passages in the letter, then, we can see that this ground will not be yet another post-Kantian account of '*the Origin*' but instead will try to articulate a novel, adequate account of inquiry, with all that that entails. Coleridge views himself as venturing into an unmapped philosophical wilderness; the lectures are an 'Introduction' to the system in that they show us what to avoid, the general direction to head, and what method we should use to explore it.

Coleridge's remark that his system is 'progressive' assumes—unwisely, it seems to me—that Southey was fully aware of that term's prominence in the 'Essays on Method' (or even in the previously published, bowdlerized 'Treatise on Method'). The whole letter—and the philosophical lectures along with it—is written under the aegis of the 'Essays on Method' that Coleridge had published in November 1818, of which he wrote just two months before his letter to Southey, and right before he began his lectures, that 'in point of value... they outweigh all my other works' (*CL* 4: 885). Coleridge had published the *Biographia Literaria* in 1817, and rejected it as 'immature' later that year when he worked through his irreconcilable problems with Schelling's subjective and absolute idealisms. In 1817 and 1818 he arrived instead at the views finally presented in the 'Essays on Method'. The upshot of the 'Essays' is an attempt to fold both the method of transcendental deduction employed by Kant and the early post-Kantians and the strictly inductive and frankly skeptical method of Hume and his followers into a single model of inquiry.

Coleridge's method distinguishes three kinds of 'relation'—those of law, theory, and the fine arts—that together encompass deduction, induction, and imagination (the last of which the founder of pragmatism, C. S. Peirce, later called 'abduction', and what Coleridge in the Southey letter calls 'production'), and that for him belong to a single, overarching method of inquiry. In their simplest terms, relations of law 'appoint to each thing its *position*' (*F* 1: 459); relations of theory focus on 'a given arrangement of many under one point of view... for the purposes of understanding, and in most instances of controlling, them' (*F* 1: 464); and relations of the fine arts 'constitute a link' (*F* 1: 464) between law and theory because 'in all, that truly merits the name of *Poetry* in its most comprehensive sense, there is a necessary predominance of Ideas (i.e. of what originates in the artist himself), and a comparative indifference of the materials' (*F* 1: 464). One notes in passing the glimpse one gets here of how philosophy can be 'productive'—poetry in this sense is its crucial facilitator. Most important for us here, though, is that each element of method is comprised of relations internally, and each stands in relation to the others: 'the RELATIONS of objects are the prime *materials* of Method, and... contemplation of relations is the indispensable condition of thinking methodically' (*F* 1: 458). Indeed, if 'METHOD...becomes natural to the mind which has been accustomed to contemplate not *things* only...but likewise and chiefly the *relations* of things' it should also be remembered that for Coleridge the atomic 'thing' is itself a fiction. As Coleridge writes in a notebook entry from within a month of the philosophical lectures: 'Atoms.—If understood and employed as xyz in Algebra, and for the purpose of scientific Calculus, as in elemental Chemistry, I see no objection to the...Fiction not overweighed by its technical utility. But if they are asserted as real and existent, the Suffiction (for it would be too complimentary to call it a Supposition) is such and so fruitful an absurdity that I can only compare it to a Surinam Toad crawling on with a *wartery* of Toadlets on its back, at every fresh step a fresh tadpole' (*CN* 4: 4518).

Thus, the single, unified method of inquiry that Coleridge develops in the 'Essays on Method' is also a holistic, relational metaphysic that is perpetually self-correcting and in principle is interminable. Inquiry never arrives at a beatific consummation—a figurative dead end—but neither does it collapse into helpless skepticism or myopic nominalism.[3] This ongoing metaphysical/scientific inquiry has two defining features: first, it begins with a 'leading thought' that launches the inquiry (the impulse to launch one having been created by an anomaly of some sort); and second, it is 'progressive'. Coleridge reminds us that 'the Greek Μεθοδος, is literally *a way*, or *path of Transit*' (*F* 1: 457), that it 'cannot...otherwise than by abuse, be applied to a mere dead arrangement, containing in itself no principle of progression' (*F* 1: 457), and that it is 'itself a distinct science, the immediate offspring of philosophy, and the link or *mordant* by which philosophy becomes scientific and the sciences philosophical' (*F* 1: 463).

Coleridge's concern with 'method' does not just underlie the lectures; it is also one of its major explicit *topoi*. Indeed, the series as a whole tends to proceed along parallel tracks: on one side, Coleridge discusses the views of historically important philosophers and movements (Plato, Aristotle, Stoicism, Scholasticism, etc.) in the first half, proceeding in the second half to analyze the role and impact of post-classical philosophy on society; on the other side, he returns time and again to certain themes, regardless of which philosopher or movement is currently under review. Beyond his stated objectives he almost reflexively expounds on progression and method, the nature of history, the relation of language to thought, and the relation of philosophy to society as a whole and religion in particular. These second-track reflections often take the form of universal, ahistorical claims embedded in whatever historical matter Coleridge is elucidating. Like Hegel and Schelling, Coleridge is acutely aware that a philosophically ambitious history of philosophy also implies a philosophy of history, and so assumes certain theories of method and language, an epistemology and metaphysics of time, and so on—the two reasons Coleridge cites for publishing the lectures and the four 'postulates'

---

[3] For further discussion of Coleridge's 'Essays on Method' see Barfield, Jackson, and Hipolito 2004.

underlying them that he mentions in his letter to Southey are never far in the background.

We can see this dual-track approach already in the 'Prospectus'. Coleridge says that previous English historians of philosophy—Stanley and Brucker in particular—collect 'sentences and extracts...with no *principle* of arrangement, with no *method*, and therefore without unity and without progress or completion' (*LHP* 1: 4). Coleridge concludes from this sorry state that the times:

> seem rather to *require* a work like the present...which...does in the main consider Philosophy historically, as an essential part of the history of man, and as if it were the striving of a single mind...at different stages of its own growth and development; but so that each change and every new direction should have its cause and its explanation in the errors, insufficiency, prematurity of the preceding, while all by reference to a common object is reduced to harmony of impression and total result.   (*LHP* 1: 5)

So while Coleridge discusses philosophy's history, he does so using the 'leading thought'—that is, the imaginative hypothesis—that it is, as it were, the outward evidence of an evolution of consciousness, and that that evolution is 'progressive' as Coleridge understood this term.

Progressive towards what, though? In the 'Prospectus' Coleridge suggests a dialectical model of continual, wholly inward, correction of philosophical error and/or 'immaturity'. Indeed, the *Biographia Literaria* and Coleridge's own later rejection of it are sufficient to show that he thought of his own changing views in these terms. If such was his initial goal, it disappears almost immediately in the lectures themselves (by the fifth one, at the latest). So how does 'progress' itself progress in subsequent lectures, and how does it culminate? A very brief comparison of the conclusions to the similar lecture series of Hegel and Schelling helps to frame clearly Coleridge's unique direction. This is especially pertinent because at least one prominent reader sees in Coleridge's lectures a 'striking similarity' to those of Hegel (*OM* cxciii), and the differences in their respective conclusions help to illustrate how far apart they really are.[4]

Hegel's lectures, the most influential history of philosophy in the nineteenth century, end on a high note. Hegel claims that:

> A new epoch has arisen in the world. It would appear as if the World-spirit had at last succeeded in stripping off from itself all alien objective existence, and apprehending itself at last as absolute Spirit, in developing from itself what for it is objective, and keeping it within its own power, yet remaining at rest all the while. The strife of the finite self-consciousness with the absolute self-consciousness, which last seemed to the other to lie outside of itself,

---

[4] McFarland's full comment is: 'Despite the striking similarity between the philosophical lectures of Coleridge and those of Hegel, on one important point they were absolutely opposed. Hegel's system constituted a form of pantheism. Coleridge, on the contrary, saw a God presiding over both a human and an external nature, but not located within those realms' (*OM* cxciii). Leaving aside whether it is accurate to describe Hegel's system as pantheistic, I hope to show that they differ on more than theology.

now comes to an end. Finite self-consciousness has ceased to be finite; and in this way absolute self-consciousness has, on the other hand, attained to the reality which it lacked before.   (3: 551)

This conclusion is, in part, the basis for the unfair but understandable caricature of Hegel as a self-aggrandizing egomaniac. Throughout the lectures he has followed the dialectical unfolding of the history of philosophy as the mediated approach of 'Geist' to self-consciousness through its overcoming of self-imposed externality. Thus Hegel himself, having articulated the true and complete history of philosophy—'the sole work of which is to depict this strife' (3: 552)—*becomes* the 'concrete universal' insofar as he instantiates the entry of the absolute itself, as a whole, into full historical self-consciousness. On his own terms he is entitled to say, perhaps with unintended irony: 'At this point I bring the history of Philosophy to a close' (3: 552).

Schelling's lectures *On the History of Modern Philosophy* are in many ways a counterpoint to Hegel's. They discuss the Rationalist/Idealist tradition from Descartes through Hegel and Jacobi, which Schelling in 1834 largely views as a consolidation of error although it includes his own early philosophy. The lectures end with the contrasting but equally inadequate philosophies of Jacobi and Hegel. For Schelling, Jacobi avows an 'empty theism' that 'in attributing to reason an *immediate*, so to speak blind *knowledge* of God, indeed of passing off reason as an immediate organ of God and divine things' gave to philosophy his 'worst present' (169). Hegel, on the other hand, 'wants the Absolute, before he takes it as a principle, as the result of a science, and this science is precisely the Logic' (153). Schelling accuses Hegel of trying to assimilate the essentially inassimilable facticity of material existence—that there is 'something' rather than 'nothing'—into the abstract, dialectical peregrinations of his *Logic*.

if... in order to get to a *creation* no more is necessary than to go back down the steps which one has climbed, and if the Absolute already becomes an effective cause simply by this reversal... so that one would come back as far as pure being, which = nothing; enough, we can see what inconsistencies the reversal would lead to if understood in this way, and see how illusory the opinion is that one could, by such a simple reversal, transform philosophy into a philosophy which could also comprehend a free creation of the world.   (158–9)

Schelling here argues that if the evolution of the world is a wholly rational process it should be reversible, but if we do that with Hegel's system we arrive at the first term of his logic, Being, which Hegel himself claims is the same as Nothing. Consequently, even if we take Hegel on his own terms we still have the basic problem of how it is that something can be generated out of nothing—the *identity* of Being and Nothing elides the supposedly inevitable next step, Becoming. For the late Schelling, modern Rationalist/Idealist philosophy culminates in the glaringly obvious need to use the most acutely rational means to forcefully assert that a bottomless gulf separates the facticity of the world from our acutely rational efforts to assimilate it—we cannot jump the gap either with Jacobi's *salto mortale* or with Hegel's dialectical pirouettes.

Coleridge's lectures predate those of Hegel or Schelling, but we might see him as a proleptic mediator of their conflict. He rejects that one can proceed 'from law to hypothesis' as this would require 'an absolute [that] is contemplable in every dependant and finite' (*LHP* 2: 533). To this extent his views coincide with Schelling's; indeed, Coleridge was singularly unimpressed by Hegel in his brief perusal of his *Logic*. Furthermore, Schelling's 'positive' philosophy, rooted in material existence, finds a corollary in what Seamus Perry describes as Coleridge's 'instinctive and complicating diversitarian love... [for] the common plural world where we... live' (291). However, he does not follow his German contemporary to the conclusion that our choice then is between 'two kinds of persons' (*AW* 103), the one who 'governs madness' or the one who 'is governed by madness' (*AW* 103–4). Either way, for Schelling, in the absence of a deductively secured absolute ground we must acknowledge that 'self-lacerating madness is still now what is innermost in all things' (*AW* 103). Instead, the conclusion that Coleridge draws from the failure of the post-Kantian use of the transcendental deduction to ground a metaphysic is the need for a new method to replace transcendental deductions without reverting to Rationalist deductions or Empiricist inductions. And that is how he presents his history of philosophy.

Thus the champion of the final lectures is Francis Bacon, not only with respect to enthusiasm but also the sheer amount of discussion—Coleridge only gives Locke more attention quantitatively, and some of that he devotes to explaining socio-economically the otherwise inexplicable: how Locke's arguments could have so misled so many otherwise intelligent people (see *LHP* 2: 563–4). Bacon, by contrast, emerges in the lectures as the pioneer of Coleridgean method, as he had in the 'Essays on Method' a month earlier (in fact, Coleridge quotes and paraphrases the 'Essays' in this part of his discussion). Bacon's philosophy 'demands, indeed, experiment as the true groundwork of all real knowledge' (*LHP* 2: 486) but that is not because he is an Empiricist *avant la lettre*. Contrary to the popular view of Bacon as the strictest adherent to pure induction, 'he requires some well-grounded purpose in the mind, some self-consistent anticipation of the result, in short the *prudens* [*quaestio*], the prudent forethought and enquiry which he declares to be [*dimidium scientiae*]' (*LHP* 2: 486). The conclusion Coleridge draws from Bacon's claim that science is founded on 'experiment' rather than the 'senses' alone is that 'our perception can apprehend through the organs of sense only the phenomena evoked by the experiment, but that same power of mind, which out of its own laws has proposed the experiment, can judge whether in nature there is a law correspondent to the same' (*LHP* 2: 487). Furthermore, according to Coleridge the '*lux intellectus*' that Bacon introduces in order to explain how errors of judgment are possible commits him to the view that there is a 'pure and impersonal reason freed from all the personal idols which this great legislator of science then enumerates' (*LHP* 2: 487).

Coleridge, then, agrees with Schelling that philosophy is rooted in facticity (without partaking of the fiction of matter existing outside relations), but the lack of an absolute is not cause for melodramatic despair; if the skeptic is willing to concede that lawful relationships can be educed (or produced?) via experiment, they must also allow what follows from that: that those lawful relationships are more than the sum of the phenomena they govern. As such, they must be known through the '*lux intellectus*' that itself must be more than a phenomenon if it is the means to perceive extra-phenomenal laws that govern relations among phenomena. As Coleridge puts it while comparing Locke and Descartes:

If you only substitute for the phrase, the ideas being derived from the senses or impressed upon the mind or in any way supposed to be brought in . . . if for this you substitute the word 'elicit', namely, that there are no conceptions of our mind relatively to external objects but what are elicited by their circumstances and by what are supposed to be correspondent to them, there would be nothing found in Locke but what is perfectly just. (*LHP* 2: 568)

Coleridge in fact begins this lecture by describing the theory of mind that he thinks follows from the Baconian model of ideas 'elicited' by experiments. He first notes that 'man, taken in the ideal of his humanity, has been not inaptly called the microcosm of the world in compendium, as the point to which all the lines converge from the circumference of nature' (*LHP* 2: 461). He then unpacks this analogy with a description of the 'threefold mind' (*LHP* 2: 461). Each of the three is typified by efforts at self-correcting experiment. The first 'beholds all things perspectively from his relative position as man'; the second 'in which those views are again modified, too often disturbed and falsified by his particular constitution and position'; and finally the third, which 'though it requires both effort from within and auspicious circumstances from without to evolve it into effect', is nevertheless his 'highest power' (*LHP* 2: 461). It is highest because 'he places himself on the same point as nature and contemplates all objects, himself included, in their permanent and universal beings and relations' (*LHP* 2: 461). Here Coleridge reverts to the traditional designation of the astronomer as the physical scientist *par excellence*:

the astronomer who places himself in the centre of the system and looks at all the planetary orbs as with the eye of the sun. Happy would it be for us if we could at all times imitate him in his perceptions—in the intellectual or the political world—I mean, to subordinate instead of exclude. Nature excludes nothing. She takes up all, still subjecting the highest to the less so and ultimately subjecting all to the lower thus taken up. But alas! The contrary method, exclusion instead of subordination, this and its results, presents the historian with his principal materials in whatever department his researches are directed. (*LHP* 2: 461)

The astronomer as exemplar of the ideal knower 'places himself on the same point as nature' only insofar as his *knowledge* of the laws that govern planetary *are* those laws, and he arrives at an understanding of those laws through the kind of 'subordination' of phenomena to physical laws that occurs in nature itself. Nor is this analysis limited to scientific method. We have already seen that for Coleridge at this time science and philosophy as reciprocal, mutually implicating endeavors—that, as he puts it in a contemporaneous notebook entry, 'Philosophy... is not a *Science*; but a Supplement of Science. Consequently Philosophy is not the same as Science; and yet cannot be wholly heterogeneous' (*CN* 4: 4517). Philosophy is similar to science insofar as both are concerned with method, but differs in that philosophy's proper metaphysical, second-order role is to fashion a method capable of inquiring into method itself. What ushers in the modern era for him, then, is not (as it is for both Hegel and Schelling) the Cartesian method of universal doubt, but the discovery by Bacon that 'the science of metaphysics [and ontology]' (*LHP* 2: 507) is inseparable from 'experiment, as [an] organ of reason' (*LHP* 2: 509).

It would be a mistake to think, based on all of this, that Coleridge faithfully traces the history of philosophy, in accordance with his method of inquiry, as the 'striving of a single mind' in which 'every new direction should have its cause and its explanation in the errors, insufficiency, and prematurity of the preceding' (*LHP* 1: 5). It is true, he does sometimes purport to show this quasi-dialectical process at work (for example, between Greek and Jewish cultures as a whole). Within philosophy proper, examples include among others Zeno and Democritus, Plato and Aristotle, the Stoics and the Epicureans, and the Scholastic Realists and the Nominalists. Nevertheless, Coleridge also maintains in the seventh lecture—that is, barely halfway through his course—that 'before the birth of our Saviour all philosophy could do or had done had been really achieved and as well achieved [if] philosophy is confined to the meaning I give it, [truth attained] by the efforts of reason itself' (*LHP* 1: 326). If attaining truth through reason and correcting errors and immaturities are coextensive enterprises, philosophical progress ends before the advent of Christianity. Indeed, philosophy reaches its apex with 'the difference between Aristotle and Plato... which will remain as long as we are men and there is any difference between man and man in point of opinion' (*LHP* 1: 230). Coleridge suggests here that all subsequent dialectical relations in philosophy relate to the basic Plato/Aristotle polarity as aftershocks to an earthquake: they may bring down more houses, but they add nothing qualitatively new. However, if the history of philosophy ceases to make progress with Aristotle, and is properly born with Pythagoras,[5] then it has a very short history indeed.

This does not mean that philosophy's history comes to an end, though; rather, for Coleridge it takes on a different importance. Philosophers subsequent to 'the Aristotelian system' may have held opinions in which 'there was nothing new', but they are still important because 'they were highly influencive and connected with the manners, nay, with the great political events of mankind' (*LHP* 1: 327). The

---

[5] 'The man to whom the name [philosopher] seems due first of all was Pythagoras, something like one of the most extraordinary human beings that has ever astonished and perplexed the world' (*LHP* 1: 64).

social effects of philosophy are 'out of sight' and 'indirect', but these are 'in almost every instance ten times more important than the direct and apparent ones' (*LHP* 1: 327). We have, then, two ways of viewing the history of philosophy, both of which have equal importance for Coleridge: the dialectical overcoming (or at least clarification) of error, which culminates in an adequate method of inquiry that ramifies to the other branches of philosophy (metaphysics, ethics, epistemology, and so on), and the relation of philosophy to society as a whole.

But what is the philosophy of history that supports this particular picture of the history of philosophy? Coleridge critics tend to emphasize Coleridge's adherence to a religious view of history as taking direction from divine Providence, and stress that for Coleridge human history involves 'the process of individuation and the role of the Logos in that process' (Kooy 728).[6] While this perspective is correct in many respects, it understates Coleridge's vigorous efforts during these years to synthesize natural philosophy and history (and, implicitly, theology insofar as for Coleridge the human sciences are also natural sciences—what Pamela Edwards well describes as 'the vibrantly organic and dynamically interdependent nature of history and life' (151). In this respect Coleridge follows no less a figure than Kant, who in his essay 'Idea for a Universal History' (1784) sets out to discover the *a priori* principles that govern history. In the essay Kant anticipates his *Critique of Judgment* (1790) by arguing that we cannot help but think of human behaviors, like all natural behaviors, as purposive though not necessarily rational:

The only way out for the philosopher since he cannot assume that mankind follows any rational *purpose of its own* in its collective actions, is for him to attempt to discover a *purpose in nature* behind this senseless course of human events, and decide whether it is after all possible to formulate in terms of a definite plan of nature a history of creatures who act without a plan of their own.   (42)

Kant views human behavior, then, as an extension of the natural world, and as such we must use alogical 'reflective' judgments—which are strictly analogous to aesthetic judgments—in order to cognize it.

Coleridge takes up this position—reading the essay on history through the third *Critique*, and incorporating aesthetic/reflective judgments into his theory of inquiry as 'relations of the fine arts'. Moreover, beyond these changes, he also adds to it the dynamic view of nature held by the *Naturphilosophen*. Raimonda Modiano has shown that 'for a decade after 1815' Coleridge pursued a 'passionate and steady interest in the inner constitution of nature and its laws of development' (138). His view of history as having an 'evolution' is rooted as much in this dynamic *Naturphilosophie* as it is in 'Providence'. The principle of polarity that underlies *Naturphilosophie* was much on Coleridge's mind during the lectures, and this contemporary notebook entry explains it concisely. Beginning with the observation

---

[6] For further discussion of Coleridge's philosophy of history see Barfield, Di Paolo, and Edwards. For discussion of British views of history in general during this period see Bann and Phillips.

that in Euclidean geometry one generates a line by extending a point in opposite directions, Coleridge says that:

Unity is manifested by Opposites. But it is equally true, that all true Opposites tend to Unity. For the further Fleeing each from the other is here precluded by the assumption of the Line as finite, i.e., the assumption of a punctum indifferentiæ midway between the extreme points, and the distance of each from the mid point is the exponent or measure of the equal *attractive* power of the mid point over each extreme... or the measure of its own projective power.   (*CN* 4: 4513)

The historical 'progress' of philosophy by means of the dynamic polarity of Plato and Aristotle has precisely the power generated by this unified opposition. From the original point of Pythagoras' foundational speculations emerges, via Sophistic skepticism, the productive, polar opposition of Plato and Aristotle.

Coleridge views Plato as holding several discernible philosophical positions. First, he sees Plato as propounding a phenomenology that generates his idealism: 'The mind always feels itself greater than aught it has done. It begins in the act of perceiving that it must go beyond it in order to comprehend it; therefore it is only to that which contains distinct conception in itself, and, thereby satisfying the intellect, does at the same time contain in it a plenitude which refuses limitation or division, that the soul feels its full faculties called forth' (*LHP* 1: 194). According to Coleridge, Plato deduces from the fact that the mind perceives itself to exceed the sum of possible phenomenal predicates that one must strive 'to contemplate things not in the phenomenon, not in their accidents or in their superficies, but in their essential powers, first as they exist in relation to other powers co-existing with them, but lastly and chiefly as they exist in the Supreme Mind, independent of all material division, distinct yet indivisible' (*LHP* 1: 193).

However, this position does not amount to a system. Indeed, Plato's 'system' is not a system at all. 'But what this philosophy is', Coleridge says, 'you look for in vain in the writings of Plato' (*LHP* 1: 191). Instead, Plato's *Dialogues* are 'all preparative, predisciplinary, tending to kindle the desire for the philosophy itself in the few minds thereto called, tending to remove the obstacles and most fitting to foster the growth of the wings of such minds fluttering, as it were, on the edge of the eagle's nest' (*LHP* 1: 216). If Plato's works have been interpreted as an attempt to build a dogmatic system, that is the fault of their interpreters, who miss completely 'the doubtful tone expressed on all these points in the dialogues of Plato himself' (*LHP* 1: 217). The emphasis on mental activity and phenomenology (as we would call it now) in Coleridge's description of Plato dovetails with the pivotal role he gives Plato as an exponent of methodical inquiry in the 'Essays on Method'. For Coleridge, Plato is most remarkable for isolating mental activity out from phenomena because that foregrounds the distinctness of the inquirer from the subject of inquiry.

Aristotle supplements and drives Platonic introspection, questioning, and ideal-ism with equal attention to the senses, experiment and generalization. Coleridge credits Aristotle, nearly a superhuman 'abstracting and generalizing power in the world' (*LHP* 1: 235), as having begun 'the science of logic itself' (*LHP* 1: 234) and 'experimental knowledge of which he was assuredly the father' (*LHP* 1: 227). Coleridge plainly privileges the Platonic tradition throughout the lectures—after all, we are all either Platonists or Aristotelians by disposition—but despite his greater enthusiasm for the former, the two must coexist: 'one stands on one point, and another on another, the objects seen are the same, they vary only according to the point of perspective' (*LHP* 1: 228). If the two are eternally locked in conflict as quasi-Blakean contraries, that is only because there can be no philosophical progress otherwise; and by progress, as we have seen, Coleridge means the gradual clarification of the method by which philosophy inquires into its fundamental, foundational premises. One goal of the lectures and of Coleridge's philosophical thought as a whole during this period is to pivot away from attempts to prove the superiority of the Platonic over the Aristotelian tradition, and to discover instead how the opposed dispositions of Plato and Aristotle unify within the larger framework of an adequate model of inquiry.

The Plato/Aristotle polarity is, as it were, the inner aspect of the history of philosophy; its outer aspect is its relation to society as a whole. More specifically, philosophy impacts on society, transforms it for better or worse, through its reaction on language and consequently on the basic, unquestioned metaphysical and cosmological assumptions of society. 'What is philosophy in one age is common sense in another, and vice-versa' because 'philosophy perpetually acts as the pioneer and purveyor of common sense' (*LHP* 1: 256).[7] Later in the course Coleridge says more about just how this occurs:

The influences of philosophy must not be sought for... in the immediate effect of their writings upon the students of speculative knowledge.... No, we must look for it every-where, only not in their own shape, for it becomes active by being diluted. It combines itself as a colour, as it were, lying on the public mind, as a sort of preparation for receiving thought in a particular way and excluding particular views, and in this way its effect has been great.   (*LHP* 2: 494)

So, it may be that 'nothing... has been really discovered in pure speculation by the moderns' (*LHP* 1: 304) but nevertheless 'I can prove [philosophy] to have exerted [an influence] upon the structure of language, moral feelings, and political opin-ions of European nations' (*LHP* 1: 304). The 'great' influence of philosophy on society occurs in and through its dilution into everyday language. Coleridge first establishes what has become familiar but was then unusual—that 'words... are the

---

[7] Coleridge suggests here that 'common sense' can affect the direction of philosophy just as philosophy can affect common sense. He does not expand on that here, but it is not hard to see that he anticipates the direction taken by Moore and Wittgenstein.

great mighty instruments by which thoughts are excited and by which alone they can be [expressed] in a remembered form' (*LHP* 1: 257). So, when 'philoso-phy...employed itself in desynonimizing words' under the scholastic realists, it 'laid the foundation of our modern languages' (*LHP* 1: 387). Insofar as philosophers affect the meanings of words—or, still more radically, affect the structure of language itself (as Coleridge suggests above, presumably having in mind the birth of Romance languages from medieval Latin)—their influence diffuses into the thoughts and the structure of the thoughts of people at large all the more powerfully for being 'hidden'.

A few pages ago I referred to a notebook entry that Coleridge wrote on polarity. Several months later he wrote another, on language, that he thought helped to explain it (which itself highlights the close connection Coleridge saw between language and natural laws). That later notebook entry also clarifies the importance of this argument for Coleridge. 'Grammar and Logic', he says, 'mutually support each other.... The result from both, or the perfect knowledge of Words and the positions and relations of Words as representing and corresponding to, the sensible Objects & the bodily, imaginative, moral and intellectual processes of Man whether active or passive, is Metaphysics, or Philosophy as far as it is Science' (*CN* 4: 4644). Metaphysics—the scientific pursuit of philosophy or, what amounts to the same thing, properly methodical inquiry into the nature of methodical inquiry—simply is the philosophy of language and logic, which are themselves ultimately identical. To bring about changes in language is therefore to refashion metaphysics itself.

The great tool for introducing such changes is 'desynonimization', which is still 'a largely neglected area of his thought' (Hamilton 1983, 4). 'There are', Coleridge says, 'few pursuits more instructive and not many more entertaining...than that of retracing the progress of a living language for a few centuries, and its improve-ments as an organ and vehicle of thought, by desynonymizing words' (*LHP* 2: 553). Coleridge again anticipates efforts by such otherwise contrary twentieth-century philosophers as Moore and Wittgenstein to find the essence of philosophy in ordinary language (though he would deny what they affirm, that it can be reduced to such language): because Plato and Aristotle exhaust all possible avenues of traditional philosophical inquiry, its proper social and historical role is to help us better understand the words we use by more sharply defining them.[8] In so doing, though, it also helps to reshape that world. Put simply, if language and thought are just as inextricable as thought and perception, to alter the first is to affect the last. Indeed, while Coleridge is exceedingly unclear on this point, it eventually becomes obvious that when in the 'Prospectus' he describes the history of philosophy as the development of a single mind, he cannot rest his claim on the dialectical

---

[8] For more detailed discussion of Coleridge's philosophy of language see Reid, 11–26, and McKusick.

overcoming of error by the triumph and defeat of philosophers. Rather, it is far more fruitful and consistent with Coleridge's practice in the lectures to view the history of language as the developmental record of a single cultural consciousness, and to see the philosopher's role as being to help society to 'progress' by methodically 'desynonimizing' words.

If the dialectical struggles of philosophers are limited on one side by 'common sense', they are bound in on the other by religion. Throughout the lectures Coleridge is at pains to distinguish the two, and to define them precisely by what separates them. So, for example, he says that 'the human mind ... never can in a civilized state be without some philosophy or other' (*LHP* 1: 326–7), but that is only because 'without a congenial philosophy there can be no general religion' (*LHP* 1: 327). Statements such as these are the reason many of Coleridge's readers have viewed him as giving up in his later years the disinterested pursuit of truth through philosophy for a dogmatic theology; at the very least, Coleridge appears to bend his philosophy to make it better conform to his theology.[9] Coleridge himself contributes to this perception. The vigor of his piety seems at times to tempt him into appalling solecisms. For example, during a discussion of 'the spread of Christianity' as arising from 'this necessity for a religion comprehending the interests of all mankind' (*LHP* 1: 308)—itself a highly dubious claim—Coleridge goes still further and says that:

For what can we ask more, what can we think more elevated, as a proof of a religion, than a demonstration of its necessity for mankind, a necessity not first felt when it was preached, but already discovered; so that, as it were, the very vices of mankind and their own sense of their utter helplessness went beforehand as a prayer for its appearance, and when it appeared and was found adapted to the heart of man in all its recesses, surely it was something more than mere human reasoning, and yet included it all, to say that a religion which so fitted the human heart must have come from that Being that made the human heart. (*LHP* 1: 308–9)

Now, this has the appearance of a deduction of the 'necessity for mankind' of Christianity. If we recast it as a syllogism, though, its inadequacy is obvious: the major premise is that a presumably supreme Being made 'the heart of man in all its recesses'. Grant this and it must be the case that the heart wants what the Creator implants in it as a desire. Thus, my vices must be prayers for salvation, and such salvation must come in the form of a religion that celebrates the Creator. Obviously, every aspect of this argument is fallacious; so far from including 'human reasoning', it seems to take leave of it.

Set against such important but relatively rare passages, though, are Coleridge's more frequent and more fruitfully nuanced accounts of the relation of religion

---

[9] The classic presentation of this view is McFarland. For a more recent elaboration of the same idea see Hamilton 2007. Of course, McFarland and Hamilton are both far more sophisticated in their arguments than I can do justice to here.

to philosophy. For example, the major premise in the above argument would seem to be an object of the crudest faith. And yet, throughout the lectures Coleridge rejects that faith should act as 'the extinguisher upon all the powers of the intellect' (*LHP* 1: 376) and defines it instead, most unusually, as 'the energies of our moral feelings' (*LHP* 1: 377), 'the moral anticipation' (*LHP* 1: 377), and 'an anticipation of knowledge by the moral will' (*LHP* 1: 280). Such an energetic unification of feeling, thought, and will should be recognized by veteran Coleridge readers as coextensive with his comments elsewhere on imagination, and forms the core of the moral philosophy and theology that Coleridge developed at much greater length in *Opus Maximum* and *Aids to Reflection*, and that are grounded in the aesthetic discourse of the sublime and the beautiful.[10] We can already see the 'relations of the fine arts'—in which the idea is 'carried' into the materials—behind his claim that 'the true problem of all true philosophy' is 'to take virtue as a precept in order to render it a nature' (*LHP* 1: 275). Everything depends, of course, on what one takes to be a precept, and how one goes about carrying it into 'nature'. For Coleridge this occurs as a sublime revelation: 'It would be in vain to seek for a proof of a perfect circle in nature.... Even so is it with all the great moral truths. They show a fitness in the human mind for religion, but the power of giving it is not in the reason; that must be given as all things are given from without, and it is that which we call revelation' (*LHP* 1: 310). Reflections such as this put us on the verge of Coleridge's immediately subsequent reflection on conscience as the 'ground of consciousness' and on the methodical articulation and implementation of moral ideas as free, imaginative acts. Coleridge will later articulate these distinctions more clearly. Already in the *Lectures*, though, the sublime ideal of religion is the limiting condition of philosophy, as it affects and is affected by society in its endless effort to articulate methodically the ground of its imaginative productivity.

WORKS CITED

BANN, STEPHEN. 1995. *Romanticism and the Rise of History*. New York: Twayne Publishers.
BARFIELD, OWEN. 1971. *What Coleridge Thought*. Middletown: Wesleyan University Press.
COLERIDGE, SAMUEL TAYLOR. 1983. *Biographia Literaria*, ed. James Engell and W. Jackson Bate. Vol. 7 of *The Collected Works of Samuel Taylor Coleridge*. Princeton: Princeton University Press. (=BL)
—— 1956–1971. *Collected Letters of Samuel Taylor Coleridge*. 6 vols., ed. Earl Leslie Griggs. Oxford: Clarendon Press. (=CL)
—— 2000. *Lectures 1818–1819: On the History of Philosophy*, ed. J. R. de J. Jackson. Vol. 8 of *The Collected Works of Samuel Taylor Coleridge*. Princeton: Princeton University Press. (=LHP)

[10] For fuller discussion of Coleridge's moral philosophy in this period see Hipolito 2005.

COLERIDGE, SAMUEL TAYLOR. 1957–2002. *The Notebooks of Samuel Taylor Coleridge.* 5 vols., ed. Kathleen Coburn. Princeton: Princeton University Press. (=*CN*)

DI PAOLO, CHARLES. 1992. *Coleridge: Historian of Ideas.* Victoria: University of Victoria Press.

EDWARDS, PAMELA. 2004. *The Statesman's Science: History, Nature and Law in the Political Thought of Samuel Taylor Coleridge.* New York: Columbia University Press.

HAMILTON, PAUL. 1983. *Coleridge's Poetics.* Stanford: Stanford University Press.

—— 2007. *Coleridge and German Philosophy: The Poet in the Land of Logic.* London: Continuum.

HEGEL, G. W. F. 1892–6. *Lectures on the History of Philosophy,* trans. by E. S. Haldane and F. H. Simson (3 vols, London: Humanities Press).

HIPOLITO, JEFFREY. 2004. Coleridge, hermeneutics, and the ends of metaphysics. *European Romantic Review,* 15 (4): 547–65.

—— 2005. The moral epistemology of Coleridge's *Aids to Reflection. Journal of the History of Ideas,* 66 (1): 455–74.

KOOY, MICHAEL JOHN. 1999. Romanticism and Coleridge's idea of history. *Journal of the History of Ideas,* 60 (3): 717–35.

MCFARLAND, THOMAS. 1969. *Coleridge and the Pantheist Tradition.* Oxford: Clarendon Press.

MCKUSICK, JAMES. 1986. *Coleridge's Philosophy of Language.* New Haven: Yale University Press.

MODIANO, RAIMONDA. 1985. *Coleridge and the Concept of Nature.* Tallahassee: Florida State University Press.

PERRY, SEAMUS. 1999. *Coleridge and the Uses of Division.* Oxford: Oxford University Press.

PHILLIPS, MARK SALBER. 2000. *Society and Sentiment: Genres of Historical Writing in Britain, 1740–1820.* Princeton: Princeton University Press.

REID, NICHOLAS. 2006. *Coleridge, Form and Symbol, or The Ascertaining Vision.* Aldershot: Ashgate.

SCHELLING, F. W. J. VON. 2000. *The Ages of the World,* trans. by Jason W. Wirth (Albany: State University of New York Press).

—— 1994. *On the History of Modern Philosophy,* trans. by Andrew Bowie (Cambridge: Cambridge University Press).

SHAFFER, E. S. 2000. Ideologies in readings of the late Coleridge: *Confessions of an Inquiring Spirit. Romanticism on the Net,* 17 [Accessed September 15, 2007] <http://users.ox.ac.uk/~scat0385/17confessions.html>

CHAPTER 14

COLERIDGE AS READER: *MARGINALIA*

H. J. JACKSON

'COLERIDGE as Reader: *Marginalia*.' Is that one topic or two? If two, which of them is the subject here? 'Coleridge as Reader' covers most of his life—for he was an early reader—and overlaps significantly with the other chapter-titles in this collection, especially the ones collected under 'Sources and Influences', whch necessarily consider what he read, how he read, and what he *made* of what he read. For almost two centuries 'Coleridge as Reader' has proved a fruitful way of getting a handle on Coleridge—both the man and the works—as we see in the approaches of critics as diverse as Charles Lamb, Thomas De Quincey, J. L. Lowes, and T. M. McFarland. Whatever his failings in other areas, Coleridge as Reader cuts a heroic figure. The consensus is that he was extraordinarily widely-read, extraordinarily adventurous in his reading, extraordinarily sensitive in his responses, and extraordinarily creative in his transformation of the materials that came his way. He acquired a name as a literary omnivore very early on, liked that image, and cultivated it. At twenty-four he said he was 'a library-cormorant' who had read 'almost every thing' (*CL* 1: 260). Attempts to describe the range and scale of his reading generally turn into enormous lists that are themselves unreadable. Lacking the full set of languages and the advanced competence in disparate fields that Coleridge acquired in the course of a lifetime, no critic or biographer has even attempted to follow his intellectual tracks in all their highroads and byways.

The common impression of Coleridge as Reader is, like most common knowledge, a partial truth. As I hope to demonstrate here, he was a remarkable reader but not beyond compare. The black sheep of a high-achieving family, in the absence of formal qualifications for a conventional career, he became a professional reader. Like other bookish children before and after, he made his living by reading, drawing on the accumulated capital of many years' practice for his own lectures and publications. Success brought its own problems and a measure of disillusionment. The library-cormorant of twenty-four, the man who at thirty-two could describe a state of blessedness as consisting in the possession of a wife and children, 'two or three friends, and a thousand Books' (*CL* 2: 1162), complained of being 'irremissibly task-worked' in his sixties (*CL* 5: 365). At the end of his life he found even the pace of his reading tediously slow, 'for alas! thro weakness of the body & over-activity of the suggestive mind I now crawl thro' a book like a fly thro a milk splash on a Tea-tray! I who 20 years ago, used to read a volume, stereotype-wise by whole pages at a glance' (*M* 4: 336–7). Nevertheless, books and reading were to him, as he acknowledged, 'the staff of life' (*CL* 6: 607)—and they were so not only in the obvious sense of a source of livelihood but also in the sense of a generally dependable support. They were his counsellors, his recreation, his comfort and refuge, as well as his bread and butter.

The topic 'Marginalia' represents a more manageable subset of the history of Coleridge's activities as a reader. For better *and* worse, Coleridge is the best-known scribbler in books in the English-speaking world, having held the title unchallenged for 170 years or more. Again, he can be seen to have himself promoted this aspect of his legend. In 1819, an edited version of a long note on Sir Thomas Browne appeared in *Blackwood's Magazine*, correctly attributed to him by name and almost certainly contributed by him directly. The introductory headnote points out that Coleridge's close friends all knew that some of his most valuable manuscript work was to be found 'in the blank leaves and margins of books; whether his own, or those of his friends, or even in those that have come in his way casually, seems to have been a matter altogether indifferent' (*M* 1: 796). *Church and State*, published in 1829, includes some notes transcribed from his copy of Isaac Taylor's recent *Natural History of Enthusiasm*, prefaced with the assurance that they had been written in pencil because the book was not his own, and with the remark that these notes might 'remind some of my old school-fellows of the habit for which I was even then noted: and for others they may serve, as a specimen of the Marginalia, which, if brought together from the various books, my own and those of a score others, would go near to form as bulky a volume as most of those old folios, through which the larger portion of them are dispersed'(*CCS* 166). This statement is a piece of defensive myth-making, addressing Coleridge's reputation as a spoiler of books (for even then it was thought wrong to write in other people's books without invitation) and an idler (but his marginalia would fill a fat folio volume). The claim that he was known as a writer of marginalia as a schoolboy is not true, and the implication that his reading was largely of a learned or antiquarian cast is an exaggeration, though both points tend to corroborate the engaging impression of Coleridge as a schoolboy and as a reader that had been created by Charles Lamb in his famous essays of 1820, 'Christ's Hospital Five and Thirty Years Ago' and 'The Two Races of Men'.

The word 'marginalia' that appears in both the *Blackwood's* article and *Church and State*, a neuter plural noun (singular *marginale*) naturalized by Coleridge from Latin, had previously been associated with scholarly commentaries on the Bible, the law, and classical literature. In applying it to his own writings it is likely that Coleridge was making a Lambish joke and having it both ways, as in mock-heroic fictions. On the one hand the term has an aggrandizing effect: Coleridge's scribbles are put in the same category with learned annotations. On the other, it is ironically self-deprecating, for there is nothing rigorous or systematic about his notes— which is just what makes them unpredictable and enjoyable.

Coleridge's will specifically provided for the publication of his marginalia. Through the loyalty and dedication of his family and executors, hundreds of pages duly appeared in various collections of his 'literary remains' between 1836 and 1853; these were incorporated in Shedd's important American edition of Coleridge's collected works and were followed in the next century by the publication of smaller sets of notes and further reprints and collections. All this exposure (documented by George Whalley as part of his extensive introduction to the Bollingen edition of the *Marginalia*) consolidated Coleridge's reputation as a brilliant writer in the minor and somewhat suspect genre of marginal commentary. The once scattered marginalia deserve to be taken into account in studies of Coleridge's life and writings, especially since they have now been conveniently and reliably brought together in six substantial volumes of the *Collected Works*.

But the marginalia are not easy to understand, partly because they are so various, partly because the legends surrounding Coleridge get in the way, and partly because current assumptions about people who write in books are at odds with those of Coleridge and his contemporaries. In what follows I aim to use Coleridge's marginalia as a window onto the larger scene of Coleridge as reader. I shall describe the extent and limitations of the marginalia, with reference specifically to the Bollingen edition; explain Coleridge's place in traditions of book use; outline the role of these notes in his personal literary economy, in which reading generates new work; and indicate ways in which the marginalia reveal Coleridge's actual reading practices and reinforce his theories about reading—for he did develop a coherent theory of reading in opposition to some educational trends of his day. Finally I shall suggest some of the opportunities for new research created by the completion of the Bollingen edition. To balance generalization with specificity, I shall take one book as a touchstone, Luther's *Table-Talk*, one of the 'old folios' that Coleridge was probably thinking of when he wrote the previously quoted passage in *Church and State*.

WHAT COLERIDGE READ

Coleridge both was and was not an exceptional reader and note-maker. Given that he lived in an age before academic specialization, when 'science' meant learning of any kind and physics and chemistry, like history, philosophy, and criticism, were written of in such a way as to be intelligible to any educated reader; in an age when, furthermore, magazines (published usually in octavo format, looking like books and often preserved for reference and rereading in personal libraries) reported on developments in fields as various as agriculture, antiquities, church history, medicine, and politics, all of which were expected to interest most of their subscribers, Coleridge's range of reading interests was not very much out of the ordinary. Even the fact that he published authoritatively in different fields is not particularly uncommon. In two or three respects, however, he stood out from his contemporaries. One was his lifelong relish for difficult books, especially difficult *old* books, the kind of which Charles Lamb, speaking for ordinary mortals, remarked that 'when one meets with it one shuts the lid faster than one opens it' (*Letters* 3: 107). The periodical reviews and magazines were not promoting them, nor were they subjects of conversation among the general reading public. But they were the reading of scholars, and Coleridge had a scholar's education: if his early life had run more smoothly, he would most probably have become a clergyman like his father, or a Fellow at a university. Another relatively arcane taste, his preference for English writers of the seventeenth century over those of the eighteenth, was one that he shared with Lamb and other non-academic literary connoisseurs as part of a minority movement that led to the editing of many such texts in the early nineteenth century: *Aids to Reflection* would have been an edition of selections from Archbishop Leighton if somebody hadn't beaten Coleridge to it. Finally, Coleridge's extensive reading of German literature and philosophy was unusual, as Rosemary Ashton has demonstrated, given common prejudices against the Germans, but it was not unknown. In his immediate circle, Henry Crabb Robinson was a better Germanist and Joseph Henry Green was a serious amateur.

Fascinated by the exceptional, commentators are generally silent about the everyday. Record-keeping, too, favours the anomalous. Although Coleridge once referred to his way of writing notes in books as 'a habit indulged by the partiality of my friends' (*M* 3: 373), it was not a 'habit' in the sense of something—a wicked thing—he couldn't help doing. Most of his notes were deliberately produced for a specific occasion and for a known audience, as the headnotes in the Bollingen edition indicate. Thus the books containing them have always been *special* volumes, and Coleridge well knew they would be. In 1811, in poor health, he remarked in the margin of one of Charles Lamb's books, 'I will not be long here, Charles!—& gone, you will not mind my having spoiled a book in order to leave a Relic' (*M* 1: 372). Most books and most readings, however, are not special but routine and ordinary.

Coleridge did not write notes impulsively or compulsively. He left unscathed the great majority of the books that passed through his hands.

As Samuel Johnson pointed out in conversation, 'We must read what the world reads at the moment' (Boswell 3: 332). That sort of reading we take for granted. Like everyone else, Coleridge absorbed fairytales and fables as a child, studied standard texts at school, and as an adult must have put in many hours a week with the ephemeral productions of newspapers, pamphlets, and periodicals. His reading career began and ended with the Bible, a daily companion for the whole of his life. He was well grounded in classical and English literature before he ever wrote a substantive note in a book of his own, yet of that early and formative reading there remains hardly a trace. Like the rest of us, he read far more books than he ever owned, drawing on various kinds of public and private collections, and sharing books with friends and acquaintances. His letters and notebooks provide a better gauge of the full extent of his reading than the volumes of marginalia do. Nevertheless there remain about 450 works with his notes in them, and more—probably not many—may surface in time. Aside from personal associations, they had commercial value even in Coleridge's time, so that sale catalogues have always made a point of the presence of notes in his hand.[1] Collectively they constitute a remarkable archive, showing the ways in which one gifted individual used and responded to his books.

THE BOLLINGEN EDITION

The Bollingen edition of the marginalia is organized alphabetically by author (or by title in the case of anonymous works). The headnote to each entry gives basic bibliographical information and outlines what is known about the circumstances under which the notes were composed. Then the marginalia, together with the passages that prompted them, are arranged following the sequence of pages in the book, with footnotes to provide translations, identifications, and cross-references.[2] An extensive analytical index in the final volume makes it possible to track specific topics through the full set of marginalia and thus (by virtue of the cross-references)

---

[1] For lists of books known to have contained notes by Coleridge but that had not been traced by 1969 see Whalley, 'Coleridge Marginalia Lost'; or go to the Table of Contents for each volume of *M*, where 'lost' titles are flagged with a dagger (†). These lists should be checked against the index to *M*, however, to bring them up to date to 2001. The marginalia of well-known figures were common stock in the sale-rooms in the late eighteenth and early nineteenth centuries: scholars' notes could be expected to serve other scholars, and there was already a thriving trade in the personal property of literary celebrities.

[2] An exception is made for notes on the fly-leaves that explicitly refer to a page within the volume; these are introduced at that point as though they had been written there.

through Coleridge's works as a whole, including the letters and notebooks. The index is an absolutely vital tool: it makes the marginalia accessible when otherwise they might prove too voluminous or too confusing to contemplate. This sensible method of presentation has nevertheless some unavoidable limitations. It violates chronology: unless the book was annotated at a sitting, there is seldom any way of telling in what order the notes were actually written, though they may represent multiple readings many years apart. Even if all the notes were written at a sitting, the first notes in the sequence, the ones on the blank front flyleaves, usually comment on the work as a whole and could not have been the first composed. On the larger scale, alphabetical order means that books that belong to one phase of Coleridge's life are likely to have as neighbours books from other phases.[3] The alphabetical arrangement also inevitably separates works of the same genre from one another. But arrangement by genre or subject would be impractical anyway, since Coleridge's notes often, indeed *character-istically* stray far from the matter at hand. He had an excursive mind.

Apart from problems arising from the way it is organized, the Bollingen edition may be innocently misleading because of things that it leaves out. Some of the books that were most important to Coleridge are not there, or if they are, the notes may be surprisingly inadequate. But he started writing notes relatively late in his career (when he was about thirty) and never did it systematically. More often than not, he wrote with a social purpose—he was going to share the book with a friend—or for professional reasons. His four annotated copies of Shakespeare illustrate both functions. Also absent from the edition are, naturally, all the pages of the book that Coleridge did not write on. Though entries in the *Marginalia* include page numbers for every note, it is not easy to reconstruct where exactly in the text the notes fall, how they are distributed, and what went unnoted if not unnoticed and possibly unread. Furthermore, the presentation does not reveal to what extent Coleridge's notes might have been influenced by text beyond the passages quoted with them. Therefore, while the edition provides convenient access to the marginalia, for close study it is advisable to consult a copy of the annotated work as well, preferably in the edition that Coleridge himself used with all the accompanying apparatus and paratext. It is better still to be able to consult the original, in the major collections of London and Toronto, or elsewhere. The Bollingen headnotes always include locations.

Coleridge's Luther

Coleridge's annotated Luther is at once unique and representative. Luther himself, Coleridge revered as a hero: the greatest of Protestant reformers, translator of and commentator on the Bible, author of hymns and sermons, a man of earthy humour

---

[3] The companion volume of selections from the marginalia, *A Book I Value*, is organized chronologically.

and huge energy. In the *Friend* he wrote about Luther's encounter with the Devil in a way that suggests sympathetic identification (*Friend* 1: 136–47). He must have read a great deal both by and about him. One of the 'lost' books, possibly annotated, is a five-volume German edition of Luther's collected works (*CM* 3: 781). But the one annotated book that has survived is the *Table-Talk*, a relatively light work, first published in German and then issued in an abridged form in English in 1652. It consists of a collection of records of Luther's conversations with his friends supplemented by extracts from his works which express his opinions on all kinds of topics from church doctrine to household management, the whole organized in short sections under separate headings (two or three to a page, the headings being included in the Bollingen edition) and then into chapters with general titles such as 'Of the Law and the Gospel', 'Of Auricular Confession', 'Of Languages'. It is a book to dip into, not to read through. Coleridge borrowed it from Charles Lamb in 1819—the year of his first publication of marginalia, in *Blackwood's*—and he never gave it back, although Lamb tried for a while to retrieve it, for it didn't belong to him either. It must have been on his mind in 1820 when he wrote the essay about book-borrowers, 'The Two Races of Men', that ended with an affectionate tribute to his old friend: 'Reader...if thy heart overfloweth to lend them, lend thy books; but let it be to such a one as S. T. C.—he will return them (generally anticipating the time appointed) with usury; enriched with annotations, tripling their value....I counsel thee, shut not thy heart, nor thy library, to S. T. C.' (*Works* 503). In keeping with this indulgent attitude, Lamb effectively surrendered Luther. After Coleridge's death nearly all the marginalia in the volume—117 notes in all, a few of them with dates from 1819, 1826, or 1829—were reproduced, only lightly edited, in *Literary Remains*, so they have been in the public domain for a long time.

   Coleridge's notes to Luther are not his best—not his most vibrant, deep, incisive, intellectually adventurous, or hilarious. But they have their merits. The original editors of *Literary Remains* and their intended audience probably appreciated their seriousness: most of the notes take up, in a spirit of earnest and pious enquiry, the matters of religion debated by Luther and his companions. (Coleridge's family, responsible for his manuscripts and his good name, hoped to demonstrate his Protestant orthodoxy.) A few notes respond to Luther's coarse jokes and comic anecdotes in a vein of forced humour that modern readers are unlikely to take much pleasure in, though the conjunction of theological cruxes with jocularity is itself incongruous and therefore interesting—as when Coleridge makes a point about the doctrine of miracles by using the example of a fart followed by a bolt of lightning (*M* 3: 721). Many notes express loving admiration of Luther even as they detect flaws or inconsistencies in his system of belief. A few while addressing spiritual or ecclesiastical issues touch upon matters of great personal concern to Coleridge, such as marital problems and opium addiction. Taken en masse they provide valuable evidence about Coleridge's opinions and attitudes during his productive middle age and dramatically represent the mental process of his reading at that time.

The content of the notes is revealing, but so are certain physical features of the book that are described, up to a point, but not explored in the Bollingen edition. Like other seventeenth-century folios, Luther's *Table-Talk* came equipped with printed marginal glosses that acted as readers' aids and implicitly as models for further, readerly intervention. By the time Coleridge acquired the volume, previous readers had already left their marks: some page references and headings in ink on the end-papers, an ownership inscription on the front flyleaf, and some brief comments in the text. His earliest notes are in the same form as the existing page references, but in pencil; his latest are unashamedly in ink. Several of the apparently early, pencilled notes, which could have been rubbed out by Coleridge or his executors, were instead overtraced in ink—a common practice when later owners wanted to preserve them. We know that Coleridge's notes were prized, for there is at least one 'manuscript facsimile', that is, another copy of the same work into which Coleridge's notes have been transcribed, probably on behalf of Henry Crabb Robinson who also preserved some of Blake's marginalia (*M* 3: 719). A note about Luther written on a loose sheet has for similar reasons been fastened into this volume with sealing-wax (*M* 3: 722). The physical evidence of use indicates that far from being disreputable or surreptitious, readers' notes were conceived by owners and annotators alike as a normal and even desirable supplement to a volume.

Other physical evidence helps us to understand Coleridge's method of reading. Though 117 notes (most of them long) sounds like a lot, and though they are scattered throughout the 542-page volume, the bulk of the annotation is at the front and many sections, especially towards the end, are left untouched. Coleridge seems to have begun at the beginning but to have run out of steam—a common pattern in his books and in those of many other readers, especially in the case of recreational reading and non-fiction works.[4] On the other hand, he read some parts of the book more than once, returning to sections that interested him and writing postscripts to his own earlier notes. On the complicated question of justification by faith, for instance, he first made a thoughtful comment, signed it with his initials as a way of taking responsibility for it, and then added this further remark: 'Mem. I should not have written the above Note in my present state of Light. Not that I find it false; but that it may have the effect of falsehood by not going deep enough' (*M* 3: 749).

COLERIDGE AND OTHER READERS

The last quotation raises an important question, which itself exposes the motivation for marginalia. For whom did Coleridge write these notes? To whom were they addressed? The answer is not simple. Nowadays we assume that marginalia are

---

[4] See my surveys in *Marginalia* and *Romantic Readers*.

private records written by and for the owner of the book. But they are responsive; they react to the words of the text; so sometimes they address the author. We write not only 'Nonsense!' to assert ourselves and express disagreement, but 'You cannot be serious', as though speaking to the writer directly. The postscript just quoted, 'Mem.', appears to be Coleridge's cautionary memorandum to himself. Lest he should think, on a further reading, that he had solved the problem about justification by faith on the first pass, he registers his current awareness of the inadequacy of his initial idea. Part of the distinctiveness of Coleridge's notes lies precisely in this, the way that they dramatize the process of *thinking through* a question. (It is also the reason for their being so often very long; whereas conventional marginalia are confined to a small space and accordingly tend to be pithy, Coleridge's notes can carry on over several pages, until he has exhausted his subject.) This note, however, only indicates an objection: the former note does not go deep enough. He does not take the time to work out a deeper, better answer. So perhaps he was writing for himself alone. It can hardly have been for Luther's benefit.

There are several notes addressed directly to Luther, however, generally in such terms as these, balancing respect and resistance: 'Nay, but dear honoured Luther! That is *not* fair!' (*M* 3: 725). This practice is consistent with Coleridge's own explanation of his reading habits, in a copy of Schelling: 'A book, I value, I reason & quarrel with as with myself when I am reasoning' (*M* 4: 453). And it is psychologically plausible, since readers tend to experience reading as a conversation with the book, or with the author as embodied in the book; and at the same time to identify themselves with the author as they read, so that—again quoting Coleridge's self-observation—'his thoughts become my thoughts' (*M* 6: 305). But not all the notes can be accounted for in this way either. It complicates matters but also clarifies them, to recall that in this case the relationship was not polar but triangular. Besides Luther the author and Coleridge the reader, there was the Other Reader, whether the donor of the volume, Charles Lamb, or the unknown owner of a future generation. And this is true of all books annotated in the early nineteenth century. Although few readers writing in books can have foreseen print publication, none of them imagined that they were alone with their books and that no other eyes would ever read them. Books are durable; they circulate; sooner or later they will be passed on to someone else. Not only was there no prospect of privacy, then, but all marginalia involved an element of performance and display. De Quincey complained that Wordsworth's marginalia were pedestrian—'such as might have been made by anybody'—as though Wordsworth owed it to his admirers to do better (*Works* 11: 118).

A few of the notes in the Luther volume are addressed to Charles Lamb by name, as Coleridge comments on or interprets Luther's words for him. Some of his jokes must have been designed for Lamb's delight, especially the puns, such as 'Foolgentius' for Fulgentius (*M* 3: 765). Other notes merely imply awareness of a nameless future reader. These occasional clues expose the underlying conditions of composition: at the back of Coleridge's mind as he communed with his books was the Other Reader for whose benefit, in part, the notes were written.[5] To the ghostly presence of that third party we owe their unusual expansiveness. Coleridge took the time to explain and develop the position he adopted, to justify himself, and to create a positive impression, for 'my nature is very social', as he rather ruefully acknowledged (*CN* 2: 2322, quoted *M* 1: lxix). Whereas most earlier readers who wrote in books did so impersonally, in order that their corrections, cross-references, updating, or scholarly additions, for example, would add value to the book whoever owned it, Coleridge put a personal stamp on his notes, knowing that his authorship would be recognized and appreciated. Long before his death, books with his notes were going the rounds of Highgate.[6] Passing remarks in letters and in the marginalia themselves bear witness to their popularity, and we know that even strangers sometimes had books conveyed to Coleridge for a written opinion (as in the case of Barry Cornwall, *M* 4: 161–3). Anne Gillman held back a copy of Maria Edgeworth's novel *Helen* so that he could write 'remarks' on it—which he scrupulously did on separate sheets of paper because the book was the property of a book society (*CL* 6: 988). In this social, communicative use of marginalia he was not alone, for other readers had shared books with friends this way; but he did it exceptionally well.[7]

To illustrate the complexity of marginalia of this period, we may consider one extended, sober reflection of Coleridge's, prompted by Luther, on the difficulty of maintaining hope of salvation along with the consciousness of sin. (Only the beginning and end are quoted.)

Oh! how true, how affectingly true is this! And when too Satan, the Tempter, becomes Satan, the Accuser, saying in my heart—This Sickness is the consequence of Sin or sinful infirmity—& thou hast brought thyself into a fearful dilemma—thou canst not hope for salvation as long as thou continuest in any sinful practice—and yet thou canst not abandon thy daily dose of this or that poison without suicide. For the Sin of thy Soul has become the Necessity of thy Body [...] O what a miserable despairing Wretch should I become, if I [...] gave up the faith, that the Life of Christ would *precipitate* the remaining dregs of Sin in the crisis of Death, and that I shall rise a pure *capacity* of Christ, blind to be irradiated by

[5] Marginalia fairly frequently anticipate such use. The first note that meets the reader's eye in Coleridge's spectacular annotated Böhme, for instance, is addressed 'To the Reader'. It begins, 'I earnestly intreat of the Reader into whose possession or under whose perusal this Copy of Jacob Behmen's Writings should happen to fall, and who should feel disposed to peruse the numerous marginal annotations added by me in my own hand-writing, that he would *first of all* read over the Note occupying the Margins of pages 125, 126, and 127—lest perchance I should lead him into errors from which I have extricated myself' (*M* 1: 556).

[6] For example, he owned 25 volumes of Scott's prose fiction, some of them annotated. They were evidently lent out in the neighbourhood: one of his notes refer to 'young Readers of this, my ever circulating Copy of Scott's Novels' (*M* 4: 612).

[7] Some of Coleridge's books and letters contain evidence suggesting that other readers, notably Green and Tulk, exchanged opinions with Coleridge by writing notes in the same books: *M* 3: 239, 6: 100 n. 7; *CL* 4: 870.

his Light, empty to be possessed by his fullness, naked of merit to be cloathed with his Righteousness! (*M* 3: 746–7)

Here the three-way act of communication is plain to see: Coleridge gratefully takes up Luther's idea, agrees with it, and expands on it, making observations that bear witness to his own convictions and offering them to other readers in spiritual distress. He is not only talking to himself. The reference to 'this or that poison' is deliberately vague, the point being a general truth, though Lamb could have been expected to understand that opium-taking was the source of the private anguish. For him this note, if he ever saw it, would be a relic indeed—a vivid reminder of his friend and of the friendship that had seen them both through periods of suffering.

FROM READING TO WRITING

A final factor in the composition of Coleridge's marginalia was the plan or possibility that the thoughts he had while reading might be turned to account in his own writings. A further 'Mem'. of 1829 in the Luther volume, for instance, lays out some ideas for the projected 'Noetic or Doctrine & Discipline of Ideas', a version of the *magnum opus* (*M* 3: 742). Yet another note, undated this time, wrestles with the distinction between reason and understanding, which formed an important part of *Aids to Reflection* in 1825. As a writer Coleridge was always on the alert for materials, whether he found them in a book or found them in himself in the process of reading, stimulated by the book. He was about mid-way through his annotating career in 1819 when he acquired the *Table-Talk*. By that point he was well aware of the potential practical value of his reading notes. An early note to Browne had just been recycled as an article for a magazine, as we have seen. Coleridge had already used annotated copies of Shakespeare as a basis for three series of lectures (*M* 4: 684). His lectures on the history of philosophy were intertwined with his reading of Tennemann (*M* 5: 691). And his publisher would soon give him a copy of Leighton to work with on what became *Aids to Reflection* (marginalia to Taylor were drafted into that project too). In 1820 he told his friend Thomas Allsop that he had five projects on the go, four of them almost complete but in 'so many scraps & *sibylline* leaves, including Margins of Books & blank Pages, that unfortunately I must be my own Scribe' (*CL* 5: 27). So while he was writing notes in Luther's *Table Talk*, he could be said to have been multi-tasking: on the one hand pleasurably engaging with Luther and Lamb, but on the other bearing in mind the claims of posterity, gathering and *generating* ideas that might be publishable.

Coleridge was not born a writer of original marginalia, he became one. His first extended notes, written for friends, appear self-conscious in the way that letters do—anxious to be useful, seeking to sustain a relationship. Memorable notes to Browne's *Religio Medici* (for Sara Hutchinson, 1802), *Anderson's British Poets* (for Wordsworth, 1803), Malthus's *Essay on the Principle of Population* (for Southey, 1804), Percival's *Account of the Island of Ceylon* (for Poole, 1807), and Daniel's *Poetical Works* (for Lamb, 1808) are all of this relatively uncomplicated kind. By 1819, however, Coleridge's practice had evolved into the more sophisticated mode that is found in the Luther. By then, too, he had come to consider his marginalia as part of a creative process, along with other methods of note-taking.

The link to the *Notebooks* is particularly significant. Coleridge's on-and-off reading in Luther's *Table Talk* left traces in the notebooks, as the headnote indicates (*M* 3: 719). What seems to have happened is that at first, when he thought the book would have to be returned to Lamb, Coleridge was careful to make his notes in pencil, and copied extracts from it into his notebooks, along with brief indications of what it was he found interesting about them. Later, not needing to copy out extracts because the book was staying on his own shelves where he could find it whenever he liked, he used the notebooks to develop ideas about specific passages. These notes show that what Coleridge was inclined to do was to apply Luther's words to the contemporary world; he would borrow Luther's authority and reshape his ideas for a different audience. In *CN* 4: 4665, tentatively dated 1820, Coleridge observes the applicability of a remark of Luther's to modern-day 'pseudo-evangelicals', and then makes a note to himself to try to read the whole of the *Table-Talk* this way, seeking analogies. Thus the marginalia and the notebooks reinforced one another, the needs of the notebooks shaping the approach to the marginalia and the marginalia providing the seeds of ideas that could be transplanted to the notebooks for fuller development.

Like other people, Coleridge read for pleasure, to pass the time, to escape from his own thoughts, for information, to have something to talk about at dinner parties, and to fuel his own writing projects. These mixed motives are reflected in the extant marginalia, and it is always wise to consider the circumstances of his reading before attributing meaning to any particular note. For example, the Luther note about the daily dose of poison vividly expresses personal guilt, but it is not only self-castigating, it is designed to bring comfort. It adds personal testimony to Luther's counsel, in order to give hope to the despairing. Coleridge must have found relief in writing it; he could also anticipate help for himself in future, as for any other reader who came upon the passage later, including those who might find it in a published form among his own works some day. He knew what he was doing. The exercise of writing marginalia was for him neither the traditional scholarly discipline of uniform commentary nor the messy, self-indulgent habit that we deplore nowadays, but a flexible method of snaring ideas for future use.

THEORY AND PRACTICE OF READING

Self-conscious in all things, Coleridge was particularly self-conscious about the process of reading. The immediacy of marginal annotation enabled him to catch his own mind in motion as he read, and many notes, as a consequence, record observations of this kind. (In George Frere's copy of the autobiography of Richard Baxter, with notes of about the same time as those in the Luther, Coleridge specifically recommended such awareness: 'Force yourself to reflect on what you read paragraph by paragraph, and in a short time you will derive your pleasure, an ample portion at least, from the activity of your own mind' (*M* 1: 280, abbreviations expanded).) Even notes that are not explicitly self-reflexive reveal trains of thought that can be fascinating both for what they tell us about Coleridge and for what they suggest about the psychology of reading in general.

The 'activity' of mind that Coleridge observed and cultivated in himself—partly through the writing of marginalia and the keeping of notebooks—became the object of a minor crusade with him, in the course of which he articulated a theory and advocated a method of reading based on his own experience. A strenuous reader himself, he deplored the evidence he saw around him of lazy, passive reading and the thoughtless writing that was both its cause and its product. While it is easy to see special pleading in his diatribes against the newspapers, magazines, and novels of the day, and to view his campaign as little more than a sour-grapes complaint about his own bad reviews and limited readership, it is important to remember that Coleridge's lifetime exactly coincided with an explosion of the market for print and a corres-pondent boom in publishing.[8] He was not alone in worrying about letting large numbers of ill-educated readers loose on printed matter, and about the likely effect of their influence on the publishers. Other intellectuals and educators, apparently afraid of losing control over the lower orders, were also roused to outrage by the sensation-alist press of the time. The snobbishly self-righteous tone of Coleridge's attack on 'the devotees of the circulating libraries' in the *Biographia* (1: 48) is regrettable. But as his note on Baxter says, and all the evidence of his own practice as a reader demonstrates, he knew that the experience of those readers could be richer than it was, and that they would find greater pleasure as well as self-improvement if they could be persuaded to change their reading habits.

Coleridge's Golden Rule for reading was a variant of the Christian doctrines of charity and humility. Readers were to give authors the benefit of the doubt, submitting—at least temporarily—to their direction. 'Until you understand a writer's ignorance, presume yourself ignorant of his understanding', was the way he phrased this Rule in the *Biographia* (1: 232). The injunction is repeated in many

[8] For important contributions to an understanding of this phenomenon see Altick and St Clair; for a short, convenient survey, see Brewer and McCalman.

forms in the marginalia. On behalf of Böhme he addresses 'the contemptuous . . . Reader', urging patience: though much in these writings is obscure or confused, they also contain moments of illumination, and repay forbearance. 'Read then in meekness', he advises, 'lest to read him at all, which might be thy folly, should prove thy Sin' (*M* 1: 558). Detecting Steffens in misrepresentation of Kant, Coleridge observes regretfully that Steffens had 'never studied Kant with that affectionate submission of mind without which no great man can be understood' (*M* 5: 243). His own notes on Kant show him prepared to go over and over the same passage until he either works out what it means or discovers the flaw in the reasoning (*CM* 3: 247–9, 272–3, 322–4). He had learnt the value of patience himself, the hard way.

Though the lesson of patient submission might seem to be a lesson in passivity, it is not. The rule is to understand a work on its own terms before venturing to criticize it. Understanding requires an effort of imagination. Coleridge's criticism, his theory of reading, and the records of his own reading are exceptional for their display of imaginative engagement, especially but not exclusively historical engagement. He urges his friends and readers to put themselves in the place of the author or of the author's contemporary readers, rather than imposing the perspectives of the present; and it is clear that he practised what he preached. Wanting to persuade Lamb to give the works of Samuel Daniel another chance, Coleridge suggests that Lamb should pretend to himself that he is 'a plain England-loving English Country Gentleman' of Daniel's generation, one whose reading hardly extends to more than a newspaper once every month or two, and consider how such a man would feel about Daniel's *Civil Wars* (*M* 2: 118). The imaginative engagement that enables a reader to understand what the work originally meant by the same token entitles that reader to criticize—to comment on its strengths and weaknesses. But the effort of understanding has to come first.

Writing marginalia actually in the margins of a book, rather than turning to notebooks or even to the blank leaves at the front and back of a book, is conducive to careful reading because it focuses attention and slows readers down. Stopping once in a while to register a reaction, readers find at last that they have accumulated a set of specific, detailed observations that might reveal a pattern or add up to a general impression. For Coleridge, the process led in most cases (not all) to *friendly*, constructive criticism. He wrote admirably about literary underdogs, urging a fair chance for writers whom it was the fashion to despise, such as Swedenborg, Böhme, and the Cambridge Platonists. In his copy of Luther, too, we find many notes that point out errors but in an indulgent spirit, as much interested in the probable reason for the error as in the lapse itself. When Luther cites Origen as one bad thing having come out of the great school of Alexandria, Coleridge comments, 'Poor Origen! Surely, Luther was put to it for an instance and had never read the Works of that very best of the old Fathers, and eminently an upright and godlie learned Man' (*M* 3: 728). Of Christ's descending into Hell, an item of belief for Luther, Coleridge wonders, 'Could Luther have been ignorant, that this clause was not intruded into the Ap[ostles'] Creed till the VIth Century P.C.?' (*M* 3: 732). A friend makes allowances: in this case, furthermore, Coleridge was right—Luther did not know this fact about the history of the Creed. By precept and example, Coleridge to this day sets a standard for sympathetic, intelligent, broad-minded reading.

DIRECTIONS FOR RESEARCH

Until now, scholarly use of the marginalia has been held back by the narrow selections available and by the lack of indexes. If the marginalia made any appearance at all in critical or biographical studies, it was usually as nuggets—quotable sentences taken out of context. Now, when it appears that almost all the books Coleridge wrote substantive notes in have been found, and the notes themselves have been accurately transcribed and printed with the appropriate apparatus, the risk is that the volume of materials will prove just too overwhelming. But the field is practically wide open and there are ways of cutting paths through it. There are four obvious approaches; beyond them, the horizon is as unlimited as human ingenuity. The first is to take Coleridge himself as a subject. Departments of English still favour author-centred research, which in any case has a natural feel to it, as we experience the past by identifying ourselves with a single figure. Coleridgean biography, especially intellectual biography, could be considerably enriched by reference to the records of his activity as a reader; after all, most of his adventures were intellectual adventures and some of his most intense relationships were with great thinkers through their books. The alphabetical order of the Bollingen edition makes this a relatively easy route to follow. As a special subset within Coleridgean biography, the records of Coleridge's reading of works by his contemporaries could provide a new perspective even on such overworked topics as his relationships with Wordsworth and Southey.

A second way is to consider the relationship from the other side. What do Coleridge's remarks about the books he read have to offer to studies about them and their authors—especially the great Germans whose writings he read so attentively? What did he notice particularly? Did he observe the qualities of the work that we consider most important today? Does he raise issues that we ought to be thinking about? Were his views typical of his time and place? Where does his reading belong in the general history of that author's reception? Could his comments be used in some way—say, as footnotes—in new editions?

A third way is by theme or topic, cutting across the full range of his reading. Anyone working on early nineteenth-century history will find fresh resources in the marginalia, though Coleridge from this angle is likely to play only a supporting role as one individual among many. His interests were not all arcane, theological, or philosophical: he wrote about schools, governments, krakens, slavery, sex, sects, hydrogen, music—see the index.

Finally, Coleridge's notes are potentially a goldmine for the history of books and reading, a scholarly area that is still under development. There is as yet no monograph dedicated to his marginalia, though the materials are certainly there. His practice could be compared with that of others, whether of his own country and era or not. How does he rate, as a reader, against others who have left comparable records, such as Gabriel Harvey, John Adams, Hester Piozzi, Vladimir Nabokov? Where do his theories of reading belong in the evolution of ideas about this central human activity? Taken by themselves or, better still, teamed up with the evidence of the letters and notebooks, the marginalia provide an unusually full record of the experience of a reader of the time—where, what, when, and most importantly how he did it.[9]

WORKS CITED

ALTICK, RICHARD D. 1957. *The English Common Reader: A Social History of the Mass Reading Public, 1800–1900.* Chicago: University of Chicago Press.

ASHTON, ROSEMARY. 1980. *The German Idea: Four English Writers and the Reception of German Thought, 1800–1860.* Cambridge: Cambridge University Press.

BOSWELL, JAMES. 1934–50. *Boswell's Life of Johnson*, ed. George Birkbeck Hill. Rev. L. F. Powell. 6 vols. Oxford: Clarendon Press.

BREWER, JOHN, and MCCALMAN, IAIN. 1999. Publishing. In *An Oxford Companion to the Romantic Age: British Culture 1776–1832*, ed. Iain McCalman. Oxford: Oxford University Press, 197–206.

COLERIDGE, S. T. 2003. *A Book I Value: Selected Marginalia*, ed. H. J. Jackson. Princeton: Princeton University Press.

—— 1853. *Collected Works*. ed. W. G. T. Shedd. 7 vols. New York: Harper.

—— 1836–1839. *Literary Remains*, ed. H. N. Coleridge. 4 vols. London: Pickering.

DE QUINCEY, THOMAS. 2000–2003. *Works*, ed. Grevel Lindop et al. 21 vols. London: Pickering and Chatto.

JACKSON, H. J. 2001. *Marginalia: Readers Writing in Books.* New Haven: Yale University Press.

—— 2005. *Romantic Readers: The Evidence of Marginalia.* New Haven: Yale University Press.

LAMB, CHARLES. 1924. Christ's Hospital Five and Thirty Years Ago. *Works*, ed. Thomas Hutchinson. Oxford: Oxford University Press, 486–98.

—— 1924. The Two Races of Men. *Works*, ed. Thomas Hutchinson. Oxford: Oxford University Press, 499–503.

LAMB, CHARLES and MARY. 1975–8. *Letters.* 3 vols. Ithaca: Cornell University Press.

[9] I am grateful to Robin Jackson and Paul Cheshire for helpful comments and suggestions on a draft version of this essay.

Lowes, J. L. 1927. *The Road to Xanadu: A Study in the Ways of the Imagination.* Boston: Houghton Mifflin.

McFarland, Thomas. 1969. *Coleridge and the Pantheist Tradition.* Oxford: Clarendon Press.

St Clair, William. 2004. *The Reading Nation in the Romantic Period.* Cambridge: Cambridge University Press.

Whalley, George. 1969. Coleridge marginalia lost. *The Book Collector,* 17 (1968): 428–42, 18 (1969): 223.

CHAPTER 15

COLERIDGE'S
NOTEBOOKS

PAUL CHESHIRE

One Habit, formed during long Absences from those, with whom I could
converse with full Sympathy, has been of Advantage to me—that of daily
noting down, in my Memorandum or Common-place Books, both Inci-
dents and Observations; whatever had occurred to me from without, and all
the Flux and Reflux of my Mind within itself. The Number of these Notices,
and their Tendency, miscellaneous as they were, to one common End ([. . .]
*what we are and what we are born to become; and thus from the End of our
Being to deduce its proper Objects*) first encouraged me to undertake the
Weekly Essay, of which you will consider this Letter as the Prospectus.

(*Friend* 2: 16–17)

THUS in his Prospectus to *The Friend* at the end of 1808, Coleridge announced to
potential subscribers the rich material that had been accumulating in his note-
books. Apart from newspaper writing, his last sustained creative effort for publi-
cation had been his 'irksome & soul-wearying Labor' (*CL* 1: 587) in 1800 on the
rushed translation of Schiller's *Wallenstein* plays.[1] It was during the subsequent
period of formal creative blockage that his informal notebook writing flourished—
a paradox which Kathleen Coburn has noted (*CN* 1, Notes, xlii). But in a previous
paragraph of this same Prospectus Coleridge had explained why he found it hard to

I am grateful to Seamus Perry for helping me gain access to the Coleridge notebook MSS, and for
invaluable conversations about the notebooks, and to Gary Herbertson for showing a way to recover
obliterated text.

  [1] *Poems* (1803) contained no poems additional to the 1797 edition.

raid these resources for publication: 'Over-activity of Thought, modified by a constitutional Indolence, [...] made it more pleasant to me to continue acquiring, than to reduce what I had acquired to a regular Form' (*Friend* 2: 16). A careful reader of the Prospectus would notice that Coleridge was still not offering to publish extracts from these notebooks, only to use them as 'encouragement' for further writing.

What were Coleridge's notebook writings? Writings that could be classed as notebook material appear under other headings because Coleridge wrote them in the margins of books (*Marginalia*) or on unbound sheets of paper (*Shorter Works and Fragments*). H. J. Jackson's chapter shows how closely related Coleridge's notebook writing and marginalia were, using the example of Coleridge's pencilled annotations in Lamb's copy of Luther's *Table Talk*. *SW&F* includes 'On the Passions', an 1828 MS written for Joseph Green, Coleridge's philosophical collaborator, that is interwoven with the informal clowning that characterizes even the most serious later notebook entries. 'Hello! YOU Sir there, looking over Mr. Green's Shoulder, like an impertinent Blackguard as you are! What are you grinning for?' (*SW&F* 2: 1434). Notebook 25 contains lecture notes that have been assigned entry numbers (*CN* 3: 4470 and others), but are printed separately in *Lectures 1818-19: On the History of Philosophy*; notes toward a Greek grammar have wobbled between exclusion (*CN* 4: 5227) and finally inclusion as Addenda to volume five of *The Notebooks*.

Contents, Development, and Structure

Contents

The practicalities of publication have helped define these boundaries, and following the 2002 publication of the final volume of the *Collected Coleridge* notebooks, it is now possible to draw up a table listing the seventy-two notebooks of various sizes and conditions contained in it (see Fig. 1). The first column on the left shows the identifying number, letter, or name of each individual notebook; these designations were not given by Coleridge. In the second column in roman numerals are the late series from 1827 onwards that Coleridge did name and number. He called these his Fly-Catchers, because they were designed to attract and trap the fly-like thoughts buzzing around his head. As the series numbering indicates, these later notebooks had a more consecutive pattern of use than the earlier ones.

The row at the bottom shows how many were in use in each year—in 1809 (a peak year) fourteen were in use. Some squares have question marks, because it is

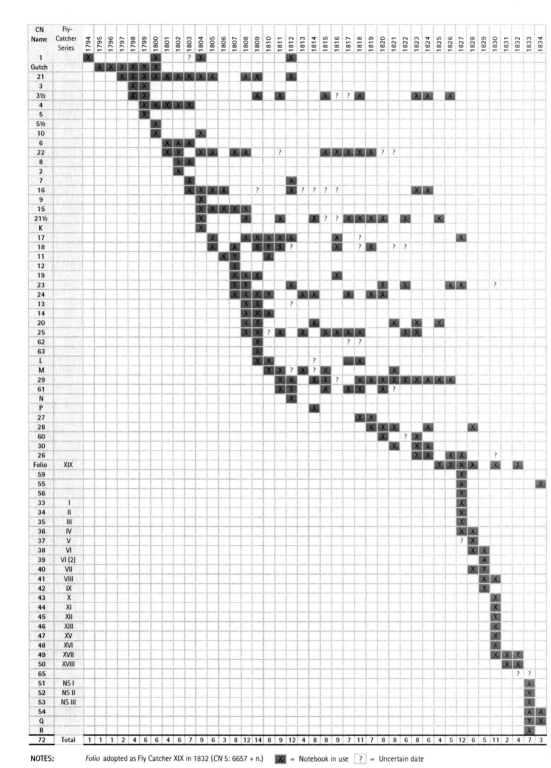

NOTES: *Folio* adopted as Fly Catcher XIX in 1832 (*CN* 5: 6657 + n.) ▨ = Notebook in use ? = Uncertain date

Fig. 1. Coleridge's Notebooks in Order of Commencement

not always possible to be certain about the dates when particular entries were written, or, in the extreme case of Notebook 65 when *any* of it was written: the editors propose 1832–3, but concede a possible seven year date range (*CN* 5, Notes, lii). Roughly one in seven of the notebook entries were dated by Coleridge; more can be dated through internal context, or external evidence, but for many entries only approximate date ranges can be given.[2] The row running horizontally from each notebook shows its period of use. Sometimes the period is due to its size: the Folio notebook was a substantial volume—others had only twenty leaves. Sometimes a long period of non-use is down to storage and rediscovery: for example the tiny Notebook 1.

The contents of these notebooks are so vast and repetitive as to be overwhelming. Like unsorted rushes shot at a ratio of fifty to one for a film that remains to be edited, they offer endless alternative takes of the 'Flux and Reflux' of Coleridge's mind engaging and re-engaging with travel, rapt attention to natural scenery, projected works, drafts of poems, metrical schemes, lecture notes, quotations in several languages, scientific, metaphysical, and theological enquiries. There is personal confession, the struggle with opium addiction, descriptions of ecstasies of love or of despair, dreams, waking dreams, altered states of consciousness fit for the diary of a mystic, self-exhortation, prayer. There are also practical memoranda: household requisites, travel costs, addresses, recipes, and debts. There are poems and other transcriptions written by the hands of others. The contents are not even limited to writing—there are logical symbols, ciphers, sketches and diagrams, newspaper cuttings, and advertisements for medicines.

Development

The period between 1794 and 1798 consisted of brief memoranda, quick jottings extracting memorable passages from his reading, a few poetical fragments, notes of projected works. When he moved to Greta Hall in 1800 the entries became richer. He arrived at the Lakes as if writing a travel journal and developed his capacity for quick natural observation of the changing light and features of a landscape by day and night. At the same time the solitary reflections and his obsessive love for Sara Hutchinson opened up layers of deep introspective feeling. In Malta the exile of imagination in his study at Greta Hall became a geographical actuality, and the occasion of the 'long Absences' mentioned in his Prospectus to *The Friend*. By the time he returned to England his notebook writing habit was well established and became an important personal psychological prop in ways I will enlarge on later.

After 1808 the notebooks also served an additional function as working notes for his lectures and for systematic personal study. The latter culminated in the final

---

[2] 1,059 entries are dated, according to Coburn's tables.

series of notebooks between 1818 and his death, many of which were dedicated to biblical and theological study, and philosophical studies that were carried on in conjunction with Joseph Green, for the eyes of whom some notebook entries were specifically written (e.g. 5: 5868). In the words of Anthony John Harding, the later notebooks were 'no longer purely private documents—his own solitary confidants—but were developing into a legacy that he would pass on to a growing circle of disciples and admirers' (*CN* 5, Text, xxi). But any outline scheme of the notebooks is a general guide, and exceptions abound. So, in the middle of the memorandum jottings that characterize the earliest period pre- 1798, there is room for a brief self-admonition: 'Mem—not to adulterize my time by absenting myself from my wife—' (1: 73). The late notebooks include an autobiographical note almost certainly for the benefit of the Gillmans with whom he lived *en famille* basking in their affection and admiration (5: 6675); humour peppers the serious study notes, and bawdy rhymes pop up occasionally (5: 6883) in close proximity to extended biblical commentary and extempore bursts of prayer.

Structure

The contents are usually divided by Coleridge's own horizontal line across the page, into distinct entries, but his divisions are not always clear cut and these have sometimes been editorially imposed in the published editions (1: 16n). The majority of entries are undated. Apart from the problematic year 1794 written next to, or as part of, an early entry (1: 6 + n.), there is no dating at all until '[Sept.] 18th, 1798', which signals the start of Notebook 3, intended as a journal of his journey to Germany (1: 335). At this stage almost all dating is in travel journal notebooks, but a practice evolves of dating entries as a form of emphasis, and this coincides with his developing technique of retrospective notebook use.

COLERIDGE AND HIS NOTEBOOKS: 'THE HISTORY OF MY OWN MIND FOR MY OWN IMPROVEMENT'

The first user of the notebooks was Coleridge himself.[3] There is much truth in the frequently quoted view of him as *writer* describing the notebooks as his 'sole-confidant', and finding solace by writing down feelings he felt unable to share with

---

[3] H. J. Jackson's chapter 'Coleridge as Reader: Marginalia', has been helpful here.

others. Also, as an exploratory thinker with few intellectual peers, he found it 'pleasant' to sketch out new ideas, and see how they worked on the page. But it is important to remember that Coleridge will have spent more time *reading* his notebooks than he did *writing* in them.

As regards others, the growing hoard of his notebook writing was a useful defence against accusations of indolence. He could tell Robert Southey, after an apparently unproductive period: 'I have filled (since I have been at Grasmere) a full Third of that *large* Metallic Pencil Pocket-book with Hints, Thoughts, Facts, Illustrations, &c &c—the greater number relating to my Comforts & Consolations' (*CL* 2: 1031). It was private and in inaccessible form so he didn't have to show anything to prove it.

But in addition to this sense of accumulation of material there was the mental space of self that writing and re-reading created. Anya Taylor anatomizes in her chapter Coleridge's different senses of self, and how these are recorded in his personal writings. Here I focus on how he *used* his notebooks to this end. Coleridge acknowledged feeling himself insubstantial in comparison to others: 'when I am in company with Mr Sharp [...] &c, I feel like a Child—nay, rather like an Inhabitant of another Planet—their very faces all act upon me, sometimes as if they were Ghosts, but more often as if I were a Ghost, among them' (3: 3324) and re-reading his old notebooks restored his sense of substance and development.[4] In 1812, for example, when a man of forty, he read an early notebook passage and commented on his younger self: 'The above written Hints were penned in this Book at the age of 24 and as I had never been prematured by Intercourse with literary men, I cannot help looking back on them as proofs of an original & self-thinking Mind' (1: 6). This use of a notebook to revisit a 'past self' to see how a mind has grown became for Coleridge part of a formal method of self-cultivation that he recommended to others. In an entry of about 1826, Coleridge advised taking books by 'two or three great writers' with

a \<separate\> note-book for each [...] in which your impressions, suggestions, Conjectures, Doubts, and Judgements are to be recorded, with the date of each, & so worded as to represent most sincerely the exact state of your convictions at the time [...] A continuity would be given to your Being, and its progressiveness ensured. All your knowledge otherwise obtained [...] would find centers round which ~~they~~ it would organize itself. And lastly, the habit of confuting your past self, and detecting the causes & occasions of your having mistaken or overlooked the Truth, will give you both a quickness and a winning kindness.   (4: 5436)

His anticipation of others reading his notebooks led him to start writing in cipher and to leave defensive messages for the imagined reader asking for charity

---

[4] See Terada for a good use of this passage in his analysis of Coleridge's problems with solidity.

'If I should perish without having the power of destroying these & my other pocket books, the history of my own mind for my own improvement' (2: 2368). His analysis of his own need to confess got subtler with time: 'my Motive or rather Impulse to do this, seems to myself an effort to eloign and abalienate it from the dark Adyt of my own Being by a *visual* Outness—& not the wish for others to see it—' (3: 4166).

Another form of concealment was obliteration of what had been written, either by removing a page or by crossing out. Many of these are done by Coleridge, but there are grounds for suspecting posthumous censorship. Ann Gillman who wrote and initialled annotations in Coleridge's notebooks after his death, certainly cut out at least one passage she considered too sensitive (*CN* 2: 2556 n.). Recently a forensic document examiner, Gary Herbertson, has demonstrated on a sample notebook entry that it is possible to recover obliterated passages that defeated Kathleen Coburn. His methodology offers hope that we can recover texts thought to be irretrievable, and learn more about the motives and hands behind their concealment.[5]

A letter to his nephew Edward in 1825 shows that Coleridge lent notebooks containing sensitive material to those he trusted:

In some of the Memorandum Books of old date, there are passages, which I do not mind your seeing—for the more *you* know what my mind has been as well as what it *is*, for strength and for weakness, the more accordant will your judgement respecting me be with my wishes—only you will read them *dramatically*—i.e. as the portrait and impress of the mood and the moment—birds of passages—or Bubbles—But I would have them sacred to your eyes.   (*CL* 5: 492-3)

This sounds relaxed enough, but he may have vetted and obliterated the worst passages before handing over these old notebooks.

Another letter from the same period gives the impression that he left his notebooks lying around in his room at Highgate while he was away (*CL* 5: 375). If there were specially designated secret notebooks that he kept concealed, they haven't survived. The first six pages of Notebook 19 are written in cipher, which might indicate it was originally earmarked as a private notebook. It was started in May 1807 at a time of great domestic tension, and the first entry is a complaint about Mrs Coleridge (*CN* 2: 3040-56, 3068). Whether the cipher was experimental or not (it hardly seems necessary to cipher four lines of a Goëthe poem) it soon stopped, and the remainder of Notebook 19 is not especially confidential.

---

[5] See Herbertson for a description of the techniques available, and Cheshire 2008 for a description of how they have been applied.

Approaching the Material

The question of genre is difficult. How can a travel journal, a transcription of Giordano Bruno, a study aid for his doctor's schoolboy son, and a ciphered confession claim any common authorial intention? A recent essay by Pamela Woof sets out the kinds of writing appropriate to journals (dated entries) and common-place books (repositories of miscellaneous notes), both of which kinds of writing can be found in Coleridge's notebooks. If the notebooks are, as Josie Dixon describes in her sensitive essay, 'private, occasional writings-without-a-genre' (77) a genre quest would seem hopeless and perhaps Seamus Perry is right to turn the problem on its head: 'The main point of the notebook as a genre is the avoidance of conclusion or closure which its *ad hoc* life allows' and adds that even in his more formal writings Coleridge liked 'mixing up his genres' (31).[6]

There are other approaches. Coleridge's practice of reading his notebooks and the method he sets out for giving 'continuity [. . .] to your 'Being' (4: 5436 quoted above) sounds exactly like the practice described by Michel Foucault in *Technologies of the Self*.[7] According to Foucault the practice of 'care of the self', which he distinguished from the cult of 'know thyself', started in Greece within the Platonic school. 'A relation developed between writing and vigilance. Attention was paid to nuances of life, mood, and reading, and the experience of oneself was intensified and widened by virtue of this act of writing' (28). There is a rich discussion to be had as to whether this 'vigilance' serves a moral or epistemic purpose, and how it relates to the puritan practice of examining conscience. A Virginia Woolf diary entry seems to cut through these layers of complicating analysis: 'I have composed myself, momentarily, by reading through this years diary. That's a use for it then. It composes' (Light, 5). This ordering notation and re-iteration, so vital for our sense of psychic equilibrium, goes deeper than the verbal; it is taken up in the practice of certain artists, whose work engages with 'themes of revisiting; collecting and re-ordering; time, journey and weathering' (Meares, 3).

Two recent essays on Coleridge's notebooks by Anthony John Harding tackle the problem of genre from the point of view of the reader's expectation. His first essay approaches the notebooks from the point of view of literary theory. He discusses their place within the 'life-writing' genre and puts forward a 'material hermeneutic' approach by arguing that the found form of the manuscript notebooks imposes a 'fore-understanding' on the reader (2000). Harding's second essay surveys the way the manuscript material in the notebooks has been changed, or 'monumentalized', by its publication in book form, and anticipates the further effect when individual notebook entries are made available through a searchable internet based format in isolated gobbets, as search 'hits' without any accompanying commentary (2004).[8]

---

[6] See also Dugas, who pursues the theme of the 'contingent' notebook writing space.

[7] I came to Foucault via Harding 2004.

[8] The much needed electronic index is in process at the University of Alberta TAPOR site.

In the next section I will follow up Harding's emphasis on the reader's 'fore-understanding' by tracing the publication history of the notebooks. I hope to show that the earliest forms of publication have shaped the way the notebooks have been presented in the *Collected Coleridge* edition and hence the way a reader views them.

Shaping our View of the Notebooks—Publication History

Robert Southey struggled to prize scraps from Coleridge's notebooks and marginalia for *Omniana* (1812), an enlarged version of a series he had published in the *Athenaeum* five years previously. Coleridge's *Omniana* contributions were expanded and included in *Literary Remains* published in 1836 two years after his death. But these were not designed to show the range of his notebook writing: the job before the editors was to foreground Coleridge the committed Christian and to keep addiction and personal troubles private.[9] Accordingly his 'Confessio Fidei' (3: 4005), which when set alongside the 'Ego-ana' written on the same day, 3 November 1810 shortly after his break with Wordsworth (3: 4006) becomes the courageous stock-taking of a man in deep despair, here appears among other statements of religious faith and turns complacent as a result; the context in which the text appears is crucial to the impression it makes on the reader (Southey 1969, 348–60).

The notebooks themselves were regarded as private and entrusted to a closed circle of friends and family. James Gillman made transcriptions for a planned second volume of his *Life of Coleridge*, and his wife Ann read and annotated them. One sole notebook escaped this custody. The Gutch notebook (*c*.1795–9), which had become the property of an old friend of Coleridge's, was acquired by the British Museum in 1868 and a transcription of it by Alois Brandl was published in Germany in 1896. The year prior to this Ernest Hartley Coleridge, the poet's grandson, had published a selection of passages from the notebooks under the title *Anima Poetae*. These two publications are interestingly complementary. Brandl's transcription of the Gutch was lightly annotated, and although his transcriptions go interestingly astray in places (1: 73, quoted above, became 'Men—hot to adulterize my time by absenting myself from my wife—') he followed the *layout* of Coleridge's pages more faithfully than Coburn, and his transcription provided the stimulus for John Livingston Lowes' groundbreaking *The Road to Xanadu*, as Lowes acknowledged (xiv). Lowes first showed the world how much could be learned by a close and thorough study of what seemed then to be memoranda of impenetrable obscurity.

---

[9] Cottle's indiscreet *Early Recollections* was anticipated. See Southey 1965, 2:444–9.

On the other side of the editorial tradition E. H. Coleridge's 1895 *Anima Poetae* was equally influential. The tone of his preface presented a Coleridge to match the *fin de siècle* theosophical *zeitgeist*: 'The half-belief that the veil of the senses would be rent in twain [...] was the breath of his soul. It was his fate to wrestle from night to morn with the Angel of the Vision' (xiii). Although EHC sensed the world was ready for a more human Coleridge, he felt bound to respect the 'sacred trust' of confidentiality. In place of notes he added a minimal amount of contextual setting in brackets, and (a gorgeous touch) marginal glosses that recall the 1817 'Ancient Mariner'; e.g., 'THE MOON'S HALO AN EMBLEM OF HOPE' (283). This was a literary rather than a scholarly text, and he polished it accordingly. If it weren't for frequent misreadings of the text, we could praise this as good copy editing.

The publication of the full text of the notebooks had to wait until Kathleen Coburn earned the goodwill of the family owners and had the tenacity and capacity to devote the rest of her life to complete a task that threatened to be infinite. She had before her the warning examples of the 'chaos' of EHC's unpublished transcripts (Coburn 1974, 5–6) and Lowes' notes towards a 'forthcoming' edition of the Gutch notebook filling 'an aged steamer trunk' that he was able to show her in 1937, but were untraced after his death (1977, 60). The time-scale speaks for itself; she obtained from Lord Coleridge exclusive editorial rights to produce an edition and had the bulk of the notebooks photographed in 1936.[10] The first volume was published in 1957, the fifth and (as it turned out) final volume in 2002, 11 years after her death. The planned sixth volume, which was to consist of a 'concordance-type subject index' and addenda and corrigenda, did not appear.[11]

Coburn's edition shows the influence of her predecessors. The depth of annotation owes a lot to Lowes, whose literary detective work connecting imagery in *Kubla Khan* with descriptions of rutting alligators in William Bartram's *Travels* showed how illuminating and attractive a pursuit of esoteric sources could be.[12] EHC's breaking up of notebook passages into discrete fragmentary entries and most importantly his chronological collation of texts from different notebooks was followed by Coburn.[13] Coburn's annotation has rightly been greeted with unanimous praise. One of the many great pleasures of reading the notebooks in her edition is to follow her discoveries of sources, and sense her revelling in Coleridge's exotic old seventeenth-century tomes. Her chronological arrangement needs a better appraisal than it has received so far.

---

[10] Following Coburn 1977, 55–6. *CN* 1, Text, xi dates the completion 1937.
[11] Projected in 1957 (*CN* 1, Text, xli); still planned in 1990 (*CN* 4, Text, xxii.)
[12] Lowes 8; Coburn 1977, 60.
[13] *CN* 1, 16 n. ff. shows how the entry divisions follow *Anima Poetae*.

The Chronological Arrangement

Turning seventy-two artefact notebooks into unified printed form is a process of realization and interpretation much like producing a play from a written text. The staging (or even the lack of staging) unavoidably shapes how it is seen. Kathleen Coburn's decision to print the notebooks in chronological order was designed to make their contents more readily available to the reader by ordering what she felt was the chaos of the source material. The Gutch notebook alone, with no dated entries, proved intractable and had to be printed en bloc (1: 9–305). Coleridge started filling many of his notebooks from the front, the back and anywhere in between; he left pages blank and filled them years later with unrelated matter; he sometimes grabbed the nearest available notebook to catch the thought of the moment.

Notebook 3½, the use of which spans 28 years, is a good example of the problem Coburn faced. It was bought in Germany, probably in 1798, as a vocabulary book for learning German. While in Germany Coleridge filled the top half of pages of about a third of the book with German vocabulary. Someone writing in Gothic script, possibly him, possibly not him, copied out extensive extracts from German books and articles, but there are also some short humorous entries in English amongst this studious German. The notebook was put away when he returned to England, until over four years later at 4 a.m. on Monday 21 November 1803, by candlelight in his study at Greta Hall, he numbered its 128 remaining blank pages and wrote that he proposed to use these to copy out notes on the picturesque and the pleasures of natural scenery (1: 1676). This intention lasted two pages. Six years later this notebook was briefly used when he was living with the Wordsworths to make notes for *The Friend* (3: 3465), and then silence until in 1823 it had a final burst of use for extended meditations in Highgate at which point Coleridge wrote in it: 'When shall I find time & *ease* to reduce my Pocket-books and Memorandums to an Index—or Memoria Memorandorum?' (4: 4946). It was the contemplation of this exceptional Notebook 3½ that gave rise to this oft repeated quotation (*AP* v; *CN* 1, Text, xviii).

Ordering such zigzagging accretions chronologically fulfils the primary need to know what Coleridge was thinking when, but its undesirable side-effects are worth noting. When the dating of entries is uncertain, as they often are, the serial sequencing can be misleading. The occasions when Coleridge did choose between particular notebooks, or allocated particular sections of a notebook to a specific purpose can be overlooked. His associative links and his dialogue with himself are cut when thematically connected entries, written adjacently, are separated on chronological grounds and printed several pages apart. All these points are made by Coburn in her introduction (*CN* 1, Text, xvii–xxxv) and her tables at the end of each volume are intended to enable readers to reconstruct the original composition of an individual notebook.

The 'Confessio Fidei' passage first published in *Literary Remains*, as mentioned above, is a good example of the effect of chronological arrangement. Although this entry and the 'Ego-ana' were both headed with the same date and written in the same notebook, Coleridge chose to keep them separate, leaving more than twenty pages between them.[14] The chronological arrangement removes Coleridge's self-created partitioning and places the striving Christian right alongside the mess of his life. One could say this suits Coburn's stated aim, which was to present a Coleridge 'very different from the historical and public perception of him—more lonely, more rebellious, more sceptical, much wider in range, and more deeply human' (Coburn 1979, 3). One could also say that such juxtapositions (and there are many of them) bring the revelations that are the strength of her chronological arrangement. If she had opted to print the notebooks 'spilled out one by one', an option she expressed a degree of sympathy for, many instances of contemporaneous writing would probably still be overlooked (Coburn 1977, 113).

After Coburn

A balanced assessment of the strengths and weaknesses of the *Collected Coleridge* edition is necessary, because it is for the foreseeable future the foundation for any serious study of the notebooks. Coburn's hope was to 'draw others unto this argument, whether they undertake a new worke or amend this...' (*CN* 1, Text, xli). Anthony John Harding's contribution to the final volume should not be overlooked. A comparison of Coburn's comments in 1974 on an entry where Coleridge claimed that the cholera epidemic was the result of savage races neglecting to cultivate their higher functions, with Harding's notes in the *Collected Coleridge* edition is instructive (Coburn 1974, 28; *CN* 5: 6660 n.). In the same year that the final volume was published, Seamus Perry's *Selection* from the notebooks appeared. There are many places where Perry takes an independent line in transcription, chronology, and in the updating of scholarship, and this welcome plurality of viewpoints stops editorial judgements from being set in stone.[15]

Awareness of and interest in the notebooks is more than healthy. It is rare to read a study of Coleridge in any depth that does not make use of them, and Perry's claim that their publication has changed the character of Coleridge scholarship is surely right (xii). For the notebooks to be read in and for themselves editions must be affordable and portable, and selection is one important way to meet the challenge of dissemination. Nicholas Halmi (who had to carry out an extreme filtration of Coleridge's miscellaneous prose) wisely pointed out that selection takes a lot of care

---

[14] Notebook M. 'Confessio Fidei', fos. 2–7v. 'Ego-ana', fos. 20–24. The intervening entries (4007–10) are not dated.

[15] For example Perry's use of James Diggle's 1998 article amending the Latin and Greek transcripts and translations.

to get right. Anthologizing brief gems 'runs the risk of representing Coleridge as something like the "wit and wisdom machine", as Samuel Beckett put it, of Boswell's Johnson' (Halmi). Such a tendency would be counterbalanced by the Brandl path: the publication of individual notebooks preferably in facsimile editions to enable a reader to see the raw material. Many new discoveries will be made when an editor has time to focus in depth on a project of manageable size.

ILLUSTRATIONS OF COLERIDGE'S NOTEBOOK USE 1800–1803

Turning away from a general discussion of the notebooks to particular examples, I have chosen extracts from Notebook 21 that show Coleridge's discovery of the uses to which he could put his notebooks.[16] Before his move to Greta Hall in Keswick the notebook writings had been mostly of a common-place book character, but the passages that follow show him writing 'for himself'; in the first illustration he is trying to build a mental haven, a place of imaginary union with Sara Hutchinson; in the second, he is using the notebook to manage his conflicted feelings towards Wordsworth.

Greta Hall and 'The Vast Structure of Recollection'

When Coleridge moved to Greta Hall in Keswick, he used Notebook 21 in his study, writing mainly in ink from his desk or his sofa bed, and this writing location makes an immediate contrast with the smaller pencil notebooks he could slip into a pocket and use in a variety of situations. As a result, it only shows a side of Coleridge. This Coleridge didn't go out walking, or go on harum scarum expeditions with Tom Wedgwood—he stayed at home, alone in his Greta Hall study, thinking, sleeping, dreaming and writing. Even his fine descriptions of the landscape and the effects of weather by day and by night are views from the two windows of this study that looked out on a 270° panorama of lakes and mountains. The interiority of the room as a mental space was just as striking to him: 'these beloved Books still before me, this noble Room, the very centre to which a whole world of beauty converges, the deep reservoir into which all these streams

---

[16] I am grateful to Graham Davidson, editor of *The Coleridge Bulletin*, for allowing use of material from my study of Notebook 21 (Cheshire 2008) in this section.

& currents of lovely Forms flow' (1: 1577). In the pages of Notebook 21, he expressed as much affection for his 'noble Room' as he did for Sara Hutchinson. If we were to form our impression from this notebook alone, it was his permanent home by day and night. Charles Lamb left a memorable description of it: 'Coleridge had got a blazing fire in his study, which is a large antique ill-shaped room, with an old fashioned organ, never play'd upon, big enough for a church, Shelves of scattered folios, an Eolian Harp, & an old sofa, half bed' (Lamb 2: 69).

This is the bed from which Coleridge wrote the following nocturne:

Oct. 19. 1802.—midnight. Sitting up in my bed, which I had drawn alongside the fire, with my head to the great Window, & the foot to the Bookcase, my candle on the green table close by me—& I was reading—a flash of Lightning came so vivid as for the moment to extinguish in appearance both the Candle & the bright Fire/it was followed by a Clap of Thunder, that made the window belly in ~~and~~ as in a violent Gust of wind—the window that looks out on Newlands, thro' which the lightning came. (1: 1251)

About a year previously he was lying in the dark on this same bed in an opiated reverie. The fire was spent—the only light source was a candle stump which provided a strange stroboscopic alternation of light and dark. He reached for his notebook, and pencilled in his experience. The use of a pencil is unusual in this notebook, and the hand seems rushed indicating a hasty improvisation:

Prest to my bosom & felt there—it was quite dark. I looked intensely toward her face—& sometimes I *saw* it—so vivid was the spectrum, that it had almost all its natural sense of *distance* & *outness*—except indeed that, feeling & all, I felt her as *part* of my being—twas all spectral—But when I could not absolutely *see* her, no effort of fancy could bring out even the least resemblance of her face. (1: 985)

The unnamed spectral figure is Sara Hutchinson and this notebook is pervaded by his obsessive love for her, and even includes some transcriptions in her hand. The experience described here seems to be a deliberate invocation. This could be a passage from John Dee's magical diary. This deliberateness is confirmed by what he goes on to write next: 'By thinking of different parts of her Dress I can at times recall her face—but not so vividly as when it comes of itself—& therefore I have ceased to try it' (1: 986). Such invocation experiments suggest that when he addressed Sara Hutchinson in his notebooks asking 'Why aren't you here?' (1: 981) it was not just as a lover missing his absent beloved. It was the complaint of a idealist metaphysician who says, if you are present as a living being in my heart, then on the deepest plane of reality you *are* here: it's the world outside that's wrong. It's also the cry of an unsuccessful magus. He has cast the spells, made the invocations: why, then, has the summoned spirit not appeared?

He also used this notebook for another form of union with Sara: the recovery and manipulation of latent memories. In October 1803 he started transcribing a long sequence of entries from an earlier notebook. At first these seem to be nothing more than extractions of interesting material but a sense develops that he is feeding on his own history. He sets off a time loop that gradually leads into the re-treading of his journey north in 1799, and reaches the vivid Sara Hutchinson moment he wants to freeze-frame. The trigger for awakening this living memory is as tangential as Proust's madeleine: a 'Print of the Darlington Ox, sprigged with Spots' recorded in that earlier notebook (1:576):

O Heaven when I think how perishable Things, how imperishable Thoughts seem to be! — For what is Forgetfulness? Renew the state of affection or bodily Feeling [...] and instantly the trains of forgotten Thought rise from their living catacombs!—Old men, & Infancy/and Opium, probably by its narcotic effect [...] produces the same effect on the *visual*, & *passive* memory/. so far was written in my b. pocket [book] Nov.25th 1799—Monday Afternoon, the Sun shining in upon the Print, in beautiful Lights—& I just about to take Leave of Mary—& having just before taken leave of Sara.   (1: 1575)

Immediately following this series of transcriptions from earlier notebooks, Coleridge left a twenty page gap; presumably this was to allow space for continuing the sequence of memories.[17] This would explain why the first entry he makes on jumping forward dwells on the subject of the necessity to relive experience in memory: 'Nothing affects me much at the moment it happens [...] For a Thing at the moment is but a Thing of the moment / it must be taken up into the mind, diffuse itself thro' the whole multitude of Shapes & Thoughts, not one of which it leaves untinged' (1: 1597).

The Cost of Praising Wordsworth: Folio 50

In addition to exploring 'the vast structure of recollection' in his Proust-like meditations on memory, Coleridge was also using this notebook to think about himself in relation to Wordsworth.[18] Notebook writing allowed him to creep up on a problem by degrees, and sometimes he seems to be hinting at things he can't quite own to. The entries 'I lay too many Eggs' (1: 1248) and 'I am sincerely glad, that [Wordsworth ...] is devoting himself to his great work' (1: 1546) are both well known, but, as far as I know, they have never been connected. This is hardly surprising; they are separated by ninety pages in the *Collected Coleridge* edition because Kathleen Coburn dated them thirteen months apart.[19]

The sequence of entries on folio 50 run as follows:

---

[17] Fos. 57–67. He started filling this gap in 1804 (2: 2117 ff.).
[18] Proust 1: 47–51. Also cit. Abrams, 80.
[19] In Cheshire 2008 I argue that these entries were both written in October 1803, but my point here does not depend on their dating, but on their written location.

I lay too many Eggs <in the hot Sands of this Wilderness, the World!> with Ostrich Carelessness & Ostrich Oblivion. The greater ~~number~~ part, I trust, are trod underfoot, & smashed; but yet no small number crawl forth into Life, some to furnish Feathers for the Caps of others, & still more to plume the Shafts in the Quivers of my Enemies, of them that lie in wait against my Soul.

I am sincerely glad, that he has bidden farewell to all small Poems—& is devoting himself to his great work—grandly imprisoning while it deifies his Attention & Feelings within the sacred Circle & Temple Walls of great Objects & elevated Conceptions. —In these little poems his own corrections, coming *of necessity* so often, at the end of every 14, or 20 lines— or whatever the poem might chance to be—wore him out—difference of opinion with his best friends irritated him / & he wrote at times too much with a sectarian Spirit, in a sort of Bravado.—But now he is at the Helm of a noble Bark; now he sails right onward—it is all open Ocean, & a steady Breeze; and he drives before it, unfretted by short Tacks, reefing & unreefing the Sails, hawling & disentangling the ropes.—His only Disease is the having been out of his Element—his return to it is food to Famine, it is both the specific Remedy, & the condition of Health.

Jalap instead of breakfast, Ipecacuanha for one's Dinner, Glauber's salts in hot water for Tea, & the whole together in their several metempsychoses, after having passed back again thro' the Mouth, or onwards thro' the Bowels, in a grand Mawwallop for one's Supper.   (*CN* 1: 1248, 1546, 1547 adding Coleridge's horizontal lines)

The first impression is of Coleridge's self-deprecation. 'I lay too many Eggs with Ostrich Carelessness', while Wordsworth is 'devoting himself to his great work— grandly imprisoning while it deifies his Attention & Feelings within the sacred Circle & Temple Walls of great Objects & elevated Conceptions'. All the imagery is of concentration and industry: Wordsworth is centred within this single great egg, and he is writing *The Recluse*, the great poem that Coleridge had conceived for him, while Coleridge is scattering eggs he doesn't even want to hatch, in the wilderness outside.

But there is an underlying identification with Shakespeare, first noted by David Chandler, that reverses Coleridge's apparent self-deprecation. His ostrich eggs passage was adapted from Edward Capell's recently reprinted preface to an edition of Shakespeare, who seemed bafflingly careless about the printing of his works. Ostrich carelessness, explained Capell, 'is a fit emblem of almost every great genius: they conceive and produce with ease those noble issues of human understanding; but incubation, the dull work of putting them correctly upon paper and afterwards publishing, is a task they cannot away with' (Chandler, 192). If Coleridge the careless ostrich is the genius, what does that make Wordsworth? Given that Coleridge felt he had conceived the plan for *The Recluse*, it follows that Wordsworth had been allocated the 'dull work of incubation'.

The ostrich allusion has other resonances. In George Sandys's *A Relation of a Journey*, which Coleridge had recently been reading, ostriches do not distinguish between their own eggs and those of others: 'When they have laid their egges [...]

they leave them; & unmindful where: sit on those they next meet with' (139). There was justifiable concern at that time that Coleridge's admiration for Wordsworth's poetry was leading him to neglect his own work in favour of his friend's. Shakespeare's Sonnet 86, which has echoes with 1: 1546 is about a poet being silenced by the greatness of a rival: 'Was it the proud full sail of his great verse [. . .] That did my ripe thoughts in my brain inhearse?' Coleridge later quoted this sonnet in *Biographia Literaria*, using it unconvincingly to show that a man of genius can feel no envy towards a rival (*BL* 1: 35).[20] The self-deprecation and the praise of Wordsworth are a gallant struggle to be noble, undermined by the underlying envious feelings that leak out. He makes these same feelings explicit a few pages later in an entry about the 'Envy' A. feels 'at the report that B. had written a new Poem'. By then he could acknowledge his true feelings, but he still couldn't put his name to them (1: 1606). In March 1805 he was still reading and mulling over the import of these passages (2: 2471).

On folio 50, Coleridge ends his praise of Wordsworth (1: 1546) by describing his new work as a 'Food' that is his 'Remedy'. The entry beneath, which qualifies as the most disgusting passage in Notebook 21, could well show the natural reaction to his attempt at noble self-effacement. Unpalatable medicine is being eaten for breakfast and the resulting vomit or excrement has to be eaten again for supper in an endless cycle *ad nauseam*.[21]

'ONE COMMON END'?

Coleridge claimed in his Prospectus to *The Friend* quoted at the head of this chapter that the notebook writings 'miscellaneous as they were' all tended towards 'one common End'. A rough paraphrase of that 'End' would be the aim to find out what the purpose of our lives is, by knowing what we are and what we could be. This may seem an extravagant claim to apply, say, to a note with incidental antimonarchical gibes about the making of ginger beer (1: 162). The way to make sense of this claim is to view Coleridge looking through his notebooks and seeing in their pages what he is from top to bottom. Although he dissociates himself when he describes their contents to his nephew 'as the portrait and impress of the mood and the moment—birds of passages—or Bubbles' (*CL* 5: 493), for himself they are food for self-observation. His high ideals, his failings, and his foolery are recorded on these pages for him to contemplate.

---

[20] *BL* ch. 2 also includes the much repeated 'I lay too many Eggs . . .' passage.
[21] In *CN* 1: 1802 (Jan. 1804) after Wordsworth has read him 'the second Part of his divine Self-biography' Coleridge writes 'Looking at obseen Picture ophthalmium venerea—'.

Private notebook writing has a cultural history with its own particular discourse, and commentators are right to say it is simplistic to think the notebooks show the 'true Coleridge' or give the inside story on what he really thought (Harding 2004, 6). The solitary writer is an aspect of self antithetical to the social figure. We pull faces in mirrors rather than at our neighbours. In real life we have little real knowledge of what anyone else is thinking, or who anyone else really is behind their social mask. However unreliable that may be, we use literature as a window into other lives. And to that end, the private writing genre in general, and a forty-year collection of the 'Flux and Reflux' of a mind as remarkable as Coleridge's in particular, are about as good as it gets.

WORKS CITED

ABRAMS, M. H. 1971. *Natural Supernaturalism: Tradition and Revolution in Romantic Literature.* New York: W. W. Norton.

CHANDLER, DAVID. 1998. Coleridge the ostrich and Capell's Shakespeare. *NQ*, NS 45: 192–3.

CHESHIRE, PAUL. 2008. From Infant's Soul to Black Book: Coleridge's Notebook 21', *Coleridge Bulletin*, NS 31 (Summer) [pages tbn].

COBURN, KATHLEEN. 1974. *The Self-Conscious Imagination.* London: Oxford University Press.

—— 1977. *In Pursuit of Coleridge.* Chatham: Bodley Head.

—— 1979. *Experience into Thought: Perspectives in the Coleridge Notebooks.* Toronto: University of Toronto Press.

COLERIDGE, S. T. 1895. *Anima Poetae*, ed. Ernest Hartley Coleridge. London: Heinemann.

—— 1836-9. *The Literary Remains*, ed. H. N. Coleridge, 4 vols. William Pickering.

—— 2000. *Coleridge's Notebooks: a Selection*, ed. Seamus Perry. Oxford: Oxford University Press.

—— 1896. Notizbuch aus den Jahren 1795–1798 [etc.], ed. Alois Brandl, *Sonderabdruck aus dem Archiv für das Studium der neueren Sprachen, und Litteraturen*, Braunschweig.

DIGGLE, JAMES. 1998. Greek and Latin in Coleridge's Notebooks. *NQ*, NS 45: 193–9.

DIXON, JOSIE. 2002. The Notebooks. In *The Cambridge Companion to Coleridge*, ed. Lucy Newlyn. Cambridge: Cambridge University Press, pp. 75–88.

DUGAS, K. 1985. Struggling with the contingent: self-conscious imagination in Coleridge's notebooks. In *Coleridge's Imagination: Essays in Memory of Pete Laver*, ed. Richard Gravil et al. Cambridge: Cambridge University Press, pp. 53–68.

FOUCAULT, MICHEL. 1988. Technologies of the Self. In *Technologies of the Self: A Seminar with Michel Foucault*, ed. by Luther H. Martin, Hugh Gutman, and Patrick H. Hutton. Amherst: University of Massachusetts Press, pp. 16–49.

HALMI, NICHOLAS. 2000. 'The Norton Critical Edition of Coleridge's Poetry and Prose.' *Romanticism On the Net* 19 August [accessed 18 October 2007] <http://users.ox.ac.uk/~scat0385/19halmi.html>

HARDING, ANTHONY JOHN. 2000. Coleridge's Notebooks and the case for a material hermeneutics of literature. *Romanticism*, 6 (1) (Spring): 1–19.

HARDING, ANTHONY JOHN. 2004. Coleridge's Notebooks: manuscript to print to database. *Coleridge Bulletin*, NS 24 (Winter): 1–10.

HERBERTSON, GARY. 2002. *Document Examination on the Computer: a Guide for Forensic Document Examiners* Berkeley: Wideline.

LAMB, CHARLES and MARY. 1976–. *Letters*, ed. Edwin W. Marrs Jr. 3 vols. Ithaca: Cornell University Press.

LIGHT, ALISON. 2007. *Composing One's Self: Virginia Woolf's Diaries and Memoirs*. Southport: Virginia Woolf Society.

LOWES, JOHN LIVINGSTON. 1955. *The Road to Xanadu*. Boston: Houghton Mifflin.

MEARES, CHARLES. 2000. *Measure and Metaphor: Art practices and the Revealing of Coastal forms* University of Plymouth M. Phil. Thesis.

PERRY, SEAMUS. 1999. *Coleridge and the Uses of Division*. Oxford: Oxford University Press.

PROUST, MARCEL. 1983. *Remembrance of Things Past*, tr. C. K. Scott Moncrieff and Terence Kilmartin. 3 vols. Harmonsdsworth: Penguin.

SANDYS, GEORGE. 1632. *A Relation of a Journey Begun An. Dom. 1610*, London: Crooke.

SOUTHEY, ROBERT. 1965. *New Letters of*, ed. Kenneth Curry, 2 vols. New York: Columbia University Press.

[SOUTHEY, ROBERT and COLERIDGE, S. T.] 1812. *Omniana, or Horae Otiosores*. 2 vols. London: Longman, Hurst, Rees, Orme, and Brown.

SOUTHEY, ROBERT and COLERIDGE, S. T. 1969. *Omniana*, ed. Robert Gittings. Carbondale: Southern Illinois University Press.

TERADA, REI. 2004. Phenomenality and dissatisfaction in Coleridge's *Notebooks*. *Studies in Romanticism*, 43 (Summer): 257–81.

WOOF, PAMELA. 2008. The uses of notebooks: from journal to album, from commonplace to keepsake. *Coleridge Bulletin*, NS 31 (Summer).

CHAPTER 16

COLERIDGE AS TALKER: SAGE OF HIGHGATE, *TABLE TALK*

DAVID VALLINS

COLERIDGE's long period of residence with the Gillmans at Highgate from 1816 onwards, and especially the period after 1829 when his celebrity as sage and conversationalist was at its height, is the context of most of the speeches reported by his nephew and son-in-law, Henry Nelson Coleridge, and his nephew, John Taylor Coleridge, in the *Table Talk*, as well as of most other surviving descriptions of his conversation. The distinctive opinions he expressed to his numerous visitors in this period will be discussed later in this chapter; yet it is perhaps worth noting, first, that even in the 1790s Coleridge's conversation seems to have had much of the fluency, expansiveness, and interconnected digressiveness with which (among other notable qualities) many of his later listeners associated it. Even one of his greatest detractors, William Hazlitt, that is, describes the remarkable continuousness of Coleridge's style of conversational lecturing, as well as its poetic intensity and seemingly transcendent movement from subject to subject, in which 'he appeared to me to float in air' (albeit also 'to slide on ice') during their first meeting in 1798 (1930–4: 17: 107, 113). While Hazlitt interprets Coleridge's apparent inability 'to keep on in a strait line' either physically (while walking) or intellectually (in conversation) as a sign of 'instability of purpose' (1930–4: 17: 113), however, most of his other listeners interpreted both the complexity and the all-inclusive nature of his conversation as signs of a Reason transcending the world of mundane understanding in which a mere superficial consistency might be sought for. Carlyle's ironical comment on how Coleridge, in his later years, was widely thought to have unique access to 'the sublime secret of believing by "the reason" what "the understanding" had been obliged to fling out as incredible', depicts as inconsistency and illogicality what more sympathetic listeners, such as De Quincey, interpreted as a comprehensiveness exceeding the attention-span of most of his listeners (Carlyle 1896–9: 11: 53). Carlyle, like Hazlitt, that is, describes Coleridge's conversation as 'not flowing anywhither like a river, but spreading everywhere in inextricable currents and regurgitations', 'terribly deficient in definite goal or aim, nay often in logical intelligibility.... So that, most times, you felt logically lost', and 'swamped' by 'a confused unintelligible flood of utterance' (1896–9: 11: 55–6). De Quincey, in contrast, interprets the common complaint of Coleridge's 'wandering' in thought or conversation as an illusion produced by the limited power of most of his listeners to follow or comprehend the breadth and subtlety of his comparisons or analogies, since 'he seemed then to wander the most when, in fact, his resistance to the wandering instinct was greatest—viz., when the compass and huge circuit by which his illustrations moved traveled furthest into remote regions before they began to revolve. Long before this coming round commenced most people had lost him, and naturally enough supposed that he had lost himself' (1896–7: 2: 152–3).

The matter-of-factness with which Carlyle detaches himself from the admirers of Coleridge's 'dusky sublime character' and transcendent meditations (1896–9: 11: 53), however, is echoed in surprising quarters—most notably, perhaps, in Samuel Rogers' report of a conversation with Wordsworth after listening to Coleridge talk 'uninterruptedly for about two hours': 'On quitting the lodging, I said to Wordsworth, "Well, for my own part, I could not make head or tail of Coleridge's oration: pray, did you understand it?" "Not one syllable of it," was Wordsworth's reply' (see Carlyle 1896–9: 11: 53; Dyce 1952: 147; and Armour 1969: 336). In the terms with which H. N. Coleridge echoes De Quincey's analysis of Coleridge's conversation, such comments would seem to amount to a confession of intellectual laziness or inadequacy: like Pindar, he says, Coleridge 'has been called a rambling rhapsodist, because the connections of his parts, though never arbitrary, are so fine, that the vulgar reader [or listener] sees them not at all' (*TT* 2: 21). Yet Carlyle's, Hazlitt's, and perhaps Wordsworth's adoption of the 'vulgar' viewpoint is clearly deliberate, implying a wish to detach themselves from the transcendental philosophy which Coleridge professed, and not to seem overly impressed by its purveyor. Again, however, De Quincey seems especially pertinent in highlighting one of the causes of Coleridge's perceived obscurity, whether that were interpreted as confused illogicality or as sublime transcendence of mundane understandings. It was not only, De Quincey writes, that 'he gathered into focal concentration the largest body of objects, apparently disconnected, that any man ever yet could assemble, or having assembled could manage', but also that the continuousness of Coleridge's talk kept his audience 'in a state of passiveness', since 'when men's minds are ... passive, when they are not allowed to react, then it is that they collapse most, and that their sense of what is said must ever be feeblest' (1896–7: 5: 204–5, 3: 331). Despite his unfavourable judgement of the discussions which produced this reaction, Carlyle's distaste for the experience of 'sit[ting] as a passive bucket and be[ing] pumped into whether you consent or not' (1896–9: 11: 55) suggests that such, partly enforced, disengagement from Coleridge's discourse may have been among the reasons for the perception of it as either excessively obscure or inconsistent. De Quincey and H. N. Coleridge, however, are emphatic in stressing that 'logic the most severe was as inalienable from his mode of thinking, as grammar from his language' (De Quincey 1896–7: 2: 153; see also *TT* 2: 11–12), while James Fenimore Cooper, who visited Coleridge in 1828, noted that though 'His utterance was slow, every sentence being distinctly given', there seemed at the same time 'to be a constant struggling between an affluence of words and an affluence of ideas, without either hesitation or repetition' (1930: 167; see also Armour 1969: 181).

Such an effortful, yet clear and fluent, process of giving voice to the interconnected multitude of Coleridge's ideas is evoked less favourably by Southey in a passage which Coleridge echoed in a letter to his son Hartley of around 1820: 'he goes to work like a hound, nosing his way, turning, and twisting, and winding, and doubling, till you get weary with following the mazy movements' (1856: 2: 189; see also Armour 1969: 339 and *CL* 5: 98). In Coleridge's own interpretation, however, the point of such a convoluted development of his ideas (implicitly associated by Southey with the motion of the 'sacred river' in 'Kubla Khan') was precisely to enjoy the 'scent' or discovery of truth rather than to possess it: the process of thinking and (re-)discovering or exploring the relations and analogies between ideas and phenomena, in other words, was at least the immediate purpose of his thought and writing, though the achievement of a sublime sense of a totality transcending complete and immediate comprehension may well have been among its secondary aims.[1] This sense of a totality transcending the details is echoed by several of his listeners, such as William Rowan Hamilton, who writes that 'I feel it almost an injury to the sense of grandeur and infinity with which the *whole* impressed me then, to try to recall the *details* now' (Graves 1882–9: 1: 538–9). The same sense of a 'universal', all-inclusive vision—not ranging over 'the particular topics in hand', but spreading its 'circumference as wide as the boundary of things visible and invisible'—is expressed by H. N. Coleridge, who connects the grandeur of the totalities invoked or implied by Coleridge's conversation both with a transcendence of the phenomenal world in which one saw 'the infirmities of the flesh shrinking out of sight, or glorified and transfigured in the brightness of the

---

[1] See *CL* 5: 98, and *PW* I. 1: 512–14; also my discussion of this and related statements by Coleridge in Vallins 79–88.

awakening spirit', and with a unifying and shaping interiority of thought and imagination, comprehending and illustrating its subject-matter 'by light from the soul' (H. N. Coleridge 1834: 3; see also Armour 1969: 144).

In addition, however, H. N. Coleridge illustrates his uncle's well-known distinction between 'talent' and 'genius' partly by paraphrasing the latter's analysis of the conversation of Sir James Mackintosh, as an example of the former, and partly by making explicit the identification of Coleridge's conversation as a prime example of the latter—a conclusion (I would argue) necessarily, but never boastfully, implied in Coleridge's critiques of the standardized and populist pedestrianism he encountered in others. Similarly, echoing Coleridge's description of Sir Humphry Davy, he comments that Coleridge 'may be slower [than Mackintosh], more rambling, less pertinent; but then, what he brings forth is fresh coined; his flowers are newly gathered . . . and, if you please, you may almost see them growing in the rich garden of his mind' (H. N. Coleridge 1834: 3–4; see also *TT* 1: 40–2). This is, indeed, essentially the same point as Coleridge made in describing his own preference of the 'chase' to the 'quarry' in intellectual pursuits—a view which his nephew more directly echoes in describing how, if Coleridge's conversation was not always the most concise way of expressing the ideas he sought to communicate, 'it was generally the most beautiful; and what you saw by the way was as worthy of note as the object to which you were journeying' (*TT* 2: 9; see also *CL* 5: 98). As noted earlier, however, this preference of the activity of developing and connecting ideas to the discovery of concrete truths was also susceptible of precisely the opposite value-judgement from listeners unsympathetic to the sense of infinitude and transcendent meaning which Coleridge's conversation encouraged, so that for Hazlitt, he resembled 'the mendicant pilgrims that travellers meet in the Desert, with their faces always turned towards Mecca, but who contrive never to reach the shrine of the prophet' (1930–4: 16: 100). Similarly, though Wordsworth is reported as describing Coleridge, after his death, as 'wonderful for the originality of his mind, and the power he possessed of throwing out in profusion grand central truths from which might be evolved the most comprehensive systems', there is still a dissatisfaction both with his interest in 'German metaphysics' and with a perceived lack of intelligibility or accessibleness in his speech and ideas, which Wordsworth feared might make his 'an influence not likely to meet with adequate recognition'.[2] Such persistent doubts from some quarters, together with the unreserved admiration and delight his conversation produced in others, again highlight a distinction or division in mental characters paralleling that which Coleridge summarized as the distinction between 'Aristotelians' and 'Platonists', the first of whom 'consider Reason a Quality or Attribute', and the latter of whom 'consider it a Power' (*TT* 1: 172–3). The frequency with which the responses of his acquaintances

---

[2] From 'a Letter to a Friend' by the Revd Robert Perceval Graves (Wordsworth 1851: 2: 288–9, quoted in Armour 379).

to Coleridge's philosophical discourse themselves appear to illustrate the dichoto-
mies and dialectical oppositions with which he analysed thought and experience,
indeed, itself seems a mark of the depth and force of his analyses.

The opinions expressed in his conversation, however, also reveal a fascinating
series of attempts to apply his philosophical principles to contemporary issues in
politics and culture, and thus often have a controversial quality reflecting Cole-
ridge's sense that most of his contemporaries were far from sharing his predom-
inantly Platonic outlook. In addition, his *Table Talk* can often seem paradoxical in
combining a vigorous critique not merely of materialism, but also of conformity
to received or conventional opinions, with a defence of established values and
institutions in religion and politics which often portrays Coleridge as an arch-
conservative in relation to the progressive or 'reform' movements of the early
nineteenth century. In the *Table Talk*, indeed, these paradoxes are perhaps more
prominent than in any of the works he published, partly because of the contem-
poraneity of many of the comments recorded by H. N. Coleridge with the debates
surrounding the eventual passage of the first Reform Act in 1832, and partly because
of their more spontaneous, and less public or 'censored' character, which gives us
more vivid and direct access to Coleridge's sentiments and opinions, as well as
requiring a continual resolution of their surface contradictions, through which the
reader is actively involved in discovering or comprehending their underlying unity.
That this does not imply a mere facile presumption of consistency in Coleridge's
thought is, I will suggest, evident from comparing his fundamentally idealist
conceptions of the church and state with his critiques of empiricist or materialist
philosophy, and of the predominance of 'understanding' and 'talent' over 'reason'
and 'genius'. The starting-point of Coleridge's reflections on politics and society in
the *Table Talk*, indeed, is also the fundamental premise of his mature thought in
general, namely 'the essential difference between the Reason and the Understand-
ing,—between a Principle and a Maxim—an eternal Truth and a mere conclusion
from a generalization of a great number of Facts' (*TT* 1: 244). Just as the interests of
the nation are, according to Coleridge, to be distinguished from the choices of the
majority of its citizens, that is, so the multitude of concrete facts cannot in
themselves reveal their underlying significance or origin. As extensively argued in
many others of his writings, the organ through which we derive the spiritual
illumination needed to appreciate such differences is the Reason; and in propor-
tion as either this organ, or the power to implement its insights—the Will—is
lacking or suspended in the individual, we are liable to become not only misguided
or deluded, but also morally degraded (see *TT* 1: 235; also *AR* 216–20).

The possession of Reason, then, is fundamental to any correct judgement in
philosophy, religion, morality, or politics; and Coleridge often distinguishes those
whose work is activated by the insights of Reason as the possessors of 'Genius', in
contrast with those activated by the merely empirical and logical powers of
'Understanding'—the possessors of 'Talent'. 'Talent, lying in the Understanding,'

he revealingly says, 'is often inherited; Genius rarely or never' (*TT* 1: 138); or, in other words, the organ which facilitates the insights of genius, and which enables us to grasp or intuit truths transcending the material realm, is itself beyond that realm, sharing much of the spiritual quality of the 'specially imbreathed' soul of man itself (see *AR* 15). The productions of the power of 'talent', however, are—he suggests—liable to be more superficially striking or impressive, being concerned with surface forms more than with profound reflection or insight. 'Few men of Genius', he says, 'are keen; but almost every man of Genius is subtle' (*TT* 1: 250). Because of its greater surface appeal and accessibleness, however, 'Talent', he argues, is often liable to bring greater worldly or material success—as, notably, in the case of the philosopher and educationalist Sir James Mackintosh (*TT* 1: 40). The large profits which Mackintosh derived from, among other appointments, his work as a judge and as an educationalist in India are noted by Coleridge elsewhere (see *CL* 1: 588 and *CL* 2: 402); but the commercial effectiveness of his conversational fluency on diverse topics is hinted at by Coleridge's well-known proposal 'to write on his forehead, "Warehouse to let"' (*TT* 1: 42). No other contemporary is so emphatically associated by Coleridge with a striking assemblage of facts and phrases entirely lacking in 'Genius', or the unifying and revelatory force of Ideas, which are uniquely the domain of Reason: however great his power and 'brilliancy', no animating idea would remain in the minds of his listeners (*TT* 1: 42). The difference between his mind and that of an individual animated by Reason, in other words, was analogous to that between 'an inorganic and an organic body...in the first ...the Whole is nothing more than a collection of the individual phaenomena; in the second...the whole...is in fact every thing and the parts nothing' (*TT* 1: 258).

In tracing the extent to which Coleridge's own opinions on topics as diverse as metaphysics and parliamentary reform reflect the informing and unifying principle of an organic unity generated by inward conviction rather than outward perception, I will suggest, we thus also discover the essence of his distinction between the shaping spirit of 'Genius', in which the insights or ideas of Reason are combined with the unifying power of imagination, and the mere superficial fluency or eloquence of 'talent', in which the focus of the discourse is primarily external, rather than constantly generated by inward conviction. Considering his consistent interpretation of such conviction, in his own writings, as founded on the insights of Reason or divine illumination, indeed, it is perhaps surprising that—in one of the most interestingly summative or synthetic passages in the *Table Talk*—Coleridge should describe both the French Revolution, and the current reform-movement in Britain, as arising from an emphasis on subjective individualism, in contrast with the 'Mechanico-corpuscular philosophy' which, he argues, dominated European culture from the late seventeenth to the late eighteenth century (*TT* 1: 280–2). Though elsewhere he argues that the 'atomistic' thought of empiricists or materialists has tended to dissolve the organic unity of societies as well as suppressing insight into religious and spiritual truths, that is, this notable passage of the *Table*

Talk ascribes the breakdown of society to the opposite tendency, whereby 'attach-
ment to mere external worldliness and to forms' was replaced by a purely 'subjective'
emphasis on the interests of individuals (*TT* 1: 280–2).[3] Such a theory may well help
us to understand how Coleridge's works—like those of several of his contemporar-
ies—could combine so vigorous an early support for revolutionary change with so
vehement an opposition to popular democracy in his later writings. The increasing
dominance of material interests and utilitarian conceptions of the individual arising
from the process of industrialization in the later eighteenth century, that is, tended—
Coleridge argues—to suppress the recognition of the human as inherently trans-
cending the mechanical or functional, necessitating a defence of the human both in
the practical form of revolutionary movements and in the metaphysical and religious
form of Coleridge's own attacks on the commercial exploitation of human beings in,
for example, 'Religious Musings' (see 'Religious Musings' lines 276–300, *PW* I.1: 185–
6). Taken to the opposite extreme, however, subjectivism without the unifying
concepts of Reason led, he argues, to a form of popular chaos, or the most extreme
degree of 'that tendency of the public mind which substitutes its own undefined
notions or persons for real objects and historical actualities' (*TT* 1: 281). Paradoxic-
ally, indeed, the effect of the predominance of such subjectivism on popular literature
(increasingly separated, he suggests, from any literature deserving of the name) was,
he argues, to produce such standardized modes of expression (especially regarding
contemporary politics) as to deprive the newspapers and reviews of any substantial
or intelligent content (see *TT* 1: 285). Hence the 'extremes' of subjectivism and
materialism ultimately 'meet' in a form of superficial populism which Coleridge
contrasts with that idealism—at once rational and intuitive—which, as he writes in
Biographia Literaria, 'is at the same time, and on that very account, the truest and
most binding realism' (*BL* 1: 260–1).[4] Only the observation of 'real objects and
historical actualities', that is, can enable us to discover the true origin and significance
of phenomena, whether physical or social. Hence the polarization which connects the
opposing extremes of subjectivism and materialism is mirrored in the polarities of
Coleridge's thought, which reconciles the extremes of objective and subjective in an
organicist critique of its irrational 'other'.

The symmetry of this relation between Coleridge's own method of thinking and
the patterns he traces in external phenomena, however, of course raises the
question of how far his interpretations of nature, society, or literature are shaped
by a primary intuition or conviction as distinct from 'objective' observation in the
conventional sense—a point he addresses directly, if scarcely apologetically, in a

---

[3] See also S.T. Coleridge, *Lects 1818–19*, 1: 239–41 on the evils of 'atomistic' thought, whether in
philosophy or politics, and *TT* 1: 260, where he notes that when the aristocracy, in Britain as elsewhere,
had 'subordinated persons to things . . . the Poor almost in self-defence, learnt to set up Rights above
Duties'.

[4] See also *Friend*, 1: 110: 'Extremes meet—a proverb, by the bye, to collect and explain all the
instances of which, would constitute and exhaust all philosophy.'

comparison of the various methods by which scholars have sought to discover the truth of any subject. Where metaphysical or ideal truths are concerned, he argues, neither the 'analytical' nor the historical method can in any way be relied on; only the 'constructive' or 'synthetic' method will suffice (*TT* 1: 364).

You must commence with the philosophic Idea of the Thing, the true nature of which you wish to find out and manifest.... If you ask me how I can know that this Idea—my own invention—is the Truth, by which the phenomena of history are to be explained, I answer, in the same way... that you know that your eyes are made to see with—and that is— because you *do* see with them.... in order to make your facts speak Truth, you must know what the Truth is which ought to be proved—the Ideal Truth—the Truth which was consciously or unconsciously, strongly or weakly, wisely or blindly intended at all times (*TT* 1: 366–7).

The evident circularity of this argument—indeed its explicit rejection of external standards or 'measures' as intrinsically irrelevant to the inner light of reason or conviction—is highly characteristic of the spirit in which, in the *Table Talk* and other later works, Coleridge rejects as essentially inappropriate the attempts both of radical politicians to 'meddle' with the constitution, and of political economists to develop theories of the operation of societies on material, rather than spiritual or ideal, grounds. This privileging of innate conviction is, in a sense, never argued beyond an appeal to divine inspiration; yet, I will suggest, neither can it simply be equated with an allegiance to the interests of the property-owning classes, as opposed to those of the 'mob' or demos, however much Coleridge decried the reduction of government to a mere 'delegation' of representatives (see *TT* 1: 220–1). If his opposition to 'reform' often seems anti-democratic, indeed, it is primarily because it proceeds from the same privileging of individual feeling or conviction over popular or conventional opinion as informs his poetry and philosophical writings. In a notable discussion of the relation between poetry and philosophy, indeed, Coleridge emphasizes the importance of the 'higher Logic which Passion articulates, and which is... often at variance with the Logic of mere Syllogism and Grammar', arguing that this 'reasonableness, as it were, of Passion' must be recognized in order to appreciate the works of any great poet (*TT* 1: 399).[5] The logic or reasonableness of passion entails that primary insight into truth which, as noted above, he argued was essential to commencing any inquiry into or illustration of the truth. Knowledge, that is, begins with a conviction or inner light to be applied in investigating the facts before us, and without such insight, which is the basis of 'method', the facts themselves can produce no knowledge worthy of the name.[6]

---

[5] See also *Lects 1808–19*, 2: 427, where Coleridge comments that 'Milton attempted to make the English language obey the logic of passion as perfectly as the Greek and Latin. Hence the occasional harshness in the construction.'

[6] See also *Friend*, 1: 454–5 on the necessity of a 'starting-post... leading thought... [or] INITIA-TIVE' to give 'method' to one's discourse, or to bring 'things the most remote and diverse in time, place, and outward circumstance... into mental contiguity and succession'.

Despite his frequent emphasis on the dialectical resolution of polarities, indeed, Coleridge's philosophy always confessedly exemplifies a distinct faction in an intellectual polarization he rarely seeks to resolve, namely that between 'Aristo-telians' and 'Platonists':

Every man is born an Aristotelian or a Platonist. I don't think it is possible that any one born an Aristotelian *can* become a Platonist, and I am sure no born Platonist *can* ever change into an Aristotelian....

Aristotle was... the sovereign lord of the Understanding—the Faculty judging by the Senses. He was a Conceptualist, but never could raise himself into that higher state, which was *natural* to Plato... in which the Understanding is distinctly *contemplated* and looked down upon, from the Throne of Actual Ideas or Living, Inborn, Essential Truths. (*TT* 1: 172–3)

That such 'Living, Inborn, Essential Truths' can never submit themselves to assessment by the standards of understanding or the senses is no less clear than that Coleridge's primary position—which organizes and interprets phenomena rather than being shaped by external impressions—is one that consistently 'looks down' on the phenomena of mere perception and on the Aristotelian or materialist who fails to enter this 'higher state' of contemplation. The latter class, however, seem almost inevitably, in Coleridge's view, to be the majority, if only because insight into higher truths requires 'methodical' thought or understanding originating in a primary conviction, rather than the mere repetition or echoing of familiar phrases and opinions which he saw as characteristic of the majority. Yet Coleridge nevertheless retains the optimistic vision of an improvement in the popular mind or vision, whereby the Platonic insights of the leaders in thought or opinion, such as himself, might (paradoxically) be propagated among those less innately tied to either Aristotelian or Platonic modes of thought. The majority of the English, he is reported as saying, are not yet able to grasp 'the essential difference between the Reason and the Understanding,—between a Principle and a Maxim—an eternal Truth and a mere conclusion from a generalization of a great number of Facts' (*TT* 1: 244). To start without a principle—or, as Carl Woodring puts it, 'an idea serving as the initiative towards progression' (*TT* 1: 269n), is in Coleridge's view the fundamental error or weakness of empirically-based thought in all periods, since it is the primary conviction or insight of Reason that 'has always pointed out to men the ultimate end of the various sciences' (*TT* 1: 269). Though often manifested or recognized through feeling or conviction, however, Reason is of course defined by Coleridge as the organ through which we intuit the insights of the divine Reason or 'Word' (see *TT* 1: 127 and *TT* 1: 333–4); and just as God himself must remain intrinsically incomprehensible, so the insights of reason in human beings involve a striving towards the expression or comprehension of a principle that always eludes complete expression, in a manner analogous to the Ideas of Reason which Kant describes as necessary to guide or direct philosophical inquiry, as well as moral action (see Walsh 1975: 208, 238–40). Another way of describing the problem of contemporary thought and culture, especially in Britain, therefore, was to say that the conceivable or comprehensible had been elevated above the transcendent or incomprehensible, in a manner which, though flattering to men's tastes or understanding, too manifestly failed to preserve a respect for any higher values or ideals (see *TT* 1: 383–4).

In addition to the proponents of a political reform based on delegations or representatives of the (unenlightened) people, those who most manifested the 'Aristotelian' failure or incapacity to rise to the 'higher' view that could distinguish 'principles' from 'maxims' deduced from an accumulation of facts notably included the political economists, who form a repeated focus of Coleridge's criticism in the *Table Talk*. Though occasionally so mild in his critique as to describe contemporary political economy as merely a 'solemn humbug' guilty of no more than making false deductions about humanity and society from fundamentally obvious or sensible premises (*TT* 1: 348–9), Coleridge's criticisms of Malthus, in particular, though also of political economy more generally, are often as vehement in their expressions of disgust as his comments on any aspects of contemporary British life. In one passage, indeed, Coleridge is reported as saying of Malthus' theory in the *Essay on the Principle of Population* that, in his view, none of 'the heresies and sects and factions which the ignorance and the weakness and the wickedness of man have ever given birth to, were altogether so disgraceful to man as a Christian, a philosopher, a statesman, or citizen as this abominable tenet'. Its evils, he suggests, should be highlighted by 'Ridicule' in the manner of Swift, though 'it is so vicious a tenet, so flattering to the cruelty, and avarice, and sordid selfishness of most men, that I hardly know what to think of the result' (*TT* 1: 323–4). Coleridge's mention of Swiftian 'ridicule'—presumably, that of 'A Modest Proposal'—as an appropriate response to Malthus suggests a close connection between his disgust at the principle of denying assistance to the poor in order to reduce the number suffering deprivation or misery, and his conviction that Mandeville's earlier recommendation of the cultivation of individual vice as a means of benefiting society as a whole must have been nothing more than 'a bonne bouche of solemn raillery' (see Swift 1984: 492–9, Mandeville 1924: 3–8, and *TT* 1: 397). So uninspired a deduction of maxims for the material benefit of the majority, without reference to any principles of intuitive or religious feeling, as Malthus' theory manifested, he implies, was almost as intolerable, except in the form of satire, as either Swift's or Mandeville's ostensible recommendations would have been.

In addition to such disgust at the privileging of a mechanical conception of humanity or society—again, involving deduction from an accumulation of 'facts'—over that which derived from a primary insight or intuition involving an influx of the divine Reason, however, some of Coleridge's criticisms of political economy reflect a similar distaste for the conversion of land or property into merely an economic phenomenon, separated from any concept of duty or of the social organism beyond that entailed in the pursuit of profit. 'When shall we return to a sound conception of the right to property', he is reported as saying, '—namely as . . . implying and demanding the performance of commensurate duties?' The 'horrible perversion of humanity and moral justice' known as political economy, he adds, has blinded people to 'this truth as to the possession of land', while the monetary and credit systems, together with the operation of the stock market, have engendered the inappropriate and selfish habit of treating land primarily as a tradeable commodity (*TT* 1: 352). The alternative to such a commercialized 'free market' in land as in other forms of property, he suggests, was a more fixed or stable system of proprietorship characteristic of an older and more hierarchical society. Yet though Coleridge may seem conservative in deprecating a mobility of landed property, and preferring a more stable 'subordination of classes and offices' (*TT* 1: 361), his reasons for opposing this contemporary trend include a sense of the desirableness of a greater unity in society, and a greater respect for humane values and ideals, than was necessarily entailed in the political economists' models of unrestricted competition. This ideal of the social organism is clearly distinguished by Coleridge from an 'absolute coordination of each to all and all to each', such as—he argues—could exist only under a system of slavery (*TT* 1: 361–2). Its essence, rather, is again the transcendent principle of both the individual human being and the society to which he or she belongs as intrinsically more than a mere accumulation of 'facts'—an ideal too obviously ignored by the calculations of political economy. Whereas, in an 'inorganic' body, 'the *Whole* is nothing more than a collection of the individual phaenomena', Coleridge notes, in an 'organic' body, such as 'a man', 'the whole is the effect of, or result [*sic*] from, the parts—is in fact every thing and the parts nothing.' A state, he continues, 'is an Idea intermediate between the two—the Whole being a result from and not a mere total of, the parts—and yet not so merging the constituent parts in the result, but that the individual exists perfectly within it' (*TT* 1: 258–9). Though society is, or should be, partially analogous to the transcendent unity of the human being, therefore, it should primarily be a system within which the human (including all forms of individuality) is cherished and respected, rather than treated as the means to any other end such as the increase of wealth or the expansion of the economy.

Coleridge's criticisms of contemporary proposals to extend free trade through the abolition of import-tariffs, particularly on wheat, moreover, appeal not only to the importance of maintaining Britain's independence and to the value of traditional agriculture as a mode of employment for its people, but also to an ideal of national unity which he feared the political economists were threatening to dissolve—not merely, as in the passages discussed above, by breaking down the social organism through an excessive emphasis on profits and the free transferability of land, but also by allowing international market forces to take precedence over national interests. The principal effect of political economy, he says in several late passages contemporary with the debate on the corn laws in 1834, is 'to denationalize mankind, and to make love of country a foolish superstition' (*TT* 1: 487, 490).

A traditional model of national unity based on hierarchy and the duties of each class towards the others, and connected by Coleridge with the central importance to the nation's interests of agriculture as against manufacturing or trading activities, is thus the immediate cause of his opposition to free international trade. Agriculture, he says, has greater importance to the nation than manufacturing not only because it allows practical self-sufficiency, but also because it avoids those forms of international competition that would be liable to excite rivalry and enmity between nations; while the promotion of manufacturing at the expense of agriculture would involve attaching greater importance to 'the luxuries or comforts of society' than to 'the necessaries of life' (*TT* 1: 476), or in other words would involve promoting the interests of the wealthiest few at the expense of the society or nation as a whole.[7]

As noted earlier, however, a further threat which Coleridge perceived to the model of social unity needed to preserve respect for Platonic ideals was the contemporary pressure for the emancipation both of Roman Catholics and of dissenting sects or churches. The Catholic Relief Act of 1829, and the subsequent pressures to admit dissenters to the universities, at times met with his forceful criticism on the grounds of their tendency to dissolve that 'national Church' or 'political establishment connected with, but distinct from, the *spiritual* Church', which, he argued, was necessary to prevent both the 'dreadful tyranny' of the papacy, and the dissolution of the church into 'a multitude of enthusiastic sects' (*TT* 1: 482–3).[8] Again, therefore, the ideal of an organically-unified nation simultaneously—and even by means of its distinctive unity—guaranteeing a greater degree of liberty to its citizens in general than would result either from the merging of the national church in a larger one, or from its fragmentation and dissolution, is fundamental to Coleridge's conservative arguments. And it is also characteristic of Coleridge's thought and mode of argument that the 'extremes' of liberty and constraint should 'meet' in this argument about the protection not only of individual freedom in a practical sense, but also of a Platonic respect for the human, by preserving laws which marginalized religious minorities. The Catholic Relief Act, he is reported as saying in June 1834, 'was in effect a Surinam toad, and the Reform Bill and the Dissenters' admission, and attacks on the Church are so many toadlets one after another detaching themselves from their parent' (*TT* 1: 484–5).[9] The maintenance of unity at the price of individual freedom seems at first glance to

---

[7] Coleridge's argument here depends partly on the view that if Britain were forced to buy corn from overseas, foreign suppliers would imediately raise the price to take advantage of this demand—a theory which diminishes the contradiction with his earlier criticism of import-tariffs as exacerbating the hardships of the poor. See *TT* 1: 476 and n.

[8] However, see also *CCS* xxxv–viii and xlii–lv on Coleridge's more ambivalent approach to the issue of Catholic Emancipation in *On the Constitution of the Church and State* and earlier writings.

[9] On Surinam toads' unique manner of reproduction and multiplication see *TT* 1: 485 n. and *CL* 3: 94–5.

be the implication of this catalogue of (to Coleridge) distastefully and inappropri-
ately radical measures advanced by contemporary governments; yet a slightly later
passage again highlights his association of the dis-unification or 'denationalization'
of England involved in this weakening of the Anglican church with another, equally
pernicious one. According to Sir Robert Peel, Coleridge notes, adherence to Roman
Catholicism is in no way incompatible with 'the duties of citizenship and allegiance
to a territorial sovereign'—a view to which Coleridge responds by adding that 'if the
religion of the majority is innocuous to the interests of the nation—the majority
have a right to be trustees of the nationalty—the property set apart for the nation's
use—and rescued from the gripe of private hands (*TT* 1:485). Though this passage is
more conversational in style than most, its meaning seems to be that if one were to
admit that the admission of Catholics to parliament does not undermine the nation,
then government by the majority, whatever their religion, should at least serve to
protect that social and economic order which prevents merely private, commercial
interests from dominating the national life. Hence, it appears, the importance for
Coleridge of maintaining the dominance of the established church was primarily to
provide a consistent defence against the 'privatization' or 'denationalization' either
of culture or of property, and the fragmentation of the 'spiritual platonic' England he
cherished through the dominance of private and sectarian interests, whether mater-
ial or religious (see *CL* 1: 2598).

Such a vision, moreover, was also at the basis of his opposition to a parliamen-
tary reform that would deliver the government of the nation into the hands of a
populace relatively little-schooled in the importance of the transcendent ideals for
which he sought to preserve a general reverence. The 'miserable' consequence of
the replacement of the traditional modes of election and representation, originally
based on the 'landed', 'manufacturing or shop-keeping', and 'mercantile' interests,
with a more equal division of electors into geographical constituencies, he is
reported as saying, 'is to destroy our Nationalty, which consisted in our Represen-
tative Government, and to convert it into a degrading Delegation of the Populace.
There is no Unity for a People but in Representation of National Interests;
a Delegation of the Passions or Wishes of the People is a rope of Sand' (*TT*
1: 220–1). Coleridge's concept of the 'Nationalty'—a term he uses in several
comments on the first Reform Act—again highlights his idea of the nation and
its values as transcending individual choices or interests, and as needing to be
protected or preserved by 'the power of the best men',[10] not in the feudalistic
sense of a combination of aristocratic and ecclesiastical powers, but rather in
the sense of a co-operation of those of wealth, traditional rank, and individual
distinction to hold in trust what was most valuable in the nation's culture, and to

---

[10] This is Colmer's translation of Coleridge's phrase in Greek: 'ἡ ἐκ τῶν ἀρίστων κρατεια'. See
TT 1:297 and n.

facilitate its improvement in accordance with Christian and Platonic principles (see *TT* 1: 266). His ideal, in other words, was one of 'permanence with progression', through a coalition of aristocratic with intellectual and spiritual influences, in which the fundamental aims and values of the nation would never be at issue, or capable of being altered by the wishes of the majority.[11] The 'progressive' influence on government, that is, should in his view originate not in a 'democracy' of mercantile or manufacturing interests, but rather in the work of inspired individuals acting to influence the more permanent centres of power. The fact that he particularly deprecates the proposal to increase the political power of 'that class— the shop keepers, which in all countries and in all ages has been . . . and ever will be the least patriotic, and the least conservative' (*TT* 1: 266), and emphasizes that he would greatly prefer 'a universal suffrage by all householders' (*TT* 1: 263), indeed, highlights the extent of his opposition to the commercial classes in particular, as distinct from the less privileged or educated population in general, though the passage immediately following the latter statement in H. N. Coleridge's notes paradoxically stresses the importance to the state of 'Classes as they represent classified property', and the consequent 'Madness' of introducing an electoral system 'which must inevitably render all discipline impossible' (*TT* 1: 263).

While recognizing the extent to which these and others of Coleridge's reflections on political and social reform are informed by the Platonic vision of a state governed by transcendent 'Ideas' rather than 'facts' or material interests, therefore, it is hard to resist the view of these comments as expressing a conception of the political means to achieve this vision which both precedes and disdains all modern conceptions of democracy. 'Democracy is no legitimate ingredient of any Government whatsoever', he is reported as saying (*TT* 1: 297); and his comments on plans to abolish slavery in British colonies further illustrate the movement in his thought from an early quest for general liberation to a later emphasis on protecting Christian or Platonic ideals and traditional hierarchies from a democratized and materialistic populace. As a 'rhetorical means' of encouraging the abolition of slavery by the British government, he says to an unidentified acquaintance, he has no objection to an emphasis on the rights of the 'Negros'. The habit of 'declaiming about their Rights to the Blacks', however, he condemns as foolishly naive, and even politically harmful, arguing that 'They ought to be forcibly reminded of the state in which their brethren in Africa still are, and taught to be thankful for the Providence which has placed them within means of grace' (*TT* 1: 386). Similarly, though describing the abolition bill as a 'tremendous . . . act of positive enhancement', Coleridge paradoxically expresses a fear that it may damage 'the concept of humanity and freedom', primarily because the importance of religious faith—and specifically the Anglican faith as against that of the

---

[11] On this point see also *CCS* 24–5, 29, 42–3, etc.

non-conformist groups most vigorously advocating this reform—has not been considered or referred to by the proponents of the bill (*TT* 1: 389–90).

Such reservations even with regard to the abolition of slavery, on the grounds that it might diminish knowledge or observance of Christian teachings, highlight the sometimes disconcerting degree to which idealist principles and a preference for the established order have displaced, in some of these late reflections, a practical sense of the circumstances and interests of individuals. What remains most stimulating in the *Table Talk*, however, is the way in which its fragmentary form involves the reader in seeking to piece together the fragments of Coleridge's thought, or in which the surface contradictions often point to a higher and transcendent resolution. In this respect, indeed, his reflections often resemble Kant's—or Plato's—antinomies, in leading the mind (as Coleridge says Plato does) to recognize that 'contradictory propositions' are both true, and that their truth can therefore only be explained by 'a higher logic—that of Ideas' (*TT* 1: 98).[12] The way in which 'extremes' continually seem to 'meet' through the action of Coleridge's 'energic' mind (*TT* 1: 464), or in which the opposites of empiricism and idealism, individualism and communitarianism, stasis and progress, etc., continually change places and form new oppositions leading to 'a higher point of view' from which we see them 'under another light and in different relations' (*TT* 1: 248–9), indeed, resembles not only Coleridge's own description of his elusive 'system' (ibid.), but also the mode of thought and creativity he described as characterizing Shakespeare, 'evolving B out of A and C out of D &c., just as a serpent moves, which makes a fulcrum of its own body, and seems for ever twisting and untwisting its strength' (*TT* 1: 464). As noted earlier, that is, the organicist and dialectical idealism Coleridge professes often resembles a description of his own mode of thinking, so that the 'androgyn[ous]' union of active and passive, or reflection and perception which he described as essential to knowledge is continually exemplified in those arguments which recommend it.[13] Whether or not by the editors' design, indeed, the *Table Talk* represents Coleridge's most substantial contribution to the genre of the Romantic fragment, continually gesturing towards a resolution only to be completed in the imagination of the reader.[14]

---

[12] On the Kantian 'antinomies of pure reason' and Coleridge's interest in these and analogous paradoxes as highlighting the inexpressible truths of Reason, see Kant 1933: 384–484 and Vallins 2000: 147–9.

[13] See *TT* 2: 190–1, where H. N. Coleridge revises Coleridge's statement in *CN* 4: 4705 that 'a Great Mind must be androgyne', and the analogous comment in *TT* 1: 268 regarding the necessity of a feminine element in 'Genius'.

[14] On the function of the Romantic 'fragment form'—particularly in the works of Jean Paul Richter, Novalis, and Friedrich Schlegel—as representing 'the incomplete nature of language, communication, and art as parts representing the unattainable perfection towards which they strove, while at the same time . . . instruct[ing] the reader in his role as actively participating to create the relations which the artifact could simulate', see Wheeler 1984: 11–17.

WORKS CITED

ARMOUR, RICHARD W. and HOWES, RAYMOND F. eds. 1969. *Coleridge the Talker: A Series of Contemporary Descriptions and Comments, with a Critical Introduction.* New Edition. New York: Johnson Reprint Corporation.

CARLYLE, THOMAS. 1896–9. *The Works of Thomas Carlyle,* ed. H. D. Traill, 30 vols. London: Chapman & Hall.

COLERIDGE, HENRY NELSON. 1834. Review of *The Poetical Works of S.T. Coleridge.* 3 vols. London: 1834. *Quarterly Review,* 52: 1–38.

COOPER, JAMES FENIMORE. 1930. *Gleanings in Europe: England,* ed. Robert E. Spiller. New York: Oxford University Press.

DE QUINCEY, THOMAS. 1896–7. *Collected Writings,* ed. David Masson, 14 vols. London: A. and C. Black.

DYCE, ALEXANDER. 1952. *Recollections of the Table Talk of Samuel Rogers, First Collected by the Revd. Alexander Dyce,* ed. Morchard Bishop. London: Richards Press.

GRAVES, ROBERT PERCEVAL. 1882–9. *Life of Sir William Rowan Hamilton,* 3 vols. Dublin: Hodges, Figgis, and Co.

HAZLITT, WILLIAM. 1930–4. *The Complete Works of William Hazlitt,* ed. P. P. Howe. 21 vols. London: Dent.

KANT, IMMANUEL. 1933. *Critique of Pure Reason,* trans. Norman Kemp Smith. London: Macmillan.

MANDEVILLE, BERNARD. 1924. *The Fable of the Bees: or, Private Vices, Publick Benefits,* ed. F. B. Kaye. 2 vols. Oxford: Clarendon.

SOUTHEY, ROBERT. 1856. *Selections from the Letters of Robert Southey,* ed. John Wood Warter. 4 vols. London: Longman, Brown, Green, and Longmans.

SWIFT, JONATHAN. 1984. *Jonathan Swift,* ed. Angus Ross and David Wooley. Oxford: Oxford University Press.

VALLINS, DAVID. 2000. *Coleridge and the Psychology of Romanticism: Feeling and Thought.* Basingstoke: Macmillan.

WALSH, W. H. 1975. *Kant's Criticism of Metaphysics.* Edinburgh: Edinburgh University Press.

WHEELER, KATHLEEN 1984, ed. *German Aesthetic and Literary Criticism: The Romantic Ironists and Goethe.* Cambridge: Cambridge University Press.

WORDSWORTH, CHRISTOPHER. 1851. *Memoirs of William Wordsworth,* 2 vols. London: Moxon.

CHAPTER 17

COLERIDGE AS THINKER: *LOGIC* AND *OPUS MAXIMUM*

MURRAY J. EVANS

COLERIDGE's *Logic* and *Opus Maximum*, while markedly different kinds of texts, also have a number of things in common. First, they are roughly contemporaneous, with *Logic* likely written across the 1820s and most of *Opus Maximum* in the period 1819–23.[1] Second, both texts were draft texts, not published in Coleridge's lifetime; both only first appeared in Bollingen editions in the last thirty years, *Logic* (hereafter *L*) in 1981 and *Opus Maximum* (hereafter *OM*) in 2002. Finally, judging by the sparse extant scholarship, the texts have attracted very few modern readers, relative to readers of the *Biographia Literaria*, for example. This is only partly for the reason of late publication, since they are both difficult texts. The *Logic* is an apparently dry treatise on an apparently unimaginative topic, and *OM* resists wholistic reading. It is, moreover, apparently irrelevant to perceived main

---

[1] *Op Max*, xx. Jackson, *Logic* (hereafter *L*), xlvii, xlix, and l writes of Coleridge's offering to present *L* to publishers in 1823, 1826, and 1829; the MS for his edition cannot, because of the evidence of watermarks, have been written out before 1827 (liv). Nicholas Halmi thus estimates the dates for the major fragments of *Opus Maximum* (hereafter *OM*): Victoria Library MS 29, parts iii and ii (McFarland's 'Fragment 1' and 'Fragment 2'), 1820–3; Huntingdon Library HM 8195 (McFarland's 'Fragment 3'), 1822–3; and VCL MS 29, part i ('Fragment 4'), 1819–21 (*Op Max*, 5, 80, 214, 291). On draft texts, see *L*, xiii and *Op Max*, xvii–xviii.

highways of Coleridge scholarship, which avoid the 'later Coleridge' in favour of 'Coleridge' of the early years and poems, except for a major forward outpost at the publication of the *Biographia* in 1817. Yet both *L* and *OM* arguably reveal to us Coleridge the thinker in uniquely rich ways, with insights that surprise and reorient our current knowledge on both Coleridge and also a number of perennial issues for Coleridge and Romantics scholarship. I begin with some contextual comments on each text and on what little scholarship exists for each. Then I discuss how aspects of *L* are developed and fulfilled in *OM*, since such an approach is proportionally fair to *OM* as the longer and, I think, more important text. For this reason, I will also review the major themes of *OM*.

In his edition of *L*, J. R. de J. Jackson reminds us that Coleridge meant the text for young upper- and middle-class men so that they might cultivate 'the development of their ability to think for themselves'. Philosophically, as 'essentially a popularisation' of Kant's *Critique of Pure Reason*, it sets out to present the three traditional divisions of logic, but only the first two are completed.[2] Part 1, 'The Canon'—a 'form to which all legitimate constructions of the understanding must correspond'—analyses and defines the syllogism, comprising the major premise, minor premise, and the conclusion. The subject of the major must be the predicate of the minor, as in Coleridge's example: 'all that common land is calcareous: but such a field is common land... [therefore] the field is calcareous'.[3] Part 2, 'The Criterion or Dialectic'—'a test for the distinguishing of truth'—presents the 'trancendental aesthetic', also termed '*critical* or judicial logic' which is restricted to the science of 'the universal forms of the pure sense', particularly time and space.[4] Here Coleridge discusses analytic judgments, by which 'we know what we know *better*', and synthetic judgments, by which 'we know more'. Part 2 is concerned, then, with 'the conditions that render experience itself possible'; its 'transcendental logic', analyzing the workings of the understanding, is not to be confused with *transcendent* knowledge.[5] In all, Coleridge emphasizes the importance, if also the limits, of logic: 'logic by itself... is but a cabinet of many drawers and pigeonholes, all empty. But are we, therefore, to procure no cabinets, and content ourselves with lumber-rooms and slut-corners?'[6] To the missing Part 3, 'The Organon', whose inclusion Coleridge predicts from the outset, would fall discovering truth or determining if metaphysics is possible. Coleridge also calls this 'the logic of ideas and first principles', and the 'noetic'.[7] As we will see, this is the territory of *OM*.

Given its greater length and scope, even though unfinished, *OM* is harder to characterize. As Thomas McFarland rehearses,[8] Coleridge wrote and re-wrote plans

---

[2] *L*, lix, lxii, and lx.
[3] *L*, 51 and 54–5.
[4] *L*, 51, 146, 149, 146, and 154.
[5] *L*, 174, 146, 149, and 147.
[6] *L*, 204; *OED* online, 14 February 2008: slut, n., a corner of a room allowed to collect filth.
[7] *L*, 52, 51, and 169.
[8] *Op Max*, xci–cv.

of its major divisions, with repeated refinements and revisions, over the first three decades of the nineteenth century. The burden of the extant work is arguably clear, through two sections of Victoria College Library MS 29 (McFarland's Fragments 1 and 2) and Huntingdon Library HM 8195, entitled 'On the Divine Ideas' (McFarland's Fragment 3). This project is to elaborate 'the one assumption, the one postulate'—'the Existence of the *Will*, which ... is the same as *Moral Responsibility*, and that again [the same as] the reality and essential difference of moral *Good* and *Evil*.[9] This early announcement in *OM* accurately predicts its generous attention to conscience and faith.[10] This aim and material develops into another, related one: the extrapolation from first philosophical principles of Coleridge's preferred formulation of the Christian Trinity—the Divine Tetractys (Absolute Will, Father, Son, and Holy Spirit). Among the other fragments of *OM*,[11] the largest one, Victoria College Library MS 29 part 1 (McFarland's Fragment 4), is an abstruse disquisition on, among other things, the process of Creation; more than the other major fragments, it appears to suffer from the absence of contextual material Coleridge never completed for *OM*.

As yet, there is no book-length study of the *Opus Maximum*, what Coleridge meant to be the culminating work of his career.[12] Of the little scholarship on the text, most includes only short illustrative excerpts for other purposes.[13] But Jeffrey Barbeau's collection of essays on the *Opus* is a welcome arrival, and with the publication of the Bollingen edition, more published work may appear. McFarland's prolegomena to that edition, while providing much contextual material, do not much engage the text itself, and his footnotes often provide comparisons to other Coleridge texts without illuminating moments in, and larger trajectories of argument.[14]

In spite of infrequent discussions of Coleridge's *Logic*, there is a surprising variety of conflicting responses. Alice Snyder, who early published excerpts of the work, opposes its entire publication, viewing it as a mere copy of Kant, best served by outline and selective quotation! Bollingen editor Robin Jackson acknowledges that the work, indebted to Kant, contains no new arguments. It is important, not for its place in the 'development of philosophy, but in the light it sheds on Coleridge's opinions in the 1820s'. Moreover, 'Coleridge's account carries an

---

[9] *Op. Max.* 11.

[10] See *Op. Max.* 57–96 and preceding passages at 21–48, 55–7.

[11] On these fragments, a number of them single leaves only, see Nicholas Halmi, 'Editorial Practice', *Op Max*, xix–xx. I share the skepticism of Halmi, 'Nicholas Halmi reads,' 49–50, about editors' uneasy inclusions/exclusions so as to constitute the Bollingen *Op Max*—to be sure, an occupational hazard of much editing.

[12] My manuscript, 'Coleridge's Sublime Rhetoric in the *Opus Maximum*: Trinity, System, and Self', is presently under consideration for publication.

[13] See, for example, Muirhead and Boulger. Mary Ann Perkins's *Coleridge's Philosophy* has the most generous selection of excerpts from *OM*.

[14] See Evans, review.

undertone of digression that bears purposefully upon our conceptions of sense experience and the pure reason', which provides 'a hint of aims in the *Logic* that have not been openly declared'. Suggesting Coleridge's 'religious motive' for repro-ducing Kant's discussion of space and time, he concludes that the 'concealed aims rather than the declared ones' make *L* 'much more than a derivative introduction to Kant'.[15] James McKusick goes farther in claiming considerable originality for the work, since it 'enacts a "linguistic turn" on Kant's philosophy'.[16] Meanwhile, in his Prolegomena to the Bollingen *Opus Maximum*, Thomas McFarland argues that Coleridge split off several discrete works, including the *Logic*, from his grandly envisaged *magnum opus*, leaving the reduced, extant *Opus Maximum*. While technically, *OM* does not include the treatise on logic envisaged in some of Coleridge's plans for it, McFarland's statement about the relationship between the two texts needs considerable qualification and expansion.[17]

Accordingly, in my presentation of points of contact between the two texts, I will not only argue that *OM* expands on mentions of the same topic in the *Logic*. My argument also qualifies McFarland's opinion that *L* split off from *OM*, in showing that the latter text fulfills and enacts many aspects of *L* in a markedly systematic way. My essay thus also means to challenge the claim that Coleridge was a failed systemizer.[18] These points of contact between the two texts also comprise high points towards a larger understanding of *OM*, a desideratum in current scholar-ship. In all, further discussion of both texts and their relations will significantly enrich our understanding of Coleridge in the 1820s and beyond.

THE 'VERB SUBSTANTIVE' IN *LOGIC* AND *OPUS MAXIMUM*

That *OM* largely jumps off from what would have been *Logic*'s missing Part 3, on the Noetic, is clear from an important assertion in *OM* concerning the relation of grammar and logic to 'primary truths'. As *OM* puts it, the 'science of grammar is but logic in its first exemplification' or 'product', 'thoughts in connexion, or connected language'. The 'primary distinctions of identity and alterity, of essence

---

[15] Snyder, 68; *Logic*, lxii–lxv, lxvii.

[16] McKusick, 120. Readers concerned, as I am, about McKusick's assumptions about the relation between language and the Word in Coleridge can read an existing critique in Reid. Further on Coleridge's originality, Merrison argues that Richard Whately's success in the revival of formal logic in England rested on Coleridge's prior work (175–6).

[17] *Op Max*, ccxxii. See also Barbeau, 25–6. McFarland himself acknowledges that *OM* is 'concerned with logic throughout' (*Op Max*, ccxxii).

[18] See, for example, Perry, 1–3.

and form, of act and of being' constitute 'the groundwork and, as it were, the metaphysical contents and preconditions of logic'. Strictly speaking, then, the 'forms of grammar or the rules of logic' derive from 'those primary truths', rather than lending them an illustration, since 'as they are the being of all beings, ens entium, so are they the form of all forms, idea idearum'. The implication here is that all discourses, including logic and grammar, are themselves illustrations of this 'idea of all ideas'.[19]

In this connection, *L*'s repeated mention of the 'verb substantive' is apposite. Coleridge comments that 'the verb substantive ("am", *sum*, εἰμι) expresses the identity or coinherence of being and act. It is the act of being.' Later he mentions that Supreme and other beings 'are not objects of logic' since 'they are of necessity presumed and presupposed in the very first step', just as his previous analysis of the syllogism demonstrated 'the force of the copula "is" in every logical position, which communicates the reality to the subject and predicate'. This, then, is 'the existence of that first and highest insight—an insight into the existence of a somewhat that is the common ground of the subject and object'.[20] *OM* makes these passing comments in *L* its own governing idea.

A passage in MS 29 confirms the centrality of this primary idea, which in the course of *OM* Coleridge calls the postulate of the Will or the idea of God. In this passage,[21] Coleridge lists various discourses in which a sense of the idea or postulate recurs. In grammar 'we begin with the verb substantive, with that which is the identity of being and action, of the noun and the verb; and we regard the noun and verb as the positive and negative poles of this identity, the Thesis and Antithesis'. Here, identity 'can be no otherwise explained than as one containing in itself the ground and power of two as their radical antecedent'. His next illustration is from geometry, concerning 'a point producing itself into a bi-polar line, when we contemplate the same as anterior to this production and as still containing its two poles, or opposites in unevolved co-inherence'. Next comes biblical discourse, first from the Old Testament. Because of the aptness of the verb substantive for expressing 'the act by which we are[,] ... we at once see the propriety with which the Hebrew Legislator named that co-inherence of act and being which is the ground and eternal power of the universe, of all things, and of all acts, and yet not included in nor the same with the sum total of these, the Absolute I AM'.[22] The passage continues with more versions of this likeness in discourses of identity. I will return to, below, the larger Pythagorean logic of the passage, by which Coleridge also calls 'the Absolute I AM', Prothesis. For the present, the grammatical, geometrical and biblical discourses of the passage clearly all sound alike logically, as versions of that prothetic 'co-inherence of act and being' characteristic of the

---

[19] *Op Max*, 208 and 207.
[20] *Logic*, 16–17, 130–1, and 145.
[21] *Op Max*, 187–9.
[22] Exodus 3: 14; *Op Max*, 188.

'Absolute I AM'—as the 'ground' of 'all things, and of all acts', but not coincident with 'the sum total' of those acts. This sense of what I have called 'prothetic repetition'[23] is confirmed later in *OM*, where Coleridge calls these dependent discourses, not 'proofs', but 'a series of exemplifications of the same truth, as if a man should demonstrate the essential properties of the triangle in a vast succession of diagrams, and in all imaginable varieties of size, and colour, and relative position: each would have the force of all'.[24]

The Charge of Obscurity, and the Main Themes of *Opus Maximum*

The importance of this kind of repetition for comprehending both ideas and also their relationships in *OM* cannot be overestimated, speaking to the intuitive coherence of Coleridge's system there. Yet this kind of argument in Coleridge's prose has obviously vexed scholars of his work. Jerome Christensen, for example, charges that 'method' in *The Friend* descends to mere chiasmus:

For the amicable chiasmus is the figure of method . . . Partaking of both poles, distinct from either, method is both the crossing plank from one side of the stream to the other and the eddy where circulates the proprieties of intention and act: *a* in *b*, *b* in *a*. Translucent, provisional, faultlessly deferential to the truth it serves—method follows the track of the chiasmus.[25]

Where every term is defined as being a form of another—'*a* in *b*, and *b* in *a*'—there is no difference, Christensen implies. Christensen's view, which I think dubious in the case of *OM* (and also *The Friend*), is worthy of careful reply.[26] The view, moreover, is a fair example of criticisms directed at Coleridge's obscurity. *OM* is a very good text in reference to which to answer such criticisms, since here Coleridge purports to lead his readers through a systematic extrapolation of higher truths from first principles. While Coleridge's method does open itself to charges such as Christensen's, the content of his argument is not obscure as a set of concepts. A summary of the main conceptual lines of argument in *OM* will confirm this point and thus begin to answer charges such as Christensen's.

---

[23] For a fuller and originating treatment of this whole context, see Evans, 'Reading "Will"', 84–9.

[24] *Op Max*, 271.

[25] Christensen, 'Method', 24.

[26] The pervasive intertextuality of *The Friend* and *OM* remains an important and unaddressed topic, which I take up in 'Coleridge's Sublime Rhetoric'.

As for the main content of *OM*, Coleridge makes it clear that his central preoccupation is with the will, both in its 'finite and creaturely' and 'absolute' senses. The first, Coleridge regards as his 'one great and inclusive postulate and moral axiom—the actual being of a *responsible Will*'. [27] In a major section of *OM* corresponding to his 'Essay on Faith', Coleridge adds numerous lengthy passages. [28] Some of these passages expand on the two major preoccupations of this part of *OM*, both having to do with conscience, what he sees as the *sine qua non* of human subjects. [29] The first is 'the underived, unconditional authority of the Conscience [in] all other things within the sphere of morals and the practical reason'. Here Coleridge's ongoing quarrel is with William Paley's doctrine of prudence and self-love. [30] Sometimes in discourse reminiscent of *L*'s technical analysis of the syllogism, Coleridge presents what is largely a logical critique of two Paleyan syllogisms. One of these syllogisms, for example, falsely states that nature can prompt 'a man to benefit himself' when in fact, Coleridge reminds us, it can only induce to gratification. The second preoccupation of this section of *OM* is that conscience is 'the root and precondition of all other consciousness ... anterior, therefore, to it in the order of thought, i.e. without reference to time'. [31] In this regard, *L* anticipates *OM* in its comment that self-consciousness cannot be ultimate: 'to affirm of any finite being that it is absolute is a contradiction in terms: in order to absoluteness there must be an "is" (*est*) which necessarily involves the "I am," and again an "I am" without which no "is" would be conceivable.' In *OM* this insight becomes a major argument against the error of conceiving of a subjectivist self that pre-exists the act of conscience; it is in what Coleridge calls the act of conscience, to treat neighbor as oneself, that self and other are together constructed. For Coleridge, there is 'no ... "*I*" ... without a "*Thou*"'. [32] This assertion that there are no single selves for Coleridge is an important corrective to some scholarship on the self in Coleridge and Romantics scholarship at large. For example, in his conclusion to the seminal *Coleridge and the Pantheist Tradition* concerning the 'Essay on Faith', McFarland asserts that a subjectivist self pre-exists the act of conscience, while Coleridge argues the opposite both in the 'Essay' and also in its extended form, in *OM*. [33] This is only one instance of how attention to *OM* allows scholars to get a more

---

[27] *Op Max*, 19 and 17. His general definition of will, more simply, is 'the *power* of *originating* a *state*' (18).

[28] I assume that the 'Essay on Faith', the shorter version, was written first, according to Jackson and Jackson, *SWF* ii, 834, in 1820; and that Coleridge used it to expand on considerably in his longer version in *OM*. These many expansions indicate that the 'Essay on Faith' is not the longer version, as previously suggested (Barth, 29, n. 38).

[29] In *Op Max*, these particular passages go from p. 59 (after 'insanity or apostasy') to p. 69 (up to 'This, I contend, ...').

[30] *Op Max*, 60. As Coleridge wrote elsewhere (*CL* 3, 153), Paley advocated the following human behavior: '*Obey* God, *benefit* your Neighbour; but *love* YOURSELVES above all'.

[31] *Op Max*, 67 and 59–60.

[32] *L*, 82; *Op Max*, 75. I have summarized a number of key passages (*Op Max*, 58–9, 72–6). For an excellent and full treatment of the argument as it appears in the 'Essay on Faith', see Cole.

[33] McFarland, *Coleridge and the Pantheist Tradition*, 238–9 and 241–2.

accurate picture of Coleridge on the self, as a more stable basis for their own work on this and related topics.

The second and related major theme of *OM* is will in its 'absolute' sense: the Absolute Will or Divine Prothesis, which Coleridge derives from the foundation of Pythagoras' 'grand system of the deity', 'the monas': 'not as the one, but as that which without any numbers and perfectly distinct from numbers was yet the ground, and, by its will, the cause of all numbers; and in the manifestation of the godhead [Pythagoras] represented it by the famous triad three'.[34] Accordingly Coleridge's preferred formulation of the Trinity is the Divine Tetractys: Absolute Will, Father, Son and Holy Spirit. Coleridge makes clear that the Absolute or Ground is not existential.[35] It is a postulate, in recognition of the limits of human logic, crucial to any thinking about God. Absolute Will 'is the abysmal depth... of the eternal act by which God as the alone causa sûi [self-caused cause] affirmeth himself eternally'. The 'depth begetteth not', Coleridge stresses, but its eternal causativeness is 'self-realized' in the persons of the Tetractys: 'the supreme mind begetteth his substantial idea, the primal Self, the adorable *I am*, its other self, and becometh God the Father, self-originant... and self-subsistent, even as the Logos or Supreme Idea is the co-eternal Son, self-subsistent but begotten by the Father.' Coleridge calls this 'the coeternal act of alterity, or the begetting of the identity in the alterity'. So much for the first two Persons of the Trinity. Coleridge extrapolates the Holy Spirit according to the traditional term, perichoresis, 'the primary, absolute, co-eternal intercirculation of Deity'. The form of the Spirit, moreover, is act, not being; in its circulation, it 'constitutes the eternal unity in the eternal alterity and distinction' of the Father and the Son. Thus is completed 'the venerable Tetractys of the most ancient philosophy, the absolute or the prothesis, the Idem, the Alter, and the Copula by which both are one, and the copula one with them'. Thus 'we have the Absolute under three distinct ideas, and the essential inseparability of these without interference with their no less essential interdistinction is the Divine Idea'.[36]

The third major, again related, idea in *OM* concerns divine ideas, whose importance is reflected in the title of one of the major manuscript fragments, the Huntington MS—'On the Divine Ideas' (hereafter *ODI*). A divine idea is 'a representation of the universal under the eminence of some form in particular'. Divine ideas are 'God's *ideas* of finite things, *the finite things*—which originate in him but acquire separate existence.'[37] Not to be confused with angels,[38] they are nonetheless 'uncreated forms

---

[34] *Lects 1818–19*, I, 79.

[35] Reid, 'Coleridge and Schelling', 472.

[36] *Op Max*, 232–3, 199, 206–7, and 209–11.

[37] *Op Max*, 236; *SWF*, I, 156. Perkins helpfully adds that for Coleridge, 'the symbol reveals the universal in the particular, the Idea is a *particular* form within the universal, the Absolute' (174). Some of this material is taken from a fuller discussion in Evans, 'The Divine Ideas'.

[38] Barth, *Coleridge and Christian Doctrine*, 106 n. 4. On the provenance of divine ideas, see Perkins, 171–3.

and eternal truths, powers, and intelligences'.[39] Indeed, in some discussions of the Trinity, divine ideas appear almost as an additional member of a Trinity itself already expanded to Tetractys. Having defined the Son as the 'ALTERITY' or 'the PLEROMA [or fullness] of Being,' for example, Coleridge in a separate category defines 'The *Object-ivity*': the 'Distinctities in the pleroma are the Eternal IDEAS—the Subsistential Truths, each considered in itself an Infinite in the form of the Finite; but all considered as one with the Unity, the Eternal Son, they are the energies of the Finific'.[40] In the Son, then, is 'the plenitude of divine forms'; in 'this other, all others are included, . . . in this first substantial intelligible distinction (= ὁ Λογος) all other distinctions that can subsist in the indivisible unity (Λογοι θειοι) or[41] contain it, are included'. Because of the finite and infinite dimensions of a divine idea, though, it possesses a 'potential duplicity of being': it 'in some sense or other is, yet is not God'. Here Coleridge's distinction between the Absolute Will and the Persons of the Trinity does him conceptual favours. For 'in the absolute Will, which abideth in the Father, the Word and the Spirit, totally and absolutely in each, one and the same in all, the ground of all reality is contained, even of that which is only possible and conditionally possible alone'. But the Persons of the Trinity, i.e., the Absolute Will self-realized, must include in themselves only the 'absolutely real, that is, as far as the reality is actual and not merely possible'. The Trinity cannot include the 'possible . . . or potential, as contra-distinguished from the actual'.[42] Coleridge rehearses this doubleness of divine ideas thus. Each divine idea is real to God, since 'it is the necessary offspring of a power, the essence of which is to be causative of reality', i.e., the Absolute Will; each idea is also actual to God, 'because and as far as it is one with the Will of the Father'. As for the idea itself, it is real 'inasmuch as a Will is its essence'; and the idea is also actual, but only inasmuch as it wills to be one with the will of God. As a will, then, a divine idea may act on its potential aberrantly, may will 'its actuality in its Self and not in God' (as proved by the fact of the existence of evil). (This insight is the basis for Coleridge's extended discussion in *ODI* on what he regards as its central problem: on how God and evil can co-exist, on the 'passage from the absolute to the separated finite'.) It is our limited understanding that necessitates these multiple vantage points for Divine ideas. Accordingly, Coleridge stipulates that divine ideas cannot be envisaged as 'actual as particular forms' in themselves.[43]

The complexity of these definitions allows Coleridge considerable dexterity to pursue related questions in *OM*.[44] One such question he only raises in *L*, since it

---

[39] *Op Max*, 233.

[40] *SWF*, 11, 1511–12.

[41] The 'or' is present in the MS but omitted in *Op Max*, 207.

[42] *Op Max*, 206–7, 246, 216, 222, 221, and 222.

[43] *Op Max*, 236, 237–8, 218, and 236. Thus for Coleridge, in the Absolute Will and divine ideas, but not the Triad, 'the potential necessarily co-exists as alternable with the actual' (232).

[44] For a full discussion of divine ideas, see Evans, 'Divine Ideas', from which I draw the example in this paragraph.

exceeds the boundaries of his present discussion, necessarily confined 'to the data presented to us by *reflection*'. Coleridge nonetheless adds the following aside:

What these laws are is a subject for future inquiry, but be they what they may, it is easy to imagine some superior being capable of contemplating at once an individual mind and its objects, of judging how far and in what manner the objects are modified for the human mind by its own mechanism, and lastly of looking at the objects independent of such modification.[45]

The 'future inquiry' that Coleridge alludes to here occurs in *ODI*, where, in rejecting the false opposition, between 'real' and 'unreal', he actually refers to 'a former work, that on Logic'.[46] Instead, he asserts that 'under the idea reality we have to find two opposites, both of which are reality, though each a form opposite to the other[:] the actual and the potential'. Only thus can there be any intelligible argument 'connected with the ideas, laws, or powers'. Coleridge then applies this notion in an analogy on the 'reality of the potential' in divine ideas.[47] He suggests that when we are sitting in a chair, or performing some other such activity, some acts and passions are 'actually present' but many others (like standing up at any moment) are also 'really potential'. Next, Coleridge uses his distinction in relation to God's knowledge of the finite, so as to counter the fallacies of Moses Mendelssohn, anima mundi, and what he calls 'the Indian... universal element'. He presumes that God as 'a being limitless' would have both 'self-comprehension' and also 'a knowledge of the finite', and of finites' knowledge of one another and other things. Not only 'would all things that are[,] have actual reality in the universal mind' (your sitting down). Their 'potential being in relation to the finite' (your standing up) would also have reality, since this potentiality 'would be affirmed in the same act that gave being to the finite, and [would] be included in the product of that act'. Here Coleridge is grounding his argument in what we have already seen is *OM*'s primary postulate of the Absolute Will, the 'act we have defined as That which is essentially causative of reality'. For this creative act—but not, as we have already seen, for the Persons of the Trinity—the potential must be 'a form of reality... no less, though a far lower form, than the actual'. Accordingly we may predicate 'both the actual and the potential of one and the same subject'.[48] Put another way, God sees both your (actual) sitting down and your (potential) standing up at any moment. In Coleridge's terms, both are 'real'. This passage, one step in a grander argument in *OM* stretching over most of its considerable

---

[45] *L*, 245.

[46] *Op Max*, 226–30. See also *L*, 129–30: 'reality can have no contrary, and in accurate language we should say that "unreal" is the contrary word to the word "real". All opposites, like the extreme points of all lines, must have a mid-term common to both.'

[47] *Op Max*, 227 and 230.

[48] *Op Max*, 227, 229, and 230.

length, is one example of where something 'easy to imagine'[49] and only mentioned in *Logic*, as outside its announced scope, is expanded systematically in *OM*.

Tentative Logic in *Logic* and *Opus Maximum*

There is another important instance in which Coleridge dilates a passage in *L*, this time into an extensive mode of argument in *OM*. *L* states that transcendental logic, based on the principles of identity and contradiction, can prove no more than 'the legitimacy of the form'. It cannot prove 'that our assertion is consistent with facts of experience, or with substantial truths, whencesoever derived'.[50] Coleridge uses this idea very effectively in *OM*, including in the section which expands the 'Essay on Faith,' frequently reminding his readers of the speculative style of his argument, its tentative logic.[51] Often these comments pertain to Coleridge's claim that his philosophical argument will not yet appeal to the authority of revelation or the Scriptures. The opening paragraph of *OM*'s 'Essay on Faith' section announces that he will proceed by the 'unaided *reason* and *understanding*' rather than argument from revelation, though we may find revelation to be the basis for the sufficiency of reason. When he occasionally cites Scripture, he specifies that he is not citing it as authoritative, but as 'fit expressions only,' as he might do from 'any other well known books'.[52] A second rhetorical aspect of Coleridge's speculative argument in this section of *OM* is his insistence that he is dealing with postulates, but not yet with fact. MS 29 part ii (Fragment 2) opens with such a careful distinction between postulates, or facts of consciousness, and any reality of perception or faith, by reminding readers that they are

still within the bounds prescribed by the mind, exerting its powers unaided on such facts[53] alone as are found within its own consciousness, and as we have been enquiring hitherto what these facts are and have not yet arrived at the point in which we can apply the deductions therefrom so as to conclude the reality of any object or article of our faith.[54]

His argument proceeds 'before we have arrived at any outward proofs, while we are yet within the limits of pure reason, and of ideas, the reality of which is still

---

[49]   *L*, 245.

[50]   *L*, 209.

[51]   *Op Max*, 208–9. I borrow the phrase from Coleridge's usage for his larger method: 'the formal algebra of dialectic, or tentative logic' (*Op Max*, 196). See also my n. 63 in its context.

[52]   *Op Max*, 57 and 88.

[53]   *Op Max* erroneously reads 'factors' here.

[54]   *Op Max*, 80.

problematic'. Importantly, we have learned 'not indeed whether a true religion exists, but what it must be, and what it cannot be, if it have, or at any future time should have, a real existence'. Such comments, all of them absent from the 'Essay on Faith', proliferate. Thus Coleridge's argument continues to proceed 'on the supposition that we shall hereafter establish the reality of a supreme being'.[55]

Both these techniques—a refusal to cite Scripture authoritatively, and a reliance on postulates and a deferral in asserting the factual reality of objects or beliefs until their ideal plausibility and coherence are established—also have a bearing on system in *OM*. Since this tentative logic is present elsewhere in *OM*,[56] these two techniques ground this section of *OM* in another aspect of this system, its pervasive style or rhetoric. The larger view of Coleridge that emerges from this rhetoric, first, complicates some stereotypes of the post-1818, 'religious Coleridge' by contesting their dogmatic implications. Religious, the content of *OM* certainly is; but these examples of the very numerous additions to a shorter, more dogmatic text, the 'Essay on Faith', underline Coleridge's larger project in *OM* as constructing a philosophy with religious implications, of presenting postulates and ideas. More doctrinal concerns are in fact put off to projected and what have proved to be, non-extant sections of *OM*.

The Absurdity of the Contrary in *Logic* and *Opus Maximum*

Negative Proof, and the Unprovable Idea of God

Another, even more complex example of Coleridge's expansion of brief passages in the *Logic* into the method of *OM* begins with his discussion of how mathematical intuitions have 'a certainty accompanied with the sense of the impossibility of the contrary'. Coleridge gives us an example: 'the perfect equality of two given [geometrical] figures' means 'that they cover each other in all points'.[57] A second and related point of contact is *Logic*'s later table of the primary conceptions of the understanding by which we perceive objects. Here Coleridge challenges the reader to find any conception prior to those listed. He continues, if the reader cannot find such,

---

[55] *Op Max*, 83 and 93; see also 95–6.
[56] See Evans, 'Reading "Will"', 92.
[57] *L*, 222.

he will by this negative proof of [the list's] completeness be disposed and prepared for proofs positive, any one of which if well grounded will in addition to the former suffice to mature the justifiable anticipation into a rational conviction, viz. that the conceptions contained in the above table *are* and are *all* the stem-conceptions of the understanding in its determination of objects and at once the necessary preconditions and the essential forms of such determination.

These two mentions in the *Logic*, of the impossibility (or absurdity) of the contrary and of negative and positive proof, blossom into a large part of the method of the argument in *OM*.[58]

An important passage in *ODI* (McFarland's Fragment 3) illuminates this practice of argument, when Coleridge refers to two kinds of negation when presenting 'ideas and conceptions, whether in the primary development of the thought or in exciting and assisting the mind of another to repeat the process'.[59] The first is negative definition—our 'negative proof'—here called 'preparative' logic, 'as in giving directions to a traveller whose immediate object lies beyond a heath where there are many paths and the one which alone he is to take is dim and unknown to him'. The first step is to 'describe the others in succession, each by some appropriate mark and still ending with "Now this you are not to take" or "None of these are your road"'. Then we may

describe the one in question positively, that is, by its proper characters, if it be in our power so to do. If not, we must leave him to find them out by himself, or to give up the object he had in view—content with having saved him in the one case from going astray, and in the other from wasting or risking the waste of his time and strength.

Coleridge calls this process 'the first use of negation'.

Coleridge uses this first kind of negation extensively in *OM*, notably in the conclusion of *ODI*.[60] Here, his strategy in proving the primacy of the idea of God is to examine each 'supposed' proof for opposing views. If he can show that each so-called proof is intrinsically false, then he can demonstrate 'our position: that there is no speculative proof, no properly scientific or logical demonstration, possible. In other words, that the idea of the Godhead is the true source and indispensable precondition of all our knowledge of God'.[61] Coleridge next goes through each purported proof concerning God and refutes it. In turn, he dismisses that we can 'know God by the *sense*' (or intuition), as if God were a geometrical figure; 'that God is space', from Rabbinical writings, where space appears as 'a symbol of God's omnipresence and infinity'; then, the view 'that we see God with our eyes', according to 'the Brahmins'. In conclusion, Coleridge previews what may be his critique of

[58] *L*, 264. The same argument reappears at *L*, 92: 'Again: there cannot be two absolutes different from each other. The supposition involves an absurdity.' I am grateful to Robin Jackson for pointing out these passages to me.

[59] *Op Max*, 253.

[60] For discussion of this passage in another context, see Evans, 'Divine Ideas', 43.

[61] *Op Max*, 273–4.

another scheme—the argument from design, proving God by His creation—and then the manuscript breaks off.[62] This series of counter-arguments exposes the impossibility or absurdity of the contrary in positions opposed to Coleridge's idea of God. Thus through this 'first use of negation', his is, by default, the last argument standing.

Tetractic Logic, Positive Proof, and Synthesis

Back, then, to our crux earlier in 'On the Divine Ideas' on two kinds of negations. The second kind he calls 'determinant' logic, 'where ... the negation is partial only, as disjunctive conjunctive', for example when 'describing the predominant hue of the opal or the occasional opalescence of the horizon at sunset': 'not a green but an intervening or combining hue, or both colours in one'. Coleridge's discourse of the 'disjunctive conjunctive' is clearly—or unclearly—exploring middle positions between two opposites. This method, Coleridge continues, is highly useful 'in all reasoning in which we proceed by antithesis, or what I have elsewhere called the logic of Trichotomy, or still more accurately, adopting both the principles and the terminology of the eldest Pythagorean school, the Tetractic'.[63] Coleridge is speaking of his adaptation of the four terms of the Pythagorean conception of God or tetractys—prothesis, thesis, antithesis, and mesothesis—to which he adds 'synthesis'. This second type of logic thus pertains to 'when we have to speak of the [point of] indifference ... of two extremes, [e.g.] in the magnet', or 'in cases of neutralization', of which there are three kinds. The first he calls indifference 'proper', as 'in water as the neutral product of oxygen and hydrogen'.[64] The second kind, what he often also calls 'synthesis', is 'a positive tertium aliquid [a "third something else"]', either a 'union of two opposites' or a 'combination with an overbalance of one component'. The last kind I have already discussed: 'prothesis', i.e., 'the identity of any two', as distinguished from the union of a thesis and antithesis—synthesis— and from their equilibrium or indifference.

In *OM*, these notions inform the highly sophisticated rhetoric of Coleridge's arguments in ways that add precision to what Seamus Perry so aptly calls the 'zigzaggery of Coleridgean prose'.[65] In this mode, Coleridge entertains a nexus of

---

[62] For each of these topics, see *Op Max*, 274–5, 275–6, 276–85, and 286–90. For a reconstruction of Coleridge's apparently missing conclusion to the MS, see Evans, 'Divine Ideas', 44–5.

[63] *Op Max*, 253, 254. He also calls this method 'the five most general Forms or Preconceptions of Constructive Logic' (*SWF*, I, 784 n. 1 and *AR*, 182) and 'the formal algebra of dialectic, or tentative logic' (*Op Max*, 196). In discussing that Coleridge sets out on 'a new triadic "logic"', Milnes mentions the Prothesis and the 'Noetic Pentad' (204–5), but his study does not examine *OM*.

[64] *Op Max*, 254. On the considerable variability of Coleridge's tetractic nomenclature, see Evans, 'Coleridge's Sublime Rhetoric'.

[65] Perry, 101. Perry is likewise interested in Coleridge's polar proclivities, but he prefers 'muddle' to 'dialectical' to label Coleridge's thinking, because the latter term's 'implications of progressively

opposites in search of a middle term, i.e., a synthesis or an indifference. He uses the two terms to generate a third.[66] For example, at the extant opening of *OM*, Coleridge uses the absurdity of the contrary as a mode of argument, beginning with a paraphrase of the point in the *Logic* on how identical figures cover the same amount of space. For geometry to proceed, we must necessarily assent to acts of imagination regarding classes of lines. If we once decide what a circle is and draw it, it would be absurd then to withhold our assent from, or imagine anything contrary to that act. For such figures, there is no opposite to their necessity. This is Coleridge's thesis. He then embeds this postulate of scientific systems in a contrast with that of his antithesis, moral systems. In these, initially there must be 'the power of withholding . . . assent'. In order to enunciate a third category of postulates, then, Coleridge suggests that we may take for granted a fact—i.e., 'an assertion respecting particulars or individuals' as contrasted with 'universal . . . positions' (as in geometry). A fact 'once taken for granted' can lead to deductions and conclusions as 'a logical truth'. He calls these conclusions 'hypothetical positions', his new, third category of postulate. Now Coleridge is ready for a genuinely new middle position. For moral truths to be, not only equal, but also superior to scientific ones, Coleridge needs an opposite of both 'hypothetical positions' grounded on fact and also 'the unconditional necessary' of the scientific position. I will not pursue Coleridge's subsequent quest for a middle position between this new thesis and antithesis, in which the moral postulate would possess some characteristics of each.[67]

To generalize, there are two benefits of his method: generating new middle terms out of existing opposites, and providing forward momentum in the construction of an argument. The vulnerability of the method is that its clarity is never crystal clear: there is always a supplement of marginal unclarity, arguably because the argument and its terminology remain on the move. In the first part of MS 29 (Fragment 4), Coleridge says as much, concerning the dynamic modification of interpenetrating and 'opposite powers', where each is 'under such a predominance of one power' that, although we may name the product, it is dynamically in 'a mid state, on tiptoe in the act of "about to pass" into the other'.[68] The remedy for lack of absolute clarity in the method is in the continuity of method: opposite terms must continue to stand 'on tiptoe', then 'pass into the other' new (and just previously latent) intermediate terms in his argument. In this technique of what Coleridge

evolving, synthetic resolution' are 'off the mark in Coleridge's case'. My discussion has suggested instead a middle position between Coleridge's 'experience and exploration of division' and 'the unity of any triumphantly pulled-off conclusion' (17).

[66] Cf. Shaffer, 'Coleridge's Revolution', 214, on Coleridge's manner of handling opposites: 'his characteristically moderate, semi-dialectical method of progressive redefinition: by multiplying slighter gradations between the two terms, they are made to approach each other'.

[67] *Op Max*, 5–8. For the larger context of argument from which this material is taken, see Evans, 'Reading 'Will'', 75–6.

[68] *Op Max*, 321.

calls 'positive proof' we can recognize his Pythagorean category of synthesis, i.e. the combination of two terms into 'a third something else'. The technique, along with the absurdity of the contrary, a species of negative proof, pervades the argument of *OM*. These modes of discourse are crucial to understanding the content of the work, particularly in its aspect as that residually 'third something else'.

The Lingering of Negative Proof: Indifference

Conceptualizing Coleridge's 'Divine Idea', then, is possible; but his presentation of it will remain unduly opaque for readers of *OM* without an appreciation of its tetractic logic in action, in the rhetoric of his argument. For example, at the end of MS 29 (Fragment 2), with great sophistication Coleridge uses absurdity of the contrary, that mention in *L* expanded in *OM* to a whole system of thought. If the opening of the MS,[69] discussed above, often uses synthesis in its discovery of new middle terms, its conclusion also uses indifference in a sometimes eerie suspension of thesis and antithesis. Here, for example, Coleridge presents two contrasting visions. The one is of a world of 'alterity', of meaningful distinctions, underwritten by the alterity of the Father and the Son:

we have only to learn that in this other [the Son] all others are included, that in this first substantial intelligible distinction (ὄ Λογος) all other distinctions that can subsist in the indivisible unity (Λογοι θειοι) or[70] contain it, are included, to see at the same moment that under the form of being [the Logos]—that is, under being as not only the essence but as the form of the essence—all is completed.[71]

In context, Coleridge urges us into a meditative state: that 'we have only to learn', and we are 'to see at the same moment' the source of all *others*, all distinctions, and all completions. With this vision he contrasts an alternate vision of the absurdity of the contrary, the absence of the positive proof of the preceding affirmations:

the very attempt to pass beyond it is to plunge instantly from light into mere unsubstantial darkness, [where] our words have not only no correspondence in reality but none in idea, conception, image, or act, that is absolute nonsense.

Here is an image of dark isolation—another invitation to a meditative state— where words have no objective purchase in so many domains: reality, idea, conception, image, act. (Coleridge's phrase elsewhere for this sort of vision is 'a – [negative] seeing'.[72]) The combination of the two contrasting views is, arguably, an 'indifference': a kind of vision, positive and negative, of otherness,

---

[69] *Op Max*, 5–11.
[70] The MS reads 'or' here, where *Op Max* omits it.
[71] *Op Max*, 207.
[72] *CN*, IV, 4855.

distinction, form and being—and of their absence. The passage is not the conclusion of his argument, but this indifference suspends the two visions for the reader's contemplation on the way to that conclusion. My larger point is that the indifference here hangs on the absurdity of the contrary and negative proof ('that is absolute nonsense'), terms from the *Logic* which Coleridge enacts in *OM* to haunting rhetorical effect.

COLERIDGE AS THINKER: RELIGION AND SYSTEM, REVISITED

In conclusion, then, McFarland's assertion is technically true, that Coleridge apparently removed *L* as logical treatise from his grand plans for *OM*. But *L*'s missing third part on the Noetic is the domain of much of *OM*; and as we have seen, *OM* fulfils *L* in a number of ways. First, *L*'s mention of the verb substantive becomes the governing idea, the Divine Idea, of *OM*, whose repetition in multifold contexts drives the 'prothetic rhetoric' of its arguments. That some, like Christensen, have found this repetition obscure in its apparent collapse of distinction is, in part, belied by our ability to conceptualize the main themes of *OM*'s argument: the finite will in conscience, Absolute Will and the Divine Tetractys, and the divine ideas. But that residual unclarity in *OM* is illuminated by two other ways in which the text fulfils *L*. First, *L*'s statement focusing on form as distinct from consistency with experience or truth becomes that recurring technique of tentative logic in *OM*, where Coleridge declines to cite Scripture authoritatively, instead relying on postulates and deferring any insistence on the factual reality of objects or beliefs until establishing their ideal plausibility and coherence. Second, *L*'s mentions of the absurdity of the contrary becomes in *OM* part of a pervasive system of rhetoric of positive and negative proof: on the indemonstrability of the idea of God in *ODI*, in the dialectical quest for the primary postulate in the opening of MS 29, and at its conclusion, in the 'indifferent' vision of alterity and its nonsensical absence.

My nuanced consideration of the relationship between *L* and *OM* has also thus yielded insights that revise our current knowledge of a number of perennial issues for Coleridge and Romantics scholarship—on Coleridge's obscurity, on his disbelief in single subjectivity, and on the status of religion and system in Coleridge. For the correspondence in different modes of passages in *L* and *OM* reveals a shared system of thought between the two texts, in spite of their different emphases. For detractors of the existence of system in Coleridge's thought, moreover, the news is not good in a broader way. There is, as I have shown, a conceptual coherence in even a fragmentary *OM*, and my examples form part of a larger and systematic sweep of argument, in MS 29 for example, beginning with Coleridge's establishing of his postulates, and culminating, step by step, in his elaboration of the Tetractys. Finally, not only the content of *OM* is systematic, but so also is its rhetoric, in the pervasive presence of its 'tetractic' logic.

So when we consider Coleridge in the 1820s as thinker in these two texts, he emerges as a much more systematic thinker than often hitherto thought. What is more, while he is certainly a *religious* thinker, obliquely in *L* and overtly in *OM*, his tentative logic complicates any stereotypes of Coleridge as dogmatic religious thinker. For at the end of his argument in MS 29, Coleridge is evidently still using indifference as a technique, with its puzzling backtracking from ultimate certainty. This recurring dynamic of negative proof is one important clue that he did not regard his philosophy as a closed system, or an ultimate one. *OM*'s combined use of the *synthetic* system-building of positive proof with the *indifferent* and agnostic effect of negative proof lets him have his cake and eat it too. His system in the *Opus Maximum* is formidable; but his rhetoric prevents us from confusing his system with the sublime realities which it enacted, and to which it finally—inadequately—pointed.[73]

WORKS CITED

BARBEAU, JEFFREY W., ed. 2006a. *Coleridge's Assertion of Religion: Essays on the* Opus Maximum. Leuven, Paris and Dudley MA: Peeters.

—— 2006b. The quest for system: an introduction to Coleridge's lifelong project. In Barbeau, *Coleridge's Assertion*, 1–32.

BARTH, J., and ROBERT, S. J. 1969. *Coleridge and Christian Doctrine.* Cambridge, Mass.: Harvard University Press.

BOULGER, JAMES D. 1961. *Coleridge as Religious Thinker.* New Haven: Yale University Press.

CHRISTENSEN, JEROME. 1995. The Method of *The Friend*. In *Rhetorical Traditions and British Romantic Literature*, ed. Don H. Bialostosky and Lawrence D. Needham. Bloomington and Indianapolis: Indiana University Press, pp. 11–27.

COLE, STEVEN E. 1991. The Logic of Personhood: Coleridge and the Production of Social Agency. *Studies in Romanticism*, 30: 85–111.

COLERIDGE, SAMUEL TAYLOR. 1959. *The Collected Letters of Samuel Taylor Coleridge. Vol. III. 1807–1814*, ed. Earl Leslie Griggs. Oxford: Clarendon Press.

—— 1993. *The Collected Works of Samuel Taylor Coleridge: Aids to Reflection*, ed. John Beer. Bollingen Series 75 (9). London and Princeton: Routledge and Princeton University Press. Cited as *AR*.

—— 1987. *The Collected Works of Samuel Taylor Coleridge: Lectures 1808–19: On Literature*, ed. R. A. Foakes. Bollingen Series 75 (5). London and Princeton: Routledge and Princeton University Press.

[73] I am grateful for the generous support of The University of Winnipeg in providing research and travel monies in support of this research.

—— 2000. *The Collected Works of Samuel Taylor Coleridge: Lectures 1818–19: On the History of Philosophy*, ed. J. R. de J. Jackson. Bollingen Series 75 (8). London and Princeton: Routledge and Princeton University Press.

—— 1981. *The Collected Works of Samuel Taylor Coleridge: Logic*, ed. J. R. de J. Jackson. Bollingen Series 75 (13). London and Princeton: Routledge & Kegan Paul and Princeton University Press.

—— 2002. *The Collected Works of Samuel Taylor Coleridge: Opus Maximum*, ed. Thomas McFarland, with the assistance of Nicholas Halmi. Bollingen Series 75 (15). Princeton NJ: Princeton University Press.

—— 1995. *The Collected Works of Samuel Taylor Coleridge: Shorter Works and Fragments*, ed. H. J. Jackson and J. R. de J. Jackson. Bolingen Series 75 (11). London and Princeton: Routledge and Princeton University Press.

—— 1990. *The Notebooks of Samuel Taylor Coleridge. 4. 1819–1826. Text*, ed. Kathleen Coburn and Merton Christensen. Bollingen Series 50. Princeton: Princeton University Press. Cited as *CNiv*.

EVANS, MURRAY J. 2003. The divine ideas in Coleridge's *Opus Maximum*. *The Coleridge Bulletin*, New Series, 22: 39–47.

—— —— Reading 'Will' in Coleridge's *Opus Maximum*: The Rhetoric of Transition and Repetition, in Barbeau, *Coleridge's Assertion*, 73–95.

HALMI, NICHOLAS. 2007. Nicholas Halmi reads *Coleridge's Assertion of Religion: Essays on the* Opus Maximum (Leuven: Peeters, 2006) by Jeffrey Barbeau. *The Coleridge Bulletin*, New Series, 30: 48–50.

McKUSICK, JAMES C. 1986. *Coleridge's Philosophy of Language*. New Haven: Yale University Press.

McFARLAND, THOMAS. 1969. *Coleridge and the Pantheist Tradition*. Oxford: Clarendon Press.

MERRISON, JOANNE. 1998. The death of the poet: Coleridge and the science of logic. *The Third Culture: Literature and Science*, ed. Elinor S. Shaffer. Berlin and New York: Walter De Gruyter, 170–81.

MILNES, TIM. 2003. *Knowledge and Indifference in English Romantic Prose*. Cambridge: Cambridge University Press.

MUIRHEAD, JOHN H. 1930. *Coleridge as Philosopher*. Repr. 1954. London and New York: George Allen & Unwin and Humanities Press.

PERKINS, MARY ANNE. 1994. *Coleridge's Philosophy: The Logos as Unifying Principle*. Oxford: Clarendon Press.

PERRY, SEAMUS. 1999. *Coleridge and the Uses of Division*. Oxford: Clarendon Press.

REID, NICHOLAS. 2006. *Coleridge, Form and Symbol, or The Ascertaining Vision*. Aldershot: Ashgate Press.

—— 1994. Coleridge and Schelling: the missing transcendental deduction. *Studies in Romanticism*, 33: 451–79.

SHAFFER, ELINOR S. 1969. Coleridge's revolution in the standard of taste. *Journal in Art and Aesthetic Criticism*, 28: 213–21.

SNYDER, ALICE D. 1929. *Coleridge on Logic and Learning, with Selections from the Unpublished Manuscripts*. New Haven: Yale University Press.

PART III

THE POETIC WORKS

CHAPTER 18

COLERIDGE ON ALLEGORY AND SYMBOL

NICHOLAS HALMI

DESYNONYMIZATION

As befits a thinker who identified social progress with linguistic precision, Coleridge was preoccupied with questions of definition and distinction in philosophical and critical terminology. Because words are not only 'the instruments of communication' but 'the only signs that a finite being can have of its own thoughts', he explained in his philosophical lecture of 8 January 1819, their signification becomes more specific as human thought becomes more complex, 'in proportion as what was conceived as one and identical becomes several' (*Lects Phil*, i. 212). Although this process occurs naturally, 'new relations' in thought necessitating 'new distinctions' in language, it gains in accuracy and clarity when it is performed actively and self-reflexively, which is to say philosophically. To 'desynonymize' words is therefore nothing less than the philosopher's social responsibility (*Lects Phil*, ii. 553–4).

It was a responsibility that Coleridge himself took seriously, formulating and defending distinctions between (to name only the better known examples) imagination and fancy, primary and secondary imagination, reason and understanding, intuitive and discursive reason, fancy and wit, genius and talent, imitation and copy, organic and mechanic form, illusion and delusion, abstraction and generalization, and not least symbol and allegory. But while these distinctions were supposed to be purely instrumental, improving the functioning of language 'as an organ and a vehicle of thought' (*Lects Phil*, ii. 553), they in fact became objects of interpretation and debate in themselves, and indeed may be said to constitute a large part of Coleridge's critical legacy. When he facetiously asked Coleridge the public intellectual to 'explain his Explanation' (*Don Juan*, dedication), Lord Byron could scarcely have imagined that critics of the following century would earnestly take it upon themselves to perform exactly that service.

Criticisms of Coleridge's desynonymizing fall under three broad categories: the empirical, the conceptual, and the ethical. The famous distinction between imagination and fancy, for example, has been discredited as an irrelevance to the explication of poetry (Hardy 1951), dismissed as an idiosyncratic juxtaposition of German idealist with British associationist terminology (both of which in any event belong to a superseded faculty psychology), and distrusted as an 'attempt to keep empirical and associationist thought undisturbed in a subordinate position below an idealist system' (Wellek 1955–92: ii. 164–5). Similar complaints of empirical unverifiability, conceptual confusion, and the ethically dubious promotion of a hierarchy under the guise of an opposition have been levelled—and not unjustly— against the Coleridgean distinction most contested in recent decades, that between the symbol, as a non-discursive and synecdochical form of representation, and allegory, as the discursive representation of abstractions through unrelated images of no inherent significance.

The handful of instances, all dating to the decade between 1816 and 1825, in which Coleridge contrasted allegory unfavourably with the symbol reflect neither the full range of his comments on allegory, for they were often sympathetic, nor his own willingness to resort to the mode (see Gatta 1977). He thought well enough of his 'Allegoric Vision' (1795), a satirical narrative involving personified abstractions, to reprint it no fewer than three times between 1811 and 1829 (the last in his *Poetical Works*), revising it as he did so in order to accommodate his changed political and religious views (*Lects 1795*, 89–93; *EOT*, ii. 262–70; *LS*, 131–7; *PW*, i. 197–203). But his subordination of allegory to the symbol has received a disproportionate amount of attention because of its conformity to a theoretical disposition that, having found its earliest expression among certain of Coleridge's German contemporaries, notably Goethe and Schelling, persisted among artists and critics well into the twentieth century. Indeed W. B. Yeats not only affirmed this disposition but assimilated to it, as had Coleridge himself in *The Statesman's Manual* (1816), the distinction between imagination and fancy: 'A symbol is indeed the only possible expression of some invisible essence, a transparent lamp about a spiritual flame; while allegory is one of many possible representations of an embodied thing, and belongs to fancy and not to imagination' (Yeats 1903: 116; see also Halmi 2007*b*: 2–3).

When Paul de Man, in his influential essay 'The Rhetoric of Temporality', criticized Coleridge for obfuscating the painful truth, supposedly enacted in Romantic allegory as a self-conscious 'distance in relation to its own origin', that a sign can never coincide temporally with its referent, the broader target of his critique was nothing less than 'wide areas of European literature of the nineteenth and twentieth centuries'—the self-styled symbolist movement—as well as the correlative criticism that accepted unquestioningly the superiority of the symbol to allegory (de Man 1969: 191). Coleridge was simply the foremost anglophone representative of this particular form of 'tenacious self-mystification'. That more is at stake in the distinction between symbol and allegory than Coleridge's perspicacity is acknowledged equally, if less explicitly, in the vehemence with which critics sympathetic to him have responded to de Man's provocation—chiefly by declaring the concept of the symbol theological in essence or provenance (or both) and therefore of no proper concern to literary critics (e.g., Abrams 1974; Barth 1977; McFarland 1990), a gesture no more effective in the event than Tosca's urging Cavaradossi to flee after what was supposed to have been his mock execution. To defend Coleridge's concept of the symbol is to affirm the vision, or at least the hope, of a world endowed with an inherent numinousness (cf. Barth 1977: 163–4).

COLERIDGE'S EARLY SYMBOLIST THEORY

Coleridge's originality having been impugned repeatedly almost from the beginning of the nineteenth century, much scholarship has been devoted to identifying, with varying degrees of plausibility, the sources of and influences on his thought. But while the parallels to Coleridge's concept of the symbol among his German contemporaries have often been noted (e.g., by Wellek 1955–92: ii. 174–5; Ward 1966; McFarland 1981: 26–34; Halmi 2007*b*: ch. 1), surprisingly little attention has been given to possible sources of his distinction between symbol and allegory, despite its relatively late appearance in his writings. It is likely that this desynonymization of two terms he had not previously treated as synonyms was intended to bring into sharper relief what he had come, by 1816, to consider the defining characteristic of the symbol: the grounding of its representational function in a relation of ontological participation. For only when he began to assert that the symbol is a *part* of what it represents did he also begin to differentiate it from allegory.

That this distinctively Romantic concept of the symbol evidently required a foil, and that the concept of allegory was available to serve as such, may be attributed to a burdensome inheritance from Enlightenment semiotics, a general anxiety about representation. An unmistakable manifestation of this anxiety, present equally in the eighteenth-century theorization of allegory and the Romantic theorization of the symbol, was the view of the relationship between sign and meaning as necessarily problematic because it straddled the ontological barrier between the realm outside the human mind and the realm inside it. The corollary of that assumption, no less compelling for its paradoxicality, was that signification could be successful only where it seemed not to occur at all—that is, where a sign became completely transparent to its meaning. Such transparency was ascribed to so-called natural signs because their signifying power, being based on causal or mimetic relations, was thought to inhere in them rather than, as in the case of artificial or conventional signs, to require a human act of institution. Natural signs were therefore, in theory, intuitively and universally recognizable. Artificial signs—a class to which eighteenth-century critics invariably assigned allegorical images—were, by contrast, culturally specific and therefore at risk of being ambiguous, incomprehensible, or simply unrecognizable.

But while the concept of the natural sign defined the ideal against which all signs were to be judged, it could not simply be invoked in reaction against the disenchantment of the world, by which I mean the loss, felt as a loss, of the sense that the natural world possesses an inherent numinousness or divinely ordained significance accessible to humanity. For natural signs revealed no more than the source of their communicative function: smoke was a sign merely of fire, a symptom a sign merely of a disease, a baby's cry a sign merely of the baby's distress. What the philosopher George Berkeley called the 'visual language' of natural signs may have been divinely ordained, in that it was grounded in the nature of things, but it possessed no metaphysical content.[1]

Already in the 1790s Coleridge began to confront the difficulty of theorizing the numinousness of nature, which is to say of reconceiving the natural sign as a natural symbol. He may have had Berkeley in mind when he declared, in a note of *c*.1795, 'We see our God everywhere—the Universe in the most literal Sense is his written Language' (*Lects 1795*, 339)—a declaration in which precisely the words *literal, written*, and *Language* cannot be taken literally—but this early conception of a universal symbolism was indebted primarily to Mark Akenside's didactic poem *The Pleasures of Imagination* (1744), which, elaborating the analogy between the human artist and the divine creator, identified the appreciation of God's handiwork with the powers of imagination. Indeed in his first 'Lecture on Revealed Religion', delivered in May 1795—the same lecture in which his 'Allegoric Vision' made its first appearance as an attack on atheism and Anglicanism—Coleridge followed Akenside almost verbatim: 'The Omnipotent has unfolded to us the Volume of the World, that there we may read the Transcript of himself. In Earth or Air the meadow's purple stores, the Moons mild radiance, or the Virgins form

---

[1] Berkeley referred to the 'language' of nature in, e.g., *A New Theory of Vision* (1709), §147, and *The Theory of Vision... Vindicated and Explained* (1733), §§38–40. See Halmi 2007*b*: 53–62, and Wellbery 1984: 24–30, for fuller analysis of the concept of the natural sign in Enlightenment semiotics.

Blooming with rosy smiles, we see pourtrayed the bright Impressions of the eternal Mind' (*Lects 1795*, 94; cf. p. 158).[2]

In poems of the 1790s, too, Coleridge emphasized the morally educative effects of learning to recognize the representation of Providence in nature. The lines he contributed to book 2 of Robert Southey's *Joan of Arc* (1795) and later republished in his own poem 'The Destiny of Nations' (1817) stated this theme forthrightly:

> For all that meets the bodily sense I deem
> Symbolical, one mighty alphabets
> For infant minds; and we in this low worlds
> Placed with our backs to bright Reality,
> That we may learn with young unwounded ken
> Things from their shadows...
>
> (2. 19–24; *PW*, i. 210; cf. p. 282)

And three years later, in 'Frost at Midnight', he promised his infant son Hartley,

> so shalt thou see and hear
> The lovely shapes and sounds intelligible
> Of that eternal language, why thy God
> Utters, who from eternity doth teach
> Himself in all, and all things in himself.
>
> (lines 63–7; Coleridge 2003: 121)

The force of this promise lay in the experience, as claimed *in propria persona* in 'Fears in Solitude' (also of 1798), of having himself learned morality from the English landscape:

> from thy lakes and mountains-hills,
> Thy clouds, thy quiet dales, thy rocks and seas,
> Have drunk in all my intellectual life,
> All sweet sensations, all ennobling thoughts,
> All adoration of the God in Nature,
> All lovely and all honourable things....
>
> (lines 181–6; Coleridge 2003: 114–15)

Yet a secondhand natural theology resting uneasily on Shaftesburian Neoplatonism, analogizing Christian apologetics, and the eighteenth-century cult of artistic genius would not suffice permanently. In 1802, criticizing the poet William Lisle Bowles (whose sonnets he had earlier admired) for an inability 'to see or describe

---

[2] Cf. *The Pleasures of Imagination*, 1.99–107: 'To these [sc. of 'higher hopes'] the sire omnipotent unfolds / The world's harmonious volume, there to read / The transcript of himself. On every part / They trace the bright impressions of his hand: / In earth or air, the meadow's purple stores, / The moon's mild radiance, or the virgin's form / Blooming with rosy smiles, they see portray'd / That uncreated beauty, which delights / The mind supreme' (Akenside 1996: 94). On Akenside's moralizing celebration of imagination (itself indebted to the third earl of Shaftesbury's *Moralists* (1711)) and its importance to Coleridge, see Engell (1981: 42–7).

any interesting appearances in nature, without connecting it by dim analogies with the moral world', Coleridge insisted that 'A Poet's *Heart & Intellect* should be *combined, intimately* combined & *unified*, with the great Appearances in Nature—& not merely held in solution & loose mixture with them, in the shape of formal Similies' (*CL*, ii. 864; cf. Wilson 1972: 44). But the poet could express this unity—'we are all *one Life*'—only so long as he was convinced of its truth, and by 1805, as a remarkable notebook entry indicates, Coleridge's conviction was evidently wavering. The language of nature had become an object of earnest hope and uncertain apprehension:

In looking at objects of Nature while I am thinking, as at yonder moon dim-glimmering thro' the dewy window, I seem rather to be seeking, as it were *asking*, a symbolical language for something within me that already and forever exists, than observing any thing new. Even when that latter is the case, yet still I have always an obscure feeling as if that new phænomenon were the dim Awaking of a forgotten or hidden Truth of my inner Nature/It is still interesting as a Word, a Symbol! It is Λογος, the Creator! <and the Evolver!>.   (*CN*, ii. 2546)

Because Akenside for his part had assumed a pre-established harmony between mind and nature as the basis of the analogy between God and artist, he regarded the natural world as significant only in so far as it stimulated the imagination to form its own world, in effect an alternative to nature. Precisely that assumption of a pre-established harmony was now in question for Coleridge, however, and in need of empirical confirmation—in nature itself and prior to any imaginative act by the observer. In the *Biographia Literaria* he would argue, following Schelling, that the original identity of subject and object must be assumed as the basis of knowledge (*BL*, i. 252–3, 271, 279, 285), but he nonetheless hoped (as Schelling too did) that it might also be realized in the sensible world. Thus the symbolic language Coleridge demanded had to be at once objectively real and subjectively meaningful, non-discursive yet expressive of something greater than itself. Such a language obviously could not consist in artificial signs, but nor could it consist in natural signs, at least as defined in Enlightenment semiotics.

A decade was to pass before Coleridge arrived at a provisional solution to the problem of conceptualizing the natural symbol, and that solution involved two categorial conflations: one of the relations part/whole and identity/difference, the other of linguistic and non-linguistic representation. The first conflation was intimated in a notebook entry of 1811 or earlier in which Coleridge struggled to decide whether 'thoughts' or 'symbols'—he used the two terms synonymously in this instance—were parts of, substitutes for, or coterminous with things (*CN*, iii. 4058). The second conflation was intimated in another notebook entry, this time of 1815, in which he defined the symbol by reference to a quotation from Phineas Fletcher's allegorical poem *The Purple Island* (1633): 'Symbols = "the whole, yet of the whole a part"' (*CN*, iii. 4253).[3] Wellek, who understood the symbol to be a figure of substitution, and hence metaphorical, noted exasperatedly that Coleridge 'seems to confuse symbol and synecdoche', the latter 'a figure of continuity from which symbol cannot even develop' (1955–92: ii. 174).

Once, however, Coleridge had settled on this basic synecdochical definition of the symbol, he tended to treat all instances of the general semiotic phenomenon (that is, whatever he labelled symbolic) as functionally equivalent, regardless of context and despite the difference in kind between linguistic and non-linguistic representation. In one of the few examples he offered of a 'symbolical Expression', 'Here comes a *Sail*—that is, a Ship' (*CN*, iii. 4503; *Lects 1808–19*, ii. 418), only the *referents* of the words *sail* and *ship* are ontologically related, while the words themselves are artificial signs with no inherent connection to one another—a fact Coleridge ignored. On the other hand, when 'a single tree or flower' is perceived to be 'a natural symbol of that higher life of reason' (*LS*, 72), the signifying function derives from the ontological connection of the visible object itself to the invisible force directing its development. Yet Coleridge's de facto dissolution of distinctions among types of semiotic operations, not to mention ontological realms (human texts, natural objects), was entirely characteristic of Romantic symbolist theory—he was no greater an offender of logic in this respect than Schelling—and reflective of an inclination to extend the symbol's domain to the whole of reality (see Halmi 2007*b*: 17–19). For naturalizing the symbol as a potentially ubiquitous mode of representation was the theoretical prerequisite to affirming nature as symbolic.

SYMBOL VS ALLEGORY

As if in agreement with Yeats's assertion that '[o]nly one symbol exists, though the reflecting mirrors make many appear and all different' (1937: 240), Coleridge did not distinguish types of symbolism when, in *The Statesman's Manual*, he sought to inform the English 'higher classes' that the correct understanding of both nature and scripture required 'the study of the science and language of *symbols*' (*LS*, 79). But he did take trouble—for the first time—to distinguish symbols from the 'phantom proxies' of allegorical imagery: 'by a symbol I mean, not a metaphor

---

[3] Strictly speaking, the term *synecdoche* may be applied to any trope in which a less inclusive stands for a more inclusive term, or vice versa (part for whole, singular for plural, species for genus, particular for general, etc.). But Coleridge implicitly included cause/effect relations in this class by defining natural phenomena as symbols of an immanently operating divine reason (*LS*, 72, 79), and the distinction between part/whole and cause/effect substitutions remains ambiguous in semiotics, though the latter are normally considered metonymical (see Eco 1984: 116–17).

of allegory or any other figure of speech or form of fancy, but an actual and essential part of that, the whole of which it represents' (*LS*, 30, 79). In other words, whereas allegories merely substitute fictional images for abstract ideas, symbols convey something beyond or greater than themselves precisely because of what they are in themselves.

That Coleridge introduced this distinction in order to clarify, in the first instance, the peculiarity of imagery in the Hebrew Bible has been interpreted as evidence of his indebtedness to the eighteenth-century bishop Robert Lowth for the concept of the symbol (Engell 1989: 95; Engell 1999: 135–9). In his Oxford lectures *On the Sacred Poetry of the Hebrews* (1753), the original Latin edition of which Coleridge borrowed from the Bristol Library in September 1796 (Whalley 1949: 123), Lowth had defined 'mystical allegory', in contradistinction to those forms of allegory in which the literal meaning serves solely as the medium of the figurative meaning, as referring equally to historical realities and sacred truths (1753: 97). For his part Coleridge maintained that the symbolism of the Old Testament possesses 'a two-fold significance, a past and a future, a temporary and a perpetual, a particular and a universal' (*LS*, 30; cf. p. 49). But if Lowth indeed influenced Coleridge, the extent of that influence is difficult to assess for several reasons.

First, Coleridge's claims for the symbol were more expansive, with respect to both their contexts and (as will be examined below) their constitution, than Lowth's for mystical allegory. Symbols, after all, were supposed to be observable not only in scripture but in nature and in secular art and literature. To be sure, Coleridge was reluctant to designate the symbol an aesthetic product. When, in *The Statesman's Manual*, he attributed their creation to the faculty of imagination, he was referring specifically to the divinely inspired prophets (*LS*, 29); and in a literary lecture of March 1819, as if to avoid impugning the objectivity of their significance, he questioned whether they could be created fully consciously: 'it is very possible that *the general truth* represented may be working unconsciously in the Poet's mind during the construction of the Symbol' (*Lects 1808–19*, ii. 418). The inadequacy of Coleridge's very few attempts to expound the concept of the symbol with illustrations from literature, such as a reference to the humour of *Tristram Shandy* (*Lects 1808–19*, ii. 417–18), suggest that he was little interested in accounting for the possible literary use of symbols.

Nonetheless, he chose to contrast the symbol with allegory, which by the eighteenth century was classified not only as a trope or an interpretive method, as had been the case since antiquity, but also as a distinct literary genre. Coleridge clearly shared Lowth's basic conception of allegory as narrative devoid of intrinsic interest, continuously directing the beholder's attention to a meaning outside itself. But he was hardly dependent on Lowth for this conception, which was a commonplace derived from classical rhetorical theory and mediated through Enlightenment semiotics. Closely identified with the use of artificial signs, allegory was held in generally low esteem in eighteenth-century criticism and was expected to compensate for the limitations of its nature by rendering its meaning as transparently as possible (see Halmi 2007*b*: 8–10). Consequently, the least interesting allegories were judged the most successful. De Man's claim that late-Enlightenment allegory soberly accepted the irrecoverable anteriority of its meaning to its narrative would have come as news to the practitioners of the genre.

Finally, notwithstanding the genuine affinities between Lowth's concept of mystical allegory and Coleridge's of the symbol, there is no evidence that Coleridge reread *De sacra poesi Hebræorum* after 1796. On the other hand, there is no question that before 1816 he read at least one work in which the symbol and allegory were explicitly contrasted, August Wilhelm Schlegel's *Lectures on Dramatic Art and Literature* (as is noted by Ward 1966: 24–5; and Halmi 2007*a*: 138–9). Although both Goethe's essay 'On the Subjects of the Fine Arts' (1797), in which the contrast was first adumbrated, and Schelling's lectures on the philosophy of art (1802–3), in which it was elaborated with Goethe's encouragement, remained unpublished till after Coleridge's death, Schlegel's lectures (published in three volumes between 1809 and 1811) had been given to him no later than December 1811 (*CL*, iii. 359–60; *Lects 1808–19*, i. 353–4) and provided him with material for his own lectures of 1812–13 (see *Lects 1808–19*, i, pp. lix–lxiv, 172–5; and Chapter 10 of this *Handbook*). Thus in so far as any text can be identified as the immediate source of Coleridge's distinction, the most plausible candidate is Schlegel's sixth lecture, in which the figures of the gods in Greek literature are described as symbolic but not allegorical: 'Allegory is the personification of an idea, a fable solely undertaken with such a view; but that is symbolical which has been created by the imagination for other purposes, or which has a reality in itself independent of the idea, but which at the same time is easily susceptible of a symbolical explanation [*einer sinnbildlichen Auslegung sich willig fügt*]; and even of itself suggests it' (Schlegel 1815: i. 105; Schlegel 1962–74: v. 81). Here too, however, the parallel is inexact, for Coleridge did not follow Schlegel in applying the distinction to Greek literature till almost a decade after he had adopted it in his biblical exegesis and natural philosophy.

TAUTEGORY

Coleridge made two principal contributions to Romantic theorization of the symbol, both made in *The Statesman's Manual* and both, characteristically, terminological. One was to coin the word *tautegorical* to emphasize the difference between the symbol and allegory; the other, which has been the source of considerable misunderstanding, was to describe the symbol as *consubstantial* with its referent. The former term, created by combining the Greek adjective *tautos* ('identical') or noun *tauto* (a contraction of *to auto*, 'the same') with the verb *agoreuein* ('to speak in the assembly')—by analogy to *allegoria* (from *allos*, 'other', + *agoreuein*)—was introduced to the world in what would have been its original form, appropriately declined, had it been a genuine Greek word.[4] By way of criticizing contemporary exegetes for failing to appreciate the nature of biblical imagery, Coleridge inserted into his explanation of the symbol a parenthesis that may be translated 'which is always tautegorical':

> Now an Allegory is but a translation of abstract notions into a picture-language which is itself nothing but an abstraction from objects of the senses . . . On the other hand a Symbol (ὅ ἐστιν ἀεὶ ταυτηγόρικον) is characterized by the translucence of the Special in the Individual or of the General in the Especial or of the Universal in the General. Above all by the translucence of the Eternal through and in the Temporal. It always partakes of the Reality which it renders intelligible; and while it enunciates the whole, abides itself a living part in that Unity, of which it is the representative.   (*LS*, 30)

Returning to this theme nine years later in *Aids to Reflection* (1825), Coleridge anglicized and defined his neologism: '*tautegorical* (i.e. expressing the *same* subject [as itself] but with a *difference*) in contra-distinction from metaphors and similitudes, that are always *allegorical* (i.e. expressing a *different* subject but with a resemblance)' (*AR*, 206). Still in 1825, in a lecture before the Royal Society of Literature, Coleridge turned from the Hebrew prophets to the Greek gods, arguing that the figure of Prometheus in Aeschylus' *Prometheus Bound* was 'tautegorical' by virtue of embodying a 'philosopheme', a proto-philosophical meaning that could neither have been expressed otherwise nor imputed arbitrarily (*SW&F*, ii. 1267–8, 1280). (This argument, influenced by Schelling's *On the Deities of Samothrace* (1815), represented a revision of his earlier, uniformly negative judgement of Greek myth (as in *CL*, ii. 865–6).) Curiously, however, Coleridge did not oppose symbol and allegory as rigorously in the lecture on Prometheus as he did in *Aids to Reflection* or as he had previously: referring to myths of 'Jove's intrigues with Europa, Io, &c.', he conceded without elaboration that the 'symbol fades away into allegory', as if they were stages along a representational continuum, although he also added that even while fading the symbol 'never ceases wholly to be a symbol or tautegory' (*SW&F*, ii. 1280; see also Harding 1995: ch. 9).

Published in 1834, 'On the *Prometheus* of Aeschylus' eventually caught the attention of Schelling, who was sufficiently impressed by Coleridge's coinage to appropriate it—with a footnote acknowledging the irony of the fact—in one of his own lectures on Greek myth: 'Mythology is not *allegorical* but *tautegorical* [*tautegorisch*].

---

[4] Hedley (2000: 134) suggests that Coleridge may have encountered the related noun *tautotès* ('identity'), used by Plato and Aristotle, in John Smith's *Select Discourses* (1660: 97), which Coleridge first read in Sicily in 1804 (*CN*, ii. 2164–7 and nn.).

In it the gods are actually existing beings whose *existence* is not different from their *meaning*, for they mean *only* what they are' (1856–61: xi. 195–6 (my trans.); see also Halmi 2005). Although by the early 1840s, when Schelling started lecturing on the philosophy of mythology, the concept of the symbol as such had long since lost its centrality in his thought, he recognized Coleridge's 'apposite term' as encapsulating what he himself now taught about the Greek gods in particular and had once taught about symbols in general: that their meaning is the same as, because it inheres in, their ontological content.

CONSUBSTANTIALITY

For Coleridge, as for Schelling, the identity of the symbol with its referent was grounded in its participation in its referent: that is, the symbol was tautegorical because it was synecdochical. But Coleridge alone, in *The Statesman's Manual*, used the theologically fraught adjective *consubstantial* as a synonym of *synecdochical*: 'Imagination . . . incorporating the Reason in Images of the Sense, and organizing (as it were) the flux of the Senses by the permanence and self-circling energies of the Reason, gives birth to a system of symbols, harmonious in themselves, and consubstantial with the truths, of which they are the *conductors*' (*LS*, 29). Since a central point of the *Manual* was to establish the equivalence of the Bible with 'another book, likewise a revelation of God—the great book of his servant Nature' (*LS*, 70; cf. pp. 49–50), in so far as both consisted in symbols, it was daring of Coleridge to apply to the symbol, and hence to the relationship of natural phenomena to divine reason, a term with exclusively Christological associations. But it was precisely because of one of those associations, if not the other, that the term was useful to him.

In the creed recited in the Anglican Communion, Christ is affirmed as 'the only-begotten Son of God, Begotten of his Father before all worlds, God of God, Light of Light, Very God of very God, Begotten, not made, being of one substance with the Father, By whom all things were made'. This periphrasis expresses the sense that the word *consubstantial* (Greek *homoousios*) had acquired in Trinitarian theology as a result of the early Church's concern to assert the orthodoxy of the doctrine of Christ's divinity. Whatever else might be said of it, the relationship between the Father and the Son was distinguishable in kind from that between the Creator and the creation: 'All Beings are *Created*', as Coleridge himself summarized the matter, 'save the Father, from whom all are, and the Son, eternally begotten of the Father, and the uncreated Spirit eternally proceeding—and the Father, the Son and the Spirit are the one only God' (*CM*, ii. 732). Thus there was no more forceful way of claiming the ontological connection of the symbol to its referent than by describing that connection as consubstantial, albeit at the cost of dissolving the distinction between *generatio ex Deo* and *creatio ex nihilo* on which Trinitarian orthodoxy was founded. (For a fuller consideration of the theological contexts and implications of Coleridge's use of the word *consubstantial*, see Halmi 2007*b*: 110–20.)

Coleridge's natural philosophy, to the extent it embraced the concept of the consubstantial symbol, might have come into open conflict with his theology if he had accepted the Lutheran doctrine of consubstantiation, according to which the body and blood of Christ coexist with the original substance of the consecrated bread and wine in the Eucharist. But while referring to the Eucharist, from the 1820s till his death, as a symbol and defining it as 'a part, or particular instance selected as representative of the whole, of which whole however it is itself an actual, or real part' (*CM*, i. 862), Coleridge steadfastly disallowed the sacramental elements the consubstantiality he attributed to scriptural and natural symbols. Indeed he lamented that Luther would never 'have had to seek a murky Hiding-hole in the figment of Consubstantiation' precisely if had understood 'the true definition of a Symbol as distinguished from the Thing on one hand, and from a mere metaphor or conventional exponent of a Thing, on the other' (*CM*, ii. 280). Consubstantial symbols were evidently to be found everywhere *except* at the altar. In that respect Coleridge may be said to have formulated two mutually exclusive concepts of the synecdochical symbol, one consubstantial and the other sacramental (see further Halmi 2007*b*: 127–32).

Yet it must be emphasized that Coleridge no more sought to reject Christian orthodoxy by appropriating the concept of consubstantiality than, as an admirer of Dante, Spenser, and Bunyan, he sought to disparage all allegorical writing by opposing allegory to the symbol. The true target of the intellectual labour represented as it were synecdochically in his theorization of the symbol was what he referred to in *The Statesman's Manual* as 'the general contagion of [the] mechanic philosophy' and 'an unenlivened generalizing Understanding' (*LS*, 28). Rejecting reductive interpretations of scripture on the one hand and reductive explanations of nature on the other, Coleridge undertook, with an accommodation to the exigencies of Enlightenment semiotics, to justify theoretically the belief in a numinousness that was no longer intuitively recognizable.

WORKS CITED

ABRAMS, M. H. 1974. Coleridge and the Romantic vision of the world. In *The Correspondent Breeze: Essays on English Romanticism*. New York: Norton, pp. 192–224.

AKENSIDE, M. 1996. *The Pleasures of Imagination*, in *The Poetical Works of Mark Akenside*, ed. R. Dix. Teaneck, NJ: Fairleigh Dickinson University Press, pp. 85–174.

BARTH, J. R. 1977. *The Symbolic Imagination: Coleridge and the Romantic Tradition*. 2nd edn. New York: Fordham University Press, 2001.

COLERIDGE, S. T. 2003. *Coleridge's Poetry and Prose*, ed. N. Halmi, P. Magnuson, and R. Modiano. New York: Norton.

DE MAN, P. 1969. The Rhetoric of temporality. In C. S. Singleton, ed., *Interpretation: Theory and Practice*. Baltimore: Johns Hopkins University Press, pp. 173–209.

ECO, U. 1984. *Semiotics and the Philosophy of Language*. London: Macmillan.

ENGELL, J. 1981. *The Creative Imagination: Hobbes to Coleridge*. Cambridge, MA: Harvard University Press.

—— 1989. *Forming the Critical Mind: Dryden to Coleridge*. Cambridge, MA: Harvard University Press.

—— 1999. *The Committed Word: Literature and Public Values*. University Park: Pennsylvania State University.

GATTA, J. 1977. Coleridge and allegory. *Modern Language Quarterly*, 38: 62–77.

HALMI, N. 2005. Greek myths, Christian mysteries, and the tautegorical symbol. *Wordsworth Circle*, 36: 6–8.

—— 2007a. Coleridge's most unfortunate borrowing from A. W. Schlegel, in Christoph Bode and Sebastian Domsch, eds., *British and European Romanticisms*. Trier: WVT, pp. 131–42.

—— 2007b. *The Genealogy of the Romantic Symbol*. Oxford: Oxford University Press.

HARDING, A. J. 1995. *The Reception of Myth in English Romanticism*. Columbia: University of Missouri Press.

HARDY, B. 1951. Distinction without difference: Coleridge's fancy and imagination. *Essays in Criticism*, NS 1: 336–44.

HEDLEY, D. 2000. *Coleridge, Philosophy and Religion: 'Aids to Reflection' and the Mirror of the Spirit*. Cambridge: Cambridge University Press.

LOWTH, R. 1753. *De sacra poesi Hebræorum*. Oxford.

McFARLAND, T. 1981. *Romanticism and the Forms of Ruin: Wordsworth, Coleridge, and Modalities of Fragmentation*. Princeton: Princeton University Press.

—— 1990. Involute and symbol in the Romantic imagination, in J. R. Barth and J. Mahoney, eds., *Coleridge, Keats, and the Imagination: Essays in Honor of Walter Jackson Bate*. Columbia: University of Missouri Press, pp. 29–57.

SCHELLING, F. W. J. 1856–61. *Sämmtliche Werke*, ed. K. F. A. Schelling. 14 vols. Stuttgart.

SCHLEGEL, A. W. 1815. *A Course of Lectures on Dramatic Art and Literature*, trans. J. Black. 2 vols. London.

—— 1962–74. *Kritische Schriften und Briefe*, ed. E. Lohner. 7 vols. Stuttgart: Kohlhammer.

SMITH, J. 1660. *Select Discourses*. London.

WARD, P. 1966. Coleridge's critical theory of the symbol. *Texas Studies in Language and Literature*, 8: 15–32.

WELLBERY, D. 1984. *Lessing's 'Laocoon': Semiotics and Aesthetics in the Age of Reason*. Cambridge: Cambridge University Press.

WELLEK, R. 1955–92. *A History of Modern Criticism 1750–1950*. 8 vols. New Haven: Yale University Press.

WHALLEY, G. 1949. The Bristol Library borrowings of Southey and Coleridge. *The Library*, 34: 114–32.

WILSON, D. B. 1972. Two modes of apprehending nature: A gloss on the Coleridgean symbol, *PMLA* 87: 42–52.

YEATS, W. B. 1903. William Blake's illustrations to the *Divine Comedy*, in *Essays and Introductions*. London: Macmillan, 1961, pp. 116–45.

—— 1937. *A Vision*. London: Macmillan, 1962.

CHAPTER 19

COLERIDGE'S EARLY POETRY, 1790–1796

DAVID FAIRER

As a body of work, Coleridge's early poetry is not easy to characterize and evaluate, and he had difficulty doing so himself. When he looked back from the vantage-point of *Biographia Literaria* it seemed that his first published collection, *Poems on Various Subjects* (April 1796), had been mere 'juvenilia', of value chiefly for offering 'buds of hope', a hint of 'better works to come'.[1] This is factually misleading but interpretationally helpful: misleading because the great majority of his 1796 *Poems* were written after the age of twenty-one (and therefore can hardly be said to represent his juvenilia), but also helpful in highlighting an image of uncertain hope that runs erratically through the volume. Coleridge appears to be projecting himself not as a young poet growing confidently towards his full powers, but as a precariously talented genius that needs careful nurturing if he is not to relapse into the juvenile. The distinction is significant. In preparing his first published volume Coleridge chose in effect to veil his own chronological development as a poet, as if to remind himself of his unsteadiness and lack of direction. A reader of the 1796 *Poems* can detect a disingenuousness in which naivety is being performed alongside self-assurance. The volume is organized so that maturity and adolescence alternate, and youthful love-verses sit alongside a politically committed public voice.[2]

[1] See *BL*, pp. 5–6.
[2] For a fuller account of this and an analysis of the 1796 *Poems*, see David Fairer, *Organising Poetry: The Coleridge Circle, 1790–1798* (Oxford: Oxford University Press, 2009), ch. 7.

Coleridge does not 'mature' as a poet in any consistent way, although he comes to have a critical awareness of where maturity might lie. But the confident poetic voice he finally projects in April 1796 through 'Religious Musings' (the final item in the collection) is not the one that will represent him to posterity. It is elsewhere in the volume that we can trace the disparate strands that will come together in the great poems of his maturity.

The 1796 volume has to accommodate a range of voices, and it does so with a degree of uneasiness. The preface appears to be offering the reader a work of late eighteenth-century Sensibility, personal poems whose expressions of suffering have worked a kind of catharsis on the poet himself:

Why then write Sonnets or Monodies? Because they give me pleasure when perhaps nothing else could. After the more violent emotions of Sorrow, the mind demands solace and can find it in employment alone; but full of its late sufferings it can endure no employment not connected with those sufferings.[3]

With a stress on the poet's *sufferings*, this passage evokes the sentimental mechanism that Charlotte Smith acknowledged in the preface to her popular *Elegiac Sonnets* (1784): 'Some very melancholy moments have been beguiled, by expressing in verse the sensations those moments brought'. And just as Smith hesitantly directed her book at a small band of sympathetic readers ('I can hope for readers only among the few, who to sensibility of heart, join simplicity of taste')[4] Coleridge wants to think of his own debut collection as speaking not to a 'public' but to individual readers who have shared his feelings:

What is the PUBLIC but a term for a number of scattered individuals of whom as many will be interested in these sorrows as have experienced the same or similar?   (1796: vii)

It seems that in putting his early verse together Coleridge was happier thinking of an individual friendly reader rather than a more judgemental 'public'; but in casting his poems in this personal way as 'sorrows' he not only underplays the elements of delight and joy they express, but also compromises those poems that are directed toward the public world.

Nevertheless, this sentimental, confessional vein does indeed run through Coleridge's early verse, and there are several poems which consciously act out the mechanisms of eighteenth-century Sensibility in this way. The concept of the 'sympathetic imagination', which had been formulated by the 1720s, involved the individual placing him/herself into the situation of another so as to feel their emotions.[5] Reinforcing this, Locke's theories of association and mental reflection

---

[3] *Poems on Various Subjects, by S.T. Coleridge, Late of Jesus College, Cambridge* (London: G. G. and J. Robinson; Bristol: J. Cottle, 1796), p. vi. Further references will be given in the form of 1796: vi.

[4] Charlotte Smith's prefaces are printed chronologically at the beginning of her *Elegiac Sonnets*, 5th edn. (London: T. Cadell, 1789), pp. iii–vii.

[5] See Walter Jackson Bate, 'The Sympathetic Imagination in Eighteenth-Century English Criticism', *ELH*, 12 (1945), 144–64.

encouraged a dynamic concept of the mind in which a self was not only projected into, but also reflected from, experience.[6] Human identity thus became located in more subjective areas of individual experience and memory. In Sensibility, reflective memory is a crucial medium for self-expression. Many of Smith's sonnets consciously move from observation to reflection of this kind, and throughout the 1796 volume we can see Coleridge handling the same idea. In 'Lines to a Beautiful Spring in a Village' (pp. 28–30), for example, he sets up a busy scene of village life (the children sailing their paper boats, etc.), only to see it dissolve the moment the speaker turns to his own memories. The turn comes when observation is replaced by memory, and the spring (no longer the focus for the villagers' activities) becomes an object of reflection, literally so in this case:

> . . . Thy fount with pebbled falls
> The faded form of past delight recalls,
> What time the morning sun of Hope arose,
> And all was joy; save when another's woes
> A transient gloom upon my soul imprest,
> Like passing clouds impictur'd on thy breast.
>
> (23–8)

The tone of the poem changes when memory distracts him from the immediate scene: he makes a 'turn' to a more intimate and personal voice, as if to draw closer to his ideal sympathetic reader. The poet offers himself as a man of romantic sensibility whose consciousness is imprinted ('imprest') by the sorrows of a friend; but at the same time it seems that what is imprest on his 'soul' might be as temporary as those passing clouds reflected in the water. Such *impressions*, as philosophers like David Hume showed, might be entirely fleeting and evanescent.[7]

By placing emphasis on the dynamics of subjectivity, Sensibility could catch the most fleeting and fluid of experiences. But the role of rational judgement, the conscious structuring of meaning, might be lacking. There are moments in Coleridge's 1796 *Poems* when the poet recognizes this and the verse conveys a sense of experience slipping away before it can be held and shaped. Towards the close of 'Lines on a Friend who Died of a Frenzy Fever' (pp. 32–5) he adopts what had long been the characteristic pose of any sentimental elegist:

> As oft at twilight gloom thy grave I pass,
> And sit me down upon its' recent grass,

---

[6] John Locke, *An Essay Concerning Human Understanding* (2nd edn, 1694), II. xxvii ('Of Identity and Diversity'). On Locke's dynamic 'grammar of reflection', see Jules David Law, *The Rhetoric of Empiricism: Language and Perception from Locke to I. A. Richards* (Ithaca and London: Cornell University Press, 1993), pp. 51–92.

[7] See Georges Dicker, *Hume's Epistemology and Metaphysics: An Introduction* (London: Routledge, 1998), pp. 5–15; and R.J. Butler, 'Hume's Impressions', in *Impressions of Empiricism*, ed. Godfrey Vesey (London: Macmillan, 1976), pp. 122–36.

> With introverted eye I contemplate
> Similitude of soul, perhaps of—Fate!
>
> (35–8)

The moment of sympathetic identification is confirmed by the dramatic catch of breath signalled by the dash. The lines are conventional and knowingly naïve: the phrase 'with introverted eye' nicely expresses the conscious way in which he is conducting his meditation and is now ready to make the turn to the self. But at this very moment there rises a kind of resistance in him, a tone of frustration, a sense of weary incapacity. The dead man is forgotten and the poet turns elegist on himself:

> To me hath Heaven with bounteous hand assign'd
> Energic Reason and a shaping mind,
> The daring ken of Truth, the Patriot's part,
> And Pity's sigh, that breathes the gentle heart—
> Sloth-jaundic'd all! and from my graspless hand
> Drop Friendship's precious pearls, like hour glass sand.
> I weep, yet stoop not! The faint anguish flows,
> A dreamy pang in Morning's fev'rish doze.
>
> (39–46)

Here the first two couplets (reminiscent of the final passage of Gray's *Elegy*) deliver his own epitaph; but the poetry gains new strength with the sudden exclamation of self-disgust. It is more than a change of tone: the genre itself seems to shift from elegy to dramatic soliloquy.[8]

These powerful lines express a sense of frustration that seems to haunt the 1796 volume and challenge the character and role of poetry: how can we grasp things of value that are not physical? How can poetry in particular do justice to truth and reality when it lives in a world of images? Can poetry embody ideas and make them real, or does it merely reflect experience in intangible ways? In the above passage the concept is expressed almost literally as a failure to grasp, to hold onto things. An idea loses its form and slips away unless it can be embodied and made real (Coleridge will explore this idea again on a larger scale in 'Kubla Khan'). Here the lines are contemptuous of the flaccid, the faint and the fluid. They challenge poetry to find a way of embodying experience so that it does not just exist within the imagination.

These questions are raised in an interesting form by the text of Coleridge's youthful signature-piece, 'Monody on the Death of Chatterton', the opening poem of the 1796 collection (pp. 1–11). This text is thoroughly re-written and extended from the original 90-line version which was composed at Christ's Hospital (and proudly included by the Headmaster in the school's *Liber Aureus*

---

[8] The final reference to 'Morning's fev'rish doze' takes us straight to the world of Pope's Belinda at the opening of *The Rape of the Lock* (1714), and the scene when the sylph Ariel appears in her half-waking morning dream.

in 1790).[9] In the original 1790 version the voice is confident, committed, and angry, and expresses the teenage Coleridge's response to the poverty and neglect that brought about the poet Chatterton's suicide at the age of 17. 'Is this the land of liberal Hearts!' (13) he demands. The poem shows us a charity boy of his own age who had dreamed of becoming the champion of the oppressed, but whose hopes had been dashed as he himself became a victim. Coleridge enters into the drama of the allegorical scene, picturing Chatterton ready to drink the bowl of poison ('Already to thy lips was rais'd the bowl', 58); The figure of Pity attempts to intervene by offering images of his home and family; but Despair and Indignation with 'Neglect and grinning Scorn, and Want combin'd' (77) finally triumph by recalling his hopeless situation. The youth takes the drink: 'Recoiling back thou sent'st the friend of Pain / To roll a tide of Death through every freezing vein' (78–9). At the end Coleridge pictures the young poet in Heaven charming the angels with his melodies. The scene fills him with poetic ambition, but also with a determination that if similar 'Waves of Woe' (88) should come, he himself will ride out the storm. In this lively poem we are part of a scenario of Sensibility in which pity and despair, sorrow and indignation, engage within us, and like the speaker we are made to visualize ('powerful Fancy evernigh / The hateful picture forces on my sight', 45–6). The poem makes abstractions palpable. It is the work of a youth who has delighted in *The Faerie Queene*, in which Spenser's poetry bodies forth an imagined world where thoughts are actively realized and humanity's inner demons have to be encountered.

Coleridge's re-written version of the 'Monody' published in the 1796 *Poems* is quite different in approach, and its stylistic changes are marked.[10] It suggests something of a crisis confronted the poet in his early twenties about the effective role of poetry in the world. Where the 1790 text opened on a note of youthful confidence ('high my bosom beats with love of Praise', 2) and brought Chatterton before us as a suffering physical presence, the 1796 version introduces another figure who scarcely registers in the physical world at all:

> When faint and sad o'er Sorrow's desart wild
> Slow journeys onward poor Misfortune's child;
> When fades each lovely form by Fancy drest,
> And inly pines the self-consuming breast...
>
> (1–4)

---

[9] The *Liber Aureus* ('golden book') was the headmaster Dr Boyer's book of poetical honours. It is now BL MS Ashley 3506. The transcript of the 'Monody' (in Coleridge's hand) is at vol. 1, ff. 44^r–46^v. The poem would accompany Coleridge through the whole of his life and be repeatedly re-cast across a span of fifty years. See I. A Gordon, 'The Case History of Coleridge's *Monody on the Death of Chatterton*', *Review of English Studies*, 18 (1942), 49–71. See also *PW*, I. i. 139–44 and II. i. 166–87.

[10] Coleridge had re-written and extended the 'Monody' for publication in Lancelot Sharpe's Cambridge edition of Chatterton's Rowley Poems (1794), pp. xxv–xxviii. The 1796 text is a light revision of this, and includes the 'Susquehanna' ending which had probably been omitted in 1794 for lack of space. See Arthur Freeman and Theodore Hofmann, 'The Ghost of Coleridge's First Effort: "A Monody on the Death of Chatterton"', *The Library*, 11 (1989), 328–35.

This new tentative opening gives us the image of a lost and wandering child. It is not, as we might think, the young Chatterton victimized by the harsh world, but an unspecific symbol of transience. It is the disembodied essence of poetry's imagined world, who fades to an appropriately melancholy tonal accompaniment. The Coleridge of 1790 had tried to look away from the scene but was forced by his imagination to confront it. In 1796 the reverse is the case: the imagination lets us luxuriate in Chatterton's spirit. He becomes a 'Sweet tree of Hope! ../. Loading the west-winds with its soft perfume!' (51–3). No longer a challenging presence, he is the emblem of a haunting absence, a magical dew-fall of imagination: 'Fancy, elfin form of gorgeous wing, / On every blossom hung her fostering dews, / That, changeful, wanton'd to the orient day!' (54–6). A sense of the poetic spirit is beautifully caught, but in the process Chatterton slips away. Once the fruit-tree image has been established it is difficult to develop it in other than awkward ways: here the tree goes on to suffer the 'sickly mildew' of 'Penury' and is finally struck by lightning.

It is clear that during 1794–7 Coleridge was struggling to find a poetic language that would not betray uncomfortable realities, and the 'Monody' became a test-case for him. In July 1797 he made it clear to Southey that he did not want the poem reprinted. He was now linking it in his mind with his early lyric poem, 'Songs of the Pixies':

Excepting the last 18 lines of the Monody, which tho' deficient in chasteness & severity of diction, breathe a pleasing spirit of romantic feeling, there are not 5 lines in either poem, which might not have been written by a man who had lived & died in the self-same St Giles's Cellar, in which he had been first suckled by a drab with milk & Gin.[11]

Coleridge's self-contempt is remarkably graphic. Indeed he is drawing on the eighteenth-century satiric powers of Hogarth, perhaps recalling the St Giles scene shown in 'Gin Lane' where the baby slips from the breast of its gin-sodden mother and tumbles down into the cellar. This lost child is closer to the world of Chatterton's garret than anything in Coleridge's poetry, and it conveys a horrified physical distaste. Coleridge's poetic ideals and his social indignation somehow could not be reconciled. In the same letter he acknowledges being trapped by 'such a high idea, of what Poetry ought to be, that he cannot conceive that such things as his natural emotions may be allowed to find place in it'. There is a problem here, evident in Coleridge's early verse and his dissatisfaction with it, of how to work between the ideal and the real, and find a 'natural' mode of writing. It brings to a head Coleridge's loss of faith in what he sees as the mistaken Parnassian strain of his youth:

[11] Coleridge–Southey, [c.17 July 1797]; CL, I, 333.

...on a life & death so full of heart-giving *realities*, as poor Chatterton's to find such shadowy nobodies, as cherub-winged DEATH, Trees of HOPE, bare-bosom'd AFFECTION, & simpering PEACE—makes one's blood circulate like ipecacacuanha.[12]

In order to understand Coleridge's early poetry we have to confront this sense of critical disgust. But it would be misleading to see it as a reaction against his early work as a whole. In fact, what Coleridge is here mocking are the dematerializing additions he added to the Chatterton monody in 1794, which had compromised the Hogarthian indignation of the earliest version.

To understand the force of Coleridge's self-criticism it is helpful to look briefly at 'Songs of the Pixies' (pp. 15–25).[13] This miniature irregular ode (a suite of nine varied lyric stanzas) is one of several pieces in the 1796 collection that play knowingly with the juvenile notes of romance. It seems naive, but is a sophisticated exercise in the early eighteenth-century romantic mode, one feature of which was what Addison called 'the Fairie way of Writing', the style mastered by Pope in the descriptions of the sylphs in *The Rape of the Lock*.[14] Coleridge enjoys returning imaginatively to the Pixies' Parlour, a small cave overlooking the River Otter where he had hidden when a child and courted when an adolescent, and he uses it to create a poetry of the disembodied imagination: 'For mid the quiv'ring light 'tis our's to play, / Aye-dancing to the cadence of the stream' (89–90). In this place the poet becomes an enchanted youth granted special favours:

> Weaving gay dreams of sunny-tinctur'd hue
> > We glance before his view:
> O'er his hush'd soul our soothing witch'ries shed,
> And twine our faery garlands round his head.

(45–8)

In the 1796 volume, 'Songs of the Pixies' becomes a continual reference-point for other poems that visit 'the Bowers of old Romance',[15] a world where Pope's Ariel sleeps in the nosegay on Belinda's breast, where Shakespeare's Puck paints the eyelids of lovers, and the Renaissance figure of Cupid generally makes mischief.

In his early poetry Coleridge has clearly mastered this playful vein; and there is an adolescent seductive intent behind poems that toy with fanciful arousals, miniature violations, and those erotic moments when the senses are sharpened by the almost audible, the scarcely tangible, and the marginally visible. Some of Coleridge's characteristic love verses play coyly along this borderline of consciousness; and his language has a pouting, whispering quality that suggests the

---

[12] Ibid.

[13] 'Songs of the Pixies' was reprinted in the 1797 second edition, but only (he told Southey in the above letter) because of 'dear Cottle's solicitous importunity' (ibid., p. 333).

[14] *Spectator*, no. 419 (1 July 1712). See David Fairer, *English Poetry of the Eighteenth Century, 1700–1789* (London: Longman, 2003), pp. 102–21 ('The Romantic Mode, 1700–1730').

[15] 'Effusion 24. In the Manner of Spenser' (1796: 73–6).

intimacies of lovers' small-talk, the kind of insinuating technique that Satan used when he crouched (as a toad) up against Eve's ear.[16] In what may at first seem flippant, adolescent writing we can detect the verbal mastery of Coleridge the enchanter, the man who knows how to weave a poetic spell:

> Too well those lovely lips disclose
> The Triumphs of the op'ning Rose:
> O fair! O graceful! bid them prove
> As passive to the breath of Love.
> In tender accents, faint and low,
> Well-pleas'd I hear the whisper'd 'No!'
> The whisper'd 'No'—how little meant!
> Sweet Falsehood, that endears Consent!
> For on those lovely lips the while
> Dawns the soft relenting smile,
> And tempts with feign'd dissuasion coy
> The gentle violence of Joy.
>
> (1796: 83, 'Effusion 28')

Spoken by Geraldine to Christabel, these lines would haunt Coleridge criticism, and Charles Lamb fondly recalled Coleridge reading them aloud.[17] There is something violent about the gentle intimacy. These devilishly spun lines are a clue to Coleridge's mature power as a poet. We notice his observant sense of how a pair of lips must unclose in order to disclose, a witty idea that is clinched by the word 'op'ning' in the next line. There is a dynamics of passivity here. She is unfolding naturally to him; her smile 'dawns', and merely her quiet breathing is an inhalation of love—though the 'Triumphs', he knows, are really his. Within the fine paradoxical thread of the poem, 'no' means 'yes', and 'Falsehood' is 'sweet' when it makes 'Consent' so endearingly reluctant. The poem clearly belongs to the libertine tradition of Rochester, but also to the 'sweet reluctant amorous delay' (*Paradise Lost*, IV, 311) of Milton's unfallen Eve. The quietness of the 'No!' was satirically picked up by Byron's rakish narrator in *Don Juan* to describe Donna Julia's seduction: 'A little still she strove, and much repented, / And whispering "I will ne'er consent"—consented' (*Don Juan*, I. cxvii, 8–9). In Coleridge's hands, however, a sense of the disembodied is never entirely lost, so that the emotional movements seem to prompt the physical ones. There is ease as well as coercion here.

In the 1796 *Poems* this item is entitled 'Effusion 28', but it is elsewhere called 'The Kiss'. A significant and unique feature of the 1796 volume is Coleridge's decision to group together into a single section thirty-six poems of different character and

---

[16] 'Assaying by his Devilish art to reach / The Organs of her Fancie, and with them forge / Illusions as he list, Fantasms and Dreams' (Milton, *Paradise Lost*, IV, 801–3). See also V, 36–53.

[17] 'When I read in your little volume your 19th Effusion. or the 28th.... I think I hear *you* again. I image to myself the little smoky room at the Salutation & Cat, where we have sat together thro' the winter nights, beguiling the cares of life with Poesy' (Lamb–Coleridge, 8–10 June 1796; Marrs, I, 18).

form (stanzaic poems, blank verse, sonnets, album verses, elegiac and meditative poetry, poems on public themes) all under the title of 'Effusion'. It was an odd thing to do, since none of the poems was composed with that title in mind, and they were never to be grouped in this way again. Young poets often like to show their mastery across different poetic forms, but Coleridge's tactic works in the opposite direction; it suggests that faced with collecting his poems together for the first time he felt some kind of loss of faith in poetic form and in his own abilities. In the preface he says that he chose the term 'in defiance of Churchill's line, "Effusion on Effusion pour away".[18] More than two-thirds of the poems in this volume are thus linked to the notion (from the Latin verb *effundere-effusum*) of 'pouring out or forth'. Here we might be reminded of 'Lines on a Friend' where he despairs of being able to hold things together: 'from my graspless hand / Drop Friendship's precious pearls, like hour glass sand'. 'Effusion' is not a containing form, and the effect of this title is especially uncomfortable for the volume's twenty-one sonnets, since a defining characteristic of the sonnet form is compression. But in his preface Coleridge maintains that 'they do not posses that *oneness* of thought which I deem indispensible in a Sonnet' (1796: x). This is a remarkable signal to his readers and suggests that at this time he was feeling his poetry lacked formal control and he was somehow wasting his talent, letting it slip away.

This idea is reinforced when the 'Effusions' section ends with what appears to be a deliberate 'throw-away' gesture of this kind, a point where Coleridge's poetic self-confidence is at its lowest ebb. The crisis comes with 'Effusion 36', deliberately placed last in the section and given the subtitle 'Written in Early Youth', which is untrue (it dates from 1793).[19] At the climax of the section therefore Coleridge is pointedly offering the reader a 'juvenile' voice, one that returns us to the 'faery' atmosphere of the Pixies' Parlour:

> To fan my Love I'd be the EVENING GALE;
> Mourn in the soft folds of her swelling vest,
> And flutter my faint pinions on her breast!
> On Seraph wing I'd float a DREAM, by night,
> To soothe my Love with shadows of delight...
>
> (66–70)

It is an exercise in disembodiment taken to an extreme, and here Coleridge prints an extraordinary note that only increases the reader's embarrassment: 'I entreat the

---

[18] Churchill uses the term satirically: 'Why may not LANGHORNE, simple in his lay, / *Effusion* on *Effusion* pour away, / With *Friendship*, and with *Fancy* trifle here' (*The Candidate* [1764], 41–4). Langhorne published *The Effusions of Friendship and Fancy* in 1763.

[19] Its placing in the 1796 volume is deliberate: the copy text carries Coleridge's written instruction: 'to be printed the last of the Effusions next to "My pensive Sara". In the Rugby MS, fol. 31ʳ, the manuscript has the concluding note: 'End of the Effusions'. The poem was first printed in *The Weekly Entertainer* (Sherborne), 28 October 1793. See *PW*, II, 101, where it is given its original title, 'Absence: A Poem'.

Public's pardon', it reads, 'for having carelessly suffered to be printed such intolerable stuff as this' (1796: 183–4). It is not an apology to a sympathetic reader, we notice, but a public retraction, and it confirms a sense that this poet is a young man who has not yet found his right path. In this way it becomes part of a pattern in his first collection, in which he projects an image of youthful uncertainty.

Looking back over the 'Effusions' section we can see that it is ordered so as to avoid indicating a growing strength and maturity. It opens with a confident, public, political voice, and ends on a note of adolescent tetchiness. In doing so it tends to muffle the impact of Coleridge's ten *Morning Chronicle* 'Sonnets on Eminent Characters' (Effusions 1–10), in which he surveys the state of the nation and rouses it to action.[20] The figures he has chosen are largely people whose *voices* move, persuade, or inspire, and the emphasis is as much on the aural as the visual. Even the quiet-toned William Lisle Bowles (the addressee of the opening 'Effusion 1') begins in the last couplet to swell into the sublime:

> As the great SPIRIT erst with plastic sweep
> Mov'd on the darkness of the unform'd deep.

Bowles is not usually identified with the primal scene, but here this climactic image sets the bass-note for the sounding sonnets that follow. Edmund Burke's political contradictions are hinted at in the second sonnet through the voice of Freedom, who speaks as a loving mother to her estranged child, disturbed by the 'alter'd voice' which she cannot recognize. In the fifth, the radical lawyer Thomas Erskine speaks out at the crucial moment just in time to prevent 'British Freedom' from flying away:

> ERSKINE! thy voice she heard, and paus'd her flight
> Sublime of hope! For dreadless thou didst stand...
> And at her altar pourd'st the stream divine
> Of unmatch'd eloquence.
>
> (3–8)

In these sonnets, 'hope' ceases to be a precarious melancholy companion and becomes a mark of optimism: the tones of sublimity emphasize the universal sweep of these poems, which stage a series of inspirational pageants of which Liberty is the theme. 'Effusion 6' celebrates Sheridan the dramatist and opposition orator ('Now patriot Rage and Indignation high / Swell the full tones!', 9–10), and no. 7 also draws on the eloquence of the public stage by catching the power of Sarah Siddons, the great tragic actress: 'Ev'n such the shiv'ring joys thy tones impart, /

---

[20] In the Gutch notebook Coleridge can be seen working out an arrangement for the 'Effusions' section, so that the 'Sonnets on Eminent Characters' will be printed in a different order from their first appearance in *The Morning Chronicle*. See *CN*, entry 305; Coleridge's jottings are re-examined by Carl R. Woodring, *Politics in the Poetry of Coleridge* (Madison: University of Wisconsin Press, 1961), pp. 226–7.

Ev'n so thou, SIDDONS! meltest my sad heart!' (13–14). In these sonnets Coleridge taps the excitement of public speech and its immediacy of effect. Rather than describe scenes, the poems seem to create and embody them like heroic painting with added sound effects, as at the end of the sonnet to Stanhope ('Effusion 10'):

> Angels shall lead thee to the Throne above:
> And thou from forth it's clouds shalt hear the voice,
> Champion of FREEDOM and her God! rejoice!

The poems reach their climax, and as a group of ten under their original title they would have made an effective section in themselves. But this poem is immediately followed by 'Effusion 11', in which all the energy that has built up is dissipated in a moment:

> Was it some sweet device of faery land
> That mock'd my steps with many a lonely glade,
> And fancied wand'rings with a fair-hair'd maid?
> Have these things been?
>
> (1–4)

It is disconcerting, and the contrast could hardly be greater. Not only does Coleridge introduce a sonnet of melancholy introspection and lost love, but he prints one by Charles Lamb. 'I forlorn do wander, reckless where', reads line 13, as if to dispel the dynamic, forward-looking impulse of the public sonnets.

Coleridge's acute critical capacity, as we have seen, could be turned against himself, and against a notion of the conventionally poetic. There are moments when he recoils from the role of youthful genius and adopts the more direct voice of the common man. One early poem that celebrates a stubborn refusal to be 'poetry' is 'Effusion 33', subtitled 'To a Young Ass, it's mother being tethered near it' (pp. 91–3). In the 1796 volume it follows a series of fanciful love lyrics, as if to disconcert the reader with an awkward revision of the traditional intimacies: 'I love the languid Patience of thy face', it remarks, 'And oft with gentle hand I give thee bread, / And clap thy ragged Coat, and pat thy head' (2–4). To befriend the 'oppressed' ass, he appears to insist, is much more than a scene from a sentimental novel. The reader soon realizes that *liberty*, *equality*, and *fraternity* are his themes:

> I hail thee BROTHER—spite of the fool's scorn!
> And fain would take thee with me, in the Dell
> Of Peace and mild Equality to dwell...
>
> (26–8)

Settled with the Pantisocrats on the banks of the Susquehanna, the ass will be no beast of burden, no servant to his human masters, but will take on a liberated life of its own: 'How thou wouldst toss thy heels in gamesome play, / And frisk about, as Lamb or Kitten gay!' (31–2). And what a relief its dissonant song would be:

> Yea! and more musically sweet to me
> Thy dissonant harsh Bray of Joy would be,
> Than warbled Melodies that sooth to rest
> The tumult of some SCOUNDREL Monarch's breast![21]
>
> (33–6)

The hint of assonance in 'Bray of Joy' belies the harsh idea and makes the paradoxical point beautifully. It is clear that the youthful Coleridge could value dissonance as well as harmony, and in this poem he offers his own antidote to the 'warbled Melodies' we have just been reading in the previous Effusions 23–32.

Readers of the 1796 *Poems* will be disappointed if they try to trace an emerging 'mature voice'. As I have been arguing, the volume does not offer a story of poetic development but a disconcerting mixture of the juvenile, the mature, and the adolescent. Coleridge is aware of performing all three roles and has the critical intelligence to understand the difference, but there is no clear trajectory. I have drawn attention to his dissatisfactions with the self-consciously 'poetic' strain: it is clear that he was ambivalent about the disembodied world of imagination, which he knew he could create with a light skilful touch. He handles it, as Pope did in *The Rape of the Lock*, with playful indulgence and an awareness that poetic 'maturity' lay elsewhere. Pope's boast 'That not in Fancy's maze he wander'd long, / But stoop'd to Truth, and moraliz'd his song' seems to have lodged in Coleridge's mind.[22] We can hear him echoing Pope's words in the sestet of 'Effusion 12':

> But ah! sweet scenes of fancied bliss, adieu!
> On rose-leaf beds amid your faery bowers
> I all too long have lost the dreamy hours!
> Beseems it now the sterner Muse to woo,
> If haply she her golden meed impart
> To realize the vision of the heart.
>
> (9–14)

But there is some uneasiness here. The poet wakes from the dream, but the antique vocabulary (*Beseems, haply, meed*) suggests that the language of old romance still lingers. The image slips into soft focus and we realize he is simultaneously dismissing and indulging the dream. There is added irony in the fact that 'Effusion 12', subscribed 'C.L.', is Coleridge's revision of a sonnet by Charles Lamb. Lamb felt awkward about Coleridge's changes: 'I had rather have seen what I wrote myself', he said, 'tho' they bear no comparison with your exquisite line, "On rose-leafd beds amid your faery bowers".'[23]

---

[21] See David Perkins, 'Compassion for Animals and Radical Politics: Coleridge's "To a Young Ass"', *ELH*, 65 (1998), 929–44 (pp. 935–6).

[22] Pope, *Epistle to Dr Arbuthnot* (1735), 340–1.

[23] Lamb–Coleridge, 8–10 June 1796 (Marrs, I, 20).

Coleridge's early poetry can buy its exquisiteness too dearly. The reader often senses a tension between elements of disembodied dream and embodied thought (it is evident, as we saw, in the revised text of the Chatterton monody). Sometimes we feel the pull towards a pure lyric strain (verbal music and 'exquisite' imagery) and at other times a rousing call to thought and action. He can react in frustration against 'shadowy nobodies', or equally against overloaded thought, from which lyric ease seems like a relief:

I cannot write without a *body* of *thought*—hence my *Poetry* is crowded and sweats beneath a heavy burthen of Ideas and Imagery! It has seldom Ease—The little Song ending with 'I heav'd the—sigh for thee! is an exception—and accordingly I like it the best of all, I ever wrote.[24]

By the Spring of 1796 Coleridge thought for a moment that he had found his true poetic voice. Returning from his *Watchman* tour on 13 February, perhaps with a new confidence in his far-reaching influence, he flung himself into the sublimities of 'Religious Musings'. The printing of the 1796 volume was held up until he had finished the 446-line poem, and it was placed at the end with a fresh title-page and an epigraph announcing his new resolve:

> What tho' first,
> In years unseason'd, I attun'd the Lay
> To idle Passion and unreal Woe?
> Yet serious Truth her empire o'er my song
> Hath now asserted....
>
> (1796: 136)

It has Akenside's name attached, but the lines are Coleridge's.[25] It is another version of Pope's boast at having left 'Fancy' for 'Truth'. Coleridge could now claim the traditional pre-eminence of the 'higher' lyric vein, and the visionary poem would be the foundation on which he would construct his reputation as a poet: 'I build all my poetic pretensions on the Religious Musings', he told John Thelwall, and he repeated the idea to others.[26]

Ostensibly a Christmas poem about God becoming man, it shifts focus from the nativity story of Luke's gospel to the Book of Revelation and the apocalyptic moment when the human 'elect' will become godlike. In the prefatory 'Argument'

---

[24] Coleridge–Southey, 11 December 1794 (*CL*, I, 137).

[25] Coleridge re-writes Akenside's *The Pleasures of the Imagination* (1772 text), I, 49–56. Akenside describes a more gradual poetic development: 'What, though first / In years unseason'd, haply ere the sports / Of childhood yet were o'er, the adventurous lay / With many splendid prospects, many charms, / Allur'd my heart, nor conscious whence they sprung, / Nor heedful of their end? Yet serious truth / Her empire o'er the calm, sequester'd theme / Asserted soon'.

[26] Coleridge–Thelwall [late April 1796]; *CL*, I, 205. Cf. 'I rest for all my poetical credit on the *Religious Musings*' (to Benjamin Flower, 1 April 1796; *CL*, I, 197); and 'I pin all my poetical credit on the Religious Musings' (to Poole, 11 April 1796; *CL*, I, 203).

its political trajectory looks clear enough: '... *The present State of Society. French Revolution. Millenium. Universal Redemption. Conclusion*' (1796: 137). As poetry it sets its sights above the things of this world and addresses itself to the higher angelic spirits:

> Contemplant Spirits! ye that hover o'er
> With untir'd gaze th'immeasurable fount
> Ebullient with creative Deity!
> And ye of plastic power, that interfus'd
> Roll thro' the grosser and material mass
> In organizing surge! Holies of God!
> (And what if Monads of the infinite mind?)
> I haply journeying my immortal course
> Shall sometime join your mystic choir!
>
> (429–37)

One wonders what the young ass would make of it all. Today, when we close the 1796 volume, this sound may be echoing in our ears ('When fiery whirlwinds thunder his dread name / And Angels shout, DESTRUCTION!', 417–18); but after a little while, another sound emerges to replace it. It is a wondering voice, and a confident (but also confiding) one. The blank verse here is not 'on the stretch',[27] and this turns out to be the voice that will prove most fruitful of any in the 1796 volume:

> The stilly murmur of the distant Sea
> Tells us of Silence. And that simplest Lute
> Plac'd length-ways in the clasping casement, hark!
> How by the desultory breeze caress'd,
> Like some coy Maid half-yielding to her Lover,
> It pours such sweet upbraidings, as must needs
> Tempt to repeat the wrong! And now its strings
> Boldlier swept, the long sequacious notes
> Over delicious surges sink and rise,
> Such a soft floating witchery of sound
> As twilight Elfins make, when they at eve
> Voyage on gentle gales from Faery Land...
>
> ('Effusion 35', 11–22)

It is as if the poetry of the Pixies' Parlour has found an expressive medium through the music. We meet again here the 'witchery' of Spenserian enchantment, the coy seductiveness of the album verses, but also hints of the bolder sweep of an ode. The verse is all the richer for being able to draw on these layers of association and link them to the human pulse that the poem's opening sets going ('My pensive SARA! thy soft cheek reclin'd / Thus on my arm...'). Here the 'delicious surges' connect

---

[27] Coleridge–Southey, [*c*.17 July 1797]; *CL*, I, 333.

the 'sink and rise' of the breeze through the casement window to the wider world of the spirit that has found its way in. Suddenly the 'organizing surge' of *Religious Musings* looks abstract in comparison, and its very totality limiting. The lines of 'The Eolian Harp' (to use the poem's later title) are the truly organic ones because of the way the words come to life among themselves, drawing out meaning from each other, so that 'clasping', 'sequacious', and 'Voyage' (to choose just three) extend their reach, and the reach of the poem, outwards. In contrast, the idea of 'Journeying my immortal course' (*RM*, 436) becomes something dogged and predictable—we even have to be told *about* the universal 'plastic' (shaping) power rather than experience directly something genuinely creative. The language of 'Effusion 35' is in conversation with itself, and its blank verse has the sinuous turns and emphases that help to shape the thought and not merely reflect (or declare) it.

The reviewers of Coleridge's *Poems on Various Subjects* (1796), however, ignored 'Effusion 35' completely, and preferred to praise the poet either for his elements of 'sweetness', 'tenderness', and 'elegance' (in 'Songs of the Pixies' and the later effusions) or for the 'boldness' and 'sublimity' of 'Religious Musings'. The old aesthetic categories still had to serve.[28] Not even John Aikin, whose review in the *Monthly* was the most perceptive, could find critical purchase on a poem that allowed itself to 'tremble into thought', and which combined familiar elements from Coleridge's youthful verse and made them into something new. It is 'Effusion 35' that locates the recognizable Coleridgean power of finding his way to sublime thoughts through human tenderness:

> And what if all of animated nature
> Be but organic Harps diversly fram'd,
> That tremble into thought, as o'er them sweeps,
> Plastic and vast, one intellectual Breeze,
> At once the Soul of each, and God of all?
>
> (36–40)

WORKS CITED

BATE, WALTER JACKSON. 1945. The sympathetic imagination in eighteenth-century English criticism. *ELH*, 12: 144–64.

BUTLER, R. J. 1976. Hume's impressions. In *Impressions of Empiricism*, ed. Godfrey Vesey. London: Macmillan.

DICKER, GEORGES. 1998. *Hume's Epistemology and Metaphysics: An Introduction*. London: Routledge.

---

[28] See *Coleridge: The Critical Heritage*, ed. J.R. de J. Jackson (London: Routledge & Kegan Paul, 1970), pp. 32–8.

FAIRER, DAVID. 2003. *English Poetry of the Eighteenth Century, 1700–1789*. London: Longman.

GORDON, I. A. 1942. The case history of Coleridge's *Monody on the Death of Chatterton*. *Review of English Studies*, 18: 49–71.

HOFMANN, THEODORE. 1989. The ghost of Coleridge's first effort: 'A Monody on the Death of Chatterton'. *The Library*, 11: 328–35.

JACKSON, J. R. DE J., ed. 1970. *Coleridge: The Critical Heritage*. London: Routledge & Kegan Paul.

LAW, JULES DAVID. 1993. *The Rhetoric of Empiricism: Language and Perception from Locke to I.A. Richards*. Ithaca and London: Cornell University Press.

PERKINS, DAVID. 1998. Compassion for animals and radical politics: Coleridge's 'To a Young Ass'. *ELH*, 65: 929–44.

WOODRING, CARL R. 1961. *Politics in the Poetry of Coleridge*. Madison: University of Wisconsin Press.

CHAPTER 20

....

COLERIDGE'S
GENRES

....

MICHAEL O'NEILL

WRITING to Aubrey de Vere in 1849, Sara Coleridge praises his article on 'Tennyson, Shelley, and Keats', but she objects to his ascription of 'versatility' to Keats and denial of the same quality to her father. Warming to her theme, Coleridge's dutiful and brilliant daughter enumerates the '*modes* of the poetical faculty' exhibited by her father:[1]

1. The love poems, as 'Lewti', and 'Genevieve', which Fox thought the finest love poem that ever was written.
2. The wild, imaginative poem, treating of the supernatural, as 'The Ancient Mariner' and 'Christabel.'
3. The grave strain of thoughtful blank verse, as 'Fears in Solitude.'
4. The narrative ballad, homely, as 'The Three Graves;' or romantic, as 'Alice du Clos.'
5. The moral and satirical poem of a didactic character, as the lines on 'Berengarius,' and those lines in which he speaks of seeing 'old friends burn like lamps in noisome air,' and 'Sancti Dominici Pallium.'
6. The high, impassioned lyric, as 'The Odes to France,' and on 'Dejection.'
7. The sportive, satirical extravaganza, as the 'War Eclogue,' 'The Devil Believes,' etc.
8. The epigram and brief epitaph.
9. The drama.

....

[1] *Memoir and Letters of Sara Coleridge*, edited by her daughter (New York and London: Harper, 1875), pp. 327–8.

Sara Coleridge's '*modes*' serve as rough-and-ready outlines of genres and remind one of her father's range. More recently, also in list-making mood, Max Schulz in *The Poetic Voices of Coleridge* (1963) grouped Coleridge's works under the following categories of poetic 'voice', as helpfully summarized by W. J. B. Owen in a review:

farrago, a rambling hotch-potch, often with a basic theme of social or political satire; *prophecy*, odes such as 'France' and 'Dejection' and the 'Hymn before Sunrise'; *ventrilo-quism*, the ballads and ballad-like poems, artificial in that they use an acquired manner markedly different from the eighteenth-century Miltonic, and eventually drifting away from the spareness of the ballad to a Spenserian development of it in 'Christabel'; *conver-sation*, the poems in the easy blank verse of the later 1790's, celebrating 'the one life' and conforming generally to a definable pattern of argument; *dream*, displaying 'the ability of the mind to transform and combine things into new forms...', 'Kubla Khan' the outstanding example; *confession*—of failure, misery, pain, 'the death agonies of Coleridge's spirit'...; *improvisation*, poems supposedly extemporized by Coleridge, 'garbed now in the robes of a semi-retired oracle'...; and *song*.

Owen concludes the list with the slightly tart comment that 'The classes overlap', as though a pack of cards were beginning to topple.[2] But it is a clue to Coleridge's generic brilliance that they should overlap, since individual poems frequently fuse possibilities originating in different kinds.

In a celebrated essay M. H. Abrams credits Coleridge with the creation of one of the most influential of Romantic kinds, the 'greater Romantic lyric'. In such a poem, as Abrams describes the matter, 'the perfect shape for the descriptive-meditative-descriptive poem was precisely the one described and exemplified in T. S. Eliot's "East Coker," which begins: "In my beginning is my end," and ends: "In my end is my beginning"'.[3] One's attention is caught by the unsolipsistic but necessarily personal burden of the pronouns in Eliot's line. In turn, Coleridgean uses of genres are always displays of and have at stake the nature of individual poetic genius: not because poetry is a form of celebrity exhibitionism, but because each poem seems to be trying to answer anew the question, 'In what way can I demonstrate the purpose of poetry?' Another way of putting this is to say that at stake is the discovery or creation of connectedness between the self and otherness, including the otherness embodied by previous works in related genres; the result-ing fusion of individual talent and tradition becomes a means by which, to adapt the German Idealist of chapter 12 of *Biographia Literaria*, the subject (here the poet dealing with genres) 'becomes a subject by the act of constructing itself objectively to itself' (*CC* 7. 1, p. 273).

---

[2] Review of Max F. Schulz, *The Poetic Voices of Coleridge* (Detroit: Wayne State University Press, 1963) and Werner W. Beyer, *The Enchanted Forest* (Oxford: Blackwell, 1963), *RES* (1965), N.S. 16, pp. 86–7

[3] M. H. Abrams, 'Structure and Style in the Greater Romantic Lyric' (1965), quoted from *Roman-ticism: Critical Concepts in Literary and Cultural Studies*, ed. Michael O'Neill and Mark Sandy, 4 vols. (London: Routledge, 2006), vol. 1, p. 201.

Drawing on Schelling's notion 'That in self-consciousness the subject and object of thought are one' (*CC* 7. 1, p. 273 n.), Coleridge elaborates a circular process which allows the subject to become a subject by virtue of its own self-objectification. But in the poetry the process is less formulaically assured, which is why Coleridge's descriptive-meditative poems are always poems about longing and love, and often address issues raised by the assertion in 'Dejection: An Ode': 'in ourselves alone does nature live' (48). It may be the case that Coleridge's imagination is more dramatic than Wordsworth's, 'more volatile' and 'protean', and that he 'tends to lose sight of the equilibrium between mind and reason', as J. C. C. Mays argues (*CC* 16. 1. 1, p. clxxi). Yet his poetic self-awareness is rarely less than vigilant. In 'Dejection: An Ode' Coleridge writes an epithalamion and an anti-epithalamion. The poem's use of wedding imagery offers itself as a covert gift to Wordsworth (the ode was published in the *Morning Post* on the day of Wordsworth's marriage), even as it reflects bitterly if indirectly on the poet's lack of such happiness. But in the very act of acknowledging a divorce between inner and outer, between an inward 'dull pain' (20) and outward objects that are 'excellently fair' (37), Coleridge pays tribute to the unions that can be or have been effected by his 'shaping spirit of Imagination' (86). His concern with the relationship between 'his shaping spirit of Imagination' and 'nature' runs parallel with his sense of the relations between individual poems and genres. It is in the life created by the former that the latter are reborn; yet unless genres are available to the poet the individual poem will be cut off, separate, alone.

Genres matter to Coleridge. In a lecture of 1819 he defends shrewdly the idiom used for the Player's speech about the killing of Priam in Act 2 of *Hamlet* in terms that show much generic know-how: the speech shows an 'admirable substitution of the Epic for the Dramatic, giving such a *reality* to the impassioned Dramatic Diction of Shakspear's own Dialogue, and authorized too by the actual style of the Tragedies before Shakspeare' (*CC* 5. 2, pp. 300–1). Much earlier, in his Preface to *Poems on Various Subjects* (1796), he offers this combative justification of poetry which might be be censured for its 'querulous egotism'. 'But', he argues, 'egotism is to be condemned then only when it offends against time and place, as in an History or an Epic Poem. To censure it in a Monody or Sonnet is almost as absurd as to dislike a circle for being round' (*CC* 16. 1. 2, p. 1194). You can see the young Coleridge trying to find a way of justifying poetry about his own feelings, and he offers a witty attack on the avoidance of the word 'I': 'With what anxiety every fashionable author avoids the word *I*!—now he transforms himself into a third person, —"the present writer"—now multiplies himself and swells into "*we*"—and all this is the watchfulness of guilt' (*CC* 16. 1. 2, p. 1195). This defence of the first person links with the suggestive Notebook entry, 'Poetry without egotism comparatively uninteresting' (*CN* 1, 62), as is noted by Mays (*CC* 16. 1. 2, p. 1195 n.), and it provides a clue to Coleridge's particular originality in his use of genres. In the 'Monody on the Death of Chatterton', the textual history of which is remarkably complex (Mays speaks of the second only of its 'three basic forms' as a 'Romantic ode written at Bristol and Cambridge in 1794 and successively expanded and modified in subsequent collections' (*CC* 16. 2. 1, p. 166)), Coleridge's 'monody'— or poem (often elegiac) spoken by a single voice—draws attention at its close to that voice. Coleridge imagines a fantasy of escape, both for Chatterton from death, and for himself into the 'sweet dream' (136) of Pantisocracy. There, in America, 'sooth'd sadly by the dirgeful wind' (142), he will 'Muse on the sore ills I had left behind' (143). What is striking about the late flowering of sensibility in this early Romantic ode is the undisguised pleasure in poetry as aesthetic rehabilitation. The 'there' (142) of the penultimate line is the monody as surely as it is the banks of the Susquehanna.

The poem is only a frail stay against 'sore ills' and in 1797 Coleridge seems to include aspects of its diction as one of the targets of his mockery in 'Sonnets Attempted in the Manner of "Contemporary Writers"', a sequence of three poems which shows Coleridge's alertness to literary fashion. Signed 'NEHEMIAH HIG-GINBOTTOM', the first poem sought to 'excite a good-natured laugh at the spirit of *doleful egotism*' (*CC* 16. 1. 1, p. 356), a spirit surely in evidence in Coleridge's own 'Monody'. 'Musing', Coleridge's final state in the 'Monody', takes an ironic battering at the start of the sonnet: 'Pensive, at eve, on the hard world I mus'd, / And my poor heart was sad', 'hard' and 'poor' being stressed to mock the habit of what Coleridge calls 'jumping & misplaced accent on common-place epithets' (*CC* 16. 1. 1, p. 355). There is a delicious sense of ego-deflating comedy at the sonnet's centre where musing is wholly sent up: 'And I did pause me on my lonely way, / And mus'd me on those wretched ones, who pass / O'er the black heath of SORROW. But alas! / Most of MYSELF I thought' (7–10). The *m*s of 'mus'd me' and 'Most of MYSELF' alliterate with mocked, complacent self-concern.

Yet for all the wit of Coleridge's recoil against songs of himself, the 1796 volume is notable for its groping towards a poetry of the self as a tide threaded through by currents of otherness. Later he would protest against William Bowles's 'blank verse poems' and their 'perpetual trick of *moralizing* everything'. By contrast, for Coleridge the ideal is that 'A Poet's *Heart & Intellect* should be *combined, intimately combined & unified*, with the great appearances in Nature—& not merely held in solution & loose mixture with them, in the shape of formal Similies' (*CL* II, 864). This assertion belongs to 1802, but in 1796, he heads towards it through his use of a form he calls the 'Effusion'. The editors of the Norton Coleridge edition suggests that the poet may be indebted for the term 'effusion' from William Preston 'who defined love poetry as a "spontaneous effusion of a mind wholly occupied by a single idea, careless of rules, little studious of poetic fame, and desirous only of expressing its emotions".[4] In 1796 Coleridge even calls some of his sonnets

---

[4] *Coleridge's Poetry and Prose*, ed. Nicholas Halmi, Paul Magnuson, and Raimonda Modiano (New York: Norton, 2004), p. 5.

'effusions', including the poem addressed 'To the Author of *The Robbers*', which concludes with a vision of Schiller as Coleridgean visionary or ideal poetic super-ego: 'Could I behold thee in thy loftier mood.../ Awhile with mute awe gazing I would brood, / Then weep aloud in a wild extacy!' (10, 13–14). The 'effusion' valorizes the expression of apparently authentic feeling. Unashamed declarations of subjectivity have for the young Coleridge an ethical value: he comments sourly that 'men old and hackneyed in the ways of the world are scrupulous avoiders of Egotism' (*CC* 16. 1. 2, p. 1196). Accordingly, he regarded the sestet of the sonnet to Schiller as 'strong & fiery' (*CC* 16. 1. 1, p. 152), and there is power in his handling of the sonnet's syntax, the final line giving the sense of release after the 'brooding' deliberation suggested by the heavily stressed penultimate line. As is evidenced by the possibility-expanding use of the conditional tense and the imagined encounter with the idealized self, communion with his own imagination in the process of thinking is beginning to establish itself as one of Coleridge's most pressing themes.

In *Biographia Literaria* he calls such communion 'the mind's self-experience in the act of thinking' (*CC* 7: I, p. 124), and its presence distinguishes his work from its eighteenth-century forerunners. In 'Effusion XXXV', later 'The Eolian Harp', Coleridge makes one of the great generic break-throughs of Romantic poetry. In 1796 the poem was a long way from achieving its completed structure, but even in this version the sense of a 'Difference of Form as proceeding and Shape as superinduced' is clear. Coleridge defines such a 'Shape' as 'either the Death or the imprisonment of the Thing' but such a 'Form' as 'its self-witnessing, and self-effected sphere of agency' (*CN* III, 4397 f. 53v). This is the side of Coleridge suspicious of mere obedience to rules: 'Could a rule be given from *without*, poetry would cease to be poetry, and sink into a mechanical art' (*CC* 7: 2, p. 83). 'The Eolian Harp' differs from one of its likely influences, Book 1 of Akenside's *The Pleasures of Imagination*, by virtue of a blank verse attuned to the 'mind's self-experience' in this particular poem. It is in this sense of writing to, from and about the apparent moment of composition that Coleridge warrants his own later 'claim to the thanks of no small number of the readers of poetry in having first introduced this species of short blank verse poems—of which Southey, Lamb, Wordsworth, and others have since produced so many exquisite specimens' (*CC* 16 1: 1, p. 232). Akenside draws an extended comparison between 'Memnon's marble harp' (109) responding 'to the quivering touch / Of Titan's ray' (110–11), and nature's ability to 'Attune the finer organs of the mind' 'To certain species of external things' (115, 114).[5] The blank verse suggests 'the interfusing of the mind and nature', as David Fairer and Christine Gerrard remark, partly by the way the comparison 'interfuses' nature and mind: nature allows the mind to be 'attuned' to nature.[6]

---

[5] Quoted from *Eighteenth-Century Poetry: An Annotated Anthology*, ed. David Fairer and Christine Gerrard (Malden, MA: Blackwell, 1999).

[6] Ibid., p. 309 n.

And it is surely the case, as George Dekker has argued, that 'it is difficult to believe that Coleridge's "organic Harps diversely fram'd" (45; qtd as in Dekker) are unrelated to Akenside's "breath / Of life informing each organic frame"' (73–4).[7] But Coleridge makes the blank-verse effusion or meditation his own by making this poem the place where 'many idly flitting phantasies, / Traverse my indolent and passive brain' (40–1). There the verb 'Traverse' evokes mental operation, without being assertive about its source and origin, while the adjectival luxuriance of 'indolent and passive' conveys the poet's enjoyment of 'the mind's self-experience'. The lines spark off the poem's central speculation: 'And what if all of animated nature / Be but organic harps diversely framed . . . ?' (44–5). The very questioning allows for doubt, riposte, backing off of a kind signalled by the final paragraph's opening: 'But thy more serious eye a mild reproof / Darts' (49–50). Although many readers dislike the crumbling of Coleridge's quasi-pantheist bravado before Sara's 'more serious eye', he has demonstrably created a form in which emotions can overlap, ensue, interrupt—and all be caught as a dynamic process enacted through the blank verse.

The poems gathered in *Sibylline Leaves* under the heading 'Meditative Poems in Blank Verse' are among Coleridge's finest generic achievements. At their centre is the cluster of poems that have come to be known as his conversation poems.[8] In his development of this kind of poem, Coleridge uses and divests himself of generic influence. The form owes much to Cowper's 'divine Chit chat' (*CL* 1, 279), as Coleridge called it, in *The Task*, a ruminative blank verse close to talk but not unMiltonic in idiom. The effect can be of a self-mocking jokiness, as in the lines from *The Task*, Book IV, which lie behind 'Frost at Midnight'. Cowper talks of spinning yarns out of the fire's 'red cinders' (289), 'while with poring eye / I gaz'd, myself creating what I saw' (289–90), or watching 'The sooty films that play upon the bars' (292) that anticipate, as in Coleridge's reworking, 'some stranger's near approach' (295).[9] Cowper is present in his poem, in a way that Akenside is not, but Coleridge wanted a more elusive, less trenchantly solid effect. Accordingly, as he revised 'Frost at Midnight' after its initial publication in 1798, he cut lines that too explicitly define the mind's activities, working 'sometimes with deep faith, / And sometimes with fantastic playfulness' and always bearing witness to 'the self-watching subtilizing mind' (*CC* 16 1. 1, p. 454 n.). Rightly, Coleridge saw these subtle lines as too schematically insisting on their subtlety. Their deletion allows for

---

[7] George Dekker, *Coleridge and the Literature of Sensibility* (New York: Barnes & Noble, 1978), p. 119.

[8] See George McLean Harper, 'Coleridge's Conversation Poems', in *English Romantic Poets: Modern Essays in Criticism*, ed. M. H. Abrams, 2nd edn (Oxford: Oxford University Press, 1975), pp. 188–201. See the useful discussion in Schulz of 'The Conversation Voice', pp. 73–99.

[9] Quoted from *The Complete Poetical Works of William Cowper*, ed. H. S. Milford (London: Frowde, 1905). For a seminal discussion of Coleridge and Cowper, see Humphry House, *Coleridge: the Clark Lectures 1951–52* (1953; London: Rupert Hart-Davis, 1969), pp. 78–83.

greater fluency and surprise as the poem contrives its transitions from present to past to future and back to the present again. The poem's mental events are no longer made allegorical of 'the self-watching self-subtilizing mind'. Rather, they are themselves the central substance of the poem, from which the reader is able to abstract a plot about how the transitions work, to meditate on and respond to, even fill in 'the interspersed vacancies / And momentary pauses of the thought' (46–7) left open in the poem, as well as divining the link between such 'vacancies' and 'pauses', and the closing 'trances of the blast' (71).

'Frost at Midnight' delights by offering itself as a process, a reverie, that with miraculous delicacy ends up as an artistically organized product. What may seem to be a mere rumination in blank verse discovers as it proceeds a 'self-witnessing' form, curving back on itself so that it ends where it starts, with the 'secret ministry of frost' (72). By the end, that 'secret ministry' has become '*combined, intimately combined & unified*' with the 'Poet's *Heart & Intellect*', so that in attending to it Coleridge concludes his poem; a secret ministry is at work, so the poem persuades us, in the natural world and in the meditation that unfolds in the poem, with its final revelation of reciprocity, the 'silent icicles, / Quietly shining to the quiet Moon' (73–4). Coleridge originally ended the piece with six lines describing his baby's response to the icicles, life kicking on beyond the formal triumph achieved by revision. With the cut of the lines comes a gain in aesthetic polish and poise. Coleridge wrote that 'The last six lines I omit because they destroy the rondo, and return upon itself of the Poem. Poems of this kind & length ought to lie coiled with its' tails round its' head' (*CC* 16. 1. 1, p. 456 n.). Yet the muffled sound of a door shut against the barbaric yawp of life may just be heard and hints at the price paid for one kind of generic triumph.

'Coleridge', writes George Dekker, 'was a deliberate artist who discovered freedom within the constraints of inherited literary conventions'.[10] Certainly his instinct is towards a highly individualized version of traditional forms: 'The Rime of the Ancient Mariner' may be, as J. C. C. Mays avers, 'an exercise in the Gothic Revival ballad' (*CC* 16. 1. 1, p. 367), a poem 'professedly written in imitation of the *style*, as well as of the spirit of the elder poets', as the Advertisement to the 1798 edition of *Lyrical Ballads* has it (*CC* 16. 1. 1, p. 367). But it transforms the balladic genre, turning it into a vessel that carries an unprecedented freight of significance. Mocked by Charles Lamb, the 1800 sub-title of the poem 'A Poet's Reverie' serves one useful function: it reminds us that the poem is generically *sui generis*, the product of 'a poet's Reverie'. Lamb was 'sorry that Coleridge has christened his Ancient Marinere "a poet's Reverie"—it is as bad as Bottom the Weaver's declaration that he is not a Lion but only the scenical representation of a Lion'; he goes on, 'What new idea is gained by this Title, but one subversive of all

---

[10] Dekker, p. 180.

credit, which the Tale should force upon us, of its Truth'.[11] Yet Coleridge's credit-subverting subtitle alerts us to his poem's self-conscious fascination with 'scenical representation'. The word 'reverie' may hedge its bets, allowing itself to be thought of in distinctly lightweight terms as meaning 'merely dreamy', but it intimates strongly that, *au fond*, the poem exists as a work of 'pure imagination' (*CC* 14. 2, 100) and demonstrates the workings of that imagination.

It is hard to feel at all comfortable in assigning a generic label to the poem. Yes, it is a ballad and imitates the ballads Coleridge read in Percy's *Reliques*. Its finger on the pulse of literary fashion, it is, in some respects, a decidedly artful piece of literary pastiche. But it is also a poem in possession of its own kingdom. From its arresting opening 'It is an ancient Mariner' (1; poem is quoted from the 1834 version), or from the early image of the 'ice, mast high' (53) that, by way of a haunting internal rhyme, 'came floating by, / As green as emerald' (53–4), the poem plunges the reader into a pellucid, hallucinatory world of the imagination and continually outsmarts our critical account. This is no ordinary ballad, the reader senses; if anything, as the great forces and laws of the universe figured in symbols of star and moon emerge as central to the poem, it seems to border on mythic exploration, at once revelatory and mysterious. God is queasily present and absent, nowhere more so than in the equivocal lines: 'Nor dim nor red, like God's own head, / The glorious Sun uprist' (97–8). Are the dimness and redness like or unlike God's own head?[12] One presumes the latter to be the case, but the negative construction allows briefly for the former view to flicker forth—and suddenly the poem is about goodness and evil, and about God's role in those things. We inhabit a poem that has the makings of a theodicy, a work that at times seeks to justify the ways of God to mariners, yet even with the addition of the religiously minded gloss in 1817 it seems calculatedly to raise as many questions as it solves about the nature of suffering and evil. The gloss is one of Coleridge's generic innovations; he allows it to reinforce yet play against the events narrated in the poem in intriguing ways and involving temporal and cultural disjunctions:

'The Ancient Mariner' leaves behind the bracing ironies of a traditional ballad as 'Sir Patrick Spens' (collected in Percy's *Reliques*), in which, as Schulz has it, 'transition and explanation are omitted; all is situation'.[13] 'Sir Patrick Spens' makes its impact through Sir Patrick's double response of laughter and weeping to the King's order that he undertakes an impossible voyage, heroic dedication in the face of likely disaster, and details that tell us of that disaster: the hats of the shipwrecked lords floating above their drowned bodies, the ladies with golden combs in the hair who must wait a long time before their dead lords will return.

---

[11] *The Letters of Charles and Mary Lamb 1796–1817*, ed. Edwin M. Marr, 3 vols. (Ithaca, NY: Cornell University Press, 1975–8), 1, p. 266. Mays argues that the word 'reverie' has 'an almost technical meaning in Coleridge's vocabulary of dreams' (*CC* 16. 1. 1, p. 365).

[12] See House, *Coleridge*, pp. 99–100.

[13] Schulz, p. 61.

The anonymous balladist is entirely silent about his poem's implications. By contrast, in some of the most memorable writing of the Romantic period, Coleridge evokes in Part III a vision of life as a near-godless, existential waste of ocean. 'Death' (189) and 'Life-in-Death' (193) play dice for the fate of the crew: the atmosphere is one of terrifying visionary chiaroscuro. 'No twilight within the courts of the sun' is Coleridge's haunting gloss on a stanza that turns the cosmos into a projection of nightmare: 'The Sun's rim dips; the stars rush out: / At one stride comes the dark; / With far-heard whisper, o'er the sea, / Off shot the spectre-bark' (199–202). Coleridge makes every syllable tell, capturing the mariner's plight as he is suspended between the dubious heavens of the 'stars' and the hell of the 'spectre-bark'. In the line, 'At one stride comes the dark', the present tense of 'comes' coincides with the metrical stress to bring the dark upon us stealthily and overpoweringly.

At such moments this 'work of…pure imagination' (CC 14. 2, 100) draws creative refreshment from two generic fountains other than narrative and ballad: namely, lyric and epic. If 'lyric' is involved with the expression of a speaker's feelings, then 'The Ancient Mariner' is deeply lyrical. In however displaced a way, Coleridge is writing the poem that defines who he was as a poet.[14] Tellingly he saw the poem in self-referential terms. Wreathed among the affecting ironies of the later 'Constancy to an Ideal Object' (1804–7? 1822?) is a concealed, conditional allusion to Coleridge as his own Ancient Mariner. Without his Ideal Object his life 'were but a becalmed Bark, / Whose Helmsman on an Ocean waste and wide / Sits mute and pale his mouldering helm beside' (22–4). In a poem whose yearning, defeated couplets bring together confession, self-critique and metaphysical inquiry, Coleridge here gives expression to the imagining of failure through the spaciously becalming influence of adjectival doublets. Rhythmically idling on its own painted ocean, the poem confers a retrospective form on 'The Ancient Mariner', converting it into a narrative that contains within itself a measure of covert and proleptic lyric autobiography. That the bestowal of such a generic identity takes place in a simile is appropriate: it suggests how, in 'The Ancient Mariner', comparisons that both pause and intensify grasp of an inner state, such as the likeness drawn between the mariner and 'one, that on a lonesome road / Doth walk in fear and dread' (446–7), quicken the poem's lyrical pulse.

That 'lonesome road' may not be entirely existential or personal. Coleridge, on recent readings, is encountering the haunting spectre (and ghastly reality) of slavery in the poem. This reading goes back to William Empson who, in William Keach's gloss, 'connects the power of neurotic guilt in the poem to disguised

---

[14] Compare Mays's comment on the poem: 'Begun as an attempt merely to earn £5 from the *Monthly Magazine*, it became a mirror in which Coleridge came to see his fate endlessly reflected' (*CC* 16. 1. 1, p. 368).

anxieties about European maritime exploitation and the slave trade'.[15] Such 'anxieties' are indeed 'disguised', and such a reading can only be speculative; but one reason for the poem's power is the way Coleridge converts balladic form into a vehicle for staging confrontation not only between the questing, suffering self and an august yet terrifying universe but also between such a self and a nightmarish Gothicized polity, where justice is inscrutable, horrors unexplained, and deliverance inexplicable. The theologico-political Coleridge is overt in many of his 1790s poems, perhaps most singularly in the near-bombastic sublimities of 'Religious Musings', but it is arguable that he manifests himself with maximum cunning in 'The Ancient Mariner'. Indeed, in the poem we encounter a Romantic version of epic or brief epic, one that can be brought into agreement with Shelley's definition of epic as poetry that bears a 'defined and intelligible relation to the knowledge, and sentiment, and religion, and political condition of the age in which [the poet] lived, and of the ages which followed it'.[16] 'The Ancient Mariner' bears out this definition with a twist. Its defined and intelligible relation' to the 'knowledge, and sentiment, and religion, and political condition of the age' may be the discovery that those things cannot finally be seen as 'defined and intelligible'. As Livingston Lowes showed in *The Road to Xanadu*, Coleridge's poem distils images drawn from many branches of knowledge. The poem seems peculiarly suited to and expressive of its age, as Coleridge at least partly suggests in his account of 'supernatural' poetry in *Biographia Literaria*, chapter 14, where he lays emphasis (and in the process brings in yet another generic category) on the 'dramatic truth' of the emotions produced by supernatural 'incidents and agents' (*CC* 7. 2, p. 6). 'The Ancient Mariner' is to the Romantic age a work that tells Coleridge's contemporaries that there are more things in heaven and earth than are dreamt of in their philosophy. So, the opening sentence of the Latin epigraph from Burnet's *Achaeologiae Philosophicae* added in 1817 reads in an eighteenth-century translation quoted by Mays: 'I can easily believe that there are more Invisible than Visible Beings in the Universe' (*CC* 16. 1. 1, p. 371). A Notebook entry of 1796, listing possible works, includes as one of items, 'The Origin of Evil, an Epic Poem' (*CN* 1, 161). 'The Ancient Mariner' might be seen as the product of that recorded aspiration.

Just as Coleridge transforms the genre of ballad in 'The Ancient Mariner', so in 'Christabel' he does something rich and strange with the genre of romance. Excluded from the 1800 edition of *Lyrical Ballads* as not being compatible with the volume's overall spirit, uncompleted, radically different in tone and atmosphere in its two parts, which do at least share a fascination with psychological trespass and possess conclusions that do little to solve or resolve, the poem has a powerfully liminal quality, as though it were on the threshold of turning into the

---

[15] Samuel Taylor Coleridge, *The Complete Poems*, ed. William Keach (London: Penguin, 1997), p. 500.

[16] Percy Bysshe Shelley, *The Major Works*, ed. Zachary Leader and Michael O'Neill (Oxford: Oxford University Press, 2003), p. 692.

poem it can never quite become. A romance, it circles round an obscure horror: that of Christabel's possession (albeit momentary) by Geraldine. But what motivates Geraldine Coleridge never quite says, nor do we find out who she is. Additions intriguingly complicate: lines which appeared in print for the first time in 1828 suggest that Geraldine herself fights with a force of evil: 'Deep from within she seems half-way / To lift some weight, with sick Assay, / And eyes the Maid and seek delay' (257–9): a triplet in deep sympathy with the poem's troubled refusal to stride purposefully forward to the accomplishment of a narrative deed. In his peroration to *The Road to Xanadu*, Livingston Lowes claims that 'the Road to Xanadu, as we have traced it, is the road of the human spirit', that poetic shapes are ' "carved with figures strange and sweet, All made out of the carver's brain" ', and that 'what the carver-creator sees . . . is the unique and lovely Form'.[17] Lowes alludes eloquently to 'Christabel', 179–80, but, in doing so, he reminds us that the 'unique and lovely Form' of the poem calls into question the independent status of unique and lovely poetic forms.

Indeed, in 'Christabel', we feel that 'All' is 'made out of the Carver's brain' (180). Many stylistic features draw attention to the tap of the verbal chisel: the question-and-answer routine of the opening, for example, or the poem's metrical cunning, which offers itself as one of the many metrical experiments Coleridge wrote. Yes, it has 'correspondence with some transition, in the nature of the imagery or passion', as Coleridge asserts in his Preface (*CC* 16. 1. 1, p. 483). But it knows it does. The poem dances to its own measure rather like 'the One red Leaf, the last of its Clan, / That dances as often as dance it can' (49–50), perilously in possession of its own continued poetic life, even as its awareness of the work done by the carver's brain seems to chime with its investigation of the way one mind can project its evil intentions into another. In 'Frost at Midnight' Coleridge perfected the poem's turn back upon itself; the snake swallows its tail as the poem's rondo corresponds to a religious vision of rare contentment, even if shadowed by a sense of having to be shaped. In 'The Ancient Mariner' worries about formal rondures are more urgent; the mariner returns to land, the poem offers us a moral, but there is a strong feeling that, fighting hard against this moral, is the unforgettable memory of a seemingly abandoned soul, 'Alone, alone, all, all alone, / Alone on a wide wide sea!' (232–3). In 'Christabel', the poem suspends itself in a mid-air of tranced vision, itself 'Fearfully dreaming, yet, I wis, / Dreaming that alone, which is' (294–5). And if it be objected that such a reflexive reading narrows the poem's scope, my point really is that by refusing to fulfil the laws of genre, backing off, as it does, from the requirements of romance, 'Christabel' exhibits Coleridge's wariness of the very formal artifice it so consummately displays. Coleridge's handling of genres displays his subtle sense of art's limits, adumbrated in an early notebook entry: 'Poetry—excites us to artificial

[17] John Livingston Lowes, *The Road to Xanadu: A Study in the Ways of the Imagination* (1927; London: Pan, 1978), p. 396.

feelings—makes us callous to real ones' (*CN* 1. 87)). Seamus Perry speculates that this is 'An effect of *bad* poetry, presumably' (*CNS*, p. 140) and quotes persuasively a number of associated passages, yet Coleridge's compressed note expresses anxiety, too, about the effect of '*good* poetry'. Aesthetically pleasing poetry might be ethically undesirable. 'Christabel' signs or breaks off with 'A very metaphysical account of Fathers calling their children rogues, rascals, & little varlets—&c —' (*CL* 2. 728), an account of 'callous' feelings caused by 'Love's Excess' (664); a contradictory state unveiling and concealing itself in a series of pell-mell enjambments. Coleridge diagnoses the reason for 'Words of unmeant Bitterness' (665) in lines that almost parody the workings of imagination: 'Perhaps 'tis pretty to force together / Thoughts so all unlike each other' (666–7). Poetic dreams of accomplishment are entoiled, for Coleridge, in 'a World of Sin' (673).

Poetic genre and poetic form might, indeed, be thought of as possessing, for Coleridge, a redemptive quality and presenting a potentially sinful temptation. 'Kubla Khan' is a Romantic lyric, disguising itself in 1816 as as 'psychological curiosity' or 'FRAGMENT' (*CC* 16. 1. 1, p. 511), in which Coleridge responds to Collins's 'Ode on the Poetical Character', a poem which he asserted 'has inspired & whirled *me* along with greater agitations of enthusiasm than any the most *impassioned* Scene in Schiller or Shakespeare' (*CL* 1, 279). Collins's musical, rhapsodic couplets ask, 'Where is the Bard, whose Soul can now / Its high presuming Hopes avow? / Where He who thinks, with Rapture blind, / This hallow'd Work for Him design'd?' (51–4).[18] Hubris threatens here, even if the work is 'hallow'd', and the close of the poem laments that 'Heav'n, and *Fancy*' 'Have now o'erturn'd th'inspiring Bow'rs, / Or curtain'd close such Scene from ev'ry future View' (74–6). These lines describe a two-pronged assault on 'th'inspiring Bowers': both religious authority and the human imagination itself chastise poetic hopes, and the last phrase, 'ev'ry future View', falls wistfully but also heavily: a nail driven deeply into the coffin of ambition. Collins gives us access to a primal poetic 'Scene' precisely by declaring himself outcast from it, and in doing so he paves the way for Coleridge's ode-like response in 'Kubla Khan': ode-like because the poem's structure shows study of an ode's turns and counterpointings. Coleridge imagines (partly by way of echoes of Collins's 'The Passions. An Ode for Music') a return to poetic paradise, in which the poet takes on the mantle of the Khan, the man of power, but supersedes him by virtue of a capacity for inclusive, unexploitative vision.[19] Khan as enforcer of order in the face of 'caverns measureless to man' (4) bears a relationship, at once ironic and more than ironic, to the poet reducing experience to order through poetic form. The hypnotic opening insists that we re-hear, as if for the first time, the potent force of poetry as magical spell; the poem's genre is, initially, incantation. Xanadu lifts

---

[18] Quoted from *Eighteenth-Century Poetry: An Annotated Anthology*, ed. David Fairer and Christine Gerrard.

[19] For the echoes of Collins, see *The Road to Xanadu*, pp. 365–6.

itself out of history into spellbinding poetic fantasy. Yet there is a price to be paid for effortless song. That quarrelsome conjunction 'But' (12), introducing the second movement, alerts us to this price as it ushers in a world of rebellious energies, sexuality, both male and female, and 'Ancestral voices prophesying war' (30). Read in Bloomian terms, those 'Ancestral voices' could be the voices of the slain poets, Collins and other distressed poets of sensibility, come back to tell Coleridge that their fears about poetic vision were not to be scorned.

In response Coleridge imagines (31–6) an idyllic interlude, a virtual poetic triumph, one that almost teases its own demonstration of imaginative delight in yoking together contraries. From Collins he takes the idea of 'mingled measure' and against Collins he asserts, with ease, his poetic achievement: 'It was a miracle of rare device, / A sunny pleasure-dome with caves of ice' (35–6).[20] Yet, affectingly, Coleridge then goes on to stage a scene of suppositious inspiration, saying what he could achieve were he to be re-inspired. Mays argues that 'the tonal significance of the word "Could" in line 42—"Could I revive with me"—is neither neutral nor unambiguous' (CC 16. 1. 1, p. 510); but it is arguable that longing for imaginative power, part of the poem's inheritance from Collins's ode, is as strong an element as any in the mix. A flurry of end-rhymes on the same sound between lines 46 and 50 ('air', 'there', 'Beware!', 'hair') suggests how much is at stake, little less than the speaker's incarnation as the inspired poet imagined by Collins, recoverer of the sacred tradition. Yet again a Coleridgean poem ends with a version of the self engaged in imagined poetic shaping. As the self takes on the form of an idealized poet, so the poem shapes itself in a completed design, albeit a design that contains within itself the turbulent drama of not fully realized aspiration. The imagined spectators merge with the speaker himself in voicing the emphatic final two lines of the poem, 'For he on honey-dew hath fed, / And drank the milk of Paradise' (53–4), but the final indicative verb takes us back to a past, even if it is one imagined in the future, and we can never wholly lose sight of the fact that behind the indicatives lies a train of what grammarians call present unreal conditionals.

Coleridge's awareness of the ode's generic possibilities, potently implicit in 'Kubla Khan', blaze out in other poems, notably 'France: An Ode'. Like 'To William Wordsworth' and 'A Tombless Epitaph', the poem uses its genre as a vehicle for poetic self-reflection. It dwells on Coleridge's poetic career, a career dialectically bound up with his political views. In a stanza form that deftly remodels the sonnet (in effect, each stanza is a sonnet and a half, twenty-one lines in the form of two alternatingly rhyming quatrains followed by a couplet, then a further alternatingly rhyming quatrain, then a final seven lines rhyming *abaccbc*), Coleridge fuses the overall high passion and transitions from stanza to stanza characteristic of the ode with an intricate way of netting the poetic winds and tides of emotional surge and counter-surge. As suggested, the form has behind it Coleridge's experimentation

---

[20] Ibid., p. 365.

with the sonnet; the subtle rhyming of 'To the River Otter', for example, illustrates his delight in cutting across expected verbal groupings, serving as an emblem of the ways in which the 'many various-fated years' (2) survive in consciousness and 'Visions of childhood' (12) cut athwart 'Lone manhood's cares' (13). Coleridge commented in his Preface to his *Sonnets from Various Authors* (1796) that 'The Sonnet . . . is a small poem, in which some lonely feeling is developed' (*CC* 16. 1. 2, p. 1205). Clearly 'France: An Ode' is a more richly orchestrated poem, but it is keenly alert to the cadences of 'lonely feeling', and its formal originality reminds us that its author wrote in the same 1796 Preface:

Respecting the metre of a Sonnet, the Writer should consult his own convenience.— Rhymes, many or few, or no rhymes at all—whatever the chastity of his ear may prefer, whatever the rapid expression of his feelings will permit;—all these things are left at his own disposal   (*CC* 16. 1. 2, p. 1206).

In the last section of 'France: An Ode', 'the rapid expression' of Coleridge's 'feelings' articulates itself in the space between the demands of form and the longing for liberty. Rhymes and metre work with particular expressiveness. Rhyme mimes the entrapped condition of those who think they can be free through mere rebellion. They cannot, the poem argues; they merely ensnare themselves, engaging in a 'mad game' (86) that is grimly mimicked by the writing in which they 'wear the name / Of Freedom graven on an heavier chain' (87–8). There, the rhymes work like manacles. But they also work to suggest how the poet can find a space where he can experience, in the terms proposed by the poem, a liberty beyond that available to 'men, as a society' (*CC* 16. 1. 1, p. 464). Around 1807 Coleridge glossed the last stanza thus: 'the Object . . . is to shew, that true political Freedom can only arise out of moral Freedom' (*CC* 16. 1. 1, p. 468). One place that such 'Freedom' seems momentarily attainable is in the territory colonized by the poem, a poem whose final seven lines make of the poem the focus of an embrace between self and 'all things':

> And there I felt thee! On yon sea-cliff's verge,
>   Whose pines just travell'd by the breeze above,
> Had made one murmur with the distant surge —
>   Yes! as I stood and gaz'd, my forehead bare,
>   And shot my being thro' earth, sea, and air,
> Possessing all things by intensest love —
>   O LIBERTY! my spirit felt thee there!
>
> (99–105)

That last line has, as its metapoetic generic sub-text, the words, 'my spirit feels thee here', here in this suddenly coalescing group of rhymes. Once more, the poet comes to the fore, announcing his entangled, productive, individual engagement with a genre, in this case the ode, into which he breathes new life by dramatizing and enacting his own poetic presence.

To think about genre, in Coleridge's case, is to think about form at the local level, the aesthetics of verbal delivery and phrasing, as his many pieces of metrical experimentation bear witness. But, as 'To Derwent Coleridge: The Chief and Most Common Metrical Feet Expressed in Corresponding Metre' illustrates, these pieces often also remind us that all questions of aesthetics, for Coleridge, are ultimately questions about ethics—about the right ways in which poems might operate. So, Coleridge, jokily rhyming on 'Poet' (14), says that, if Derwent aspires to the name, he will need 'these metres to shew it' (13). But he will also and simultaneously need to be 'innocent, steady, and wise, / And delight in the Things of Earth, Water, and Skies' (11–12), and have 'sound Sense in his Brains' (14). A central ethical issue for a poet whose response to past genres is to dramatize his heightened awareness of such response concerns poetic self-representation. In 'To William Wordsworth', tribute, appropriately couched in a blank verse that out-Wordsworths Wordsworth as it mirrors the Miltonic ambitions of *The Prelude*, threatens to topple over into self-pity. Indeed, the genre of this poem comes close to poetic self-elegy, even as it gazes beyond itself towards a new genre inaugurated by Wordsworth: that of 'orphic song' (45), in which a poem becomes its own self-involved, self-created 'song divine of high and passionate thoughts, / To their own Music chaunted!' (46–7). At the heart of Coleridge's engagement with genre is this glimpse of poetry as a form of 'orphic song'. At the end of 'To William Wordsworth', having temporarily but valiantly turned away from the 'unhealthful road' (79) of 'self-harm' (80), he constructs, yet again, an image of himself in the throes of possible creation as he evokes the 'momentary Stars of my own birth, / Fair constellated Foam, still darting off' (98–9). There, the exquisite tension between 'still' (at once meaning 'always' and 'motionless', as though perfected) and 'darting' emblematizes, in little, the tension between the poem in process and the poem as product.

Genres, one may think, exist in a symbiotic relationship with genius; poetic traditions are mansions that await the arrival of the unexpected guest, the individual talent. As a glance at the index of the Bollingen edition of *Biographia Literaria* reveals, poetic genius was much in Coleridge's thoughts. Chapter 15 of *Biographia* analyses Shakespeare's poetry in order to set out 'characteristics of original poetic genius in general' (*CC* 7. 2, 19) and lays emphasis on the poet's command, his superiority, so to speak, over his materials (including, if only implicitly, the genre in which he is working): 'the sense of musical delight' (*CC* 7. 2, 20), for instance, bespeaks the presence (though Coleridge does not force this link) of 'a superior spirit more intuitive, more intimately conscious' (*CC* 7. 2, p. 21) than anything or anyone else in the poem. The poet's personality in art transmutes itself into something close to Olympian serenity. Yet Coleridge also knows how to transmute the self so that it seems untransmuted, and this, my chapter has argued, is one of the characteristics of his own form of 'original poetic genius'. In his epitaphic 'S. T. C.', composed between 1803 and 1833 (see *CC* 16. 1. 2, p. 1145), the poem reaches out to the 'viator', the traveller, in the traditional manner of epitaphic poems, here a 'Christian Passer-by' (1), and pleads for 'one thought in prayer' (4). Only eight lines in length, the poem mimes expression of hesitant spiritual hope that adapts itself to, strains against, but finally acquiesces in, the chiselled constraints of the epitaphic form, always brief, terse, and striving for impersonality. And yet Coleridge brings, as so often in his poetry, the drama of his career to the poem's centre, alluding to one of the most famous passages in 'The Ancient Mariner', the encounter between Death and Life-in-Death, when he prays 'That he who many a year with toil of Breath / Found Death in Life, may here find Life in Death' (5–6). Superbly he betters his earlier lines, makes them assume a new Christianized version of the kind glossed well by Paley's reference to John 12: 13: 'He that loveth his life shall lose it; and he that hateth his life in this world shall keep it unto life eternal'.[21] It is intriguing and affecting that the transaction described at the poem's close is ambiguous: 'to be forgiven for Fame, / He ask'd, and hoped, thro' Christ' (7–8). Coleridge explained that 'for' in the phrase 'for Fame' means 'instead of' (*CC* 16. 1. 2, p. 1146), but another meaning, to be forgiven on account of his fame, refuses wholly to be banished. This seems appropriate as an ending to a career whose dealings with genre supply, in a creatively impressive sense, one of the most powerful if covert examples of egotistical sublimity in the Romantic period.

Works Cited

ABRAMS, M. H. 2006. Structure and style in the greater Romantic lyric (1965), quoted from vol. 1 of *Romanticism: Critical Concepts in Literary and Cultural Studies*, ed. Michael O'Neill and Mark Sandy, 4 vols. London: Routledge.

COLERIDGE, SAMUEL TAYLOR. 1997. *The Complete Poems*, ed. William Keach. London: Penguin, 1997.

—— 2004. *Poetry and Prose*, ed. Nicholas Halmi, Paul Magnuson, and Raimonda Modiano. New York: Norton.

COLERIDGE, SARA. 1875. *Memoir and Letters of Sara Coleridge*, ed. her daughter. New York and London: Harper.

COWPER, WILLIAM. 1905. *The Complete Poetical Works*, ed. H. S. Milford. London: Frowde.

DEKKER, GEORGE. 1978. *Coleridge and the Literature of Sensibility*. New York: Barnes & Noble.

Eighteenth-Century Poetry: 1999. An Annotated Anthology, ed. David Fairer and Christine Gerrard. Malden, MA: Blackwell.

[21] Quoted in Morton D. Paley, *Coleridge's Later Poetry* (1996; Oxford: Clarendon, repr. 1999 (with corrections)), p. 124. Paley also notes the allusion to 'The Ancient Mariner' and offers an indispensable discussion of the various versions of the poem.

HARPER, GEORGE MCLEAN. 1975. Coleridge's Conversation Poems. In *English Romantic Poets: Modern Essays in Criticism*, ed. M. H. Abrams, 2nd edn. Oxford: Oxford University Press, pp. 188–201.

HOUSE, HUMPHRY. 1969. *Coleridge: the Clark Lectures 1951–52*. First publ. 1953; London: Rupert Hart-Davis.

LAMB, CHARLES. 1975–8. *The Letters of Charles and Mary Lamb 1796–1817*, ed. Edwin M. Marr, 3 vols. Ithaca, NY: Cornell University Press.

LOWES, JOHN LIVINGSTON. 1978. *The Road to Xanadu: A Study in the Ways of the Imagination*. First publ. 1927; London: Pan.

OWEN, W. J. B. 1963. Review of Max F. Schulz, *The Poetic Voices of Coleridge* (Detroit: Wayne State University Press, 1963) and Werner W. Beyer, *The Enchanted Forest* (Oxford: Blackwell). *RES* (1965), N.S. 16: 86–7.

PALEY, MORTON D. 1996. *Coleridge's Later Poetry*. Repr. 1999 (with corrections). Oxford: Clarendon.

SCHULZ, MAX F. 1963. *The Poetic Voices of Coleridge*. Detroit: Wayne State University Press.

SHELLEY, PERCY BYSSHE. 2003. *The Major Works*, ed. Zachary Leader and Michael O'Neill. Oxford: Oxford University Press.

CHAPTER 21

COLERIDGE AS PLAYWRIGHT

GEORGE ERVING

SAMUEL Taylor Coleridge's influence as a dramatic critic has, understandably, overshadowed his reputation as a playwright.[1] He completed four plays: *The Fall of Robespierre, an Historic Drama* (1794), co-authored with Robert Southey, never performed, and printed for limited distribution; *Osorio, A Tragedy* (1797), begun at the behest of Richard Brinsley Sheridan but also rejected by him; *Remorse, A Tragedy* (1813), a revision of *Osorio* that made an extraordinarily successful opening run at Drury Lane but languished thereafter; and *Zapolya: A Christmas Tale*, in Two Parts (1817), which, having been rejected by Drury Lane, played for ten evenings at the less prestigious Surrey Theatre before disappearing altogether.[2] As with Romantic period drama in general, which until recently has been ignored as the poor stepchild of its Elizabethan and Jacobean forebears, all Coleridge's plays largely faded from view. Beginning in the 1980s, however, the historicist turn in Romantic criticism has excited interest in the theatre's cultural authority during the Revolutionary period, wherein current events were discussed as drama and

---

[1] See contributions by Matthew Scott and Charles Mahoney in this volume for Coleridge as dramatic critic.

[2] Coleridge also left several dramatic fragments: *The Spell; or, Laugh Till You Lose Him!* (1800–15?), *The Triumph of Loyalty, an Historic Drama in five Acts* (1801), and *Didaste; or The Bait without the Hook* (1811–12? 1815?). For details relating to sources, dating, textual variants, dramaturgy, production, and reception of each play, see J. C. C. Mays' introductions in Samuel Taylor Coleridge, *Poetical Works*, The Collected Works of Samuel Taylor Coleridge, ed. J. C. C. Mays, vol. 16, Bollingen Series 75, 16 vols. (Princeton: Princeton University Press, 2001), 1: 57–65.

dramatic representations of current events in turn shaped political opinion. As Gillian Russell points out, the London patent theatres at Covent Garden and Drury Lane, as well as their provincial counterparts, wielded enormous influence as *de facto* 'representative assemblies or national "houses"' and the drama's elevated authority as an unofficial medium for shaping public opinion during an era troubled by frequent food riots, reform agitations, war protests, and invasion scares, marked it as an important target for government surveillance and super-vision.[3] Consequently, the Stage Licensing Act of 1737, which called upon the Lord Chamberlain's Examiner of Plays to censor political content in all manuscripts intended for the London patent theatres, was enforced with special rigor after the outbreak of war in 1793. This in turn transformed the drama, as playwrights often sought to circumvent censorship by producing figural rather than explicit repre-sentations of contemporary events, and plays increasingly demonstrated a reflexive concern for the relationship between fiction and reality.[4]

Conditioned by these factors, critical interest in Romantic period theatre has brought resurgent attention to Coleridge's dramatic practice and raised a new set of interpretive problems.[5] While Carl Woodring long ago recognized that Coleridge's plays were implicitly political, more recent research has sought to understand their political subtexts and dramaturgical strategies with greater precision.[6] The effort requires a more nuanced understanding of how each work comments upon contemporary social, political, and religious issues, how each

---

[3] Gillian Russell, *The Theatres of War: Performance, Politics and Society, 1793–1815* (Oxford: Oxford University Press, 1995), 15–18. For an excellent introduction to the theatre's cultural role during the Romantic period, see Gillian Russell, 'Theatre', *An Oxford Companion to the Romantic Age, British Culture 1776–1832*, ed. Iain McCalman (Oxford: Oxford University Press, 1999), 223–31.

[4] See also, Terrence Allen Hoagwood, 'Romantic Drama and Historical Hermeneutics' with greater precision, *British Romantic Drama: Historical and Critical Essays*, ed. Terrence Allan Hoagwood and Daniel P. Watkins (Madison, N.J.: Fairleigh Dickinson University Press, 1998), 25. As Jeffrey Cox has shown, strategies of displacement entailed scripting plays that presented historical parallels to the French Revolution (rarely successful), neoclassical tragedies portraying the demise of tyranny, or gothic dramas whose stock themes were of incarceration in castle-prisons or monasteries at the hands of cruel aristocrats and or hypocritical monks (though by the late 1790s these often reflected an ambivalence regarding the energies liberated by the Revolution). See Jeffrey N. Cox, 'The French Revolution in the English Theatre', *History and Myth: Essays on English Romantic Literature*, ed. Stephen C. Behrendt (Detroit: Wayne State University Press, 1990), 33–52. For censorship of theatre at this time, see 'The Suppression of Political Comment on the Stage during the French Revolution and Napoleonic Wars', in L.W. Conolly, *The Censorship of English Drama, 1737–1824* (San Marino, CA: Huntington Library, 1976), 83–112. For a comprehensive list of British plays written in the 1790s, sorted by political their themes and attitudes, see Theodore Grieder, 'Annotated Checklist of the British Drama, 1789–99', *Restoration and 18th Century Theatre Research* 4 (1965): 21–47.

[5] These primarily treat individual plays. Julie Carlson's *In the Theatre of Romanticism: Coleridge, Nationalism, and Women*, Cambridge Studies in Romanticism, ed. Marilyn Butler and James Chandler, vol. 5 (Cambridge University Press, 1995) is the only book-length study to date of Coleridge's plays.

[6] Carl Woodring, *Politics in the Poetry of Coleridge* (Madison: University of Wisconsin Press, 1961), 194–219.

relates to Coleridge's non-dramatic writings, and how each may attempt to manipulate dramatic and literary conventions so as to conceal controversial content from censorship without sacrificing intelligibility or the power to delight and instruct.[7] Critical research must also attempt to account for the apparent conflict between Coleridge's dramatic practice and dramatic criticism. In the 1790s, for example, he inveighs against the Gothic as a low-class art form imported from Germany yet he scripts *Osorio* as a Gothic melodrama explicitly indebted to Schiller's Gothic drama *The Robbers* and ghost story *Der Geisterseher*. In the 1810s, he condemns Gothic drama as 'Jacobinical' yet retains *Osorio*'s gothic features as he positioned *Remorse* for the London stage.

With these critical concerns in mind, this essay introduces Coleridge's dramas in light of a signal paradox between their political affiliations and their thematic preoccupations. Written over a twenty-three-year period, the plays reflect the evolution of Coleridge's political outlook from radical to reactionary, and his theological transformation from Unitarian to Trinitarian, yet they retain a surprising degree of thematic consistency. Each is concerned with the usurpation and recovery of rightful authority, with the misrecognition and revelation of sovereign identity, and with the dangers of demagoguery, hypocrisy, despotism, atheism, and materialism. What changes, therefore, is not, Coleridge's dramatic preoccupation with moral, political, and religious issues, but the elements in British society he assigns to the roles of hero and villain.

THE FALL OF ROBESPIERRE, AN HISTORIC DRAMA (1794)

Coleridge's first venture as a playwright was to pen Act I and edit Southey's work on Acts II and III of *The Fall of Robespierre*, which the two produced as a means of raising funds for their 'Pantisocracy' scheme to establish in Pennsylvania, along with their small circle of disaffected radicals, a society based upon the abolition of private property. Written hurriedly in late August and early September 1794, the play closely follows British newspaper accounts of the discursive events leading to Robespierre's overthrow and execution on 28 July 1794, though Coleridge's contribution takes far more artistic license than Southey's near-verbatim conversion of

---

[7] For an excellent example of how *Osorio* encodes Coleridge's political ideas, see Marjean D. Purinton, 'The English Pamphlet War of the 1790s and Coleridge's *Osorio*', *British Romantic Drama: Historical and Critical Essays*, ed. Terence Allan Hoagwood and Daniel P. Watkins (Madison, NJ: Fairleigh Dickinson University Press, 1998), 159–81.

journalistic prose to dramatic verse. Their drama thus demonstrates the close connection that Lucyle Werkmeister and Matthew Buckley have noted between newspapers and the theatre in the early 1790s, but at the same time, it is unusual in its direct representation of the Revolution, which by 1794 would have prevented its being performed on any major stage.[8] It seems likely for this reason and for its preference for dialogue over action (Southey's acts consist entirely in public oratory), that the authors intended it as a closet drama to be circulated among the dissenting readership of its radical Unitarian publisher, Benjamin Flower.

This raises the question, however, as to what appeal Coleridge expected it to have for such readers, since the play does not betray an obvious pro-revolutionary bias toward the events of Thermidor that was likely to gratify republican sentiment or to have aroused reactionary censure.[9] It is, however, a play about conspiracy, written on the eve of the Treason Trials and in the midst of the Pitt Ministry's sharp step-up of counter-revolutionary measures during the summer and fall of 1794. Act I, in particular, imagines the psychology of suspicion and fear that must have existed amidst the inner circles of the French leadership when it remained uncertain as to who would dare support, and who betray the plot to depose Robespierre 'The Incorruptible'. Such imaginings bore tacit relevance for the British radical movement that had been infiltrated by government spies. Coleridge's dedicatory preface, stating that the play is an attempt 'to imitate the empassioned and highly figurative language of the French Orators, and to develope the characters of the chief actors on a vast stage of horrors', further suggests its relevance for a Britain polarized by fiery declamation. *The Fall of Robespierre* thus underscores Coleridge's sense of politics as drama and drama as politics by representing their discursive similarity. Consequently, the play is concerned less with the portrayal of tragic characters than with the means by which fear and discourse operate upon one another in shaping the momentous political events of the day. As William Jewett has argued, Coleridge dramatizes how terror

---

[8] Lucyle Werkmeister, *A Newspaper History of England 1792–1793* (Lincoln: University of Nebraska Press, 1967), 42. Matthew Buckley, ' "A Dream of Murder": *The Fall of Robespierre* and the Tragic Imagination', *Studies in Romanticism* 44(4) (2005): 515–49. Buckley provides a detailed analysis of how *The Times'* reporting of events leading up to Thermidor shaped Robespierre's character for its British readership, including Coleridge, by drawing analogies between his character and Shakespeare's Macbeth and Julius Caesar. Regarding direct representations of the Revolution, see Cox, 'The French Revolution in the English Theatre', 34–8.

[9] Nicholas Roe and Matthew Buckley provide a possible answer in arguing that the play reveals Coleridge's guiltily sympathetic identification with Robespierre as a tragic hero and commanding genius, but Coleridge's portrayal of an arrogant and remorseless tyrant who gloats over having purged the Girondins, with whom British dissenters such as Coleridge's tutor William Frend considered friends and political allies, makes this argument problematic. See Nicholas Roe, *Wordsworth and Coleridge: The Radical Years* (Oxford: Clarendon Press, 1988), 210–23; Buckley, ' "A Dream of Murder": *The Fall of Robespierre* and the Tragic Imagination', 524–8.

produced by the collective imagination speaks through political leaders to their empowerment or ruin.[10] For Jewett the play thus exposes the processes that generate (and later demystify) Robespierre as the embodiment of terror occasioned by contagious fear, especially the fear of another's fear. Barrere fears Robespierre, so Tallien and Legendre fear Barrere; all fear the mob, whether it assumes the form of a sudden consensus in the Assembly that turns upon one or more of its own members, or that of the Parisian citizens taken to the streets, whose ever-present clamor, we are to imagine, threatens to overwhelm the voices of the chief actors in the Assembly in a decisive moment of sublime violence.

Similarly for Reeve Parker, Coleridge's Robespierre is 'less a dramatization of a tragic "character" than of the tragic nature of political discourse itself, [wherein Robespierre] represents a particularly virulent node'.[11] It is the language of republican virtue that sustains Robespierre's self-presentation as the hypostasis of Truth and of the Republic in its call for the sacrifice of private attachment to the demands of the general will (Parker, 12). Coleridge's concern, then, is with the reciprocal relation between political power and popular sovereignty when demagoguery that claims to represent the will of the people shapes and is shaped by popular fear. Robespierre's fall from power thus occurs in the moment he ceases to elicit awe, the moment his own agency visibly emerges from its former transparency as the *vox populi*. However, as the victorious Barrere's closing speech in the final act indicates, one demagogue merely takes up the position of another while the discourse of fear remains intact. The play does not offer even a glimpse of the rhetoric of civility and 'candour' that Coleridge's Dissenting readership held up as the appropriate means of aligning political policy with popular sovereignty. Instead, Tallien's wife Adelaide complains, 'O this new freedom! At how dear a price / We've bought the seeming good! The peaceful virtues / And every blandishment of private life, / The father's cares, the mother's fond endearment, / [Are] All sacrificed to liberty's wild riot.'[12] Her song's wistful search for 'domestic peace' in some 'cottag'd vale' that shelters love ('the sire of *pleasing* fears') voices the appeal of Pantisocracy for the young Coleridge, who viewed with alarm the emergence in Britain of what *The Fall of Robespierre* portrays in France. Nor was it to be a passing concern for the fear of demagoguery remains a central theme in his subsequent plays.

---

[10] William Jewett, *Fatal Autonomy: Romantic Drama and the Rhetoric of Agency* (Ithaca: Cornell University Press, 1997), 30.

[11] Reeve Parker, 'Cutting Off Robespierre: Coleridge's Thermidorean Coup,' unpublished MS (2002).

[12] Coleridge, *PW* I (*CC*), 21.

OSORIO, A TRAGEDY (1797)

Subsequent to *The Fall of Robespierre*, Coleridge turned his creative energies toward poetry, journalism, and political oratory, and might never have composed another play had he not in February of 1797 received from Richard Brinsley Sheridan, the celebrated playwright, liberal Whig MP, and manager of the Drury Lane Theatre, an invitation to compose for the London stage 'a tragedy on some popular subject'. The offer must have been as flattering to the young and relatively unknown Bristol radical as it was exciting, given that a successful run at Drury Lane would be far more lucrative than the pittance he was scraping together as lecturer, journalist, and poet. Moreover, the request suggested a unique opportunity to disseminate his political and theological views in the great metropolis where they might gain maximum exposure. Thus encouraged, Coleridge set to work for the ensuing seven months on a drama entitled, *Osorio, The Sketch of a Tragedy*. Despite these incentives, however, the writing proved arduous.[13] Writing for the London stage meant addressing a more ideologically diverse audience than the reform-minded group of provincial dissenters and radicals to whom he had pitched his Bristol lectures (1795), *The Watchman* (1796), and demanding theologico-political poems like 'Religious Musings' (1794–6). He could not expect London theatre-goers to sympathize so unreservedly with his anti-ministerial and anti-clerical views, nor could he assume that a manuscript expressing such opinions would pass inspection by the Lord Chamberlain's Examiner of Plays. The challenge was especially severe during the period of *Osorio*'s composition, given that threats of a French invasion and recent naval mutinies among the Channel and North Sea fleets had galvanized popular support for the government against its perceived enemies, Dissenters and radicals chief among them. Coleridge thus needed to be quite clever if he were to succeed in evading censorship, yet still make his political meaning intelligible and persuasive.

Coleridge met the challenge by attiring his political tragedy in the costume of a Gothic romance. Set in sixteenth-century Granada during the Inquisition's expulsion of the Moors, *Osorio* describes a rivalry between two brothers of Spanish nobility, Albert (the returning hero/outcast) and Osorio (the villain/usurper), who vie for the affection of their foster-sister Maria, the heroine. The action turns on Osorio's attempts to convince Maria that Albert has drowned in a shipwreck, though he believes (mistakenly) that he has had Albert secretly murdered. Albert, however, has returned to Granada disguised in the outlawed robes of a Moorish chieftain, and intends not to seek blood revenge, but to force Osorio to feel remorse for his fratricidal intentions. In the denouement, Osorio finally recognizes Albert as his brother but experiences self-loathing so intense that he begs for death and

---

[13] For letters referring to *Osorio*'s composition, see *CL* 1: 313, 316, 318, 320, 324, 325, 326, 327, 344, 349–50, 352, 355–6.

willingly submits to his fate at the hands of a rebel band of Moors led by Alhadra, whose husband Osorio had murdered.

Numerous cues signal the play's Gothic posture. The setting in Inquisitorial Spain follows the Gothic vogue for depicting Roman Catholic Southern Europe as the bastion of popery and repression. Italy and Spain in particular were commonly portrayed in terms of the foreign and forbidden—the location of excessive passions, religious superstition, and dark intrigues carried out with ruthless malevolence. Coleridge's chief villain, Osorio, fits the stereotype of the tyrant/usurper that populated Gothic narratives. Together with Francesco the Inquisitor, another archetypal villain, Osorio forces the heroine, Maria, to make the generic choice of 'virtue in distress', that of marriage without love or life in a convent. The hero, Albert, conforms to the Gothic role of the returned outcast in the mold of Karl Moor from Schiller's *The Robbers*. Alhadra, Ferdinand's avenging wife and leader of the Moorish band, functions symbolically as the leader of the oppressed masses commonly portrayed in Gothic narratives as outcast robber bands or *banditti*, such as those featured in *The Robbers* and William Godwin's 'Jacobin novel' *Caleb Williams*. Finally, the play invokes the Gothic's trademark aesthetic of the sublime in its use of such stock *topoi* as the castle, the cave, and the dungeon, and in its engagement with the supernatural through clairvoyant premonitions, prophetic dreams, and spiritual channeling.

While Coleridge's decision to employ the Gothic makes sense insofar as he would be meeting demand for a popular form of entertainment, the choice nonetheless comes as something of a surprise given his critical appraisals of the genre. In the *Critical Review* (February 1797) he decried Matthew Lewis's best-selling *The Monk* (1796) for its violent and sexual sensationalism and for its infidelity to 'moral truth', which he argued must ultimately be the criterion that sustains the reader's interest.[14] Coleridge's reviews of Ann Radcliffe's *The Mysteries of Udolpho* (1794) and *The Italian* (1797) were hardly less censorious, though here his attack focused on the tedious predictability of her trademark device of the 'explained supernatural', which introduced mysterious events and spectral appearances only to explain them away in the denouements by revealing their natural causes.[15] Moreover, the moral tenor of his remarks regarding the Gothic's treatment of mystery was also implicitly religious and political, for they were homologous with his Unitarian censure of 'mystery' as the manipulative obfuscations practiced by the Anglican priesthood and by the Pitt ministry in their attempts

---

[14] See Samuel Taylor Coleridge, *Shorter Works and Fragments*, The Collected Works of Samuel Taylor Coleridge, ed. J. Jackson and J. de J. Jackson, vol. 11, Bollingen Series 75, 16 vols. (Princeton: Princeton University Press, 1995), 1: 57–65.

[15] For a useful discussion of the explained supernatural, see E. J. Clery, *The Rise of Supernatural Fiction 1762–1800*, Cambridge Studies in Romanticism, ed. Marilyn Butler and James Chandler, vol. 12 (Cambridge: Cambridge University Press, 1995), 539–43.

to maintain authority.[16] In sum, Britain's taste for the Gothic appeared to Coleridge as an alarming symptom of an infirm nation grown addicted to sensationalism false forms of mystery.

Why then did Coleridge make such liberal use of the Gothic in *Osorio*? How are we to account for the contradiction between his dramaturgical and critical practices? While the possibility that he was willing to sacrifice principles for cash cannot be dismissed, the artistry of *Osorio* suggests another reason—that his objections were not so much with the Gothic *per se* as with the ways in which it was being employed. Additionally, the Gothic's popularity and frequent use as a vehicle for veiled political commentary made it attractive. Though often set in the feudal past of a 'forbidden' foreign culture such as Catholic Spain or Italy, Gothic romances were increasingly received in the politically charged climate of the 1790s as oblique commentary upon contemporary events. How they reflected those events from a political standpoint, however, was open to interpretation. Conservative appropriations of the Gothic looked back nostalgically in the manner of Burke's *Reflections* at a feudal past to argue for the restoration of violated property rights and a perpetuation of the class and gender values of feudal patriarchy. The radical Gothic, by contrast, asked its readers to condemn such a world and reform its entrenched systems of inequality.[17] By 1797 and the writing of *Osorio*, multiple interpretive possibilities were available. If the Gothic romance was seen as a vehicle for exploring the question of what it meant to be English in terms of one's moral values, aesthetic taste, religious faith, and political heritage, then it could be manipulated to suit Coleridge's ambitions for propagating the tenets of Unitarian ideology. Thus despite his critical misgivings, Coleridge found good reasons to employ the Gothic in his tragedy: its popularity increased the chances of success, its concern with 'mystery' provided an opening for his criticisms of the religious and political establishment, and its ideological ambiguity suggested a means of encoding his radical politics and heterodox theology so as to protect the play from government censorship, yet allow its messages to find audience.

Coleridge's chief means of achieving these aims was to reverse Radcliffe's explained supernatural by creating scenes that expose false mystery but that then replace it with a 'legitimate' mysticism deserving of reverence. We first see this in the play's pivotal séance scene (III.i), which closely followed Schiller's recently translated *Der Geisterseher* (1788, trans. 1795): seeming to suggest the triumph of informed skepticism over base superstition, the audience is made aware at the beginning that Osorio has employed an alleged 'sorcerer' (though unbeknownst to him this is Albert in disguise) to 'channel' Albert's spirit in order to convince Maria of his death. The sham backfires, however, for Albert's invocation has the effect of

[16] For radical vs. conservative gothic, see Miall, D. S. 'Gothic Fiction.' *A Companion to Romanticism*, Ed. Duncan Wu (London: Blackwell, 1998) 345.

[17] See, for example, Samuel Taylor Coleridge, *Lectures 1795 on Politics and Religion*, The Collected Works of Samuel Taylor Coleridge, ed. Lewis Patton and Peter Mann, vol. 1, Bollingen Series 75, 16 vols. (London: Routledge & Kegan Paul; Princeton University Press, 1971), 210.

reducing Osorio to fits of paralyzing guilt, while it increases the swooning Maria's sense of mystical connection with Albert's 'departed' spirit.

The reversal also seeks to unsettle the audience. While Albert's invocation of spirits is a Gothic commonplace, his language echoes that of 'Preternatural Agency' and 'Religious Musings', Coleridge's most ambitious Unitarian poems. What particularly distinguishes *Osorio's* supernaturalism from the Gothic prototype is the ontological status of the 'spirit' Albert summons from an 'innumerable company' that encircle the earth, causing ominous whirlwinds and maelstroms, commonplace symbols of apocalyptic retribution during the revolutionary decade. Coleridge's major poems of 1795–6 feature such spirits as 'powers' that animate the natural order and guide the unfolding of human history toward its millennial destiny. These poems are concerned, moreover, with the epistemological possibility of apprehending such powers and they valorize an 'elect band of patriot-sages' (such as the Unitarian scientist and political radical Joseph Priestley) as the true seers of the contemporary age, who have succeeded in reclaiming 'Man's free and stirring spirit that [otherwise] lies entranced'. The spirit world Albert presumes to command thus recalls the natural world that Coleridge's Unitarian poems find to be alive with spiritual powers that hold revolutionary potential, and his invocation thus blurs the customary boundaries that distinguish the natural and the supernatural, science and magic, the secular and the sacred. From this perspective, Albert's persona as sorcerer subsumes the roles of natural philosopher, metaphysician, theologian, and poet, the same combination of identities that Coleridge had been assimilating as his own since his move to Bristol in 1794.[18]

Albert's spiritual affiliations with nature support his moral vocation as one who seeks to reform rather than avenge his murderous brother. One sees this, for example, in the soliloquy that Coleridge later excerpted as 'The Dungeon' for *Lyrical Ballads*, where Albert expostulates upon nature's ability, to quell rather than inflame the impulse toward revenge, unlike incarceration. Like the elect of Heaven and Unitarian Christ of 'Religious Musings', the 'Despised Galilaean [who] Self regardless [. . .] Mourns for th' Oppressor' (*PW* I (*CC*), 174–5), Albert's ability

---

[18] Critical commentary has for the most part viewed Albert as a one-dimensional character typical of contemporary melodramas. William Jewett is the only critic to my knowledge who links Albert's heroism with the ideology of Coleridge's Unitarian poems. See Jewett, *Fatal Autonomy: Romantic Drama and the Rhetoric of Agency*, 99–131. Marjean Purinton identifies Albert with aspects of Coleridge's political radicalism. See Purinton, 'The English Pamphlet War of the 1790s and Coleridge's *Osorio*', 159–81. Donald Priestman has seen Albert's heroism as a response to the evils Coleridge saw in Godwin's *Political Justice*. See Donald G. Priestman, 'Godwin, Schiller, and the Polemics of Coleridge's *Osorio*', *Bulletin of Research in the Humanities, Stoney Brook, NY*, 82 (1979): 236–48. Reeve Parker calls into question Albert's putative virtue by arguing that he is in fact Osorio's double, and that the brothers are more alike than would appear. Parker's provocative essay suggests that Albert is a kind of poltergeist returning to avenge himself under the pretext of heartfelt concern for Osorio. See Reeve Parker, '*Osorio's* Dark Employments: Tricking Out Coleridgean Tragedy', *Studies in Romanticism* 33 (Spring 1994): 119–60.

to commune with 'Nature's Essence, Mind, and Energy' results in a refusal to 'imbosom' contempt or revenge. When questioned by Osorio's agents as to his identity, Albert cryptically replies that he is one who can 'bring the dead to life again' (*PW* III (*CC*), 87). At one level, the remark refers to his own status as one who, though believed dead, will reveal himself to be alive in the play's denouement. At another, it bespeaks his Christ-like intent to bring about his brother's spiritual resurrection. These multiple meanings underscore the aptness of Albert's chosen disguise as a sorcerer, that is as one who, though mortal, 'sees into the life of things' more deeply than others, and by virtue of his participation in the divinity of nature refuses hatred and vengeance.

The reversal of the explained supernatural in the séance scene thus aims at two effects. Intratextually, it chastens Osorio's smug materialism that would dismiss the possibility of a moral and spiritual order while it also signals Albert's eventual return from the dead as a living husband, brother, and son. Extratextually, it links Albert's apparent identity as a conventional hero/outcast of Gothic romance to a politically mysterious persona who uses the language of Coleridge's Unitarian poems.

A second key instance of Coleridge's reversal of the 'explained supernatural' takes place in the denouement, where having revealed his true identity and Osorio's fratricidal plot, Albert appeals to the God of mercy on his brother's behalf. Osorio, however, seeks divine retribution and begs for punishment rather than salvation. His entreaty is immediately answered by Alhadra and her band of Moors, who burst in to avenge the murder of her husband, Ferdinand. To his horror, Albert realizes not only that his mission to secure Osorio's spiritual salvation has been thwarted, but also that his séance performance has unwittingly contributed to Osorio's demise. His despairing final words, 'O horrible!' acknowledge these failures as the Moors carry Osorio offstage to his death and Alhadra delivers an impassioned, curtain-closing soliloquy thanking 'Heaven' for its wise assistance in meeting extreme despotism with extreme vengeance, and pledging her further assistance as an instrument of divine retribution that would 'shake the kingdoms of this world . . . Till desolation seemed a beautiful thing'. An audience accustomed to conventional Gothic dramas, in which good is ultimately rewarded and evil clearly punished, could be expected to cheer Osorio's downfall, but must also find itself puzzled over Alhadra's apparent triumph and Albert's failure peacefully to bring about his brother's spiritual reformation.

It would be especially disconcerting given that Alhadra's avenging band appears to conform to the stock Gothic feature of the 'crowd', which as Ronald Paulson notes, had come to signify the threat of revolutionary anarchy uncontained.[19] Her curtain-closing soliloquy, however, takes on apocalyptic overtones, suggesting that

---

[19] Ronald Paulson, 'Gothic Fiction and the French Revolution', *ELH* 48 (3) (1981): 539–43.

underlying the apparent disorder of crowd violence there operates the plan of providence. *Osorio's* conclusion thus fits the eschatological theme that Morton Paley has identified in Coleridge's writings in the 1790s where an early emphasis on millennial peace gives way to preoccupation with God's retributive vengeance.[20] Albert's stunned silence as Alhadra calls for a cleansing of the established political and religious order mimes the astonishment that accompanis the Burkean sublime. How far would the apocalyptic cleansing reach? Would it result in a millennial future for the peaceful 'elect' like Albert, or rather for religious militants like Alhadra? Does the healing power of nature suggested by the example of Albert's refusal to seek blood revenge win the day? Or do the ending's apocalyptic overtones suggest that human society is so tainted by self-interest and so doomed to fractiousness that only God's wrath can rectify it? Rather than provide Radcliffean closure, the text does not decide.

Precisely why Sheridan pocketed the manuscript of *Osorio*, failing even to acknowledge its receipt, is unclear, but Coleridge's humorous remark to Thelwall is telling: 'I received a letter from Linley, the long & the short of which is that Sheridan rejects the Tragedy—his *sole* objection is—the obscurity of the three last acts' (*CL* 1: 213). Certainly the strategy of reversing the explained supernatural jeopardized the play's intelligibility, though to have made his political and theological beliefs explicit would surely have meant rejection by the censors. Perhaps Coleridge hoped, that *Osorio* might nonetheless communicate a plea for tolerance and Christian forbearance at a time when the fears of clandestine enemies within, Dissenters and radicals in particular, were escalating. Perhaps given the challenges he faced he felt it would be enough to create a hero merely suggestive of Unitarian values with whom the Drury Lane audience might sympathize. The irony in this, however, is that the strategy of advancing Dissenting ideology under the camouflage of the Gothic, were it known, undermines the play's of dispelling reactionary fears that Unitarians were covertly working to foment revolution. In this sense, the tragic irony of *Osorio* is that it reveals how the censure of Unitarians, which had gained momentum throughout the decade and had become particularly acute during the invasion scare of 1797, became self-fulfilling, for as objects of widespread distrust their cause could only advance by means of dissimulation. Sheridan's indictment regarding 'the obscurity of the three last acts' thus speaks more to the nature of the undertaking itself than to Coleridge's dramaturgical abilities. By attempting to insinuate beliefs he dared not make explicit, his drama languished from an obscurity that was, after all, its necessary condition.

---

[20] Morton Paley, *Apocalypse and Millennium in English Romantic Poetry* (Oxford: Oxford University Press, 1999), 100, 115, 139–40.

REMORSE, A TRAGEDY (1813)

More than fifteen years separate the completion of *Osorio* from its reincarnation as *Remorse*, which ran for twenty nights at Drury Lane in January of 1813 and netted Coleridge more in revenues than all his other literary productions combined.[21] While it is no small irony that the failure of nine months' labor in 1797 should provide the foundation for his largest commercial success, it is all the more surprising given the dramatic change in his political and religious views over the intervening years. Coleridge renounced his Unitarianism in 1805 and increasingly sought to dismiss or deny his earlier radical involvement, while over the same interval, his criticism of the Gothic as symptomatic of the nation's spiritual, moral, and aesthetic malady intensified and turned politically conservative: Gothic drama, which he now called 'Jacobinical drama', was infecting the British body politic with morally enervating ideas from the Continent by locating, goodness only in lower class characters and vice only in aristocrats and prelates. Just as the 'low' art of the Gothic was usurping the 'high' tradition of Elizabethan and Jacobean drama, so it inverted what Coleridge now took to be the natural social order.[22]

Osorio's resurrection as *Remorse* thus poses several interpretive problems: first, how is it that a play rejected by Sheridan for its obscurity should later become one of Drury Lane's more successful productions? Was Sheridan merely mistaken, or did its positive reception reflect changes in the political environment, or changes in theatrical taste, or changes in the manuscript, or some combination of these? Second, how did Coleridge reconcile his conservative theological and political views with a play that was rooted in the soil of his earlier heterodoxies, and how did he reconcile his critical hostility to Gothic drama with *Remorse*'s Gothic credentials? Is *Remorse* an act of hypocrisy?

J. D. Moore has argued that the political ambiguity of the Gothic, especially with respect to its representation of the central conflict between hero and villain, made it an easy matter to transform the aristocratic tyrant of the *ancien regime* into the usurping tyrant of the new order.[23] Whereas an audience in 1797 might have interpreted Coleridge's villain as representing William Pitt, his ministers, or his aristocratic supporters, audiences in 1813 would be more likely to find the likeness of Napoleon. Moore also sees *Remorse* as an attempt to elevate the Gothic's

---

[21] For *Remorse*'s production history, revisions of *Osorio*, and textual variants (stage, Larpent, and print versions), see Mays' introductions in *PW* III (*CC*), 1027–59; 1136; 1229–36.

[22] Coleridge applies the term 'Jacobin' to theatrical taste in his critique of Charles Robert Maturin's play *Bertram*, where he defines 'Jacobinical Drama' as consisting in 'the confusion and subversion of the natural order of things in their causes and effects' by representing virtue in lower class characters and vice exclusively in the upper class (*BL* (*CC*), 269).

[23] John David Moore, 'Coleridge and the "Modern Jacobincal Drama": Osorio, Remorse, and the Development of Coleridge's Critique of the Stage, 1797–1816', *Bulletin of Research in the Humanities, Stoney Brook, NY*, 85 (1982): 443–64.

aesthetic respectability through the aristocratic and moral valor of the hero Alvar (Albert of *Osorio*). Thus, according to Moore, Coleridge saw *Remorse* as a corrective to the 'Jacobinical Drama' he reviled, and as a positive example of what Gothic drama might become when crafted by morally and politically responsible playwrights. Yet while these explanations are surely correct, they don't go far enough. First, villainy in both plays is not so much political (signifying Pitt or Napoleon) as theological; the hero's struggles are with a zealous Inquisitor and an atheistic materialist. Second, whatever may be said about Alvar as a proper example of moral heroism may also be said of Albert. In each case, the hero is an aristocrat who overcomes the temptation to seek revenge with a Christ-like will to forgive his brother's fratricidal transgressions and heal his diseased soul.

Several small but highly significant changes to *Osorio*'s manuscript suggest how Coleridge sought to reshape *Remorse* so that it would coincide with his changed theological, political, and critical views. In particular, the extraction of two short passages known as 'The Foster Mother's Tale' and 'The Dungeon' (appropriated as stand-alone pieces for *Lyrical Ballads*), and the diminution of Alhadra's character distinguish *Remorse* from *Osorio* to a greater degree than has been recognized. Critical opinion that 'The Foster Mother's Tale' was easily omitted misses its structural and political role in providing the psychological motivation for Maria to free the sorcerer (the disguised Albert) from incarceration in the dungeon, an act that sets up the final scene's revelations.[24] *Remorse* struggles to fill the gap left by its removal: Teresa (Maria in *Osorio*) leaves the séance determined to find Alvar's grave where she intends to join him by committing suicide. Inexplicably, however, we find that she has sought out her Foster Mother in order to gain possession of the dungeon keys. In *Osorio*, Maria follows the sorcerer's instructions to seek out the Foster Mother, who cooperatively provides the dungeon keys and a tale that helps Maria make an intuitive connection between Albert and the sorcerer. Thus in addition to its structural function, the passage associates Albert with the tale's nature-boy protagonist and thus reinforces Albert's heterodox religious identity as a votary of nature and as the victim of political and religious persecution. The piece thus works suggestively to underscore the play's central themes—the superiority of spiritualized nature as a moral guide, over the Established Church and the plight (incarceration or escape to the New World) of those who dare to say so. The deletion of 'The Foster Mother's Tale' in *Remorse* thus generates a new political reading that, unlike *Osorio*, does not valorize religious heterodoxy as the victim of Anglican tyranny.

The removal of Albert's prison soliloquy, 'The Dungeon', has a similar effect, by calling attention away from a standard Gothic symbol of *ancien regime* tyranny

---

[24] Coleridge omitted 'The Foster Mother's Tale' in all versions of *Remorse*, though he appended it to the second and subsequent print editions. While Mays suggests that it was omitted without consequence, Reeve Parker calls attention to its structural role in motivating Maria to spring Albert from his dungeon captivity. See Parker, '*Osorio*'s Dark Employments: Tricking Out Coleridgean Tragedy', 148–52.

while also eliminating Albert's eloquent claim (as in 'The Foster Mother's Tale') that nature chastens and reforms the transgressor (whose transgressions are in any event the result of 'ignorance and parching poverty' perpetrated by aristocratic privilege) far more effectively than incarceration (*habeas corpus* was in suspension) prescribed by the 'pamper'd Mountebanks' of the judicial and ecclesiastical systems. The result is that *Remorse* offers a less theologically and politically radical hero, one more likely to be seen as an Anglican victim of the traditional Catholic enemy or the new breed of utilitarian atheists than as a Dissenter persecuted by the British government.

Coleridge also changes the political tenor of *Remorse* by diminishing the role and simplifying the character of Alhadra, to whom he had given considerable attention in *Osorio* as a representation of the masses oppressed under the *ancien regime* who were observed to have usurped the tyrannical roles of their overthrown masters. As the victim of brutal incarceration at the hands of the Inquisition and having witnessed her husband's murder by Osorio, Alhadra has good reason to seek revenge, but demonstrates instead a remarkably complex response, one that likely reflects Coleridge's own ambivalence about the course of the Revolution during *Osorio*'s composition. At times she feels impotent outrage, especially when she considers her children's fatherless future; at others a dutiful responsibility to her comrades and to her religious principles to seek revenge. For a brief moment, she becomes receptive to a Christian appeal for forgiveness urged by Albert's close associate and moral surrogate Maurice, but then rejects such 'puny precepts' as incompatible with 'the soul of Man', which rightly desires 'Ambition, Glory, thirst of Enterprize— / The deep and stubborn purpose of revenge' (*PW* III (*CC*), 137). At one point, weary from persecution and the prospect of vengeance that she feels called upon to commit, she lapses into a desire for oblivion that Coleridge referred to as his own 'Brahman Creed', in a letter to Thelwall (*CL* 1: 350, 14 Oct. 1797). Coleridge might not have condoned Revolutionary violence, but in Alhadra he demonstrates a sympathetic understanding of the dilemma faced by the oppressed. Eliminating these scenes in *Remorse* makes Alhadra a less complex and less sympathetic character, and suggests a less tolerant attitude toward the restive masses. Perhaps most significantly, he eliminates Alhadra's curtain-closing soliloquy that calls for apocalyptic vengeance and that appears to signal the defeat of Albert's aims at peaceful reform. Instead, Coleridge inserts for the stage version of *Remorse* a joyful family reunion and gives Alvar the play's final words—a pat moral that Heaven justly brings remorse to those who ignore their conscience. *Remorse* thus offers closure where *Osorio* had refused it; whereas in the earlier play, persecuted Unitarians needed to await a vindicating apocalypse, in the latter, the hero, now more Anglican than Unitarian, experiences the certainty of triumph over the villain's tyranny and atheism. The explained supernatural is re-reversed.

Taken altogether, *Remorse*'s erasures of these key passages in *Osorio* make it a less religiously heterodox, less politically radical and altogether less complex drama. Perhaps this goes some way towards explaining its success, for *Remorse* gave its audiences the exaggerated moral stereotypes and the final triumph of virtue over vice that they had come to expect. Whether it succeeded in achieving the moral penetration of Elizabethan drama that Coleridge admired is doubtful but by eliminating *Osorio*'s Dissenting voices, one may see how Coleridge sought to reconcile *Remorse* with his censure of the 'Jacobinical Drama'.

ZAPOLYA, A CHRISTMAS TALE (1817)

Encouraged by Byron to build upon the success of *Remorse*, Coleridge wrote what became his last play, *Zapolya*, in December 1815 and January 1816. Drury Lane rejected it, however, and it was not published until 1817, nor did it see the stage until February 1818 when it ran for ten nights at the Surrey Theatre before disappearing altogether, perhaps, as The *Theatrical Review* suggested, because it was 'of too serious a cast for the frequenters of this Theatre, and...too good [or] at any rate...Too poetical' (*PW* III (*CC*), 1331).

Though he began *Zapolya* as a tragedy, Coleridge shifted course to produce a Shakespearean romance in the manner of *The Winter's Tale*, with twenty years separating its two parts and with thematic emphasis on the ability of pious and long-suffering patience to overcome political and familial divisiveness. As with *Osorio* and *Remorse*, *Zapolya* offers oblique commentary upon contemporary events by setting them in a remote and foreign historical past. Set (probably) during the civil wars of seventeenth-century Hungary, its first part, 'The Prelude, entitled "The Usurper's Fortune"', puts the heroic military commander, Rab Kiuprili, who has returned from the front upon learning of the king's death, in dramatic confrontation with the usurping King Emerick and with Kiuprili's son Casimir, who has been duped by Emerick into believing that his bid for the throne is legitimate. Kiuprili is thrown in prison for challenging Emerick's authority, but escapes with the deposed Queen, Zapolya, and her infant Andreas, the rightful heir. The second part, 'The Sequel, entitled "The Usurper's Fate"', unfolds in four acts, culminating with the overthrow of Emerick, Andrea's ascendancy, reconcilement between Kiuprili and Casimir, and the reunion of Zapolya and Andreas, who had been separated from one another since his infancy, she having been forced to live as a forest savage to avoid capture and execution by Emericks forces, and he having been raised by a peasant foster-father.

Critics have sometimes viewed the play as a celebration of Napoleon's final defeat in June 1815, but by the time of *Zapolya*'s composition a half year later, Coleridge's focus was upon post-war economic dislocations and social unrest, conditions that also prompted his *Lay Sermons*, written immediately after *Zapo-lya*.[25] The second of these begins with the observation that 'Peace has come without the advantages expected from Peace, and on the contrary, with many of the severest inconveniences usually attributable to War' (*LS* (*CC*), 141). Coleridge's diagnosis of the nation's ills is less concerned with the problems of economic recession *per se*, than with the serious threat to peace posed by restive, unemployed workers and soldiers recently returned from war, who were susceptible, to the inflammatory rhetoric of 'vile demagogues' spreading 'political calumny [and] private slander' (*LS* (*CC*), 151). Such false physicians, 'Mountebanks and Zanies of Patriotism' (he doesn't name names, but his letters suggest Cobbett, Hazlitt, and Leigh Hunt, among others) destroy 'every principle, every feeling, that binds the citizen to his country, the spirit to its Creator' (*LS* (*CC*), 151). However, Coleridge's fears of mass uprisings are concerned not only with fear-mongering demagogues, but also with the impoverished conditions of moral and spiritual awareness that must be in place for demagoguery to gain credence and for tyranny to take hold.

Part I of *Zapolya* dramatizes these concerns. As with the earlier plays, the action occurs in a climate of fear that forces men to conceal their true identities. In the opening scene, the patriot Chef Ragozzi warns Kiuprili, in a manner reminiscent of *The Fall of Robespierre*'s first act, to 'fear the worst. / [for] Mystery is contagious. All things here / Are full of motion: yet all is silent: / And bad men's hopes infect the good with fears' (*PW* (*CC*), 3.2, 1342). Emerick has won popular support through bribery and false rumors that malign the throne's rightful claimants. Mobs cheer him and denounce the innocent Queen. Kiuprili also finds that his son, Casimir, has mistaken the favor of the duped multitude for evidence of Emerick's legitimacy, a view made more attractive by Emerick's having secured the wealthy heiress Sarolta as Casimir's bride. Casimir's inability to see through Emerick's designs is for Kiuprili an unforgivable transgression against family, country, and heaven that anticipates Coleridge's anxieties in the *Lay Sermons* regarding Britain's fragile state as a nation susceptible to deceitful promises.

Illyrians lack sufficient religiosity to resist Emerick's false rumors, bribes, and scare tactics, for as Ragozzi remarks, 'Doubtless they deem Heaven too usurp'd! Heaven's justice / Bought like themselves!' (*PW* III (*CC*), 1345). This deficiency of what Coleridge would refer to as the necessary 'counter-weight' to Britain's 'over-balance of the commercial spirit' (*LS* (*CC*), 169) becomes apparent in the early confrontation between Kiuprili and Emerick. Refusing attempts to placate his suspicions regarding Emerick's secret designs for usurping the throne, Kiuprili warns that 'with the soul, the conscience is co-eval, / Yea, the soul's essence' (*PW* III (*CC*), 1352). Emerick's reply that conscience 'is but the pulse of reason' establishes a central ideological tension between the 'shallow sophisms' of utilitarian reasoning

---

[25] See, for example, Woodring, *Politics in the Poetry of Coleridge*, 217.

that, as Emerick demonstrates, can be used to manipulate the gullible masses, and the proper authority of moral conscience that obeys the imperatives of the innocent heart. It is precisely this tension that Coleridge sought to resolve by prescribing a transformation of national consciousness from one infected by 'the commercial spirit' of economic calculation (its preoccupation with advantage gained through trade, colonization, and military superiority), to one concerned foremost with moral and spiritual rectitude as prescribed by biblical example and Anglican doctrine.

Part II stages the eventual realization of the latter in its final reunion of parent and child, of true monarch and loyal subject, and it thus follows *Remorse* in providing optimistic closure where *The Fall of Robespierre* and *Osorio* ended ominously. *Zapolya's* reconciliations, however, must be seen as prescriptive, given Coleridge's appraisal of contemporary conditions. In this regard, the play further anticipates the *Lay Sermons* in suggesting the means by which the nation should find its way home, for it promotes 'the principles, taught by God's word, exampled by God's providence, commanded by God's law, and recommended by promises of God's grace, [which] alone can form the foundations of a Christian community... [and by] which the true friend of the people is contradistinguished from the factious demagogue' (*LS* (*CC*), 130–1). As J. D. Coates has argued, *Zapolya's* ending imagines the ideal state as a moral organism that depends upon the moral choices of its members properly guided by a transcendent metaphysic of Christian goodness.[26] This logic finds expression in the play's emphasis on instinctual sympathy, intuition, and feeling as infallible gauges of moral truth and natural law. At each turn, the beleaguered and oppressed are sustained by a 'strange and hidden power of sympathy', a 'hidden light', and a 'heaven guarded instinct' that supportively binds them to one another during the years of exile, as well as by a faith that 'look[s] to heaven rather than the corrupt court'. Moreover, though the villains mask their despotic intentions, and the innocents protect themselves by means of disguise, innocence intuitively sees through deception, where wickedness does not.

Zapolya's implicit argument for the authority of sensibility over intellect is not new to Coleridge's drama; in each of his plays, innocent intuition is able to recognize virtue and vice where reason, often led astray by deceitful language, fails. The acuity of sympathy in discerning moral truth was also a commonplace motif in melodrama and Gothic romance, and carried political resonance insofar as 'sensibility' remained a contested concept in the rhetoric of revolution, as it had in the pamphlet wars of the 1790s. What appears to be different about the role of feeling and instinct in *Zapolya* is that it draws upon a more traditional Christian piety than it does in *Osorio*, where innocent sensibility is linked closely with spiritualized nature. 'The Foster Mother's Tale' here again provides a useful

---

[26] J. D. Coates, 'Coleridge's Debt to Harrington: A Discussion of Zapolya', *Journal of the History of Ideas* 38 (3) (1977): 505.

point of comparison. In *Osorio*, the story of the nature boy's mistreatment by the aristocracy and clergy, followed by his subsequent escape to the wilds engages Maria's sympathy and prompts her to free the incarcerated 'sorcerer' whom she intuitively identifies with the boy. In *Zapolya*, however, primitive nature is no longer presented as a desirable haven. Zapolya and Raab Kiuprili are reduced to a desperate state of bare survival during their prolonged exile in a forest cave, and their sustaining faith is not in natural religion, but in a protective heaven. The foundling nature boy in *Osario*, we are to assume, will find happiness among the New World savages, but the foundling Prince Andreas becomes the restorer of a just and harmonious polity.

The twenty-year interval that separates the play's two parts underscores the importance of patience in bringing about such a restoration. *Zapolya*'s victims of tyrannical oppression sustain an unfaltering faith in Heaven's wisdom and an unfailing loyalty to the ideal of the rightful king, though none know for sure until the denouement whether he is even alive. Zapolya's advice to her son to 'Leave then to Heaven / the work of Heaven: and with a silent spirit / Sympathize with the powers that work in silence!' (*PW* III (*CC*), 1397–8) clearly anticipates Coleridge's counsel in the second *Lay Sermon* that Britain's moral transformation into a truly 'Christian nation' must come gradually. Again, as with his use of sensibility, Coleridge imbues new meaning to a familiar position, for he had pleaded similarly for patience in 'A Moral and Political Lecture' (1795), and in his Unitarian manifesto 'Religious Musings', wherein he beseeches the oppressed to 'rest awhile, / Children of Wretchedness! More groans must rise, / More blood must stream, or ere your wrongs be full' (*PW* I (*CC*), 186). But whereas these earlier exhortations urged patience to the disenfranchised and Unitarian 'patriot-sages' with the assurance that their sufferings would be vindicated by imminent apocalyptic revenge associated with the French Revolution, patience in *Zapolya* suggests political docility and conformity to Anglican precepts, for it is these that the reformed Coleridge has now concluded will purge the state of materialism and irreligion.

Whatever critics may decide about *Zapolya*'s intrinsic merits, the play offers useful insights regarding Coleridge's dramatic practice when placed in relation to the earlier plays. It allows us to see that, despite the significant changes that took place in Coleridge's political and religious views between *The Fall of Robespierre* and his composition of *Zapolya*, his chosen themes remain remarkably constant. The action in each is set against a background of fear and suspicion that requires characters to conceal their true identities and purposes; villains and heroes alike wear masks that are often retained until the final scenes. Each play is concerned with tyranny and demagoguery, and thus with questions of rightful versus usurped political sovereignty. Similarly, each, with perhaps the exception of *The Fall of Robespierre*, seeks to distinguish true from false religion, often through its treatment of mystery. Each, of course, though set in a foreign country, and often in a remote past, offers indirect commentary upon the contemporary state of British politics and society. What changes, then, is the political employment of these themes. Coleridge's villains in the first two plays (a category that includes virtually all of the characters in *The Fall of Robespierre*, who rise and fall as they manipulate and are manipulated by the discourse of fear) are readily associated with what he viewed to be the undesirable extremes of atheism (*Robespierre and Osorio*) and Anglican orthodoxy (*Osorio*), each of which offered a specious form of enslaving idolatry. In *Zapolya*, however, the chief villain remains an atheist, but his villainy threatens the position, not of a Unitarian such as Albert, but of the restorer of Anglican orthodoxy. Reciprocally, Coleridge's hero in *Osorio* loses his Unitarian credentials through the manuscript cuts that produced *Remorse*, and is replaced altogether by the more traditionally devout character of Andreas in the final play. Perhaps most tellingly, the battle cry for apocalyptic vengeance against tyrants that closes *Osorio* gives way to a call for loyalty to the established order in *Zapolya*, whose vision of a restored Christian nation warrants celebration in no small part because it has silenced the spirit of Dissent that animated *Osorio*.

WORKS CITED

BUCKLEY, MATTHEW. 2005. 'A Dream of Murder': *The Fall of Robespierre* and the tragic imagination. *Studies in Romanticism*, 44 (4): 515–49.

CARLSON, JULIE. 1995. *In the Theatre of Romanticism: Coleridge, Nationalism, and Women*. Cambridge Studies in Romanticism, ed. Marilyn Butler and James Chandler, vol. 5. Cambridge: Cambridge University Press.

CLERY, E. J. 1995. *The Rise of Supernatural Fiction 1762–1800*. Cambridge Studies in Romanticism, ed. Marilyn Butler and James Chandler. Vol. 12. Cambridge: Cambridge University Press.

COATES, J. D. 1977. Coleridge's debt to Harrington: a discussion of *Zapolya*. *Journal of the History of Ideas*, 38 (3) 501–8.

COLERIDGE, SAMUEL TAYLOR. 1971. *Lectures 1795 on Politics and Religion*. The Collected Works of Samuel Taylor Coleridge, ed. Lewis Patton and Peter Mann. Vol. 1, Bollingen Series 75. 16 vols. London: Routledge & Kegan Paul; Princeton University Press.

—— 2001. *Poetical Works*. The Collected Works of Samuel Taylor Coleridge, ed. J. C. C. Mays. Vol. 16, Bollingen Series 75. 16 vols. Princeton: Princeton University Press.

—— 1995. *Shorter Works and Fragments*. The Collected Works of Samuel Taylor Coleridge, ed. J. J. Jackson and J. R. de J. Jackson. Vol. 11, Bollingen Series 75. 16 vols. Princeton: Princeton University Press.

CONOLLY, L.W. 1976. *The Censorship of English Drama, 1737–1824*. San Marino, CA: Huntington Library.

COX, JEFFREY N. 1990. The French Revolution in the English Theatre. In *History and Myth: Essays on English Romantic Literature*, ed. Stephen C. Behrendt. Detroit: Wayne State University Press, 33–52.

GRIEDER, THEODORE. 1965. Annotated checklist of the British Drama, 1789–99. *Restoration and 18th Century Theatre Research*, 4: 21–47.

HOAGWOOD, TERRENCE ALLEN. 1998. Romantic drama and historical hermeneutics. In *British Romantic Drama: Historical and Critical Essays*, ed. Terrence Allan Hoagwood and Daniel P. Watkins. Madison, N.J.: Fairleigh Dickinson University Press.

JEWETT, WILLIAM. 1997. *Fatal Autonomy: Romantic Drama and the Rhetoric of Agency*. Ithaca: Cornell University Press.

MOORE, JOHN DAVID. 1982 Coleridge and the 'Modern Jacobincal Drama': Osorio, Remorse, and the development of Coleridge's critique of the stage, 1797–1816. *Bulletin of Research in the Humanities, Stoney Brook, NY*, 85: 443–64.

PALEY, MORTON. 1999. *Apocalypse and Millennium in English Romantic Poetry*. Oxford: Oxford University Press.

PARKER, REEVE. 2002. Cutting off Robespierre: Coleridge's thermidorean coup. MS, 2002.

—— 1994. *Osorio*'s dark employments: tricking out Coleridgean tragedy. *Studies in Romanticism* 33 (Spring): 119–60.

PAULSON, RONALD. 1981. Gothic fiction and the French Revolution. *ELH* 48 (3): 532–54.

PRIESTMAN, DONALD G. 1979. Godwin, Schiller, and the polemics of Coleridge's *Osorio.*' *Bulletin of Research in the Humanities, Stoney Brook, NY*, 82: 236–248.

PURINTON, MARJEAN D. 1998. The English pamphlet war of the 1790s and Coleridge's *Osorio*. In *British Romantic Drama: Historical and Critical Essays*, ed. Terence Allan Hoagwood and Daniel P. Watkins. Madison, NJ: Fairleigh Dickinson University Press, 159–81.

ROE, NICHOLAS. 1988. *Wordsworth and Coleridge: The Radical Years*. Oxford: Clarendon Press.

RUSSELL, GILLIAN. 1995. *The Theatres of War: Performance, Politics and Society, 1793–1815*. Oxford: Oxford University Press.

—— 1999. Theatre. In *An Oxford Companion to the Romantic Age, British Culture 1776–1832*, ed. Iain McCalman. Oxford: Oxford University Press, 223–31.

WERKMEISTER, LUCYLE. 1967. *A Newspaper History of England 1792–1793*. Lincoln: University of Nebraska Press.

WOODRING, CARL. 1961. *Politics in the Poetry of Coleridge*. Madison: University of Wisconsin Press.

CHAPTER 22

....

COLERIDGE AS TRANSLATOR

....

FREDERICK BURWICK

WITH his English version of Friedrich Schiller's *Wallenstein* in 1800, Coleridge established himself as translator early in his career. Throughout the following years he continued in his role as interpreter and commentator on German literature and philosophy. J. C. C. Mays's edition of Coleridge's *Poetical Works* identified over a hundred translations among Coleridge's poems, half of them from the German.[1] Some of the translations are no more than a couple of lines, a brief distich or epigram. Some, like the *The Piccolomini* and *The Death of Wallenstein*, are several thousand lines. It is an easy matter to count lines, but a far more difficult task to count the poems. Determining the boundaries separating a translation from a variation on a theme is complicated when a poem has more than one source, or when a borrowed poem is integrated into the poet's own work. Coleridge himself suggests that we distinguish what is 'translated' from what is 'transferred'. He introduces this distinction between 'translated' and 'transferred' in talking about the importation of oriental tales into European literature during the period of the Crusades.[2] By 'transferred' Coleridge means a re-telling, such as was presumed to be at work in the transmission of folk tales and ballads.

During his walking tour of Wales in 1794, Coleridge became interested in Welsh popular ballads, and recorded this 'translation':

---

[1] *Poetical Works* (= *PW*), ed. J. C. C. Mays, *The Collected Works of Samuel Taylor Coleridge*, 16 (Princeton: Princeton University Press, 2001), 3: 1558, 1563, 1581, 1639.

[2] *Lectures 1808–1819: On Literature* (= *Lects 1808–19*), 2 vols., ed. Reginald Foakes, *The Collected Works of Samuel Taylor Coleridge*, 5 (Princeton: Princeton University Press, 1987) 2: 402–3.

> If, while my Passion I impart,
>   You deem my words untrue,
> O place your Hand upon my Heart—
>   Feel how it throbs for *You*.
> Ah no!—reject the thoughtless Claim
>   In pity to your Lover!
> That thrilling Touch would aid the flame
>   It wishes to discover!
>
> (*PW* 1: 124)

As J. C. C. Mays points out, 'It is possible that C[oleridge] heard it sung [...]. But it is more likely that he worked from the translated version in Edward Jones's *Musical and Poetical Relicks of the Welsh Bards*' (1784; 2nd edn 1794). In other words, the poem may not be translated directly but rather adapted from a translation. In terms of Coleridge's distinction, not 'translated' but 'transferred'. When Coleridge in 1800 noted his intent to produce 'Translations of the Volkslieder of all countries', including 'Welsh poets' and a 'Series of true heroic Ballads from Ossian', it would seem likely that he had in mind poetic retelling rather than strictly literal 'word for word' renditions ('Memoranda for a History of English Poetry' (1800); *SW&F* 1: 108).

In translating *Wallenstein*, Coleridge claimed a strict fidelity to the original:

In the translation I endeavoured to render my Author *literally* wherever I was not prevented by absolute differences of idiom; but I am conscious, that in two or three short passages I have been guilty of dilating the original; and, from anxiety to give the full meaning, have weakened the force.   (*PW* 3: 205)

Because J. C. C. Mays's dual-language edition makes the comparison easy, it can be quickly discovered that Coleridge's claim is more than his actual practice reveals, and rightly so. Indeed, the merit of Coleridge's translation is that he is not bound by too strict an adherence to the original. Coleridge himself calls attention the liberties he takes with Thekla's song (II. vi) and offers a prose translation as a footnote to his verse translation (*PW* 3: 378–81).

When Coleridge claimed in the *Biographia Literaria* to translate 'as nearly as possible, word for word', his purpose was to refute Abraham Cowley's advice against attempting a literal translation of a Pindaric ode:

If (says Cowley) a man should undertake to translate Pindar, word for word, it would be thought that one madman had translated another; as it may appear, when he, that understands not the original, reads the verbal traduction of him into Latin prose, than which nothing seems more raving.[3]

---

[3] *Biographia Literaria* (= *BL*), 2 vols., ed. W. J. Bate and James Engell, *The Collected Works of Samuel Taylor Coleridge*, 7 (Princeton: Princeton University Press, 1983), 2: 86.

Upon hearing lines from Cowley's translation of Pindar's 'Olympian Ode 2', Coleridge's audience agreed 'that if the original were madder than this, it must be incurably mad'. Coleridge then gave his own literal translation of the same lines, 'and the impression was, that in the general movement of the periods, in the form of connections and transitions, and in the sober majesty of lofty sense, it appeared to them to approach more nearly, than any other poetry they had heard, to the style of our bible in the prophetic books' (*BL* 2: 86–7; *PW* 1: 926–7). Coleridge modestly presents himself as superior to Cowley in translating Pindar, but his caution is against the mistake of poets in thinking they must aggrandize the style of the original.

The test of good style, Coleridge argued in his Lectures on European Literature of 1818, 'is whether you can translate the phrase into simpler terms, regard being had to the feeling of the whole passage'. In a well crafted style it should not be possible to 'substitute other simpler words in any given passage without a violation of the meaning or tone' (*Lects 1808–19* 2: 237). Coleridge considered it a rule 'that whatever is translatable into other language in simple terms ought to be so in the original or it is not good' (*Lects 1808–19* 2: 451). The best style, however, is perfection in its own language: 'one criterion of style is that it shall not be translatable without injury to the meaning' (*Lects 1808–19* 2: 237). He asserted the same principle in the *Biographia*: 'the infallible test of a blameless style; namely, its untranslatableness in words of the same language without injury to the meaning' (*BL* 2: 142; cf. *BL* 1: 23). Or even earlier in the Lectures of 1811–12: 'whatever without injury could be translated into a foreign language in simple terms ought to be so in the original or it is not good' (*Lects 1808–19* 1: 366).

The measure of a good translation is its degree of invisibility, the degree, Coleridge argues, that intervention of a mediating language vanishes and leaves the reader with the sense of responding directly to the original. Coleridge praises Johann Heinrich Voss for just such achievement as translator.

Voss, scarcely less celebrated as a Scholar & Philologist, than as an original Poet, & combining both excellencies as the first of Translators—His versions of Homer & Virgil are such that his countrymen may fairly claim the *unique* glory of having the Iliad and the Georgics in German; for you have only to abstract your conscious attention from the different sound of the words themselves, in order to forget that it is a Translation which you are reading.   ('On Greek Metre' (1820), *SW&F* 2: 863)

In letter to William Blackwood (October 1821), Coleridge proposed writing 'The Life of Hölty, a German poet, of true genius, who died in early manhood; with specimens of his poems, translated, or freely imitated in English verse' (*SW&F* 2: 916–17).

Responding to John Murray's request to translate Goethe's *Faust*, Coleridge declared that 'A large portion of the work cannot be rendered in blank Verse, but must be in wild lyrical metres'(to John Murray, 31 August 1814; *CL* 3: 523). Six years later, when Thomas Boosey solicited Coleridge to translate *Faust*, Coleridge again declared that it must be 'translated in the manner & metre of the original: as far as would be acceptable to the English Ear'.[4] Most 'acceptable to the English Ear', in drama and in epic narrative, was the blank verse of Shakespeare and Milton. Coleridge's conviction of the superiority of blank verse in English poetry is evident again in his enthusiastic endorsement of Henry Francis Cary's translation of Dante's *Divina Commedia*.[5] Avoiding the challenges of Dante's terza rima,[6] Cary conducted his translation in blank verse. 'Those only who see the difficulty of the Original,' Coleridge wrote, 'can do justice to Mr Cary's Translation—which may now & then not be Dante's *Words*, but always, always *Dante*.' The translator must enter into and become the poet.

Genius is not alone sufficient—it must be present, indeed, in the Translator, in order to supply a *negative* Test by its Sympathy; to feel that it has been done well. But it is *Taste, Scholarship, Discipline,* TACT, that must do it.[7]

Lecturing on Dante at the Royal Institution in March 1819, Coleridge quoted from Cary's translation, again bestowing praise on the quality of his rendition (*Lects 1808–19* 2: 401).

The good style requires of the translator a high degree of rigor. A lesser style allows the translator more freedom. For example, 'Johnson's style has pleased many from the very fault of being perpetually translatable; he creates an impression of cleverness by never saying any thing in a common way' (*Lects 1808–19* 2: 237). This distinction between 'translated' and 'transferred', however, does not necessarily carry with it an implicit appraisal of the merit of the original. Hölty is 'a true genius', his poems are nevertheless to be 'freely imitated'. The better the style the more untranslatable it becomes. Therefore a superior style resists direct translation and can only be adapted. Nevertheless, as Coleridge also asserts, the superior translation ought to adhere to its source in order to recreate the impression that one is reading the original. Bad poetry, on the other hand, is readily translatable and may actually be transformed into good poetry. It should be kept in mind that Coleridge also

---

[4] To Thomas Boosey and Sons (10 May 1820), *CL* 5: 43. As relevant to his negotiations with Boosey, Griggs inserts 'My Advice and Scheme', a proposal for translating *Faust*; single sheet dated 12 May 1820. Huntington Library MS accession number 131334.

[5] Henry Francis Cary, *The Inferno of Dante Alighieri: canto I–XXXIV, with a translation in English blank verse, notes, and a life of the author*, 2 vols. (London: Printed for J. Carpenter, 1805–6); *The vision, or, Hell, Purgatory, and Paradise, of Dante Alighieri*, 3 vols. (London: Printed for Taylor and Hessey, 1814; 2nd corrected edition, 1819).

[6] Geoffrey Chaucer used terza rima for his *Complaint to His Lady*; in the Romantic period it was used by Byron in his *Prophecy of Dante*, and by Shelley in his *Ode to the West Wind* and *The Triumph of Life*.

[7] Coleridge, *Marginalia*: Part 2, ed. George Whalley, *The Collected Works of Samuel Taylor Coleridge*, Volume 12 (Princeton: Princeton University Press, 1984), p. 136.

intended to write 'a History of bad Poetry in all ages of our literature'.[8] Although he claimed it as *desideratum*, Coleridge seldom strove for 'word for word' rendition of a foreign poem. On a few occasions, apparently hoping to turn 'a sow's ear into a silk purse', he expended his efforts on adapting bad poetry.

The distinction between 'translated' and 'transferred', is a curious variation of Coleridge's desynonymization of 'copy' and 'imitation'.[9] A 'copy', after all, would entail 'word for word' fidelity, while 'imitation' would include a broad range of variations. Coleridge's practice was very much involved with the latter, which includes a spectrum of nuances—such as 'influenced by', or 'inspired by', or 'adapted from'. Coleridge's 'The Picture; or, The Lover's Resolution' is 'influenced' by Salomon Gessner; his 'The Blossoming of the Solitary Date-tree' is 'Influenced by medieval German love poetry'; his 'The Wanderings of Cain' is an 'imitation'of Gessner's *The Death of Abel*, his 'Homesick' is 'adapted' from Samuel Gottlieb Bürde. Indeed, Coleridge wrote a whole series of 'Adaptations': of Daniel's 'Musophilus', of Daniel's 'Epistle to Sir Thomas Egerton', of Donne's 'To Sir Henry Goodyere', of Donne's 'Eclogue 1613, December 26'. A more complicated composition is the poem which began with lines which the poet 'involuntarily poured forth' from the top of Scafell, then recognizing that 'the Ideas &c' were 'disproportionate to our humble mountains' and 'accidentally lighting on a short Note in some swiss poems', he claimed that he 'transferred myself thither, in the Spirit, & adapted my former feelings to these grander external objects' (*CL* 2: 864–5).[10] Coleridge did not acknowledge that 'short Note' accompanied Friedericke Brun's 'Chamounix beym Sonnenaufgange' which enabled Coleridge to transform his effusion on Scafell into 'Hymn before Sun-rise in the Vale of Chamouny' (*PW* 2: 717–23). By this account, her poem was not 'transferred' into his, but rather he was 'transferred . . . in the Spirit' into the scene described in her poem.

Among Coleridge's translations are translations of translations, for example his 'Lines from the *Bhagavad-Gita*, from Creuzer'. On occasion, Coleridge himself is the author of the source text and the author of the translation into the target language. These acts of self-translation pose a different set of questions about authorial mediation. On the birth of Hartley Coleridge, he wrote 'Sonnet: to a Friend, who asked how I felt, when the Nurse first presented my Infant to me'. Two years later he wrote to his wife from Ratzeburg that he had translated his sonnet into German:

---

[8] 'Memoranda for a History of English Poetry' (1800), *Shorter Works and Fragments* (= *SW&F*), 2 vols., ed. H. J. Jackson and J. R. de J. Jackson, *The Collected Works of Samuel Taylor Coleridge*, 11 (Princeton: Princeton University Press, 1995), 1: 108.

[9] In English 'translated' and 'transferred' have drifted apart semantically, but in Latin, as James McKusick reminded me, 'translatio' and 'transfero' were interchangeable as synonyms.

[10] *Collected Letters of Samuel Taylor Coleridge* (= *CL*), 6 vols., ed. Earl Leslie Griggs (Oxford: Clarendon Press, 1956–71), 2: 864–5.

The Gentry and Nobility here pay me an almost adulatory attention—there is a very beautiful little Woman, less I think than you—[...] I have quite won her heart by a German Poem which I wrote. It is that sonnet 'Charles! My slow heart was only sad when first'—& considerably dilated with new images & much superior in the German to it's former dress—It has excited no small wonder here for it's purity and harmony.

(20 October 1798; *CL* 1: 429)

The conciliatory 'less I think than you' may not have appeased Sara, but even if the German woman was less beautiful, Coleridge readily claimed that his German translation was more beautiful. In comparing the original to the translation, and finding the translation superior, Coleridge affirms an 'Open Sesame' that allowed him to enter the cavern of a poem and emerge with a treasure superior to the poem as he found it.

COLERIDGE'S TRANSLATION/ ASSIMILATION OF GESSNER

Coleridge also indulged a peculiar genre of metrical meddling, translating the rhythms not the language. He performed this revision on a passage from Salomon Gessner's *Daphnis* (1754), supposedly sung by Phillis to the flute:

Du brauner Hirt, der du die Lämmer in dem Buchen-Thal hütest; ach! wann ich bei dir vorübergeh, und ein nicht verlornes Schaf suche, wann ich dann unter dem Blumen-Kranz hervor dich seitwarts anblike, und so freundlich-lächelnd dich grüße, ach! warum verstehst du mich dann nicht? Heut sah ich mich im klaren Wasser und blikte unter dem Blumen-Kranz hervor, wie ich dich anblike, und lächelte, wie ich dir zulächle; ich muß es nur selbst gestehn, mein kleiner Mund lächelte lieblich, und mein braunes Auge sollte dir viel viel sagen, und doch du blöder Hirt! und doch verstehst du mich nicht.   (*Schriften* 5 vols. Zurich 1770–2, II: 38; *PW* 1: 542)

While in Göttingen during the early months of 1799, Coleridge transformed Gessner's prose into fourteen lines of verse:

> Du brauner Hirt, der du die Schafe
> Zum Buchenhaine treibst,
> Ich gehe gern bey dir voruber
> Und such ein nicht verlornes Lamm;
> Dann blick ich unter meinem Kranze
> Dich seitwarts freundlich an.
> Warum willst du mich nicht verstehen
> Ich sehe mich in klarem Bache

> Und lächle so mir zu,
> Als unter meinem Rosenkranze
> Mein Auge dir zu lächeln pflegt,
> Wie vieles sagt dir doch mein Auge?
> Ach! Allzublöder Hirt!
> Warum willst du mich nicht verstehen?

(*PW* 1: 542–3)

A similar metrical adaptation, 'Pastoral from Gessner', Coleridge also translated into English and published in the *Morning Post* (21 December 1821; *CN* 1: 396;[11] *PW* 1: 673–4). Always attentive to the rhythms of language, Coleridge may have indulged this experiment simply to exercise his German. His metrical paraphrase, however, is also a critique of Gessner's passage, introduced as a song yet unable to become one. Coleridge noted elsewhere that 'a true poet will never confound verse and prose, whereas it is almost characteristic of indifferent prose writers that they directly but silently, should be constantly slipping into scraps of metre' (*Lects 1808–19* 2: 236). Matthew Scott, in his essay on Coleridge's *Wallenstein*, comments on the 'Master/ Slave dialectic that translators must naturally fall into'.[12] Coleridge often rebelled against that subservience, discovering his dislike for the poet and assuming authority over the poem. Coleridge would grow discontent with the process of translating, sometimes shifting from the 'word for word' rigor to a free adaptation, other times abandoning the project altogether, protesting against the faults of the original. An example of the former is the translation of E. T. A. Hoffmann's *Der goldne Topf* which Coleridge transformed into 'The Historie and Gests of Maxilian'.[13] An example of the latter is the translation of Salomon Gessner that he undertook in July 1802. Coleridge had completed translating about half of Gessner's prose poem, *Der este Schiffer*, into blank verse, 'but gave it up under the influence of double disgust, moral & poetical' (March 1811; *CL* 3: 313). J. C. C. Mays estimates that Coleridge must have completed the first book and then left the second as a draft (*PW* 2: 900–1). The moral disgust was aroused by Gessner's eroticism; the poetical simply by the realization that his translation was significantly superior to the original.

---

[11] *The Notebooks of Samuel Taylor Coleridge* (= *CN*), ed. Kathleen Coburn (Princeton: Princeton University Press, 1957–2002), 1: 396.

[12] Matthew Scott, 'The Circulation of Romantic Creativity: Coleridge, Drama, and the Question of Translation', *Romanticism on the Net*: An Electronic Journal Devoted to Romantic Studies, vol. 2, May 1996. See also: Joyce Crick, 'Coleridge's *Wallenstein*: Two Legends', *The Modern Language Review*, vol. 83, no. 1 (Winter 1988): 76–86; and Joyce Crick, 'Some Editorial and Stylistic Observations on Coleridge's Translation of Schiller's *Wallenstein*', *Publications of the English Goethe Society*, vol. 54 (1984): 37–75.

[13] Julian Knox, 'Coleridge's "Cousin-German": Narrative Alter-Egos in the "The Satyrane Letters" and "The Historie and Gests of Maxilian"', paper presented at the Coleridge Summer Conference, Cannington, 20–6 July, 2006.

His conviction that in translating he was creating a work better than the original provided an easy transition into assuming full authorial control. Two of Coleridge's poems had their origin in a similar process of disaffection with Gessner's work. One of these was 'The Wanderings of Cain', which commenced as a translation of Gessner's *Der Tod Abels* ('The Death of Abel'; *PW* 1: 358–9). The second was 'The Picture; or, The Lover's Resolution', influenced by Gessner's 'Der feste Vorsatz' ('The Fixed Resolution'; *PW* 1: 711–17).[14] Again, it is a case of translating prose into blank verse, or, to resort again to counting, Gessner's 45 lines are transformed into Coleridge's 186 lines. Part of that amplification, as J. C. C. Mays notes, is Coleridge's echoing of lines from a poem by Anna Letitia Barbauld. In Gessner's erotic idyll, the wandering narrator, indulging in the lush delights of erotic melancholy, follows the course of a stream through a landscape strikingly similar to that which Coleridge describes. Bidding farewell to the dark and the fair, to stately Melinde and 'kleine Chloe', Gessner's narrator comes upon a maiden's footprint in the sand; melancholy vanishes, and he follows the maiden's trace ('Spur'), thinking how passionately, if he finds her, he will embrace and kiss her ('O! wenn ich dich fände, in meinen Arm würd ich dich drüken, und dich küssen!'), ('Oh! If only I found you, how I would hug you and kiss you!').[15] From Gessner, Coleridge develops the motif of a self-reflexive landscape, at once exterior and yet also a mirror of the narrator's mood and desires. His longing for a 'stately virgin's' presence becomes exteriorized. The scene also seems to replicate memories, as in Gessner's lines: 'noch gestern hüpftest du froh im weissen Sommer-kleid um mich her, wie die Wellen hier im Sonnen-Licht hüpfen' ('yesterday you danced happily about me in your white summer dress, just as the waves here in the water dance in the sun light'). As in Gessner's poem, Coleridge's trope is that the very act of abjuration becomes a conjuration. The lovelorn narrator seeks refuge from his self-torment in the wild depths of the woods:

> here will I couch my limbs,
> Close by this river, in this silent shade,
> As safe and sacred from the step of man
> As an invisible world—unheard, unseen
>
> (lines 51–4)

Even in this 'invisible world' he is pursued by the very images that he strives to negate.

> The breeze, that visits me
> Was never Love's accomplice, never raised
> The tendril ringlets from the maiden's brow,

---

[14] For the comparison of Gessner's poem and Coleridge's, I am indebted to Susan Luther, 'Coleridge, Creative (Day)Dreaming, and "The Picture"', *Dreaming* Vol. 7, No. 1 (March 1997); Salomon Gessner, *Sämtliche Schriften in Drei Bänden* (1762), ed. Martin Bircher (Zürich: Orell Füssli, 1972–4).

[15] Gessner, 'Der feste Vorsatz', *Sämtliche Schriften*, 120–4.

> And the blue, delicate veins above her cheek;
> Ne'er played the wanton—never half disclosed
> The maiden's snowy bosom, scattering thence
> Eye-poisons for some love-distempered youth.
>
> (lines 58–64)

Coleridge did not need to derive from Gessner the strategy of reaffirming presence while insisting upon its absence, for he had used the same abjuration/conjuration in 'Lewti, or The Circassian Love-Chant', Coleridge's reworking of Wordsworth's 'Beauty and Midnight: An Ode' (*PW* 1: 457–61)[16] The 'eye-poisons' of wanton images arise in spite of disclaiming their truth. The stream, too, is said *not* to reflect the teasing images which torment the fictional lover, who, of course, is *not* the narrator. The absent images are nevertheless described in attentive detail:

> no pool of thine,
> Though clear as lake in latest summer-eve,
> Did e'er reflect the stately virgin's robe,
> The face, the form divine, the downcast look
> Contemplative! Behold! her open palm
> Presses her cheek and brow! her elbow rests
> On the bare branch of half-uprooted tree,
> That leans towards its mirror!
>
> (lines 72–9)

So insistent is the mind's projection that lover cries out, 'Behold!' As if it were not enough to delineate the very look and gesture of the image that is not there, he has the phantom image return his gaze and then teasingly cast flowers into the water, dispelling her own non-existent presence:

> he now
> With steadfast gaze and unoffending eye,
> Worships the watery idol, dreaming hopes
> Delicious to the soul, but fleeting, vain,
> E'en as that phantom-world on which he gazed,
> But not unheeded gazed: for see, ah! see,
> The sportive tyrant with her left hand plucks
> The heads of tall flowers that behind her grow,
> Lychnis, and willow-herb, and fox-glove bells:
> And suddenly, as one that toys with time,
> Scatters them on the pool! Then all the charm
> Is broken—all that phantom-world so fair
> Vanishes, and a thousand circlets spread,
> And each mis-shape the other.
>
> (lines 81–94)

---

[16] *PW* I: 254; *CN* 3708, 315 n., 218 n.

The lovelorn poet, like a mime who manipulates imaginary objects, has played with images which he has mentally projected onto the surface of the pool. The image of the maiden, too, becomes a mime whose gesture, plucking 'the heads of tall flowers that behind her grow', acts out the beholder's desire for her touch. Since she exists here only as image of his unrequited love, she naturally re-enacts the lover's recollected experience of a 'sportive tyrant' who even as a merely mental phenomenon disrupts his image of her. The poet advises his alter ego, the 'poor youth' who has witnessed his dream dashed, to wait and watch.

> The stream will soon renew its smoothness, soon
> The visions will return! And lo! he stays:
> And soon the fragments dim of lovely forms
> Come trembling back, unite, and now once more
> The pool becomes a mirror
>
> (lines 96–100)

The 'half-uprooted tree' and 'each wild-flower' reappear as inverted images, but the image of the maiden is no longer there. Although neither she nor her image were present in the first place, only now does the lover confront the visual evidence of her absence: 'He turns, and she is gone!' As if she had just at this moment fled through the 'woodland maze', he runs off to seek her vanished form in vain. His fictional counterpart, the poet declares, may well devote his 'mad love-yearning' to the vacant pool, which will no doubt requite his 'sickly thoughts' with a bewitching image of his beloved, 'her shadow still abiding there, / The Naiad of the mirror!' (lines 110–11). At the close of this digression, the narrator repeats his denial of its truth: 'Not to thee, / O wild and desert stream! belongs this tale' (lines 111–12). The stream, as reflector of images, thus becomes a personified poet. Since the wild stream has had 'no loves', it could scarcely be guilty of generating false images. This denial not only continues the imaginary projection, it also strangely implicates narrator's own lovelorn lot.

If Coleridge had adhered more closely to Gessner's conventional trope, he would have described the maiden casting her flowers into the pond then leaving her lover alone in the woods. To narrate the same events as seen reflected in the water might call attention to the mimetic description. The latter strategy, even as metaphor for poetic representation, could nevertheless reinforce, rather than undermine, the claims of visual presence. The phenomena of reflected images, after all, could effectively enhance descriptive verisimilitude. The poet might thus have it both ways. And Coleridge certainly does retain this double advantage even when he proceeds to negate the entire scene and all of its participants: there is no lover, no mistress, no reflection, no river. A positive narration presents absences as if they were present. Coleridge presents absences and insists upon their absence. The net result, as Coleridge well knows, is much the same: we 'believe' the latter neither more nor less than the former. The negation, however, deftly calls attention to that process of indulging illusion which Coleridge referred to as 'the willing suspension of disbelief for the moment which constitutes poetic faith'. As he distinguished it from delusion, illusion involves self-awareness. By allowing his fictional lover to lapse into 'sickly thoughts', he thematizes both illusion and delusion.

Having unfolded and refolded the redoublings of the absent image, Coleridge goes on in this poem to reaffirm the illusions of presence. 'This be my chosen haunt,' he declares, 'emancipate / From passion's dreams' (lines 118–19). The river inside his text is now said to be real, and inside his text he commences to 'trace its devious course' as if the traces were the thing itself. Not surprisingly, his tracing leads him through a terrain in which the supposedly objective representation is transformed by subjective response. The reflection of a 'soft water-sun' is said to be 'throbbing' as if it were 'heart at once and eye' of the imagined river. Overshadowed by clouds, the reflected images become 'the stains and shadings of forgotten tears, / Dimness o'erswum with lustre'. The river is then described as running through a 'circular vale', with a cottage 'close by the waterfall'. Here the poet claims to discover at his feet a picture of the very scene he has just described.

> But what is this?
> That cottage, with its slanting chimney-smoke,
> And close beside its porch a sleeping child,
> His dear head pillowed on a sleeping dog—
> One arm between its fore-legs, and the hand
> Holds loosely its small handful of wild-flowers,
> Unfilletted, and of unequal lengths.
> A curious picture, with a master's haste
> Sketched on a strip of pinky-silver skin,
> Peeled from the birched bark!
>
> (lines 152–61)

The ekphrastic description of the 'curious picture' is more minutely detailed than the poet's description of the 'original' scene in the lines immediate preceding. Coleridge thus makes the painted image seem more real than reality, in marked contrast to the emphatic unreality of the phantom reflections in the imaginary river. The depicted image is no will-o'-the-wisp, and the painting itself is a palpable object.

> Yon bark her canvass, and those purple berries
> Her pencil! See, the juice is scarcely dried
> On the fine skin! She has been newly here;
> And lo! yon patch of heath has been her couch—
> The pressure still remains!
>
> (lines 162–7)

Reversing his rhetorical tactic, Coleridge affirms the picture as strongly as he previously had denied the reflection. Yet even this latter image is revealed amidst absences and traces. Only the signs remain behind. The poem ends with the poet, now with picture in hand as well as image in mind, in quest of a maiden who still is no longer there.[17]

In giving close attention to 'The Picture', a translation that ceased to be a translation, and became very much Coleridge's own poem, I delineate the characteristics of one species of Coleridgean composition: Gessner's theme and imagery are retained but amplified. As he sought to gain access to the untranslatable, Coleridge generated an entire spectrum of poetic strategies with varying degrees of appropriation and intervention: from translated to transferred, seldom word-for-word, more often freely adapted. To some degree acts of appropriation intrude in all his translation, even where he claims to adhere closely to the original. Much of his translation is self-translation, asserting his identity into the alterity of the text. He was less pre-emptive when he sought to communicate lines that he regarded as cultural artefacts, a drinking song or a nursery rhyme. For Coleridge, all translation and adaptation was a cultural enrichment. In the presence of a strong poet, such as Schiller or Goethe, he overcame the sense of subjugation, through his subjective 'entering into' the mind of the other, his creative empathy or *Mitgefühl*. With a lesser poet, such as Gessner, he simply made the poem his own. But even here, in the 'transferred poem', there was a cultural exchange, a shared awareness.

COLERIDGE AND CONTEMPORARY TRANSLATION THEORY

In order to fulfill its potential for cross-cultural mediation, translation must reach beyond the self and convey larger movements of the *Zeitgeist* from one country to another. In spite of this advocacy of translation as a step toward international communication, the period was nevertheless one of colonization, of imposing the dominant language on the occupied people as a tool of exploitation, undermining their own culture. Few proponents of translations as cultural exchange were more influential than Germaine de Staël, who early in her career wrote on the interaction between social conditions and literature (*De la littérature considérée dans ses rapports avec les institutions sociales*, 1800). Her principal work, *De l'Allemagne* (1810), drew not only from her extensive reading of German literature, but also her tour through Germany, her interviews with Goethe and Schiller in Weimar, and the suggestions of August Wilhelm Schlegel. Perceiving her praise of German literature and philosophy as an affront against French culture under his leadership, Napoleon

---

[17] *PW* I: 369–74; *CN* 3708, 3995, 4227.

ordered the destruction of the entire first edition (1811). Napoleon's reaction supported Staël's contention that literature exercised social, cultural, and political power. John Murray commissioned the English translation published in 1813,[18] and her work triggered in Britain an expanding interest, not just in Goethe and Schiller, but in previously neglected authors such as Zacharias Werner and Jean Paul.

In 'The Spirit of Translations' (1816), a study of Italian literature, de Staël criticized the practice during the Renaissance of writing in Latin. The rationale, of course, was that Latin was supposedly a universal language of scholars throughout Europe. But it was 'dead and artificial', capable of bearing allusions of the past, but bereft of any vitality of the present. Worse, it was inaccessible to the larger population. Translations would be unnecessary if all people knew all languages, or if only one language were spoken by all people. Since neither of those conditions prevail, Staël argued that translation must strive to fulfill a more important function of mediating among different cultures. To negotiate intercultural communication, translation must reflect both cultural constituencies:

Ultimately, it is the universal to which one must aspire in attempting to do good for the human race. I would go even further: even if one had a good understanding of foreign languages, a successful translation of a work into one's own language would provide a more familiar and intimate pleasure than the original. The imported beauty that a translation brings with it gives the national style new turns of phrase and original expressions. To preserve a country's literature from banality, a sure sign of decadence, there is no more effective means than translating foreign poets.[19]

In declaring that the original is more familiar and more intimately pleasing in translation, Staël is not merely repeating the earlier rationale for classical Greek and Latin translations. She is not referring, after all, to resuscitating historical antiquity, but to creating passageways between present day communities. Translation is a cross-pollenation that brings about a richer bloom, 'new turns of phrase and original expressions'. A literature cannot thrive without this sort enrichment; cultural isolation ends in 'banality'. Translation does more than reflect the source language's idiomatic originality, it also generates expressive originality within the language and culture into which a text is translated. Only by participating in a transcultural dialogue can cultural originality be sustained.

---

[18] *Germany*, by the Baroness Staël Holstein. Translated from the French. 3 vols. (London: John Murray, 1813). The unnamed translator was Francis Hodgson, whose French was inadequate to the task, and was therefore edited and corrected by William Lamb. Lady Caroline Lamb, in a letter to John Murray (October 1813; Murray Archive), pointed out the inaccuracies and recommended that her husband correct the text; cited in Paul Douglass, *Lady Caroline Lamb, A Biography* (London: Palgrave Macmillan, 2004), p. 154.

[19] Germaine de Staël, 'The Spirit of Translation', trans. Doris Y. Kadish, in *Translating Slavery: Gender and Race in French Women's Writing, 1783–1823*, ed. Doris Y. Kadish and Françoise Massardier-Kenney (Kent, Ohio: Kent State University Press, 1994), 163; in *Melanges, Oeuvres complètes de Madame la baronne de Staël-Holstein*, ed. Auguste de Staël (Paris: Treuttel and Wurtz, 1820–1), 17: 387–99.

In proposing excerpts rather than a full translation of *Goethe's Briefwechsel mit einem Kinde*, Sarah Taylor Austin may well have been concerned for Goëthe's reputation.[20] Although also a member of the well-known Taylor family of Norwich, she was no direct relation of William Taylor, but like him she translated numerous works from German and was influential in the reception of German literature in Britain. Her fullest exposition of her theory of translation appeared in the introduction to her three-volume publication of the *Characteristics of Goethe*.[21] Following Goëthe's death on 22 March 1832, Austin's work was among the first full accounts of his career to appear in English, translated from contemporary biographies with passages from Goethe's *Kunst und Alterthum* (Art and Antiquity).[22] Austin endorses Goëthe's own belief that translation should reveal rather than conceal the attributes of the original language. 'In translating,' Goethe wrote, 'one must confront the untranslatable; only then will one become aware of a foreign nation and a foreign language.'[23] The theories of Goethe, de Staël, and Austin coincide on this point: a translation does not usurp and colonize, but seeks to establish communication and trade.[24] Rather than domesticating the foreign, the translation retains the integrity and authenticity of the foreign. Preconceptions of the nature of the foreign bring about the fake and counterfeit foreign, the restatement of a stereotype.[25] The foreign must be introduced, not isolated; respected, not camouflaged. Translation must thus balance familiarizing and defamiliarizing. Austin presented her own translation as deliberately drawing attention to linguistic differences and keeping national distinctions in play. Her work thus serves as a 'plaidoyer in favour of the Germanisms with which I have made bold to affright English readers'.[26]

Although 'glad to refer unconditionally to the writings of my friend Mr. Carlyle', Austin makes it clear that she disagrees with some of Carlyle's views on Goethe, especially those concerning translation.[27] In his review of William Taylor's

[20] Janet Ross, *Three Generations of English women. Memoirs and Correspondence of Mrs. John* [Susannah] *Taylor, Mrs. Sarah Austin, and Lady Duff Gordon* (London: John Murray, 1888).

[21] Sarah Taylor Austin, *Characteristics of Goethe. From the German of Falk, von Müller, etc. with notes, original and translated, illustrative of German literature*. 3 vols. (London: Effingham Wilson, 1833).

[22] Austin's sources were Johann Daniel Falk, *Goethe aus nähern persönlichen Umgange dargestellt* (Leipzig: F. A. Brockhaus, 1832); Friedrich von Müller, *Goethe in seiner practischen Wirksamkeit* (Weimar: W. Hoffmann, 1832); Müller, *Goethe in seiner ethischen Eigenthümlichkeit* (Weimar: W. Hoffmann, 1832); extracts from the posthumous issue of *Kunst und Alterthum* (1832).

[23] Goethe, *Gesamtausgabe*, 45 vols., ed. Peter Boerner (Munich: dtv, 1961–3); *Maximen und Reflexionen*, 'Beim Übersetzen muß man bis ans Unübersetzliche herangehen; alsdann wird man aber erst die fremde Nation und die fremde Sprache gewahr', 18: 518.

[24] For an account of the translation theories of Sarah Austen, Germaine de Staël, and Margaret Fuller, see Colleen Glenney Boggs, 'Margaret Fuller's American Translation', *American Literature* 76. 1 (2004), 31–58.

[25] Austin, Preface, *Characteristics of Goethe*, xxx.

[26] Ibid., xxxvii.

[27] Ibid., xvi.

Historic Survey of German Poetry,[28] Carlyle praised Taylor for the literal bias of his translations:

Compared with the average of British Translations, they may be pronounced of almost ideal excellence. [...] One great merit Mr. Taylor has: rigorous adherence to his original; he endeavors at least to copy with all possible fidelity the turn of phrase, the tone, the very metre, whatever stands written for him.[29]

In his admiration of Goëthe, Carlyle readily endorsed Goethe's concept of World-Literature (Weltliteratur):

do not many other indications, traceable in France, in Germany, as well as here, betoken that a new era in the spiritual intercourse of Europe is approaching; that instead of isolated, mutually repulsive National Literatures, a World-Literature may one day be looked for? The better minds of all countries begin to understand each other, and, which follows naturally, to love each other.[30]

World-Literature, according to Goethe, was not to be achieved through translation; rather, authors must gather together and communicate among themselves.[31] Taylor's literary particularity, as Carlyle recognized, belonged to the elder generation of translators. Yet even the practice of the present day was far removed from the future era of World-Literature. On the other hand, Austin's Germanisms drew attention to the importance of national linguistic distinctions. She also reaffirmed Goethe's own translation practices:

It appears to me that Goethe alone... has solved the problem.... 'There are two maxims of translation,' says he, 'the one requires that the author of a foreign nation be brought to us in such a manner that we may regard him as our own; the other, on the contrary, demands of us that we transport ourselves over to him and adopt his situation, his mode of speaking, his peculiarities.[32]

---

[28] William Taylor, *Historic Survey of German Poetry, interspersed with various translations,* 3 vols. (London, Treuttel and Würtz, Treuttel jun. and Richter, 1830).

[29] Thomas Carlyle, 'Taylor's *Historic Survey of German Poetry* (1830)', *Edinburgh Review* 53 (1831): 151–80; *Complete Works of Thomas Carlyle,* 20 vols. (New York, Collier, 1901), 15: 338.

[30] Carlyle, 'Taylor's *Historic Survey*', *Works,* 15: 341–2.

[31] Goethe, *Die Zusammenkunft der Naturforscher in Berlin* (1828), *Gesamtausgabe,* 18: 392. 'Wenn wir eine europäische, ja eine allgemeine Weltliteratur zu verkündigen gewagt haben, so heißt dieses nicht, daß die verschiedenen Nationen von einander und ihren Erzeugnissen Kenntnis nehmen, denn in diesem Sinne existiert sie schon lange, setzt sich fort und erneuert sich mehr oder weniger. Nein! hier ist vielmehr davon die Rede, daß die lebendigen und strebenden Literatoren einander kennenlernen und durch Neigung und Gemeinsinn sich veranlaßt finden, gesellschaftlich zu wirken. Dieses wird aber mehr durch Reisende als durch Korrespondenz bewirkt, indem ja persönlicher Gegenwart ganz allein gelingt, das wahre Verhältnis.' See Hans Joachim Schrimpf, *Goethes Begriff der Weltliteratur* (Stuttgart: Metzler, 1968).

[32] Austin, Preface, *Characteristics of Goethe,* xxxii–iii. Goethe, 'Zum brüderlichen Andenken Wielands' (1813), *Goethes Sämtliche Werke,* Jubiläums-Ausgabe, 40 vols., ed. Eduard von der Hellen (Stuttgart und Berlin: Cotta, 1902–7), 37: 22.

Both maxims are concerned with encountering 'Fremdheit'. The first maxim addresses the translator whose task is to make the foreign author available to the reader, so that the reader may view him as his own; the second puts the responsibility on the reader who must approach the position and point of view of the foreign author.[33]

Schleiermacher, in *On the Different Methods of Translation* (1813), also described these same two tasks but emphasized that neither offers any guidance for the translator. One might agree that the translator ought to convey not just the words, but the cultural context (*Zustände, Sprachweise, Eigenheiten*), but how that aim is to be accomplished is more than the first maxim explains. The second maxim involves a hermeneutic rather than a translating task, for the reader is expected to cross the textual threshold to comprehend the foreign author. The key to successful translation, Schleiermacher argued, lies in recognizing and exploiting the inherent plasticity of language. Even if the current usage of words in the target language are incommensurable with the foreign author's, the translator may nevertheless 'bend the language of the translation as far possible towards that of the original in order to communicate as far as possible an impression of the system of concepts developed in it.' The language into which the foreign author is introduced is therefore altered and enriched.[34]

Schleiermacher's antitheses of identity and alterity prevail as well in the problem of assimilating or preserving. Austin endeavored to represent the foreign text without sacrificing its linguistic and national specificities to her own English. Schleiermacher referred to 'bending' language to accommodate foreign concepts and phrases.[35] Lawrence Venuti, in *The Translator's Invisibility* (1995), reformulated Schleiermacher's distinction as familiarizing translations (which obscure the particularities of the foreign text) and foreignizing translations (which reveal the unfamiliar aspects).[36] For Venuti, these were opposite methods between which a translator must choose. Goethe and Austin understood the merit of each approach in relation to its purpose, indeed Austin regarded them more as modes that could be used intermixed, interchanged, in varying degrees.

During the first half of the eighteenth century, the Swiss critics Johann Jakob Bodmer and Johann Jakob Breitinger argued that successful translation replicated the original in another language.[37] In Leipzig, Johann Christoph Gottsched countered that the obligation of the translator was not to counterfeit, but to enrich his

---

[33] Manfred Fuhrmann, 'Goethes Übersetzungsmaximen,' *Goethe Jahrbuch* 117 (2000): 26–45.

[34] Schleiermacher, *Sämmtliche Werke*, 30 vols. (Berlin: G. Reimer, 1835–64.), Part 3, Vol. II, pp. 207–45.

[35] Susan Bernofsky, 'Schleiermacher's Translation Theory and Varieties of Foreignization: August Wilhelm Schlegel vs. Johann Heinrich Voss, *The Translator* (1997), 3 (2): 175–92.

[36] Venuti, *The Translator's Invisibility: A History of Translation* (London: Routledge, 1995).

[37] Johann Jakob Breitinger, *Critische Dictkunst: Worinnen die Poetische Mahlerey in Absicht auf die Erfindung im Grunde untersuchet und mit Beyspielen aus den berühmtesten Alten und Neuern erläutert wird* (Zurich: Orell, 1740), p. 139.

own language. The translator must 'teach his language to speak foreign thoughts'.[38] Georg Venzky, translator of Sir Thomas Browne's *Religio Medici* (1746) and advocate of Gottsched's position, identified four sorts of translation: the 'natural' translation is word-for-word, as in interlinear texts; the 'free' translation captures the sense; the augmented (*vermehrte*) translation incorporates explanatory words or phrases; its opposite is the condensed (*verstümmelte*) translation; the most complete (*vollständigste*) translation integrates commentary and exegesis and may thus improve upon the original.[39] Whether the translator should render the foreign work in the polished manner and style of the native literary tradition, or should introduce and interpret the foreign elements, clearly anticipates the debate in the Romantic period on whether a translator should strive to make the foreign familiar or preserve the foreignness of the original.[40]

How early nineteenth-century theories depart from those of their eighteenth-century predecessors can be demonstrated in the ways in which Novalis and Goethe delineate the three sorts of translation. Once again, Sarah Taylor Austin is the crucial mediatrix. In *Characteristics of Goëthe*, Austin translated Novalis on translation.

A translation... is either grammatical, or paraphrastic (*verändernd*, altering), or 'mythic'. By 'mythic' translation, Novalis means a textualization of natural phenomena. Grammatical translations, for Novalis, strive for strict verbal and stylistic equivalence. While they depend on great erudition, they do not require 'the highest poetical spirit' required by paraphrastical translations, if they are 'to be genuine'. Paraphrastic translations easily 'degenerate into travesties', like Pope's translation of Homer, so 'the true translator in this kind must, indeed, be himself the Artist, and be able to give the Idea of the Whole, thus or thus, at his pleasure. He must be the poet of the poet, and thus be able to make him speak at once after his own original conception, and after that which exists in his (the translator's) mind.'[41]

Novalis's recommendation shifts the significance from textual accuracy to the evocation of belief. Rather than thinking of the original as a linguistic construct, he suggests that it belongs to a cultural system of belief, trust, or faith. The translator must share that cultural credence and reflect it through the artistry of the translated language. The 'Idea of the Whole' ('poetischer Geist und philosophischer Geist in ihrer ganzen Fülle') is dynamic interaction. While such a

---

[38] Johann Jakob Brucker, 'Abhandlung von einigen alten deutschen Übersetzungen der heiligen Schrift', *Beyträge zur Critischen Historie der deutschen Sprache, Poesie und Beredsamkeit*, ed. Johann Christoph Gottsched (Leipzig, 1738; rpt. Leipzig, 1732–1744, Hildesheim: Olms, 1997), p. 11.

[39] Georg Venzky, 'Das Bild des geschickten Übersetzers' (The Image of the capable Translator), *Beyträge zur Critischen Historie der deutschen Sprache, Poesie und Beredsamkeit* (Leipzig, 1734; rpt. Hildesheim: Olms, 1997), p. 64.

[40] Gundula-Ulrike Fleischer, 'Übersetzungstheorien und -praxis im 16.–19. Jahrhundert (Ein entwicklungsgeschichtlicher Abriß)', *Jahrbuch der Ungarischen Germanistik* (1996), pp. 159–72.

[41] Austin, Preface, *Characteristics of Goethe*, xxx. Austin translated from Novalis, *Blüthenstaub*, HKA Bd. 2, S. 439–41.

translation remains an ideal rather an actual accomplishment, the desire to 'grasp the whole' leads the way to a more fulfilling understanding.

Goethe, too, in notes appended to his *West-östlicher Divan*, identified three sorts of translation. The first, a 'prosaic translation', is similar to what Novalis called a 'grammatical translation', a translation that is content to give the meaning of the original in terms of close verbal equivalencies or approximations. Such a translation works best in prose. The second sort, a 'parodistic translation', is similar to that suggested in the first of his two 'Übersetzungsmaximen', and closely parallels what Austin, citing Novalis, called a 'paraphrastical translation'. The translator attempts to identify with the foreign conditions in order to adopt, emulate, and reproduce those conditions. The third sort of translation creates, in a new language, a work identical with the original, a work that recreates all the meaning and power of the original. These three sorts of translation may coexist, but they also mark three epochs in the historical advance of translation. The signal accomplishment of the first epoch was Luther's bible translation; Voss's translation of Homer was the crowning achievement of the second epoch; and as an event of the third epoch Goethe offers his own translation of the Sufi poet Hafiz in his *West-östlicher Divan*.[42]

Translation for the theatre was dictated primarily but a sense of box-office attraction. But there were expectations. Friedrich Schiller was typically treated with literary respect, as in Tytler's *The Robbers* (1799),[43] Coleridge's *Wallenstein* (1801), and Mellish's *Mary Stuart* (1801).[44] Unlike the school-boy prize competitions for the best Greek or Latin poem, self-translation in the period was typically autobiographical or confessional, and offered an opportunity for subjective exploration as well as finding a voice in another culture. Popularization may have marked an extreme in Romantic translation, but even in advocating greater fidelity to the original, there was a sense that translation ought to make foreign culture broadly accessible. During the period of revolution and international turmoil, translation could scarcely escape the polemics of competing ideologies and rivaling nationalism. Foreignizing translation—allowing the features of the source language to show through—was the most prominent issue in the translation theory of the Romantics, evident in arguments of de Staël and Austin for translation as cultural enrichment. As dedicated purveyors of foreign culture, de Staël and Austin joined the ranks of other major translators and interpreters, from Tytler, Taylor, and Coleridge, to De Quincey and Carlyle. Part of their endeavor as mediators of a

---

[42] Goethe, 'Noten und Abhandlungen zu besserem Verständnis des west-östlichen Divans', *Gesamtausgabe*, 3: 307–9.

[43] Peter Mortensen, 'Robbing *The Robbers*: Schiller, Xenophobia and the Politics of British Romantic Translation', *Literature and History*, vol. 11, no. 1 (Spring 2002): 41–61.

[44] Elke H. M. Ritt, *Mary Stuart: A tragedy (1801) von Joseph Charles Mellish: die autorisierte englische Blankversübersetzung von Schillers Maria Stuart; Analyse und Text, nebst einer Biographie des Übersetzers und handschriftlichem Dokumentationsmaterial* (Munich: tuduv-Verlag, 1993).

broader community of European thought was evident in their affirmation of the translation theories of those whom they were translating: Novalis, Goethe, Schleiermacher.

When he pursued a familiarizing rather than foreignizing mode of translation, Coleridge's practice was directed by assimilating and subsuming the foreign text into his own poetic voice. Cary may become Dante, but Coleridge would transform Gessner, Goethe, and Hoffmann into Coleridge, so that his own poetic idiom was prominent. In his translation of *Faust*, he frequently relied on his own phrasing and imagery rather than adhere strictly to Goethe's.[45] As soon as the translation of Goethe was published (September 1821), Coleridge commenced his negotiations with Blackwood for further translations from the German (*CL* 19 September and *c*.19 September 1821). In November 1821, he recorded in his notebook the phrase, 'Twixt thro'—twixt in—Zwischen Branches—Swelling Branches' (*CN* 4738),[46] referring to Anselmus's vision of the Serpent Daughters ('Zwischen durch—zwischen ein—zwischen Zweigen, zwischen schwellenden Blüten') in E. T. A. Hoffmann's *Der goldne Topf*. When it appeared in *Blackwood's Edinburgh Magazine* (January 1822), however, the translation had been thoroughly assimilated into Coleridge's adaptation, 'The Historie and Gests of Maxilian' (*SW&F* 2 963–87), with an excuse that a 'pre-existant' version of this tale had awakened in the mind of a Prussian or Saxon, who managed to write it down 'before I had put a single line on paper' (*SW&F* 2:975).[47] Similar coincidences occur throughout Coleridge's work.

Works Cited

Austin, Sarah Taylor. 1833. *Characteristics of Goethe. From the German of Falk, von Müller, etc. with notes, original and translated, illustrative of German literature.* 3 vols. London: Effingham Wilson.

Bernofsky, Susan. 1997. Schleiermacher's translation theory and varieties of foreignization: August Wilhelm Schlegel vs. Johann Heinrich Voss. *The Translator*, 3 (2): 175–92.

Boggs, Colleen Glenney. 2004. Margaret Fuller's American translation. *American Literature*, 76(1): 31–58.

Breitinger, Johann Jakob. 1740. *Critische Dictkunst: Worinnen die Poetische Mahlerey in Absicht auf die Erfindung im Grunde untersuchet und mit Beyspielen aus den berühmtesten Alten und Neuern erläutert wird.* Zurich: Orell.

Brucker, Johann Jakob. 1997. Abhandlung von einigen alten deutschen Übersetzungen der heiligen Schrift. *In Beyträge zur Critischen Historie der deutschen Sprache, Poesie und*

---

[45] *Faustus, translated by Samuel Taylor Coleridge from the German of Goethe*, ed. Frederick Burwick and James McKusick (Oxford: Oxford University Press, 2007).

[46] The editors of the Notebook do not identify Hoffmann's *Der goldne Topf* as source for this entry.

[47] See note 9 above.

Beredsamkeit, ed. Johann Christoph Gottsched. Leipzig, 1738; rpt. Leipzig, 1732–1744, Hildesheim: Olms.

CARLYLE, THOMAS. 1901. Taylor's *Historic Survey of German Poetry* (1830), *Edinburgh Review* 53 (1831): 151–80; *Complete Works of Thomas Carlyle*, 20 vols. New York: Collier, 15: 338.

CARY, HENRY FRANCIS. 1805–6. *The Inferno of Dante Alighieri: canto I–XXXIV, with a translation in English blank verse, notes, and a life of the author.* 2 vols. London: Printed for J. Carpenter.

—— *The Vision, or, Hell, Purgatory, and Paradise, of Dante Alighieri.* 3 vols. London: Printed for Taylor and Hessey, 1814; 2nd corrected edition.

COLERIDGE, SAMUEL TAYLOR. 1983. *Biographia Literaria* (= *BL*). 2 vols., ed. W. J. Bate, and James Engell, *The Collected Works of Samuel Taylor Coleridge*, 7. Princeton: Princeton University Press.

—— 1956–1971. *Collected Letters of Samuel Taylor Coleridge* (= *CL*). 6 vols. ed. Earl Leslie Griggs. Oxford: Clarendon Press.

—— 2007. *Faustus, translated by Samuel Taylor Coleridge from the German of Goëthe*, ed. Frederick Burwick and James McKusick. Oxford: Clarendon Press.

—— 1987. *Lectures 1808–1819: On Literature* (= *Lects 1808–19*), 2 vols. ed. Reginald Foakes, *The Collected Works of Samuel Taylor Coleridge*, 5. Princeton: Princeton University Press.

—— 1984. *Marginalia*, ed. George Whalley. *The Collected Works of Samuel Taylor Coleridge*, 12. Princeton: Princeton University Press.

—— 1957–2002. *The Notebooks of Samuel Taylor Coleridge* (= *CN*), ed. Kathleen Coburn. Princeton: Princeton University Press.

—— 2001. *Poetical Works* (= *PW*), ed. J. C. C. Mays, *The Collected Works of Samuel Taylor Coleridge*, 16. Princeton: Princeton University Press.

—— 1995. *Shorter Works and Fragments* (= *SW&F*), 2 vols., ed. H. J. Jackson and J. R. de J. Jackson, *The Collected Works of Samuel Taylor Coleridge*, 11. Princeton: Princeton University Press.

CRICK, JOYCE. 1988. Coleridge's *Wallenstein*: two legends, *The Modern Language Review*, 83 (1) (Winter): 76–86.

—— 1984. Some editorial and stylistic observations on Coleridge's translation of Schiller's *Wallenstein*,' *Publications of the English Goëthe Society*, 54: 37–75.

DOUGLASS, PAUL. 2004. *Lady Caroline Lamb, A Biography*. London: Palgrave.

FALK, JOHANN DANIEL. 1832. *Goethe aus näherm persönlichen Umgange dargestellt*. Leipzig: F. A. Brockhaus.

FLEISCHER, GUNDULA-ULRIKE. 1996. Übersetzungstheorien und -praxis im 16.–19. Jahrhundert (Ein entwicklungsgeschichtlicher Abriß). *Jahrbuch der Ungarischen Germanistik*, pp. 159–72.

FUHRMANN, MANFRED. 2000. Goethes Übersetzungsmaximen, *Goëthe Jahrbuch* 117: 26–45.

GESSNER, SALOMON. 1972–74. *Sämtliche Schriften in Drei Bänden* (1762), ed. Martin Bircher. Zürich: Orell Füssli.

GOËTHE, JOHANN WOLFGANG VON. 1961–3. *Gesamtausgabe*, 45 vols. ed. Peter Boerner. Munich: dtv.

—— 1902–1907. *Goethes Sämtliche Werke*, Jubiläums-Ausgabe, 40 vols., ed. Eduard von der Hellen. Stuttgart und Berlin: Cotta.

Knox, Julian. 2006. Coleridge's 'Cousin-German': Narrative Alter-Egos in the 'The Satyrane Letters' and 'The Historie and Gests of Maxilian', paper presented at the Coleridge Summer Conference, Cannington, 20–26 July.

Luther, Susan. 1997. Coleridge, Creative (Day)Dreaming, and 'The Picture'. *Dreaming* 7 (1) (March).

Mortensen, Peter. 2002. Robbing *The Robbers*: Schiller, Xenophobia and the Politics of British Romantic Translation. *Literature and History*, 11 (1) (Spring): 41–61.

Müller, Friedrich von. 1832. *Goethe in seiner practische Wirksamkeit*. Weimar: W. Hoffmann.

—— 1832. *Goëthe in seiner ethischen Eigenthümlichkeit*. Weimar: W. Hoffmann.

Novalis. 1977–2001. (= Friedrich con Hardenberg) *Blüthenstaub*, in *Novalis Schriften: die Werke Friedrich von Hardenbergs/Novalis*, ed. Paul Kluckhohn, Richard Samuel; unter mitarbeit von Heinz Ritter und Gerhard Schülz. 6 vols Stuttgart: Kohlhammer. 2, pp. 439–41.

Ritt, Elke H. M. 1993. ed. *Mary Stuart: A tragedy (1801) von Joseph Charles Mellish: die autorisierte englische Blankversübersetzung von Schillers Maria Stuart; Analyse und Text, nebst einer Biographie des Übersetzers und handschriftlichem Dokumentationsmaterial.* Munich: tuduv-Verlag.

Ross, Janet. 1888. *Three Generations of English women. Memoirs and Correspondence of Mrs. John* [Susannah] *Taylor, Mrs. Sarah Austin, and Lady Duff Gordon*. London: John Murray.

Schleiermacher, Friedrich. 1835–1864. *Sämmtliche Werke*, 30 vols. Berlin: G. Reimer.

Schrimpf, Hans Joachim. 1968. *Goethes Begriff der Weltliteratur*. Stuttgart: Metzler.

Scott, Matthew. 1996. The circulation of Romantic creativity: Coleridge, drama, and the question of translation, *Romanticism On the Net*: An Electronic Journal Devoted to Romantic Studies, vol. 2, May.

Staël, Germaine de. 1813. *Germany*. Translated from the French. 3 vols. London: John Murray.

—— 1820–1. *Melanges, Oeuvres complètes de Madame la baronne de Staël-Holstein*, ed. Auguste de Stael. Paris: Treuttel and Wurtz.

—— 1994. The spirit of translation, trans. Doris Y. Kadish. In *Translating Slavery: Gender and Race in French Women's Writing, 1783–1823*, ed. Doris Y. Kadish and Françoise Massardier-Kenney. Kent, Ohio: Kent State University Press.

Taylor, William. 1830. *Historic Survey of German Poetry, interspersed with various Translations*, 3 vols. London: Treuttel and Würtz, Treuttel jun. and Richter.

Venzky, Georg. 1997. Das Bild des geschickten Übersetzers [The Image of the Capable Translator], *Beyträge zur Critischen Historie der deutschen Sprache, Poesie und Beredsamkeit*. Leipzig, 1734; rpt. Hildesheim: Olms.

Venuti, Lawrence. 1995. *The Translator's Invisibility: A History of Translation*. London: Routledge.

PART IV

SOURCES AND
INFLUENCES

CHAPTER 23

COLERIDGE AND
PLAGIARISM

ANDREW KEANIE

THE sources of Coleridge's writings have long fascinated critics, and the commentary has ranged from praise for myriad-minded weaving together of manifold cultural materials to condemnation for plagiarism. Coleridge's kindest critics have disentangled the components of what Kelvin Everest has called his 'eclectically derivative' corpus and 'compulsively devious'[1] practice with sensitive fingers. In his remarkable book, *The Road to Xanadu: A Study in the Ways of the Imagination* (1927), John Livingston Lowes 'made us all familiar with the picture of Coleridge as a man with a wonderfully capacious memory coupled with poetic powers that allowed him to refine from the raw material of his reading gems of the purest quality'.[2]

Coleridge's unkindest critic, Norman Fruman, has reacted against what in his view is the canonical sentimentality that has transmogrified the real Coleridge, the chronic liar (who claimed to be translating Schiller before he knew any German, and who criticized Italian poets before he knew Italian), into 'the Da Vinci of literature'.[3] Fruman's landmark study of Coleridge's plagiarisms, *Coleridge: The Damaged Archangel* (1970), was brash and profound, and the following general observation is typical of the book:

---

[1] Kelvin Everest, 'Coleridge's Life', *The Cambridge Companion to Coleridge* (Cambridge, 2002), pp. 17–31, at p. 26.

[2] W. Schrickx, 'Coleridge and the Cambridge Platonists', *A Review of English Literature* (edited by A. Norman Jeffares), vol. VII, no. 1, January 1966, p. 71.

[3] Norman Fruman, *Coleridge: The Damaged Archangel* (1970), p. 292.

Since Coleridge is considered a speculative genius of the first rank, even one of the seminal minds of history, we are certainly not disposed to accuse him either of literary theft or conscious deception. It has become distinctly unfashionable to speak of literary ethics where important writers are involved, especially poets. In fact, the case of Coleridge's extensive silent borrowings has gone far towards changing contemporary attitudes toward such practices.[4]

Fruman's book was published a year after Thomas McFarland's *Coleridge and the Pantheist Tradition* (1969), which contains a chapter on Coleridge's borrowings,[5] including the view that

the concept of 'plagiarism' cannot stand the stress of historical examination. We encounter the term so rarely that we are perhaps not so critical of it as we should be. It applies mainly to the stricken efforts of undergraduates to meet demands far beyond either their abilities or their interests. But it has no proper applicability to the activities, however unconventional, of a powerful, learned, and deeply committed mind.[6]

Fruman must have either read McFarland's apposite book but decided not to include consideration of it in his own, or not read it (deliberately ignoring or genuinely unaware of the competition). At any rate, Fruman did seem (coincidentally or not) to take issue with McFarland's broadly benevolent view of Coleridge's borrowings: 'The word "plagiarism" itself is vaguely discredited.'[7] Despite (or because of) the invaluable insights they have provided for a general readership, some late twentieth-century investigations into Coleridge's borrowings have been characterized by the bites and feints of competitive academics. Fruman and McFarland polarized Coleridge studies.

Coleridge crossed a qualitative line, that intangible border that separates plagiarists from the other writers who have their secrets, but seem to lack the tendency towards dependency: Coleridge had, as John Beer (himself borrowing and adapting Harold Bloom's phrase) has said, an 'anxiety to be influenced'.[8] His 'nature require[d] another Nature for its support, & repose[d] only in another form the necessary Indigence of its being'.[9]

Spoken plagiarism is more difficult to detect than written plagiarism. It was as a speaker that Coleridge impressed his contemporaries the most. In his tart essay, 'Mr Coleridge' (1825), Hazlitt would draw attention to what he considered the

---

[4] Norman Fruman, *Coleridge: The Damaged Archangel* (1970), pp. 69–70.

[5] Thomas McFarland, *Coleridge and the Pantheist Tradition* (Oxford University Press, 1969), ch. 1, 'The Problem of Coleridge's Plagiarisms', pp. 1–52.

[6] *Coleridge and the Pantheist Tradition*, p. 45.

[7] *Coleridge: The Damaged Archangel*, p. 70.

[8] John Beer, 'Coleridge and Wordsworth: Influence and Confluence', in Donald Sultana (ed.), *New Approaches to Coleridge: Biographical and Critical Essays* (1981), pp. 192–211, p. 193.

[9] *CN* II, 2712.

disappointing skimpiness of Coleridge's finished, written, and published output,[10] but in an earlier essay (first published in the *Liberal*, no. 3, April 1823, although some passages had appeared in Hazlitt's letter to the *Examiner* of 12 January 1817)[11] he had recollected Coleridge's style of preaching with particular fondness:

the organ was playing the 100th psalm, and, when it was done, Mr Coleridge rose and gave out his text, 'And he went up into the mountain to pray, HIMSELF, ALONE'. As he gave out his text, his voice 'rose like a stream of rich distilled perfumes', and when he came to the two last words, which he pronounced loud, deep, and distinct, it seemed to me, who was then young, as if the sounds had echoed from the bottom of the human heart, and as if that prayer might have floated in solemn silence through the universe.[12]

Coleridge uttered the words so thrillingly that the seventeen-year-old Hazlitt (until that moment despondent as a failed painter) was electrified into lifelong productivity as an essayist:

Poetry and Philosophy had met together. Truth and Genius had embraced, under the eye and with the sanction of Religion. This was even beyond my hopes. I returned home well satisfied... there was a spirit of hope and youth in all nature, that turned everything into good.[13]

It was essentially Coleridge's passionate, personal delivery of another man's words that made the life-changing impact on the young Hazlitt. There lies a Coleridgean rub. 'And he went... HIMSELF, ALONE' is from John 6: 15. Hazlitt would have known as much without Coleridge acknowledging the source. As a speaker, Coleridge made others' words his own by redeploying them with a difference; and in this case, according to Hazlitt, Coleridge redeployed the words of John in the context of a sermon 'upon peace and war; upon church and state—not their alliance, but their separation—on the spirit of the world and the spirit of Christianity, not as the same, but as opposed to one another'.[14]

The instance is representative of Coleridge's disinclination (in writing and in person) to break the continuity, or weaken the radiance and rhapsody, of a passion. The instance also shows that it did not occur to Hazlitt (whose bitterness is unmistakable in his later essay, 'Mr Coleridge') to disapprove of, or seek to create a climate of opprobrium around, Colerdge's borrowing. Why should Coleridge— who could make 'the whole material universe look like a transparency of words' when 'holding forth to a large party of ladies and gentlemen... on the Berkeleian

---

[10] 'What is become of all this mighty heap of hope, of thought, of learning and humanity? It has ended in swallowing doses of oblivion and in writing paragraphs in the *Courier*' (*Selected Essays of William Hazlitt*, ed. Geoffrey Keynes, London: The Nonesuch Press, 1970, p. 733).

[11] *William Hazlitt: Selected Writings* (ed. Jon Cook, Oxford University Press, 1991), p. 395.

[12] Ibid., pp. 12–13.

[13] Ibid., p. 213.

[14] Ibid.

Theory'[15]—punctuate the flow of his talk or prose with the typographical marks of quotation? To do so would only remind the auditor of the printed book which was the source of the speaker's inspiration.

Michael John Kooy has remarked that there is in the community of Coleridge scholars a 'nervous fixation on sources' that has left scholars 'unaccustomed, even unwilling to think of Coleridge's relationship with other thinkers except in terms of either slavish dependence or absolute ignorance'.[16] Such scholarly nervousness may have spoiled Coleridge enthusiasts' appetite for the necessarily sweet and sour portions of one of the most penetrating assessments of Coleridge's writing habits—by Thomas De Quincey:

Had, then, Coleridge any need to borrow from Schelling? Did he borrow *in forma pauperis*? Not at all: there lay the wonder. He spun daily, and at all hours, for mere amusement of his own activities, and from the loom of his own magical brain, theories more gorgeous by far, and supported by a pomp and luxury of images, such as neither Schelling—no, nor any German that ever breathed, not John Paul—could have emulated in his dreams. With the riches of El Dorado lying about him, he would condescend to filch a handful of gold from any man whose purse he fancied, and in fact reproduced in a new form, applying itself to intellectual wealth, that maniacal propensity which is sometimes well known to attack proprietors and millionaires for acts of petty larceny.[17]

The simultaneity of De Quincey's approval and opprobrium is prodigious. Even as De Quincey (a plagiarist[18]) called Coleridge a plagiarist, he seems to have tried to generate a general mood of ambivalence about questions as thorny for himself as they were for Coleridge, such as: is reading ex-nihilo composition an inalienable right? McFarland has recognized De Quincey's kinship with Coleridge:

De Quincey's accusation was ameliorated by an acute and sympathetic analysis of the possible psychological explanation for Coleridge's actions, by a favourable attitude towards Coleridge's intrinsic originality, and finally, by a casualness that led him into citing Coleridge's source as Schelling's 'Kleine Philosophische Werke' (the work in question is actually the *System des transscendentalen Idealismus*).[19]

---

[15] *William Hazlitt: Selected Writings* (ed. Jon Cook, Oxford University Press, 1991), p. 220.

[16] John Michael Kooy, *Coleridge, Schiller, and Aesthetic Education* (London: Palgrave Macmillan, 2002), p. 96.

[17] Thomas De Quincey, *Reminiscences of the English Lake Poets* (ed. David Wright, Harmonsworth, 1970; repr., 1986), pp. 8–9.

[18] 'In 1965 appeared a book which severely damages De Quincey's reputation for encyclopedic learning. Albert Goldman's *The Mine and the Mint: Sources for the Writings of Thomas De Quincey* (Carbondale, Ill.) establishes beyond reasonable doubt the following "general rule": "namely, that in any matter requiring merely intellectual ability De Quincey is not likely to have plagiarized; but when it is a question of special knowledge, facts and ideas that can only be obtained by thorough research, then in almost every instance he is dependent on a single source" (p. 81)' (*Coleridge: The Damaged Archangel*, p. 469).

[19] *Coleridge and the Pantheist Tradition*, p. 3.

Coleridge's daughter, Sara Coleridge, seems to have had the same sort of intellectual sympathy for her father's writing methods as De Quincey:

At all times [Coleridge's] incorrectness of quotation and of reference, and in the relation of particular circumstances, was extreme; it seemed as if the door betwixt his memory and imagination was always open, and though the former was a large strong room, its contents were perpetually mingling with those of the adjoining chamber. I am sure that if I had not had the facts of my Father's life at large before me, from his letters and the relations of friends, *I should not have believed such confusions as his possible in a man of sound mind.*[20]

So too it seems that with a close comprehension of his father's practice that Hartley Coleridge, in his essay, 'Ignoramus on the Fine Arts' (1831), would ask a rhetorical question as if seeking to settle a family concern:[21] 'What extempore preacher would expose . . . his note-book to his congregation?'[22]

[20] *The Complete Works of Samuel Taylor Coleridge*, ed. W. G. T. Shedd, 7 vols. (New York, 1853–4), vol. III, p. xxxvi n.

[21] Hartley Coleridge's reputation would also be tainted by the accusation of plagiarism, which, as Elizabeth Story Donno has argued in her article, 'The Case of the Purloined Biography: Hartley Coleridge and Literary Protectivism' (*Bulletin of Research in the Humanities* 1979, 82, pp. 458–86), mobilized the 'family concern' (p. 459) in such a way that Hartley's brother (and posthumous editor), Derwent Coleridge, and Hartley's cousin (and anonymous reviewer), Henry Nelson Coleridge, would seek to conceal the extent of Hartley's debts to John Dove and Henry James Monk. Hence, the phrase, 'fraternal protectivism' (p. 463).

[22] *Hartley Coleridge: Essays and Marginalia* (2 vols., Edward Moxon, London, 1851), vol. I, p. 180. Fruman has written provocatively about how certain phrases taken from the Bible came to be included in Coleridge's notebooks in the way they did:

Those inclined to view the activity in the mind of a poet as governed by the inscrutable 'hooks and eyes' of association and imagination are content to suppose that Coleridge was at random jotting down phrases which his astonishingly retentive memory had retained from his reading. But this supposition requires a taxing degree of credulity. Consider the order of the 'remembered' phrases:

(1) Ps. 44:25;

(2) Ps. 64;

(3) Wisdom of Solomon 12:26;

(4) Ps. 38:8;

(5) Ps. 38:8;

(6) Ps. 41:3 and 42:4;

(7) Ps. 49:4;

(8) Ps. 55:8;

(9) Ps. 22:3;

(10) Ps. 88:13;

(11) Judith 16:11;

(12) Wisdom of Solomon 8:3;

(13) Ecclus. 16:9.

An odd pattern of memory, surely. And if it were merely a matter of memory, why would Coleridge, or anybody else, remember from the vast tract of the Bible only bits and snatches from the Psalms and

Less interested in the Coleridge family concern, and with more of the instinct of the ruthless journalist than Hartley Coleridge, De Quincey revealed S. T. Coleridge's silent debt to the Danish-German poet, Friederica Brun. Sympathetically, De Quincey said that Coleridge had taken Brun's poem, which was just twenty lines long, and made it more than four times longer, awakening 'the dry bones of the German outline... into the fullness of life'; less sympathetically, De Quincey said that in 'mere logic... and even as to the choice of circumstances, Coleridge's poem is a translation'.[23] The Coleridge children did not relish their father's *modus operandi* being illuminated so flamboyantly for the readers of *Tait's Magazine*, but, worse, they were revolted by the additional personal comments De Quincey had included (be it remembered, just after Coleridge's death, in 1834) in order to create a sensation. De Quincey's biographer, Grevel Lindop, has summarized the burden of De Quincey's other *épingles*:

De Quincey gave the public a great deal of exciting gossip. 'Coleridge's marriage', he explained, 'had not been a very happy one.' Indeed, 'Coleridge... assured me that his marriage was not his own deliberate act; but was in a manner forced upon his sense of honour, by the scrupulous Southey, who insisted that he had gone too far in his attentions to Miss F[ricker], for any honourable retreat.' Mrs Coleridge's jealousy of 'a young lady... intellectually very much superior to her'—Dorothy Wordsworth—was described in some detail, as was Coleridge's addiction to opium, which, wrote De Quincey reprovingly, 'he first began... not as a relief from any bodily pains or nervous irritations—for his constitution was strong and excellent—but as a source of luxurious sensations'. He also laughed at Coleridge's incompetence in conducting *The Friend*—insisting on dwelling so far from the printer, handling subscriptions and mailing lists so badly.[24]

Sara Coleridge recognized De Quincey's fundamental sympathy with her father's mode of composition. However, she sorrowed over the way De Quincey had blended his insights with scurrilous matter:

We have been much hurt with our former friend, Mr De Quincey... for publishing so many personal details respecting my parents in *Tait's Magazine*... He has characterized my father's genius and peculiar mode of discourse with great eloquence and discrimination... I cannot believe that he had any enmity to my father, indeed he often speaks of his

---

comparatively so much from the much more limited and obscure Apocrypha? It seems neither reasonable nor helpful to posit the preternatural flashings of the creative imagination as lying behind these entries. Much more reasonable is the supposition that in the cold light of common day Coleridge had his Bible and Apocrypha open before him and that he was flipping pages back and forth between them, pen in hand, picking up phrases which might prove useful. (*Coleridge: The Damaged Archangel*, pp. 237–8)

[23] Thomas De Quincey, *Recollections of the Lake Poets* (ed. Edward Sackville West, London, 1948), p. 24.

[24] Grevel Lindop, *The Opium-Eater: A Life of Thomas De Quincey* (New York: Taplinger Publishing Co., 1981), p. 315.

kindness of heart; but 'the dismal degradation of pecuniary embarrassment', as he himself expresses it, has induced him to supply the depraved craving of the public for personality.[25]

But Sara would have noticed, too, how De Quincey, the nimble wordsmith, could illustrate the necessity of his tools of analysis in unearthing the grandeur of Coleridge's conception from the medium of Coleridge's almost primitive clumsiness.

The piquant views of Hazlitt and De Quincey square broadly with the idea that Coleridge somehow failed to transmit the full value of his personality via the printed page. The experience of listening to Coleridge speak was analogous to the experience of passing through Paradise in a dream, having a flower presented to you as a pledge that your soul had really been there, but not finding that flower in your hand (in Coleridge's published work) when you awoke.[26] However hurtfully—and, sometimes, hatefully—De Quincey and Hazlitt wrote about Coleridge, it can be seen that in the fullness of time their words did help in the weaving of the spell of Coleridgean enchantment. Yet in the meantime the discardable minutiae that De Quincey included in his account of Coleridge, understandably, inflated obnoxiously in the mind of a daughter offended: Sara Coleridge would have perceived with alarm the journalistic looseness with which De Quincey was handling her father's newly posthumous reputation.[27] De Quincey did not look as if he would shun being acknowledged as the critic who had punctured the stately pleasure dome (which might have begun to fly about like a slipped balloon in the public perception, losing its mystique in farts and whistles).

De Quincey's charge that Coleridge was a 'conversational plagiarist, given to trumpeting other men's bright ideas as his own',[28] was a point well-aimed by a fellow-plagiarist protected by something Coleridge never had: the ease, the luxury, the ability to live out the dream we all have that if we ignore our annoyances, they will go away. In short, De Quincey had a peculiarly robust conscience. Walter Jackson Bate has said that Coleridge 'could not . . . be even mildly conscience-free about [his plagiarisms] as De Quincey was able to be'.[29] De Quincey claimed that he discussed with Poole 'Coleridge's manner of spinning brilliant impromptu theories on philosophical themes in the course of conversation'. According to De Quincey, Poole

---

[25] Sara Coleridge, *Memoir and Letters of Sara Coleridge, Edited by her Daughter*, 2 vols. (London: Henry S. King and Co, 1873), I, p. 109.

[26] 'If a man could pass through Paradise in a dream, and have a flower presented to him as a pledge that his soul had really been there, and if he found that flower in his hand when he awoke—Aye! and what then?' (*CN* 4287)

[27] 'Five of [De Quincey's] "Autobiographical Sketches" had appeared when, on 25 July 1834, Coleridge died. For De Quincey this was an event of immediate practical importance for he knew quite well that his reminiscences of Coleridge were a rich vein which he could mine as soon as S.T.C. himself was safely past objecting.' (*The Opium-Eater*, p. 314)

[28] Grevel Lindop, *The Opium-Eater: A Life of Thomas De Quincey*, p. 314.

[29] Walter Jackson Bate, *Coleridge* (1968), p. 137.

came round to confessing that he suspected Coleridge of 'borrowing' some of his theories from little-known authors and passing them off, with a great show of brilliance, as his own. As a case in point, Poole recalled that a few days previously [Coleridge] had been holding forth on the subject of the Pythagorean philosophy, and he ventured to offer his own explanation of the well-known enigma as to why Pythagoras had forbidden his disciples to eat beans. To put it plainly, 'Coleridge', said Poole, 'gave us an interpretation which, from his manner, I suspect to have been not original. Think, therefore', he challenged De Quincey, 'if you have anywhere read a plausible solution'. De Quincey, according to his own testimony, had the answer ready at once. Yes: in a minor German writer ('a poor stick of a man', he hastened to add, 'not to be named on the same day with Coleridge') he had come across such a theory: beans in ancient Greece were used as tokens in voting, and the prohibition had referred not to eating but to meddling in politics. 'By Jove', was Poole's reply, 'that is the very explanation he gave us!'[30]

One must be wary of any anecdote from De Quincey,[31] but one might still find the above passage irresistibly illuminating when considered alongside, say, the furtive reverberation of Coleridge's 'Deeds to be hid which were not hid',[32] in 'The Pains of Sleep' (1803). Furthermore, Coleridge's confession in 'Dejection: an ode' (1802), though impressionistic, seems to illustrate the point even less equivocally:

> And fruits and foliage not my own seemed mine...
> For not to think of what I needs must feel...
> And haply by abstruse research to steal
> From my own nature all the natural man—
> This was my sole resource, my only plan:
> Till that which suits a part infects the whole,
> And now is almost grown the habit of my soul.[33]

Coleridge's borrowed ideas flourished most felicitously (and least detectably) amongst the contingencies of spontaneous utterance. The music of Coleridge's talk enchanted many of his auditors, a number of whom would prove eloquently inarticulate about what it was that had enchanted them. 'I can give no idea of the beauty and sublimity of his conversation. It resembles the loveliness of a song,'[34] said Anne Chalmers. Remembering nothing of what Coleridge had actually said to bring about his listeners' raptness, Thomas Hood did remember the diminishing bump back to the ordinary world:

I had been carried, spiralling, up to heaven by a whirlwind intertwisted with sunbeams, giddy and dazzled, but not displeased, and had then been rained down again with a shower

---

[30] Grevel Lindop, *The Opium-Eater: A Life of Thomas De Quincey*, pp. 141–2.

[31] In *A Flame in Sunlight: The Life and Work of Thomas De Quincey* (1936), Edward Sackville-West has recognized De Quincey's ability to 'defend [him]self against remorse' (p. 50), and his ability 'to create... self-justifying illusions round... dark... and... perplex[ing] episode[s] in his life' (p. 51).

[32] *Samuel Taylor Coleridge: Poetical Works* (edited by E. H. Coleridge, 1912), p. 390.

[33] Ibid., pp. 366–7.

[34] *S.T. Coleridge: Interviews and Recollections*, ed. Seamus Perry (Basingstoke and New York: Palgrave, 2000), p. 272.

of mundane stocks and stones that battered out of me all recollection of what I had heard, and what I had seen![35]

Julius Charles Hare found himself similarly frustrated when he tried to recollect what Coleridge had actually said:

When I look upon the scanty memorial, which I have alone preserved of this afternoon's converse, I am tempted to burn these pages in despair. Mr. Coleridge talked a volume of criticism that day, which, printed verbatim as he spoke it, would have made the reputation of any other person [Schelling? Or the 'poor stick of a man' mentioned by De Quincey?] but himself. He was, indeed, particularly brilliant and enchanting, and I left him at night so thoroughly *magnetized*, that I could not for two or three days afterwards reflect enough to put anything on paper.[36]

Many of Coleridge's contemporaries felt that they had failed to record any satisfactory sense of the stratosphere to which his talk could help them mount, in imagination, before the moment melted away. One of the more capable contenders, Hazlitt, said that he (at 17 years old) 'could not have been more delighted if [he] had heard the music of the spheres'[37] (but, as mentioned earlier, the older Hazlitt would be less prepared to produce such encomia).

Coleridge the talker could be so impressive that impressed individuals tended to conceptualize Coleridge as at the centre of some Ptolemaic system, shedding Coleridgean light through the intellectual universe. It would be more appropriate to envisage Coleridge's elliptical orbit in a *Copernican* system, with Coleridge periodically vivified by bright, if borrowed, light. J. C. C. Mays would agree with the Copernican view, finding it no less impressive than the Ptolemaic: when Mays says that Coleridge's 'texts . . . are unstable, subject to revision, the limits of what is his are endlessly negotiable, so much being made up of adaptations, borrowings, "quotations," '[38] he values Coleridge's mastery born of his lifelong practice.

When one remembers that Coleridge was in the habit of dictating his formal works to an amanuensis rather than actually writing them down himself, one may discern the difficulty of his intellectual identity: as an agglomeration of others' scattered or scarcely known concepts and ideas, Coleridge could exhibit the spectrum of himself (including the spectra of others) less culpably when viva voce than in writing. Having claimed that Coleridge was merely responsible for '*legitimately* unconscious' plagiarism when borrowing from Brun and Shelvocke,[39]

---

[35] Ibid., p. 217.

[36] Ibid., p. 252.

[37] *William Hazlitt: Selected Writings* (ed. Jon Cook), p. 213.

[38] J. C. C. Mays, 'Coleridge's "Love": "All he can manage, more than he could"', *Coleridge's Visionary Languages: Essays in Honour of John Beer*, ed. Tim Fulford and Morton D. Paley (Cambridge: D.S. Brewer, 1993), pp. 49–66, at p. 57.

[39] Tilar J. Mazzeo, *Plagiarism and Literary Property in the Romantic Period* (Philadelphia: University of Pennsylvania Press, 2006), p. 20. 'The Rime of the Ancient Mariner' took (claimed De Quincey) its 'original hint' from the shooting of an albatross in Shelvocke's *Voyage Around the World* (1726).

De Quincey would become more strident with regard to Coleridge's 'barefaced' plagiarisms[40] in chapter 12 of the *Biographia Literaria*, 'literally translated from the German, and stretching over some pages'.[41] Coleridge wished to borrow so harmoniously, and so winningly, that he would transcend altogether any allegation of plagiarism. But he was more harmonious and winning as a talker than a doer, and Hazlitt made the point depreciatingly explicit:

if Mr Coleridge had not been the most impressive talker of his age, he would probably have been the finest writer; but he lays down his pen to make sure of an auditor, and mortgages the admiration of posterity for the stare of an idler.[42]

He succeeded in captivating Keats (no idler), who, unlike the others who found Coleridge impressive in person, appeared to be able to keep his memory under control. Keats actually remembered a number of the topics, though he did not record anything beyond the headings, which themselves could not implicate Coleridge as an 'intellectual kleptomaniac':[43]

I walked with him at his alderman—after dinner pace for near two miles I suppose. In these two miles he broached a thousand things.—let me see if I can give you a list.—Nightingales, Poetry—on Poetical sensation—Metaphysics—Different genera and species of Dreams— Nightmare—a dream accompanied by a sense of Touch—single and double Touch—A dream related—First and Second Consciousness—the difference explained between Will and Volition—so many metaphysicians from a want of smoking the second Consciousness—Monsters—the Kraken—Mermaids—Southey believes in them—Southey's belief too much diluted—A Ghost Story—Good morning.—I heard his voice as he came towards me—I heard it as he moved away—I heard it all the interval—if it may be called so.[44]

Hazlitt heard the music of the spheres in Coleridge's talk. Keats's appreciation of the rich, resounding silence just after, and since, the Coleridgean symphony may be indicated by his revaluation of the word 'interval'. Correspondingly, Hartley Coleridge would be lastingly impressed by his father's capacity to witch the air with dreams turned inside out:

with an eloquence of which the Notes published in his Remains convey as imperfect an impression as the score of Handel's Messiah upon paper compared to the Messiah sounding in multitudinous unison of voices and instruments beneath the high embowered roof of some hallowed Minster.[45]

And yet for all this, Coleridge reduced the idea of himself to the heat of performances, to the vanished intimacies of particular occasions. Perhaps (as

---

[40] Mazzeo, *Plagiarism and Literary Property in the Romantic Period*, p. 23.
[41] Ibid.
[42] E. D. Mackerness (ed.), *Spirit of the Age* (Northcote House, Plymouth, 1991), pp. 55–6.
[43] Grevel Lindop, *The Opium-Eater: A Life of Thomas De Quincey*, p. 142.
[44] *Letters of John Keats* (ed. Robert Gittings, Oxford, 1970), p. 237.
[45] *Dramatic Works of Massinger and Ford, with an introduction by Hartley Coleridge* (1840), p. xxxvi.

Fruman thinks) it was precisely in this way that he meant to render undetectable
the maximum number of his unacknowledged intellectual debts. At any rate, print
would be the medium that would impose incriminating limitations on Coleridge.
Fruman insists that in print 'Coleridge left himself... tiny escape hatch[es] in the
event of... plagiarism charge[s] during his lifetime',[46] or 'safety valve[s], however
small, for [his] anxiet[ies] about... intellectual debt[s] he was so carefully sup-
pressing'.[47] Many more of Coleridge's debts became checkable once in print and
extant, and he would have to defend or, as the passage below illustrates, deny them:

In Schelling's 'NATUR-PHILOSOPHIE', and the 'SYSTEM DES TRANSCENDENTALEN
IDEALISMUS', I first found a genial coincidence with much that I have toiled out for
myself... It would be but a mere act of justice to myself, were I to warn my future readers,
that an identity of thought, or even similarity of phrase will not be at all times a certain
proof that a passage has been borrowed from Schelling, or that the conceptions were
originally learned from here. In this instance, as in the dramatic lectures of Schlegel to
which I have before alluded, from the same motive of self-defence against the charge of
plagiarism, many of the most striking resemblances, indeed all the main and fundamental
ideas, were born and matured in my mind before I have ever seen a single page of the
German Philosopher... Let it be not charged on me as ungenerous concealment or
intentional plagiarism. I have not indeed... been hitherto able to procure more than two
of his [Schelling's] books, viz. The 1st volume of his collected Tracts, and his System of
Transcendental Idealism... [48]

Thoughts airborne in talk can lose all their grace and charm on the flat of the page
('similarity of phrase will not be at all times a certain proof' of plagiarism). The statement
clatters across the page like an albatross denied, at least for now, the freedom of the
deep sky. In the verbal, spontaneous and tangential setting that Coleridge preferred,
he could have manoeuvred the momentary dynamics of, say, his facial expressions
and spoken nuances to carry the odour of his mendacity downwind from his auditors.
However, in print, and therefore uninformed by Coleridge's happiest psychic principles,
the dead argument has developed cracks and fissures, and the vapours from Coleridge's
central iniquity steam unmistakably through the formal protest.

He did, however, eventually invent a way to spirit more of the energy of his
speaking self down to the realm of ink and paper. By the time he came to write 'The
Reproof and Reply' in 1823, he had essentially re-edited the reality of his methods of
composition; the whole shrill story had had enough time to acquire in his mind the
colours and lineaments of a lighter lay:

> But most of *you*, soft warblings, I complain!
> 'Twas ye that from the bee-hive of my brain
> Did lure the fancies forth, a freakish rout,
> And witch'd the air with dreams turn'd inside out.[49]

[46] *Coleridge: The Damaged Archangel*, p. 450.
[47] Ibid., p. 451.
[48] *Samuel Taylor Coleridge* (ed. H. J. Jackson, Oxford University Press, 1985), pp. 235–7.
[49] *Samuel Taylor Coleridge: Poetical Works*, p. 442.

The legend of Coleridgean whimsy, which Coleridge's subconscious mind had been so painfully building up through the years in order to cover 'the [real] habit of [his] soul',[50] now slipped into place as though it had always been there:

> All Nature *day-dreams* in the month of May.
> And if I pluck'd 'each flower that *sweetest* blows',—
> Who walks in sleep, needs follow must his *nose*.
> Thus, long accustom'd on the twy-fork'd hill,
> To pluck both flower and floweret at my will;
> The garden's maze, like No-man's-land, I tread,
> Nor common law, nor statute in my head;
> For my own proper smell, sight, fancy, feeling,
> With autocratic hand at once repealing
> Five Acts of Parliament 'gainst private stealing!
>
> For Chisholm speaks, 'Poor youth! he's but a waif!
> The spoons all right? the hen and chickens safe?
> Well, well, he shall not forfeit our regards—
> The Eighth Commandment was not made for Bards!'[51]

Holmes has said that 'no one plagiarized like Coleridge',[52] but it may also be the case that no one defended his own plagiaristic methods with the same ingenuity as Coleridge in 'The Reproof and Reply'.

Some critics believe that the real attack on Coleridge's plagiarism commenced in 1840. James Frederick Ferrier discovered Coleridge's use of passages from Schelling while he was busily borrowing from the same source in his work, 'The Philosophy of Consciousness' (1838/39). Without a trace of the ambivalence that informed De Quincey's commentary, Ferrier published a zero-tolerance critique of Coleridge in *Blackwood's Magazine*, in March 1840:

all the real information and learning put forth in *Biog. Lit.*, Chap. V., is stolen bodily from [Maass] . . . a considerable show of learning is exhibited on the subject of the association of ideas; and of course the reader's impression is, that Coleridge is indebted for the learning here displayed to nothing but his own researches. But no such thing—he is indebted for it entirely to Maasz [*sic*]. He found all the quotations, and nearly all the observations connected with them, ready-made to his hand in the pages of that philosopher.[53]

Ferrier's straightforwardly angry assertion that the sage of Highgate was a thief would prove a trailblazing one for future critics tone deaf beyond the theme that all plagiarism is automatically wrong. Such critics would therefore remain unimpressed by the needy charmer of 'The Reproof and Reply' (a narrator whose motto could have been: 'Robbery is no sin if it is whimsical').

---

[50] *Samuel Taylor Coleridge: Poetical Works*, p. 367.

[51] Ibid., pp. 442–3.

[52] Richard Holmes, *Coleridge: Darker Reflections* (1998), p. 280 n.

[53] J. F. Ferrier, 'The Plagiarisms of S.T. Coleridge', *Blackwood's Edinburgh Magazine* 47 (March 1840), pp. 287–99, at pp. 296–7. (Quoted in *Coleridge: The Damaged Archangel*, p. 76.)

Through the nineteenth century, and much of the twentieth, articles by (among others) J. M. Robertson, John Sterling, James Stirling, René Wellek, and Joseph Warren Beach would appear, disclosing this or that unacknowledged borrowing in Coleridge. As a result, it would become natural for the Coleridge enthusiast to acknowledge the presence of an anomaly or two without the need to become too defensive. Writing in 1961, Carl Woodring would say that Coleridge (as the young editor of *The Watchman*) 'ransacked many ... sources for scraps to imitate, adapt or plagiarize ... The scramble for copy banished joy, creativity, and honesty.'[54] Critics had admired the soaring, swooping albatross so often that they felt they could afford also to observe, with morbid fascination, that same bird's more grotesque pedestrian conduct. The terminology of the new world of Coleridge studies gave a patina of deliberative action to Coleridge's behaviour that, before there was iconoclasm (a representative instance of which is quoted below), there were critics such as Lowes and Abrams to elucidate:

Coleridge's dazzling effect on friends and acquaintances is well known and easily understood. His brilliance was manifest. The combination of learning, extreme quickness of mind, and moral idealism was irresistible in a man so young, so accomplished, so blessed with enthusiasm, energy, and eloquence. The occasional sceptics among the crowds of admirers Coleridge left behind were few and inconsequential. He seemed to exude good nature, and his need for friendship and approval was such that his affections sometimes seemed to bubble up like a great fountain washing over those he loved or whom he wanted to love him.[55]

Coleridge found—or seemed to find—his reason for borrowing in the deep structure of the universe, as if it were one of the eternal antimonies that have to be accepted: 'I regard truth as a divine ventriloquist: I care not from whose mouth the sounds are supposed to proceed, if only the words are audible and intelligible.'[56] Fruman's attack rendered the claim controversial. If Fruman has been impressed at all by Coleridge's apologia, it is only for the reason that it has (to borrow Julius Charles Hare's word again) '*magnetized*'[57] so many leading scholars away from the 'plain'[58] truth that Coleridge was a compulsive liar: 'Scholars have often quoted Coleridge's phrase ["divine ventriloquist"] to account for his apparently dreamy indifference to such terrestrial activities as citing specific authorities.'[59] Fruman has argued that Coleridge was accomplished and charismatic enough to manage the reception of the misbehaviour he was unable to hide. Coleridge made it public knowledge (or, in Fruman's view, misinformed the public) that his mind,

---

[54] Carl Woodring, *Politics in the Poetry of Coleridge* (University of Wisconsin Press, 1961), p. 21.

[55] *Coleridge: The Damaged Archangel*, p. 266.

[56] *Biographia Literaria* I (eds. James Engell and W. Jackson Bate, Bollingen Series 75, Princeton University Press, 1983), p. 164.

[57] *S.T. Coleridge: Interviews and Recollections*, p. 252.

[58] *Coleridge: The Damaged Archangel*, p. xix.

[59] Ibid., p. 91.

'*habituated to the Vast*,'[60] was in joyous syncopation with the rhythms and contingencies of the flow of (his and others') thoughts through it; if Coleridge claimed he had read 'everything', did it not follow that he had special dispensation to write[61] and talk about everything? Coleridgean fun characterizes the claim. (How could he, or indeed anybody, have read everything?) The drollery emerges from the combination of Coleridge's obsessive intonation and the hundred percent banality of almost every word he uses, the fond hope being that his hostile critics' best barbs would skid off the high gloss of his stylish horseplay.[62] In short, or—given that 'Mr Coleridge... has only to draw the sliders of his imagination, and a thousand subjects expand before him'[63]—in long, Coleridge spirited himself idiomatically into many of the divine ventriloquist's dummies (if poets including Akenside[64] and Jonson,[65] and philosophers including Schelling[66] and Schlegel[67] may with justice be referred to as such).

Imagine a Coleridge living chastely, fighting off covetous inclinations and practising instead intellectual abstinence and fasting. What would have been the result? No plagiarism, which, however, like all forms of nature has its right to existence and continuance. The squandered flowing of the precious fountains of knowledge and wisdom would spell no new contribution to literature but the reverse. In *The Road to Xanadu*, Lowes revealed that 'Kubla Khan' was an encyclopaedic repository of sources, but (as with Hazlitt) it did not occur to Lowes to disparage Coleridge on that score. It would be Fruman who would use Lowes's findings against Coleridge:

> Coleridge himself, though directing attention to Purchas, said nothing about drawing upon any other sources in 'Kubla Khan', not even Milton. Yet he could not have supposed that Mount Amara as a place-name came out of the void. He certainly knew its origin in *Paradise Lost*, a poem that dominated his imagination for most of his life.[68]

One literary theorist and biographer unhampered by strong feelings for or against Coleridge, Richard Bradford, has explained how the component parts of 'Kubla Khan' are held in one harmony:

---

[60] *CL*, I, 354.

[61] Reviewing Fruman's *Coleridge: The Damaged Archangel*, McFarland argued that 'Coleridge marginally annotated a vast number of books—many hundreds of them. Far more were read than were annotated, and not all those known to have been annotated can be found... There is nothing to equal this in the entire history of culture. (*Yale Review* 62 (1974), pp. 252–86, p. 275.)

[62] As Fruman has pointed out, Ferrier's intense moral indignation (for example: 'Let all men know and consider that plagiarism, like murder, sooner or later *will out*') looks rather unsophisticated beside Coleridge's (and many Coleridge scholars') urbane modes of writing. (*Coleridge: The Damaged Archangel*, p. 463.)

[63] *Hazlitt's Selected Essays* (ed. Geoffrey Keynes, 1970), p. 726.

[64] *Coleridge: The Damaged Archangel*, pp. 38–40.

[65] Ibid., pp. 40–2.

[66] Ibid., pp. 80–3.

[67] Ibid., pp. 155–6.

[68] Ibid., p. 344.

It is virtually impossible to isolate a single word or syllable that is not linked phonetically with at least two others: Xana*d*u, *d*i*d*, *d*ome, *d*ecree, *D*own; *st*ately, *s*acred, *s*unless, *s*ea; *K*ubla *K*han, de*c*ree, *s*a*c*red, *c*averns. Such a listing could be extended and supplemented by an almost infinite series of permutations in which alliteration connects with stress pattern, semantic foregrounding, syntactical structure and rhyme scheme.[69]

Bradford's view of 'Kubla Khan' is more disinterested than, say, M. H. Abrams's view:

if Plato's dialectic is a wilderness of mirrors, Coleridge's is a very jungle of vegetation. Only let the vehicles of his metaphors come alive, and you see all the objects of criticism writhe surrealistically into parts of plants, growing in tropical profusion. Authors, characters, poetic genres, poetic passages, words, metre, logic become seeds, flowers, blossoms, fruit, bark, and sap.[70]

Yet the two critics' views can both corroborate an important point: Coleridge was spellbound and through his own interior infrastructure of echoes by his own lonely, fantastic game of solitaire. (Holmes has thrown 'some sympathetic light into the lonely darkness of [Coleridge's] solitary study and the endless, sometimes desperate, "night-conversations" with his fellow authors'.[71]) He raced after his (and others') thoughts, constructing lines, choosing among a flood of associations, angling persistently for the suitable word; while he sought to choose the single word among three that presented themselves, at the same time he struggled to hold the feeling and tone of the whole piece he was constructing—while forging the sentence into the selected structure and tightening the bolts of the edifice, he strove at the same time to keep in mind the tone and proportion of the whole piece—the whole fine network of intersecting vibrations. 'Kubla Khan' has a sort of verbal micro-climate, and its own eco-system of interconnected, interdependent reverberations that can know nothing of propriety or intellectual property. Hazlitt's idea (of a Coleridge having only to draw the sliders of his imagination for a thousand subjects to expand before him) may thus be redeployed in another context, without Hazlitt's rancour: the concept of Coleridge's practice is metaphysical and Platonic, and Shakespeare could have illustrated it with airy sprites. Blake could have illustrated it with angels. I. A. Richards could have illustrated it with little drawings of electric wires, switches and boxes meant to represent communication from an unknown source to an unknown recipient—a process often (despite Fruman's many withering sallies) beginning and ending in mystery.

There is another way of getting to grips with why Coleridge was often 'wilfully obscure, bittily disorganized, eclectically derivative and compulsively devious in [his] constant rhetorical manoeuvring':[72] Coleridge is the example, *par excellence*,

---

[69] Richard Bradford, *A Linguistic History of English Poetry* (London: Routledge, 1993), p. 124.

[70] M. H. Abrams, *The Mirror and the Lamp*, p. 169.

[71] Richard Holmes, *Coleridge: Darker Reflections* (1998), p. 281 n.

[72] Kelvin Everest, 'Coleridge's Life', *The Cambridge Companion to Coleridge* (Cambridge, 2002), pp. 17–31, at p. 26.

of the writer developing by inspissation—showing a steady thickening of the qualities of vision and method (of, say, 'Kubla Khan') over the original framework (of, say, *Purchas His Pilgrimes*)—the common-denominational factors, the general colour of which is borrowed from other writers (such as Samuel Purchas)—until the process of saturation is complete and the mature work is left perfectly opaque with its author's organically evolved quality. The result is, therefore, something new; its success is proportionate to the writer's skill in adapting his personal material to the old framework, or in shrewdly underpinning it in order to conceal the fact that he is really demolishing the framework itself. The process may be compared to the substitution, in an existing building, of a new façade for the original one, without pulling down and rebuilding the whole. Scaffolding is erected, props are introduced before mullions are withdrawn, no piece can be moved without the substitution of another; but in the end the scaffolding disappears to reveal the new façade complete. When one compares Coleridge's 'Frost at Midnight'—

> the thin blue flame
> Lies on my low-burnt fire, and quivers not;
> Only that film, which fluttered on the grate,
> Still flutters there, the sole unquiet thing.
> Methinks, its motion in this hush of nature
> Gives it dim sympathies with me who live,
> Making it a companionable form,
> Whose puny flaps and freaks the idling Spirit
> By its own moods interprets, every where
> Echo or mirror seeking of itself,
> And makes a toy of Thought.
>   But O! how oft,
> How oft, at school, with most believing mind,
> Presageful, have I gazed upon the bars,
> To watch that fluttering *stranger!*[73]—

with the 'Winter Evening' section of Cowper's *Task*—

> In the red cinders, while with poring eye
> I gazed, myself creating what I saw.
> Nor less amused have I quiescent watched
> The sooty films that play upon the bars,
> Pendulous, and foreboding, in the view
> Of superstition, prophesying still,
> Though still deceived, some stranger's near approach[74]—

one may discern Coleridgean inspissation. Whether one is censorious about it or not is another matter.

[73] *Samuel Taylor Coleridge: Poetical Works*, pp. 240–1.
[74] Roger Lonsdale (ed.), *Eighteenth Century Verse* (Oxford University Press, 1984), p. 599.

Keeping Coleridge's behaviour in proportion, Mazzeo has called Fruman's book 'monumental'[75] while at the same time she has referred to McFarland's work as a guiding light. In doing so, Mazzeo has dropped the Fruman–McFarland debate into the most appropriate pocket of literary critical history:

His [Coleridge's] alleged plagiarisms continue to occasion controversy, and this is often productive. However, unless the controversy is framed by a historical context, the debate is senseless; judged by modern standards, Coleridge is obviously guilty.[76]

In composing chapter 12 of his *Biographia Literaria*, Coleridge must have had Wordsworth's writings, or detailed notes taken directly from them, before him. The chapter is cumulatively enthusiastic on the subject of Wordsworth's poetry. Coleridge points readers in the direction of particularly beautiful passages from 'Intimations of Immortality' and *The White Doe*. Coleridge's admiration for the poetry of his former collaborator is indicated, as the chapter progresses, by the increasing length at which he quotes from it, and the decreasing sense of the necessity of his literary-critical intervention. It is as if Coleridge, at the beginning of the chapter, holds his reader balanced on the two-wheeled simplicity of Wordsworthianism. The reader is held tight for a while, like a child being helped to ride a grown-up's bicycle, and being given the time, love and support to pick up a feel for the unsettling absence of impediments. Soon, even as the reader's handling of Wordsworthianism is closely superintended, the Coleridgean stabilizers are almost imperceptibly removed by their progenitor—the flawed, unthanked father who, having let go, watches (with powerful concern in his eyes) cultural England pedal towards the light of (Wordsworthian) refinement, growth and development.

Yes, Coleridge *is* 'guilty' (to borrow Mazzeo's sympathetic irony) of plagiarism (and other sins), and the spirit of his shame has the power to secure possession of readers whose minds involuntarily dilate in Romantic gloom. Coleridge's shame inhabits the *Biographia Literaria* as a troubled, maundering soul that cannot refine itself into consistent invisibility. It haunts certain corridors and passageways of the prose's rickety structure. Here, it clanks along, brazenly offering German philosophers' ideas. There, it slips through what looks to the reader like a conversational brick wall (but is a communicating door to the ghost) with diffident gestures. Marilyn Butler has defined what it is that propelled the book's reputation beyond the atmosphere of reproach:

What does emerge . . . most brilliantly with and through Coleridge, is a new recognition of the distinctiveness of the poet as a type. It was Coleridge who in the second decade of the century, that Restoration era when so many German and French painters were creating

---

[75] Tilar J. Mazzeo, *Plagiarism and Literary Property in the Romantic Period* (Philadelphia: University of Pennsylvania Press, 2006), p. 17.
[76] Ibid., p. 45.

soulful, alienated portraits of themselves and one another, produced his English writerly equivalent, the *Biographia Literaria*.[77]

Coleridge advertised his '*friable* intellect',[78] implying that German philosophers' ideas could trickle imperceptibly, yet inevitably, into his own writings through the felicitous convolutions in the *Zeitgeist*. Fruman was 'right' to point out the sheer extent of Coleridge's dependence on others. But the independence of Coleridge's emotional appeal remains extraordinarily renewable. Fruman's elaborate, glacial correctness was destined, even from its conception, to melt and dribble into a puddle of unintentional drollery. After all, Fruman constructed his thesis out of the melange of echoes from past critics, whose books, or detailed notes from them, *he* must have had in front of *him*. For example, he drew on Sara Coleridge,[79] Ferrier,[80] Orsini[81] and Wellek.[82] Coleridge did not seek the protection of an academic environment whose rules he could practice and proclaim. He was caught in the toils of life, and his words—including the words he silently lifted from others—remain peculiarly vascular with his life and his sensation.

[77] Marilyn Butler, *Romantics, Rebels & Reactionaries: English Literature and its Background 1760–1830* (Oxford University Press, 1981), p. 92.

[78] *CL* IV, 685.

[79] Sara Coleridge said that her father 'could hardly have been aware how many of the German critics' sentences he had repeated in those latter lectures, how many of his illustrations had intertwined themselves with his own thoughts' (*Coleridge: The Damaged Archangel*, p. 158.)

[80] 'Now, how Coleridge could reconcile with ordinary faith his statement, that a paragraph, consisting of forty-nine lines, to which his own contribution was six, was only *in part* translated from a foreign work—how he could outrage common sense, and the capacities of human belief, by saying that he might have transcribed 'the substance of it from memoranda of his own, written many years before Schelling's pamphlet was given to the world'—how could he have the cool assurance to tell us that he 'prefers another's words to his own'—not, mark you, because these words belong to that other man, and not to him—but *as a tribute due to priority of publication*—and how he could take it upon him to say that in this case nothing more than coincidence was *possible*, (except on the ground that it was impossible for any human being to write anything but what he had written before!)—how he could do all these things, entirely baffles our comprehension.' (Quoted in *Coleridge: The Damaged Archangel*, 465.)

[81] In his essay, 'Coleridge and Schlegel Reconsidered' (*Comparative Literature* 16, 1964), pp. 101–2, Orsini has identified parallel passages:

The reader can see for himself that Coleridge was following Schlegel step by step, sentence by sentence, and finally word for word. The all-important definition of organic form in the last paragraph is a faithful translation from Schlegel, with the alteration of only one word of the original; 'soft mass' (*weichen Masse*) in Schlegel is replaced by 'mass of wet clay'. No doubt the change from the abstract to the concrete is a stylistic improvement. But, if the argument for Coleridge's independence from Schlegel is to rest upon this single and unimportant word, it rests on thin ground indeed. Can it honestly be doubted that Coleridge here had Schlegel's text in front of him and made a translation of it?

[82] Wellek's earlier argument had been that Coleridge was more a failed principle of literary organization than a single successful voice—'no doubt a great mediator of ideas' with 'in most of what he wrote a certain unifying temperament which cannot be mistaken, but if we look more closely we find that Coleridge has built a building of no style'. (René Wellek's *Kant in England 1793–1838* (Princeton University Press, 1931), pp. 66–8). See also, Wellek's 'Coleridge's Philosophy and Criticism', *The English Romantic Poets; A Review of Research* (ed. T. M. Raysor, New York, 1950), p. 96.

Works Cited

Abrams, M. H. 1953. *The Mirror and the Lamp*. Oxford: Oxford University Press.

Bate, Walter Jackson. 1968. *Coleridge*. Cambridge, MA: Harvard University Press.

Beer, John. 1981. Coleridge and Wordsworth: influence and confluence. In Donald Sultana, ed., *New Approaches to Coleridge: Biographical and Critical Essays*. London and New Jersey: Vision Press, Barnes and Noble.

Bradford, Richard. 1993. *A Linguistic History of English Poetry*. London: Routledge.

Butler, Marilyn. 1981. *Romantics, Rebels, and Reactionaries: English Literature and its Background 1760–1830*. Oxford: Oxford University Press.

Coleridge, Hartley. 1851. *Hartley Coleridge: Essays and Marginalia*, 2 vols. London: Edward Moxon.

—— 1840. ed. *Dramatic Works of Massinger and Ford, with an introduction by Hartley Coleridge*, London: Moxon.

Coleridge, S. T. 1912. *Samuel Taylor Coleridge: Poetical Works* ed. E. H. Coleridge.

—— 1983. *Biographia Literaria* I eds. James Engell and W. Jackson Bate, Bollingen Series 75, Princeton University Press.

—— 1985. *Samuel Taylor Coleridge* ed. H. J. Jackson. Oxford: Oxford University Press.

—— 1853–1854. *The Complete Works of Samuel Taylor Coleridge*, ed. W. G. T. Shedd. 7 vols. New York.

Coleridge, Sara. 1873. *Memoir and Letters of Sara Coleridge*, 2 vols. London: Henry S. King and Co.

Cook, Jon 1991. ed., *William Hazlitt: Selected Writings*, Oxford University Press.

De Quincey, Thomas. 1986 *Reminiscences of the English Lake Poets* ed. David Wright, Harmonsworth, 1970; repr.

—— 1948. *Recollections of the Lake Poets* ed. Edward Sackville West, London.

Donno, Elizabeth Story. 1979. The case of the purloined biography: Hartley Coleridge and literary protectivism. *Bulletin of Research in the Humanities*, 82: 458–86.

Everest, Kelvin. 2002. Coleridge's Life, *The Cambridge Companion to Coleridge*. Cambridge: Cambridge University Press.

Ferrier, J. F. 1840. The plagiarisms of S. T. Coleridge. *Blackwood's Edinburgh Magazine*, 47 (March): 287–99.

Fruman, Norman. 1970. *Coleridge: The Damaged Archangel*. London: George Braziller.

Hazlitt, William. 1991. *Spirit of the Age*, ed. E. D. Mackerness, Northcote House, Plymouth.

Holmes, Richard. 1998. *Coleridge: Darker Reflections*. London: HarperCollins.

Keats, John. 1970. *Letters of John Keats*, ed. Robert Gittings. Oxford: Oxford University Press.

Keynes, Geoffrey. ed. 1970. *Selected Essays of William Hazlitt*. London: The Nonesuch Press.

Kooy, John Michael, 2002. *Coleridge, Schiller, and Aesthetic Education*. London: Palgrave Macmillan.

Lindop, Grevel. 1981. *The Opium-Eater: A Life of Thomas De Quincey*. New York: Taplinger Publishing Co.

Lonsdale, Roger. ed. 1984. *Eighteenth Century Verse*. Oxford: Oxford University Press.

Lowes, John Livingston. 1927. *The Road to Xanadu: A Study in the Ways of the Imagination.* Boston and New York.

Mays, J. C. C. 1993. Coleridge's 'Love': 'All he can manage, more than he could'. In *Coleridge's Visionary Languages: Essays in Honour of John Beer,* ed. Tim Fulford and Morton D. Paley. Cambridge: D. S. Brewer, pp. 49–66.

Mazzeo, Tilar J. 2006. *Plagiarism and Literary Property in the Romantic Period.* Philadelphia: University of Pennsylvania Press.

McFarland, Thomas, 1969. *Coleridge and the Pantheist Tradition.* Oxford: Oxford University Press.

—— 1974. Coleridge's plagiarisms once more. *Yale Review,* 62: 252–86.

Orsini, G. N. G. 1964. Coleridge and Schlegel reconsidered. *Comparative Literature,* 16: 101–2.

Perry, Seamus ed. 2000. *S. T. Coleridge: Interviews and Recollections.* Basingstoke and New York: Palgrave.

Sackville West, Edward. 1936. *A Flame in Sunlight: The Life and Work of Thomas De Quincey.* London: Cassell.

Schrickx, W. 1966. Coleridge and the Cambridge Platonists. *A Review of English Literature* (ed. by A. Norman Jeffares), VII (1) (Jan).

Wellek, René, 1931. *Kant in England 1793–1838.* New Jersey: Princeton University Press. pp. 66–8.

—— 1950. Coleridge's philosophy and criticism. In *The English Romantic Poets; A Review of Research,* ed. T. M. Raysor, NY.

Woodring, Carl 1961. *Politics in the Poetry of Coleridge.* London: University of Wisconsin Press.

CHAPTER 24

COLERIDGE: BIBLICAL AND CLASSICAL LITERATURE

ANTHONY JOHN HARDING

COLERIDGE'S LIFELONG IMMERSION IN BIBLICAL AND CLASSICAL LITERATURE

Until the full text of Coleridge's surviving notebooks and marginalia began to appear in print, few scholars would have considered Coleridge a figure of much importance in classical studies, and assessments of his importance as a biblical critic were largely based on one work, the posthumously published *Confessions of an Inquiring Spirit*.[1] His lecture 'On the Prometheus of Aeschylus' had drawn some attention, as had his remarks about both biblical and classical literature in the literary lecture series and the 1818–19 philosophical lectures. Very few scholars realized, however, that these public statements grew out of a large accumulation

---

[1] J. H. Green's 1853 edition of *Confessions of an Inquiring Spirit* was republished in 1956 with a new introduction by H. St. J. Hart. In *Nineteenth-Century Studies* (1949), Basil Willey remarked on Coleridge's advanced views about the inspiration of the Scriptures (pp. 46–52). The first work to give extensive consideration to Coleridge's views on the Bible was J. Robert Barth's *Coleridge and Christian Doctrine* (Cambridge, MA: Harvard University Press, 1969).

of commentary and criticism in the notebooks and marginalia; or that, in these mainly private records, Coleridge had felt himself free to pursue a number of original ideas and speculations about the ancient world, many of which his English contemporaries would have found surprising or even shocking.

Some of the ideas explored in the notebooks and marginalia were of course communicated to the select circle that gathered around him during the Highgate years—the *Table Talk* gives some indication of how frequently and eagerly Coleridge spoke about biblical and classical literature at his Thursday evening soirées— and many of his disciples and correspondents later became writers of some significance in Victorian Britain. An assessment of Coleridge's influence on other thinkers is beyond the scope of this chapter, but it is important to recall that we have yet to grasp the full extent of his influence on his younger contemporaries, especially as it relates to how the ancient world was understood and interpreted.

Coleridge came of age in a decade when, in the wake of deist and rationalist challenges to the credibility of the Bible, and the rise of a new kind of Hellenistic humanism, historicist scholarship was setting about the task of approaching both the Bible and the oldest classical Greek texts—particularly those of Homer, Aeschylus, and Pindar—in a new way. From his early acquaintance with William Frend and John Jebb at Cambridge, and J. P. Estlin and others in the West Country, Coleridge knew that there was work to be done towards a more thorough, historically-grounded understanding of the literature of the ancient world. His 1795 lectures 'On Revealed Religion', indeed, tried to refute Paine's attacks on the Bible by showing how Paine had misrepresented Deuteronomic law. Coleridge saw it as an integral part of his vocation as thinker to move beyond the deists' critiques and discover new ways of comprehending the vitality of the biblical canon and Greek and Latin classic literature, and their intimate connection with modern Europe. He stressed the centrality of biblical and classical (particularly Greek) literature to the development of the consciousness of the human race, envisaging its world-historical role. In this respect, Coleridge was self-consciously a man of the nineteenth century, and one who was more open to European perspectives than most of his compatriots were, even though he remained a distinctly 'English' thinker. Crabb Robinson's remark about Coleridge's mind being 'much more German than English' (quoted *Lects 1808–19* I, 259) has some colouring of truth, but needs to be counter-balanced by the recollection that, despite his use of and borrowings from Schiller, Heyne, Hermann, and Schlegel on ancient literature, Tennemann on philosophy, Creuzer and Schelling on mythology, and Michaelis, Semler, Lessing, Eichhorn, Schleiermacher, and others on the biblical canon, he frequently criticized what he took to be the narrowness and reductiveness of their interpretations, and accused them of mistaking the spirit of the ancient authors they cited. Though a post-Kantian, he repudiated the 'Conflict of the Faculties': that is, he did not consistently separate his biblical-theological studies from his work on classical literature, nor either of these from his philosophical interests. At a time when the modern historicist study of classical literature was in the process of formation under C. G. Heyne at Göttingen and F. A. Wolf at Halle and Berlin, and historicist study of the Bible was beginning to take shape through the work of J. G. Eichhorn at Göttingen and W. M. L. de Wette at Heidelberg and then Berlin, Coleridge remained unconfined by disciplinary boundaries, in this respect, at least, harking back to the era of Richard Bentley, the Cambridge classicist and biblical scholar to whose views on Homeric verse, on the Book of Daniel, and on the text of the New Testament Coleridge often referred.[2]

The best evidence of how intensely Coleridge valued Greek and Latin literature may be this margin note written in or around 1807:

when I recollect, that I have the whole works of Cicero, [of] Livy, and Quintilian, with many others, the whole works of each in a single Volume...I...feel the liveliest Gratitude for the Age, which produced such Editions, and for the Education, which by enabling me to understand and taste the Greek and Latin Writers, has ~~likewise~~ thus put it in my power to collect on my own shelves <for my actual use> almost all the best Books in spite of my so small Income.   (*CM* IV, 99–100)

Precisely because it *is* a margin note, this is probably more revealing about Coleridge's lifelong engagement with classical literature than the much better-known comment in *Biographia Literaria* about James Boyer, the 'very severe master' at Christ's Hospital who taught him to prefer Demosthenes to Cicero, and Homer and Theocritus to Virgil (*BL* I, 8). The reminiscence of Boyer is the public man paying homage to his *alma mater*, and perhaps exorcising his childhood terror of an irascible master, while the notebooks and marginalia rather more convincingly testify to the development of his tastes and interests over more than three decades.[3] This note shows how Coleridge thought of himself as having benefited from a peculiar conjunction of circumstances: the charity-boy who, by the privilege of good schooling, had been granted admission to the select company of those who could aspire to genuine learning in the tradition of Bentley and Porson, and permitted by the economics of contemporary print production to assemble a substantial library. In Coleridge's case, too, knowledge of the languages combined with two rarer gifts: the ability to develop strong intuitions about those parts of ancient texts that appeared psychologically authentic or (sometimes)

---

[2] For Bentley see *CN* II, 2120; IV, 4615; V, 5752, 5792, 5831, 6026, 6824; *CM* I, 376; III, 421; VI, 217. On Heyne and Wolf, see Ulrich von Wilamowitz-Moellendorf, *History of Classical Scholarship*, trans. Alan Harris, ed. Hugh Lloyd-Jones (Baltimore: The Johns Hopkins University Press, 1982), pp.101–2, 108. On Eichhorn (who was Heyne's pupil) and de Wette, see Thomas Albert Howard, *Religion and the Rise of Historicism* (Cambridge: Cambridge University Press, 2000), pp. 36, 43.

[3] His low opinion of Virgil seems to have remained unchanged: in 1832, he remarked that Virgil was a poet 'in *no* sense but that of having a good ear' (*CM* II, 88). Nevertheless, in 1833, at a moment of extreme pessimism about the future of England, it was some lines from the *Aeneid* that came to his mind (*CM* III, 153). On her wedding-day, he gave his daughter a polyglot edition of the *Georgics* (*CM* VI, 30).

inauthentic for their supposed authors; and a poet's ear for the pronunciation of both Latin and Greek. When, late in life, Coleridge engaged in a friendly dispute with his son Hartley about the origin of the Greek digamma, and Bentley's argument about the authenticity of those lines in the *Iliad* that seem to call for it (*CM* II, 53), he wrote as a poet, rather than merely as a scholar.[4]

While hostile to the prevailing scepticism of the Enlightenment, Coleridge was active in engaging with its historical discoveries and pursuing the questions it raised. He had a sense of the ancient writers striving to wrench their language towards subtler distinctions and profounder concepts; and like his contemporary F. D. E. Schleiermacher, he understood how dynamically languages might interact with each other.[5] In Theocritus, Coleridge pointed out in a notebook entry of 1810, 'Every ten lines almost furnish one or more instances of Greek words, whose specific meaning is not to be found in the best Lexicons' (*CN* III, 3780). Similarly, in a margin note on Thomas Gray's commentary on Plato, he chided Gray for being too much of a Lockean to understand how the notion of a 'general Idea' might have presented an intellectual challenge to most of Socrates' contemporaries (*CM* II, 869). This sense of the dynamism of ancient languages—the sense of language as *parole* striving to convey something that lies just beyond the present capacity of language as *langue*—is one of the many elements that connect Coleridge's almost professional interest in classical literature with his dedication to the close study of the Bible.

What Coleridge called 'the reciprocal oppositions and conjunctions of Philosophy, Religion, and Poetry...in the Gentile World, and in early Greece more particularly' (*CL* V, 344) became the principal theme of his work on classical literature after 1817. It was during this period that he turned decisively away from Spinozism, though still feeling the need to articulate, from the perspective of one who had fully experienced its persuasiveness, the ways in which it was deficient as a philosophy and an ethics—an agenda that is apparent in the 1818–19 philosophical lectures. This period also saw the beginning of his friendship and collaboration with the London rabbi and Hebrew scholar Hyman Hurwitz, and of his sustained study of the Bible. Coleridge's wish to prove the fallaciousness of pantheism, and its complicity with a debasing polytheism, provided him with a strong motive to link the two interests, in ancient Greek literature and in the development of the Bible. The Greek texts he most returned to were those that could most persuasively be read as conveying or (as he put it) 'refracting' the monotheistic faith of the Hebrew patriarchs. The key premise of the 1825 lecture—that Greek tragedy, most especially

---

[4] Coleridge thought the manner of pronouncing Greek taught at Eton and Westminster 'cacophonous' (*CM* II, 66). See also *CM* II, 760–2, 1089–90; V, 690.

[5] On the intermingling of Hebrew, Aramaic, and Greek in the multilingual society in which the New Testament originated, see Schleiermacher's *Hermeneutics and Criticism and Other Writings*, trans. Andrew Bowie (Cambridge: Cambridge University Press, 1998), pp. 40–3. He asked the key theological question: 'was Christianity something new or not?' (p. 43).

the plays of Aeschylus, helped to protect the Greek city-states from the worst consequences of a debasing and sensual polytheism—was already adumbrated in the 1808 Lectures 'On the Principles of Poetry' ('the <earliest> History of ~~Gree~~ Greece was combined with its Religion—and then Tragedies formed a sort of Bible or biblical Instruction for the People'—*Lects 1808–19* I, 46). Pantheism, Coleridge had come to believe, was a creed of the intellectual elite in the ancient world, and in both Egypt and Greece fostered polytheism as the popular faith or state religion, a religion that encouraged sensuality and even depravity. Yet, in Greece, there existed a force that countered the bad effects of polytheism: the mystery religions. Though the existence of a connection between the monotheistic faith of the ancient Hebrews and the mystery religions of Samothrace had been suggested by George Stanley Faber in 1803, and by Friedrich Schelling in 1815, Coleridge's search for a sustaining personal creed gave him particularly urgent reasons for wanting to clarify the relationship; and the case of Aeschylus provided the perfect *topos* for such an investigation. The 1825 lecture on Aeschylus demonstrates better than any other single work how closely classical and biblical studies were related, both for Coleridge himself and for his contemporaries.

His only work on biblical topics to find its way into print in the last few years of his life was *On the Constitution of the Church and State* (1829), an extended essay on a fundamental political problem: how can a state provide for its own permanence, while allowing for progress and development? As in the 1795 lectures, he turned to the Hebrew Commonwealth as a model, taking it as an example of the idea that a polity should set aside a portion of its wealth, which he terms the 'Nationalty', specifically to support a class of individuals who will teach and interpret the law and history of the state.

The 'True Homer': Historicism and the Homer Debate

The view that the *Iliad* did not have one individual author, but was a compilation of poems from oral sources first assembled in the sixth century BCE, had been put forward early in the eighteenth century. Giambattista Vico had considered Homer not as an individual genius possessed of esoteric wisdom, but as a 'man of the people'. [6] Later eighteenth-century critics increasingly understood the epic as a product of its culture, and ascribed it to a group of bards or 'rhapsodes', sometimes suggesting that the name 'Homer' was actually a collective title for these poets.

---

[6] Kirsti Simonsuuri, *Homer's Original Genius: Eighteenth-Century Notions of the Early Greek Epic (1688–1798)* (Cambridge: Cambridge University Press, 1979), p. 95.

Wolf's *Prolegomena ad Homerum* (1795), which was informed by serious textual scholarship, turned the 'multiple Homers' theory from a speculative insight to a serious critical approach (see Wilamowitz-Moellendorf, p. 108, and *Lects Phil* I, 53 n.). In 1787, it was still just possible for Eichhorn to argue that, as the Greeks never doubted Homer was the author of the *Iliad* and *Odyssey*, so there was no reason to question the Jewish tradition that Moses was the sole 'author' of the Pentateuch. (Eichhorn did accept, however, that more ancient sources lay behind the Mosaic books.) Coleridge's margin note, written 1810–12, astutely pointed out how quickly German scholarship had moved on after 1787 (*CM* II, 397). A further note, in Gottfried Hermann's 1806 edition of the Homeric Hymns, adds the suggestion that the name Homer may come from the use of 'Homereuomenoi', or 'stitchers-together', in a title attached to one version of the *Iliad* (*CM* II, 1130). As early as 1808, Coleridge referred to the existence of an individual named Homer as 'more than problematic' (*CM* II, 1126). However, despite this evident interest in the 'multiple Homers' theory, in his 1818–19 lectures Coleridge went only so far as to state that 'Homer' was probably a name for the vocation of poet, or for 'a fraternity of men who had wandered through the countries and, by the charms of music and whatever else could work upon the minds of a rude people, gradually introduced those traditions or this, properly speaking, poetic and sensuous mode of propagating truths which Herodotus attributes to Homer' (*Lects Phil* I, 54).

Admittedly, this judgement about the authorship of the *Iliad* is that of an admiring student of Greek language and literature rather than that of a classicist. For all his interest in philology and textual scholarship, Coleridge's readings of classical literature retain their value now principally because they are informed by a keen poetic sensibility and a characteristic kind of psychological insight. For example, what particularly interested him in contrasting the poetry of the *Iliad* with that of the *Odyssey* was the disparity between the complete *absence* of subjectivity in the former poem, and its strong *presence* in the latter. The *Odyssey*, Coleridge felt, exhibited what he called 'a Subjectivity of the Persona or Character', distantly anticipating the subjectivity of a Hamlet, which was a dimension the *Iliad* completely lacked. 'The Iliad has no subjectivity whatever; it is a clear stream which reflects on its bosom the heaven and the trees and flowers and men on its banks— every thing but itself. In the Lyric Poets, Individuality begins to appear; but we have so little that we cannot fully judge. In the Dramatists, the Individual and the Subjective are intense' (*TT* I, 130). A passage such as that in Book IV of the *Odyssey*, where Helen is imagined as standing near the wooden horse, tempting the warriors concealed in it by seductively imitating the voices of their wives, evoked (Coleridge felt) quite a different concept of subjectivity, and quite a different worldview, from that present in the *Iliad*, which could suggest that this is 'one of the Passages, which justify the suspicion that the Iliad & Odyssey were not of the same Author or (perhaps) Age' (*CM* II, 1124). These insights—even if they are indebted to Schiller's *Ueber naïve und sentimentalische Dichtung*—allow us a glimpse into Coleridge's developing sense of how modern forms of subjectivity emerged gradually, over centuries of cultural and social change.

COLERIDGE'S IMAGINATIVE UNDERSTANDING OF THE ANCIENT WORLD: A SELF-CONSCIOUSLY POST-ENLIGHTENMENT OUTLOOK

If Coleridge was indebted to Wolf, Eichhorn and the late-eighteenth-century emphasis on the creativity of a *people*, expressed through its institutions and rituals, as opposed to the creativity of the individual poet-sage, he nevertheless distanced himself from the Enlightenment's rationalistic stance towards the supernatural, its drive to discover naturalistic explanations for narratives of spiritual experience, and its general hostility towards religion. As he remarked in a notebook entry of 1826, 'Eichhorn pretends to no *faith* in *spiritual* Christianity' (*CN* IV, 5334 f. 32ᵛ). Where Eichhorn treated claims of supernatural events with consistent scepticism, and tried to show how such claims might be elaborations of natural occurrences, Coleridge developed a fuller imaginative grasp of what might have been the needs—not only religious, but legal and military—of the ancient community: its rituals, legal system, military organization, and cultural practices. Occasionally, he censured Eichhorn's attitude of haughty condescension towards the biblical writers (see for instance *CN* V, 6056, 6284, 6374), but he reserved particular scorn for Herder's reductive humanizing of the Bible in *Briefe, das Studium der Theologie betreffend* and *Von der Auferstehung*. On Herder's 'Menschlich muss man die Bibel lesen' ('The Bible must be read in a human way'), Coleridge remarked: 'A famous word, a serviceable and accomodating word is that menschlich/human, or rather human-natural! . . . how can man reason otherwise? Can he reason göttlich [divinely]?—If he can, ought he not?' (*CM* II, 1051). Herder's praise of the Greeks he thought equally empty: Herder merely 'ranted' about Homer, and had 'no feeling of Reality, no collation of these Fineries with the real *History* of these eulogized Greeks' (*CM* II, 1071).

These criticisms of Herder give us a clue to what Coleridge saw as the urgent need for the early nineteenth century: to work out a better understanding of the way in which modern human consciousness emerged from and was formed by the disciplining power of history.[7] For Coleridge 'the human' was always a goal—

---

[7] Here, he built on Lessing's 'Die Erziehung des Menschengeschlechts' (see *SW&F* II, 1155 n.), but was also responding to the views of Rousseau (whom he critiqued in *The Friend*), and of his sometime mentor Joseph Priestley, whose views had influenced the 1795 Lectures.

something in the process of being realized—rather than a starting-point, a *datum*. Typically, where a late-Enlightenment writer such as Lessing or Eichhorn offered a naturalistic explanation for a supernatural event, Coleridge sought for an explanation in the beliefs or religious practices characteristic of the time. So, when Lessing suggested that the star that led the Wise Men to Bethlehem might have been 'a fiery phenomenon of the atmosphere' ('eine feurige Lufterscheinung'), Coleridge in a margin note offered a notably more interesting suggestion, with a specific connection to the cultural history of Asia Minor: 'Much more probably the Star of St Matthew originated in some *astrological* inference. Such a Planet in such a quarter of such a House (i.e.—one of the 12 Houses of the Star-mongers) might signify the Birth of a great Monarch, & in what country' (*CM* III, 653).

From the time of his first sustained investigations into ancient philosophy and history—that is, about the time of his work on the 1809–10 *Friend*—Coleridge started to build a comprehensive theory of the development of human culture, based on the hypothesis of two divergent strands in human history. One strand was the persistence of an originary monotheism, consolidated among the ancient Hebrews by the revelation of divine law to Moses, preserved in Judaism, and inherited by Christianity and Islam. The other was the deterioration of the high philosophic pantheism of the Egyptians (itself an inferior form of monotheism) into increasingly superstitious and sensual forms of polytheism. As Coleridge sets out this theory in the 1818–19 lectures on philosophy, the crucial distinction is not geographical or political, but moral-psychological. One people,

attending more to their moral feeling and to the manifest good consequences of it in the world, yielded to the traditions of their ancestors and found themselves happy.... To know that a thing was right and congruous to their moral nature they held as the evidence of its truth, and this by a most excellent logic; for unless they supposed themselves to be either infinite, in one extreme, or beasts in the other, they must believe themselves to be progressive. But whatever is progressive must have a dim horizon as well as a clear vicinity, and what truth has more right to be obscure to us than that which, when we arrive at [it], will be the very perfection of our being... (*Lects Phil* I, 56)

It is worth pointing out how this emphasizes not the obedience of the ancient Hebrews to Deuteronomic law, nor even their monotheistic faith as such, but their forward orientation, the 'dim horizon' of a higher perfection towards which the law was directed. The contrast is of course with the Greek path towards polytheism:

The other race determined that their imagination, as the Scriptures properly call it, but which they deemed their understanding or their reason, should be the judge of all things... they followed the natural leadings of the imagination or fancy governed by the law of association... Wherever, therefore, they saw motion, they supposed that in some way or other there was a vital or motive power; and... conceived that the whole world, every thing, must have a motive power. (*Lects Phil* I, 57)

Theologically, one consequence of this mode of belief was that where Judaism posited a benevolent Creator who 'saw every thing that he had made, and behold, *it was* very good' (Genesis 1:31), in pagan theologies 'good came out of evil, the better out of the worse' (*Lects Phil* I, 58).

The distinction between a culture focused on the regularizing of morals and a culture based on the impressions of the 'understanding' was not of course so absolute as to exclude the possibility that a man brought up in a polytheistic culture, governed by the 'leadings of the imagination or fancy', might discover within himself a 'reverence of that something which instinctively we must conceive of as greater than ourselves' (*Lects Phil* I, 130). Coleridge's interest in Greek literature and philosophy focused on what he saw as evidence of such religious feeling persisting in esoteric forms, and in opposition to the official public worship of Zeus, Dionysus, and other gods and goddesses. In an early margin note (1808) written in Chapman's translation of Homer, Coleridge remarked on the way in which Proclus and Porphyry attempted to turn the *Iliad* and *Odyssey* into a kind of Bible or Koran for the Greek people. He took these attempts as proof that at least some educated Greeks considered that their culture lacked a sacred text: 'They felt the immense power of a *Bible*, a Shaster, a Koran / there was none in Greece or Rome / & they tried therefore by subtle allegorical accomodations to conjure the poems of Homer into the βιβλιον θεοπαραδοτον [book handed down from God] of Greek Faith' (*CM* II, 1123). From the 1812 lectures on drama, it is clear that Coleridge knew of, indeed borrowed, Friedrich Schlegel's judgement that the ancient Greeks owed their education wholly to Nature ('Die Bildung der Griechen war vollendete Naturerziehung'). As he repeated and elaborated on this judgement, however, he also echoed Schlegel's reference to the exceptions from the rule, the occasional flashes of poetic insight and philosophic 'presentiments...of after times' to be found in Greek literature (*Lects 1808–19* I, 438–9).

In the 1818–19 'philosophical lectures', Coleridge considerably developed this theme, interweaving it with a more fully theorized account of the deleterious effects of polytheism, and of the subterranean connections between polytheism and its older, more respectable relative, pantheism: 'the effect of [polytheism] in all ages has been, in the under states of life, cruelty and brutality, in the higher states, selfishness and sensuality...[Yet] there will be [moments] when the reverence of that something which instinctively we must conceive of as greater than ourselves, and then all the aggregate of things that we behold will excite feelings of devotion and awe, and these will produce fragments of true religious feeling but for a few philosophers...' (*Lects Phil* I, 130). A few months after giving the concluding lecture of this series, Coleridge resumed studying what he had referred to as his two dominant lines of enquiry: the 'traditions and oracles of the Greeks' and 'the history and prophecies of the Jews' (*Lects Phil* I, 108). The notebooks and marginalia reveal a sustained and thorough programme of reading in both biblical and classical studies, though he also absorbed contemporary reports of archaeological discoveries, and was interested in noting how they appeared to confirm Herodotus's accounts of the ancient world (*CM* I, 771, VI, 173). He regarded it as a given that any thoughtful reader, whether of the Bible or of a secular text, must have 'imagination enough to *live* with his forefathers', as he remarked in relation to the reading of Milton, and not '[read] a work meant for immediate effect on one age, with the notions & feelings of another' (*CM* II, 969).

Coleridge never lost sight of the social and political context of ancient literature, but his primary focus was increasingly on the intersection of poetry, religion, and philosophy, with a particular emphasis on the workings of myth. A notebook entry written in 1822 shows that he found in Origen some authorization for his own sense that the opening chapters of Genesis were to be interpreted as mythic. Origen's phrase '$\mu\nu\theta\upsilon\varsigma$ $\kappa\alpha\iota$ $\gamma\rho\alpha\mu\mu\alpha\tau\alpha$' (in *Contra Celsum*) referred not to 'Fabeln und Schriften' ('fables and letters'), as one anonymous scholar had suggested, but 'symbolic Stories and sacred Books': 'Thus too', Coleridge continues, 'in Origen's belief the transgression of Adam and Eve was a Muthos . . . —An Idea shadowed out in an individual Instance, imaginary or historical—the truth remains the same' (*CN* IV, 4899 f. 44). In Coleridge's understanding, Origen was also more respectful of the Greek mystery religions and their use of 'symbolic Stories' than were other apologists for Christianity, treating them as '*refractions* of the Light of the ante-Mosaic or Patriarchal Revelation' (*CN* IV, 4900).

At a time when scholars were beginning to investigate the possibility, partly suggested by analogy with the *Iliad*, that the Pentateuch was assembled from several different pre-existing documents that incorporated more ancient oral traditions—but before this notion had been fully formalized [8]—Coleridge was not only willing to entertain such a possibility, but astute in seeing the new kind of historical understanding that would be necessary. He readily drew on analogies between the biblical canon and the canon of Greek and Latin literature to assist his theorizing. He certainly understood how many apparent inconsistencies and contradictions in the Genesis and Exodus narratives might be accounted for by the hypothesis of numerous source-documents. When for example the seventeenth-century divine Thomas Fuller pointed out how the number of Canaanite nations varies from two to eleven in different parts of Genesis and Exodus, and remarked 'Now how come they to be so differently computed where one and the

---

[8] Eichhorn posited that there were two sources for the Book of Genesis, distinguished by the two different names used for God: in one, 'Elohim' (a plural) was used, in the other, 'Jahweh'. However, Eichhorn and other members of the 'mythological school' (J. P. Gabler and G. L. Bauer) rejected the notion that Moses was not, at least, *compiler* of the Pentateuch. This view was challenged in 1806–7 by de Wette, who concluded that the Pentateuch in its present form must be dated much later than Moses' time, and read it as an expression of the religious spirit and practices of the Israelites, not as a source of historical information. De Wette's 'fragment' hypothesis evolved into the 'documentary' hypothesis principally associated with the German biblical scholar Julius Wellhausen. See Howard, pp. 38–41, and John Rogerson, *Old Testament Criticism in the Nineteenth Century: England and Germany* (London: SPCK, 1984), pp. 32–5.

same Spirit is the Auditour...?', Coleridge commented: 'What wild work we should have, were this theory carried into Ancient Records universally! If for instance the Volumes of Herodotus, Thucydides, Xenophon, Dyonisius Halic. &c were all gravely assumed to have been written by the Historic Muse!' (*CM* II, 831). Coleridge followed Eichhorn in deducing that Genesis chapters 1–10 must have been assembled from two different documents. By 1819, however, he had rejected Eichhorn's view that Moses could have been responsible for combining these documents, and noted: 'the present form of the whole Pentateuch I cannot help thinking later than Moses' (*CM* II, 390). In an important notebook entry of 1816 or 1817, he put forward the idea that the account of the creation and fall of man in Genesis 2 might reflect hieroglyphic markings on a column or stele (*CN* III, 4325). Later, he advanced a similar explanation for the story of the Flood, seemingly a blend of myth and history that was developed in order to establish certain symbols in the nation's consciousness: 'is it partly mythical, partly historical—the historical *facts* having been employed as Symbols?' (*CN* V, 6145). The way in which Coleridge seized on the idea that such narratives were intended as symbolic rather than as literal history, and that they embodied philosophical and religious teachings in narrative form, shows how readily he advanced beyond both Lessing and Eichhorn.

In 1822, beginning the study of Exodus, Coleridge made use of analogies with the rhapsodes (or 'Homereuomenoi'), and with the popular fables incorporated into the narratives of Christ's birth and infancy in Matthew and Luke, to suggest that Exodus 1–11 was a traditionary 'Life' that might have been assembled by Samuel and David: 'a distinct Book, a traditional Life of Moses and his Brother Aaron, previously to the commencement of his Legislatorship—of far higher value indeed, but still analogous to the Gospels of the Infancy' (*CN* IV, 4897). Some years later, his conviction on this point was even stronger: 'the first 11 or 12 Chapters of Exodus could not have been, in their present form & language at least, written by Moses or a Contemporary of Moses... [but] to call these Chapters an *interpolation* would mislead and convey a false and *modern* association—almost as soon should I call the Life of Homer, that goes under the name of Herodotus, an interpolation of the Iliad, because it is prefixed to some old Manuscripts of the Poem' (*CN* V, 6248). These investigations into the original context and function of the documents that make up the Hebrew Bible and the New Testament make him an intellectual contemporary of de Wette and a precursor of later nineteenth-century schools of biblical criticism, though few of his judgements found their way into print during his lifetime.[9]

---

[9] Coleridge was aware of de Wette's reputation, and wrote extensive critical marginalia on his fictionalized memoir, *Theodor* (*CM* II, 181–209). In 1825, Coleridge asked Carl Aders to obtain a copy of de Wette's introduction to the Old Testament, but there is no evidence that Aders was able to comply with the request (see *CM* II, 181 headnote).

COLERIDGE'S HERMENEUTICS

If Coleridge's investigations of biblical literature place him, in one sense, on the side of those who adopted an historicist approach, particularly the German Higher Critics, and if, like them, he freely used analogies between the redaction, transmission, and reception of texts in the pagan world and the redaction, transmission, and reception of texts in Jewish and early Christian communities, he nevertheless refused to follow the historical approach to its most radical conclusions by historicizing or relativizing foundational beliefs. The line of demarcation between response to the Bible and response to Homer, Pindar, Virgil, and Cicero is an essential element of Coleridge's hermeneutic.[10] While accepting that human agency was involved in the creation and transmission of biblical texts, and that interpreters of these texts must be alert to the likelihood of errors and inconsistencies in them, even whole sections (such as the Infancy narratives) that were little more than popular fables, Coleridge was critical of the way in which more radical commentators went from questioning the integrity of the *texts* to questioning the integrity of biblical *authors*—the prophets, apostles, and evangelists. Coleridge remained more conservative than Schleiermacher or H. E. G. Paulus in distinguishing between the kind of authorial status he would wish to grant to a canonical writer such as St Matthew or St Paul, where the authority imputed to the work is intimately connected with the sacredness of its author, and the status that accrues to the authors of imaginative works, even a Homer, an Aeschylus, or a Pindar: 'Homer, Eschylus, Pindar are for us the *names* of the Iliad & Odyssey; of the Prometheus &c; and of the Prize-Odes. . . .—But this dare not be applied to a charter or code, where the Author gives the authority to the Work—Whoever wrote the Iliad, was Homer; but it must have been *Matthew* who wrote the Gospel attributed to him—The work derives its Authority from the Author' (*CM* II, 892–3). Religious faith, in other words, links the canonical biblical writers, and such crucial non-canonical figures in Jewish and early Christian tradition as Philo of Alexandria, to each other and to their readers in a way that cannot be true of any secular writer (see *CN* IV, 5071). Though the margin note just quoted is late (1833), it is consistent with many earlier remarks about both biblical writers and such classical thinkers as Plato and Cicero, to whom Coleridge did ascribe a *moral* authority comparable to that of a St John or a St Paul, even while denying them comparable spiritual authority. Indeed, Coleridge thought the moral and spiritual feeling of the writer of the fourth Gospel to be so inimitably distinctive as to make it his primary reason for rejecting Eichhorn's argument that St John was also author of the Apocalypse: 'The entire absence of all *spirituality* [from the

---

[10] For the distinction between reading 'by the light of the Spirit' and reading 'historically and philologically', see *CN* IV, 5337 f. 35.

Apocalypse] perplexes me, it forms so strong a contrast with the Gospel & I Epistle of John...' (*CM* III, 922; see also *CN* V, 5976, f. 14). Similarly, in 1825 Coleridge drew on an analogy with the letters of Cicero and Pliny to suggest that the genuine epistles of Paul (that is, not the Epistle to the Hebrews, which he conjectured might be by Apollos, nor those to Timothy or Titus) could be proven genuine by their 'character of individual Genius' (*CM* I, 512).[11] The same literary sense of an individual author's 'genius' could of course be evidence *against* the genuineness of parts of a work. This hermeneutic principle, the individual character that marks the style and the moral and spiritual feeling of many books of the New Testament, gave him reason for doubting the authenticity of some parts of the first three gospels, in particular the Infancy narratives of Matthew and Luke, while maintaining (against Eichhorn's views) the genuineness of Luke 14–23 (*CM* II, 36–7).

Coleridge's consistent opposition to the superstitious veneration of the biblical text (which he called 'bibliolatry', taking this term from Lessing) found its fullest formulation in the 'Letters on the Inspiration of the Scriptures', written for the general public but not published in his lifetime, probably from fear that a hostile reception of the 'Letters' might damage the chances of *Aids to Reflection* receiving a sympathetic hearing (see *CN* IV, 5323). The 'Letters' argue strongly for our being responsive to the individual humanity of the voices we hear in biblical texts, not in the minimal sense of Herder's 'menschlich' but in the stronger sense that powerful expressions of faith should be received as such, not diluted or robbed of their human qualities by the notion that all such utterances were somehow dictated by a supernatural intelligence. As Coleridge put it in the 'Letters', the doctrine of plenary inspiration 'demands of me ~~the~~ to belie~~f~~ve, that not only whatever finds me but all that exists in the sacred Volume, and which I am bound to find therein, was—not alone *inspired by*, i.e. composed by men under the actuating influence of, the Holy Spirit; but likewise—dictated by an Infallible Intelligence...' (*SW&F* II, 1123). Such a doctrine actually nullified the 'rule of faith' that, over many centuries, established the biblical canon, and made the Bible 'the only *adequate* Organ' for the 'moral and intellectual cultivation of the species' (*SW&F* II, 1155).

COLERIDGE ON THE FUNCTION OF MYTH

What emerges most strongly from Coleridge's public utterances on classical and biblical literature is his belief in the power of narrative, including mythic narrative, to raise human communities to a higher sense of their responsibilities: in short, the

---

[11] For the conjecture (first suggested by Luther) about Apollos' authorship of Hebrews, see *CN* V, 5753, 5876, 6048; on the Epistles to Timothy and Titus, see *CM* I, 459, V, 128.

power of certain myths to function as what Coleridge named 'philosophemes'. This term, adapted from a German word used by both Schelling and Creuzer (see *CM* II, 389 n.), became crucial to his discussions of both biblical and classical literature. In a note (written probably before 1820) about the first three chapters of Genesis, he suggested that Genesis 2 and 3 contained 'the moral or spiritual theory or philosopheme of Man' (*CM* II, 389). The term was also central to his lecture on Aeschylus, which he delivered at a meeting of the Royal Society of Literature on 18 May 1825, and which was subsequently published in the Society's *Transactions*.

Coleridge's particular interest in the *Prometheus* of Aeschylus as offering clues to possible connections between the patriarchal faith of the Hebrews and the mystery religions of ancient Greece dates from 1820, when his son Hartley (then a probationary Fellow at Oriel College, Oxford) reported that he was planning to write a prize-essay on Aeschylus that would include a section on the 'sacerdotal religion of Greece, and on the sources and spirit of mythology' (quoted *SW&F* II, 1252). Though the College did not renew Hartley's fellowship, his hopes of establishing himself as a scholar were not wholly quashed, and his father encouraged him in this project, lending assistance by assembling a substantial body of notes and research materials on the mystery religions. As we have seen, Coleridge's interest in the more general topic of Greek religion dated back at least to 1808. His annotations on two key studies of the mystery religions, George Stanley Faber's *Dissertation on the Mysteries of the Cabiri* and Friedrich Schelling's *Ueber die Gottheiten von Samothrace*, probably date from 1817–19,[12] and Notebook 29, in use from 1817 to 1825, contains much material on the topic. Hartley's essay was published in 1822, and when Coleridge *père* was elected Associate of the Royal Society of Literature in 1824, he took up the subject again, proposing it to the Society's secretary, Richard Cattermole, as one of his two proposed areas of enquiry (*SW&F* II, 1252).

Referring in his lecture to the Prometheus myth, Coleridge argued that 'The most venerable, and perhaps the most ancient, of Grecian mythi, is a philosopheme, the very same in subject-matter with the earliest record of the Hebrews, but most characteristically different in tone and conception...' (*SW&F* II, 1267). Evidently, the distinction already outlined in the 1818–19 Lectures between those ancient peoples that 'followed the natural leadings of the imagination or fancy' and those that '[attended] more to their moral feeling and to the manifest good consequences of it in the world' (*Lects Phil* I, 56–7) remain relevant here, but Coleridge is now more interested in the way that both Greek philosophy and what was known or inferred about the mystery religions constituted a counter-culture, opposing and correcting both the general Greek tendency towards a pantheistic identification of God with the world and the polytheism of the official (state) religion. Coleridge followed Schelling in suggesting that, as it was the Phoenicians

---

[12] Coleridge was scathing, however, about Faber's etymological 'proofs'. See *CM* II, 574, 580, 581–2 and *CN* V, 5761.

who brought the Cabiric mysteries to Greece, it was through the Phoenicians that the doctrines of the Hebrew patriarchs and a version of the Jewish cosmogony—both somewhat altered in the process of transmission—found their way into the teachings of the mystery religions, which fostered the cultivation of the mind and the spirit rather than the senses and instincts. As Coleridge had noted in the 1818–19 lectures, though Heraclitus and Pythagoras may themselves have learned from these 'patriarchal Doctrines' (and thus thought of God as pure spirit separate from nature), their utterances were 'understood...according to the common opinion', and their disciples 'took for granted the identity of God and the world' (*Lects Phil* I, 126). But for Coleridge, the importance of Pythagoras was precisely that he was the first philosopher to begin with the mind itself, with the Νοῦς, or pure reason, rather than with sense impressions; he 'sought in his own mind for the laws of the universe' (*Lects Phil* I, 75). Plato, too, would have been aware, through the mystery religions, of the more spiritual tradition associated with a monotheistic faith. Agreeing with a Dutch scholar who denied that Pythagoras, Heraclitus, and Plato could have known the Pentateuch, Coleridge noted: 'I find nothing in Plato that requires us to suppose him acquainted with the Books of Moses, or which may not be sufficiently accounted for by the patriarchal Doctrines *refracted* thro' the Phœnician Pantheism or Theophysy, in the Cabiric Mysteries instituted by Phœnician Navigators in Samothrace' (*CM* VI, 5). The persistence of the Prometheus myth in Greek culture was a providential corrective to what might otherwise have been the catastrophic effects of pantheism among the elite and its even more dangerous progeny, polytheism, among the common people. By the same means, Coleridge came to believe, Aeschylus could also have learned from the Phoenician theology and cosmogony. He was one of those far-seeing poets whose work—as Coleridge had argued in the 1818 *Friend*—developed the esoteric beliefs expressed in the mystery religions, beliefs which 'prevented Polytheism from producing all its natural barbarizing effects' (*Friend* I, 504).

The fundamental 'philosopheme' of the 'Aeschylian mythology', then, was 'The generation of the Νοῦς, or pure reason in man'. This 'reason' is not the false rationality which sets man at enmity with the divine order, but on the contrary that which most closely connects him to it. Reason is the divine spark that '*potenziates*, ennobles, transmutes' what is merely physical and animal. The first important quality of Prometheus is not, then, his defiance of Zeus, but the fact that he is 'a God of the race before the *dynasty* of Jove...and linked of yore in closest and friendliest intimacy with him' (*SW&F* II, 1268). This element of the myth signifies that the Nous, or pure reason, is pre-existent to all material forms: 'derivation of the spark from above, and from a God anterior to the Jovial dynasty (*i.e.* to the submersion of spirits in material forms), was intended to mark the *transcendency* of the Nous, the contra-distinctive faculty of man, as timeless (ἄχρονον τὶ), and in this *negative* sense *eternal*' (*SW&F* II, 1268–9). As Coleridge read the conflict between Zeus and Prometheus, then, Zeus was not (as he was for

Shelley) 'the Oppressor of mankind'; and Prometheus was mankind's 'Champion' in a spiritual sense, the bringer of Mind or Reason—that which is most godlike in man.[13] This reading enabled Coleridge to link the Prometheus myth to Semitic traditions, and to portray Aeschylus as a poet who transmitted to Greek culture the doctrine of the 'supersensuous and divine' origin of things (*SW&F* II, 1271), even though, like the Phoenician belief-system through which it reached Greece, this teaching did not fully distinguish between the Creator who willed the world into existence and the continuing material substance that now makes up the visible world.

LATER STUDIES IN THE BIBLE: THE PROPHETIC INTENT OF BIBLICAL TEXTS

Clearly, Coleridge's immersion in biblical studies was not that of a dispassionate historian. What he particularly sought to grasp in his Old Testament reading was in what sense the texts could be understood as having prophetic intent, both as calling the people of Israel to be worthy of the faith entrusted to them, and as anticipating the advent of a Messiah. His studies of the New Testament similarly emphasized the prophetic: not the foretelling of a future event (the kind of millennialist reading for which he excoriated the preacher Edward Irving), but the sense that these writings were meant to work an effective change on their auditors and readers, a '*Passing into a new mind*' (*AR*, p. 132).[14] At the same time, however, Coleridge deplored the low level of knowledge, both in the Established Church and among Dissenters, about the social and cultural context from which the biblical text emerged, an ignorance too often accompanied by strident insistence on the infallibility of Scripture.

Understanding the Bible as prophetic meant accepting that the meaning of any part of it was contained in it 'by Involution' (*CM* III, 102). The meaning is only partially understood at first, but as an individual or community continues to reflect on and reinterpret the sense, a fuller meaning begins to disclose itself. This process Coleridge characterized with a phrase from Pindar's Olympian Odes, 'συνετοῖσι Φωνοῦντα' ('speaking to the enlightened'), applying it for instance to certain

---

[13] For further comparison of Coleridge's reading of the Prometheus myth with Shelley's, see Anthony John Harding, *The Reception of Myth in English Romanticism* (Columbia, MO: University of Missouri Press, 1995), pp. 246–57.

[14] Coleridge had seen Irving become (as he thought) seriously led astray by a simplistic form of millenialism (*CN* IV, 5323 f. 28ᵛ). In 1833, Coleridge firmly warned himself against imagining that recent events in Europe were anticipated in biblical prophecy (*CN* V, 6815).

utterances of Jesus that '*involved* . . . the . . . affirmation of his Jehovahood' (*CM* II, 486). The very fact that successive books of the Bible are redacted documents, documents that have been discovered to have new meaning at a period several centuries later than their point of origin, indicates the prophetic intent or 'forward orientation' of Scripture. As Coleridge put it in a notebook entry of 1829: 'Is not the true Meaning of the words of the Prophets, and of the Old Testament generally, their applicability? Or—is not the meaner application of the words & sentences if not superseded yet over-built by the more important?' (*CN* V, 6069). The concept of 'Involution' adapted from Leibniz's monadology, is thus central to Coleridge's understanding of prophecy.

CONCLUSION

It is important to locate Coleridge's engagements with classical and biblical literature at a particular historical juncture, and within the ideological force-field of the late Enlightenment. He was drawn to the writings of the ancients by an entirely contemporary need to investigate what the nineteenth century came to regard as world-historical questions. In the wake of deist and rationalist questioning of the credibility of the Bible, and the rejection of older ideas about the authority of classical texts, historicist scholarship was setting about the task of approaching both the Bible and the oldest classical Greek texts—Homer, Aeschylus, Pindar—in a new way. From Coleridge's lectures, notebooks, marginalia, and fragmentary writings, it is evident that he developed a consistent hermeneutic and his own variant of historicism: a non-Hegelian, but distinctively nineteenth-century concept of continuity and development in human history.

WORKS CITED

BARTH, J. ROBERT, S.J. 1969. *Coleridge and Christian Doctrine*. Cambridge, MA: Harvard University Press.

HARDING, ANTHONY JOHN. 1995. *The Reception of Myth in English Romanticism*. Columbia: University of Missouri Press.

HOWARD, THOMAS ALBERT. 2000. *Religion and the Rise of Historicism: W. M. L. de Wette, Jacob Burckhardt, and the Theological Origins of Nineteenth-Century Historical Consciousness*. Cambridge: Cambridge University Press.

ROGERSON, JOHN W. 1984. *Old Testament Criticism in the Nineteenth Century: England and Germany*. London: SPCK Press.

SCHLEIERMACHER, FRIEDRICH DANIEL ERNST. 1998. *Hermeneutics and Criticism and Other Writings*. Trans. Andrew Bowie. Cambridge: Cambridge University Press.

SIMONSUURI, KIRSTI. 1979. *Homer's Original Genius: Eighteenth-Century Notions of the Early Greek Epic (1688–1798)*. Cambridge: Cambridge University Press.

WILAMOWITZ-MOELLENDORF, ULRICH VON. 1982. *History of Classical Scholarship*. Trans. Alan Harris, ed. Hugh Lloyd-Jones. Baltimore: The Johns Hopkins University Press.

WILLEY, BASIL. 1964. *Nineteenth-Century Studies*. Harmondsworth: Penguin.

CHAPTER 25

COLERIDGE AS A
THEOLOGIAN

DOUGLAS HEDLEY

It is perhaps surprising to the uninitiated that Coleridge was so serious in his theology. A poet of genius in an age of magnificent English poets, a most distinguished man of letters and critic, and a philosopher of rare insight and learning, but he was *primarily* a theologian. He veritably wrestles with questions of the status of Scripture, doctrines of the Fall, justification and sanctification, the personality and infinity of God. His theology remains deeply metaphysical. He was convinced that theology requires philosophical explication and thus Coleridge stands at odds with that great strand in Christian thought from Tertullian to Pascal, Kierkegaard, and Barth that revels in paradox. Coleridge is not a fideist; but neither is he a dry rationalist in his theology.

The term 'theology' has its ambiguities. It is used by Aristotle as a first philosophy and was generally avoided by the Western Church Fathers. Even Aquinas speaks of sacred doctrine (*sacra doctrina*) rather than theology. One ought to avoid anachronism, as if theology or philosophy were neatly circumscribed, as it is in Western universities. Schleiermacher is known today as a theologian and Hegel as a philosopher, but Hegel was trained as a theologian and exerted a great influence upon nineteenth-century theology. Schleiermacher translated Plato into German, wrote purely philosophical works, and influenced philosophers like Dilthey, Heidegger, and Gadamer. This issue is complicated by the fact that Coleridge belongs to that Augustinian Christian Platonic strand of thought that tends to merge the philosophical and the theological. Whereas St Thomas and later Thomists distinguished neatly between truths of natural reason and revealed truths, the Christian Platonists like Augustine, Bonaventura, or Nicholas of Cusa tended to merge the two. Whereas, for example, the doctrine of the Trinity is a revealed truth and inaccessible to natural reason for St Thomas, the Christian Platonists look for enigmatic signs of the Trinity in self-consciousness or mathematical analogies.

It is easy to overlook the deep theological influence upon much philosophy up to the nineteenth century (and beyond). German Romantic and Idealistic thought, in particular, had a powerful theological component: Nietzsche remarked in his *Anti-Christ* that the Lutheran Parsonage was the home of German philosophy: One need only say 'Tübingen Stift' to understand what German philosophy basically is—a cunning theology.[1] Hence it is far from surprising that Coleridge should have found elective affinities in German idealism.

A Trinitarian Theology of the Spirit

We do not possess a comprehensive systematic theology like Schleiermacher's *The Christian Faith*. The recently published *Opus Maximum* has much of interest but remains a large fragment. This was clearly not Coleridge's intention. However, we may agree with the acute observation of F. D. Maurice:

> The real Logo-Sophia of Coleridge is constained in his Lay Sermons... [and] in his Aids to Reflection, wherein he awakens young men to ask themselves whether that divine Wisdom is not speaking to them... whether there is not a will in them which can only be free when it is obeying the motions of a higher Will.[2]

S. T. Coleridge, the son of a Church of England parson, was educated at a Church of England school and a Church of England university, latterly as a scholar at Jesus College, Cambridge. This was England prior to the Reform Act and the Catholic Emancipation Act, caught in the tumult of the French Revolution and the Napoleonic war. Born in 1772, the revolution exploding in 1789 was formative for the young Coleridge. The Revolution overturned monarchy, aristocracy, and Church for citizenship, nation, and rights. Thomas Paine published the Rights of Man in 1791. From 1791–4 Coleridge was certainly a supporter of the French revolutionary cause. As an undergraduate he burnt Liberty and Equality on to the lawns of

---

[1] Der protestantische Pfarrer ist Grossvater der deutschen Philosophie, der Protestantismus selbst ihm peccatum originale. Definition des Protestantismus: die halbseitige Lähmung des Christentums—*und* der Vernunft... Man hat nur das Wort 'Tübinger Stift' auszusprechen, um zu begreifen, *was* die deutsche Philosophie im Grunde ist,—eine *hinterlistige* Theologie...

[2] Beer, cxxxvi.

St John's and Trinity Colleges in Cambridge with gunpowder,[3] supported the Unitarian Frend, became a Unitarian preacher, and was suspected of being a French spy while discussing Spinoza with Wordsworth; the young man who dreamed of Pantiscocracy in Pennsylvania turned back to the Church of England and became one of its most seminal (and reforming) thinkers. The *Biographia Literaria* of 1817 describes (and to some extent denies) the shift in opinions. There is humour in his depiction of the official scrutiny of Coleridge and Wordsworth as spies; yet clearly the two were perceived as dangerous supporters of the revolutionary cause. It is a work of genius but Coleridge was evidently disguising—perhaps even to himself— the extent of his change of heart. The idea of reversal, repentance, and renewal are at the heart of Coleridge's theology—the decisive moment in the 'Mariner' when he blesses the snakes and the albatross falls from his neck. Behind the then fashionably mysterious and Gothic aspect of the 'Rime' is a view of the human condition quite at odds with the rationalism and optimism of the French Enlightenment and the ideals of Revolution. We find his poetry foreshadowing elements of his mature theology. In true Augustinian fashion, this suggests that the heart knows more than it can articulate. It is also an index of the Augustinian side to Coleridge's thought that the doctrine of the Trinity plays a very central role. This doctrine is the key to Coleridge's theology.

THE SEVENTEENTH CENTURY

The Reformation began in 1517, with Luther nailing his 95 theses to the door of the Wittenberg castle Church, but the settlement of the peace of Westphalia was not finalized until 1648, with its principle of *cuius regio, eius religio.* The seventeenth century was a momentous period for theology. Formerly, Western Christendom, both Protestant and Catholic, employed its scholastic theology throughout the great European universities. The new science radically challenged the Post Reformation settlements. Philosophers like Descartes and Hobbes were responding both to the wars of religion and to the challenge of the new science. Atheism was rare, but Renaissance figures like Vanini drew upon ancient Epicurean positions, and later Spinoza's radically deterministic pantheism seemed identical to, or at least very close to atheism. Henry More and Cudworth saw themselves duelling with atheism. Various heresies like Arianism and Socinianism were gaining momentum.

Coleridge was fascinated by the seventeenth century. Not only was it the greatest age of English literature, but the defining period of English theology. After the

---

[3] James Gillman, *The Life of Samuel Taylor Coleridge* (London, 1838), pp. 49–50.

moderate Protestantism of the Elizabethan settlement and Elizabeth's avowed determination not to 'make windows into men's souls', there ensued a battle between those Anglicans like Milton, who wished to continue the work of the Reformation and purify the Church of England from residual pre-Reformation inheritance, and those who wished to consolidate episcopacy and even forge links with Catholic Europe. Many of the main figures of the age, like Cromwell, were independents. And, after the Glorious Revolution of 1688 and the Act of Uniformity, came the expulsion of dissenting Protestants from the English Church.

Theological heresies abounded, and in particular forms of Anti-Trinitarian theology. Socinianism, with its roots in Renaissance Italy and its success in Poland and Transylvania, was a powerful force in the Low Countries and exerted an influence upon major English intellectuals, not least John Locke. In the 1790s there was a particularly virulent debate about the doctrine of the Trinity. The rationalist Socinianian influence, spearheaded by early polemicists such as John Biddle (1615–62) became manifest in the Unitarianism of figures like Priestley (1733–1804). This was a mixture of rationalism and a biblically based critique of dogmas such as original sin and the Trinity, which were deemed by the Socinians unscriptural. But Socinian influence was also evident in those Divines within the Church of England who were influenced by Locke, especially William Paley. The rise of English pietism in John Wesley is another important source of Coleridge's theology, the emphasis upon the heart and its proper affections remained a powerful force in Coleridge's theology. Young Coleridge was clearly deeply influenced by the rationalism of 'Socinian moonlight' and the passionate religion of the Methodist stove. He retained throughout his career a combination of the desire to understand religious belief while retaining a deep sense of the *properly* passionate nature of that belief. This is not least because Coleridge's theological interests and obsessions can be linked so intimately to his own biography.

THE LOGOS

By 1795 Coleridge was no longer a political radical, but was still very closely linked to radical religion. By 1797 he had moved to Nether Stowey. It was here that he produced much of his great poetic oeuvre. Yet he was troubled by theological problems. As Richard Holmes notes, he uses the language of the seafarer or mariner in his later reminiscences as an image of this spiritual or theological quest.

I retired to a cottage in Somersetshire at the foot of the Quantock, and devoted my thoughts and studies to the foundations of religion and morals. Here I found myself all afloat. Doubts rushed in; broke upon me from the fountains of the great deep and fell from the windows of heaven. The frontal truths of natural religion and the books of Revelation alike contributed to the flood; and it was long ere my ark touched upon an Ararat and rested.[4]

He claims a difference in his metaphysical opinions from those of the Unitarians, that is, while a zealous adherent to Unitarian Christianity, he was a Trinitarian *ad normam Platonis* (p. 180). This was the man whom Charles Lamb described to the young Coleridge at Christ's Hospital as the captivating young 'Mirandula', who unfolded 'deep and sweet intonations, the mysteries of Jamblichus, or Plotinus'.[5]

Coleridge is claiming that the idea of a Divine logos or cosmic word or rationality predisposed him to a return to Trinitarian theology. In his early notebooks we can find reference to such a principle that forms the basis of the idea of a correspondence between internal human reality and external transcendent spiritual reality:

In looking at objects of Nature while I am thinking, as at yonder moon dim-glimmering thro' the dewy window-pane, I seem rather to be seeking, as it were *asking*, a symbolical language for something within me that already and forever exist, rather than observing anything new. Even when that latter is the case, yet still I have always an obscure feeling as if that new phaenomenon were the dim Awakening of a forgotten or hidden truth of my inner nature/ It is still interesting as a Word, a Symbol! It is Λογοω, the Creator! And the Evolver![6]

The Logos in Middle Platonism and in ancient Hellenism (Plutarch and Philo designate that creative dimension of Deity, the designation of the consubstantiality of the logos with the Father in Christian theology) expressed the idea that this creative dimension was identical and in no way inferior to the true essence of the Godhead. Importantly, the idea of the Logos was identified by Socinians like Priestley as the main vehicle of the infection of Scriptural Christianity by pagan philosophy.

Christian theology had semitic roots but developed within the Hellenic context forged by Alexander the Great's conquests and transmission of Greek *paideia* with the ancient near East. St John's prologue has resonance of the Platonic Jewish thinker Philo. Yet the Graeco Roman dimension is less the Apolline rationalism of the ancient Hellenes or the sturdy pragmatism of the Romans than the mystical phase of Platonism inaugurated by Plotinus.

The formative period of its theology—the shaping of the Nicea and Constantinople—was a period in which the dominant philosophical school was the Platonism that emerged in the wake of Plotinus (204–70). The leading Platonists from Porphyry to Proclus and Simplicius regarded Christianity as a barbarous development. In the period of Julian the Apostate, Platonism became the official religion of

---

[4] Coleridge, *Biographia*, I, 200.
[5] Charles Lamb, 'Christ's Hospital Five and Twenty Years Ago', 1820, *Essays of Elia: First Series* (Moxon, 1840), p. 13.
[6] Coleridge, *CN*, ii, 2546.

the state, and the Emperor Justinian closed down the Platonic Academy in Athens in 529. At one level, Christian theology and Neoplatonism were opposing forces. However, Christian theology drew much from Platonism. Augustine and Gregory of Nyssa drew deeply from Plotinus and shared much in common with the Platonists. Conversely, the pagan Platonists imitated Christian theology and terminology. The deep proximity and mutual hostility between Neoplatonism and Christian theology is pivotal for an appreciation of Coleridge's theology. Coleridge is a Christian Platonist, an inheritor of the complex and ambiguous attempt to reconcile Christian kerygma with Platonic metaphysics evident in writers like Clement and Justin, Origen, Gregory of Nyssa, and Augustine.

Florentine Christian Neoplatonism, with its spiritus rector Marsilio Ficino (1433–99) revived and promulgated the Christian Platonic synthesis with great energy and power. But it was ultimately suppressed by the Counter Reformation. The ideas it promulgated survived more powerfully outside the orbit of the counter-Reformation and the next great centre of Christian Neoplatonic speculation in the seventeenth century was England, and Cambridge in particular. Through influential eighteenth-century thinkers and scholars like Shaftesbury and Mosheim, the legacy of the Cambridge Platonists continued to exert an influence on the continent of Europe.[7]

THE CABBALISTIC TURN

We need first to consider Coleridge's theology in the context of the Pantheism controversy (*Pantheismusstreit*). This was the celebrated and momentous debate between F. H. Jacobi (1743–1819) and Moses Mendelssohn (1729–86) concerning Lessing's alleged pantheism. It took place while Schelling and Hegel were students of theology in the Tübingen Stift. Jacobi published (rather scandalously) a conversation he had enjoyed with Lessing in which Lessing openly avowed his 'Spinozism'. Jacobi was intent upon contrasting Lessing's Spinozism with Christian theism: the former as deterministic nihilism, the latter presupposing inexplicable freedom.[8] Spinoza was, indeed, a vital part of the development of German Idealism. Jacobi's interpretation of Spinoza is coloured by a particular 'cabbalistic' context. Coleridge himself in the *Philosophical Lectures* speaks of Spinoza as holding 'the opinions of the most learned Jews, particularly the Cabbalistic philosophers'.[9]

---

[7] See Douglas Hedley, 'Cudworth, Coleridge and Schelling', *The Coleridge Bulletin*, 16 (2000), pp. 63–70.

[8] Friedrich Heinrich Jacobi, *Über die Lehre des Spinoza* (Hamburg: Felix Meiner, 2000), p. 3.

[9] Coleridge, *OM*, cxcv.

The cabbalistic Spinoza points to F. H. Jacobi: he uses the Cabbalistic term 'Das Immanente Ensoph' or the cabbalistic concept of immanent Ensoph in order to expound Spinoza.[10] The Ensoph is the equivalent of the Logos—the creative principle within the divine that is the fountain of productive divine energy. Jacobi's intention is manifestly polemical, but it reveals a very interesting aspect of the interpretation of Spinoza, which became a cardinal element in the Romantic-idealistic reception of Spinoza.[11] The 'substance' of Spinoza's *Ethics* as it is interpreted via the Cabbalistic Ensoph draws Spinoza into an orbit of Neoplatonic Mysticism. Spinoza comes to be seen as much closer to the *philosophus teutonicus* Jacob Boehme. The substance of Spinoza becomes a dynamic source of cosmic processions.

In *Uber die Lehre des Spinoza* Jacobi describes how, before he realized the nature of Lessing's pantheism, he was puzzled by a passage in Lessing's *Education of the Human Race* ¶ 73 which identifies the Father of the Christian Trinity *with natura naturans* and the Son of the Christian Trinity with *natura naturata*.[12] Lessing in *Die Erziehung des Menschengeschlechts* ¶ 73 actually writes:

On the doctrine of the Trinity—if we try to sort out intellectually this doctrine after infinite confusions left and right, that God cannot be one object—that his unity is a transcendent unity that does not exclude plurality. Does not God require a representation of himself? That is to say a representation in which all that constitutes him is contained... how better and more concrete than by calling this representation the son, Divine begotten from eternity?[13]

---

[10] Friedrich Heinrich Jacobi, *Über die Lehre des Spinoza* (Hamburg: Felix Meiner, 2000), p. 182.

[11] *Kabbala und die Literatur der Romantik: zwischen Magie und Trope*, ed. Eveline Goodman-Thau, Gert Mattenklott, Christoph Schulte (Tübingen: M. Niemeyer, 1999).

[12] Ehe mir Lessings Meinungen auf die bisher erzählte Weise bekannt geworden, und in der festen Überzeugung, die sich auf Zeugnisse stützte; Lessing sei ein rechtgläubiger Deist, war mir in seiner Erziehung des Menschengeschlechtes einiges ganz unverstandlich, besonders der 73 ¶. Ich. mochte wissen, ob jemand diese Stelle anders, als nach Spinozistischen Ideen deutlich machen kann. Nach diesen aber wird der Kommentar sehr leicht. Der Gott des Spinoza, ist das lautere principium der Würklichkeit in allem Würklichen, das Seins in allem Dasein, durchaus ohne individualitat, und schlechterdings unendlich. Die Einheit dieses Gottes beruhet auf der Identitat des nicht zu unterscheidenden, und schließet folglich eine Art der Mehrheit nicht aus. Bloß in dieser transcendentalen Einheit angesehen, muß die Gottheit aber schlechterdings der Würklichkeit entbehren, die nur im bestimmten Einzelnen sich ausgedruckt befinden kann. Diese, die Würklichkeit mit ihrem Begriffe, beruhet also auf der Natura naturata (dem Sohne von Ewigkeit); so wie jene, die Möglichkeit, das Wesen, das substantielle des Unendlichkeit, mit seinem Begriffe, auf der Natura naturanti (dem Vater).

[13] Z. E. die Lehre von der Dreienigkeit.—Wie, wenn diese Lehre den menschlichen Verstand, nach unendlichen Verirrungen rechts und links, nur endlich auf den Weg bringen sollte, zu erkennen, daß Gott in dem Verstande, in welchem endliche Dinge *eins* sind, unmöglich *eins* sein könne; daß auch seine Einheit eine transcendentale Einheit sein müsse, welche eine Art von Mehrheit nicht ausschließet? Muß Gott wenigstens nicht die vollständige Vorstellung von sich selbst haben? d.i. eine Vorstellung, in der alles befindet, was in ihm selbst ist....so viel bleibt doch immer unwidersprechlich, daß diejenigen, welche die Idee davon populär machen wollen, sich schwerlich faßlicher und schicklicher hätten ausdrücken können, als durch die Benennung eines *Sohnes*, den Gott von Ewigkeit zeugt.

This 'christological' passage is linked by Jacobi to Spinoza's metaphysics. Such a christological reading of Spinoza via Lessing is quite incredible, apart from the view of Spinozist as a Cabbalist propagated by Johann Georg Wachter at the beginning of the eighteenth century, in which the relationship between Substance and modes is linked to a Christian Neoplatonic logos speculation. On this reading, the Spinozistic (and pantheistic) idea of modifications of the one Substance is mysteriously interpreted as procession or emanation from the first cause. Of primary importance is the role of the Cabbalistic figure Adam Kadmon, who stands for the Christ-logos figure.[14] The immediate source of Wachter's Christian Cabbalism was the remarkable friend and pupil of Henry More: Anne Conway and her *Principia Philosophiae Antiquissimae & Recentissimae*.[15] Wachter tells us that the Cabbalists speak of two principles within the Deity, the second of which is called variously Adam Kadmon, the Logos, or the Word and mentions in this connection expressly Spinoza.[16] Wachter sees Spinoza as presenting an intellectually rigorous exposition of a Christian metaphysics of a fundamentally Neoplatonic kind in which the Logos stands for the Divine intellect.[17] Hence Wachter was convinced that in this manner he could acquit Spinozism of the twin accusations: pantheism and materialism. Wachter's speculative Spinozistic christology is not completely absurd: in Spinoza's *Short Treatise natura naturata* is described as the 'son'. However, Wachter did not know this text.[18] Furthermore, in a letter to Heinrich Oldenburg Spinoza says that his theory of God as the immanent rather than transcendent cause of the world is akin to ideas of St Paul in Apostles 17 and 28, various antique philosophers, and 'the ancient Hebrews', in as far one as can infer their views from the corrupted traditions.[19] Wachter did not, however, think that Spinozism was compatible with the personality of the Divine or the immortality of the soul. Winfried Schröter observes that Wachter had no illusions about Spinoza as 'Spinoza Christianus', or even 'christianissimus' (Goethe).[20] Brucker in his celebrated *Historia critica*

---

[14] Wilhelm Schmidt-Biggemann, *Philosophia perennis Historische Umrisse abendländischer Spiritualität in Antike, Mittelalter und Früher Neuzeit* (Frankfurt am Main, 1998), pp. 304 ff.

[15] Anne Conway, *The Principles of the Most Ancient and Modern Philosophy*, eds Allison P. Coudert and Taylor Corse (Cambridge: Cambridge University Press, 1996).

[16] The Cabbalists "loquuntur de principiato quodam primo, quod Deus immediate ex se effluere fecere, & quo mediante caetera in series & ordine sint producta, idque variis nominibus salutare solent, qualia sunt, Adam Kadmon, Messias, Christus, Logos, verbum, Filius, Primogenitus, Homo primus, Homo Coelestis, Dux, Pastor, Mediator, & reliqua... rem ipsam agnovit SPINOZA, ut praeter nomen nihil desiderare possis'. Johann Georg Wachter, *Elucidarius cabalisticus*, p. 49, ed. W. Schröter in: *Dokumente: Johann Georg Wachter: De primordiia Christianae religionis, Elucidarius cabalisticus, Origines juris naturalis* (Stuttgart-Bad Cannstatt: frommann-holzboog, 1995).

[17] Et de intellectu quidem divino (cujus modo mentio facta) plane ad mentem Cabalististarum philosophatur, qui duplicem lógon DEI, statuunt, unum DEO internum, alternum.

[18] Schröter, *Spinoza in der deutschen Frühaufklärung* (Würzburg: Königshausen und Neumann, 1987), p. 99.

[19] Baruch de Spinoza, *Briefwechsel*, trs. into German by C. Gebhardt (Hamburg: Felix Meiner, 1986), p. 276.

[20] Schröter, *Spinoza in der deutschen Frühaufklärung* (Würzburg: Königshausen und Neumann, 1987), pp. 101–2.

philosophiae knew that 'the difference between modifications and emanations is far greater than the famous Wachter admits; modifications are within in the Substance, emanations proceed without'. [21]

Jacobi's pantheism polemic depends upon his bizarre interpretation of Spinoza. Jacobi insists: The Cabbalistic philosophy as far as research reveals, and according to the best commentators like the younger van Helmont and Wachter, is nothing but an under-developed or newly confused Spinozism'.[22] These works which Jacobi refers to as Cabbalistic, are in fact Christian. Henry More, Anne Conway, Van Helmont, and Wachter were all Christian thinkers, and Jacobi's polemical identification of Cabbala and Spinozism as forms of pantheism was not based on any direct knowledge of Jewish sources. The Spinoza at the heart of the Pantheism controversy was not the cool headed, Stoicizing pantheist that one encounters in his Ethics, but a Spinoza transformed—quite crassly—into a Neoplatonist.

PANTHEISM AND IDEALISM

In Fragment 2 of the *Opus Maximum* Coleridge is dismissive of 'the recent writings of Schelling and his followers, as often as they attempt to clothe the skeleton of the Spinozistic pantheism and breathe a life thereunto' (*OM*, p. 205). Yet Crabb Robinson was quite correct when he observed that Coleridge 'metaphysicized à la Schelling while he abused him'.[23] An investigation of the topics of the later works of Coleridge shows a profound proximity to these 'recent writings of Schelling' in his Munich phase: Divine Will, evil, freedom, system, etc.

The question of the Divine will and potentiality is *the* problem which Schelling after 1809 is attempting to answer. This is not a question that a *genuine* pantheist like Spinoza (unlike perhaps his cabbalistic alter ego) would regard as worth contemplating. Indeed, Spinoza is quite adamant that the religious imagination is the source of such an absurd anthropomorphism as a belief in a *personal* Deity.[24]

Coleridge's intellectual proximity to Schelling can be explained in terms of a *shared* Neoplatonic tradition. But these shared ideas were often transmitted via the

---

[21] 'Longius inter se distant modificationes et emanationes, quam uult cl. Wachterus; modificationes enim substantiae immanent, emanationes progrediuntur', Vol. 4/2, p. 695.

[22] Die Kabbalistische Philosophie, so viel davon der Untersuchung offen liegt, und nach ihren besten Kommentatoren, von Helmont dem Jüngeren, und Wachter, ist als Philosophie, nichts anders, als unterentwickelter, oder neu verworrener Spinozismus. *Friedrich Heinrich Jacobi, Über die Lehre des Spinoza*, p. 182 (Hamburg: Felix Meiner, 2000), p. 120.

[23] Henry Crabb Robinson, *Diary*, ed. T. Sadler (London, 1869), ii, p. 273.

[24] See the scarcely veiled contempt for the idea of the personality of the deity in the appendix to book one of Spinoza's *Ethics*.

Christian cabbala. When Coleridge refers to the 'Hebrew sages' or 'the Rabbinical writings' (*OM*, p. 275), McFarland refers to the possible influence of Hyman Hurwitz (*OM*, p. 275 n. 183). But we should not ignore the role of Henry More, whose deeply Neoplatonic *Psychozoia* is quoted on p. 244 of the *Opus Maximum*. I do not wish to suggest that Coleridge is merely repeating Cabbalistic lore. However, we clearly have clues about the provenance of his thought. This provenance is far closer to what McFarland summarily describes as the 'pantheistic tradition' than Jacobi's own Pascalian philosophy of faith.

Schelling's Christian Neoplatonism is deeply rooted in a South West German mystical tradition.[25] But he was also influenced by this Christian cabbalism which can be traced to Henry More and Anne Conway. This son of a professor of oriental languages, who knew Persian and Arabic as well as Hebrew, Schelling never studied the Jewish Cabbala. But he was influenced by *Christian* Cabbalistic ideas mediated by figures such as More and Conway—a system of Christian Neoplatonism revolving around the logos concept. The decisive shift in Schelling's thought was in 1809 and onwards. At this point Schelling was, for the first time, in the physical proximity of Jacobi himself and Franz von Baader, an exponent of Christian cabbala and great admirer of Boehme.[26] Schelling's *On Human Freedom* reflects this influence; as does *Über die Gottheiten von Samothrace* of 1815.

TRINITY AND UNITY

Coleridge's speculations about the triune identity of God as ipseity, altereity, and community seems puzzling. But we do not need to confine ourselves to the esoteric parameters of Western intellectual history to discover precedents. His thought has its clear precedent among genuinely philosophical theologians of Platonic provenance. Nicholas of Cusa speaks of the '*unitas, aequalitas et conexio*' in his *De Docta Ignorantia* 1 VIII 21 or '*unitas, iditas, identitas*' in *De Docta Ignorantia* I IX 25. Both Coleridge and Cusa are metaphysicians of unity and their theological speculation concerning the Trinity belong within this Pythagorean–Parmenidean–Platonic framework. Coleridge inherited this tradition from seventeenth-century divines like Thomas Jackson and the Cambridge Platonists. This was reinforced by his reading of German writers like Lessing and Schelling.

Plato's dialogues raised the problem of how realms of being and becoming relate. Are ideas ultimate reality? How do the forms relate to the form of the Good?

---

[25] Ernst Benz, *The Mystical Sources of German Romantic Philosophy*, translated by Blair R. Reynolds and Eunice M. Paul (Allison Park, Pa.: Pickwick Publications, 1983).

[26] Ernst Benz, *Die Christliche Cabbala. Ein Stiefkind der Theologie* (Zürich, 1958).

In *Theaetetus* 183 he refers to the great Eleatic monist Parmenides as 'venerable and awesome'. Plato refers to the good beyond Being (*Rep.* 509). Later Platonists identified the Good with Unity. The general tendency of Christian theology was to identify the 'forms' with the mind of God. The transcendent Godhead becomes the locus of manifold ideas within one transcendent principle. Quite how this one principle can contain plurality without compromising its unity was a puzzle for the more metaphysically minded Divines of the Church.

Aristotle rejected the hypostasing of the Parmenidean–Pythagorean–Platonic strand—unity is not an entity beyond concrete unities. The One means 'continuous' or 'the whole', the 'individual' or the 'universal'. These are all one because they are indivisible (*Metaphysics* XI 1–5). But in Neoplatonism, the second part of Plato's dialogue *Parmenides* was interpreted as providing an ontology in which the three hypostases become a descending hierarchy of unity. Incorporeal reality has three levels—One, Intellect and Soul like concentric circles around the One, the ineffable 'One' or 'Good' is the transcendent principle of all being (Plotinus VI 9, 5, 30). In Christian theology the doctrine of the Trinity embraced, modified and perpetuated this pagan speculation concerning the nature of transcendent unity. Coleridge stands within this tradition of speculation about the Trinity in relation to a metaphysics of unity. This Patristic 'Henological' tradition was developed by John Scot Eriugena in 810–77. With the Scholastic revival of Aristotle (and Arabic influence) and Aquinas (1225–74) we find the Aristotelian sense of each sensible object is a being and a unity, and rejection of any special dignity accorded to *unum*. This was reinforced in later scholasticism: the great Iberian scholastic Francisco Suárez (1548–1617) argued for the Aristotelian priority of being. But Platonic *henological* strand of metaphysics was not extinguished by the Aristotelians. In the High Middle Ages it resurfaced through the translation of Proclus' *Parmenides Commentary* and *Elements of Theology*. This can be seen clearly in Eckhart (1260–1328). God is *unum* as radically different from all particular items. Negation of the negation. Esse fundatur et figitur in uno et per unum. Being is founded and made possible by unity. For Nicholas of Cusa (1401–1461) God as *non aliud*, the 'not other', indicates his preference of *unum* over *ens*.

A most distinguished English representative of this henological tradition of Eckhart and Cusa was Thomas Jackson (1579–1640), friend of Herbert and Nicholas Ferrar. His *A Treatise of the Divine Essence and Attributes* of 1628 was a sustained attempt to employ Neoplatonic metaphysics in the service of Christian theology. [27]

The special theological and metaphysical role of the concept of unity can be clearly seen in the famous passage about the distinction between primary and secondary imagination and fancy in the *Biographia*. Imagination is a 'repetition in the finite mind of the eternal act of creation in the infinite I AM'. This is a reference

---

[27] See P. White, *Conflict and Consensus in the English Church from the Reformation to the Civil War* (Cambridge, 1992), pp. 256–71.

to Exodus 3.14 where God tells Moses 'I am Who I am.' This passage was the subject of much later Hellenic and medieval speculation about the Divine nature. But one should note that the repetition is of the eternal self constitition of the Deity:

The Will, the absolute Will, is that which is essentially causative of reality, essentially and absolutely, that is boundless from without and within. This is our first principle' (p. 220) and he explicitly refers to the tenet of God as *causa sui* throughout his mature writings, that 'which admits of no question out of itself, acknowledges no predicate but the I AM IN THAT I AM'. [28]

Thus, for Coleridge, finite creativity is the image of that supreme perfection who is, in his essence, creative self-constitution. The parallel is not between God's making of the world and the artistic or poetic making, but between the auto-constitution of the Godhead and the radical and free spontaneity of the creative artist. And through radical self constitution we come to the doctrine of the Trinity.

TRINITY AND PERSONALITY: GOD AS ABSOLUTE WILL

The appeal to the God of Abraham and Isaac is also to the God of Exodus 3.14, 'I am who I am', as grounded in the absymal *causa sui*. This appeal is not, for Coleridge, a sacrificium intellectus since 'true metaphysics are nothing else but true divinity'.[29] It is entirely of a piece with Coleridge's metaphysical and empirical reflections upon the unfathomable mystery of the finite imagination as the image of its transcendent divine source. The *Biographia* recounts how Coleridge could not 'reconcile personality with infinity',[30] since being a 'person' conceptually involves distinction from other persons. Thus an infinite person could have no 'other'. The Trinity solves the problem in so far as the Godhead is constituted precisely by the interactions of the persons or hypostases. But Coleridge is keen to avoid the charge of tritheism. The three persons are three in one. Coleridge's Trinitarian resolution to the conflict between personality and infinity is to see personeity (as the root of personality) as essentially relational. The idea of God as *causa sui* is that of the *abysmal* (without bottom or ground) relationality of the first Principle. Our modern word person comes from the Latin *Persona*—which originally meant an actor's mask or role—and from this to mean one's role or character. Boethius

---

[28] Coleridge, *Friend*, I p. 519.
[29] Coleridge, *Biographia*, p. 291.
[30] Coleridge, *Biographia*, I, p. 204.

(480–525) defined a person as *naturae rationalis individua substantia* (individual substance of a rational nature), a definition of personal identity that arose out of debates concerning the Trinity (one substance and three persons).

Coleridge is linking 'self-existence' with 'Spirit' by the 'Fathers and the School divines' (p. 188). Yet this is, *prima facie*, an odd claim. Certainly he cannot mean Augustine or Aquinas. The most important of the Fathers, St Augustine in *De Trinitate* says explicitly

> those who suppose that God is of such power that he actually begets himself, are . . . wrong, since not only is God not like that, but neither is anything in the world of body or spirit. There is absolutely no thing whatsoever that brings itself into existence.[31]

The most influential Schoolman, St Thomas Aquinas, in his *Summa contra Gentiles* is equally adamant.

> The existence of the cause is prior to that of the effect. If, then something were its own cause of being, it would be understood to be before it had being—which is impossible . . .[32]

Aquinas is making the common-sense point that causation presupposes a distinction between cause and that which is caused, and hence the idea of self causation is a contradiction in terms. Needless to say, the concept of *causa sui* is utterly meaningless to Kant—though for more complex reasons. On the basis of his Transcendental Idealism causality is a concept which cannot be legitimately employed beyond the limits of possible experience. *Causa prima* may be vacuous for Kant, but *causa sui* unintelligible.

Of course, the immediate source of the language of *causa sui* is that of Spinoza, and his enormous influence upon the eighteenth century. Yet self generation or auto-constitution of the Divine is not problematic for a pantheist. If the world is identical with the Divine and vice versa, then the creator creates himself in the generation of the cosmos. Hence a Stoic like Seneca can happily say that *deus ipse se fecit*, but this is merely expressing conceptual truth within pantheistic parameters. Such a position would be untenable for Coleridge, or any pagan Platonist who holds to a self-generating transcendent god, and a radical distinction between God and world.

Hence our puzzle. Coleridge is claiming as a tenet, his central tenet, furthermore, a principle which is clearly *rejected* by the great theological authorities and Coleridge's own much-admired Kant. It is also a tenet *accepted* by pantheists such as the ancient Stoics or Spinoza. Is this an instance of Coleridge vacillating between pantheism and theism?

---

[31] Saint Augustine, *The Trinity* Book 1, 1 (Hyde Park, NY: New York City Press, 1991), p. 66.
[32] Thomas Aquinas, *Summa Contra Gentiles* 1. 22, trans. A. C. Pegis, Book One: God (London, Notre Dame: Notre Dame Press, 1975), p. 119.

PLOTINUS AND THE WILL OF THE ONE

Nor can we attribute the concept of the *causa sui* to Neoplatonic lore. Proclus, who exerted an enormous influence upon Christian theologians such as Denys the Areopagite, Thomas Aquinas or Nicholas of Cusa, writes:

For some want to say that the first principle is self-constituted, arguing that even as the first principle of moving things is the first moved, even so the first principle of all those things which have any sort of existence is self constituted; for all things subsequent to the first principle also derive from the first principle. [33]

Proclus' own typically measured opinion is that the One is 'superior to all such causality'.[34] Dillon suggests that Plotinus is probably the target of Proclus' rejection of the doctrine of *causa sui* for the First Principle.[35] In his Commentary on the Republic Proclus argues that the One is above self generation since he is transcends any kind of multiplicity.[36]

Plotinus in *Ennead* VI 8 argues that the One is 'the father of reason and cause and causative substance, which are certainly all far from chance, he would be the principle and in a way the exemplar of all things which have no part in chance, truly and primarily, uncontaminated by chances and coincidence and happening, cause of himself and himself from himself and through himself; for he is primarily self and self beyond being'.[37]

If then the Good is established in existence, and choice and will join in establishing it—for without these it will not be—but this Good must not be many, its will and substance must be brought into one; but if its willing comes from itself, it is necessary that it also gets its being from itself, so that our discourse has discovered that he has made himself. For if his will comes from himself and is something like his own work, and this will is the same thing as his existence, then in this way he will have brought himself into existence; so that he is not what he happened to be but what he himself willed. [38]

Coleridge takes up the ancient tenet that an ultimate principle must be postulated in order to avoid an infinite regress—'we must be whirl'd down the gulph of an infinite series. But this would make our reason baffle the end and purpose of all reason, namely unity and system. Or, we must break off the series arbitrarily, and

---

[33] Proclus, *Commentary on Plato's Parmenides*, trans. G. R. Morrow and J. M. Dillon (Princeton: Princeton University Press, 1987), p. 505.

[34] Ibid., p. 506.

[35] Ibid., p. 505.

[36] Proclus, *Commentaire sur la Timée*, tr. and notes by A. J. Festugière (Paris: Vrin, 1967), Vol. II, book 2, p. 59.

[37] Plotinus, *Ennead* VI 8, 14, 40 ff.

[38] Plotinus, *Ennead* VI 8, 13, 50 ff.

affirm an absolute something that is in and of itself at once cause and effect (*causa sui*), subject and object, or rather the absolute identity of both.[39]

The link between Trinitarian self realization and the concept of *causa sui* is strikingly evident in the hymns of Synesius of Cyrene, which Coleridge quotes in the *Biographia Literaria*:

Thus the true system of natural philosophy places the sole reality of things in an ABSO-LUTE, which is at once *causa sui* et effectus—in the absolute identity of subject and object, which it calls nature, and which in its highest power is nothing else but self-consciousness or intelligence.[40]

In Coleridge's Pythagorean terminology, the 'abysmal Ground of the Trinity' is the One which is the prothesis, which logically (though not temporally) proceeds the Trinity of Father, Son, and Spirit. The model is that of Neoplatonic–Neopythagorean series of numbers being generated from a primordial one. Moreover, Coleridge's speculation about the 'tetractys of the most ancient philosophy' (*OM* p. 209, cf. 259) draws on a tradition of Pythagorean–Cabbalistic numerology. Schmidt-Biggeman writes of Reuchlin's cabbalistic use of the four: 'The Four is the order, which neighbours upon the Trinity—this is the last number before the divine number three: it is the number of wisdom.'[41]

A good instance of Coleridge's use of the Patristic tradition is the quotation of the hymns of Synesius. [42]

God is one, but exists or manifests himself to himself, at once in a threefold Act, total in each and one in all. [43]

He wishes to avoid Sabellianism (the doctrine that there are merely three modes, not three persons, of one God), Tritheism (three Gods!) and Subordinationism in which there exists a hierarchy within the Divine. The three persons of the Godhead are one, Coleridge affirms, but their unity is not grounded in the Father (hence avoiding subordinationism). The One or Monad (prothesis) of the primordial Godhead expresses itself eternally as the triad of thesis qua Father—(Ipseity), antithesis qua Son (Alterity) and synthesis qua Spirit (copula) which is 'the identity of object and subject fit alter et idem'.[44]

Coleridge is attempting to express the central Christian idea of the absolute divine subjectivity (the great I AM) as constituted by the substantial *relation*

[39] Coleridge, *Biographia*, I, p. 285.

[40] Coleridge, *Biographia*, I, 284.

[41] 'Die Vier ist die Ordnung, die der Trinität benachbart ist, es ist die letzte—vor—der göttlichen Zahl Drei, es ist auch die Zahl der Weisheit.' Wilhelm Schmidt-Biggemann, *Philosophia Perennis*, p. 181. In the Pythagorean tradition Tetrad and the Decad are closely related: $10=1+2+3+4$. See K. S. Guthrie, *The Pythagorean Sourcebook and the library* (Grand Rapids, 1987), pp. 27 ff.

[42] Samuel Vollenweider, *Neuplatonischer und christliche Theologie bei Synesios von Kyrene* (Göttingen: Vandenhoeck and Ruprecht, 1985).

[43] Coleridge, *Collected Notes*, III, 4427.

[44] Coleridge, *Biographia* I, 279.

between the hypostases of the Father, Son and Spirit. Whereas Neoplatonism, whether of Plotinian or the post-Iamblichean (e.g. Proclus) form, sees a hierarchy of descending levels of unity in the divine, Christian Trinitarian theology sees the unity of the Godhead as defined by the relation of the three.

It is an eternal and infinite self-rejoicing, self loving, with a joy unfathomable, with a love all comprehensive. It is absolute; and the absolute is neither singly that which affirms, nor that which is affirmed; but the identity and living copula of both.'

Coleridge's daring speculations about the Trinity contain the proviso that all attempts to express the Godhead are deeply inadequate. 'In the philosophy of ideas our words can have no meaning for him that uses and for him that hears them, except as far as the mind's eye in both kept fixed on the idea' (OM p. 226). Coleridge discusses the 'ground or the nature of Deity', but 'we nevertheless abjure the rash and dangerous expressions that the depth begetteth the paternal Deity, or that a Not-Good, which yet is not Evil, a Not-Intelligent...' (OM p. 232). This is a critique of Boehme and Schelling's attempt to posit a grim or inscrutable aspect of the Divine nature. Coleridge wishes to maintain the personal nature of the Deity through his emphasis upon will. However, he refuses to suggest any dark or surd element in the Godhead.

The relevance of Coleridge's Trinitarian speculations to the rest of his thought may seem hard to fathom. If one considers his famous definition of imagination as a 'repetition in the finite mind of the eternal act of creation in the infinite I AM',[45] however, it becomes apparent that the creative act which is the paradigm of artistic activity is the creation of the cosmos but the self generation of the Godhead. Creation of the cosmos for Christians is not, as it is for pagan Platonists, eternal. The self generation of the adorable of 'adorable tetractys' is the theory of the 'infinite yet self-conscious Creator'.[46] The fusing power of the imagination is a vital and original agency—it cannot be reduced to mechanical aggregation and association of images (fancy). The finite I Am, for Coleridge, is the manifestation of the Infinite I AM and as such is an inferior reflection of the absolute subjectivity of the Triune Godhead.[47] When Coleridge says in the *Biographia* that Spirit is the 'mediation of subject and object' and that this self representation implies 'an act, and it follows therefore from that intelligence or self-consciousness is impossible, except by and in a will. The self-conscious spirit is therefore a will; and freedom must be assumed as a *ground* of philosophy, and can never be deduced from it',[48] he is fusing his Trinitarian speculations with his metaphysics of mind. Coleridge reflects upon the aporetic nature of self-consciousness—to what does the personal

---

[45] Coleridge, *Biographia*, I, 304.

[46] Coleridge, *Biographia*, I, p. 203.

[47] See Friedrich Uehlein's magnificent *Die Manifestation des Selbsbewustseins im konkrten 'ich bin'* (Hamburg: Felix Meiner, 1982).

[48] Coleridge, *Biographia*, I, p. 279.

pronoun 'I' refer? This aporia drives Coleridge to the self generating, a-bysmal or groundless, transcendent I AM of Christian theology. The primary imagination as the aboriginal and unconscious power of perception is a faint imitation of the groundless creativity of the Godhead. Like 'Bottom's Dream' *in A Midsummer Night's Dream* 4.1, 'it hath no bottom'.

THE ONE AND THE MANY

Coleridge attacks inadequate conceptions of unity—the unity of naturalism which limits all knowledge to those phenomena bound together by inexorable laws of experimental method or the unity of pantheism which presents all specific items in the world as the necessary manifestation of one true essence. These accounts of unity, the mechanistic and the pantheistic unities cannot explain our consciousness of responsibility, finitude, evil, and death. They cannot explain our awareness of alienation. Coleridge's own theology of unity forms the basis of his radically metaphysical aesthetics. Beauty cannot, he thinks, be understood in empirical terms but as the embodiment of intelligible order and unity: ultimately as the Divine splendour. Whereas the merely agreeable is simply 'congruous with the primary constitution of our senses', the beautiful is 'multeity in unity', and that unity points to the Divine triune Unity. In *The Statesman's Manual* a symbol . . . is characterized by a translucence of the special in the individual, or of the general in the special, or of the universal in the general: '. . . the translucence of the eternal through and in the temporal.' For Coleridge true science is contained in the doctrine of those Symbols forming a Correspondence between the physical and the spiritual worlds. The key to this correspondence is Scripture. The Bible 'contains a Science of *Realities*: and therefore each of its Elements is at the same time a living GERM, in which the Present involves the Future'[49]. Scriptures provides the symbolic articulation of 'great PRINCIPLES' and 'Sublime IDEAS'.

This is required as a counterblast to the 'unenlivened, generalizing Understanding. Prophecy shows things and events in the world as symbols of 'living ideas'—idea in the mind of God who 'as the One and Absolute, at Once the Ground and the Cause, . . . alone containeth in himself the ground of his own nature, and therein of all natures'.[50] It is only on the basis of Coleridge's deeply metaphysical and Trinitarian theology that we can appreciate properly his equally adamant insistence upon the *existential* dimension of religious faith. The human condition is determined by alienation from its Divine source. The soul's dissatisfaction with the

---

[49] Coleridge, *Statesman's Manual*, (in *LS*), p. 49   [50] Ibid.

senses and the soul's inner discord both constitute evidence of its higher vocation and its longing for a transcendent unity. The heart is restless until it rests in God.

THEOLOGY AND SPIRITUALITY: FAITH AS THE LOVE THAT UNITES THE SOUL TO GOD

Coleridge's theology is radically doctrinal. To read his work is to sense his conviction that Christianity is the mechanism of the salvation of the soul through Christ's death. Deeply influenced by his reading of Scripture and in particular St Paul, Coleridge came to see Unitarianism as failing to grasp the 'good news' of the Christian Gospel. Hence the emphasis of contemporary Unitarianism upon the resurrection rather than the crucifixion was a failure to grasp the nature of the specifically Christian dispensation and hope.

Among the theologians who exerted an influence upon Coleridge the place of Robert Leighton (1611–84), Bishop of Dunblane and Glasgow, must be emphasized. Leighton seems to have been decisive for Coleridge at the nadir of his relationship with Wordsworth and with Sara Hutchinson in 1813/14. Leighton's strong theology of grace appealed to Coleridge at this period of personal wretchedness and depression.

Talking about the problem of the efficacy of prayer Coleridge says that the Christian should not wait for '...outward or sensible Miracles from Prayer—It's [*sic*] effects and it's [*sic*] fruitions are spiritual, and accompanied (to use the words of that true *Divine*, Archbishop Leighton) not by Reasons and Arguments; but by an inexpressible kind of Evidence, which they only know who have it.'

Leighton was an Augustinian who thought that the most significant evidence for the Divine was to be found within the soul's awareness of its own contingency; its guilt and remorse pointed beyond itself to the transcendent Divine source. Christian theology must be based upon this 'spiritual evidence' rather than the apparent order of the physical cosmos, or the external miracles performed by Christ; the latter two from of evidence providing the foundations of much Unitarian apologetic and the work of William Paley.

Coleridge wrote in 1822 words about Leighton that constitute remarkably apt self-description:

Leighton has by nature a quick and pregnant Fancy: and the august Objects of his habitual Contemplation, and their remoteness from the outward senses; his constant endeavour to see or to bring all things under some point of Unity; but above all, the rare and vital Union of Head and Heart, of Light and Love, in his own character;—all these working conjointly could not fail to form and nourish in him the higher power, and more akin to Reason—the power, I mean of Imagination.[51]

For Coleridge the life of a Christian is not based merely upon the historical memory of Christ but upon a real contact with the risen Christ. The Spirit is the vehicle through which the resurrected Christ becomes present and manifold in the believers. '*Evidences* of Christianity! I am weary of the WORD. Make a man feel the *want* of it; rouse him, if you can, to the self-knowledge of his *need* of it; and you may safely trust it to its own EVIDENCE.'[52]

This is the sense in which Coleridge's theology was deeply existential while deeply Platonic. His nemesis was William Paley with his frankly Utilitarian and crypto-Unitarian Theology. While for Paley theology is grounded upon the *do, ut des* between God and the soul, for Coleridge Christian theology can only have a true foundation upon the pure love of God. Thus Coleridge sides with the mystics such as Fénelon. Yet Coleridge's own experience of frailty and suffering led him to an almost Augustinian emphasis upon sin and the human need for redemption. The apparent rigour of Augustinianism, Coleridge came to believe, was ultimately comforting for those aware of the real state of humanity on account of its assurance of unmerited grace. By way of contrast the seemingly blithe optimism of semi-Pelagianism masked a cruelty in presenting humanity with practically unattainable goals. This can be seen most clearly in his great works *Aids to Reflection* (1825, 1831) and his sustained critique of Jeremy Taylor's semi-Pelagianism..

SCRIPTURE AND THE SENSE OF HISTORY

One of the essential shifts of consciousness in the eighteenth and nineteenth century was the development of truly historical sense. Ancient writers have little awareness of the shift of meanings of words and even questions of historical evidence play very little role in their thought. Plotinus will happily quote the word of philosophers dead for 600 years or more as if they were contemporaries. Lessing's famous ditch between eternal truths of reason and contingent facts of history did not worry Aquinas or Scotus. This a-temporal mode of thought persisted in the minds of luminaries like Pope. Many Enlightenment thinkers envisaged the culture of France as a universal norm. The Romantic era reacted to this 'timeless' universalism and regarded different historical phases as possessing distinctive principles and norms. It was also marked, understandably, in a era of revolutions from 1789 to 1848 by scepticism about the abiding force of political and social forms. Coleridge was one of the first thinkers in England to grasp this radical

---

[51] John Beer, Editor's Introduction, liii.
[52] *Aids to Reflection*, pp. 405–6.

sense of history and its implications for the authority of Scripture and ecclesiastical tradition. The Socinian attempt to base Christian theology upon miracles looked increasingly question-begging in the light of heightened awareness of the diverse assumptions and reasoning practices of differing cultures. Quite apart from the strictly philosophical questions of how any event deemed supernatural can be judged an act of the Divine, the widespread acceptance of miracles in the ancient world looks increasingly like a cultural and historical phenomenon.

Robert Lowth (1710–87) exerted an enormous impact upon German biblical scholarship in his defence of the 'Sacred Poetry of the Hebrews' (Latin 1754, English 1787) as possessing its own beauties and structures which should not be confused with the Hellenic paradigms. Herder's own momentous defence of the particularity and historical conditioned nature of human cultures was deeply influenced by Lowth. Coleridge only seems to have become aware of Vico (1668–1744) rather late in his career, but Vico's sense that each age has its own distinctive principles and political and social structures must have reinforced Coleridge's strong historical sense.

Yet Coleridge also possessed a powerful sense of the importance of recognizing the difference of the past through a powerful imaginative sympathy and appreciation. In *Confessions of an Enquiring Spirit*, posthumously published by his nephew in 1840, he writes: 'In the Bible there is more that *finds* me than I have experienced in all other books put together; . . . the words of the Bible find me at greater depths of my being; and . . . whatever finds me brings with it an irresistible evidence of its having proceeded from the Holy Spirit.' The emphasis is upon both inward experience and the Trinity. It is often misunderstood as a 'liberal' anti-dogmatic subjectivism. This is quite clearly not the case. In this text we have a brave and lucid attempt to avoid the extremes of bibliolatry, on the one hand, and a corrosive scepticism on the other.

THEOLOGY AND SOCIETY

One of the most important of Coleridge's writings is his *On the Constitution of the Church and State*. In this work Coleridge presents a defence of the Church within society. Coleridge desynonymized 'culture' and 'civilization', a distinction which has inspired critics of Utilitarianism such as Carlyle, Matthew Arnold, T. S. Eliot, and Raymond Williams.[53] *On the Constitution of the Church and State* (1830) is a

---

[53] The distinction is derived from Rousseau via German Philosophy. It was Rousseau in his prize essay 'First Discourse' who had argued that science and the arts had not merely failed to improve but had corrupted mankind.

work on the nature and history of the English constitution, which is a response to the contractualism of French and Scottish Enlightenment.[54] Coleridge saw the State as based upon a dynamic and irresolvable tension between permanence (the landed aristocracy) and progression (manufacturing and professions). The constitution is formed by the 'law of balance' between these principles, and change in the constitution is best understood, Coleridge thinks, as an organic process rather than the mechanical substitution of one system of government with another. Yet he importantly included a third principle which he calls the 'National Church', a group of teachers called the 'clerisy' distributed throughout the land. Mill claims that Coleridge 'vindicated against Bentham and Adam Smith and the whole eighteenth century, the principle of an endowed class, for the cultivation of learning, and for diffusing its results among the community.'[55] This should not be confused with the Christian Church, but represents a common trust of the nation which serves the cultural and spiritual growth of the population.[56] The National Church, constituted by the clerisy, serves to cultivate 'the harmonious development of those qualities and faculties that characterize our *humanity*'. Human minds are not inert instruments which respond passively to stimulus from without, but the discipline and cultivation of the mind is the educating of souls. Culture, as opposed to mere civilization, is the formation of self-conscious reflective rational beings capable of contemplating eternal truths through the symbols of religion.[57] On the other hand, unity is not to be confused with mere uniformity. Society is not merely the sum of individuals but also spiritual community in which eternal values constitute an essential component.

Coleridge's plea is for a group of teachers whose major task is not merely to instruct with facts or information but to educate and cultivate the rational spirit in the young. This education provides contemplative detachment from immediate concerns and needs, and the capacity for contemplation of—and assent to—those immaterial values and principles that distinguish man from beast: 'Civilization is itself but a mixed good, if not far more a corrupting influence . . . where (it) is not grounded in *cultivation*, in the harmonious development of those qualities and faculties that characterize our *humanity*. We must be men in order to be citizens.'[58] Coleridge agrees with Rousseau that 'whatever law or system of law compels any other service, disennobles our nature, leagues itself with the animal against the godlike, kills in us the very principle of joyous well doing, and fights against humanity'.[59]

[54] S. T. Coleridge, *On the Constitution of the Church and State* (Princeton: Princeton University Press, 1976).

[55] See J. S. Mill, 'Coleridge', in *Utilitarianism and Other Essays* (Harmondsworth: Penguin, 1987), p. 212.

[56] See Mill, 'Coleridge', p. 208.

[57] Coleridge, *On the Constitution of Church and State*, pp. 42–3.

[58] Ibid.

[59] Coleridge, *Friend* I, p. 191.

The theory of the clerisy is ostensibly anti-Rousseauian (the view expressed in *Emile* is that clergy should play no role in education) Coleridge's own view of the ideal constitution of the Church and State is a scathing critique (Mill says the 'severest satire') of the Church's *de facto* arrangements.[60]

In the *Table Talk* of September 1830, Coleridge refers to the bitter error of the Church 'clinging to the court and state instead of cultivating the people'. He argues that the state regards people as groups rather than as individuals, such as with regard to birth and property. The (ideal) Church operates from the reverse perspective—treating people as individual persons without gradation of rank: 'A Church is therefore in Idea the only pure Democracy.'[61]

AFTERLIFE AND INFLUENCES: BROAD CHURCH MOVEMENT

After Coleridge's death in 1834, Hare and F. D. Maurice were prominent among those who felt the influence that Coleridge's famous talk—snuffling '*tawlk*', as Carlyle sneeringly noted—was having on the Cambridge writers and members of the Society of Apostles at Trinity College. Tennyson was a member, and encountered Arthur Hallam's enormous interest in Coleridge. John Sterling, later frequently a guest of Coleridge at Highgate, and F. D. Maurice, who dedicated *The Kingdom of Christ* to Coleridge in 1846, were key figures.[62] Both were taught by J. C. Hare, lecturer in Classics at Trinity (1822–32), who himself imbibed 'the life-giving words of the poet-philosopher'. After Coleridge's death, Julius Hare wrote to William Whewell, the Master of Trinity to suggest that a Coleridge memorial prize be established at Cambridge, for essays 'in the philosophy of Christianity'. Whewell eventually put Hare's proposal to the authorities, but it was rejected, and Whewell reported back: 'With our governors, it seems, the vagaries of [Coleridge's] earlier years are better known than the Christian philosophy, which he has impressed on so many in his riper years.' The Cambridge Triumvirate, Westcott, Lightfoot, and Hort showed the effect of his influence, as did the Scottish theologian, Thomas Erskine of Linlathen.[63]

---

[60] J. S. Mill, 'Coleridge', p. 211.

[61] S. T. Coleridge, *Table Talk*, I (Princeton: Princeton University Press, 1990), p. 189.

[62] C. R. Sanders, *Coleridge and the Broad Church Movement: Studies in S.T. Coleridge, Dr Arnold of Rugby, J. C. Hare, Thomas Carlyle, and F. D. Maurice* (Durham: Duke University Press, 1942).

[63] D. Horrocks, *Laws of the Spiritual Order: Innovation and Reconstruction in the Soteriology of Thomas Erskine of Linlathen* (Paternoster, 2005).

The publication of Coleridge's *Aids to Reflection*, with a 'Preliminary Essay' by James Marsh, was a decisive event in nineteenth-century American intellectual history. Through his edition, Marsh aimed to heal the schism between 'old light' Calvinists and 'new light' revivalists among the Congregational clergy. Instead, the work was most effective in Concord, Massachusetts, subject of the first meeting of what became called the Transcendental Club. Here Ralph Waldo Emerson acquired Coleridge's distinction between the Reason and the Understanding that would inform such writings as his 'Divinity School Address'. Ironically, despite his invectives against Unitarianism Coleridge exerted a influence upon American Unitarians, especially Emerson. In 1833 Frederic Henry Hedge, erstwhile professor of logic at Harvard, and then minister in West Cambridge, published an article in The Christian Examiner, 'Coleridge', expounding the latter acutely as relying upon a correspondence between internal human reality and external spiritual reality. In 1836, Emerson published 'Nature', and American Transcendentalism had a deep debt to Coleridge. The seminal religious thought of William James bears the marks of Coleridge via this Harvard Unitarian/transcendentalist tradition. William Greenough Thayer Shedd (1820–94) was one of the leading Presbyterian theologians of nineteenth-century America. Shedd studied at the University of Vermont and was heavily influenced by his mentor, James Marsh (professor of philosophy and disciple of Samuel Taylor Coleridge). Shedd graduated from the University of Vermont in 1839 with a theology and philosophy that exhibited a great sympathy and affinity with Coleridge's thought.

TWENTIETH-CENTURY ENGLISH THEOLOGY

William Temple (1881–1944) is a notable instance of Coleridge's afterlives. (His father Frederick was a contributor to *Essay and Reviews* and was a central member of the Broad Churchmen.) William Temple is one of the most distinguished Archbishops of Canterbury since Anselm, and his works—*Mens Creatrix* (1917), *Christus Veritas* (1924), and *Nature, Man and God* (1934)—bear a Coleridgean strain. Arguably two of the most important post-war theologians in Great Britain in the second half of the twentieth century have been Daniel Hardy (1930–2007) and Colin Gunton (1941–2003). Dan Hardy was an American Episcopalian who taught for much of his life in England, at the Universities of Birmingham and Durham and, although nominally in retirement, at Cambridge (*God's Ways With the World: Thinking and Practising Christian Faith*, September 1996). Colin Gunton was a Reformed English theologian (*The One, the Three and the Many*, 1993). Both developed a distinctively Trinitarian theology with explicit reference to Coleridge, and a deep sense of Coleridge's continuing relevance for contemporary thought.

CONCLUSION

Coleridge has impressed many subsequent theologians through his determination to spiritualize Christian theology: to present an account of the mechanics of salvation worthy of the Christian view of God as good and immaterial. He is also relentless in his refusal to pander to superstition or supernatural materialism.

There are many contemporary critics of religion who see religion as the baneful product of a false belief in a transcendent God. Yet such cultured despisers are inclined to overlook the deep roots of a sense or intimation of both transcendence and 'fallenness' (guilt or sin) in the human condition. Coleridge's starting point, however lofty and arcane his subsequent speculations, is always the human condition: infinite domain of the human soul and its infinite longing for redemption and salvation. As such he will continue to impress those who reflect upon their inner lives and provoke them to reflect. More broadly, Coleridge represents a rich and distinctive tradition of theology, both strongly poetic and metaphysical at the same time. Just as Henry More could draw on Spenser, Coleridge naturally drew upon the poets. He also represents a crucial juncture because of his deep knowledge of German literature and the developments in the theology of his age. Unlike Pusey, or even Newman, Coleridge was aware of the most corrosive German attacks upon the warrant of Scripture. Unlike George Eliot's fictional Mr Casaubon, Coleridge was not merely massively learned and dedicated: he could draw on deep theological resources with which to question the very questions of the Enlightenment. Coleridge was uniquely equipped to consider the implications of the crisis of theology in the nineteenth century and yet also uniquely equipped to construct a productive and constructive response. Coleridge's enduring legacy has been the combination of an inquiring Christian liberality combined with a profound knowledge of the doctrinal tradition.

WORKS CITED

Primary Sources

BARUCH DE SPINOZA. 1986. *Briefwechsel,* trans.into German by C.Gebhardt. Hamburg: Felix Meiner.

CONWAY, ANNE. 1996. *The Principles of the Most Ancient and Modern Philosophy,* eds. Coudert, Allison and Corse, Taylor. Cambridge: Cambridge University Press.

CRABB ROBINSON, HENRY. 1869. *Diary,* ed. T. Sadler. London.

GILLMAN, JAMES. 1838. *The Life of Samuel Taylor Coleridge.* London.

JACOBI, FRIEDRICH HEINRICH. 2000. *Uber die Lehre des Spinoza* Hamburg: Felix Meiner.

LAMB, CHARLES. 1840. Christ's Hospital five and twenty years ago, 1820. In *Essays of Elia: First Series.* Moxon.

MILL, J. S. 1987. Coleridge. In *Utilitarianism and Other Essays*. Harmondsworth: Penguin.

PLOTINUS. 1967–84. *Enneads*, trans. by A.H. Armstrong, 7 vols., Cambridge, MA. and London: Heinemann.

PROCLUS. 1987. *Commentary on Plato's Parmenides*, trs. G. R. Morrow and J. M. Dillon. Princeton: Princeton University Press, p. 505.

—— 1967. *Commentaire sur la Timée*, trans. and notes by A. J. Festugiere. Paris: Vrin.

SAINT AUGUSTINE. 1991. *The Trinity*. Hyde Park, NY: New York City Press. p. 66.

The Collected Works of Samuel Taylor Coleridge, general editor Kathleen Coburn, 16 vols. in 34, Bollingen Series (Princeton, New Jersey: Princeton University Press, 1971–2002).

THOMAS AQUINAS. 1975. *Summa Contra Gentiles* 1. 22, trs. A. C. Pegis, Book One: *God*. London, Notre Dame: Notre Dame Press, p. 119.

WACHTER, GEORG. 1995. *Elucidarius cabalisticus, ed.* W. Schröter in: *Dokumente: Johann Georg Wachter: De primordiia Christianae religionis, Elucidarius cabalisticus, Origines juris naturalis*. Stuttgart-Bad Cannstatt: frommann-holzboog.

Secondary Sources

BENZ, ERNST. 1983. *The Mystical Sources of German Romantic Philosophy*, trans. by Blair R. Reynolds and Eunice M. Paul. Allison Park, Pa: Pickwick Publications.

BENZ, ERNST. 1958. *Die Christliche Cabbala. Ein Stiefkind der Theologie*. Zürich.

GOODMAN-THAU, EVELINE. MATTENKLOTT, GERT SCHULTE, CHRISTOPH, (eds). 1999. *Kabbala und die Literatur der Romantik: zwischen Magie und Trope,*. Tübingen: M. Niemeyer.

HEDLEY, DOUGLAS. 2000. Cudworth, Coleridge and Schelling. *The Coleridge Bulletin*, 16: 63–70.

—— 2000. *Coleridge, Philosophy and Religion*. Cambridge: Cambridge University Press.

—— 2008. *Living Forms of the Imagination*. London: T&T Clark.

HORROCKS, D. 2005. *Laws of the Spiritual Order: Innovation and Reconstruction in the Soteriology of Thomas Erskine of Linlathen*. Paternoster.

SANDERS, C. R., 1942. *Coleridge and the Broad Church Movement: Studies in S.T. Coleridge, Dr Arnold of Rugby, J. C. Hare, Thomas Carlyle, and F. D. Maurice*. Durham: Duke University Press.

SCHMIDT-BIGGEMANN, WILHELM. 1998. *Philosophia perennis Historische Umrisse abendländischer Spiritualität in Antike, Mittelalter und Früher Neuzeit*. Frankfurt am Main.

SCHRÖTER. 1987. *Spinoza in der deutschen Frühaufklärung* Würzburg: Königshausen und Neumann.

UEHLEIN, FRIDERICH, 1982. *Die Manifestation des Selbsbewustseins im konkrten 'ich bin'*. Hamburg: Felix Meiner.

VOLLENWEIDER, SAMUEL 1985. *Neuplatonischer und christliche Theologie bei Synesios von Kyrene*. Göttingen: Vandenhoeck and Ruprecht.

WHITE, P. 1992. *Conflict and Consensus in the English Church from the Reformation to the Civil War*. Cambridge.

CHAPTER 26

....

COLERIDGE AND SHAKESPEARE

....

CHARLES MAHONEY

An endless activity of Thought, in all the possible associations of Thought with Thought, Thought with Feelings, or with words, or of Feelings with Feelings, & words with words—

(*CN* III, 3246 (1808))

Whenever I am reading Shakespear, scarce three pages together can I read but spite of myself I sink back in my Chair, & and cannot go on for the fullness, the overflowingness of Thought & Feeling awakened by the last or by some passage that throws a Light on all the Past—

('On Reading Shakespeare' [1813], *SW&F* I, 345)

WALKING from his lodgings on the Strand to the Royal Institution on 30 March 1808, on the way to deliver the third of his *Lectures on the Principles of Poetry*, Coleridge had his pocket picked, and thereby lost most of his notes for the lecture. Or so he said. Though De Quincey and others corroborated this claim,[1] it is nonetheless almost too good, too Coleridgean to be true—as if the Man from Porlock or the writer of the 'judicious letter' in chapter 13 of the *Biographia* had suddenly materialized to derail another promising Coleridgean scheme. In poor health and perilous financial straits, Coleridge had been invited by Humphry Davy

---

[1] Writing to his sister later in the spring, De Quincey noted that Coleridge 'had his pocket picked of the main part of his lecture as he walked from the Strand; but, having notes, he managed to get through very well' (cited in *Lects 1808–19* (CC) I, 15; see also the account of Edward Jerningham, cited in *Lects 1808–19* (CC) I, 145).

to deliver a course of 25 lectures, for which he was to be paid £140, only to lose his notebook on the evening of the third lecture and thus resume more-or-less extemporaneously. Though such an account may make the 1808 lectures sound like but another Coleridgean fragment, the story of Coleridge's lost notebook is in fact of far more than merely anecdotal interest, for it draws our attention to many of the abiding difficulties attendant upon any attempt to evaluate Coleridge's role as a critic of Shakespeare. In the notes that do remain for this lecture, Coleridge instructs himself at one point to 'read from Pocket book' (*Lects 1808–19* (CC) I, 67), which of course he cannot do—just as his own readers cannot even now turn to one integrated, canonical account of Coleridge's criticisms of Shakespeare.[2] Though this criticism is certainly not lost to us, neither is it immediately accessible, scattered as it is over notes for lectures (there is not a complete text for even one of Coleridge's lectures on Shakespeare), observations collected in the *Table Talk*, marginalia in his various editions of Shakespeare, sundry comments in his letters, numerous notebook entries, and two brief publications assembled from lecture notes (chapter 15 of the *Biographia* [1817] and an excerpt from the 'Essay on the Principles of Method', written for *The Friend* [1818]). Coleridge's lost pocket book, it would appear, presents only too apt a figure for the loss at which readers of Coleridge may find themselves when they attempt to assemble a coherent account of his criticisms of Shakespeare.

Between 1808 and 1819, Coleridge offered a total of eight courses of lectures which were either wholly or partially devoted to considerations of Shakespeare.[3] Of these, the most significant were arguably the first series of 1808 (*Lectures on the Principles of Poetry*), which established much of the critical lexicon and many of the general principles to which Coleridge would return for the next eleven years; the 1811–12 series (*Lectures on Shakespeare and Milton*), for which the most detailed accounts remain (courtesy of the notes and letters of John Payne Collier, Henry Crabb Robinson, and J. Tomalin), the 1813 series in Bristol (*Lectures on Shakespeare and Education*), which most prominently reflects the influence of August Wilhelm Schlegel; and the late series of 1818–19 (*Lectures on Shakespeare*), with its new

---

[2] The definitive texts of the lectures are to be found in *Lects 1808–19* (CC), painstakingly established by R. A. Foakes. But given the fragmentary and sometimes contradictory nature of these notes and records, it is not possible to establish a canonical text for any of the lectures.

[3] *Lectures on the Principles of Poetry* (1808, Royal Institution); *Lectures on Shakespeare and Milton in Illustration of the Principles of Poetry* (1811–12, London Philosophical Society); *Lectures on European Drama* (1812, Willis's Rooms, London); *Lectures on Belles Lettres* (1812, Surrey Institution); *Lectures on Shakespeare and Education* (1813, White Lion, Bristol); *Lectures on the Principles of Judgement, Culture, and European Literature* (1818, London Philosophical Society); *Lectures on Shakespeare* (1818–19, Crown and Anchor, Strand); *Lectures on Shakespeare, Milton, Dante, Spenser, Ariosto, and Cervantes* (1819, Crown and Anchor, Strand). For a more detailed account of this trajectory, see *Lects 1808–19* (CC) I, xxxix–xliv.

attention to what Coleridge had come to denominate 'particular and practical criticism'.[4]

Though the lectures are not the only way to negotiate Coleridge's criticisms of Shakespeare, they provide a coherent narrative around which to organize an account of what many have found to be not merely the most important Romantic criticism of Shakespeare, but the most dynamic, influential analysis of Shakespeare between Samuel Johnson and A. C. Bradley—if not the most indispensable criticism of Shakespeare in English.[5] It is in the lectures that Shakespeare is celebrated as 'the myriad-minded man' (*Lects 1808–19* (CC) II, 112), as the Protean poet 'who now flowed, a river; now raged, a fire; now roared, a lion' (*Lects 1808–19* (CC) I, 225). It is here as well that Iago's Act III soliloquy ('Thus do I ever make my fool my purse') is famously characterized as 'the motive-hunting of motiveless Malignity' (*Lects 1808–19* (CC) II, 315), and Hamlet is said to be 'a man living in meditation . . . , continually resolving to do, yet doing nothing but resolve' (*Lects 1808–19* (CC) I, 390).[6] As unsystematic as it may be, part of the impact of this criticism derives from the fact that so many of the larger critical insights for which Coleridge is justly celebrated find their initial formulation in his lectures on Shakespeare. For example, when in the *Biographia* Coleridge defines 'poetic faith' as 'that willing suspension of disbelief for the moment' (*BL* (CC) II, 6), he may be heard to be drawing on notes for the 1808 lecture series, where he writes of stage presentations that they 'are to produce a sort of temporary Half-Faith, which the Spectator encourages in himself & supports by a voluntary contribution on his own part, because he knows that it is at all times in his power to see the thing as it really is' (*Lects 1808–19* (CC) I, 134).[7] Similarly, when Coleridge later argues that for any poet to be celebrated for genuine poetic power, he must demonstrate 'multeity'—Coleridge's term for the 'power of reducing multitude into unity of effect, and modifying a series of thoughts by some one predominant thought or feeling' (*BL* (CC) II, 20)—he again draws on notes from the lectures of 1808, where he defines poetic beauty as 'a pleasurable sense of the Many . . . reduced to unity by the correspondence of all the component parts to each other & the reference of all to one central Point' (*Lects 1808–19* (CC) I, 35).[8] Such

---

[4] See Coleridge's 1818 prospectus for a course of lectures on Shakespeare, where he proposes not a reflection on general principles but a scene-by-scene analysis (*Lects 1808–19* (CC) II, 34). See also chapter 15 of the *Biographia*, with its initial attention to the 'purposes of practical criticism' (*BL* (CC) II, 19). The phrase was later adopted and given greater currency by I. A. Richards in *Practical Criticism* (1929).

[5] See, for example, Harbage's praise for Coleridge as 'the greatest of Shakespearean critics' (*Coleridge's Writings on Shakespeare* 25, 22).

[6] Here and throughout, cancellations in Coleridge's notes have been silently elided.

[7] See also Coleridge's letter to Daniel Stuart of 13 May 1816 (*CL* IV 642), and his notes on stage 'delusion' apropos *The Tempest* (*CM* (CC) IV, 781).

[8] See also Coleridge's definition of the imagination in lecture 4 of the 1811–12 series (*Lects 1808–19* (CC) I, 249) and his definition of beauty in 'Principles of Genial Criticism' (*SW&F* (CC) I, 369, 372).

instances abound. Whatever their announced topic, the literary lectures were principally concerned with Shakespeare.[9] And it was in thinking, writing, and lecturing about Shakespeare that Coleridge came to formulate the opinions on poetry that inform not merely *Biographia Literaria* but also the 'Essays on the Principles of Genial Criticism' (*SW&F* I, (CC) 353–86), the 'Treatise on Method' (*SW&F* I, (CC) 625–86), and the oracular pronouncements collected in *Table Talk*.

Though he was not approached by Davy to lecture at the Royal Institution until 1806, Coleridge appears to have been thinking about a detailed analysis of Shakespeare's plays as early as 1804, under the aegis of a wide-ranging consideration of morality and English literature with Shakespeare as the centerpiece. In a letter to Sir George Beaumont from February, 1804, Coleridge outlines a plan which in both its general concerns and its specific procedures bears startling resemblance to his eventual treatment of Shakespeare over the course of his lectures between 1808 and 1819:

In explaining what I shall do with Shakespere I explain the nature of the other five. Each scene of each play I read, as if it were the whole of Shakespere's Works—the sole thing extant. I ask myself what are the characteristics—the Diction, the Cadences, and Metre, the character, the passion, the moral or metaphysical Inherencies, & fitness for theatric effect, and in what sort of Theatres—all these I write down with great care & precision of Thought & Language—and when I have gone thro' the whole, I then shall collect my papers, & observe, how often such & such Expressions recur & thus shall not only know what the Characteristics of Shakespere's Plays are, but likewise what proportion they bear to each other. Then, not carelessly tho' of course with far less care I shall read thro' the old Plays, just before Shakespere's Time, Sir Phillip Sidney's Arcadia—Ben Johnson [sic], Beaumont & Fletcher, & Massinger in the same way—so as to see & to be able to prove what of Shakespere belonged to his Age, & was common to all *the first-rate* men of that true Saeculum aureum of English Poetry, and what is his own, & his only—Thus I shall both exhibit the characteristics of the Plays—& of the mind—of Shakespere.... (*CL* II 1054)[10]

Reading each scene as if it were the whole not merely of the play but of Shakespeare's entire *oeuvre*, Coleridge aspires to balance the local insight with the general observation, anticipating the synecdochic reading strategy he would develop in the 1810s, in which he put a great deal of pressure on the opening scenes as representative of the 'judgement with which Shakespear always in his first scenes prepares, & yet how naturally & with what a concealment of art, for the Catastrophe—how he presents the *germ* of all the after events' (*Lects 1808–19* (CC) I, 559). Enumerating the 'characteristics' of Shakespeare's plays, Coleridge attends to

---

[9] See Coleridge's 1807 letter to Davy before undertaking to lecture at the Royal Institution (*CL* III, 29–30), and his 1818 letter to William Mudford, recollecting the same series of lectures (*CL* IV, 839).
[10] Compare the prospectus to the 1811–12 lecture series, *Lects 1808–19* (CC) I, 179.

matters as seemingly minute as diction, cadence, and metre, as all-encompassing as 'moral or metaphysical Inherencies', as imaginative as character and passion, as dramaturgical as a play's 'fitness for theatric effect', and as historical as Shakespeare's relation to the Elizabethans—all concerns of his later analyses of Shakespeare.

Shakespeare's diction is a constant preoccupation of Coleridge's, and nowhere is it more apparent than in Coleridge's marginalia in his various editions of Shakespeare, such as when he observes of Mercutio's last words in *Romeo and Juliet*, 'The wit and raillery habitual to Mercutio struggling with the pain giving so fine an effect to Romeo's Speech, & the whole so completely justifying him' (*M* (CC) IV, 832). Coleridge's attention to metre also manifests itself throughout his marginalia, such as in his list of simple and composite feet in his copy of Theobald's *The Works of Shakespeare* (*M* (CC) IV, 686–7) or in his claim that 'Shakespeare never introduces a catalectic line without intending an equivalent to the foot omitted in the pauses, or the dwelling emphasis, or the diffused retardation' (*M* (CC) IV, 844). Such detailed observations—or what Coleridge termed 'hypercriticism'—correspond throughout this period with his conviction as to 'how little instructive any criticism can be which does not enter into minutiae' (*CN* III, 3970).

Under the heading of 'moral or metaphysical Inherencies' Coleridge may be seen to organize three possibilities: the relation (the relative 'grossness' or high-mindedness) of Shakespeare's manners and morality to that of other Renaissance dramatists (*Lects 1808–19* (CC) I, 521–2); the moral disposition of a play, such as in his criticisms of *Measure for Measure* for being 'degrading to the character of Woman' (*M* (CC) IV, 693); or the 'moral conceptions' that inform his depictions of character, such as in his observations regarding 'the innocent mind of Othello plunged by its own unsuspecting and therefore unwatchful confidence, in guilt and misery not to be endured' (*SW&F* (CC) I, 655). Closely related to Coleridge's interest in moral inherencies and conceptions is his exploration of the 'psychological', a new term at the time which Coleridge deploys to denominate a method both of organizing Shakespeare's works psychologically rather than historically ('flow[ing] from the progress & order of his mind'; *Lects 1808–19* (CC) I, 253) and of describing his development of dramatic character in terms of 'psychologic portraiture' (*Lects 1808–19* (CC) I, 126).[11] Integral to such portraiture is Coleridge's conviction that Shakespeare develops his characters not from observation but from meditation; thus it may be said that they are not copies so much as imitations. As he writes in a letter dating from 1802, 'It is easy to cloathe Imaginary Beings with our own Thoughts & Feelings; but to send ourselves out of ourselves, to *think* ourselves in to the Thoughts and Feelings of Beings in circumstances wholly and strangely different from our own / hoc labor, hoc

[11] See Coleridge's apology for using the term 'psychology' in the 'Treatise on Method' (*SW&F* (CC) I, 655).

opus / and who has atchieved it? Perhaps only Shakespere' (*CL* II, 810). Coleridge's construction of Shakespeare as the Protean poet *par excellence* is predicated upon a conviction of precisely this ability to send himself out of himself, thus 'becom[ing] by power of Imagination another Thing' (*Lects 1808–19* (CC) I, 69).

Coleridge's attention to 'fitness for theatric effect' has less to do with dramaturgy and matters of staging than with what he terms Shakespeare's judgement, or his ability to construct and arrange his plays in accord with the limitations of 'poetic faith' and the demands of 'taste'. Coleridge is concerned in this regard to demonstrate that Shakespeare's judgement (his powers of discrimination and arrangement) was equal to his genius (understood in this context as the power of execution), that Shakespeare was not a 'delightful Monster—wild indeed, without taste or Judgement' (*Lects 1808–19* (CC) I, 79) but, rather, a deliberate, meditative poet, one whose work 'gave proof of a most profound, energetic & philosophical mind' (*Lects 1808–19* (CC) I, 82).[12] In making this argument, Coleridge seeks to overturn two commonplaces of eighteenth-century criticism: not merely that Shakespeare was 'an ignorant man, a child of nature, a wild genius, a strange medley' (*Lects 1808–19* (CC) I, 274–5), but also that the age of Elizabeth was one in which England was struggling to define itself against the darkness, chaos, and relative barbarity of its own past. Rather, according to Coleridge, the reign of Elizabeth witnessed 'a great activity of mind and a passion for thinking & making words to express the objects of thought & invention' (*Lects 1808–19* (CC) II, 287–8), produced such men of genius as Edmund Spenser and Sir Philip Sidney, Sir Walter Raleigh and Lord Bacon, and was in this regard 'favourable to the existence & full developement of Shakespeare' (*Lects 1808–19* (CC) II, 287). And it is in this context that Coleridge constantly attempts to adjudicate 'what of Shakespeare belonged to his Age . . . and what is his own, & his only'.

Coleridge's 1804 letter to Beaumont thus serves as a prologue of sorts to his later, professional interest in Shakespeare over the course of his lectures, and underscores at the outset his multifaceted reading strategies—his attention to textual minutiae as well as historical speculation, to his own critical vocabulary as well as Shakespeare's individual lexicon, to the particular as well as the universal. Appropriate to the first act of one of Shakespeare's plays, it 'presents the *germ* of all the after events' and prompts us to read for a similar vocabulary of organic growth throughout the lectures.

Although not formally announced as a series of lectures on Shakespeare, the 1808 lectures appear to have been conceived of in Shakespearean terms. As Coleridge wrote to Davy, after introducing general, philosophical principles and the principles of poetry, he anticipated that he would then turn directly to 'the genius

---

[12] Compare Coleridge's formulation in chapter 15 of the *Biographia*: 'No man was ever yet a great poet, without being at the same time a profound philosopher' (*BL* (CC) II, 25–6). See also the 1802 letter to Sotheby (*CL* II, 810).

& writings of Shakespere, relatively to his Predecessors & Contemporaries, so as to determine not only his merits [and] defects, the proportion that each merit bears to the whole, but what of his merits & defects belong to his age, as being found in contemporaries of Genius, [and] what belong to himself' (*CL* III, 29–30). There remain detailed notes and records for the first four lectures.[13] Of these, the first addresses the principles of taste (in relation to the principles of poetry), the second sketches the history of the drama before Shakespeare, the third examines Shakespeare's power as a poet, and the fourth initiates Coleridge's examination of Shakespeare as a dramatist. Although this may appear at first to be a disappointingly scant record, it nonetheless provides a crucial foundation for Coleridge's ensuing engagements with Shakespeare in at least three important ways: first, Coleridge's establishment of his own general principles and critical lexicon allows him to move increasingly from the general and abstract to the particular and descriptive in subsequent courses of lectures; second, his analysis of Shakespeare initially as a poet (and only subsequently as a dramatist) not only distinguishes his treatment from most eighteenth-century and Romantic critics,[14] but also foregrounds his later, close readings of Shakespeare's language as decidedly literary (or as he will put it, 'practical') criticism; third, the materials for these lectures form the basis of Coleridge's best-known account of Shakespeare, the analysis of his poetic power in chapter 15 of *Biographia Literaria*.

Coleridge begins the first lecture with a long disquisition on taste, both in its primary sense (tasting a ragout, or mutton) and its metaphorical sense (having a taste for Milton or Shakespeare), in order then to define taste as

> . . . a distinct Perception of any arrangement conceived as external to us co-[existent] with some degree of Dislike or Complacency conceived as resulting from that arrangement. . . . And in this Definition of Taste is involved the definition of the Fine Arts, as being such whose especial purpose is to gratify to the Taste—that is, not merely to adjoin but to combine and unite a sense of immediate pleasure in ourselves with the perception of external arrangement. (*Lects 1808–19* (CC) I, 30)

Such a definition inflects 'taste' as a matter both of pleasure (complacency) and of judgement (perception—here, the ability 'to combine & unite a sense of immediate pleasure in ourselves with the perception of external arrangement' (*Lects 1808–19* (CC) I, 37)). Coleridge's point is twofold: to demonstrate the necessity of defining one's

---

[13] For a representative account of the difficulty of assembling these materials, see Foakes's notes on the texts for the third lecture of the 1808 series (*Lects 1808–19* (CC) I, 60–1).

[14] Schlegel, for example, entirely neglects Shakespeare's poetry, while Hazlitt relegates it to a brief, concluding chapter of *The Characters of Shakespear's Plays*, which he begins by observing that 'Our idolatry of Shakespear . . . ceases with his plays. In his other productions, he was a mere author, though not a common author' (*Works* IV, 357). Remarking that recent claims for the equality of the poems to the plays are but the fashionable and 'desperate cant of modern criticism' (a jab at Coleridge?), he then blithely characterizes *Venus and Adonis* and *The Rape of Lucrece* as 'a couple of ice-houses. They are about as hard, as glittering, and as cold' (*Works* IV, 358).

terms when those terms are so susceptible to being misunderstood and misapplied, and to establish the necessity of doing the same for 'beauty' ('generally admitted as the direct & peculiar Object of the Taste'; *Lects 1808–19* (CC) I, 31), a term similarly susceptible to various inflections. When Coleridge eventually defines beauty as 'a pleasurable sense of the Many... reduced to unity by the correspondence of all the component parts to each other & the reference of all to one central Point' (*Lects 1808–19* (CC) I, 35), he once again incorporates the criteria of pleasure and judgement. Although Shakespeare is nowhere mentioned by name in this first lecture, Coleridge's definitions here make possible numerous later arguments he will make regarding Shakespeare's judgement in relation to his genius. In other words, if Shakespeare gratifies the taste of his readers, it is not merely because of his imagination and inventiveness (genius) but also because of his ability to select and arrange his materials in reference to one central point or principle (judgement)—to 'present a Whole to us combined with a consciousness of its parts' (*Lects 1808–19* (CC) I, 35).

The third and fourth lectures of the 1808 series are similarly critical to our understanding of several larger terms and themes—in this case not only Shakespeare's 'power' as a poet, but also Coleridge's important distinctions between and definitions of fancy and the imagination, which he would later rework in chapters 12 and 13 of the *Biographia*. Drawing repeatedly upon *Venus and Adonis*, Coleridge argues in both lectures that 'Shakespeare appears—from his poems alone, apart from his great works—to have possessed all the conditions of a true Poet' (*Lects 1808–19* (CC) I, 78) due to his numerous 'powers', prominent amongst which is that protean ability 'to become by power of Imagination another thing' (*Lects 1808–19* (CC) I, 69). In addition, 'fancy' here names 'the aggregative Power... the bringing together Images dissimilar in the main by some one point or more of Likeness' (*Lects 1808–19* (CC) I, 67), while 'imagination' names the 'power of modifying one image or feeling by the precedent or following ones' as a result of which 'many circumstances [combine] into one moment of thought to produce that ultimate end of human Thought, and human Feeling, Unity' (*Lects 1808–19* (CC) I, 68), or 'the power by which one image or feeling is made to modify many others, & by a sort of *fusion to force many into one*' (*Lects 1808–19* (CC) I, 81).[15] The absolute essential of poetry, according to Coleridge, is 'to make every thing present by a Series of Images' (*Lects 1808–19* (CC) I, 68), which he illustrates with reference to Wordsworth's lyric 'I wandered lonely as a cloud',[16] and to one couplet in *Venus and Adonis*, 'Look! how a bright star shooteth from the Sky, / So glides he in the night from Venus' Eye' (lines

---

[15] Compare Coleridge's definitions in chapter 12 of the *Biographia* (*BL* (CC) I, 293).

[16] Wordsworth was in fact in attendance at the third and fourth lectures of this series, spent the night with Coleridge, and (according to Richard Holmes) reaped the benefits of these lectures and Coleridge's conversation apropos the 'habits of exalted Imagination' in his lines on St Paul's; see Holmes, *Coleridge: Darker Reflections*, 126–7.

815–16).

Consistent with his conclusions in the 1808 series, Coleridge continues to argue in his 1811–12 lectures that Shakespeare must be understood as a 'two-fold Being...the Poet & the Philosopher', and that he availed himself of it 'to convey profound Truths in the most lively Images, and yet the whole faithful to the character supposed to utter the lines & a further development of that character' (*Lects 1808–19* (CC) I, 267). What is new in these lectures is Coleridge's detailed attention to Shakespeare's characters, as is evident above (an observation made apropos *Love's Labour Lost*, which Coleridge believed to have been Shakespeare's first play) as well as in the prospectus to the course of fifteen lectures on Shakespeare and Milton which Coleridge initiated in November 1811, where he promises 'a philosophic Analysis and Explanation of all the principal *Characters* of our great Dramatist' (*Lects 1808–19* (CC) I, 179), including Othello, Falstaff, Richard III, Iago, and Hamlet. Though he did not begin really to analyse characters until the seventh lecture, the notes and accounts which remain show Coleridge to have given a good deal of attention in the remaining lectures to characterization (Shakespeare's 'psycological genius' (*Lects 1808–19* (CC) I, 306)), dialogue, and plotting in *Romeo and Juliet*, *The Tempest*, and *Hamlet*.

In the 1811–12 series of lectures, Coleridge proceeds first to *Romeo and Juliet*—not because it was among the earliest of Shakespeare's works, but because 'in it were to be found all his excellencies such as they afterwards appeared in his more perfect Dramas but differing from them in being less happily combined: all the parts were present but they were not united with the same harmony' (*Lects 1808–19* (CC) I, 303). The want of harmony here indicates a want of taste, or judgement, which Shakespeare will add once he has been 'disciplined by experience' and thus able to add 'to genius that talent by which he knows what part of his genius he can make intelligible to that part of mankind for whom he writes' (*Lects 1808–19* (CC) I, 304). Of far greater interest to Coleridge than the construction of the play is its characterization. Observing that the principal characters in *Romeo and Juliet* may be divided into two types—those which may be said to be 'representatives of classes which he had observed in society' (*Lects 1808–19* (CC) I, 318), and those which are clearly 'drawn rather from meditation than observation' (*Lects 1808–19* (CC) I, 306)[17]—Coleridge cites Tybalt and Capulet as representative of the former: common characters under the sway of one particular passion who, though deserving of little interest in themselves, 'derive it from being instrumental in those situations in which the most important personages develope their thoughts & passions' (*Lects 1808–19* (CC) I, 305). And it is in developing such characters that Shakespeare explores 'all the minutiae of the human heart' (*Lects 1808–19* (CC) I, 306). Of an entirely different order is Mercutio, 'one of the truly Shakespearean

---

[17] As Coleridge remarks in a subsequent lecture, 'Shakespeare's characters from Othello or Macbeth down to Dogberry are ideal: the are not <the> things but the abstracts of the things which a great mind may take into itself and naturalize to its own heaven' (*Lects 1808–19* (CC) I, 351).

characters' in that he was 'drawn rather from meditation than from observation, or rather by observation that was the child of meditation' (*Lects 1808–19* (CC) I, 306).

Hence it was that Shakespeare's favourite characters are full of such lively intellect. Mercutio was a man possessing all the elements of a Poet: high fancy; rapid thoughts: the whole world was as it were subject to his law of association: whenever he wished to impress anything, all things became his servants: all things told the same tale, and sound as it were in unison: this was combined with a perfect gentleman himself unconscious of his powers[.] It was by his Death contrived to bring about the whole catastrophe of the Play. It endears him to Romeo and gives to Mercutio's death an importance which it otherwise could not have acquired. (*Lects 1808–19* (CC) I, 307).

Arguing that it is on the fate of a poet that the catastrophe depends, Coleridge simultaneously underscores Shakespeare's genius (his creation of such a lively poetic intellect in Mercutio)[18] and his judgement (the connection of Mercutio's death with Romeo's resolve and consequent demise). As he concludes, 'Had not Mercutio been made so amiable and so interesting an object to every reader we could not have felt so strongly as we do the necessity of Romeo's interference or connecting it so passionately with the future fortunes of the lover & the Mistress' (*Lects 1808–19* (CC) I, 307).

Over the course of the remaining lectures in the 1811–12 series, Coleridge entered into extended considerations of *The Tempest, A Midsummer Night's Dream, Richard II, Richard III*, and *Hamlet*. Of these, the detailed records of the lectures on *The Tempest* and *Hamlet* are of particular note. In the former, Coleridge made an important distinction between Shakespeare's real and his ideal plays ('Shakespeare's plays might be separated into those where the real is disguised in the ideal & those where the ideal is hidden from us in the real' (*Lects 1808–19* (CC) I, 357)) before turning to *The Tempest* as representative of the ideal, as a play in which Shakespeare appeals to the imagination since 'the principal and only genuine excitement ought to come from within,—from the moved and sympathetic imagination' (*Lects 1808–19* (CC) II, 268–9). For Coleridge, the sympathetic imagination works hand-in-hand with what he repeatedly terms 'Poetic Faith[,] before which our common notions of philosophy give way' (*Lects 1808–19* (CC) I, 362). Poetic faith is voluntary—as he puts it famously in the *Biographia*, it is constituted by a 'willing suspension of disbelief ' (*BL* (CC) II, 6)—and in *The Tempest* it may be seen to be at work in concert with Shakespeare's judgement, his preparation of the scene for such unreal possibilities as a supernatural tempest, an unflappable boatswain whose demeanor is 'perfect gallows', a marooned magician, an ethereal sprite, and a 'monster' who speaks in blank verse. Arguing again that Shakespeare's genius is integral to his judgement, Coleridge here locates that judgement in such moments as 'the admirable gradations by which the supernatural powers of *Prospero* were disclosed' (*Lects 1808–19* (CC) I, 369),

---

[18] Much as Coleridge will later remark that Prospero is 'the very Shakespeare himself, as it were, of the tempest' (*Lects 1808–19* (CC) II, 269).

and in the introduction of Ariel, at which point Shakespeare 'makes' the reader 'wish that if supernatural agency were employed it should be used for a being so lovely' (*Lects 1808–19* (CC) I, 362). Here, Shakespeare's preparation of the reader is a sign for Coleridge of his abiding judgement, while the reader's willingness to exert his imagination (a product of this preparation) is a sign of his own poetic faith. Indeed, the nebulous nature of Ariel represents precisely this poetic challenge, for he is sufficiently disembodied that both judgement and faith must work in concert: 'In air he lives, and from air he derives his being . . . hence all that belongs to Ariel is all that belongs to the delight the mind can receive from external appearances abstracted from any inborn or [individual] purpose' (*Lects 1808–19* (CC) I, 363). And although Caliban seemingly represents a stark antithesis to Ariel, his intro-duction also represents for Coleridge another instance of Shakespeare's 'admirable judgement and preparation' and a similar challenge to poetic faith, for despite his brutish appearance he is still 'a noble being: a man in the sense of the imagination, all the images he utters are drawn from nature & are highly poetical; they fit in with the images of Ariel: Caliban gives you images from the Earth—Ariel images from the air' (*Lects 1808–19* (CC) I, 364–5). Thus it is that *The Tempest* emerges in Coleridge's reading as an exemplary test for his renewed sense of the operations of stage illusion, in relation to the spectator's 'poetic faith' on the one hand and the poet's judgement on the other.

With regard to *Hamlet*, Coleridge takes it upon himself to demonstrate Shake-speare's judgement in the introduction of the Ghost of Hamlet's father. As is the case in the dagger scene in *Macbeth*, 'the reader is totally divested of the notion that the vision is a figure in the <highly wrought> imagination (*Lects 1808–19* (CC) I, 387), for neither Hamlet nor Macbeth is in any way morbidly preoccupied with the apparition he is about to witness. In Coleridge's words, 'How admirable is the judgment of the poet! Hamlet's own fancy has not conjured up the Ghost of his father: it has been seen by others: he is by them prepared to witness its appearance, & when he does see it he is not brought forward as having long brooded on the subject' (*Lects 1808–19* (CC) I, 386). Because the Ghost is not presented as a product of Hamlet's own distempered imagination, the reader is prepared to exert his imagin-ation, his poetic faith, in countenancing it. Another potential challenge confronting the reader here is that of Hamlet's seeming indecision, his inconsistency, with regard to avenging the death of his father. According to Coleridge, however, 'There was no indecision about Hamlet' (*Lects 1808–19* (CC) I, 387): he knew very well what it was incumbent upon him to do, and he continually resolved to do it. Yet as often as he resolved to act, just as often did he fail to do so. In Coleridge's reading, the entire play turns upon the call to action and the individual mind's response to this exhortation. Thus, in his concluding remarks, Coleridge dilates upon this dilemma in a way that, however obliquely, would appear to comment upon his own notorious irresolution:

Shakespeare wished to impress upon us the truth that action is the great end of existence—that no faculties of intellect however brilliant can be considered valuable, or otherwise than as misfortunes, if they withdraw us from or render us repugnant to action, and lead us to think and think of doing, until the time has escaped when we ought to have acted. In enforcing this truth Shakespeare has shewn the fulness, and force of his powers: all that is amiable and excellent in nature is combined in Hamlet, with the exception of this one quaity: he is a man living in meditation, called upon <to act> by every motive human & divine but the great purpose of life defeated by continually resolving to do, yet doing nothing but resolve.[19] (*Lects 1808–19* (CC) I, 390)

Coleridge too emerges in many contemporary accounts as a man living in meditation, one who can (for example) write a prospectus for a series of lectures far more effectively than he can deliver them or even refrain from digressing as he proceeds through the course. The potential likeness between Hamlet and Coleridge comes even more to the fore in Coleridge's 1813 lectures, where he emphasizes Hamlet's 'enormous intellectual activity, and a consequent proportionate aversion to real action' (*Lects 1808–19* (CC) I, 539), as well as his penchant for 'running into long reasonings—carrying off the impatience and uneasy feeling of expectation by running away from the *particular* in the *general*[;] this aversion to personal, individual, concerns and escape to Generalization and general reasonings a most important characteristic' (*Lects 1808–19* (CC) I, 541).

Another similarity that becomes legible at this period is that between some of Coleridge's arguments regarding Shakespeare (including those pertaining to the relation between his genius and his judgement) and those made by the German critic August Wilhelm Schlegel in his *Über dramatische Kunst und Litteratur* (*On Dramatic Art and Literature*, 3 vols, 1809–11; translated into English in 1815 as *A Course of Lectures on Dramatic Art and Literature*).[20] Sometime between the eighth and ninth lectures of the 1811–12 series, Coleridge appears to have received a copy of at least one of Schlegel's volumes, and Schlegel's influence is immediately discernible in the remaining lectures in this series,[21] as well as in those he gave at the Surrey Institution in 1812 and in Bristol in 1813 (at which point he was reportedly bringing his copy of Schlegel into the lecture room with him). While much has been made of Coleridge's alleged 'plagiarism' from Schlegel,[22] what is finally at stake here is

---

[19] See Crabb Robinson's letter of 3 January 1812, where he observes apropos these concluding remarks, 'Somebody said to me, this is a Satire on himself; No, said I, it is an Elegy. A great many of his remarks on Hamlet were capable of a like application' (cited in *Lects 1808–19* (CC) I, 391)

[20] See Hazlitt's review (*Works* XVI, 57–99), where he notes that 'It is indeed by far the best account which has been given of the plays of that great genius by any writer, either among ourselves, or abroad' (*Works* XVI, 59).

[21] See, for example, Lecture 9, where Coleridge refers to 'a Work by a German writer' and goes on to make a decidedly Schlegelian distinction between 'mechanic and organic regularity' (*Lects 1808–19* (CC) I, 353, 358). For further details pertaining to Coleridge's first acquaintance with Schlegel, see *Lects 1808–19* (CC) I, 172–5, as well as an important letter from December 1811 in which, ironically, Coleridge defends Walter Scott against charges of having plagiarized from *Christabel* (*CL* III, 354–61).

[22] As Foakes notes, what is at stake in aligning Coleridge and Schlegel is not *whether* Coleridge borrowed from Schlegel, but *when*: beginning in December, 1811, the impact of Schlegel 'was so strong in the next few years that all Coleridge's general comments in his lectures, as distinct from his practical criticism, tend to bear the marks of his close reading in Schlegel's lectures. Conversely, then, the lack of

something else entirely: the critical value of the language of 'organic form' for our understanding of both Shakespeare and romantic criticism. Coleridge in no way sought to suppress his indebtedness to a certain 'Work by a German writer', as he termed Schlegel's lectures just before citing his crucial distinction between 'mechanic and organic regularity' (*Lects 1808–19* (CC) I, 353, 358), and he subsequently drew on him almost verbatim in an important lecture given at the Surrey Institution in December, 1812. Arguing again that 'the Judgement of the great Poet [is] not less deserving of our wonder than his Genius' (*Lects 1808–19* (CC) I, 494), Coleridge explains that he is not about to suggest that genius was immune to rules or regulation, but wants to suggest instead that genius (here, poetic spirit) is better understood as being governed by its own internal rules—'the power of acting creatively under laws of its own origination' (*Lectures 1808–19* (CC) I, 494–5)—rather than by such externally imposed criteria as, for example, the three unities or any other arbitrary critical dicta.[23]

Imagine not I am to oppose Genius to Rules—No!—the Comparative value of these Rules is the very cause to be tried.—The Spirit of Poetry like all other living Powers, must of necessity circumscribe itself by Rules, were it only to unite Power with Beauty. It must embody in order to reveal itself; but a living Body is of necessity an organized one—& what is organization, but the connection of Parts to a whole, so that each Part is at once End & Means!   (*Lects 1808–19* I, (CC) 494; compare Schlegel II, 94)

Allowing that poetic genius must be circumscribed by rules, Coleridge argues (following Schlegel) that it is to abide by those rules which arise internally, rather than those rules or criteria which have been externally imposed. No work of art is formless; what is at stake is the agency of shaping and forming the material. Alluding once more to Schlegel, here 'a Continental Critic', Coleridge sets forth the difference between mechanical and organic regulation in decidedly Schlegelian terms:

The form is mechanic when on any given material we impress a predetermined form, not necessarily arising out of the properties of the material—as when to a mass of wet clay we give whatever shape we wish it to retain when hardened[.]—The organic form on the other hand is innate, it shapes as it developes itself from within, and the fullness of its developement is one & the same with the perfection of its outward Form.   (*Lects 1808–19* (CC) I, 495; compare Schlegel II, 94–5)

Thus it is that Coleridge repeatedly observes of Shakespeare that the logic of his plays arises from within their own structure, their own 'nature'.

---

any such influence in lecture-notes that on other grounds appear to be early tends to confirm that they belong to the period before he read Schlegel' (*Lects 1808–19* (CC) I, lxii). Part of the appeal for Coleridge of Schlegel's lectures, according to Foakes, was that he found there 'echoes of his own thought, but well articulated and more coherently set forth' (*Lects 1808–19* (CC) I, lxiii). See also Raysor, I, xxvi–xxviii. For a less accommodating account of Coleridge's use of Schlegel, see Fruman, 141–64.

[23] See Coleridge's disagreement with Johnson's observations on what it would take to make *Othello* into a 'regular' tragedy, *CM* (CC) IV, 863.

Integral to this inflection of the organic is that the form is innate and indwelling. As he remarks elsewhere, in a lengthy metaphor of the poetic process as a living plant, 'the vital principle of the Plant can make itself manifest only by embodying itself in the materials that immediately surround it'; then, once it has done so, 'it takes them up into itself, forces them into parts of its own Life, modifies & transmutes every power by which it is itself modified: & the result is, a living whole' (*Lects 1808–19* (CC) I, 447). In Coleridge's reading of Shakespeare, the surrounding materials are often construed as the politics, literature, and intellectual 'genius' of the age in which he lived, while the modification of these materials may be read in Shakespeare's depiction not of 'individual' characters but of 'classes' of characters, finally the process less of obser-vation than of meditation. Incorporating character, story, and invention into his own work, then, the poet endows them with an agency of their own, such that they—in the end, the words of the plays—generate and modify the play in which they appear. Accordingly, it is because Shakespeare puts on display 'the life and principle of the being, with organic regularity' that 'the separate speeches do not appear to be produced the one by the former but to arise out of the peculiar character of the speaker'—as, for example, the Boatswain in the opening scene of *The Tempest*, when 'a sense of danger impresses all and the bonds of reverence are thrown off and he gives a loose to his feelings and thus to the old Counsellor pours forth his vulgar mind' (*Lects 1808–19* (CC) I, 358). Similarly (and, not coincidentally, once again in relation to the opening scene of a play), Coleridge observes of the 'Weird Sisters' that they establish the 'Key-note of the character of the whole play' ('the invocation is made at once to the Imagination, and the emotions connected therewith'; *M* (CC) IV, 786)—their im-portance confirmed (I.iii) 'after such an order of the King's as establishes their supernatural powers of information' (*M* (CC) IV, 787). What Coleridge here terms 'Key-note' he elsewhere denominates 'germ', a formulation which more aptly captures the 'vital principle' which Coleridge habitually views as representative of Shakespeare's judgement.

In the first of his 1818–19 lectures on Shakespeare, Coleridge quickly distanced himself from Schlegel with the announcement that 'I am proud that I was the first in time who publicly demonstrated to the full extent of the position, that the supposed Irregularity and Extravagances of Shakespear were the mere dreams of... Pedan-try',[24] clarifying that his principal object in these lectures would be 'to prove that in all points from the most important to the most minute, the Judgement of Shake-spear is commensurate with his Genius' (*Lects 1808–19* (CC) II, 263). While such broad claims are familiar, Coleridge's procedure here differs from that of earlier lectures in an important way. Rather than beginning with a discourse on general principles or on the history of the drama, Coleridge adopts what he hopes will be 'a more instructive form' (*Lects 1808–19* (CC) II, 263) of criticizing Shakespeare's plays

---

[24] See also Coleridge's 1818 letters to James Perry (*CL* IV, 831) and William Mudford (*CL* IV, 839).

in a more 'minute' or 'practical' fashion, proceeding scene by scene through the plays under consideration.[25] In support of this critical method, Coleridge did not rely on notes from earlier courses of lectures but instead brought into the lecture hall with him his copy of *The Dramatic Works of William Shakespeare* (ed. Samuel Ayscough, 2 vols, 1807), which he had had rebound with interleaved blank sheets on which he had written prefatory essays and detailed commentary on the texts (*Lects 1808–19* (CC) II, 257; *CM* (CC) IV, 778–9). Reflecting Coleridge's annotations and local concerns, these lectures concentrate throughout on what he elsewhere termed 'hypercriticism' (*CN* III, 3970)—in this case close critical attention to such seeming 'minutiae' as meter, rhyme, personae, diction, 'quibbles', and imagery in support of the organic development and unity of the play under scrutiny. Take, for example, Coleridge's reflections on Mowbray's challenge to Bolingbroke in the first scene of *Richard II* ('To prove myself a loyal gentleman / Even in the best blood chamber'd in his bosom; / In haste whereof, most heartily I pray / Your highness to assign our trial-day' (I.i.148–51):

Q[uer]y. The occasional interspersion of rhymes and the more frequent winding up of a Speech therewith—what purpose was this to answer? In the earnest Drama, I mean.— Deliberateness? An attempt as in Mowbray to collect himself and *be cool* at the close? I can see that in the following Speeches the rhyme answers the purposes of the Greek Chorus, and distinguish[es] the *general* truths from the passions of the Dialogue—but this is not exactly to *justify* the practice which is unfrequent in proportion to the excellence of Sh[akespeare]'s Plays.—One thing, however, is to be observed—they are *historical, known,* & so far *formal* Characters, the reality of which is already a *fact.* (*M* IV, 797)

Attending to something as seemingly innocuous as the transition from blank verse to a closed couplet, Coleridge reads there not only a formal pattern (its repetition in numerous speeches early on in the play) but also an insight into the formality of the characters themselves (for whom unrhymed verse may be too colloquial), the tension between the 'deliberateness' of the versification and the passions of the characters themselves, and, as a cumulative result, the mood created by what he elsewhere terms 'intercurrent verse' (*M* (CC) IV, 795). In this way, a minute observation prompts more comprehensive speculations regarding versification, character, and tone, all potentially to be assembled in support of the play's organic unity.

Similar observations abound throughout Coleridge's marginalia, such as in his commentary on Horatio's remarks, 'Let us impart what we have seen to-night / Unto young Hamlet' (I.i.169–70)—'the unobtrusive and yet fully adequate mode of introducing the main Character, *Young* Hamlet, upon whom transfers itself all the interest excited for the acts & concerns of the King, his Father' (*M* (CC)

---

[25] See Coleridge's 1818 prospectus for a series of lectures on Shakespeare, in which he designates his method 'particular and practical criticism' with a scene-by-scene analysis of the plays under consideration (*Lects 1808–19* (CC) II, 35).

IV, 841)—or his commentary shortly thereafter when the King addresses Laertes, 'And now, Laertes, what's the news with you? / You told us of some suit; what is't, Laertes?' (I.ii.42–3)—'Shakespear's art in introduc[ing] a most important but still subordinate character first.... So Laertes—who is yet thus graciously treated from the assistance given to the election of the King's Brother instead of Son by Polonius' (*M* (CC) IV, 841). As slight as these observations may appear, they nonetheless may be seen to remind us simultaneously of the priorities of Coleridge's critical method at this period and of many of the headings of his evaluation of Shakespeare. '*Young* Hamlet', for example, underscores both what Coleridge elsewhere celebrates as 'Shakespear's *instinctive* propriety in the choice of Words' (*CM* (CC) IV, 799) and his judgement in introducing the main character in such an unobtrusive yet 'fully adequate' manner. And Shakespeare's judgement is similarly on display in representing the King's interest in Laertes (that is to say, Hamlet's rival) before there is any indication of his disposition toward his stepson Hamlet. In Coleridge's hands, all such details contribute to the 'living whole' that is the play, 'in which we may in thought & by artificial Abstraction distinguish the material <Body> from the indwelling Spirit, the contingent or accidental from the universal & essential, but in reality, in the thing itself, we cannot separate them' (*Lects 1808–19* (CC) I, 447).

However arbitrary and accidental Coleridge's marginalia and incomplete notes may sometimes sound, more often than not they will be found to participate in the 'living whole' that is Coleridge's unique style of Shakespeare criticism, at once abstract and particular, equal parts practical and speculative intervention. Due in part to his insistence on Shakespeare as a poet, Coleridge's criticism of Shakespeare repeatedly reveals many of his steadfast beliefs about the necessary 'powers' of great poetry: the power of making everything present by a series of images; the power of fancy in bringing together dissimilar images; the power of imagination in modifying these images and forcing the many into one; the Protean power of the poet in sending himself out of himself; the power of the poet to imitate (rather than copy) nature; and the power of the poem, understood as an organic form, in relating all of the parts to the whole. Coleridge's critical dicta also often underscore what he himself aspires to achieve in his lectures on Shakespeare: to bring into the fullest play the imagination and reason of his auditors, and to make his auditors better as well as wiser (*Lects 1808–19* (CC) I, 515, 522). Although Coleridge did not lecture or publish on Shakespeare after 1819, his continued preoccupation with him is evident most memorably in his conversation, as recorded in the *Table Talk*. It is here that Coleridge designates Shakespeare 'the Spinozistic deity, an omnipresent creativeness', further remarking that 'Shakespeare's rhymed verses are excessively condensed; epigrams with the point every where; but in his blank verse, he is diffused with a linked sweetness long drawn out' (*TT* (CC) I, 125), and it is here as well that he observes of Shakespeare that 'one sentence begets the next naturally; the meaning is all inwoven. He goes on kindling like a meteor through the dark atmosphere' (*TT* (CC) I, 356). Finally, in one of the final conversations recorded in *Table Talk*, Coleridge describes Shakespeare thus:

> Shakespeare is of no age.... The construction of Shakespeare's sentences, whether in verse or prose, is the necessary and homogenous vehicle of his peculiar manner of thinking. His style is not the style of the age....
>
> I believe Shakespeare was not a whit more intelligible in his own day than he is now to an educated man, except for a few local allusions of no consequence. As I said, he is of no age— nor of any religion, or party, or profession. The body and substance of his own works came out of the unfathomable depths of his own oceanic mind—his observation and reading supplied him with the drapery of his figures.   (*TT* (CC) I, 467–8)

Perhaps something similar might be said of Coleridge:[26] the innovations of his criticism came out of the depths of his own mind and years of thinking on the principles of poetry, while his close reading in Shakespeare provided him with the necessary figures, accidents, and minutiae to substantiate his claims. 'Shakespeare' names not merely the poet who exceeded his own age and genius, but also the occasion of Coleridge's most important literary criticisms.

WORKS CITED

FOAKES, R. A., ed. 1989. *Coleridge's Criticism of Shakespeare*. Detroit: Wayne State University Press.

FRUMAN, NORMAN. 1971. *Coleridge, The Damaged Archangel*. New York: George Braziller.

HARBAGE, ALFRED. 1959. Introduction to Terence Hawkes, ed., *Coleridge's Writings on Shakespeare*. New York: Capricorn Books.

HAZLITT, WILLIAM. 1930–4. *The Complete Works of William Hazlitt*, ed. P. P. Howe. London and Toronto: J. M. Dent and Sons.

HOLMES, RICHARD. 1998. *Coleridge: Darker Reflections, 1804–1834*. New York: Pantheon.

RAYSOR, T. M., ed. 1960. *Coleridge's Shakespearean Criticism*. 2 vols. 2nd edn rev. London: Dent, Everyman's Library.

SCHLEGEL, A. W. 1815. *A Course of Lectures on Dramatic Art and Literature*. trans. John Black. 2 vols. London.

[26] Henry Nelson Coleridge makes a similar observation in the first (1835) collection of Coleridge's *Table Talk*; see *TT* (CC) I, 468 n. 9.

CHAPTER 27

COLERIDGE AND THE ENGLISH POETIC TRADITION

CHRISTOPHER R. MILLER

WHEN he was a university student, Coleridge was visited in his rooms by a ghost—or so he later jokingly reported in a letter to a friend. It was the shade of Thomas Gray, who urged the budding poet to 'write no more verses—in the first place, your poetry is vile stuff'.[1] The choice of Gray as messenger of discouragement was particularly apt, for this popular eighteenth-century poet had not only preceded Coleridge at Cambridge, he had also wondered in his ode 'The Progress of Poesy' (1757) who would become the legitimate successor to Shakespeare, Milton, and Dryden. Voicing a common concern about the continuing vitality of the English poetic tradition, Gray poses the unanswered question, 'Oh! lyre divine, what daring spirit / Wakes thee now?' It is not likely that he would have recognized the young Coleridge as that daring spirit; nor, for that matter, did Coleridge think of himself in this way, either early or late in his career.

And yet if a 'progress of poesy' were written in the twenty-first century (perhaps in critical prose rather than in verse) it would certainly include Coleridge in its

[1] *Collected Letters of Samuel Taylor Coleridge*, ed. Earl Leslie Griggs (Oxford: Clarendon Press, 1956), 1: 27.

ranks. It would do so in part because in 1798 he collaborated with his friend and rival William Wordsworth on *Lyrical Ballads*, one of the single most important collections of poetry in the English canon. By the later accounts of both men, the plan was that Coleridge's poems would emphasize the marvelous or supernatural, and Words-worth's the common and everyday. That division of mimetic labor is manifest in the difference between Coleridge's major contribution, 'The Rime of the Ancient Mariner', and the poem that concludes the collection, Wordsworth's 'Lines Composed a Few Miles Above Tintern Abbey'. The first is a long allegorical ballad about a seemingly deathless sailor condemned to tell the story of how he wantonly killed an albatross at sea and suffered ghoulish punishments as a result; the second is a meditative lyric in which the poet revisits a beloved spot with his sister, to whom he addresses a fond wish for future contentment under the genial influences of nature. It would be misleading, however, to use this contrast to make a larger generalization about Coleridge's poetry—misleading because Coleridge himself was disposed to write about ordinary settings and situations; and because his poem, 'Frost at Midnight', which did not appear in *Lyrical Ballads*, profoundly shaped Wordsworth's poetic approach in 'Tintern Abbey'. In 'Frost at Midnight' and other poems, Coleridge developed a lyric form whose influence can be felt to this day; and his ideas about poetry have had a lasting effect on Anglo-American literary criticism.

In essence, Coleridge advanced the tradition envisioned by Gray by departing from the kind of ode that his predecessor exalted. From the Greek for 'song', the word 'ode' denotes a poem on some lofty or serious theme, often addressed to a deity or personified abstraction. English odes were generally not meant to be sung as their ancient Greek precursors were, but they often alluded to song, for they aspired to something of the aural immediacy and emotional pulse of vocal music; and in their tones of solemn celebration, they functioned as secular counterparts to the religious hymns sung by a church choir or congregation. In the mid-eighteenth century, no worthy epic successor to Milton had emerged, and in that gap, the shorter lyrical form of the ode occupied a place of prestige. It is for this reason that Gray includes John Dryden and not Alexander Pope in his pantheon of immortals: Dryden wrote, among other things, the odal 'Song for St Cecilia's Day' (1687) which celebrated the patron saint of music; but while Pope wrote his own 'Ode for Music' on the same occasion, he was better known for his work in less soleman poetic genres. Pope's *Essay on Man* (1733–4), for instance, treats serious philosoph-ical themes, but it does so with urbanely conversational leisure rather than hymnal ardency. In Dryden's ode, the first voice is that of the divine Creator calling a primordial chaos of atoms into a new harmony ('Arise, ye more than dead' (7)); but the first (and only) voice of Pope's poem is unmistakably that of the author himself, who teasingly urges a friend to set aside worldly concerns to muse with him upon the mystery of that creation ('Awake, my St John! Leave all meaner things / To low ambition, and the pride of kings' (1–2)). Both poems notably begin with a brisk act of awakening, but the relationships implied by that act dramatically differ: the first implies a vertical hierarchy between deity and creation, whereas the second constructs a horizontal rapport between peers; the first is a mystical invocation, the second a social invitation.

In his own poetic style, Coleridge hovered between these two modes; and to appreciate that balance, it is useful to consider the differences between two poems that Coleridge wrote in 1796: the 'Ode to the Departing Year' and 'The Eolian Harp'. Like 'The Progress of Poesy', both of them invoke symbolic lyres, but only the first is written in the eighteenth-century vein of sublimity exemplified by Gray; the second is decidedly not an ode, but rather something Coleridge vaguely called an 'effusion'. Like Gray's poem, Coleridge's ode is about a 'progress' of sorts—the passage of time rather than a succession of poets—and it represents that passage as a solemn procession:

> Spirit who sweepest the wild harp of Time!
> It is most hard, with an untroubled ear
> Thy dark inwoven harmonies to hear!
> Yet, mine eye fixed on Heaven's unchanging clime,
> Long had I listened, free from mortal fear,
> With inward stillness, and a bowèd mind;
> When lo! its folds far waving on the wind,
> I saw the train of the departing Year!
> Starting from my silent sadness
> Then with no unholy madness
> Ere yet the entered cloud foreclosed my sight,
> I raised the impetuous song, and solemnized his flight.
>
> $(1-12)^2$

The 'Spirit' hailed in this ode is Divine Providence, the mysterious power that impels the turning year and plays the 'harp of Time.' In a twist on the conventional trope in Gray's ode, Coleridge's harp represents time rather than poetry, but the metaphor is still apt: music is a temporal art, its successive notes standing for the lapse of hours and days; and its major and minor modes and various styles might suggest the diversity of events, both joyous and tragic, in a single year.

There is a dark undersong to this harp-music, which the poet hears in a kind of nightmare; it is full of 'women's shrieks and infants' screams' (51), 'the Earth's unsolaced groaning' (82), and a voice foreboding 'years of havoc yet unborn' (86). In essence, the poem recounts a dream-vision of the passing year as a 'train' of personified abstractions—Hope with her 'wishful gaze' (20), 'young-eyed Joys' (22), 'Ambition in his war-array' (38), Death wielding his 'mortal mace'—mingled with more particular scenes of human suffering. At the temporal cusp of his 'Progress', Gray worries about the fate of the English poetic tradition, but in the

---

[2] Samuel Taylor Coleridge, *The Complete Poems*, ed. William Keach (London: Penguin, 1997). All quotations of Coleridge's poetry refer to this edition.

fiercely apocalyptic mode of a biblical prophet, Coleridge is anxious about the fate of the country as a whole. His tranquil 'mother Isle' (122) may be an Edenic sanctuary set apart from the violence of the French Revolution and European battlefields, but it is not impervious to the world's turmoil. More specifically, Coleridge implies that England could suffer divine retribution for its continued profiting from the slave trade, which it did not outlaw until 1807. This was a provocative, even dangerous, statement to make, and Coleridge circumspectly avoids uttering it directly: instead, he draws on the multivocal resources of the ode, delegating his grim prophecy to the year's 'fervent Spirit' to utter; and he frames the whole poem as a troubling dream or hallucination from which he wakes with relief.

Gray and his contemporaries had never put the ode to such politically contentious uses. In many ways, the dire tenor of Coleridge's poem echoes the strains of William Collins' 'Ode to Fear' (1746) which hails a terrible deity whose 'ghastly train' features the stalking figures of Danger and Vengeance; but unlike Coleridge's allegorical fiends, these powers remain generalized and abstract, and are never directed at anyone or anything in particular. Collins wishes to channel the sublime emotion of Fear into his own art, treating it as a daemonic Muse that once possessed Shakespeare in the most chilling passages of his tragedies. It is customary in the English ode to ask the deified subject for instruction, and Collins accordingly wishes to be tutored in what he sees as the fundamental impulse in Shakespeare's art: 'Teach me but once like him to feel' (69). Coleridge's Spirit of the Departing Year functions as a similar tutelary figure, but its lessons are more dire, with more immediate bearing on the poet's own historical moment. Here, no fictive pretext needs to be invented to excite the emotion of fear; History itself is the presiding muse, and creates plenty of reasons to be afraid.

The formality and elaborate artifice of the ode might seem ill-suited to Coleridge's political purposes, but these features offered a few advantages. Since it traditionally observed or defined a solemn occasion, the ode was a fitting lyric genre for a sober year-end meditation; and its abstract language enabled the poet to universalize his commentary. Rather than specifically mentioning England's slave trade, for instance, Coleridge laments 'Afric's wrongs, / Strange, horrible, and foul!' (88–9), and rather than blaming an impassive and corrupt parliament or church, he refers, in elevated diction, to a 'deaf Synod, "full of gifts and lies"' (91). In practical terms, such generalization veils Coleridge's social protest, but it also gives the poem a biblical grandeur and trans-historical scope: the sufferings of a whole continent are mourned, and the guilt is laid upon generations of deliberative bodies as well as all who have profited from slavery.

Coleridge valued many features of the ode—its quasi-religious solemnity, its passionate intensity, its rhythmic irregularity—and he learned much from predecessors such as Gray and Collins; but his best poetic work lay elsewhere, in a new lyric form that has come to be known as the 'conversation poem'. Coleridge himself coined this epithet to describe 'The Nightingale' (1798), but an influential 1928 essay by G. M. Harper applied that label to a handful of other poems, the earliest being 'The Eolian Harp' (1795).[3] In broadening the descriptive scope of the term, Harper meant to praise something new and admirable in Coleridge's poetry, but the poet himself used it in a more apologetic way. As someone who had considered pursuing a career as a Unitarian minister and thought of himself as a philosopher, journalist, and lecturer, Coleridge was always rather tentative about his role as poet, especially in the shadow of Wordsworth; and so the term 'conversation' was meant as a kind of disclaimer for informality and improvisational looseness. The point is made even more strongly in 'Reflections on Having Left a Place of Retirement' (1796), to which Coleridge added the subtitle, 'A Poem which affects not to be Poetry', and a Latin motto, *sermoni propriora* ('more suitable as prose').

How are we to understand Coleridge's place in the poetic tradition when the author himself so emphatically insists that he is barely writing poetry at all? Though Coleridge was genuinely unsure of his poetic powers, it should be kept in mind that he had a wry and self-deprecating sense of humor; moreover, in declaring a break from or variation on generic conventions, he was implicitly asserting his own originality. In 'The Eolian Harp', Coleridge plays on the same trope that animates Gray's ode—the inspired and inspiring music of the lyre—but with a dramatically different opening gesture and setting. Gone is the artificially induced phantasmagoria of the 'Ode on the Departing Year':

> My pensive Sara! thy soft cheek reclined
> Thus on mine arm, most soothing sweet it is
> To sit beside our cot, our cot o'ergrown
> With white-flowered jasmin, and the broad-leaved myrtle,
> (Meet emblems they of Innocence and Love!)
> And watch the clouds, that late were rich with light,
> Slow saddening round, and mark the star of eve
> Serenely brilliant (such should wisdom be)
> Shine opposite! How exquisite the scents
> Snatched from yon bean-field! and the world so hushed!
> The stilly murmur of the distant sea
> Tells us of silence.
>
> (1–12)

Rather than beginning with the titular harp or some other symbolic abstraction, the poet affectionately addresses his fiancée, Sara Fricker; rather than setting his poem in a mythical landscape, he locates himself in Somerset, in south-west England, where he had rented a cottage. In the spirit of that personal and

---

[3] Harper's 1928 essay was the first to apply the term 'Conversation Poem' to lyrics other than 'The Nightingale'. The essay is collected in *English Romantic Poets: Modern Essays in Criticism*, ed. M.H. Abrams (London: Oxford University Press, 1975, 2nd edn), 188–201.

geographical specificity, Coleridge describes his surroundings with observational precision, noting the time of day, the kind of vegetation growing on the property, the look of the sky, the far-off sound of waves in the Bristol Channel.[4] The speaker of an ode is usually alone and nearly invisible, a disembodied voice or priest-like celebrant; Coleridge, on the other hand, appears very much in the flesh. More shockingly, so does his beloved: the two recline together in an embrace involving the frankly erotic contact of cheek and arm; and they do nothing more momentous than watch the day pass into night. Though lofty abstractions are invoked (innocence, love, wisdom), they are mentioned in parenthetical asides rather than odal apostrophes, as if Coleridge were writing a letter or journal entry, or simply musing aloud in the presence of a companion.

While the exclamatory fervor of the poem recalls eighteenth-century odes on sublime subjects, Coleridge significantly departs from that tradition in choosing blank verse rather than rhyming stanzas—thus following in the footsteps of Shakespeare, who wrote his plays largely in unrhymed iambic pentameter, and Milton, who chose that poetic form for *Paradise Lost*. Coleridge would later write a play with strong Shakespearean overtones, and 'The Eolian Harp' might be thought of as free-standing soliloquy, an extended dramatic speech that creates its own situation and setting. He was also a great admirer of Milton, and though he never fulfilled his ambition to write a Miltonic epic on the origin of evil, Coleridge shared his predecessor's sentiments about the expressive possibilities of blank verse. In the preface to *Paradise Lost*, Milton defended his choice of poetic form by citing the precedent of Shakespearean tragedy and denouncing rhyme on both aesthetic and moral grounds: the 'jingling sound of like endings' was not only 'of no musical delight' but also a form of 'bondage' that compelled the poet to choose words for their sound more than their sense.[5] Rather than being shaped by rhyming phrases, blank verse lines are typically structured as prose sentences, and enjambed rather than end-stopped, so that the sense of a line can, in Milton's phrase, be 'variously drawn out'. Coleridge would later suggest in the *Biographia Literaria* (1817) that the reader of blank verse 'should be carried forward, not merely or chiefly by the mechanical impulse of curiosity, or by a restless desire to arrive at a final solution; but by the pleasurable activity of the mind excited by the attractions of the journey itself'. Poetic lines, he insisted, should seem naturally fluent, '[l]ike the motion of a serpent...or like the path of sound through the air'. Though Milton's and Coleridge's preferences for blank verse were informed by somewhat different motives,

---

[4] Jack Stillinger has suggested that Coleridge's new domestic situation—the companionship of friends, marriage to Sara Fricker in 1795, the pleasant influence of rural Somerset—significantly contributed to the poet's creative inspiration. In essence, Stillinger argues that Coleridge wrote better poems in the country than in the city. See Stillinger, 'Pictorialism and Matter-of-Factness in Coleridge's Poems of Somerset', in *The Wordsworth Circle*, 20:2 (1989), 62–8.

[5] John Milton, *Paradise Lost*, ed. David Scott Kastan, based on the edition of Merritt Y. Hughes (Indianapolis: Hackett Publishing, 2005), 5. All quotations of the poem refer to this edition.

both insisted on its emancipatory quality, its capacity to register sinuous move-
ments of thought.

For Coleridge's purposes, the most influential eighteenth-century heir of
Milton's blank verse was William Cowper, who adopted the form for his long
poem, *The Task* (1785). A widow by the name of Lady Austen who befriended the
poet requested a poem in blank verse on the whimsical subject of the sofa; and what
began as a mock-epic and quasi-odal tribute to a piece of furniture grew into a six-
book poem exalting the pleasures of quiet domestic life over the busy affairs of the
world, the country over the city. The poem was both about leisure and enabled by
leisure, for in a prefatory remark Cowper explains that it was by virtue of having
time on his hands that he could relax and pursue the 'winding train of thought to
which his situation and turn of mind led him'.[6] Rather than following a predeter-
mined plan or structure, the poem was supposed to grow organically out of the
rhythms of thought, and what Milton saw as the freedom of blank verse enabled
that fluidity.

Cowper's poem enjoyed great popularity, and Coleridge was not alone in his
appreciation when he praised 'the divine chit-chat of Cowper' (*CL*, I. 197)—that is,
a poetic mixture of Miltonic solemnity and conversational informality. By 'divine,'
Coleridge primarily meant 'delightful'; but the adjective also tacitly alludes to
Cowper's fame as the author of religious hymns. By writing informal, unrhymed
'chit-chat', Cowper was far from rejecting stanzaic form or more serious verse; he
was simply exploring the possibilities of a flexible and intimate poetic idiom. In his
varied poetic output, he was capable of writing both personal reminiscences about
collecting blackberries as a child and public declarations of faith in a God who
'plants his footsteps in the sea, / And rides upon the storm'. That versatility
certainly appealed to Coleridge, and Cowper's blend of the solemn and the playful
can be recognized in the colloquial yet philosophically serious tones of 'The Eolian
Harp'.

In 'The Progress of Poesy', Gray begins with a formal command to the emblem-
atic harp: 'Awake, Eolian lyre, awake, / And give to rapture all thy trembling strings'
(1–2). In Coleridge's poem, on the other hand, the poet himself seems awakened by
an actual harp, startled by its sudden burst of sound:

> And that simplest lute,
> Placed length-ways in the clasping casement, hark!
> How by desultory breeze caressed,
> Like some coy maid half yielding to her lover,
> It pours such sweet upbraiding, as must needs
> Tempt to repeat the wrong!

---

[6] See *The Poems of William Cowper*, 2 vols., vol. 2, ed. John D. Baird and Charles Ryskamp (Oxford: Clarendon Press, 1995).

The eolian harp was a musical novelty-instrument played by the wind moving through its strings, so that its weirdly throbbing notes were purely random, never to be repeated in the same way twice. Like Gray, Coleridge draws connections between the lyre and his own poetic art, but the first association that comes to mind is a mischievous comparison between the instrument and Sara Fricker: one is mounted in a window-frame to catch passing breezes, the other is clasped in her lover's arms; both audibly respond when provoked, whether by a gust of air or by a companion's teasing remark. This idea of dynamic response becomes the governing theme of the poem, as Coleridge's true philosophical concern emerges: what, in short, is the human mind like? Perhaps it could be compared to the eolian harp, since both are finely sensitive to external stimuli. If the mind could be likened to a natural phenomenon, perhaps the reverse equation could also be made: perhaps all living things—birds, flowers, trees—'tremble into thought' under the sway of 'one intellectual breeze, / At once the Soul of each, and God of All' (46–8).

There were a few problems with this speculation, however. From a metaphysical standpoint, it could account for the way the mind *responds* to the world but not for how it actually *originates* thought. From Coleridge's Christian perspective, the metaphor was also troubling, for it raised the unorthodox premise that the soul was not an exclusively human property, and that God was not so much the divine creator and redeemer of biblical tradition as an animating current running through all things. Here is where the flexibly conversational form of Coleridge's poem was especially useful: instead of making definitive declarations, the poet could write as if he were thinking out loud; and since he was addressing Sara, he could use her as sounding-board and skeptic. Though Sara never actually speaks in the poem, the 'mild reproof' from her 'more serious eye' (49) says enough to make the poet retreat from his extravagant musings. Coleridge had his own doubts about his ideas, but by expressing them through Sara's disapproving glance, he turned a philosophical monologue into an intimate dialogue, thus once more sounding the theme of dynamic response—the give and take of conversation, the teasing repartee of a romantic couple, the rhetorical pulse of statement and counter-statement. Rather than seeing the notion of the 'conversational' in dismissive terms, later twentieth-century critics have valued Coleridge's poetic mode for precisely this dialogic nature. Since his lyrics are heard and sometimes responded to by some addressee or auditor, Coleridge can ironize his thoughts and statements—to see them as provisional, potentially flawed, and subject to critique or retraction.[7]

---

[7] For a discussion of irony in Coleridge's poetry, see Anne Mellor, *English Romantic Irony* (Cambridge: Harvard University Press, 1980), 137–64. Mellor describes a tension between the vision of a world in constant flux and the 'demand for coherent meaning'. Mellor focuses mainly on the 'Rime of the Ancient Mariner', 'Kubla Khan', and the Dejection Ode; but in a contemporaneous study, Kathleen Wheeler makes similar arguments about 'The Eolian Harp', describing a species of Romantic irony without specifically invoking the term. See Wheeler, *The Creative Mind in Coleridge's Poetry* (London: Heinemann, 1981), 65–91.

Though Coleridge cannot adequately answer his question about the nature of the mind, he does manage to suggest the ongoing, associative flow of thought. When Gray begins his ode at 'Helicon's harmonious springs' (3), he invokes a mythical point of origin for poetry, but when Coleridge refers to 'vain Philosophy's aye-babbling spring', he means something else entirely (57): he is likening thoughts to '[b]ubbles that glitter as they rise and break' from that ever-ending mental flow. The bubble was a traditional emblem of vanity and transience, and by invoking the metaphor, Coleridge seems to dismiss his own passing thoughts; but in their ebullient glittering, the river-bubbles also suggest the beauty and wonder of human cognition.

In his offhand way, Coleridge thus introduced a significant innovation on the eighteenth-century ode. 'The Eolian Harp' places itself in a topographically real setting while harking back to a mythical landscape of poetic inspiration; it addresses both intangible abstractions ('O the one life within us and abroad') and an intimate companion ('And thus, my love!'); and it moves between solemn and playful modes, between Philosophy and Eros, between daring speculation and orthodox piety. In many ways, Coleridge's poem amplifies and refines characteristics and tendencies of poetry of previous decades. Elaborately descriptive landscape poems, such as James Thomson's *The Seasons*, were enormously popular; and Gray himself had written the site-specific 'Ode on a Distant Prospect of Eton College', in which he revisits his old school and nostalgically reflects on his vanished youth. The sonnet form, which enjoyed a revival in the late eighteenth-century in the work of such poets as William Lisle Bowles and Charlotte Smith, had often been used for solitary meditations in natural settings, such as a riverbank or shoreline, often at dusk. Coleridge had attempted several sonnets himself, and he valued the form for its economy of expression in articulating a single feeling. He was not so happy with his efforts, however. 'I love Sonnets', the poet wrote in a letter, 'but *upon my honour* I do not love *my* Sonnets' (*L* I. 287). In frustration with the clichés of the sonnets of Bowles that he had once admired, Coleridge even wrote a parody under the pseudonym of Nehemiah Higginbottom. With exaggerated self-pity, the poem begins, 'Pensive at eve, on the *hard* world I mused, / And *my poor* heart was sad; so at the Moon / I gazed, and sighed, and sighed' (1–3). The extra sigh wittily suggests the exhaustion of a poetic vocabulary: Coleridge himself was not above musing on the world or gazing on the moon in his own poetry, but he hated the emotional clichés that went along with such activities. In both emulating and writing against the poetry of his eighteenth-century predecessors, Coleridge created his own distinct idiom and form.

We can see the interplay of tradition and innovation in 'The Nightingale', which first appeared in *Lyrical Ballads*. Nothing could be more traditional than writing a poem about a nightingale: it was a perennial emblem of the poet pouring out beautiful music in the dark; and it inevitably recalled the Greek myth of Philomela, who was raped, silenced by the removal of her tongue, and finally turned into a nightingale to lament her misfortune in an endless song without words. Read as an allegory of poetry, the story of Philomela represents a counter-myth to the legend of the Hippocrene: rather than being drawn from a magical stream, artistic inspiration comes out of suffering and hard experience. When Coleridge listens to the nightingale in his poem, he inevitably thinks of this tradition:

> And hark! the Nightingale begins its song,
> 'Most musical, most melancholy' bird!
> A melancholy bird! Oh! idle thought!
> In nature there is nothing melancholy.
>
> (12–15)

Coleridge's term 'conversation poem' refers primarily to the fact that he is speaking to Sara, now his wife, as well as William and Dorothy Wordsworth; but he is also engaged in a dialogue with poetic tradition and with himself. In describing the nightingale as 'most musical, most melancholy', he is quoting Milton's epithet for the bird in 'Il Penseroso' (1631); but in the next moment he overhears himself making the allusion and retracting it. Coleridge is not directly rebuking Milton—he knew that 'Il Penseroso' was deliberately written from the perspective of a melancholy man—but rather satirizing the impulse to imitate a poetic idiom and frame of mind. In essence, he traces a progress of poesy in miniature, which runs from the originary Milton to 'many a poet' who 'echoes the conceit', and finally to the 'youths and maidens most poetical' who 'must heave their sighs / O'er Philomela's pity-pleading strains' (35, 38–9). This genealogy is not so much a progress, however, as a story of decline—from a true poet to merely 'poetical' devotées. In the guise of writing a poem about listening to a nightingale, Coleridge performs an act of literary criticism akin to Wordsworth's Preface to the 1800 edition of *Lyrical Ballads*. Wordsworth here rejects what he calls 'poetic diction'—the use of outworn mythical figures, formulaic metaphors, allegorical personification—in favor of simpler and more direct language. Though the two poets had philosophical disagreements about the nature of poetic language, Coleridge fundamentally shared Wordsworth's aversion to the artificial and stilted; both in their own ways purported to reinvigorate the English poetic idiom.

In his insistence on departing from the melancholic tradition of nightingale poetry, Coleridge devotes the second half of his poem to three scenes of listening to the bird's song, each of which might be described as a happily sociable conversation. In the first, Coleridge hears a whole chorus of nightingales who 'answer and provoke each other's song, / With skirmish and capricious passagings' (58–9), not unlike the flirtatious banter between the poet and his fiancée in 'The Eolian Harp'; and in the second, a 'gentle Maid' (probably Wordsworth's sister Dorothy) hearkens to a similar chorus awakened into song by a breeze, '[a]s if some sudden gale had swept at once / A hundred airy harps' (81–2). Finally, in the present moment of utterance, the poet imagines that his own baby son Hartley would, if he were not sleeping indoors, place his hand to his ear and bid his elders, loitering in the night air, to listen to the nightingale. In a poem that begins with a reflection on the problem of perceiving the world through rote poetic formulas, it is apt that Coleridge ends with a scene of preverbal sensation. Though Hartley is 'capable of no articulate sound,' he 'knows well / The evening-star' (92, 97–8) and 'laughs most silently' (103) at the play of moon-beams; blissfully ignorant of the poetic tradition of nocturnal melancholy, he might, in his father's hopes, come to associate the night with joy rather than sorrow.

Like 'The Eolian Harp', and distinctly unlike the 'Ode to the Departing Year', 'The Nightingale' purports to be a site-specific utterance that takes place within a particular lapse of time. As much as Coleridge's ode concerns the thematic *idea* of time, it does not mimetically register the experiential *passage* of time. When, in the last strophe of the ode, the poet hears a brood of vultures portending disaster for England ('And hark! I hear the famished brood of prey / Flap their lank pennons on the groaning wind' (151–2)), he invokes a sound that is as purely notional and symbolic as the 'wild harp of Time' that opens the poem. But when Coleridge exclaims toward the end of 'The Nightingale', 'That strain again! / Full fain it would delay me!' (90–1), he implies a spontaneous response to an actual bird, which repeats a song-phrase heard in the beginning of the poem. The sensory fact of that echo—the sheer awareness of repetition—suggests the passage of time, and the duration of the poem itself as an utterance in time.

By implication, the form of the poem is shaped not by a predetermined structure but rather by the vagaries of natural phenomena and the meandering course of the poet's own mental associations. Though Coleridge begins the final verse paragraph with a formal gesture of leave-taking ('Farewell, O Warbler!' (87)), the resurgence of the bird's song inspires the affectionate digression on Hartley and affords an excuse to linger among friends a while longer; and in the end, the goodbye must be reiterated, this time with conclusive force ('Once more, farewell, / Sweet Nightingale!' (109–10)). In light of the eighteenth-century odal tradition in which Coleridge was steeped, it was odd to write a lyric poem that emphasized its inability or unwillingness to end, and its responsiveness to external stimuli rather than internal structural principles.

Though a poems such as 'The Eolian Harp' and 'The Nightingale' might seem formless, critics have identified an underlying pattern or shape in them. Most saliently, M. H. Abrams has credited Coleridge with inventing what he calls the 'greater Romantic lyric', a poetic form in which a solitary speaker stations himself in a particular place, figuratively departs in a reverie of recollection or anticipation, and finally 'returns' with a new sense of his situation.[8] In geometric terms, such a

---

[8] M. H. Abrams, 'Structure and Style in the Greater Romantic Lyric', in *From Sensibility to Romanticism*, ed. Frederick Hilles and Harold Bloom (New York: Oxford University Press, 1965), 527–60. In his 1928 essay on Coleridge, G. M. Harper noticed a closural gesture in the conversation

poem might be described as a circle, always coming back to where it began; and in musical terms, it might be likened to a sonata, with its threefold process of exposition, development, and recapitulation. With reference to Coleridge's predecessors, Abrams cogently identified the way that the Romantic lyric abstracted the spatial excursions of eighteenth-century landscape poetry into mental movements. In this way, Abrams helps us to see how poems such as 'The Nightingale' addressed and at least partially solved the aesthetic problem that Samuel Johnson identified in the popular topographical poetry of his time: a 'want of method'—that is, the lack of a coherent narrative and perceptual order to 'appearances subsisting all at once.'[9] In a natural world of endless variety and countless things, how should the poet proceed? Poems such as *The Seasons* suggested the rambling itinerary of a long walk (or several walks), but Coleridge typically situates himself in one spot and wanders only in his imagination; and no matter how far his thoughts take him, he always ends up centripetally drawn back to that starting-point.

The situation of being confined and stationary informs two of Coleridge's finest conversation poems, 'This Lime-Tree Bower My Prison' (1797) and 'Frost at Midnight' (1798)—both of which find liberation in purely imaginative movement. In the first, he finds himself unable to join his friends on a country walk after an injury to his foot, and must content himself with sitting in a grove of trees instead; and in the second, he keeps an insomniac vigil in a draughty cottage while his son sleeps peacefully nearby. The metaphor of imprisonment is a knowingly melodramatic and self-pitying gesture—Coleridge had a flair for such hyperbole—but it aptly suggests the challenge that the poet poses for himself: overcoming the limitations of being in one time and place rather than another, bridging the distance between the solitary self and others. In 'This Lime-Tree Bower', Coleridge's approach to the problem can be tracked through grammatical changes of addressee: the poem begins with a soliloquy-like statement heard by no one ('Well, they are gone, and here must I remain' (1)); it speculatively charts, in third-person description, the friends' course ('Now, my friends emerge / Beneath the wide wide Heaven' (20–1)); it singles out one of those friends and affectionately apostrophizes him ('My gentle-hearted Charles!' (28)); it ecstatically ascends to an odal fiat

poems that he called 'the return'; and W. J. Bate (*Coleridge* (New York: Macmillan, 1968)) suggested that this feature reflected an impulse 'to return home—return to the hearth, the domestic and simple virtues, the humanly direct and unpretentious' (49). Bate takes Coleridge's lyrics to be so 'open' that they lack a 'protective superimposed form' (48), but Abrams' articulation of the structure of the 'greater Romantic lyric' corrects that notion. Albert Gérard offered a corollary to Abrams' formula when he suggested the metaphor of systole (contraction) and diastole (expansion) to describe the progress of Coleridge's lyrics. See Gérard, 'The Systolic Rhythm: The Structure of Coleridge's Conversation Poems', in *Coleridge: A Collection of Critical Essays*, ed. Kathleen Coburn (Englewood Cliffs, N.J.: Prentice-Hall, 1967).

[9] See Johnson's essay on James Thomson in *Lives of the English Poets*, ed. George Birkbeck Hill (Oxford: Clarendon Press, 1905), 3: 299–300.

('Ah! slowly sink / Behind the western ridge, thou glorious sun!' (32–3)); and it concludes with a benediction on the friend. Meanwhile, in the course of these shifts, time visibly passes, as late afternoon deepens into twilight, a bat '[w]heels silent by' (56–7), and a last lone rook flies 'along the dusky air / Homewards' (68–9). These movements form the backdrop for Coleridge's own mental shift from self-pity to ecstatic communion.

In the previous century, evening—the temporal threshold between day and night—had become the emblematic moment of lyric utterance, under the strong influence of several lyrical descriptions of twilight in *Paradise Lost*. This time of day was especially associated with a contemplative or melancholy mood, a sense of the ephemeral, an effort of perceptual adjustment in a darkening world. Collins' 'Ode to Evening' (1747) exemplifies this moment; and within the odal tradition it is peculiar in treating its subject as both a muse-like deity *and* as the specific moment of utterance. It is only in this atmosphere of calm, when 'Air is hushed' and the 'bright-haired Sun' yet lingers in the west, that the poet can receive inspiration from his goddess, and an urgently reiterated 'now' emphasizes that point: 'Now teach me, Maid composed, / To breathe some soften'd strain.' The opening of Gray's highly influential 'Elegy Written in a Country Churchyard' (1751) features a similarly contemplative twilight setting, and it, too, associates the poetic vocation with this time of day:

> The curfew tolls the knell of parting day,
> The lowing herd wind slowly o'er the lea,
> The plowman homeward plods his weary way,
> And leaves the world to darkness and to me.
>
> (1–4)[10]

In the crossed paths of lyric speaker and plowman at dusk, Gray marks a symbolic intersection between the material labor of the field and the invisible work of poetic thought. The 'parting' of day, herd, and plowman serves as fugal counterpoint to the speaker's activity, which is to linger in a churchyard reading tombstones in the waning light; while the rest of the world heads home to sleep, the poet lingers outdoors, lost in thought.

Coleridge adopts this temporal setting in several of his conversation poems, but his version of evening tends to be a more dynamic and processual one. Far more than his predecessors, and even more than Wordsworth, he registered complex, wayward, ephemeral thoughts and sensations in time. 'This Lime-Tree Bower', for instance, arrives at evening in the course its utterance; and in the poem's artfully composed atmosphere of spontaneity, events are observed as they pass, including the poet's own mental adjustments and serendipitous discoveries. In this way,

---

[10] Thomas Gray, *The Complete Poems*, ed. H. W. Starr and J. R. Hendrickson (Oxford: Clarendon Press, 1966).

Coleridge is capable of surprising himself, as the act of describing his friends' walk comes to serve as vicarious enjoyment of it: 'A delight / Comes sudden on my heart, and I am glad / As I myself were there!' (43–5). As the sun goes down, the poet traces his own arc of thought.

'Frost at Midnight' is set in the middle of the night and thus lacks that measure of time; but the sleepless poet finds an external counterpoint to his oscillating thoughts in the regular breathings of his infant son and the fluttering of an ember in the fire-grate. The imaginative task of describing thought still preoccupies Coleridge, but unlike 'The Eolian Harp', this poem does not propose a single unifying emblem for it. We might expect the titular frost to perform a symbolic role akin to that of the harp, but it is more subtle and mysterious than that—a force that 'performs its secret ministry / Unhelped by any wind' (1–2). The frost might represent the mind's gradual accretions and fractal branchings; or it might suggest natural forces beyond the mind's control or ken, 'the numberless goings on of life, / Inaudible as dreams' (12–13). It is not even clear whether the word 'frost' denotes the active agency of cold or its visible and tangible effect on the surfaces of the world; and that ambiguity itself reflects the imaginative challenge of representing thought as both activity and thing, both contemplation and its object.

The primary act of thought in the poem is association, the drawing of connections between things on the basis of perceived likenesses. The poet's restless mind finds 'dim sympathies' and a 'companionable form' in the flickering ember, since it, too, stirs within a still and silent room. By another association, the reverie of watching the fluttering film in the fire-grate—what Coleridge calls, in folk parlance, a 'stranger'—brings back the memory of similar daydreams during his school days in London, when he gazed at a waning fire and recalled summer days of his earlier childhood in the Devonshire countryside. Even amid that nostalgic recollection of the past, the boy's mind would anticipate the near future: as he pretends to read his book, he indulges the superstition that a 'fluttering stranger' in the fireplace portends the arrival of an actual stranger or visitor who would change the shape of a routine day in some unpredictable way; and the occasional opening of the schoolroom door continually raises these hopes. The random, back-and-forth swaying of a door, with its afforded glimpses of a world elsewhere, makes an apt metaphor for the poem's mental movements—between past and present, present and future, country and city, adult and child. For Coleridge, any single moment of thought was really a complex manifold: watching an ember or learning a lesson in school was anything but a single-focused activity; a sight is interleaved with a sound, one scene superimposed upon another. 'Who ever felt a single sensation?' the poet once wrote. 'Is not every one at the same moment conscious that there co-exist a thousand others, a darker shade, or less light, even as when I fix my attention on a white house or a grey bare hill or rather long ridge that runs out of sight each way.'[11]

---

[11] Samuel Taylor Coleridge, *Anima Poetae*, ed. E. H. Coleridge (London: Heinemann, 1895), 102–3.

In the climactic turn of 'Frost at Midnight', Coleridge watches Hartley sleeping in his cradle and projects happy scenes of the child's future in the natural world: 'But thou, my babe! shalt wander like a breeze / By lakes and sandy shores' (54–5). Like all parents who imagine their children as better versions of themselves, Coleridge here draws a contrast between the memory of his own tedious school-room lessons and an anticipated sensory education in the 'eternal language' (60) of nature uttered by God. Before this point, the poet has been musing silently to himself, but as in his other conversation poems, he cannot resist the social impulse to imagine an audience; and the gesture is all the more touching for being addressed to a sleeping infant who can neither hear nor respond to the apostrophe. (A few months after Coleridge wrote the poem, Wordsworth would imitate this gesture in 'Tintern Abbey', turning midway through the poem to address his sister Dorothy and express his hopes for *her* future.) Coleridge does not speak to his son as one would to a baby, of course. His diction is pitched between odal sublimity and conversational familiarity, and within a few lines, he addresses both his child ('My babe so beautiful!' (48)) and God ('Great universal Teacher!' (63)) with the same vocative intensity. The final verse paragraph, a kind of prayer for the child, is a marvel of closural eloquence, for it brings the poem back to its starting point even as it looks ahead to winter midnights (and spring days) yet to come:

> Therefore all seasons shall be sweet to thee,
> Whether the summer clothe the general earth
> With greenness, or the redbreast sit and sing
> Betwixt the tufts of snow on the bare branch
> Of mossy apple-tree, while the nigh thatch
> Smokes in the sun-thaw; whether the eve-drops fall
> Heard only in the trances of the blast,
> Or if the secret ministry of frost
> Shall hang them up in silent icicles,
> Quietly shining to the quiet moon.

The declarative statement that begins the poem ('The frost *performs* its secret ministry') is here transposed into the subjunctive future ('*if* the secret ministry of frost *shall* hang them'), so that the present moment of poetic utterance is carried into Hartley's adulthood; and father and son stand, figuratively speaking, at the same window. What Coleridge notices this time that he had not mentioned before is the 'silent icicles' under the eaves, as well as the moon itself; and that difference registers both a shifting focus of attention and ongoing changes in the world outside the window—droplets that lengthen into icicles, a moon that rises and sets. Two lapses of time are represented here: the hour of the poet's nocturnal musing and the larger future span of seasons and years.

Without mentioning the divine agency of the previous verse paragraph, Coleridge's description presents a benevolent force of nature that clothes the world with vegetation and adorns it with glistening ice. It is as if the poet were writing a child's primer on seasonal variety, with iconic pictures of summer greenery and winter snow, thawing and freezing, robin and apple-tree. It is a deliberately naïve and childlike view of the world, but also an Edenic one, with a strong echo of Eve's tribute to Adam in *Paradise Lost*: 'With thee conversing I forget all time', she says in a kind of love-lyric to her mate, 'All seasons and their change; all please alike' (4. 638–9). And because her experience has been entirely in Adam's companionate presence, Eve adds that no time—whether morning or evening, rain or shine—'without thee is sweet' (4. 656). Coleridge, on the other hand, insists that all moments in nature will be sweet to his son regardless of whether the two are together to share them. It is striking that a lyric poem that begins with a solitary speaker ends with the projection of a solitary listener out in the world; and Wordsworth emulates this gesture at the end of 'Tintern Abbey' when he imagines a happy future for his sister even in his absence.

All of the conversation poems register the poet's solitude and stationary position, but none with so much anguish as 'Dejection: An Ode' (1802), one of the last great lyrics Coleridge would write. Coleridge first composed the poem as a verse-letter to Sara Hutchinson, the sister of Wordsworth's fiancée Mary Hutchinson, and the woman for whom he had an adulterous and unconsummated longing. In revising the first version, Coleridge eliminated some of the more painfully revealing hints of that desire, including the recipient's name; and in these changes, an intensely personal 'Letter' became a more generalized (though no less anguished) 'Ode'. Though it formally addresses Sara (anonymously hailed as 'Lady' and 'friend devoutest of my choice' (47, 148)), the poem is also implicitly directed at Wordsworth, who was in the midst of writing his own ode, subtitled 'Intimations of Immortality'. In that poem, Wordsworth poses the troubling question of what happens to the 'visionary gleam' of childhood—the freshness and wonder of the world—when one becomes an adult. His ultimate answer is that while the gleam can never be fully recovered, the loss is compensated by a gain in imaginative power (the poetic capacity to invent metaphors) and stoic wisdom (a tragic but ennobling sense of mortality). Coleridge did not dispute the appeal of Wordsworth's solution to the crisis, but he was less sure of its application. Far more acutely than his friend and poetic rival, Coleridge broods over the problems that thwart his imaginative powers and emotional well-being: unspecified 'afflictions' (82), which in his case included insomnia, various physical ailments, and an addiction to opium; the futile attempt to find solace in 'abstruse research' (89); the deadening effect of habit; and morbid 'viper thoughts' (94) that prey on his mind.

If Coleridge's ode strictly followed its eighteenth-century predecessors, it might invoke Dejection as a presiding spirit, a muse-like figure akin to Collins' Fear. Instead, Dejection is nowhere deified, nor even mentioned by name except in the title itself. As if to suggest the inadequacy of odal abstraction, Coleridge attempts several times to articulate the nature of his own dejection, describing it as a 'dull pain' (20), a 'grief without pang, void, dark, and drear' (21), an aching gap between seeing beauty and feeling it, the failure of his 'genial spirits' (39), and a 'smothering weight' (41) on his breast. In the most typically odal moment in the poem, the poet declares the antidote to his problem:

> Joy, virtuous Lady! Joy that ne'er was given,
>   Save to the pure, in their purest hour,
> Life and Life's effluence, cloud at once and shower...

> (64–6)

The declamatory exuberance echoes the tenor of eighteenth-century odes, but Joy is not deified or asked for inspiration; Coleridge knows that he can only describe it as a vital life-force, not summon it at will. Since Joy is vaguely personified as a 'sweet voice' (71), we might suspect that Coleridge was thinking of the unnamed Lady herself as a giver of joy; but the poet never goes so far as to ask her for anything. Indeed, in a rare moment of odal personification, he asks for a blessing on *her*: 'Visit her, gentle Sleep! With wings of healing' (128). Like 'Frost at Midnight', the poem ends with a prayer for another person's well-being, but with a desolate sense that the poet has no part in that blessing.

Like 'Frost at Midnight', the Dejection Ode is a nocturnal vigil that measures the duration of its utterance: it begins by describing a tranquil evening in which the poet has been 'gazing on the western sky, / And its peculiar tint of yellow green' (28), anticipates an impending storm, and finally marks the harbinger of that storm in a fierce 'wind / Which long has raved unnoticed' (96–7). The participle 'unnoticed', without the explicit agency of a perceiver, suggests that the poet has become so absorbed in contemplation that he has become temporarily oblivious to the outside world. Coleridge's turn to the weather suggests the ongoing nature of thought itself—a silent, invisible, and continuous activity anterior to the writing (or speaking) of the poem. Beyond measuring a span of time, the advent of the storm signifies a hoped-for revival of the poet's spirits. Recalling the vitalizing power of the wind in 'The Eolian Harp', Coleridge begins the Ode with the hope for renovation:

> Those sounds which oft have raised me, whilst they awed,
>   And sent my soul abroad,
> Might now perhaps their wonted impulse give,
> Might startle this dull pain, and make it move and live!

> (17–20)

Not only does the wind fail to signify the universal and divine spirit that animates 'The Eolian Harp', it cannot even perform this hoped-for salutary function: it might startle the poet out of his musings, but it cannot truly lift him out of his depression. Coleridge's poetic habit of representing the duration of lyric utterance here acquires special poignancy, because this temporal interval cannot be made to coincide with a revival of the spirit. Though Coleridge's 'dull pain' might 'move and live' in poetic language, it is no less vexing by the end of the poem; and no odal gesture of invocation or banishment can alleviate the problem. The enabling fiction of many conversation poems is that lyric utterance is therapeutic, in that it allows the speaker space and time to work through a problem and emerge with a new perspective on the world. This is painfully not the case in the Dejection Ode. Seventeen years after Coleridge wrote this poem, John Keats composed his own dejection-ode, the 'Ode to a Nightingale'; and its time-hauntedness—its conceit of an opiate drunk 'one minute past', its temporal reference to 'this passing night', its aural measure of the nightingale's receding song—owes something to Coleridge's acute temporal reckonings. Indeed, many of Keats's poems bear genetic traces of his predecessor's poetry, and scholars have noted other poets' debts to Coleridge.[12] While lyric form alone could not revivify Coleridge's spirits, it indisputably invigorated the English poetic tradition.

WORKS CITED

Primary Texts

COLERIDGE, SAMUEL TAYLOR. 1895. *Anima Poetae*, ed. E. H. Coleridge. London: Heinemann.

—— 1956. *Collected Letters*, ed. Earl Leslie Griggs. Oxford: Clarendon Press.

—— 1997. *The Complete Poems*, ed. William Keach. London: Penguin.

COLLINS, WILLIAM. 1979. *The Works of William Collins*, ed. Richard Wendorf and Charles Ryskamp. Oxford: Clarendon Press.

COWPER, WILLIAM. 1995. *The Poems*, 2 vols., vol. 2, ed. John D. Baird and Charles Ryskamp. Oxford: Clarendon Press.

GRAY, THOMAS. 1996. *The Complete Poems*, ed. H. W. Starr and J. R. Hendrickson. Oxford: Clarendon Press.

MILTON, JOHN. 2005. *Paradise Lost*, ed. David Scott Kastan, based on the edition of Merritt Y. Hughes. Indianapolis: Hackett Publishing.

POPE. ALEXANDER. 1963. *The Poems of Alexander Pope*, ed. John Butt. New Haven: Yale University Press.

Secondary Texts

ABRAMS, M. H. 1965, Structure and style in the Greater Romantic lyric. In *From Sensibility to Romanticism*, ed. Frederick Hilles and Harold Bloom. New York: Oxford University Press, 527–60.

BATE, W. J. 1968. *Coleridge*. New York: Macmillan.

GÉRARD, ALBERT. 1967. The Systolic Rhythm: The Structure of Coleridge's Conversation Poems. In *Coleridge: A Collection of Critical Essays*, ed. Kathleen Coburn. Englewood Cliffs, N.J.: Prentice-Hall.

---

[12] In Jack Stillinger's estimation, Coleridge 'exerted a powerful influence on the language of subsequent English poetry, right up to our own time'. See Stillinger, *Romantic Complexity: Keats, Coleridge, and Wordsworth* (Urbana and Chicago: University of Illinois Press, 2006), 153.

JOHNSON, SAMUEL. 1905. James Thomson. In *Lives of the English Poets*. ed, George Birkbeck Hill. Oxford: Clarendon Press.

MELLOR, ANNE. 1980. *English Romantic Irony.* Cambridge, Mass.: Harvard University Press.

HARPER, G. M. 1975. Coleridge's conversation poems. In *English Romantic Poets: Modern Essays in Criticism*, ed. M.H. Abrams. London: Oxford University Press.

STILLINGER, JACK. 1989. Pictorialism and matter-of-factness in Coleridge's poems of Somerset. *The Wordsworth Circle*, 20 (2): 62–8.

—— 2006. *Romantic Complexity: Keats, Coleridge, and Wordsworth.* Urbana and Chicago: University of Illinois Press.

WHEELER, KATHLEEN. 1981. *The Creative Mind in Coleridge's Poetry.* London: Heinemann.

CHAPTER 28

COLERIDGE AND EUROPEAN LITERATURE

MATTHEW SCOTT

COLERIDGE conceived of English Literature both as a discrete national tradition, one whose two very different peaks were Milton and Shakespeare, and also as an integral part of a wider western European enterprise with a heritage that is predominantly classical. He was then, as in so many areas of his thought, a somewhat divided man but one at least who remained relatively untroubled by this apparent contradiction. More important in any case, he was a literary enthusiast throughout his life, gobbling up a diverse diet of reading from various European traditions, in oddments that are now lost to all but the specialist as well as in works of canonical significance. As a lecturer and talker, he was central to defining the terms under which British readers in the nineteenth century discovered European, and especially German literature. Meanwhile, however, although it is not our subject here, he played a supreme role in the construction of the canon of English literature and was, in the Romantic sense at least, a nationalist of sorts. Indeed, one of his most telling contributions to the national literary culture is surely the creation in *Biographia Literaria* of practical criticism, the close empirical study of literary texts, which has remained at the heart of Anglo-American letters ever since. But in that very book, he also pioneered a form of study in which literature is read as philosophy, or the former considered in light of the latter: a kind of cultural analysis that seems to herald the influence of continental literary theory before the fact. The two, very different volumes of *Biographia* are the most succinct manifest-ation of our complex critical debt to Coleridge and they are testament to a legacy that must place him amid a very select group of writers, such as John Dryden, George Eliot, and Ezra Pound, who did much to advance the historical terms under which literary culture in English understood itself as a separate, on-going tradition while also facilitating the means by which that culture could see itself as part of a larger international project. He shares, in common with those other writers, a commitment to the task of translation as well as to the critical appraisal of the English literature of his time, one that is alive to its foreign influences and prophetic about its future international character. This essay will seek to explain the ways in which these apparently opposing aspects of his literary enthusiasm grew together and remained fundamental to one another, while also pointing to the most important connections to European literature within Coleridge's oeuvre.

Coleridge's Reading

Coleridge's own famous description of his reading self was as a 'library-cormorant', an early epithet employed during a letter from Bristol to John Thelwall in Novem-ber 1796:

I am, & ever have been, a great reader—& have read almost every thing—a library-cormorant—I am *deep* in all out of the way books, whether of the monkish times, or of the puritanical æra. I have read & digested most of the Historical Writers—; but I do not *like* History. Metaphysics, & Poetry, & 'Facts of mind'—(i.e. Accounts of all the strange phantasms that ever possessed your philosophy-dreamers, from Tauth, the Egyptian, to Taylor, the English Pagan), are my darling Studies. (*CL*, 1, 260)

The letter speaks to us immediately of a rather overwhelming desire to impress an elder but even allowing for this it provides a useful sense of the breadth of Coleridge's interests. As a unique category, literature—understood in the terms of the traditional academy—was, of course, of central importance to Coleridge but it was never really a free-standing field, being always closely related to other arenas of intellectual endeavour. Elinor Shaffer, among others, has demonstrated that his early literary ambitions were epic in scope, if unrealized, and they were as such deeply inclusive, pretending to incorporate the study of history, theology and philosophy. Here it is worth noting that poetry is sandwiched between two other disciplines that are quasi-philosophical in nature. The first of these, metaphysics, is relatively easy to define as an academic subject, if anything but straightforward in practice. The second (facts-of-mind) is far more obscure and yet it remains an obsession, at the core of Coleridge's lifelong intellectual project. If we turn to his marginalia then we can find plenty of evidence to suggest that one of his on-going interests, in which European figures played a huge part, was indeed in this strange body of writing that tells of the mysterious space at the limits of consciousness, where material reality and mental life exist in unsettling relation with one another. Some of his most annotated books are works of mysticism or early pseudo-science by German authors who are lost to all but the specialist now, works dealing with the nature of light and the universe, with dreams, illusions and half-understood phenomena such as magnetism. It can seem pretty baffling that Coleridge gave such time to figures like Jakob Böhme, Hermann Boerhaave, Gotthilf Heinrich von Schubert, Lorenz Oken, and Karl Alexander Friedrich Kluge but we must, I think, see this as forming part of a continuum with his apparently unrelated literary interests. For one thing, historical study of the ineffable aspects of mind allowed Coleridge access to a developed tradition of writing that attempted to explain problems, which his own investigations into the literary imagination had already touched upon, about the ways in which the individual consciousness can appear to shape and even recreate what seems like external reality in ways that are subjective and unique. At the same time, however, these continental writers played a part in opening up an intellectual heritage that was increasingly central to him from the end of the 1790s onwards. The German philosophical and theological tradition conditioned so much of Coleridge's thought that it is hard to overstate its impact. Many of his longest and most engaged annotations draw squarely on the works that remain key to understanding his engagement with idealism, the self, the beautiful and sublime, pantheism, the higher biblical criticism; with Kant, Fichte, Schelling, Herder, Jacobi, and Eichhorn.

The marginalia, however, tell an incomplete story because they do not adequately relate the tale of Coleridge's more distinctly literary reading. And inevitably they only provide a rough guide to the ways in which that reading influenced his own diverse output. Certain key figures are just missing or are incompletely represented in the texts available to us, and for evidence of their influence we will need to look further afield. First, however, it is worth making some general suggestions about Coleridge's interest in European literature, which can be categorized under several clear headings, each of which intersects, to a greater or lesser degree, with the others. The first of these, his longest-standing interest, is in the writing of ancient Greece and Rome. One of his earliest literary productions in verse was an ancient Greek ode written at Cambridge for which he was awarded a college medal, and indeed his interest in classical verse and especially in Greek metre persists throughout his life. Notably, of course, it is in the form of the ode that Coleridge, building upon late eighteenth-century innovations, produced some of his most innovative poetry, not least the disarming mature poem 'Dejection'.

Schooling in the classics must be traced back to his education at Christ's Hospital, where Coleridge came under the strict tutelage of James Boyer who influenced his taste in ways that he describes vividly in *Biographia*:

He early moulded my taste to the preference of Demonsthenes to Cicero, of Homer and Theocritus to Virgil, and again of Virgil to Ovid. He habituated me to compare Lucretius. (in such extracts as I then read) Terence, and above all the chaster poems of Catullus, not only with the Roman poets of the, so called, silver and brazen ages; but with even those of the Augustan era: and on grounds of plain sense and universal logic to see and assert the superiority of the former, in the truth and nativeness, both of their thought and diction. At the same time that we were studying the Greek Tragic Poets, he made us read Shakspeare and Milton as lessons: and they were the lessons too, which required most time and trouble to *bring up*, so as to escape his censure. (*BL*, 1, 8–9)

Boyer instilled one of the precepts that Coleridge would take forward into his collaboration with Wordsworth, namely that poetry should be seen as a science of language in which convention is always tested against the fitness of idiom. It is significant that he should value a quality of linguistic authenticity in classical poetry, and implicitly find a connection in this to the greatest models in the English tradition. But once again, *Biographia* only gives a partial sense of Coleridge's on-going engagement with the classical tradition.

Mention of Thomas Taylor, the translator of Plato, in the above letter to Thelwall, points to the arena within which this engagement persisted most productively for Coleridge's intellectual development. The increasing popularity of Platonism in the late eighteenth century had much to do with its renewed importance for philosophers and theologians who were challenging orthodox Christian conceptions of the place of God within the material world. The largely German, Spinozistic tradition that questioned the make-up of Nature was of immeasurable importance to Coleridge as he wrestled with heterodox religious beliefs that grew out of his own Unitarianism, some of which bordered upon a pantheism with which he toyed uncomfortably, as Thomas McFarland has shown. But his reading ranged very widely, as is evident from the Notebooks, and many of the works that Coleridge returned to over the course of his life were of Hellenistic Neoplatonism or from the Christian classical tradition of Renaissance Italy that was so heavily influenced by that earlier movement.

An important late poem of Coleridge is 'The Garden of Boccaccio' and this, as well as the many references to Dante in the literary lectures, serves to remind us of the importance to him of the literature of Italy. If he was first drawn to European literature as a result of his classical schooling, a second and still more lasting pull towards the Latinate culture of Italy and to a lesser extent Spain, grew out of his Christianity, and indeed Coleridge's interest in European literature must to a large extent be seen within this context. His ongoing concerns about the heresy of pantheism find a natural outlet in his disparagement of classical mythology (as a religion of the supernatural) and his celebration of Hebraic monotheism. And yet, related to this, a sense emerges in Coleridge's thought of there being an aesthetic as well as a spiritual teleology to the adoption by Christian poets of classical forms. In chapter 18 of *Biographia*, he celebrates the use of classical machinery in poets of the Renaissance such as Petrarch, precisely because it is, within the Christian context, an exploded mythology, a linguistic and figurative growth of the European poetic tradition out of its secular past, rather than a challenge to the Christian faith. This is an important qualification because, for Coleridge, classical mythology may have provided a model for later poets, but a secular conception of a *Weltliteratur*, such as Goethe's for example, which incorporated Christian Europe and its classical past with the Islamic East, was not one that he could follow in good faith.[1] His notion of European literature is one conditioned by a common classical heritage that has become decently Christianized; the discomfort that he felt increasingly for *Faust*, for example, must be seen within this purview, and indeed it conditioned his complex, changing response to the most important body of European writing to interest him: the emerging literature of Germany.

COLERIDGE AND THE GERMAN LITERARY TRADITION

One of Coleridge's greatest literary heroes was Milton, *the* national poet of Christian classicism. It is unsurprising, then, that when he began to look for contemporary models in European literature he was drawn to two writers both of whom engaged directly with their combined Christian and classical heritage and who did so within the searching context of the late enlightenment. They are Gotthold Ephraim Lessing and Friedrich Gottlieb Klopstock, authors respectively of the drama *Nathan der Weise* (1779) and the epic *Messias* (1748–72). Together they assume an eminent place among the European writers who first excited the adult Coleridge even if they are, in some ways, rather unlikely influences. Already in his own lifetime, Klopstock, in spite of his reputation as the German Milton, had become something of by-word for sheer unreadability, the butt of Lessing's humour as a poet more admired than known, and he inspired a strange cocktail of emotions in Coleridge. It was to Klopstock that he and Wordsworth made a

---

[1] See Fritz Strich, *Goethe and World Literature* (London, Routledge, 1949), 32.

form of quasi-pilgrimage during their 1798 trip to Germany and we have a full account of their meetings in the odd appendix that appears as 'Satyrane's Letters' in *Biographia*. In fact, Coleridge was only present for the first of three meetings that Wordsworth had with Klopstock and the account is derivative of Wordsworth's notes, expanding a version that first appeared in the 1809 *Friend*. It is fascinating nevertheless. Like so many pilgrimages, theirs is a tissue of emotions whose predominant note is disappointment. Prepared for a marvellous moment, a touching of the hem of the garment, Coleridge is initially alive to the historical significance of the meeting, but his narrative soon runs over into bizarre banality as his idealized conception of the poet becomes confounded by physically embodied reality:

I looked at him with much emotion—I considered him as the venerable father of German poetry; as a good man; as a Christian, seventy-four years old; with legs enormously swoln; yet active, lively, cheerful, and kind, and communicative. My eyes felt as if a tear were swelling into them. In the portrait of Lessing there was a toupee periwig, which enormously injured the effect of his physiognomy—Klopstock wore the same, powdered and frizzled. By the bye, old men ought never to wear powder—the contrast between a large snow-white wig and the colour of an old man's skin is disgusting, and wrinkles in such a neighbourhood appear only channels for dirt. It is an honour to poets and great men, that you think of them as parts of nature; and any thing of trick and fashion wounds you in them as much as when you see venerable yews clipped into miserable peacocks.—The author of the Messiah should have worn his own grey hair. (*BL*, 1, 196–7)

At the end of the letter, Coleridge cannot resist having a jibe at Klopstock's reputation as only a very *German* Milton, and there is a real ambiguity in the last sentence quoted above: the author of the *Messiah* simply cannot disguise his grey hair beneath make-up because the poem is itself so dated and remote from the modern reader. In his odd physical appearance then, there is serious underlying significance since it reveals Klopstock to be of another era, that of the artifice of pre-revolutionary Europe. Klopstock is not the sublime, Romantic man of elemental nature, who has formed in Coleridge's mind as the quintessential poet, but instead he sinks into the bathos of barely disguised physical decay, a figure reminiscent of Visconti's made-up Von Aschenbach melting in the Venetian sun. Earlier in the meeting, there is a moment of almost tragicomic disagreement, where Klopstock suggests that the blank verse of the long-forgotten Richard Glover is superior to that of Milton and, although this is soon cleared up as a matter of that which has been lost in translation, it is hard not to see a persistent disparagement of the *Messias* when compared with *Paradise Lost* in Coleridge's critical writings as something of its legacy.

Earlier on in *Biographia*, Coleridge hints that Klopstock's epic breaks down because, unlike *Paradise Lost*, it fails to achieve a sense of artistic illusion and attempts instead to trick us into the delusion of believing in it as fact. This is one of his slipperiest critical distinctions but it takes us back to one of the key elements that has already emerged in his description of Klopstock the man; namely, that he is not of nature but unnatural and artificial. Rather than allowing his characters to grow into lives of their own that are separate from their mere biblical personae and hence alive on their own terms, Klopstock's 'are derived from Scripture history [...] and not merely suggested by it as in the Paradise Lost of Milton' (*BL*, 11, 133–4). The result is a heightened sense of artifice that strengthens rather than reduces the sense of the work's fictionality. As readers we are, Coleridge seems to suggest, unable to succumb to a sense of the natural mimesis of a work that grows organically but are instead forced to give ourselves up to the whole production or nothing at all. This famously difficult aesthetic dyad, illusion versus delusion, is elsewhere worked out in relation to the project of *Lyrical Ballads* but the inclusion of Klopstock at such a significant moment in *Biographia*, when Coleridge is outlining the chief defects of Wordsworth's poetics is worth noting, not least because the *Messias* seems to serve as a focus against which to sharpen his specific critique of his former collaborator. Klopstock, an ambivalent figure in his earlier literary development, clearly remains as a minor antagonist, a counter presence to his aesthetic credo.

Ernest Bernhardt-Kabisch has argued that Coleridge's meeting with Klopstock did have an unexpected effect on the latter in that it served to a certain degree to stimulate his thoughts about poetic metre and in particular about the use of the hexameter in English.[2] It is clear that their discussion did turn for a moment around the matter of different national metres and the legacy of the classical hexameter. Coleridge's friend William Sotheby had recently translated into English another contemporary German epic attempt, Christoph Martin Wieland's *Oberon* (which became better known in Britain as the basis for Weber's Covent Garden opera), and the business of adapting foreign stanzaic and metric forms appears to have been prominent in his mind at the time. Undoubtedly, Coleridge maintained an on-going fascination with the connections between German and Greek metre. He read widely in German poetics, citing Christian Garve (the translator of Edmund Burke) in *Biographia* in support of his claim that poetry is a species of philosophy, and struggled later on for a time with an essay on Greek metre in which he followed the German metric theorist Johann August Apel, who is best known as the librettist of Weber's *Der Freischütz*. Most of all, however, we should see the meeting with Klopstock as a watershed moment in Coleridge's intellectual life

---

[2] See Ernest Bernhardt-Kabisch, ' "When Klopstock England Defied": Coleridge, Southey, and the German/English Hexameter', *Comparative Literature*, 55 (2003), 130–63.

because the discussions opened up a conduit to other German writers, such as Schiller, Goethe, Nicolai, and Kant, whom he had only just begun to discover. It is with this visit that the balance of Coleridge's intellectual loyalty shifts with permanent effect to Germany, and somewhat paradoxically, given the impression made upon him by Klopstock, his first, naïve responses to its literature gradually harden into a set of literary values that remain with him during the period of his greatest critical achievement. Fundamental to these is the concept of literary genius as being at one with nature, possessing an authenticity that follows from the growth of natural, organic form.

In Klopstock and Lessing, Coleridge found his two principle Latinate influences—Christianity and classicism—combined in a new northern European tradition, but the latter offered him something else besides this. His play, *Nathan der Weise*, whose Jewish hero is based upon Moses Mendelssohn, offers a view of religion that is based upon the principles of enlightenment rationalism but it also presages the drama of *Sturm und Drang* that would have a considerable impact upon the English literary culture of the 1790s. Lessing provided a way for Coleridge of conceiving of drama in neo-Shakespearean terms, which is to say without the burden of a legacy from the classical French drama that dominated eighteenth-century taste. In both *Biographia* and his literary lectures, Coleridge is frequently rude about the French stage, which he held to be mannered and servile to obsolete rules. Lessing, whose biography Coleridge toyed with writing, was responsible for allowing German drama to free itself from this influence and that he was able to do so followed specifically from his reading of Shakespeare. In his interesting 'Critique of *Bertram*' that is appended to *Biographia*, Coleridge makes the bold claim that Lessing was at least in part responsible for reintroducing Shakespeare to the English and whether we see this as anything more than the product of a remembered enthusiasm for his first German model, it is worth pointing out that Shakespeare is consistently associated with the canon of German writing that Coleridge most admired.

For all that his literary achievements are diverse, Lessing remains a figure of the Enlightenment; it was from other German writers, Herder, Bürger, Goethe, Schiller, and Tieck that he drew inspiration for his championing of a national literary tradition that was local and eschewed the classical past. Coleridge's interest in Kant, Schelling, Schlegel, and the like is well covered elsewhere in this volume. These are specific traceable debts that illuminate aspects of his philosophical or critical endeavours. More interesting in many ways are those literary relationships that have been less adequately reviewed but which nevertheless lend us an impression of the ways in which Coleridge employed his reading of European literature to inform upon both the English tradition and his various critical and intellectual projects. For the remainder of this chapter, I would like to consider two figures in particular, Friedrich Schiller and Ludwig Tieck.

COLERIDGE AND SCHILLER

Michael John Kooy has argued impressively for the latent presence of Schiller in a great deal of Coleridge's thought. Nevertheless, of all Schiller's works, it is clearly from the two great plays at either end of his career—*Die Räuber* and *Wallenstein*—that Coleridge learnt most. In her important work on the Romantic stage moreover, Julie Carlson has suggested that Coleridge's translation of the latter in 1800 shortly after his return from Germany (a historiographical drama dealing implicitly with the development of nationalism), is replete with all the political implications of rediscovering a nationalistic, even Shakespearean, dramatic language. We need only turn to what Coleridge himself says about Schiller and in particular about *Wallenstein* to see that Carlson is justified in equating the project with both nationalistic and Shakespearean motives. At the various points in his career when Coleridge comments upon Schiller, it is often with an eye to Shakespeare. Although Schiller comes off unfavourably by comparison, the very fact that the two are dealt with together there shows Coleridge's admiration for his writing. In the Preface to the second of his translations, *The Death of Wallenstein*, he writes:

> Few, I trust, would be rash or ignorant enough to compare Schiller with Shakespeare, yet, merely as illustration, I would say that we should proceed to the perusal of Wallenstein, not from Lear or Othello, but from Richard the Second, or the three parts of Henry the Sixth. (*PW*, 111, 620)

It is significant that Coleridge offers this comparison, especially given the fact that the authenticity of the early Histories was under question as is clear from Malone's essay in the collected works. The implication seems to be that the mature Schiller can bear comparison only with the style of a lesser Shakespeare, and this is a point taken up and developed by unfavourable contemporary reviewers. The *British Critic*, in an unsigned review, comments that:

> For the tediousness of most of the scenes and speeches in the dramas, the translator, Mr. Coleridge, makes the best apology in his power, comparing them to Shakespeare's three historical plays of Henry the Sixth. But, not to mention that a very small part of those plays is supposed, by the best critics, to have been the work of Shakespeare, is not this comparison to the worst of our bard's historical dramas, somewhat like that of the actor, who assured himself of success, 'because he was taller than Garrick, and had a better voice than Mossop'?[3]

Nevertheless, this is a fair comparison since Schiller's *Wallenstein*, like Shakespeare's Histories, opens itself readily both to questions of historiography and of inscribing a national literature written out of collective history. This is something that Coleridge himself expresses much later in his *Table Talk* of 1833:

---

[3] *British Review*, November 1801, xvii, 542–5.

The young men in Germany and England who admire Lord Byron prefer Goethe to Schiller; but you may depend upon it, Goethe does not, nor ever will, command the mind of the people of Germany as Schiller does. Schiller had two legitimate phases. The first as author of the Robbers, which must not be considered with reference to Shakespeare, but as a work of the material sublime—and in that line it is undoubtedly very powerful indeed. It is quite genuine and deeply imbued with Schiller's own soul. After this, Schiller outgrew the composition of such plays as the Robbers and at once took his true and only rightful stand in the grand historical drama the *Wallenstein*. Not the intense drama—he was not master of that—but of the diffused drama of history, in which alone he had ample score for his varied powers. This is the greatest of his works—not unlike Shakespeare's historical plays—a species by itself. (*TT*, 1, 339–41)

Coleridge had complained to Josiah Wedgwood during the translation of the 'dull heavy play', but whether we should take this seriously, or as merely an expression of temporary exasperation in the face of an extraordinary project, is hard to say. (*CL*, 1, 610) Given the results, one would probably tend in favour the latter. In his *Table Talk*, Coleridge describes the play as a nationalist work, implying that the incorporation of history works to capture the national imagination. Nevertheless, *Wallenstein* is not a work which speaks of a political or radical agenda but rather deals with the specific question of the aesthetic as a realm which may incorporate, as E. S. Shaffer puts it, epic issues concerned with 'the nature of leadership, with the peculiar conjunction of religious superstition, personal ambition, and national achievement'.[4]

Coleridge himself has an ambiguous and troubled reaction to the stage. Early on he clearly thought that it could be an arena for suggesting political action. As his career continues he develops a critique of the stage, which will ultimately become an opposition towards it. John David Moore, in his useful essay, 'Coleridge and the "modern Jacobinical Drama"', suggests that this process can be explained by reference to both an increasing reaction against political reform, as well as a belief in the moral ambiguousness of much of the drama of the period. Nevertheless, there is another element at work, which brings us round to a discussion of the collaboration between Coleridge and Schiller that culminates in his translations of *Wallenstein* in 1800. This is the sense of the denigration of an art form that Coleridge felt in the cheap Drury Lane theatre of the day. Carlson picks up upon this to suggest that within Coleridge's sense of the need to re-invigorate the writing of drama as high art, lies a nationalism whose impulse goes back to an appreciation of the golden age of English drama in Elizabethan and Jacobean England. From this point of view, it is hardly surprising that Coleridge looks to Germany and Schiller, in particular, when he begins his play-writing career, for Schiller had found a language and a style which seemed able to appropriate Shakespeare, in formal and linguistic terms, while all the while remaining faithful to the concerns of the day.

---

[4] E. S. Shaffer, *'Kubla Khan' and The Fall of Jerusalem* (Cambridge, 1975, p. 56).

Coleridge was obviously aware of having taken liberties with the prompt book text that he used for the translation of the plays, and he certainly remains conscious of having appropriated another artist's work in order to promote his own poetic imagination. Both Tieck and August Wilhelm Schlegel claimed to prefer Coleridge's version to the original, and although he came to dislike it for a time after the realism of failure in the reviews (the *British Critic* called his translations 'devoid of harmony or elegance'), his confidence was renewed by later praise from Shelley amongst others. In his preface to *The Piccolomini* he writes:

> In the translation I endeavoured to render my Author *literally* wherever I was not prevented by absolute differences of idiom; but I am conscious, that in two or three short passages I have been guilty of dilating the original; and from anxiety to give the full meaning, have weakened the force. (*PW*, 111, 205)

Coleridge's advice to us to look back to Shakespeare's early history plays as a key to the trilogy is not without foundation. Like *Henry VI Parts Two and Three*, the drama is unremitting in its seriousness, while at the same time it incorporates vast rhetorical passages and curiously astrological imagery. The action of the drama is not succinctly political, but inexorably historical. As such we do not respond irrationally in Schiller's terms by becoming politically engaged but are instead indifferent to the action, because it is history, and yet it is only a semblance of the reality with which we are presumably familiar. This explains Coleridge's remarks in the preface: 'It was my intention to have prefixed a Life of Wallenstein to this translation; but I found that it must either have occupied a space wholly disproportionate to the nature of the publication, or have been merely a meagre catalogue of events narrated not more fully than they are already in the Play itself.'

Both Coleridge and Schiller suggest that in order for art to have the effect that it can, it must appeal to something other than our base nature. For Schiller, this is a belief that is integrally bound into his own movement away from radical drama. I would suggest that this is a further interesting link between the two thinkers. For Coleridge, too, the late wish to disassociate himself from an early interest in radical drama, and belief in its power to influence politics, informs directly upon his critical theory. Important in this is his late disavowal of 'Jacobinical' drama, and belief in the importance of the creation of a nationalist theatre. The interesting link between the writers is, of course, the fact that *Die Räuber* had such an effect on both the British and German stage.[5] Coleridge's movement away from Schiller's early play may in some sense account for his comparative silence regarding Schiller's other work in his later career.

---

[5] The radical reaction in Germany was very marked. Goethe tells of meeting a German Prince who said that if he had been God and had known that the creation would result in the writing of *Die Räuber*, he would never have created the world. See Georg Lukács, *Goethe and his Age*, trans. Robert Anchor (London: Merlin, 1968), 43.

On 13 November 1794, Coleridge wrote to Southey, asking, 'My God! Southey! Who is this Schiller? This convulser of the heart? Did he write his Tragedy amid the yelling of Fiends?... Why have we ever called Milton sublime?'(*CL*, 1, 122) He adheres to this belief in the sublimity of Schiller's early period until late in life, when he categorizes Schiller's corpus into two periods, that of 'the material sublime', and that of 'the diffused drama of history'. (*TT*, 1, 339; 41) Hazlitt makes a similar distinction in *Lectures on Elizabethan Literature*, and provides us with a wonderful, if hyperbolical, appraisal of the play: '*The Robbers* was the first play I ever read: and the effect it produced upon me was the greatest. It stunned me like a blow, and I have not recovered enough from it to describe how it was. There are impressions which neither time nor circumstances can efface.'[6] The appeal of the play to Coleridge may be seen to exist upon two levels: first, there is the political nature of the drama, but second, and more important are the formal qualities of the work. Largely, the play succeeds in these terms because of three separate elements. First, and most important, is the extreme naturalism of the piece, which has characters speaking in believable voices, and thinking about real issues in reasoned terms. Second, there is an appeal to the contemporary taste for Gothic elements in staging, and plot development. Third, and this may be the crucial point for Coleridge, Schiller manages to begin his task of re-invigorating drama in classical tragic terms by taking stock set-pieces from Shakespeare and giving them a definitively modern feel. For Coleridge, schooled in Shakespeare from an early age, Schiller's drama is sufficiently Shakespearean to make him feel at home, but is not so linguistically in debt to a former idiom to feel like mere pastiche.

For Coleridge in *Biographia*, however, the play is responsible for the worst excesses of recent theatre. Charging *Bertram* with a gothicized melodrama, he writes, 'Bertram disarmed, out-heroding Charles de Moor in the Robbers, befaces the collected knights of St. Anselm (all in complete armour) and so, by pure dint of black looks, he outdares them into passive poltroons' (*BL*, 11, 233) This comment contains something of a double-charge. Not only does *Bertram* pastiche *Die Räuber*, it also goes in for excessive stage machinery. The criticism of Schiller lies in the arbitrary nature of the revenge motive of the play, which is, he writes, 'a monster not less offensive to good taste than to sound morals'. (*BL*, 11, 210) Nevertheless, Coleridge's charge is not specifically directed at Schiller, it seems, or at least certainly not solely at it: he attacks both the play itself and the imitations that it spawned, involving himself in the process in a discussion that takes us back to the relationship between Schiller and Coleridge, in terms of their aesthetics.

The British reception of *Die Räuber* in the 1790s had been enthusiasm among those who were looking for a dramatic form that enabled both speed of action and

---

[6] *The Complete Works of William Hazlitt*, ed. P. P. Howe, 21 vols. (London: Dent, 1930–4), vi, 362.

revolutionary sentiment in drama. The radical reception was of course tempered somewhat by those who saw the play as scandalously revolutionary, in particular *The Anti-Jacobin*, who exaggerated and the mocked the Gothic elements in their parody *The Rovers* (1798). However, it is apparent that in general, the play was either welcomed or attacked in terms of its apparent political nature. Furthermore, political accounts of the play ranged from those which saw Karl's revolt as some-how prophetic of the revolution in France, to those who saw the form of the play as a direct attack upon the rules of French classicism, which were somehow figures, in hindsight, for the aristocratic ruling class in France. Such views of the revolution as theatre are of course familiar from Burke and Paine. John David Moore points out that in the exchange between Burke and Paine, there is a theatrical use of tropes which suggests that Burke saw the revolution as a tragedy followed by a terrible burlesque acted out by the masses, while Paine saw the whole thing as revivifying comedy.[7]

Nevertheless, where the politics of the play were seen to be unacceptable, the dramatic quality may have proved enticing. *The Red-Cross Knights. A Play in Five Acts* [...] *Founded on The Robbers of Schiller* (1799), by J. G. Holman, takes the play and turns it into a Christian work about the Spanish crusades against the Moors, while remaining self-consciously indebted to the original. Like Coleridge, Holman borrows the brothers plot from Schiller in Roderic and Ferdinand, and incorporates a mutual love interest in Eugenia. In the 'Advertisement', Holman explains that he had become 'captivated' by the 'beauties' of Schiller's play, and he describes a curious creative process in which he had originally intended merely to prepare the piece for the stage, but found that his work was prohibited by the licenser. He goes on:

On a more dispassionate investigation of the play, I found much to justify the licenser's decision ... Still unwilling to abandon a favourite object, I determined on forming a Play, which should retain as much of the original, with the omission of all that seemed objectionable.[8]

The final result excises the unacceptable radicalism of the Ur-play, but nevertheless incorporates whole scenes from Tytler's translation. In the context of *Osorio*, Coleridge's own Schillerian drama of 1797, the transposition of the action from Germany to medieval Spain is interesting, but the excision of the modern and by implication of the real from the play lies in contravention to Schiller's intention. He refers to Karl as a modern Don Quixote figure in his original Preface to the play.

---

[7] John David Moore, 'Coleridge and the "modern Jacobinical Drama": *Osorio, Remorse,* and the Development of Coleridge's Critique of the Stage, 1797–1816', *Bulletin of Research in the Humanities,* 85 (1982), 443–64.

[8] J. G. Holman, *The Red Cross Knights* (London, 1799), 'Advertisement'.

Moreover, he was extremely disinclined to transpose the action to the medieval era, in the process emphasizing the role of Amalia for sentimental effect, and removing the priest of Act III, turning him into a local magistrate. It was under these conditions, laid down by Dahlberg, director of the Mannheim Theatre, that the play's reputation in Germany was initially made. For Schiller, the play was modern, and should be seen as such.

Coleridge's charge against Maturin rests upon a similar basis. The play attempts to be too close to life. In *The Friend* of 1809, Coleridge constructs a dialogue between himself and an imaginary play-goer, who is eager to see more 'Jacobin' drama: 'Is it your own poor pettifogging nature then, which you desire to see represented before you then? not human nature in all its health and vigour?' he asks. (*Friend*, 11, 220; *BL*, 11, 189) Jacobin drama combines, for Coleridge, the worst of both worlds. On the one hand, it aims to be true to life, and represents ordinary people in ordinary situations, combined with excessive staging, in order to draw the audience into the sensuous belief that they are watching the real. On the other hand, it displays a morality and society that is, on his terms, far removed from that which we know from our own personal experience. As such any moral purpose that the dramas may have rests upon a 'gross self-delusion' that we are seeing reality. Coleridge's critique relies upon a renewed belief in the ideal over the material in theatre. This is combined with a romanticized nostalgia for the kind of theatrical experience that he supposed audiences to have enjoyed in Shakespeare's day. In Lecture XI of the 1811–12 Lectures on Shakespeare and Milton, he writes of the Shakespearean stage: 'The stage had nothing but curtains for its scenes, and the Actor as well as the author were obliged to appeal to the imagination & not to the senses.' (*LL*, 1, 350) This is the true theatre of the mind.

In the 'Critique of *Bertram*', Coleridge contrasts the Maturin play with the *Atheista Fulminato* of Tirso de Molina. This is admittedly an unfair comparison, but it bears out Coleridge's point rather well. Both plays present us with a situation requiring us to come to terms with the immoral behaviour of the protagonist. Coleridge's criticism of *Bertram*, however, is that it demands that we sympathize with the real immorality of the events that we see because we are led towards a conclusion in which we are to identify directly with the hero. By contrast, in the character of *Don Juan*, reality is so far removed from the play, that we see nothing but a type or symbol on stage, which is entirely incredible in real terms. We are asked to believe in the character for the duration of the play, and this ideal quality actually increases the moral force of the play. The audience is asked to make an imaginative leap of faith in coming to terms with the fiction before them, and in so doing, by implication, the imagination is moved to discover the ethical value of the work for itself.

COLERIDGE AND LUDWIG TIECK

Coleridge's reading of Schiller provides us with extraordinary evidence of his use of German literature in his wider literary and aesthetic projects. The writer with whom I should like to conclude is a closer associate and one who illuminates both his interest in William Shakespeare and other aspects of his intellectual life in the middle of the Romantic period. This is Ludwig Tieck.

Tieck and Coleridge were close associates in June 1817, when they met in London to discuss the editing of Shakespeare and disagreed over the attribution of some of the apocryphal works. They then corresponded, having exchanged suggestions for reading material. Over the following eighteenth months, Coleridge would deliver three of his most important series of literary lectures, in which he made some of his most substantial contributions to aesthetic theory. A shared interest in Shakespeare and the nature of dramatic illusion was then the essential common ground between the two men. Yet there is a further reason for our interest in their relationship, and this follows from the fact that both sustained an increased interest in animal magnetism or mesmerism at exactly this point in their intellectual lives, being determined to establish the truth or falsity of the phenomenon.[9]

Coleridge and Tieck had in fact already met at the house of the Humboldts in Rome during 1806, but it was the later encounter that was clearly more fruitful. Henry Crabb Robinson records Tieck's impression of Coleridge in his diary entry for 29 June 1817:

I had more conversation with Tieck this evening than before on general literary subjects. He is well read in the English plays which were accessible in Germany; and has a decision of opinion which one wonders at in a foreigner. He has no high opinion of Coleridge's critique, but he says he has learned a great deal from Coleridge, who has glorious conceptions about Shakespeare (*herrliche Ideen*). Coleridge's conversation he very much admires, and thinks it superior to any of his writings. But he says there is much high poetry in 'Christabel'.[10]

By July 1817, Coleridge felt sufficiently well versed in Tieck's literary achievements to recommend him to Southey 'as a Poet, Critic, and Moralist [who] stands (in *reputation*) next to Goethe'. (*CL* § 1069, IV, 754) In fact, he must have engaged in a

---

[9] Kathleen Wheeler, Earl Leslie Griggs, and Edwin Zeydel have all examined the relationship between Tieck and Coleridge, and have exposed its intellectual foundations in these two separate and apparently unrelated areas. See Kathleen Wheeler, 'Coleridge's Friendship with Ludwig Tieck', in *New Approaches to Coleridge: Biographical and Critical Essays*, ed. Donald Sultana (New York: Barnes and Noble, 1981), 96–112; Earl Leslie Griggs, 'Ludwig Tieck and Samuel Taylor Coleridge', *Journal of English and German Philology*, 54 (1955), 262–8; Edwin H. Zeydel, *Ludwig Tieck and England: A Study in the Literary Relations of Germany and England during the Early Nineteenth Century* (Princeton: Princeton University Press, 1931), 68–79; 93–6.

[10] *Diary, Reminiscences, and Correspondence of Henry Crabb Robinson*, ed. Thomas Sadler, 3 vols. (Macmillan, 1869), II, 62–3.

pretty heroic act of reading because this letter is dated by Griggs to around 20 June 1817 and a mere month earlier he had written to his bookseller, Thomas Boosey, to order 'all the works, you may have of Ludwig Tieck' as well as works by Schelling, Steffens, and Solger. (*CL*, § 1060, IV, 738) Although he makes no specific mention of it, it is therefore extremely likely that Coleridge would have looked at Tieck's translation of *The Tempest*. A reading of Solger's *Erwin*, meanwhile, gives rise to an interesting note of Coleridge's, in which he is critical of the application of abstract meaning to critical terms, suggesting instead that the criticism should proceed according to the appropriate application of a language of critical response:

Generally indeed I complain of the German Philosophers (as we are most apt to complain of our dearest Friends)—of the Post-Kantian at least—that for the precipitance with which they press to their own determinations of what the *thing* is, without having first enquired what the *word* means when it is used *appropriately*. Whenever I can convince a man that another term would express his meaning far more unexceptionably, the term used was not *appropriate*—but the rule is that the same word should not have heterogeneous, <or even disparate> senses. Thus instead of asking, Was Schönheit sey? I would enquire what schöne properly meant—i.e. what men mean when they use the word schön in preference to any other epithet. A rose is a pleasing sight: and so to a hungry man is a Hogspudding. But a Rose is beautiful—ergo, beautiful means something else or something more than pleasing. The difference is not in the *degree*—for add to a keen appetite a long and involuntary abstinence from animal food, and a particular predilection, the Hogspudding will become tenfold more pleasing without advancing a single Step towards Beauty. (*SW&F*, 1, 598)

We know that Tieck had suggested the reading of Solger to Coleridge. This reaction is interesting not least because it is demonstrative of the fact that Coleridge remains concerned to apply critical language carefully and pragmatically, without reaching forward into mere abstract speculation. As in so many things, he is of course rather contradictory in this regard. Nevertheless, Roger Paulin has suggested that in his discussions with Tieck, Coleridge would have become acquainted with someone for whom the process of textual scholarship far outweighed the aims of mere abstract theory.[11] Coleridge's debt to the later Tieck may be slight in terms of his own aesthetic theory, but there is nevertheless the trace of the latter's practical criticism in this kind of statement.

Immediately prior to the note on Solger and dated 8 July 1817, some nine days after his last acquaintance with Tieck in London, Coleridge wrote the long and detailed note on the subject of animal magnetism, in which he addresses the verity of the phenomenon with renewed rigour.[12] H. J. and J. R. de J. Jackson note that this is the first substantial treatment of the subject by Coleridge, which is not inhabited

[11] Roger Paulin, *Ludwig Tieck: A Literary Biography* (Oxford: Clarendon Press, 1985), 211.
[12] 'On Animal Magnetism', *SW&F*, 1, 588–95.

by more or less complete scepticism. They suggest that he is appealing for a 'suspension of disbelief' in regard to the claims of the magnetists.[13] The essay seeks above all to question the validity of a materialist theory of the will, arguing from the evidence provided by magnetism, which suggests that an external force may control our power of volition from without. 'For myself', Coleridge concludes, 'I shall even say—I will try it when I have them the opportunity, myself [. . .] and till then I will be neutral.'[14] Still, his argument is full of contradictory turns because as much as he is determined to establish the sovereignty of the individual will, he has to admit that it is potentially affected by external forces:

> The only position, I say, asserted by all Magnetists as Magnetists is, that the will or (if you prefer it the vis vitae in man as even less theoric) ~~the vis vitae of Man~~ is not confined in its operations to the Organic Body, in which it appears to be seated; but under certain <previously defined> Conditions of distance and position, of and above all of the relation to the Patient to the Agent, and of the Agent to the Patient, is capable of acting and producing certain <pre-defined> Effects on the <human> living Bodies external to it.[15]

If Coleridge is to accept this, then it must have enormous consequences for his conception of the rational will in terms that have a profound impact upon any dependence placed upon the will in other activities. The subject can, in the example of mesmerism, find itself affected by external phenomena in ways that alter our conception of individual choice, and this attendant effect is manifest in bodily as well as mental states that result from the interaction.

John Beer has suggested that an arcane reference to Tieck in Coleridge's marginalia to Karl Christian Wolfart's *Erläuterungen zum Mesmerismus*, suggests that their meeting had rekindled speculations that he had earlier entertained about the relationship between human volition and magnetism.[16] Besides referencing Tieck, Coleridge suggests that a passage in Wolfart reminds him of a long held theory that volition is a mode of double Touch.[17] (*CM*, 111, 868) Beer has defined this latter theory as an analysis 'of physical touch and sensation, including the ways that children learn by touch and the phenomenon of 'seeing double'. Magnetism appeared to lend Coleridge further evidence at this time that there were modes of consciousness in which the will could not be controlled internally by the mind alone, but was subject to a form of external force. Beer goes on:

---

[13] *SW&F*, 1, 588.

[14] *SW&F*, 1, 595.

[15] *SW&F*, 1, 590.

[16] John Beer, *Coleridge's Poetic Intelligence* (Houndsmills: Macmillan, 1997), 85–6.

[17] Coleridge mentions that Tieck 'attested the fact of Wolfart's power of fixing the needle in the Mariner's Compass by pointing his finger on it'. He goes on, 'I think it probable, that An. Magnetism will be found connected with a Warmth-Sense: & will confirm my long long ago theory of Volition as a mode of *double Touch*.'

Supposing that developed human consciousness had not one pole (that by which we make contact with the outside world, of which touch is the final arbiter) but two: an outer sense of touch and an inner sense which was in direct communication with the inner life-forces of the universe? The first could be said to govern waking-life, in which the external world was perceived, and finally tested, by touch; the second would be more operative in states of dream or hypnotism or somnambulism or trance. (86)

The question of the connection between this second state and that of aesthetic experience is one that is rich. The reason for turning to Tieck's presence in Coleridge's thought is not simply to suggest that the two states are the same, nor indeed that they are necessarily similar, but rather to point out that it is in a concern with the quality of the attention experienced by the human subject when confronted by aesthetic phenomena that we find interesting questions asked in the Romantic period. If there is a connection to be made out of this coincidence, it is not to suggest that both form part of some larger system, rather that they provide evidence of the intrusion of some central questions about the state of the active mind into very different areas of investigation.

The connection between the two areas of interest is vivid enough if we turn to Coleridge's most significant epistolary reflection upon Tieck. The key letter is to John Hookham Frere, 27 June 1817. Coleridge begins by detailing Tieck's 'ASTON-ISHING' intimacy with British writers and lists his manifold accomplishments as a translator and scholar before suddenly breaking off: 'I put a question to him concerning the present convictions of scientific men in Germany respecting Animal Magnetism—and at length asked him—Have you yourself seen any of these wonder-works?' (*CL*, §1065, IV, 744–5) Tieck, he explains, enjoyed a close connection to Wolfart, and much of the letter concerns the divisions between the various factions of Materialists, Magnetists and Spiritualists, giving their rival views. 'What a strange co-incidence', Coleridge reflects, 'that utterly without any design or connection the phaenomenon of Magnetism as a physiological Power [...] should have risen just as the Doctrine of the τὸ θεῖόν or the Absolute as the ground or basis, and the ὁ θεός, or the Living and Tri-une God as the Summit and Result of all Philosophy has been revived under all the advantages of modern physical discoveries—and soon after Schelling and Steffens had demonstrated the necessary existence of such a faculty in the human Will independently of the facts that have realized it!' (*CL*, §1065, IV, 745) His reference to Schelling pinpoints the precise grounds for his attraction to and problems with animal magnetism in his later thought. In its favour, magnetism suggests that there is one principle that connects all of organic nature. This is a view that Schelling had espoused in the preface to his treatise on the *Weltseele*, which suggests that there is an electrically charged magnetic polarity present throughout nature. Dale E. Snow notes that, 'This world principle must be capable of encompassing and giving rise to life as well as every other living level of being. He refers to it as 'an eternal and infinite willing-in-itself... in all forms, grades, and potencies of reality'. This great chain of being is variously described as 'a constant chain of life [*Lebenskette*] returning into itself', and a 'god-like unity... of all life'.[18] Animal magnetism, as much as it complicates any theory of the will, provides nevertheless further potential evidence of the existence of a totality, or Absolute in which the subject becomes known to itself in relation to the other objects in the universe.[19]

The difficulties with magnetism are, nevertheless, easy to understand. Frederick Burwick has evinced the analogous example of Fichte to explicate the problem. For Fichte, magnetism seriously compromises our sense of a unified and independent subjectivity if its implications are sustained, because then the 'will and thoughts of another [...] overwhelm an individual's consciousness and rule in regency'.[20] His way out of this difficulty is to suppose that the Ego is not actually suppressed but that the subject willingly acquiesces to the magnetic influence, falling thereby into a form of *volitional* trance. The relevance of such an explanation is apparent if we turn to Coleridge's first recantation of his earlier denunciation of magnetism. This occurs in *The Friend*, 7 September 1809, and takes the form of a marginal note in which he defines 'The Problem' as 'whether the nervous system of one body can, under certain circumstances, act physically on the nervous system of another living body?' (*Friend*, 1, 59) Trevor Levere has proposed that mesmerism suggested to Coleridge that, 'there was a higher power of life, manifested through the exertion of the will and perhaps one with the imagination'.[21] The very question of the role of individual agency is, nevertheless, precisely that which continues to haunt him in his reflections upon the matter, and it is so to the extent that the will of the patient appears to become hostage to that of another, whose own power is dependent upon the suspension of agency in that patient. The fact that this may not be a willing suspension lies at the heart of the problem.

The evidence of Coleridge's letters demonstrates that he had begun to reconsider his position on magnetism in the period immediately before his meeting with Tieck. The spur to this was a further reflection upon the nature of the uncon-sciousness mind in its dream-state. On 20 May 1817, he wrote to Thomas Boosey to question the nature of the supposed 'luminous Fluid' connecting the mesmerist to his patient. He goes on to describe a dream vision in which he appears to sense the effects of electricity over his own body:

---

[18] Dale E. Snow, *Schelling and the end of Idealism* (Albany: SUNY Press, 1996), 85.

[19] For a useful summary of Schelling's *Identitätsphilosophie*, which strongly influences Coleridge in this letter, see Andrew Bowie, *Schelling and Modern European Philosophy: An Introduction* (Routledge, 1993), 55–91, esp. 60–2.

[20] Frederick Burwick, 'Coleridge, Schlegel and Animal Magnetism', in *English and German Roman-ticism. Cross-Currents and Controversies*, ed. James Pipkin, Heidelberg: Carl Winter Verlag, 275–300, 298.

[21] Trevor H. Levere, *Poetry Realized in Nature: Samuel Taylor Coleridge and Early Nineteenth-Century Science*, Cambridge: Cambridge University Press, 1981, 246–61.

I have myself once seen (i.e. appeared to see) my own body under the Bed cloaths flashing silver Light from whatever part I prest it—and the same proceed from the tips of my fingers. I have thus written, as it were, my name, Greek words, cyphers &c on my Thigh: and instantly seen them together with the Thigh in brilliant Letters of silver Light. *CL*, §1056, IV, 731)

Adducing his statement upon stage illusion to Daniel Stuart, written only one year earlier, 'We neither believe it or disbelieve it—with the will the comparing power is suspended', Burwick suggests that Coleridge's understanding of the dream state is at one with his conception of the ground of aesthetic engagement: 'The facility of dreaming Coleridge defined in terms very similar to his *dictum* on "poetic faith" as the "willing suspension of disbelief".' (*CL*, §1010, IV, 641–2; Burwick (1985), 281) On Burwick's account, Coleridge adheres to a theory of the power of the will in both regards. The subject remains master in his own mind, even as he appears to be affected by external forces because there has been a volitional act of self-suspension. If the connection between mesmerism and aesthetic engagement seems incredible then it is worthwhile to reflect upon the fact that in the later letter to Frere, mentioned above, Coleridge moves with ease from the discussion of magnetism back to the central concern of Shakespeare:

But these Tieckiana have seduced me from Mr Tieck himself and the purpose of this letter.—For the last 15 years or more he has devoted the larger portion of his Time and Thoughts to a great Work on Shakespear, in 3 large Volumes Octavo. (*CL*, §1065, IV, 745)

There is a delicious sense of Coleridgean connectivity in the ease with which he slips from the detailed discussion of magnetism to reflect upon Shakespeare scholarship. We might find it difficult to follow him in this fluid intellectual process but his reading of Tieck, at once a close associate and interlocutor, lends a sense of how closely Coleridge's reading of German literature intersects with his fundamental literary, philosophical and scientific concerns.

WORKS CITED

BEER, JOHN. 1977. *Coleridge's Poetic Intelligence*. Houndsmills: Macmillan.

BERNHARDT-KABISCH, ERNEST. 2003. 'When Klopstock England defied': Coleridge, Southey, and the German/English hexameter. *Comparative Literature* 55: 130–63.

BOWIE, ANDREW. 1993. *Schelling and Modern European Philosophy: An Introduction*. London: Routledge.

BRITISH REVIEW, The, 1801.

BURWICK, FREDERICK. 1985. Coleridge, Schlegel and animal magnetism. In *English and German Romanticism: Cross-Currents and Controversies*, ed. James Pipkin. Heidelberg: Carl Winter Verlag, pp. 275–300.

GRIGGS, EARL LESLIE. 1955. Ludwig Tieck and Samuel Taylor Coleridge. *Journal of English and German Philology*, 54: 262–8.

HAZLITT, WILLIAM. 1930–4. *The Complete Works of William Hazlitt*, ed. P. P. Howe, 21 vols. London: Dent.

HOLMAN, J. G. 1799. *The Red Cross Knights*.

KOOY, MICHAEL JOHN. 2002. *Coleridge, Schiller and Aesthetic Education*. Houndsmills: Palgrave.

—— 1995. The end of poetry: aesthetic and ethical investigations in Coleridge and Schiller. *The Wordsworth Circle*. 26: 23–6.

LEVERE, TREVOR H. 1981. *Poetry Realized in Nature: Samuel Taylor Coleridge and Early Nineteenth-Century Science*. Cambridge: Cambridge University Press.

LUKÁCS, GEORG, 1968. *Goethe and his Age*, trans. Robert Anchor. London: Merlin.

MOORE, JOHN DAVID. 1982. Coleridge and the 'modern Jacobinical Drama': *Osorio, Remorse*, and the Development of Coleridge's Critique of the Stage, 1797–1816.' *Bulletin of Research in the Humanities*, 85: 443–64.

PAULIN, ROGER. 1985. *Ludwig Tieck: A Literary Biography*. Oxford: Clarendon Press.

ROBINSON, HENRY CRABB, 1869. *Diary, Reminiscences, and Correspondence of Henry Crabb Robinson*, ed. Thomas Sadler, 3 vols. London: Macmillan.

SCHILLER, FRIEDRICH. 1904–5. *Schillers Sämtliche Werke (Säkular-Ausgabe)*, ed. E. van der Hellen, 16 vols. Stuttgart.

SCOTT, MATTHEW. 1996. The circulation of Romantic creativity: Coleridge, drama, and the question of translation, in *Romanticism On the Net 2*.

SHAFFER, E. S., 1975. *'Kubla Khan' and The Fall of Jerusalem* Cambridge: Cambridge University Press.

SNOW, DALE E., 1996. *Schelling and the End of Idealism*. Albany: SUNY Press.

STRICH, FRITZ, 1949. *Goethe and World Literature*. London: Routledge.

WHEELER, KATHLEEN. 1981. Coleridge's friendship with Ludwig Tieck. In *New Approaches to Coleridge: Biographical and Critical Essays*, ed. Donald Sultana. New York: Barnes and Noble, 96–112.

ZEYDEL, EDWIN H. 1931. *Ludwig Tieck and England: A Study in the Literary Relations of Germany and England during the Early Nineteenth Century*. Princeton: Princeton University Press.

CHAPTER 29

COLERIDGE'S DIALOGUES WITH GERMAN THOUGHT

ELINOR SHAFFER

THE German renaissance of culture in the late eighteenth century, leading to the high period of German literature and thought embracing both 'die Klassik', the classical period, and 'die Romantik', the Romantic period, was an immensely heady and rich time, when a host of major writers and thinkers was active. It is entirely to Coleridge's credit that he was deeply engaged in this major intellectual movement which has such far-reaching consequences for literature, aesthetics, and philosophy. His reading was wide and deep, including literature, travels, history, philosophy, theology, and natural sciences, ranging from the classics (he was a Greek scholar at Cambridge) to the major English and Continental thinkers of the modern period. Coleridge's early interest in German (his German grammar book of the mid-1790s contains his neatly turned translation of a poem by the popular poet K.W. Ramler, his first known translation from the German), his appreciation of Schiller as a playwright (whom he compared to Shakespeare), his reading of contemporary poets such as Friedrich Gottlieb Klopstock (1724–1803) and Salomon Gessner, before his meeting with Klopstock (by then the grand old man of

German letters) on his journey with Wordsworth to Germany in 1798, all exhibit his keen interest.

The literary projects which he planned to carry out in Germany, a biography of Lessing, and translations of Schiller, were both ambitious and apposite. His interest never abated, but led to a lifetime of dialogue with the issues and the actors of the Enlightenment and of the new movement that would become known as Romanticism.[1] Indeed, his dialogues with these figures, in whom leading ideas and individual talent met, illustrate and embody an aspect of the new hermeneutical thinking that developed out of new approaches to understanding the Bible in which Coleridge participated, and that became a discipline of the higher criticism and later of the new social sciences.

His engagement was not only with poetry (though in Germany he was already known as the author of *Religious Musings* (1795)), but with the challenging thought of the time. His intention when he set out for Germany was to write a biography of G. E. Lessing (1729–81), the renowned Enlightenment dramatist, critic, and theologian, one of the most influential writers of the eighteenth century. Lessing's brother had in the early 1790s published a biography together with an edition of his works, which had given rise to much interested comment. This was Coleridge's stimulus.

Coleridge's early engagement with Lessing was of the utmost importance, for many of the major developments of his own intellectual and cultural lifetime still built on Lessing's work, both in literary and in theological controversy. Lessing's dramatic writings—and Coleridge in 1796 identified him first to a correspondent as 'the author of *Emilia Galotti*'[2] (one of his best-known plays)—included his ground-breaking drama criticism which broke the long hold of the French unities over the stage. His *Hamburg Dramaturgy* (*Hamburgische Dramaturgie*) (1767–8) for the first time raised Shakespeare to the level of the Greeks, arguing for frank acknowledgement that the great Greek tragedians, like Shakespeare, displayed acts and characters deemed unfit for the stage by the French 'rules'. These writings underpin the attempts to meld Shakespeare and the Greeks by Friedrich Schiller (1759–1805), whose plays Coleridge commented on favourably in the 1790s and whose historical tragedy *Wallenstein*, Schiller's masterpiece in this genre, received its enthusiastic première during Coleridge's stay in Germany.

---

[1] Eichner (2007) shows that the terminology of 'Romantic', 'Romanticist', and 'Romanticism' was first adopted in Germany by 1805. In England 'romantic' as an adjective referring to certain landscapes and paintings was common in the eighteenth century; but the full vocabulary of a new movement was not in place until the 1860s.

[2] *CL* I, 'To Benjamin Flower', 1 April 1796.

COLERIDGE'S DIALOGUE WITH
SCHILLER: TRAGIC FREEDOM

The extent of Coleridge's knowledge of Schiller is one of the major new findings of the last few years.[3] He knew all four of Schiller's early plays in English; only his early comments on *The Robbers* (*Die Räuber*) have been widely quoted. But crucially he also knew more of Schiller's aesthetic ideas than had been fully traced. The major essays 'On the Danger of Aesthetic Morals'('Ueber die Gefahr aesthetischer Sitten') and 'On Spontaneous and Reflective Poetry'('Ueber naïve und sentimentalische Dichtung'), were published in Schiller's journal *The Horae* (*Die Horen*) in 1795–6, and had been reviewed by Coleridge's friend and mentor Thomas Beddoes in the *Monthly Review* before his departure for Germany.[4] He also makes an early mention of the essay 'On Grace and Dignity'('Ueber Anmut und Würde'). Although there is no direct proof of his reading of Schiller's *The Aesthetic Education of Man* (*Die Aesthetische Erziehung des Menschen*), Schiller's impressive didactic poems freighted with his aesthetic insights into the role of the 'free play'of the imaginative faculty in moral life were published in the journal 'The Muses'Almanac'(*Musenalmanach*) during Coleridge's stay in Göttingen, and his interest is reflected in his Notebooks from 1800 on.[5] Coleridge not only read this journal but owned Schiller's *Poems* (*Gedichte*) and his collected *Essays* (1792–1802).This is of major significance, for Schiller's aesthetic insights, in both essays and poems, form the essential bridge between Kant's *Critique of the Power of Judgement* (*Critik der Urteilskraft*) (1790), the third of the Critiques that transformed German and European philosophy, supplying a crucial argument for the new discipline of aesthetics and the new literary movement that would be known as Romanticism. Schiller's aesthetic essays interpreted Kant's aesthetic thought in more accessible terms closer to those of literature itself, and this literary transposition was carried out by a major writer who had already earned his credentials as a force in poetry and in theatre. Kant's crucial claim in the *Critique of the Power of Judgement* that those ideas that could no longer claim to be demonstrable—the ideas of God, the soul, and freedom—could nevertheless find some kind of realization in the arts was the driving force behind the Romantic movement and the sudden increase in the power and significance of art. Where theology and metaphysics (such as the traditional proofs of the existence of God) had fallen to the scepticism of Hume and to Kant's *Critique of Pure Reason* (1780), backed by the new science, art could

---

[3] Kooy (2002) carries out a detailed reassessment of the evidence. See also *PW* for Joyce Crick on Coleridge's translation of *Wallenstein*.

[4] Kooy, pp. 28–30.

[5] Ibid., ch. 4.

step in to salvage these values that had been and remained essential for the humanity of the race. It was this discovery, and this conviction, that animated the post-Kantian philosophers, among them Coleridge. Schiller embodies his aesthetic convictions in other ways in the series of plays which began with *Wallenstein*. As he wrote in the introduction to his last play *The Bride of Messina* (*Die Braut von Messina*), 'It is through the aesthetic illusion of tragic action that we are brought to realize our moral freedom' (a Kantian road to a Kantian goal).[6] Schiller like Coleridge as a major poet was able, as Fichte or Schelling could not, to carry out in artistic form the demonstration that Schiller following Kant demanded: that art works could embody and carry the values signified by 'God', 'the soul', and 'freedom' even though there could be no valid proof of their existence. It was this insight, embodied in Kant's *Critique of the Power of Judgement* (*Critik der Urtheilskraft*) (1790), especially in the section on the 'Critique of the Teleological Power of Judgment', and carried out more accessibly in Schiller's aesthetic essays, poems, and dramas that Coleridge took with him into his major works, both in poetry and criticism. As we know, he did not while in Germany undertake his full study of Kant's own difficult texts, but he sent them home, and embarked on them after his return; as usual with Coleridge, he read with intensity and an unquenchable urge to comprehend even what might not be welcome or accessible ideas, and he continued to grapple with them in detail for the remainder of his life, as his marginalia and his Notebooks show, and as his major critical works—the *Biographia Literaria* (1817) and the *Aids to Reflection* (1825)—amply demonstrate. But equally characteristically he had already grasped the essentials for his own imaginative use from Schiller's attempts to come to grips with Kant and to convey the aesthetic message that was a culmination of the eighteenth-century evolution of the new aesthetics. He also grasped the crux; how could 'free play', even that leading to the 'harmony of the faculties', be bonded to moral action? Both the speed of his imaginative grasp, and the searching quality of his sustained attempts to plumb the depths of the works that grounded the new teachings were characteristic of him. These early readings of Schiller's plays, his philosophical essays and poetry, paved the way for grappling with the more technical language of Kant, and his own intensive labours at his verse translation of *Wallenstein* (1800) were essential for his response to the new aesthetics of Kant and the post-Kantians. Coleridge's major contributions as a thinker lie in aesthetics (a new field in philosophy in the eighteenth century) and in literary theory and criticism (seen as a discipline, not as *belles-lettres*), and this larger acquaintance with the heady and provocative new German work of his day gives the full context of his own contributions.

Coleridge figures in Schiller's letters as the playwright sought an English translator, though the two writers were never in direct contact.[7] Coleridge carried out

---

[6] Kooy, p. 22.   [7] Ibid., p. 38.

his blank verse translation of the two major parts of the trilogy just after his return to England. In his 1800 preface to his translation he held that Schiller could rank with Shakespeare (*PW* II, 724–5), certainly for historical tragedy, and he had voiced this view several times in the 1790s (*PW* I, 73). His translation of Schiller's hexameters into Shakespearian blank verse brought them even closer. The groundwork for Coleridge's and A.W. Schlegel's Shakespeare lectures of the first decade of the nineteenth century was already laid.

These were among his earliest dramatic and aesthetic concerns; but they were also among his most abiding, as his continued praise of Schiller in his *Table Talk* shows. This dialogue, although it was brought to an end by Schiller's early death, reflected the intimate relationship between translator and translated that would be a feature of Romantic hermeneutics. Between them they imaged a modern Shakespeare.

Lessing and the 'Search for the Historical Jesus'

Although Coleridge never completed his projected Life of Lessing (one of those formidable tasks he rightly perceived the need of but could not always carry through), his early awareness of Lessing, and the notices of the biography and edition of his works published by his brother, an occasion for considerable fresh comment on the great Enlightenment figure, provided the basis for many of the inquiries that concerned Coleridge all his life. His main source of information was Dr Thomas Beddoes, the Unitarian and former reader in chemistry at Oxford, a supporter of the French Revolution, who had like Coleridge settled in Bristol, and having berated the Librarian of the Bodleian for failing to acquire important contemporary books, collected an extensive private library of writings in biblical criticism and current controversy to which Coleridge had access. Coleridge soon came to know Lessing as 'the most formidable infidel of them all', as he put it, whose 'Fragments of an Anonymous Author' was not yet translated.[8] His concern with the issues posed by these *Wolfenbüttel Fragments*, a probing account of the

---

[8] *CL* 1, To Benjamin Flower, 1 April 1796. For a full account of Coleridge's knowledge of Lessing, the higher criticism, and the mythological school of Biblical criticism before he went to Germany, see Shaffer (1975), pp. 17–51.

circumstances surrounding the death of Jesus, the nature of religious leadership (the disciples were alleged to have concocted the story of the Resurrection in order to seize power), and the reliability of reported testimony and witness, which founded the long 'quest for the historical Jesus', led him (for a moment) to consider translating and commenting on them. The 'Fragments', in particular the 'Acts of the Disciples of Jesus', had actually been written in large part by H. S. Reimarus, but Lessing appeared as 'Editor', and most had believed him responsible. The book had unleashed furious controversy in Germany in the 1780s and laid the groundwork for the later and even greater scandal occasioned by D. F. Strauss's *Life of Jesus* (*Das Leben Jesu*) (1835).

Coleridge pursued these matters eagerly in Göttingen, where he attended lectures by J. G. Eichhorn, the noted higher critic of the bible: well known for his work on the Old Testament, and having recently extended his treatment of Genesis as oriental myth to certain parts of the New Testament he was now lecturing over this dangerous ground. He did not publish these lectures on the New Testament until 1804–18; so Coleridge had the excitement of hearing the work before publication and debating with the eminent scholar. He also attended the famous seminar of C. G. Heyne, whose work on mythology set off a train leading to Coleridge's dialogue with the later Schelling on the philosophy of mythology. The stimulation of these contacts with other minds, whether on the page, in the lecture theatre, or in the seminar room, suggests the aura of the Socratic model that played a role in the new hermeneutics. Friedrich Schlegel and Schleiermacher had already embarked on their translation of all of Plato's dialogues, which Schleiermacher would finish only well into the nineteenth century.

Coleridge had read Lessing's probing *Essays on Theology* in 1795, which challenged the right to claim that Christianity was a historical (rather than a mythological) religion. The historical evidences for the events recounted in the bible had been shown to be thoroughly unreliable. Given the evidence for the lateness of the existing Gospels (so late they could not have been written by the Apostles) he nevertheless still had hopes for the discovery of an *Urevangelium* or early form of the gospel story, which led to Schleiermacher's (negative) analysis (1808) of existing evidence before the earliest Gospel. These essays set Coleridge a lifelong task: how religious believers who were also men of modern times fully aware of new thinking could most intelligently and effectively stand by their faith.

In short, Lessing founded or made significant and much discussed contributions to the main lines of inquiry in controversial literary, aesthetic and religious questions that were carried further after his death by Coleridge and many others well beyond the death of Coleridge himself. The dialogue across the grave was an intense one.

COLERIDGE, SCHELLING, AND THE
PHILOSOPHY OF MYTHOLOGY

Schelling's *Philosophy of Mythology*, a series of lectures begun in Munich in 1837–42 and carried further in his last appointment in Berlin, is often given scant attention, as it is felt that other kinds of philosophy were pushing forward in the old Romantic philosopher's later years—the Hegelians of the right and the left, including Marxism, and new currents leading to Nietzsche. Moreover, the current edition of Schelling's works has so far progressed only through nine volumes, completing his early philosophy culminating in the *System of Transcendental Idealism* (*System des transcendentalen Idealismus*) (1800) that Coleridge drew on for the *Biographia*.

Today Schelling's own reputation is rising again, and he is credited with being right as against Hegel in some important respects. This need not concern us here. But there are two main lines of thought that developed from the 'philosophy of mythology' that help us to see what modern traditions Coleridge belongs to and why Schelling recognized him as a 'remarkably gifted man' and a 'congenial spirit' who had contributed to his own thinking on mythology and literary art (as well as drawing constructively in *BL* on his earlier work). The links between Coleridge's and Schelling's early works have been much discussed; but there is a complex and equally interesting set of links between Coleridge's and Schelling's late works, which has gone largely unnoticed.[9]

The most important line is the further development of the response to the Higher Criticism that embraced (instead of rejecting) the idea that all religions represented mythological modes of thought and experience. This insight had been used for the critique of religious claims, especially claims to the uniqueness of Christian or Judaeo-Christian belief systems; under the pressure of the higher-critical analysis of the Biblical narratives, it could, with the right redefinition of 'mythological', be turned into a defense.[10] A mythology properly understood could not be undermined by the discrediting of documents treated as historical. But 'mythology' would have to be taken seriously, not dismissed in the spirit of levity and jeering that had been directed by Bayle, Voltaire, and Reimarus at all Oriental religions (among which were numbered Islam, Christianity, and Judaism).

Friedrich Schleiermacher, a major force in the history of Biblical and classical studies and Romantic religious views, worked powerfully on the development of these possibilities. As in Schleiermacher's treatise *On Luke*, which Coleridge read

---

[9] McFarland (1969) for example argued that the attack on Schelling as a 'pantheist' turned Coleridge from him by 1810. However, Hamilton (2007) has called attention to some of Schelling's later references to Coleridge.

[10] See Shaffer (1975) for a detailed account of this process.

in the excellent translation by Connop Thirlwall, with Thirlwall's clear and ample 100-page introduction (1825), he carefully unpicked any claim to the existence of any extant first-hand account of the events of the life of Jesus before the earliest Gospel (dated to *c.*65 AD); and he effectively denied the authenticity of three letters claimed to have been written by Paul. Schleiermacher's Lectures on the Life of Jesus, which he began to give in 1818, although they were not published until much later, were heard by D. F. Strauss, whose own *Life of Jesus* (*Das Leben Jesu*), translated by George Eliot three years after Coleridge's death, gained as much notoriety as the *Wolfenbüttel Fragments* and a still wider hearing.[11]

The mythological interpretation could be used for the defense of religious claims, on the grounds that such mythological thinking was natural and necessary to the human mind. It could also be understood as requiring a mode of interpretation of meaning in communications between humans. This was an extension of known textual methods, but took on further depth in the analysis of exchanges between humans, of which the privileged model was two human beings in personal contact who were capable of understanding one another. Schleiermacher developed a hermeneutic method which was carried out in his late lectures on hermeneutics. This both resided in, and became the model of, the Romantic communication between two 'geniuses'. This was one of the most productive new lines of thought struck out from the mythological school of Biblical criticism.[12] It led on, in Dilthey's profound and original *Life of Schleiermacher* (1869), the biography not of a man but of a discipline, to the development of hermeneutics from their use in classical and biblical exegesis, and in Romantic literature (as proposed by Schleiermacher himself together with Friedrich Schlegel) to their transformation into the modern methods of the social sciences, carefully compared and contrasted to the methods of the natural sciences. It was in this tradition, which sets forth from Vico (whom Coleridge read), whose Autobiography (*Vita di Giambattista Vico*) is that of the sciences of the human, rather than of a single individual, which fed into Herder's *Humanitätsbriefe* (the link between Vico and Herder has been shown), and Lessing's *The Education of the Human Race* (*Die Erziehung des Menschengeschlechts*), and into Coleridge's *Biographia Literaria*. That work has often been misconstrued, and broken down into disparate fragments, with bits of autobiography and biography (of himself and of Wordsworth) separated from the criticism and the philosophical backing, a procedure which shows no understanding of the aim of a biography of a discipline, not of an individual. As Coleridge's 'Literary

---

[11] For the impact of George Eliot's translation of Strauss on her fiction see Shaffer (1975). For the continuing impact of these issues on writers throughout the Victorian period see Shaffer, 'Irony in Biblical Criticism' (2007).

[12] For a reading of the *Biographia Literaria* in terms of the hermeneutic procedures rooted in the dialogue of the leading minds of the present and the past, see Shaffer, 'The Hermeneutic Community: Coleridge and Schleiermacher', *The Coleridge Connection* (1990).

Biography' introduces the formative spirit of the Romantic literary vocation, as Vico's autobiography represented that of the study of human history, Wilhelm Dilthey, through his *Life of Schleiermacher* (1869), was the major architect of the hermeneutic method characterizing the human sciences as opposed to the natural sciences.

One of Coleridge's most underrated and least discussed works, his 'On the Prometheus of Aeschylus', his Royal Institution lecture (1825), perhaps the most carefully and elaborately planned and 'finished' of all his public lectures, returns to his earliest concern with Greek studies, to 'the noblest Subject that perhaps a Poet ever worked on—the Prometheus', and the 'most pregnant and sublime Mythos and Philosopheme', and follows a main pathway of commentary on Greek tragedy, philosophy, and mythology.[13] Moreover, this lecture, published in the *Transactions of the Royal Institution* only in 1834, was read and referred to by Schelling in his own attempts to formulate a Philosophy of Mythology.

Schelling's Lectures on the Philosophy of Mythology given in Munich in 1837–42 refer explicitly to Coleridge's 'Prometheus' lecture as a source, and also to Coleridge's request for a copy of his own essay 'Die Gottheiten von Samothrace'. His lectures on the *Philosophy of Mythology* in Berlin go further. He finds Coleridge a 'remarkably gifted man' ('ein sonderlich begabte Mann') who understood him very well in previous works (and here he can only be referring to *Biographia Literaria*). He now proceeds to borrow in turn from Coleridge the idea of 'tautegory' used in his 'Prometheus' Lecture (and as his modern editors have shown also in his notebooks). 'Tautegory' may be defined as the mode of passage of permanent ideas of value through their multiplicity of historical embodiments, that is, as maintaining the mythology at the centre of any system of thought. These lectures by the two men—the 'Prometheus' lecture and the lectures in the Philosophy of Mythology—show that not only did Coleridge and Schelling develop elements from one another at several stages in their thinking, they were here moving on to a new phase. Both Coleridge and Schelling sought a way past but also through Kant; if they had found one route through imaginative art, the philosophy of mythology would offer another enabling mode for their age. This was an ambitious programme, and they were both drawing on a broad range of shared sources from classical to contemporary times, from Homer, Hesiod, and Herodotus to Sir William Jones, Hume's essay on *The Natural History of Religion* (1757), which raised the question of the order of historical succession of monotheism and polytheism, the recent work on Homeric epic (1795) by F. A. Wolf showing that the 'epic' could be seen as a series of 'folk lays' or songs, Volney's *Ruins of Empire* (1792), Dupuis' *Origine de tous les cultes* (1791), and Creuzer's *Symbolik und Mythologie der alten*

---

[13] Coleridge, *CL* v, 142–3 (16 May 1821). Coleridge had annotated a borrowed copy of a new edition of the *Prometheus* in 1817, and put together a number of notes for the benefit of his son Hartley in 1821 (*SW&F* v. 2, 1252–3). He had also concerned himself with *Naturphilosophie* and read Genesis in Hebrew as a creation myth in 1818–19.

Völker (1821) (*Symbolism and Mythology of the ancient peoples*).[14] All these works were read by both of them.[15] Moreover, both were fully cognizant of the developments in the Higher Criticism from Eichhorn to Schleiermacher. Coleridge's reading just at this time of Vico's *Scienza Nuova* and of Connop Thirlwall's excellent 100-page introduction to his translation of Schleiermacher's *On Luke* (1825)—an essay first written in 1808—brought him up to date and gave him crucial material for the lecture.

Finally, this programme is the culmination of Coleridge's exploration in *Aids to Reflection*—his finest and most telling philosophical essay—of a border area beyond the strict Kantian 'Limits of Reason Alone', which he had shown that even Kant had to resort to in order for the religion of morality to work. That area just beyond the limits of reason where 'aids to reflection' may be permitted— by Kant, reluctantly, by Coleridge, sympathetically—is the area of the imagination in which Coleridge is at home.[16] It is also the new ground that the Higher Criticism of the Bible moved onto, the latest phase of the insight of Lessing, Eichhorn, and Schleiermacher that to admit religion as mythology (rather than continuing to claim it as revelation or history) could represent not a defeat but a defensible ground. The relation of Greek tragedy to religion, the mutual relations of monotheistic and polytheistic religion, the role of myth in both, and the diversifying development of early social groupings are shared European topics. Even while he praises Coleridge for having previously demonstrated his understanding of Schelling in the construction of his theses in the *Biographia*, with these late lectures Schelling has in fact moved from idealist method: 'mythology' understood as tautegory becomes a symbolic mode of representing permanent values that ever changed their phenomenological aspect in history.

Coleridge's late *annus mirabilis*, the year 1825—the equivalent in his maturity to the youthful *annus mirabilis* of 1798—homed in on the major texts of the culture, the Bible and the Greeks, the main texts on which hermeneutics was at work, and their interpretation through the modern philosophy most to be reckoned with, Kant's placing of the bounds of reason. Coleridge's *annus mirabilis*

---

[14] For Schelling's sources see the three sets of annotated student notes on his *Philosophie der Mythologie*, the Munich lectures 1837/42. Coleridge had of course known Schelling's early essay on Philosophemes from the two-volume collected *Abhandlungen* of 1808; had read Creuzer's *Symbolik und Mythologie* and Schelling's 'Die Gottheiten von Samothrake'; for his part, Schelling at the time he embarked on the series of lectures on the Philosophy of Mythology had read Coleridge's 'Prometheus' lecture, to which he refers explicitly both in the lectures and in his notes ('Mitschrift Chováts' (Berlin 1842), in *Philosophie der Mythologie*, pp. 153–4; see also *Schriften* XI, 196 Anm. 1).

[15] Another work that was influential on Schelling's early formation, and could have been known to Coleridge during his Göttingen stay, was C. G. Heyne, *De origine et causis Fabularum Homericarum* (Göttingen 1778). Heyne, still teaching his seminar on mythology in Coleridge's time, saw philosophers as originators of mythology through philosophemes and images out of cosmogony. Coleridge may simply have worked from Schelling's own formulation of the philosopheme.

[16] See Shaffer, 'Coleridge and Kant's "giant hand" ' (2004) for an explication of Coleridge's *Aids to Reflection* in relation to Kant's *Religion within the Limits of Reason Alone*.

brought a harvest of three major works, the *Confessions of an Inquiring Spirit* (1824), *Aids to Reflection* (1825), and the Royal Institution lecture 'On the Prometheus of Aeschylus' (1825). The connections between these works have not been fully recognized, despite their having been written so close together in time. *Confessions* had been written in 1824, to serve as an introduction to *Aids to Reflection*, but was not published with it for reasons never wholly clarified, and it appeared only posthumously; in the *Collected Coleridge* it appears only in *SW&F*, still separated from *Aids*. The title was drawn from Goethe's *Confessions of Beautiful Soul* (*Bekenntnisse einer schönen Seele*), a section of the novel *Wilhelm Meister*, of which Carlyle had sent Coleridge his translation.[17] Materials used in the 'Prometheus' lecture had partly been prepared for Coleridge's son Hartley in 1820. Despite these various circumstances, the three works are closely related, and together represent Coleridge's most complete and effective statements.

Coleridge chose Kant's most tightly limited definition of 'religion within the limits of reason alone', while exploring and pressing towards the wider possibilities of the Kantian 'aid' as he envisaged them. The wider possibilities of the Kantian 'aid' include those of the reconstitution and reimagining of religion as a mythological phase of human history and a continuing resource of the human imagination. The necessary reformulation through various phases of human development is an example of tautegory.

Thus the 'Prometheus' lecture explores the possibility of the mythological 'aid to reflection' in explicating the Greek moment in the history of the divine in terms of the philosophy of mythology of his own time. This lecture was related to the Schelling essay that Coleridge drew upon, 'The Gods of Samothrace' ('Die Gottheiten von Samothrake'), which fed into Coleridge's far-ranging cultural exposition of the emergence of Greek tragic literature and philosophy.[18] These were not merely antiquarian or proto-anthropological ruminations, but took place in a period of intense conflict over the ownership and decipherment of the Egyptian cult objects (including the Rosetta Stone) first claimed by Napoleon. The interpretation of the nature of Egyptian religion and mythology was of crucial concern for the relation of mythology to religion.

Coleridge's lecture may be seen as an interpretation of Aeschylus' play, whose theme was so important to the period, whether in Goethe's poem 'Prometheus', which applauds man defiantly seizing fire, or in Shelley's verse play *Prometheus Unbound*, in which the god-bound titan finally finds liberty. In Aeschylus' play the earliest Greek tragic dramatist invents or invests his invention with the values of Greek culture, whether these are in fact the 'significances' of the Eleusinian Mysteries which Aeschylus in his lifetime was accused of revealing, or an enactment

---

[17] On the 'Confessions' see Shaffer (2004).
[18] One of the transcripts of Schelling's Munich lectures cites him as saying that Coleridge had requested a copy of the essay on 'The Gods of Samothrace' from him.

of the birth of reason or philosophy in its human form, in which the supreme god Jove represents Law, and Prometheus the assertion of the right to separate Reason from Law. Coleridge's lecture needs to be placed in the full context of the development of tragic theory in the period, in Schiller's enactments of irreconcilable tragic conflict in modern history, in Hegel's unfolding of meaning through history in the *Phenomenology*, or in his *Aesthetics* on the ethical conflict between two 'rights' (the Hegelian reading of *Antigone* is not far from Coleridge's of *Prometheus*, a drama in which Jove as Law stands implacably opposed to Prometheus as Reason, as in Hegel's view of *Antigone* (state) Law on traitors is opposed to the equally binding personal obligation to bury one's dead), in A.W. Schlegel's, Goethe's and Coleridge's own views of Shakespeare, and in the later development of all these ideas in Nietzsche's *Birth of Tragedy*. Coleridge's inventive philological imagination is also at work on the relation between the roots of language and the thought that developed from it, including the tragic experience of the Greeks and the religious vision of the Orient. It has never been shown that Coleridge was familiar with Hölderlin yet there is a ghostly dialogue between them. In his later years in medical care, Hölderlin had been the school friend of Schelling and Hegel, and is credited today with being the author or co-author of the 'First Programme of German Idealism' (*Erstes Systemprogramm des deutschen Idealismus* (1795)), as well of course as perhaps the major German Romantic poet, and a brilliant innovator in the translation of Greek tragedy (Sophocles) and poetry (Pindar). It was on the basis of Hölderlin's translations of Sophocles' *Antigone* (as well as Schleiermacher's own arduous experience of translating the dialogues of Plato into German over fifteen years) that Schleiermacher based his ground-breaking essay of 1813 'On Difficulty in Translation', which broke decisively with the dominant French cultural practice of '*les belles infidèles*', the 'beautiful unfaithful ones', that is of 'improving' the language of the translated work and bringing it over smoothly into the style and manner of the target language. Instead, Schleiermacher demanded that the foreign text in translation retain its difficulties and peculiarities thus enriching the target language. This reflected new thinking about translation of the Bible as well as the Greeks. Coleridge was acting in this contemporary and challenging spirit in interpreting Aeschylus via the less familiar and more barbarous myths of the 'gods of Samothrace'. He was also acknowledging the Oriental mythologies attendant on the characteristically Greek discovery of reason, or philosophy.

Schelling in his *Philosophy of Mythology* of the Berlin period rightly gives Coleridge further credit, both as a kindred spirit and as a source of a crucial idea for the new philosophy. Schelling in these lectures had moved on from his attempts in *The Ages of the World* (*Die Weltalter*) to derive everything from an original unity. As Andrew Bowie has put it, 'The interest of the idea of the "new mythology" in Schelling, and in that part of Schlegel's argument which stresses the need for a new synthesis of the tendencies of modernity, lay in the fact that it did not have recourse to a philosophy of pure origins, and saw the task of synthesis as our task.'[19] Here, Coleridge can help with a concept of his own, tautegory, which is historical and aesthetic, rather than idealist-philosophical. Both Coleridge and Schelling hold Kant's attempt in *Religion within the Limits of Reason Alone* to locate principles in the structure of the consciousness itself to be impossible. Schelling's debt to Coleridge's idea of tautegory is considerable, then, for it allows the human race to pass from mythological phase to historical without losing the religious encounters of their past. This is an exploration of the possible uses of the Kantian 'aid to reflection' when it is released from the artificial shackles binding reason, in short, when Prometheus is unbound.

Coleridge's *Confessions of an Inquiring Spirit*, when they were finally published in 1840, did indeed show him at the cutting edge of new thinking, while returning to one of his earliest dialogue partners, Lessing. When the essay drew attacks, in which Coleridge figures as the founder of an English school of biblical interpretation that would lead to 'complete Infidelity',[20] J. H. Green, his companion and actual *Gesprächspartner* through the productive 1820s, now professor of anatomy, provided an excellent introduction to the second edition (1849), which firmly and frankly admits Coleridge's lifelong concern with Lessing's work, especially the *Wolfenbüttel Fragments* and the *Essays on Theology*. The *Confessions* draw upon Lessing to relinquish any claim to the 'inspired' nature of the biblical texts and to suggest a modern, non-literal mode of reading the bible. So familiar is the reading of the Bible as literature now both inside and outside religious establishments that readers in the twenty-first century may find it very difficult to understand how shocking it seemed then to read the Bible as literature. Coleridge compared the Bible's standing as literature with that of Shakespeare. This shocking procedure too is now so familiar as to pass without remark.

MAX MUELLER AND THE NAMES OF NUMINOUS EXPERIENCE

Looking beyond Schelling's *Philosophy of Mythology* into the later nineteenth century to see where the 'Germano-Coleridgean' tendency so shrewdly identified by J. S. Mill went, we can identify three streams to all of which Coleridge was a contributor and participant: the mythological trend that emerged from the higher

---

[19] Bowie, p. 225.
[20] An anonymous essay 'On Tendencies towards the Subversion of the Faith' appeared in *The English Review*, x (1848), 399–444 (*SW&F* II, 1114–15).

criticism of the Bible into a defense (rather than a critique) of the mythological groundwork of religion; the hermeneutic interpretative methods which enabled the reinterpretation and the renewal of ancient texts in modern contexts, of which Schleiermacher was the major exponent, especially as later interpreted by the great historian and social scientist Wilhelm Dilthey in his monumental study of *Schleiermacher* (1869) which founded the modern methods of the humanistic and social sciences over against those of the natural sciences; and we perceive that these trends were also integral to the growth of the philological branch of thought that distinguished German nineteenth-century studies. In England the representative of this philological approach to matters of mythology was Max Mueller (1823– 1900), whose mode of thought displays and encapsulates the whole history of modern German idealism as it found a form in the historical study of languages from the Indo-European root to the modern European languages.

Max Mueller offers a very good insight into the German thought that both Coleridge and he were heir to, and represents in his own work one vital pathway along which it developed. Mueller was greatly struck by Schelling's late Lectures on the Philosophy of Mythology, which he had the opportunity of hearing in Berlin when (having already written a thesis on Spinoza's *Ethics*) he was a young student of Sanskrit. This set him on his course for life. In 1841 Schelling had been appointed professor in Berlin, and at his inaugural in 1844 his audience included Marx, Engels, Kierkegaard and Bakunin, as well as Jacob Burkhardt. The whole cycle of lectures on the Philosophy of Mythology was given in 1845–6. Numbers at his lectures fell off, but among those who still listened in 1846 was Max Mueller, who was fascinated by the parallels between the natural history and philosophy of mythology as Schelling described them and the history of language, and visited the philosopher a number of times to discuss these matters with him.[21] Schelling's Berlin Lectures were published only posthumously, but Mueller was established in Oxford by 1848, where he edited the Sanskrit *Rigveda*, was elected a Fellow of All Souls in 1858 and Deputy Taylorian Professor of Modern Languages, and finally Professor of Comparative Philology in 1868, a chair founded for him.

In his own lecture on 'The Philosophy of Mythology', Mueller outlined the philosophical background very clearly:

That stream of philosophic thought springing from Descartes had two branches, the idealistic (for example, Spinoza), and the sensualistic (for example, Hume), which came together again in Kant: 'and the full stream was carried on by Schelling and Hegel . . . This stream of modern philosophic thought has ended in a Philosophy of Mythology, which . . . forms the most important part of Schelling's final system, which he called his positive philosophy, given to the world after the death of that great thinker and poet, in 1854.'[22]

---

[21] Stone (ed.), p. 12.
[22] Mueller, 'On the Philosophy of Mythology', in Stone (ed.), pp. 145–6.

Schelling had attempted to create a literary-philosophical version of religion in *The Ages of the World* (*Die Weltalter*), which proliferated into many versions, and remained unfinished, the many MSS finally destroyed in a bombing raid on Munich in the Second World War. *The Philosophy of Mythology* represents a more concrete and anthropological approach to the definition of god and the gods; indeed, he felt it incumbent on him to explain why a philosopher should treat the subject, giving as his explanation that it was as appropriate as the time-honoured subject of 'nature'.

Mueller then developed his own philological version of the philosophy of mythology, which erected an imaginative account of the creation of myths of the gods through the names of elemental experiences, and these gods were (from the proto-Sanskrit roots) those of the Indian, the Greek and the Roman deities. Coleridge too had been familiar with the early phases: he had read Sir William Jones, and Friedrich Schlegel's *The Wisdom of the Indians* (*Die Weisheit der Indier*); it is not known whether he had become aware of the lectures of Franz Bopp from 1805, in comparative philology.

Despite Mueller's stress on the history of language, he also undertook to use his philological insights to illuminate a variety of religious topics, 'the discovery of the soul', 'what was thought about the departed', and 'the divine and the human'. While he called these topics 'anthropological', in a lecture like 'The Perception of the Infinite' (1878) he is still explicitly concerned with philosophical problems handed down from Kant through Schelling. From the start, like Coleridge, he was concerned with the limited scope of the reason as described in Kant's *Critique of Pure Reason* (*Kritik der reinen Vernunft*). He held that Kant in his denial of direct apprehension of religious entities, had instead in the *Critique of Practical Reason* 'opened a side door' (the moral law) through which to apprehend the sense of the Divine. Like Schelling and Coleridge he was not satisfied with this 'side door' (though Coleridge found Kant's *Metaphysics of Morals* one of the most sublime treatises he had ever read), and sought a 'direct faculty with which to apprehend the Infinite'.[23] In the event, however, as Schiller found another side door (the way via tragic freedom), as did Schelling (the way via art, in the *System des Transcendentalen Idealismus*), as did Coleridge (the way via imagination, in the *Biographia*), so Mueller found his way via the reconstitution of mythic names in an ancient language.

In all these cases, the problem for religion was set by the Higher Criticism: the text of the Scriptures could no longer be regarded as inspired by a Holy Spirit, and the events told in the sacred text could not form the basis of a historical religion, for they were shot through with mythological references and betrayed the hands of a variety of compilers. As Mueller put it succinctly, 'Higher critical scholarship now applied to all religious texts. Only this makes comparative mythology possible.'[24]

---

[23] Ibid., p. 146.   [24] Ibid., p. 115.

This excursus into the future of German movements of thought shows that Coleridge had early in the century engaged in the major movements and continued to be in dialogue with the leading minds of the time. Returning to this after Mueller allows us to see that Coleridge used Naturphilosophie, as Mueller used Sanskrit names, to breathe life into a mythology of science which was that of a human experience of nature.

Works Cited

Primary Sources

Creuzer, Friedrich. 1819–23. *Symbolik und Mythologie der alten Völker, besonders der Griechen.* 7 vols, rev. edn. Leipzig/Darmstadt.

Dilthey, Wilhelm. 1869. *Das Leben Schleiermachers.*

Hume, David. 1757. *The Natural History of Religion.* Oxford: Oxford University Press.

Kant, Immanuel. 1994. *Critik der Urtheilskraft.* Berlin und Libau: bei Lagarde und Friederich, 1790. Facsimile reprint, with a brief introduction by Lewis White Beck, London: Routledge/Thoemmes Press.

—— 2000. *Critique of the Power of Judgment,* ed. Paul Guyer. Trans. Paul Guyer and Eric Matthews. Cambridge: Cambridge University Press.

—— *Religion within the Limits of Reason Alone.* Cambridge: Cambridge University Press. With an introduction and notes by Paul Guyer.

Mill, John Stuart. 1950–1980. *Mill on Bentham and Coleridge,* intro. F. R. Leavis. Chatto and Windus; repr. 1980, Cambridge: Cambridge University Press.

Mueller, Max. 2002. *The Essential Max Mueller: On Language, Mythology and Religion,* ed. Jon Stone. New York: Palgrave Macmillan.

Schelling, Friedrich Wilhelm Joseph. 2000. *Das System der transzendentalen Naturphilosophie. The Ages of the World.* (Fragment) Translated, with an Introduction by Jason M. Wirth from the handwritten remains Third Version (*c.*1815). State University of New York Press.

—— 1994. *On the History of Modern Philosophy.* Munich Lectures (*c.* 1833–4). Translation, Introduction, and Notes by Andrew Bowie. Cambridge: Cambridge University Press.

—— 1856–8. 'Historisch-Kritische Einleitung in die Philosophie der Mythologie', Vol. XI, *Sämmtliche Werke,* 14 vols, Stuttgart and Augsburg.

Schiller, Johann Christoph Friedrich. 1967. *Letters on the Aesthetic Education of Man,* trans. L.A. Willoughby and Elizabeth M. Wilkinson. Oxford: Oxford University Press.

Schleiermacher, Friedrich. 1982. On the different methods of translation [1813]. In *German Romantic Criticism,* ed. A. Leslie Willson. New York: Continuum.

—— 1825. *On Luke,* trans. Connop Thirlwall.

—— 1975. *Das Leben Jesu.* Lectures first given 1819; published 1864, ed. Jack C. Verheyden. Philadelphia: Fortress Press.

—— 1977. On the concept of hermeneutics, with reference to F. A. Wolf's Instructions and Ast's Textbook. In *Hermeneutics: The Handwritten Manuscripts,* ed. Heinz Kimmerle, trans. James Duke and Jack Forstman. Missoula, Montana: Scholars Press.

Secondary Works

BOWIE, ANDREW. 1990. *Aesthetics and Subjectivity from Kant to Nietzsche*. Manchester: Manchester University Press.

EICHNER, HANS W. 2007. *Romanticism and its Cognates. The European History of a Word.*?

FRANK, MANFRED. 1975. *Der unendliche Mangel an Sein*. Frankfurt.

—— 1985. *Eine Einführung in Schellings Philosophie*. Frankfurt.

—— 1989. *Einführung in der frühromantische Aesthetik*. Frankfurt.

HAMILTON, PAUL. 2007. *Coleridge and German Philosophy*. Continuum.

—— 2001. Coleridge as Philosopher. In *The Cambridge Companion to Coleridge*, ed. Lucy Newlyn. Cambridge: Cambridge University Press.

HOUGH, BARRY and DAVIS. 2009. *Coleridge's Laws: A Study of Coleridge in Malta*, with an Introduction by Michael John Kooy: Open Book Publishers.

KOOY, MICHAEL JOHN. 2002. *Coleridge, Schiller and Aesthetic Education*. Palgrave.

KUEHN, MANFRED. 2005. The reception of Hume in Germany. In Peter Jones, ed., *The Reception of David Hume in Europe. Reception of British and Irish Authors in Europe*. Series Editor: Elinor Shaffer. Continuum Books, pp. 98–138.

—— 2001. *Kant. A Biography*. Cambridge: Cambridge University Press.

MCFARLAND, THOMAS. 1969. *Coleridge and the Pantheist Tradition*. Oxford.

MOMIGLIANO, ARNALDO D. 1966. *Studies in Historiography*. London.

SHAFFER, ELINOR S. 1983. Aspects of Coleridge's Aesthetics, unpub. Ph.D. thesis, Columbia University, 1966; summarized and quoted in Catherine Miles Wallace, *The Design of 'Biographia Literaria'*. London: Allen and Unwin, 1983.

—— 1975. *'Kubla Khan' and The Fall of Jerusalem. The Mythological School in Biblical Criticism and Secular Literature 1770–1880*. Cambridge: Cambridge University Press.

—— 1990. The hermeneutic community: Coleridge and Schleiermacher. In *The Coleridge Connection*, ed. Richard Gravil and Molly Lefebure. Macmillan, pp. 200–29.

—— 2000. Religion and literature. In *The Cambridge History of Literary Criticism*, vol. 5, 'Romanticism', ed. Marshall Brown. Cambridge: Cambridge University Press, pp. 138–61.

—— 2002. The 'Confessions' of Goethe and Coleridge: Goethe's *Bekenntnisse einer Schönen Seele* ('Confessions of a Beautiful Soul') and Coleridge's *Confessions of an Inquiring Spirit*, in *Goethe and the English-Speaking World*, ed. Nicholas Boyle and John Guthrie. London: Camden House, pp. 145–58.

—— 1970. Metaphysics of culture: Kant and Coleridge's *Aids to Reflection*. *Journal of the History of Ideas*, 31(2) (April–June): 199–218.

—— 'Coleridge and Kant's 'Giant Hand'. In Rüdiger Görner, ed., *Anglo-German Affinities and Antipathies*. Munich, pp. 39–56.

—— 2007. Irony and Biblical criticism. In *Samuel Butler: Victorian Against the Grain*, ed. James G. Paradis. Toronto, Buffalo, and London: Toronto University Press, pp. 58–90.

—— ed. 1983. *Comparative Criticism*. Vol 5, 'Hermeneutic Criticism'. Cambridge: Cambridge University Press.

SHAFFER, ELINOR and ZUCCATO, EDOARDO, eds. 2007. *The Reception of S.T. Coleridge in Europe*. London: Continuum.

SZONDI, PETER. 1975. *Einführung in die literarische Hermeneutik*. Vorlesungen Bd. 5. Frankfurt a.M.: Suhrkamp taschenbuch, pp. 7–192.

CHAPTER 30

COLERIDGE AND LANGUAGE THEORY

JAMES C. MCKUSICK

THROUGHOUT his career, Coleridge was persistently engaged with the question of the relation between language and thought. In a letter of September 1800 to William Godwin, Coleridge formulates this question as follows:

'Is Logic the *Essence* of Thinking?' in other words—Is *thinking* impossible without arbitrary signs? &—how far is the word 'arbitrary' a misnomer? Are not words &c parts & germinations of the Plant? And what is the Law of their Growth?—In something of this order I would endeavor to destroy the old antithesis of *Words & Things*, elevating, as it were, words into Things, & living Things too. (*CL* 1, 625)

Although in this letter he is ostensibly asking Godwin to grapple with these challenging topics, at a deeper level Coleridge is setting forth the agenda for much of his own future speculation on the nature and origin of language. Specifically, Coleridge is pondering whether words are merely arbitrary signs, or whether they can be described as 'living Things' with their own vital process of historical development. This question is a central one for Coleridge; it recurs at several crucial moments in his intellectual career. His youthful enthusiasm for the poetry of Bowles, for example, is largely motivated by his perception that Bowles is 'the only always-natural poet in our Language' (*CL* 1, 278). His eventual rejection of Berkeley's idealist philosophy is prompted by his dissatisfaction with its doctrine of linguistic arbitrariness.[1] His critique of Wordsworth in the *Biographia Literaria* (chapters 17–22) grows out of a controversy over what constitutes a truly 'natural' poetic diction. His oft-quoted distinction between symbol and allegory in *The Statesman's Manual* (30) is phrased as a distinction between natural and merely conventional modes of signification. These few examples may serve to indicate that Coleridge's quest for a criterion of linguistic 'naturalness' is a persistent element in his poetical, critical, and philosophical endeavors. The purpose of this essay is to trace the development of Coleridge's theory of language and to situate that development in the intellectual climate of his era.

Coleridge's engagement with what A. C. Goodson terms 'the problem of language' (*Coleridge's Writings: On Language* 1) spans several decades and encompasses all of his major published works. Coleridge also reflects on the problem of language in his more personal and private writings—his letters, marginalia, fragmentary essays, and most notably his lifetime production of bescribbled 'flycatchers'. The incredible variety of Coleridge's achievement and the incomplete or provisional state of most of his writings pose an enormous problem for scholars who seek to comprehend the significance of his thought. One of the most important and least understood historical determinants of Coleridge's textual practice is the new conception of language that emerged in England during the Romantic period. Coleridge himself contributed to the development of this fundamental shift in linguistic understanding, most overtly in *Lyrical Ballads* and the *Biographia Literaria*, but also in *The Friend* and *Aids to Reflection*. Indeed, virtually all of Coleridge's writings reflect his lifelong engagement with linguistic theory. Coleridge's articulation of a distinctively Romantic conception of language, progressively formulated and modified throughout his career, provides a coherent, though constantly evolving, thread of discourse in his poetry, criticism, and philosophy.

Coleridge's *Notebooks* furnish a lively introduction to his fascination with language and linguistic theory. The first volume of the *Notebooks* (covering the period 1794–1804) is especially remarkable for its frothy verbal texture, its odd juxtapositions and seminal conjunctions, and the many voices that ventriloquize in its various transcriptions from other works. Throughout the early *Notebooks*, Coleridge investigates the nature and origin of language, as for example in an entry (dating perhaps from the mid-1790s) that combines etymological speculation with observations of infant language: 'Smile from subrisus. B and M both labials / hence Infants first utter a, Ba, pa, ma, milk' (*CN* 1, 4).[2] What is the implied relation between etymology and the acquisition of language? Evidently both provide

---

[1] In a notebook entry of July–September 1809, Coleridge says that 'words have a tendency to confound themselves & co-adunate with the things [they signify]—Berkeley's System thence only unbelievable' (*CN* 3, 3542). Coleridge is here objecting to Berkeley's assertion that language is composed of arbitrary signs.

[2] This notebook passage is corrected from Add. MS. 47496, fo. 1ᵛ, in the British Library (the manuscript reads 'ma' for 'a' in the published version).

evidence concerning the ultimate origin of language; the babble of infants can tell us something about the *Ursprache*. Subsequent notebook entries explore the significance of infant language from this point of view. Coleridge notes that 'Children in making new Words always do it analogously' (*CN* 1, 867), implying a general principle of analogy in the formation of language. Later he describes how his infant son Hartley used stones to signify 'fire' in a scene of aboriginal naming (*CN* 1, 914).

All of these early notebook entries bear witness to Coleridge's fascination with infant language, regarded as a source of information about the prehistoric origin of language, and, more generally, the origin of human consciousness. The careful study of these notebook passages adds a linguistic dimension to the Romantic *topos* of the wise infant and offers a plausible justification for Coleridge's otherwise rather doting portrayal of his son Hartley in 'The Nightingale', or for Wordsworth's paean to the 'blessed babe' in *The Prelude* (2, 232). Coleridge's linguistic speculations derive from the Enlightenment tradition of inquiry into the origin of language, an inquiry that was reflected in a widespread European fascination with the Wild Boy of Aveyron, a child who was found wandering alone in the forest near Toulouse, France in 1797. The Wild Boy lacked the ability to speak in any known language, but in his expressive grunts and howls, he spoke eloquently to the French *philosophes* in their quest to discover the ultimate origin of language (Lane 73–95; Newton 98–127). Many European intellectuals of the 1790s imagined that the Wild Boy of Aveyron might provide clues concerning the primordial language spoken by Adam and Eve in the Garden of Eden, in words believed to express the essential nature of things. Coleridge was deeply intrigued by the story of the Wild Boy of Aveyron; he referred to Jean Itard's account of the boy's education shortly after its 1802 publication in English (*CN* 1, 1348), and in 1809 he pondered the suitability of this topic for Wordsworth's unfinished poem, *The Recluse*:

A fine subject to be introduced in William's great poem is the Savage Boy of Aveyron in Itard's account—viz—his restless joy & blind conjunction of his Being with natural Scenery; and the manifest influence of Mountain, Rocks, Waterfalls, Torrents, & Thunderstorms—Moonlight Beams quivering on Water, &c on his whole frame. (*CN* 3, 3538)

For Coleridge, the story of the 'Savage Boy' offers a contemporary means of inquiry into the origin of language, as he envisions the boy's first utterances emerging through passionate engagement with 'natural Scenery'. For such 'savage' speakers, words have a vital connection with the natural objects that they signify.

The question of the relation between words and things has a distinguished history, extending as far back as Plato and Aristotle.[3] Are words purely conventional signs, or is their lexical form in some way motivated by the things they

---

[3] Plato's views concerning the relation between words and things are to be found in his *Cratylus* and *Phaedo*. He may be considered the progenitor of the doctrine that words are natural signs, although his argument is typically hedged with Socratic irony. Aristotle, on the other hand, argues that words have meaning 'not as an instrument of nature (φύσει) but by convention' (*De Interpretatione*, 17a.1). Aristotle is thus an early advocate of the view that words are conventional signs.

signify? This ancient philosophical conundrum took on a renewed immediacy in the sixteenth and seventeenth centuries, partly due to the rise of Protestantism and its need to validate the interpretation of Scriptural language, and partly due to the rise of the natural sciences and their promise of a wholly deterministic psychology. The theological aspect of the controversy is best exemplified by the doctrines of Jakob Boehme (1575–1624) and Faustus Socinus (1539–1604). Boehme advanced the doctrine of an ancient, God-given Adamic language, in which words expressed the true essences of things. Socinus, on the other hand, rejected the Adamic language doctrine, while also denying the consubstantiality of God and the Word. Already in the early seventeenth century, a doctrine of mystical essentialism was opposed to one of more skeptical conventionalism.[4]

The scientific aspect of this controversy is best exemplified by the contrasting doctrines of John Locke (1632–1704) and Gottfried Wilhelm von Leibniz (1646–1716). Locke asserted that any language, even the supposed original Adamic language, was only an imperfect human instrument; he regarded language in general as a collection of purely arbitrary signs.[5] Some of Locke's followers, notably Étienne Bonnot de Condillac (1715–80) and John Horne Tooke (1736–1812), held the more extreme position that language actually determines the progress of understanding, and hence that thought is constituted by language. Language, in this view, is not just a convenient tool, but a pair of spectacles we can never remove. Horne Tooke made extensive use of etymology to prove his thesis that all words originate in the 'names of things', which in turn was supposed to demonstrate that the human mind is entirely governed by the impressions of material objects.

Leibniz, in an extended critique of Locke's position, advanced a carefully qualified theory of linguistic rationalism.[6] He avoided the extreme (Boehmean) view that particular words phonetically express the 'signatures' of things, and emphasized instead the existence of an immanent ordering principle in language, whereby language is not only the tool, but actually the mirror of thought. This doctrine of linguistic harmony became crucial to eighteenth-century efforts to investigate the motivated character of linguistic signs; it was typically expressed in the quest for a universal grammar that would systematize all linguistic phenomena (Essick, 56–61). James Harris's *Hermes* (1751) is the classic English example of universal grammar. Lord Monboddo's *On the Origin and Progress of Language* (1773–92) is perhaps the most thorough and systematic exposition of linguistic rationalism ever produced

---

[4] For the Boehme–Socinus controversy, see Hans Aarsleff, *From Locke to Saussure*, 59-60, 80. The relevant texts are Boehme's *Aurora* (1614) and *De Signatura Rerum* (1622), and Socinus's *De Statu Adami ante Lapsum* and *Explicatio Primae Partis Primi Capitis Evangelistae Johannis* (1562). Coleridge was familiar with both of these authors; see *Marginalia* 1, 553-696, *Aids to Reflection*, 338.

[5] Locke's view of Adamic language is given in his *Essay Concerning Human Understanding* (1690), III, vi, 44-51.

[6] Leibniz's critique of Locke is given in his *Nouveaux essais sur l'entendement humain* (composed in 1704, and first published in 1764).

in England. He defines language as 'the expression of the conceptions of the mind by articulate sounds', thereby ruling out the possibility that the mind's conceptions may themselves be determined by language. Monboddo's book is unique in that it gives exhaustive etymological evidence for its theses, thus demonstrating that linguistic rationalism need not be limited to a synchronic or taxonomic mode of analysis, as exemplified by universal grammar.

Monboddo's book fared poorly in England, where linguistic materialism prevailed; it fared better in Germany, where it was translated with a preface by Johann Gottfried Herder, one of the progenitors of the 'new philology'. This new philology, comprised in the work of such linguists as Friedrich Schlegel, Franz Bopp, Jacob Grimm, and Rasmus Rask, was grounded in the historical study of Germanic languages within the larger context afforded by the discovery of Sanskrit and the systematic development of the Indo-European hypothesis of linguistic origin. Hans Aarsleff has traced the role of linguistic historicism, and specifically the Adamic language doctrine, in the rise of interest in Sanskrit, Persian, and other ancient languages in the German universities (*Study of Language in England*, 143–61). However, the seminal role of Coleridge in the development of language theory in Britain has not been widely recognized. After a youthful flirtation with the associationist doctrines of David Hartley, Coleridge set himself the task of advancing linguistic rationalism; this meant the espousal of rigorously systematic doctrines of linguistic 'harmony' (on the Leibnizian model) as well as more local efforts to combat Horne Tooke on his home turf, etymology. In the context of the ongoing controversy over the essential nature of language, Coleridge's scattered exercises in etymology fall into place as part of a more rigorously conceived program of scholarly inquiry, and need not be dismissed as 'unscientific' merely because they do not conform to modern canons of correctness. Coleridge himself distinguished between a reductive linguistic historicism, such as that espoused by Horne Tooke, and a more speculative philosophy of language: 'Horne Tooke, in writing about the formation of words only, thought he was explaining the philosophy of language, which is a very different thing' (*Table Talk*, 2, 83).

In his later philosophical writings, Coleridge offers a systematic and distinctively original approach to the problem of the origin of language. He is clearly in sympathy with the post-Lockean tradition of linguistic speculation in England and France, especially in the work of Condillac, Hartley, Monboddo, and George Berkeley; yet he also evinces strong affinities with the major figures of the German Enlightenment, such as Herder, Gotthold Ephraim Lessing, Johann David Michaelis, and Wilhelm von Humboldt. All of these writers were united by a common fascination with the question of the origin of language: did language arise from arbitrary signs (as Locke and Condillac supposed), or were the first human words connected in some essential way with their referents? Coleridge addressed this question in a variety of ways throughout his career, and he evidently intended to write a treatise on the subject of linguistic origin. In a notebook entry of 1803 he indicates his plans to write a 'philosophical Romance to explain the whole growth of Language' (*CN* 1, 1646). Although he never got around to writing such a treatise, he was constantly gathering materials for it in his notebooks, which thereby became a storehouse of information on etymology, language acquisition, and comparative linguistics.

The *Notebooks* provide a significant historical and intellectual context for Coleridge's poetry of the 1790s, particularly for his revolutionary linguistic practice in the conversation poems. Coleridge's speculation on language provides an illuminating context for the verbal texture of these poems, their abrupt shifts in tone and subject matter and their frequent use of quotation and allusion. Coleridge's theoretical understanding of language, as expressed in the notebooks and elsewhere, can furnish the basis for a detailed analysis of the phonetic, lexical, and syntactic features of these poems. In particular, these poems serve to elucidate a distinction between 'ordinary language', a term that Coleridge often mentions with contempt (*CL* 2, 699), and 'natural language', a term that meets with his highest approbation (*BL* 1, 22). Although they are firmly grounded in 'the language really used by men' (as Wordsworth described the predominant idiom of *Lyrical Ballads*), the conversation poems clearly deviate from the norms of actual spoken discourse, especially in those climactic moments that evoke the 'lovely shapes and sounds intelligible / Of that eternal language, which thy God / Utters' ('Frost at Midnight', 59–61). Coleridge regarded this 'eternal language' as 'natural' by virtue of its immediacy to the feelings of the human heart and the objects of the natural world, all pervaded by 'the one Life within us and abroad' ('The Eolian Harp', 26).

Coleridge's own endeavor to employ the 'language of nature' in his poetry establishes a theoretical context for his critique of Wordsworth's Preface to *Lyrical Ballads*. As I have argued in *Coleridge's Philosophy of Language* (100–18), the entire controversy between Wordsworth and Coleridge arises from their very different conceptions of natural language. For Wordsworth, 'natural language' is synonymous with 'ordinary language' because only in everyday conversation can the referents of words be determined sufficiently to make communication possible. The process of communication, in his essentially Lockean view, requires the presence of unchanging natural objects to provide objective standards of usage. For Coleridge, however, 'the best part of human language, properly so called, is derived from reflection on the acts of the mind itself' (*BL* 2, 54). In Coleridge's view, if there is any linguistic structure held in common by all speakers of a given language, it will be formed through the process of education, by which the mind's innate faculties are 'educed' and made available to conscious reflection. Only in this way can the 'voluntary appropriation of fixed symbols to internal acts' (*BL* 2, 54) become intelligible to readers of poetry. Ordinary conversation, being unreflective, is not particularly conducive to the communication of ideas. Coleridge regards the words of ordinary language as mere '*arbitrary marks* of thought, our smooth market-coin of intercourse with the image and superscription worn out by currency' (*BL* 2, 122). Coleridge's predilection for individual forms of expression stands in stark opposition to Wordsworth's dream of a common language.

Coleridge's supernatural poems may likewise be examined in the linguistic context established by the *Biographia Literaria* and the *Notebooks*. In the *Biographia*, Coleridge claims that the poet should not simply copy 'the sort and order of words which he hears in the market, wake, high-road, or plough-field' (2, 81), but should exercise his own creative powers by coining new words or reviving ancient usages. The notebooks exemplify this radical linguistic doctrine in their odd textual juxtapositions and their eccentric deviations from ordinary English usage. 'The Rime of the Ancient Mariner', with its strange words and its intrusive, hypnotic narrator, may be regarded as an extension of this linguistic experiment, particularly in the version of this poem first published in *Lyrical Ballads* (1798), with its deliberately archaic diction and spelling. As John Livingston Lowes points out in *The Road to Xanadu* (296–310), this version of the poem is more than just a fake antique ballad on the model of Percy's *Reliques* and Chatterton's 'Rowley' poems. Lowes demonstrates that Coleridge combines three fairly distinct types of archaic usage: first, the traditional ballad lexicon (*pheere, eldritch, beforne, I ween, sterte, een, countrée, withouten, cauld*); second, the diction of Chaucer and Spenser (*ne, uprist, I wist, yspread, yeven, n'old, eftsones, lavrock, jargoning, minstralsy*); and third, seafaring terminology (*swound, weft, clifts, biscuit-worms, fire-flags*). All three types of archaic usage are severely curtailed in the 1800 edition of the poem, perhaps in response to a reviewer in the *British Critic* (October 1799) who denounced the poem's 'antiquated words', citing *swound* (line 397) and *weft* (line 83) as flagrant examples of nonsensical diction. Coleridge omitted the vivid seafaring term *weft* in 1800, along with most of the other words listed above. The merits and demerits of Coleridge's 1800 modernization and his later addition of a marginal gloss in *Sibylline Leaves* (1817) have been widely debated; Lowes regards Coleridge's revision of 'The Rime of the Ancient Mariner' as a definite improvement, and more recent critics have tended to accept this established opinion. However, I am inclined to agree instead with critics like William Empson who prefer the poem's original version, not for its consistent adherence to any discrete type of usage, but precisely for its multifaceted syncretic quality, which bespeaks the author's desire to reassemble the surviving fragments of archaic language into an older, more natural mode of poetic discourse (see Empson's 'Introduction' to *Coleridge's Verse*). The poem's archaic language harks back to the *Ursprache*, presumed by Enlightenment linguists to exist at the primeval origin of human consciousness and the misty dawn of civilization.

A similar criterion of linguistic naturalness seems to be at work in 'Kubla Khan'. The realm of the emperor is a world of beginnings, where Alph, the sacred river, bursts from a mysterious cleft in the rock, where walls and towers rise silently from the earth at a single word of command. The magical powers of language result from the very priority or firstness of the names by which the objects in this landscape are known. The proper name *Alph* suggests an etymological relation to *alpha* or *aleph*, the first letter of the Greek or Hebrew alphabet and thus a figure for absolute linguistic origin. The name *Abora* is more complex in its associations, but they all have to do with the idea of firstness. *Abora* suggests *Amara*, the exotic pleasure-garden mentioned in *Paradise Lost* (book 4, line 281). The word *Abora* may also allude to the *aborigines*, or indigenous people of Italy (prior to the Roman conquest); moreover, according to John Beer (*Coleridge the Visionary*, 256), the word *Abor* is a name for the sun in some ancient mythologies. In addition, *Bethabara* is the name of the place where Christ was baptized; Coleridge probably noticed this word in Joseph Cottle's poem 'John the Baptist' (1796). The name *Abora* thus adds a whiff of pagan ritual and a hint of Christian revelation to the scene of poetic inspiration portrayed in the poem's closing lines. It ties together a web of intralinguistic associations that evoke absolute scenes of origin.

Throughout his career as a poet and philosopher, Coleridge's quest for linguistic naturalness is fundamentally motivated by a pervasive nostalgia for the alleged transparency of primitive language, the immediacy of relation between the linguistic sign and its referent. Coleridge's distaste for ordinary language is motivated by a corresponding reaction against the defacement of words in the tawdry transactions of everyday life. If words are mere arbitrary signs, then they cannot possibly be misused, because any enunciation, no matter how deviant from normal discourse, can eventually be assimilated to existing usage. But if words have a single natural or 'root' signification, then any change in their meaning threatens the entire delicate fabric of the English language. Coleridge's early journalism and political lectures complement the linguistic texture of his poetry by engaging in a systematic critique of the contemporary abuse of words, especially in the windy rhetoric of parliamentary politics. Coleridge's 1795 *Lectures on Politics and Religion* (*CC* 1) and the first volume of *Essays on His Times* (*CC* 3) establish the primary historical determinants of Coleridge's linguistic theory. Coleridge's radical political views are closely related to his quest for the radical origins of the English language.

In the 1795 lectures, Coleridge repeatedly criticizes the abuse of language perpetrated by his 'aristocratic' adversaries; he gives several examples of names arbitrarily imposed upon objects or events for nefarious purposes. The aristocratic appeal to 'Church and Constitution' (*CC* 1, 38) only serves as a smokescreen for irreligious and unlawful purposes; and the dubious equation of 'Illumination and Sedition' (*CC* 1, 52) stifles any criticism of the established political order. The hated aristocrats rely on slogans and catch-words that acquire 'almost a mechanical power' over the minds of the common people (*CC* 1, 53). Coleridge deplores the plight of his fellow-radical, John Horne Tooke, who was put on trial for sedition because of his writings in defense of liberty (*CC* 1, 19). Horne Tooke, who was both a political agitator and a renowned etymologist, experienced at first hand the tyranny exerted by the political establishment in its power to alter and misconstrue the meaning of words. Only by attending carefully to the meaning of words can we resist the insidious rhetoric of the politicians; otherwise we may be 'hurried away by names of which we have not sifted the meaning' (*CC* 1, 33). The ringleader of this abuse of language, according to Coleridge, is Prime Minister William Pitt, whose false eloquence masks the utter vacuity of his discourse. Pitt's speeches consist of 'words on words, finely arranged, and so dexterously consequent, that the whole bears the semblance of argument, and still keeps awake a sense of surprise—but when all is done, nothing rememberable has been said; no one philosophical remark, no one image, not even a pointed aphorism' (*Essays on His Times*, 1, 224). Such rhetorical deception threatens the entire structure of language with a collapse of meaning, a descent into darkness.

In the prevailing climate of deceptive and misleading political discourse, *The Friend* takes on a renewed immediacy and interest for readers of Coleridge. From the perspective of his lifelong inquiry into the nature and origin of language, *The Friend* emerges not simply as a miscellaneous collection of essays, but as a coherent and many-faceted attempt to remedy the contemporary abuse of language by reestablishing the proper meaning of words. Coleridge declares the purpose of his periodical in an eloquent defense of his 'metaphysics', which he uses 'to expose the folly and legerdemain of those who have thus abused the blessed machine of language' (*Friend*, 1, 108). He proceeds to make a series of precise verbal distinctions, showing how the often abstruse terminology of politics, economics, ethics, and religion can be demystified and elucidated by careful linguistic analysis. The *Essays on the Principles of Method* furnish a more general statement of the analytic method employed throughout *The Friend*. This method consists in the incremental elaboration of linguistic distinctions, either in relation to abstract ideas or to 'the truths which have their signatures in nature' (*Friend*, 1, 492). In either case, the progress of human understanding requires the precise conformity of words with the concepts they signify.

Coleridge's method of linguistic analysis enables him to distinguish between words that are closely related in meaning and often regarded as synonymous in ordinary usage. This is his technique of 'desynonymization', a term he devised in 1803 to denote the act of distinguishing between apparent synonyms (*CN* 1, 1336). In the *Biographia* he describes the contribution of this process to the historical evolution of language, arguing that 'in all societies there exists an instinct of growth, a certain collective, unconscious good sense working progressively to desynonymize those words originally of the same meaning' (*BL* 1, 82). He suggests that this gradual process of differentiation can account for the entire formation of a lexicon, from a few simple sounds to an immense nomenclature. Coleridge's critical and philosophical vocabulary derives largely from his own frequent habit of desynonymizing. Several of his most crucial distinctions—between fancy and imagination, genius and talent, symbol and allegory, copy and imitation—result from this technique of linguistic analysis. Coleridge's practice of desynonymization can be observed throughout the *Biographia*, the *Notebooks*, and *The Friend*. The distinctions created by means of desynonymization play a major role in the formation of Coleridge's critical and philosophical discourse.

The constitutive role of desynonymization in Coleridge's intellectual development raises a larger set of questions concerning the relation between language and thought. Is language merely the dress of thought, the means by which we express our knowledge of things? Or does language actually determine the process of thought by circumscribing the range of possible concepts? Coleridge addresses the problem of linguistic relativity in the *Logic* (*CC* 13), a work that languished in undeserved obscurity until its publication in 1981. The *Logic* is the most coherent and systematic exposition of Coleridge's philosophy of language, and it contains the fullest articulation of his views on the origin and acquisition of language, the relation between grammar and logic, and the role of language in thought. More than just a paraphrase of Kant's *Critique of Pure Reason*, it enacts a linguistic turn upon Kant's philosophy.

Coleridge's revision of Kant's philosophy is grounded in his assertion that logical categories in fact presuppose grammatical categories, and for this reason Coleridge affirms that grammar is prior to logic. More specifically, Kant argues that every logical proposition entails the assertion that 'I think', which he terms the 'transcendental unity of apperception' (Kant, 132). Coleridge agrees that all propositions entail the assertion 'I think,' but he parts company with Kant in the logical priority that he attributes to such an assertion. For Kant, the assertion 'I think' is itself an ultimate principle, 'the highest point with which . . . the whole of transcendental philosophy must be connected' (Kant, 134 n.), whereas for Coleridge the individual unity of apperception is 'secondary or derivative, and we must first secure an absoluteness, an independency, to the position "I am" before we can communicate certainty to other positions' (*Logic* 82). Coleridge discovers such certainty in 'the absolute Self, Spirit, or Mind, the underived and eternal "I am"' (*Logic* 85). This position in turn finds support in the science of grammar:

The title 'I Am' attributed to the Supreme Being by the Hebrew Legislator must excite our admiration for its philosophic depth, and the verb substantive or first form in the science of grammar brings us the highest possible external evidence of its truth. For what is a fact of all human language is of course a fact of all human consciousness. (*Logic* 82)

According to Coleridge, the science of grammar, by positing the verb substantive ('I am') as a foundation for all human language, tends to corroborate the philosophical position that the absolute 'I am' is a fact of all human consciousness. In this sense, for Coleridge, grammar is prior to logic.

Coleridge's assertion that grammar is prior to logic has important ramifications in his subsequent interpretation of Kant's philosophy. For Coleridge, language actually constitutes the structure of the human understanding. Coleridge follows Kant in describing logical categories as 'predicaments', and their corresponding acts of judgment as '*predicabilia*, that is, the characters predicable, or which may be affirmed respecting objects in consequence of the predicaments' (*Logic* 268). For Coleridge, however, there is a deeper sense in which logical categories are 'linguistic': they are derived from language and constitute a way of formalizing its possibilities. All logical propositions, in Coleridge's view, are acts of judging; and in order to specify these acts it is necessary to substantiate 'the acts of judging into logical entities and to contemplate the act as a product, the judging as a judgment' (*Logic* 240). This conversion of an act into a product is essentially a linguistic operation, since 'it lies at the bottom of universal grammar as well as of logic' (*Logic* 240). Consequently, the *Logic* argues that epistemological questions cannot be resolved without a prior analysis of linguistic structures, since language itself constitutes the only possible medium of intellectual inquiry. Coleridge seeks to rewrite Kant's philosophy in such a way as to reveal its dependence on lexical and grammatical categories that, as innate modes of conception, determine our perception of reality. The activity of thought, in this view, is wholly constituted by the activity of language.

By enacting a linguistic turn on Kant's *Critique of Pure Reason*, the *Logic* articulates a coherent and original philosophy of language. Considered in relation to Coleridge's earlier works, the *Logic* offers a provisional resolution of key issues concerning the role of language in the formation of human consciousness and ethical values. Moreover, Coleridge's engagement with the theory of language, and especially his concept of desyonymization, played an essential role in the subsequent development of linguistics and lexicography in Britain.

As Coleridge gathered the etymological materials for his intended treatise on language, he became ever more acutely aware of the inadequacies of existing English dictionaries and the need for a new dictionary that would reflect the latest philological discoveries. In the *Biographia Literaria*, he sternly denounced Samuel Johnson's dictionary on the grounds of its incompleteness and inaccuracy (1, 237 n.) and issued his own proposal for a new English dictionary embodying the latest findings in comparative and historical linguistics:

> Were I asked, what I deemed the greatest and most unmixt benefit, which a wealthy individual, or an association of wealthy individuals could bestow on their country and on mankind, I should not hesitate to answer, 'a philosophical English dictionary; with the Greek, Latin, German, French, Spanish and Italian synonimes, and with correspondent indexes'. (*BL* 1, 239 n.)

In the following year, Coleridge entered into a contractual agreement with the publishers of the *Encyclopedia Metropolitana* to prepare an etymological dictionary of the English language. Coleridge described the plan for this new 'Philosophical and Etymological LEXICON of the English Language' in terms that strikingly foreshadow the plan that was later devised for the *Oxford English Dictionary* (OED): each word would be accompanied by illustrative citations in chronological order, with 'every attention to the independent beauty or value of the sentences chosen ... consistent with the higher ends of a clear insight into the original and acquired meaning of every word' ('Treatise on Method', *Shorter Works and Fragments*, 687). Coleridge's historical approach to lexicography becomes even more explicit in the *Logic*, which calls 'for a dictionary constructed on the only philosophical principle, which regarding words as living growths, offlets, and organs of the human soul, seeks to trace each historically through all the periods of its natural growth and accidental modifications' (*Logic* 126).

Like so many of Coleridge's overly ambitious projects, this proposed dictionary was never completed. Yet Coleridge's dream of a new English dictionary lived on in the minds of his younger contemporaries, many of whom remembered his call for a new dictionary and cherished his inspiring remarks on the fundamental knowledge revealed in the history of words. Among these admirers of Coleridge was Julius Charles Hare, an occasional visitor to Coleridge at Highgate during the 1820s and a lifelong advocate of Coleridge's views in philosophy, politics, and theology. During the early 1830s, Hare was an active member of the Etymological Society at Cambridge, an informal association of scholars interested in classical and modern philology. A major objective of this society was to publish 'a new Etymological Dictionary of the English language; of which one main feature was to be that the three great divisions of our etymologies, Teutonic, Norman, and Latin, were to be ranged under separate alphabets'; but this project never got beyond the early planning stages (Aarsleff, *Study of Language in England*, 217). Hare nevertheless did much to popularize Coleridge's linguistic theories during the early Victorian period, particularly in his best-selling book, *Guesses at Truth* (1827). As an example of Coleridge's talent for innovation, Hare mentions that his word 'to *desynonymise* ... is a truly valuable one, as designating a process very common in the history of language, and bringing a new thought into general circulation' (178). This particular term came to be commonly used by the early editors of the OED. Frederick James Furnivall, for instance, in an article of 1860–1, argues that the new English dictionary should record all variant forms of a word, in order 'that others coming after might see which prevailed, or whether both continued to exist, becoming desynonymized or not' (Furnivall, 43–4). In this way, Coleridge's concept of desynonymization came to justify the OED's broad inclusion of variant forms and its precise discrimination of closely related words and senses.[7]

The most significant of these younger admirers of Coleridge in the later history of the OED was Richard Chenevix Trench, a graduate of Trinity College, Cambridge, and a close associate of Hare. Trench visited Coleridge in 1832 and had a lively discussion with him on issues of biblical hermeneutics. During the 1840s Trench also became acquainted with Sara Coleridge, the daughter of Samuel Taylor

---

[7] OED credits Coleridge, *BL* 1, 82, with the first recorded usage (in 1817) of the word 'desynonymize', although in fact Coleridge used the word earlier (in 1803) in *CN* 1, 1336. Coleridge is credited with the first recorded usage for over 600 words in the OED; for a list of these coinages, see McKusick, '"Living Words": Samuel Taylor Coleridge and the Genesis of the OED', 23–45.

Coleridge and (together with her husband, Henry Nelson Coleridge) the main editor of his works and guardian of his posthumous reputation. As a member of the Coleridge circle, Trench was fully conversant with his works and deeply influenced by his ideas on the history of language. The Coleridgean view of words as 'living powers' runs as a leitmotif through Trench's writing on language, particularly his book entitled *On the Study of Words* (1851). This enormously popular work, which went through fourteen editions by 1872, consists mainly of examples of the knowledge and instruction contained in the history of individual words. Trench's reliance on Coleridge's inspiration is apparent:

It is to Coleridge that we owe the word 'to desynonymize'... and his own contributions direct and indirect in this province are both more in number and more important than those of any other English writer; as for instance the disentanglement of 'fanaticism' and 'enthusiasm', of 'keenness' and 'subtlety', of 'poetry' and 'poesy;' and that on which he himself laid so great a stress, of 'reason' and 'understanding'. (Trench 98 n.)

Trench also relies on Coleridge in his discussion of specific etymologies, particularly in his analysis of the word 'education,' which, he reminds his readers, involves a process of 'drawing out' (Latin *educere*) what is already present in the mind of the student, rather than merely pouring knowledge into an empty vessel (Trench, 111). This view of education as 'educing' is a favorite topic of Coleridge, who recurs to it at least half a dozen times in his lectures and published works (see, for example, *Lay Sermons* 40, *Friend* 1, 540 n., *Logic* 9). Like Coleridge, Trench reveals a moralizing tendency in his etymological analyses, a tendency that, for better or worse, would later prove congenial to the compilers of the OED, despite their avowed scientific objectives.

As editor for the new dictionary, the Philological Society chose a man who was thoroughly grounded in the new Germanic philology, highly talented in the field of lexicography, and young enough to see the project through to completion. This man was Herbert Coleridge, the grandson of Samuel Taylor Coleridge, and only 27 years old when he first became associated with the dictionary project in 1857. He was the son of Sara Coleridge and Henry Nelson Coleridge, who spent most of their adult lives editing Coleridge's posthumous works, and thus he grew up in a home that was virtually a shrine to the memory of his grandfather. Herbert Coleridge was deeply instilled with a knowledge of his grandfather's accomplishments and determined to carry on his legacy in the field of historical linguistics. By 1860 the dictionary was well underway, as Herbert Coleridge corresponded with scholars throughout Britain and North America, constructed a set of 54 wooden pigeonholes to receive their quotation slips, and published a list of formal guidelines, entitled *Canones Lexicographici* (Craigie and Onions, vii–x). Herbert Coleridge promised to be a competent and highly resourceful editor of the dictionary that his grandfather had first conceived almost half a century before.

Tragically, however, Herbert Coleridge died of consumption in April 1861, at the age of 31, leaving the dictionary project in disarray and resulting in a delay of almost two decades before a suitable replacement could be found. In the meantime, the editorial process ground to a halt, slips were misplaced, readers lost interest, and the entire project came to be regarded as a hopeless enterprise by all but the most ardent of its supporters. In 1878, however, a brash, self-educated school-teacher from the Scottish border country resumed the task of editing the dictionary. The new editor, James Murray, proved to be not only a brilliant lexicographer but a shrewd publicist, and under his leadership the project flourished, attracting hundreds of volunteer readers in England and America (Murray 305–8). Finally completed in 1928, the OED is still regarded as a uniquely authoritative accomplishment of Victorian scholarship. Both in design and execution, the OED owes much to the influence of Samuel Taylor Coleridge, and it remains the most enduring legacy of his fascination with the history and structure of the English language.

Although speculation concerning the origin of language was a banned topic of professional discourse during the reign of the 'new philology' in the later nineteenth century, the influence of Coleridge's concept of desynonymization on the makers of the *Oxford English Dictionary* assured that the project would pervasively reflect Coleridge's important insight into the historical evolution of language. Coleridge's theory of desynonymization provides a central focus for all of his speculations on language theory. It enables him to describe the evolution of language as a process involving both conscious volition and the merely functional responses of ordinary discourse to the exigencies of everyday life. Coleridge most clearly describes the relation between autonomic lexical evolution in 'common language' and the self-conscious innovations of 'active philosophical language' in his *Lectures on the History of Philosophy*:

As society introduces new relations it introduces new distinctions, and either new words are introduced or different pronunciations. Now the duty of a philosopher is to aid and complete this process as his subject demands, and a distinction has perhaps already begun to carry an adjective to a substantive. We should say, and be perfectly intelligible, that Cowley was [a] fanciful, Milton [an] imaginative poet. The philosopher proceeds and establishes the same meaning, in fancy and imagination; for active philosophical language differs from common language in this only, or mainly at least, that philosophical language does that more accurately and by an express compact which [is] unconsciously and as it were by a tacit compact aimed at and in part accomplished by the common language, though with less precision and consistency.   (*Lects Phil*, 554)

Coleridge evidently conceives of language as a set of semantic oppositions that are gradually accumulated as society becomes more complex. At any given time, this set of oppositions constitutes a synchronic system, but it is always evolving and changing as new distinctions arise. His methodological originality consists in his perception that the diachronic aspect of language is not exhausted by tracing etymologies (Horne Tooke's method) or by discovering patterns of sound change (the method of the comparative grammarians). He seeks to account for linguistic change in terms of the accommodation of an existing system to an influx of new semantic relationships. The evolution of language, according to this view, occurs by the conscious ascription of distinctive meanings to previously insignificant phonetic differences. Sound change provides only the raw material for semantic innovation, which occurs both through the collective 'common sense' of ordinary speakers and through intentional acts by poets and philosophers.

Coleridge's engagement with language theory was vitally important to the intellectual culture of its own time, and it remains as a seminal instance of nineteenth-century speculation on the nature and origin of language. William Keach has noted that Coleridge's speculation on linguistic universals anticipates Chomsky's theory of generative grammar: 'Coleridge is by implication already anticipating generative grammarians like Chomsky and Pinker, with their methodological preferences for transformational "roots" and "trees"' (Keach, 18). Coleridge's hypothesis that all human languages emerge from a primordial 'verb substantive' (*Logic* 82) has much in common with Chomsky's putatively universal 'deep structure' that underlies all human utterance. Although subsequent linguistic research has cast substantial doubt upon Chomsky's utopian quest for linguistic universals, the emergence of such a quest in twentieth-century linguistics nevertheless suggests the endurance of a fundamentally Romantic (and Coleridgean) set of assumptions about the nature and origin of language. According to this Coleridgean view, any given language expresses certain universal aspects of human cognition, and if we could only discover the remote origin of all human languages, we would learn something fundamental about human nature. Coleridge's questing spirit, his vision of the sacred river Alph, his fascination with the Wild Boy of Aveyron, and his recurrent interest in English etymology and universal grammar, all converge in his utopian dream of discovering the ultimate origin of human language.

WORKS CITED

AARSLEFF, HANS. 1982. *From Locke to Saussure: Essays on the Study of Language and Intellectual History.* Minneapolis: University of Minnesota Press.
—— 1967. *The Study of Language in England, 1780–1860.* Princeton: Princeton University Press.
BEER, JOHN B. 1959. *Coleridge the Visionary.* London: Chatto & Windus.
COTTLE, JOSEPH. 1796. John the Baptist. In *Poems*, 2nd edn. Bristol.
CRAIGIE, WILLIAM A., and ONIONS, CHARLES T. 1933. Historical introduction to *Oxford English Dictionary Supplement.* (Oxford: Oxford University Press, pp. vii–x.
EMPSON, WILLIAM. 1973. Introduction, in *Coleridge's Verse: A Selection*, ed. William Empson and David Pirie. New York: Schocken Books.

ESSICK, ROBERT N. 1989. *William Blake and the Language of Adam*. Oxford: Clarendon Press.

FURNIVALL, FREDERICK JAMES. 1860–1. Response to Herbert Coleridge, On the exclusion of certain words from a dictionary, *Transactions of the Philological Society*: 43–4.

GOODSON, A. C. 1998, ed. *Coleridge's Writings, Volume 3: On Language*. New York: St Martin's Press.

HARE, JULIUS CHARLES, and HARE, AUGUSTUS WILLIAM. 1827. *Guesses at Truth, by Two Brothers*. London: James Taylor.

ITARD, JEAN MARC GASPARD. 1802. *De l'éducation d'un homme sauvage, ou des premiers développements physiques et moraux du jeune sauvage de l'Aveyron*. Paris: Gouyon, 1801; trans. Nogent, *An Historical Account of the Discovery and Education of a Savage Man, of the First Developments, Physical and Moral, of the Young Savage Caught in the Woods near Aveyron, in the Year 1798*. London: Richard Phillips.

KANT, IMMANUEL. 1787. *Kritik der reinen Vernunft*. Second edition. Riga.

KEACH, WILLIAM. 2004. *Arbitrary Power: Romanticism, Language, Politics*. Princeton: Princeton University Press.

LANE, HARLAN. 1975. *The Wild Boy of Aveyron*. Cambridge: Harvard University Press.

LEIBNIZ, GOTTFRIED WILHELM VON. 1981. *Nouveaux essais sur l'entendement humain* (1764); trans. Peter Remnant and Jonathan Bennett, *New Essays on Human Understanding*. Cambridge: Cambridge University Press.

LOCKE, JOHN. 1690. *An Essay Concerning Human Understanding*. London: Printed by Eliz. Holt, for Thomas Basset.

LOWES, JOHN LIVINGSTON. 1927. *The Road to Xanadu: A Study in the Ways of the Imagination*. Boston: Houghton Mifflin.

MCKUSICK, JAMES C. 1986. *Coleridge's Philosophy of Language*. New Haven: Yale University Press.

—— 1992. 'Living words': Samuel Taylor Coleridge and the genesis of the OED. *Modern Philology*, 90: 1–45.

MURRAY, K. M. ELISABETH. 1977. *Caught in the Web of Words: James Murray and the Oxford English Dictionary*. New Haven: Yale University Press.

NEWTON, MICHAEL. 2002. *Savage Girls and Wild Boys: A History of Feral Children*. New York: St Martins Press.

PERCY, THOMAS. 1765. *Reliques of Ancient English Poetry*. 3 vols. London: Dodsley.

TRENCH, RICHARD CHENEVIX. 1927. *On the Study of Words: Five Lectures* (1851); reprinted together with *English Past and Present: Five Lectures* (1855), ed. George Sampson. London and Toronto: J. M. Dent & Sons.

COLERIDGE AND PHILOSOPHY

CHRISTOPH BODE

ALTHOUGH he did not leave behind an original, coherent philosophical system or a single finished book that could be called, without qualification, a philosophical work, Samuel Taylor Coleridge has somehow acquired the reputation of being the most philosophical of the British Romantic poets. However, this seeming consensus dissolves once we take a closer look at what different people mean by this accolade (if an accolade it is). For some, it simply means that all or most of his major poetry is philosophically informed in one way or another. For others, it means that he tried to base his literary criticism on philosophical principles, which helped him become 'one of the most original thinkers on the imagination'[1] or 'the most profound of English critics'.[2] For others still, it means—and this is borne out by his letters, notebooks, and marginalia—that he thought and read a great deal about philosophical matters and tried to communicate them to others, however successfully. And for some, he is a philosopher in his own right, with a coherent body of philosophical thought,[3] even though others had to pick up and arrange the body parts for him, since he, sadly and for whatever reasons, proved habitually incapable of doing so himself.

There is a double problem here. If, in the case of Coleridge, philosophy pervades all of his writerly activities, then all he ever wrote or was recorded to have said falls

---

[1] Engell, *The Creative Imagination*, 366.
[2] McFarland, *Pantheist*, 23.
[3] Cf. Muirhead, *Philosopher*, 15.

under the heading of 'Coleridge and Philosophy'. It is extremely helpful for the present writer (and for prospective readers of this handbook, I presume, as well) that there are separate chapters on the *Biographia Literaria*, the *Logic*, and the *Opus Maximum*, the *Philosophical Lectures*, and so on. But the basic challenge remains: since not all can be covered, there has to be a rigorous selection not only of texts but of key issues.

The other problem is even greater. It is extremely controversial whether Coleridge can be regarded as an original philosophical thinker. Some have questioned his basic qualifications. René Wellek, an authority one should not disregard too easily, remarked on the 'fundamental weakness, incoherence and indistinctness of thought'[4] and considered 'the study of Coleridge's philosophy to be "futile" because of the jumble of different kinds of thinking, and because he uses Kantian terminology in a non-Kantian sense'.[5] Thomas McFarland and the editors of the *Biographia Literaria* in the *Collected Works* series believed Wellek judged too harshly. But Paul Hamilton, too, has doubts about Coleridge's systematics and consistency;[6] Norman Fruman, the untiring *advocatus diaboli* in matters of plagiarism, cites Mary Warnock's severe judgement that because of his 'unintellectual attitude to philosophy Coleridge can never be taken seriously by professionals';[7] the editor of Coleridge's *Logic*, J. R. de J. Jackson, unrestrainedly says that the book, part of Coleridge's mirage-like *magnum opus* project, 'is essentially a popularization of the *Critique of Pure Reason*' and then continues: 'The philosophical arguments of the *Logic* are often complex and subtle; the complexity and the subtlety are Kant's. Coleridge is a faithful interpreter of his master in the field of logic, and he does not at any point attempt to revise, refute, or refine [...]. It is very difficult to improve on Kant. There is no evidence to suggest that Coleridge was capable of this sort of sustained thinking or that he ever attempted it' (lxii). And even the basically well-disposed I. A. Richards found, 'Coleridge was not, I suppose, a good Philosopher; he made too many mistakes *of the wrong kind*'.[8] Add to these fundamental doubts, shared by some, the basically uncontested fact that Samuel Taylor Coleridge 'regularly cannibalized the works and ideas of others and employed the results quite opportunistically',[9] and it is obvious that—no matter whether one calls this 'plagiarism' (Fruman) or 'a mode of composition' (McFarland)—nothing short of a complete tracing of his sources and influences could do full justice to the patchwork quilt of what could only be tentatively called 'the philosophy of Samuel Taylor Coleridge'. This, the respective editors of the

---

[4] Wellek, *Kant*, 68.
[5] Emmett in Brett (ed.), *Writers and their Background*, 206.
[6] Cf. Hamilton, *Coleridge's Poetics*, 1.
[7] Fruman in Gallant (ed.), *Theory of Imagination*, 57, and Warnock, *Imagination*, 108.
[8] Cited by Emmett in Brett (ed.), *Writers and their Background*, 196.
[9] Appleyard, *Philosophy of Literature*, x.

Bollingen *Works* have attempted to do, with varying success. But, of course, it cannot possibly be replicated here.

Again, the solution must be a rigorous selection, and one that does not totally ignore the development (a sometimes contradictory development) of Coleridge's thought (as does Barfield, for example), although the systematic aspect must be in the foreground. In 1808 Robert Southey commented upon Coleridge's fashions in philosophy: 'Hartley was ousted by Berkeley, Berkeley by Spinoza, and Spinoza by Plato; when I last saw him Jacob Behmen had some chance of coming in.' But Southey did grant Coleridge originality of a kind: 'The truth is that he plays with systems and any nonsense will serve him for a text from which he can deduce something new and surprising.'[10] Unfortunately, Samuel Taylor Coleridge himself is not a very reliable witness regarding the evolution of his own religious, political and philosophical thinking.[11] For example, with some impudence he declared he had never been a Jacobin. He claimed to have developed the same ideas as Friedrich Schelling before Schelling even published them (between 1797 and 1800), though there is absolutely no evidence for this in Coleridge's writing and, what is more, what Coleridge *did* write during this period (and before) stands in marked opposition to Schelling's *Transendental-* and *Naturphilosophie* and to other forms of German Idealism as well.[12] He also lied about his acquaintance with August Wilhelm Schlegel's *Vienna Lectures* and about the extent of his familiarity with Schelling's post-1800 writings, from which he helped himself copiously, either totally without or with misleading acknowledgments. What is more: rather than stating his own ambivalences about certain philosophical positions as unequivo-cally as possible, Coleridge sometimes tended to *act them out*. Spinoza is a case in point. Fascinated by Spinoza's geometrical clarity, Coleridge was however deeply afraid of his seeming denial of free will (although why a philosopher who denies free will should write an *Ethics*, Coleridge could never quite resolve) and of the atheism he saw lurking behind Spinoza's pantheism. Torn between attraction and repulsion ('my head was with Spinoza, though my whole heart remained with Paul and John', *BL* I, 201), Coleridge could never quite make up his mind whether Spinozism inevitably leads to atheism or not: in the *Biographia Literaria* he says, after some wavering, that it does not (I, 152–3); in a letter he says it does (*CL* VI, 853) and likewise in the *Opus Maximum* (278), the implication seems to be it does, but when Jacobi accuses Spinoza of atheism, Coleridge comes to his defence,[13] although elsewhere he would reiterate that all pantheisms are practically atheistic:

---

[10] Cited by Appleyard, *Philosophy of Literature*, 52.

[11] See generally Fruman, *Archangel*; but also Fruman in Burwick (ed.), *Coleridge's* Biographia Literaria, 16, 19.

[12] Cf. Fruman, *Archangel*, 120.

[13] Cf. McFarland, *Pantheist*, 187–9; see also Berkeley, *Coleridge and the Crisis of Reason*, 34, 47, 52.

The inevitable result of all consequent reasoning, in which the intellect refuses to acknow-ledge a higher or deeper ground than it can itself supply [...] is—and from Zeno the Eleatic to Spinoza, and from Spinoza to the Schellings [...] of the present day, ever has been—pantheism, under one or other of its modes [...] and in all alike [...] practically atheistic.   (*OM* 106–7)

And yet again, he admitted that had he 'either the strength of mind or goodness of heart to be an atheist, [...] I should be an atheist with Spinoza' (quoted in McFarland, *Pantheist*, 251).

Is it any wonder, then, that critics come to radically different conclusions about Coleridge's convictions, fluid and contradictory as they are? The following passage is often cited in support of Coleridge's pantheist leanings:

In looking at objects of nature what I am thinking [...] I seem rather to be seeking, as it were *asking*, a symbolical language within me that already and forever exists, than observing anything new. Even when that latter is the case, yet still I have always an obscure feeling as if that new phaenomenon were the dim Awaking of a forgotten or hidden Truth of my inner Nature. It is still interesting as a Word, a Symbol! It is *Logos*, the Creator! and the Evolver!
(*CN* II, 2546).

But John Beer says that Coleridge was never a pantheist (*AR* lxii), whereas the basic hypothesis of Thomas McFarland's *Coleridge and the Pantheist Tradition* is that Coleridge had an almost lifelong struggle with it. The famous 'O! the one Life' lines of 'The Eolian Harp' were only inserted in 1817,[14] and Seamus Perry rightly points out that 'the doctrine of a universal One Life originates in Coleridge's Unitarianism, encountered at Jesus College through the Don Frend',[15] so that Jonathan Wordsworth seemed justified in concluding, 'Coleridge remains a Uni-tarian until after 1817.'[16] But in 1814 Coleridge had stated that Socinianism, another name for Unitarianism, 'is not only not Christianity, it is not even a Religion' (*CL* III, 479). One last instance: in the winter of 1794, Coleridge professes to be a Necessitarian, a follower of David Hartley.[17] In November 1796, both Hartley and George Berkeley, the Bishop of Cloyne, 'are *my men*'—a puzzling combination. Then Berkeley alone seems to take over, 'I am a Berkeleian', 'you remember, I am a *Berkeleian*' (quoted in Appleyard, *Philosophy of Literature*, 48). Appleyard dates Coleridge's rejection of Hartley in 1801 and holds that generally Hartley had very little influence on Samuel Taylor Coleridge,[18] except perhaps that he named his first son after him (and the second after Berkeley). But Christensen, on the contrary, cites Coleridge's letter to Southey from 1803—a rebuttal of Hartley's basic assump-tions[19]—and states that 'Coleridge never successfully completed the overthrow of

---

[14] Cf. Abrams, *The Correspondent Breeze*, 163.
[15] Perry, *Uses of Division*, 70.
[16] Wordsworth in Wu (ed.), *Companion to Romanticism*, 490.
[17] Cf. Christensen, *Machine of Language*, 62.
[18] Cf. Appleyard, *Philosophy of Literature*, 35–8.
[19] Cf. Christensen, *Machine of Language*, 82.

association which he proclaimed in 1801'.[20] Still, Hamilton quotes Samuel Taylor Coleridge as speaking, in 1804, of 'the pernicious Doctrine of necessity' (Hamilton, *Colerige's Poetics*, 78). It is certainly true that Necessitarianism does not exactly put a strong emphasis on free will, sinfulness, and inherent depravity[21]—things that were evidently close to Coleridge's heart—and he may therefore not have found it congenial to him in the long run. But how long, exactly, was that run?

In view of all this, it seems reasonable to choose, as an instrument to locate Coleridge's philosophical positions and their trajectory and as a gauge to measure some of Coleridge's changes and developments, a philosopher whom Samuel Taylor Coleridge held in exceptionally high esteem ever since he seriously encountered his writings in 1801, a philosopher, who is, indeed, central for Samuel Taylor Coleridge (cf. *BL* I, cxxxvi), to whom he never gave up allegiance[22] and who, in having written an epistemology, an ethics, and an aesthetics which, in a way, defined the age,[23] offers a *system* of philosophy to which Coleridge's varying positions can be related. That philosopher is Immanuel Kant.

It seems likewise reasonable to follow up Coleridge's relation to Kant's Critical Philosophy with a sketch of Coleridge's relationship to the philosopher who, amongst the German Idealists who built upon and responded to Kant, is of the greatest importance to Coleridge, namely Friedrich Schelling. By doing this, one can see to what degree Coleridge's deviations from Kant are original or merely epigonal and derivative. Rosemary Ashton once confidently announced, 'Coleridge knew his Kant.'[24] If so, he struggled hard to understand him. In December 1796, he found him 'most unintelligible' (quoted in McFarland, *Pantheist*, 214 and Muirhead, *Philosopher*, 50). In another instance, he complains about the 'impenetrable obscurity', which Kant, however, shares 'with every great discoverer and benefactor of the human race' (quoted in Coburn, *Experience into Thought*, 40). In the *Marginalia*, he confesses, 'Kant I do not understand' (*M* II, 249). So, in how far do his 'discrepancies' betoken 'a confusion',[25] a lack of grasp, or, on the contrary, an original and creative development of Kant's ideas? We do not have to accept without examination Warnock's verdict that Coleridge simply failed to understand Kant's Copernican Revolution.[26]

Kant's Copernican Revolution, as explicated in the *Critique of Pure Reason* (1781), is basically a reversal of the assumption that our knowledge (*Erkenntnis*) has to conform to the objects of our knowledge. Kant argues that, in order to find out what our mind (and its different faculties) can do and what it cannot do, one

---

[20] Cf. Christensen, *Machine of Language*, 17.
[21] Cf. McFarland, *Pantheist*, 224.
[22] Cf. ibid., 93.
[23] Cf. Shaffer, 'Coleridge and Kant's "Giant Hand"'.
[24] Ashton, *The German Idea*, 3.
[25] Barfield, *What Coleridge Thought*, 177.
[26] See Warnock, *Imagination*, 95–6.

first has to ask how it is equipped, what are the necessary *a priori* conditions of our understanding, what is—if you will—our basic software that *precedes* any experience and necessarily limits and structures both what we experience and how it is further processed by our minds. Once one has identified the basic, immutable forms in which we experience ourselves and the world, the '*reine Anschauungsformen*' of time and space, which are not derived from experience but rather the inevitable precondition of any experience, and once one has identified certain core categories, or pure concepts of understanding, such as the idea of causality, which likewise make experience possible in the first place and cannot be deduced from it, it becomes obvious why the objects, as we know them, follow the structure of our mind, rather than the other way round.

This Copernican Revolution of Kant's Critical Philosophy is primarily a revolution in epistemology, but it has far-reaching consequences for the possibility of any metaphysics, ethics, and aesthetics, and it is necessary to at least sketch them, so that Coleridge's handling of them, which is sometimes original, sometimes idiosyncratic, but certainly unique, can be understood. The first of these consequences is that, since we have only access to reality *as we understand it* within the frame of the possibilities of our mind, we can, by definition, never know what reality is 'really' like. All we *can* say is that reality as such, the realm of the *Dinge an sich*, is 'out there' but remains inaccessible to us. It is beyond our experience and beyond our possibilities of knowing. And therefore it is inadmissible to speculate with ideas of the Understanding, which at once constitute and limit the possibilities of our experience, about realms which are by definition beyond our knowing. There are large areas about which it is not possible to say anything, let alone to argue rationally, and philosophy must confine itself to the other ones, which are its proper and only realm. Kant radically delimits the reach of metaphysics, but by doing so, by throwing untenable claims overboard, he makes it very strong in its core business.

Now Kant was not simply sceptically advising against the extension of the mind's faculties beyond the sphere in which they are applicable. He could show that if this is ignored, one ends up with paradoxical results and irresolvable contradictions, with paralogisms and the so-called antinomies. For example, it can be both proven conclusively that the world has a beginning in time and that it has not. And it can be both proven conclusively that it is spatially limited and that it is not. Such nonsensical results prove that the software has been misapplied. It is not designed to solve such problems. Worse was to come: one cannot logically prove the existence of God. True, one cannot logically prove his (or her) non-existence either. But that is small comfort because it does not mean that there is a good fifty-fifty chance. It means that God is not an object of rational inquiry. Key concepts of metaphysics, like 'God', 'freedom of the will', 'immortality' are *regulative* ideas only, i.e., they do *not* have a truth value and they are *not* constitutive of knowledge. They only function as objectives or principles of pure reason in our processing of whatever we process. They are useful assumptions—it makes sense (in every sense of the phrase) to act *as if* they were true and real, but they are still only assumptions, which for categorical reasons can never be proven but can only be surmised.

Of the three basic human faculties it is the Understanding which processes the data delivered by Sensibility. It forms conceptions and rules, it analyzes, abstracts, orders, and explains, but it does so according to the precepts and principles of the highest human faculty, which is Reason. Reason does not add anything to the store of our knowledge, but, reflecting upon the principles and the limits of our Understanding and our knowledge, it controls the Understanding in its operations and scope. Itself not constitutive of knowledge, Reason can only postulate ideas like 'God', 'freedom of the will', or 'immortality', which are, it bears repetition, useful assumptions. The prime function of Reason, however, is to warn the Understanding not to overstep its limits and to wisely restrict itself to its own sphere.

Many followers of Kant were not willing to accept these radical consequences, and Samuel Taylor Coleridge, for all his admiration of Kant, was one of them. In fact, considering how often he expressed his highest respect for the sage from Königsberg, it is surprising how few of Kant's key concepts and ideas he was willing to accept unaltered. And the drift and pattern of his deviations from Kant are significant, telling, and characteristic of him. The major points can be subsumed under six different headings:

1. THE *A PRIORI* AND THE CATEGORIES

Coleridge seems to have had some difficulty in grasping that the categories of the Understanding are *a priori* and therefore not dependent on, but constitutive of experience, and it seems that this was not only a problem for him when he began his Kant studies in 1801.[27] In the *Biographia Literaria* (I, 293) Coleridge writes:

This phrase, *a priori*, is in common most grossly misunderstood, and an absurdity burthened on it, which it does not deserve! By knowledge, *a priori*, we do not mean, that we can know any thing previously to experience, which would be a contradiction in terms; but that having once known it by occasion of experience (i.e. something acting upon us from without) we then know, that it must have pre-existed, or the experience itself would have been impossible.

And the editors of the *Biographia Literaria* explain another passage as follows (*BL* I, 270, n. 1): '[*a priori*] truths must first be perceived and conceived by something

---

[27] Cf. Christensen, *Machine of Language*, 77.

or—according to C's point of view—by some being. And therefore some act, apparently willed by this being, causes such truths to exist and to be thought of.' Orsini draws attention to yet another passage in *The Friend*: '*a priori* (that is from those necessities of the mind or forms of thinking which, though first revealed to us by experience, must yet have pre-existed to make experience itself possible)'.[28] But *a priori* forms of knowledge can neither be 'revealed' nor can they be confirmed by empirical experience. If we experience the world as time and space, this does not show that our categories are *chronologically* prior to our experience; it shows that this is the way we experience the world, and necessarily so, i.e., *independent* of all empirical experience. Coleridge seems to be amazed at a wonderful coincidence of forms of the understanding with the 'laws of nature', when these supposed laws are nothing but the forms in which the human understanding comprehends nature. To quote Kant:

Die Ordnung und Regelmäßigkeit also an den Erscheinungen, die wir *Natur* nennen, bringen wir selbst hinein, und würden sie auch darin nicht finden können, hätten wir sie nicht, oder die Natur unseres Gemüts ursprünglich hineingelegt.

So übertrieben, so widersinnig es auch lautet, zu sagen: der Verstand ist selbst der Quell der Gesetze der Natur, und mithin der formalen Einheit der Natur, so richtig und dem Gegenstande, nämlich der Erfahrung angemessen ist gleichwohl eine solche Behauptung.[29]

Compare this to Coleridge's sense of wonder in *The Statesman's Manual*: 'The fact therefore that the mind of man in its own primary and constituent forms represents the laws of nature is a mystery which of itself should suffice to make it religious; for it is a problem of which God is the only solution, God, the one before all, and of all, and through all!' (quoted in Orsini, *Coleridge and German Idealism*, 113–14).

2. *ANSCHAUUNGSFORMEN* AND 'INTELLECTUAL INTUITION'

It is notoriously difficult to find a good translation for *Anschauungsformen*. It is certainly not 'forms of perception', but neither is the established 'forms of intuition' a fortunate solution, as has been observed before.[30] Since 'intuition' is commonly

---

[28] Orsini, *Coleridge and German Idealism*, 78.

[29] Kant, *Kritik der Urteilskraft*, A 125, A 127.

[30] Cf. Hume, 'Kant and Coleridge on Imagination', 495, and Orsini, *Coleridge and German Idealism*, 91.

defined as 'knowledge or perception not gained by reasoning and intelligence; instinctive knowledge or insight', this translation of Kant's *Anschauungsformen* is even downright misleading: Kant's *Anschauungsformen* do not yield any kind of knowledge about anything, they are the necessary form or mode in which we experience everything (necessary because we cannot choose to experience the world outside time and space). Coleridge knew the difficulty of translating *Anschauungsformen* and yet chose a misleading translation that allowed him to radically break away from Kant, while claiming he was only extending the meaning of the term:

> I take this occasion to observe, that here and elsewhere Kant uses the terms intuition, and the verb active (Intueri, *germanice* Anschauen) for which we have unfortunately no correspondent word, exclusively for that which can be represented in space and time. He therefore consistently and rightly denies the possibility of intellectual intuitions. But as I see no adequate reason for this exclusive sense of the term, I have reverted to its wider signification authorized by our elder theologians and metaphysicians, according to whom the term comprehends all truths known to us without a medium. (*BL* I, 289)

'That which can be represented in time and space' is, of course, already a misrepresentation of Kant; it should read, 'that which by necessity is experienced as time and space'. There is no mysticism in Kant and no intellectual intuition, no immediate knowledge of higher truths. No matter whether Coleridge obtained this from 'our theologians and metaphysicians' or from Fichte or Schelling (see corresponding *BL* note),[31] this mystical backlash has nothing to do with Kant's *Critique of Pure Reason*.

3. *Ding an sich*

In the *Biographia Literaria* (I, 155), Coleridge cannot bring himself to believe that Kant only meant what he said about the *Noumenon* or *Ding an sich* and then goes on to parrot Schelling: 'In spite therefore of his own declarations, I could never believe, it was possible for him to have meant no more by his *Noumenon*, or THING IN ITSELF, than his mere words express; or that in his own conception he confined the whole *plastic* power to the forms of the intellect, leaving for the external cause, for the *materiale* of our sensations, a matter without form, which is doubtless inconceivable.' The first part of the sentence we can only take at face value. Kant's

---

[31] Also Berkeley, *Coleridge and the Crisis of Reason*, 71, 82–4, 89.

deduction is as clear as can be: if reality is only accessible for us through pure concepts of Understanding, which, as it were, frame our experience and knowledge of it, then the realm of *Noumena*, or the *Dinge an sich*, is beyond the reach of our knowledge. We do not know what 'reality as such' is like, but we do know that reality as we experience it is *not* 'reality as such'.

This seems clear enough, but when critics such as Basil Willey declare that Kant's *Ding an sich* is 'not directly approachable'[32] or when Jim McKusick speaks of 'Kant's difficulty in arriving at the *Ding an sich*,'[33] it is evident that the concept is perhaps difficult to grasp: for the *Ding an sich* is not like some geographical location that can be reached only by balloon, neither is it like the South Pole that one explorer failed to reach though others were later to succeed. And when Tom McFarland puzzles over the question 'whether Kant meant, by his conception of *Ding an sich* to imply the existence of a God supramundane', only to resign, 'neither commentary nor his own words supplies a wholly unambivalent answer',[34] it might help to reiterate that Kant did not '*concede* [. . .] the absolute unknowability of positive *Noumena*' (on the contrary, that is the very point he makes), and neither did he fill, in the *Critique of Pure Reason*, 'this "empty space" [. . .] protected by the first *Kritik* [. . .] with freedom, immortality, and God'.[35] The *Dinge an sich* are categorically distinct from Kant's *regulative Ideen*, and, of course, *they* can never the 'objects of religious hope' that McFarland wishes to thematize.

To return to Coleridge's fundamental problems with the *Ding an sich*, as opposed to objects as we know them: in the *Biographia Literaria* (I, 262–3), Coleridge advocates a 'true and original realism'. 'This believes and requires neither more nor less, than that the object which it beholds or presents to itself, is the real and very object. In this sense, however much we may strive against it, we are all collectively born idealists, and therefore and only therefore are we at the same time realists'. But not, it is clear, *Critical Philosophers*.[36] Coleridge neither understood why one should not speculate about the *Ding an sich* (why, for example, it should not have a form) nor why the object we perceive should not be 'the real and very object'. Perhaps needless to underline, the point here is not to accusingly labour the fact that Coleridge is not a proper Kantian—why should he be? The point is that, yet again, he has simply no use for another of Kant's key concepts.

---

[32] Willey, *Coleridge*, 89.
[33] McKusick, 'Coleridge's "Logic"', 487.
[34] McFarland, *Pantheist*, 368, n. 56.
[35] Ibid., emphasis added.
[36] Cf. Appleyard, *Philosophy of Literature*, 185, 186, 194.

4. ANTINOMIES

Orsini is rather harsh on Coleridge when, in the *Logic* manuscripts, Coleridge assigns the Kantian antinomies to the Understanding, rather than to Reason, as Kant had done.[37] But this mistake, if mistake it is and not a mere consequence of Coleridge's re-evaluation of the Understanding (see below), seems negligible. If the categories as concepts of the Understanding are misapplied to objects which are beyond experience, one can, of course, blame Reason for not having exerted proper control (it is duly punished by a conflict within itself). One could also, as Coleridge does, blame the Understanding, which, unsupervised and uncontrolled, applies its *Anschauungsformen* and its categories to spheres 'contradistinguished from phenomena' (*Logic* 139–140). The far more basic re-interpretation of Kant's antinomies, which are a warning sign to return to one's proper sphere and not speculate about, say, God, immortality, or free will, is that for Coleridge the antinomies play a totally different role:

> Yet there had dawned upon me, even before I had met with the *Critique of the Pure Reason*, a certain guiding light. If the mere intellect could make no certain discovery of a holy and intelligent first cause, it might yet supply a demonstration, that no legitimate argument could be drawn from the intellect *against* its truth. And what is this more than St. Paul's assertion, that by wisdom (more properly translated by the powers of reasoning) no man ever arrived at the knowledge of God? (*BL* I, 201–2)

Apart from the fact that, as Berkeley says, Coleridge's claim to have intuited a central point of the first *Critique* before he even read it is wildly implausible,[38] the *Kritik der reinen Vernunft* draws no such comfort from the impossibility of proving God's existence and from the concomitant impossibility to disprove God's existence. As René Wellek put it very succinctly: 'Kant is put to strange uses: His doctrines on the limits of our knowing power become a sort of back-door through which the whole of traditional theology is admitted.'[39]

5. REGULATIVE IDEAS

As concepts of reason (*Vernunftbegriffe*), regulative ideas, unlike the categories (*reine Verstandesbegriffe*) or the *Anschauungsformen*, are not necessary to make

[37] Cf. Orsini, *Coleridge and German Idealism*, 138, 142, 148; see also Berkeley, *Coleridge and the Crisis of Reason*, 149.

[38] Cf. Berkeley, *Coleridge and the Crisis of Reason*, 99.

[39] Wellek, *Kant*, 115.

any experience, but they can be used to organize experience into a meaningful whole. No objective reality appertains to them, but they are powerful and they have an effect. Coleridge was not quite willing to accept this drastic restriction.[40] It is true that time and again he repeated that no logical proof of the existence of God was possible (e.g. *Logic* 329),[41] that it would indeed be a misuse of logic to even attempt it (cf. *Logic* 131): 'We do not win Heaven by logic.' (*TT* I, 278). On the other hand, he disagreed with Kant's position that ideas of reason are merely regulative and not also constitutive of knowledge:

[T]here neither are, have been, or ever will be but two essentially different Schools of Philosophy: the Platonic and the Aristotelian. To the latter, but with a somewhat nearer approach to the Platonic, Emanuel Kant belonged; to the former Bacon and Leibniz & in his riper and better years Berkley—and to this I profess myself an adherent. [. . .] He for whom Ideas are constitutive, will in effect be a Platonist—and in those, for whom they are regulative only, Platonism must be a hollow affectation. (*CL* V, 13–14, 15, cf. also last appendix to *The Statesman's Manual*)

This is not only 'one of Coleridge's unhistorical projections' because it assumes that 'the regulative-constitutive dichotomy was present in ancient thought',[42] but it also has wider implications for Coleridge's theory of the consubstantiality of the symbol: what Wellek calls Coleridge's strange confusion of symbol and synecdoche[43] is ultimately religiously motivated.[44] The fact that in 1809 Coleridge took a note on the error of 'taking God, i.e. a Spirit, as *a thing*—the subject of the Categories' (see *N* III, 3575) does, of course, not mean that he was a Kantian after all—God as a regulative idea is not an object of the Understanding anyway. Rather, it indicates again that Coleridge reshuffled Kant's faculties, and considerably so: clinging to the possibilities of intuitive, immediate knowledge of higher truths (which, of course, would be difficult to communicate),[45] Coleridge held that ideas of Reason were somehow constitutive of knowledge—an option categorically denied by Kant.

6. REASON AND UNDERSTANDING

In 1825, Coleridge wrote to his nephew, J. T. Coleridge: 'In Kant's *Critique of the Pure Reason* there is more than one fundamental error; but the main fault lies in the Title-page, which to the manifold advantage of the Work might be exchanged

---

[40] See Muirhead, *Philosopher*, 90, 91, and Emmett in Brett (ed.), *Writers and their Background*, 203.
[41] See also Muirhead, *Philosopher*, 223, 234, 235, and Willey, *Coleridge*, 219.
[42] Orsini, *Coleridge and German Idealism*, 137.
[43] Cf. Wellek, *Romantic Age*, 174.
[44] See also Berkeley, *Coleridge and the Crisis of Reason*, 191–2.
[45] See Hamilton, *Colerige's Poetics*, 196–7.

for—an Inquisition respecting the constitution and limits of the Human Understanding' (*CL* V, 421). This passage testifies the complete divergence of Coleridge from Kant. Certainly, the *Critique of Pure Reason* proved the limitations of both Understanding *and* Reason—but, as much as Coleridge was ready to accept anything that led to a depreciation of the former, he was unwilling to accept any conclusions that assigned a limited role to Reason: 'Coleridge was never prepared to admit that the deliverances of the reason had subjective value alone, nor that the reason was bereft of all contact with external reality. This was why he ultimately sided with Plato against Kant.'[46] Like Kant, Coleridge insisted upon a clear distinction between Reason and Understanding (see *AR* 8), but not so much because he wanted to separate it from empirical reality—rather because he wanted to upgrade it to some power or faculty that gave access to an even more important reality: 'Reason is to Coleridge an organ of faith'.[47]

Summarizing all this in a kind of interim report, it is safe to say that Samuel Taylor Coleridge either failed to grasp or refused to accept *any* of the key elements of Kant's *Critical Philosophy*. To all intents and purposes, Kant's Copernican Revolution was lost on him. Why then did he repeatedly express his highest respect for the 'all-becrushing' Kant (*BL* II, 89), most impressively so in the following passage from the *Biographia Literaria* (I, 153)?

The originality, the depth, and the compression of the thoughts; the novelty and subtlety, yet solidity and importance, of the distinctions; the adamantine chain of the logic; and I will venture to add (paradox as it will appear to those who have taken their notion of IMMANUEL KANT, from Reviewers and Frenchmen) the *clearness* and *evidence*, of the '*Critique of the Pure Reason*,' of the JUDGMENT; of the 'METAPHISICAL ELEMENTS OF NATURAL PHILOSOPHY,' and of his 'RELIGION WITHIN THE BOUNDS OF PURE REASON,' took possession of me as with a giant's hand.

How can one praise all these qualities in a philosopher and yet refuse to accept a single one of his philosophical principles or concepts? Coleridge's undifferentiated praise for the first *Critique* and, at the same time, for Kant's pre-critical inaugural dissertation of 1770 (see *BL* I, 288, *Logic* 243–4),[48] his praise for the second *Critique* and, at the same time, for Kant's pre-critical *Der einzig mögliche Beweisgrund zu einer Demonstration des Daseins Gottes* (1763)[49] suggest that he was totally indifferent to Kant's *critical* revolution in philosophy and there are very good reasons to

---

[46] Appleyard, *Philosophy of Literature*, 121.

[47] Wellek, *Kant*, 105; see also 91, 93.

[48] 'Thus, if Coleridge seriously sought to offer the *idées maîtrises* of Kant's system as his own, he would never have allowed himself continually to suggest that the *Inaugural Dissertation* presented in concentrated summary the central theses of the *Critique of Pure Reason*. Whereas, the philosopher who seeks to come to terms with Coleridge's understanding of Kant may find that what puzzles him and interests him most is just this obstinate insistence on the part of the poet that the *Inaugural Dissertation* does contain the very marrow or substance of Kant's mature thought.' (McKinnan in Beer (ed.), *Coleridge's Variety*, 184)

[49] See Engell in Gravil and Lefebure (eds.), *The Coleridge Connection*, 168.

suppose that he, in a way, found some of the *pre-critical* Kant more consoling than the rest.[50]

It could be that Kant came in useful to drive out Newton, Locke, Hume, Priestley, Hartley, and even Berkeley, or to lay to rest (although never definitively so) the spectre of atheism Coleridge suspected behind pantheism and Spinozism.[51] And if we are to believe in the three phases of his philosophical development as constructed in the *Biographia Literaria* (materialism, idealism, and critical philosophy), Kant has undoubtedly such a *negatively* critical function for him. But on the *constructive* side he seems to have been of absolutely no use whatsoever to Samuel Taylor Coleridge, except perhaps for the *Logic*. But had not Kant himself said in the preface to the second edition of the *Critique of Pure Reason* (1787) that 'though metaphysics cannot be the foundation of religion, it must always continue to be a bulwark of it' (quoted from *Opus Maximum* lxi–lxii) and that the *Critique* was written against materialism, fatalism, atheism, free-thinking unbelief, fanaticism, superstition, idealism, and scepticism?[52]

This prompts us, in order to complete the picture, to take a brief look at Kant's and Coleridge's respective philosophical views on religion and ethics, and finally at a key concept of Kant's aesthetics, the sublime, which, like in a burning glass, focuses the aesthetic implications of his critical turn.

Kant's categorical imperative contains his ethics in a nutshell: it places the responsibility for ethically correct behaviour solely on the individual and their powers of reasoning. Consonant with the main thesis of 'Was ist Aufklärung?', it is the individuals' courage to make use of their own understanding and the public use of reason that will eventually erode the bastions of irrationality, obscurantism, and political oppression. It is true that, as Kant demonstrates in his second *Critique*, the fact of a moral conscience points to the necessary assumption of a free will (of which, Kant says, if we study mankind from outside, there is no indication), and that once free will is accepted as an 'as if' regulative idea, the ideas of 'God' and 'immortality' follow suit. But religion remains an affair of the individual, of his or her conscience, and *practically* of the *practical* exercise of reason (which, after all, gives Kant's second *Critique* its title). *Religion within the Bounds of Reason Alone* (1793) tries to show that the Christian religion contains elements of a reasonable religion (*Vernunftreligion*) and that, thus interpreted, it is a rationally acceptable form of religion. The King of Prussia responded quickly: Kant was ordered to keep his mouth shut on matters of religion. He complied, but after the king's death he published *Der Streit der Fakultäten* (1798), in which he reiterated his position and even went further in his claim that the Faculty of Philosophy had the right to critically examine the statutes of the Faculty of Theology, not the other way round.

---

[50] See Loades in Watson (ed.), *An Infinite Complexity.*

[51] See Willey, *Coleridge*, 87, Berkeley, *Coleridge and the Crisis of Reason*, 42, and McFarland, *Pantheist*, 89, 90.

[52] See Ashton, *The German Idea*, 39.

The implied synecdoche was obvious.

Coleridge knew Kant's categorical imperative well; he gave it in different versions, sometimes watered down to a 'Do unto others…' truism, and when he once gave an accurate, verbatim translation, he failed to make clear that it was Kant's and not his idea and formulation.[53] Apart from that, Coleridge was living in a different moral universe. Tortured by feelings of guilt, remorse, and a general sense of insufficiency and inferiority, Coleridge felt the existential reality of Original Sin, inherent moral depravity, and irredeemable weakness, which all cried out for redemption, grace, and salvation. 'I believe most steadfastly in original Sin […] and for this inherent depravity, I believe, that the *Spirit* of the Gospel is the sole cure.' (*CL* I, 396) The systematic absence in Kant of ideas of grace, redemption, and so on contrasts vividly with their central place in Coleridge's religious thinking, which in turn was alien to Kant's *Vernunftreligion*. How Coleridge's belief in a need for a doctrine of 'Salvation by the Cross of Christ' (*CL* II, 1192) 'was notably enhanced […] by Kantian analysis'[54] must remain a mystery. Accepting Kant's dictum that nothing in the world is truly good but a good will, Coleridge was yet dissatisfied with Kant's 'cold', rational ethics with moral obligation and duty as its pillars, and he deplored the lack of importance given to the affections.[55] In absolute contrast to the Kant of the *Streit der Fakultäten*, Coleridge saw philosophy not only as a handmaiden to Christian religion, but Christian religion as the culmination of all philosophy: 'Religion therefore is the ultimate aim of philosophy' (*M* III, 317). At one point in time, his projected *Logosophia* was to bear the title of 'Christianity the one true Philosophy' (*CL* III, 533–4). Somehow reversing the order of the human faculties and redefining their respective powers, Coleridge explains in a note on *Aids to Reflection* (469):

N.B. The Practical Reason alone *is* Reason in the full and substantive Sense. It is Reason in its own sphere of *perfect freedom*, as the source of *IDEAS*, which *Ideas* in their conversion to the responsible Will become *Ultimate* Ends. On the other hand, Theoretic Reason, as the ground of the Universal and Absolute in all Logical *Conclusion*, is rather the *Light* of Reason in the Understanding and known to be such by its contrast with the contingency and particularity which characterize all the proper & indigenous growths of the Understanding.

Wellek comments: 'The Kantian scale which rises from Sense to Understanding and then to Reason has changed. Understanding has dropped to the lowest place and the intuitions of Sensibility have been put next to the intuitions of Reason, though on a lower plain.'[56]

Coleridge's unique use of Reason and Understanding has been remarked upon before, but, in this context here, the motivation for this usage is strikingly

---

[53] See Orsini, *Coleridge and German Idealism*, 155.
[54] McFarland, *Pantheist*, 226.
[55] See Wellek, *Kant*, 88.
[56] Ibid., 127, 128.

obvious: wedged between a pressing need for salvation and the reassurances of established Christian religion, Coleridge redefined Reason in such a way that it included the doctrines of Christianity as necessary and eternal truths of reason (cf. *Opus Maximum*, lxi), historically revealed and accessible to intuitive knowledge. Reading Kant's pre-critical *Träume eines Geistersehers* (1766), Coleridge commented:

I cannot conceive a supreme moral Intelligence, unless I believe in my own immortality—for I must believe in a whole system of apparent means to an end, which end had no existence—my Conscience, my progressive faculties, &c.— But give up this, & Virtue wants all reason—. (*M* III, 317)

How deeply the Kant of the *Critiques* must have disappointed him in this respect—especially since Kant travels the same road, but never fails to point out that these are only 'as if' assumptions. By way of contrast, in Coleridge's Christianity, 'God was the anchor of the whole system'.[57] The difference is fundamental, as Coleridge himself pointed out in the *Opus Maximum*: 'The points in which I disagree with the illustrious sage of Königsberg—*those, namely, in which he differs from the Christian code*—and the philosophical grounds of my disagreement will appear in its own place in another part of this work.' (*Opus Maximum* 39–40, emphasis added) What it boils down to is the difference between a philosophy that is not afraid of its own consequences and a philosophy that serves a religion. Some may call the latter bad philosophy or no philosophy at all (I reserve my judgement until the very end), but the inconsistencies are palpable:

The dualism of faith and reason or as Coleridge would say of reason and understanding, goes sometimes to amusing length in the *Aids to Reflection*. [...] It is a truly Coleridgean inconsistency that he still asserts subjective idealism side by side with a belief in the Triune God and the historical creed of Christianity. [...] All controversy is simply closed and mankind has to receive the revelation of God in a spirit of humility. Coleridge does not mind that this amounts to a formal abdication of philosophy, a declaration of bankruptcy, a final surrender to a view of the universe which is fundamentally incoherent as it contains the stupendous contradiction between our understanding and the reason imposed upon us.[58]

After all this, it cannot come as a surprise that Coleridge has no use for Kant's critical redefinition of the sublime. In the Kantian sublime we do not encounter God in all his grandeur and might, nor is it explained in physiological terms as in Burke, but in the Kantian sublime we encounter *ourselves* in a confrontation with something that is immeasurably great or violent—because it is then that we realize that as *rational* beings we can grasp infinity as an idea, although as *sensuous* beings we are overwhelmed by it, and furthermore, that the *idea* of a rational being in this universe can never be annihilated by the physical annihilation of one particular

---

[57] McFarland, *Pantheist*, 222.
[58] Wellek, *Kant*, 129, 124, 131.

being. In the sublime, we experience respect for our own vocation, apropos of natural objects to which we mistakenly ascribe sublimity. In the sublime we stand in awe before our possibilities and destiny. Although he added some interesting touches to Friederike Brun's 'Chamonix beim Sonnenaufgange',[59] there is nothing like this in the Coleridgean sublime, and it could not be otherwise.[60] True, for Coleridge as for Kant, the sublime is subjective, but it is then absorbed into the beautiful[61] and it is bereft of its self-reflexive grandeur.

It is likewise with Kant's definition of the work of art as offering 'purposefulness without purpose'.[62] Even the purposefulness of nature, which offers a model for that of art, is only an idea that we ascribe to it; in ascribing the same to a work of art, all the while recognizing that it does not serve a purpose, we are operating with an 'as if' at two removes. Coleridge's idea of 'ideas' allows no systematic place for such unrestrained free play of the powers of the mind, as is perpetually provoked by the 'ästhetische Ideen', to which no concept can ever be adequate. Sooner or later an aesthetics that *serves* will have to meet the higher demands of ulterior truth. But that is a matter of Coleridge's criticism. Before we move on, one can only underline John Muirhead's assessment, made some 80 years ago: 'There is a sense in which Coleridge's whole philosophy was a Philosophy of Religion'.[63] All his divergences from his greatest philosophical hero, Immanuel Kant, can be explained as divergences caused by Coleridge's religious needs and convictions.

Just as Immanuel Kant in the preceding pages was not introduced in order to test whether Coleridge was a good Kantian, but as a point of reference that is stable and permanent enough to help locate and trace Samuel Taylor Coleridge's philosophical drift, so Friedrich Schelling will not be used in the following pages in order to demonstrate to what degree Coleridge owed his deviations from Kant to the architect of *Transzendental-* and *Naturphilosophie*. We know already that he owed a great deal to him and to other German Idealists. We know he rejected him in 1818, and later still deplored the use he had made of him in the *Biographia Literaria*. And we think we know this had something to do with charges of pantheism (and/or Catholicism) against Schelling (who, throughout his career, had been plagued with charges that he was an atheist, *and* a Catholic (!), or failing that, a pantheist. Blessed with foresight, Schelling commented ironically in the *Freiheitsschrift* that it could not be denied that such general names as 'pantheism' were of great advantage in such smear campaigns since they covered whole philosophical schools, irrespective of all their differences).

---

[59] See Reinfandt in Bode and Rennhak (eds.), *Romantic Voices*, and Esterhammer, 'Coleridge's "Hymn before Sun-rise"'.

[60] Cf. Kant, *Kritik der Urteilskraft*, §§ 27–9; see also Bode, 'And what were thou...?'.

[61] See Shaffer, 'Coleridge's Revolution in the Standard of Taste'.

[62] Kant, *Kritik der Urteilskraft*, § 11.

[63] Muirhead, *Philosopher*, 217.

In the following, a look will be taken at Coleridge's 'transcendental deduction' of the imagination in chapter 12 of the *Biographia Literaria*. The twelve postulates, or twelve theses, largely follow Schelling—that Coleridge in writing them helped himself generously to principally three *different* texts by Schelling, instead of just one,[64] does not only show that Coleridge was a master *collagiste*, it also shows that up to 1809, contrary to what his detractors said, the body of Schelling's work was coherent enough to allow such a cut and paste technique without glaring inconsistencies between the passages thus assembled.

Four preliminary points: the following does not even attempt to critique the *Biographia Literaria* as a whole; it is not a discussion of the imagination and fancy in Coleridge either; it largely ignores Coleridge's 'borrowings' from Kant, Leibniz, Fichte, Jacobi, et al.; and it does not discuss the matter of Coleridge's plagiarisms and 'borrowings'—although it could be said that, thanks to the labours of the editors of the *Biographia Literaria* volume in the Bollingen edition, all the evidence is now in the open, even if it is sometimes, and in strategic places, presented and commented in a way that seems either evasive and noncommittal or apologetic, tendentious, partisan, and downright misleading.[65] Rather, the following will determine, taking chapters 12 and 13 of *Biographia Literaria* as a paradigmatic example, the distances Coleridge walked with Schelling and where exactly he parted company with him. It promises also to eventually offer a new, radical reading of the famous 'gap' in chapter 13.

The third paragraph of chapter 12 contains, of course, one of the heaviest ironies in Coleridge's overall œuvre. For, when he says that 'the fairest part of the most beautiful body will appear deformed and monstrous, if dissevered from its place in the Organic whole' (*BL* I, 234), this rings the bell for an absolutely unique orgy of disseverings of textual parts from a plethora of sources—it opens a *tour de force* collage of acknowledged and unacknowledged quotations, paraphrases, 'borrowings', and condensations.[66] The irony cannot have been lost on Coleridge, although the original reader was hardly in a position to share his mirth. One may call this dubious practice merely an 'unorthodox and disingenuous mode of composition',[67] but it remains slightly embarrassing that what McFarland held up as a prize specimen of mosaic composition is a passage taken *in toto* from Jacobi. What Jacobi leaves untranslated, Coleridge does not translate either (cf. *BL* 244–7).[68]

---

[64] These texts are *Vom Ich* (1795), *Abhandlungen zur Erläuterung des Idealismus* (1797), and *System des transzendentalen Idealismus* (1800).

[65] See Fruman, 'Review Essay'; also Shaffer in Pape (ed.), *A View in the Rear-mirror*, with regard to the *Opus Maximum*.

[66] See Haeger in Burwick (ed.), *Coleridge's* Biographia Literaria, 79.

[67] McFarland, *Pantheist*, 29.

[68] Cf. McFarland, *Pantheist*, 135–6, and Fruman, 'Review Essay', 142.

After some preliminaries, the bulk of chapter 12 is devoted to an exposition of the subject–object relationship according to Friedrich Schelling. The positing of the objective pole, or nature, and of the subjective pole, or self or intelligence, leads to two basically opposed ways of grounding a philosophy (*BL* I, 255, 257), depending on whether one begins with the objective or with the subjective pole. This is pure Schelling. And Coleridge follows Schelling in claiming that, for the transcendental philosopher, the 'I AM' always already posits the objects and that the task is to show that the existence of things without us and our own immediate self-consciousness are actually identical and only seemingly opposite (*BL* I, 260). Coleridge took this from *System des transzendentalen Idealismus*, but the merging of *Natur-* and *Identitäts-* or *Transzendentalphilosophie* was already indicated in Schelling's *Ideen zu einer Philosophie der Natur* (1797): 'Die Natur soll der sichtbare Geist, der Geist die unsichtbare Natur seyn.' Nature is posited as the visible part of spirit, spirit the invisible part of nature—spirit and nature are one and the same, we have only come to call the visible part of the spectrum 'nature' and the invisible one 'spirit', an arbitrary distinction.[69] It is an arbitrary distinction which philosophy must expose: 'Philosophie ist Naturlehre des Geistes', 'das System der Natur ist zugleich das System unseres Geistes'.[70] Or, two years later, in the *Einleitung zu dem Entwurf eines Systems der Naturphilosophie* (1799): 'Nach dieser Ansicht, da die Natur nur der sichtbare Organismus unseres Verstandes ist, kann die Natur nichts anderes als das Regel- und Zweckmäßige produziren, und die Natur ist gezwungen es zu produziren. Aber kann die Natur nichts als das Regelmäßige produziren [...], so folgt dass [...] also das Ideelle auch hinwiederum aus dem Reellen entspringen und aus ihm erklärt werden muss.'[71] Theoretical philosophy, Schelling concludes in the *System*, is the reconstruction of the evolution of self-consciousness.[72] It is in this context, in the context of Absolute Idealism, that Coleridge, immediately before Thesis I, declares that the object we behold 'is the real and very object' (*BL* I, 263, see also *BL* I, 134). Discarding Kant's *Ding an sich* with Schelling's help, it is not yet obvious that Coleridge has something entirely different in mind.[73] As he assembles Theses I through VI from various Schelling texts, carefully identified by the latest editors of the *Biographia Literaria*, the decisive break occurs between Thesis VI and its Scholium,[74] when Coleridge, expanding on the SUM or I AM, introduces 'sum quia deus est' and 'sum quia in deo sum' (*BL* I, 274). As the editors discretely point out on the same page,

---

[69] The English standard translation 'Nature is to be regarded as visible mind, mind as invisible nature' is somewhat inaccurate because it would be a good translation of 'Natur soll unsichtbarer Geist, Geist unsichtbare Natur sein'—which Schelling did not write.

[70] Schelling, *Schelling*, 128–9.

[71] Ibid., 134.

[72] Ibid., 167.

[73] See Orsini, *Coleridge and German Idealism*, 197, 203.

[74] See Wallace in Burwick (ed.), *Coleridge's* Biographia Literaria, 58.

'C intentionally affirms and expands a position that Schelling fully explains but sets aside as untenable "in theoretical philosophy" [...]. Schelling states that theoretical philosophy cannot, given its own criteria, successfully assert that God is the ground of our *knowledge* [...], nor can it identify God with the *Ich*; God is an object determined by the *Ich*, an object whose *existence* cannot be proved ontologically [...].' Schelling is here absolutely at one with Kant's first *Critique*. What is striking in Samuel Taylor Coleridge is the total absence of an awareness of the systematic incongruity and incompatibility, not of the pieces he has assembled, because they cohere perfectly, but of his own *addition* to what he has assembled. There is a certain lack of understanding of the consistency and inner logic of philosophical systems. *Pace* the editors of the *Biographia Literaria* (*BL* I, 274, n. 2, right column), Coleridge *is* disagreeing with the Schelling he had read, for whom such effusions had no place in theoretical philosophy.

It happens again at the end of Thesis IX: Coleridge has been translating from Schelling's *System* about the principle of transcendental philosophy and then he adds an afterthought of his own: 'In other words, philosophy would pass into religion, and religion become inclusive of philosophy. We begin with the I KNOW MYSELF, in order to end with the absolute I AM. We proceed from the SELF, in order to lose and find all self in GOD' (*BL* I, 283). 'God' is simply grafted onto Schelling's texts, but the break is painfully obvious and the editors' attempt to gloss it over only makes matters worse: 'Schelling, Kant, Fichte, Jacobi, and others likewise carried philosophy into religion and vice versa [...]. C is not stepping outside the mainstream of transcendental philosophy *as a whole*; and he is within a great philosophic tradition centuries long.' The first part is patently wrong (with the possible exception of Jacobi), and the second part is beside the point. The point is: what Coleridge adds in no way follows from what he had cribbed from Schelling.

But was Coleridge not ingenuous, was he not original, did he not know exactly what he was doing? Obviously not. For in Thesis X, he continues to translate from Schelling that speculations about a higher consciousness are *not* the business of the transcendental philosopher (*BL* I, 284–5)—but that is exactly what Coleridge had done in the preceding thesis—and then, as if to prove for a third time that he had no clue what the passages he had been transcribing mean in their original systematic context, he does it again: translating from Schelling's *System* he writes, 'Thus the true system of natural philosophy places the sole reality of things in an ABSOLUTE [...], in the absolute identity of subject and object, which it calls nature, and which in its highest power is nothing else but self-conscious will or intelligence', only to add an incompatible idea of his own: 'in this sense the position of Malbranche, that we see all things in God, is a strict philosophical truth' (*BL* I, 285). Haeger has drawn attention to the fact that immediately before this, Coleridge had inserted another two sentences of his own: 'Should we attempt it, we must be driven back from ground to ground each of which would cease to be a ground the moment we pressed on it. We must be whirl'd down the gulph of an infinite series.'[75] It may be that this almost physical horror of losing ground prompted Coleridge to a leap of faith that *logically* was not necessary (there is no infinite regress at this point in Schelling). But whatever the ultimate motivation—religious *Angst* or an astonishing lack of consecutive reasoning, or both of them—the fact is that Coleridge substituted the idealistic ABSOLUTE, which is, in its highest power or potency, self-consciousness, with the personal God of Christianity. As Orsini has it, Coleridge lapsed into traditional theodicy.[76] It is true that, for example in the *Systemschrift* and in Schelling's 'Philosophie der Kunst', there are passages in which Schelling seems to say that all art derives from God or that the universe is identical with God or that all thinking is in God. But invariably he clarifies that, e.g., 'unter Universum ist nicht das reale oder ideale All, sondern die absolute Identität beider verstanden',[77] or that God *as identity* of the real and the ideal is the source of all art because it defines 'the final possibility of art'.[78] But this identity is not transcendent. And this may explain a puzzle that is more astonishing and ultimately more interesting than why Coleridge grafted 'God' onto Schelling's *Natur- und Transendentalphilosophie*: Why did he not make any use of Schelling's transcendental deduction of the supreme importance of *Kunst* (which is both art, and literature, and possibly musical composition as well)? He had it right there in his hand while he was dictating the *Biographia Literaria*. And his refusal to take it over may be one way to explain the 'débâcle' of chapter 13.[79]

As early as in the *Ältestes Systemprogramm des deutschen Idealismus* (1796/7) Schelling and Hegel had postulated that the highest act of reason had to be an aesthetic act.[80] But it was in the *System des transzendentalen Idealismus* that he deduced why the work of art is the culmination of a process that is at once natural and spiritual: it is only in the work of art that the *identity* of the spheres of nature and spirit is not only deduced (as in philosophy) but actually represented. Only the work of art can *show* the factual identity of that which is separated in nature and art, namely the identity of conscious and unconscious, of freedom and necessity, of nature and spirit. The aesthetic activity of the genius, in whose imagination the conscious and the unconscious merge,[81] results in a product that reflects for me (because *it is*!) 'jenes absolute Identische, was selbst im Ich schon sich getrennt hat'.[82] *Natur-* and *Transzendentalphilosophie* are forever running on parallel tracks and can never be *one*,[83] but the latter can *point* to a phenomenon that proves the

---

[75] Haeger in Burwick (ed.), *Coleridge's Biographia Literaria*, 86.

[76] Cf. Orsini, *Coleridge and German Idealism*, 205; see also 224–5, 237.

[77] Schelling, *Schelling*, 229.

[78] Ibid., 230.

[79] Cf. Hamilton, *Colerige's Poetics*, 23.

[80] Cf. Schelling, *Schelling*, 95–7.

[81] Cf. ibid., 156–9, 184–7.

[82] Ibid., 191; see also Burwick in Gravil and Lefebure (eds.), *The Coleridge Connection*, 178–80, and Ferris, 'Coleridge's Ventriloquy', 63.

[83] Cf. Schelling, *Schelling*, 147.

absolute indifference, or identity, of the real and the ideal: art.[84] The Philosophy of Art is the true organon of philosophy.[85] But the Philosophy of Art can never *be* the thing for which it prepares the way of understanding. Art, says Schelling in the *System*, is the only and eternal revelation that there is ('die Kunst [ist] die einzige und ewige Offenbarung, die es gibt'[86]). The only and eternal revelation that there is. Art, not God. Of course, this would be totally unacceptable to Coleridge. But he must have seen it coming. Why did he step on the brakes only when it was too late—so that he had to introduce the hoax letter from a friend in chapter 13 and then present a lame conclusion without a deduction? As they say, if he did not want to go to Philadelphia, why did he board the train? McFarland, who seems to be inordinately worried on Coleridge's behalf, is puzzled by 'Coleridge's utilization in the *Biographia* of what we consider the fundamentally alien thought of Schelling',[87] 'alien to Coleridge's most deeply cherished philosophical and religious convictions'.[88] Why, if Coleridge, as McFarland sees it, preferred Jacobi to Schelling, did he plagiarize from the latter? Or, as the editors of the *Biographia Literaria* wonder, why did he use Schelling when he could have used Fichte (*BL* I, cxxvi)? Even granted that Coleridge 'was badly off his philosophical form when he wrote the *Biographia*',[89] it is difficult to believe that *as he translated from Schelling* it dawned upon him that this was 'alien to his own' thought: 'He therefore had no choice but to terminate his exposition of Schelling's transcendental idealism and proceed to other matters.'[90] Jonathan Wordsworth comments wryly: 'If at the climax of the metaphysical section of *Biographia* he was truly surprised by the pantheist tendency of his own thinking, he must have been writing in his sleep since 1795.'[91] Or at least he had been asleep since he began to dictate the *Biographia Literaria*.

On the other hand, Orsini's hypothesis lacks credentials, too: 'Coleridge had reached the brink of the absolute subjectivism which was at the centre of Schelling's idealism. This idealism would have done without the personal God whom Coleridge could not give up. So he stopped here in the *Biographia*.'[92] But Coleridge had inserted passages about an apparently Christian, personal God three times before, although they never fitted systematically—why not do it a fourth time? Because this time the inconsistency would have been too obvious, even by Coleridge's standards? *Biographia Literaria* 'is a religious testament', say its editors (*BL* I, cxxxv), and

---

[84] Ibid., 224.

[85] Ibid., 161.

[86] Ibid., 189.

[87] McFarland, *Pantheist*, 132–3.

[88] Ibid., 40.

[89] Ibid., 41.

[90] Ibid., 42; see also McFarland, *Coleridge and the Pantheist Tradition*, 152, and McFarland in Bloom (ed.), *Coleridge*, 119. His breaking off of his translation is even presented by McFarland (*Pantheist*, 42) as ultimate proof that Coleridge was not plagiarizing. He had convictions, after all.

[91] Wordsworth in Gravil and Newlyn (eds.), *Coleridge's Imagination*, 46.

[92] Orsini, *Coleridge and German Idealism*, 214–15.

Coleridge's 'philosophical and religious thoughts are deeply inseparable and can be discussed only as one large unit or not at all' (*BL* I, cxxxvi), as he 'tried to find an anchorage for his philosophy in the bottomless sea of faith' (*BL* I, lxxiii). Schelling, by contrast, had written in the *Systemschrift* that once the work of philosophy was done, it would return to the ocean of poesy,[93] and, to repeat it once more, that *art* was the only and eternal revelation there was. And yet, it could be argued that by breaking off where he did—*and in the act of breaking off*—Coleridge proved that, for once, he had entirely understood what Schelling meant.

Let us, however, put this on the back-burner for a moment and consider what we have so far: Every time Coleridge deviates from his philosophical sources and breaks away from his philosophical heroes, every time there are inconsistencies in his own philosophical reasoning and systematic incompatibilities between the philosophical building blocks he uses, one major reason can be given for these faultlines: Coleridge's religious views and needs. The problem is not that Coleridge evidently had a strong personal need for a religious view of life;[94] neither is it that religion for Samuel Taylor Coleridge was 'the *raison d'être* of everything else';[95] and neither is it in itself problematical that Coleridge's mature philosophical thought was identical with Christian doctrine.[96] Rather the problem seems to be that (a) these religious convictions are basically, that is to say, *systematically*, incompatible with the philosophical materials Coleridge assembled from various sources to give substance to his own deliberations or to impress his audiences and readership; *and* that (b) Coleridge was either unaware of these incompatibilities or chose to obfuscate the contradictions. This is not simply a matter of Coleridge's avowed objective 'to reduce all knowledges into harmony' (*Friend* I, 108).[97] When even Muirhead says that 'Coleridge's thought [. . .] was too much dominated by the religious interest',[98] this is not only confined, it seems to me, to ethics (as Muirhead will have it), but it is true for the whole of his philosophy. Religiosity overrides philosophical consistency, and this leads to glaring contradictions and non-sequiturs, time and again: it is an inbuilt, irresistible force that leads to foreseeable faultlines in his arguments, as faith and logic pull into different directions.

His rejection of Schelling in 1818 is a good example for this. Schelling may have been suspect for Coleridge because of his alleged 'pantheist tendencies'. But when Coleridge wrote to J. H. Green on 30 September 1818 (*CL* IV, 854), rejecting Schelling downright, he gave as the first reason Schelling's willingness to give nature full priority over the self.[99] Now, for everybody who has ever read a single

---

[93] Cf. Schelling, *Schelling*, 194.

[94] See Appleyard, *Philosophy of Literature*, 8.

[95] Willey, *Coleridge*, 69.

[96] See Gregory, *Coleridge and the Conservative Imagination*, vii.

[97] See Wallace (ed.), *The Design of* Biographia Literaria, 68, and Barfield, *What Coleridge Thought*, 158.

[98] Muirhead, *Philosopher*, 160.

[99] Cf. Modiano, *Concept of Nature*, 168–71.

line of Schelling, this is sheer nonsense. The core of Schelling's whole *Transzen-dental- und Naturphilosophie* is the absolute *identity* of nature and self. It is a wilful misrepresentation of a philosophy, simply because Coleridge had no *religious* use for it. Oddly enough, when dictating the *Biographia Literaria* two years earlier, Coleridge had radically deviated from his appropriation of Schelling when he said that the imagination 'subordinates art to nature' (*BL* II, 17) (something unheard of in Schelling)—surely not a pre-emptive strike against Schelling's alleged willing-ness to give nature priority over the self, but a most telling reaction on the part of Coleridge since even Schelling's *balanced* view was obviously too much for him, as it gave art far too great a say.[100] Later, in his *Philosophical Lectures*, he has nothing to say of any substance on Schelling (see Lecture 13), although he had announced as late as in Lecture 12 that he would treat him next time. Instead, he practically denies him any originality and calls him a 'Roman Catholic pantheist' (II, 589), which is not only absurd but 'vicious'[101] and slanderous: Schelling never converted to Catholicism. Habitually uninterested in philosophical systems *as systems*, Cole-ridge appropriated more or less randomly what he thought fit—and discarded or misrepresented what was of no use to him:

But even if Coleridge had not become disenchanted with Schelling, the use he was likely to have made of him in the lecture would have resembled the use he made of Kant; he was interested only in showing their contributions to the confutation of modern materialism. It was never his intention to conclude by presenting a version of philosophy that could stand alone, only one that might be a worthy partner of religion. (*Lects Phil* I, cxlii)

Of course, in this case, Coleridge knew exactly what he was doing. In the same year, and in spite of the bogeymen of pantheism and atheism, Coleridge correctly identifies Schelling's philosophy as not of the Spinozistic or 'it is' kind, but as a system in its own right:[102]

In an 'examination of all the Systems', as he writes in 1818, Coleridge clearly reveals his hopes, for he identifies three systems as stemming 'from the pure Reason': the first is '*Objective*', that is, as we see from our previous discussions, the philosophy of 'it is', which Coleridge therefore quite properly equates with 'Spinoza'; the second is 'Subjective' and is equated with 'Berkeley, Fichte'; the third is '. . . the Identity of both', which equals 'Schelling'.

And earlier the same year, he had no qualms about translating Schelling's rightly famous Munich academic lecture 'Über das Verhältnis der bildenden Künste zur Natur' (1807) and passing it off as his own ('On Poesy or Art').[103] No wonder the editors of the *Biographia Literaria* find the piece 'Schellingesque' (I, cv). So much

---

[100] Cf. Fruman in Gallant (ed.), *Theory of Imagination*, 56.

[101] Wellek, *Romantic Age*, 154.

[102] The irony implied in quoting from McFarland (*Pantheist*, 158) is not accidental. The source is *CL* IV, 863.

[103] See Hamilton, *Coleridge and German Philosophy*, 23, Fruman, *Archangel*, 168, 169, Hamilton, *Colerige's Poetics*, 88 and Appleyard, *Philosophy of Literature*, 239.

for the supposed radicality of Coleridge's fundamental rift and disagreement with Schelling in 1818—it appears to have been highly selective and dictated, on Coleridge's part, alternately by opportunism and religious zealotry.

Coleridge's *Philosophical Lectures*, whose major source is Wilhelm Gottlieb Tennemann's unacknowledged *Geschichte der Philosophie*, from which he deviates mostly when Tennemann is too Kantian for him, is interesting because of the emphases he changes or because of the conspicuous absences: 'Any member of Coleridge's audience who came to his lectures expecting to receive a survey of modern German philosophy would have been disappointed, and indeed a modern reader hoping for clarification of Coleridge's views on Leibniz, Kant, and Schelling is likely to feel disappointed too' (*BL* I, cxxxvi). As in other places, some of Coleridge's characterizations and assessments may be called 'highly unorthodox', such as when he sees Lord Bacon as a 'British Plato' (*BL* II, 484–95), 'a thinker for whom ideas, and not randomly derived facts, were paramount' (*BL* I, cxxix)— which is puzzling because Plato, in turn, is once identified (see *Friend* I, 482) as empirical and inductive throughout.[104] And since we have already learnt that Kant was closer to Aristotle than to Plato, it is curious to learn in addition that Coleridge saw Bacon also as a forerunner to Kant.[105] But then, Coleridge had at least once ascribed a purely Kantian passage, the starting point of the *Critique of Pure Reason*, to Plato;[106] he had opined that Berkeley's philosophy was 'most inappropriately called Idealism' (*Logic* 128); had told his audience in Lecture 9 that the radical nominalist William of Occam, of all people, deserved admiration for his fine balance of reason and faith (*BL* I, 392) (a most telling misreading) and that Schelling's philosophy was little more than that of the early seventeenth-century German mystic, Jakob Böhme (*CL* IV, 883). Nobody can deny the originality of all this. But more important is the pervading ahistoricity of the *Philosophical Lectures*. Holding that 'all forms of philosophy that are proper philosophy [...] had been developed previous to the appearance of our Lord' (*Lects Phil* I, 261, compare also *Lects Phil* I, 326), Coleridge presents the later history of philosophy as repeated attempts to come close, in its own field, to a truth that had already been revealed to mankind in a different form, viz. in the form of Christian religion—a truth that, deplorably enough, is unattainable to philosophy. This already indicates what would be the role of philosophy in the aspired unity of religion and philosophy: an inferior, serving one (cf. *BL* I, c–cx). Note here that religion in Coleridge holds the same *systematic* place as art in Schelling—but art in Schelling is not a *transcendent* revelation.

In the context of this chapter, it seems inappropriate to devote much space to the *Aids to Reflection* (1825), since what started out as his reflections on Archbishop

---

[104] Cf. McFarland, *Pantheist*, 58.
[105] See Wellek, *Kant*, 74.
[106] See Fruman, *Archangel*, 172.

Leighton remains essentially an assertion of Christian religion. Its opposition to Kant's *Über Religion innerhalb der Grenzen der bloßen Vernunft* has been remarked upon above, and its use of Prothesis, Ground, and the Will can easily be subsumed under the discussion of the *Opus Maximum*, which is soon to follow.

But the *Logic* is a different matter, because here is least and, paradoxically, most powerful interference from religion, as Coleridge faithfully follows and expounds Kant's *Logik*, the *Kritik der reinen Vernunft* and other sources. J. R. de J. Jackson is absolutely right in observing that were the *Logic* only a popularization of the *Critique of Pure Reason*, written for young students, it would be less interesting: 'But it is the concealed aims rather than the declared ones that make the book much more than a derivative introduction to Kant.' (*Logic* lxvii) If it is true that it is these concealed aims that ultimately justify the publication of what Alice D. Snyder considered 'masses of unorganized, unfocused material' (vii) that should not be 'foist[ed] on the world in their entirety', it is a pity that the religious core of Coleridge's *Logic*—the keystone he added—has been overlooked in some quarters. The core of Coleridge's *Logic* is that he derives language and reason from the *verb substantive* (*sum*, I am), which posits at one and the same time subject and object:

But to affirm of any finite being that it is absolute is a contradiction in terms: in order to absoluteness there must be an 'is' (*est*) which necessarily involves the 'I am', and again an 'I am' without which no 'is' would be conceivable. This therefore and this alone can be the *principium essendi et sciendi* or the perfect identity of being and knowing and therefore the ground and source of both. Without any present reference to any religious or superhuman authority the title 'I Am' attributed to the Supreme Being by the Hebrew legislator must excite our admiration for its philosophic depth, and the verb substantive or first form in the science of grammar brings us the highest possible external evidence of its truth. For what is a fact of all human language is of course a fact of all human consciousness. (*Logic* 82)

It is obvious that the *logos* here is *not* solely a linguistic category, but a philosophical and a religious category at the same time.[107] Therefore, it is misleading to speak of a *linguistic turn* and to make Coleridge the forerunner of twentieth-century linguistic and philosophical thought.[108] Rather, what we have here is the exact opposite of a linguistic turn, it is a *metaphysical turn*, because language, grammar, and reason are all derived from a divine ground (the divine Logos is an outerance of the divine Will),[109] which, as Coleridge knows, cannot be proven, but only be posited. Coleridge does not revise Kant's *Critique of Pure Reason* in the light of linguistic

---

[107] Cf. Perkins, *Coleridge's Philosophy*.

[108] See, however, McKusick, *Coleridge's Philosophy of Language*, or McKusick, 'Coleridge's "Logic"', 480: 'Coleridge's intention in the *Logic* is to formulate a post-Kantian theory of language. Much more clearly than Kant, Coleridge sees that epistemological questions cannot be resolved without a prior analysis of the linguistic structures that themselves constitute the means of intellectual inquiry. The *Logic* seeks to revise Kant's *Critique of Pure Reason* in the light of linguistic theory. I will describe Coleridge's "linguistic turn" in the remainder of this paper.'

[109] Cf. Perkins, *Coleridge's Philosophy*, 35.

theory; rather, he puts it on a religious foundation, and the reason he begins his *Logic* with an exposition of language is a purely didactic one. Language *reflects* the rules of reasoning (cf. *Logic* 13). There is no indication that Coleridge believed that language, taken as *langue* or *parole*, 'determines' or even 'constitutes' thought.[110] '[Grammar] therefore takes the lead in the scheme of artificial education because it reflects the form of the human mind, and gradually familiarizes the half-conscious boy with the frame and constitution of his own intellect' (*Logic* 18). Perkins observes: 'the initial premiss of his theory of language is an underlying act of faith'.[111] For Coleridge, Perkins says, grammar and logic are products of *immutable* laws[112]—the *linguistic turn* of the twentieth century goes into the diametrically opposed direction. And likewise it is not correct to say that in his *Logic*, 'Coleridge revises Kant's doctrine of time and space [...] by pointing out that even these supposedly immediate intuitions are at least partially constituted by the structure of language'[113] or, even more radically, 'he seeks to rewrite Kant's doctrine of the categories in such a way as to reveal their dependence on prior structures of grammar which, as innate modes of conception, determine our perception of reality. The activity of thought, in this view, is wholly constituted by the activity of language.'[114] For once, Coleridge takes over Kant's *a priori* categories as they are; he only gives linguistic *illustrations* for them (see, for example, *Logic* 261). Coleridge's theologically founded belief in a universal language and in universal grammar by no means covers the claim, 'it follows that what we call "reality" is to some extent the result of linguistic choice. We construct our own world by language.'[115] This, it seems to me, is an anachronistic misreading that ignores the metaphysical meaning of Coleridge's *logos*, which is that, just like the ultimate reason for my existence is God (cf. *Logic*, 84–5), so there can be no language without a God who says 'I am that I am'. Coleridge's linguistics, remarks Essick, 'was always a theology'.[116]

To what extent is the picture drawn here modified by the publication of Coleridge's *Opus Maximum*, like his *Logic* another tranche of the prospective overall *magnum opus* (an established terminology that seems to have it the wrong way round)? Hardly at all. Planned as a work in the service of the Christian religion, 'to the Glory of God in the advancement of the Truth in Christ' (*OM* civ, cf. 152), it contains few, if any, surprises. No logical proof of the existence of God is possible, 'the idea of the Godhead is the true source and indispensable precondition of all

---

[110] See, however, McKusick, 'Samuel Taylor Coleridge', 96, or McKusick, 'Linguistic Approaches to Teaching Coleridge', 55.

[111] Perkins, *Coleridge's Philosophy*, 46.

[112] Cf. ibid., 44.

[113] McKusick, *Coleridge's Philosophy of Language*, 143.

[114] Ibid., 147.

[115] McKusick, 'Coleridge's "Logic"', 287.

[116] Essick in Burwick (ed.), *Coleridge's* Biographia Literaria, 74.

our knowledge of God' (*OM* 274). And this idea can only be inferred (though not in a logically compelling way) from the fact of conscience (he is here again close to the Kant of the *Kritik der praktischen Vernunft*). The Will, which is identical with Moral Responsibility (cf. *OM* 11, see also *OM* cxix–cxxv), points to the existence of an absolute Will, which, together with the idea of universal Reason, is 'peculiar to the idea of God' (*OM* 81, cf. 195, 220). At the basis of this philosophical system, there lies an act of faith. As Hamilton comments: 'It is only if religion is asserted that the rest follows.'[117] The sanctions, if one does not follow this, are dreadful because—the admonishment has been quoted before—'the inevitable result of all *consequent* Reasoning, in which Speculative intellect refuses to acknowledge a higher or deeper ground than it can itself supply' (*OM* 106) is pantheism and ultimately 'practical Atheism' (*OM* 107), for, as Coleridge had noted in the *Marginalia*, 'Pantheism, trick it as you will, is but painted Atheism' (*M* III, 1083). Perhaps it is needless to point out: this is only a fearsome option to people who are not already pantheists or atheists. But once accepted, the 'incarnation of the Logos in Jesus' (*OM* ciii) or the underlying chiasm that 'Reason is *subjective* revelation, Revelation objective reason' (*CL* VI, 895) are beautiful figures of thought.

What is striking about the *Opus Maximum* is the ongoing struggle with Schelling who refuses to be exorcised.[118] Coleridge may have had fundamental difficulties with Schelling's attempt, in the *Freiheitsschrift*, to explain the origin of evil and especially with Schelling's (as Coleridge saw it) positing of God as absolute Will that separates itself from the undifferentiated *Ungrund* (which implies a *temporal* nature of God). But Coleridge's Will is not so different from Schelling's *Wollen*, Coleridge's Ground has the same *systematic* place as Schelling's *Grund* and *Ungrund* (although the concept of Prothesis might here come into play as well). As Richard Berkeley has summarized after an ambitious discussion of the matter: 'Coleridge's conception of the Trinity is [. . .] heavily informed by Schelling, Spinoza and even Mendelssohn. The similarities have always been reasonably obvious, since Coleridge's inclusion of a ground to Trinity has obvious pantheistic implications, and bears a blatant resemblance to Schelling's conception of the *Ungrund*.'[119] Even the (strictly speaking, inconceivable) initial breaking into existence is imagined in similar terms:

Now here is what was with no unseemly fear and inward trembling named the abyss of abysmal mystery, that there is in the causative Allmight of God (who shall dare utter it? or if he feel permitted, in what terms shall he utter it? Shall he say a more than God, or a less than God, and yet more in the sense other, a somewhat that God did not realize in himself; for the real containeth both the actual and the potential, but in God as God by the necessity of his absolute perfection there is no potentiality). When, therefore, we speak of the Will as the

[117] Hamilton, *Colerige's Poetics*, 132.
[118] Cf. ibid., 189.
[119] Berkeley, *Coleridge and the Crisis of Reason*, 179; see also 67 and 118–26.

ground of the divine existence, from which it indeed would be more wise to abstain, or when we meet with it in the mystic passages of writers of deserved name and undoubted piety, it will be highly expedient to bear in mind that the words are used prolepticè or by anticipation, i.e. the Will contemplated after we have [. . .] beheld its self-realization, as the necessary being, ens entium, or Supreme Mind. (*OM* 231)

The dissimilarities, of course, cannot be overlooked either: Coleridge's God is unmistakably the personal God of the Trinity, and his starting point, both philosophically and psychologically, is totally at odds with Schelling's. To quote an early letter (1802):

My Faith is simply this—that there is an original corruption in our nature, from which & from the consequences of which, we may be redeemed by Christ. . . . and this I believe—not because I *understand* it, but because I *feel*, that it is not only suitable to, but needful for, my nature. (*CL* II, 807)

Philosophically, the whole *magnum opus* project is, of course, backward-looking and anachronistic (cf. *OM* clxiv).[120] 'For the rest of his life the investigation and defense of religion, and the synthesis of it with his metaphysics, were Coleridge's principal concerns.'[121] 'There is', says McFarland as editor of the *Opus Maximum*, 'a sense of desperation, a last-ditch quality, about Coleridge's effort' (*OM* cliv). One can only concur. At a time when Coleridge tried to prove time and again that reason and faith could be reconciled, if only one were willing to accept the ulterior superiority of faith, this was less and less seen as a helpful operation. Western civilization went down a different path and reserved for religion a more confined and a more specific cultural space.

I had promised to show that the 'gap', the breaking off in chapter 13 of Coleridge's *Biographia Literaria* can be read as a gesture that acknowledges Schelling's philosophy of art—I might add, even practises what Schelling preaches. The philosophy of art can always only *point* to the fact that in art we encounter the identity of nature and spirit, of conscious and unconscious, of freedom and necessity as actualized—a deductive philosophy of art can never *be* what it points to, it can only be a signpost. The moment Coleridge stops his deduction (*Unterbrechung der Succession* is, according to Schelling's *System*, the key operation of reflexivity)[122] and introduces the fictive 'Letter from a Friend', a second kind of reflexivity becomes possible: his text becomes what it had hitherto only been talking about—*Kunst*, art, fiction. It is exactly this deliberate gap, the missing deduction, that draws our attention to that other gap that can never be bridged: the ontological gap between the philosophy of art and its object. It is not so much the meagre conclusion at the end of chapter 13 that is of import in this reading than

---

[120] See also McFarland, *Romanticism and the Forms of Ruin*, 368.
[121] Appleyard, *Philosophy of Literature*, 254.
[122] Cf. Schelling, *Schelling*, 169.

the knowledge that even if it had been conclusively deduced, it still would not have been *the thing*. In breaking off and inserting the hoax letter, Coleridge gives us *the thing*. Only that in order to recognize it, we have to make a leap; not a leap of faith this time, but a leap of the imagination. This is not a Sternean hoax,[123] it is an instance of Romantic Irony. Kathleen Wheeler is right: Schlegel would have loved it,[124] though Friedrich Schlegel more than August Wilhelm. It is the fragment that points to the necessarily finite presentation of the infinite and that opens up, at the same time, the space for the endless activity of its readers, as they explore the concrete dynamics of a subject–object polarity that is constitutive of *everything*. Iser's gaps of indeterminacy [125] are characteristic of fictional texts; they are what makes them work. In non-fictional texts they are either not recognized or a nuisance. I suggest reading the *Biographia Literaria* as an exemplification of Schelling's philosophy of art, indeed, as *fiction*.

If this is not the only way to read it, it is at least a possibility. And it would resolve many controversies. After all, 'it is neither possible or necessary for all men, or for many, to be PHILOSOPHERS' (*BL* I, 236). Whether or not it was intentional (according to Schelling, it defines a genius that this does not matter), at least in the *Biographia Literaria*, that supreme mix of genres and styles, but possibly also in all his tales about the *magnum opus*, Coleridge proved to be a supreme novelist and storyteller. The gaps he left behind, all the pointers to texts he never wrote (see, for example, *BL* I, 304, n. 2 and 306, n. 1), his fragments and strategic interruptions, his frantic inventions: all prove him to be a great poet and fiction writer, who happened to mistake himself for a profound philosopher. As philosopher, he must, I think, be regarded as a 'hopeless anachronism'.[126] And the finest and most tragic failures are, of course, necessary ones. But to end on an upbeat note: as Hegel once remarked, showing a surprisingly un-teleological side: 'Every philosophy has been, and still is necessary. None has passed away, but all are affirmatively contained as elements in a whole. [...] No philosophy has ever been refuted. What has been refuted is not the principle of this philosophy, but merely the fact that this principle should be considered final and absolute in character.' (Quoted in *OM* cxciii.) However, there is reason to believe that Coleridge, the philosopher, would have violently rejected this possibility to be saved.

---

[123] Cf. Hume, 'Kant and Coleridge on Imagination', 496, n. 36, and Willey, *Coleridge*, 215.

[124] Cf. Wheeler in Gallant (ed.), *Theory of Imagination*, 94.

[125] For a different take on Iser's gaps of indeterminacy in connection with the *Biographia Literaria*, see Hamilton, *Colerige's Poetics*, 14; on readers' activity as subject in *Biographia Literaria*, see Wheeler in Orr (ed.), *Coleridge*, 148.

[126] Abrams in Beer (ed.), *Coleridge's Variety*, 124.

Works Cited

ABRAMS, M. H. 1984. *The Correspondent Breeze: Essays on English Romanticism.* New York and London: Norton.

APPLEYARD, J. A. 1965. *Coleridge's Philosophy of Literature: The Development of a Concept of Poetry 1791–1819.* Cambridge, MA: Harvard University Press.

ASHTON, ROSEMARY. 1994. *The German Idea: Four English Writers and the Reception of German Thought, 1800–1860.* London: Libris.

BARFIELD, OWEN. 1971. *What Coleridge Thought.* Middletown, CN: Wesleyan University Press.

BEER, JOHN, ed. 1974. *Coleridge's Variety: Bicentenary Studies.* London and Basingstoke: Macmillan.

BERKELEY, RICHARD. 2007. *Coleridge and the Crisis of Reason,* New York and Basingstoke: Palgrave Macmillan.

BLOOM, HAROLD, ed. 1986. *Samuel Taylor Coleridge: Modern Critical Views.* New York and Philadelphia: Chelsea.

BODE, CHRISTOPH. 1992. *'And what were thou...?' Essay über Shelley und das Erhabene.* Essen: Blaue Eule.

——, and RENNHAK, KATHARINA. eds. 2005. *Romantic Voices, Romantic Poetics: Selected Papers from the Regensburg Conference of the German Society for English Romanticism* Trier: wvt.

BRETT, R. L., ed. 1971. *Writers and their Background: S. T. Coleridge.* London: Bell & Sons.

BURWICK, FREDERICK ed. 1989. *Coleridge's* Biographia Literaria: *Text and Meaning.* Columbus: Ohio State University Press.

CHRISTENSEN, JEROME. 1981. *Coleridge's Blessed Machine of Language.* Ithaca and London: Cornell University Press.

COBURN, KATHLEEN. 1979. *Experience into Thought: Perspectives in the Coleridge Notebooks.* (Toronto, Buffalo and London: University of Toronto Press.

ENGELL, JAMES. 1981. *The Creative Imagination: Enlightenment to Romanticism.* Cambridge, MA and London: Harvard University Press.

ESTERHAMMER, ANGELA. 2001. Coleridge's 'Hymn before Sun-rise' and the Voice Not Heard. In *Samuel Taylor Coleridge and the Sciences of Life,* ed. Nicholas Roe. Oxford: Oxford University Press, 224–345.

FERRIS, DAVID S. 1985. Coleridge's ventriloquy: the abduction from the *Biographia Studies in Romanticism,* 24(1) (Spring): 41–84.

FRUMAN, NORMAN. 1971. *Coleridge, the Damaged Archangel.* New York: Braziller.

—— 1985. Review essay: aids to reflection on the New *Biographia. Studies in Romanticism,* 24 (Spring): 141–75.

GALLANT, CHRISTINE, ed. 1989. *Coleridge's Theory of Imagination Today.* New York: AMS.

GRAVIL, RICHARD, and LEFEBURE, MOLLY. eds. 1990. *The Coleridge Connection: Essays for Thomas McFarland.* London and Basingstoke: Macmillan.

GRAVIL, RICHARD, NEWLYN, LUCY. and ROE, NICHOLAS. eds. 1985. *Coleridge's Imagination: Essays in Memory of Pete Laver.* Cambridge: Cambridge University Press.

GREGORY, ALAN P. R. 2003. *Coleridge and the Conservative Imagination.* Macon, GA: Mercer University Press.

HAMILTON, PAUL 1983. *Colerige's Poetics.* Oxford: Blackwell.

—— 2006. *Coleridge and German Philosophy: The Poet in the Land of Logic.* London: Continuum.

HUME, ROBERT D. 1970. Kant and Coleridge on imagination. *Journal of Aesthetics and Art Criticism*, 28: 485–96.

KANT, IMMANUEL. 1924. *Kritik der Urteilskraft.* Hamburg: Meiner.

MCFARLAND, THOMAS. 1969. *Coleridge and the Pantheist Tradition* Oxford: Clarendon.

—— 1981. *Romanticism and the Forms of Ruin: Wordsworth, Coleridge, and the Modalities of Framentation.* Princeton, NJ: Princeton University Press.

MCKUSICK, JAMES C. 1986. *Coleridge's Philosophy of Language* New Haven: Yale University Press.

—— 1987. Coleridge's 'Logic': a systematic theory of language. In *Papers in the History of Linguistics: Proceedings from the Third International Conference on the History of the Language Sciences*, ed. Hans Aarsleff, Louis G. Kelly, and Hans-Josef Niederehe. Amsterdam Philadelphia: John Benjamins. 479–487.

—— 1991. Samuel Taylor Coleridge. *Dictionary of Literary Biography*, vol. 107. Detroit: Gale, 68–105.

—— 1991. Linguistic approaches to teaching Coleridge. In *Approaches to Teaching Coleridge's Poetry and Prose*, ed. Richard E. Matlak. New York: MLA, 49–56.

MODIANO, RAIMONDA, 1985. *Coleridge and the Concept of Nature.* London and Basingstoke: Macmillan.

MUIRHEAD, JOHN H. 1970. *Coleridge as Philosopher.* London: Allen and Unwin, New York: Humanities Press, 1930, third impression.

ORR, LEONARD, ed. 1994. *Critical Essays on Samuel Taylor Coleridge.* New York: G. K. Hall.

ORSINI, G. N. G. 1969. *Coleridge and German Idealism: A Study in the History of Philosophy with Unpublished Materials from Coleridge's Manuscripts.* Carbondale/Edwardsville: Southern Illinois University Press.

PAPE, WALTER, ed. 2006. *A View in the Rear-mirror: Romantic Aesthetics, Culture, and Science Seen from Today: Festschrift for Frederick Burwick.* Trier: wvt.

PERKINS, MARY ANNE. 1994. *Coleridge's Philosophy: The Logos as Unifying Principle.* Oxford: Clarendon.

PERRY, SEAMUS. 1999. *Coleridge and the Uses of Division.* Oxford: Clarendon.

SCHELLING, FRIEDRICH WILHELM JOSEPH. 1995. *Schelling*, ed. Michael Boenke. Munich: Diederichs.

SHAFFER, ELINOR. 1969/70. Coleridge's revolution in the standard of taste. *Journal of Aesthetics and Art Criticism*, 28: 213–21.

—— 2004. Coleridge and Kant's 'Giant Hand'. In *Anglo-German Affinities and Antipathies*, ed. Rüdiger Görner. Munich: Iudicium, 39–56.

WALLACE, CATHERINE MILES, ed. 1983. *The Design of* Biographia Literaria. London and Boston, Sydney: Allen and Unwin.

WATSON, J. R., ed. 1983. *An Infinite Complexity: Essays in Romanticism.* Edinburgh: Edinburgh University Press.

WARNOCK, MARY, 1976. *Imagination.* London: Faber and Faber.

WELLEK, RENÉ. 1931. *Immanuel Kant in England 1793–1838.* Princeton, NJ: Princeton University Press.

—— 1955. *A History of Modern Criticism 1750–1950, Vol. 2: The Romantic Age.* London: Cape.

WILLEY, BASIL. 1972. *Samuel Taylor Coleridge.* London: Chatto and Windus.

WU, DUNCAN, ed. 1998. *A Companion to Romanticism* (paperback edn. 1999). Oxford: Blackwell.

CHAPTER 32

COLERIDGE AND THE ARTS

JULIAN KNOX

ADEPT as Coleridge was in the art of mastering foreign languages such as German and Italian (not to mention his schoolboy Latin and Greek), one of the lingering desires which surfaces time and again in his notebooks, letters, and published works is that of learning the language of art: 'I wish very much I could draw—how many awkward and round about Sentences which after all convey no true ideas, would three lines with a pencil save me' (*CL* 1, 440). Coleridge writes this from Ratzeburg in 1798, and it is telling that at the same time he was reaching proficiency in German, he should also meditate on the limitations of verbal communication as such. Coleridge was embarking on new ground, not only linguistically but also culturally, and he recognizes on the way that spoken and written language can only express so much in regards to these fresh, not-quite-English surroundings. Words might effectively capture the feelings, but they fall short of seizing what Coleridge calls the 'distinct image', as he laments upon beholding a group of German women sowing fir-seed:

Never did I behold aught so impressively picturesque, or rather *statue*-esque, as these Groups of Women in all their various attitudes—The thick mist, thro' which their figures came to my eye, gave such a soft *Unreality* to them! . . . What can be the cause that I am so miserable a Describer? Is it that I understand neither the practice nor the principles of Painting?—or is it not true, that others have really succeeded?—I could half suspect that what are deemed fine descriptions, produce their effects almost purely by a charm of words, with which & with whose combinations, we associate *feelings* indeed, but no distinct *Images*. (511)

Is it that Coleridge wished he were a painter rather than an author, or is he holding out a more complex hope that he might incorporate the 'principles of Painting' into the representational strategies of writing that gets beyond a mere 'charm of words'? In the notebooks Coleridge would often sketch a scene, if only in rough outline. Taken together, his collected works reveal a conscientious effort not only to attain fluency in the language of the visual arts, but also to bring the visual and the verbal into conversation in the space of the text.

In addition to the essays and public lectures on aesthetic principles that Coleridge delivered throughout the 1810s, his deep consideration of the arts informs other areas of his thought as well, including his political writings at the turn of the century, his arguments on the history of philosophy, and his later spiritual writings, to name a few. In a related sense, the conversation between the visual and the verbal comes unmistakably to bear on the mode of Coleridge's writing—the shape he gives to a text and the nature of his voice within it—be it the turns of ekphrastic description in his notebooks or the caricaturizing aspirations of 'Satyrane's Letters', the playful visuality of 1828's 'The Garden of Boccaccio' or the more reverent play of voices in 1825's *Aids to Reflection*. For Coleridge, of course, the issue of aesthetic principles is by no means divorced from the progress of philosophy,[1] nor are the explicitly spiritual writings of his later years anomalous to these other regions of his thought. While to most readers such interconnectedness is a given, essential characteristic of his literary persona ('everything is connected with everything else'), what is perhaps less clear is the extent to which Coleridge's experience and consideration of the arts[2] feeds into each of these areas.

With a few exceptions, critical treatments of Coleridge on the arts have generally looked at the issue from the other way around, and in this respect they have indeed provided an invaluable resource for understanding (to borrow the title of Carl Woodring's 1978 essay) 'what Coleridge thought of pictures'. In broad strokes, Woodring covers the major bases in Coleridge's experience of graphic arts: the relationship with the painter Sir George Beaumont, the voyage to Malta and Italy, the persistence of aesthetic categories such as the 'picturesque' and 'sublime' in training Coleridge's eye for art as well as for nature, and the various collections and collectors, patrons and painters that crossed Coleridge's path. Edoardo Zuccato and J. B. Bullen provide illuminating accounts of Coleridge and Italian art, the former placing the fine arts in the context of Coleridge's Italian voyage and his investment in Italian poetry and philosophy, the latter arguing for Coleridge as a

---

[1] In addition to Lectures 4 and 5 of the 1818 *Lectures on the History of Philosophy*, see the opening lectures of the 1808 series 'On the Principles of Poetry' for a cogent instance of this (*Lects 1808–19* 1, 24–57).

[2] My usage of the term 'arts' in this essay will refer to the visual arts unless otherwise noted. Music was by no means unimportant to Coleridge, as Kevin Barry has shown in his study *Language, Music and the Sign*, though I agree with Edoardo Zuccardo that Barry's study prioritizes the role of music in Coleridge's aesthetic thought at the expense of reductively consigning the visual arts to 'the negative side of his epistomology' (Barry, 152).

proto-Ruskin through his sensitive response to fourteenth-century Italian painting and his recognition of its ideological dimensions. In addition to her analyses of Coleridge's aesthetic principles as they developed through his grapplings with Kant, Schelling, Gilpin, and Knight, Elinor Shaffer also gives insightful appraisals of Coleridge's foundational visits to the Campo Santo at Pisa and his friendship with the American painter Washington Allston.

Each of these accounts of Coleridge and the arts tend to subscribe to Woodring's claim that 'the graphic arts came into full existence for Coleridge [...] from acquaintance with Sir George Beaumont in 1803' (91). This is true to the extent that Beaumont's collection brought Coleridge into sustained contact with works by such Old Masters as Peter Paul Rubens, Claude Lorrain, and Nicolas Poussin—the standard-bearers, as it were, of artistic taste in England at that time. This is not to mention the other major collections in London, such as those of Lord Ashburnham and J. J. Angerstein to which Beaumont, as far as we know, also introduced Coleridge. But Coleridge was no neophyte to art collections: in 1796 he writes Tom Poole about his visit, with the Evanses, to Oakover, home of 'a few first-rates of Raphael & Titian' (*CL* 1, 231). Two years prior to this, he informs Southey of his hopes to write a '*wild* Ode [...] when I am in the Humour to *abandon* myself to all the Diableries, that ever met the Eye of a Fuseli' (135). As Woodring and Bullen both suggest, the impression given by these early references is that Coleridge's under- standing of the visual arts up to 1803 was nothing more than conventional. This may be accurate in terms of how many artistic names, movements and terms Coleridge would have been able to produce from the top of his head, but the situation changes when one considers the rich ways Coleridge conceived of paint- ing and its possibilities well before his entry into Beaumont's circle.

The 1798–9 voyage to Germany found Coleridge wishing that he were a painter, or that he could somehow incorporate the 'principles of Painting' into his own writerly techniques. Yet to say that Coleridge had had his eyes opened to art in Germany would be to overlook what had been an ongoing interest in the possibil- ities of visual representation since his Cambridge days and his elegant imitation of Anachreon, 'To a Painter'. J. C. C. Mays' edition of the *Poetical Works* supplies a contrast between Coleridge's version of the poem and that of his friend Robert Allen, which begins thus: 'O skilld each mimic grace to wake / Thy all-creative pencil take—' (*PW* 1, 1, 104). Coleridge's take begins similarly enough, but with a key difference: 'O skill'd the mimic form to wake!' (1). The disparity appears negligible at first, but in choosing 'mimic form' over 'mimic grace' the young Coleridge introduces a sophisticated theme of form as it relates to content that he continues to develop over the course of the poem, which closes on a remarkably suggestive note:

> Ah baffled Artist! could thy toil
> Depaint the light'ning of her smile,

> Her soften'd sense, her wit refin'd,
> The blameless features of her *mind*,
> Not such should Titian's colors shine,
> Nor Rafael's magic equal *Thine*
> Whose art could breathe along the canvass warm
> An *Angels Soul* in *Nesbitt's* kindred Form!—
>
> (19–26)

Where Allen keeps his attention on the physical features of the 'picturd Maid', suggesting the intangible only through the 'graces' flying about her 'polishd neck', Coleridge concludes his poem with the question of how the painter might represent those non-material entities of '*mind*' and '*Soul*'. Underlying this is a meditation on the spirit and the letter (2 Cor 3:5), through which Coleridge recognizes that attention only to the letter or 'mimic form' is a certain death on canvas. To capture fully the radiant beauty that is 'Nesbitt',[3] the painter's art must 'breathe along the canvass warm / An *Angels Soul*', which may well be the painter's own, considering that it is *his* art that must 'breathe' this soul onto the canvas.[4] While Coleridge was yet to articulate fully his distinction between copy and imitation, here he reaches an anticipatory position. If art is to be nothing more than a *copy* of reality, then reality is much more gratifying than even the most accurate reproduction. An imitation, on the other hand, acknowledges an essential difference from the thing represented. In 1808 Coleridge refers to 'Imitation' as 'the universal Principle of the Fine Arts' (*Lects 1808–19* 1, 83–4): instead of a replica of the represented object, what is at stake for the artist is a disclosure of his own soul or 'Spirit' as it relates to that object. Hence Coleridge repeatedly refers to Shakespeare as a 'Proteus', 'a river, a lion, yet still the God felt to be there' (69). In the final line of 'To a Painter', Coleridge recognizes that the viability of the imagined painting depends on the infusion of a living spirit into the otherwise static outlines of its subject matter.

Even if Coleridge in the 1790s had only a rudimentary knowledge of art, he was already invested in exploring its philosophical underpinnings. Such is the case in the 1797 play, *Osorio*, which concerns a bizarre love triangle between two brothers and their shared love interest, Maria, in Inquisition-era Spain. Osorio vies unsuccessfully for the affections of Maria, whose lover Albert she believes to have died in a shipwreck while battling the Moorish armies. Osorio also believes Albert has died, albeit from different causes: he arranged for Albert's assassination. What

---

[3] Probably Molly Nesbitt, and if so, this is a later addition to the poem; cf. Coleridge's letter to his brother George on 5 August 1793: 'Do you know Fanny Nesbitt? She was my fellow-traveller in the Tiverton diligence from Exeter.—I think a very pretty Girl.—' (*CL* 1, 60).

[4] See also *AR* 15: 'Life is the one universal soul, which, by virtue of the enlivening Breath, and the informing Word, all organized bodies have in common, each *after its kind*. This, therefore, all animals possess, and man as an animal. But, in addition to this, God transfused into man a higher gift, and specially imbreathed:—even a living (that is, self-subsisting) soul, a soul having its life in itself. "And man became a living soul." '

Osorio fails to realize is that Albert talked down his assailants and gave them a portrait of Maria as proof of 'mission accomplished'. After Osorio unwittingly buys into his returned brother's disguise as a Moorish conjurer, he hires Albert to stage a spectacle meant to prove (via the production of the portrait) Albert's death to Maria, leaving her no choice but to wed the surviving brother. Albert, however, is also a painter, and in place of producing said portrait at the end of the 'incantation scene' he reveals his own painting depicting the assassination attempt. In her analysis of *Osorio*'s 1813 incarnation as *Remorse*, Sophie Thomas argues that Coleridge centralizes issues of visuality in an exploration of the interrelations between history, dramatic illusion, and truth: 'A picture that conceals a deception, is to be supplanted by one that reveals it: the conflict between the brothers becomes a contest of images over their power to maintain competing views of history' (550). As Thomas indicates, Coleridge invests the painted images in *Osorio/Remorse* with an almost supreme authority to shape their viewers' understanding of history. What remains to be considered, however, are the fascinating ways in which Coleridge explores his characters' perception of those powerful images, ways that reveal much about Coleridge's complex attitude towards the visual image as such.

In Act 2, Osorio describes Maria as a perfect candidate to be fooled by a finely wrought illusion (one wonders if the following is a submerged satire on contemporary theater-goers):

> She is a lone Enthusiast, sensitive,
> Shivers, and cannot keep the tears in her eye.
> Such ones do believe the marvellous too well
> Not to believe it. We will wind her up
> With a strange music, that she knows not of—
> With fumes of Frankincense, and mummery—
>
> (*Osorio* II.1.32–7)

Osorio bargains here on Maria's extreme sensibility as a means to achieve tyranny over her mind. Music, incense and 'mummery' play a crucial part in manipulating her constitution so as to render her uncritical of the grand finale, the unveiling of her own portrait. In short, Osorio aims to destroy the boundaries between image and reality, thereby impairing the reflective action that Coleridge came to regard as vital to the experience of art. If in 1818 Coleridge theorizes art as 'of a middle nature between a Thought and a Thing' (*LL* 2, 218),[5] then Osorio designs to have Maria respond to the portrait as *only* a 'Thing', as a false proof of history rather than as a means of reflection, of '*looking down into* [herself]' (*AR* 30). In Coleridge's later spiritual thought, this reflective process will reveal 'the living fountain and spring-head of the evidence of the Christian faith in the believer himself' (30); in the

---

5 See also *CN* 3, 4397.

context of *Osorio*, it would affirm Maria in her refusals of Osorio by prioritizing her conscience over her consciousness.[6] As Coleridge defines it in 1818, art works not as a copyist, but instead as the 'imitratress of Nature' (*LL* 2, 219); likewise, its effects are produced not by its proximity to an actual 'Thing', but instead by 'the congruity of the animal impression with the reflective Powers of the mind' (218).

Coleridge had already exhibited his deep distrust of sensibility in the previous year's *Watchman*,[7] and by 1825 he was explicitly dissociating it from the understanding and condemning it as a 'passive' principle that 'in its mere self [...] proves little more than the coincidence or contagion of pleasurable or painful Sensations in different persons' (*AR* 58). As an aesthetic response, this is what Coleridge discourages when he writes of the 'LUST OF THE EYE' (*OM* 85–6) a phrase which some critics have taken as proof that visuality belongs to the negative side of Coleridge's epistemology. On the contrary, Coleridge recognizes that the eye is a dynamic organ: the mind acts *on* it, mediates it, as much as the eye acts on the mind. In other words, the eye must not be regarded only as a passive receptor of stimuli—this is the problem Coleridge locates in associationist philosophy, and it is also the foundational assumption of most bad art, as well as art criticism (*SW&F* 1, 359). Hence in the lectures on Shakespeare Coleridge develops his parallel desynonimizations of delusion and illusion, copy and imitation as a means of counteracting the tendency he saw on the contemporary stage for productions to attempt tricking the eye into submission through visual gimmickry.

The eye might be lustful in threatening to condition a subject into a state of sensual overreliance, but Coleridge also recognizes—and this is one of the linchpins of his thinking on visual art—that good art counteracts the tyranny of the eye by bringing it into conjunction with the higher faculties of the mind. Art challenges the spectator to reach beyond surface appearances to discover a unity amidst the diversity of visual information entering the eye, '[...] so that not the Thing presented, but that which is *re*-presented, by the Thing, is the source of the Pleasure' (*Lects 1808–19* 2, 218). The 'Thing' itself would suffice in pleasing the lustful eye, but the re-presentation of that 'Thing' in the work of art constitutes a productive difference through which 'Thought' intervenes, leading the spectator out of rudimentary sense-perception into the higher realms of understanding and reason. If the understanding is the faculty by which the 'phaenomena of perception' are brought to bear on one another and organized into rules of experience (*Friend* 1, 156), and the reason is the 'scientific Faculty' that uncovers the essential properties of things by subordinating these rules of experience to 'ABSOLUTE PRINCIPLES' (157), then the experience of art straddles the two. On one level, art addresses the understanding by inviting us to connect the dots, as it were, between the diverse

---

[6] For the connection between conscience and reflection, see Aphorisms 43–46 in the 'Moral and Religious Aphorisms' of *Aids to Reflection*.

[7] Issue number 160. See *Watchman* 139.

components of the piece. But art functions on another level, that of 'essential properties' or pure ideas discernible only by the reason. Like nature is to a religious observer the 'Art of God' (*LL* 2, 218), a true work of art is a source of permanent ideas that transcend both the transient dictates of style and subject-matter, as well as to some extent the material circumstances of the composition itself: 'For in all, that truly merits the name of *Poetry* in its most comprehensive sense, there is a necessary predominance of the Ideas (i.e. of that which originates in the artist himself), and a comparative indifference of the materials' (*Friend* 1, 464). This might well describe Albert's approach to representation in *Osorio*. In a touch of supreme irony, Coleridge has Osorio tell Albert that 'You are no *dullard* / But one that strips the outward rind of things!' (II.2.57–8), invoking issues of form and content that Coleridge has already begun to explore in his earlier poems and lectures.

In the 'Allegoric Vision' that opens the 1795 *Lectures on Revealed Religion*, Coleridge's speaker enters the Temple of Religion, a 'large and gloomy pile' whose frenzied inhabitants occupy the extremes of sensibility, engaging either in 'antic merriment' and 'mad Melancholy'. Presiding over this chaos is the Goddess Religion: 'her features blended with darkness rose to my view terrible yet vacant' (*Lects 1795*, 90). The vacancy of the Goddess's features corresponds to the empty rituals carried out at her feet. Such a situation certainly appeals to the 'lust of the eye': everything in and about the temple smacks of sensuality, ritual, and servitude to external form. And yet despite its negative connotations at this stage of the allegory, visuality is instrumental in rescuing Coleridge's speaker from this nest of folly. When the 'Woman clad in white' leads the deserters of the temple to high land overlooking the valley, they are able to 'observe the Relation of its different Parts, each one to the other' (91).[8] She then furnishes them with an 'optic Glass which assisted without contradicting our natural vision and enabled us to see far beyond the Valley' (91).[9]

Such oppositions between form and content, letter and spirit, 'rind' and substance, are a mainstay in Coleridge's thinking on the arts and—like his idea that art addresses both the understanding and the reason, that it appeals to the senses at the same time that it impels the viewer to pass beyond them—their oppositional nature is mutually constitutive. Hence even though Coleridge refers to the 'indifference of the materials' alongside the presiding 'Ideas' that constitute '*Poetry*' in

---

[8] This might be the first inkling of Coleridge's definition of beauty as 'Multëity in Unity,' a major aesthetic criterion that, once he fully articulates it in the 1808 lectures, informs much of his subsequent thought (*LL* 1, 35 and n.). In the version of the 'Allegoric Vision' that appears in the *Lay Sermon* of 1817, Coleridge accordingly appends the phrase 'and of each to the whole, and of all to each' to this sentence (*LS* 136).

[9] This device may well be a version of the 'Claude Glass', a tinted convex mirror then in vogue as a means of attaining a picturesque perspective of a landscape, similar to those painted by Claude. In lecture 6 of the same course, Coleridge alludes again to the Claude Glass, this time in the context of the town/country divide (*Lects 1795*, 224).

its comprehensive sense, he also recognizes that materials are essential to the production of such poetry and inseparable from the viewer's contemplation of it, as in his response to Michelangelo's Sistine Chapel frescos:

Ideal = the subtle hieroglyphical *felt*-by-all though not without abstruse and difficult analysis detected & understood, consonance of the *physiognomic* total & substance (Stoff) with the obvious *Path*ognomic / herein equi-distant from Opie-ism, i.e passions planted in a common face, <or portrait> that might equally well have been the accidental Substrate of any other Passion [...] Take as an instance the true Ideal Michael Angelo's despairing Woman at the bottom of the Last Judgment.   (*CN* 2, 2838)

Here, Coleridge regards the 'Ideal' as inextricable from the material qualities of the work: the proper convergence of the '*physiognomic*' (the physicality of depicted figures) with the '*Path*ognomic' (the passions those figures express) will elucidate that which is 'felt by all'. This Coleridge opposes to the paintings of John Opie, whom he claims merely superimposes such passions on generic figures. That Coleridge instances Michelangelo's *Last Judgement* as an illustration of the 'true Ideal' is telling when one compares his account with that of Hazlitt: 'Those near the bottom of the Last Judgment are hideous, vulgar caricatures of demons and cardinals, and the whole is a mass of extravagance and confusion' (*Works* 10, 241). Even in Michelangelo's moments of grotesquery, Coleridge recognizes a 'mighty spirit' taming the 'untractable matter' and 'reducing external form to a symbol of the inward and imaginable beauty' (*Lects 1808–19* 2, 711). It is this struggle between spirit and matter that lends Michelangelo's works their electricity and their permanence, that even in his wrestlings with his own untractable body reminds Coleridge of a 'divine something corresponding to within' (711). Conversely, he recognizes that the Ideal relies on the materiality of the body in order to express itself; that without engaging with the physical, experiential world, the Ideal threatens to render all appearances deformed and monstrous: 'A Man melancholy mad with the Ideal—his contemplation of human faces, all warped, & all detestibly ugly' (*CN* 1, 1306).

We are now in aesthetic territory that appears quite distant from 1797's *Osorio* and, while it may be true that Coleridge's knowledge of art history was still in its infancy at this juncture, his major ideas on the topic had taken root. In *Osorio* Coleridge has already started to think about the ideological dimensions of visual representation insofar as it provides a means of 're-presenting' reality, and he has also launched his exploration into the complex relationship between the work of art and the human senses. Moreover, each of the aforementioned 1790s texts find Coleridge considering the oppositional yet symbiotic relationship between form and content that would soon engender further diametric pairings such as matter and spirit, thought and thing, and ideas and materials. In this sense the 1790s were a critical period in Coleridge's thinking on the arts, and it is fitting that he should close the decade with a German voyage that not only found him increasingly attentive to the various works of art that crossed his path, but that also witnessed him reflecting on 'What an enviable Talent it is to have [a G]enius in Painting!' (*CL* 1, 507).

When passing through Helmstedt in July 1799, Coleridge engaged in 'three hours' Picture-seeing' with the doctor, physicist, and chemist Gottfried Christoph Beireis, whose collection contained 'The earliest attempts by Holbein, Michael Angelo, Raphael, Correggio, &c' (*CL* 1, 522). Among this assortment of Old Masters, what especially impressed Coleridge were Beireis' 'German Pictures [...] in my opinion, the most valuable' (522). Even though Italian painters figure into the bulk of his subsequent writing on art, Coleridge was remarkably perceptive when it came to appreciating the differences between the Northern and the Italian Renaissance: 'The Italian masters differ from the Dutch in this that ages in their pictures are perfectly ideal: the infant that a Madonna holds in her arms cannot be guessed of any particular age—it is humanity in infancy. The babe in the manger in a Dutch painting is a fac simile of some real new born bantling' (*TT* 1, 229). Despite the negative implications that 'fac simile' carries in Coleridge's vocabulary, his admiration of Beireis' German paintings reflects a willingness to approach such works on their own terms, as is also clear in his *Table Talk* account of Rubens' *Triumph of Silenus*:

But Oh! what a wonderful picture is that of Rubens' [...] It is the very revelry of Hell; every evil passion is there that could in any way be forced into juxta position with joyance—Lust and hard by it see the Hate; every part is pregnant with libidinous Nature without one spark of the Grace of Heaven. The Animal is triumphing—not over—but in the absence, in the non-existence of, the Spiritual part of Man. I could fancy that—

> all the souls that damned be,
> Leapt up at once in anarchy,
> Clapped their hands and danced for glee.

(228)

Coleridge certainly has problems with viewers responding to art only on sensual terms, but when a work such as Rubens' playfully ironizes that very aesthetic response by presenting *nothing but* 'libidinous Nature', Coleridge is gleeful enough in his appreciation of the painting to recall apposite lines of his own poetry (namely, 'Fire, Famine and Slaughter').

The extent of Coleridge's fascination with the sensuous, even grotesque dimensions of visual art is one that few critics have taken into serious account: it begins with the 1798–9 trip to Germany, where it takes the form of a growing interest in caricature. During the voyage to Hamburg, Coleridge finds himself almost at a loss for words to describe the cartoonish absurdity of his fellow-passengers—in addition to a drunken Dane who has taken a disgraced Swedish noble into virtual bondage, also on board is a Prussian merchant who unites the characters of a 'buffoon' and a 'Mountebank' (*CL* 1, 423)—and so, Coleridge writes in terms that conscientiously draw from the visual arts. If less than a decade later Coleridge would define 'imitation' in terms of the essential difference from the thing it represents, then in caricature he finds a prototype of this concept. As Ernst Kris has put it, the caricaturist 'consciously alters his model, distorts it, plays with its features, and thus shows the power of his imagination—which can exalt as well as degrade. Instead of an objective portrayal of the outer world he substitutes his subjective vision.' Such is Coleridge's own endeavour in the letters from Germany, which find him repeatedly seeking out the '*one* look' of the characters he encounters. As Coleridge writes of the Prussian, 'Amid all his droll looks and droll gestures, there remained *one* look, in his face, that never laughed—and that one look was the Man—the other looks were but his Garments' (*CL* 1, 423). This effort to cut through the 'Garments' and other embellishments of a persona to discover its one true 'look' Coleridge also directs at his other fellow-travelers. Hence in a rare state of sobriety the Dane's 'character' still 'oozed out at every pore'; likewise, the German tailor and his wife 'were both Characters' (425, 427). Coleridge also capitalizes on caricature's political dimensions. As late as 1826 he was writing to the art-collector Charles Aders about commissioning 'what seems to me no bad subject for a Caricature—viz. the REFORM BILL' (*CL* 6, 882). Less than a year after returning from Germany, Coleridge's prior experimentation with verbal caricature pointedly manifests itself in his essay on the character of Pitt for the 19 March 1800 issue of *The Morning Post*:

As his reasonings, even so is his eloquence. One character pervades his whole being. Words on words, finely arranged, and so dexterously consequent, that the whole bears the semblance of argument, and still keeps awake a sense of surprise—but when all is done, nothing rememberable has been said; no one philosophical remark, no one image, not even a pointed aphorism.   (*EOT* 1, 224)

Coleridge's method of description here is unmistakably that of caricature—his simultaneously exaggerative and reductive language aligns his narrative method with the visual techniques of a Gillray or a Rowlandson. Where Coleridge might even have an advantage over visual caricaturists is in his focus on Pitt's empty rhetoric, of which he need not provide a visual representation, but which he can instead mock in its own medium—after all, Pitt's speeches are such that produce 'no image'.

In a conversation of 1811, Coleridge tells Crabb Robinson that 'ideal beauty' in art involves 'taking away from each individual that which is the result of *accident* in him', to which Robinson replies that caricature displays the 'converse of the ideal, being the individuality of the thing caricatured without the general character' (Morley, 1, 34). While Robinson may be correct to assert that caricature exploits the accidental in its portrayal of an individual, for Coleridge the resulting 'one look' is not necessarily limited to the particular figure it depicts. In his portrayal of the Dane, for instance, Coleridge shows us more than a singular ridiculous individual, but also points up the inherently addled and self-contradictory nature of jacobinical ideology. As Coleridge conceives it, a caricature's capacity for illuminating universals is not necessarily precluded by its primary objective of capturing 'individuality'. In its best instances, a caricature provides both.[10] For Coleridge, no artist better exemplifies this fluidity between the individual and the universal more than William Hogarth, whose presence pervades the German letters and their subsequent revision as 'Satyrane's Letters'. To his description of a German card-party featuring two men with enormous pipes (*CL* 1, 461), Coleridge adds in 1809 a paean to Hogarth that highlights his countryman's ability to combine the absurd with the beautiful:

> Hogarth himself never drew a more ludicrous distortion both of attitude and physiognomy, than this effort occasioned: nor was there wanting beside it one of those beautiful female faces which the same Hogarth, in whom the Satyrist never extinguished that love of beauty which belonged to him as a Poet, so often and so gladly introduces as the central figure in a crowd of humourous deformities, which figure (such is the power of true genius!) neither acts, nor is *meant* to act as a contrast; but diffused through all, and over each of the group, a spirit of reconciliation and human kindness [...]   (*Friend* 2, 213).

In emphasizing that the woman's beauty works its effects through diffusion rather than through contrast, so that the humanity of the deformed figures encircling her is heightened rather than compromised, Coleridge draws attention to Hogarth's integration of caricatural specificity and harmonizing ideality. In Hogarth, the universal emerges not at the expense of the particular, but instead emanates out of it. During his stopover at Gibraltar in 1804, Coleridge recalls Hogarth when musing on the cosmopolitan nature of the town: 'I could fill a fresh sheet with a description of the singular faces, dresses, manners, &c &c of the Spaniards, Moors, Jews [...], Greeks, Italians, English, &c that meet in the hot crowded streets [...]. But words would do nothing. [...] A dozen Plates by Hogarth from this Town!' (*CL* 2, 1134). Why, after providing this formidable list of the various nationalities and ethnicities that populate Gibraltar, would Coleridge assert 'words would do nothing'? Coleridge has all the variety a travel-writer could hope for, but he also recognizes that only a Hogarth could depict such a profusion of diverse characters and at the same time amplify the ideal of humanity in which they participate.

Despite his insistence on the inadequacy of words to capture such a scene, for Coleridge Hogarth's productions are themselves uniquely 'verbal'. In considering *The Rake's Progress*, he isolates the 'Spider-web on the Poor-Box' in Plate v as 'one proof of a hundred that every thing in Hogarth is to be translated into *Language—*

---

[10] Coleridge would have thought quite poorly of a caricature that attempted to elicit reflection on spiritual matters (the highest domain of the ideal), much in the same way that whenever Rubens attempts 'anything involving or presuming the spiritual' he renders his characters 'beasts, absolute unmitigated beasts' (*TT* 1, 230).

words—& to act as words, not as Images' (*CN* 3, 4096). Lamb expresses a similar idea in his essay on Hogarth, claiming that 'Other pictures we look at,—his prints we read' (*Works* 1, 89);[11] yet what distinguishes Coleridge's account from Lamb's is its emphasis on translation. Hogarth might be singular among artists in his ability to present a scene in which 'every thing' calls for a verbal correspondent, but for Coleridge the issue of the *translatability* of the visual image informs nearly all of his encounters with visual art. It also informs his experiences of nature, as evidenced by his numerous attempts at picturesque landscape description.[12] These two strands join in 1801's 'The Picture' (itself an expanded translation of Salomon Gessner's 'Der Feste Vorsatz'), the narrator of which seeks to translate nature into an image of his mind by haphazardly projecting the latter onto the former. It is not until he discovers a drawing left behind by his beloved that the narrator initiates a mode of translation that effectively mediates between the subjective and the objective. In integrating this image into the poem the narrator, as Modiano has recognized, describes the content of the picture 'before we are even aware of it' as a drawing (92), thereby mimicking the image's seamless conjoining of mind and nature. While in *Osorio* such obfuscation of the borders between artistic image and historical reality yields potentially pernicious consequences, even here Coleridge locates a corrective in Albert's counter-image of the assassination attempt. Similarly, if the narrator's main flaw in 'The Picture' is his unbridled fancy, then the fluid manner with which he integrates the picture into the landscape is not evidence of further folly but is instead an affirmation of objectivity (Modiano 92), of the mind in reflective harmony with nature rather than ensnared in its own projections. In 'The Picture', then, the translation of visual art into narrative discovers something akin to what John Beer has termed 'an intuition of permanent illumination in the midst of flux' (*AR* xcv), much in the same way that the 'disparted waves' of the river 'dart off asunder' before a mossy rock glistening in the sun, only to meet again,

> Each in the other lost and found: and see
> Placeless, as spirits, one soft water-sun
> Throbbing within them, Heart at once and Eye!
>
> (124–9)

Even though Coleridge would assert in his 1808 lectures that the term 'Poetry', while inclusive of painting and music, 'is rightly applied by eminence to measured *words*, only because the sphere of their action is far wider, the power of giving permanence to them much more certain' (*LL* 1, 76), much of this arises out of his realization in Italy that paintings degrade over time, that they are easily lost to posterity, and that their range of influence is limited to those fortunate enough to

---

[11] For more information on the Coleridge–Lamb–Hogarth nexus, see *CN* 3, 4096 n.
[12] For the best account of Coleridge and the picturesque, see Modiano 8–27.

behold them (*CN* 2, 2759, *Lects 1808–19* 1, 208). If writing is more 'permanent' than visual representation, the latter is nonetheless more immediate in its effect, and consequently Coleridge's translations of image into word find him invested in combining these qualities. In 1803, Coleridge would confess to his notebook that 'Without Drawing, I feel myself but half invested in language' (*CN* 1, 1554). The figure most instrumental in bolstering Coleridge's fluency in visual language at this time was Beaumont. As Woodring has shown, Beaumont opened Coleridge's eyes to an unprecedented range of paintings, but even more important was the sense of excitement and purpose Beaumont inspired in his new friend towards articulating the latent poetry in visual art. In a letter of 22 September 1803, Coleridge promises to send Beaumont 'three Specimens of my *Translations* from your Drawings. If you should really like them, I will go on & make a Volume' (995). Like scores of other projects Coleridge proposed, this volume never fully materialized, but those parts of it that exist—namely, a series of notebook descriptions of thirty-one Beaumont landscapes—are fascinating for the ways in which they reproduce the journey of the eye through the various components of the pictures, lending poetic resonance to their compositional flow. Before one of Beaumont's drawings of Conwy Castle in North Wales, Coleridge offers the following description: 'Conway Castle, seaward— Sea—& on the steep Bank below the Castle wall Trees, under the Shadow of which a Bark is building.—a beautiful Thought' (*CN* 2, 1899 *f93*). Coleridge sets his course through the drawing with one word, 'seaward', and as his eye pans the landscape it also hones in on it, resting finally on a vessel under the shade of trees. He casts his own master-stroke in his judgement of the drawing, 'a beautiful Thought', which joins the realism of the piece with the conscious artistry involved in its production; nature gives way to mind, and disparate details dissolve themselves into unity in such a way that, as Coleridge would define it in 1808, constitutes the 'beautiful'.

Beaumont's ability to synthesize a 'oneness' from the diverse elements of a visual scene, as in the aforementioned drawing's seamless, almost cyclical movement from the ancient, towering castle walls down to the bark nestled as if *in utero* amongst the trees, is one upon which Coleridge meditated further as he sailed to the Mediterranean in the spring of 1804: 'Sir G. Beaumont found great advantage in learning to draw from Nature thro' Gause Spectacles' (*CN* 2, 1973).[13] The harmonizing vision afforded by such spectacles, a sort of ocular relative to the aforementioned Claude Glass, is one that Coleridge sought to replicate during the long days at sea which found him contemplating, among other things, the picturesque

---

[13] In a political sense, Coleridge would don 'Gause Spectacles' of his own in his letters to the Beaumonts, particularly that of 1 October 1803. It is here that Coleridge launches into the infamous recantation/papering-over of his earlier radical sentiments, an apology that takes up the bulk of the letter, and which has been a major fulcrum of judgment for critics such as E. P. Thompson, who writes with perhaps more severity than is necessary that Coleridge 'was a man whose intellect was only fitfully within his own control. But we cannot forgive any critic or historian who accepts such a letter as this as a true record of any part of his evolution' (Thompson, 40).

elements of ships, 'this phantom of complete visual wholeness in an object, which visually does not form a whole' (2012). When Coleridge arrived at Gibraltar, he discovered phantoms of another sort in St Michael's Cave, an immense cavern that reminded him of *Osorio*, and more generally of gothic architecture: 'excepting that there were no Saints or Angels, it was perfect Gothic Extravaganza' (2045). During his second visit to the cavern, these gothic associations came into starker relief: 'the obelisks, the pillars, the rude statues of strange animals, episcopal Thrones, conical church yard monuments [...] in short, such a very populousness of forms so very various, yet combined by the sameness of the material' (2050). Such comments are of a piece with the 'Multëity in Unity' that Coleridge had begun to articulate via Hogarth and Beaumont, yet in their context here there is a spiritual dimension that hearkens back to 1795's 'Allegoric Vision'. Where earlier Coleridge locates a harmonious variety not in the 'gloomy pile' but rather in the landscape surrounding it, here he discerns in the cave a structural fluidity of 'populousness' and 'sameness' that he would later develop into an architectural metaphor for Christianity: 'the Gothic architecture impresses the holder with a sense of self-annihilation; he becomes, as it were, a part of the work contemplated. An endless complexity and variety are united into one whole, the plan of which is not distinct from the execution. A Gothic cathedral is the petrifaction of our religion' (*Lects 1808–19* 2, 59).

As his experiences in St Michael's Cave illustrate, the journey to the Mediterranean is a nexus-point in Coleridge's thinking on the arts that finds him revisiting earlier formulations and developing them with an eye toward their more programmatic manifestation in the lectures and published writings of the ensuing decade. Alongside Coleridge's practice of visual–verbal translation, he is also interested in the conjunction of the arts with history; how they shape history, as he had explored in *Osorio*, but also how the course of history coincides with that of the arts. In 1799, Coleridge had already considered art's historical value while touring the churches of Lübeck: 'Every picture, every legend cut out in gilded wood-work, was a history of the manners & feelings of the ages, in which such works were admired & executed' (*CL* 1, 461). Coleridge revisits this idea in the 1818 *Lectures on the History of Philosophy*, where he employs the progress of the arts as an analogue for the historical development of 'speculative opinion, especially of the Platonic idea[s]' (*Lects Phil* 1, 195). The difference between these two articulations stems from Coleridge's Italian experience. In addition to the fact that nearly all of the schools and works mentioned in this lecture Coleridge encountered in Italy, what stands out among them is the Campo Santo, the cemetery at Pisa whose fresco cycle *The Triumph of Death* he regarded as a watershed in the history of art and philosophy. If for Coleridge the paintings produced in the wake of the fall of Rome find every figure 'imprisoned within its own outline' (195) while Michelangelo and Rafael, on the other end of the spectrum, represent the artistic apotheosis of the 'mighty spirit [...] reducing external form to a symbol of the inward and imaginable beauty' (2, 712), then the frescos in the Campo Santo reveal the first blooming of that spirit out of the rude mass of 'stiff, lifeless divisions and subdivisions *ad infinitum*' (1, 195). This 'awkwardness of composition and stiffness of outline' is still extant in the work of Giotto and his associates, to whom Coleridge attributes *The Triumph of Death*,[14] but the key point is that spirit is no longer wholly subservient to matter, 'idea' no longer shackled by 'outline'. Indeed, in the *Triumph of Death* 'it was one mighty idea that spoke to you, everywhere the same' (196). These frescos are not just exemplary of their time and place, as with the woodcuts at Lübeck, but they re-enact the struggle of human consciousness to break out of mechanical Aristotelian thinking towards a Platonic contemplation of things 'not in their accidents or superficies, but in their essential powers' (193).

Coleridge might have chosen Michelangelo and Raphael, whose productions he considered 'mightier' than Giotto's (*Lects 1808–19* 2, 59), as the centerpieces of this lecture, but aside from the importance of the Campo Santo frescos as initiating a sea-change in painting that culminated in those two artists, what captivates him is the frescos' palpable sense of process, of materials *translating* into 'idea' in a way that had not yet been attempted in the medium. Coleridge accordingly invokes metaphors of language in his explication of *The Triumph of Death*: 'it was the adoption of a symbol, which, though not in as polished a language as could be wished for, which though in a hoarser voice and less tempered modulation uttered the same words to that mind which is the source of all that we really enjoy or that is worth enjoying' (*PL* 1, 196). Where in his translations of Beaumont's drawings and elsewhere Coleridge strives to synthesize a language accommodative of visual representation, in the Pisan frescos he locates an endeavour to visualize that which defies visuality *and* words altogether, the 'presence we cannot explain' (195). While 'form' is necessary to the disclosure of this 'presence', it is ultimately a vehicle that at best resembles 'mere words unnoticed in that which they convey' (196), in a similar way that Coleridge's own visual–verbal translations seek, despite their medium, to avoid a mere 'charm of words'.

If *The Triumph of Death* is paradigmatic of the struggle between 'Free Life' and 'confining Form' (*SW&F* 1, 374) that characterizes the best specimens of visual art, then Coleridge also found works in the Campo Santo that exhibited no such dynamism. Among these were the sculptures at 'Algarotti's Tomb', which featured 'inveterate likenesses of periwigs in marble' (*TT* 1, 170). When in Lecture 5 Coleridge charts the decline of philosophy from Platonism down to the 'merely mechanical' or Atomistic School, he points to these 'great marble wigs' as an artistic example of the last, in which 'the effect of outward form or symbol was more noble than the cause which produced it' (*Lects Phil* 1, 239). Again, the seeds of this idea originate in the 1790s, where during a visit to Klopstock's residence Coleridge notices in a portrait of Lessing 'a Toupee Periwig which enormously injured the

---

[14] As Shaffer has pointed out, more recent scholarship has attributed this cycle to Francesco Traini, 'the finest Pisan painter of the fourteenth century' ('Infernal Dreams', 13).

effect of his Physiognomy' (*CL* 1, 443). It seems felicitous indeed that at the same site at which Coleridge discovered in Giotto/Traini a perfect instantiation of his nascent thinking on matter and spirit, he would also find an occasion to theorize his longstanding aversion to the periwig. Such, however, is the nature of the Pisan experience that, as Shaffer has put it, furnished Coleridge with 'the precise location, recognition and realization in his own time of empirical examples of the art his aesthetics called for' ('Infernal Dreams', 10).

Important as Italy's artistic monuments were to Coleridge—they include, besides the Campo Santo, Michelangelo's Sistine Chapel frescos and the adjoining Stanze and Loggia by Raphael, the church of S. Paolo fuori le Mura in Rome, and the Uffizi Gallery in Florence[15]—it is not these alone that define his aesthetic experience. Additionally, it was the circles of expatriate artists with whom he mingled at Wilhelm von Humboldt's house on Trinità de' Monti, and at the Café Greco in Rome, that helps explain how a visit intended to last three days turned into a sojourn of over four months. These figures include the British painters George Wallis and Thomas Russell;[16] the Danish sculptor Bertel Thorwaldsen; the German painters Asmus Jakob Carstens, Gottlieb Schick and Joseph Anton Koch, as well as the writer Ludwig Tieck; and not least, the American painter and sometime-poet Washington Allston. Among these contacts, it was in Allston that Coleridge found a kindred spirit. Not only had Allston already painted subjects of interest to Coleridge, such as various scenes from Schiller, Milton, and the Bible, but both men had the reputation of being 'talkers', both were Romantic 'Renaissance men' adept at multiple forms of creative expression, and both were Icarian overreachers whose soaring expectations of their respective 'great work' resulted in self-recrimination and a growing sense of 'work without hope'.[17] In addition to maintaining close contact with Coleridge during his subsequent stay in London, Allston also befriended Beaumont, who commissioned his *Angel Releasing St Peter from Prison* for the parish church of Ashby-de-la-Zouch in north-west Leicestershire. In Rome, however, Coleridge had already found in Allston some reminders of his English friend's aesthetic principles. Whether or not he employed 'Gause Spectacles', Allston also approached his art with an emphasis on the unifying power of the eye, as he expresses to Coleridge before an unfortunately unnamed painting: "He works too much with the Pipe in his mouth—looks too much at the particular Thing instead of overlooking—ubersehen.'—*Alston*' (*CN* 2, 2794).

---

[15] Coleridge purchased 'Prints from the Fresco Works of Raphael' while in Rome (*CL* 2, 1190). For more on the church of S. Paolo fuori le Mura see *CL* 2, 569, and Zuccato, 73–4. For the Uffizi, see *CN* 2, 2853 and n., and Sultana, 395.

[16] Joseph Farington notes in his diary of 1810 that 'Whilst [Russell] was at Rome Coleridge arrived there from Malta, in a destitute condition, His money being expended. Mr. Russell became his friend & protector, & relieved [him] from His difficulties, which had reduced His mind to such a state, as to cause Him to pass much of his time in bed in a kind of despairing state' (6, 167).

[17] For more on the shared cast of mind between Allston and Coleridge, see *CN* 2, 2704 n., and Johns, 3–6.

Such *übersehen* is a practice Coleridge sought to replicate in his picturesque description of the vale of Olevano (*CN* 2, 2796) and also in his ekphrastic translation of Allston's *Diana and the Nymphs in the Chase*. Though correct to indicate the holistic nature of Coleridge's theoretical priorities, Zuccato is perhaps overly reductive in his claim that Coleridge's investment in 'the idea embodied in form' compromised his eye for the compositional interrelations within paintings: 'His comments on painting often seem to disembody the image, to atomize it into its components: he considers colour, or form, or drawing, but seldom the relations among them' (75). Not only would Coleridge explicitly shun such atomizing tendencies in his 1818 philosophical lectures, but his description of Allston's painting reveals him at pains to verbalize the harmonic congruency of its component parts. Coleridge's priority is to give a sense of the image's immediate effect on the viewer, but his medium leaves him at a disadvantage by compelling him to represent this effect in temporal terms by traversing the composition from left to right. Coleridge overcomes this difficulty as best he can, by treating details as paradigmatic of the whole, as in his description of the stones in the middle-ground of the painting:

But the right hand of the Picture, the tree with its cavern-making roots stretching out to some faintly purplish Stones that connect the right extremity with the purple rock on the left extremity [...] & how by small stones, scattered at irregular distances along the foreground even to one in the very centre or bisection of the foreground, which seems to balance & hold even all the tints of the whole picture, the keystone of its colors—so aided by the bare earth breaking in & making an irregular road to the Lake on which that faery figure shoots along as one does in certain Dreams, only that it touches the earth which yet it seems to have no occasion to touch [...]   (*CN* 2, 2831 *f*96–7)

Coleridge's articulation of the compositional and coloristic unity of the piece leads him into an explication of its human interest—that which is 'felt by all'—through his reference to 'certain Dreams', which becomes a portal into the psychological landscape of the painting. In addition, then, to giving what Shaffer has appositely termed 'a direct experience of walking in the scene depicted' ('Coleridge's Ekphrasis', 119), Coleridge also evokes those intangible, universal qualities that—as in the best specimens of visual art—rise gracefully out of the material trappings of a work. The next entry of his notebook finds Coleridge meditating on 'The quiet circle in which Change and Permanence *co-exist*, not by combination or juxtaposition, but by an absolute annihilation of difference/column of smoke, the fountains before St Peters, waterfalls/God!—Change without loss' (*CN* 2, 2832). It is this cycle of 'Change and Permanence', of absolute intuition in the midst of flux, that Coleridge locates in Allston's painting and replicates in his own 'translation'.

Coleridge would again invoke this 'quiet circle' in his *Essays on the Principles of Genial Criticism*, intended to promote Allston's 1814 Bristol exhibition. In his assessment of Allston's *Dead Man Restored to Life*, Coleridge presents his friend as more than a mere follower of Michelangelo and Raphael, but indeed as the spirit of those artists 'restored to life':

You will find, what you had not suspected, that you have before you a circular groupe. But by what variety of life, motion, and passion, is all the stiffness, that would result from an obvious regular figure swallowed up, and the figure of the groupe as much concealed by the action and passion, as the skeleton which gives the form of the human body, is hidden by the flesh and its endless outlines!   (*SW&F* 1, 373)

In addition to echoing his earlier notebook entry on Michelangelo's Sistine Chapel, and prefiguring his lecture remarks on the Campo Santo frescoes, this comment parallels his description in the next paragraph of Raphael's *Galatea*, in which 'the circle is perceived at first sight' (374). Underlying these comments, then, is another 'circular group' consisting of none other than Allston, Raphael, and Coleridge himself. One might agree with Woodring that 'Had Coleridge known no painters and seen few paintings, his theories of art might have been scarcely different' (95), but this is to impose a mechanical superstructure onto a development that is decidedly more organic than Coleridge has been credited for. If the seeds of his theories were planted in the poetry, lectures and philosophical inquiries of the 1790s, then it was in his experiences of art and his relationships with painters from the turn of the century onwards that those seeds took root and flourished into the mature principles of the 1810s. Moreover, it was in his friend Allston that Coleridge found a definitive convergence of those principles, be it the way in which his works embodied the electric dynamism of form and content, matter and spirit that for Coleridge marked the apotheosis of visual representation—in place since the early Renaissance but seldom achieved since—or the occasion his paintings provided for Coleridge to execute the grandest of his numerous visual–verbal 'translations'.

   While the second decade of the nineteenth century finds Coleridge synthesizing these ideals into a critical system (if so it may be termed) that spans the course of his public lectures and publications, they would continue to exert considerable influence on his writings of the 1820s. When devising his plans for the *Aids to Reflection*, which on the surface has little to do with visual art, Coleridge conceives of his text in terms of a painting. Voicing his reservations about the prospect of simply providing a collection of highlights or 'Beauties' of Archbishop Leighton's *Works*, Coleridge tells the publishers Taylor and Hessey that such a procedure would be 'almost as injurious to the Original, as the taking out of the Lights of a Titian or a Correggio & presenting them apart from the Shades would be, con-sidered as a specimen of the Picture' (*CL* 5, 289). In other words, Coleridge worries that his latest work will be the literary equivalent of a painting composed of mere outlines, which may be 'wonderfully vivid at times, but [with] no life' (*PL* 1, 195). Consequently, Coleridge invokes the metaphor of painting to justify the infusion of his own voice into Leighton's so as to illuminate and personalize what he fears will otherwise be dead, decontextualized fragments. This serves as a pre-emptive apology for the obfuscation of the boundaries between his voice and Leighton's that constitutes the narrative fabric of the *Aids*, in which Coleridge has taken the 'Lights' of the Titian and Correggio and intermixed them, as it were, with the 'Shades'.

While metaphors of visuality inform Coleridge's practice of 'translating' Leighton's works into a spiritual philosophy that is uniquely his own, visual art itself remained for Coleridge an occasion for translation. In his 1828 poem 'The Garden of Boccaccio', such translation finally assumes the form of the extended lyric, which finds him reflecting on his experience of the Tuscan countryside in 1806, and with it his feelings of dejection and 'vacancy' arising from the impossible love for Asra that had haunted him at the time. What lifts him out of this Keatsian 'dull continuous Ache' is an 'exquisite Design' that a friend, presumably Anne Gillman, places on his desk of 'Boccaccio's Garden and its Faery, / The Love, the Joyaunce and the Gallantry!' (*PW* 1. 2. 9, 14–16). The 'Design' is none other than Thomas Stothard's 1825 watercolor depicting a scene from the *Decameron*, and what the poem goes on to convey is an ekphrastic self-narrative in which Coleridge projects himself onto Boccaccio ('With old Boccaccio's Soul I stand possest, / And breathe an Air like life, that swells my Chest') at the same time that he locates himself in the painting ('I see no longer! I myself am there') (71–2, 65). What is doubly fascinating about this poem is that while Coleridge was preparing it for publication in F. M. Reynolds' *Keepsake* annual, the accompanying engraving (evidently produced concurrently with Coleridge's writing process) modified Stothard's original so as to accord with the images in the poem. This piece exhibits, then, that organic reflexivity between word and image that Coleridge had, in various ways, striven to articulate since the 1790s.

WORKS CITED

BARRY, KEVIN. 1987. *Language, Music and the Sign: A Study in Aesthetics, Poetics, and Poetic Practice from Collins to Coleridge*. Cambridge: Cambridge University Press.

BULLEN, J. B. 1993. Coleridge and early Italian art. In *English Studies in Transition: Papers from the ESSE Inaugural Conference*, ed. Robert Clark and Piero Boitani. London: Routledge, pp. 196–207.

FARINGTON, JOSEPH. 1926. *The Farington Diary*, ed. James Grieg. 8 vols. London: Hutchinson.

HAZLITT, WILLIAM. 1933. *The Complete Works*, ed. P. P. Howe. 21 vols. London and Toronto: J. M. Dent.

JOHNS, ELIZABETH. 1979. Washington Allston and Samuel Taylor Coleridge: a remarkable relationship. *Archives of American Art Journal*, 19 (3): 2–7.

KRIS, ERNST. 2008. The Principles of Caricature. *The Gombrich Archive.* 22 January < http://www.gombrich.co.uk/showdoc.php?id=85>.

LAMB, CHARLES. 1818. *The Works of Charles Lamb.* 2 vols. London: C. and J. Ollier.

MODIANO, RAIMONDA. 1985. *Coleridge and the Concept of Nature.* London: MacMillan.

MORLEY, EDITH J., ed. 1938. *Henry Crabb Robinson on Books and their Writers.* 3 vols. London: J. M. Dent, 1938.

SHAFFER, E. S. 1993. Coleridge's ekphrasis: visionary word-painting. In *Coleridge's Visionary Languages: Essays in Honour of J. B. Beer*, ed. Tim Fulford and Morton D. Paley. Cambridge: D. S. Brewer. pp. 111–21.

—— 1989. 'Infernal Dreams' and Romantic art criticism: Coleridge on the Campo Santo, Pisa. *The Wordsworth Circle* 20 (1): 9–19.

SULTANA, DONALD. 1969. *Samuel Taylor Coleridge in Malta and Italy.* Oxford: Basil Blackwell.

THOMAS, SOPHIE. 2004. Seeing things ('as they are'): Coleridge, Schiller, and the play of semblance. *Studies in Romanticism*, 43: 537–55.

THOMPSON, E. P. 1997. *The Romantics: England in a Revolutionary Age.* New York: New Press.

WOODRING, CARL. 1978. What Coleridge thought of pictures. In *Images of Romanticism: Verbal andVisual Affinities*, ed. Karl Kroeber and William Walling. New Haven: Yale University Press, pp. 91–106.

ZUCCATO, EDOARDO. 1996. *Coleridge in Italy.* Cork: Cork University Press.

CHAPTER 33

COLERIDGE AND SCIENCE

ERIC G. WILSON

In 1816, Coleridge moved in with Dr James Gillman, a surgeon living in Highgate. Coleridge hoped that the young physician could help him control his opium intake. But Coleridge was also probably excited to be sharing a dwelling with a bona fide man of science. Coleridge for most of his adult life had been an assiduous student of several scientific disciplines, ranging from geology to chemistry to physiology. Whether he was keen on increasing his 'stock of metaphors'[1] or bent on discovering the principle of life itself, Coleridge never separated his poetical and philosophical efforts from ongoing commitment to the hard facts of nature. In fact, right around the time Coleridge took his new address at Gillman's home, he published a riveting description of photosynthesis (*LS* 6, 72). This process— revealed, as Coleridge knew, by Joseph Priestley during the last quarter of the eighteenth century—suggested this to Coleridge: the ability of the plant to vacillate between inhalation and exhalation might blur the line between nature and human, object and subject. But the respiration of plants also intimated to Coleridge another possibility: that all of nature is but a symbol of human consciousness—a consciousness that oscillates between passive reception and active projection. Such polarized thinking—the breathing leaves are intrinsically valuable complements to human inhaling; these same organs are valuable only as revelations of the human activity—is typical of Coleridge. The obvious questions arising from this polarity center on the possibility of reconciliation. Can the panting plant be both opaque

---

[1] John Ayrton Paris, *The Life of Sir Humphry Davy*, i. 138.

fact and transparent vision? Can this vacillating greenery simultaneously function as necessary fact and sign of fantasy? Such inquiries cut to the strange heart of Coleridge's life-long passion for scientific inquiry.[2]

This division between proto-ecological vision and Platonic hope for transcendence is the appropriate context for thinking about Coleridge's interest in science. Ultimately, Coleridge turned to science in hopes of reconciling these two poles and thus marrying spirit and matter, mind and body. But, as Coleridge knew well, this blending is difficult, perhaps impossible, to accomplish: ephemeral bodies are resilient to the dictates of the mind.[3] Hoping to overcome these intractable facts and consequently to synthesize visible data and invisible laws, Coleridge entered into numerous scientific debates. In a full exposition of Coleridge's interests in science, one could easily provide a detailed section on the poet's interest in geology, especially in the controversy between Neptunists, who believed that the earth was shaped by water, and Vulcanists, who held that the globe was formed through fire.[4] One could also focus on Coleridge's entry into the so-called science of race, his place in the debate, racist on both sides, between those who believed in hierarchical gradations among the races and those who maintained that a unified human species developed different races through degeneration.[5] One could further discuss Coleridge's participation in the science of dreaming, divided between those who claimed that dreams are transcendental visitations and those who argued that dreams are physiological phenomena.[6] Other sciences could be chosen as well, including ecological sciences[7] and social sciences.[8]

---

[2] Several excellent studies of Coleridge's passion for science have been published in the past thirty-five years or so. The definitive early book on Coleridge and science is Trevor H. Levere's *Poetry Realized in Nature*. Important earlier studies that laid the general intellectual groundwork for Levere's fine work include Thomas McFarland's *Coleridge and the Pantheist Tradition*, Owen Barfield's *What Coleridge Thought*, M. H. Abrams's 'A Light in Sound': Science, Metascience, and Poetic Imagination', Kathleen Coburn's 'Coleridge: A Bridge Between Science and Poetry', John Beer's *Coleridge's Poetic Intelligence*, and Timothy J. Corrigan's '*Biographia Literaria* and the Language of Science'. More recent work on Coleridge's general relationship to science—work following that of Levere—includes Raimonda Modiano's *Coleridge and the Concept of Nature* and Ian Wylie's *Young Coleridge and the Philosopher's of Nature*.

[3] For a study of Coleridge's fundamentally divided mind, see Seamus Perry, *Coleridge and the Uses of Division*. Also see Eric G. Wilson, *Coleridge's Melancholia: An Anatomy of Limbo*.

[4] See James M. McKusick's ' "Kubla Khan" and the Theory of the Earth'.

[5] See Peter J. Kitson's 'Coleridge and "the Ouran utang Hypothesis": Romantic Theories of Race' and Tim Fulford's 'Theorizing Golgotha: Coleridge, Race Theory and the Skull Beneath the Skin'.

[6] See Jennifer Ford's *Coleridge on Dreaming*.

[7] See Tim Fulford's 'Coleridge, Darwin, Linnaeus: The Sexual Politics of Botany' and James C. McKusick's 'Coleridge and the Economy of Nature'.

[8] See Elinor Shaffer's 'Myths of Community in the *Lyrical Ballads* 1798–1998: The Commonwealth and the Constitution', Kenneth R. Johnston's 'The Political Sciences of Life: From American Panitsocracy to British Romanticism', and Susan Manly's 'Jews, Jubilee, and Harringtonianism in Coleridge and Maria Edgeworth: Republican Conversions'.

Being unable to discuss all of Coleridge's scientific interests, I have decided to hone in on those concerns that occupied him the most. To this end, I will discuss, in this order, Coleridge's interests in chemistry, physiology, cognition, mesmerism, optics, and pathology. In the case of each of these sciences, Coleridge predictably was of two minds, vacillating between the spiritual and the physical.

CHEMISTRY

The young Coleridge was passionate about chemistry. This interest initially grew out of his contact with Priestley, Thomas Beddoes, and Erasmus Darwin. Priestley not only attempted to reveal the inner workings of plants; he also tried to grasp the nature of matter itself, equating spirit with electricity and concluding that matter is a manifestation of this divinely ordained galvanic power. The youthful Coleridge embraced Priestley's idea that God and matter are one, claiming that he was a 'compleat Necessitarian' (*CL* 1, 137). Coleridge met Beddoes, a chemist, soon after moving to Bristol in 1795. Beddoes had recently established there a Pneumatic Medical Institution. The study of air fascinated Coleridge—it suggested the mutual interdependence between human and nature. This fascination got Coleridge reading scientific texts, especially those of Darwin. Darwin's poem *The Botanic Garden* (1791) proved a compendium of the scientific knowledge of Coleridge's day. It was perhaps his wonderment at the polymathic Darwin that led Coleridge in 1797 to state that he 'should not think of devoting less than 20 years to an Epic poem'. He would need '[t]en to collect materials and warm [his] mind with universal science'. He 'would be a tolerable mathematician, [he] would thoroughly know Mechanics, Hydrostatics, Optics and Astronomy, Botany, Metallurgy, Fossilism, Chemistry, Geology, Anatomy, Medicine—then the mind of man—then the minds of Men—in all Travels, Voyages and Histories'. So he 'would spend ten years; the next five in the composition of the poem and the five last in the correction of it' (*CL* 1, 320). While such a plan seems outlandishly grandiose, Coleridge almost, in the end, achieved it.[9]

Coleridge's contact with Priestley, Beddoes, and Darwin constituted a backdrop for Coleridge's meeting with Humphry Davy. Soon after his return to England from a trip to Germany in 1799—a trip that introduced him to German science and philosophy and thus led him to reject his youthful determinism—Coleridge ended up once more in Bristol. Davy was there too, working as the chemical superintendent of Beddoes' Pneumatic Institution. Coleridge and Davy soon become fast friends. The two men complemented each other. Davy, a chemist who wrote

---

[9] See Levere, 9–16, and Wylie, *passim*.

poetry, was keen on discovering the basic constituents of matter and the ways in which these elements combine. Coleridge, a poet hot for chemistry, was bent on understanding the powers underlying the mind and the ways that these powers connect to matter.[10]

Stoked by Davy, Coleridge became fascinated by chemistry. Soon after leaving Bristol for the Lakes—he moved to Keswick to be near Wordsworth—he said that he would 'attack chemistry, like a Shark' (*CL* 1, 605). Coleridge quickly revealed the reason for this fervor. He believed that Davy's scientific studies—his delvings into the basic principles of matter—might provide the foundations for a metaphysical scheme capable of including the natural world. He wished to measure Davy's perspectives against those idealistic systems of Spinoza and Leibniz. Coleridge at this time indeed believed that Davy had turned science into metaphysics. In his mind, Davy was 'the Father and Founder of philosophic Alchemy, the Man who *born* a Poet first converted Poetry into Science and *realized* what few men possessed Genius enough to *fancy*' (5, 309). Such a perception suggested that Davy had substantiated the dreams of the alchemists—those visions of a cosmos ruled by a pervasive and intelligent spirit, a universe in which everything manifests the 'one Life within us and abroad'.

It is no wonder, then, that Coleridge in 1802 left his haven in the Lakes to come to London to hear Davy's lecture at the Royal Institution. By attending to Davy's lectures on the history and nature of chemistry, Coleridge wished to add to his collection of metaphors. The specificity of Coleridge's lecture notes is striking, beautiful.[11] As he watched Davy demonstrate the various properties of the chemical elements, he found himself fascinated with the display of combination and color. This fascination had not waned by 1806, the year that Davy made his great scientific breakthrough. In that year, Davy began to wonder if the very make-up of matter is electromagnetic, if material things are not solid substances at all but fields of polarized forces. In this paradigm, the Newtonian view of matter—things are composed of imponderable atoms pressed together or pulled apart by gravity— would be obsolete. Replacing this view would be a more dynamic vision: natural events are combinations of invisible spheres inhabited by positive and negative powers. Davy thought he had found sufficient evidence to predict this new picture. He announced that the Newtonian universe might well be a thing of the past and that a new, more active cosmos would soon emerge, a cosmos in which every creature would be a pattern, in varying degrees of density or rarefaction, of one power.[12]

---

[10] See Levere, 20–35; Coburn; Molly Lefebure, 'Humphry Davy: Philosophic Alchemist'; and Mark Kipperman, 'Coleridge, Shelley, Davy, and Science's Millennium'.

[11] Nicholas Roe notes the beauty of Coleridge's descriptions in his introduction to his edition, *Samuel Taylor Coleridge and the Sciences of Life*, 12.

[12] See Levere, 32–3.

Instead of taking Davy's work at face value, Coleridge tried to appropriate it into his growing metaphysical system. By 1806, he had renounced the Unitarianism of his youth and was moving rapidly toward a Trinitarian view. To accomplish such a view, he had to reject his earlier passion for material particulars and hold hard to immaterial generalities. He was especially taken by the philosophies of Kant, Johann Gottlieb Fichte, F. W. J. Schelling, and Henrik Steffens, each of whom, in his own way, argued that the cosmos is a polarized manifestation of a numinous principle. Versed in these thinkers, Coleridge increasingly rejected empiricism and moved inexorably toward idealism. He believed that electromagnetism, far from being the sole power behind material existence, is but one of many forces manifesting absolute spirit.[13] He suggests this idea in his 1825 *Aids to Reflection*. In the conclusion of this book, Coleridge attacks Newton and his 'corpuscular school' for being overly materialistic and thus leaving no place for transcendent spirit or its attendant intellectual freedom. To this dangerous worldview, Coleridge contrasts the 'increasingly *dynamic* spirit of the physical sciences'. If one looks at the scientific ideas of men like Davy, one will find that visible objects are powerful manifestations of invisible and purposeful laws. Physical events are revelations of the 'combining and constitutive power'. As such, these palpable occurrences are like 'the pulses of air to the voice of a discourser'—symbols of an organizing intelligence. In this way, material elements further resemble 'the column of blue smoke from a cottage chimney in the breathless summer noon, or the steadfast-seeming cloud on the edge-point of a hill in the driving air-current' (*AR* 9, 398–9). They, these flashes of matter, are lubricious wisps of the universal mind, quick scintillations of the enduring invisible potency.

Note the tension in Coleridge's descriptions. He of course most loves the synthetic power that brings together and pulls apart earth's polarities—its formless forms, its patterned turbulences. But, at the same time, he clearly revels in these same celeritous structures. Note the lyrical attention he gives to the smoke and the cloud. This strain between antinomies appears in full relief in what follows, when Coleridge praises the 'unseen agency' that 'weaves its magic eddies'. Doing so, this intelligent power generates increasingly complex organic forms: the 'foliage becomes indifferently the bone and its marrow, the pulpy brain, or the solid ivory'. These physical occurrences, Coleridge emphasizes, are real. What we see when we look at the grass, the ox, and the elephant '*is* blood, *is* flesh, is itself the work, or shall I say, the translucence, of the invisible energy which soon surrenders or abandons them to inferior powers' (*AR* 9, 398–9). Such interplay between active principle and palpable precipitation is not, Coleridge urges, a mere conjecture or hypothesis. This interaction is fact: organs are both opaque and transparent, poems and poets, valuable beings and portals to something beyond.

---

[13] Levere, 58–81.

PHYSIOLOGY

Coleridge's polarized view of chemistry—the science can reveal the ultimate principle of life; the science is but one manifestation of cosmic consciousness—of course provides a fascinating context for several of Coleridge's poems, especially 'The Rime of the Ancient Mariner' (1798), in which the living things emerge in the form of tense eddies. These eddies could well prove to be manifestations of a polarized physical power; but they could also be exhibitions of a spiritual potency. These duplicities encourage both ecological and transcendental readings of the poem—is it a paean to thriving bodies or a celebration of the Christian soul? In the end, one is hard pressed to tell the difference.

This same duplicity controls Coleridge's abiding interest in physiology.[14] In 1816, Coleridge composed *Hints Toward the Formation of a More Comprehensive Theory of Life*, a meditation on vitality. In his *Theory*, Coleridge enters into nineteenth-century physiological debates on the nature of life, all the while keeping in mind the idealism of Schelling and Steffens. During the early years of the nineteenth century, the most important theoretician of life was John Hunter, the eighteenth-century surgeon. In his *Treatise on Blood* (1794), Hunter attempted to discover the difference between living and non-living beings by finding a power common to all animated creatures. In undertaking this exploration, Hunter opened the door to both transcendentalist and materialist interpretations of his work. He seemed to conclude that life is a potency that thrives independently of organization. Apparently for Hunter, life is a creative force generating endlessly varied organisms. In ostensibly developing this view, Hunter behaved as if he were a vitalist, someone holding that life is an ungraspable, almost spiritual principle existing beyond the matter that it enlivens. The two most important nineteenth-century interpreters of the ambiguous Hunter were John Abernathy and Sir William Lawrence. Abernathy championed Hunter's spiritualist notions while Lawrence took an opposing view, arguing that Hunter really believed that life is dependent upon organization. In Coleridge's mind, this debate was best defined in spiritualist and materialist terms: Abernathy, endorsing Hunter's spiritualist current, was on the side of dynamic spirit; Lawrence, finding Hunter a materialist, was on the side of inert matter.[15]

Coleridge in the essay aligns himself with Abernathy. He claims that 'Life is not a *Thing*—a self-sufficient *Hypostastis*—but an *Act* and a *Process*' (*SW&F* 11. 1, 557). Arrangements of atoms cannot, in the end, account for life. For Coleridge, life is the '*power* that which discloses itself from within as a principle of *unity* in the many' (510). Though Coleridge certainly drew this definition from Abernathy, he

---

[14] See Levere, 45–52, and Corrigan, 402–4. See also 'The Rime of the Ancient Mariner and Frankenstein', Angela Esterhammer's 'Coleridge's "Hymn before Sun-rise" and the Voice Not Heard', and Seamus Perry's 'Coleridge and the End of Autonomy'.
[15] See Alan Richardson, *British Romanticism and the Science of the Mind*, 24–9.

found in Abernathy what he had already discovered in Schelling and Steffens. This connection is immediately shown by Coleridge's rewording of this definition: 'I define life as the *principle of individuation*, or the power which unites a given *all* into a *whole* that is presupposed by its parts' (510).[16] With Schelling and Steffens clearly in mind, Coleridge demonstrates how this principle functions through the chain of being. Metals, in his mind, prove the 'simplest form of unity, namely, the unity of powers and properties' (514). Crystal constitutes the next scale, manifesting not only a union of powers but also 'of parts' (515). Geological phenomena appear next, illustrating 'the tendencies of the Life of Nature to vegetation or animalization' (516). Finally, Coleridge states, we rise to the 'present order of vegetable and animal Life' (516).

In this ascent of the chain of being—an ascent characterized by increasingly complex and autonomous forms of life—each major category manifests a particular polarity even as it shares qualities with the rungs below and above. The inanimate scale is driven by the primary polarity of magnetism: attraction and repulsion. The next category, the animate, links with the inanimate in its lower levels. While the lower forms of life manifest magnetism, they also exemplify the polarity of reproduction and irritability. The next scale of animated being demonstrates increasing individuation. These forms share with the lower rungs reproduction and irritability, but they also feature a new polarity: sensibility, or the interplay between pleasure and pain. As the ladder ascends, it becomes characterized by increasingly complex forms of individualized sensibility, moving from consciousness to self-consciousness. At the top of this ladder is the human being, a blending of idiosyncratic and unrepeatable inward meditation and unrepeatable and idiosyncratic outward expression (*SW&F* 11. 1, 535–51). In thinking about his own thoughts, in reflecting while transcending nature, the human being is 'a revelation of Nature'. He 'is referred to himself, delivered up to his own charge; and he who stands the most on himself, and stands the firmest, is the truest, because the most individual, Man' (551). This individual self-confidence gives rise to increasingly complex modes of polarity, and ultimately to the greatest polarity of all—genius, a blending of originality and sympathy (551).

Still, though the human is ascendant, this same human being is dependent for his existence on each preceding rung of the ladder. In Coleridge's scheme, each being is twofold, both an integral whole and a part of a larger whole—intrinsically valuable as a fact and mere cipher of the next level. In this 'holarchy'—as opposed to a hierarchy—every creature is a component of a cosmic manifold, a system in which each rung is dependent on those below it and subsumed by those above it.[17] This tense vision provides a rich context for thinking about Coleridge's ideas on

---

[16] See Levere, 50.

[17] 'Holarchical' is a term used by Arthur Koestler in his 1967 *Ghost in the Machine* to detail organic homologies, 45–58.

organicism and the poetics that grow out of it. Is Coleridge's organicism finally an appeal to life as a physical power or is it ultimately an invocation of a transcendent spirit? Is a symbol a synecdoche, a part standing for the whole that it constitutes, or is it a place of irony, a visible entity that is made meaningless when the invisible realm to which it points is ascendant?

SCIENCES OF THE MIND

During the first part of the nineteenth century, scientists were for the first time exploring the idea that the mind might not be a transcendental power at all, a component of the soul, but rather a faculty located within the brain, an aspect of the body. These developers of this anti-dualistic account of the mind—including Erasmus Darwin, F. J. Gall, P. J. Cabanis, Charles Bell, J. C. Spurzheim, and William Lawrence—all believed that the embodied mind is an active organ, not a passive machine. As such, the mind perpetually processes sensual data. Doing so, the mind is a complex manifold, composed of numerous parts and circuits, all of which might well be dependent upon the power of electricity. Possessing material minds, humans are little different from animals—distinct only in degree and not kind. Both human being and animal alike, organic as they are, are shaped by their palpable environments. Thus, the early neuroscientists mentioned above persistently studied the mind in ecological terms. Focusing on interactions between human minds and environments, these proto-neurologists showed an interest in adaptation. This focus led to evolutionary accounts of human development.[18]

Fascinated by the facts of the mind, Coleridge exhibited a keen interest in these scientific developments. He was a deep student, as we know, of Darwin, and he knew the work of Gall and Lawrence. Early in his intellectual life, Coleridge, steeped in Priestley as well as in Darwin, was firmly in a materialist camp when it came to neuroscience. He believed in the corporeality of thought, calling it motion.[19] However, after being schooled in Kant and the German idealists, he pulled away from the concept of an embodied mind. He became increasingly convinced that the mind is a transcendental power, a faculty not dependent upon physical organization. Still, even though Coleridge professed a passion for metaphysics—and thus a spiritualist notion of mind—he throughout his life remained ambivalent about the embodied mind, especially in his thinking on the emotions and the unconscious. For instance, in 1816, Coleridge took a positive view

---

[18] See Richardson, 5–38.   [19] Ibid., 40–4.

on Spurzheim's 'Anatomical Demonstrations of the Brain' (*SW&F*, 540). About a year later, he praised the 'splendor and originality' of Spurzheim's and Gall's theories of the physical mind (*CN* 3, 4355). However, at another juncture Coleridge criticized Spurzheim for being 'dense' and 'ignorant' for believing that the brain is an amalgamation of distinct components (*TT* 183). Coleridge also struck an ambiguous stance on Darwin. Though Coleridge as a young man admired Darwin's ideas and even as a mature thinker endorsed Darwin's notion of an actively organic mind, the poet could also express disdain for the natural philosopher's atheism and his seeming adherence to blind nature over a purposeful God.[20] This duplicity in regard to Darwin and Spurzheim informed Coleridge's meditations on the mind throughout his life. When he was attempting to synthesize Platonism, Christianity, and German idealism into a transcendental theory of consciousness, he was also wishing for an anti-Cartesian system that wouldn't separate physiology and psychology. Contemplating this latter possibility, Coleridge in 1821 wondered if the mind might produce changes in the body without any act of individual will. Given this consideration, it makes sense that Coleridge coined the terms 'neuropathology' and 'psychosomatic'—words that suggest linkage between body and mind.[21]

Coleridge explores this linkage—a linkage, again, that runs counter to idealism—in his speculations on dreams. In several places he suggests that dreams arise from bodily conditions that have nothing to do with the will. Such a theory would intimate that the mind is a manifestation of the body's involuntary nerves. For instance, in 1803, Coleridge broods over how difficult it is for conscious thinking, driven by reason, to curb the mind's seemingly involuntary stream of thought. Dreams, he concludes, form an especially good example of the notion that the mind is generated by bodily desires (*CN* 1, 1770). In 1818, Coleridge continued to be preoccupied by this idea, wondering if dreaming occurs only when the 'voluntary. . .power' is suspended and the mind, like an involuntary organ, acts of its own accord (*Lects 1808–19*, 266). Coleridge was clearly concerned over these possibilities because they would, if true, undercut his highest hopes for the mind's ability to transcend the body. This concern was possibly behind his decision not to publish 'Kubla Khan' (1797, 1816) for almost twenty years. In the context of early nineteenth-century theories of mind, the poem's famous introduction was an especially powerful description of the embodied mind, a picture of a mental constitution thoroughly controlled by bodily dispositions. The dreamer in the little farmhouse is but a vessel for opium driven nerves.[22]

[20] Richardson, 41–3.
[21] Ibid., 43; Coburn, 85.
[22] In this paragraph, I follow Richardson, 45–8, 57–65.

MESMERISM

Connected to Coleridge's interest in scientific theories of mind was his enduring engagement with mesmerism, a phenomenon that in Coleridge's day still seemed worthy of scientific meditation. In 1778, Anton Mesmer unveiled his theory of animal magnetism. He claimed that a principle of attraction harmonizes nature and human alike. The medium of this attraction is animal magnetism, a universal fluid. All diseases result from disequilibrium in magnetic flow. Mesmer's cure involved putting the patient through a 'crisis'. He massaged the patient's magnetic 'poles' until he induced a trance. Bereft of self consciousness and will, the patient lived in a violent moment what had been enervating him for weeks. After this convulsion, the perverse forces were exorcised.[23]

A delegation led by Benjamin Franklin in 1784 concluded that Mesmer's magnetic fluid does not exist and that his cures issue from imagination. However, mesmerism nonetheless exerted a strong influence on serious thinkers in the late eighteenth and early nineteenth centuries. One group of thinkers, exemplified by the *Naturphilosoph* Schelling, thought that the galvanic fluid was a manifestation of the world soul. The 'rapport' between patient and healer was, for these thinkers, simply a recognition and manipulation of the spiritual power coursing through the cosmos, unifying subject and object, human and nature.[24] Another group of theorists, instanced by Gall, believed that the animal fluid was a physical force somehow inhering in the embodied mind. The phenomenon of the magnetic sleep was simply a result of the manipulation of the body's nerves.[25]

Coleridge was deeply versed in this primary debate concerning animal magnetism. He was of course deeply familiar with the works of Schelling, but he was also versed in the texts of Gall.[26] In addition, he had read detailed studies of animal magnetism by C. A. F. Kluge, K. C. Wolfart, and J. P. F. Deleuze.[27] In sum, he was thoroughly informed on the nature of mesmerism and the problems surrounding the movement. These problems inspired in Coleridge a mixed response to the magnetic sleep. On the one hand, Coleridge saw Mesmer's idea of a universal power as a version of the universal soul of the Platonists, Christians, and German idealists. In an 1821 notebook entry, Coleridge wonders if animal magnetism might be the key to the transcendental imagination. He wrote, 'If the Zoo-magnetic influx be only the influence of the Imagination, the active Imagination may be a form of

---

[23] See Eric G. Wilson, 'Matter and Spirit in the Age of Animal Magnetism', Tim Fulford, 'Conducting the Vital Fluid: the Politics and Poetics of Mesmerism in the 1790's', and Ford, 102–7.

[24] Glenn Alexander Magee, *Hegel and the Hermetic Tradition*, 215–19.

[25] Robert W. Rieber, *The Bifurcation of Self*, 38–41.

[26] Richardson, 44–6.

[27] Frederick Burwick, *The Damnation of Newton*, 236–54. See also Charles J. Rzepka, 'Re-collecting Spontaneous Overflows'. See also Ford, 103–7. See also Beer, 221–2, 279–81.

Zoo-magnetic Influence' (*CN* 4, 4806). The imagination might be an inflection of a ubiquitous power. The mind might be capable of harnessing this potency and sending the power in new directions. These altered currents might be able to produce in those present a hypnotic effect, producing in them fresh insights into the force unifying the universe. In this scenario, the mind might prove itself capable of two things—overcoming the split between subject and object and altering the disposition of those objects on which it focuses. Coleridge suggests this possibility in an earlier meditation on animal magnetism, claiming that the basis of mesmerism is not far-fetched. 'Magnetists' simply assert that the 'will...of Man is not confined in its operations to the Organic Body' but under certain 'Conditions' is 'capable of acting and producing' 'Effects' on the 'living bodies external to it' (*SW&F*, 590). The will of one mind might be able to transcend its bodily container and alter the makeup of external objects. As Coleridge asserts in an 1817 work, one intoning a poem might affect his audience in the same way that a magnetist might impact his patients. When one recites a poem, the transmission between speaker and auditors is 'a species of animal magnetism, in which the enkindling reciter, by perpetual comment of looks and tones, lends his own will and apprehensive faculty to his auditors. They live for a time in the dilated sphere of his own being' (*BL*, 39).

In other places, though, Coleridge intimates the opposite—that animal magnetism is a materialist phenomenon. In an 1816 essay, he wonders if 'Mesmer's Gesticulations' are on par with other instances of quackery, including the idea that scrofula can be cured by royal touch (*SW&F*, 470). Such a skeptical utterance suggests that mesmerism is not a valid form of spiritual transcendence at all but rather, perhaps, just a psychosomatic manipulation of the nerves. Coleridge expands this criticism in his marginalia to Kluge, jotted around the same time as the piece on scrofula. Like Kluge, Coleridge claims that under certain circumstances one person can act on the body and mind of another so as to 'produce a morbid Sleep'. But in this case Coleridge wonders if the magnetic trance occurs when the 'Brain' of the patient 'awakes while the organs of sense remain in stupor'. If this statement is true, then animal magnetism is a matter purely of the body—of the physical brain continuing to function while the other parts of the anatomy sleep. Indeed, Coleridge in the same set of marginalia asserts that the magnetic sleep is the same as dreaming or as drug-induced hallucinations. In 'certain states of mind', he notes, when the 'will and attention' are 'concentered to an Object', the 'human Body transpires a virus in its *form*' analogous to 'the Galvanic Effluence'. This concentration generates effects like 'those of Opium' or '*the Dream*' (*M*, 371). The body can become so worked up that its brain can produce illusions, deceptions, wispy images.[28]

---

[28] Frederick Burwick, *The Haunted Eye*, 116–18.

OPTICS

So fascinated was Coleridge with the animal magnetism that he invoked it in two of his most powerful poems, 'The Rime of the Ancient Mariner' and 'Christabel' (1798, 1816). In the former, he features the Mariner's 'glittering eye' as a hypnotic power capable of putting those present into a trance. In the latter, Coleridge writes of Geraldine's commanding eye, able to overpower Christabel and make her engage in actions beyond her control. In both cases, Coleridge is interested in the link between galvanism and the eye. This is fitting, for Coleridge during his mature years was fascinated by optics, the science of vision. At times, he wondered if sight is a vessel of supernatural witness, a revelation of cosmic polarity. Other times, he felt that seeing is a purely biological phenomenon, an event dependent on material process.

In the early part of the nineteenth century, there still thrived a centuries-old debate on the nature of light and thus of color. When Newton in the early years of the eighteenth century passed a beam of white light through a prism, he noticed that the light divided into the seven colors of the spectrum. Newton concluded that light is made of indivisible atoms that fragment, when refracted, into different hues. White light, then, is not homogenous. It is, like everything else in Newton's cosmos, an amalgamation of material parts pressed together or pulled apart by gravity.

In the early years of the nineteenth century, Goethe countered Newton's materialist claims.[29] He focused on a distinction overlooked by Newton—between 'physiological colours' and 'physical colours'. The former kind of colors refers to subjective perceptions of hues, on how the eye processes lights and shadows and mixtures of the two. The later sort of colors points to objective occurrences of color, to how color might arise when no perceiver is around. Goethe is interested in how these two kinds of colors work together—in how the eye bridges the gap between the interior and the exterior. In focusing on this interaction, Goethe supposed that colors are composed not of discrete particles but of dynamic interactions between darkness and light. For Goethe, the colors that form when light is passed through a prism are dependent upon the semi-opacity, or the darkness, of the glass. The colors created by the prism are mixtures of whiteness, or visible light, and blackness, or visible darkness. This vision opposes Newton's materialist and quantitative analysis. It assumes that color is a manifestation of ungraspable powers—powers that can be accessed only through their qualitative mergers, their palpable overlaps.[30]

---

[29] Burwick, *Damnation*, 9–53.
[30] Ibid., 9–79. See also Levere, 149–56.

Goethe's ideas shared affinities with the optical theories of the *Naturphilosophen*, namely those of Schelling and Lorenz Oken. In the late eighteenth century, Schelling had proposed that the absolute spirit manifests in various polarized forces. One result of these forces' pulsations is light, a plus–minus vibration of oxygen flowing through ether. In this way, light is but one of many polarized expressions of a ubiquitous consciousness. Schooled in Schelling, Oken in 1808—two years before Goethe published in color theory—released his own anti-Newtonian account of light. Oken argued that the sun causes tension in the pervasive either and that this tension manifests itself as light, a current that travels in straight lines. According to the nature of the ether—sometimes it is indifferent to bodies and sometimes it is dynamically related to bodies—these lines appear as darkness or light. These pervasive cosmic lines—either dark or light—generate blackness and whiteness. All other colors are dependent upon interactions between these two hues.[31]

Coleridge was interested in light and color from a very early age. Even before the turn of the nineteenth century, he was experimenting with a prism, attempting to understand and reject Newton's optics. Around this time, he claimed that a 'clear and sober Confutation of Newton's... {Theory of} Colors... is practicable, the exceeding unsatisfied state, in which Sir I. Newton's first Book of Optics leaves my mind—strongly persuades me' (*M* 12. 3, 1014). Coleridge also asserted that Newton's theory was a 'Fiction', mainly because it fragmented light into seven different parts. Questioning Newton's materialist stance, Coleridge said that he adopted' the doctrine of Pythagoras [!] respecting Colors, as arising from Light and Shadow'[32]. Leaning toward a polarized theory of color, Coleridge in 1812 was anxious to read Goethe. After having read the German poet, Coleridge in 1817 proposed, in opposition to Newton, that light is 'nothing but *visibility* under certain conditions'. He confesses that as early as 1798, he believed—partly based on his reading of Boehme—that 'Sound was = Light under the praepotence of Gravitation, and Color = Gravitation under the praepotence of Light' (*CL* 4, 750–1). Color is not a gathering of distinct bits—it is an attractive and repulsive power manifested by the potency of light. Coleridge expanded this theory in 1820, when he claimed that the Newtonian prism, as a 'dense and semi-opake Whole', casts a shadow. Doing so, it casts whiteness 'by its total *energy*, as qualifying (not intercepting) Light: i.e. the Prism generates *White* within itself'. Likewise, it generates colors 'by the polarizing energies of its parts acting on the White'[33]. Such a vision would intimate that the healthy eye would act as an intermediary between its own interior organization and the external world, that it would synthesize objective darkness and brightness into the various hues of the spectrum and thus overcome the split between subject and object.

Still, although Coleridge generally challenged Newton's theory of color and light, he was not nearly as dogmatic in his criticisms as were Goethe and Oken. Reading

---

[31] Burwick, *Damnation*, 55–8.
[32] Quoted in Levere, 151.
[33] Quoted in Levere, 151.

Oken's attacks on Newton, Coleridge wrote in the margins that the he was skeptical of the philosopher's 'mountebank Boasting and Threatening'. Coleridge even questioned Goethe. Though he lauded the poet's 'impeachment of Newton's experiments' 'by Counter-experiments of his own', he also noted that Goethe 'had not succeeded in convincing or converting a single Mathematician' (*M*, 1014). In fact, Coleridge wondered if Goethe and Oken might be wrong in proposing their dynamic theories of color and if Newton might be right in forwarding his atomic hues. Having studied a French chemist who claimed that the plant's greenness is not a mixture of yellow and blue but homogeneous, Coleridge praises this 'very noticeable fact' as the strongest datum he had yet heard 'in favour of the Newtonian Chromatology'. Open to the possibility that Newton's materialist theory might be right, Coleridge believed that the 'Prismatic Spectrum is a highly complex phaenomenon—so that, in the present state of our knowledge, the same appearance is susceptible to several Solutions' (*CN* 3, 3606). But, in the end, Coleridge would likely recoil from a primary consequence of Newton's color theory: each of us is a material fragment ultimately disconnected from other material parts; hence, we are all of us forever divorced from what we see.[34]

PATHOLOGY

Coleridge's meditations on light are important for reading key moments in his poetry, especially those instances dealing with sight. We think in this regard of 'Dejection: An Ode' (1802) or of 'Constancy to an Ideal Object' (1804–7? 1823? 1826?) or of 'Limbo' (1811). Each of these poems deals with the opposition between successful vision, when the subject and the object interact to produce a synthetic perception, and unsuccessful sight, occurring when the subject and object are divorced and thus devoid of valid perception. In the first instance, we can imagine that the dynamic theory of light holds sway—polarized powers mesh to produce colors that are manifestations of a unifying spirit. In the second, we can suppose that the materialist idea of color lurks—each element in the universe is a fragment alienated from other parts.

This latter scenario—the body divorced from the thriving world—suggests yet another of Coleridge's scientific interests: pathology. In the late eighteenth and early nineteenth centuries, two schools of pathological medicine ruled Europe. The source of both schools was John Brown, the eighteenth-century Scottish physician. Brown's system was appealing to medical thinkers because it was based

---

[34] Ibid., 54–8; Levere, 149–56.

on induction. No more did doctors have to rely on invisible powers such as ethers and fluids. After Brown, who published his masterwork in 1780, doctors could feel comfortable diagnosing the visible symptoms of their patients. Moreover, doctors were empowered to treat disease systematically and not locally—the whole body, Brown thought, needed proper stimulation if diseases were to be assuaged. In addition, doctors found encouragement for treating disease quantitatively; that is, for measuring degrees of excitability in order to ascertain the correct treatment for calming the patient. Finally, Brown's system was not dogmatic—it endorsed neither mechanism, the idea that life is constituted by organization, nor vitalism, the notion that life is a power beyond organization. Such ambiguity allowed scientists to read Brown—as they read Hunter—in divergent ways, with some believing him to be a materialist and others holding that he was an idealist. Coleridge throbbed between these two poles.[35]

The main impetus behind Coleridge's divided sense of pathology was the thought of Beddoes. Almost as myriad minded as Coleridge himself, Beddoes at different times embraced the materialist and the idealist sides of Brunonian medicine. The materialist side of Beddoes—one he shared with Erasmus Darwin—applied Brown's ideas in his Pneumatic Institute. He thought that he could heal physical symptoms by exposing patients to proper combinations of air. An overexcited patient might be breathing too much oxygen—the most vital part of air. For a cure, this patient might sit in a sealed area largely devoid of oxygen. But Beddoes, studied in Kant, read Brown at other times as a transcendentalist. This interpretation came in the form of 'mentalism', based on the assumption that the mind is above the body and controls the body. Such a presupposition might lead to mind-centered therapies. A patient might change his psychological stance toward his disease. This change might alter the symptoms. If depression can cause disease, tranquility can cure it.[36]

Coleridge shared his friend's duplicity toward Brown. As early as 1796, Coleridge exhibited a keen interest in Brown's theories. At this early juncture, under the sway of Priestley and Darwin, Coleridge tended to put a materialist spin on the ideas of the Scottish physician. He wondered if a friend might be 'so weakened by exertion and anxiety, as to make stimulants . . . necessary' to health (CL 1, 154). In the same year, Coleridge showed an awareness of the primary debate raging over Brown. He noted that his friend John Thelwall, as a materialist sharing affinities with Beddoes and Darwin, believes that life is nothing but 'organized matter acted on by external stimuli'. While admitting that this system is just as likely to be valid as any other, Coleridge also forwarded the vitalist position, invoking the notion that life arises from 'a plastic immaterial Nature—all-pervading' (1, 294–5). This ambiguity signals Coleridge's simultaneous fascination with the mentalist position, grounded,

[35] Neil Vickers, *Coleridge and the Doctors*, 43–6.
[36] Ibid., 43–78.

again, on the idea that a power lies outside of matter and controls matter. In 1796, the same year that Coleridge mentioned the materialist take on Brown, he extolled the virtues of the mentalist reading. In a letter to the father of a sick friend, Coleridge claimed that a 'knowledge of the *Mind* is essentially requisite to the well-treating' of the son's malady. The young man need not treat the body proper, but rather he should aspire to 'Sympathy and Calmness' (1, 154). Around the same time, Coleridge speculated on the causes of his own disease—neuralgia. In a letter to another friend, Coleridge asserted that his illness originated in excessive anxiety'. His 'ever-shaping and mistrustful mind' has mingled with 'gall-drops, till out of the cup of Hope' he has '*almost poisoned* [himself] with Despair' (1, 249–50). It is Coleridge's mood that generates his bodily disease—his physical symptoms grow directly from his mental constitution.

Coleridge for the remainder of his years vacillated between materialist and mentalist accounts of his diseases. This duplicity of conviction provides a rich context for understanding the two poems in which Coleridge is the most candid about his maladies: the 1802 'Dejection: An Ode' and the 1803 'The Pains of Sleep'. In both, Coleridge meditates on the causes of his pathologies, both mental and physical. The question in both is this: is the body a mere machine that becomes ill when the parts grow faulty, or is the sick anatomy a manifestation of the diseased soul?

By now the impulse behind Coleridge's heterogeneous interest in science should be clear. Coleridge never wished to specialize in only one scientific discipline. Rather, he desired a universal system of knowledge in which science would play a major role. First and foremost, recall, Coleridge hoped to be a metaphysician. He yearned for a grand philosophical paradigm that would include not only all scientific disciplines but also all art forms. Such a longing led Coleridge in his later years—right around the time that he was brooding on photosynthesis—to search for a method of thought that would synthesize all knowledge. The result of this search is his 'metascientifical' 'Essay on the Principles of Method', from 1818. In this piece, Coleridge establishes the basis of a proper method of inquiry: recognition of the fundamental interaction between mind and matter. For Coleridge, the only way a human being can discover himself in nature is to 'comprehend nature in himself, and its laws in the ground of his own existence'. To look within is to look without. When the thinker activates his Reason, he intuits universal principles that generate the physical world. He realizes a continuity between internal constitution and external process. In the mind, one finds a mirror in which matter is reflected; in matter, one discovers a looking glass in which mind appears. When one apprehends the potencies unifying human and nature, one can then 'reduce Phaenomena to Principles'. One can encounter an 'idea of the common centre, of the universal law, by which all power manifests itself in opposite yet interdependent forces'. Witnessing this spirit, one 'gradually and progressively' comprehends 'the relation of each to the other, of each to all, and of all to each' (*Friend*, 511).

Such supposed interactions between mind and nature led Coleridge elsewhere in the essay to claim that the ideal scientist and the ideal poet are virtually inseparable. In Coleridge's eyes, the proper poet and the proper scientist alike intuit with their Reason the universal law and accordingly then translate events into symbols of that law. Just as the 'lunatic, the lover, and the poet' are to Shakespeare's mind different versions of one universal form, so 'water and flame, the diamond, the charcoal, and the mantling champagne, with it ebullient sparkles' are all metaphors of a principle of unity. Coleridge admits that the propensity of chemistry toward spirit is 'the first charm of [this science] and the secret of the almost universal interest excited by its discoveries'. In this sense, chemistry is not so much a hard science as an artistic endeavor, a revelation of 'the sense of a principle of connection given by the mind, and sanctioned by the correspondancy of nature'. Chemistry reveals the analogical nature of the universe, a field in which everything is a metaphor for everything else, with each somehow manifesting the power of the all. Hence, if 'in Shakespeare we find nature idealized into poetry...so through the meditative observation of a Davy...we find poetry, as it were, substantiated and realized in nature' (*Friend*, 471). Shakespeare translated natural events into symbols of the laws of his mind, thus transforming all of nature into a vast poem. Davy and his scientific colleagues transposed the insights of their imaginations into the laws of nature, therefore turning the poetic mind into a mirror of nature. Taken together, Coleridge's scientist and poet both reveal the cosmos as a poet and a poem, as a creative interaction between intuition and realization, imagination and fact, power and form. Such is Coleridge's dream of a vast synthesis, inside and outside as one.

Works Cited

Abrams, M. H. 1972. 'A light in sound': science, metascience, and poetic imagination. *Proceedings of the American Philosophical Society*: 458–76.

Barfield, Owen. 1971. *What Coleridge Thought*. Middletown, CT: Wesleyan University Press.

Beer, John. 1977. *Coleridge's Poetic Intelligence*. New York: Barnes and Noble.

Burwick, Frederick. 1986. *The Damnation of Newton: Goethe's Color Theory and Romantic Perception*. Berlin and New York: Walter de Gruyter.

—— 1987. *The Haunted Eye: Perception and the Grotesque in English and German Romanticism*. Heidelberg: Carl Winter Universitätsverlag.

Coburn, Kathleen. 1974. Coleridge: a bridge between science and poetry. In *Coleridge's Variety: Bicentenary Studies*, ed. John Beer. Intro. L. C. Knights. Pittsburgh, PA: University of Pittsburgh Press, pp. 81–100.

CORRIGAN, TIMOTHY J. 1980. *Biographia Literaria* and the language of science. *The Journal of the History of Ideas*, 41: 399–419.

ESTERHAMMER, ANGELA. 2001. Coleridge's 'Hymn before Sun-rise' and the Voice Not Heard. In *Samuel Taylor Coleridge and the Sciences of Life*, ed. Nicholas Roe. Oxford: Oxford University Press. 224–5.

FORD, JENNIFER. 1998. *Coleridge on Dreaming: Romanticism, Dreams and the Medical Imagination*. Cambridge: Cambridge University Press.

FULFORD, TIM. 1997. Coleridge, Darwin, Linnaeus: the sexual politics of botany. *The Wordsworth Circle*, 28: 124–30.

—— 2003. 'Conducting the Vital Fluid: The Politics and Poetics of Mesmerism in the 1790's', *Studies in Romanticism*, 43: 57–78.

—— 2001. Theorizing Golgotha: Coleridge, race theory and the Skull Beneath the Skin. In *Samuel Taylor Coleridge and the Sciences of Life*, ed. Nicholas Roe. Oxford: Oxford University Press. 117–33.

JOHNSTON, KENNETH R. 2001. The political sciences of life: From American Panitsocracy to British Romanticism. In *Samuel Taylor Coleridge and the Sciences of Life*, ed. Nicholas Roe. Oxford: Oxford University Press, 47–68.

KIPPERMAN, MARK. 1998. Coleridge, Shelley, Davy, and science's millennium. *Criticism*, 40 (Summer): 409–37.

KITSON, PETER J. 2001. Coleridge and 'the Ouran Utang hypothesis': Romantic theories of race. In *Samuel Taylor Coleridge and the Sciences of Life*, ed. Nicholas Roe. Oxford: Oxford University Press, 91–116.

KOESTLER, ARTHUR. 1967. *Ghost in the Machine*. New York: Macmillan.

LAU, BETH. 2001. The Rime of the Ancient Mariner and Frankenstein. In *Samuel Taylor Coleridge and the Sciences of Life*, ed. Nicholas Roe. Oxford: Oxford University Press, 207–23.

LEFEBURE, MOLLY. 1990. Humphry Davy: philosophic alchemist. In *The Coleridge Connection: Essays for Thomas McFarland*, ed. Richard Gravil and Molly Lefebure. London and Basingstoke: MacMillan, 83–110.

LEVERE, TREVOR H. 1981. *Poetry Realized in Nature: Samuel Taylor Coleridge and Early Nineteenth-Century Science*. Cambridge: Cambridge University Press.

MAGEE, GLENN ALEXANDER. 2001. *Hegel and the Hermetic Tradition*. Ithaca, NY: Cornell University Press.

MANLY, SUSAN. 2001. Jews, Jubilee, and Harringtonianism in Coleridge and Maria Edgeworth: Republican conversions. In *Samuel Taylor Coleridge and the Sciences of Life*, ed. Nicholas Roe. Oxford: Oxford University Press, 69–90.

McFARLAND, THOMAS. 1969. *Coleridge and the Pantheist Tradition*. Oxford: Oxford University Press.

McKUSICK, JAMES C. 1996. Coleridge and the economy of nature. *Studies in Romanticism*, 33: 375–92

—— 2001. 'Kubla Khan' and the theory of the Earth. In *Samuel Taylor Coleridge and the Sciences of Life*, ed. Nicholas Roe. Oxford: Oxford University Press, 134–54.

MODIANO, RAIMONDA. 1985. *Coleridge and the Concept of Nature*. London and New York: Palgrave Macmillan.

PARIS, JOHN AYRTON. 1831. *The Life of Sir Humphry Davy*. 2 vols. London: H. Colburn and R. Bentley.

PERRY, SEAMUS. 1999. *Coleridge and the Uses of Division*. Oxford and New York: Oxford University Press.

PERRY, SEAMUS. 2001. Coleridge and the end of autonomy. In *Samuel Taylor Coleridge and the Sciences of Life*, ed. Nicholas Roe. Oxford: Oxford University Press, 246–270.

RICHARDSON, ALAN. 2001. *British Romanticism and the Science of the Mind*. Cambridge: Cambridge University Press.

RIEBER, ROBERT F. 2007. *The Bifurcation of the Self: The History and Theory of Dissociation and Its Disorders*. New York: Springer.

ROE, NICHOLAS. 2001. Coleridge and the sciences of life. In *Samuel Taylor Coleridge and the Sciences of Life*, ed. Nicholas Roe. Oxford: Oxford University Press, 1–21.

RZEPKA, CHARLES J. 2007. Re-collecting spontaneous overflows: Romantic passions, the sublime, and Mesmerism. *Romantic Circles Praxis Series*. http://www.rc.umd.edu/praxis/passions/rzepka/rzp.html-64KB—15 February.

SHAFFER, ELINOR. 2001. Myths of community in the *Lyrical Ballads* 1798–1998: The Commonwealth and the Constitution. In *Samuel Taylor Coleridge and the Sciences of Life*, ed. Nicholas Roe. Oxford: Oxford University Press, pp. 25–46.

VICKERS, NEIL. 2004. *Coleridge and the Doctors: 1795–1806*. Oxford: Clarendon Press.

WILSON, ERIC. 2004. *Coleridge's Melancholia: An Anatomy of Limbo*. Gainesville, FL: University Press of Florida.

—— 2006. Matter and spirit in the age of animal magnetism. *Philosophy and Literature*, 30 (2): 329–45.

WYLIE, IAN. 1989. *Young Coleridge and the Philosophers of Nature*. Oxford: Oxford University Press.

PART V

RECEPTION

CHAPTER 34

COLERIDGE'S LITERARY INFLUENCE

SEAMUS PERRY

THE achievement is so various, and the literary influence so diverse, that no generalization here can be useful: there is no single distinctive 'Coleridgean' idiom or manner for later poets to appropriate or to reject (which might help explain the absence of decent parodies). Neither are the lines of influence always clearly defined: no subsequent ballad can hope to escape the example of 'The Ancient Mariner'; and for some, such as Wilde's *Ballad of Reading Gaol*, its example is unhelpfully overwhelming;[1] but it would be tendentious to find in all modern balladry a series of re-written Mariners.

Among his contemporaries, it is of course Wordsworth who felt the impact most momentously: he would not have become Wordsworth, most particularly not the author of *The Prelude*, had he evaded Coleridge's sway, even if what he became was never quite what Coleridge had envisaged for him; but to say so is to broach a vast and intricate subject, ranging widely beyond the merely literary, and a proper treatment requires space of its own.[2] Beyond Wordsworth, the pattern of influence within Coleridge's own lifetime is already extremely varied, and complicated by the roundabout ways in which some of the most important works made their way out

---

[1] The proximity of Wilde's poem to Coleridge's is briefly and trenchantly dealt with by Harold Bloom, *The Anxiety of Influence: A Theory of Poetry* (New York, Oxford University Press, 1973), 6.

[2] The topic is discussed in this volume by Richard Gravil.

to the public. 'Christabel', for example, originally written between 1797 and 1803, did not appear in print until 1816, but the poem acquired great manuscript celebrity in the meantime. ('We had frequently heard of Mr Coleridge's manuscript of "Christabel"', said one reviewer in 1816, readying himself for disappointment.)[3] Coleridge's performance of the poem had long been a party piece, and a party piece for others as well: it was through John Stoddart's striking recitation that Scott learned of the poem, an exposure which decisively shaped his *Lay of the Last Minstrel* (1805).[4] The Wordsworths thought the likeness improperly close: 'I fear it is to be accounted for by Mr Scotts having heard Christabel repeated more than once...having been exceedingly delighted with C's poem he was led by it insensibly into the same path' (*Early Years*, 632). The indebtedness to Coleridge is indeed sometimes startling, as Byron robustly observed: 'But for him, perhaps, "The Lay of the Last Minstrel" would never have been thought of', Medwin reported in *Conversations of Lord Byron*, 'The line "Jesu Maria shield thee well!" is word for word from "Christabel".'[5] Scott was evidently stung by the publication of such remarks and subsequently offered acknowledgment to Coleridge, handsomely, as that 'due from the pupil to his master' (*Poetical Works*, vi. 24). Coleridge himself protested Scott's honesty, perhaps a little too much (*CL* iii. 355–61). But if at times the dependency of the *Lay* is too plain, other passages show how astutely Scott grasped the potential in Coleridge's experiment with metre—what Scott called 'the singularly irregular structure of the stanzas, and the liberty which it allowed the author to adapt the sound to the sense' (*Poetical Works*, vi. 24). Coleridge advertised his audacity in the preface to the poem, claiming its metre to be founded on 'a new principle: namely, that of counting in each line the accents, not the syllables', with the variation in the number of syllables managed 'in correspondence with some transition in the nature of the imagery or passion'.[6] Whether the metrical principles (or indeed the practice) of Coleridge's poem were quite as revolutionary

[3] *Coleridge: The Critical Heritage*, ed. J. R. de J. Jackson (2 vols.; London, Routledge & Kegan Paul, 1970–1991), 209. (Hereafter *Critical Heritage*.)

[4] See *The Letters of William and Dorothy Wordsworth. The Early Years*, ed. Ernest de Selincourt, revised Chester L. Shaver (Oxford, Clarendon Press, 1967), 633. (Hereafter *Early Years*.) And see Scott's recollections in his 'Introduction' (1830–1) to *The Lay of the Last Minstrel: The Poetical Works of Sir Walter Scott, Bart.* (Edinburgh, Cadell and Whittaker, 1833–4), vi. 23–4. (Hereafter *Poetical Works*.) It was through a recital by John Hookham Frere, similarly, that Scott picked up on Coleridge's poem 'The Knight's Tomb', which he then quoted in *Ivanhoe* (1819) as the work of 'a contemporary poet, who has written but too little': *Ivanhoe*, ed. Graham Tulloch (Edinburgh, Edinburgh University Press, 1998), 79. Coleridge identifies Frere as the mediator (*CL* iii. 381); and see the account, evidently based on Coleridge's own recollections, in James Gillman, *The Life of Samuel Taylor Coleridge* (1 vol. only published; Pickering, 1838), 277–8.

[5] Actually, 'Jesu Maria, shield us well!' (i, l. 5), echoing 'Jesu, Maria, shield her well!' ('Christabel', i, l. 54). Thomas Medwin, *Journal of the Conversations of Lord Byron: Noted during a Residence with his Lordship at Pisa in the years 1821 and 1822* (2nd. edn; Colburn, 1824), 309. Elsewhere in the book (261), Byron is reported to say, '"Christabel" was the origin of all Scott's metrical tales'.

[6] *Christabel: Kubla Khan, A Vision; The Pains of Sleep* (London, Murray, 1816), vii. (Hereafter *Christabel*.)

as he claimed remains a doubtful point: there are many precursors, including Burns and Chatterton and the ballads.[7] Nevertheless, there was something provocative about the movement of the verse: Donald Davie has given a fine account of the rhythmical vitality of Scott's *Lay*, at its best, in which 'the wandering of the stress keeps us alert so as to find it, never in each new line quite where it was in the line before'; and the excellence he describes there is one that emulates a Coleridgean example (though such emulation was only possible, as Davie rightly maintains, thanks to the 'aliveness to verse-movement' that Scott had possessed already).[8] The free or improvisatory quality to the metre looks forward to later departures; and, in particular, commentators have often noted a kinship between Coleridge's claims for metrical innovation and those more famous pronouncements made by Hopkins about 'sprung rhythm' (the novelty of which has been similarly disputed).[9] Hopkins himself discussed the distinction he recollected from Coleridge between 'accent' and 'quantity' (though Coleridge said 'syllables'), and wondered if it did not anticipate his own principle:[10] Ted Hughes, for one, found the two to be 'the very same thing'.[11]

Byron was sensitive to Scott's undisclosed debt, no doubt, because his own *Siege of Corinth* leant on 'Christabel' too: 'I am partly in the same scrape myself', he admitted gamely to Coleridge.[12] Byron's note to *The Siege* confessed 'a close, though unintentional, resemblance': 'Was it the wind, through some hollow stone, / Sent that soft and tender moan? / He lifted his head, and he looked on the sea, / But it was unrippled as glass may be ....'.[13] The lines don't have much of the original's metrical fizz, but they show the influence all the same. Byron had heard the poem recited by Scott, and the impact was startling:

Last Spring I saw W[alte]r Scott—he repeated to me a considerable portion of an unpublished poem of yours—the wildest & finest I ever heard in that kind of composition—the title he did not mention—but I think the heroine's name was Geraldine—at all events—the 'toothless mastiff bitch'—& the 'witch Lady'—the descriptions of the hall—the lamp suspended from the image—& more particularly of the *Girl* herself as she went forth in the evening—all took a hold on my imagination which I never shall wish to shake off.

(*Letters*, iv. 318–19)

---

[7] See J. C. C. Mays's discussion: *CPW* i. 482, n.

[8] 'The Poetry of Sir Walter Scott (Chatterton Lecture on an English Poet)', *Proceedings of the British Academy*, 47 (1961): 61–75, 68.

[9] See, for example, Karl Shapiro, 'English Prosody and Modern Poetry', *ELH* 14 (1947): 77–92, 87–9.

[10] *The Correspondence of Gerard Manley Hopkins and Richard Watson Dixon*, ed. Claude Colleer Abbott (London, Oxford University Press, 1935), 18.

[11] *Winter Pollen: Occasional Prose*, ed. William Scammell (London, Faber, 1994), 329.

[12] *Byron's Letters and Journals*, ed. Leslie A. Marchand (12 vols.; London, Murray, 1973–94), iv. 321. (Hereafter *Letters*.)

[13] 'The Siege of Corinth', lines 476–9, and Byron's note: *The Complete Poetical Works*, ed. Jerome J. McGann (7 vols.; Oxford, Clarendon Press, 1980–93), iii. 338; 486.

It is very nice that he should remember the *heroine* as Geraldine. 'Christabel' is one of several works that helped shape Byron's literary wickedness: as one commentator puts it (with *Mazeppa* in view) Coleridge's vision of 'evil in the world as a positive and powerful force whose agent is, however unwittingly man himself, as seen in the [Ancient] Mariner's motiveless crime and in Christabel's transformation, clearly had a profound effect upon Byron's mind'.[14] The remark suggests, additionally, that what mattered to Byron more than the metrical experimentalism of the poem was its atmosphere; and Byron is not peculiar here: George Watson is right to say that the 'real successors to "Christabel" are not direct metrical successors' but other poems of the nineteenth century 'that have nothing to do with the rhyming four-footer'.[15] Keats's 'The Eve of St Agnes' is perhaps the most prominent example: Thomas McFarland has even suggested than Keats wrote his poem with 'Coleridge's poem open before him'.[16] Charles Lamb greatly admired Keats's desciption of Madeline (lines 208–43) in which he found 'a delicacy worthy of Christabel':[17] the poem tiptoes about the erotic reality of Madeline's preparations for bed with rapt but discreet attention: one thing that Keats had learnt from Coleridge's poem was a lovely tact in leaving things unsaid, or half-said ('and sees, / In fancy, fair St Agnes in her bed, / But dares not look behind, or all the charm is fled').[18] But often in 'Christabel', of course, leaving things unsaid, or half-said, works to a different, more insinuating, gothic effect—what Coleridge himself called 'witchery by daylight' (*Table Talk*, i. 410): 'Behold! her bosom and half her side— / A sight to dream of, not to tell!' (i, lines 252–3). Reviewers at the time offered laboriously puzzled paraphrases of the story and complained that they could not make anything of it: 'we are wholly unable to divine the meaning of any portion of it', Thomas Moore boasted, of the 'Conclusion' to the second part, scarcely an impenetrable piece of writing (*Critical Heritage*, i. 231); and the poem's purposeful obscurity provoked some obvious, dull parodies.[19] Hazlitt was mischievous but far from obtuse when he speculated about the poem's murky secrets: 'There is something disgusting at the bottom of his subject, which is but ill glossed over by a veil of Della Cruscan sentiment and fine writing—like moon-beams playing on a charnel house, or flowers strewed on a dead body' (*Critical Heritage*, i. 207). The Della Cruscan jibe is pretty off the point; but Hazlitt is nevertheless on to something important

---

[14] Robert F. Gleckner, *Byron and the Ruins of Paradise* (Baltimore, MD, Johns Hopkins University Press, 1967), 308.

[15] George Watson, *Coleridge the Poet* (London, Routledge & Kegan Paul, 1966), 110.

[16] Thomas McFarland, *Originality and Imagination* (Baltimore, MD, Johns Hopkins University Press, 1985), 143. The parallels are noted in detail by Jack Stillinger, *Romantic Complexity: Keats, Coleridge, and Wordsworth* (Urbana, IL, University of Illinois Press, 2006), 47–52.

[17] *Lamb as Critic*, ed. Roy Park (London, Routledge & Kegan Paul, 1980), 243.

[18] Lines 232–4: *The Poems of John Keats*, ed. Miriam Allott (London, Longman, 1970), 468.

[19] The several parodies are cited in Chris Koenig-Woodyard, 'sex—text: "Christabel" and the Christabelliads', *Romanticism On the Net* 15 (August 1999) [26 February 2008]. http://users.ox.ac.uk/~scat0385/parodyxtabel.html.

about the way the verse plays at keeping secrets, and more receptive souls found the effect positively thrilling: it was hearing Byron read of 'A sight to dream of, not to tell' that sent Shelley screaming from the room. Later in the century, it was 'Christabel' that Swinburne singled out as the 'loveliest' of Coleridge's poems, though loveliness in this case keeps some characteristically rum company: 'The very terror and mystery of magical evil is imbued with ... sweetness.' 'Christabel' is cast as the precursor of Swinburne's own dark songs of troubling pleasure: 'That sensuous fluctuation of soul, that floating fervour of fancy, whence his poetry rose as from a shifting sea'.[20] It is not hard to make out a connection between the sexy ambivalence of Geraldine and the intoxicating danger of Swinburne's women ('Cold eyelids that hide like a jewel / Hard eyes that grow soft for an hour', 'Curled snakes that are fed from my breast', and the rest of it):[21] 'the ultimate source' for Sappho in 'Anactoria', says Camille Paglia, most plausibly, is the Coleridge poem, partly mediated through the French Romantics 'via his artistic heirs, Byron and Poe'.[22] Swinburne was not shy of his debt: Coleridge was, he said in a late letter, 'the greatest poet ever born into this world'.[23] No wonder that the name of Hazlitt was not to be uttered in The Pines.[24]

'Kubla Khan', which appeared in the same volume as 'Christabel', enjoyed a similar notoriety as a private recital piece long before it became a published text. A poem by Mary Robinson (to whom Coleridge addressed his Skiddaw poem, 'A Stranger Minstrel') responded to a hearing with verses 'To the Poet Coleridge' which give some dim sense of the extraordinariness of the show.[25]

> Now by the source, which lab'ring heaves
>   The mystic fountain, bubbling, panting,
> While Gossamer its net-work weaves,
>   Adown the blue lawn, slanting!
> I'll mark thy *sunny dome*, and view
> Thy *Caves of Ice*, thy fields of dew!

---

[20] *Swinburne as Critic*, ed. Clyde K. Hyder (London, Routledge & Kegan Paul, 1972), 139. (Hereafter *Swinburne*.) Swinburne's essay appears as the introduction to his selection from Coleridge: *Christabel and the Lyrical and Imaginative Poems of S. T. Coleridge* (London, Sampson Low, Son, and Marston, 1869).

[21] 'Dolores', lines 1–2; 26: *The Poems of Algernon Charles Swinburne* (6 vols.; London, Chatto and Windus, 1904), i. 154; 155.

[22] Camille Paglia, *Sexual Personae: Art and Decadence from Nefertiti to Emily Dickinson* (1990; repr., New Haven, CT, Yale Nota Bene, 2001), 477. For Poe and Coleridge, see in the first instance Floyd Stovall, 'Poe's Debt to Coleridge', *Studies in English* 10 (1930), 70–128.

[23] See Earl Leslie Griggs, 'Swinburne on Coleridge', *Modern Philology* 30 (1932) 215–16, 216.

[24] The house where Swinburne lived for many years in the care of Theodore Watts-Dunton: *The Letters of Algernon Charles Swinburne, with Personal Recollections*, ed. Thomas Hake and Arthur Compton Rickett (London, Murray, 1918), 183–4.

[25] *The Poetical Works of the Late Mrs. Mary Robinson, including many pieces never before published* (3 vols.; London, Phillips, 1806), i. 226–9.

Coleridge refers self-deprecatingly to his poem in the preface as 'a psychological curiosity', which might contain an element of bluff, but seems to suggest, too, some genuine blindness on his part to the full significance of the piece: the poem only appeared in print at all because, like 'Christabel', it had struck Byron so much in the performance: the preface alludes to 'the request of a poet of great and deserved celebrity' (*Christabel*, 51). As it happens, Leigh Hunt seems to have been next door during the reading in question: 'He recited his "Kubla Khan," one morning, to Lord Byron, in his Lordship's house in Piccadilly, when I happened to be in another room', Hunt recollected in *Lord Byron and Some of his Contemporaries*: 'I remember the other's coming away from him, highly struck with his poem, and saying how wonderfully he talked.'[26]

The wonderfulness of his utterance matches a wonder in the poem: the main narrative business is an exotic piece of estate management, but its suggestive power lies in the confrontation Coleridge sets up between a tremendous act of human creativity and the world outside. It predates by several years Coleridge's abstract speculations about the marriage of art and nature, of 'subjective' and 'objective'; but those concerns are stirring within the poem in a symbolic form. The opening verse describes the appearance of the pleasure dome upon the Khan's 'decree'; the second turns, in a striking alteration of perspective, to depict the unconstrained sublimities of the surrounding landscape; and the third, in a moment of fleeting synaesthesis, manages to splice the two realms in a 'mingled measure'. Kubla's creativity feels divine and miraculous; but, even without knowing that Coleridge associated the Khan with Cain, the dome is the work of a despot and anyway its achievement already overshadowed by the threatened destruction of 'war'.[27] Coleridge would later theorize the dubious power of such a figure as 'commanding genius' (*Biographia*, i. 32–3); but the moral ambiguity of genius is already powerfully, if implicitly, established within the poem: that would no doubt have been one of the things about it to appeal so powerfully to Byron—rather as it spoke, over a century later, to Orson Welles in *Citizen Kane*.

A modern tradition of poems about poetry stems from 'Kubla Khan', in which a palace or house, or some enclosed territory, represents what's aesthetic, and is placed in contrast with whatever rougher world lies without. Wordsworth's 'Elegiac Stanzas', written after the death of his brother, would be an early and striking example of a poem written in revisionary response: the 'treasure-house divine' in that case is Peele Castle which begins the poem in a moment of breathless wonder, reflected, like the dome, on the water ('Thy Form was floating on a glassy sea'), an altogether appropriate subject for 'the Poet's dream'. But the stanzas, like many of

---

[26] Leigh Hunt, *Lord Byron and Some of his Contemporaries* […] (London, Colburn, 1828), 304.

[27] For Khan and Cain, see John Beer, *Coleridge the Visionary* (London, Chatto and Windus, 1959), 222.

the greatest Wordsworth poems, mistrust the aesthetic that they envisage so beautifully: the serenity of the scene ('Housed in a dream') is abruptly renounced as illusory, and the poem steels itself instead for a future of 'fortitude, and patient cheer, / And frequent sights of what is to be borne'.[28] To say so is to embrace a life without art in a spirit of tragic humanism, regretful but resolved: Tennyson, in his early poem 'The Poet's Mind', regards that life with comical disdain, but recognizes its insistence all the same. The poet's mind is both an unmistakably Xanaduvian landscape ('All the place is holy ground'; 'In the middle leaps a fountain') and the river that runs through it: 'Clear and bright it should be ever, / Flowing like a crystal river; / Bright as light, and clear as wind'. (The rhyme 'ever'/'river' is from Coleridge's poem: lines 23–4.) What impinges upon the poet's mind is not the disturbing natural energy imagined in 'Kubla Khan' but the 'frozen sneer' of some non-specifically sophistical 'sophist'; but it is the fact of impingement at all that matters, registering an unignorable reality without poetry which is in some way inimical to it.[29] The mind-garden is luxuriant but, like the Khan's garden with its 'walls and towers... girdled round', curiously embattled too: Tennyson regards it with wonder and misgiving in equal measure—as he does the analogous aesthetic retreats that feature in 'The Palace of Art' or 'The Lady of Shalott'. Among the modern poets it is Yeats who relived these Romantic dilemmas with the greatest vigour: his masterpieces discover a Coleridgean ambivalence in the aesthetic removal after which his lesser poems hanker. Byzantium is another version of the special, artistic place, sparkly but chilly: the connection with Coleridge's poem was yet clearer in an earlier draft in which the poet longed to see 'St Sophia's sacred dome / Mirrored in water'.[30]

In the fourth and final verse of 'Kubla Khan' Coleridge begins to undo all the good work: without warning, he steps out of his own myth and imagines, within the tentative space of the conditional grammar, as though much more in hope than certain prospect, the possibility of recapturing the vision he has just lost—'Could I revive within me / Her symphony and song...'. You become habituated to the effect of the transition, but it is a startling change of mood from the proclaimed miracle of the third stanza; and although the poem ends with great rhythmic aplomb, a suggestion of something unfinished or unresolved still hangs powerfully in the air. Coleridge went out of his way to stress that in his elaborate choice of title for the 1816 printing: 'Kubla Khan Or, A Vision in a Dream. A FRAGMENT'; and the emphasis is entirely characteristic. Much of Coleridge's intellectual life was devoted to the end of unity and harmony, 'the balance or reconciliation of opposite or discordant qualities' (*BL* ii. 16); and it is a paradox not lost on commentators

---

[28] William Wordsworth, *The Major Works*, ed. Stephen Gill (Oxford, Oxford University Press, 1984; 2000), 326–8.

[29] *The Poems of Tennyson*, ed. Christopher Ricks (London, Longmans, 1969), 224–5.

[30] Jon Stallworthy, *Between the Lines. Yeats's Poetry in the Making* (Oxford, Clarendon Press, 1963; corr. repr., 1965), 95.

that so many of his own poems, 'Kubla Khan' included, should exemplify with such magnificence, rather, fragmentariness and incompletion. Eliot, for one, thought 'Kubla Khan' a poem insufficiently 'written' and lacking 'organization';[31] but Eliot's sharpest responses are often reserved for the poems in which he has the deepest personal interest, and the uncertain play in 'Kubla Khan' between organization and fragmentation resembles more than anything else the mode of a modernist work such as his own 'The Waste Land'. (Yeats, who found much to admire in Coleridge, considered 'Kubla Khan' 'typical' of modern verse.[32]) Eliot's poem works by juxtaposition, an unexplained sequence of voices and landscapes; and among its obvious precursors is Coleridge's 'mosaic technique':[33] 'Kubla Khan', as Rosemary Ashton says, is 'perhaps the first great non-discursive poem' in the language.[34] Eliot, like Coleridge, is drawn to seeing the poet's mind as a place where disparate experience comes together to form new wholes;[35] while, like Coleridge too, his imagination in practice finds a stimulus in the reality of disparateness as much as it finds a serenity in the achievement of order.

The tenacity of 'Kubla Khan' within the literary memory is due in no small part to the inspired invention of the 'person on business from Porlock' with which Coleridge prefaced it. The person from Porlock is one of the great modern myths, a Pooter-like representative of the prosaic and ordinary world, stumbling uncomprehendingly into the special space of genius, like Rosencrantz and Guildenstern in Stoppard's play. Coleridge is attempting to transcribe his amazing and inward creativity, the fruit of 'three hours in a profound sleep, at least of the external senses', when he finds his space overtaken by something alien: so, in a comical and rueful way, the anecdote anticipates the dualisms (between creativity and world, mind and external nature) of the poem to come. In her delightful response, 'Thoughts about the Person from Porlock', Stevie Smith scolds Coleridge for putting the blame for failure on the hapless man; and the question she asks is indeed an excellent one: 'Then why did he hurry to let him in? / He could have hid in the house'.[36] Smith descends with disarming waywardness into the historical details of the person (his name turns out to be Porson), including the doubtful

[31] T. S. Eliot, *The Use of Poetry and the Use of Criticism: Studies in the Relation of Criticism to Poetry in England* (London, Faber and Faber, 1933), 146.

[32] W. B. Yeats, *Essays and Introductions* (London, Macmillan, 1961; 1980), 222. For an enlightening account of Yeats's response to Coleridge, see Matthew Gibson, *Yeats, Coleridge and the Romantic Sage* (Basingstoke, Macmillan, 2000).

[33] Elinor Shaffer's phrase: *'Kubla Khan' and The Fall of Jerusalem: The Mythological School in Biblical Criticism and Secular Literature, 1770–1880* (Cambridge, Cambridge University Press, 1975), 250.

[34] Rosemary Ashton, *The Life of Samuel Taylor Coleridge* (Oxford, Blackwell, 1996), 116. I draw here on some points made in 'Eliot and Coleridge', in *Coleridge's Afterlives*, ed. James Vigus and Jane Wright (Basingstoke, Palgrave, 2008).

[35] See, e.g., 'The Metaphysical Poets': *Selected Prose of T. S. Eliot*, ed. Frank Kermode (London, Faber and Faber, 1975), 64.

[36] *The Collected Poems of Stevie Smith*, ed. James MacGibbon (London, Allen Lane, 1975), 385–6. I draw here on examples discussed in 'Tennyson and the Legacies of Romantic Art', *Romanticism* 14 (2008).

gentility of his ancestors and the name of his cat (it is Flo): the charm of the thing lies in what seem such firmly counter-Coleridgean instincts for the merely common or garden. For Coleridge's popular reputation (which he did much himself to cultivate) was, on the contrary, as a figure of colossal introversion, hardly at home in the common world of families and cats at all. In his adulatory *Life of Coleridge*, James Gillman reproduced some of Coleridge's own notes, in which he cast himself as an archetypically dreamy youth, father to the man: 'My whole being was, with eyes closed to every object of present sense, to crumple myself up in a sunny corner, and read, read, read' (*Life*, 20). Swinburne says, admiringly: 'Coleridge was the reverse of Antæus: the contact of earth took all strength out of him' (*Swinburne*, 137). Writing just after Coleridge's death, in one of several memoirs at once perceptive and impish, De Quincey describes their first meeting, portraying a man only imperfectly alive in the world at large:

I examined him steadfastly for a minute or more; and it struck me that he saw neither myself nor any other object in the street. He was in a deep reverie; for I had dismounted, made two or three trifling arrangements at an inn door, and advanced close to him, before he had apparently become conscious of my presence. The sound of my voice, announcing my own name, first awoke him: he started, and, for a moment, seemed at a loss to understand my purpose or his own situation; for he repeated rapidly a number of words which had no relation to either of us. There was no *mauvaise honte* in his manner, but simple perplexity, and an apparent difficulty in recovering his position amongst day-light realities.[37]

De Quincey assumes a Porlockian role here, intruding upon a consciousness ill-disposed to external objects: there is an immense gallery of Coleridgean portraiture that works variations upon the theme, and the stories (Lamb's especially) are often very funny. More importantly, they help to establish a myth of the artist, one which persists influentially through to the modern period: the historical importance of the legendary Coleridge lies in the way that he exemplifies, or caricatures, an idealist tendency within post-Romantic literary thinking. In his *Romantic Image* Frank Kermode cites a *New Yorker* cartoon joke about a gaunt artist proclaiming 'I paint what I *don't* see':[38] it is a gag primarily about the pretensions of the post-war avant-garde, but the cliché about artists upon which it depends is a thoroughly nineteenth-century invention, and the mythologized Coleridge plays a central part in its establishment. Coleridge himself memorably ascribes to modern poetry 'a fleeting away of external things, the mind or subject greater than the object' (*Lectures 1808–19*, ii. 427–8), a quality he associates especially with the genius of Milton, who, he says in *Biographia*, 'attracts all forms and things to himself, into

---

[37] Thomas De Quincey, 'Samuel Taylor Coleridge: By the English Opium Eater', *Tait's Edinburgh Magazine* NS i (1834), 509–20, 51X.

[38] Frank Kermode, *Romantic Image* (London, Routledge & Kegan Paul, 1957), 4. (Hereafter *Romantic Image*.)

the unity of his own IDEAL' (ii. 27–8). The rhetoric is unmistakably his own; but the underlying assumption—that the poet's mind remakes its raw materials into new kinds of aesthetic reality—might be shared by most of the great moderns; and its foundational principle is the superiority of consciousness (and, specifically, of poetic consciousness) to the crude and lifeless stuff of mere material existence. A disparagement of 'external things' is a key part of the tradition here: 'The wrong of unshapely things is a wrong too great to be told', Yeats wrote, 'I hunger to build them anew';[39] and that disparagement had received its most memorable expression in Coleridge's 'Dejection':

> O Lady! we receive but what we give,
> And in our life alone does Nature live:
> Ours is her wedding garment, ours her shroud!
>   And would we aught behold, of higher worth,
> Than that inanimate cold world allowed
> To the poor loveless ever-anxious crowd,
>   Ah! from the soul itself must issue forth
> A light, a glory, a fair luminous cloud
>   Enveloping the Earth—

The way that such a position anticipates the aesthetic *contemptus mundi* of the symbolists was most compellingly set out by Kermode: a writer such as Wilde might seem spectacularly remote from Coleridge; but, as Kermode persuasively argues, lines run surely from the one literary epoch to the other, linking 'the best writing between Coleridge and Blake at the outset and Pound and Eliot in our own time' (*Romantic Image*, 44).

The person from Porlock would appear, in such an idealist light, the unmitigated villain of the piece: for his arrival shatters the unity of the 'ideal' into fragments; but then, on second thoughts, within a more encompassing Coleridgean context, the disaster of his arrival may not be so clear-cut after all. For 'things' are regarded in quite a different way elsewhere within Coleridge's literary thinking, one very far from the belittlement that anticipates Yeats's distaste before 'uncomely things'.[40] The *locus classicus* for this Coleridgean voice comes in chapter four of *Biographia*, a passage that originally appeared in *The Friend*:

To carry on the feelings of childhood into the powers of manhood; to combine the child's sense of wonder and novelty with the appearances, which every day for perhaps forty years had rendered familiar...this is the character and privilege of genius, and one of the marks which distinguish genius from talents. And therefore is it the prime merit of genius and its most unequivocal mode of manifestation, so to represent familiar objects as to awaken in

---

[39] 'The Lover Tells of the Rose in his Heart': *The Collected Poems of W. B. Yeats* (London, Macmillan, 1950; 1958), 62.

[40] I draw in this part of the essay on some material I have also discussed in 'Coleridge's English Afterlife', in *The Reception of S. T. Coleridge in Europe*, ed. Elinor Shaffer and Edoardo Zuccato (London, Continuum, 2007), 14–26, 24–6.

the minds of others a kindred feeling of sensation concerning them and that freshness of sensation which is the constant accompaniment of mental, no less than of bodily, convalescence. Who has not a thousand times seen snow fall on water? Who has not seen it with a new feeling, from the time he has read Burns' comparison of sensual pleasure

> To snow that falls upon a river
> A moment white—then gone for ever!
>
> (*BL* i. 80–1)

Coleridge is gathering himself to describe the genius of Wordsworth, but the praise answers to something in his own mind too: it is what Coleridge calls elsewhere 'delight in little things, / The buoyant child surviving in the man'.[41] Such perception depends upon a quality of mind, though it does not merely discover a quality of mind ('freshness') but rather a quality of the 'objects': it sets out an aesthetic, to speak in the broadest terms, which regards the world as a proper object of wonder, rather than something 'inanimate' and 'cold'. The relevant theological corollary to this wondering realism is Coleridge's early quasi-pantheism, which looked upon natural scenes with a thrilling awe; and if the place of worldly 'things' in the rich complexity of Coleridge's philosophy of art is an increasingly marginal or troubled one, then that would parallel the fate of an enthusiasm for 'outward forms' within his religious thinking. But the recuperative imagination that he attributes in *Biographia* to Burns long remains an important part of the mix; and it stands at the head of a tradition of nineteenth- and twentieth-century writing in which the character of the poet is principally defined by his ability to defeat habit and to reacquaint his readers with the marvellousness of the commonplace. Carlyle can be especially remorseless on the subject: 'universal Wonder', as the fictive editor writes in *Sartor Resartus*, is 'the only reasonable temper for the denizen of so singular a Planet as ours';[42] but the position occurs in all kinds of temper. Browning, for example, whose Coleridgean credentials otherwise might not look promising, writes in his 'Essay on Shelley' of 'objective' and 'subjective' poets (the terminology itself has a strong tang) and seeks to vindicate the objective, who deals with 'things external': 'it is with world, as starting point and basis alike, that we shall always have to concern ourselves: the world is not to be learned and thrown aside, but reverted to and relearned'. After a protracted period of subjectivity, the objective poet offers 'a supply of the fresh and living swathe'.[43] The defence of art mustered by Fra Lippo Lippi suggests that he has been reading *Biographia*: 'we're made so that we love / First when we see them painted, things we have passed / Perhaps a hundred times nor cared to see; / And so they are better, painted—better to us'.[44]

---

[41] 'The Blossoming of the Solitary Date-Tree', lines 58–9.

[42] Thomas Carlyle, *Sartor Resartus. The Life and Opinions of Herr Teufelsdröckh in three books* (1831; Centenary Edition; London, Chapman and Hall, 1904), 53.

[43] *Peacock's Four Ages of Poetry, Shelley's Defence of Poetry, Browning's Essay on Shelley*, ed. H. F. B. Brett-Smith (Oxford, Blackwell, 1921; 1972), 63–83, 67; 68.

[44] 'Fra Lippo Lippi', lines 300–3: Robert Browning, *Poetical Works 1833–1864*, ed. Ian Jack (Oxford, Oxford University Press, 1970, 1980), 576. (Hereafter *Browning*.)

Thomas Hardy, a great admirer of Browning, similarly defines an artist by his ability to notice 'things' otherwise unremarked, such as fresh foliage in the Spring ('the May month flaps its glad green leaves like wings, / Delicate-filmed as new-spun silk'): '"He was a man who used to notice such things"', Hardy imagines the neighbours saying after his death—rather as the uncomprehending citizens in Browning's 'How It Strikes a Contemporary' remark the fascination with which the poet in their midst scrutinizes humdrum realities.[45] The young Auden was much shaped by Hardy, and his greatest poetry depends upon (in John Bayley's words) 'vivid personal apprehensions of things';[46] while, to come to the contemporary, the poetry of Heaney (one of whose books is entitled *Seeing Things*) partly stems from the conviction that 'Description is revelation!'[47]—a phrase which formed a sort of manifesto for 'Martian' poetry.[48]

Coleridge's own descriptive powers are best displayed in the 'conversation' poems ('Pale beneath the blaze / Hung the transparent foliage': 'This Lime-Tree Bower', lines 47–8); and these poems represent Coleridge's artistic interest in ordinary experience in another influential way too, which is (as their normal generic grouping implies) the experience of ordinary language. The conversation poem builds on the important example of Cowper, but Coleridge recognized that he had done something innovative and influential with his precursor: 'I have some claim to the thanks of no small number of the readers of poetry in having first introduced this species of short blank verse poems—of which Southey, Lamb, Wordsworth, and others have since produced so many exquisite specimens' (*CPW* i. 232). In Coleridge's hands, the conversation poem does not stay levelly 'conversational': as critics have often observed, while it begins within the domestic and familiar, even colloquial in idiom ('Well, they are gone, and here must I remain': 'This Lime-Tree Bower', 1), it typically raises itself to a poetry of vibrant religious experience or introspection, before returning to the quotidian all over again. M. H. Abrams offers the most inclusive account of the genre to which Coleridge's conversation poems prominently belong, 'the greater Romantic lyric', and he mentions its afterlife in works by Arnold, Whitman, Stevens and Auden.[49]

Coleridge once described 'Fears in Solitude' as 'perhaps not Poetry—but rather a sort of Middle thing between Poetry & Oratory—*Sermoni propior*' (*PW* i. 469);

---

[45] 'Afterwards', lines 2–3; 4: *The Complete Poems of Thomas Hardy*, ed. James Gibson (New Wessex Edition; London, Macmillan, 1976), 553. Browning, 633–6.

[46] John Bayley, *The Romantic Survival. A Study in Poetic Evolution* (London, Constable, 1957), 156.

[47] Seamus Heaney, *Seeing Things* (London, Faber, 1991). 'Fosterage', in *North* (London, Faber, 1975), 71.

[48] Craig Raine, whose *A Martian Sends a Postcard Home* (Oxford, Oxford University Press, 1979) gives its name to the 'school', once said in interview, 'Heaney has a poem of which the first line is '"Description is revelation!"', and I believe that': *Viewpoints. Poets in Conversation with John Haffenden* (London, Faber, 1981), 179.

[49] M. H. Abrams, 'Structure and Style in the Greater Romantic Lyric', in *The Correspondent Breeze. Essays on English Romanticism*, ed. Jack Stillinger (New York, Norton, 1984) 75–108, 75–8.

and the conversation poems occupy a similarly flexible and ambiguous space between 'Poetry' and what Wordsworth called in the 'Preface' to *Lyrical Ballads*, 'language really used by men'.[50] 'Sermoni propiora' is Horatian (*Satires* 1. 4. 42), meaning 'closer to common speech', and Coleridge used it, or at least a variation upon it, 'Sermoni proprioria' ('Belonging, rather, to common speech'), as the epigraph to 'Reflections on having left a Place of Retirement' (*PW* i. 260; 261): he offered as his own joky translation, '*Properer for a Sermon*' (*CL* ii. 864). The idiomatic vitality of the poems grows from the shifting rapport they strike up with the un-'poetic' and ordinarily discursive, and in this they anticipate a wholly characteristic modern manner, in which the relationship between verse and prose is of central concern. Eliot once recollected of his generation: 'it was one of our tenets that verse should have the virtues of prose, that diction should become assimilated to cultivated contemporary speech, before aspiring to the elevation of poetry'.[51] A living connection with speech was crucial to the healthiness of poetry, but the poetry could not seek merely to replicate speech. A modern meditative poem would not normally adopt blank verse, but it would, exemplarily, emulate a Coleridgean 'Middle thing', existing self-consciously between the voices of elevated lyric and of personal address, positioning itself between the purer languages of art, on the one side, and of life, on the other:

> If it form the one landscape that we, the inconstant ones,
>   Are consistently homesick for, this is chiefly
> Because it dissolves in water.[52]

'Reflections on having left a Place of Retirement' had a subtitle in its original appearance: '*A Poem, which affects not to be* POETRY' (*PW* ii. 353). You might affect your poem not to be 'POETRY' for reasons of gracious self-deprecation; alternatively, it might be a sign that you have lost your nerve; and in nothing more does Coleridge's poetry anticipate the literary moderns than in the acknowledgement it sometimes makes of its own inadequacy or falling-short. Poetic inadequacy can take a showily textual form, as in 'The Blossoming of the Solitary Date-Tree', in which some 'lost' verses are printed as prose paraphrases with the invitation to the reader to render them into metre, or (as we have already seen) in 'Kubla Khan', where an elaborate paratextual frame advertises the poem as a failure; elsewhere, it expresses itself as a more tacit, often comical ruefulness about proceedings ('Well!— / It is a father's tale': 'The Nightingale', lines 105–6); and sometimes it can emerge in full-blown crisis, as, most influentially, in 'Dejection: An Ode', a poem Eliot knew well.[53] 'Dejection' is the forerunner of the modern lyric of

---

[50] *Lyrical Ballads*, ed. Michael Mason (Harlow, Longman, 1992), 59.

[51] T. S. Eliot, *On Poetry and Poets* (London, Faber, 1957), 160.

[52] 'In Praise of Limestone', in W. H. Auden, *Collected Poems*, ed. Edward Mendelson (London, Faber, 2007), 538.

[53] I gather together some bits of evidence in 'Eliot and Coleridge', 230–1.

desolation, in which poetry manages to get itself written within some paradoxical space which poetry has long forsaken. In his prose, Matthew Arnold criticized Coleridge as an admirable failure; but his failure was a positively enabling example for Arnold's poems, which self-consciously inhabit a time after the potential for true poetry has come to an end—with the death of Wordsworth, for example ('Memorial Verses, April 1850'). And Arnold is not alone: modern writing is often making a Coleridgean discovery and finding life in the last embers of imagination, by imagining the imagination's last gasp—*Imagination Dead Imagine*, Beckett instructs us.[54]

Works Cited

Abrams, M. H. 1984. *The Correspondent Breeze. Essays on English Romanticism*, ed. Jack Stillinger. New York: Norton.

Ashton, Rosemary. 1996. *The Life of Samuel Taylor Coleridge*. Oxford: Blackwell.

Auden, W. H. 2007. *Collected Poems*, ed. Edward Mendelson. London: Faber.

Bayley, John. 1957. *The Romantic Survival. A Study in Poetic Evolution*. London: Constable.

Beckett, Samuel. 1984. *Collected Shorter Prose 1945–1980*. London: John Calder.

Beer, John. 1959. *Coleridge the Visionary*. London: Chatto and Windus.

Bloom, Harold. 1973. *The Anxiety of Influence: A Theory of Poetry*. New York: Oxford University Press.

Browning, Robert. 1921. Essay on Shelley. In *Peacock's Four Ages of Poetry, Shelley's Defence of Poetry, Browning's Essay on Shelley*, ed. H. F. B. Brett-Smith. Oxford: Blackwell, 1972, 63–83.

—— 1980. *Poetical Works 1833–1864*, ed. Ian Jack. Oxford: Oxford University Press, 1970.

Byron, George Gordon, Lord. 1973–1994. *Byron's Letters and Journals*, ed. Leslie A. Marchand. 12 vols.; London: Murray.

—— 1980–1993. *The Complete Poetical Works*, ed. Jerome J. McGann. 7 vols.; Oxford: Clarendon Press.

Carlyle, Thomas. 1904. *Sartor Resartus. The Life and Opinions of Herr Teufelsdröckh in three books*. 1831; Centenary Edition; London: Chapman and Hall.

Coleridge, S. T. 1816. *Christabel: Kubla Khan, A Vision; The Pains of Sleep*. London: Murray.

Davie, Donald. 1961. The poetry of Sir Walter Scott: Chatterton Lecture on an English Poet. *Proceedings of the British Academy* 47: 61–75.

De Quincey, Thomas. 1834. Samuel Taylor Coleridge: By the English opium eater. *Tait's Edinburgh Magazine*, NS i: 509–20.

Eliot, T. S., 1957. *On Poetry and Poets*. London: Faber.

1975. *Selected Prose of T. S. Eliot*, ed. Frank Kermode. London: Faber and Faber.

—— 1933. *The Use of Poetry and the Use of Criticism: Studies in the Relation of Criticism to Poetry in England*. London: Faber and Faber.

Gibson, Matthew. 2000. *Yeats, Coleridge and the Romantic Sage*. Basingstoke: Macmillan.

---

[54] Samuel Beckett, *Collected Shorter Prose 1945–1980* (London, John Calder, 1984), 145.

GILLMAN, JAMES. 1838. *The Life of Samuel Taylor Coleridge*. 1 vol. only published; Pickering.

GLECKNER, ROBERT F. 1967. *Byron and the Ruins of Paradise*. Baltimore, MD: Johns Hopkins University Press.

GRIGGS, EARL LESLIE. 1932. Swinburne on Coleridge. *Modern Philology* 30: 215–16, 216.

HAFFENDEN, JOHN. 1981. *Viewpoints. Poets in Conversation with John Haffenden*. London: Faber, 179.

HARDY, THOMAS. 1976. *The Complete Poems of Thomas Hardy*, ed. James Gibson. New Wessex Edition; London: Macmillan.

HEANEY, SEAMUS. 1975. *North*. London: Faber.

—— 1991. *Seeing Things*. London: Faber.

HOPKINS, G. M. 1935. *The Correspondence of Gerard Manley Hopkins and Richard Watson Dixon*, ed. Claude Colleer Abbott. London: Oxford University Press.

HUGHES, TED. 1994. *Winter Pollen: Occasional Prose*, ed. William Scammell. London: Faber.

HUNT, JAMES HENRY LEIGH. 1828. *Lord Byron and Some of his Contemporaries*. London: Colburn.

JACKSON, J. R. de J., ed. 1970–1991. *Coleridge: The Critical Heritage*. 2 vols.; London: Routledge & Kegan Paul.

KEATS, JOHN, 1970. *The Poems of John Keats*, ed. Miriam Allott. London: Longman.

KERMODE, FRANK. 1957. *Romantic Image*. London: Routledge & Kegan Paul.

KOENIG-WOODYARD, CHRIS. sex—text: 'Christabel' and the Christabelliads. *Romanticism On the Net* 15 (August 1999). http://users.ox.ac.uk/-scato385/parodyxtabel.html.

LAMB, CHARLES. 1980. *Lamb as Critic*, ed. Roy Park. London: Routledge & Kegan Paul.

McFARLAND, THOMAS. 1985. *Originality and Imagination*. Baltimore, MD: Johns Hopkins University Press.

MEDWIN, THOMAS. 1824. *Journal of the Conversations of Lord Byron: Noted during a Residence with his Lordship at Pisa in the years 1821 and 1822*. 2nd.edn.: Colburn.

PAGLIA, CAMILLE. 2001. *Sexual Personae: Art and Decadence from Nefertiti to Emily Dickinson*. 1990; repr., New Haven, CT: Yale Nota Bene.

PERRY, SEAMUS. 2007. Coleridge's English afterlife. In *The Reception of S. T. Coleridge in Europe*, ed. Elinor Shaffer and Edoardo Zuccato. London: Continuum, 14–26.

—— 2008. Eliot and Coleridge. In *Coleridge's Afterlives*, ed. James Vigus and Jane Wright. Basingstoke: Palgrave, 224–51.

—— 2008. Tennyson and the legacies of Romantic art. *Romanticism*, 14: 1–13.

RAINE, CRAIG. 1979. *A Martian Sends a Postcard Home*. Oxford: Oxford University Press.

ROBINSON, MARY. 1806. *The Poetical Works of the Late Mrs. Mary Robinson, including many pieces never before published*. 3 vols.; London: Phillips.

SCOTT, WALTER. 1833–1834. *Ivanhoe*, ed. Graham Tulloch. Edinburgh: Edinburgh University Press, 1998.

—— *The Poetical Works of Sir Walter Scott, Bart.* 12 vols. Edinburgh: Cadell and Whittaker.

SHAFFER, ELINOR. 1975. *'Kubla Khan' and The Fall of Jerusalem: The Mythological School in Biblical Criticism and Secular Literature, 1770–1880*. Cambridge: Cambridge University Press.

SHAPIRO, KARL. 1947. English prosody and modern poetry. *ELH* 14: 77–92.

SMITH, STEVIE. 1975. *The Collected Poems of Stevie Smith*, ed. James MacGibbon. London: Allen Lane.

STALLWORTHY, JON. 1965. *Between the Lines. Yeats's Poetry in the Making*. Oxford: Clarendon Press, 1963; corr. repr.

STILLINGER, JACK. 2006. *Romantic Complexity: Keats, Coleridge, and Wordsworth* Urbana, IL: University of Illinois Press.

STOVALL, FLOYD. 1930, Poe's debt to Coleridge. *Studies in English,* 10: 70–128.

SWINBURNE, ALGERNON CHARLES. 1869. ed., *Christabel and the Lyrical and Imaginative Poems of S. T. Coleridge.* London: Sampson Low, Son, and Marston.

—— 1972. *Swinburne as Critic,* ed. Clyde K. Hyder. London: Routledge & Kegan Paul.

—— 1904. *The Poems of Algernon Charles Swinburne.* 6 vols.; London: Chatto and Windus.

TENNYSON, ALFRED. 1969. *The Poems of Tennyson,* ed. Christopher Ricks. London: Longmans.

WATSON, GEORGE. 1966. *Coleridge the Poet.* London: Routledge & Kegan Paul.

WATTS-DUNTON, THEODORE. 1918. *The Letters of Algernon Charles Swinburne, with Personal Recollections,* ed. Thomas Hake and Arthur Compton Rickett. London: Murray.

WORDSWORTH, WILLIAM. 2000. *The Major Works,* ed. Stephen Gill. Oxford: Oxford University Press, 1984.

—— and COLERIDGE, S. T. 1992. *Lyrical Ballads,* ed. Michael Mason. Harlow: Longman.

—— and WORDSWORTH, DOROTHY. 1967. *The Letters of William and Dorothy Wordsworth. The Early Years,* ed. Ernest de Selincourt, revised Chester L. Shaver. Oxford: Clarendon Press.

YEATS, W. B. 1961, 1980. *Essays and Introductions.* London: Macmillan.

—— 1950, 1958. *The Collected Poems of W. B. Yeats.* London: Macmillan.

CHAPTER 35

···

COLERIDGE'S EARLY BIOGRAPHERS

···

MORTON D. PALEY

THE biography of Samuel College published soonest after his death (not counting obituaries)[1] was Thomas De Quincey's *Samuel Taylor Coleridge*. This appeared in sections in *Tait's Edinburgh Magazine* from September 1834, hardly a month after the poet's death, to January 1835. (It was re-published in De Quincey's *Literary Reminiscences* in 1854.) De Quincey tells how, as a twenty-two-year-old Oxford undergraduate, he sought Coleridge out during the summer of 1807, and gives a memorable image of him: 'his person was broad and full, and tended even to corpulence; his complexion was fair...associated with black hair; his eyes were large and soft in their expression; and it was from the peculiar appearance of haze or dreaminess, which mixed with their light, that I recognized my object' (295). The two men became close for a short time, but their closeness did not last beyond 1810, so the part of De Quincey's narrative that involves first-hand knowledge is limited to a very few years. Of the Coleridges' marriage De Quincey testifies that Sara Coleridge was 'a virtuous wife, and a conscientious mother', but that she 'wanted the original basis for affectionate patience and candour' (301). De Quincey thought this was the reason for Coleridge's frequent 'expression of cheerless despondency' at that time. The Coleridges were, in De Quincey's view, simply incompatible in

---

[1] The obituaries are listed in Haven pp. 78–83.

temperament. This seems a fair assessment, but as De Quincey's narrative continues, we sense a spirit of vindictiveness at times scarcely hidden, as for example, in his description of Coleridge lecturing at the Royal Institution in 1808: 'His lips were baked with feverish heat, and often black in colour; and in spite of the water which he continued drinking through the whole course of the lecture, he often seemed to labour under an almost paralytic inability to raise the upper jaw from the lower' (320). Surely this is not Coleridge but one of those 'With throats unslaked, with black lips baked' in 'The Rime of the Ancient Mariner'.[2] Indeed the Coleridge of de Quincey's account often appears like a fictive construction.

De Quincey's *Coleridge* is chiefly remembered for charging Coleridge with plagiarism, a subject discussed elsewhere in this volume. It also damaged Coleridge's reputation in another way. Coleridge's opium addiction had been known to the members of his immediate circle, to whom he maintained that he had started to take opium as a painkiller and had consequently become dependent on the drug. A few of them were recipients of letters expressing the guilt Coleridge felt and the anguish of his unsuccessful attempts at withdrawal. De Quincey, however, states to a wide reading public 'I believe it to be notorious that he first began the use of opium, not as a relief from any bodily pains or nervous irritations, but as a source of luxurious sensations' (318). Some nineteenth-century readers who might forgive a man who had become a victim of opium out of pain might not have sympathized with one who had turned to it for pleasure. De Quincey, with the air of authority he had assumed on opium-taking—even this article bears the cognomen of 'the English Opium-Eater'—is likely to have been believed on the subject. The biography that came next reinforced that belief.

Joseph Cottle wrote his *Early Recollections Chiefly Relating to the Late Samuel Taylor Coleridge* (1837) because, he said (1: vii), Coleridge had in the *Biographia Literaria* 'passed over, in silence all distinct reference to BRISTOL' (and, it might be added, to Cottle as well). Cottle, a Bristol bookseller in the 1790s, certainly deserved credit for his literary acuteness in appreciating the poetry of Coleridge and Wordsworth at that early time; if for nothing else, he would have gone down in literary history as the original publisher of the *Lyrical Ballads*. He not only paid Coleridge £30 for the second edition of his *Poems on Various Subjects* (1797) but also loaned the poet money for, among other things, his wedding-ring, and advanced the funds (never fully repaid) with which Coleridge bought the paper for *The Watchman*. As a publisher Cottle was patient as well as generous. Coleridge's marked proof pages of the 1797 volume (British Library), more of a palimpsest manuscript than a set of proofs, testify to that. The great value of Cottle's *Early Recollections* (1837) and its successor *Reminiscences* (1847) lies in his close association with Coleridge as friend and publisher during his years in and around Bristol. Cottle publishes many letters for the first time, gives eyewitness accounts of Coleridge preaching and lecturing,

---

[2] *Poetical Works*, Vol. 1, part 1, p. 385, line 356.

and prints recollections of conversations that would otherwise be entirely lost. Cottle says that when Coleridge lectured on Shakespeare at the White Lion in Bristol, his lectures had a 'conversational character', and showed 'little of the toil of preparation'. As a preacher, according to Cottle, Coleridge was more of a lecturer. At Bath he 'wore his blue and white waistcoat' (rather than a clergyman's trad-itional black) and, says Cottle, '... the whole discourse consisted of little more than a Lecture on the Corn Laws!... which... he laboured to show... were cruelty to the poor, and the alone cause of the prevailing suffering, and popular discontent' (1: 118). Invited to preach a second time, Coleridge sent word that he 'would give the congregation another sermon... on the Hair Powder Tax!' Of course in 1796 many men who opposed war taxes refused to powder their hair, and in 1837 the Corn Laws, which kept the price of bread high, were still being debated. But Cottle—like the later Coleridge himself—wants to make Coleridge's political and religious concerns—they were really the same—appear trivial. His first volume concludes with the publication of *Lyrical Ballads* 'about Midsummer, 1798', the departure of Coleridge and the Wordsworths for Germany, and Cottle's ending his business as a bookseller.

Coleridge visited Bristol in 1807, and to Cottle's 'unspeakable pleasure', said that he had renounced Socinianism (i.e., Unitarianism) and declared 'his deepest conviction, of the truth of Revelation; of the Fall of Man; of the divinity of Christ, and redemption alone through his blood' (2: 76). There was then a gap of some seven years before the two met again. Coleridge spent a considerable time in Bristol in 1814–15, which is the only other period of his subject's life on which the author had first-hand knowledge.[3] Cottle gathered many anecdotes from Coleridge during this period, and appears to have accepted them uncritically. For example, he tells how Coleridge left Rome in 1806, after being warned by the Prussian Minister Alexander von Humboldt that he was in danger from Napoleon, given a passport and a carriage by the pope, and exited in the entourage of Napoleon's uncle Cardinal Fesch. Coleridge had given a variant of this story in *BL* (1: 216), and Cottle's credulous re-telling of it continued its plausibility for a long time to come. It was, however, neither Cottle's strengths nor the weaknesses as a biographer, nor his complete indifference to textual accuracy, that attracted attention. What created a sensation was Cottle's giving the public a detailed account of Coleridge's opium habit in Coleridge's own words.

Cottle had foreseen this reaction. In his preface he declares that some will 'denounce all reference to Mr. Coleridge's unhappy passion for *Opium*' (xvii), but says that he will give not 'a fictitious display' but 'a faithful exhibition of the life of the individual'. The extent to which a biographer was privileged to include the details of his or her subject's personal life was yet to be agreed on. Cottle's introducing the subject of Coleridge's addiction to a wide readership upset

---

[3] The last letter Cottle received from Coleridge was dated 10 March 1815.

Coleridge's relatives and close friends.[4] In defending this, Cottle asserted that his subject was 'a man who, from his intellectual eminence, ceases to be private property, but is transferred, with all his appendages, to the treasury of the public' (1: 18). There was also a confessional letter that Coleridge had left (with his friend Josiah Wade), with the intention, says Cottle, of presenting himself as a cautionary example after his death. Cottle prints this letter, as well as a long expostulation from himself to Coleridge, commencing 'I am afflicted to perceive that Satan is so busy with you, but God is greater than Satan' (1: 159). As a reviewer of Cottle's second edition wrote in *The Times* in 1847: 'It is astonishing how much you may abuse a man if you will but do it in a reverent spirit, and, as it were, for the good of the object abused'.

Although Cottle knew that the probable origin of Coleridge's opium habit was the relief of physical pain, he did not see fit to mention this in the course of 38 pages devoted to Coleridge's addiction. Yet James Gillman had sent him this information on 2 November 1835:

After Mr Coleridge's decease, his body was inspected by two able anatomists, appointed by Mr Green: a task too painful for either him or me to perform. The left side of the chest was nearly occupied by the heart, which was immensely enlarged, and the sides of which were so thin as not to be able to sustain it's weight when raised. The right side of the chest was filled with a fluid enclosed in a membrane having the appearance of a cyst, amounting in quantity to upwards of three quarts, so that the lungs on each side were completely compressed—This will account sufficiently for his bodily sufferings, which were almost without intermission during the progress of the disease, and will explain to you the necessity of subduing these sufferings by narcotics, and of driving on a most feeble circulation by stimulants—which his case had imperatively demanded—This disease, which is generally of slow progress, had it's commencement in Coleridge more than 30 years before his death. (*CL* 6: 992).

Perhaps Cottle did wish to deter other sufferers from chronic pain from following Coleridge's example, but his omission of Gillman's information hardly accords with his prefatory statement that he was attempting 'to exhibit what Biography *ought to be*, in order to redeem its character, an undisguised portrait of the man...' (1: xxv).

Shortly after its publication, Henry Nelson Coleridge ferociously attacked Cottle's *Early Recollections* in an anonymous (as all reviews of course were) review in the *Quarterly*. 'The refuse of advertisements and handbills, the sweepings of a shop, the shreds of a ledger, the rank residuum of a life of gossip,—this forty-years' deposit of Bristol garbage, smeared in the very idiocy of anecdote-mongering on a shapeless fragment, and a false name scratched in the filth', H. N. Coleridge called it (25). Refusing to believe that Coleridge had meant his confessional letter to be

---

[4] Ironically, none of these took legal action, but Cottle, who had represented the servants of Hannah More in, to say the least, an unflattering light, was subjected to a series of lawsuits by Charles Tidy, More's former coachman; the upshot was that Cottle had to pay nearly £1000 (B. Cottle, 21).

published, he angrily questions Cottle's claim that a man like Coleridge becomes public property. 'Does a great man cease to be a man?' asks Coleridge's son-in-law (30). Whatever the personal feelings unleashed in this dispute, this is the nub of the question. Cottle was hardly a disinterested biographer, but even if he had been, the same question would have been raised.

Cottle's second edition, now entitled *Reminiscences of Samuel Taylor Coleridge and Robert Southey*, appeared in 1847. There are indeed some important differences between it and its predecessor. *Reminiscences*, as its full title indicates, contains much more material on Southey than the first. Cottle reduced to a footnote a detailed account (1: 157–75) of how Sir Herbert Croft obtained Chatterton's letters from the poet's sister under false pretences and used them in *Love and Madness*, leading Cottle and Southey to bring out *The Works of Thomas Chatterton* (Longman and Rees, 1803) for the benefit of the sister and her daughter (145–7 n.). *Recollections* had also included a long reply in prose and verse (1: 111–23) to Byron's satirical lines on Joseph and his brother Amos, published in *English Bards and Scotch Reviewers* in 1809, which concluded:

> Had Cottle bent o'er the desk, or, born to useful toils,
> Been taught to make the paper which he soils,
> Ploughed, delved, or plied the oar with lusty limb,
> He had not sung of Wales, nor I of him.[5]

(lines 406–10)

Probably Cottle realized that calling attention to Byron's satire was not in his own best interest. In any event, he eliminated his response. But on the subject of Coleridge and opium Cottle stuck to his guns. In the Introduction that replaced and drew material from the former Preface, he stated: 'In preparing the following work, I should gladly have withheld that one letter of Coleridge to Mr. Wade (p. 394) had not the obligation to make it public have been imperative; concealment would have been injustice to the living, and treachery to the dead' (vii), and he was indeed true to his word. No doubt those who took Henry Nelson Coleridge's side would have agreed with Miss Bordereau in Henry James's *The Aspern Papers*, who, on discovering the narrator about to search her desk for the love letters of the poet Jeffrey Aspern 'hissed out passionately, furiously: "Ah you publishing scoundrel!"' (James, 118).

The second biography to appear, just a year after Cottle's *Early Recollections*, was *The Life of Samuel Taylor Coleridge* by James Gillman, published by William Pickering (who had also published all three three-volume editions of the *Poetical Works*). As Coleridge had lived with Gillman and his wife Anne from 1816 until his death, and Gillman had been Coleridge's doctor as well, this book could have been

---

[5] 'Wales' refers to *The fall of Cambria: A Poem By Joseph Cottle* (London: Longman, Hurst, Rees, and Orme, 1808).

rich in information about its subject's later life. However, Gillman's *Life* was intended as the first volume of a work whose second volume never appeared, and the narrative stops in 1819. For all but three years of it, Gillman had to rely on Coleridge's memories, those of mutual friends and acquaintances, and published material.

Early on we have anecdotes of Coleridge's childhood, most of them familiar from the *Biographia Literaria* (from which Gillman quotes at great length) and sources such as Charles Lamb's 'Christ's Hospital Five and Thirty Years Ago': Coleridge's schooling, his friendship with Lamb, his chance encounter with a man in the street who bought him a membership in a circulating library in Cheapside, floggings by his schoolmaster James Boyer, and the like. On Coleridge's time at Cambridge, Gillman quotes at length from the account published by Coleridge's Jesus College friend Val le Grice in the *Gentlemen's Magazine*. Gillman is inclined to take a rosy view of incidents in Coleridge's life, as when he says that Coleridge gave all his cash to beggars in Chancery Lane before enlisting in the dragoons, with no mention of the lottery ticket on which Coleridge had pinned his hopes. Coleridge's release from the army is effected in *The Life* without any expenditure by his relatives. His leaving Cambridge is explained by his own genius: 'However excellent for the many, the system adopted by our universities was ill suited for a mind like Coleridge's, and there were some who felt that a College routine was not the kind of education which would best evolve, cultivate, and bring into training powers so *unique*' (63). Without at all disputing the general truth of this statement in view of the moribund state of both Oxford and Cambridge at the time, we have to ask what insight it gives us into Coleridge. Both Wordsworth and Byron completed their Cambridge degrees and nevertheless did some soaring. Gillman even says of the Pantisocracy scheme 'it is doubtful whether he [Coleridge] and Southey were really in earnest at the time it was planned' (69). Perhaps Coleridge intentionally gave his future biographer this impression. Gillman does not deny the influence of William Frend on Coleridge, or the sincere conviction of Coleridge's political addresses in Cambridge and Bristol, but he does reprint the long passage from the *Biographia* in which Coleridge makes fun of his younger self selling *The Watchman*, thus collaborating with his subject in trivializing his earlier political commitments.

Gillman covers Coleridge's years in Bristol and its vicinity without even mentioning Joseph Cottle, not even in connection with *Religious Musings*, which Cottle had done so much to encourage. He lets the *Biographia* tell the genesis of the *Lyrical Ballads*, and for Coleridge's preaching he reprints several pages of Hazlitt's 'My First Acquaintance with Poets'. For Coleridge's time in Germany Gillman extracts a considerable part of 'Over the Brocken', originally published in *The Amulet* for 1828. One can of course understand why Gillman fell back on such sources. Although Gillman had won a prize from the Royal College of Surgeons for his *Dissertation on the Bite of a Rabid Animal* (London, 1812), he knew himself no literary man, and so reached out for support to the writings of those who were, especially those of his subject. We do sense Coleridge's presence at times, as when Gillman writes of how Coleridge felt oppressed by 'the monotonous sameness of the blue sky' of Malta, and of the terrible pain in the bowels that Coleridge suffered there, 'which neither opium, ether, nor peppermint, separately or combined, could relieve' (171). The 'gap in his [Coleridge's] minutes' for Coleridge's residence in Rome, Gillman says, 'is partly filled up by his own verbal account, repeated at various times to the writer of this memoir', and continues: 'While in Rome, he was actively employed in visiting the great works of art, statues, pictures, buildings, palaces, &c. &c. observations on which he minuted down for publication' (179). Gillman accepts a version of Coleridge's departure from Italy only slightly different from Cottle's. In Gillman's narrative (as in Cottle's) the American ship on which Coleridge traveled 'was chased by a French vessel, which caused Coleridge to throw his papers overboard', but Gillman adds 'and thus to his great regret, were lost the fruits of his literary labors in Rome'. The pursuing ship was, according to Coleridge's letter to Daniel Stuart of 22 August 1806, a 'Spanish Privateer Ruffian' (*CL* 2: 1177), but this could involve only a later slip of memory on Coleridge's part. More important, were the writings of Coleridge's stay in Italy indeed lost in this manner? As Kathleen Coburn puts it, 'Perhaps we shall never know; it is difficult to believe that the only memorials of his weeks in Naples, Rome, and Florence were those that have survived to us' (*CN* 2: xvi).

Gillman asserts that De Quincey 'made several mistakes' in his memoir of Coleridge published in *Tait's Magazine*. One of these is 'of Coleridge's so borrowing the property of other writers as to be guilty of "petty larceny"'. To this Gillman replies with an excuse that can no longer be maintained seriously: 'with equal justice might we accuse the bee which flies from flower to flower in quest of food, and which, by means of the instinct bestowed upon it by an all-wise Creator in quest of food, extracts its nourishment from the field and from the garden, but *digests* and *elaborates* it by its own *native* powers.' Gillman is on firmer ground, being the close friend best qualified on the subject, in arguing that Coleridge became addicted to opium as a result of trying to alleviate the pain of rheumatism (not for pleasure, as De Quincey had said) 'till he had acquired a habit too difficult to control' (245–6).

In chapter 4 Gillman at last reaches the events about which he knew most. On 9 April 1816 a doctor named Joseph Adams wrote to Gillman about an unnamed literary man who had unsuccessfully tried to break his opium habit, and who 'has proposed to me to submit himself to any regimen, however severe' (271). The unfortunate literary man wished to domicile himself with a doctor who would prevent him from taking opium. 'As he is desirous of retirement, and a garden, I could think of no one so readily as yourself'. Out of 'commiseration and interest' Gillman went to see Adams the following day. He learned that several doctors had actually advised Coleridge against discontinuing opium! Gillman and Adams agreed that Adams would drive Coleridge to Highgate that evening, but in the event Coleridge came alone. Gillman well conveys the intensity he felt after their meeting: 'We parted with each other, understanding in a few minutes what perhaps under different circumstances, would have cost many hours to arrange; and I looked with impatience for the morrow, still wondering at the apparent chance that had brought him under my roof. I felt indeed almost spell-bound, without the desire of release' (273). When Coleridge came next he bore with him perhaps the most unusual precious gift ever brought by a new lodger—the proof sheets of *Christabel*!

In defense of Gillman's book, it must be said that biographical literature in his time was still often made up largely of extracts from the subject's writings, and also that he did a real service in printing letters and other manuscript material not hitherto seen by the reading public. Some of Coleridge's printed material was difficult to obtain, and some—the prospectuses of some of Coleridge's lectures, for example—had never been in print except in the most literal sense. The frustrating thing about Gillman's *Life* is that he was in a position to say so much! No one had lived with Coleridge for anything like the time that the Gillmans did. No doubt volume 2 would have told us a great deal about Coleridge's daily life during that period, although it would have been out of character for Gillman to reveal anything to Coleridge's detriment. We must be very grateful to him for what he preserved, as well as for his kindness to a man who at times could be a very difficult genius.

Sara Coleridge, deeply devoted to the absentee father who had not even attended her wedding, wrote an Introduction to the new edition of the *Biographia Literaria* prepared by her late husband and herself and published in 1847 by William Pickering. Although not a book in its own right, this lengthy introduction, considering its source, deserves mention here. An astute and learned scholar, Coleridge's daughter begins with a rebuttal to the charges of plagiarism brought by James Frederick Ferrier in 1840, a subject discussed elsewhere in the present volume. However, the 60 pages following this are on other subjects. Sara Coleridge pictures her father as having had an affectionate spirit, and says that some friendships slipped away from him 'because he lacked resolution to hold them fast' (xlvii). She defends him against charges from various sources that he was not Catholic or orthodox enough (lx), or that he once engaged in heretical teaching, or that *Aids to Reflection* was 'a half-way house to Anglo-Catholic orthodoxy' (lx–lxx). On the subject of Unitarianism, she is more convincing than was Coleridge himself, saying that 'his Unitarianism was . . . not a satisfaction in the positive divinity of the Unitarians, but . . . a revulsion from certain explanations of the Atonement commonly received as orthodox . . . .' Her very extensive exposition and defense of Coleridge's religious views testifies the extent to which they still provided material for controversy near the mid-century. The last part of the

Introduction begins with the reasons for withdrawing a paragraph of text concerning Wordsworth's detractors because 'those passages contain *personal* remarks, right or wrong, they were anomalies in my Father's writings' (clviii). Sara Coleridge also admits that her father was capable of 'flights of extravagant satire' (clxxvii), perhaps a quality more valued in him today than in 1847. Nevertheless, as far as Coleridge's relations with the established critical journals of his day are concerned, one may easily agree with the author 'that my Father, upon the whole, was more sinned against than sinning' (clxxxi).

Almost immediately after its publication, the second edition of the *Biographia* was reviewed along with Cottle's 1847 *Reminiscences* in a long essay by one of the great American scholars of the time, Charles Eliot Norton.[6] Published anonymously in the *North American Review,* this was, as Richard Haven (128) puts it, 'in effect a biographical monograph', and was later adapted for the memoir of Coleridge prefixed to *The Poetical Works of Coleridge and Keats with a Memoir of Each* (Boston: Houghton Mifflin, 1854). Norton almost immediately states his principle of preferring for the sake of biography *nil de mortuis nisi verum* to *nil de mortuis nisi bonum.* After summarizing Coleridge's life up to his departure from Cambridge, Norton gives an ingenious explanation of how Coleridge could later say that he had never been a Unitarian:

It seems to us that Coleridge was accustomed to adopt opinions of the highest importance, rather from the coincidence with certain temporary theories of his own, than from such a thorough analysis and examination of their foundations, as every reflection man is called upon to make for himself. Of course nothing was more likely than that, with advance in life, his theories should undergo a change, and consequently the opinions founded upon them, until by degrees, by a further process of self-deception, he persuaded himself, that he never had held such opinions, but that there had always been in his mind some reserved clause, as it were, which had given a different character to the whole. (408)

This is an acute observation, and Norton continues that it 'will . . . explain numerous inconsistencies in his character and writings, otherwise unintelligible . . .'. After further summarizing some of the events in Coleridge's life, Norton comes to the question of when he first took opium. Differing with Sara Coleridge, who believed, on the basis of one of her father's letters to Thomas Poole, it was in November 1796, Norton thinks 'it must have commenced still earlier, but he disagrees with De Quincey as to the cause, believing 'his [Coleridge's] repeated asseverations, that bodily pain first led him to use opium' (423). As illustrations of Coleridge's suffering caused by the drug, Norton prints a passage from *The Friend* and the poem 'The Visionary Hope'. He also uses information from sources other than those he is reviewing, such as Le Grice's article, letters by Charles Lamb published by Thomas Noon Talfourd, letters by Coleridge that had appeared in Allsop's 1836 *Letters, Conversations and Recollections of S. T. Coleridge* ('worthless' except for these,

---

[6] For the identification of the author, Haven cites Cushing.

436), and an anonymous account of Coleridge's conversation in 1822, published in *The Gentleman's Magazine*[7] a year before Norton's review.

Norton loses sympathy with his subject after 1816 and never finds it again. Although he remarks on the scarcity of information about Coleridge's later years, he does not attempt to fill this gap by discussing his subject's late works. *Aids to Reflection* is given one sentence, and all that is said of *On the Constitution of the Church and the State* is that it is one of 'three publications that we consider least valuable from Coleridge's pen' (434), the others being the two *Lay Sermons*. His account ends on a strangely condemnatory note. After quoting Coleridge as having said 'By what I *have* effected am I to be judged by my fellow-men; what I *could* have done is a question for my own conscience',[8] Norton sternly disagrees (440). 'Every man', he writes, 'is accountable to his fellow-men for the use which he makes of the talents which are intrusted to his charge. The greater those talents, the greater becomes his responsibility. No one has a right to say, my fellow-men shall not question me. Before the solemn tribunal of the present and the future all men must stand, and according to their works shall they be judged.' This condemnation of Coleridge according to the standard of a sort of secularized Calvinism is at variance with the enlightened tone of most of what preceded it.

Norton's essay reappeared as 'Memoir of the Author' in an 1855 reprint of Derwent and Sara Coleridge's edition of *The Poems of Samuel Taylor Coleridge*, originally published in 1852. There Norton added a long passage from notes taken of his first talk with Coleridge by John Sterling, first published by Archdeacon Hare in his preface to John Sterling's *Essays and Tales* (1848). Sterling shows Coleridge to be, as Mme de Staël had observed before him, incapable of dialogue, but maintains 'On the whole his conversation, or rather monologue, is by far the most interesting I ever heard or heard of' (ci). By far the longest addition is nearly seven pages from Thomas Carlyle's *Life of John Sterling*, published in 1851. Carlyle's famous description of Coleridge on Highgate Hill begins the long excerpt, which is at the same time vivid and disapproving.

> Brow and head were round, and of massive weight, but the face was flabby and irresolute. The deep eyes, of a light hazel, were as full of sorrow as of inspiration; confused pain looked mildly from them, as in a kind of mild astonishment. The whole figure and air, good and amiable otherwise, might be called flabby and irresolute; expressive of weakness under possibility of strength. (civ)

In concluding his essay, Norton removed his severe judgement of 1847, and wrote that 'though his prose works will not, it is probable, be widely read hereafter' (cx), Coleridge had a great influence on the next generation of thinkers. The new memoir nobly ends:

---

[7] The anonymous author says he 'looked for the light of genius which had exercised such influence on his age, but I could not find it' (Norton, 440).

[8] This sentence is from *Biographia Literaria*, 1: 221.

His influence on thought has been transmitted through the lives and works of many men, who, though not to be classed as his disciples, yet received from him intellectual stimulus and fertilization. From Carlyle to Stuart Mill there is scarcely one of the English thinkers of the present day who does not owe much, directly or indirectly, to the teachings of Coleridge. (cxi)

H. D. Traill's *Coleridge* (1884) pulls together what was then known of Coleridge and presents it in concise, readable form. Traill had the advantage a number of printed publications, including Thomas Allsop's Letters, *Conversations, and Recollections of S. T. Coleridge* (1836), as well as *The Life and Correspondence of Robert Southey* (1849), and Christopher Wordsworth's *Memoirs of William Wordsworth* (1851). Traill asserts in his Prefatory Note that there was as yet no complete biography of Coleridge of any appreciable length, and no critical study of Coleridge's works as a whole, and asks the reader's 'infinite indulgence' for his attempt to do both within the confines of the English Men of Letters series. However, the limitations of Traill's *Coleridge* are not altogether externally imposed.

Traill is at his best in writing of Coleridge as a poet. There his appreciation is limited to poems originally written from 1797 to 1802; he dislikes Coleridge's poems of the early and middle 1790s, and discusses no poem later than 'To William Wordsworth' (1807). These are, however, limitations that Traill shared with his contemporaries. Although he dismisses 'Kubla Khan' as 'hardly more than a psychological curiosity' (56), his discussion of other major poems is intelligent and lucid. Of 'Dejection' he makes the interesting suggestion that, had not Coleridge's health dictated otherwise, this ode could have been 'the cradle-cry of a new-born poetic power, in which imagination, not annihilated but transmigrant, would have splendid proved its vitality through other forms of song' (65–6). On Coleridge as a critic, Traill praises the *Biographia* especially for its discussion of Wordsworth's poetry, and he says of the 1811 Shakespeare lectures 'Coleridge . . . is in the domain of Shakespearean commentary absolute king' (156). Coleridge the journalist compels the author's admiration to the point of his saying that 'among the articles in the *Morning Post* between 1799 and 1802 may be found some of the finest specimens of Coleridge's maturer prose style'(81). He accepts Coleridge's view of his importance to the *Morning Post* and the *Courier*, and doesn't appear to have read Daniel Stuart's articles, or at least takes no account of them.

Any biographer's account of Coleridge's personal life would be hampered, as is Traill's, by his necessary ignorance of Coleridge's hopeless love for Sara Hutchinson and of the break, never entirely healed, with Wordsworth in 1810. Traill does discuss the circumstances of Coleridge's marriage, following De Quincey in asserting that the couple loved each other early on and that this continued for at least six years, but that their estrangement was complete by 1806. The story of Coleridge's addiction is treated with sympathy, and Traill dismisses the 'comical malice' (89) of De Quincey's account of its origin. Like Gillman, Traill has no doubt that Coleridge first turned to opium as an anodyne. Coleridge's rheumatic condition and other

688   MORTON D. PALEY

illnesses were the cause, and the climate of the Lake District was further detrimental to his health.

Only the last three of the book's twelve chapters are devoted to Coleridge's life and thought after 1818. *Aids to Reflection* and *On the Constitution of the Church and the State* are given short shrift, and what Traill calls 'the Coleridgean philosophico-theology' (178) is presented out of what appears to be a sense of duty. At last, after a lengthy summary of Joseph Henry Greene's *Spiritual Philosophy*, he exclaims 'It is like offering a traveler a guide-book written in hieroglyphics' (183). Traill was hardly alone in his view of the late Coleridge, but his closing chapter on Coleridge's influence on contemporary thought does a disservice to both subject and reader, entirely omitting, for example, Coleridge's effect on later religious thinking. This is hardly the complete biography and critical study that Traill set out to deliver.

To the German professor Alois Brandl belongs the distinction of having written the first book on Coleridge to be published in a foreign language. *Samuel Taylor Coleridge und die Englische Romantik* (Berlin: R. Oppenheim, 1886) was translated into English by Lady Eastlake with Brandl's assistance and published by John Murray in 1887. Brandl says that for him 'to undertake the life of a man without interweaving a history of his literary development was "out of the question"' (viii), although this was 'usual in England'. He did research on Coleridge's manuscripts and early printed editions at the British Museum and in Lord Coleridge's collection, and he examined the Crabb Robinson diaries in Dr Williams' Library.

It is true that *Samuel Taylor Coleridge and the English Romantic School* is in some ways too much of its time. William Blake, for example, is characterized as 'a demented genius'. There is an unfortunate tendency to use the term 'The Romantic School' as if it were an entity, as in 'The Romantic School provided him with...' (57). Source-hunting is at times nearly obsessive. Some assertions are made without any production of evidence, as when we are told that Mary Evans broke off with Coleridge, 'under the pretext of prudence, not without a coquettish assumption of compassion' (75), and that 'There was no quarrel, no harshness, no bitter word' between the Coleridges during the decline of their marriage (273). Brandl also tends to view Coleridge's radical expressions either as youthful indiscretions or, in the instance of 'Fire, Famine, and Slaughter', as not really meant to be believed (15). Such condescension can lead to misinterpretation. Brandl mistakenly thinks 'Recantation Illustrated in the Story of the Mad Ox' a 'humorous apology for Coleridge's earlier revolutionary rage' (179) when it is actually is a fable showing how revolutionary rage is produced by society. However, the importance of this book is not in its defects but in its positive achievements.

In discussing Coleridge's early poems Brandl has an excellent sense of the literary traditions behind the poetry and also of Coleridge's development as a poet. Brandl declares 'He is first and foremost a landscape elegist; he cultivates also a lofty lyrical style, and tries his hand in the epic direction' (41). Brandl discusses the tradition of such poets as Akenside, Mallet, Dyer, and Gray as determining choices of subject and style, all against a background of Milton's shorter poems, and he considers in some detail the example William Lisle Bowles, whose influence Brandl comprehends but does not praise. He links 'Songs of the Pixies' to 'L'Allegro', 'Il Penseroso', and 'Comus' (84–5), and says the first revision of the 'Monody on the Death of Chatterton' displays a Spenserian mode, and that 'a heightening of the imagination is here and there evident' (89). No earlier writer had given Coleridge's early poems such sympathetic and discerning attention. Brandl even defends the much-derided 'To a young ass, its mother being tethered near it' as an example of Coleridge's power of sympathy with all life.

Brandl gives a pertinent description of the state of Bristol in the mid-1790s, although his view of Coleridge's political writings of that period is nevertheless condescending. He calls the political sonnets published in the *Morning Post* in 1794–5 'rather fanatic "Abdiel warnings", addressed to the foes of freedom' (95). Improvements in style in the *Poems* of 1797 are equated with revisionary politics: 'And as he pruned away his excrescences in style, so did he his political exaggerations'(178). Brandl is clearly more satisfied when he can say of Coleridge in 1799 'He had become, in the English acceptation, a tolerably moderate Conservative' (252).

At his critical best when he recognizes 'Frost at Midnight' as one of 'Coleridge's most original and finished works' (189), Brandl is at his worst when he says things like 'The Romantic school . . . failed from not being critical enough, and nowhere less so than in "Kubla Khan".' For Christabel he perceptively draws the parallel Christabel/Una and Geraldine/Duessa, but on the whole delivers a very literal-minded exposition the poem. He finely appreciates 'The Eolian Harp', observing that 'The different situations are arranged according to the divisions of the day:— like Milton, Coleridge's lark sings in the morning, the waters murmuring in noonday, while musical sounds—there, of clanging bells, here, of vibrating strings—are heard in the evening' (130). He is full of expert praise for the poetic and dramatic values of Coleridge's translation of Schiller's *Wallenstein*.

Observing that the English speak of addiction as 'a sin and not an illness' (187), this biographer has a humane attitude toward Coleridge's addiction. He says Coleridge began to take opium in November 1796 to relieve the pain of 'the chronic inflammation of the joints he inherited from his father, which had attacked him . . . in Christ's Hospital, and which he had never gotten rid of' (182). Without harping on the subject, Brandl make it clear that opium severely affected the rest of Coleridge's life.

With other early critics, Brandl believes that Coleridge's poetic impulse died with 'Dejection', which 'may be considered as the poet's dirge to his own imagination' (278). He does not attempt to disguise his 'sense of weariness' (360) with most of Coleridge's later prose writings, and he only glances at the later poetry. An exception to the former is *Aids to Reflection* (1825), which Brandl praises for being free of the theological speculation that generally occupied Coleridge at this time, and the later influence of which he recognizes. Of Coleridge and Carlyle he says 'the two were too much akin to learn from each other' (370), and he pithily observes that in Edward Irving Coleridge saw the 'shadow side of his labors' (372).

Coleridge enters the Gillmans' household on page 342 and dies on page 384, with his last eighteen years flying by the reader. The biographer who would give serious attention to the later Coleridge was yet to come. However, Brandl introduced several important elements into writing the life of Coleridge. For the part of Coleridge's career that he covers in detail, he gives scrupulous attention to matters of style and revision; he makes use of the manuscripts known to him, and he includes opium in the story of Coleridge's life without moral condemnation. His was the first scholarly biography of Coleridge.

The most thorough, comprehensive, and trustworthy account of Coleridge's life to date was given by Leslie Stephen is his *DNB* article of 1887. True, there are a few minor errors, easy to spot in the light of later knowledge. John Thelwall hardly deserves to be characterized as an 'agitator'. Stephen takes the then general view that Coleridge's 'poetic impulse... almost expired" with *Dejection: An Ode*, which he calls 'Ode to Dejection'. He too accepts one of Coleridge's versions of his departure from Italy saying that Coleridge was warned by the Prussian ambassador Wilhelm von Humboldt 'that he was a marked man' because of articles he had written in the *Morning Post*. (As Stephen rightly points out, Napoleon's treatment of some journalists was notorious, but those journalists were French, or, in the case of Mme de Staël, Swiss.) He thinks Washington Allston's 1806 portrait of Coleridge (Harvard University Art Museums), then in a private collection in America, non-existent. These are at most venial sins in a nineteenth-century biography of Coleridge. The virtues of Stephen's account are on the other hand major. It has the great quality of informative succinctness (which may be why Stephen succeeded so admirably with the entire *DNB* project). In particular, Coleridge's years in Cambridge and Bristol are covered in detail as they deserve, as is his career as a journalist.

Stephen displays a sense of justice not always found in earlier biographers, who often tend to be exculpatory or condemning. Stephen calls De Quincey's characterization of Coleridge's opium dependency 'cruel levity', and he conveys the drug's terrible effects without taking Cottle's high moral tone. Coleridge's financial dealings are also treated fairly. Although he accepted gifts and loans (many of which turned out to be gifts) from his friends, until his death, Coleridge kept up his insurance for his wife's benefit, and when his friends the Morgans needed help he gave them the £80 he had received from John Murray for *Christabel*. (Of John Morgan, one of the friends who had not thrust himself forward after Coleridge's death, Stephen remarks that his friendship 'has hardly received justice from Coleridge's biographers', something certainly true at that time and still to some extent today.)

Stephen gives a detailed account of the publication of Coleridge's poetry, though he is more concerned with its reception than with the poetry itself. Nevertheless he is on target when he says 'his early poems are marked by a kind of platonic pantheism oddly combined with the materialism of Hartley and Priestley'. Of 'The Rime of the Ancient Mariner' and 'Kubla Khan', among others, Stephen finely declares 'his best poems are all really dreams or spontaneous reveries showing a nature of marvelous richness and susceptibility, whose philosophic temperament only appears in the variety and vividness of the scenery'. Stephen also appreciates Coleridge as a critic. Those who attended Coleridge's lectures on Shakespeare and other poets in 1811–12 'were listening to the greatest of English critics'. Hazlitt and Carlyle 'failed to perceive' that in conversation 'his apparent rambling was governed by severe logical purpose'. Stephen goes so far as to say 'Coleridge alone among English writers is in the front rank at once as poet, as critic, and as philosopher'. However, he almost immediately qualifies the last. Stephen does not think that Coleridge created a 'philosophical system', and he recognizes the important position of unacknowledged translations from Schelling in the 'metaphysical exposition' of the *Biographia Literaria*. What Coleridge 'undoubtedly deserves' is 'the honour of having done much to stimulate thought'.

At the end of his article Stephen acknowledges help from his friend J. Dykes Campbell, and also says 'A Life with new materials is in preparation by Mr. Ernest Hartley Coleridge'. That life was never to be written. Instead, James Dykes Campbell in editing his important edition of *The Poetical Work of Samuel Taylor Coleridge* (1893) found that 'As ... no authoritative biography of Coleridge existed, I was obliged to construct a narrative for my own purpose' (v). Campbell revised and to some extent augmented his introduction, and it was published in 1894 as *Samuel Taylor Coleridge, a Narrative of the Events of His Life*, followed in 1896 by a second edition featuring Leslie Stephen's 'Memoir' of Campbell. Campbell was an able and assiduous scholar of manuscripts and rare books, and with the co-operation of other scholars and collectors, he produced a study that considerably extended the knowledge of its subject's life and writings. As Stephen says, he also, 'felt the peculiar charm of Coleridge's character' (xxxvii) and as a result his biography, neither idealizing nor moralistic, was the best to date.

Campbell was able to use some resources not available to his predecessors. Among these were William Knight's *Memorials of Coleorton* (1887), *Thomas Poole and His Friends* by Mrs Henry Sandford (1888), Alfred Ainger's edition of *The Letters of Charles Lamb* (1888), *The Life of William Wordsworth* by William Knight (1889), and E. H. Coleridge's privately printed *Letters from the Lake Poets* (1889). Campbell also consulted manuscripts owned by E. H. Coleridge and others, which enabled him to correct some of Cottle's gross textual errors and misrepresentations. Most important, he brought to his materials an acute and discriminating intelligence.

Campbell reconstructs Coleridge's relationship with the Evans family, and is the first to recognize that 'On a Discovery made too late' (1794), published in 1796 as

'Sonnet: to My Own Heart'[9] (38), has to do with the crisis in his feelings for Mary Evans. He prints part of Thomas Poole's amateurish but feelingful verses on Coleridge to show, in Mrs Sandford's words, 'Coleridge as he was in the first early freshness of the dawn of his marvelous powers' (47–8). In Campbell's judgement one indication of this is 'To the Reverend George Coleridge', largely ignored by previous critics, but in Campbell's judgement a 'beautiful and touching poem'.

An example of Campbell's judiciousness concerns Coleridge's claims that he had considerably raised the circulation of the *Morning Post* and that Daniel Stuart had offered him a partnership in *The Courier*, which would have been worth £2000 a year. Both Brandl (236) and Traill (77) accept this. Yet Stuart's published account is not brought in by either, as it is by Campbell. Coleridge, wrote Stuart, 'could not write daily on the occurrences of the day', and proved useless as a Parliamentary reporter when Stuart took him to the gallery of the House of Commons. According to Stuart, Coleridge was unable to produce anything on schedule, accepted pay for articles that he did not deliver, and did the general circulation of the either publication (Stuart, 485–92). Nevertheless, Stuart admits of Coleridge's essay on William Pitt and his poem 'The Devil's Thoughts', 'I never knew two pieces of writing so wholly unconnected with daily occurrences, produce so lively a sensation. Several hundred sheets extra were sold by them, and the paper was in demand for weeks and weeks afterwards.' But the Pitt essay was supposed to be followed by one on Napoleon that never materialized, and Stuart's account of Coleridge's relations with him is mostly of the author's reneging on promised material. Campbell highly praises the quality of Coleridge's journalism and says that the reputation of both newspapers must have been raised by Coleridge's contributions, but tends to trust Stuart's memory of the details better than Coleridge's.

Campbell's account of Coleridge's exit from Rome is less histrionic than his predecessors'. He also gives a balanced explanation of the rupture with Wordsworth that ensued after Basil Montagu, that perfect Godwinian, repeated to Coleridge what Wordsworth had told him in confidence about what a difficult house-mate Coleridge could be (179–80). Previous biographers had ignored this subject, important not only in itself but also for understanding Coleridge and Wordsworth's relations in later years. The story of Coleridge's addiction, instead of assuming center stage as in Cottle's books, is made part of an ongoing narrative that culminates, at least for a time, with Coleridge's putting himself under Dr Gillman's care in Highgate. Campbell is not under the illusion that Coleridge's consumption of laudanum then ceased, but he is probably correct in thinking that it was for the most part controlled. The *Christabel* volume was in the press when Coleridge took up residence with the Gillmans household in April 1816. During the three years that immediately followed, Coleridge published *The Statesman's Manual*, the *Biographia Literaria, Sibylline Leaves, Zapolya* (written in 1815), a ten-thousand-word essay on

---

[9] *PW* no. 83, Campbell 38.

Method in the *Encyclopaedia Metropolitana*, and the three-volume 'Refacimento' of *The Friend*, and resumed writing for *The Courier* with what Campbell calls 'prodigious' industry (229). He also lectured on the principles of judgement, culture, and European literature from 27 January to 13 March 1818, and from December 1818 to March 1919 gave alternating lectures on the history of philosophy and on literature.[10] This is a remarkable record of accomplishment for a frequently ill man beset by problems with publishers.

Coleridge's later years were, as Campbell observes, marked by new friendships—most notably with the surgeon Joseph Henry Green, who became his disciple and then literary executor; Thomas Allsop, who after Coleridge's death published letters that are 'our main authority for the details of Coleridge's life from 1820 to 1826' (237); and the Swedenborgian theologian Charles Augustus Tulk. Campbell makes it clear that Coleridge was appreciated late in life by old friends and new, some of who regularly attended his Thursday evenings at Highgate. Campbell says *Aids to Reflection* (1825) 'became the most popular of all Coleridge's prose works', and he credits *On the Constitution of the Church and the State* (1830) with having given the initial impulse for the Oxford Movement. Nor does he think Coleridge wrote no interesting poetry during these years. He mentions seven of the late poems by name, prints all of the published 'Work without Hope', and remarks: 'although now, "a common greyness silvers everything", the old magic still mingles with the colours on the palette' (266–7). Campbell compares 'Work without Hope' to Robert Browning's 'Andrea del Sarto' (from which the quotation is taken), in which the artist watches the lights of Fiesole die out one by one. In addition to its many other excellent qualities, Campbell's book is provided with a detailed index of 30 double-columned pages. The best Coleridge biography of the nineteenth century, its aims and methods look forward to the best scholarship of the twentieth.

WORKS CITED

ANON. 1846. Extracts from the Portfolio of a Man of the World—1822. *Gentlemen's Magazine*, 26: 570–4.
—— 1847. *Reminiscence of Coleridge and Southey by Joseph Cottle. Times* no. 19697, 3 November, pp. 6–7.
ALLSOP, THOMAS, ed. 1836. *Letters, Conversations and Recollections of S. T. Coleridge*. 2 vols. Edward Moxon.
BRANDL, ALOIS. 1887. *Samuel Taylor Coleridge and the English Romantic School*. Trans. Lady Eastlake. London: John Murray.

---

[10] See Coleridge, *Lectures 1818–1819 On the History of Philosophy*, ed. J. R. de J. Jackson. 'Chronological Table,' p. xxxiii. The editor points out (lxvii) that Campbell did not know whether more than two of the lectures ever had been given.

BYRON, GEORGE GORDON, LORD. 1986. *Byron*, ed. Jerome J. McGann. Oxford: Oxford University Press.

CAMPBELL, JAMES DYKES. 1896. *Samuel Taylor Coleridge: A Narrative of the Events of his Life...with a Memoir of the Author by Leslie Stephen*. 2nd edn. London: Macmillan.

CERGIEL, C. V. LE GRICE. 1834. College reminiscences of Mr Coleridge. *Gentleman's Magazine*, NS 2: 605–7.

COLERIDGE, HENRY NELSON. n.d. *Early Recollections...by Joseph Cottle*. *Quarterly Review*, 69: 25–32.

COLERIDGE, SAMUEL TAYLOR. 1983. *Biographia Literaria*, ed. James Engell and W. Jackson Bate. Vol. 7 of *The Collected Works of Samuel Taylor Coleridge*. Princeton: Princeton University Press.

—— 1956–71. *Collected Letters of Samuel Taylor Coleridge*. 6 vols., ed. Earl Leslie Griggs. Oxford: Clarendon Press.

COTTLE, BASIL. 1987. *Joseph Cottle of Bristol*. Bristol: Bristol Branch of the Historical Association.

COTTLE, JOSEPH. 1837. *Early Recollections Chiefly Relating to the Late Samuel Taylor Coleridge. During His Long Residence in Bristol*. 2 vols. London: Longman, Rees.

—— 1847. *Reminiscences of Samuel Taylor Coleridge and Robert Southey*. London: Houlston and Stoneman.

CUSHING, WILLIAM. 1878. *Index to the North American Review: Volumes I–LXXXV, 1815–1877*. Cambridge, Mass.: John Wilson.

DE QUINCEY, THOMAS. 1834–8. Samuel Taylor Coleridge by the English Opium-Eater. In *The Works of Thomas De Quincey*. Gen. ed. Grevel Lindop. Vol 10. *Articles from Tait's Edinburgh Magazine*. ed. Alina Clej, pp. 287–347.

FERRIER, JAMES FREDERICK. The plagiarisms of S. T. Coleridge. *Blackwod's Magazine*, 47: 287–99.

GILLMAN, JAMES. 1836. *The Life of Samuel Taylor Coleridge*. London: Pickering.

HARE, JULIUS CHARLES, ed. 1848. *Essays and Tales by John Sterling...with a Memoir of His Life*. 2 vols. London: John W. Parker.

JAMES, HENRY. 1908. *The Aspern Papers*. New York: Charles Scribners's Sons.

LAMB, CHARLES. 1820. ['Elia']. Christ's Hospital five-and-thirty years ago. *London Magazine*, 2: 483–90.

—— 1848. *Final Memorials of Charles Lamb: Consisting Chiefly of his Letters not Before Published, with Sketches of Some of His Companions*, ed. Thomas Noon Talfourd. London: Moxon.

LE GRICE, CHARLES VALENTINE ['Cergiel']. College reminiscences of Mr Coleridge. *Gentleman's Magazine*, NS 2: 605–7.

LOWES, J. LIVINGSTON. 1986. *The Road to Xanadu: A Study in the Ways of the Imagination*. Princeton: Princeton University Press [1927].

MULLAN, JOHN, ed. 1997. *Lives of the Great Romantics* II: *Keats, Coleridge, and Scott by Their Contemporaries*. London: Pickering and Chatto.

NORTON, CHARLES ELIOT. Reminiscences of Samuel Taylor Coleridge.... *North American Review*, 65: 401–40.

—— 1855. Memoir of the Author. *The Poetical Works of Coleridge and Keats*. 4 vols. in 2. Boston. Little, Brown, pp. xxix–cxi.

PALEY, MORTON D. 1999. *Portraits of Coleridge*. Oxford: Oxford University Press.

SANDFORD, MARGARET E. 1888. *Thomas Poole and His Friends*. London: Macmillan. 2 vols.

STEPHEN, LESLIE. 1887. Coleridge, Samuel Taylor. *DNB* vol. 11. New York: Macmillan, pp. 302–17.

STUART, DANIEL. 1838. Anecdotes of the Poet Coleridge. *Gentlemen's Magazine*, NS 9: 485–92, 577–90, NS 10, 23–7, 124–8.

TRAILL, H. D. 1884. *Coleridge.* New York: Harper.

CHAPTER 36

....

COLERIDGE'S RECEPTION ON THE CONTINENT

....

ELINOR SHAFFER

BRITISH writers have often been very well known and highly influential on the Continent, but their reception abroad has not been considered part of their 'afterlife', which is taken to refer only to their reputation in English. This keeps a considerable part of their nature and influence concealed or unsuspected. There are cases where a writer's workings abroad have become known to his countrymen, but these have often been to the detriment of his standing at home—for example, Byron's notorious self-exile abroad after bad behaviour, his dangerous tendency to become embroiled in foreign quarrels and foreign amours, often taken to be all too justly represented in poor prose translations into a range of languages other than his own.

In Coleridge's case, however, his reputation abroad has been largely ignored for quite special reasons: first, his *oeuvre* in English has only very recently been established through the long labours on the richly annotated *Collected Coleridge*, the *Letters* and the *Notebooks*, which have at last allayed the sense of Coleridge as a fragmentary, even a failed writer, or one who did not fulfil his promise; and second, his relations with the Continent have, unusually, been viewed through the other end of the lens: his own borrowings from European thinkers. These two notions have been connected; that is, Coleridge's various disabilities, which made it difficult to carry out his grand projects, led him to 'borrow' from foreign sources. The fact and extent of his borrowings are now established in detail, and it is possible not only to assess the creative manner of his dealings with the new transcendentalist and idealist philosophy, but to see how this affected his recognition abroad, where these philosophies have often been more influential or more highly thought of than in England.

To go back to his own lifetime to see how, or indeed whether, his reputation made its way across the Channel is, however, to be agreeably surprised by how early it was established, through his first book of poetry *Religious Musings* (1795), now perhaps little read; the current notion that the anonymously issued *Lyrical Ballads* (1798) is the manifesto of English Romanticism tends to weight the reception towards Wordsworth, who notoriously excluded 'Christabel' from the 1800 edition and identified the author of 'The Ancient Mariner' merely as 'a friend'. It has recently been shown that the publishers of the *Lyrical Ballads* had actually already set 'Christabel' in type when the demand came for it to be excised. Moreover, the early association between Coleridge and Southey, known in his own right, has a very considerable presence in the reception, and their joint productions such as *Wat Tyler* and *The Fall of Robespierre*, as well as the communitarian politics of Pantisocracy are noticed. The political works are valued in relation to the politics of the receiver, and vary with the temper of the times.

The first mentions of him in public records are also very early. Coleridge gains a place in the German *Lexikon* by J. D. Reuss, *Das Gelehrte England* (1804), a Who's Who of eminent Englishmen, where all his works to date are listed (though *Lyrical Ballads* is listed under Wordsworth's name), culminating in his translation of Schiller's important historical tragedy, *Wallenstein*, whose opening in 1798 coincided with Coleridge's stay in Göttingen. Reuss, a librarian at the University of Göttingen, the major German university in the eighteenth century, with an outstanding collection of English books, probably met Coleridge, as well as doing a thorough job of research into his publications.[1] Approached by Schiller's agents (as Schiller's correspondence shows), though the two did not meet while Coleridge was in Germany, he carried out the translation and it was published in England, with his Introduction, in 1800. This work gave him a permanent place in German literary history; its blank verse rendering of Schiller's hexameters carried the national poet—as Schiller quickly became after his death in 1805—further back to one of his inspirations in Shakespeare, translations and acting versions and new critical valuations of whom were gathering weight and pace in Germany. It would not be too much to claim that this major translation of a recognized European writer gave him a place early on—he was still under thirty—in Continental literary circles.

---

[1] On Reuss see Frederick Burwick, 'The Reception of Coleridge in Germany to 1939', *The Reception of S. T. Coleridge in Europe*, eds. Elinor Shaffer and Edoardo Zuccato (London: Continuum, 2007), p. 89.

The sense of crisis and delay in his poetical and personal life so familiar in his English biographers' accounts does not affect his steady advance in Continental recognition. The collection of Coleridge's poems in *Sibylline Leaves* (1817) led to his inclusion (with five poems) in *The Living Poets of England* in 1827, published in English by the French publishers Baudry and Galignani. The enterprising 'pirate' houses of Baudry and the better known Galignani played an immense role in the reception and circulation of all the Romantic poets: they were enterprising and quick off the mark, and they undercut the prices of the English publishers and circulated their books in England as well as on the Continent. When Coleridge's *Poetical Works* (1828) appeared, it was quickly followed in the same year by J. W. Lake's *The British Poets of the Nineteenth Century*, including no fewer than 42 poems by Coleridge, mainly from *Sibylline Leaves*. Significantly, this book was published simultaneously in Paris and Frankfurt. In 1829, when the second edition of Coleridge's *Poetical Works* appeared in England, published by Pickering, Galignani published Coleridge's collected poems in *The Poetical Works of Coleridge, Shelley and Keats*. This shows their enterprise and good judgement, for the poems of Keats and Shelley were not then easily accessible, and they added to the poems of Coleridge in his *Poetical Works* by publishing 'The Tale of the Dark Ladie', which had appeared only in a newspaper, the 'Morning Post' (1799), and epigrams from *The Keepsake* (1829).[2] Coleridge, represented by both early and late work, takes his place already as the senior poet to the second generation of Romantics. Moreover, by adding *The Fall of Robespierre* (1794) attention was drawn to Coleridge's radical youth, and this had considerable positive impact on his reception in Europe, standing him in good stead with radical movements and giving a fuller sense of his trajectory than he might have liked at the end of his life.[3] Moreover, the works received good distribution: J. W. Lake's anthology, *The British Poets of the Nineteenth Century* (1829), a ringing title, containing 42 poems by Coleridge, was published simultaneously in Paris and Frankfurt in 1828. Galignani's editions also contained biographical memoirs of the authors, and they circulated a journal 'Galignani's Messenger' making their authors known throughout Europe. When the third edition of Coleridge's *Poetical Works* appeared in the year of his death, 1834, he was already established on the Continent as a leading poet of his nation and of his century.[4]

These publications were enough to ensure that poems of Coleridge were included in anthologies of English and Romantic poetry both in English and in

---

[2] Michael John Kooy, 'Coleridge's Early Reception in France', pp. 37–8.

[3] On the interest of the German liberals and radicals, including Marx, Engels and Coleridge's translator Ferdinand Freiligrath, see Burwick, pp. 97–9, and 101–4; on the interest of the Italian nationalists, seeking an independent state of Italy, see Nasi 2007, p. 213. *The Fall of Robespierre* was the second work of Coleridge's to be translated into Italian (after his poem 'Love').

[4] See *The Reception of S. T. Coleridge in Europe*, eds. Elinor Shaffer and Edoardo Zuccato (Continuum, 2007) for a more detailed account of the reception and for extensive bibliographies.

translations throughout the century, although not on the scale of Byron. One of the most often cited was 'Glycine's Song', from the verse play *Zapolya* (1817); this 'Song' was in fact Coleridge's excellent rendering of Ludwig Tieck's fine Romantic lyric 'Herbstlied', or Autumn Song, a copy of which, Kathleen Coburn speculated, had probably been given to Coleridge by Tieck himself on their first meeting in Rome in 1805.

If the keen Continental publishers pressed on with publication in various forms, hard on the heels of the English publishers, and often outselling them, the reviewing establishment on the Continent, in particular the French-language periodicals, were quick to review the works, often also translating essays or comment from British journals, and journals such as the *Revue Britannique* regularly published translations of new work. Such was the dominance of France in cultural institutions that these journals (like French translations generally) reached a large literate French-reading public all over Europe; one could argue that the literary network was more effective then than now, and it is little wonder that Coleridge among many other writers became known abroad. Coleridge's play *Zapolya* was reviewed in *Annales encyclopédiques* in 1818, the year after its London staging; the favourable if mixed review (the author despite some 'obscure [*recherchées*] ideas' showed 'traces of a brilliant imagination') is Coleridge's first known review in France.

Another route by which writers became known abroad was through the correspondence of publishers, writers and translators, a good deal of which has survived from the period, and this provides a fascinating trail through the creative process by which books get written and published. In Coleridge's case, for example, one can find details of his proposals to publishers, and theirs to him. Writers abroad of the eminence of Goethe keep *Tagebücher*, diaries, in which they inscribe lists of well-known writers in other countries, and they receive reports and correspondence from publishers abroad on their own reputations, the likelihood of translations or performances of their works, the news and critical comment surrounding them, the market, and the press reception.

Louis Simond, a Frenchman who had gone into exile in America at the time of the Revolution, published his travels in England (1817), describing meetings with Wordsworth, Southey and Coleridge among others, and literary travels were quite popular both with those who made them and those who read them. More important than these earliest references were certain individual critics who played a major role in the reception of virtually all English-language authors in the early nineteenth century, not only the poets including Coleridge and his contemporaries, but also the novelists, Walter Scott and Jane Austen, as well as a host of other writers such as Mrs Radcliffe, Matthew 'Monk' Lewis, Maria Edgeworth, Fanny Burney, and Lady Morgan.[5] The major critics were often writers as well as critics, translators,

---

[5] See *The Reception of Walter Scott in Europe*, ed. Murray Pittock (Continuum, 2006) and *The Reception of Jane Austen in Europe*, ed. Anthony Mandal and Brian Southam (Continuum, 2007), both in the Series on the Reception of British and Irish Authors, Series Editor: Elinor Shaffer.

journal editors and later university professors, such as Philarète Chasles (1798–1873) and Amédée Pichot (1795–1877). These critics' essays found their way across Europe, where they were read in French, and with little delay translated into other languages—Chasles' 1821 'Essai historique sur la poésie anglaise et sur les poètes anglaises vivantes' (Historical essay on English poetry and on the living English poets), for example, was translated into both Russian and Polish by the following year. A later essay by Chasles, 'De La Littérature anglaise actuelle' (On current English literature), which appeared in 1838 in the *Revue des Deux Mondes* (Review of two worlds), one of the leading journals reporting on European literature and society from its founding in 1828 to the First World War (and still in existence), was translated (for example) into Czech in 1839, Chasles' earlier views now amplified by comments on the decline of English (Victorian) letters since that halcyon time.[6] Current Continental literary journalism was up to date with the work of contemporary writers in England as elsewhere. Critical material was often translated from British journals. It is worth stressing this Europe-wide network of current information if only because it is not normally part of the literary education even of specialists in these English writers to know these facts, often relegated to 'history of the book' studies.[7]

Pichot published his memoir of his travels in Britain during the early 1820s in a three-volume *Voyage historique et littéraire en Angleterre et en Ecosse* (1825) (Historical and literary voyage to England and Scotland), in which while showing his awareness of the current view in England of Coleridge as a 'dreamer' and one given to mesmerizing if possibly empty conversational flights, addresses the work seriously, with notable analyses of 'The Ancient Mariner' (in the context of his other poems), his affecting love poetry, and his dramas, including *Zapolya, Remorse,* and his *Wallenstein* translation.[8] He devoted another book to Coleridge in 1827, and later (1860) wrote a biography.

Coleridge's encounters abroad, most often treated as part of his own biography and formation, were also of immense significance for his reception, then and later. Although Coleridge did not carry on correspondence with major European figures (as Carlyle did with Goethe in the 1820s), yet he was known to them. He had personal contact with a range of figures through his own travels on the Continent, which were far from following the ordinary patterns of the Grand Tour or the later tourism which began with the train over the Alps, or the European pilgrimages to

---

[6] Martin Procházka, 'A Spectre or an Unacknowledged Visionary? Coleridge in Czech Culture', in Shaffer and Zuccato, eds., pp. 254–74.

[7] It is now possible to assess the numbers of copies published, the number of reprintings and the extent of the distribution; see, for example, William St Clair's important study, *The Reading Nation in the Romantic Period* (Cambridge University Press, 2004).

[8] Pichot has been shown not to have spent as much time as he claimed in Britain, and to have lifted some of his ostensibly first-hand reporting of meetings with the poets from other sources. See Pichois 1965 and Kooy 2007.

Sir Walter Scott's Scotland. Coleridge went to Germany in 1798; then to Malta and Italy in 1804–5. In Germany he was an already published poet and a keen student, who attended the lectures and seminars of eminent professors in a range of fields and had personal contacts with them; in Italy, he held the post of Under-Secretary to the British Commissioner of Malta. While his time in Malta in 1804–5 had been given some attention earlier, recent work has opened the archives of the British and the Maltese to inquire much more closely into Coleridge's duties and experiences as part of a colonial administration.[9] He travelled widely from Malta, first to Sicily, and then northwards to Rome, where he stayed for five months, and on to Pisa and Florence, taking ship for England from Livorno; that experience was highly unusual in every way, and evaded the Grand Tour stereotype of the well-to-do sons of the rich travelling southwards across the Alps to broaden their worldly knowledge.

Coleridge and Wordsworth setting out together for Germany in 1798 made a pilgrimage to Hamburg to meet the *éminence grise*, Germany's major eighteenth-century poet, Friedrich Gottlieb Klopstock (1724–1803); if Wordsworth carried on a conversation in French with the grand old man, Coleridge had begun to learn German and was familiar with Klopstock's odes and his epic *Der Messias* (The Messiah). Coleridge's account of their journey has been translated into German more than once.[10] If Wordsworth spent the winter in Goslar (not a simple mountain village but the centre of court life), Coleridge threw himself into the intellectual life of the University of Göttingen, the leading university, especially notable for its English collections, met and heard the lectures of the eminent naturalist J. F. Blumenbach (whose ideas on animal magnetism were to play a role in his later thinking), and the leading higher critic of the Bible, J. G. Eichhorn, who having published groundbreaking studies of the dating and authorship of the books of the Old Testament was just entering the more risky territory of the New Testament and its mythological bases.[11] J. G. Heyne's seminar on mythological studies was still flourishing in Göttingen, a major influence also on the Schlegel brothers and Schelling. Later he met Ludwig Tieck, poet, novelist, playwright, and Shakespeare critic, one of the most attractive and congenial spirits among the German Romantics, in Rome in 1805, where there were sizeable English and German communities, and again in London, in 1817; Tieck later noted his sorrow at Coleridge's death. He met Mme de Staël, in the London offices of the publisher Murray in 1813; her book *De l'Allemagne* (*On Germany*), first published in 1810, but destroyed by order of Napoleon, was published by Murray in England in 1813 in French and English, and was to spread appreciation of the new German Romantic movement across Europe. Other English critics who had come into contact with Germany at that period were

---

[9] Donald J. Sultana, *Coleridge on Malta* (1969), a pioneering study, is now outdated. See the more recent work by Barry Hough and Howard Davis (2007 and 2008).

[10] See Breunig 2007.

[11] Shaffer, 1975 pp. 22–3.

also drawn upon by Mme de Staël for insights into the new movement.[12] Mme de Staël famously reported to her lover A. W. Schlegel, the critic and translator of Shakespeare, that she had met the Coleridge 'whom you admire so much' ('qui vous admire tant'), but that Coleridge understood monologue, but not dialogue ('Avec M. Coleridge, c'est tout a fait un monologue'); as she herself was well known for her flow of conversation, there must have been a splendid double monologue.[13] It is important to note these personal encounters, for they convey the sense of how much travel, study, and introductions made the spread of a reputation easier. How significant they were felt to be may be measured by Chasles' having exaggerated the length of his stay in England, and the number of notables he met. He even fabricated a persuasive account of meeting Coleridge, describing him 'as a kind of mystical Diderot'.[14] Travel was more difficult than now, we may think; but there was a great deal of it, and stays abroad were much longer and often more productive. Writing one's travels (true or fictitious) was also an effective way of establishing one's credentials.

Undoubtedly, however, the greatest impact on European readers came through translations of 'The Ancient Mariner', and in particular through Gustave Doré's illustrations to the poem.[15] This grand volume, *The Rime of the Ancient Mariner, Illustrated by Gustave Doré*, first published in London in 1876 and then in Paris, travelled all over Europe, carrying a French translation; but the rather mediocre prose translation by Auguste Barbier often gave rise to a demand for a better one in the local language, including a number of better ones by other French writers. The illustrations themselves represented an interpretation of the poem in the sense of a medievalizing, visionary, anti-classical text. Doré became celebrated and successful, and his illustrated volumes of Dante, Cervantes, and Tennyson's *Idylls of the King*, as well as Coleridge's 'Mariner', were widely distributed, the national poets in the lead—Dante especially in Italy, Cervantes understandably in Spain—but all of them became well known and special editions were produced as elegant gifts for Christmas and the New Year well into the twentieth century. In Germany the finest translation, agreed to be that by the Romantic poet and translator Ferdinand Freiligrath (1810–76), first published in 1831 in a periodical, and published in his *Gedichte* (Poems) in 1838, in a section devoted to his translations, was printed with Doré's illustrations (1878). In Italy the most acclaimed translation, by the fine poet and translator Enrico Nencione, with many English contacts, was printed with Doré's illustrations in 1889; and in the twentieth century the rendering by the symbolist poet Mario Luci (1985) appeared with Doré's illustrations. Luci also

[12] Vigus 2007 describes in detail Mme de Staël's meetings with Henry Crabb Robinson while he was a student at Jena, in order to glean information about Schelling's philosophy which she deployed in *De l'Allemagne*.

[13] Burwick 2007, p. 93.

[14] Pichois 1965 revealed the deception for the first time.

[15] Soubigou 2007, pp. 61–87.

placed 'Kubla Khan' at the head of a book devoted to Symbolist poetry. Thus Coleridge's poem received the attention of the best translators of the time, who also translated other English poetry of note—Freiligrath translated Felicia Hemans, Letitia Landon, Southey, Tennyson, and Longfellow; Nencione translated Tennyson and Yeats as well as the Romantics. A stream of French poets translated, interpreted or were stimulated to their own recreations: Sainte-Beuve, whose two early translations in the 1830s of 'The Eolian Harp' and 'Fears in Solitude' and his recommendation of Coleridge to Baudelaire, were an augury of Coleridge's attractions, as of Sainte-Beuve's own critical ascendancy.[16] Baudelaire's creative response came in 'L'Albatros' in *Les Fleurs du Mal* (1861) (*Flowers of Evil*)—and through Baudelaire's championship of Edgar Allan Poe, Poe's master the sound poet Coleridge also found his way by another route into the mainstream.[17] Coleridge also made his way obliquely via the success of De Quincey's *Opium-Eater* in France, which carried with it an unwilling Coleridge (who concealed rather than writing about his addiction). These are complex matters of indirect reception which still need further investigation. But the *poète maudit* in France became fashionable, reaching back to Chatterton, on whom Coleridge had written a sympathetic ode, and at the end of the 1820s became the subject of Alfred de Vigny's play of that name. Later Rimbaud's creative response to the 'Mariner' in *Le Bateau ivre* (*The drunken ship*) (1871) seems also to draw on the imagery of intoxication as well as of the sea. At any rate, Coleridge's predilections, which drew down moral opprobrium in England, became part of his aura as a Romantic poet. Later still Antonin Artaud, the founder of the 'Theatre of Cruelty', became identified with Coleridge as an artist figure of extravagant intoxications.[18]

Another major French translation of 'The Ancient Mariner' followed early in the twentieth century by Valery Larbaud, an influential and fertile writer, critic and translator, perhaps best known today for his translation of Joyce's *Ulysses*. Again a work of Coleridge's became interwoven with the best poetic and illustrative talent of the major literary communities and itself formed a supranational reference point. 'The Ancient Mariner' was an international classic by the end of the nineteenth century and moved on into a new key in the twentieth.

The reception of a writer may point not only to the recognition elsewhere of his major works, but also to more surprising concatenations with his less familiar works. *Zapolya* is one example; another is the early, unfinished prose poem, written just before 'The Ancient Mariner', 'The Death of Cain', though this was known only later. It was sufficiently evident that the 'Mariner' was linked with the figure of the

---

[16] See Kooy, 2007, pp. 27–60.

[17] On the close link between Coleridge and Poe, see Floyd Stovall, 1969 and Bate 1990. For the importance of Poe in France see Quinn 1971 and Eliot 1949.

[18] Jonathan Pollock, 'Opium and the Occult: Antonin Artaud and Samuel Taylor Coleridge', *Revue de la literature comparée*, 300 (October–December 2001), 567–77.

guilty man who fled from his crime, or was forced to wander as a consequence of his crime, and this was a theme that had many echoes throughout the century, whether in Victor Hugo's subterranean flights of a supposed criminal in *Les Misérables* and his remote seamen of *Les Travailleurs du mer* (The Toilers of the Sea) (another work illustrated by Doré), or in the labyrinthine toils of Eugène Sue's popular *Les Mystères de Paris*, and his novel *Le Juif errant* (1844–5) (the 'Wandering Jew') (a theme also illustrated by Doré), and the theme of the Ghost Ship in *Der Fliegende Holländer*, 'The Flying Dutchman', that captured Wagner's imagination. Here 'reception' opens out beyond personal contacts, publishing, reviewing, sales and readership networks, author or publisher and translator links, individual criticism and biography, and the taste of illustrators, into more complex and far-reaching patterns of comparative literary criticism. Coleridge had touched a nerve of the age and tapped into an archetypal theme.

The exploration of Coleridge's reception in France, Germany, and Italy may seem to be on familiar ground, even if the scope and firm advance of the recognition is unexpected, and the poets, translators, and critics in those countries, as well as the infrastructure of publishers and journals, are less well known than they should be to English speakers; but his reception in other countries is quite unfamiliar, and here Spain in particular is a new and fertile territory.[19] Yet Coleridge's reception in Spain is one of the earliest, in that it was effected by the group of Spanish Liberals in exile in London whose interest in English social and literary developments was quickly reflected in their own periodicals and in Spain. The largest exodus of the defeated Liberals was between 1823 and the death of the King of Spain ten years later. The activity of exile communities in spreading ideas and texts, both by importing their own cultural products into their new environment, and in their transmission of the new environment back to the homeland, has been considerably investigated, though detailed work on the Spanish Liberal group is currently being extended. Periodicals, translations, and accounts of both worlds, together with the setting up of small publishing houses, as well as the continuation of old battles in new terms, are familiar elements of these transplanted communities and are well documented in exile studies.

This general effect was in the case of Coleridge's reception intensified by the personal contact between Coleridge and one of the leading members of the exile community, Joseph Blanco White, as he became known in Britain. Blanco White had actually come earlier than the main wave of exiles, having arrived by 1810, and he stayed until his death in 1841. As a convert to Anglicanism in 1814, ordained in London, he had put down further roots. He and Coleridge met over four years

---

[19]   Here the pioneering research of Eugenia Perojo Arronte must be gratefully acknowledged; see her two chapters on Spain in *The Reception of S. T. Coleridge in Europe*, on the Nineteenth Century, pp. 135–66, and on the Twentieth Century, pp. 167–96.

from 1825, and there are expressions of warm friendship and respect on both sides. While the community in general was more interested in Scott, a more nuanced literary relationship flourished between Coleridge and Blanco White, who wrote poetry in both Spanish and English with Coleridge as a model and mentor. He wrote at least seven poems in English in 1825–6. When his poetry reached Spain, the glimpse of another, more direct style of observation was able to supply a new possibility to poets like Bécquer and Campoamor.

In the twentieth century Coleridge's most fascinating Spanish reader was Unamuno.[20] Miguel de Unamuno (1864–1936) is a figure of European stature and significance, as a philosopher and critic, as well as a poet who exerted a powerful influence on the course of Spanish poetry. It is again characteristic of Coleridge, as we review his Continental reception, that he is taken up by figures such as Unamuno, Croce, and Gabriel Marcel.

Unamuno, professor of Greek at Salamanca, is best known outside of Spain for his essay *The Tragic Sense of Life* (*Del Sentimiento tragico de la vida*) (1913). This, together with other works, put him in the line of Schopenhauer, Kierkegaard, and Nietzsche as forerunners of modern existentialism. He wrote novels closely linked with his existentialist philosophy, for example *Mist* (*Niebla*) (1914). He came late to poetry, and his first collection in 1907 occasioned surprise amongst his acquaintances. But he felt that his poetry was most important to him, and would 'furnish contemporary literature with something new'. He described it as most akin to 'the English "musings", to English meditative poetry, that of Wordsworth, Coleridge, Browning . . .'[21]

Like the earlier Spanish poets influenced by English, he felt that Spanish poetry badly needed a new direction, a new rhetoric, or rather a movement away from rhetoric and bombast towards the natural. Already in 1899 he had written: 'In no other European language do words have such a degree of concretion, such a graphic and precise sense, such a sharply bounded shape as they have in English.'[22] He began to translate poems, including Coleridge's 'Reflections on Having Left a Place of Retirement'. The use of enjambment, and of a plain spare style, puzzled his contemporaries; only the fine poet Juan Ramón Jiménez understood.[23] Unamuno began to use this style, found through translation, in his own writing too.

But Unamuno also concerned himself with Coleridge's prose, his criticism and thought. He owned and annotated the *Biographia Literaria* (1906 edition), and was

---

[20] Flores, 2007. I am grateful to Cristina Flores Moreno for her further research into Unamuno's interest in Coleridge, including a detailed examination of his library and marginalia.

[21] Perojo Arronte, p. 169. In Spanish the very phrase is English, 'los "musings" inglesas'.

[22] Unamuno used a title in English for his article, 'The English-speaking Folk', in the journal *La vida literaria* (1899).

[23] Perojo Arronte, p. 170.

particularly struck by passages on the relation between poetry and philosophy. He lectured that year on the need for imagination. At the same time the imagination must have a place, a spatial localization. He also put explicit references to Coleridge into some of his verse. It was the 'Meditative Poems' that were his main model, as identified in his edition of the poems (1893); many of those poems were afterwards called 'conversation poems', by G. M. Harper. Unamuno's first volume contained a section called 'Meditaciones', in which the conception of the poetic genre was reinforced by his discovery of the *Biographia*.

Unamuno seems to comprehend and put into effect Coleridge's combination of an unadorned (in Spanish terms) style, a precise localization and a profound imagination. Unamuno's championship of Coleridge took time to be assimilated, but finally further translations of his prose as well as his poetry have come out, to general approbation. Unamuno's intense interest in Coleridge, his sense that this is the way forward for a whole national poetry, and for himself as a poet and philosopher, provides a fresh insight into Coleridge's qualities. This, of course, is one of the great gains from reception studies: that the familiar acquires the intensity of a longed-for transformation.

This is not just a case of reception as transmission by translation, publication, and critical notice, it is a full-blown case of reception by one mind of another, a hermeneutic encounter and dialogue between two creative minds in which a new way of thinking and writing is engendered, and one culture opens to another. Unamuno's understanding of the link between Coleridge's poetic style and his mode of critical and philosophical thinking is genuinely illuminating for others too. 'Reception' can also be a form of defamiliarization (to use the Russian Formalist term). When after reading Unamuno's comments, and his translation of the poem, I returned to Coleridge's familiar poem 'Reflections on Having Left a Place of Retirement' I felt that I saw for the first time what a very remarkable poem it is, intricate in the realization of simplicity. 'Reception' abroad can also return a poet to his home.

The paradigmatic case of Unamuno, philosopher as well as poet, also opens the question of the reception of Coleridge's prose, his thought, more generally. In one sense, his prose writings were not received early nor were they widely diffused. Often they circulated only in extracts or fragments; the form of the 'Aphorism' became associated with his name, partly because of the wide circulation of the fine selection of his thought under the title of *Anima Poetae* (1895). His *Table Talk*, which was widely praised, was also treated as a source of aphorisms. This may also have been owing to the awareness on the Continent of the aphorism as a Romantic form, so effectively and creatively deployed by Friedrich Schlegel in the early critical writings that established the new movement of Romanticism, and by Novalis (1771–1801), a major German Romantic writer, author of the novel *Heinrich von Ofterdingen* (the quest for the 'blaue Blume') and of the collection of aphorisms known as *Blütenstaub*, 'pollen' or 'seed'—not system, but germinating thoughts. The Polish critic Zygmunt Kubiak carried this out even more fully, not only organizing his selections under the title of aphorisms (*Aforyzmy*, 1975) but arguing that Coleridge is not limited to the Romantic aphorism or philosophical framework but presents a 'panorama' resembling ancient Greek collections of epigrams.[24] This is one productive way of looking at Coleridge's prose, and perhaps seems all the more so now that we have his splendid Notebooks and marginalia. Certainly the nineteenth-century array of 'Biographia' in its diverse parts, the *Table Talk*, the *Literary Remains* edited by his nephew, and lecture notes by other hands, not to mention rumours of unfinished works, seemed to call for anthologizing rather than for complete and faithful reproduction.

Yet the 'pollen' fell on some surprising soil. Tolstoi, for example, read the *Aids to Reflection* in 1890, and quoted it in his own defence (in English) when he was accused of blasphemy.[25] *Aids to Reflection* (1825) is Coleridge's most finished work of prose, presenting a powerful argument using Kant's own weapons against him; but it is also offered in the form of 'aphorisms', both those of the seventeenth-century Anglican Robert Leighton, and Coleridge's own. It is thus a complex piece of work in which the very form is a comment on the argumentative style of current philosophers. Tolstoi read it in English, the book having been lent to him by a friend (and reception studies of 'distribution' must not forget the importance of books simply carried home by visitors to foreign parts). Tolstoi faced charges of religious unorthodoxy, and sought aid; in the end he decided that Coleridge was too much embedded in his own English and Anglican context to offer much direct help in his own predicament, but he quoted Coleridge nevertheless, in a pithy aphorism: 'He who begins by loving Christianity better than Truth will proceed by loving his own Sect or Church better than Christianity, and end in loving himself better than all.'

However, Coleridge's thought also found a serious reception by thinkers who like Unamuno stood in the same line of development from German thought from Kant and the post-Kantians. One important line is eastern European, from the Austro-Hungarian Empire and the Czech lands where German thought was a strong presence; another is Spanish, as we have seen in part, where Romanticism had some early German roots in Böhl von Faber and some important twentieth-century philosophers notably Ortega y Gasset (1883–1955), best known in English for *The Revolt of the Masses* (1932), who studied in Germany; and another is Italian, where the idealist tendency took strong root and issued in a major school of aesthetics of which the best known representative is Benedetto Croce (1866–1952). In Spain, the criticism of Cervantes' *Don Quixote*, including that of Coleridge, and Schlegel, is closely bound up with philosophical currents, and is a rich vein down to Ortega's *Meditation on Quixote* (Eng. trans. 1964) and Madariaga's

[24] Coghen, 2007, pp. 293–5.
[25] Volkova, 2007, pp. 314–15. *Aids to Reflection* has still not been translated into Russian.

influential German-tinged reading of the 'dialectical' relationship between Quixote and Sancho Panza.

In Italy the aesthetic movement started in the nineteenth century by Francesco De Sanctis (1817–83) came to an important peak with Croce's *Estetica* (*Aesthetics as the Science of Expression and General Linguistics*) (1902). Croce commented directly on Coleridge's historical importance in this work and more extensively in his *Nuove Pagine Sparse* (New scattered pages) (1948–9), where he deals with the distinction between Imagination and Fancy. While filling in the antecedents of this distinction (Jean Paul, Schelling, Solger), he gives Coleridge credit for applying it sharply in his own critical practice.[26] Virtually none of this rich material has been considered in English Coleridge studies.

Moreover, many of the twentieth-century literary critics who have concerned themselves with Coleridge's philosophy have come from these Continental backgrounds, notably René Wellek, who wrote his habilitation thesis at the Charles University of Prague in 1930, known in its English version as *Kant in England* (1931), and who emigrated to the United States shortly afterwards; and Gian Orsini, an Italian academic who worked in the United States after the Second World War, whose *Coleridge and German Idealism* (1969) sympathetically constructed a view of his organic thought.[27] Wellek's knowledge of the background, derived from the strongly German-oriented teaching of the University of Prague, led him to find Coleridge inconsistent in the way he deployed British empirical philosophers in conjunction with Kant and German idealism and at times seemed to try to put them together in a kind of bricolage or 'mosaic' pattern (as McFarland later called it, referring rather to specific borrowings from different sources). A knowledge of this intellectual background through reception studies might have allayed the tendency of the editors of the *Collected Coleridge* to view Wellek as a kind of enemy against whom Coleridge had to be protected. Wellek did, however, succeed in suggesting 'a second England', a non-empirical line of philosophers including the seventeenth-century Cambridge Platonists, Ralph Cudworth and Henry More, among others, an idealist stream he saw as revived through Kant in the eighteenth century.[28] The Cambridge Platonists have sometimes in English been seen as a 'native' stream available to Coleridge which made Kant unnecessary to him or to us. Academic studies on the Continent as in Britain continue to explore these multiple traditions.[29] Once again, it is clear that exile communities play a very considerable role in reception; in these cases, it is the critics and academics who continue in their new environment to pursue the lines of thought opened to them

---

[26] Croce, 1949, pp. 187–8. Quoted and translated in full in Nasi, 2007.

[27] For other Italian critics and academics working in exile after the Second World War see Nasi, 2007.

[28] On Wellek see Procházka, 2007, pp. 262–71.

[29] See for example the recent Spanish thesis on Coleridge and Cudworth (Flores Moreno 2007).

by their original training. They may be of immense help in stimulating new thinking in English studies, but may also be misunderstood. It is as important to place the critics and academics in their milieu as the writers themselves.

Coleridge's relation to Continental idealist movements needs further investigation, and should prove as vital as the new work on Coleridge and Unamuno. But it is also the case that Continental like British philosophy has moved on, and there is a whole new phase of philosophical thinking in which Coleridge is also finding a place and benefiting from new thinking. In both cases, the need to justify Coleridge in terms of consistent, systematic thinking has receded. One of the most interesting recent lines of thought has been opened by Luciano Anceschi, who has moved away from idealist to phenomenological aesthetics. He argued that Coleridge is as important as a philosopher as he is as a poet, and called him 'undoubtedly the highest figure of that intellectual movement that we agree in calling *English Romanticism*'.[30] He traces the idea of 'pure poetry' from Sir Philip Sidney to Coleridge, Poe, and 'that great nexus of modern poetic culture, that of Poe-Baudelaire'.[31] Most importantly, he formulates a new conception of Coleridge's philosophical method: Coleridge relates style and logic in an unusual way. The apparently inconsistent 'composite shape' of many of his texts, and especially the *Biographia*, represents not a rhetoric imposed on a thought, but an intimate way that thought structures itself and offers 'a continuous revelation of a process of growth of a mental position, a spiritual attitude'.[32]

Thus Coleridge has had an extraordinarily rich and positive reception on the Continent, in many ways different from that he has had at home. The *Collected Coleridge* has now opened the way to fuller and more integral citation and commentary especially on the prose; only last year the complete works were translated into Italian.

Perhaps we can close with the words of that excellent Italian critic, well-known to English readers, Mario Praz, and still suggestive of the further reaches of Coleridge reception that open out before us:

A glacier, a mysterious shimmering azure crystal formed by layer upon layer of ancient snow—readings upon readings of innumerable books—but not a text so perfect as to exclude detritus and deposits, not defined by its own outline, lying down, its passive form modelled by the ribs of the mountains, but just the same endowed with its own inert energy, a thrust derived from its very immensity: like Chaos, rich with latent lives, first seed of the gods, formless and venerable.[33]

---

[30] Anceschi, 1992, p. 36. Quoted in Nasi 2007, p. 223.
[31] Ibid., xix.
[32] Anceschi, 1992, pp. 33–4. Quoted in Nasi 2007, p. 224. This is my brief paraphrase.
[33] Praz, 'Introduzione', *La Ballata del vecchio marinaio*, p. 9.

Works Cited

Barber, Giles. 1961. Galignani's and the publication of English books in France from 1800 to 1852. *Library: The Transactions of the Bibliographical Society* [London], 16 [December]: 267–86.

Barnaby, Paul (compiler). 2007. Timeline: The European reception of S. T. Coleridge. In *The Reception of S. T. Coleridge in Europe*, ed. Elinor Shaffer and Edoardo Zuccato. The Reception of British and Irish Authors in Europe, Series Editor: Elinor Shaffer. London: Continuum, pp. xviii–lx.

Bate, Jonathan. 1990. Edgar Allan Poe: a debt Repaid. *The Coleridge Connection*, ed. Richard Gravil and Molly Lefebure. London: Macmillan, pp. 255–70.

Brandes, Georg. 1872–91. *Die Hauptströmungen der Literatur des neunzehnten Jahrhunderts;* 6 vols. Berlin: F. Duncker. These lectures were given in Danish in Copenhagen and translated into German within a year. Coleridge appears in Vol. II. Engl. trans: *Main Currents in Nineteenth-Century Literature*, Heinemann, 1904.

Brandl, Alois. 1886. *Samuel Taylor Coleridge und die Englische Romantik.* Strassburg: Karl Trübner; Berlin: Oppenheim 1886. Engl. trans. by Lady Elizabeth Rigby Eastlake, *Samuel Taylor Coleridge and the English Romantic School.* London: John Murray, 1887.

Breunig, Hans Werner. 2007. Coleridge's German reception after 1945. In *The Reception of S. T. Coleridge in Europe*, ed. Elinor Shaffer and Edoardo Zuccato. London: Continuum, pp. 113–34.

Burwick, Frederick. 2007. The reception of Coleridge in Germany to World War II. In *The Reception of S. T. Coleridge in Europe*, ed. Elinor Shaffer and Edoardo Zuccato. London: Continuum, pp. 88–112.

Cardwell, Richard, ed. 2005. *The Reception of Lord Byron in Europe*, 2 vols. The Reception of British and Irish Authors in Europe, Series Editor: Elinor Shaffer. London:Continuum.

Casanova, Pascale. 2005. *The World Republic of Letters*. Engl. trans. by M.B. Debevoise of *La République mondiale des lettres* (1999). Harvard: Harvard University Press.

Chasles, Philarète. 1850. Portraits contemporains: Jerémie Bentham, Coleridge, Foscolo, *Etudes sur les hommes et les moeurs du XIXe siècle*, Paris: Amyot.

Coghen, Monika. 2007. Coleridge's Polish reception. In *The Reception of S. T. Coleridge in Europe*, ed. Elinor Shaffer and Edoardo Zuccato. London: Continuum, pp. 275–96.

Earle, Peter G. 1960. *Unamuno and English Literature*. New York: Hispanic Institute in the United States.

Eliot, T. S. 1949. From Poeto Valéry. New York: Harcourt Brace & Company.

Flores Moreno, Cristina. 2009. Nature imagined in S. T. Coleridge's 'Meditative Poems' and Miguel de Unamuno's *Poesías*: A study on reception. *Comparative Critical Studies*, 6 (1).

—— 2008. *Plastic Intellectual Breeze. The Contribution of Ralph Cudworth to S. T. Coleridge's Early Poetics of the Symbol.* Bern: Peter Lang.

Furman, Nelly. 1971. *'La Revue des Deux Mondes et le romantisme' (1831–1848).* Geneva: Droz.

Hough, Barry and Howard, Davis. 2007. Coleridge's Malta. *Coleridge Bulletin*, NS 29 (Summer): 81–95.

—— —— 2008. Coleridge as Public Secretary in Malta: the surviving archives *Coleridge Bulletin*, NS 31 (Summer): 90–101.

—— —— 2009. Coleridge's Laws: A Study of Coleridge in Malta. Open Book Publishing.

JONES, KATHLEEN. 1939. *'La Revue Britannique': son histoire et son action littéraire 1825–1840*. Paris: Droz.

KLESSE, ANTJE. 2001. Illustrationen zu S. T. Coleridge's 'The Rime of the Ancient Mariner'. Eine Studie zur Illustration von Gedichten, Memmingen: Curt Visel.

KOOY, MICHAEL JOHN. 2007. Coleridge's early reception in France, from the First to the Second Empire. In *The Reception of S. T. Coleridge in Europe*, ed. Elinor Shaffer and Edoardo Zuccato. London: Continuum, pp. 27–60.

NASI, FRANCO. 2007. Coleridge's aesthetic philosophy and critical writings in Italy. In *The Reception of S. T. Coleridge in Europe*, ed. Elinor Shaffer and Edoardo Zuccato. London: Continuum, pp. 213–41.

PEROJO ARRONTE, EUGENIA. 2007a. Imaginative Romanticism and the search for a transcendental Art: Coleridge's poetry and poetics in nineteenth-century Spain. In *The Reception of S. T. Coleridge in Europe*, ed. Elinor Shaffer and Edoardo Zuccato. London: Continuum, pp. 135–66.

—— 2007b. Coleridge's poetry and poetics in twentieth-century Spain. In Elinor Shaffer and Edoardo Zuccato, eds., *The Reception of S. T. Coleridge in Europe*. London: Continuum, pp. 167–96.

PICHOIS, CLAUDE. 1965. *Philarète Chasles et la vie littéraire au temps du romantisme*. 2 vols. Paris: Librairie José Corti.

PRAZ, MARIO. 1947. Introduzione, *La ballata del vecchio marinaio*, Florence: Fussi.

QUINN, PATRICK. 1971. *The French Face of Edgar Poe*. Carbondate and London: Southern Illinois University Press.

SCHMID, SUSANNE and ROSSINGTON, MICHAEL, eds. 2008. *The Reception of P. B. Shelley in Europe*. The Reception of British and Irish Authors in Europe, Series Editor: Elinor Shaffer. London: Continuum.

SHAFFER, ELINOR. 1975. *'Kubla Khan' and The Fall of Jerusalem. The Mythological School in Biblical Criticism and Secular Literature*. Cambridge: Cambridge University Press.

—— and EDOARDO, ZUCCATO. eds. 2007. *The Reception of S. T. Coleridge in Europe*. London: Continuum. With Timeline of Coleridge's reception in Europe by Paul Barnaby and an extensive bibliography.

SOUBIGOU, GILLES. 2007. The reception of *The Rime of the Ancient Mariner* through Gustave Doré's illustrations. In Elinor Shaffer and Eduardo Zuccato, eds., *The Reception of S. T. Coleridge in Europe*. London: Continuum, pp. 61–87.

ST CLAIR, WILLIAM. 2004. *The Reading Nation in the Romantic Period*. Cambridge: Cambridge University Press.

STOVALL, FLOYD. 1969. Poe's debt to Coleridge. *University of Texas Studies in English*, x (1930): 70–127, Repr. in *Edgar Poe the Poet*. Charlottesville: University Press of Virginia.

SULTANA, DONALD J. 1969. *Coleridge on Malta*. Oxford: Blackwell.

VIGUS, JAMES. 1804. Zwischen Kantianismus und Schellingianismus: Henry Crabb Robinsons Privatvorlesungen über Philosophie für Madame de Staël 1804 in Weimar. Appendix: Mme de Staëls Marginalien zu Henry Crabb Robinsons Manuskripten. Germaine de Stael und ihr erstes deutsches Publikum, ed. Gerhard R. Kaiser and Olaf Muller. Heidelberg: Winter 2009: 357–93.

VIGUS, JAMES and WRIGHT, JANE, eds. 2008. *Coleridge's Afterlives.* Basingstoke: Palgrave Macmillan.

VOLKOVA, ELENA. 2007. The albatross in Russia: praised, shot and repented. *The Reception of S. T. Coleridge in Europe,* ed. Elinor Shaffer and Edoardo Zuccato. London: Continuum, pp. 297–317.

WELLEK, RENÉ. 1931. *Immanuel Kant in England, 1793–1838.* Princeton: Princeton University Press.

ZUCCATO, EDOARDO. 1996. *Coleridge in Italy.* Cork: Cork University Press.

—— 2007. 'The Translation of Coleridge's Poetry and his Influence on Twentieth-Century Italian Poetry', *The Reception of S. T. Coleridge in Europe,* ed. Elinor Shaffer and Edoardo Zuccato. London: Continuum, pp. 197–212.

CHAPTER 37

WRITING ABOUT
COLERIDGE

ROBERT M. MANIQUIS

> We await ... the great genius who shall triumphantly succeed in believing
> *something.* For those of us who are higher than the mob, and lower than
> the man of inspiration, there is always *doubt*; and in doubt we are living
> parasitically (which is better than not living at all) on the minds of the
> men of genius of the past who have believed something.
>
> T. S. Eliot, *A Note on Poetry and Belief* (1927)

CRITICAL writing about Coleridge is labyrinthine, not unlike Coleridge's own
prose, but no serious reader of Coleridge disdains a labyrinth. Reading his best
poems, his lectures and essays, his letters and notebooks, we, like the Wedding
Guest in 'The Rime of the Ancient Mariner', are led to cryptic halts, which, to invert
Keats's phrase, tease us into thought. Coleridge tells us that thinking demands
physical energy, that there is no thinking without deep feeling, and that 'by deep
feeling, we make our ideas *dim,* and this is what we mean by *our life, ourselves*' (*CN*,
I, 921). As in our lives, light alternates with dimness in many of Coleridge's texts.
We continuously wonder, for instance, why the Mariner kills the albatross or what
Geraldine is up to in *Christabel*—is there something divine or lurid going on there?
And we are often not above looking in Coleridge for darkness within darkness.
DeQuincey, Baudelaire, and Jack London have taught us that completely drugged
or drunken oracles speak twaddle, and yet we are still tempted by the false idea that
Kubla Khan is only an opium revelation, which only further obscures a magnifi-
cently dark poem.

If Coleridge's poems bristle with interpretive puzzles, his prose has provided a problematic base for modern interpretation itself. He wrote, indeed, the most obscure and—perhaps because it is obscure—the most influential critical paragraph in English literature, that which defines Imagination and Fancy in Book XIII of the *Biographia Literaria* (*BL*, 304–5.) That one passage has been explained by erudite commentators, working in holes and corners, famous poets, speaking to the wide world, and professors brandishing belief in a cultural *something* that seems to bear some resemblance to God. Together they have invoked everything under the sun, in order to make sense of what once was indispensable to English-speaking culture, the grand open secret of the Imagination. To unpack this idea, explicators invoke the ancient philosophers and Church fathers, old and new psychic theories, Enlightenment and modern theories of language, German idealism, Higher Criticism of the Bible, mythological criticism, mysticism and theosophy, Christian heresies, and Greek drama. The list of what is used to explain Coleridge's poetry and his ideas could go on much longer. But the reader is perhaps already wary of this critical mass and is looking here, not for another list of its variety, but for guidance to it. Because too many interpretations jostle about in too many excellent books and essays, no simple guide to criticism of Coleridge is possible here or, for that matter, anywhere else. Nor will there be here talk of the excellent biographies of Coleridge or studies of his theology, his politics, his poetic techniques, his plagiarism, his relationship with Wordsworth, or to continental literature. For these topics, the reader may go to other essays in this very handbook. Rather, what follows are sketches of where a few critics have laid out paths towards Coleridge—paths then trod by many others. Because I can, in a few pages, signal only some points of entry into this criticism, my descriptions will be rapid and my preferences will simply have to show through. With, then, neither completeness nor justifications of my tilt towards or away from any given idea, here are some twists and turns in the matter of Coleridge—twists and turns that I personally find interesting.

Interesting moments abound in Coleridge. Consider, for instance, a sentence from his *Notebooks* about a pot of urine, which is neither a trivial nor an irreverent topic. American readers especially will remember the shock of Cotton Mather, colonial Puritan divine, when, as he was making water against a wall, he noticed a dog likewise emptying the 'Cistern of Nature'. This unpleasant epiphany of the beast within forced Mather to resolve that while evacuating, he would henceforth turn his mind away from the waste that unites him with the dog, and upwards towards God (Mather, 1: 357 (June, 1700)). Much like Cotton Mather and Samuel Johnson and even John Bunyan, Coleridge was commonly wracked with guilt. But it was certainly not urine that would send him into fear and trembling—quite the opposite. He enjoyed, on at least one occasion, looking, much as children do, at the contents of a chamber pot. In 1953 Humphrey House, in an elegant series of lectures entitled simply *Coleridge*, cited the following sentence from the *Notebooks*:

What a beautiful Thing Urine is, in a Pot, brown yellow, transpicuous, the Image, diamond shaped of the of the [*sic*] Candle in it, especially, as it now appeared, I having emptied the Snuffers into it, & the Snuff floating about, & painting all-shaped Shadows on the Bottom.

(*CN*, Dec. 1803, I, 1766, quoted by House, 48)

House wanted to recall and emphasize Coleridge's fascination with physical sensations and impressions, which he balances against overemphasis on Coleridge the critical thinker. Sensual exploration and metaphysical theory are poles of attraction between which Coleridge moved, sometimes preoccupied with such sensations as, for instance, pinching himself in 'double touch', and thinking about the line between simultaneous sensations— or are they simultaneous?—of touch feeling itself. Beginning, however, at the other end of things; he also strung together theories of theology, imagination, culture, education, the state, and he thought long about how to explain the *Logos* that holds the universe of mind and things together in time and space. It is reasonable, then, to think of two Coleridges, the empiricist sensualist and the theorizer, keeping in mind Coleridge's maxim that 'extremes meet' and that these two Coleridges are really only one. Although there is no privileged way to navigate through criticism on Coleridge, a critic's emphasis on either the explorer of sensations or the theorizer of concepts is a simple but reliable way to gauge where a book or essay on Coleridge may ultimately lead. On the one hand, there are the oppositions of *subject* and *object*, contraries that Coleridge described in unity or opposition, but also further below them, simple *haeccitas*, thingness, the small, the concrete, the sensual, the surprising, the anecdotal, the epiphanic, the unique. And then there are the epistemological, metaphysical, theological, taxonomic, historical, and critical ideas. Pointing to these contemplative tiers in Coleridge may seem banal, for we all move between subject and object, concrete and abstract, inductive and deductive, and do we not all feel our double natures, our bodily and mental selves, our masculine and feminine traits, the right and left sides of our brains? Doubling and merged dualities provide our psychic commonplaces, from Dostoevskian, Stevensonian, and Freudian doppelgängerish personalities, to pairings of the Dionysian and the Apollonian, to Kafkaesque transformations, by which, like Hieronymus Bosch, we blend man and insect or smile at Clark Kent's transparent disguise of an American übermensch. Such contraries as were once found in medieval dialogues of the body and the soul or in philosophy's mind–body problem were amalgamated by Coleridge into broad alternations between the sensual and the mental. His is a case of a deeply religious man who periodically falls from holistic Christian paradox of the human and the divine into conflicting mental dualities. He is a writer whose ideal of subject and object unified is often pierced by polarities of the particular and the universal, whose ripping apart or collapsing together can *both* threaten momentary—or final—disintegration. No sensible critic or biographer of Coleridge of whom I am aware has imagined that Coleridgean contraries can be separated one from the other. And a good number of writers enjoy exploring both sides of Coleridge. But critics quite often tip in one direction or the other, and even when the critic knows *both* the phenomenalist and the noumenalist in Coleridge, *where that critic puts the emphasis makes all the difference.* What Humphry House was doing in 1954, in citing such passages as that on the pot of urine, was bringing us back to Coleridge the sensual explorer. But why did House think that the emphasis should be pulled that way and back from what? The beginnings of an answer to this question lie in the differences between the two most influential books ever written on Coleridge, both published about twenty years before Humprhy House's book: John Livingston Lowes's *The Road to Xanadu: A Study in the Ways of the Imagination* (1927) and I. A. Richards's *Coleridge on the Imagination* (1934). Their emphases and hence their effect upon subsequent ideas about Coleridge could not be more different.

The Road to Xanadu is one of the best books about poetry ever written in English. To be sure, Lowes's prose is overwrought. His swirling names of animals, things, colors, shapes, smells, and various material stuff may take us aback. His poetic prose flirts with the wondrous in lyrical flights, exotic diction, orchestrated tonalities, and occasional organ chords. None of this, however, interferes with the tough-minded parts of his enquiry. His ornate prose counterpoints the hard intelligence of the critic who, like a stubborn detective, traces sources of Coleridge's poetry in his reading. Not that one must agree with what Lowes says about poetry or imagination to enjoy the book. Agreement with him often seems beside the point as he draws us into semantic delight. Furthermore, making correct or incorrect assertions is not really the way a critical position wields influence. The power to impose a reading of poetry or a theory about it demands logical plausibility. But critical power derives as much from a striking mental style, an imposing attitude, the impressive nature of the assertions themselves, and values already shared by one's readers. In these respects, however loose Lowes's ideas, his book is seductive. At times he seems to be trying to imitate the ways of Coleridgean imagination in the way he writes about it. Here he is on one of the *Notebooks*:

It is a mirror of the fitful and kaleidoscopic moods and a record of the germinal ideas of one of the most supremely gifted and utterly incalculable spirits ever let loose upon the planet. And it is nothing else in the world so much as a jungle, illuminated eerily with patches of phosphorescent light, and peopled with uncanny life and strange exotic flowers. But it is teeming and fecund soil, and out of it later rose, like exhalations, gleaming and aërial shapes. (6)

When House, twenty years or so later, leaned towards the shore where Lowes describes Coleridge, he was less betwitched than Lowes by the magical poet of association. But House leaned more in that direction than he did towards I. A. Richards's sense of things in *Coleridge on the Imagination*. In order to appreciate House's balancing act, we need to consider why Richards rejected Lowes's version of the Coleridgean imagination.

Before he published his book on Coleridge in 1934, Richards had begun fighting, not long after the First World War, the good fight for poetry against the exclusive attribution of truth or falsity to scientific discourse. His emphasis was not, like that of Lowes, on Coleridge's accretive mind out of which flowed musically associated images in poems like *Kubla Khan*, which Lowes considered magical but uninterpretable and perhaps meaningless. Meaning was not the concern of Lowes as it was for Richards, who after all, was the author of *The Meaning of Meaning* (1923). Although he explains in that book that the concept *meaning* itself keeps slipping away from us in the complex 'behavior' of words, Richards went to Coleridge for principles by which to interpret something he would not be embarrassed to call the meaning of a poem. He left to Lowes that version of Coleridge imaged as the phenomenalist *promeneur* ambling about in dreamy associations. It was Coleridge the discriminating critical theorist whom Richards sought. What he hoped for was enough psychological coherence with which to counter the associationism celebrated by Lowes, to correct the sloppy emotionalism indulged in by many readers, and to point out the mistake in the scientific dismissal of poetic emotion as a form of knowledge. In *Practical Criticism* (1929) he analyzed hundreds of anonymous readings, which he called 'protocols', by students of dozens of good and not so good poems. In these readings, he found gross mis-reading caused mostly by slippage from the poem being read into associations from other remembered poems. No such haphazard reading could be respected by anyone who respected the ideals of scientific discipline, for, despite its limitations in exploring mind and language, science, however difficult its topic, is usually clear about what it is talking about and *how* it is talking about it. Shoddy literary reading is usually unclear and never really knows what it is talking about. Richards wanted to replace it with ways to agree on at least the immediate things a poem was asserting or describing. He also wanted ways to identify carefully the tone and apparent intention of the poetic speaker. And he wanted ways to evaluate emotive statements. He called these *pseudo-statements* in order to specify that poetry conveyed truths and perhaps falsities quite special to its way of speaking, but not therefore less important than scientific statements, whose truth and falsity were available in science's way of speaking. What was implied by value in emotive statements was its quotient of psychological force and its capacity to affect the reader's feelings and to connect them to behavior, something that science cannot always do. The structured emotional expression of poems, he argued, could relay information, determine attitudes, and modify feeling, thinking, and actual living. Richards was not given to purple flourishes, but his cultural purpose is clear. What he wrote and what he taught, at Cambridge and later at Harvard, had to do with forming the mind within a surrounding mass culture and an elite, emotive literary culture both of which had disabled even educated readers.

In considering the difference between Richards and Lowes it is not necessary to think of disciplined thought versus associative effusion. Lowes was anything but sloppy. His tracing of the accumulated images from Coleridge's reading that formed associative hooks and eyes demanded careful discriminations. Although he does not interpret *The Rime of the Ancient Mariner* or *Kubla Khan*, there is the implication that in order to engage poems produced by the associative power, the reader must receive both the associations in the poem and even mix them with his own. This is exemplified by Lowes's enfolding of his personal, anecdotal associations in demonstrating how Coleridge's associations must have worked. Actually Lowes demonstrates less precisely how Coleridge writes than how he reads. He reminds us, of course, that there is no poem built upon associations without will, judgement, and disciplined selection (90–2). He says in so many words, as any teacher of poetry might, that a poem is not a bucket of randomly connected thoughts. But concentrating on what happens before and during the writing of a poem produces an emphasis and an accumulative effect on 'creative energy' in *The Road to Xanadu*. This creative energy and celebration of associations spills over into his notion of the imagination of Coleridge, as well as of Chaucer, of the mathematician Poincaré, and of Darwin. To be consistent with this timeless imagination as the creative power of association Lowes revises Coleridge's definition in the *Biographia Literaria*, claiming that it is wrong to distinguish Fancy from Imagination, which he asserts is only one process working in different degrees of intensity (103).

Richards considered this description of Coleridgean imagination quite mistaken (31–8). The collapsing of Fancy and Imagination into one agency of different intensities he saw as one source of the mis-readings he had discovered in *Practical Criticism*. In writing *Coleridge on the Imagination* in part to counter such mistakes, he did not produce, like Lowes, an enthralling book, but a rather difficult psychological essay. Still, *Coleridge on the Imagination* is as enjoyable to read as *The Road to Xanadu*, the enjoyment coming not in a phenomenological dance but in closely argued textual interpretation and epistemological distinctions. He quotes from and tries to force into theory and practice what Coleridge does in comparing various lines from Shakespeare's *Venus and Adonis* (*Lects 1808–19*, 5, I, 67, 81). One set of lines arises from mere fancy, another from the height of intense imagination. Coleridge was obviously distinguishing good poetry from poetry not quite as good. But how is it that one set of lines is better than another—how exactly do we distinguish Fancy from Imagination, upon what basis, implying what knowledge, and, most important, to what end? What Coleridge says about those sets of lines in *Venus and Adonis* is sensitive and sensible. But what is to be extracted from such interpretations of poetic lines in the way of arguable principles with which to measure mental phenomena as difficult to define as *feelings*?

For early twentieth-century readers, nothing was available to meet such critical *desiderata*, except in the books that Richards had himself already authored. The principles one could derive from reading Dryden, Pope, or Johnson—all instructive readers of poetry—were not suited to nineteenth- and early twentieth-century poetic diction, tone, subject, audience, genres, and newly figured presences of the poet in the poem. Most important, classical critics could not answer new cultural needs in a rapidly de-Christianizing mass society. Nor was there, at least for Richards, anything like a native version of Aristotle's *The Poetics*, adaptable to the reading of English poetry. Richards's calling upon Coleridge seems inevitable. No writer other than Coleridge had been such a prolific and influential interpreter of texts, especially those of Shakespeare and of Wordsworth, who had come to be seen as the best English poet since Milton. Matthew Arnold was the other looming nineteenth-century sage, known, like Coleridge, for inculcating a bourgeois idea of culture cultivated in a cross-breeding of religion and literature. Arnold offered a Victorian version of the *clerisy*, the educated class imagined by Coleridge as an intellectual elite in a projected 'National Church' (*CCS*, 50–60). But his elite is even more diffuse than Coleridge's, a mythical classless class that would help to culturally embody and yet rise above the political and the social. To accompany this grand idea there were Arnold's famous 'touchstones', the best that has been thought and said in the language of the tribe. Touchstones were honored utterances by which the disinterested classless class could sense what was well from what was badly thought and said (Arnold, 161–88). But there was no principle within the touchstones discernable except by appealing to the mind that could, without laboriousness, understand their significance, where *understanding* actually meant *feeling* their talismanic *aura* and their inspiring or, one could also say, their obfuscating power. The touchstones reposed upon a grand *petitio principii*, to wit, the cultured mind recognizes itself in recognizing the best that has been thought and said by the cultured mind. Touchstones were feeble imitations of what Coleridge was trying to show in practical interpretation, that is, the difference between those lines of Fancy and those lines of Imagination in *Venus and Adonis*. In the midst of the still powerful presence of the Arnoldian in English literary culture, Richards, if he were to invoke any critical authority at all, looked past Arnoldian religiose culture back to the psychologized religion of Coleridge, someone he thought more likely to exemplify precise reading while transmitting an arguable theory of how imagination works.

Two problems had to be confronted in looking beyond Arnold to Coleridge. The first is that, if Arnold's system of touchstones went round and round in defining culture, Richards wielded his own hermeneutic circle. Trying to avoid, he says, the collapse of descriptive analysis into the thing described, he falls into one of his moments of idealistic faith:

Fortunately we have a more direct and surer method of identifying the work of the Imagination; namely, through the Imagination itself. In spite of all aberrations there is a persistent tradition...which recognizes acts of Imagination. Literally they are *recognized*: the *all in each* finds again in them the same enlargement. Arnold said that great poetry interests the permanent passions; but this, as so often happens, splits what is one into two.

For the passions are *in* the poetry and the poetry is only the way this interest and these passions go in it. No description of Imagination is of any use to those who do not otherwise sometimes know this way—as poets; or know when they are in it, as readers; yet it is the way—however often fashion, miscomprehension, obstructive pre-possessions, or dullness may hide it from us (98).

This beggars the begging of the question in Arnold's touchstones. And it comes close to the kind of identification of poet and reader that Lowes insists upon. It is one of those passages in Richards's writing—others occur in *Principles of Criticism* and *Practical Criticism*—in which we catch more than a glimpse of attachment, not only to a scientific or psychological, but also to an essentialist, Romantic notion of the mind. This is the mind de-Christianized, celebrating its own aesthetically disciplined order.

In carrying this Coleridgean self-recognition of imagination forward into the twentieth century Richards had also to confront the problem that, however psychologized they were, Coleridge's religious ideas were central to his concept of the imagination. This religious aura had to be stripped away or at least roughened against the more hesitant, self-conscious reaching out of the mind toward order. That is why for Richards, as for many subsequent readers of chapter XIII in *Biographia Literaria*, the orders of the Primary and Secondary Imagination undergo a shift of emphasis. What Coleridge calls 'the living Power and the prime Agent of all human perception, and as a repetition in the finite mind of the eternal act of creation in the infinite I AM' takes second place in interest to the Secondary Imagination, which 'dissolves, diffuses, dissipates, in order to recreate, or where this process is rendered impossible, yet still at all events it struggles to idealize and to unify' (*BL* 304–5). Just as Lowes had collapsed Fancy, the predominantly associative faculties, into both the Primary and Secondary Imagination, Richards collapsed the Primary into the Secondary. In the Secondary Imagination he tried to systematize the principles of Coleridgean imagination by psychologizing them even more than Coleridge did. He was aware of Freud and suspected that much must be bubbling in that mysterious—or as many think today—that fictional psychoanalytic unconscious. Richards did not, however, call for psychoanalytic interpretation, but a general psychologism quite as mysteriously operative as the suffusion of Coleridge's Secondary Imagination by the Primary. He sought something like a taxonomy or what he calls an 'inventory' of the emotions rather than their anthropological origins.

Two of the most important immediate reactions to Richards's project came in the writings of F. R. Leavis and T. S. Eliot. Leavis had great respect for Coleridge, but was alarmed at Richards's scientific leanings. Defender of literary against mass culture, Leavis suspected that Richards was giving in to the vulgar myth of access to truth only in science. Leavis considered analogies to science in reading poetry a mistake in the war against science's intellectual provincialism and the manufactured emotional effusion he despised and traced to bad Romantic habits (Leavis, 336–57). But the ooze of emotion in both mass and educated culture was what Richards also considered an immense danger and which, with the aid of disciplined, scientifically inspired precision, might be fought off. By enlisting Coleridge Richards sought to lead unorganized minds into principled arguing of how emotion worked in good poetry, how it was organized, what its value was as knowledge, how it could be a guide to action and, as Richards dramatically puts it, the working out of one's 'freedom'. Leavis and Richards were, after all, fighting the same battle. T. S. Eliot, a good friend of Richards, invokes Coleridge in a few of his own essays, but Eliot also saw in Richards and elsewhere the humanist project by which stripping the Coleridgean of its religious aura and driving it towards the organized free mind was only another maneuver of literary Protestantism, of which, it can be said, Romanticism is the supreme example. Eliot tended to see most literature that followed upon Romanticism as decaying Protestantism (Eliot, 1934: 39). Like Coleridge, he had gone from Unitarianism to Anglican Orthodoxy, and while he could not imagine his poetry completely separate from his beliefs (Eliot, 1927: 59–62), he preferred distinguishing religious belief from its *simulacra* as poetry, and although Richards did not call for belief in God but in a humanly imagined order recognizing itself, that was still an act of belief. Eliot preferred to avoid these literary forms of decaying religion. He disliked the humanist substitute: 'Nothing in this world or the next is a substitute for anything else; and if you find you must do without something, such as religious faith or philosophic belief, then you must just do without it' (Eliot, 1933: 133). Leavis and Eliot, on several issues, then, parted ways with Richards on the subjects of science and belief. But it was Richards's instrumentalizing of Coleridge that turned out to be the greater influence. His suggestion that reading should imitate at least the rigor of science and find psychological ways to describe the emotions, with his appeal to Coleridgean imagination, was a pioneering project. His many books devoted to disciplining the reading of literature are still as important in understanding Coleridge as is *The Road to Xanadu*. Lowes seemed not to doubt the eternal power of human imagination to inspire either a Coleridge or a Darwin nor the eternal power of poems to work their magic on the reader. Richards seriously doubted the power of poetry to convey truths in a scientific or imperfectly educated literary culture if it could no longer be read, not only with magic, but with discipline. That a critic as brilliant as Richards undertook to teach anew the reading of poetry and that he called on Coleridgean complexity to help him did not bode well for the reading of poetry in the twentieth century. Be that as it may, the propulsion of Coleridge directly into the center of modern English criticism was both critically and, as we shall see, ideologically imposing. By the end of the Second World War, where students in high school or graduate school earnestly studied a poem, the ideas of Coleridge, refracted by Richards, hovered in the classroom.[1]

The most obvious influence of those ideas was, especially in America, in the so-called New Criticism, a way of reading that converted old religious tendencies of high culture into a new humanist sensibility and intelligence trained upon the work of art itself. This had nothing to do, I hasten to add, with anything like the idea of art for art's sake. New Criticism was, in fact, culturally and political tendentious. Following the critical example of Richards, it developed further the principle that the poem's unifying tensions, ambiguities, ironies, and paradoxes had the effect of organizing the mind and the emotions into a sense of freedom. This was naturally to be pinned to nothing more explicit than the freedom of the trained, sophisticated reader from the stock responses, the sentimentalities, the historically anecdotal, the Romantically corrupted understanding of poetic emotion and its connection to ideas. But the underlying connections between such interpretive freedom and that, in the outside world, from political doctrines and battles, shared something of Coleridge's and Arnold's ideas of a clerisy or a disinterested readership, a privileged intelligentsia that could identify its members at least by the way they read texts. The New Critics were not members of a uniformed brigade. Each critic connected with it—Empson, Brooks, Blackmur, Tate, Ransom—developed their own critical style and specific interpretations of literary works. But it is not difficult to see in all these critics an attitude toward literature and reading sponsored by Richards in his appeal to Coleridge's Secondary Imagination. Furthermore New Critics were eclectic and could be as inspired by Richards's intellectual critics as much as they were by Richards himself. Whether it was Eliot expiating on the 'dissociation of sensibility' by which Romanticism separated the emotive from the intellectual or Leavis's praise of D. H. Lawrence as an authentic purveyor of intelligence combined with feeling or I. A. Richards finding a special status for the 'truth' of emotive statements, such critics sought, in their different ways, to save aesthetic expression of emotion from absorption by the manufactured emotions of an invasive, romantically generated mass culture. The irony, of course, is how often a romantic Coleridgean idea about the mind authorizes this cultural critique of Romanticism and the reading program that it empowered...

The reading program was that of mentality seeking wholeness, order, balance, and consoling poetic form in the midst of modern disorder. Paul Fussell in *The Great War and Modern Memory* (1975) describes how the unspeakable horror of the First World War drove literary expression of emotion into ironic, tangential rubbing up against terror, a distancing that kept the mind from endless darkness

---

[1] The influence of I. A. Richards on twentieth-century criticism is recounted in many books and articles. A useful place to begin such reading is with A. C. Goodson, *Verbal Imagination: Coleridge and the Language of Modern Criticism* (New York and Oxford: Oxford University Press, 1988), 3–55. For excellent introductions to Richards and his works, see John Constable, *I. A. Richards, Selected Works: 1919–1938* (London and New York, 2001), 10 vols.

of the soul. Another warding off of that darkness is there in Richards's *Coleridge on the Imagination*, in the armament of ambiguities, rounded ironies, paradoxes, all these and many more structural stresses balanced in the unity of a poem. A poem's clashes of thought and feeling could be, if the poem was good, held together in the stressed tensional and mutual clasp of emotion and intellect. This wholeness was attractive compared to the disintegrating impression carried in sensations from a brutal, real world. Like all the irony-wielding poets and novelists pointed to by Fussell, New Critical writers lived under the historical image of the First World War and later the Second World War. Though these critics were not given to the reducing of poems to the Freudian family romance, they certainly knew what Freud was talking about in *Civilization and its Discontents* (1930), an essay every bit as affected by the brutalities of 1914 to 1918 as any novel or poem had been by its horrors. The New Critics were not simply escapists. Poetic tension, holding the mind in place, was not an isolated aesthetic concept. If, for Freud, neurosis held in permanent tension destructive instincts and the moral censure within the self, critics under the aegis of the Coleridgean, organically unified poem found in the tensions, ambiguities, and paradoxes ways to hold in place at least reflections of the world's internecine violence. This poetic unity was grounded, without reductive Freudian psychologizing and with those principles of imagination adumbrated by Coleridge, instrumentalized by Richards, and driven by the New Critics into particular poems and the rigorous reading of them.

Not all critics thought, however, that one could look for rigor either in Richards's theories, in his use of Coleridge's, or in New Critical interpretations. In discussing Richards's recalling of Coleridge as a guide to a modern concept of imagination, I suggested there was for Richards no more obvious guide than Coleridge and that no one resembling Aristotle was suitable to Richards's cultural purpose. But another group of critics, disciplined readers like Richards and the New Critics, chose indeed to follow, not Coleridge, but Aristotle. This group emerged in the 1930s at the University of Chicago and were known ultimately as Neo-Aristotelians. They took a stance against a creature they called the 'Coleridgean critic'. More than a straw man and less than any individual critic, the Coleridgean critic, in the eyes of the Neo-Aristotelians was a 'type', an amalgamation of Romantic, deductive practices of humanist essentialism by which something universal called 'poetry' or 'imagination' was imposed on aesthetic objects called 'poems'. In one of his first descriptions of what the Neo-Aristotelian criticism took to be wrong with contemporary criticism, R. S. Crane described as 'Coleridgean' the obvious suspects, I. A. Richards, Cleanth Brooks, John Crowe Ransom, and Allen Tate, but also included T. S. Eliot, as critics who assuming,

as nearly all critics since Coleridge have done, that poetry is a single essence reflecting in its peculiar medium the unity of experience or of the mind or of human speech, and hence that the knowledge of poetry is one and is inseparable in its ultimate principles from knowledge of psychology or language, they have aimed at the kind of organic treatment of poems which is possible only when the terms used to effect it are broader in their signification not only than particular varieties of poems but also than poetry itself. (Crane, 199)

The New Critics, in fact, did not read poems, it was argued; rather they looked for 'touchstones' of that universal abstract called 'poetry', itself the reflection of some other undefined order, a *something* to stimulate or simulate belief. Referring to the 'touchstones' in New Critical interpretation was, of course, meant to be derogatory. Far from being precise readers, the New Critics, it was argued, were 'amateur philosophers' who obscured intrinsic forms of poems by forcing into them ideas about imagination and 'organic' unity. These deleterious effects upon literary criticism were attributable to the influence of the earliest semantic theories of Richards, capped off by the importation of Coleridge's theories in his 1934 book and its pervasive influence. The Neo-Aristotelians—R. S. Crane, Elder Olsen, Richard McKeon, and others—rightly identified the dominance of Coleridge in the New Criticism, which they also rightly identified as the dominant practice of American and, to a lesser extent, British criticism. This clash between the Chicago and the New Critical schools of criticism suggests how culturally hegemonic the Coleridgean had become. Coleridge was by the middle of the twentieth century just as pervasive as he had been through the last half of the nineteenth, beginning in 1839 to 1840 with the publication of Mill's famous essays on Bentham and Coleridge. By reaching back beyond Coleridge to Aristotle, just as Richards had reached past Arnold to Coleridge, the Neo-Aristotelians invoked the rhetorical analysis of genre and the developing 'action' of a poem, play, or novel by which aesthetic devices found their 'intrinsic' form. In *that* analysis, the individual poem would shed those pieces of Coleridgean cultural baggage that obscured the ideas of such unjustly honored critics as Empson and Brooks. Kenneth Burke, the American critic, whose eclecticism makes him difficult to label, defended the Coleridgean critic against these attacks. He compared the different starting points of both kinds of critics and argued that it hardly matters from which point one starts, for both the Neo-Aristotelians and the Coleridgeans were deductive when inductive and vice versa (Burke, 465–84).[2] Burke himself turns to Coleridge frequently in his many provocative rhetorical works, which suggests that Coleridge in the twentieth century was not only the occasion for the making of critical schools and their clashes, but that even for someone like Burke—rhetorician, grammarian, sometime Freudian, sometime Marxist, sometime structuralist critic—Coleridge offered

---

[2] Burke is responding to Crane's preface to essays by Norman MacLean and Elder Olsen, which appeared in *The University Review*, University of Kansas City in 1942 (Crane, 1942) and in which Crane's critique of Coleridgean critics is succinctly stated. Ten years later the critique was expanded in *Critics and Criticism* (Crane, et al., 1952), especially in the 'Introduction,' 1–24, and in the chapters 'I. A. Richards on the Art of Interpretation', 27–43 and 'The Critical Monism of Cleanth Brooks', 83–107. The terms used by Crane and others, quoted in my discussion, are all to be found in Crane's Introduction and these chapters, *passim*.

places from which to launch a definition, an idea, a nuance. Burke's defense of the Coleridgean critics, however, seems today hardly to have been crucial since the Neo-Aristotelian critics, although they made incisive interpretations of texts and brilliant critiques of the New Critics, would never have anything like the influence of the Coleridgean humanists.

It is important to remember that all through the decades of critical dispute that I have described, many scholars continued about their business unengaged in fierce critical battles, content to explain the complex contexts of Coleridge's social, political, philosophical, and theological worlds. For although it may seem that the period 1770 to 1830 is neatly summed up in platitudes about Romanticism, the work of many scholars like Beer, Schaffer, McFarland, to mention just a few, suggest how much there is still to debate, to suspect, to learn. Even Norman Fruman, whose preoccupation with Coleridge's plagiarisms made him seem to over-reverential Coleridgeans no more than a bull in a china shop, had things to teach to those who disapproved of him. The emphasis in this and other useful intellectual history tends to be on Coleridge the thinker and theorist, but usually not at the expense of Coleridge the associationist and sensual explorer. Scholarly books of this period are certainly not sheltered from contemporary critical clashes. Some participate, if only indirectly in them, and display no more political innocence than purely polemical books. But most scholars during these productive decades rarely emphasize extremes for purely cultural and political purposes. They usefully poke about in all corners of Coleridge's writing in search of significant patterns. In any case, as such scholarly work proceeded in the last half of the twentieth century, along with the publication of the gigantic *Collected Works*, critical polemics changed. They would no longer be concerned with reading the phenomenalist or the noumenalist Coleridge, as in the different reading practices of Lowes and Richards. The clash of the Neo-Aristotelians and the New Critics faded away, and the arc of competing emphases began to bend differently in politically disruptive years from the 1970s on. Revisions and attacks came from both traditional and radical quarters. From one direction the humanist version of Coleridgean imagination was, by religious-minded critics, pulled back into attenuated Christian discourse. It could be said that one tendency was to re-Christianize Coleridge. Another group of critics attacked that same humanist imagination, with an eye to dismantling what they considered tendentious, even nefarious, Romantic ideology.

Consider first the re-Christianizing of Coleridge. Discontent had been at work in some critics, ever since the 1930s with what Richards and the New Critics had achieved—the removal of the Yahwistic 'I am that I am', and by implication the Christological presence, in Coleridgean imagination. A number of books, from the 1960s on, attempted to put Christianity or at least its urbanely described beliefs back into the reading of Coleridge, some of which, despite their thinly disguised theological leanings, can still be read, even by atheists, with profit (Barth). A concentrated sense of the insistence, in many such books, can be got by reading a fierce essay by Jonathan Wordsworth in which he, as Coleridge might say, *de-synonymizes* the famous definition of the Imagination in the *Biographia Literaria*. He argues that the Coleridgean world had been turned upside down, and, indeed, as we have seen in discussing Richards, what was Primary was de-emphasized in favor of the Secondary Imagination, transformed into a shibboleth of purely humanist imagination, not as Coleridge thought, imagination within a universe organized by God. Putting the emphasis back on Christianity in Coleridge continues to this day, and quite recently has even taken a sharp turn from urbanity into a kind of primitive Christian joy in revelation theology thought to be shining out of Coleridge's mind (Barbeau). Of all those books that attempt to describe the place of Christianity in Coleridge's texts the most subtle, interesting, and useful is Owen Barfield's *What Coleridge Thought* (1971). There can be no doubt that, enclosed within Christian paradigms, Coleridge, both as the young Unitarian and the old Anglican, strived to think about the nature of thought itself. Barfield's commentary on Coleridge's epistemological excursions within a Christian matrix are richly thick with implications about religious and mythological thinking reaching beyond the 'tyranny of the eye'.

Coleridge as Christian, even the most subtle of Christians, is, however, a secondary subject to those writers (Williams, McGann, Eagleton, Leask, Pyle), who, from the late 1960s through the 1990s, confront the humanistic deployment of Coleridge's Christianity. Some of these critiques have the air about them of the *exposé*, and what is exposed is intellectual corruption. For these writers, discussing the relation of Coleridge's Christianity to his ideas is no more useful than debating consubstantiation versus transubstantiation. Their central subject is the nature of the hermeneutic circle by which Romantic literature has all through the twentieth century been evaluated by Romantic theory, and then transmitted as an exclusive way of reading identical with an assumed form of knowledge. This was, for such interpreters of cultural power, to use an economic metaphor, a cultural bubble. The bubble had long endured and in some places still does, but for many readers the bubble burst in the political world of things as they are. Could one continue to turn one's attention to irony, paradox, ambiguity, tension in poems in the face of intensifying ideological contradictions, not to mention horrors, of the Vietnam war, the hypocrisy of CIA assassinations and *coups d'état*, American economic hegemony, the unsettling dissolutions of the USSR and the growth of Chinese communist capitalism? The planet had come to seem much too complicated to be confronted by the holistic reading of dazzling metaphoric, tonal, paradoxical, and ironically structured unities. Post-colonial history, the increasing presence of Nietzsche in post-modernist thought, the Western adaptations of Marxism, however genteel, into what came to be called the New Historicism, pushed Romantically inspired principles of Richards and the New Criticism to the side. In disestablishing Romantic ideology by pointing out either the naiveté or the bad faith of its professorial practitioners, the Coleridgean infusions in literary criticism suffered a damaging blow. Romantic orthodoxies, like the self-sufficient freedom of the organic poem, have been unsettled. Textbooks, once scaffolded with ideas inherited from Romantic theories of the imagination, are rare today. Flooding into the canon of Romantic literature, once dominated by Coleridgean critical order, are poetic and narrative texts of women, slaves, and popular political writers. Analyzing these texts alongside poems of the established literary canon, the so-called New Historical critics often read poems with the same sense of attention to poetic and rhetorical devices as New Critics used to. But they turn also to the historical moment in which the poem is framed, and there the critic looks for unresolved contradictions, not that which Coleridge thought the imagination, within the text, resolved and as the New Critics emphasized, unified in stressed tension. Something of a critical rumble occurred in Romantic studies when one critic, reading Wordsworth's *Lines Written Above Tintern Abbey,* insisted on discussing not how the poem was held organically together but what was *not* said in the poem about the social conditions in which the poem's mentally restorative pastoral was idealized (Levinson, 37–46). Breaking open the poem to let in a silenced history obviously exploded both the Wordsworthian and the Coleridgean imaginative core by which the poem's ordering of disorder had to be respected over the knowledge of disorder in the world.

This is not to say that all the ideas of any major critical path to Coleridge have been abandoned or are not still useful. Again, it is the emphases and the mixing of the ingredients that we must look to. The critic must make use of what seems at least technically accurate and avoid what has been exaggerated into falsity. In a recent review of a translation of Baudelaire, for instance, the reviewer remarks that in his poems Baudelaire 'seems to be weighing contrary ideas and resolving them', and goes on to say further that 'such tensions are integral to our idea of modern art' (Stein, 51). The ears of anyone who has followed twentieth-century literary criticism, especially as it concerns the legacy of Coleridge, will prick up at such a sentence. The very concept of poetic 'tensions', as we have seen reflected from Coleridge's Secondary Imagination and then alchemized by Richards and the New Critics, has behind it a long history of critical practice that both informs and deforms the act of reading. It is not that there are or are not obvious tensions, paradoxes, ambiguities, and what not in poems; the question is what does the critic infer from their presence and how he thinks the poem deploys them—and to what end? As soon as one imagines an aesthetic, cultural, moral, political, religious end, the act of reading turns into something wider in which there is more at stake than the act of reading a single poem. When the book reviewer says of Baudelaire, as Richards, following Coleridge, says of lines of Shakespeare, or the New Critics said of hundreds of poems, that the poet puts contradictions or tensions before us and he 'resolves' them, immense critical assumptions about the power of poetic form as an example of the poetic mind and finally of the mind itself are at stake. That is why Coleridge's theories of the imagination, right or wrong, Christian or humanist, have been crucial for so long, for his theory asserts that indeed the mind can unify, order, make sense of things, even the most contrary things, and when it feels itself inadequate to do so, it finds, even in idealizing, some sense, not only of poetic order, but of real order. This was no small claim in the de-Christianizing processes of modern culture. It was, indeed, an immense claim of the greatest import, seriously entertained all through the twentieth century until punctured in the jagged mentality of a post-modern, and completely disunified intellectual and political world.

We may now think of it as a time long past when poets and novelists as important as W. H. Auden, Robert Penn Warren, Malcolm Lowry, or William Gass made practical use of Coleridge and when his ideas thrived in university courses. But writing about and invoking Coleridge will certainly not end and so we can try to guess what twists and turns such writing may take, in the future. If we can judge by two recent books—David Haney's *The Challenge of Coleridge* and Seamus Perry's *The Uses of Division*—there may be a return to perennial, alternating emphases discussed at the beginning of this essay, either emphasis on Coleridge the abstract thinker or Coleridge, ever thinking, but gazing into the concrete, sensual world and paused in reflection between the dualities of body and mind. Haney draws Coleridge into abstractions not even imagined by Richards or House. He invites to his book all readers familiar with such French and German theorists as Hans Georg Gadamer, Paul Ricoeur, or Emmanuel Levinas. For the reader without such acquaintance, the interesting imaginary conversation engineered by Haney between Coleridge and these moderns will be mostly incomprehensible. Perhaps as the discourse of hermeneutics—for that is the realm in which Coleridge may well be refashioned—becomes more widely known, Coleridge the *hermeneut* will replace Coleridge the metaphysician.[3] Perry's book brings us round to a portrayal of Coleridge similar to that which opened this essay—Coleridge fallen from the paradoxes of Christianity into a shuffling between contraries, extremes, dualities. I described this movement within dualities as endemic to the mind of a tormented Coleridge, and he was certainly often tormented. Perry, in his artful book, interestingly portrays Coleridge in a less violent way, more suitable perhaps to our contemporary acceptance of fractures, fissures, oppositions, and dualities. Rather than seek an emphasis on this or that side of Coleridge's manner of thinking or within the topics of his thought, Perry aims at showing the dance of dualities in Coleridge, a dance that has no final step in a world with no coherent world-view and no essential unity. This is a world in which Coleridge might have been much more anguished than he was in his own, but it is one in which, once again, Coleridge reflects what we ask him to reflect. And whether it is to be Coleridge conversing with modern hermeneuts, Coleridge riding a pendulum amongst the

---

[3] See, in addition to Haney, the interesting essay by E. S. Shaffer, 'The Hermeneutic Community: Coleridge and Schleiermacher', in Gravil, 200–2.

dualities, or some other Coleridge now being designed for us in some dark library or on some shiny shore, we shall surely continue to read him with all the pleasure we have come to expect in both the light and the dimness of his writing.

WORKS CITED

ARNOLD, MATTHEW. 1973. The study of poetry [1880], *The Complete Prose Works of Matthew Arnold*, Vol. 9, *English Literature and Irish Politics*, ed. R. H. Super. Ann Arbor, Mich.: The University of Michigan Press.

BARBEAU, JEFFREY W. 2008. *Coleridge, The Bible, and Religion*. New York and Hampshire: Palgrave Macmillan.

BARFIELD, OWEN. 1971. *What Coleridge Thought*. Middletown, Conn.: Wesleyan University Press.

BARTH, JOHN. 2001. *The Symbolic Imagination: Coleridge and the Romantic Tradition*. 2nd edn. New York: Fordham University Press.

BEER, JOHN B. 1959. *Coleridge the Visionary*. London: Chatto and Windus.

BLACKMUR, RICHARD. 1961. *Language as Gesture*. London: G. Allen.

BROOKS, CLEANTH. 1968. *The Well-Wrought Urn*. London: Dobson [1949].

BURKE, KENNETH. 1952. *A Grammar of Motives*. New York: Prentice-Hall.

COLERIDGE. SAMUEL TAYLOR. 1983–2001. *The Collected Works of Samuel Taylor Coleridge*. Princeton: Princeton University Press.

—— *Lectures 1808–1819: On Literature*, ed. R. A. Foakes, Vol. 5 (=*Lects*)

—— *Biographia Literaria*, ed. James Engell and W. Jackson Bate, Vol. 7. (=*BL*)

—— *On the Constitution of the Church and State*, ed: J. Colmer, Vol. 10 (=*C&S*)

—— *The Notebooks of Samuel Taylor Coleridge*, ed. Kathleen Coburn. Bollingen Series. 1957. New York: Pantheon Books. (=*NB*)

CRANE, R. S. 1942. Two essays in Practical Criticism: prefatory note. *University Review*, University of Kansas City, 8 (3) (Spring): 199–202.

—— 1952. et. al. *Critics and Criticism: Ancient and Modern*. Chicago: The University of Chicago Press.

EAGLETON, TERRY. 1991. *Ideology: An Introduction*. London and New York: Verso.

—— 1976. *Marxism and Literary Criticism*. London: Methuen.

—— 1933. *The Use of Poetry and the Use of Criticism: Studies in the Relation of Criticism to Poetry in England*. Cambridge, Mass;: Harvard University Press.

ELIOT, T. S. 1934. *After Strange Gods: A Primer of Modern Heresy. The Page–Barbour Lectures at the University of Virginia*. London: Faber and Faber [1934].

—— 2001. A note on poetry and belief [1927]. In John Constable, ed., *I. A. Richards, Selected Works*. London and New York: Routledge, Vol. 10: 59–62.

EMPSON, WILLIAM. 1977. *Seven Types of Ambiguity*. New York: New Directions [1953].

FREUD, SIGMUND. 1989. *Civilization and Its Discontents*. New York: W. W. Norton [1930], trans. and ed. James Strachey.

FRUMAN, NORMAN. 1971. *The Damaged Archangel*. New York: G. Braziller.

FUSSELL, PAUL. 2000. *The Great War and Modern Memory*. New York: Oxford University Press [1975].

GRAVIL, RICHARD. and LEFEBURE, MOLLY. 1990. *The Coleridge Connection: Essays for Thomas McFarland*. London: The Macmillan Press.

HOUSE, HUMPHRY. 1953. *Coleridge*. London: Rupert Hart Davis.

HANEY, DAVID P. 2001. *The Challenge of Coleridge: Ethics and Interpretation in Romanticism and Modern Philosophy*. University Park, Pa: The Pennsylvania State University Press.

LEASK, NIGEL. 1988. *The Politics of Imagination in Coleridge's Critical Thought*. New York: St. Martin's Press.

LEAVIS, F. R. 1955. *D. H. Lawrence, Novelist*. New York: Knopf; First American Edition.

—— 2001. Dr. Richards, Bentham, and Coleridge [1935]. In John Constable, ed., *I. A. Richards, Selected Works*. London and New York: Routledge, Vol. 10: 336–57.

LEVINSON, MARJORIE. 1986. *Wordsworth's Great Period Poems: Four Essays*. Cambridge and New York: Cambridge University Press.

LOWES, JOHN LIVINGSTON. 1927. *The Road to Xanadu: A Study in the Ways of the Imagination*. London: Constable.

McFARLAND, THOMAS. 1969. *Coleridge and the Pantheist Tradition*. Oxford: Clarendon Press.

McGANN, JEROME J. 1983. *The Romantic Ideology: A Critical Investigation*. Chicago and London: The University of Chicago Press.

MATHER, COTTON. 1957. *The Diary of Cotton Mather*. 2 vols. New York: Frederick Ungar Publishing Company.

MILL, JOHN STUART. 1950. *On Bentham and Coleridge* [1839–40] with an introduction by F. R. Leavis. New York: G. W. Stewart.

PERRY, SEAMUS. 1999. *Coleridge and The Uses of Division*. Oxford: Clarendon Press.

PYLE, FOREST. 1995. *The Ideology of Romanticism: Subject and Society in the Discourse of Romanticism*. Stanford: Stanford University Press.

PYM, DAVID. 1979. *The Religious Thought of Samuel Coleridge*. New York.: Harper & Row.

RANSOM, JOHN CROWE. 1941. *The New Criticism*. Norfolk, Conn.: New Directions.

RICHARDS, I. A. 1934. *Coleridge on the Imagination*. London: K. Paul, Trench, Trubner & Co.

—— 1927 (with C. K. Ogden). *The Meaning of Meaning: A Study of the Influence of Language upon Thought and the Science of Symbolism*. London: K. Paul Trench, Trubner & Co.

—— 1930. *Principles of Criticism*. New York: Harcourt, Brace and Company.

—— 1929. *Practical Criticism: A Study of Literary Judgement*. London: K. Paul, Trench, Trubner & Co.

SHAFFER, E. S. 1975. '*Kubla Khan*' and the Fall of Jerusalem: The Mythological School in Biblical Criticism and Secular Literature, 1710–1880. Cambridge and New York: Cambridge University Press.

STEIN, LORIN. 2008. Beauty's law. *The New Republic*. Vol. 238, No. 4,831, 12 March: 50–5.

TATE, ALLEN. 1968. *Essays of Four Decades*. Chicago: Swallow Press.

WILLIAMS, RAYMOND. 1958. *Culture and Society: 1780–1850*. New York: Columbia University Press.

WORDSWORTH, JONATHAN. The infinite I AM: Coleridge and the ascent of being. In *Coleridge's Imagination: Essays in Memory of Pete Laver*, ed. Richard Gravil, Lucy Newlyn, and Nicolas Roe. Cambridge: Cambridge University Press, 22–52.

INDEX